J. W. Gott
479 C. C.

W9-DDK-802

Theodora Gott

THE MISCELLANEOUS WORKS

OF

OLIVER GOLDSMITH

MACMILLAN AND CO., Limited
LONDON . BOMBAY . CALCUTTA . MADRAS
MELBOURNE

THE MACMILLAN COMPANY
NEW YORK . BOSTON . CHICAGO
DALLAS . SAN FRANCISCO

THE MACMILLAN CO. OF CANADA, Ltd.
TORONTO

The Globe Edition

THE MISCELLANEOUS WORKS

OF

OLIVER GOLDSMITH

WITH BIOGRAPHICAL INTRODUCTION

BY

PROFESSOR MASSON

MACMILLAN AND CO., LIMITED
ST. MARTIN'S STREET, LONDON
1925

COPYRIGHT

First Edition (Globe 8vo) ,1868.
Reprinted, 1871, 1874, 1878, 1881, 1884, 1889 (Crown 8vo), 1895,
1899, 1902, 1904, 1907, 1908, 1912, 1915, 1919 1923, 1925

PRINTED IN GREAT BRITAIN

CONTENTS.

ESSAYS.

THE BEE:

A SELECT COLLECTION OF ESSAYS ON THE MOST INTERESTING AND ENTERTAINING SUBJECTS.

AN INQUIRY INTO THE PRESENT STATE OF POLITE LEARNING.

BIOGRAPHIES.

POEMS.

DRAMAS.

MISCELLANEOUS POEMS.

INDEX OF FIRST LINES TO SMALLER POEMS.

MEMOIR OF GOLDSMITH.

THE *Life of Oliver Goldsmith* by Mr. (now Sir James) Prior, published in 1837, in two volumes 8vo, was the first really careful biography of a writer who had already for seventy years been among the most popular and fascinating of our English classics. To the results of Mr. Prior's researches it can hardly be said that there has been any material addition. Mr. John Forster's well known *Life and Adventures of Oliver Goldsmith*, published in 1848, superseded, however, for most purposes, the work of Mr. Prior, and from its greater vivacity and its abundant deliciousness of literary anecdote, will probably remain the standard biography of Goldsmith to all time coming. Washington Irving's *Oliver Goldsmith: A Biography*, published in 1849, was avowedly a compilation from Prior and Forster, but has an independent interest, as the work of one who delighted, all his life, in acknowledging Goldsmith as his literary master, and has been named, in consequence, "The American Goldsmith." Of smaller memoirs of Goldsmith the number is past counting. Perhaps, therefore, no better reason can be given for here adding one more than that it will be convenient for possessors of this edition of Goldsmith's Works to have some account of the Author bound up with it.

Oliver Goldsmith was born, on the 10th of November, 1728, at the obscure, and then almost inaccessible, village of Pallas, or Pallasmore, in the county of Longford, in the very midmost solitude of Ireland. His father, the Rev. Charles Goldsmith, was the poor Protestant clergyman of that Irish parish. He was one of a family of Goldsmiths, noted for worth and goodness of heart rather than worldly prudence, who were originally from the South of England, and in whom, since their first coming to Ireland, the clerical profession, in its Protestant form, had been almost hereditary. Goldsmith's mother, Ann Jones, was also of a clerical and Protestant family that had been naturalized in Ireland. She was one of the daughters of the Rev. Oliver Jones, master of the diocesan school of Elphin in Roscommon. From this maternal grandfather young Oliver derived his Christian name. He used afterwards to maintain, however, that it had come into the line of his maternal ancestry through some connexion with Oliver Cromwell.

Four children, three of them daughters, and one a son, named Henry, had been born to the clergyman of Pallasmore and his wife before the appearance of the

"Oliver" that was to make them famous; and the family was ultimately completed by the birth of three sons younger than Oliver, named Maurice, Charles, and John. The eldest of this family of eight (a daughter), and this last-named John, died in childhood. Effectively, therefore, Oliver grew up as one of a family of six, three of whom were older, and two younger, than himself.

A native of the rural heart of Ireland, Goldsmith, till his seventeenth year, received his entire education, whether of scenery and circumstance, or of more formal schooling, within the limits of that little-visited region. Not, however, without some changes of spot and society within those limits. In 1730, while he was yet but an infant, his father, after having been about twelve years minister of Pallas, removed to the better living of Kilkenny West, a parish some miles south of Pallas, and situated not in the county of Longford, but in the adjacent county of West Meath. Thenceforward, accordingly, the head-quarters of the family were no longer at Pallas, but at Lissoy, a quaint Irish village within the bounds of the new parish. Here, in a pretty and rather commodious parsonage-house, on the verge of the village, and on the road between Athlone and Ballymahon, the good clergyman set himself to bring up his children on his paltry clerical income, eked out by the farming of some seventy acres of land. He was himself a mild eccentric of the Dr. Primrose type, kindly to all about him, and of pious, confused ways. But the immortal oddity of Lissoy, and the incarnation of all that had been peculiar for some generations in the race of the Goldsmiths, was the parson's young son, Oliver. In book-learning, for one thing, he was, from the first, a little blockhead. "Never was so dull a boy" was the report of a kinswoman, who, having lived in the Lissoy household, had been the first to try to teach him his letters, and who afterwards, under her married name of Elizabeth Delap, kept a small school at Lissoy, and survived to be proud of her pupil, and to talk of him in her extreme old age, after he was dead. Hardly different seems to have been the report of the Lissoy schoolmaster, Thomas Byrne, more familiarly known as "Paddy Byrne,"—a veteran who had returned to his original vocation of teaching after having served in the wars under Marlborough and risen to the rank of quartermaster to a regiment in Spain. And yet of this "Paddy Byrne" Goldsmith seems to have retained to the last an affectionate recollection:—

A man severe he was, and stern to view;
I knew him well, and every truant knew.
Well had the boding tremblers learnt to trace
The day's disasters in his morning face:
Full well they laughed with counterfeited glee
At all his jokes, for many a joke had he;
Full well the busy whisper, circling round,
Conveyed the dismal tidings when he frowned.
Yet he was kind, or, if severe in aught,
The love he bore to learning was in fault:
The village all declared how much he knew;
'Twas certain he could write, and cypher too;
Lands he could measure, terms and tides presage;
And even the story ran that he could gauge.

Better than all, he had a stock of tales, not only of his own campaigning adventures, but also from old Irish ballads, chap-books, and fairy lore, and a knack of versifying, which he was fond of exercising in the form of extempore Irish translations from Virgil. From this "Paddy Byrne," in short, if from any one, Goldsmith caught his first notions of literary invention and rhyming. But the poor little fellow was always unfortunate. Hardly had he become aware of the wealth that was in Paddy Byrne, and hardly had Paddy Byrne had time to discern the spark of genius that lay somewhere in his awkward little pupil, when the two were separated. The boy was not more than nine years of age when an attack of confluent small-pox stopped his attendance at Lissoy school; and, when he recovered, it was with his naturally plain face disfigured into such a grotesque of ugliness that it was difficult to look at him without laughing. Whether to get him out of sight for a time, or because better instruction than Paddy Byrne's was now thought necessary for him, he was sent away from Lissoy to Elphin, a distance of about thirty miles. The purpose was that he should attend the school at Elphin which had formerly been taught by his grandfather, the Rev. Oliver Jones, but was now under the care of a Rev. Mr. Griffin. For about two years, accordingly, he did attend this school, boarding all the while with his uncle, Mr. John Goldsmith of Ballyoughter, who lived near Elphin. But in 1739, when he was eleven years old, he was brought back to a school of some reputation nearer home—one which had been set up in Athlone, about five miles from Lissoy, by a Rev. Mr. Campbell. Two years here, and four years more at the school of a Rev. Patrick Hughes at Edgeworthstown, county Longford, some seventeen miles from Lissoy, completed his school education and brought him to his seventeenth year.

The accounts of young Goldsmith during this time when he was tossed about from school to school in his native part of Ireland, generally coming home to Lissoy and its neighbourhood for the holidays, correspond singularly with what he was all through life. At every school we hear of him as a shy, thick, awkward boy, the constant butt of his companions because of his comically ugly face, and thought by most of them to be "little better than a fool." And yet everywhere there seems to have been a liking for him as an innocent simple-hearted fellow, who, though sensitive to the jokes made at his expense, and liable to fits of the sulks on account of them, would be all right again on the least beckoning of kindliness, and capital company in the playground at fives or ball with those who had been his tormentors. Of his success in school-work we hear little. We are to suppose him gradually getting on in Latin and other things in preparation for the University; and something is said as to his fondness for Ovid and Horace, his peculiar delight in Livy, his liking for Tacitus after a while, and his little care for Cicero. There are hints also to the effect that he excelled in the style of his translations, and that he had more credit for talent with the masters than among the boys. On the whole, Johnson's often-quoted saying about Goldsmith, "He was a plant that flowered late: there was nothing remarkable about him when young," seems true only in a very obvious and rough sense. The "flower" of Goldsmith was the exquisite variety of English writing which eventually he gave to the world; and, till this came, there *was* nothing "remarkable" about him to those who could not discern that it might come, unless they chose, with his schoolfellows, to think his very queerness and confused-headedness remarkable. What Goldsmith was as a man, we repeat, he was as a boy. The amount of difference produced in his case by growth and experience was even less than is usual. What was the opinion of him among his schoolfellows at Elphin, Athlone, and Edgworthstown, but an anticipation, even to identity in the mode of its expression, of that opinion which Johnson, Burke, Garrick, and others avowed they would have been obliged to form of Goldy in all his glory, if they had judged of him personally and apart from his writings? "He is little better than a fool," they all said; and yet they liked him. Nor were there wanting, in his boyhood, any more than in his manhood, those occasional gleams and flashes which challenged the current verdict, drew sudden attention to the absurd creature with the scarred face, and made people wonder whether, if he were a fool, he might not be a fool extraordinary, an inspired fool, one of Shakespeare's fools. Without insisting on the fact that the earliest letters of Goldsmith extant (not written till several years after our present date) have all the easy humour and grace of style of his later writings, we might revert to the tradition of the superior finish of his boyish exercises in translation. But there is more than this. All through his school-days, it is known, young Goldsmith remembered the trick of rhyming which he had learnt from Paddy Byrne, and not only read such English poetry as came in his way, but wrote verses of his own, which made his mother and others think that something after all might be made of "Noll." None of these verses, of any value for comparison with what he wrote afterwards, have been preserved. But there is an extempore metrical repartee of his, attributed to the time when he was at Elphin, and not more than eleven years of age, which shows that there was wit in the little fellow even thus early. At his uncle's house, it seems, as Oliver was dancing a hornpipe to the violin-playing of a certain Mr. Cumming, his droll face and figure so struck the player that he burst into laughter and pointed to the dancer as a fac-simile of "ugly Æsop." Æsop at once retorted by calling out this couplet:—

> Our herald hath proclaimed this saying:
> "See Æsop dancing, and his monkey playing."

Now that he was come to the age of seventeen, what was to be done with this lumpish, ill-favoured lad, whom everybody laughed at as a fool, and who yet was evidently no fool? The understanding had been that he was to go to the University of Dublin, where his elder brother, Henry, had already concluded his course with credit. But there were difficulties in the way. The family circumstances, never very good, had been recently much straitened by a particular cause. Goldsmith's eldest sister, Catherine, having been privately married to a Mr. Daniel Hodson, to whom Henry Goldsmith was then acting as tutor, and who was the son of a gentleman of good property, her father thought himself bound to prove that her family had not meanly brought about the match for their own interests. Accordingly, he entered into an engagement, Sept. 1744, to pay 400*l.* as her marriage-portion. By this arrangement for the credit of Mrs. Hodson all the rest of the family were pinched at the time, and some of them permanently. If Oliver were to go to the University now, it must be not as a "pensioner," like his brother Henry, but in the lower grade of a "sizar" or "poor scholar," wearing a coarse stuff gown and a red cap, and performing menial offices about college in return for his tuition and board. At this prospect Goldsmith recoiled. He would rather, he declared, be bound to some trade. At length, however, the remonstrances of a relative, whom he had every reason to respect, persuaded him to yield. This was "Uncle Contarine"—*i.e.* the Rev. Thomas Contarine (originally Contarini, for his grandfather was a refugee from Venice), clergyman of Oran, near Roscommon. This worthy man, who had been the college-companion of Bishop Berkeley, had married a sister of Goldsmith's father; and, during her life, Oliver had been a frequent visitor at their house. No one had liked the boy better all along, or better discerned what was in him, than Uncle Contarine. Already he had helped to maintain him at school; and, the recent death of his wife having left him a widower with one daughter, whatever affection would have gone to a son of his own was transferred to his nephew Oliver. He insisted that Oliver must go to college. What mattered being a sizar? He had been a sizar himself, and had he fared the worse for it?

After some kind of examination, Goldsmith was admitted at Trinity College, Dublin, on the 11th of June, 1745, the last in a list of eight sizars, of whom a John Beatty, his school-fellow at Edgeworthstown, was another. These two chummed together during the entire four years of Goldsmith's college-course. Among fellow-students who knew him well at college were Lauchlan Macleane, and some others who afterwards rose to some distinction in politics or in the church: Flood and Edmund Burke were both then in the college, but barely remembered, in after life, having seen Goldsmith there. No contrast can have been greater than between the college-life of Burke and that of Goldsmith. There was nothing, indeed, very distinguished, according to formal academic estimation, in Burke's college-career; but we have glimpses of him as a "terrible fellow" in a set of his own, domineering in a private debating society, and storing his ample mind with all sorts of information, acquired in his own way. In poor Goldy's case we find what might have been expected—"no specimens of genius," according to the report of one of his college-acquaintances, but "only squalid poverty, and its concomitants, idleness and despondence." He was better known as "lounging about the college-gates," and getting into any row that was at hand, or as playing the flute and singing Irish songs in his rooms, than as making any figure in the classes. Two causes probably contributed to make his college career more reckless and miserable than it need have been. One was that he had for his tutor a strong-bodied brute, named Wilder, of whose savageness to all about him there are yet traditions, and who seems to have had all the more delight in tormenting the poor sizar because he had come from his own part of the country and had been specially recommended to him. "*Male*,

male," he would say when Oliver was under examination, though sometimes he was forced to end with "*Valde bene.*" But the death of Oliver's father early in 1747, in the very middle of Oliver's college-course, was a greater cause of break-down than Wilder's rough tutorship. The main income of the family thus failed, and the family-group was scattered—Mr. and Mrs. Hodson remaining, indeed, in possession of the house at Lissoy; but Goldsmith's mother settling in Ballymahon, and his brother Henry taking the curacy of his father's old parish of Pallasmore, with 40*l.* a year of salary and the chance of pupils. In these circumstances, such small supplies as had till now reached Oliver from home were no longer forthcoming. Uncle Contarine seems to have done what he could; but, with such lax husbandry as Oliver's, it was like putting water in driblets into a sieve. The latter half of his stay at the University was, consequently, worse than the first. It was one series of mishaps and hardships. In May 1747, a month or two after the death of Oliver's father, there was a college riot in Dublin against the police, in retaliation for the arrest of a student; and it ended in an attempt to break open the prison and the deaths of several townsmen. Four of the ringleaders were expelled from the University; and among four others who were publicly rebuked for their share in the affair was Oliver Goldsmith—the Latin record in the University-books bearing that he had "favoured the sedition and given aid to the rioters." The next month he tried for a scholarship and failed. He did obtain a small exhibition, worth about thirty shillings a year, but even this he lost by subsequent negligence. He had to pawn his books, and resort to every other haggard shift for raising now and then a half-crown. Nothing can be more doleful than the account of the poor sizar's life at this time. But he was blessed, as he himself said afterwards, with "a knack at hoping." A copy of Scapula's Greek Lexicon, which was one of his college class-books, and is still preserved somewhere, attests this very characteristically. It is scribbled over with his signature in various forms, and especially in such forms as these—"*Free: Oliver Goldsmith.*" "*I promise to pay, &c.: Oliver Goldsmith*"—showing how, in his college-rooms, the poor fellow would dream of one day being a member of Parliament and being able to frank letters, or of being in a position to be accommodated easily with any desired sum. Meanwhile, too, at least one of his actual shifts for instant money-making had a relish of superior pleasure in it. This was the writing of ballads, to be sold, at a particular shop he knew of, for five shillings each, and thence retailed, in coarse print, to the Dublin ballad-singers. Every five shillings was something in itself; but to go out at nights, and, leaning against a lamp-post, feel one of the shillings still in your pocket, and at the same time hear a ballad of your own sung to a ragged crowd of men and girls, and be able to buy a copy of it for a penny—this was a delight worth all the pains of sizarship, and the tyranny of ten Wilders! So sometimes Oliver felt; but the one Wilder had almost proved more than enough. One evening, in the flush of some little success, Oliver was giving a supper and a dance in his rooms to "a party of young friends of both sexes from the city," when the tutor, hearing of the breach of rule, burst in, and not only abused him in gross terms before his guests, but actually collared and thrashed him. Next day Oliver was off. He sold his books and spare clothes, hung about Dublin till he had but a single shilling left, and then set out to walk to Cork, meaning to get to America. He subsisted on the shilling for three days; after which he wandered about, living no one knows how—save that he used afterwards to tell that the most delicious meal he had ever tasted was a handful of grey peas given him in this wild walk by a girl at a wake after twenty-four hours of fasting. At length he was sensible enough to think of going home; his brother Henry met him by appointment; and after a little time they went back to Dublin together, and made it up so far with Wilder that Oliver was re-admitted into college. Things then went on very much as before—Oliver again and again "cautioned," and fines appearing against him in the buttery-books. Once more we hear of an encounter between him and Wilder, and not so unsuccessfully for Goldsmith this time. The tutor had been lecturing on the subject of the Centre of Gravity, and had asked Goldsmith for a restatement of what had been said. Utterly in the dark, Goldsmith had groped in vain for some answer that would pass, when the tutor took the trouble to go over the explanation again, winding up, "And now, you blockhead, where is *your* centre of gravity?" As if not doubting that the question was intended literally, "Why, Doctor, from your definition," said Goldy in a slow voice, "I should think—" and he went on to *name*, in the frankest possible manner, the supposed whereabouts of the point required. There was a roar of laughter from the class; and, furious as Wilder was, he could only call Oliver impertinent as well as ignorant, and turn him down to the lowest place. The date of this incident, which Goldsmith used afterwards to relate with glee, is ascertained to have been May 9, 1748. Less than a year afterwards, *i.e.* in February 1749, he reached the end of his University-course and was admitted to the B.A. degree. He was the lowest in the list of those who took the degree. The wonder is that, having been so often in the black books, he obtained it at all.

And now, at the age of one-and-twenty, Goldsmith could go forth to the world as a graduate of Trinity College, Dublin. Of what use had his four years at the University been to him? Apparently, in his own opinion, of very little. Not only did he never forget the indignities attached to sizarship in those days, but he seems to have formed a theory that much of the education received at Universities was quite unnecessary. "A boy," he afterwards wrote, "who understands perfectly well Latin, French, arithmetic, and the principles of civil law, and can write a fine hand, has an education that may qualify him for any undertaking." And yet, with all his hardships at college and all his indolence, he had probably got a good deal there that remained useful to him. In mathematics he did nothing, consoling himself with the odd opinion that "this seems a science to which the meanest intellects are equal;" and to all forms of metaphysical or philosophical study—"the cold logic of Burgersdicius, or the dreary subtleties of Smiglesius"—he professed a dislike. But in scholarship and general literary accomplishment he cannot have been among the worst. He could "turn an ode of Horace into English better than any of them," he afterwards told Malone, and there is no reason to doubt it.

In Greek, too, he must have sometimes been rewarded with a *Valde bene*. In short, at college, as previously at school, though the general opinion of Goldsmith always expressed itself in the phrase, quoted by himself more than once, "that he was very good-natured and had not the least harm in him," there must have been occasional flashes from him causing people to doubt whether he was not a much cleverer fellow than he looked. And then there were his private scribblings in prose and verse for his own amusement at nights, and those precious and now unknown ballads that were hawked about the Dublin streets.

For about two years, after leaving college, Goldsmith led what Thackeray calls "the life of a buckeen," hanging on his relatives. He lived chiefly in his mother's house in Ballymahon—close to which there was a convenient inn, where he could be jovial in the evenings, and sing songs and tell stories to the choice rustic spirits that gathered round him. But sometimes he was with his sister and brother-in-law at Lissoy, fishing, otter-hunting, or lounging about the farm; and at other times he went over to his brother Henry's at Pallasmore, and tried his hand for a week or two at helping that good man with his pupils. This vagabondage of Oliver seems to have been a sore trouble to all the family. They had looked forward to his taking holy orders; but, to his own secret satisfaction, that project had failed through the refusal of the Bishop of Elphin to ordain him. Some said the refusal was because of reports of his conduct that had reached the bishop; others thought it was because he had stupidly gone to the bishop in flaming scarlet breeches. Anyhow, the Established Church of Ireland lost the services of Oliver Goldsmith. Uncle Contarine, who had been the chief hand in persuading him so far to the clerical project, next suggested a tutorship, and did at length get him, as tutor, into the family of a Mr. Flinn in Roscommon county. Here he seemed to be all right for about a year; but, suddenly tiring of the work, or quarrelling with the family, he set out, on a good horse and with thirty pounds in his pocket, bound a second time (so he gave out) for America *viâ* Cork. Nothing was heard of him for six weeks, when unexpectedly he turned up at his mother's door, without a penny, and riding on a bony animal which he called Fiddleback. He gave his mother a long rigmarole account of his adventures—how he had gone to Cork, taken his passage and sent his kit on board, and how, the captain having sailed without him, he had had to sell his good horse, buy the wretched beast Fiddleback, and all but beg his way through the country to Ballymahon. "And now, my dear mother," he ended, seeing the old lady's face gloom, "after having struggled so hard to come home to you, I wonder you are not more rejoiced to see me." Little wonder that, from this moment, there was a coolness on Mrs. Goldsmith's part to her young prodigal, and a wish to get rid of him anyhow. Even his good brother Henry ceased to have anything to say to him. Only Uncle Contarine stuck by him. He suggested that Oliver should go to London and study law at the Temple; and Oliver, having readily acquiesced, was provided with 50*l*. by Uncle Contarine for his first expenses, and duly set off. But he never got any farther than Dublin. Falling into bad hands there, he lost all he had by gambling and what not, and had to return with real shame and contrition. He was forgiven, again provided with some outfit of money, and again sent off—not, however, this time to London to study law; but to Edinburgh, to qualify himself for the medical profession. And this time Ireland and the circle of Irish relatives did get rid of their troublesome Oliver—rid of him for ever. He was but four-and-twenty years of age, and he lived twenty years longer; but he never again saw Ireland, or the face of any one of his family, save when, some five years afterwards, his younger brother Charles, a lad of twenty, knocked at the door of the wretched London garret in which he then was, and came in ruefully to spend a day or two with him on his way to Jamaica. All through Oliver's future life, however, there was a warm corner in his heart for recollections of his native Ireland, and those he had left there—his mother, his brother Henry, Uncle Contarine, and the rest. He would think of them often till the tears came; he never quite ceased to correspond with them; and he had a cherished dream of revisiting them all some day, and again resting his eyes on dear Lissoy and the green landscape round it, "the most pleasing horizon in Nature." Ere the dream could be accomplished, the mother, Uncle Contarine, and brother Henry were all dead, and it was no longer worth while.

Goldsmith as a medical student in Edinburgh might be a good theme for a little semi-historical novel to any one who chose to write a variation of some of the chapters of *Guy Mannering*, twining the quaint traditions and queer social habits of the picturesque old Scottish capital, in the middle of the eighteenth century, round the figure of the humorous Irish lad, of subsequent celebrity, who had come into the midst of them. He was there for about eighteen months, or from the autumn of 1752 to the beginning of 1754. He was boarded and lodged, no doubt, high up some stair in one of the unsavoury old courts, going off from the High Street, that still amaze the stranger in Edinburgh. His letters do not tell the exact spot—the address "Student in Physic, in Edinburgh," being enough to ensure that return-letters would reach him at the University; but he gives a satirical description in one of them of his landlady and her economical style of cookery. There were other Irish students of medicine in the town besides himself; for the Edinburgh School of Medicine was then famous throughout the world and drew students from all countries. Much of this fame depended on the great reputation of Dr. Alexander Monro, Professor of Anatomy—the first of three Alexander Monros (grandfather, father, and son) who held the same Professorship in succession from 1720 to 1846. The other medical Professors were Dr. Charles Alston (Botany and Materia Medica), Robert Whytt (Institutes of Medicine), Dr. John Rutherford (Practice of Physic), Dr. Andrew Plummer (Chemistry), and Dr. Robert Smith (Midwifery). There is proof that Goldsmith, during the two sessions of his stay in Edinburgh, attended all the medical classes, or all but the last. Of most of the Professors he did not think highly, but he was enthusiastic in praise of Monro. "This man," he writes, "has brought the science he teaches to as much perfection as it is capable of; 'tis he, I may venture to say, that draws hither such a number of students from most parts of the world, even from Russia." That Goldsmith, while thus attending Monro's lectures, really took some interest in medical studies generally, is proved by the fact that he was a member of the "Medical Society"—an association of the young hopes of the profession, for medical debate and dissertation, which still exists in Edinburgh in high repute. His admission into this society is entered in its books under the date Jan. 13, 1753. The future great chemist, Dr. Joseph Black, was one of Goldsmith's fellow-students at Edinburgh, and remembered him well; and other fellow-students with him, afterwards more or less known, were Dr. William Farr, Dr. Joseph Fenn Sleigh, and Lauchlan Macleane, his former co-mate at Trinity College, Dublin, and now also thinking of medicine as a profession. But, as may be supposed, it was not all medical study and preparation for the profession with Goldy in Edinburgh. We hear of him, naturally enough, as gathering the young Irishmen of the University about him, and leading in their suppers and their songs. He must have got somehow also into what was then the more select and stately society of the Scottish metropolis; for there is a letter of his to a friend in Ireland giving an amusing description of the fashionable Edinburgh balls and assemblies—the deathlike solemnity of the dancers of both sexes, the leanness and high cheek-bones of the men, and the ravishing effect of the Scottish dialect when spoken by a Scottish belle. "For instance, teach one of *your* young ladies to pronounce 'Whoar wull I gong?' with a becoming widening of the mouth, and I'll lay my life she'll wound every hearer." There is something also about some brief and unsuccessful connexion of his, or proposal of connexion, in some capacity, with the household of the Duke of Hamilton; and he had leisure for at least one walking-tour into some part of the Scottish Highlands. Very probably, by some exertions of his own, in teaching or the like, he helped to pay his expenses in Edinburgh, though obliged to draw now and then on Uncle Contarine for 6*l.* or 4*l.* His last draft on the excellent man was late in the winter of 1753. "As I shall not have another opportunity of receiving money from your bounty," he writes to Uncle Contarine about that date, "so I have drawn for the last sum that I hope I shall ever trouble you for; 'tis 20*l.* And now, dear Sir, let me here acknowledge":—what is acknowledged may be easily guessed—eternal sense of obligation to the good uncle. The 20*l.* were wanted, as he explains in the same letter, to carry him to the Continent, for the completion of his medical education. "I have seen all that this country can exhibit in the medical way, and therefore intend to visit Paris, where the great M. Farhein, Petit, and Du Hammel de Monceau, instruct their pupils in all the branches of medicine." That the lectures in Paris were in French, which he understood perfectly, and not in Latin, as the lectures at most other foreign Universities were, would, he hinted, be of great advantage to him; and this was the reason for his determining on Paris, rather than on Leyden, which he had also been thinking of on account of *its* "great professor," Albinus. The fact is, it was restlessness, restlessness. He had always had a desire to travel, and "the great M. Farhein" and "the great Albinus" were convenient as an excuse.

Of course, as it was Paris that Goldsmith wanted to go to, it was at Leyden that he arrived. He explains, rather confusedly, how this occurred, in a letter to his uncle from Leyden, in April or May 1754, in which he draws a humorous contrast between the Hollanders he was now among and the Scotch he had just left. "Scotland and this country bear the highest contrast. There hills and rocks intercept every prospect; here 'tis all a continued plain. There you might see a well-dressed duchess issuing from a dirty close, and here a dirty Dutchman inhabiting a palace." The "great Albinus," it would appear, had dwindled in Goldsmith's view on nearer inspection; for he goes on to say, "Physic is by no means taught so well here as in Edinburgh; and in Leyden there are but four British students, owing to all necessaries being so extremely dear, and the professors so very lazy, the chemical professor excepted." With this chemical professor, named Gaubius, he formed some real acquaintance. But, though he remained about ten months in Leyden, and learnt something there, it was only to set out from that town on a strange roving tour through the Continent. The notion of the possibility of such a tour to one without finances appears to have been put into his head by accident. Just before his arrival in Leyden there had died in that town the famous Danish humorist and miscellaneous author, Baron Holberg (1684—1754), and there seems to have been much talk in Leyden circles about this remarkable man, the reputed creator of modern Danish literature, and especially about the hardships and adventures of his early life. A Norwegian by birth, he had come, after a boyhood of great privation, to Copenhagen, and had struggled on there in singular ways. "But his ambition," as Goldsmith himself tells us, "was not to be restrained, or his thirst of knowledge satisfied, till he had seen the world. Without money, recommendations, or friends, he undertook to set out upon his travels and make the tour of Europe on foot. A good voice and a trifling skill in music were the only finances he had to support an undertaking so extensive; so he travelled by day, and at night sang at the doors of peasants' houses, to get himself a lodging." With great admiration Goldsmith goes on to tell what countries young Holberg travelled through, and how at length, returning to Copenhagen, he became popular as an author, was honoured with a title and enriched by the king, "so that a life begun in contempt and penury ended in opulence and esteem." What Holberg had done Goldsmith resolved to do; and the description he gives of Holberg's tour and his means of subsistence during it is almost an exact description of his own tour and its shifts. Leaving Leyden in February 1755, he contrived, we cannot tell how, to visit Louvain, Antwerp, Brussels, and Maestricht, and other towns of Flanders, remaining some little while in each. Then, passing into France, he seems to have fluted his way through the provincial villages of that country, much as Holberg had done, greatly charmed with the gay and simple sociability of the poor French peasants, and making himself at home among them with Irish ease. Reaching Paris, he remained there some time, attending the chemical lectures of M. Rouelle, and had the honour of seeing Voltaire, and listening to a splendid conversation in which the great Frenchman, then past his sixtieth year, took the chief part. It was an argument about England and the English, in which Voltaire, after being long silent burst into a magnificent defence of them against Diderot and Fontenelle, "his meagre face" gathering beauty as he spoke, "his eye beaming with unusual brightness," and "strokes of the finest raillery falling from him thick and fast." So Goldsmith afterwards described the interview, the scene of which he certainly makes to have been Paris, though Mr. Forster thinks this a mistake, and that it must have been in Switzerland. Through Switzerland, at all events, with a touch of Germany on the way, Goldsmith did go, visiting Geneva, Basle, and Berne, and making foot-excursions among the hills and valleys. Then, crossing the Alps, he descended into Italy by Piedmont and went to Florence, Verona, Mantua, Milan, Venice, and Padua; at which last city, on account of the reputation of its medical school, he remained some time. In Italy, he gives us incidentally to understand, his flute-playing stood him in less stead than in France, every peasant in Italy being a better musician than himself; but he had another resource in the old custom of philosophical disputations at universities and convents, followed by dinner, a night's lodging, and a small gratuity to the successful disputant. But, indeed, the mode of Goldsmith's existence during his extraordinary tour is a mystery. Letters he had sent to Ireland once or twice for remittances appear to have brought no reply; borrowings from Irish friends, met casually in Paris or elsewhere, may have helped; gambling, in which Goldsmith always did a little, is mentioned as probably helping too; and once or twice he seems to have hooked himself on to somebody, travelling like himself, who did not object to a companion. There is a dim tradition that he had committed to him in Switzerland the charge of a young gentleman, the son of a wealthy London pawnbroker, who had been sent abroad for mental improvement, and that the young gentleman, preferring cash to the mental improvement he was getting, cut the connexion rather suddenly. Back through France, at any rate, Goldy seems to have made his return journey quite alone, fluting gaily as he had come. On the 1st of February, 1756, he landed at Dover, after an absence of nearly two years in all. Having, it is believed, not a farthing in his pockets, it took him about a fortnight, and some comic singing in country barns, to pull himself on to London. He was twenty-seven years and three months old when he first set his foot in the London streets, and he was to be a Londoner and nothing else all the rest of his life.

Ah! London, London! thou breaker of hearts from of old, thou wrecker of generations of lives, thou insatiable maw of the bones and brains of men, vast over thy flat acres, then as now, spread thy fabric of brick and stone, of squares and alleys and streets, with rising steeples among them and iron-railed church-yards—divided, then as now, by the flowing and ebbing river, and on either side the river the same roar of traffic and wheels, and the same rush and skurry of myriads, all competing for existence, and some for its prizes and sweets! Didst thou note, thou half-brutal London of that day, a certain few of those myriads, on either bank of the river, whose occupation seemed to be the most foolish and peculiar of any—a constant coming down to the river with lighted matches, papers, tapers, torches, oil-pots, and all sorts of combustibles, in their hands, and trying to set the moving tide on fire? Not one of them succeeded; and the Thames flows yet an unburnt, and apparently unburnable, river, hissing at the biggest torch that can be flung into it. But the attempt to set it on fire has been a traditional employment from time immemorial, and so fascinating that Englishmen born far away from London, and even Scotchmen and Irishmen, have left their own native, and probably more combustible, streams, and set themselves down, each with his new trick for inflaming water, on the banks of this large one. Poor fellows ! it does the Thames no harm, and it amuses *them!* Strange, however, that it is precisely those Londoners, native or naturalized, who have been engaged in this hopeless occupation, that the world cares to remember afterwards ! All their contemporary myriads, otherwise occupied, are forgotten; and the very history of London is a record of the successive groups of men that have laboured at setting fire to the Thames. Well, thou big half-brutal London of February 1756, here is another young fellow, footsore from Dover, on his return from a wild continental tour, who enters thee on thy south side, and is staring about him confusedly. He has himself no notion in the world what he is to do; but, from his looks, one may prophesy that he will have to attach himself to your existing group of Thames-kindlers. He seems fit for nothing else. True, he has a diploma of M.B. from some foreign University (whether Leyden, Louvain, or Padua, no one knows), and may practise medicine, and even call himself, by courtesy, "Dr." Goldsmith. But who would trust such a short, mean-visaged, odd-looking fellow, to bleed him or prescribe for him? Clearly, whatever he may try, he can be nothing else eventually than one of the lucifer-match brigade. Meanwhile receive him as gently as you can! He is one of the best-hearted creatures that ever came out of Ireland, without a bit of harm in him, and indeed a great deal wiser and cleverer than he looks.

A little information will be more welcome than farther exclamation or the overworking of a hackneyed image.—Well, the population of London in 1756 was about 700,000. The reign of George II., which had already extended over nearly thirty years, was approaching its close. In home-politics what was chiefly interesting was the persistence in office of the Duke of Newcastle's unpopular ministry—opposed, however, by Pitt (afterwards Lord Chatham), and soon to give way before the genius of that statesman, and to be succeeded by that blaze of Pitt's ascendancy which makes the last years of George II. so brilliant a period in British annals. For Britain and Frederick the Great of Prussia were already on an understanding with each other, and the Seven Years' War was beginning. Not till 1757, indeed, when Pitt became Prime Minister, did the alliance begin to promise its splendid results—Clive's conquests in India, Wolfe's in America, &c. Just at present, while Newcastle was in power, things had a blacker look. Byng's blundering at Minorca, the all but certain loss of Hanover, and the like—these were the topics for the 700,000 Londoners; unless they chose to talk rather of such matters nearer home, as the building of the new chapel for Whitefield in Tottenham Court Road, or the opening of the Foundling Hospital, or the proposed taking down of the old houses on London Bridge. To assist them to proper opinions on these and all other subjects, there were the London newspapers of that date—daily, weekly, and bi-weekly, Whig, Tory, and what not; and, in addition to the newspapers, quite an abundance of critical journals, reviews, and magazines. For it was beginning to be a very busy time in British literature. That organization of literature into a commerce which the Tonsons may be said to have commenced had now been pretty well improved and regularized. It was no longer on the Court, or on Whig and Tory Ministers, or on the casual patronage of noblemen of taste, that men of letters depended, but on the demand of the general public of readers and book-purchasers, as it could be ascertained and catered for by booksellers making publishing their business. The centre of this book-trade was naturally London; and here, accordingly, hanging on the booksellers, and writing for the newspapers and magazines, but with side-glances also to the theatres and their managers, were now congregated such a host of authors and critics by profession as had never been known in London before. To borrow from Mr. Forster a convenient list of those whom we have now dismissed into oblivion as the smaller fry of this Grub Street world of London in the latter days of George II., there were the "Purdons, Hills, Willingtons, Kenricks, Kellys, Shiels, Smarts, Bakers, Guthries, Wotys, Ryders, Collyers, Joneses, Francklins, Pilkingtons, Huddleston Wynnes, and Hiffernans." They did not consider themselves small fry, but were busy and boisterous enough—the Irish among them fighting with the Scotch, and both with the English; and perhaps the last-named Irishman, Hiffernan, ought to have a place in literary history still, as the inventor of the grand word "impecuniosity." But in the midst of these less-known or forgotten one would seek out now the figures of those who were undoubtedly the Thames-kindlers in chief. And first among these comes Johnson, now forty-seven years of age, and a Londoner already for nearly twenty years—not yet "Dr.," and not in possession of his literary dictatorship, though advancing towards it. The poet Young was alive in old age, and at least occasionally in London; and Londoners confirmed were Richardson, approaching his seventieth year, and with all his novels published, and Smollett, not past his thirty-seventh year, but with some of his best novels published, and now working hard at histories, reviews, and all sorts of things. Fielding had been dead two years, and Sterne, though some years over forty, had not yet been heard of. The poet Collins was dying, in madness, at Chichester. Slump together the veteran and not much-liked Mallet, and Armstrong, Glover, Akenside, Garrick, Foote, Murphy, and the Wartons, without being too particular in inquiring whether they were all in London habitually at the exact time under consideration; remember also that Chesterfield, Warburton, Dyer, Shenstone, Gray, Horace Walpole, and Mason were alive here or there in England, and could be in London if they liked, and that away in Scotland, only dreaming of London in the distance, were a few northern lights, with Allan Ramsay still surviving among them; finally imagine Burke, who was Goldsmith's junior, already an adventurer in London, and such other men of about Goldsmith's own age as Percy of the Ballads, the satirist

Churchill, and the elder George Colman, either come to London or tending thither;—and you will have an idea of the state of the world of British letters at the end of the Second George's reign, and also some rough notion of the extent to which that world and its interests interpenetrated London when Goldsmith first gazed about in the crowded streets. And who was the nominal chief or laureate? Who but Colley Cibber, of whom Johnson had written—

> Great George's acts let tuneful Cibber sing,
> For Nature formed the poet for the king.

But Cibber, who was now eighty-four years of age, did not live beyond 1757. He was succeeded by a William Whitehead, whose laureateship extended from 1757 to 1788. The whole of Goldsmith's literary career, as it happened, and large portions also of the lives of Johnson, Smollett, Burke, Garrick, Reynolds, and others whom we now associate with Goldsmith, fell within the laureateship of this memorable Whitehead.

We have been attaching Goldsmith to the London world of letters somewhat in anticipation of his own efforts at any such connexion. Not to set the Thames on fire, but to get anything whatever to do by which he could earn sheer bread for his own teeth and mouth, with a daily gulp of beer, was the poor fellow's one object during a whole year after his arrival in London. It was desperate work, and the details were locked up, for the most part, in his own memory, and never told connectedly to anybody. "When I lived among the beggars in Axe Lane," he would sometimes afterwards say with a laugh; and there are traces of him in various capacities just above Axe Lane and its beggars. He was, for some time, an usher somewhere under a false name; he was then employed in the shop of a druggist in Fish-street Hill; next he is heard of as having set up for himself as a physician among the poor of Bankside, and as wearing a miserable second-hand suit of green and gold; and again he is found as reader for the press to Richardson, the novelist and printer, in his printing-office in Salisbury Court, Fleet Street. Of this last connexion, in which one might have fancied some likelihood, nothing more came than some acquaintance with Richardson himself and a sight of the poet Young; and Goldsmith had some glorious project of getting appointed to go out to the East, on a salary of 300*l.* a year, to decipher the inscriptions on "the Written Mountains" (the necessary Arabic to be learnt in the process), when an ushership in a boarding-school of the better sort turned up at Peckham. Here he lived for some time with Dr. Milner, a Dissenting minister, the proprietor of the school, and was apparently not worse off than other ushers. One day, however, Griffiths, the bookseller of Paternoster Row, dined with the Milners, and, from something he saw or had heard of the Irish usher, fancied he might be useful for hackwork on the *Monthly Review*—a periodical which had been started by Griffiths in 1749 on Whig principles, but against which a Tory rival had recently been set up in the *Critical Review*, edited by Smollett. After getting some specimens of what Goldsmith could do in the kind of work wanted, Griffiths was discerning enough to engage him. Accordingly, in April 1757, he took up his quarters in the house of Griffiths, over the shop in

Paternoster Row, on the understanding that, for board, lodging, and some small salary besides, he was to write such articles and reviews of books as might be required from him. Griffiths, and (what was worse for Goldy) Mrs. Griffiths, were to be judges of the articles, and were to clip and doctor them to suit.

Behold Goldsmith at last with the pen put into his hand—his one predestined instrument in the world! In the circumstances, however, he does not seem to have taken to it kindly. For five months, indeed, he sat daily in his room in the bookseller's house from nine o'clock till two, and sometimes later, writing, or supposed to be writing, notices of books and such-like for the *Monthly Review.* His contributions, longer and shorter, in the successive numbers of the *Review* from April to September 1757, have been picked out from among the articles supplied by other members of the Griffiths staff—Griffiths himself, Ruffhead, Grainger, Ralph, Kippis, Langhorne, &c. They include a paper on Mallet's "Mythology of the Celts," and reviews of Home's "Douglas," Burke's "Essay on the Sublime and Beautiful," Smollett's "History of England," Voltaire's "Universal History," Wilkie's "Epigoniad," and the "Odes" of Gray. They were fair magazine-articles of the kind then going, and something of Goldsmith's lightness and ease of style is discernible in all or most of them. But, whether because Goldsmith's rate of industry did not satisfy the methodical bookseller, or because Mrs. Griffiths did not like his ways, or because the tampering of both with what he wrote and their general treatment of him hurt his sensitiveness, the engagement, which had been for a year, was broken short at the end of the five months. A new hand, named Kenrick, took Goldsmith's place as Griffiths's resident hack; and Goldsmith was again adrift—not absolutely cashiered by Griffiths, and indeed still writing for him, though they were not on the best of terms, but at liberty to take other work.

Why dwell over the particulars of the next year or two of Goldsmith's anonymous drudgery? Let the merest sketch suffice:—In or about September 1757, after leaving Griffiths, he went into a garret somewhere near Salisbury Square; and here it was that his youngest brother, Charles, came in upon him, and lived for a day or two with him ruefully, on his way to Jamaica. He was then living on translations from the French and other things, still chiefly for Griffiths, with the Temple Exchange Coffee House, near Temple Bar, as his daily house of call, where letters could be addressed to him, and where he could meet and talk with a few fellow-craftsmen like himself, or somewhat more flourishing. Then he is traced going back for a little while, in his despair, to his ushership at Peckham—only, however, to emerge again and resume literary hackwork. In 1758 he is found living in No. 12, Green Arbour Court, Old Bailey—a dingy little old square, approached from Farringdon Street by a passage called Break-Neck Steps, now all demolished, and surviving only in Washington Irving's description of it when he visited it for Goldsmith's sake, and found it a colony of washerwomen, and slovenly with wash-tubs on the pavement and clothes hung to dry on lines from the windows. Here, when it was much in the same state, Goldsmith lived from some time in 1758 till late in 1760—*i.e.* till George II. was king no longer, but young George III. reigned in his stead. Here, through part of 1758 and part of 1759, he was at his very worst. Never having quite ceased to hope something from his medical studies and his degree of M.B., he had set his heart on going out to India as a medical officer in the Company's service, and had actually, through Dr. Milner, obtained the promise of some such appointment on the Coromandel coast. This prospect failing in some unexplained way, he resolved to try for an appointment as surgeon's mate in the Army or Navy. The result appears from an entry in the books of the College of Surgeons. At a Court of the Examiners for the College, held on the 21st of December, 1758, in the Old Bailey, not far from Goldsmith's lodging, various candidates were found qualified for appointments. Among them was a James Barnard, who passed as "mate to an hospital;" after the record of which fact there is this brief entry, "Oliver Goldsmith, found not qualified for ditto." It was a dreadful blow, not only on account of the shame should the fact become known (it was pretty well kept secret during Goldy's lifetime), but also on account of some immediate consequences. To appear becomingly before the examiners he had wanted a new suit of clothes; and, though by this time he had begun to have dealings with other publishers than Griffiths—with Newbery, the proprietor of the *Literary Magazine*, and with Archibald Hamilton, the proprietor of the *Critical Review*, which Smollett edited—yet it was to Griffiths that he had applied in his difficulty. For four articles contributed in advance for the *Monthly Review* Griffiths had become his security to the tailor for the new suit, on condition that the suit should be returned or paid for within a certain time. But, four days after Goldsmith's rejection at Surgeons' Hall, his landlord, to whom he was in arrears, was hauled off to prison for debt, and, to help somewhat in the landlady's distress, not only the new suit went into pawn, but the books of Griffiths which Goldsmith had for review. Griffiths, learning the fact, and probably all the angrier with Goldsmith because he had written for Hamilton and the rival Review, demanded his books, called Goldsmith a "sharper" and a "villain," and threatened all sorts of horrors. "Sir," wrote Goldsmith in reply, "I know of no misery "but a jail to which my own imprudences and your letter seem to point. I have "seen it inevitable these three or four weeks, and, by heavens! request it as a "favour—as a favour that may prevent somewhat more fatal. I have been some "years struggling with a wretched being, with all that contempt which indigence "brings with it, with all those strong passions which make contempt insupportable." But Griffiths's bark was worse than his bite, and Goldsmith was let live on in Green Arbour Court.

An extract or two from letters written by him to his Irish relatives and friends, either shortly before or shortly after his rejection by the College of Surgeons, will picture him better in this time of his deepest distress than any mere description. "Whether I eat or starve," he writes to his brother-in-law Hodson at Lissoy, "live "in a first floor or four pair of stairs high, I still remember them [his Irish friends] with "pleasure; nay, my very country comes in for a share of my affection. Unaccountable "fondness for country, this *maladie du pays*, as the French call it! Unaccountable "that *he* should still have an affection for a place who never, when in it, received "above common civility; who never brought anything out of it but his brogue and "his blunders! Surely my affection is equally ridiculous with the Scotchman's, who "refused to be cured of the itch, because it made him unco' thoughtful of his wife "and bonny Inverary." He goes on to say that, if he went to the opera, where Signora Columba was pouring forth all the mazes of melody, it only made him sigh for Lissoy fireside and "Johnny Armstrong's Last Good Night" from the lips of Peggy Golden, and that, if he climbed Hampstead Hill, the magnificent prospect thence only made him think of the dearer landscape from the little mount before Lissoy Gate. Again in a letter to an old college friend, Bryanton, whom he jocosely takes to task for having forgotten him: "God's curse, Sir! who am I? Eh! what "am I? Do you know whom you have offended? A man whose character may "one of these days be mentioned with profound respect in a German comment or "Dutch Dictionary; whose name you will probably hear ushered in by a 'doctis- "simus doctissimorum,' or heel-pieced with a long Latin termination. . . . There will "come a day, no doubt it will—I beg you may live a couple of hundred years longer "only to see the day—when the Scaligers and Daciers will vindicate my character, "give learned editions of my labours, and bless the times with copious comments on "the text. You shall see how they will fish up the heavy scoundrels who disregard "me now, or will then offer to cavil at my productions. How will they bewail the "times that suffered so much genius to lie neglected! If ever my works find their "way to Tartary or China, I know the consequence. Suppose one of your Chinese "Owanowitzers instructing one of your Tartarian Chianobacchi—you see I use "Chinese names to show my erudition, as I shall soon make our Chinese talk like "an Englishman to show his. This may be the subject of the lecture, 'Oliver "Goldsmith flourished in the 18th and 19th centuries. He lived to be an hundred "and three years old, and in that age may be justly styled the Sun of Literature and "the Confucius of Europe,'" &c. Again, in a letter to his cousin, Uncle Contarine's daughter, now Mrs. Lauder: "Alas! I have many a fatigue to encounter before that "happy time arrives when your poor old simple friend may again give a loose to the "luxuriance of his nature, sitting by Kilmore fireside, recount the various adventures "of a hard-fought life, laugh over the follies of the day, join his flute to your harp- "sichord, and forget that ever he starved in those streets where Butler and Otway "starved before him." And, best of all, in a long letter to his brother Henry: "It "gives me some pain to think I am almost beginning the world at the age of thirty- "one. Though I never had a day's illness since I saw you, I am not that strong active "man you once knew me. You scarcely can conceive how much eight years of "disappointment, anguish, and study, have worn me down. If I remember right, "you are seven or eight years older than me; yet I dare venture to say that, if a "stranger saw us both, he would pay me the honours of seniority. Imagine to your- "self a pale melancholy visage, with two great wrinkles between the eyebrows, with "an eye disgustingly severe, and a big wig; and you have a perfect picture of my "present appearance. . . . I can neither laugh nor drink; have contracted a hesi-

"tating, disagreeable manner of speaking, and a visage that looks ill-nature itself; "in short, I have thought myself into a settled melancholy, and an utter disgust of "all that life brings with it. . . . Your last letter, I repeat it, was too short; you "should have given me your opinion of the design of the heroi-comical poem which "I sent you. You remember I intended to introduce the hero of the poem as lying "in a paltry alehouse. You may take the following specimen of the manner, which "I flatter myself is quite original. The room in which he lies may be described "somewhat in this way—

"'The window, patched with paper, lent a ray
"That feebly showed the state in which he lay;
"The sanded floor that grits beneath the tread,
"The humid wall with paltry pictures spread;
"The game of goose was there exposed to view,
"And the twelve rules the royal martyr drew;
"The Seasons, framed with listing, found a place,
"And Prussia's monarch showed his lamp-black face.
"The morn was cold; he views with keen desire
"A rusty grate unconscious of a fire;
"An unpaid reckoning on the frieze was scored,
"And five cracked teacups dressed the chimney-board.'"

This last letter was written in February 1759, and within a month or two after that date things took a turn for the better with Goldsmith. His writings, hitherto, had been but anonymous hackwork in the *Monthly Review*, the *Literary Magazine*, and the *Critical Review*, with two translations from the French, both for Griffiths—one a novel; the other entitled "Memoirs of a Protestant condemned to the Galleys of France for his Religion," published in two volumes in February 1758, under the borrowed name of James Willington. But one consequence of his quarrel with Griffiths had been an engagement to pay off his unsettled score with that bookseller for the suit of clothes, and earn something besides, by writing *A Life of Voltaire*, to be published along with a new translation of the Henriade. The life and the translation were advertised by Griffiths in February 1759, as then about to appear; and, though this intention was not carried into effect, and both remained to be published in another form, the Life was probably ready by March, if not earlier. But, better still, Goldsmith had for some time been engaged on a little treatise of his own designing, which he intended to be his first avowed publication, and on which, accordingly, he was bestowing pains. The batch of letters to his Irish friends and relatives from which we have quoted had been in great part occasioned by his desire to announce to them this forthcoming performance, and to obtain through them Irish subscribers for English copies in advance, so as to prevent the Dublin booksellers from reprinting it and thus depriving him of the benefits of an Irish sale. Little or nothing seems to have been done in the desired way by his Irish friends when, in April 1759, the book was published in London by the Dodsleys, in a respectable duodecimo, and with the title "*An Inquiry into the Present State of Polite Learning in Europe.*" It is the first publication of Goldsmith's in which one need now look for anything of his real mind, and is still well worth reading. Though his name did not appear on the title-page, he had no wish to conceal the authorship, but quite the contrary; and, as the notices of it that immediately or soon appeared were on the whole very favourable (with the exception of one in Griffiths's *Monthly Review*, written by Kenrick, his successor as the hack for that periodical, and full of personal scurrility), the publication attracted attention to Goldsmith and won him some reputation even in the crowded London market of letters. From that date his connexion with Hamilton, the publisher of the *Critical Review*, and with Smollett, its editor, became closer, and his services as a contributor more in demand with them; and towards the end of the year 1759 there appears even to have been some competition by knowing ones in "the trade" for the use of the light and easy pen which Griffiths had not sufficiently valued. Thus, when in October 1759, the bookseller Wilkie started *The Bee*, a weekly periodical of essays, dramatic criticisms, &c., price 3*d.*, and also a new magazine called *The Lady's Magazine*, nominally intended chiefly for lady-readers, who but Goldsmith was the chief essayist and critic in the one, and the principal writer in the other? Not the less for this association with Wilkie in these two periodicals was he a contributor to a third periodical, *The Busy Body*, started at the same time by another bookseller, Pottinger, and published thrice a week. To be sure, both *The Bee* and *The Busy Body* were short-lived—the one reaching but its eighth number, and the other its twelfth. But Goldsmith's papers in them were noted at the time, and those in *The Bee* were in such demand afterwards that they had to be reprinted; and, after both periodicals had ceased, there were still the *Critical Review* and the *Lady's Magazine* to write for.

Acquaintances, too, were multiplying round Goldsmith. Even in his worst distress the sociable creature had made himself at home with his landlord's family; his flute, and sweetmeats, when he had them, were at the service of the children of Green Arbour Court, some of whom grew up to remember him and tell anecdotes of him; and we hear of one person, an ingenious watchmaker of the neighbourhood, who used to spend evenings with him. Then, according to Thackeray's observation that there never was an Irishman so low in circumstances but there was some other Irishman lower still and looking up to him and going errands for him, there were several fellow-countrymen of Goldsmith clinging to him, to be helped by him when he could hardly help himself—especially a certain Ned Purdon, who had been his schoolfellow. At the Temple Coffee House, also, there were opportunities for something like general society. But in the course of 1759 we have more distinct traces of Goldsmith's contact with known men in London. It was in March in that year, just before the publication of Goldsmith's *Inquiry into the State of Polite Learning*, that the Rev. Mr. Percy, afterwards Bishop Percy of the Ballads, paid that first memorable visit to him in Green Arbour Court, the queer incidents of which he used afterwards to describe. From that day Percy and Goldsmith were friends for life. Garrick's first encounter with Goldsmith was several months later, and much less pleasant. The secretaryship of the Society of Arts being vacant,

Goldsmith was anxious to obtain the post, and waited on the great actor to solicit his vote and interest. Garrick, it is said, reminded him of a passage in his *Polite Learning*, and asked how he could expect his support after that. It was a passage in which, while discussing the prospects of the drama, Goldsmith had expressed rather sharply the common complaint then made against theatre-managers, that they neglected contemporary talent and lived on old stock-plays which cost them nothing. "Indeed," said Goldy bluntly, "I spoke my mind, and believe I said what was very right." And so they parted civilly, and it was long before Garrick and Goldsmith came really together. Quite otherwise it was between Goldsmith and Smollett. It is pleasant to think of these two, perhaps the most strongly contrasted humorists and men of genius of their day—the simple, gentle-hearted, sweet-styled Irishman, and the bold, splenetically-independent, irascible, richly-inventive, rough-writing, but sombre and melancholic Scotchman—to think of these two as knit together by some mutual regard, when Smollett was already in the full bustle of his fame and industry, and Goldy was struggling and needed employment. During the whole of 1759, as we have seen, they had been, to some extent, fellow-workmen. And in the end of that year there was a visit of Smollett, along with the bookseller Newbery of St. Paul's Churchyard, to Goldsmith's lodgings in Green Arbour Court, which led to important results.

Though London already swarmed with periodicals, the indefatigable Smollett, then recently released from his three months' imprisonment for libel, had projected a new sixpenny monthly, to be called *The British Magazine;* and Newbery, besides having an interest in this magazine, had resolved on the larger attempt of a daily newspaper, price 2½*d.*, to be called *The Public Ledger*. It was to secure Goldsmith's services in both these undertakings that they had called upon him. Accordingly, from the first appearance of the *British Magazine*, on the 1st of January, 1760, with a fervid dedication to Pitt, and the unusual distinction of a royal licence to Dr. Smollett as its editor, Goldsmith was a regular contributor to its pages – his essays and criticisms forming perhaps the chief attraction of the magazine after Smollett's novel of "Sir Lancelot Greaves," which appeared there in successive instalments till its conclusion in December 1761. Goldsmith's contributions to this magazine extended even into 1762, and included at least twenty separate essays, of which some were in his most charming style. But it was in the *Public Ledger* that he made his great hit. He had been engaged by Newbery to furnish for this newspaper an article of some amusing kind twice a week, to be paid for at the rate of a guinea per article. He had already written one or two articles to suit, when the idea struck him of bringing on the scene an imaginary philosophic Chinaman, resident in London after long wanderings from home, and of making the adventures of this Chinaman, and his observations of men and things in the Western world, as recorded in letters supposed to be written by him to friends in China, together with the replies of these friends, the material for a series of papers which should consist of character-sketches, social satire, and whimsical reflection on all sorts of subjects, connected by a slight thread of story. He had always had a fancy for China and the Chinese, and an anticipation of this idea will be found in one of his letters from which we have already quoted. The first of Goldsmith's "Chinese Letters," as they came soon to be called, appeared in the *Ledger* on the 24th of Jan. 1760, with no intimation that there was to be a series of them; the second appeared on the 29th; the third on the 31st; and from that date so eagerly were they expected, and so much did they contribute to the sale of the *Ledger*, that Newbery gave them the most conspicuous place in the paper. Ninety-eight letters in all appeared in the course of 1760; and these, completed by subsequent stragglers in the *Ledger*, and by the incorporation of other papers in the same vein published elsewhere, formed eventually that delightful, if somewhat too lengthy, *Citizen of the World*, whose place among our English classics is now sure after more than a hundred years. It was while all London was reading the "Chinese Letters" and becoming fond of the philosophic Chinaman, and his friends, the Gentleman in Black, Beau Tibbs, and the rest, that George II. died, and his grandson, George III., began his reign. The glorious ministry of Pitt was brought to an abrupt end soon after, and the favourite Bute came into power, drawing Scotchmen in his train, and rousing the unanimous execration of all England against everything that was or could be called Scottish.

A change probably as important to Goldsmith personally as the change of king and of ministry was his removal, towards the end of 1760, from Green Arbour Court to superior lodgings in Wine Office Court, Fleet Street. Here, through the rest of 1760 and through 1761 and 1762, his work for the *Public Ledger* and the *British Magazine* continued to be a considerable part of his occupation. Not the whole, however. He had not quitted his hold of the *Lady's Magazine;* of which periodical, indeed, he appears to have become virtual editor some time in 1760. Among his contributions to it in 1761 were successively-published portions of that *Life of Voltaire* which he had written for Griffiths two years before, but which had, for some reason or other, remained in manuscript. But, naturally, it was for Newbery that Goldsmith's literary services were now chiefly reserved. This worthy publisher, whose red face, bustling benevolence, and zeal in getting up nice children's books, Goldsmith has celebrated in a well-known passage, did not confine himself merely to children's books and periodicals, but had a flourishing general business besides. He had been for many a year paymaster and advancer of loans to needy men of the literary tribe, including his own son-in-law Christopher Smart, and also Johnson. He was not the man to let Goldsmith, who had done such a stroke of work for him in the *Ledger*, rust for want of employment. He seems, indeed, to have taken Goldy under a kind of charge, partly for Goldy's benefit, and partly with a view to his own profit. The very lodging in Wine Office Court to which Goldy had removed was in a house the tenant of which was a relative of Newbery's. Here Newbery could have him at command, not only for the *Ledger*, but for all kinds of miscellaneous work—compilations, pamphlets on this and that, revisions of other people's books, prefaces to such, abridgments of such books as Plutarch's Lives, conclusions of historical manuals left unfinished, translations from the French, and even occasional moral articles for the *Christian's Magazine*, then edited for Newbery, for circulation among the religious, by poor, unhanged Dr. Dodd. The amount of such work done for Newbery by Goldsmith between 1760 and 1763, and traceable still in cash-accounts between them, is very large; and much remains untraceable. On the whole, though it was dreadful task-work, Goldy found it worth while, in respect of the money it brought him. His receipts at this time, and chiefly from Newbery, may be calculated at what would be equivalent now to about 250*l.* or 300*l.* a year; and, though he was generally on the debtor side in Newbery's books, for work paid for in part beforehand, there is yet evidence that the Goldsmith of Wine Office Court was, socially, in a different plight from the Goldsmith of Green Arbour Square. Not only does he frequent the theatres and taverns, attend meetings of the Society of Arts, and drop in on Monday evenings at the famous Robin Hood Debating Society in Butcher Row, where, under the presidency of "the eloquent baker" Caleb Jeacocke, young lawyers and fledgling wits discussed religion and politics; he even "receives" in his own lodging, is sponged upon there for guineas and half-guineas by rascals that know his good nature, and sometimes gives literary suppers. One such supper, given by him in Wine Office Court, is memorable. It was on the 31st of May, 1761. Whether Johnson had met Goldsmith before is uncertain; most probably he had, for the author of the *Inquiry into Polite Learning* and the *Chinese Letters* can hardly have remained a stranger to him; but this, at all events, was their first meeting not merely casual. Johnson had accepted Goldsmith's invitation to meet a largish party of friends, and Percy was to accompany him. As the two were walking to Wine Office Court, Percy observed, to his surprise, that Johnson had on "a new suit of clothes," with "a new wig nicely powdered," and everything in style to match. Struck with such a variation from Johnson's usual habits, he ventured a remark on the subject. "Why, sir," said Johnson in reply, "I hear that Goldsmith, who is a very great sloven, justifies his disregard of cleanliness and decency by quoting my practice, and I am desirous this night to show him a better example." And so the two went to Goldy's rooms, and the door was shut behind them and the others; and there was, no doubt, much noise and splendid talk far into the night; but it has not been reported, for there was no Boswell there. But from that day began the immortal intimacy of the gentle Goldsmith with the great Johnson, and all that peculiar radiance over the London of the eighteenth century which we still trace to the conjunction of their figures in its antique streets. Of only three of his contemporaries in the English world of letters had Goldsmith written with admiration approaching to enthusiasm—Smollett, the poet Gray, and Johnson. A recluse at Cambridge, Gray was inaccessible. With Smollett an acquaintance had already been established; but the resident London life of the overworked and melancholic novelist was nearly over, and he was about to be a wanderer thenceforth in search of health. But at last Goldsmith had happened on that most massive and central of the three, towards whom in any case all intellectual London consciously or unconsciously gravitated. Johnson was then in his fifty-second year, living in chambers in Inner Temple Lane—not yet "Dr.," and not yet pensioned, though on the point of being so; but already with much of his greatest work done, and firm in his literary dictatorship. Goldsmith was nineteen years younger, and with the best of his work before him.

The convenient bondage of Goldsmith to the bookseller Newbery continued till the end of 1764, or even beyond that. In May 1762 Newbery published the *Citizen of the World* in its completed form, giving Goldsmith five guineas for the new copyright. Somewhat later in the same year Goldsmith, whose health had suffered from his recent laboriousness, went to Tunbridge and Bath for recreation; and from Bath he brought back to London materials for a memoir of Beau Nash, the famous master of the ceremonies or King of the Fashion at Bath, then just dead. This curious and rather amusing little book, for which Newbery gave him fourteen guineas, was published in October 1762, under the title of *The Life of Richard Nash, Esq.* It was immediately popular; Johnson, who was by no means a book-buyer, is found purchasing a copy; and there was a second edition in December. By this time Goldsmith had made a new arrangement in the matter of domicile, or Newbery had made a new arrangement for him. The lodging in Wine Office Court was either given up or retained for occasional use only, and apartments were taken in the suburban neighbourhood of Canonbury, Islington, in the house of a Mrs. Elizabeth Fleming, close to Canonbury House, where Newbery himself resided. The terms with Mrs. Fleming were to be 50*l.* a year for Goldsmith's board and lodging—equivalent to about 100*l.* a year now; and Newbery undertook to make the regular quarterly payments, deducting them from whatever might be Goldsmith's earnings. Thus saved all trouble on the main point, and with only his incidental expenses to care for—which, however, were considerable enough, for a guinea could never remain a day whole in his pocket, and he had begun to have a gaudy taste in dress, and to have extensive dealings with Mr. Filby, the tailor, at the Harrow in Water Lane—Goldsmith went on compiling for Newbery, touching up books for him, writing prefaces where they were wanted, and furnishing papers for his magazines. For each bit of work so done Goldsmith was credited for so much in Newbery's books—one guinea, two guineas, three guineas, or higher sums, according to the extent of the work; and Goldsmith drew, or overdrew, for what he wanted as he went along, leaving the bookseller to look at the state of affairs every quarter when he came to pay Mrs. Fleming her 12*l.* 10*s.*, together with any little extras for wine, sassafras, cakes, &c., incurred with her by Goldsmith. That lady, to do her justice, kept most punctual accounts, and does not seem to have been at all exacting in the extras; for, when Goldsmith brought a friend home to dinner and tea, especially if it was the Irish physician Dr. Redmond, her practice was to charge nothing on that account, but only to make such an entry as this in the bill—"Dr. Reman's dinner and tea, 0*l.* 0*s.* 0*d.*" There is some reason to believe that among the friends who sometimes visited Goldsmith in his Islington lodgings, but are not recorded to have had gratis dinners from Mrs. Fleming, was the painter Hogarth, then in the last years of his life. Altogether, in these lodgings Goldsmith seems to have been tolerably comfortable and tolerably industrious through 1763 and 1764.

Among the fruits of his industry, in addition to a great deal of miscellaneous work which need not be inquired after particularly (though, if *Goody Two Shoes* were really his, one would like to know it), was a *History of England in a series of Letters from a Nobleman to his Son.* This work, which must not be confounded with a subsequent History of England from his pen, was published by Newbery in two pocket volumes in June 1764. The title was a *ruse* to attract attention to the book, and it succeeded. It was attributed to Lord Chesterfield or Lord Orrery, and then very generally to Lord Lyttelton, and became very popular. Goldsmith, having received 21*l.*, which remained as the balance due to him for the work, did not wish to undeceive the public. He had, indeed, by him, finished or nearly finished, certain things of his own, not written to Newbery's order, but for private pleasure, and for which he cared more than for any compilation. But of these presently.

Islington, though more out of the bustle of central London then than it is now, was not so far off but that a walk every other day would bring Goldsmith into Fleet Street and its purlieus. And more and more now there were attractions for Goldsmith tn that cosy heart of London. His acquaintance with Johnson had led to his introduction to Mr. (not yet Sir Joshua) Reynolds, then forty years of age, living in his mansion in Leicester Square, and hospitable, with his kind serenity of disposition and his 6,000*l.* a year of income, to the largest circle of attached friends that any man ever drew around him. At those *noctes cœnæque Deûm* at Reynolds's in Leicester Square, long afterwards remembered with such relish by Boswell, Goldsmith was certainly welcome even thus early. Here he would meet Burke, who barely remembered him at Trinity College, Dublin; and sometimes he and Johnson, leaving Reynolds's, and parting with Burke at the door, would go down the Strand to Johnson's chambers in Inner Temple Lane, or perhaps (for Johnson hated early hours) drop in, for more talk, at the Mitre Tavern in Fleet Street. Just at this time, too, Boswell's visage does begin to be seen on the skirts of the group of which he was to be so singularly intimate a member, and whose history he was to write for the whole world. He had been up to London for the first time in 1760, a mere lad of twenty years, but already a devoted worshipper of Johnson, and possessed with a passion for being introduced to him. He had failed in that object then; but in the end of 1762 he was again in London on his way to Utrecht to study law. Two chapters in his "Life of Johnson"—two as interesting chapters of anecdote as ever man wrote—preserve the particulars of that visit, which extended over more than six months, or to August 1763. Early in the visit, it appears, he met Goldsmith at dinner at the house of Thomas Davies, the ex-actor and bookseller, in Russell Street, Covent Garden—whose shop was perhaps then the most noted afternoon rendezvous in London for poets, wits, dramatists, and literary gossips. Improving this meeting, he had even, he tells us, become "pretty well acquainted" with Goldsmith before he made that greater acquaintanceship for which his soul panted. What mattered it to know Goldsmith, with Wilkes, Churchill, Lloyd, Robert Dodsley, and others—to all of whom the eager young fellow had somehow pushed his way—so long as Johnson was unknown? At last the momentous day came—Monday the 16th May, 1763. Boswell was sitting with Mr. and Mrs. Davies in the back-parlour behind their shop, where indeed he seems to have been for some time on the watch for the apparition that now presented itself. It was Johnson at last, rolling into the shop, as large as life, to have a talk with Davies. "Mr. Davies," says Boswell, "mentioned my name "and respectfully introduced me to him. I was much agitated; and, recollecting "his prejudice against the Scotch, of which I had heard much, I said to Davies, "'Don't tell him where I come from.' 'From Scotland,' cried Davies, roguishly. "'Mr. Johnson,' said I, 'I do indeed come from Scotland, but I cannot help it.' "'That, Sir, I find, is what a very great many of your countrymen cannot help.' "This stroke stunned me a good deal; and, when we sat down, I felt myself "not a little embarrassed, and apprehensive of what might come next. He then "addressed himself to Davies, 'What do you think of Garrick? He has refused "me an order for the play for Miss Williams, because he knows that the house "will be full, and that an order will be worth three shillings.' Eager to take "any opening to get into conversation with him, I ventured to say, 'O Sir, I "cannot think Mr. Garrick would grudge such a trifle to you.' 'Sir,' said he "with a stern look, 'I have known David Garrick longer than you have done, "and I know no right you have to talk to me on the subject.'" Here was a knock-down for the young enthusiast—only two-and-twenty years of age, it is to be remembered in his favour. But one of the best things ever said of Boswell was what Goldsmith said of him not long afterwards. Some one had called him a "Scotch cur." "No, no," replied Goldsmith, "you are too severe; he is only a Scotch *bur*. Tom Davies threw him at Johnson in sport, and he has the faculty of *sticking*." He showed this faculty by the way in which he took Johnson's first rebuff. Much as it discomposed him, it did not prevent him from calling on Johnson a week afterwards; he called again on the 13th of June, and was delighted to hear Johnson ask why he had not returned sooner; and, in fact, within a week or two from that time the queer Scotch lad had wound himself into Johnson's affections in a way that surprised everybody. Sixteen different meetings and conversations with Johnson, besides those already mentioned, are duly chronicled by Boswell as having made him happy during the six or seven weeks longer he remained in town—some in Johnson's chambers, some in Boswell's, some at supper at the Mitre or another tavern, and one, which lasted a whole day, at Greenwich down the river. At most of these meetings Boswell kept Johnson all to himself; but on the 1st of July Goldsmith was with them at the Mitre; and on the 6th, when Boswell gave Johnson a formal supper at the Mitre, Goldsmith was again there, with two other guests. Something like a jealousy of Goldsmith, indeed, on account of his established intimacy with Johnson, and Johnson's professed regard for him, seems to have mingled with the pleasure of Bozzy's first revel of six weeks in Johnson's society. It is exactly at this point of his "Life of Johnson," at all events, that he introduces his general sketch of Goldsmith with a view to his frequent appearances thereafter in the narrative; and in the depreciating tone of this sketch, with its often-quoted statements as to Goldsmith's vanity and his ridiculous ways of showing it, we have the anticipation of all that Boswell would let himself feel or think about Goldsmith to the very end. With Boswell, Goldsmith was but the foil to Johnson. And yet—for, though jealous, Bozzy could not but be honest—there are passages, even in this first sketch he gives of Goldsmith, which make amends. He tells us what Johnson said to him of Goldsmith when his name was first mentioned between them. "Dr. Goldsmith," said Johnson, "is one of the first men we now have as an author, and he is a very worthy man too"—praise which, as Goldsmith was then known only or chiefly by his *Inquiry into the State of Polite Learning* and his *Citizen of the World*, seemed rather over the mark to the hearer. Again he informs us how "Goldsmith's respectful attachment to Johnson" equally struck him, and how Goldsmith's incidental remarks about Johnson increased his admiration of Johnson's goodness of heart. For example, when some reference was made to Mr. Levett, whom Johnson maintained as a pensioner under his own roof, Goldsmith said to Boswell, "He is poor and honest, which is recommendation enough to Johnson;" and again, when Boswell referred to some man of known bad character with surprise that Johnson should be kind to such a person, "He is now become miserable," said Goldsmith, "and that ensures the protection of Johnson." On the whole, the relations between Johnson and Goldsmith were so cordial that Boswell must have thought with a pang how much they would be together, and what talk of Johnson's Goldsmith would hear, when *he* should be in London no longer to partake of such happiness, but away in Utrecht, studying law. If anything could have reconciled him to the coming absence, it was the extraordinary proof given, before he went, how thoroughly he, an unknown Scotch lad, whom Johnson had never seen till he met him in Davis's shop, had won the big man's heart. To have heard Johnson say to him, "There are few people whom I take so much to as you," was much; but to hear him farther say, as the day for his departure approached, "I must see thee out of England; I will accompany you to Harwich," was sheer ecstasy. And actually to Harwich Johnson, while all London wondered, did accompany the young cub, giving him good advices all the way, and at last seeing him off. "My revered friend," says Boswell, "walked down with me to "the beach, where we embraced and parted with tenderness, and engaged to "correspond by letters. I said 'I hope, Sir, you will not forget me in my "absence.' 'Nay, Sir, it is more likely you should forget me than that I should "forget you.' As the vessel put out to sea, I kept my eyes upon him for a "considerable time, while he remained rolling his majestic frame in his usual "manner; and at last I perceived him walk back into the town, and he "disappeared."

An event of real importance in the Johnsonian world, which happened shortly after Johnson's return from seeing Boswell off at Harwich, and the rumour of which, if it reached Utrecht, must have greatly interested Boswell, was the foundation of the famous club, unnamed at first, but afterwards called "The Literary Club," which met at the Turk's Head, in Gerrard Street, Soho. The original members of this club were Johnson, Reynolds, Burke, Goldsmith, Topham Beauclerk, Bennet Langton, Sir John Hawkins, and Dr. Nugent—to whom were soon added Mr. Chamier, Mr. Dyer, and others. They met one evening a week—Monday evening at first, but it was changed to Friday evening—for supper and talk. The club may have been founded in 1763, but it was certainly in full operation in 1764. From that date, accordingly, Goldsmith's attendances at its meetings, and his enjoyment of what passed there, have to be remembered in our imaginations of the routine of his life. It appears even that, for the convenience of these attendances, or for other reasons, Goldsmith, early in 1764, had a share of some rough chambers in the Temple, "on the library staircase," in addition to his Islington lodging. Possibly, this was by way of removal from the rooms in Wine Office Court, hitherto retained for sleeping purposes when he was in town.

It was either at some now unknown lodging in town, occupied for some little time, or, more probably, at the Islington apartments in Mrs. Fleming's house, that there occurred, late in 1764, an incident in Goldsmith's life, of which very varying versions have been given, but of which the true account is indubitably Dr. Johnson's. "I "received one morning," Johnson long afterwards told Boswell, "a message from "poor Goldsmith that he was in great distress, and, as it was not in his power to "come to me, begging that I would come to him as soon as possible. I sent him a "guinea, and promised to come to him directly. I accordingly went as soon as I "was dressed, and found that his landlady had arrested him for his rent, at which he "was in a violent passion. I perceived that he had already changed my guinea, and "had got a bottle of Madeira and a glass before him. I put the cork into the "bottle, desired he would be calm, and began to talk to him of the means by "which he might be extricated. He then told me that he had a novel ready for "the press, which he produced to me. I looked into it, and saw its merit; told the "landlady I should soon return; and, having gone to a bookseller, sold it for 60*l.* "I brought Goldsmith the money, and he discharged his rent, not without rating his "landlady in a high tone for having used him so ill." If, as appears all but certain, it was to Islington that Johnson had trudged, and the harsh landlady was Mrs. Fleming, the explânation probably is that, owing to some break-down between Goldsmith and Newbery, Mrs. Fleming saw no chance of getting her last quarter's rent and board paid her in the usual manner. What renders this likelier is that Newbery's advances to Goldsmith are found about this date dwindling to very small sums, and that, as if Newbery were proving a broken reed, Goldsmith had recently been negotiating, or proposing to negotiate, with other booksellers, such as Dodsley, Tonson, and Griffin. It was, possibly, for this last bookseller, whose shop was the Garrick's Head in Catherine Street, Strand, and who speculated in music, that the libretto for an intended *Oratorio*, on the subject of the Captivity in Babylon, was originally written by Goldsmith early in 1764, although afterwards it was sold by him to Dodsley and Newbery conjointly. But what most confirms the conjecture of some coolness between Goldsmith and Newbery at the time in question is that the bookseller to whom Johnson carried the manuscript was not Newbery himself—who, if all had been right between him and Goldsmith, would naturally have been first applied to—but his nephew, Francis Newbery, of Paternoster Row. In giving 60*l.* for it this younger bookseller must have been influenced as much by Johnson's recommendations as by any notion he could have had for himself of the worth of what he had bought. For, though it was the manuscript of the *Vicar of Wakefield*, it was thrown aside as soon as purchased, to wait young Mr. Newbery's convenience. For the present, therefore, all the satisfaction Goldsmith derived from the exquisite little tale which for a year or two he had been quietly and carefully writing at intervals, by way of relief from his compilations and task-work, was the immediate 60*l.* brought him by Johnson. Fortunately, however, he had another thing by him, similarly written for his own pleasure, and according to his own best ideas of literary art. This was his poem of the *Traveller*, the idea of which had occurred to him nine years before during his own continental wanderings, and some fragments of which he had then written and sent home from Switzerland to his brother Henry. On this poem, as well as on the *Vicar of Wakefield*, he had been for some time engaged in his Islington lodgings, writing it slowly, and bringing it to the last degree of finish, but so diffident of its success as to say nothing about it to his friends. Reynolds, indeed, once visiting him, found him bending over something at his desk, and at the same time holding up his finger in rebuke every now and then to a little dog he was teaching to sit on its haunches in a corner of the room; and, on looking over his shoulder at the manuscript, he could see that it was a poem and was able to read and remember one couplet. At length, probably at the very time of Johnson's visit of rescue, Goldsmith took Johnson into his confidence in the matter of the poem too. It was highly approved by that judge, who even added a line or two of his own; the elder Newbery, who may already have been spoken to about it, did not mind promising twenty guineas for it; and on the 19th of December, 1764, it was published, price one shilling and sixpence, with this title, "*The Traveller; or a Prospect of Society: A Poem. By Oliver Goldsmith, M.B.*" It was the first publication of Goldsmith's that bore his name, and it was dedicated, in terms of beautiful affection, to his brother, the Rev. Henry Goldsmith.

The publication of the *Traveller* was an epoch in Goldsmith's life. Now, at last, at the age of six-and-thirty, he stood forth, not as an essayist, compiler, and miscellaneous prose-humorist, half-hidden by a habit of the anonymous, but avowedly as a candidate for those higher and finer honours that belong to the name of English Poet. The time was unusually favourable. Poor as Britain had been, during the whole of the preceding portion of the eighteenth century, in poetry, as it had once been understood and as it came to be understood again—with Pope as its all-ruling tradition in the world of verse, and only Thomson and one or two more recollected as powers of variation—there was perhaps no point in the century when the British Muse, such as she had come to be, was doing less, or had so nearly ceased to do anything, or to have any good opinion of herself, as precisely about the year 1764. Young was dying; Gray was recluse and indolent; Johnson had long given over his metrical experimentations on any except the most inconsiderable scale; Akenside, Armstrong, Smollett, and others less known, had pretty well revealed the amount of their worth in poetry; and Churchill, after his ferocious blaze of what was really rage and declamation in metre, though conventionally it was called poetry, was prematurely dead and defunct. Into this lull came Goldsmith's short, but carefully-finished, poem. It was no innovation in apparent form, for the verse was that heroic rhymed couplet which the eighteenth century had adopted as the one and only true form, save for such lesser themes as would run into stanzas or gurgle into the mechanical paroxysms that were called Pindarics. But Goldsmith, as the dedication to his brother shows, really meant the poem as something new in spirit and in style—a return to simplicity and truth of feeling, and, above all, a protest against Churchill, and the wretched reduction of poetry, as in his case, to the one principle, "*indignatio facit versus.*" And the public was wonderfully ready for such an appeal to its finer literary instincts, and welcomed Goldsmith's poem beyond his utmost expectations. It was widely and highly praised in the Reviews, the general verdict being that there had been nothing so fine in verse since the time of Pope; even poems were published in commendation of it; and the author's high-mindedness in dedicating it to his brother, a poor Irish parson, rather than to any noble or wealthy patron, did not escape notice. A second edition was called for in March 1765, and a third in the following August; and, before Goldsmith died, he was to revise it again and again, with slight corrections throughout, till it reached its ninth edition. Of course, by all this Goldsmith benefited socially. The author of the *Traveller* was not a man to be thought of or looked at with indifference. People who had known him before, but to whom he had been little more than a laughing-stock, began to see what it was in him that deeper observers, like Johnson and Burke, had all along recognised. "I shall never more think Mr. Goldsmith ugly," said Miss Reynolds, Joshua's sister, after Johnson had read the poem aloud in her hearing from beginning to end. But even the deeper observers themselves were roused to a higher opinion of Goldy's genius. When Reynolds afterwards hinted to Johnson that perhaps the warm reception of the poem was due to the partiality of Goldsmith's friends, "Nay, Sir," said Johnson candidly, in a reply which reflected even on himself, "the partiality of his friends was always against him: it was with difficulty we could give him a hearing." Johnson's own opinion of Goldy from this time forward was that he was distinctly one of the chiefs of British Literature.

While the *Traveller* was passing through the press, Goldsmith had written his pretty ballad of "Edwin and Angelina," afterwards introduced into the *Vicar of Wakefield*, under its present title of "The Hermit." This little composition was occasioned by his interest in the collection of ballads and other old English poems which his friend, the Rev. Thomas Percy, was then busy with, and which was published in 1765 under its ever famous name of *The Reliques.* Goldsmith had shown his ballad to Percy, who was then chaplain to the Earl, afterwards Duke, of Northumberland; and the Countess of Northumberland had taken such a fancy to it as to have copies privately printed for herself and her friends. It was expected that something advantageous to Goldy might arise from this introduction to the Northumberland family—especially as the Earl was Lord Lieutenant of Ireland, had all sorts of offices on the Irish establishment at his disposal, and might easily, with public approval, have given some sinecure to one who was not only a popular author, but an Irishman to boot. Goldsmith did have an interview with the Earl at Northumberland House, received compliments from him on his *Traveller*, and was informed that the Earl had heard he was a native of Ireland, and would be glad to do him any kindness. Instead of improving the occasion for himself, "this idiot in the affairs of the world," as Sir John Hawkins calls him, only told the Earl he had a brother in Ireland, a poor clergyman, who stood in much need of help. "As for myself," he said afterwards in telling the story to Sir John, "I have no dependence on the promises of great men: I look to the booksellers for support." This was no mere affectation on Goldy's part; it was really true. With the exception of Mr. Robert Nugent, afterwards Lord Nugent, Viscount Clare and Earl Nugent—a jovial, elderly Irishman, of great wealth, and free-and-easy politics, who admired Goldsmith, and was always glad to see him at his seat at Gosfield Hall, Essex—Goldsmith never cared to trouble any of the "great people" with his intimacy. And the utmost that came to him from this friendship, besides a week of country air now and then, was the appearance, once or twice, of a haunch of venison in his chambers in town. For, of course, Goldsmith was now done with Islington and Mrs. Fleming. The Temple, now and thenceforth, was his established place of residence. He had had rough temporary accommodation here, as we have seen, "on the library staircase," in 1764; and this he is found exchanging, in or about 1765, for superior chambers in the same court—*i.e.*, Garden Court. These he retained till 1768.

In June 1765 Goldsmith, to take advantage of his new popularity, published, with hisname, and under the title of *Essays*, and with the motto "Collecta Revirescunt," a selection from his anonymous papers in the *Bee*, the *Busy-Body*, the *Lady's Magazine*, the *British Magazine*, &c. Other people, he says in the preface, had been reprinting these trifles of his, and living on the pillage, and now he reclaimed the best of them. The republication was in one duodecimo volume, for which Newbery and Griffin, who were the joint-publishers, gave him ten guineas each. Then, again, through the rest of that year and the whole of 1766 and 1767,—his *Traveller* having brought him more applause than cash—he relapses, for cash-purposes, into hackwork, compilation, and translation. He thought of translating the Lusiad, but, his ignorance of Portuguese being a slight obstacle, left that undertaking for Mickle. Among the compilations which he did execute we hear of such things as *A Survey of Experimental Philosophy* and a *Short English Grammar* for Newbery, a translation of a French *History of Philosophy* (Physical Speculations) for Francis Newbery, a collection of *Poems for Young Ladies* for Payne of Paternoster Row, and another poetical collection in two volumes for Griffin called *Beauties of English Poetry*. For this last, to which he gave his name, he received a considerable sum; but the sale of the collection, which was otherwise a tasteful one, is said to have suffered from the admission into it of two pieces of Prior not deemed fit for family reading. And what, all this while, had become of the *Vicar of Wakefield?* It emerged from the younger Newbery's shop in the very midst of the compilations just named—viz. on the 27th of March, 1766, or fifteen months after the *Traveller* had been out. *The Vicar of Wakefield: A Tale; supposed to be written by himself*—such was the title under which the little prose masterpiece announced itself. With less of acclamation than had hailed the *Traveller*, but gently, quietly, and surely, as it was read in households, and its charming sweetness felt wherever it was read, the Tale made its way. There was a second edition in May, a third in August, and before Goldsmith died the sixth edition was in circulation.

As, by his *Traveller*, Goldsmith had taken his place among English poets, so by the *Vicar of Wakefield* he took a place, if not as one of the remarkable group of English "novelists" that distinguished the middle of the eighteenth century (for *they* had all been voluminous in this department), at least, with peculiar conspicuousness, near that group. Richardson had been five years dead; Fielding twelve years; only Smollett of the old three remained, with his *Humphry Clinker* still to be written. But Sterne, the fourth of the group, had recently flashed into notice—eight volumes of his *Tristram Shandy*, published between 1759 and 1765, having taken the literary world by storm, and made their strange author, then a middle-aged clergyman of loose notions, the lion of London society for the time being, with dinner engagements always fourteen deep. Not the radiance of *Tristram Shandy* itself, however, diamond-darting in all colours athwart the literary heaven, could hide the pure soft star of Goldsmith's new creation. How simple this *Vicar of Wakefield* was, how humorous, how pathetic, how graceful in its manner, how humane in every pulse of its meaning, how truly and deeply good! So said everybody; and gradually into that world of imaginary scenes and beings made familiar to British readers by former works of fiction, and the latest additions to which had been Smollett's and Sterne's inventions, a place of especial regard was found for the ideal Wakefield, the Primrose family, and all their belongings. Moses, with the gross of green spectacles and shagreen cases for which he sold the horse; the philosophical wanderer George; the two daughters, Olivia and Sophia; the bouncing Flamborough girls; Miss Carolina Wilhelmina Amelia Skeggs, and the other fine lady from London; the rogue Jenkinson and his repentance; the rascally Squire; and the good uncle, Sir William, *alias* Burchell—who could forget any of them? Above all the good clergyman himself, with his punctilious honour, his boundless benevolence, and his one or two foibles! Who could help laughing over that passage in which he tells how the rogue Jenkinson, in proceeding to swindle him, assails his weak point by asking if he is the great Dr. Primrose who had written so learnedly in favour of monogamy and against second marriages? "Never did my heart feel sincerer rapture than at this moment. "'Sir,' cried I, 'the applause of so good a man as I am sure you are adds to "that happiness in my heart which your benevolence has already excited. You "behold before you, Sir, that Dr. Primrose, the monogamist, whom you have been "pleased to call great. You here see that unfortunate divine, who has so long, "and, it would ill become me to say successfully, fought against the deuterogamy "of the age.'" And the description of the family picture, executed by the travelling painter who took likenesses at fifteen shillings a head! Their neighbours, the Flamboroughs, had been painted, seven of them in all, each holding an orange; but the Primroses would not be painted that way. "We desired to have "something in a brighter style; and, after many debates, at length came to a "unanimous resolution of being drawn together, in one large historical family "piece. This would be cheaper, as one frame would serve for all, and it would "be infinitely more genteel; for all the families of any taste were now drawn in the "same manner. As we did not immediately recollect an historical subject to hit "us, we were contented each with being drawn as independent historical figures. "My wife desired to be represented as Venus, and the painter was desired not to be "too frugal of diamonds in her stomacher and hair. The two little ones were to "be as Cupids by her side; while I, in my gown and band, was to present her "with my books on the Whistonian controversy. Olivia would be drawn as an "Amazon sitting upon a bank of flowers, dressed in a green joseph richly laced "with gold, and a whip in her hand. Sophia was to be a shepherdess, with as "many sheep as the painter could put in for nothing; and Moses was to be dressed "out with a white hat and feather. Our taste so much pleased the Squire that he "insisted on being put in as one of the family, in the character of Alexander the "Great, at Olivia's feet." But there was no end to the passages that people quoted and continued to quote. Nay, not to Britain alone was the renown of the story confined. There had been French translations of one or two of Goldsmith's anonymous writings before; but the *Vicar of Wakefield* ran, almost at once, over the Continent. It was four years after its first publication when young Herder in Strasburg read a German translation of it to young Goethe. Every reader of Goethe's Autobiography knows what an impression the beautiful prose-idyll, as he called it, made on the heart and imagination of the glorious youth, and how he used its names and fancies to invest with a poetic haze the realities of his own early German loves. To the end of his days, and after he had long been the monarch of German literature, Goethe retained his affection for the book, and spoke of it as having been an influence of subtle spiritual blessing to him at an important moment of his mental history. Here was praise, indeed, could Goldsmith have heard of it! But Goethe was but twenty years of age when he first read the *Vicar of Wakefield*, and it is doubtful whether, when Goldsmith died, he knew that there was such a person as Goethe in the world!

On the strength of his increasing literary reputation, Goldsmith, even before the publication of his *Vicar*, had made one more attempt to get into practice as a London physician. He had been advised to this by Reynolds, who thought there were a good many families that might rather like to have the author of the *Traveller* for their medical man, and was anxious to see his friend in the receipt of a less precarious income than he received from the booksellers. It went so far that Goldsmith actually donned a splendid professional suit made for him by Filby—"purple silk small-clothes, a handsome scarlet roquelaure (*i.e.* short mantle) buttoned to his chin," with a full-dress wig, a sword, and a gold-headed cane. The top of this last he was to put to his mouth when meditative in the approved fashion at the bedsides of his patients. One hears, however, but of one patient of any consequence that he ever had. It was a Mrs. Sidebotham; and he did not keep *her* long. He had prescribed some dose for her, the terrific nature of which so stunned the apothecary that he refused to make it up; and, as the lady chose to trust the apothecary rather than the physician, Goldsmith went off in a huff, and vowed he would practise physic no more. Accordingly, though from this time the name of "Dr. Goldsmith" was more firmly attached to him than it had been, he fell back for the rest of his life on literature exclusively. A distinction between two kinds of his literary labours will have already amply presented itself in the course of our memoir so far; and this distinction has to be carried on in the reader's mind as applying even more conspicuously to what of his life remains. We have brought him to the year 1767, when he was thirty-eight years of age, spoken of with admiration as the author of the *Inquiry into the State of Polite Learning*, the *Citizen of the World*, the *Traveller*, a volume of *Essays*, and the *Vicar of Wakefield*, but known also to have written no end of compilations and done an immense amount of obscure hackwork for publishers. Well, he was to live seven years more; and during these seven years his life was still to distribute itself as before, and to exhibit a few finer occasional performances at the bidding of his own genius gleaming over a vast basis of sheer drudgery in compilation. "It is surely to be regretted," wrote one of his critics, "that the "author of the *Traveller*, one of the best poems that have appeared since those of "Mr. Pope, should not apply wholly to works of imagination." It was easy to say this, but how could it be helped? He found it impossible to live by poems and novels done as he would like to do them. By hackwork alone could he live; and, if he died of hackwork, you must blame the system?

One chance of escape there was, and Goldsmith had it shrewdly in view. The DRAMA was still a form of English literature in which one might follow the bent of one's genius, and yet hope for sufficient remuneration. If one could write a really successful play, and so establish a permanent connexion with the theatres! So had Goldsmith been thinking ever since the publication of the *Vicar;* and not merely thinking, for in the spring of 1767 he had finished the manuscript of his comedy, *The Good-Natured Man*, and, through Reynolds's introduction, had submitted it to Garrick, with a view to its production at Drury Lane. He had spent pains on the comedy, and had taken the liberty, in it also, of differing from the prevalent taste. The kind of comedy then in fashion was "Genteel Comedy" or "Sentimental Comedy," as it was called; and there was a special horror, on the part of theatre managers and critics, of what might be considered "low" or too broadly farcical. Goldsmith, prepossessed in favour of the older dramatists of the century, and especially of his countryman Farquhar, whom he justly reckoned the best of them all, had ventured on a return to the style of free and natural humour. Whether on this account, or for other reasons, Garrick did not like the play; and, after much hesitation on his part, and suspense on Goldsmith's, it was put into the hands of Colman, the Covent Garden manager. Neither was Colman in any hurry; and poor Goldsmith, while waiting for the result, had to betake himself for immediate supplies to his alternative of compiling. Not with his old employer, Newbery of St. Paul's Churchyard (who, indeed, died in 1767), but with Thomas Davies of Russell Street, he made an agreement to write a compendium of "Roman History," to be ready in two years, and for which he was to receive 250 guineas. And so, with a portion of this money advanced him, he lived through 1767, and at length, on the 29th of January, 1768, had the satisfaction of seeing his *Good-Natured Man* produced at Covent Garden. Satisfaction is too strong a word. Colman had had no great hopes of the piece; the actors, with one or two exceptions, were cool about it; through a great part of the performance the audience were little moved; at the famous scene of the bailiffs hisses were heard, and cries of "low," "low," from the partisans of Genteel Comedy in the pit; and not till the fourth act was the house fairly conquered into laughter and approbation. Goldsmith, who had been accompanied to the house by Johnson, Burke, and others of the Gerrard Street Club, had suffered dreadfully. It was the club night; and though, when all was over, he took the congratulations offered him, and went back to the club with his friends, and seemed in riotously high spirits, and sang his comic song of the "Old Woman tossed in a Blanket," it was only make-believe. "All the while," he said, telling the story afterwards at a dinner-table, "I "was suffering horrid tortures; and verily believe that, if I had put a bit into my "mouth, it would have strangled me on the spot, I was so excessively ill; but I made "more noise than usual to cover all that, and so they never perceived my not eating, "nor, I believe, at all imagined to themselves the anguish of my heart. But, when "all were gone except Johnson here, I burst out a-crying and even swore by —— that "I would never write again." "All which, Doctor," said Johnson, who had been listening with amazement to this frank public confession of Goldy, "I thought had "been a secret between you and me; and I am sure I would not have said anything "about it for the world." After all, however, the comedy might be called a success. With the offending scene of the bailiffs cut out, it ran a due number of nights; it brought Goldsmith between 300*l.* and 400*l.*; on its publication by Griffin, with the offending scene restored "in deference to the judgment of a few friends who think in a particular way," it had a considerable sale; and Johnson, who had stood by it manfully all through, and written the Prologue, pronounced it the best comedy that had appeared since the *Provoked Husband.*

All this time, of the writing of the *Good-Natured Man*, and the trouble in getting it brought out, Goldsmith had continued a tenant of his chambers in Garden Court, Temple, where latterly he had kept a man-servant. The success of his play, however, such as it was, induced him to a still farther promotion of himself in the matter of domicile and housekeeping. He purchased, for 400*l.*, the lease of new chambers in "No. 2, Brick Court, Middle Temple, up two pair of stairs," and furnished them in what was thought a decidedly luxurious style—"Wilton carpets," "mahogany sofas," "card-tables," "looking-glasses," &c. These chambers, consisting of three apartments, were to be his fixed London residence for the rest of his life. For neighbour, and occasional money-lender, on the same floor, he had a jolly barrister named Bott, also from the Green Island; and in the rooms underneath was the great lawyer Blackstone, dreadfully disturbed in the composition of his Commentaries, every other night, when Goldy had friends with him, by the singing and stamping and general hulla-baloo overhead. Two nights every week, however, were club-nights with Goldy, when he met company out of his own chambers. Monday evening for some time, as has been already mentioned, and then Friday evening, was the fixed evening of meeting with his more celebrated friends of the Gerrard Street Club. But for homelier jollity, and especially for the pleasures of song along with conviviality, he belonged, it appears, to another club, called the Wednesday's Club, which met at the Globe Tavern in Fleet Street. In addition to persons now unknown, this club numbered among its members Kelly the dramatist, King the comedian, Thompson the song-writer and editor of Andrew Marvel, an Irish medical man and ex-actor named Glover, and a certain William Ballantyne. Some manuscript memoranda by this last of the proceedings of the club, and of the songs sung in it, came into Mr. Forster's hands, and enabled him, in his *Life of Goldsmith*, to recover more of the history of the club and of Goldsmith's connexion with it than had been previously known.

From such a trial of the nerves as the comedy had been it was almost a relief to toil on at compilation. And here it will be as well to give an account at once of all of this sort that Goldsmith was occupied with during the last years of his life, including the undertaking that was largest of all and that hung like a millstone about his neck almost to the day of his death. Contributions to the *Gentleman's Journal*, started by Griffin in November 1768, and to a *Westminster Magazine*, begun in 1772, are hardly worth mentioning; a *Life of Parnell*, prefixed to an edition of Parnell's Works, published by Davies in 1770, was but by-play; and a *Life of Bolingbroke*, prefixed to a reprint by Davies, in the same year, of some of Bolingbroke's pamphlets, is perhaps the poorest compilation that came from Goldsmith's pen, if not the most featureless thing that ever called itself a biography. It was on his more extensive compilations of an historical kind that Goldsmith depended. His *Roman History*, which he had promised Davies in two years, and shares in which had been assigned to other publishers, duly appeared in two volumes 8vo. in May 1769, leaving him free for a greater compilation which he had just agreed for with Griffin. It was to be a huge Natural History, or *History of the Earth and of Animated Nature*, in eight volumes, the payment to be 800 guineas for the whole, or at the rate of 100 guineas a volume. It was the most magnificent-looking engagement that Goldsmith had ever made; but it proved, as has been said, a millstone hung round his neck. For, five hundred guineas of the price having been paid ere the work had been well begun, and the whole before June 1772—

by which time Griffin, to raise the money, had transferred his right to others—Goldsmith, while employed on the undertaking, was in the condition rather of one working off a heavy debt than one working for expected wages. Hence the necessity of other labours to be carried on collaterally. These were—a *History of England* in 4 vols., promised to Davies in June 1769, for 500*l.*, and finished and published in August 1771; a school-abridgment for Davies, in 1772, of the *Roman History* already published; and a *History of Greece*, begun for Griffin in 1773, but not published till after the author's death. Add a translation of Scarron's "Comic Romance," and perhaps other things of the same kind of which no account has been kept, and Goldsmith's miscellaneous literary industry from 1769 onwards will not appear inconsiderable. Deserving particular mention is a project of his, in 1773, of a "Dictionary of Arts and Sciences," or, as we should now say, an Encyclopædia, to be edited by himself, and for which he had promises of contributions from Johnson, Burke, Reynolds, Garrick, Burney, and others. He had drawn up a prospectus of this really promising scheme, and made other preparations, when the impossibility of finding capital obliged him to desist.

Amid all this toil for the Muse of hackwork (what a hag she must be!) Goldsmith did not quite neglect the finer and dearer Muse of his own affections. On the 26th of May, 1770, there appeared, published by Griffin, at his shop in Catherine Street, price two shillings, *The Deserted Village: A Poem: By Dr. Goldsmith.* This poem, dedicated to Sir Joshua Reynolds, and for the copyright of which Goldsmith had received one hundred guineas from Griffin, was instantaneously popular. Two new editions of it were called for in the following month, and a fourth in August; and through the rest of that year the lovely village of Auburn was in all men's fancies, passages from the poem were in every mouth, and the topics, which it suggested, of depopulation, luxury, and landlordism, were discussed in connexion with it. Whatever reputation Goldsmith had won as an English poet by his *Traveller* was now more than confirmed, and people were only anxious to have more in the verse-form from one who managed that form with so perfect a mastery. As a writer of verse, however, Goldsmith was too fastidious, too careful of every line and phrase, to be very productive. *The Haunch of Venison: A Poetical Epistle to Lord Clare,* written in 1771, but not published till after his death, and *Threnodia Augustalis,* "rather a compilation than a poem," as he himself says, written to be set to music on the death of the Princess Dowager of Wales, and actually recited and sung at a public commemoration of that event in February 1772 in the rooms of Mrs. Cornelys, in Soho—these, with one remarkable exception, to be mentioned in due time, are the only pieces of verse of any length that came from Goldsmith's pen after *The Deserted Village.* But, to make amends for his sparingness in the article of verse, he gave the world a second comedy, richer and better every way than his first, and indeed about the best thing of its kind in the English literature of the eighteenth century. He was busy with this comedy in 1771, and seems to have had it by him finished before the end of that year; but there was the usual, or even more than the usual, delay and difficulty in getting it accepted and brought on the stage. Not till the 15th of March, 1773, was it brought out at Covent Garden by Colman, under the name *She Stoops to Conquer; or the Mistakes of a Night*, which Goldsmith had happily adopted for it at the last moment. Colman himself was dead against it, and had spread about dismal forebodings of its failure. But the triumph was immediate and complete. It was performed every possible night for the rest of the season, and once by royal command; all the town rang with it; and the humours of the immortal Tony Lumpkin raised such roars of laughter that good hearty laughter came again into fashion on the stage, the deathblow was given to prim "Sentimental Comedy," and the practitioners and partisans of that style of drama were beaten off the field. Goldsmith's receipts from the theatre may have been between 400*l.* and 500*l.*; and as when the play was published, 6,000 copies were sold within a year, he must have received something additional on that account. It was dedicated to Dr. Johnson, in words admirably chosen. "By inscribing this "slight performance to you," said Goldsmith, "I do not mean so much to compliment "you as myself. It may do me some honour to inform the public that I have lived "many years in intimacy with you. It may serve the interests of mankind also to "inform them that the greatest wit may be found in a character without impairing the "most unaffected piety." What could be better expressed? Pen in hand, as one here sees, Goldy could do anything of this kind more beautifully and delicately than any one else.

And now, having, with one exception, completed our inventory of Goldsmith's writings, whether of the compilation kind or of the finer and more permanent kind, during the last years of his life, we are free for a look at the dear fellow himself, and his habits and circumstances socially, during all this exercise of his pen.

His head-quarters were his chambers in No. 2, Brick Court, Middle Temple. Not only had he furnished them expensively; but the breakfasts, dinners, and suppers which he frequently gave in them, whether to his friends of the Johnson and Reynolds set, or to the needier Hiffernans, Glovers, Kellys, and other literary Irishmen, of whom he had always a retinue attached to him, were extravagantly lavish. This, with his perpetual giving away of guineas to poor blackguards, or better fellows, who wanted them, and his general carelessness of money, kept him always poorer than, with his receipts, he need have been. His receipts during the last six years of his life may be calculated at between 3,000*l.* and 4,000*l.* in all, which was worth in those days about double what such a sum would be worth now; and yet he was always in debt. Something may have gone to his relations in Ireland—to his much-loved brother Henry, before his death in May 1768; to his mother, who survived till 1770, and was blind in her old age; and then to his younger brother Maurice, to whom at any rate we find him resigning a small legacy that had been left him by Uncle Contarine. Some expense to Goldsmith was also caused by the arrival in London of his nephew Hodson, and his residence there for some time without means of his own. Goldsmith's famous accounts with his tailor, Filby, which ran high

—one year as high as 70*l.*—were swelled by orders of clothes for this inconvenient young gentleman. But, on the whole, his general recklessness in his Brick Court Chambers, where he never kept a drawer locked, and let his man Dennis manage everything—this and his open-handedness to all about him in the London streets account sufficiently for his expenditure. Often, however, he was out of London, taking his open-handedness with him to the fields, or along country roads, and into roadside inns or country houses. He was particularly fond of starting with one or two Irish friends, after breakfast in Brick Court, on a ramble to Islington, Kilburn, Hampstead, or some other suburb, returning late or not till next day. He and his friend Bott rented together for some time in 1768, and again in 1769, a convenient cottage eight miles from London on the Edgeware Road; and in this "Shoemaker's Paradise," as Goldsmith called it in honour of the trade of its builder, he worked away for weeks together, in those years, at his *Roman History* and other things, running up to London when he liked. The neighbourhood was a favourite one with him, for he returned to it during portions of 1771 and 1772, for greater leisure to write his *Animated Nature*—not this time to the "Shoemaker's Paradise," or with Bott, but to a farm-house, in Hyde Lane, near the six-mile stone on the same Edgeware Road. Here, occupying a single room, and boarding with the farmer's family, who became exceedingly fond of him, he wrote not only a good portion of his *Animated Nature*, but also, it is said, *She Stoops to Conquer*. Of course, in addition to these occasional retirements to the quiet of the Edgeware Road, there were longer journeys at intervals into various parts of England. He is traced into Hampshire, Sussex, Suffolk, Derbyshire, Leicestershire, Lincolnshire, and Yorkshire; and in 1771 he was, for a good while together, with his friend Lord Clare at Bath. Some of these country excursions appear to have been undertaken in the interests of his *Animated Nature;* at all events, in the course of the excursions, he now and then jotted down an observation for use in that compilation. More purely for pleasure was a visit of six weeks to France in the autumn of 1770—his only visit to the Continent since his long and strange vagabond ramble in it fifteen years before. On this occasion he went as one of a family-party, with Mrs. Horneck, a widow lady, whose acquaintance he had recently made through Sir Joshua Reynolds, and her two daughters, beautiful girls of twenty and eighteen respectively. The elder, for whom Goldsmith had invented the playful name of "Little Comedy," was engaged to be married to a Mr. Bunbury; the younger, Mary Horneck, or "The Jessamy Bride," as Goldsmith called her, was unengaged, and——! Well, who knows? Of no feminine creature, at all events, save this "Jessamy Bride," do we hear, in all Goldsmith's life, so near to him, and in such circumstances, that the world can fancy he was in love with her and can wish that they had wedded. "The Jessamy Bride!" what a suggestion of the jasmine-flower, of gracefulness and white muslin, in the very sound of her name! Poor, plain, mean-looking Goldy!—two-and-forty years of age, too!—did he only look and sigh, and know it to be hopeless? Everything was against him even in this journey. For example, there was that wretched Hickey, the attorney, who joined the party in Paris, and would make a butt of Goldy even in the presence of the ladies, and came back with the story how, maintaining a certain distance from one of the fountains at Versailles to be within reach of a leap, he made a jump to prove his assertion and his muscular power to the Jessamy, and tumbled into the water. Who could marry a man like that? One comfort is that she did not marry Mr. Hickey. When she was engaged, which was not till a year after Goldsmith's death, it was to a Colonel Gwyn, whose wife she became about three years after that. She was alive as late as 1840, having survived Goldsmith sixty-six years. She talked of him fondly to the last.

The reader may remember a certain Kenrick, who succeeded Goldsmith as Griffiths's hack on the *Monthly Review* in 1757, and who had ever since been, for some reason, his deadly enemy. In March 1773, when Goldsmith had reached the very height of his living reputation, and *She Stoops to Conquer* was winning the plaudits of the town, this envious brute, who was editing the *London Packet* newspaper, inserted in its columns an anonymous letter of abuse against Goldsmith and all that he had done. Not content with condemning all Goldsmith's writings and especially his last comedy, as worthless, flimsy, and what not, he ventured on such elegancies as this : "Your poetic vanity is as unpardonable as your personal : would "man believe it, and will woman bear it, to be told that for hours the *great* "Goldsmith will stand surveying his grotesque orang-outang figure in a pier-glass? "Was but the lovely H——k as much enamoured, you would not sigh, my gentle "swain, in vain!" When Goldsmith read this, his blood was properly up ; and, accompanied by Captain Horneck of the Guards, the brother of the lady whose name had been dragged in, he was off to the bookseller Evans's in Paternoster Row, where the newspaper was published. What passed was described to Mr. Prior, when he was writing his Life of Goldsmith, by Mr. Harris, the publisher of St. Paul's Churchyard, who had been in Evans's employment at the time in question, and was a witness to the scene. "I have called," said Goldsmith to Evans, "in "consequence of a scurrilous attack in your paper upon me (my name is Goldsmith), "and an unwarrantable liberty taken with the name of a young lady. As for myself "I care little, but her name must not be sported with." Evans, professing that he knew nothing of the matter, stooped down as if to look for the offensive article in a file of the newspaper, when Goldsmith, unable to resist the sight of the big Welsh back so temptingly exposed, came down upon it with a whack of his cane. Instantly it was big Welshman against little Irishman ; a lamp which hung overhead was broken in the scuffle, and they were both drenched with the oil ; one of the shopmen ran for a constable, and the sneak Kenrick himself, coming out from his editor's room, helped Captain Horneck to separate the combatants, and send Goldsmith home in a coach. For a week the town was merry over the affray, chiefly at Goldy's expense ; who had, moreover, to pay 50*l.* to a Welsh charity, to avoid an action by Evans. One's wish now is that time could be rolled back to the moment of the scuffle, so that the lamp-oil that was spilt might have been poured down Kenrick's throat.

There is an abundance of stories of Goldsmith in his last years, his ways in society, and his table-talk. They are all to the same effect—what a sensitive, guileless, tender-hearted, and really high-minded, creature he was, so that everybody that knew him liked him; and yet how absurd, blundering, alternately consequential and bashful, so that everybody took liberties with him, and it was only when people remembered what a writer he was, or now and then when his wits did clear in the course of talk, and he flashed out a brilliancy as keen as any in his books, that he was looked at with adequate respect. "Dr. Goldsmith," said some one, "is this sort of man: when he comes into a room, if you have not seen "him before, you look at him with reverence because of his writings; but, before "he leaves the room, you may be riding on his back." Again, when the poet Rogers asked Conversation Cooke, as he was called, who had known Goldsmith well and been much with him, what he really was in talk, this was the answer he received, "Sir, he was a fool. The right word never came to him. If you gave "him back a bad shilling, he'd say, 'Why, it is as good a shilling as ever was *born.*' "You know he ought to have said *coined*. *Coined*, Sir, never entered his head. "He was a fool, Sir." Or take Boswell's report of one of his conversations with Johnson. "Of our friend Goldsmith he said, 'Sir, he is so much afraid of being "unnoticed that he often talks merely lest you should forget that he is in the "company.' BOSWELL—'Yes, he stands forward.' JOHNSON—'True, Sir; but, "if a man is to stand forward, he should wish to do it not in an awkward "posture, not in rags, not so that he shall only be exposed to ridicule.' BOSWELL "—'For my part, I like very well to hear honest Goldsmith talk away carelessly.' "JOHNSON—'Why, yes, Sir; but he should not like to hear himself.'" To the same purpose is another conversation of Goldsmith's friends about him, recorded by Boswell. "Goldsmith being mentioned, JOHNSON—'It is amazing how little "Goldsmith knows. He seldom comes where he is not more ignorant than any "one else.' SIR JOSHUA REYNOLDS—'Yet there is no man whose company is "more liked.' JOHNSON—'To be sure, Sir. When people find a man of the "most distinguished abilities as a writer their inferior while he is with them, it "must be highly gratifying to them. What Goldsmith comically says of himself "is very true—he always gets the better when he argues alone; meaning that he "is master of a subject in his study, but, when he comes into company, grows "confused, and unable to talk.'"

Among the best stories of Goldsmith are certainly those preserved by Boswell. The young Scotchman, it is to be understood, whom Johnson had seen off at Harwich on his way to Utrecht, had returned from abroad in February 1766, with his head full of a new enthusiasm for Corsica and Paoli. He at once renewed his intimacy with Dr. Johnson, whom he found now residing in Johnson's Court, Fleet Street; and, as during his absence Goldsmith had published his *Traveller* and other things, he no longer wondered at finding Johnson and Goldsmith so much together. The three again supped at the Mitre, and met once or twice at Johnson's, before Boswell's return to Edinburgh to begin the practice of law. But in 1768 Boswell was again in London for a considerable time; again in 1769; again in 1772, having in the meantime married; and again in 1773, when he had the honour of being elected a member of the Gerrard Street Club, already reinforced since its commencement by some other new members, among whom were Percy, Chambers, Colman, and Garrick. In Boswell's pages, accordingly, and chiefly in the form of his own recollections of those visits to London, we have a pretty continuous history, from 1768 to 1774, of that Johnsonian world which so fascinated him. It was the time, in general politics, of the continued fame of Wilkes and Liberty—the time of Chatham's obscuration, of the Grafton and other unpopular ministries, of the Letters of Junius, and of those discontents in the American colonies which led to the War of American Independence. Nor, amid these public events, were matters stationary in private with the members of the Johnsonian group. Burke's political career as a Rockingham Whig had begun in 1766, and his voice was now powerful in the House of Commons. Johnson had added his edition of Shakespeare to his many previous publications, had had his famous interview with young George III. in the royal library, had begun his intimacy with the Thrales, and had entered on his sixties. The Royal Academy having been founded in 1768, Reynolds had become its first President, and received his knighthood. What Goldsmith had been doing has been already told—save that we have yet to advert to an honour that came to him, in association with Johnson, in consequence of this last-mentioned fact of the foundation of the Royal Academy. "Dr. Johnson," says the *Public Advertiser* of December 22, 1769, "is appointed Professor of Ancient Literature, and Dr. Goldsmith Professor of History, to the Royal Academy. These titles are merely honorary, no salary being annexed to them." It was Reynolds who had arranged these distinctions for his friends in connexion with the new institution. About the same time he painted his well-known portrait of Goldsmith, engravings from which were to be seen in 1770 in the windows of all the print-shops. Its only fault is that it represents Goldsmith without a wig, whereas he invariably wore one. Reynolds, doubtless, foresaw that posterity would like to know the real shape of the head.

And now, with these preliminaries, let Boswell tell some of his stories of Goldsmith's ridiculous ways.——*Goldy's Envy of Johnson on account of his Interview with the King:*—"During all the time in which Dr. Johnson was "employed in relating to the circle at Sir Joshua Reynolds's the particulars of "what passed between the King and him, Dr. Goldsmith remained unmoved "upon a sofa at some distance, affecting not to join in the least in the eager "curiosity of the company. He assigned as a reason for his gloom and seeming "inattention that he apprehended Johnson had relinquished his purpose of "furnishing him with a Prologue to his play, with the hopes of which he had "been flattered; but it was strongly suspected that he was fretting with chagrin "and envy at the singular honour Dr. Johnson had lately enjoyed. At length, "the frankness and simplicity of his natural character prevailed. He sprung from "the sofa, advanced to Johnson, and, in a kind of flutter, from imagining himself

" in the situation which he had just been hearing described, exclaimed, 'Well, " you acquitted yourself in this conversation better than I should have done; for " I should have bowed and stammered through the whole of it.' "——*Goldy's Bloom-Coloured Coat*:—" He (Dr. Johnson) honoured me with his company at " dinner on the 16th of October (1769) at my lodgings in Old Bond Street, with " Sir Joshua Reynolds, Mr. Garrick, Dr. Goldsmith, Mr. Murphy, Mr. Bickerstaff, " and Mr. Thomas Davies. . . . One of the company not being come at the " appointed hour, I proposed, as usual on such occasions, to order dinner to " be served; adding, 'Ought six people to be kept waiting for one?' 'Why, " yes,' answered Johnson, with a delicate humanity, 'if the one will suffer more " by your sitting down than the six will do by waiting.' Goldsmith, to divert " the tedious minutes, strutted about, bragging of his dress, and I believe was " seriously vain of it, for his mind was wonderfully prone to such impressions. " 'Come, come,' said Garrick, 'talk no more of that. You are perhaps the " worst—eh, eh!' Goldsmith was eagerly attempting to interrupt him, when " Garrick went on, laughing ironically, 'Nay, you will always *look* like a " gentleman; but I am talking of being well or ill *drest*.' 'Well, let me tell " you,' said Goldsmith, 'when my tailor brought home my bloom-coloured coat, " he said, "Sir, I have a favour to beg of you. When anybody asks you who " made your clothes, be pleased to mention John Filby, at the Harrow, in Water " Lane."' JOHNSON—'Why, Sir, that was because he knew the strange colour " would attract crowds to gaze at it, and thus they might hear of him, and see " how well he could make a coat even of so absurd a colour.' "——*Goldy's Facts in Natural History*:—" On Thursday, April 29 (1773), I dined with him " (Johnson) at General Oglethorpe's, where were Sir Joshua Reynolds, Mr. Langton, " Dr. Goldsmith, and Mr. Thrale. . . . GOLDSMITH—'There is a general abhor- " rence in animals at the signs of massacre. If you put a tub full of blood into a " stable, the horses are like to go mad.' JOHNSON—'I doubt that.' GOLDSMITH— " 'Nay, it is a fact well authenticated.' THRALE—'You had better prove it before " you put it into your book on Natural History. You may do it in my stable " if you will.' JOHNSON—'Nay, Sir, I would not have him prove it. If he is " content to take his information from others, he may get through his book with " little trouble, and without much endangering his reputation. But, if he makes " experiments for so comprehensive a book as his, there would be no end to them; " his erroneous assertions would then fall upon himself.' "——*Goldy trying to shine, and resenting familiarity*:—" Goldsmith's incessant desire of being conspicuous " in company was the occasion of his sometimes appearing to such disadvantage " as one should hardly have supposed possible in a man of his genius . . . (Once) " when (he was) talking in a company with fluent vivacity, and, as he flattered " himself, to the admiration of all who were present, a German who sat next " him, and perceived Johnson rolling himself, as if about to speak, suddenly stopped " him, saying, 'Stay, stay—Toctor Shonson is going to say something.' This " was, no doubt, very provoking, especially to one so irritable as Goldsmith, who "frequently mentioned it with strong expressions of indignation. It may also be "observed that Goldsmith was sometimes content to be treated with an easy "familiarity, but upon occasions would be consequential and important. An "instance of this occurred in a small particular. Johnson had a way of contracting "the names of his friends: as Beauclerk, Beau; Boswell, Bozzy; Langton, Lanky; "Murphy, Mur; Sheridan, Sherry. I remember, one day when Tom Davies was "telling that Dr. Johnson said, 'We are all in labour for a name to *Goldy's* play,' "Goldsmith seemed much displeased that such a liberty should be taken with "his name. 'I have often desired him not to call me *Goldy.*'"

The foregoing are from Boswell's "Life of Johnson," where there is more of the same sort; but other stories, as good, have come down by other channels of tradition. One or two of these may be added to the string.——*Gibbon making game of Goldy:*—While Goldsmith was busy with his 'Grecian History,' Gibbon is said to have called upon him at his chambers in Brick Court. "You are the very person I wanted to see," said Goldsmith, "for I can't remember the name of that Indian king who gave Alexander the Great so much trouble." "Montezuma," said Gibbon mischievously; till, perceiving that Goldsmith took the information in good faith, and was making a note of it, he thought the jest might go too far, and added, "No, I mistake: it was not Montezuma; it was Porus."——*Burke making game of Goldy:*—Burke, and his friend Mr. (afterwards Colonel) O'Moore, were walking together to Sir Joshua Reynolds's to dine, when they saw Goldsmith, who was also going there, standing near a crowd that had gathered to stare and shout at some foreign women who were looking out from the windows of a house in Leicester Square. "Observe Goldsmith," said Burke to his companion, "and mark what passes between him and me at Sir Joshua's." They arrived at Sir Joshua's before Goldsmith; and, when he appeared, Burke received him with a grave face, as if seriously offended. When Goldsmith had pressed some time for an explanation, Burke, with seeming reluctance, said it was really too much to expect that one could continue to be intimate with him after the indiscreet way in which he had been behaving in the square. With great earnestness Goldsmith professed his ignorance of having done anything wrong, and asked what it was. "Why," said Burke, "did you not exclaim, as you were looking up at those women, what stupid beasts the people must be for staring with such admiration at those painted Jezebels while a man of your talents passed by unnoticed!" "Surely I did not say that," said the astonished Goldsmith. "Nay, if you had not said so," replied Burke, "how should I have known it?" "That's true," said Goldsmith humbly; "I am very sorry—it was very foolish; I do recollect that something of the kind passed through my mind, but I did not think I had uttered it."——*Goldy and the Pig-Butcher:*—At the humble Wednesday's Club at the Globe in Fleet Street, according to Mr. Forster, no less than at the Gerrard Street Club and the parties at Sir Joshua's, Goldsmith was the subject of practical jokes. Mr. Forster tells some of these and adds this story: A frequent attendant at the Club was "a certain Mr. B., described as a good sort of man and an eminent pig-"butcher, who piqued himself very much on his good fellowship with the author of the

"*Traveller*, and whose constant manner of drinking to him was, 'Come, Noll, here's "my service to you, old boy!' Repeating this one night after the comedy (*the Good-"Natured Man*) was played, and when there was a very full club, Glover went over "to Goldsmith, and said in a whisper that he ought not to allow such liberties. "'Let him alone,' answered Goldsmith, 'and you'll see how civilly I'll let him "down.' He waited a little; and, on the next pause in the conversation, called out "aloud, with a marked expression of politeness and courtesy, 'Mr. B., I have the "honour of drinking your good health.' 'Thankee, thankee, Noll,' returned "Mr. B., pulling the pipe out of his mouth, and answering with great briskness."

Enough in this vein! Quite as numerous are the anecdotes of Goldsmith's extreme tenderness of nerve, his generosity, his quick sympathy with all kinds of distress. Once, at a whist-table, we are told, hearing a woman sing in the streets, and struck by something peculiarly mournful in the tones of her voice, he could not rest till he had run out, given her some silver, and sent her away. In his own poverty he was ready with help and kind words not only for the Purdons, Hiffernans, and other poor Grub Street hacks, personally known to him, but also for any unknown young fellow he might casually encounter walking about the Temple Gardens and looking aimless and woe-begone. Remembering this, one cannot help wondering sometimes what might have happened or been prevented, if the boy Chatterton, during his fatal three months in London (May—August 1770) had chanced upon Goldsmith in his weary ramblings. One cannot but imagine, at all events, a certain sad significance in the fact that the hour of the last agony of that marvellous young life, the hunger-and-arsenic agony in the dreadful garret in Brooke Street, Holborn, coincided with the time of Goldsmith's absence from London on his Paris journey. As it was, he was one of the first, on his return, to hear of Chatterton's fate, and to talk of him and the Rowley Poems. But what more is needed to attest the essential goodness of Goldsmith's heart, his singular unselfishness and placability than the story which Boswell tells of his momentary quarrel with Johnson? "I dined with him (Johnson) this day (May 7, 1773)," says Boswell, "at the house of my friends, Messrs. Edward and Charles Dilly, book-"sellers, in the Poultry: there were present—their elder brother, Mr. Dilly of "Bedfordshire; Dr. Goldsmith; Mr. Langton; the Rev. Dr. Mayo, a Dissenting "minister; the Rev. Mr. Toplady; and my friend, the Rev. Mr. Temple." There was much talk; they came at last on the subject of toleration; and Johnson, whom the presence of a Dissenting minister made unusually loud and pugnacious, was hammering away on this subject, without much success against Dr. Mayo's calm stolidity in the common opinion. "During this argument," continues Boswell, "Goldsmith sat in restless agitation, from a wish to get in and *shine*. Finding "himself excluded, he had taken his hat to go away, but remained for some time "with it in his hand, like a gamester, who, at the close of a long night, lingers for a "little while, to see if he can have a favourable opening to finish with success. "Once when he was beginning to speak, he found himself overpowered by the loud "voice of Johnson, who was at the opposite end of the table and did not perceive

"Goldsmith's attempt. Thus disappointed of his wish to obtain the attention of "the company, Goldsmith in a passion threw down his hat, looking angrily at "Johnson, and exclaimed in a bitter tone, "*Take it.*' When Toplady was going to "speak, Johnson uttered some sound, which led Goldsmith to think that he was "beginning again, and taking the words from Toplady. Upon which he seized "this opportunity of venting his own envy and spleen, under the pretext of "supporting another person: 'Sir,' said he to Johnson, 'this gentleman has heard "you patiently for an hour; pray allow us now to hear *him.*' JOHNSON "(sternly)—'Sir, I was not interrupting the gentleman; I was only giving him a "signal of my attention. Sir, you are impertinent.' Goldsmith made no reply, "but continued in the company for some time." After he had gone, the rest talked a while longer; but at last, it being the club night, the company broke up. "He "(Johnson), and Mr. Langton, and I," says Boswell, "went together to the club, "where we found Mr. Burke, Mr. Garrick, and some other members, and amongst "them our friend Goldsmith, who sat silently brooding over Johnson's reprimand "to him after dinner. Johnson perceived this, and said aside to some of us, 'I'll "make Goldsmith forgive me;' and then called to him in a loud voice, 'Dr. "Goldsmith, something passed to-day where you and I dined; I ask your pardon.' "Goldsmith answered placidly, 'It must be much from you, Sir, that I take ill.' "And so at once the difference was over, and they were on as easy terms as ever, "and Goldsmith rattled away as usual."

Goldsmith, as Boswell had to admit, did not always drivel in conversation. Forked lightnings now and then came out of the fog, and he said excellent and memorable things. We have already quoted his definition of Boswell's main faculty, and Boswell has himself honestly recorded two or three sallies of Goldsmith at his expense. "One evening, in a circle of wits, he found fault with me for talking of Johnson as "entitled to the honour of unquestionable superiority. 'Sir,' said he, 'you are for "making a monarchy of what should be a republic.'" Again, in 1773, when Boswell had booked Johnson for his three months' tour that autumn in Scotland and the Hebrides, and it was more than flesh and blood could stand to hear him exulting in the prospect and talking of the matchlessness of his great man, "Is he like Burke, who winds into a subject like a serpent?" said Goldsmith angrily. Even Johnson himself was occasionally outwitted by Goldy, and took it good-humouredly. "JOHNSON—I remember once being with Goldsmith in West-"minster Abbey. While we surveyed the Poets' Corner, I said to him,—

'Forsitan et nostrum nomen miscebitur istis.'

"When we got to Temple Bar, he stopped me, pointed to the heads upon it, and "slyly whispered me,

'Forsitan et nostrum nomen miscebitur *istis.*'

Again, when Goldsmith, in talk with Johnson and Reynolds, spoke of the difficulty of fable-writing, and gave as an instance "the fable of the little fishes who saw birds fly over their heads, and, envying them, petitioned Jupiter to be changed into birds." While he was dilating on this and pointing out very earnestly that the skill consisted in "making them talk like little fishes," Johnson's laughter roused him. "Why, Dr. Johnson," he proceeded smartly, "this is not so easy as you seem to think; for, if *you* were to make little fishes talk, they would talk like *whales*." Again, these two often-quoted sayings about Johnson are Goldsmith's: "There is no arguing with Johnson; for, when his pistol misses fire, he knocks you down with the butt-end of it;" and, "Johnson, to be sure, has a roughness of manner, but no man has a better heart: he has nothing of the bear but his skin." Finally, take the story of the *tête-à-tête* supper of Johnson and Goldy off rumps and kidneys at Jack's Coffee House in Dean Street:—"Sir," said Johnson, "these rumps are pretty little things, but then a man must eat a great many of them before he is satisfied." "Ay, but how many of these would reach to the moon?" said Goldsmith. "To the moon!" echoed Johnson; "that, sir, I fear, exceeds your calculation." "Not at all," said Goldy firmly; "I think I could tell." "Pray then let us hear?" "Why," said Goldy slowly—and Mr. Forster must be right in supposing that here he edged off as far as possible from Johnson—"one, if it were long enough." "Sir, I have deserved it," gasped Johnson at last.

Poor Goldsmith's successes in this way, however, bore no proportion to his failures. "I have been but once at the club since you left England," wrote Beauclerk to Lord Charlemont, another member of the club, on the 5th of July, 1773; "and we were entertained as usual by Dr. Goldsmith's absurdities." This had become the common way of talking of him. More especially since Garrick, with his love of mimicry and mischief, had become a member of the club, it had become the fashion there to laugh at Goldy and all he said and did. But the fashion extended beyond the club; and, whenever Goldy's friends met together, and Garrick chanced to be among them, Goldy's "absurdities" were sure to be the theme. One such place was St. James's Coffee House in St. James's Street, where for some time a company of persons, partly belonging to the club and partly not, had been in the habit of dining together periodically. Here, one day in February 1774, when Goldy was absent, it was proposed to write jocular epitaphs upon him. Several such were written, and among them this by Garrick:—

> "Here lies Poet Goldsmith, for shortness called Noll,
> Who wrote like an angel, but talked like poor Poll."

But it was not very safe to challenge Goldsmith at this kind of sport, as Garrick and others found to their cost when, in the course of the next month, fragments of Goldsmith's little poem called *Retaliation* began to be whispered about. Who does not know this exquisite masterpiece of satire, or rather of humorous character-painting? For there is not a touch of malice or mere caricature in it, but only the keenest and kindliest observation, and the quintessence of happy expression? How all the friends that had been laughing at him are paid off, one by one, with what is at once most gracious compliment and most delicate banter, so that they must have both liked it and not liked it, and must have known that the tables were turned upon the whole pack of them, by this one retort of Goldy, for all time to come!

Especially what three portraits in miniature are those of Burke, Garrick, and Reynolds! Burke lived five-and-twenty years longer, and was to be and do during those five-and-twenty years a great deal more than he had yet been or done; but it is Goldsmith's character of him that we always quote when we want epigram or epitome. In vain Garrick tried, by subsequent verses, not in the best taste, to out-epitaph Goldy after he was dead; his clever "Poor Poll" couplet does last, but Goldy's thirty-two lines on Garrick in his *Retaliation* last also, and are a settlement for ever of the account between them. And what portrait of any one has come to us from the pencil of Reynolds more graphic than the unfinished pen-and-ink sketch of Reynolds himself with which *Retaliation* ends?

> To coxcombs averse, yet most civilly steering,
> When they judged without skill, he was still hard of hearing;
> When they talked of their Raphaels, Correggios, and stuff,
> He shifted his trumpet, and only took snuff.
> By flattery unspoilt . . . .

So, with this loving tribute to Sir Joshua, the poem breaks off. He had more to say in honour of the great painter who had been so truly his friend. Did he contemplate the addition of a portrait of Johnson? Most probably not. "It must be much from you, Sir, that I take ill," the gentle creature had said to the terrible Samuel on receiving his apology for a gross insult; and, notwithstanding his tetchy observation about Johnson to Boswell, "Is he like Burke, who winds into a subject like a serpent?" it is clear that there was no human being for whom Goldsmith felt so profound and absolute a regard.

They were not to be troubled, any of them, with poor Goldy much longer. His *Animated Nature* and his *Grecian History*, though not published, were off his hands; and except that *Retaliation* may have been lying on his desk to have a few lines added to it now and then when he was in the humour, we hear of nothing particular that was occupying him in the months of February and March 1774. He had come to the end of some years of labour in compiling; and now, if ever, was the time for carrying into effect the resolution, to which he had been persuading himself, of retiring permanently into some quiet part of the country and coming to London only for two months every year. But, in fact, either to go or stay would have been difficult for him. All his resources were gone; his feet, as he walked in the streets, were in a meshwork of debt, to the extent of about 2,000*l.*; and all that he could look forward to, with any promise of relief in it, was the chance of a new stretch of some ten thousand acres of additional ditch-work and compilation, for some bookseller who would not mind prepaying for the labour in part. He did talk of something of the kind to the publisher Nourse, into whose hands the property of the *Animated Nature* had passed, and who had it now at press. What would Mr. Nourse say to taking shares with Griffin in a large sequel to the *Animated Nature*, in the form of a work on the "*vegetable* and *fossil* kingdoms?" Mr. Nourse does not appear to have had time to consider this proposal when, as far as Goldsmith was concerned, it became unnecessary for him to think more about it. Goldy had gone in March, for a week or two, to his retreat at Hyde on the Edgeware Road, when an attack of a local complaint to which he had for some time been subject brought him back to his chambers in the Temple. The immediate illness passed off, but a kind of nervous fever followed; and at eleven o'clock at night on the 25th of March, Mr. Hawes, an apothecary and a friend of Goldsmith's, was sent for. He found Goldsmith very ill, and bent on doctoring himself with "James's fever-powders," a patent medicine the property in which had belonged to Newbery the publisher, and in which Goldsmith had great faith. In spite of all that Mr. Hawes could say, he would take one of these powders; after which he became worse and worse. Dr. Fordyce, who had been just elected a member of the Gerrard Street Club, and Dr. Turton, another physician of celebrity, were called in to assist Mr. Hawes, but without avail. "Your pulse," said Dr. Turton to his patient, "is in greater disorder than it should be from the state of your fever: is your mind at ease?" "It is *not*," said Goldsmith. And so, with varying symptoms, he lay on in his chambers in Brick Court till Monday, the 4th of April, 1774, on which day it was known through town that Goldsmith was dead. He died at half-past four that morning in strong convulsions. When Burke was told the news, he burst into tears. When Reynolds was told it, he left his painting-room, where he then was, and did no more work that day. How Johnson was affected at the moment we can only guess; but three months afterwards he wrote as follows to Bennet Langton, in Lincolnshire: "Chambers, you find, is gone far, and poor "Goldsmith is gone much farther. He died of a fever, exasperated, as I believe, by "the fear of distress. He raised money and squandered it by every artifice of "acquisition and folly of expense. But let not his frailties be remembered; he "was a very great man." When Goldsmith died he was forty-five years and five months old. His body was buried, on the 9th of April, in the burying-ground of the Temple Church. The monument to him in Westminster Abbey, with the Latin inscription by Johnson, was erected in 1776.

About Goldsmith personally we can add but few particulars to those already given. As is implied by the very name "Goldy," so persistently attached to him in spite of his remonstrances, he was a little man,—not above five feet five inches high, it is said, though stout and thick about the chest and limbs. To have seen him walking down Fleet Street, with the gigantic Johnson by his side, must have been a sight indeed. His pale and pitted face taken along with his figure, people thought him one of the plainest little bodies that ever entered a room; they even called his appearance "mean." Looking at his portrait now, and knowing what he was, we do not find this, but only a certain oddness, caused by the outbulging forehead, the lax mouth and chin, and in general the pouting, sulky, "You don't sufficiently respect me," expression. Though sociable and convivial, and lavishly expensive in his style of entertaining others, he seems himself to have had simple enough tastes in eating and drinking; he never had a habit of excess in wine, and he was fond of a bowl of milk to the last. One of his peculiarities—he himself notes it as a peculiarity in one who professed to write on Natural History—was a strong antipathy to mice, eels, and most little animals of the crawling kind, such as worms and caterpillars. Of all the rest of that strange mixture, or jumble, of qualities that went to make Goldy, a sufficient account has already been given ; and, if one were bent on summing it all up in some one general idea or impression, to be easily remembered, it must be that impression or idea in which his contemporaries concurred unanimously through every period of his life, and which has been transmitted to us in so many forms, viz. that he was one of the best-hearted creatures ever born, but a positive idiot except when he had the pen in his hand.

Except when he had the pen in his hand! Ay! there has been his power with the world! And what shall one say now of Goldsmith's writings? Take four brief remarks :—(1) Not to be forgotten is that division of them, already dwelt on, into two distinct orders—*compilations* and *original pieces*. As the division was a vital one to Goldsmith himself—for his literary life consisted, as we have said, of a succession of glitterings of spontaneous genius amid dull habitual drudgery at hackwork—so it is of consequence in our retrospect of him. Probably much that Goldsmith did in the way of anonymous compilation lies buried irrecoverably in the old periodicals for which he wrote, and which are now little better than lumber on the shelves of our great libraries. But his compilations of English, Roman, and Grecian History, and his *Animated Nature*, once so popular, are still known, and are to be distinguished from that class of his writings of which the present volume is a collection. Even in the present volume there are some small things that must be regarded as mere compilations, and may serve as minor specimens of Goldsmith in that line—the wretched shred called a *Life of Bolingbroke*, for example, and the better, but still poor, *Life of Parnell*, if not indeed also the *Memoir of Voltaire*, and the *Life of Beau Nash*. Deduct these, and in the *Inquiry into the State of Polite Learning*, the *Essays*, the *Bee*, the *Citizen of the World*, the *Vicar of Wakefield*, and the *Poems and Plays*, you have, in various forms, the pure and real Goldsmith. (2) In all that he wrote, his compilations included, there was the charm of his easy, perspicuous style. This was one of Goldsmith's natural gifts; with his humour, his tenderness, and his graceful delicacy of thought, he had it from the first. No writer in the language has ever surpassed him, or even equalled him, in that witching simplicity, that gentle ease of movement, sometimes careless and slip-shod, but always in perfect good taste, and often delighting with the subtlest turns and felicities, which critics have admired for a hundred years in the diction of Goldsmith. It is this merit that still gives to his compilations what interest they have, though it was but in a moderate degree that he could exhibit it there. "*Nullum ferè scribendi genus non tetigit; nullum quod tetigit non ornavit*" ("There was no kind of writing almost that he did not touch ; none that he touched that he did not adorn,") said Johnson of him in his epitaph in Westminster Abbey ; and the remark includes his compilations. In *matter*, his History of England, for example, has become quite worthless ; and if you want a good laugh over Goldy's notion of what sort of thing a battle might be, open the book at his descriptions of the battles of Cressy and Agincourt. What "letting fly" at the enemy! and how it is the Black Prince in the one case, and Henry V. in the other, that settles everything with his own hand, and tumbles them over in droves! But read on, and you will see how the style could reconcile people to the meagreness of the matter, and keep the compilation so long popular. And so with his *Animated Nature.* Johnson prophesied that he would make the work as pleasant as a Persian tale; and the prophecy was fulfilled. The "style" of Goldsmith—which includes, of course, the habitual rule of sequence in his ideas, his sense of fitness and harmony, the liveliness of his fancy from moment to moment, and his general mental tact—this is a study in itself. (3) In his original writings, where the charm of his style is most felt, there is, with all their variety of form, a certain sameness of general effect. The field of incidents, characters, sentiments, and imagined situations, within which the author moves, is a limited one, though there is great deftness of recombination within that horizon. We do not mean merely that Goldsmith, as an eighteenth-century writer, did not go beyond the intellectual and poetic range to which his century had restricted itself. This is true; and though we discern in Goldsmith's writings a fine vein of peculiarity, or even uniqueness, for the generation to which they belonged, there is yet abundant proof that his critical tenets did not essentially transcend those of his generation. Even more for him than for some of his contemporaries, Pope was the limit of classic English literature, and the older grandeurs of Shakespeare and Milton were rugged, barbaric mountain-masses, well at a distance. But, over and above this limitation of Goldsmith's range by essential sympathy with the tastes of his time, there was a something in his own method and choice of subjects causing a farther and inner circumscription of his bounds. All Goldsmith's phantasies, whether in verse or prose—his *Vicar of Wakefield*, his *Traveller*, his *Deserted Village*, his *Good-Natured Man* and *She Stoops to Conquer*, and even the humorous sketches that occur in his *Essays* and *Citizen of the World*—are phantasies of what may be called *reminiscence.* Less than even Smollett, did Goldsmith *invent*, if by invention we mean a projection of the imagination into vacant space, and a filling of portion after portion of that space, as by sheer bold dreaming, with scenery, events, and beings, never known before. He drew on the recollections of his own life, on the history of his own family, on the characters of his relatives, on whimsical incidents that had happened to him in his Irish youth or during his continental wanderings, on his experience as a literary drudge in London. It is easy to pick out passages in his *Vicar*, his *Citizen*, and elsewhere, which are, with hardly a disguise, autobiographical. Dr. Primrose is his own father, and the good clergyman of the *Deserted Village* is his brother Henry; the simple Moses, the Gentleman in Black, young Honeywood in the *Good-Natured Man*, and even Tony Lumpkin in *She Stoops to Conquer*, are so many reproductions of phases of himself; the incident on which this last play turns, the mistake of a gentleman's house for an inn, was a remembered blunder of his own in early life; and more than once his device for ending all happily is a benevolent uncle in the background. That of these simple elements he made so many charming combinations, really differing from each other, and all, though suggested by fact, yet hung so sweetly in an ideal air, proved what an artist he was, and was better than much that is commonly called invention. In short, if there is a sameness of effect in Goldsmith's writings, it is because they consist of poetry and truth, humour and pathos, from his own life, and the supply from such a life as his was not inexhaustible. (4) Though so much of Goldsmith's best writing was generalized and idealized reminiscence, he discharged all special Irish colour out of the reminiscence. There are, of course, Irish references and allusions, and we know what a warm heart he had to the last for the island of his birth. But in most of his writings, even when it may have been Irish recollections that suggested the theme, he is careful to drop its origin, and transplant the tale into England. The ideal air in which his phantasies are hung is an English air. The *Vicar of Wakefield* is an English prose-idyll ; *She Stoops to Conquer* is a comedy of English humour, and Tony Lumpkin is an English country-lout ; and, notwithstanding all the accuracy with which Lissoy and its neighbourhood have been identified with the Auburn of the *Deserted Village*, we are in England and not in Ireland while we read that poem. Goldsmith's heart and genius were Irish ; his wandering about in the world had given him a touch of cosmopolitan ease in his judgment of things and opinions, and especially, what was rare among Englishmen then, a great liking for the French ; but in the form and matter of his writings he was purposely English.

DAVID MASSON.

August 1868.

THE MISCELLANEOUS WORKS

OF

OLIVER GOLDSMITH

THE VICAR OF WAKEFIELD.

(1766.)

ADVERTISEMENT.

There are an hundred faults in this thing, and an hundred things might be said to prove them beauties. But it is needless. A book may be amusing with numerous errors, or it may be very dull without a single absurdity. The hero of this piece unites in himself the three greatest characters upon earth ; he is a priest, an husbandman, and the father of a family. He is drawn as ready to teach, and ready to obey ; as simple in affluence, and majestic in adversity. In this age of opulence and refinement, whom can such a character please? Such as are fond of high life will turn with disdain from the simplicity of his country fireside ; such as mistake ribaldry for humour will find no wit in his harmless conversation ; and such as have been taught to deride religion will laugh at one whose chief stores of comfort are drawn from futurity.

OLIVER GOLDSMITH.

CHAPTER I.

The Description of the Family of Wakefield, in which a kindred Likeness prevails, as well of Minds as of Persons.

I WAS ever of opinion, that the honest man who married and brought up a large family did more service than he who continued single, and only talked of population. From this motive, I had scarce taken orders a year before I began to think seriously of matrimony, and chose my wife, as she did her wedding-gown, not for a fine glossy surface, but for such qualities as would wear well. To do her justice, she was a good-natured notable woman ; and, as for breeding, there were few country ladies who could show more. She could read any English book without much spelling ; but for pickling, preserving, and cookery, none could excel her. She prided herself also upon being an excellent contriver in housekeeping ; though I could never find that we grew richer with all her contrivances.

However, we loved each other tenderly, and our fondness increased as we grew old. There was, in fact, nothing that could make us angry with the world or each other. We had an elegant house situated in a fine country, and a good neighbourhood. The year was spent in a moral or rural amusement, in visiting our rich neighbours, and relieving such as were poor. We had no revolutions to fear, nor fatigues to undergo ; all our adventures were by the fireside, and all our migrations from the blue bed to the brown.

As we lived near the road, we often had the traveller or stranger visit us to taste our gooseberry wine, for which we had great reputation ; and I profess, with the veracity of an historian, that I never knew one of them find fault with it. Our cousins, too, even to the fortieth remove, all remembered their affinity, without any help from the heralds' office, and came very frequently to see us. Some of them did us no great honour by these claims of kindred ; as we had the blind, the maimed, and the halt amongst the number. However, my wife always insisted that, as they were the same *flesh and blood*, they should sit with us at the same table. So that, if we had not very rich, we generally had very happy friends about us ; for this remark will hold good through life, that the poorer the guest, the better pleased he ever is with being treated: and as some men gaze with admiration at the colours of a tulip, or the wing of a butterfly, so I was, by nature, an admirer of happy human faces. However, when any one of our relations was found to be a person of very bad character, a troublesome guest, or one we desired to get rid of, upon his leaving my house I ever took care to lend him a riding-coat, or a pair of boots, or sometimes an horse of small value, and I always had the satisfaction of finding he never came back to return them. By this the house was cleared of such as we did not like; but never was the family of Wakefield known to turn the traveller or the poor dependant out of doors.

Thus we lived several years in a state of much happiness, not but that we sometimes had those little rubs which Providence sends to enhance the value of its favours. My orchard was often robbed by schoolboys, and my wife's custards plundered by the cats or the children. The Squire would sometimes fall asleep in the most pathetic parts of my sermon, or his lady return my wife's civilities at church with a mutilated curtsey. But we soon got over the uneasiness caused by such accidents, and usually in three or four days began to wonder how they vexed us.

My children, the offspring of temperance, as they were educated without softness, so they were at once well-formed and healthy; my sons hardy and active, my daughters beautiful and blooming. When I stood in the midst of the little circle, which promised to be the supports of my declining age, I could not avoid repeating the famous story of Count Abensberg, who, in Henry the Second's progress through Germany, while other courtiers came with their treasures, brought his thirty-two children, and presented them to his sovereign as the most valuable offering he had to bestow. In this manner, though I had but six, I considered them as a very valuable present made to my country, and consequently looked upon it as my debtor. Our eldest son was named George, after his uncle, who left us ten thousand pounds. Our second child, a girl, I intended to call after her aunt Grissel; but my wife, who during her pregnancy had been reading romances, insisted upon her being called Olivia. In less than another year we had another daughter, and now I was determined that Grissel should be her name; but a rich relation taking a fancy to stand godmother, the girl was, by her directions, called Sophia; so that we had two romantic names in the family; but I solemnly protest I had no hand in it. Moses was our next, and, after an interval of twelve years, we had two sons more.

It would be fruitless to deny exultation when I saw my little ones about me; but the vanity and the satisfaction of my wife were even greater than mine. When our visitors would say, "Well, upon my word, Mrs. Primrose, you have the finest children in the whole country;"—"Ay, neighbour," she would answer, "they are as Heaven made them, handsome enough, if they be good enough; for handsome is that handsome does." And then she would bid the girls hold up their heads; who, to conceal nothing, were certainly very handsome. Mere outside is so very trifling a circumstance with me, that I should scarce have remembered to mention it, had it not been a general topic of conversation in the country. Olivia, now about eighteen, had that luxuriancy of beauty with which painters generally draw Hebe; open, sprightly, and commanding. Sophia's features were not so striking at first, but often did more certain execution; for they were soft, modest, and alluring. The one vanquished by a single blow, the other by efforts successfully repeated.

The temper of a woman is generally formed from the turn of her features: at least it was so with my daughters. Olivia wished for many lovers; Sophia to secure one. Olivia was often affected, from too great a desire to please; Sophia even repressed excellence, from her fears to offend. The one entertained me with her vivacity when I was gay, the other with her sense when I was serious. But these qualities were never carried to excess in either, and I have often seen them exchange characters for a whole day together. A suit of mourning has transformed my coquette into a prude, and a new set of ribands has given her younger sister more than natural vivacity. My eldest son George was bred at Oxford, as I intended him for one of the learned professions. My second boy Moses, whom I designed for business, received a sort of miscellaneous education at home. But it is needless to attempt describing the particular characters of young people that had seen but very little of the world. In short, a family likeness prevailed through all, and, properly speaking, they had but one character,—that of being all equally generous, credulous, simple, and inoffensive.

CHAPTER II.

Family Misfortunes. The Loss of Fortune only serves to increase the Pride of the Worthy.

THE temporal concerns of our family were chiefly committed to my wife's management; as to the spiritual, I took them entirely under my own direction. The profits of my living, which amounted to but thirty-five pounds a year, I made over to the orphans and widows of the clergy of our diocese; for, having a fortune of my own, I was careless of temporalities, and felt a secret pleasure in doing my duty without reward. I also set a resolution of keeping no curate, and of being acquainted with every man in the parish, exhorting the married men to temperance, and the bachelors to matrimony: so that in a few years it was a common saying, that there were three strange wants at Wakefield, a parson wanting pride, young men wanting wives, and ale-houses wanting customers.

Matrimony was always one of my favourite topics, and I wrote several sermons to prove its happiness: but there was a peculiar tenet which I made a point of supporting; for I maintained with Whiston, that it was unlawful for a priest of the Church of England, after the death of his first wife, to take a second; or, to express it in one word, I valued myself upon being a strict monogamist.

I was early initiated into this important dispute, on which so many laborious volumes have been written. I published some tracts upon the subject myself, which, as they never sold, I have the consolation of thinking were read only by the happy *few*. Some of my friends called this my weak side; but, alas! they had not, like me, made it the subject of long contemplation. The more I reflected upon it, the more important it appeared. I even went a step beyond Whiston in displaying my principles; as he had engraven upon his wife's tomb that she was the *only* wife of William Whiston, so I wrote a similar epitaph for my wife, though still living, in which I extolled her prudence, economy, and obedience till death; and having got it copied fair, with an elegant frame, it was placed over the chimney-piece, where it answered several very useful purposes: it admonished my wife of her duty to me, and my fidelity to her; it inspired her with a passion for fame, and constantly put her in mind of her end.

It was thus, perhaps, from hearing marriage so often recommended, that my eldest son, just upon leaving college, fixed his affections upon the daughter of a neighbouring clergyman, who was a dignitary in the Church, and in circumstances to give her a large fortune. But fortune was her smallest accomplishment. Miss Arabella Wilmot was allowed by all (except my two daughters) to be completely pretty. Her youth, health, and innocence, were still heightened by a complexion so transparent, and such an happy sensibility of look, as even age could not gaze on with indifference. As Mr. Wilmot knew that I could make a very handsome settlement on my son, he was not averse to the match; so both families lived together in all that harmony which generally precedes an expected alliance. Being convinced, by experience, that the days of courtship are the most happy of our lives, I was willing enough to lengthen the period; and the various amusements which the young couple every day shared in each other's company seemed to increase their passion. We were generally awaked in the morning by music, and on fine days rode a-hunting. The hours between breakfast and dinner the ladies devoted to dress and study; they usually read a page, and then gazed at themselves in the glass, which, even philosophers might own, often presented the page of greatest beauty. At dinner, my wife took the lead; for, as she always insisted upon carving everything herself, it being her mother's way, she gave us, upon these occasions, the history of every dish. When we had dined, to prevent the ladies leaving us, I generally ordered the table to be removed; and sometimes, with the music-master's assistance, the girls would give us a very agreeable concert. Walking out, drinking tea, country dances, and forfeits, shortened the rest of the day, without the assistance of cards, as I hated all manner of gaming, except backgammon, at which my old friend and I sometimes took a twopenny hit. Nor can I here pass over an ominous circumstance that happened, the last time we played together. I only wanted to fling a quatre, and yet I threw deuce ace five times running.

Some months were elapsed in this manner, till at last it was thought convenient to fix a day for the nuptials of the young couple, who seemed earnestly to desire it. During the preparations for the wedding, I need not describe the busy importance of my wife, nor the sly looks of my daughters: in fact, my attention was fixed on another object,—the completing a tract, which I intended shortly to publish, in defence of my favourite principle. As I looked upon this as a masterpiece, both for argument and style, I could not, in the pride of my heart, avoid showing it to my old friend Mr. Wilmot, as I made no doubt of receiving his approbation: but not till too late I discovered that he was most violently attached to the contrary opinion, and with good reason; for he was at that time actually courting a fourth wife. This, as may be expected, produced a dispute, attended with some acrimony, which threatened to interrupt our intended alliance; but, on the day before that appointed for the ceremony, we agreed to discuss the subject at large.

It was managed with proper spirit on both sides; he asserted that I was heterodox; I retorted the charge: he replied, and I rejoined. In the meantime, while the controversy was hottest, I was called out by one of my relations, who, with a face of concern, advised me to give up the dispute, at least till my son's wedding was over. "How," cried I, "relinquish the cause of truth, and let him be a husband, already driven to the very verge of absurdity? You might as well advise me to give up my fortune as my argument."—"Your fortune," returned my friend, "I am now sorry to inform you, is almost nothing. The merchant in town, in whose hands your money was lodged, has gone off, to avoid a statute of bankruptcy, and is thought not to have left a shilling in the pound. I was unwilling to shock you or the family with the account till after the wedding: but now it may serve to moderate your warmth in the argument; for, I suppose, your own prudence will enforce the necessity of dissembling, at least till your son has the young lady's fortune secure."—"Well," returned I, "if what you tell me be true, and if I am to be a beggar, it shall never make me a rascal, or induce me to disavow my principles. I'll go this moment and inform the company of my circumstances: and, as for the argument, I even here retract my former concessions in the old gentleman's favour, nor will allow him now to be a husband in any sense of the expression."

It would be endless to describe the different sensations of both families when I divulged the news of our misfortune: but what others felt was slight to what the lovers appeared to endure. Mr. Wilmot, who seemed before sufficiently inclined to break off the match, was, by this blow, soon determined: one virtue he had in perfection, which was prudence, too often the only one that is left us at seventy-two.

CHAPTER III.

A Migration. The fortunate Circumstances of our Lives are generally found at last to be of our own procuring.

THE only hope of our family now was, that the report of our misfortune might be malicious or premature; but a letter from my agent in town soon came, with a confirmation of every particular. The loss of fortune to myself alone would have been trifling; the only uneasiness I felt was for my family, who were to be humbled without an education to render them callous to contempt.

Near a fortnight had passed before I attempted to restrain their affliction; for premature consolation is but the remembrancer of sorrow. During this interval, my thoughts were employed on some future means of supporting them; and at last a small cure of fifteen pounds a year was offered me, in a distant neighbourhood, where I could still enjoy my principles without molestation. With this proposal I joyfully closed, having determined to increase my salary by managing a little farm.

Having taken this resolution, my next care was to get together the wrecks of my fortune; and, all debts collected and paid, out of fourteen thousand pounds we had but four hundred remaining. My chief attention, therefore, was now to bring down the pride of my family to their circumstances; for I well knew that aspiring beggary is wretchedness itself. "You cannot be ignorant, my children," cried I, "that no prudence of ours could have prevented our late misfortune; but prudence may do much in disappointing its effects. We are now poor, my fondlings, and wisdom bids us conform to our humble situation. Let us then, without repining, give up those splendours with which numbers are wretched, and seek in humbler circumstances that peace with which all may be happy. The poor live pleasantly without our help; why, then, should not we learn to live without theirs? No, my children, let us from this moment give up all pretensions to gentility: we have still enough left for happiness if we are wise, and let us draw upon content for the deficiencies of fortune."

As my eldest son was bred a scholar, I determined to send him to town, where his abilities might contribute to our support and his own. The separation of friends and families is, perhaps, one of the most distressful circumstances attendant on penury. The day soon arrived on which we were to disperse for the first time. My son, after taking leave of his mother and the rest, who mingled their tears with their kisses, came to ask a blessing from me. This I gave him from my heart, and which, added to five guineas, was all the patrimony I had now to bestow. "You are going, my boy," cried I, "to London on foot, in the manner Hooker, your great ancestor, travelled there before you. Take from me the same horse that was given him by the good bishop Jewel, this staff, and take this book, too, it will be your comfort on the way: these two lines in it are worth a million,—'I have been young, and now am old; yet never saw I the righteous man forsaken, or his seed begging their bread.' Let this be your consolation as you travel on. Go, my boy; whatever be thy fortune, let me see thee once a year; still keep a good heart, and farewell." As he was possessed of integrity and honour, I was under no apprehensions from throwing him naked into the amphitheatre of life; for I knew he would act a good part whether vanquished or victorious.

His departure only prepared the way for our own, which arrived a few days afterwards. The leaving a neighbourhood in which we had enjoyed so many hours of tranquillity was not without a tear, which scarce fortitude itself could suppress. Besides, a journey of seventy miles, to a family that had hitherto never been above ten from home, filled us with apprehension; and the cries of the poor, who followed us for some miles, contributed to increase it. The first day's journey brought us in safety within thirty miles of our future retreat, and we put up for the night at an obscure inn in a village by the way. When we were shown a room, I desired the landlord, in my usual way, to let us have his company, with which he complied, as what he drank would increase the bill next morning. He knew, however, the whole neighbourhood to which I was removing, particularly Squire Thornhill, who was to be my landlord, and who lived within a few miles of the place. This gentleman he described as one who desired to know little more of the world than its pleasures, being particularly remarkable for his attachment for the fair sex. He observed that no virtue was able to resist his arts and assiduity, and that scarce a farmer's daughter within ten miles round but what had found him successful and faithless. Though this account gave me some pain, it had a very different effect upon my daughters, whose features seemed to brighten with the expectation of an approaching triumph: nor was my wife less pleased and confident of their allurements and virtue. While our thoughts were thus employed, the hostess entered the room to inform her husband that the strange gentleman, who had been two days in the house, wanted money, and could not satisfy them for his reckoning. "Want money!" replied the host, "that must be impossible; for it was no later than yesterday he paid three guineas to our beadle to spare an old broken soldier that was to be whipped through the town for dog-stealing." The hostess, however, still persisting in her first assertion, he was preparing to leave the room, swearing that he would be satisfied one way or another, when I begged the landlord would introduce me to a stranger of so much charity as he described. With this he complied, showing in a gentleman who seemed to be about thirty, dressed in clothes that once were laced. His person was well formed, and his face marked with the lines of thinking. He had something short and dry in his address, and seemed not to understand ceremony, or to despise it. Upon the landlord's leaving the room, I could not avoid expressing my concern to the stranger at seeing a gentleman in such circumstances, and offered him my purse to satisfy the present demand. "I take it with all my heart, sir," replied he, "and am glad that a late oversight in giving what money I had about me has shown me there are still some men like you. I must, however, previously entreat being informed of the name and residence of my benefactor, in order to repay him as soon as possible." In this I satisfied him fully, not only mentioning my name and late misfortunes, but the place to which I was going to remove. "This," cried he, "happens still more luckily than I hoped for, as I am going the same way myself, having been detained here two days by the floods, which I hope by to-morrow will be found passable." I testified the pleasure I should have in his company, and my wife and daughters joining in entreaty, he was prevailed upon to stay supper. The stranger's conversation, which was at once pleasing and instructive, induced me to wish for a continuance of it; but it was now high time to retire and take refreshment against the fatigues of the following day.

The next morning we all set forward together: my family on horseback, while Mr. Burchell, our new companion, walked along the footpath by the road-side, observing with a smile that, as we were ill mounted, he would be too generous to attempt leaving us behind. As the floods were not yet subsided, we were obliged to hire a guide, who trotted on before, Mr. Burchell and I bringing up the rear. We lightened the fatigues of the road with philosophical disputes, which he seemed to understand perfectly. But what surprised me most was, that though he was a money borrower, he defended his opinions with as much obstinacy as if he had been my patron. He now and then also informed me to whom the different seats belonged that lay in our view as we travelled the road. "That," cried he, pointing to a very magnificent house which stood at some distance, "belongs to Mr. Thornhill, a young gentleman who enjoys a large fortune, though entirely dependent on the will of his uncle, Sir William Thornhill, a gentleman who, content with a little himself, permits his nephew to enjoy the rest, and chiefly resides in town."—"What!" cried I, "is my young landlord then the nephew of a man, whose virtues, generosity, and singularities are so universally known? I have heard Sir William Thornhill represented as one of the most generous yet whimsical men in the kingdom; a man of consummate benevolence."—"Something, perhaps, too much so," replied Mr. Burchell; "at least he carried benevolence to an excess when young; for his passions were then strong, and as they were all upon the side of virtue they led it up to a romantic extreme. He early began to aim at the qualifications of the soldier and the scholar: was soon distinguished in the army, and had some reputation among men of learning. Adulation ever follows the ambitious; for such alone receive most pleasure from flattery. He was surrounded with crowds, who showed him only one side of their character; so that he began to lose a regard for private interest in universal sympathy. He loved all mankind; for fortune prevented him from knowing that there were rascals. Physicians tell us of a disorder, in which the whole body is so exquisitely sensible that the slightest touch gives pain: what some have thus suffered in their persons, this gentleman felt in his mind: the slightest distress, whether real or fictitious, touched him to the quick, and his soul laboured under a sickly sensibility of the miseries of others. Thus disposed to relieve, it will be easily conjectured he found numbers disposed to solicit; his profusions began to impair his fortune, but not his good-nature—that, indeed, was seen to increase as the other seemed to decay: he grew improvident as he grew poor; and, though he talked like a man of sense, his actions were those of a fool. Still, however, being surrounded with importunity, and no longer able to satisfy every request that was made him, instead of *money* he gave *promises*. They were all he had to bestow, and he had not resolution enough to give any man pain by a denial. By this he drew round him crowds of dependants, whom he was sure to disappoint, yet wished to relieve. These hung upon him for a time, and left him with merited reproaches and contempt. But, in proportion as he became contemptible to others, he became despicable to himself. His mind had leaned upon their adulation, and, that support taken away, he could find no pleasure in the applause of his heart, which he had never learnt to reverence. The world now began to wear a different aspect: the flattery of his friends began to dwindle into simple approbation; approbation soon took the more friendly form of advice; and advice, when rejected, produced their reproaches. He now therefore found that such friends as benefits had gathered round him, were little estimable: he now found that a man's own heart must be ever given to gain that of another. I now found that—that—I forget what I was going to observe: in short, sir, he resolved to respect himself, and laid down a plan of restoring his falling fortune. For this purpose, in his own whimsical manner, he travelled through Europe on foot; and now, though he has scarce attained the age of thirty, his circumstances are more affluent than ever. At present, his bounties are more rational and moderate than before; but still he preserves the character of an humorist, and finds most pleasure in eccentric virtues."

My attention was so much taken up by Mr. Burchell's account, that I scarce looked forward as he went along, till we were alarmed by the cries of my family; when, turning, I perceived my youngest daughter in the midst of a rapid stream, thrown from her horse, and struggling with the torrent. She had sunk twice, nor was it in my power to disengage myself in time to bring her relief. My sensations were even too violent to permit my attempting her rescue: she must have certainly perished had not my companion, perceiving her danger, instantly plunged in to her relief, and, with some difficulty, brought her in safety to the opposite shore. By taking the current a little farther up, the rest of the family got safely over, where we had an opportunity of joining our acknowledgments to hers. Her gratitude may be more readily imagined than described: she thanked her deliverer more with looks than with words, and continued to lean upon his arm, as if still willing to receive assistance. My wife also hoped one day to have the pleasure of returning his kindness at her own house. Thus, after we were refreshed at the next inn, and had dined together, as Mr. Burchell was going to a different part of the country, he took leave, and we pursued our journey; my wife observing, as he went, that she liked him extremely, and protesting, that if he had birth and fortune to entitle him to match into such a family as ours, she knew no man she would sooner fix upon. I could not but smile to hear her talk in this lofty strain; but I was never much displeased with those harmless delusions that tend to make us more happy.

CHAPTER IV.

A Proof that even the humblest Fortune may grant Happiness, which depends, not on Circumstances, but Constitution.

THE place of our retreat was in a little neighbourhood, consisting of farmers, who tilled their own grounds, and were equal strangers to opulence and poverty. As they had almost all the conveniences of life within themselves, they seldom visited towns or cities in search of superfluity. Remote from the polite, they still retained the primeval simplicity of manners; and, frugal by habit, they scarce knew that temperance was a virtue. They wrought with cheerfulness on days of labour; but observed festivals as intervals of idleness and pleasure. They kept up the Christmas carol, sent true love knots on Valentine morning, ate pancakes on Shrovetide, showed their wit on the first of April, and religiously cracked nuts on Michaelmas eve. Being apprised of our approach, the whole neighbourhood came out to meet their minister, dressed in their finest clothes, and preceded by a pipe and tabor. A feast also was provided for our reception, at which we sat cheerfully down; and what the conversation wanted in wit was made up in laughter.

Our little habitation was situated at the foot of a sloping hill, sheltered with a beautiful underwood behind, and a prattling river before; on one side a meadow, on the other a green. My farm consisted of about twenty acres of excellent land, having given an hundred pounds for my predecessor's good-will. Nothing could exceed the neatness of my little enclosures, the elms and hedge-rows appearing with inexpressible beauty. My house consisted of but one story, and was covered with thatch, which gave it an air of great snugness; the walls, on the inside, were nicely whitewashed, and my daughters undertook to adorn them with pictures of their own designing. Though the same room served us for parlour and kitchen, that only made it the warmer. Besides, as it was kept with the utmost neatness, the dishes, plates, and coppers being well scoured, and all disposed in bright rows on the shelves, the eye was agreeably relieved, and did not want richer furniture. There were three other apartments; one for my wife and me, another for our two daughters within our own, and the third, with two beds, for the rest of the children.

The little republic to which I gave laws, was regulated in the following manner: By sunrise we all assembled in our common apartment, the fire being previously kindled by the servant. After we had saluted each other with proper ceremony—for I always thought fit to keep up some mechanical forms of good breeding, without which freedom ever destroys friendship—we all bent in gratitude to that Being who gave us another day. This duty being performed, my son and I went to pursue our usual industry abroad, while my wife and daughters employed themselves in providing breakfast, which was always ready at a certain time. I allowed half an hour for this meal, and an hour for dinner; which time was taken up in innocent mirth between my wife and daughters, and in philosophical arguments between my son and me.

As we rose with the sun, so we never pursued our labours after it was gone down, but returned home to the expecting family, where smiling looks, a neat hearth, and pleasant fire, were prepared for our reception. Nor were we without guests: sometimes farmer Flamborough, our talkative neighbour, and often the blind piper, would pay us a visit, and taste our gooseberry wine, for the making of which we had lost neither the receipt nor the reputation. These harmless people had several ways of being good company; while one played, the other would sing some soothing ballad,—Johnny Armstrong's Last Good-Night, or the Cruelty of Barbara Allen. The night was concluded in the manner we began the morning, my youngest boys being appointed to read the lessons of the day; and he that read loudest, distinctest, and best, was to have a halfpenny on Sunday to put into the poor's box.

When Sunday came, it was indeed a day of finery, which all my sumptuary edicts could not restrain. How well soever I fancied my lectures against pride had conquered the vanity of my daughters, yet I still found them secretly attached to all their former finery: they still loved laces, ribands, bugles, and catgut; my wife herself retained a passion for her crimson paduasoy, because I formerly happened to say it became her.

The first Sunday, in particular, their behaviour served to mortify me. I had desired my girls the preceding night to be dressed early the next day; for I always loved to be at church a good while before the rest of the congregation. They punctually obeyed my directions; but when we were to assemble in the morning at breakfast, down came my wife and daughters, dressed out in all their former splendour; their hair plastered up with pomatum, their faces patched to taste, their trains bundled up in a heap behind, and rustling at every motion. I could not help smiling at their vanity, particularly that of my wife, from whom I expected more discretion. In this exigence, therefore, my only resource was to order my son, with an important air, to call our coach. The girls were amazed at the command; but I repeated it with more solemnity than before. "Surely, my dear, you jest," cried my wife; "we can walk it perfectly well: we want no coach to carry us now."—"You mistake, child," returned I, "we do want a coach; for if we walk to church in this trim, the very children in the parish will hoot after us."—"Indeed," replied my wife, "I always imagined that my Charles was fond of seeing his children neat and handsome about him."—"You may be as neat as you please," interrupted I, "and I shall love you the better for it; but all this is not neatness, but frippery. These rufflings, and pinkings, and patchings will only make us hated by all the wives of our neighbours. No, my children," continued I, more gravely, "those gowns may be altered into something of a plainer cut; for finery is very unbecoming in us, who want the means of decency. I do not know whether such flouncing and shredding is becoming even in the rich, if we consider, upon a moderate calculation, that the nakedness of the indigent world might be clothed from the trimmings of the vain."

This remonstrance had the proper effect: they went with great composure, that very instant, to change their dress; and the next day I had the satisfaction of finding my daughters, at their own request, employed in cutting up their trains into Sunday waistcoats for Dick and Bill, the two little ones; and, what was still more satisfactory, the gowns seemed improved by this curtailing.

CHAPTER V.

A new and great Acquaintance introduced. What we place most Hopes upon, generally proves most fatal.

At a small distance from the house, my predecessor had made a seat, overshadowed by a hedge of hawthorn and honeysuckle. Here, when the weather was fine and our labour soon finished, we usually sat together, to enjoy an extensive landscape in the calm of the evening. Here, too, we drank tea, which now was become an occasional banquet; and, as we had it but seldom, it diffused a new joy, the preparations for it being made with no small share of bustle and ceremony. On these occasions, our two little ones always read for us, and they were regularly served after we had done. Sometimes, to give a variety to our amusements, the girls sang to the guitar; and while they thus formed a little concert, my wife and I would stroll down the sloping field, that was embellished with blue-bells and centaury, talk of our children with rapture, and enjoy the breeze that wafted both health and harmony.

In this manner we began to find that every situation in life may bring its own peculiar pleasures: every morning waked us to a repetition of toil; but the evening repaid it with vacant hilarity.

It was about the beginning of autumn, on a holiday—for I kept such as intervals of relaxation from labour—that I had drawn out my family to our usual place of amusement, and our young musicians began their usual concert. As we were thus engaged, we saw a stag bound nimbly by, within about twenty paces of where we were sitting, and by its panting it seemed pressed by the hunters. We had not much time to reflect upon the poor animal's distress, when we perceived the dogs and horsemen come sweeping along at some distance behind, and making the very path it had taken. I was instantly for returning in with my family; but either curiosity, or surprise, or some more hidden motive, held my wife and daughters to their seats. The huntsman who rode foremost passed us with great swiftness, followed by four or five persons more, who seemed in equal haste. At last, a young gentleman of more genteel appearance than the rest came forward, and for a while regarding us, instead of pursuing the chase, stopped short, and giving his horse to a servant who attended, approached us with a careless superior air. He seemed to want no introduction, but was going to salute my daughters as one certain of a kind reception; but they had early learnt the lesson of looking presumption out of countenance. Upon which he let us know that his name was Thornhill, and that he was owner of the estate that lay for some extent round us. He again therefore offered to salute the female part of the family, and such was the power of fortune and fine clothes, that he found no second repulse. As his address, though confident, was easy, we soon became more familiar; and, perceiving musical instruments lying near, he begged to be favoured with a song. As I did not approve of such disproportioned acquaintances, I winked upon my daughters in order to prevent their compliance; but my hint was counteracted by one from their mother; so that, with a cheerful air, they gave us a favourite song of Dryden's. Mr. Thornhill seemed highly delighted with their performance and choice, and then took up the guitar himself. He played but very indifferently; however, my eldest daughter repaid his former applause with interest, and assured him that his tones were louder than even those of her master. At this compliment he bowed, which she returned with a curtsey. He praised her taste, and she commended his understanding; an age could not have made them better acquainted: while the fond mother too, equally happy, insisted upon her landlord's stepping in, and tasting a glass of her gooseberry. The whole family seemed earnest to please him: my girls attempted to entertain him with topics they thought most modern; while Moses, on the contrary, gave him a question or two from the ancients, for which he had the satisfaction of being laughed at. My little ones were no less busy, and fondly stuck close to the stranger. All my endeavours could scarce keep their dirty fingers from handling and tarnishing the lace on his clothes, and lifting up the flaps of his pocket-holes, to see what was there. At the approach of evening he took leave; but not till he had requested permission to renew his visit, which, as he was our landlord, we most readily agreed to.

As soon as he was gone, my wife called a council on the conduct of the day. She was of opinion, that it was a most fortunate hit; for she had known even stranger things than that brought to bear. She hoped again to see the day in which we might hold up our heads with the best of them; and concluded, she protested she could see no reason why the two Miss Wrinklers should marry great fortunes, and her children get none. As this last argument was directed to me, I protested I could see no reason for it neither, nor why Mr. Simpkins got the ten thousand pound prize in the lottery, and we sat down with a blank. "I protest, Charles," cried my wife, "this is the way you always damp my girls and me when we are in spirits. Tell me, Sophy, my dear, what do you think of our new visitor? Don't you think he seemed to be good-natured?"—"Immensely so, indeed, mamma," replied she: "I think he has a great deal to say upon everything, and is never at a loss; and the more trifling the subject, the more he has to say."—"Yes," cried Olivia, "he is well enough for a man; but, for my own part, I don't much like him, he is so extremely impudent and familiar; but on the guitar he is shocking." These two last speeches I interpreted by contraries. I found by this, that Sophia internally despised, as much as Olivia secretly admired him. "Whatever may be your opinions of him, my children," cried I, "to confess the truth, he has not prepossessed me in his favour. Disproportioned friendships ever terminate in disgust; and I thought, notwithstanding all his ease, that he seemed perfectly sensible of the distance between us. Let us keep to companions of our own rank. There is no character more contemptible than a man that is a fortune-hunter; and I can see no reason why fortune-hunting women should not be contemptible too. Thus, at best, we shall be contemptible if his views are honourable; but if they be otherwise!—I should shudder but to think of that. It is true, I have no apprehensions from the conduct of my children; but I think there are some from his character." I would have proceeded, but for the interruption of a servant from the Squire, who, with his compliments, sent us a side of venison, and a promise to dine with us some days after. This well-timed present pleaded more powerfully in his favour than anything I had to say could obviate. I therefore continued silent, satisfied with just having pointed out danger, and leaving it to their own discretion to avoid it. That virtue which requires to be ever guarded is scarce worth the sentinel.

CHAPTER VI.

The Happiness of a Country Fireside.

As we carried on the former dispute with some degree of warmth, in order to accommodate matters, it was universally agreed that we should have a part of the venison for supper; and the girls undertook the task with alacrity. "I am sorry," cried I, "that we have no neighbour or stranger to take part in this good cheer: feasts of this kind acquire a double relish from hospitality."—"Bless me," cried my wife, "here comes our good friend Mr. Burchell, that saved our Sophia, and that run you down fairly in the argument."—"Confute me in argument, child!" cried I. "You mistake there, my dear; I believe there are but few that can do that: I never dispute your abilities at making a goose-pie, and I beg you'll leave argument to me." As I spoke, poor Mr. Burchell entered the house, and was welcomed by the family, who shook him heartily by the hand, while little Dick officiously reached him a chair.

I was pleased with the poor man's friendship for two reasons: because I knew that he wanted mine, and I knew him to be friendly as far as he was able. He was known in our neighbourhood by the character of the poor gentleman, that would do no good when he was young, though he was not yet thirty. He would at intervals talk with great good sense; but, in general, he was fondest of the company of children, whom he used to call harmless little men. He was famous, I found, for singing them ballads, and telling them stories, and seldom went out without something in his pockets for them—a piece of gingerbread, or an halfpenny whistle. He generally came for a few days into our neighbourhood once a year, and lived upon the neighbours' hospitality. He sat down to supper among us, and my wife was not sparing of her gooseberry-wine. The tale went round; he sung us old songs, and gave the children the story of the Buck of Beverland, with the history of Patient Grissel, the adventures of Catskin, and then Fair Rosamond's Bower. Our cock, which always crew at eleven, now told us it was time for repose; but an unforeseen difficulty started about lodging the stranger—all our beds were already taken up, and it was too late to send him to the next alehouse. In this dilemma, little Dick offered him his part of the bed, if his brother Moses would let him lie with him: "And I," cried Bill, "will give Mr. Burchell my part, if my sisters will take me to theirs."—"Well done, my good children," cried I, "hospitality is one of the first Christian duties. The beast retires to its shelter, and the bird flies to its nest; but helpless man can only find refuge from his fellow-creature. The greatest stranger in this world was He that came to save it. He never had a house, as if willing to see what hospitality was left remaining among us. Deborah, my dear," cried I to my wife, "give those boys a lump of sugar each; and let Dick's be the largest, because he spoke first."

In the morning early I called out my whole family to help at saving an after-growth of hay, and our guest offering his assistance, he was accepted among the number. Our labours went on lightly; we turned the swath to the wind. I went foremost, and the rest followed in due succession. I could not avoid, however, observing the assiduity of Mr. Burchell in assisting my daughter Sophia in her part of the task. When he had finished his own, he would join in hers, and enter into a close conversation; but I had too good an opinion of Sophia's understanding, and was too well convinced of her ambition, to be under any uneasiness from a man of broken fortune. When we were finished for the day, Mr. Burchell was invited as on the night before, but he refused, as he was to lie that night at a neighbour's, to whose child he was carrying a whistle. When gone, our conversation at supper turned upon our late unfortunate guest. "What a strong instance," said I, "is that poor man of the miseries attending a youth of levity and extravagance. He by no means wants sense, which only serves to aggravate his former folly. Poor forlorn creature! where are now the revellers, the flatterers, that he could once inspire and command! Gone, perhaps, to attend the bagnio pander, grown rich by his extravagance. They once praised him, and now they applaud the pander: their former raptures at his wit are now converted into sarcasms at his folly: he is poor, and perhaps deserves poverty; for he has neither the ambition to be independent, nor the skill to be useful." Prompted perhaps by some secret reasons, I delivered this observation with too much acrimony, which my Sophia gently reproved. "Whatsoever his former conduct may have been, papa, his circumstances should exempt him from censure now. His present indigence is a sufficient punishment for former folly; and I have heard my papa himself say, that we should never strike one unnecessary blow at a victim, over whom Providence holds the scourge of its resentment."—"You are right, Sophy," cried my son Moses; "and one of the ancients finely represents so malicious a conduct, by the attempts of a rustic to flay Marsyas, whose skin, the fable tells us, had been wholly stripped off by another. Besides, I don't know if this poor man's situation be so bad as my father would represent it. We are not to judge of the feelings of others by what we might feel in their place. However dark the habitation of the mole to our eyes, yet the animal itself finds the apartment sufficiently lightsome. And, to confess a truth, this man's mind seems fitted to his station; for I never heard any one more sprightly than he was to-day, when he conversed with you."—This was said without the least design; however, it excited a blush, which she strove to cover by an affected laugh, assuring him that she scarce took any notice of what he said to her, but that she believed he might once have been a very fine gentleman. The readiness with which she undertook to vindicate herself, and her blushing, were symptoms I did not internally approve; but I repressed my suspicions.

As we expected our landlord the next day, my wife went to make the venison pasty. Moses sat reading, while I taught the little ones. My daughters seemed equally busy with the rest; and I observed them for a good while cooking something over the fire. I at first supposed they were assisting their mother, but little Dick informed me, in a whisper, that they were making a wash for the face. Washes of all kinds I had a natural antipathy to; for I knew that, instead of mending the complexion, they spoil it. I therefore approached my chair by sly degrees to the fire, and grasping the poker, as if it wanted mending, seemingly by accident overturned the whole composition, and it was too late to begin another.

CHAPTER VII.

A Town Wit described. The dullest Fellows may learn to be comical for a Night or Two.

When the morning arrived on which we were to entertain our young landlord, it may be easily supposed what provisions were exhausted to make an appearance. It may also be conjectured that my wife and daughters expanded their gayest plumage on this occasion. Mr. Thornhill came with a couple of friends, his chaplain and feeder. The servants, who were numerous, he politely ordered to the next alehouse: but my wife, in the triumph of her heart, insisted on entertaining them all; for which, by the by, our family was pinched for three weeks after. As Mr. Burchell had hinted to us the day before, that he was making some proposals of marriage to Miss Wilmot, my son George's former mistress, this a good deal damped the heartiness of his reception: but accident in some measure relieved our embarrassment; for one of the company happening to mention her name, Mr. Thornhill observed with an oath, that he never knew anything more absurd than calling such a fright a beauty; "For, strike me ugly," continued he, "if I should not find as much pleasure in choosing my mistress by the information of a lamp under the clock of St. Dunstan's." At this he laughed, and so did we: the jests of the rich are ever successful. Olivia, too, could not avoid whispering, loud enough to be heard, that he had an infinite fund of humour.

After dinner, I began with my usual toast, the Church: for this I was thanked by the chaplain, as he said the Church was the only mistress of his affections. "Come, tell us honestly, Frank," said the Squire, with his usual archness, "suppose the Church, your present mistress, dressed in lawn sleeves, on one hand, and Miss Sophia, with no lawn about her, on the other, which would you be for?"—"For both, to be sure," cried the chaplain. "Right, Frank," cried the Squire; "for may this glass suffocate me, but a fine girl is worth all the priestcraft in the creation! For what are tithes and tricks but an imposition, all a confounded imposture, and I can prove it."—"I wish you would," cried my son Moses; "and I think," continued he, "that I should be able to answer you."—"Very well, sir," cried the Squire, who immediately smoked him, and winked on the rest of the company to prepare us for the sport; "if you are for a cool argument upon that subject, I am ready to accept the challenge. And, first, whether are you for managing it analogically or dialogically?"—"I am for managing it rationally," cried Moses, quite happy at being permitted to dispute. "Good again," cried the Squire; "and, firstly, of the first, I hope you'll not deny, that whatever is, is. If you don't grant me that, I can go no further."—"Why," returned Moses, "I think I may grant that; and make the best of it."—"I hope, too," returned the other, "you'll grant that a part is less than the whole."—"I grant that too," cried Moses; "it is but just and reasonable."—"I hope," cried the Squire, "you will not deny, that the two angles of a triangle are equal to two right ones." —"Nothing can be plainer," returned t'other, and looked round with his usual importance. — "Very well," cried the Squire, speaking very quick, "the premisses being thus settled, I proceed to observe, that the concatenation of self-existences, proceeding in a reciprocal duplicate ratio, naturally produce a problematical dialogism, which, in some measure, proves that the essence of spirituality may be referred to the second predicable." — "Hold, hold!" cried the other, "I deny that: do you think that I can thus tamely submit to such heterodox doctrines?"—"What!" replied the Squire, as if in a passion, "not submit! Answer me one plain question: Do you think Aristotle right when he says that relatives are related?"—"Undoubtedly," replied the other.—"If so, then," cried the Squire, "answer me directly to what I propose: Whether do you judge the analytical investigation of the first part of my enthymem deficient secundum quoad, or quoad minus; and give me your reasons —give me your reasons, I say, directly." —"I protest," cried Moses, "I don't rightly comprehend the force of your reasoning; but if it be reduced to one simple proposition, I fancy it may then have an answer."—"Oh, sir," cried the Squire, "I am your most humble servant; I find you want me to furnish you with argument and intellects too. No, sir, there I protest you are too hard for me." This effectually raised the laugh against poor Moses, who sat the only dismal figure in a group of merry faces; nor did he offer a single syllable more during the whole entertainment.

But though all this gave me no pleasure, it had a very different effect upon Olivia, who mistook it for humour, though but a mere act of the memory. She thought him, therefore, a very fine gentleman; and such as consider what powerful ingredients a good figure, fine clothes, and fortune are in that character, will easily forgive her. Mr. Thornhill, notwithstanding his real ignorance, talked with ease, and could expatiate upon the common topics of conversation with fluency. It is not surprising then, that such talents should win the affections of a girl who by education was taught to value an appearance in herself, and consequently to set a value upon it in another.

Upon his departure, we again entered into a debate upon the merits of our young landlord. As he directed his looks and conversation to Olivia, it was no longer doubted but that she was the object that induced him to be our visitor. Nor did she seem to be much displeased at the innocent raillery of her brother and sister upon this occasion. Even Deborah herself seemed to share the glory of the day, and exulted in her daughter's victory as if it were her own. "And now, my dear," cried she to me, "I'll fairly own, that it was I that instructed my girls to encourage our landlord's addresses. I had always some ambition, and you now see that I was right; for who knows how this may end?"—"Ay, who knows that indeed!" answered I, with a groan: "for my part, I don't much like it; and I could have been better pleased with one that was poor and honest, than this fine gentleman with his fortune and infidelity; for depend on't, if he be what I suspect him, no freethinker shall ever have a child of mine."

"Sure, father," cried Moses, "you are too severe in this; for Heaven will never arraign him for what he thinks, but for what he does. Every man has a thousand vicious thoughts, which arise without his power to suppress. Thinking freely of religion may be involuntary with this gentleman; so that, allowing his sentiments to be wrong, yet, as he is purely passive in his assent, he is no more to be blamed for his errors than the governor of a city without walls for the shelter he is obliged to afford an invading enemy."

"True, my son," cried I; "but if the governor invites the enemy there, he is justly culpable. And such is always the case with those who embrace error. The vice does not lie in assenting to the proofs they see; but being blind to many of the proofs that offer. So that, though our erroneous opinions be involuntary when formed, yet as we have been wilfully corrupt, or very negligent in forming them, we deserve punishment for our vice, or contempt for our folly."

My wife now kept up the conversation, though not the argument; she observed that several very prudent men of our acquaintance were freethinkers, and made very good husbands; and she knew some sensible girls that had skill enough to make converts of their spouses. "And who knows, my dear," continued she, "what Olivia may be able to do: the girl has a great deal to say upon every subject, and, to my knowledge, is very well skilled in controversy."

"Why, my dear, what controversy can she have read?" cried I. "It does not occur to me that I ever put such books into her hands: you certainly overrate her merit."—"Indeed, papa," replied Olivia, "she does not; I have read a great deal of controversy. I have read the disputes between Thwackum and Square; the controversy between Robinson Crusoe and Friday, the savage; and I am now employed in reading the controversy in Religious Courtship."—"Very well," cried I, "that's a good girl; I find you are perfectly qualified for making converts, and so go help your mother to make the gooseberry pie."

CHAPTER VIII.

An Amour, which promises little good Fortune, yet may be productive of much.

THE next morning we were again visited by Mr. Burchell, though I began, for certain reasons, to be displeased with the frequency of his return; but I could not refuse him my company and fireside. It is true, his labour more than requited his entertainment; for he wrought among us with vigour, and, either in the meadow or at the hay-rick, put himself foremost. Besides, he had always something amusing to say that lessened our toil, and was at once so out of the way, and yet so sensible, that I loved, laughed at, and pitied him. My only dislike arose from an attachment he discovered to my daughter. He would, in a jesting manner, call her his little mistress, and when he bought each of the girls a set of ribands, hers was the finest. I knew not how, but he every day seemed to become more amiable, his wit to improve, and his simplicity to assume the superior airs of wisdom.

Our family dined in the field, and we sat, or rather reclined, round a temperate repast, our cloth spread upon the hay, while Mr. Burchell gave cheerfulness to the feast. To heighten our satisfaction, two blackbirds answered each other from opposite hedges, the familiar redbreast came and pecked the crumbs from our hands, and every sound seemed but the echo of tranquillity. "I never sit thus," says Sophia, "but I think of the two lovers so sweetly described by Mr. Gay, who were struck dead in each other's arms. There is something so pathetic in the description, that I have read it an hundred times with new rapture."—"In my opinion," cried my son, "the finest strokes in that description are much below those in the Acis and Galatea of Ovid. The Roman poet understands the use of contrast better; and upon that figure, artfully managed, all strength in the pathetic depends."—"It is remarkable," cried Mr. Burchell, "that both the poets you mention have equally contributed to introduce a false taste into their respective countries, by loading all their lines with epithet. Men of little genius found them most easily imitated in their defects; and English poetry, like that in the latter empire of Rome, is nothing at present but a combination of luxuriant images, without plot or connexion—a string of epithets that improve the sound without carrying on the sense. But perhaps, madam, while I thus reprehend others, you'll think it just that I should give them an opportunity to retaliate; and, indeed, I have made this remark only to have an opportunity of introducing to the company a ballad, which, whatever be its other defects, is, I think, at least free from those I have mentioned."

A BALLAD.

"Turn, gentle Hermit of the dale,
And guide my lonely way
To where yon taper cheers the vale
With hospitable ray.

"For here forlorn and lost I tread,
With fainting steps and slow,
Where wilds, immeasurably spread,
Seem length'ning as I go."

"Forbear, my son," the Hermit cries,
"To tempt the dangerous gloom;
For yonder faithless phantom flies
To lure thee to thy doom.

"Here to the houseless child of want
My door is open still;
And, though my portion is but scant,
I give it with good will.

"Then turn to-night, and freely share
Whate'er my cell bestows;
My rushy couch and frugal fare,
My blessing and repose.

"No flocks that range the valley free
To slaughter I condemn;
Taught by that Power that pities me,
I learn to pity them:

"But from the mountain's grassy side
A guiltless feast I bring;
A scrip with herbs and fruits supplied,
And water from the spring.

"Then, pilgrim, turn; thy cares forego;
All earth-born cares are wrong:
Man wants but little here below,
Nor wants that little long."

Soft as the dew from heaven descends
His gentle accents fell:
The modest stranger lowly bends,
And follows to the cell.

Far in a wilderness obscure
The lonely mansion lay,
A refuge to the neighbouring poor,
And strangers led astray.

No stores beneath its humble thatch
Required a master's care;
The wicket, opening with a latch,
Received the harmless pair.

And now, when busy crowds retire
To take their evening rest,
The hermit trimm'd his little fire,
And cheer'd his pensive guest:

And spread his vegetable store,
And gaily press'd, and smiled;
And, skill'd in legendary lore,
The lingering hours beguiled.

Around, in sympathetic mirth,
Its tricks the kitten tries,
The cricket chirrups on the hearth,
The crackling fagot flies.

But nothing could a charm impart
To soothe the stranger's woe;
For grief was heavy at his heart,
And tears began to flow.

His rising cares the Hermit spied,
With answering care oppress'd:
And "Whence, unhappy youth," he cried,
"The sorrows of thy breast?

"From better habitations spurn'd,
Reluctant dost thou rove?
Or grieve for friendship unreturn'd,
Or unregarded love?

"Alas! the joys that fortune brings
Are trifling, and decay;

And those who prize the paltry things,
More trifling still than they.

"And what is friendship but a name,
A charm that lulls to sleep;
A shade that follows wealth or fame,
But leaves the wretch to weep?

"And love is still an emptier sound,
The modern fair one's jest;
On earth unseen, or only found
To warm the turtle's nest.

"For shame, fond youth, thy sorrows hush,
And spurn the sex," he said;
But while he spoke, a rising blush
His love-lorn guest betray'd.

Surprised he sees new beauties rise,
Swift mantling to the view;
Like colours o'er the morning skies,
As bright, as transient too.

The bashful look, the rising breast,
Alternate spread alarms:
The lovely stranger stands confess'd
A maid in all her charms.

And, "Ah! forgive a stranger rude—
A wretch forlorn," she cried;
"Whose feet unhallow'd thus intrude
Where Heaven and you reside.

"But let a maid thy pity share,
Whom love has taught to stray;
Who seeks for rest, but finds despair
Companion of her way.

"My father lived beside the Tyne,
A wealthy lord was he;
And all his wealth was mark'd as mine,
He had but only me.

"To win me from his tender arms
Unnumber'd suitors came,
Who praised me for imputed charms,
And felt, or feign'd, a flame.

"Each hour a mercenary crowd
With richest proffers strove;
Amongst the rest, young Edwin bow'd,
But never talk'd of love.

"In humble, simple habit clad,
No wealth nor power had he;
Wisdom and worth were all he had,
But these were all to me.

"And when, beside me in the dale,
He caroll'd lays of love,
His breath lent fragrance to the gale,
And music to the grove.

"The blossom opening to the day,
The dews of heaven refined,
Could nought of purity display
To emulate his mind.

"The dew, the blossom on the tree,
With charms inconstant shine:
Their charms were his, but, woe to me,
Their constancy was mine.

"For still I tried each fickle art,
Importunate and vain;
And, while his passion touch'd my heart,
I triumph'd in his pain:

"Till, quite dejected with my scorn,
He left me to my pride;
And sought a solitude forlorn,
In secret, where he died.

"But mine the sorrow, mine the fault,
And well my life shall pay;
I'll seek the solitude he sought,
And stretch me where he lay.

"And there, forlorn, despairing, hid,
I'll lay me down and die;
'Twas so for me that Edwin did,
And so for him will I."

"Forbid it Heaven!" the Hermit cried,
And clasp'd her to his breast:
The wondering fair one turn'd to chide—
'Twas Edwin's self that press'd!

"Turn, Angelina, ever dear,
My charmer, turn to see
Thy own, thy long-lost Edwin here,
Restored to love and thee.

"Thus let me hold thee to my heart,
And every care resign:
And shall we never, never part,
My life—my all that's mine?

"No, never from this hour to part,
We'll live and love so true,
The sigh that rends thy constant heart
Shall break thy Edwin's too."

While this ballad was reading, Sophia seemed to mix an air of tenderness with her approbation. But our tranquillity was soon disturbed by the report of a gun just by us, and, immediately after, a man was seen bursting through the hedge, to take up the game he had killed. This sportsman was the Squire's chaplain, who had shot one of the blackbirds that so agreeably entertained us. So loud a report, and so near, startled my daughters; and I could perceive that Sophia in the fright had thrown herself into Mr. Burchell's arms for protection. The gentleman came up, and asked pardon for having disturbed us, affirming that he was ignorant of our being so near. He therefore sat down by my youngest daughter, and, sportsman-like, offered her what he had killed that morning. She was going to refuse, but a private look from her mother soon induced her to correct the mistake, and accept his present, though with some reluctance. My wife, as usual, discovered her pride in a whisper, observing, that Sophy had made a conquest of the chaplain, as well as her sister had of the Squire. I suspected, however, with more probability, that her affections were placed upon a different object. The chaplain's errand was to inform us, that Mr. Thornhill had provided music and refreshments; and intended that night giving the young ladies a ball by moonlight, on the grass plat before our door. "Nor can I deny," continued he, "but I have an interest in being first to deliver this message, as I expect for my reward to be honoured with Miss Sophia's hand as a partner." To this my girl replied, that she should have no objection, if she could do it with honour; "But here," continued she, "is a gentleman," looking at Mr. Burchell, "who has been my companion in the task for the day, and it is fit he should share in its amusements." Mr. Burchell returned her a compliment for her intentions, but resigned her up to the chaplain; adding, that he was to go that night five miles, being invited to a harvest supper. His refusal appeared to me a little extraordinary; nor could I conceive how so sensible a girl as my youngest could thus prefer a man of broken fortunes to one whose expectations were much greater. But as men are most capable of distinguishing merit in women, so the ladies often form the truest judgments of us. The two sexes seem placed as spies upon each other, and are furnished with different abilities, adapted for mutual inspection.

CHAPTER IX.

Two Ladies of great Distinction introduced. Superior Finery ever seems to confer superior Breeding.

MR. BURCHELL had scarce taken leave, and Sophia consented to dance with the chaplain, when my little ones came running out to tell us, that the Squire was come with a crowd of company. Upon our return, we found our landlord, with a couple of under gentlemen and two young ladies richly dressed, whom he introduced as women of very great distinction and fashion from town. We happened not to have chairs enough for the whole company; but Mr. Thornhill immediately proposed, that every gentleman should sit in a lady's lap. This I positively objected to, notwithstanding a look of disapprobation from my wife. Moses was therefore dispatched to borrow a couple of chairs; and as we were in want of ladies to make up a set at country dances, the two gentlemen went with him in quest of a couple of partners. Chairs and partners were soon provided. The gentlemen returned with my neighbour Flamborough's rosy daughters, flaunting with red top-knots; but an unlucky circumstance was not adverted to,—though the Miss Flamboroughs were reckoned the very best dancers in the parish, and understood the jig and roundabout to perfection, yet they were totally unacquainted with country dances. This at first discomposed us: however, after a little shoving and dragging, they at last went merrily on. Our music consisted of two fiddles, with a pipe and tabor. The moon shone bright. Mr. Thornhill and my eldest daughter led up the ball, to the great delight of the spectators; for the neighbours, hearing what was going forward, came flocking about us. My girl moved with so much grace and vivacity, that my wife could not avoid discovering the pride of her heart by assuring me that, though the little chit did it so cleverly, all the steps were stolen from herself. The ladies of the town strove hard to be equally easy, but without success. They swam, sprawled, languished, and frisked; but all would not do: the gazers indeed owned that it was fine; but neighbour Flamborough observed that Miss Livy's feet seemed as pat to the music as its echo. After the dance had continued about an hour, the two ladies, who were apprehensive of catching cold, moved to break up the ball. One of them, I thought, expressed her sentiments upon this occasion in a very coarse manner, when she observed, that, "by the living jingo, she was all of a muck of sweat." Upon our return to the house, we found a very elegant cold supper, which Mr. Thornhill had ordered to be brought with him. The conversation at this time was more reserved than before. The two ladies threw my girls into the shade; for they would talk of nothing but high life, and high-lived company; with other fashionable topics, such as pictures, taste, Shakespeare, and the musical glasses. 'Tis true they once or twice mortified us sensibly by slipping out an oath; but that appeared to me as the surest symptom of their distinction (though I am since informed that swearing is perfectly unfashionable). Their finery, however, threw a veil over any grossness in their conversation. My daughters seemed to regard their superior accomplishments with envy; and what appeared amiss, was ascribed to tip-top quality breeding. But the condescension of the ladies was still superior to their accomplishments. One of them observed, that had Miss Olivia seen a little more of the world, it would greatly improve her; to which the other added, that a single winter in town would make her little Sophia quite another thing. My wife warmly assented to both; adding, that there was nothing she more ardently wished than to give her girls a single winter's polishing. To this I could not help replying, that their breeding was already superior to their fortune; and that greater refinement would only serve to make their poverty ridiculous, and give them a taste for pleasures they had no right to possess. "And what pleasures," cried Mr. Thornhill, "do they not deserve to possess, who have so much in their power to bestow? As for my part," continued he, "my fortune is pretty large; love, liberty, and pleasure are my maxims; but curse me, if a settlement of half my estate could give my charming Olivia pleasure, it should be hers; and the only favour I would ask in return would be to add myself to the benefit." I was not such a stranger to the world as to be ignorant that this was the fashionable cant to disguise the insolence of the basest proposal; but I made an effort to suppress my resentment. "Sir," cried I, "the family which you now condescend to favour with your company has been bred with as nice a sense of honour as you. Any attempts to injure that may be attended with very dangerous consequences. Honour, sir, is our only possession at present, and of that last treasure we must be particularly careful." I was soon sorry for the warmth with which I had spoken this, when the young gentleman, grasping my hand, swore he commended my spirit, though he disapproved my suspicions. "As to your present hint," continued he, "I protest nothing was farther from my heart than such a thought. No, by all that's tempting! the virtue that will stand a regular siege was never to my taste; for all my amours are carried by a coup-de-main."

The two ladies, who affected to be ignorant of the rest, seemed highly displeased with this last stroke of freedom, and began a very discreet and serious dialogue upon virtue: in this, my wife, the chaplain, and I, soon joined; and the Squire himself was at last brought to confess a sense of sorrow for his former excesses. We talked of the pleasures of temperance, and of the sunshine in the mind unpolluted with guilt. I was so well pleased, that my little ones were kept up beyond the usual time to be edified by so much good conversation. Mr. Thornhill even went beyond me, and demanded if I had any objection to giving prayers. I joyfully embraced the proposal; and in this manner the night was passed in the most comfortable way, till at last the company began to think of returning. The ladies seemed very unwilling to part with my daughters, for whom they had conceived a particular affection, and joined in a request to have the pleasure of their company home. The Squire seconded the proposals, and my wife added her entreaties; the girls, too, looked upon me as if they wished to go. In this perplexity, I made two or three excuses, which my daughters as readily removed; so that at last I was obliged to give a peremptory refusal, for which we had nothing but sullen looks and short answers the whole day ensuing.

CHAPTER X.

The Family endeavour to cope with their Betters. The Miseries of the Poor, when they attempt to appear above their Circumstances.

I NOW began to find that all my long and painful lectures upon temperance, simplicity, and contentment were entirely disregarded. The distinctions lately paid us by our betters awakened that pride which I had laid asleep, but not removed. Our windows, again, as formerly, were filled with washes for the neck and face.

The sun was dreaded as an enemy to the skin without doors, and the fire as a spoiler of the complexion within. My wife observed that rising too early would hurt her daughter's eyes, that working after dinner would redden their noses; and she convinced me that the hands never looked so white as when they did nothing. Instead therefore of finishing George's shirts, we now had them new-modelling their old gauzes, or flourishing upon catgut. The poor Miss Flamboroughs, their former gay companions, were cast off as mean acquaintance, and the whole conversation ran upon high life, and high-lived company, with pictures, taste, Shakespeare, and the musical glasses.

But we could have borne all this, had not a fortune-telling gipsy come to raise us into perfect sublimity. The tawny sibyl no sooner appeared, than my girls came running to me for a shilling a-piece to cross her hand with silver. To say the truth, I was tired of being always wise, and could not help gratifying their request, because I loved to see them happy. I gave each of them a shilling; though for the honour of the family it must be observed, that they never went without money themselves, as my wife always generously let them have a guinea each, to keep in their pockets, but with strict injunctions never to change it. After they had been closeted up with the fortune-teller for some time, I knew by their looks, upon their returning, that they had been promised something great. "Well, my girls, how have you sped? Tell me, Livy, has the fortune-teller given thee a pennyworth?"—"I protest, papa," says the girl, "I believe she deals with somebody that's not right; for she positively declared, that I am to be married to a Squire in less than a twelvemonth!"—"Well, now, Sophy, my child," said I, "and what sort of a husband are you to have?"—"Sir," replied she, "I am to have a Lord soon after my sister has married the Squire."—"How," cried I, "is that all you are to have for your two shillings? Only a Lord and a Squire for two shillings? You fools, I could have promised you a Prince and a Nabob for half the money."

This curiosity of theirs, however, was attended with very serious effects: we now began to think ourselves designed by the stars to something exalted, and already anticipated our future grandeur.

It has been a thousand times observed, and I must observe it once more, that the hours we pass with happy prospects in view, are more pleasing than those crowned with fruition. In the first case, we cook the dish to our own appetite; in the latter, Nature cooks it for us. It is impossible to repeat the train of agreeable reveries we called up for our entertainment. We looked upon our fortunes as once more rising; and, as the whole parish asserted that the Squire was in love with my daughter, she was actually so with him; for they persuaded her into the passion. In this agreeable interval my wife had the most lucky dreams in the world, which she took care to tell us every morning with great solemnity and exactness. It was one night a coffin and cross-bones, the sign of an approaching wedding; at another time she imagined her daughters' pockets filled with farthings, a certain sign of their being shortly stuffed with gold. The girls themselves had their omens. They felt strange kisses on their lips; they saw rings in the candle; purses bounced from the fire, and true love-knots lurked in the bottom of every teacup.

Towards the end of the week we received a card from the two ladies, in which, with their compliments, they hoped to see all our family at church the Sunday following. All Saturday morning I could perceive, in consequence of this, my wife and daughters in close conference together, and now and then glancing at me with looks that betrayed a latent plot. To be sincere, I had strong suspicions that some absurd proposal was preparing for appearing with splendour the next day. In the evening they began their operations in a very regular manner, and my wife undertook to conduct the siege. After tea, when I seemed in spirits, she began thus:—"I fancy, Charles, my dear, we shall have a great deal of good company at our church to-morrow."—"Perhaps we may, my dear," returned I, "though you need be under no uneasiness about that;

you shall have a sermon whether there be or not."—"That is what I expect," returned she; "but I think, my dear, we ought to appear there as decently as possible, for who knows what may happen?"—"Your precautions," replied I, "are highly commendable. A decent behaviour and appearance in church is what charms me. We should be devout and humble, cheerful and serene."—"Yes," cried she, "I know that; but I mean we should go there in as proper a manner as possible; not altogether like the scrubs about us."—"You are quite right, my dear," returned I, "and I was going to make the very same proposal. The proper manner of going is to go there as early as possible, to have time for meditation before the service begins."—"Phoo, Charles," interrupted she, "all that is very true; but not what I would be at: I mean, we should go there genteelly. You know the church is two miles off, and I protest I don't like to see my daughters trudging up to their pew all blowzed and red with walking, and looking for all the world as if they had been winners at a smock race. Now, my dear, my proposal is this: there are our two plough horses, the colt that has been in our family these nine years, and his companion Blackberry, that has scarcely done an earthly thing for this month past. They are both grown fat and lazy. Why should not they do something as well as we? And let me tell you, when Moses has trimmed them a little, they will cut a very tolerable figure."

To this proposal I objected that walking would be twenty times more genteel than such a paltry conveyance, as Blackberry was wall-eyed, and the colt wanted a tail; that they had never been broke to the rein, but had a hundred vicious tricks; and that we had but one saddle and pillion in the whole house. All these objections, however, were overruled; so that I was obliged to comply. The next morning I perceived them not a little busy in collecting such materials as might be necessary for the expedition; but, as I found it would be a business of time, I walked on to the church before, and they promised speedily to follow. I waited near an hour in the reading desk for their arrival; but not finding them come as I expected, I was obliged to begin, and went through the service, not without some uneasiness at finding them absent. This was increased when all was finished, and no appearance of the family. I therefore walked back by the horse-way, which was five miles round, though the footway was but two, and, when got about half-way home, perceived the procession marching slowly forward towards the church; my son, my wife, and the two little ones exalted on one horse, and my two daughters upon the other. I demanded the cause of their delay; but I soon found by their looks they had met with a thousand misfortunes on the road. The horses had at first refused to move from the door, till Mr. Burchell was kind enough to beat them forward for about two hundred yards with his cudgel. Next, the straps of my wife's pillion broke down, and they were obliged to stop to repair them before they could proceed. After that, one of the horses took it into his head to stand still, and neither blows nor entreaties could prevail with him to proceed. He was just recovering from this dismal situation when I found them; but perceiving everything safe, I own their present mortification did not much displease me, as it would give me many opportunities of future triumph, and teach my daughters more humility.

CHAPTER XI.

The Family still resolve to hold up their Heads.

MICHAELMAS-EVE happening on the next day, we were invited to burn nuts and play tricks at neighbour Flamborough's. Our late mortifications had humbled us a little, or it is probable we might have rejected such an invitation with contempt: however, we suffered ourselves to be happy. Our honest neighbour's goose and dumplings were fine, and the lamb's-wool, even in the opinion of my wife, who was a connoisseur, was excellent. It is true, his manner of telling stories was not quite so well. They were very long, and very dull, and all about himself, and we had laughed at them ten times before: however, we were kind enough to laugh at them once more.

Mr. Burchell, who was of the party, was always fond of seeing some innocent amusement going forward, and set the boys and girls to blind man's buff. My wife, too, was persuaded to join in the diversion, and it gave me pleasure to think she was not yet too old. In the meantime, my neighbour and I looked on, laughed at every feat, and praised our own dexterity when we were young. Hot cockles succeeded next, questions and commands followed that, and, last of all, they sat down to hunt the slipper. As every person may not be acquainted with this primeval pastime, it may be necessary to observe, that the company in this play plant themselves in a ring upon the ground, all except one, who stands in the middle, whose business it is to catch a shoe, which the company shove about under their hams from one to another, something like a weaver's shuttle. As it is impossible, in this case, for the lady who is up to face all the company at once, the great beauty of the play lies in hitting her a thump with the heel of the shoe on that side least capable of making a defence. It was in this manner that my eldest daughter was hemmed in, and thumped about, all blowzed, in spirits, and bawling for "fair play" with a voice that might deafen a ballad-singer; when, confusion on confusion! who should enter the room but our two great acquaintances from town, Lady Blarney and Miss Carolina Wilhelmina Amelia Skeggs! Description would but beggar, therefore it is unnecessary to describe, this new mortification. Death! To be seen by ladies of such high breeding in such vulgar attitudes! Nothing better could ensue from such a vulgar play of Mr. Flamborough's proposing. We seemed stuck to the ground for some time, as if actually petrified with amazement.

The two ladies had been at our house to see us, and finding us from home, came after us hither, as they were uneasy to know what accident could have kept us from church the day before. Olivia undertook to be our prolocutor, and delivered the whole in a summary way, only saying, "We were thrown from our horses.' At which account the ladies were greatly concerned, but being told the family received no hurt, they were extremely glad; but being informed that we were almost killed by the fright, they were vastly sorry; but hearing that we had a very good night, they were extremely glad again. Nothing could exceed their complaisance to my daughters: their professions the last evening were warm, but now they were ardent. They protested a desire of having a more lasting acquaintance. Lady Blarney was particularly attached to Olivia; Miss Carolina Wilhelmina Amelia Skeggs (I love to give the whole name) took a greater fancy to her sister. They supported the conversation between themselves, while my daughters sat silent, admiring their exalted breeding. But as every reader, however beggarly himself, is fond of high-lived dialogues, with anecdotes of lords, ladies, and knights of the Garter, I must beg leave to give him the concluding part of the present conversation.

"All that I know of the matter," cried Miss Skeggs, "is this, that it may be true or may not be true; but this I can assure your Ladyship, that the whole rout was in amaze: his Lordship turned all manner of colours, my Lady fell into a *sound*, but Sir Tomkyn drawing his sword, swore he was hers to the last drop of his blood."

"Well," replied our Peeress, "this I can say, that the Duchess never told me a syllable of the matter, and I believe her Grace would keep nothing a secret from me. This you may depend upon as fact, that the next morning my Lord Duke cried out three times to his valet-de-chambre, Jernigan! Jernigan! Jernigan! bring me my garters."

But previously I should have mentioned the very impolite behaviour of Mr. Burchell, who, during this discourse, sat with his face turned to the fire, and, at the conclusion of every sentence, would cry out "Fudge!" an expression which displeased us all, and, in some measure, damped the rising spirit of the conversation.

"Besides, my dear Skeggs," continued our Peeress, "there is nothing of this in the copy of verses that Dr. Burdock made upon the occasion."—"Fudge!"

"I am surprised at that," cried Miss

Skeggs; "for he seldom leaves anything out, as he writes only for his own amusement. But can your Ladyship favour me with a sight of them?"—"Fudge!"

"My dear creature," replied our Peeress, "do you think I carry such things about me? Though they are very fine, to be sure, and I think myself something of a judge—at least I know what pleases myself. Indeed, I was ever an admirer of all Dr. Burdock's little pieces; for, except what he does, and our dear Countess at Hanover Square, there's nothing comes out but the most lowest stuff in nature; not a bit of high life among them."—"Fudge!"

"Your Ladyship should except," says the other, "your own things in the Lady's Magazine. I hope you'll say there's nothing low-lived there? But I suppose we are to have no more from that quarter?"—"Fudge!"

"Why, my dear," says the lady, "you know my reader and companion has left me, to be married to Captain Roach, and as my poor eyes won't suffer me to write myself, I have been for some time looking out for another. A proper person is no easy matter to find; and, to be sure, thirty pounds a year is a small stipend for a well bred girl of character, that can read, write, and behave in company: as for the chits about town, there is no bearing them about one."—"Fudge!"

"That I know," cried Miss Skeggs, "by experience. For of the three companions I had this last half year, one of them refused to do plain work an hour in the day; another thought twenty-five guineas a year too small a salary; and I was obliged to send away the third, because I suspected an intrigue with the chaplain. Virtue, my dear Lady Blarney, virtue is worth any price; but where is that to be found?"—"Fudge!"

My wife had been, for a long time, all attention to this discourse, but was particularly struck with the latter part of it. Thirty pounds and twenty-five guineas a year, made fifty-six pounds five shillings English money, all which was in a manner going a begging, and might easily be secured in the family. She for a moment studied my looks for approbation; and, to own a truth, I was of opinion, that two such places would fit our two daughters exactly. Besides, if the Squire had any real affection for my eldest daughter, this would be the way to make her every way qualified for her fortune. My wife, therefore, was resolved that we should not be deprived of such advantages for want of assurance, and undertook to harangue for the family. "I hope," cried she, "your ladyships will pardon my present presumption. It is true, we have no right to pretend to such favours; but yet it is natural for me to wish putting my children forward in the world. And, I will be bold to say, my two girls have had a pretty good education and capacity; at least the country can't show better. They can read, write, and cast accompts; they understand their needle, broadstitch, cross and change, and all manner of plain work; they can pink, point, and frill, and know something of music; they can do up small clothes, and work upon catgut; my eldest can cut paper, and my youngest has a very pretty manner of telling fortunes upon the cards."—"Fudge!"

When she had delivered this pretty piece of eloquence, the two ladies looked at each other a few minutes in silence, with an air of doubt and importance. At last Miss Carolina Wilhelmina Amelia Skeggs condescended to observe, that the young ladies, from the opinion she could form of them from so slight an acquaintance, seemed very fit for such employments. "But a thing of this kind, madam," cried she, addressing my spouse, "requires a thorough examination into characters, and a more perfect knowledge of each other. Not, madam," continued she, "that I in the least suspect the young ladies' virtue, prudence, and discretion; but there is a form in these things, madam—there is a form."

My wife approved her suspicions very much, observing that she was very apt to be suspicious herself, but referred her to all the neighbours for a character; but this our Peeress declined as unnecessary, alleging that our cousin Thornhill's recommendation would be sufficient; and upon this we rested our petition.

CHAPTER XII.

Fortune seems resolved to humble the Family of Wakefield. Mortifications are often more painful than real Calamities.

When we were returned home, the night was dedicated to schemes of future conquest. Deborah exerted much sagacity in conjecturing which of the two girls was likely to have the best place, and most opportunities of seeing good company. The only obstacle to our preferment was in obtaining the Squire's recommendation; but he had already shown us too many instances of his friendship to doubt of it now. Even in bed, my wife kept up the usual theme: "Well, faith, my dear Charles, between ourselves, I think we have made an excellent day's work of it." —"Pretty well!" cried I, not knowing what to say. "What, only pretty well!" returned she: "I think it is very well. Suppose the girls should come to make acquaintances of taste in town! This I am assured of, that London is the only place in the world for all manner of husbands. Besides, my dear, stranger things happen every day: and as ladies of quality are so taken with my daughters, what will not men of quality be? *Entre nous*, I protest I like my Lady Blarney vastly—so very obliging. However, Miss Carolina Wilhelmina Amelia Skeggs has my warm heart. But yet, when they came to talk of places in town, you saw at once how I nailed them. Tell me, my dear, don't you think I did for my children there?" —"Ay," returned I, not knowing well what to think of the matter; "Heaven grant they may be both the better for it this day three months!" This was one of those observations I usually made to impress my wife with an opinion of my sagacity: for if the girls succeeded, then it was a pious wish fulfilled; but if any thing unfortunate ensued, then it might be looked upon as a prophecy. All this conversation, however, was only preparatory to another scheme; and indeed I dreaded as much. This was nothing less than that, as we were now to hold up our heads a little higher in the world, it would be proper to sell the colt, which was grown old, at a neighbouring fair, and buy us a horse that would carry a single or double upon an occasion, and make a pretty appearance at church, or upon a visit. This at first I opposed stoutly; but it was stoutly defended. However, as I weakened, my antagonist gained strength, till at last it was resolved to part with him.

As the fair happened on the following day, I had intentions of going myself; but my wife persuaded me that I had got a cold, and nothing could prevail upon her to permit me from home. "No, my dear," said she, "our son Moses is a discreet boy, and can buy and sell to a very good advantage: you know all our great bargains are of his purchasing. He always stands out and higgles, and actually tires them till he gets a bargain."

As I had some opinion of my son's prudence, I was willing enough to entrust him with this commission: and the next morning I perceived his sisters mighty busy in fitting out Moses for the fair; trimming his hair, brushing his buckles, and cocking his hat with pins. The business of the toilet being over, we had at last the satisfaction of seeing him mounted upon the colt, with a deal box before him to bring home groceries in. He had on a coat made of that cloth they call thunder-and-lightning, which, though grown too short, was much too good to be thrown away. His waistcoat was of gosling green, and his sisters had tied his hair with a broad black riband. We all followed him several paces from the door, bawling after him, "Good luck! good luck!" till we could see him no longer.

He was scarce gone, when Mr. Thornhill's butler came to congratulate us upon our good fortune, saying that he overheard his young master mention our names with great commendation.

Good fortune seemed resolved not to come alone. Another footman from the same family followed, with a card for my daughters, importing that the two ladies had received such pleasing accounts from Mr. Thornhill of us all, that after a few previous inquiries they hoped to be perfectly satisfied. "Ay," cried my wife, "I now see it is no easy matter to get into the families of the great; but when one once gets in, then, as Moses says, one may go to sleep." To this piece of humour, for she intended it for wit, my daughters assented with a loud laugh of pleasure. In short, such was her satisfaction at this message, that she actually put her hand in her pocket, and gave the messenger sevenpence halfpenny.

This was to be our visiting day. The next that came was Mr. Burchell, who had been at the fair. He brought my little ones a pennyworth of gingerbread each, which my wife undertook to keep for them, and give them by letters at a time. He brought my daughters also a couple of boxes, in which they might keep wafers, snuff, patches, or even money, when they got it. My wife was usually fond of a weasel-skin purse, as being the most lucky; but this by the by. We had still a regard for Mr. Burchell, though his late rude behaviour was in some measure displeasing; nor could we now avoid communicating our happiness to him, and asking his advice: although we seldom followed advice, we were all ready enough to ask it. When he read the note from the two ladies, he shook his head, and observed, that an affair of this sort demanded the utmost circumspection. This air of diffidence highly displeased my wife. "I never doubted, sir," cried she, "your readiness to be against my daughters and me. You have more circumspection than is wanted. However, I fancy when we come to ask advice, we will apply to persons who seem to have made use of it themselves."—"Whatever my own conduct may have been, madam," replied he, "is not the present question: though, as I have made no use of advice myself, I should in conscience give it to those that will." As I was apprehensive this answer might draw on a repartee, making up by abuse what it wanted in wit, I changed the subject, by seeming to wonder what could keep our son so long at the fair, as it was now almost nightfall. "Never mind our son," cried my wife; "depend upon it he knows what he is about. I'll warrant we'll never see him sell his hen of a rainy day. I have seen him buy such bargains as would amaze one. I'll tell you a good story about that, that will make you split your sides with laughing.—But, as I live, yonder comes Moses, without a horse, and the box at his back."

As she spoke, Moses came slowly on foot, and sweating under the deal box, which he had strapt round his shoulders like a pedlar. "Welcome, welcome, Moses! well, my boy, what have you brought us from the fair?"—"I have brought you myself," cried Moses, with a sly look, and resting the box on the dresser. "Ay, Moses," cried my wife, "that we know; but where is the horse?"—"I have sold him," cried Moses, "for three pounds five shillings and twopence."—"Well done, my good boy," returned she; "I knew you would touch them off. Between ourselves, three pounds five shillings and twopence is no bad day's work. Come, let us have it then."—"I have brought back no money," cried Moses again. "I have laid it all out in a bargain, and here it is," pulling out a bundle from his breast: "here they are; a gross of green spectacles, with silver rims and shagreen cases."—"A gross of green spectacles!" repeated my wife, in a faint voice. "And you have parted with the colt, and brought us back nothing but a gross of green paltry spectacles!"—"Dear mother," cried the boy, "why won't you listen to reason? I had them a dead bargain, or I should not have brought them. The silver rims alone will sell for double the money."—"A fig for the silver rims," cried my wife, in a passion: "I dare swear they won't sell for above half the money at the rate of broken silver, five shillings an ounce."—"You need be under no uneasiness," cried I, "about selling the rims, for they are not worth sixpence; for I perceive they are only copper varnished over."—"What!" cried my wife, "not silver! the rims not silver?"—"No," cried I, "no more silver than your saucepan."—"And so," returned she, "we have parted with the colt, and have only got a gross of green spectacles, with copper rims and shagreen cases? A murrain take such trumpery! The blockhead has been imposed upon, and should have known his company better."—"There, my dear," cried I, "you are wrong; he should not have known them at all."—

"Marry, hang the idiot!" returned she, "to bring me such stuff: if I had them I would throw them in the fire."—"There again you are wrong, my dear," cried I; "for though they be copper, we will keep them by us, as copper spectacles, you know, are better than nothing."

By this time the unfortunate Moses was undeceived. He now saw that he had been imposed upon by a prowling sharper, who, observing his figure, had marked him for an easy prey. I therefore asked the circumstances of his deception. He sold the horse, it seems, and walked the fair in search of another. A reverend-looking man brought him to a tent, under pretence of having one to sell. "Here," continued Moses, "we met another man, very well dressed, who desired to borrow twenty pounds upon these, saying that he wanted money, and would dispose of them for a third of the value. The first gentleman, who pretended to be my friend, whispered me to buy them, and cautioned me not to let so good an offer pass. I sent for Mr. Flamborough, and they talked him up as finely as they did me; and so at last we were persuaded to buy the two gross between us."

CHAPTER XIII.

Mr. Burchell is found to be an Enemy, for he has the confidence to give disagreeable Advice.

OUR family had now made several attempts to be fine; but some unforeseen disaster demolished each as soon as projected. I endeavoured to take the advantage of every disappointment to improve their good sense, in proportion as they were frustrated in ambition. "You see, my children," cried I, "how little is to be got by attempts to impose upon the world in coping with our betters. Such as are poor, and will associate with none but the rich, are hated by those they avoid, and despised by those they follow. Unequal combinations are always disadvantageous to the weaker side: the rich having the pleasure, and the poor the inconveniences that result from them. But come, Dick, my boy, and repeat the fable that you were reading to-day, for the good of the company."

"Once upon a time," cried the child, "a Giant and a Dwarf were friends, and kept together. They made a bargain, that they would never forsake each other, but go seek adventures. The first battle they fought was with two Saracens, and the Dwarf, who was very courageous, dealt one of the champions a most angry blow. It did the Saracen very little injury, who, lifting up his sword, fairly struck off the poor Dwarf's arm. He was now in a woful plight; but the Giant, coming to his assistance, in a short time left the two Saracens dead on the plain, and the Dwarf cut off the dead man's head out of spite. They then travelled on another adventure. This was against three bloody-minded Satyrs, who were carrying away a damsel in distress. The Dwarf was not quite so fierce now as before; but for all that struck the first blow, which was returned by another that knocked out his eye; but the Giant was soon up with them, and, had they not fled, would certainly have killed them every one. They were all very joyful for this victory, and the damsel who was relieved fell in love with the Giant, and married him. They now travelled far, and farther than I can tell, till they met with a company of robbers. The Giant, for the first time, was foremost now; but the Dwarf was not far behind. The battle was stout and long. Wherever the Giant came, all fell before him; but the Dwarf had like to have been killed more than once. At last the victory declared for the two adventurers; but the Dwarf lost his leg. The Dwarf had now lost an arm, a leg, and an eye, while the Giant was without a single wound. Upon which he cried out to his little companion, 'My little hero, this is glorious sport! let us get one victory more, and then we shall have honour for ever.'—'No,' cries the Dwarf, who was by this time grown wiser, 'no, I declare off; I'll fight no more: for I find in every battle that you get all the honours and rewards, but all the blows fall upon me.'"

I was going to moralize this fable, when our attention was called off to a warm dispute between my wife and Mr. Burchell, upon my daughters' intended expedition to town. My wife very strenuously insisted upon the advantages that would result from it: Mr. Burchell, on the contrary, dissuaded her with great ardour; and I stood neuter. His present dissuasions seemed but the second part of those which were received with so ill a grace in the morning. The dispute grew high; while poor Deborah, instead of reasoning stronger, talked louder, and at last was obliged to take shelter from a defeat in clamour. The conclusion of her harangue, however, was highly displeasing to us all: she knew, she said, of some who had their own secret reasons for what they advised; but, for her part, she wished such to stay away from her house for the future. "Madam," cried Burchell, with looks of great composure, which tended to inflame her the more, "as for secret reasons you are right: I have secret reasons, which I forbear to mention, because you are not able to answer those of which I make no secret: but I find my visits here are become troublesome; I'll take my leave therefore now, and perhaps come once more to take a final farewell when I am quitting the country." Thus saying, he took up his hat, nor could the attempts of Sophia, whose looks seemed to upbraid his precipitancy, prevent his going.

When gone, we all regarded each other for some minutes with confusion. My wife, who knew herself to be the cause, strove to hide her concern with a forced smile, and an air of assurance, which I was willing to reprove: "How, woman," cried I to her, "is it thus we treat strangers? Is it thus we return their kindness? Be assured, my dear, that these were the harshest words, and to me the most unpleasing, that ever escaped your lips!"—"Why would he provoke me then?" replied she; "but I know the motives of his advice perfectly well. He would prevent my girls from going to town, that he may have the pleasure of my youngest daughter's company here at home. But, whatever happens, she shall choose better company than such low-lived fellows as he."—"Low-lived, my dear, do you call him?" cried I; "it is very possible we may mistake this man's character, for he seems, upon some occasions, the most finished gentleman I ever knew. Tell me, Sophia, my girl, has he ever given you any secret instances of his attachment?"—"His conversation with me, sir," replied my daughter, "has ever been sensible, modest, and pleasing. As to aught else—no, never. Once, indeed, I remember to have heard him say, he never knew a woman who could find merit in a man that seemed poor."—"Such, my dear," cried I, "is the common cant of all the unfortunate or idle. But I hope you have been taught to judge properly of such men, and that it would be even madness to expect happiness from one who has been so very bad an economist of his own. Your mother and I have now better prospects for you. The next winter, which you will probably spend in town, will give you opportunities of making a more prudent choice."

Wnat Sophia's reflections were upon this occasion I cannot pretend to determine; but I was not displeased at the bottom that we were rid of a guest from whom I had much to fear. Our breach of hospitality went to my conscience a little; but I quickly silenced that monitor by two or three specious reasons, which served to satisfy and reconcile me to myself. The pain which conscience gives the man who has already done wrong is soon got over. Conscience is a coward; and those faults it has not strength enough to prevent, it seldom has justice enough to accuse.

CHAPTER XIV.

Fresh Mortifications, or a Demonstration that seeming Calamities may be real Blessings.

THE journey of my daughters to town was now resolved upon, Mr. Thornhill having kindly promised to inspect their conduct himself, and inform us by letter of their behaviour. But it was thought indispensably necessary that their appearance should equal the greatness of their expectations, which could not be done without expense. We debated therefore in full council what were the easiest methods of raising money, or, more properly speaking, what we could most conveniently sell. The deliberation was soon finished: it was found that our remaining horse was utterly useless for the plough without his companion, and equally unfit for the road, as wanting an eye: it was therefore determined that we should dispose of him for the purpose above mentioned, at the neighbouring fair; and, to prevent imposition, that I should go with him myself. Though this was one of the first mercantile transactions of my life, yet I had no doubt about acquitting myself with reputation. The opinion a man forms of his own prudence is measured by that of the company he keeps: and as mine was most in the family way, I had conceived no unfavourable sentiments of my worldly wisdom. My wife, however, next morning, at parting, after I had got some paces from the door, called me back to advise me, in a whisper, to have all my eyes about me.

I had, in the usual forms, when I came to the fair, put my horse through all his paces, but for some time had no bidders. At last a chapman approached, and after he had for a good while examined the horse round, finding him blind of one eye, he would have nothing to say to him; a second came up, but observing he had a spavin, declared he would not take him for the driving home; a third perceived he had a windgall, and would bid no money; a fourth knew by his eye that he had the botts; a fifth wondered what a plague I could do at the fair with a blind, spavined, galled hack, that was only fit to be cut up for a dog kennel. By this time, I began to have a most hearty contempt for the poor animal myself, and was almost ashamed at the approach of every customer: for though I did not entirely believe all the fellows told me, yet I reflected that the number of witnesses was a strong presumption they were right; and St. Gregory, upon Good Works, professes himself to be of the same opinion.

I was in this mortifying situation, when a brother clergyman, an old acquaintance, who had also business at the fair, came up, and, shaking me by the hand, proposed adjourning to a public-house, and taking a glass of whatever we could get. I readily closed with the offer, and entering an alehouse, we were shown into a little back room, where there was only a venerable old man, who sat wholly intent over a large book, which he was reading. I never in my life saw a figure that prepossessed me more favourably. His locks of silver grey venerably shaded his temples, and his green old age seemed to be the result of health and benevolence. However, his presence did not interrupt our conversation: my friend and I discoursed on the various turns of fortune we had met; the Whistonian controversy, my last pamphlet, the archdeacon's reply, and the hard measure that was dealt me. But our attention was in a short time taken off, by the appearance of a youth, who, entering the room, respectfully said something softly to the old stranger. "Make no apologies, my child," said the old man; "to do good is a duty we owe to all our fellow-creatures: take this, I wish it were more; but five pounds will relieve your distress, and you are welcome." The modest youth shed tears of gratitude, and yet his gratitude was scarce equal to mine. I could have hugged the good old man in my arms, his benevolence pleased me so. He continued to read, and we resumed our conversation, until my companion, after some time, recollecting that he had business to transact in the fair, promised to be soon back; adding, that he always desired to have as much of Dr. Primrose's company as possible. The old gentleman, hearing my name mentioned, seemed to look at me with attention for some time; and when my friend was gone, most respectfully demanded if I was any way related to the great Primrose, that courageous monogamist, who had been the bulwark of the Church. Never did my heart feel sincerer rapture than at that moment. "Sir," cried I, "the applause of so good a man as I am sure you are, adds to that happiness in my breast which your benevolence has already excited. You behold before you, sir, that Dr. Primrose, the monogamist, whom you have been pleased to call great. You here see that unfortunate divine, who has so long, and it would ill become me to say, successfully, fought against the deuterogamy of the age."—"Sir," cried the stranger, struck with awe, "I fear I have been too familiar, but you'll forgive my curiosity, sir: I beg pardon."—"Sir," cried I, grasping his hand, "you are so far from displeasing me by your familiarity, that I must beg you'll accept my friendship, as you already have my esteem."—"Then with gratitude I accept the offer," cried he, squeezing me by the hand, "thou glorious pillar of unshaken orthodoxy! and do I behold ——" I here interrupted what he was going to say; for though, as an author, I could digest no small share of flattery, yet now my modesty would permit no more. However, no lovers in romance ever cemented a more instantaneous friendship. We talked upon several subjects: at first I thought he seemed rather devout than learned, and began to think he despised all human doctrines as dross. Yet this no way lessened him in my esteem, for I had for some time begun privately to harbour such an opinion myself. I therefore took occasion to observe, that the world in general began to be blameably indifferent as to doctrinal matters, and followed human speculations too much. "Ay, sir," replied he, as if he had reserved all his learning to that moment, "Ay, sir, the world is in its dotage; and yet the cosmogony, or creation of the world, has puzzled philosophers of all ages. What a medley of opinions have they not broached upon the creation of the world! Sanchoniathon, Manetho, Berosus, and Ocellus Lucanus, have all attempted it in vain. The latter has these words, *Anarchon ara kai atelutaion to pan*, which imply that all things have neither beginning nor end. Manetho also, who lived about the time of Nebuchadon-Asser — Asser being a Syriac word, usually applied as a surname to the kings of that country, as Teglat Phäel-Asser, Nabon-Asser—he, I say, formed a conjecture equally absurd; for, as we usually say, *ek to biblion kubernetes*, which implies that books will never teach the world; so he attempted to investigate—— But, sir, I ask pardon, I am straying from the question."—That he actually was; nor could I, for my life, see how the creation of the world had anything to do with the business I was talking of; but it was sufficient to show me that he was a man of letters, and I now reverenced him the more. I was resolved, therefore, to bring him to the touchstone; but he was too mild and too gentle to contend for victory. Whenever I made an observation that looked like a challenge to controversy, he would smile, shake his head, and say nothing; by which I understood he could say much, if he thought proper. The subject, therefore, insensibly changed from the business of antiquity, to that which brought us both to the fair: mine, I told him, was to sell a horse, and very luckily, indeed, his was to buy one for one of his tenants. My horse was soon produced; and, in fine, we struck a bargain. Nothing now remained but to pay me, and he accordingly pulled out a thirty pound note, and bid me change it. Not being in a capacity of complying with this demand, he ordered his footman to be called up, who made his appearance in a very genteel livery. "Here, Abraham," cried he, "go and get gold for this; you'll do it at neighbour Jackson's, or anywhere." While the fellow was gone, he entertained me with a pathetic harangue on the great scarcity of silver, which I undertook to improve, by deploring also the great scarcity of gold; so that, by the time Abraham returned, we had both agreed that money was never so hard to be come at as now. Abraham returned to inform us, that he had been over the whole fair, and could not get change, though he had offered half-a-crown for doing it. This was a very great disappointment to us all; but the old gentleman, having paused a little, asked me if I knew one Solomon Flamborough in my part of the country. Upon replying that he was my next door neighbour: "If that be the case, then," returned he, "I believe we shall deal. You shall have a draft upon him, payable at sight; and, let me tell you, he is as warm a man as any within five miles round him. Honest Solomon and I have been acquainted for many years together. I remember I always beat him at three jumps; but he could hop on one leg farther than I." A draft upon my neighbour was to me the same as money; for I was sufficiently convinced of his ability. The draft was signed, and put into my hands, and Mr. Jenkinson, the old gentleman, his man Abraham, and my horse, old Blackberry, trotted off very well pleased with each other.

After a short interval, being left to reflection, I began to recollect that I had done wrong in taking a draft from a stranger, and so prudently resolved upon following the purchaser, and having back my horse. But this was now too late; I therefore made directly homewards, resolving to get the draft changed into money at my friend's as fast as possible. I found my honest neighbour smoking his pipe at his own door, and informing him that I had a small bill upon him, he read it twice over. "You can read the name, I suppose," cried I,—"Ephraim Jenkinson."—"Yes," returned he, "the name is written plain enough, and I know the gentleman too,—the greatest rascal under the canopy of heaven. This is the very same rogue who sold us the spectacles. Was he not a venerable-looking man, with grey hair, and no flaps to his pocket-holes? And did he not talk a long string of learning about Greek, and cosmogony, and the world?" To this I replied with a groan. "Ay," continued he, "he has but that one piece of learning in the world, and he always talks it away whenever he finds a scholar in company; but I know the rogue, and will catch him yet."

Though I was already sufficiently mortified, my greatest struggle was to come, in facing my wife and daughters. No truant was ever more afraid of returning to school, there to behold the master's visage, than I was of going home. I was determined, however, to anticipate their fury, by first falling into a passion myself.

But, alas! upon entering, I found the family no way disposed for battle. My wife and girls were all in tears, Mr. Thornhill having been there that day to inform them that their journey to town was entirely over. The two ladies, having heard reports of us from some malicious person about us, were that day set out for London. He could neither discover the tendency nor the author of these; but whatever they might be, or whoever might have broached them, he continued to assure our family of his friendship and protection. I found, therefore, that they bore my disappointment with great resignation, as it was eclipsed in the greatness of their own. But what perplexed us most, was to think who could be so base as to asperse the character of a family so harmless as ours; too humble to excite envy, and too inoffensive to create disgust.

CHAPTER XV.

All Mr. Burchell's Villany at once detected. The Folly of being overwise.

THAT evening, and a part of the following day, was employed in fruitless attempts to discover our enemies: scarcely a family in the neighbourhood but incurred our suspicions, and each of us had reasons for our opinions best known to ourselves. As we were in this perplexity, one of our little boys, who had been playing abroad, brought in a letter-case, which he found on the green. It was quickly known to belong to Mr. Burchell, with whom it had been seen, and, upon examination, contained some hints upon different subjects; but what particularly engaged our attention was a sealed note, superscribed, "The copy of a letter to be sent to the ladies at Thornhill Castle." It instantly occurred that he was the base informer, and we deliberated whether the note should not be broken open. I was against it; but Sophia, who said she was sure that of all men he would be the last to be guilty of so much baseness, insisted upon its being read. In this she was seconded by the rest of the family, and at their joint solicitation I read as follows:—

"Ladies,—The bearer will sufficiently satisfy you as to the person from whom this comes: one at least the friend of innocence, and ready to prevent its being seduced. I am informed for a truth, that you have some intention of bringing two young ladies to town, whom I have some knowledge of, under the character of companions. As I would neither have simplicity imposed upon, nor virtue contaminated, I must offer it as my opinion, that the impropriety of such a step will be attended with dangerous consequences. It has never been my way to treat the infamous or the lewd with severity; nor should I now have taken this method of explaining myself, or reproving folly, did it not aim at guilt. Take, therefore, the admonition of a friend, and seriously reflect on the consequences of introducing infamy and vice into retreats where peace and innocence have hitherto resided."

Our doubts were now at an end. There seemed, indeed, something applicable to both sides in this letter, and its censures might as well be referred to those to whom it was written, as to us; but the malicious meaning was obvious, and we went no farther. My wife had scarcely patience to hear me to the end, but railed at the writer with unrestrained resentment. Olivia was equally severe, and Sophia seemed perfectly amazed at his baseness. As for my part, it appeared to me one of the vilest instances of unprovoked ingratitude I had ever met with; nor could I account for it in any other manner, than by imputing it to his desire of detaining my youngest daughter in the country, to have the more frequent opportunities of an interview. In this manner we all sat ruminating upon schemes of vengeance, when our other little boy came running in to tell us that Mr. Burchell was approaching at the other end of the field. It is easier to conceive than describe the complicated sensations which are felt from the pain of a recent injury, and the pleasure of approaching vengeance. Though our intentions were only to upbraid him with his ingratitude, yet it was resolved to do it in a manner that would be perfectly cutting. For this purpose we agreed to meet him with our usual smiles; to chat in the beginning with more than ordinary kindness, to amuse him a little; and then, in the midst of the flattering calm, to burst upon him like an earthquake, and overwhelm him with a sense of his own baseness. This being resolved upon, my wife undertook to manage the business herself, as she really had some talents for such an undertaking. We saw him approach: he entered, drew a chair, and sat down. "A fine day, Mr. Burchell."—"A very fine day, Doctor; though I fancy we shall have some rain by the shooting of my corns."—"The shooting of your horns!" cried my wife, in a loud fit of laughter, and then asked pardon for being fond of a joke. "Dear madam," replied he, "I pardon you with all my heart, for I protest I should not have thought it a joke had you not told me."—"Perhaps not, sir," cried my wife, winking at us; "and yet I dare say you can tell us how many jokes go to an ounce."—"I fancy, madam," returned Burchell, "you have been reading a jest book this morning, that ounce of jokes is so very good a conceit; and yet, madam, I had rather see half an ounce of understanding."—"I believe you might," cried my wife, still smiling at us, though the laugh was against her; "and yet I have seen some men pretend to understanding that have very little."—"And no doubt," returned her antagonist, "you have known ladies set up for wit that had none." I quickly began to find that my wife was likely to gain but little at this business; so I resolved to treat him in a style of more severity myself. "Both wit and understanding," cried I, "are trifles, without integrity; it is that which gives value to every character. The ignorant peasant without fault, is greater than the philosopher with many; for what is genius or courage without an heart?

"'An honest man's the noblest work of God.'"

"I always held that hackneyed maxim of Pope," returned Mr. Burchell, "as very unworthy a man of genius, and a base desertion of his own superiority. As the reputation of books is raised, not by their freedom from defect, but the greatness of their beauties; so should that of men be prized, not for their exception from fault, but the size of those virtues they are possessed of. The scholar may want prudence, the statesman may have pride, and the champion ferocity; but shall we prefer to these the low mechanic, who laboriously plods through life without censure or applause? We might as well prefer the tame correct paintings of the Flemish school to the erroneous but sublime animations of the Roman pencil."

"Sir," replied I, "your present observation is just, when there are shining virtues and minute defects; but when it appears that great vices are opposed in the same mind to as extraordinary virtues, such a character deserves contempt."

"Perhaps," cried he, "there may be some such monsters as you describe, of great vices joined to great virtues; yet, in my progress through life, I never yet found one instance of their existence: on the contrary, I have ever perceived, that where the mind was capacious, the affections were good. And indeed Providence seems kindly our friend in this particular, thus to debilitate the understanding where the heart is corrupt, and diminish the power where there is the will to do mischief. This rule seems to extend even to other animals: the little vermin race are ever treacherous, cruel, and cowardly, whilst those endowed with strength and power are generous, brave, and gentle."

"These observations sound well," returned I, "and yet it would be easy this moment to point out a man," and I fixed my eye stedfastly upon him, "whose head and heart form a most detestable contrast. Ay, sir," continued I, raising my voice, "and I am glad to have this opportunity of detecting him in the midst of his fancied security. Do you know this, sir, this pocket-book?"—"Yes, sir," returned he, with a face of impenetrable assurance, "that pocket-book is mine, and I am glad you have found it."—"And do you know," cried I, "this letter? Nay, never falter, man; but look me full in the face: I say, do you know this letter?"—"That letter?" returned he; "yes, it was I that wrote that letter."—"And how could you," said I, "so basely, so ungratefully presume to write this letter?"—"And how came you," replied he, with looks of unparalleled effrontery, "so basely to presume to break open this letter? Don't you know, now, I could hang you all for this? All that I have to do is to swear at the next Justice's that you have been guilty of breaking open the lock of my pocket-book, and so hang you all up at his door." This piece of unexpected insolence raised me to such a pitch, that I could scarcely govern my passion. "Ungrateful wretch! begone, and no longer pollute my dwelling with thy baseness! begone, and never let me see thee again! Go from my door, and the only punishment I wish thee is an alarmed conscience, which will be a sufficient tormentor!" So saying, I threw him his pocket-book, which he took up with a smile, and shutting the clasps with the utmost composure, left us, quite astonished at the serenity of his assurance. My wife was particularly enraged that nothing could make him angry, or make him seem ashamed of his villanies. "My dear," cried I, willing to calm those passions that had been raised too high among us, "we are not to be surprised that bad men want shame: they only blush at being detected in doing good, but glory in their vices.

"Guilt and Shame, says the allegory, were at first companions, and, in the beginning of their journey, inseparably kept together. But their union was soon found to be disagreeable and inconvenient to both. Guilt gave Shame frequent uneasiness, and Shame often betrayed the secret conspiracies of Guilt. After long disagreement, therefore, they at length consented to part for ever. Guilt boldly walked forward alone, to overtake Fate, that went before in the shape of an executioner; but Shame, being naturally timorous, returned back to keep company with Virtue, which in the beginning of their journey they had left behind. Thus, my children, after men have travelled through a few stages in vice, Shame forsakes them, and returns back to wait upon the few virtues they have still remaining."

CHAPTER XVI.

The Family use Art, which is opposed with still greater.

WHATEVER might have been Sophia's sensations, the rest of the family was easily consoled for Mr. Burchell's absence by the company of our landlord, whose visits now became more frequent, and longer. Though he had been disappointed in procuring my daughters the amusements of the town, as he designed, he took every opportunity of supplying them with those little recreations which our retirement would admit of. He usually came in the morning; and, while my son and I followed our occupations abroad, he sat with the family at home, and amused them by describing the town, with every part of which he was particularly acquainted. He could repeat all the observations that were retailed in the atmosphere of the playhouses, and had all the good things of the high wits by rote, long before they made their way into the jest books. The intervals between conversation were employed in teaching my daughters piquet, or sometimes in setting my two little ones to box, to make them *sharp*, as he called it: but the hopes of having him for a son-in-law in some measure blinded us to all his imperfections. It must be owned, that my wife laid a thousand schemes to entrap him; or, to speak more tenderly, used every art to magnify the merit of her daughter. If the cakes at tea eat short and crisp, they were made by Olivia; if the gooseberry wine was well knit, the gooseberries were of her gathering: it was her fingers which gave the pickles their peculiar green; and, in the composition of a pudding, it was her judgment that mixed the ingredients. Then the poor woman would sometimes tell the Squire, that she thought him and Olivia extremely of a size, and would bid both stand up to see which was tallest. These instances of cunning, which she thought impenetrable, yet which everybody saw through, were very pleasing to our benefactor, who gave every day some new proofs of his passion, which, though they had not arisen to proposals of marriage, yet we thought fell but little short of it; and his slowness was attributed sometimes to native bashfulness, and sometimes to his fear of offending his uncle. An occurrence, however, which happened soon after, put it beyond a doubt that he designed to become one of our family; my wife even regarded it as an absolute promise.

My wife and daughters happening to return a visit at neighbour Flamborough's, found that family had lately got their pictures drawn by a limner, who travelled the country, and took likenesses for fifteen shillings a head. As this family and ours had long a sort of rivalry in point of taste, our spirit took the alarm at this stolen march upon us; and, notwithstanding all I could say, and I said much, it was resolved that we should have our pictures done too.

Having, therefore, engaged the limner, —for what could I do?—our next deliberation was to show the superiority of our taste in the attitudes. As for our neighbour's family, there were seven of them, and they were drawn with seven oranges, —a thing quite out of taste, no variety in life, no composition in the world. We desired to have something in a brighter style; and, after many debates, at length came to a unanimous resolution of being drawn together, in one large historical family piece. This would be cheaper, since one frame would serve for all, and it would be infinitely more genteel; for all families of any taste were now drawn in the same manner. As we did not immediately recollect an historical subject to hit us, we were contented each with being drawn as independent historical figures. My wife desired to be represented as Venus, and the painter was desired not to be too frugal of his diamonds in her stomacher and hair. Her two little ones were to be as Cupids by her side; while I, in my gown and band, was to present her with my books on the Whistonian controversy. Olivia would be drawn as an Amazon, sitting upon a bank of flowers, dressed in a green joseph, richly laced with gold, and a whip in her hand. Sophia was to be a shepherdess, with as many sheep as the painter could put in for nothing; and Moses was to be dressed out with a hat and white feather. Our taste so much pleased the Squire, that he insisted on being put in as one of the family, in the character of Alexander the Great, at Olivia's feet. This was considered by us all as an indication of his desire to be introduced into the family, nor could we refuse his request. The painter was therefore set to work, and, as he wrought with assiduity and expedition, in less than four days the whole was completed. The piece was large, and, it must be owned, he did not spare his colours; for which my wife gave him great encomiums. We were all perfectly satisfied with his performance; but an unfortunate circumstance which had not occurred till the picture was finished, now struck us with dismay. It was so very large, that we had no place in the house to fix it. How we all came to disregard so material a point is inconceivable; but certain it is, we had been all greatly remiss. The picture, therefore, instead of gratifying our vanity, as we hoped, leaned, in a most mortifying manner, against the kitchen wall, where the canvas was stretched and painted, much too large to be got through any of the doors, and the jest of all our neighbours. One compared it to Robinson Crusoe's longboat, too large to be removed; another thought it more resembled a reel in a bottle: some wondered how it could be got out, but still more were amazed how it ever got in.

But though it excited the ridicule of some, it effectually raised more malicious suggestions in many. The Squire's portrait being found united with ours was an honour too great to escape envy. Scandalous whispers began to circulate at our expense, and our tranquillity was continually disturbed by persons, who came as friends, to tell us what was said of us by enemies. These reports we always resented with becoming spirit; but scandal ever improves by opposition.

We once again, therefore, entered into a consultation upon obviating the malice of our enemies, and at last came to a resolution which had too much cunning to give me entire satisfaction. It was this: as our principal object was to discover the honour of Mr. Thornhill's addresses, my wife undertook to sound him, by pretending to ask his advice in the choice of a husband for her eldest daughter. If this was not found sufficient to induce him to a declaration, it was then resolved to terrify him with a rival. To this last step, however, I would by no means give my consent, till Olivia gave me the most solemn assurances that she would marry the person provided to rival him upon this occasion, if he did not prevent it by taking her himself. Such was the scheme laid, which, though I did not strenuously oppose, I did not entirely approve.

The next time, therefore, that Mr. Thornhill came to see us, my girls took care to be out of the way, in order to give their mamma an opportunity of putting her scheme in execution; but they only retired to the next room, from whence they could overhear the whole conversation. My wife artfully introduced it, by observing, that one of the Miss Flamboroughs was like to have a very good match of it in Mr. Spanker. To this the Squire assenting, she proceeded to remark, that they who had warm fortunes were always sure of getting good husbands: "But Heaven help," continued she, "the girls that have none! What signifies beauty, Mr. Thornhill? or what signifies all the virtue, and all the qualifications in the world, in this age of self-interest? It is not, What is she? but, What has she? is all the cry."

"Madam," returned he, "I highly approve the justice, as well as the novelty, of your remarks; and if I were a king, it should be otherwise. It should then, indeed, be fine times with the girls without fortunes: our two young ladies should be the first for whom I would provide."

"Ah, sir," returned my wife, "you are pleased to be facetious: but I wish I were a queen, and then I know where my eldest daughter should look for a husband. But, now that you have put it into my head, seriously, Mr. Thornhill, can't you recommend me a proper husband for her? She is now nineteen years old, well grown and well educated, and, in my humble opinion, does not want for parts."

"Madam," replied he, "if I were to choose, I would find out a person possessed of every accomplishment that can make an angel happy. One with prudence, fortune, taste, and sincerity; such, madam, would be, in my opinion, the proper husband."—"Ay, sir," said she, "but do you know of any such person?"—"No, madam," returned he, "it is impossible to know any person that deserves to be her husband: she's too great a treasure for one man's possession; she's a goddess! Upon my soul, I speak what I think—she's an angel!"—"Ah, Mr. Thornhill, you only flatter my poor girl: but we have been thinking of marrying her to one of your tenants, whose mother is lately dead, and who wants a manager; you know whom I mean,—Farmer Williams; a warm man, Mr. Thornhill, able to give her good bread, and who has several times made her proposals" (which was actually the case); "but, sir," concluded she, "I should be glad to have your approbation of our choice."—"How, madam," replied he, "my approbation!—my approbation of such a choice! Never. What! sacrifice so much beauty, and sense, and goodness, to a creature insensible of the blessing! Excuse me, I can never approve of such a piece of injustice. And I have my reasons."—"Indeed, sir," cried Deborah, "if you have your reasons, that's another affair; but I should be glad to know those reasons."—"Excuse me, madam," returned he, "they lie too deep for discovery" (laying his hand upon his bosom); "they remain buried, rivetted here."

After he was gone, upon a general consultation, we could not tell what to make of these fine sentiments. Olivia considered them as instances of the most exalted passion; but I was not quite so sanguine: it seemed to me pretty plain, that they had more of love than matrimony in them; yet, whatever they might portend, it was resolved to prosecute the scheme of Farmer Williams, who, from my daughter's first appearance in the country, had paid her his addresses.

CHAPTER XVII.

Scarcely any Virtue found to resist the Power of long and pleasing Temptation.

As I only studied my child's real happiness, the assiduity of Mr. Williams pleased me, as he was in easy circumstances, prudent, and sincere. It required but very little encouragement to revive his former passion; so that in an evening or two he and Mr. Thornhill met at our house, and surveyed each other for some time with looks of anger; but Williams owed his landlord no rent, and little regarded his indignation. Olivia, on her side, acted the coquette to perfection, if that might be called acting which was her real character, pretending to lavish all her tenderness on her new lover. Mr. Thornhill appeared quite dejected at this preference, and with a pensive air took leave, though I own it puzzled me to find him in so much pain as he appeared to be, when he had it in his power so easily to remove the cause, by declaring an honourable passion. But whatever uneasiness he seemed to endure, it could easily be perceived that Olivia's anguish was still greater. After any of these interviews between her lovers, of which there were several, she usually retired to solitude, and there indulged her grief. It was in such a situation I found her one evening, after she had been for some time supporting a fictitious gaiety. "You now see, my child," said I, "that your confidence in Mr. Thornhill's passion was all a dream: he permits the rivalry of another, every way his inferior, though he knows it lies in his power to secure you to himself by a candid declaration."—"Yes, papa," returned she; "but he has his reasons for this delay: I know he has. The sincerity of his looks and words convinces me of his real esteem. A short time, I hope, will discover the generosity of his sentiments, and convince you that my opinion of him has been more just than yours."—"Olivia, my darling," returned I, "every scheme that has been hitherto pursued to compel him to a declaration has been proposed and planned by yourself; nor can you in the least say that I have constrained you. But you must not suppose, my dear, that I will ever be instrumental in suffering his honest rival to be the dupe of your ill-placed passion. Whatever time you require to bring your fancied admirer to an explanation shall be granted; but at the expiration of that term, if he is still regardless, I must absolutely insist that honest Mr. Williams shall be rewarded for his fidelity. The character which I have hitherto supported in life demands this from me, and my tenderness as a parent shall never influence my integrity as a man. Name, then, your day; let it be as distant as you think proper; and in the meantime, take care to let Mr. Thornhill know the exact time on which I design delivering you up to another. If he really loves you, his own good sense will readily suggest that there is but one method alone to prevent his losing you for ever." This proposal, which she could not avoid considering as perfectly just, was readily agreed to. She again renewed her most positive promise of marrying Mr. Williams, in case of the other's insensibility; and at the next opportunity, in Mr. Thornhill's presence, that day month was fixed upon for her nuptials with his rival.

Such vigorous proceedings seemed to redouble Mr. Thornhill's anxiety: but what Olivia really felt gave me some uneasiness. In this struggle between prudence and passion, her vivacity quite forsook her, and every opportunity of solitude was sought, and spent in tears. One week passed away; but Mr. Thornhill made no efforts to restrain her nuptials. The succeeding week he was still assiduous; but not more open. On the third, he discontinued his visits entirely, and instead of my daughter testifying any impatience, as I expected, she seemed to retain a pensive tranquillity, which I looked upon as resignation. For my own part, I was now sincerely pleased with thinking that my child was going to be secured in a continuance of competence and peace, and frequently applauded her resolution, in preferring happiness to ostentation.

It was within about four days of her intended nuptials, that my little family at night were gathered round a charming fire, telling stories of the past, and laying schemes for the future: busied in forming a thousand projects, and laughing at whatever folly came uppermost. "Well, Moses," cried I, "we shall soon, my boy, have a wedding in the family: what is your opinion of matters and things in general?"—"My opinion, father, is, that all things go on very well; and I was just now thinking, that when sister Livy is married to Farmer Williams, we shall then have the loan of his cider-press and brewing-tubs for nothing."—"That we shall, Moses," cried I, "and he will sing us 'Death and the Lady,' to raise our spirits into the bargain."—"He has taught that song to our Dick," cried Moses; "and I think he goes through it very prettily."—"Does he so?" cried I; "then let us have it: where is little Dick? let him up with it boldly."—"My brother Dick," cried Bill, my youngest, "is just gone out with sister Livy: but Mr. Williams has taught me two songs, and I'll sing them for you, papa. Which song do you choose, 'The Dying Swan,' or the 'Elegy on the Death of a Mad Dog?'"—"The elegy, child, by all means," said I; "I never heard that yet: and Deborah, my life, grief, you know, is dry; let us have a bottle of the best gooseberry wine, to keep up our spirits. I have wept so much at all sorts of elegies of late, that without an enlivening glass I am sure this will overcome me; and Sophy, love, take your guitar, and thrum in with the boy a little."

AN ELEGY ON THE DEATH OF A MAD DOG.

Good people all, of every sort,
Give ear unto my song,
And if you find it wondrous short,
It cannot hold you long.

In Islington there was a man,
Of whom the world might say,
That still a godly race he ran,
Whene'er he went to pray.

A kind and gentle heart he had,
To comfort friends and foes;
The naked every day he clad,
When he put on his clothes.

And in that town a dog was found,
As many dogs there be,
Both mongrel, puppy, whelp, and hound,
And curs of low degree.

This dog and man at first were friends;
But when a pique began,
The dog, to gain some private ends,
Went mad, and bit the man.

Around from all the neighbouring streets
The wond'ring neighbours ran,
And swore the dog had lost his wits,
To bite so good a man.

The wound it seem'd both sore and sad
To every Christian eye;
And while they swore the dog was mad,
They swore the man would die.

But soon a wonder came to light,
That show'd the rogues they lied:
The man recover'd of the bite—
The dog it was that died.

"A very good boy, Bill, upon my word; and an elegy that may truly be called tragical. Come, my children, here's Bill's health, and may he one day be a bishop!"

"With all my heart," cried my wife: "and if he but preaches as well as he sings, I make no doubt of him. The most of his family, by the mother's side, could sing a good song: it was a common saying in our country, that the family of the Blenkinsops could never look straight before them, nor the Hugginsons blow out a candle; that there were none of the Grograms but could sing a song, or of the Marjorams but could tell a story."—"However that be," cried I, "the most vulgar ballad of them all generally pleases me better than the fine modern odes, and things that petrify us in a single stanza,—productions that we at once detest and praise.—Put the glass to your brother, Moses.—The great fault of these elegiasts is, that they are in despair for griefs that give the sensible part of mankind very little pain. A lady loses her muff, her fan, or her lap-dog, and so the silly poet runs home to versify the disaster."

"That may be the mode," cried Moses, "in sublimer compositions: but the Ranelagh songs that come down to us are perfectly familiar, and all cast in the same mould: Colin meets Dolly, and they hold a dialogue together; he gives her a fairing to put in her hair, and she presents him with a nosegay; and then they go together to church, where they give good advice to young nymphs and swains to get married as fast as they can."

"And very good advice too," cried I; "and I am told there is not a place in the world where advice can be given with so much propriety as there: for as it persuades us to marry, it also furnishes us with a wife; and surely that must be an excellent market, my boy, where we are told what we want, and supplied with it when wanting."

"Yes, sir," returned Moses, "and I know but of two such markets for wives in Europe,—Ranelagh in England, and Fontarabia in Spain. The Spanish market is open once a year; but our English wives are saleable every night."

"You are right, my boy," cried his mother; "Old England is the only place in the world for husbands to get wives."—"And for wives to manage their husbands," interrupted I. "It is a proverb abroad, that if a bridge were built across the sea, all the ladies of the Continent would come over to take pattern from ours; for there are no such wives in Europe as our own. But let us have one bottle more, Deborah, my life; and, Moses, give us a good song. What thanks do we not owe to Heaven for thus bestowing tranquillity, health, and competence! I think myself happier now than the greatest monarch upon earth. He has no such fireside, nor such pleasant faces about it. Yes, Deborah, we are now growing old; but the evening of our life is likely to be happy. We are descended from ancestors that knew no stain, and we shall leave a good and virtuous race of children behind us. While we live, they will be our support and our pleasure here; and when we die, they will transmit our honour untainted to posterity. Come, my son, we wait for a song: let us have a chorus. But where is my darling Olivia? that little cherub's voice is always sweetest in the concert." Just as I spoke Dick came running in. "O papa, papa, she is gone from us, she is gone from us; my sister Livy is gone from us for ever!"—"Gone, child!"—"Yes, she is gone off with two gentlemen in a post-chaise, and one of them kissed her, and said he would die for her: and she cried very much, and was for coming back; but he persuaded her again, and she went into the chaise, and said, 'Oh, what will my poor papa do when he knows I am undone!'"—"Now, then," cried I, "my children, go and be miserable; for we shall never enjoy one hour more. And oh, may Heaven's everlasting fury light upon him and his!—thus to rob me of my child! And sure it will, for taking back my sweet innocent that I was leading up to Heaven. Such sincerity as my child was possessed of! But all our earthly happiness is now over! Go, my children, go and be miserable and infamous; for my heart is broken within me!"—"Father," cried my son, "is this your fortitude?"—"Fortitude, child?—yes, ye shall see I have fortitude! Bring me my pistols. I'll pursue the traitor—while he is on earth I'll pursue him. Old as I am, he shall find I can sting him yet. The villain—the perfidious villain!" I had by this time reached down my pistols, when my poor wife, whose passions were not so strong as mine, caught me in her arms. "My dearest, dearest husband!" cried she, "the Bible is the only weapon that is fit for your old hands now. Open that, my love, and read our anguish into patience, for she has vilely deceived us."—"Indeed, sir," resumed my son, after a pause, "your rage is too violent and unbecoming. You should be my mother's comforter, and you increase her pain. It ill suited you and your reverend character thus to curse your greatest enemy: you should not have cursed him, villain as he is."—"I did not curse him child, did I?"—"Indeed, sir, you did; you cursed him twice."—"Then may Heaven forgive me and him if I did! And now, my son, I see it was more than human benevolence that first taught us to bless our enemies: Blessed be His holy name for all the good He hath given, and for all that He hath taken away. But it is not—it is not a small distress that can wring tears from these old eyes, that have not wept for so many years. My child! to undo my darling!—May confusion seize——Heaven forgive me! what am I about to say!—you may remember, my love, how good she was, and how charming: till this vile moment all her care was to make us happy. Had she but died! But she is gone, the honour of our family contaminated, and I must look out for happiness in other worlds than here. But, my child, you saw them go off: perhaps he forced her away? If he forced her, she may yet be innocent."—"Ah, no, sir," cried the child; "he only kissed her, and called her his angel, and she wept very much, and leaned upon his arm, and they drove off very fast."—"She's an ungrateful creature," cried my wife, who could scarcely speak for weeping, "to use us thus. She never had the least constraint put upon her affections. The vile strumpet has basely deserted her parents without any provocation, thus to bring your gray hairs to the grave; and I must shortly follow."

In this manner that night, the first of our real misfortunes, was spent in the bitterness of complaint, and ill-supported sallies of enthusiasm. I determined, however, to find out our betrayer, wherever he was, and reproach his baseness. The next morning we missed our wretched child at breakfast, where she used to give life and cheerfulness to us all. My wife, as before, attempted to ease her heart by reproaches. "Never," cried she, "shall that vilest stain of our family again darken these harmless doors. I will never call her daughter more. No, let the strumpet live with her vile seducer: she may bring us to shame, but she shall never more deceive us."

"Wife," said I, "do not talk thus hardly: my detestation of her guilt is as great as yours; but ever shall this house and this heart be open to a poor returning repentant sinner. The sooner she returns from her transgressions, the more welcome shall she be to me. For the first time the very best may err; art may persuade, and novelty spread out its charm. The first fault is the child of simplicity, but every other, the offspring of guilt. Yes, the wretched creature shall be welcome to this heart and this house, though stained with ten thousand vices. I will again hearken to the music of her voice, again will I hang fondly on her bosom, if I find but repentance there. My son, bring hither my Bible and my staff: I will pursue her, wherever she is; and though I cannot save her from shame, I may prevent the continuance of iniquity."

CHAPTER XVIII.

The Pursuit of a Father to reclaim a Lost Child to Virtue.

Though the child could not describe the gentleman's person who handed his sister into the post-chaise, yet my suspicions fell entirely upon our young landlord, whose character for such intrigues was but too well known. I therefore directed my steps towards Thornhill Castle, resolving to upbraid him, and, if possible, to bring back my daughter: but before I had reached his seat, I was met by one of my parishioners, who said he saw a young lady resembling my daughter in a post-chaise with a gentleman, whom by the description I could only guess to be Mr. Burchell, and that they drove very fast. This information, however, did by no means satisfy me. I therefore went to the young Squire's, and, though it was yet early, insisted upon seeing him immediately. He soon appeared with the most open familiar air, and seemed perfectly amazed at my daughter's elopement, protesting, upon his honour, that he was quite a stranger to it. I now therefore condemned my former suspicions, and could turn them only on Mr. Burchell, who, I recollected, had of late several private conferences with her; but the appearance of another witness left me no room to doubt his villany, who averred, that he and my daughter were actually gone towards the Wells, about thirty miles off, where there was a great deal of company. Being driven to that state of mind in which we all are more ready to act precipitately than to reason right, I never debated with myself whether these accounts might not have been given by persons purposely placed in my way to mislead me, but resolved to pursue my daughter and her fancied deluder thither. I walked along with earnestness, and inquired of several by the way; but received no accounts, till, entering the town, I was met by a person on horseback, whom I remembered to have seen at the Squire's, and he assured me that if I followed them to the races, which were but thirty miles farther, I might depend upon overtaking them; for he had seen them dance there the night before, and the whole assembly seemed charmed with my daughter's performance. Early the next day, I walked forward to the races, and about four in the afternoon I came upon the course. The company made a very brilliant appearance, all earnestly employed in one pursuit,—that of pleasure: how different from mine,—that of reclaiming a lost child to virtue! I thought I perceived Mr. Burchell at some distance from me; but, as if he dreaded an interview, upon my approaching him he mixed among a crowd, and I saw him no more.

I now reflected that it would be to no purpose to continue my pursuit farther, and resolved to return home to an innocent family, who wanted my assistance. But the agitations of my mind, and the fatigues I had undergone, threw me into a fever, the symptoms of which I perceived before I came off the course. This was another unexpected stroke, as I was more than seventy miles distant from home: however, I retired to a little alehouse by the roadside; and in this place, the usual retreat of indigence and frugality, I laid me down patiently to wait the issue of my disorder. I languished here for nearly three weeks; but at last my constitution prevailed, though I was unprovided with money to defray the expenses of my entertainment. It is possible the anxiety from this last circumstance alone might have brought on a relapse, had I not been supplied by a traveller, who stopped to take a cursory refreshment. This person was no other than the philanthropic bookseller in St. Paul's Churchyard, who has written so many little books for children: he called himself their friend, but he was the friend of all mankind. He was no sooner alighted, but he was in haste to be gone; for he was ever on business of the utmost importance, and was at that time actually compiling materials for the history of one Mr. Thomas Trip. I immediately recollected this good-natured man's red pimpled face; for he had published for me against the Deuterogamists of the age; and from him I borrowed a few pieces, to be paid at my return. Leaving the inn, therefore, as I was yet but weak, I resolved to return home by easy journeys of ten miles a day. My health and usual tranquillity were almost restored, and I now condemned that pride which had made me refractory to the hand of correction. Man little knows what calamities are beyond his patience to bear, till he tries them: as in ascending the heights of ambition, which look bright from below, every step we rise shows us some new and gloomy prospect of hidden disappointment; so in our descent from the summits of pleasure, though the vale of misery below may appear at first dark and gloomy, yet the busy mind, still attentive to its own amusement, finds, as we descend, something to flatter and to please. Still as we approach, the darkest objects appear to brighten, and the mental eye becomes adapted to its gloomy situation.

I now proceeded forward, and had walked about two hours, when I perceived what appeared at a distance like a waggon, which I was resolved to overtake; but when I came up with it, found it to be a strolling company's cart, that was carrying their scenes and other theatrical furniture to the next village, where they were to exhibit. The cart was attended only by the person who drove it, and one of the company, as the rest of the players were to follow the ensuing day. "Good company upon the road," says the proverb, "is the shortest cut." I therefore entered into conversation with the poor player; and as I once had some theatrical powers myself, I disserted on such topics with my usual freedom: but as I was pretty much unacquainted with the present state of the stage, I demanded who were the present theatrical writers in vogue—who the Drydens and Otways of the day?—"I fancy, sir," cried the player, "few of our modern dramatists would think themselves much honoured, by being compared to the writers you mention. Dryden's and Rowe's manner, sir, are quite out of fashion: our taste has gone back a whole century; Fletcher, Ben Jonson, and all the plays of Shakespeare are the only things that go down."—"How," cried I, "is it possible the present age can be pleased with that antiquated dialect, that obsolete humour, those overcharged characters, which abound in the works you mention?"—"Sir," returned my companion, "the public think nothing about dialect or humour, or character, for that is none of their business; they only go to be amused, and find themselves happy when they can enjoy a pantomime, under the sanction of Jonson's or Shakespeare's name."—"So then, I suppose," cried I, "that our modern dramatists are rather imitators of Shakespeare than of nature."—"To say the truth," returned my companion, "I don't know that they imitate anything at all; nor, indeed, does the public require it of them; it is not the composition of the piece, but the number of starts and attitudes that may be introduced into it, that elicits applause. I have known a piece, with not one jest in the whole, shrugged into popularity, and another saved, by the poet's throwing in a fit of the gripes. No, sir, the works of Congreve and Farquhar have too much wit in them for the present taste; our modern dialect is much more natural."

By this time, the equipage of the strolling company was arrived at the village, which, it seems, had been apprised of our approach, and was come out to gaze at us; for my companion observed, that strollers always have more spectators without doors than within. I did not consider the impropriety of my being in such company, till I saw a mob gather about me. I therefore took shelter, as fast as possible, in the first alehouse that offered; and being shown into the common room, was accosted by a very well-dressed gentleman, who demanded whether I was the real chaplain of the company, or whether it was only to be my masquerade character in the play? Upon informing him of the truth, and that I did not belong, in any sort, to the company, he was condescending enough to desire me and the player to partake in a bowl of punch, over which he discussed modern politics with great earnestness and interest. I set him down, in my own mind, for nothing less than a parliament-man at least; but was almost confirmed in my conjectures, when, upon asking what there was in the house for supper, he insisted that the player and I should sup with him at his house; with which request, after some entreaties, we were prevailed on to comply.

CHAPTER XIX.

The description of a person discontented with the present Government, and apprehensive of the loss of our liberties.

THE house where we were to be entertained lying at a small distance from the village, our inviter observed, that as the coach was not ready, he would conduct us on foot; and we soon arrived at one of the most magnificent mansions I had seen in that part of the country. The apartment into which we were shown was perfectly elegant and modern: he went to give orders for supper, while the player, with a wink, observed that we were perfectly in luck. Our entertainer soon returned; an elegant supper was brought in; two or three ladies in easy dishabille were introduced, and the conversation began with some sprightliness. Politics, however, was the subject on which our entertainer chiefly expatiated; for he asserted that liberty was at once his boast and his terror. After the cloth was removed, he asked me if I had seen the last Monitor? to which, replying in the negative, "What! nor the Auditor, I suppose?" cried he. "Neither, sir," returned I. "That's strange, very strange!" replied my entertainer. "Now, I read all the politics that come out: the Daily, the Public, the Ledger, the Chronicle, the London Evening, the Whitehall Evening, the seventeen Magazines, and the two Reviews; and, though they hate each other, I love them all. Liberty, sir, liberty is the Briton's boast! and, by all my coal-mines in Cornwall, I reverence its guardians."—"Then, it is to be hoped," cried I, "you reverence the king?"—"Yes," returned my entertainer, "when he does what we would have him;

but if he goes on as he has done of late, I'll never trouble myself more with his matters. I say nothing. I think, only, I could have directed some things better. I don't think there has been a sufficient number of advisers : he should advise with every person willing to give him advice, and then we should have things done in another guess manner."

"I wish," cried I, "that such intruding advisers were fixed in the pillory. It should be the duty of honest men to assist the weaker side of our constitution, that sacred power that has for some years been every day declining, and losing its due share of influence in the state. But these ignorants still continue the same cry of liberty, and, if they have any weight, basely throw it into the subsiding scale."

"How!" cried one of the ladies, "do I live to see one so base, so sordid, as to be an enemy to liberty, and a defender of tyrants? Liberty, that sacred gift of Heaven, that glorious privilege of Britons!"

"Can it be possible," cried our entertainer, "that there should be any found at present advocates for slavery? Any who are for meanly giving up the privileges of Britons? Can any, sir, be so abject?"

"No, sir," replied I, "I am for liberty! that attribute of gods! Glorious liberty! that theme of modern declamation! I would have all men kings! I would be a king myself. We have all naturally an equal right to the throne : we are all originally equal. This is my opinion, and was once the opinion of a set of honest men who were called Levellers. They tried to erect themselves into a community, where all should be equally free. But, alas! it would never answer: for there were some among them stronger, and some more cunning, than others, and these became masters of the rest; for, as sure as your groom rides your horses, because he is a cunninger animal than they, so surely will the animal that is cunninger or stronger than he, sit upon his shoulders in turn. Since, then, it is entailed upon humanity to submit, and some are born to command and others to obey, the question is, as there must be tyrants, whether it is better to have them in the same house with us, or in the same village, or, still farther off, in the metropolis. Now, sir, for my own part, as I naturally hate the face of a tyrant, the farther off he is removed from me the better pleased am I. The generality of mankind also are of my way of thinking, and have unanimously created one king, whose election at once diminishes the number of tyrants, and puts tyranny at the greatest distance from the greatest number of people. Now, the great, who were tyrants themselves before the election of one tyrant, are naturally averse to a power raised over them, and whose weight must ever lean heaviest on the subordinate orders. It is the interest of the great, therefore, to diminish kingly power as much as possible; because, whatever they take from that is naturally restored to themselves; and all they have to do in the state is to undermine the single tyrant, by which they resume their primeval authority. Now, the state may be so circumstanced, or its laws may be so disposed, or its men of opulence so minded, as all to conspire in carrying on this business of undermining monarchy. For, in the first place, if the circumstances of our state be such as to favour the accumulation of wealth, and make the opulent still more rich, this will increase their ambition. An accumulation of wealth, however, must necessarily be the consequence, when, as at present, more riches flow in from external commerce than arise from internal industry; for external commerce can only be managed to advantage by the rich, and they have also at the same time all the emoluments arising from internal industry; so that the rich, with us, have two sources of wealth, whereas the poor have but one. For this reason, wealth, in all commercial states, is found to accumulate; and all such have hitherto in time become aristocratical. Again, the very laws also of this country may contribute to the accumulation of wealth; as when, by their means, the natural ties that bind the rich and poor together are broken, and it is ordained that the rich shall only marry with the rich; or when the learned are held unqualified to serve their country as counsellors, merely from a defect of opulence, and wealth is thus made the object of a wise man's ambition: by these means, I say, and such means as these, riches will accumulate. Now, the possessor of accumulated wealth, when furnished with the necessaries and pleasures of life, has no other method to employ the superfluity of his fortune but in purchasing power. That is, differently speaking, in making dependants, by purchasing the liberty of the needy or the venal, of men who are willing to bear the mortification of contiguous tyranny for bread. Thus each very opulent man generally gathers round him a circle of the poorest of the people; and the polity abounding in accumulated wealth may be compared to a Cartesian system, each orb with a vortex of its own. Those, however, who are willing to move in a great man's vortex, are only such as must be slaves, the rabble of mankind, whose souls and whose education are adapted to servitude, and who know nothing of liberty except the name. But there must still be a large number of the people without the sphere of the opulent man's influence; namely, that order of men which subsists between the very rich and the very rabble; those men who are possessed of too large fortunes to submit to the neighbouring man in power, and yet are too poor to set up for tyranny themselves. In this middle order of mankind are generally to be found all the arts, wisdom, and virtues of society. This order alone is known to be the true preserver of freedom, and may be called THE PEOPLE. Now, it may happen that this middle order of mankind may lose all its influence in a state, and its voice be in a manner drowned in that of the rabble: for, if the fortune sufficient for qualifying a person at present to give his voice in state affairs be ten times less than was judged sufficient upon forming the constitution, it is evident that great numbers of the rabble will thus be introduced into the political system, and they, ever moving in the vortex of the great, will follow where greatness shall direct. In such a state, therefore, all that the middle order has left is to preserve the prerogative and privileges of the one principal governor with the most sacred circumspection. For he divides the power of the rich, and calls off the great from falling with tenfold weight on the middle order placed beneath them. The middle order may be compared to a town of which the opulent are forming the siege, and of which the governor from without is hastening the relief. While the besiegers are in dread of an enemy over them, it is but natural to offer the townsmen the most specious terms; to flatter them with sounds, and amuse them with privileges; but if they once defeat the governor from behind, the walls of the town will be but a small defence to its inhabitants. What they may then expect, may be seen by turning our eyes to Holland, Genoa, or Venice, where the laws govern the poor, and the rich govern the law. I am then for, and would die for monarchy, sacred monarchy: for if there be anything sacred amongst men, it must be the anointed SOVEREIGN of his people; and every diminution of his power, in war or in peace, is an infringement upon the real liberties of the subject. The sounds of Liberty, Patriotism, and Britons, have already done much; it is to be hoped that the true sons of freedom will prevent their ever doing more. I have known many of these pretended champions for liberty in my time, yet do I not remember one that was not in his heart and in his family a tyrant."

My warmth, I found, had lengthened this harangue beyond the rules of good breeding; but the impatience of my entertainer, who often strove to interrupt it, could be restrained no longer. "What!" cried he, "then I have been all this while entertaining a Jesuit in parson's clothes! But, by all the coal-mines of Cornwall, out he shall pack, if my name be Wilkinson." I now found I had gone too far, and asked pardon for the warmth with which I had spoken. "Pardon!" returned he, in a fury: "I think such principles demand ten thousand pardons. What! give up liberty, property, and, as the Gazetteer says, lie down to be saddled with wooden shoes! Sir, I insist upon your marching out of this house immediately, to prevent worse consequences: sir, I insist upon it." I was going to repeat my remonstrances, but just then we heard a footman's rap at the door, and the two ladies cried out, "As sure as death, there is our master and mistress come home!" It seems my entertainer was all this while only the butler, who, in his master's absence, had a mind to cut a figure, and be for a while the gentleman himself; and, to say the truth, he talked politics as well as most country gentlemen do. But nothing could now exceed my confusion upon seeing the gentleman and his lady enter; nor was their surprise, at finding such company and good cheer, less than ours. "Gentlemen," cried the real master of the house to me and my companion, "my wife and I are your most humble servants; but I protest this is so unexpected a favour, that we almost sink under the obligation." However unexpected our company might be to them, theirs, I am sure, was still more so to us, and I was struck dumb with the apprehensions of my own absurdity, when whom should I next see enter the room but my dear Miss Arabella Wilmot, who was formerly designed to be married to my son George, but whose match was broken off, as already related. As soon as she saw me, she flew to my arms with the utmost joy. "My dear sir," cried she, "to what happy accident is it that we owe so unexpected a visit? I am sure my uncle and aunt will be in raptures when they find they have the good Dr. Primrose for their guest." Upon hearing my name, the old gentleman and lady very politely stepped up, and welcomed me with most cordial hospitality. Nor could they forbear smiling, upon being informed of the nature of my present visit: but the unfortunate butler, whom they at first seemed disposed to turn away, was at my intercession forgiven.

Mr. Arnold and his lady, to whom the house belonged, now insisted upon having the pleasure of my stay for some days; and as their niece, my charming pupil, whose mind in some measure had been formed under my own instructions, joined in their entreaties, I complied. That night I was shown to a magnificent chamber; and the next morning early Miss Wilmot desired to walk with me in the garden, which was decorated in the modern manner. After some time spent in pointing out the beauties of the place, she inquired with seeming unconcern, when last I had heard from my son George.—"Alas! madam," cried I, "he has now been nearly three years absent, without ever writing to his friends or me. Where he is I know not; perhaps I shall never see him or happiness more. No, my dear madam, we shall never more see such pleasing hours as were once spent by our fireside at Wakefield. My little family are now dispersing very fast, and poverty has brought not only want, but infamy upon us." The good-natured girl let fall a tear at this account; but as I saw her possessed of too much sensibility, I forebore a more minute detail of our sufferings. It was, however, some consolation to me to find that time had made no alteration in her affections, and that she had rejected several matches that had been made her since our leaving her part of the country. She led me round all the extensive improvements of the place, pointing to the several walks and arbours, and at the same time catching from every object a hint for some new question relative to my son. In this manner we spent the forenoon, till the bell summoned us in to dinner, where we found the manager of the strolling company that I mentioned before, who was come to dispose of tickets for the Fair Penitent, which was to be acted that evening: the part of Horatio by a young gentleman who had never appeared on any stage. He seemed to be very warm in the praise of the new performer, and averred that he never saw any who bid so fair for excellence. Acting, he observed, was not learned in a day; "but this gentleman," continued he, "seems born to tread the stage. His voice, his figure, and attitudes are all admirable. We caught him up accidentally in our journey down." This account in some measure excited our curiosity, and, at the entreaty of the ladies, I was prevailed upon to accompany them to the play-house, which was no other than a barn. As the company with which I went was incontestably the chief of the place, we were received with the greatest respect, and placed in the front seat of the theatre, where we sat for some time with no small impatience to see Horatio make his appearance. The new performer advanced at last; and let parents think of my sensations by their own, when I found it was my unfortunate son! He was going to begin; when, turning his eyes upon the audience, he perceived Miss Wilmot and me, and stood at once speechless and immoveable.

The actors behind the scene, who ascribed this pause to his natural timidity, attempted to encourage him; but instead of going on, he burst into a flood of tears, and retired off the stage. I don't know what were my feelings on this occasion, for they succeeded with too much rapidity for description; but I was soon awaked from this disagreeable reverie by Miss Wilmot, who, pale and with a trembling voice, desired me to conduct her back to her uncle's. When got home, Mr. Arnold, who was as yet a stranger to our extraordinary behaviour, being informed that the new performer was my son, sent his coach and an invitation for him; and as he persisted in his refusal to appear again upon the stage, the players put another in his place, and we soon had him with us. Mr. Arnold gave him the kindest reception, and I received him with my usual transport; for I could never counterfeit false resentment. Miss Wilmot's reception was mixed with seeming neglect, and yet I could perceive she acted a studied part. The tumult in her mind seemed not yet abated: she said twenty giddy things that looked like joy, and then laughed loud at her own want of meaning. At intervals she would take a sly peep at the glass, as if happy in the consciousness of unresisted beauty; and often would ask questions without giving any manner of attention to the answers.

CHAPTER XX.

The History of a philosophic Vagabond, pursuing Novelty, but losing Content.

AFTER we had supped, Mrs. Arnold politely offered to send a couple of her footmen for my son's baggage, which he at first seemed to decline; but upon her pressing the request, he was obliged to inform her, that a stick and wallet were all the moveable things upon this earth that he could boast of. "Why, ay, my son," cried I, "you left me but poor, and poor I find you are come back: and yet I make no doubt you have seen a great deal of the world."—"Yes, sir," replied my son, "but travelling after Fortune is not the way to secure her; and, indeed, of late I have desisted from the pursuit."—"I fancy, sir," cried Mrs. Arnold, "that the account of your adventures would be amusing; the first part of them I have often heard from my niece; but could the company prevail for the rest, it would be an additional obligation."—"Madam," replied my son, "I promise you the pleasure you have in hearing will not be half so great as my vanity in repeating them; yet in the whole narrative I can scarcely promise you one adventure, as my account is rather of what I saw than what I did. The first misfortune of my life, which you all know, was great; but though it distressed, it could not sink me. No person ever had a better knack at hoping than I. The less kind I found Fortune at one time, the more I expected from her another; and being now at the bottom of her wheel, every new revolution might lift, but could not depress me. I proceeded, therefore, towards London in a fine morning, no way uneasy about tomorrow, but cheerful as the birds that carolled by the road; and comforted myself with reflecting, that London was the mart where abilities of every kind were sure of meeting distinction and reward.

"Upon my arrival in town, sir, my first care was to deliver your letter of recommendation to our cousin, who was himself in little better circumstances than I. My first scheme, you know, sir, was to be usher at an academy; and I asked his advice on the affair. Our cousin received the proposal with a true sardonic grin. 'Ay,' cried he, 'this is indeed a very pretty career that has been chalked out for you. I have been an usher at a boarding-school myself; and may I die by an anodyne necklace, but I had rather be an under-turnkey in Newgate. I was up early and late: I was browbeat by the master, hated for my ugly face by the mistress, worried by the boys within, and never permitted to stir out to meet civility abroad. But are you sure you are fit for a school? Let me examine you a little. Have you been bred apprentice to the business?'—'No.'—'Then you won't do for a school. Can you dress the boys' hair?'—'No.'—'Then you won't do for a school. Have you had the smallpox?'—'No.'—'Then you won't do for a school. Can you lie three in a bed?'—

'No.'—'Then you will never do for a school. Have you got a good stomach?'—'Yes.'—'Then you will by no means do for a school. No, sir: if you are for a genteel, easy profession, bind yourself seven years an apprentice to turn a cutler's wheel: but avoid a school by any means. Yet come,' continued he, 'I see you are a lad of spirit and some learning; what do you think of commencing author, like me? You have read in books, no doubt, of men of genius starving at the trade. At present I'll show you forty very dull fellows about town that live by it in opulence; all honest jog-trot men, who go on smoothly and dully, and write history and politics, and are praised: men, sir, who, had they been bred cobblers, would all their lives have only mended shoes, but never made them.'

"Finding that there was no great degree of gentility affixed to the character of an usher, I resolved to accept his proposal; and having the highest respect for literature, hailed the *antiqua mater* of Grub-street with reverence. I thought it my glory to pursue a track which Dryden and Otway trod before me. I considered the goddess of this region as the parent of excellence; and however an intercourse with the world might give us good sense, the poverty she entailed I supposed to be the nurse of genius! Big with these reflections, I sat down, and finding that the best things remained to be said on the wrong side, I resolved to write a book that should be wholly new. I therefore dressed up three paradoxes with some ingenuity. They were false, indeed, but they were new. The jewels of truth have been so often imported by others, that nothing was left for me to import but some splendid things that at a distance looked every bit as well. Witness, you powers, what fancied importance sat perched upon my quill while I was writing! The whole learned world, I made no doubt, would rise to oppose my systems: but then I was prepared to oppose the whole learned world. Like the porcupine, I sat self-collected, with a quill pointed against every opposer."

"Well said, my boy," cried I: "and what subject did you treat upon? I hope you did not pass over the importance of monogamy. But I interrupt: go on. You published your paradoxes; well, and what did the learned world say to your paradoxes?"

"Sir," replied my son, "the learned world said nothing to my paradoxes; nothing at all, sir. Every man of them was employed in praising his friends and himself, or condemning his enemies; and unfortunately, as I had neither, I suffered the cruelest mortification,—neglect.

"As I was meditating, one day, in a coffee-house, on the fate of my paradoxes, a little man happening to enter the room, placed himself in the box before me; and after some preliminary discourse, finding me to be a scholar, drew out a bundle of proposals, begging me to subscribe to a new edition he was going to give to the world of Propertius, with notes. This demand necessarily produced a reply that I had no money; and that concession led him to inquire into the nature of my expectations. Finding that my expectations were just as great as my purse,—'I see,' cried he, 'you are unacquainted with the town: I'll teach you a part of it. Look at these proposals,—upon these very proposals I have subsisted very comfortably for twelve years. The moment a nobleman returns from his travels, a Creolian arrives from Jamaica, or a dowager from her country seat, I strike for a subscription. I first besiege their hearts with flattery, and then pour in my proposals at the breach. If they subscribe readily the first time, I renew my request to beg a dedication fee: if they let me have that, I smite them once more for engraving their coat of arms at the top. Thus,' continued he, 'I live by vanity, and laugh at it. But, between ourselves, I am now too well known: I should be glad to borrow your face a bit. A nobleman of distinction has just returned from Italy; my face is familiar to his porter; but if you bring this copy of verses, my life for it you succeed, and we divide the spoil.'"

"Bless us, George," cried I, "and is this the employment of poets now? Do men of exalted talents thus stoop to beggary? Can they so far disgrace their calling, as to make a vile traffic of praise for bread?"

"Oh no, sir," returned he, "a true poet can never be so base; for wherever there is genius, there is pride. The creatures

I now describe are only beggars in rhyme. The real poet, as he braves every hardship for fame, so he is equally a coward to contempt; and none but those who are unworthy protection condescend to solicit it.

"Having a mind too proud to stoop to such indignities, and yet a fortune too humble to hazard a second attempt for fame, I was now obliged to take a middle course, and write for bread. But I was unqualified for a profession where mere industry alone was to ensure success. I could not suppress my lurking passion for applause; but usually consumed that time in efforts after excellence which takes up but little room, when it should have been more advantageously employed in the diffusive productions of fruitful mediocrity. My little piece would therefore come forth in the midst of periodical publications, unnoticed and unknown. The public were more importantly employed than to observe the easy simplicity of my style, or the harmony of my periods. Sheet after sheet was thrown off to oblivion. My essays were buried among the essays upon liberty, Eastern tales, and cures for the bite of a mad dog; while Philautos, Philalethes, Phileleutheros, and Philanthropos, all wrote better, because they wrote faster than I.

"Now, therefore, I began to associate with none but disappointed authors like myself, who praised, deplored, and despised each other. The satisfaction we found in every celebrated writer's attempts was inversely as their merits. I found that no genius in another could please me. My unfortunate paradoxes had entirely dried up that source of comfort. I could neither read nor write with satisfaction; for excellence in another was my aversion, and writing was my trade.

"In the midst of these gloomy reflections, as I was one day sitting on a bench in St. James's Park, a young gentleman of distinction, who had been my intimate acquaintance at the university, approached me. We saluted each other with some hesitation; he almost ashamed of being known to one who made so shabby an appearance, and I afraid of a repulse. But my suspicions soon vanished; for Ned Thornhill was at the bottom a very good-natured fellow."

"What did you say, George?" interrupted I. "Thornhill, was not that his name? It can certainly be no other than my landlord."—"Bless me," cried Mrs. Arnold, "is Mr. Thornhill so near a neighbour of yours? He has long been a friend in our family, and we expect a visit from him shortly."

"My friend's first care," continued my son, "was to alter my appearance by a very fine suit of his own clothes, and then I was admitted to his table, upon the footing of half friend, half underling. My business was to attend him at auctions, to put him in spirits when he sat for his picture, to take the left hand in his chariot when not filled by another, and to assist at *tattering a kip*, as the phrase was, when he had a mind for a frolic. Besides this, I had twenty other little employments in the family. I was to do many small things without bidding: to carry the corkscrew; to stand godfather to all the butler's children; to sing when I was bid; to be never out of humour; always to be humble, and, if I could, to be very happy.

"In this honourable post, however, I was not without a rival. A captain of marines, who was formed for the place by nature, opposed me in my patron's affections. His mother had been laundress to a man of quality, and thus he early acquired a taste for pimping and pedigree. As this gentleman made it the study of his life to be acquainted with lords, though he was dismissed from several for his stupidity, yet he found many of them who were as dull as himself, that permitted his assiduities. As flattery was his trade, he practised it with the easiest address imaginable; but it came awkward and stiff from me: and as every day my patron's desire of flattery increased, so, every hour, being better acquainted with his defects, I became more unwilling to give it. Thus, I was once more fairly going to give up the field to the captain, when my friend found occasion for my assistance. This was nothing less than to fight a duel for him with a gentleman, whose sister it was pretended he had used ill. I readily complied with his request; and though I see you are displeased at my conduct, yet, as it was a debt indispensably due to friendship, I could not refuse. I undertook the affair, disarmed my antagonist, and soon after had the pleasure of finding, that the lady was only a woman of the town, and the fellow her bully and a sharper. This piece of service was repaid with the warmest professions of gratitude; but, as my friend was to leave town in a few days, he knew no other method of serving me but by recommending me to his uncle, Sir William Thornhill, and another nobleman of great distinction, who enjoyed a post under the government. When he was gone, my first care was to carry his recommendatory letter to his uncle, a man whose character for every virtue was universal, yet just. I was received by his servants with the most hospitable smiles; for the looks of the domestic ever transmit the master's benevolence. Being shown into a grand apartment, where Sir William soon came to me, I delivered my message and letter, which he read, and, after pausing some minutes,—'Pray, sir,' cried he, 'inform me what you have done for my kinsman to deserve this warm recommendation? But I suppose, sir, I guess your merits: you have fought for him; and so you would expect a reward from me for being the instrument of his vices. I wish—sincerely wish, that my present refusal may be some punishment for your guilt; but still more, that it may be some inducement to your repentance.' The severity of this rebuke I bore patiently, because I knew it was just. My whole expectations now, therefore, lay in my letter to the great man. As the doors of the nobility are almost ever beset with beggars, all ready to thrust in some sly petition, I found it no easy matter to gain admittance. However, after bribing the servants with half my worldly fortune, I was at last shown into a spacious apartment, my letter being previously sent up for his lordship's inspection. During this anxious interval, I had full time to look round me. Every thing was grand and of happy contrivance: the paintings, the furniture, the gildings, petrified me with awe, and raised my idea of the owner. Ah, thought I to myself, how very great must the possessor of all these things be, who carries in his head the business of the state, and whose house displays half the wealth of a kingdom! sure his genius must be unfathomable!—During these awful reflections, I heard a step come heavily forward. Ah, this is the great man himself! No; it was only a chambermaid. Another foot was heard soon after. This must be he! No; it was only the great man's valet-de-chambre. At last his lordship actually made his appearance. 'Are you,' cried he, 'the bearer of this here letter?' I answered with a bow. 'I learn by this,' continued he, 'as how that,'—But just at that instant a servant delivered him a card, and, without taking farther notice, he went out of the room, and left me to digest my own happiness at leisure. I saw no more of him, till told by a footman that his lordship was going to his coach at the door. Down I immediately followed, and joined my voice to that of three or four more, who came, like me, to petition for favours. His lordship, however, went too fast for us, and was gaining his chariot door with large strides, when I hallooed out to know if I was to have any reply. He was, by this time, got in, and muttered an answer, half of which only I heard, the other half was lost in the rattling of his chariot-wheels. I stood for some time with my neck stretched out, in the posture of one that was listening to catch the glorious sounds, till, looking round me, I found myself alone at his lordship's gate.

"My patience," continued my son, "was now quite exhausted: stung with the thousand indignities I had met with, I was willing to cast myself away, and only wanted the gulf to receive me. I regarded myself as one of those vile things that Nature designed should be thrown by into her lumber-room, there to perish in obscurity. I had still, however, half-a-guinea left, and of that I thought Nature herself should not deprive me; but in order to be sure of this, I was resolved to go instantly and spend it while I had it, and then trust to occurrences for the rest. As I was going along with this resolution, it happened that Mr. Crispe's office seemed invitingly open to give me a welcome reception. In this office, Mr. Crispe kindly offers all his Majesty's subjects a generous promise of £30 a year, for which promise all they give in return is their liberty for life, and permission to let him transport them to America as slaves. I was happy at finding a place where I could lose my fears in desperation, and entered this cell (for it had the appearance of one) with the devotion of a monastic. Here I found a number of poor creatures, all in circumstances like myself, expecting the arrival of Mr. Crispe, presenting a true epitome of English impatience. Each untractable soul at variance with Fortune wreaked her injuries on their own hearts: but Mr. Crispe at last came down, and all our murmurs were hushed. He deigned to regard me with an air of peculiar approbation, and indeed he was the first man who, for a month past, had talked to me with smiles. After a few questions, he found I was fit for everything in the world. He paused a while upon the properest means of providing for me: and slapping his forehead as if he had found it, assured me that there was at that time an embassy talked of from the synod of Pennsylvania to the Chickasaw Indians, and that he would use his interest to get me made secretary. I knew in my own heart that the fellow lied, and yet his promise gave me pleasure, there was something so magnificent in the sound. I fairly therefore divided my half-guinea, one half of which went to be added to his thirty thousand pounds, and with the other half I resolved to go to the next tavern, to be there more happy than he.

"As I was going out with that resolution, I was met at the door by the captain of a ship with whom I had formerly some little acquaintance, and he agreed to be my companion over a bowl of punch. As I never chose to make a secret of my circumstances, he assured me that I was upon the very point of ruin, in listening to the office-keeper's promises; for that he only designed to sell me to the plantations. 'But,' continued he, 'I fancy you might, by a much shorter voyage, be very easily put into a genteel way of bread. Take my advice. My ship sails to-morrow for Amsterdam: what if you go in her as a passenger? The moment you land, all you have to do is to teach the Dutchmen English, and I'll warrant you'll get pupils and money enough. I suppose you understand English,' added he, 'by this time, or the deuce is in it.' I confidently assured him of that; but expressed a doubt whether the Dutch would be willing to learn English. He affirmed, with an oath, that they were fond of it to distraction; and upon that affirmation I agreed with his proposal, and embarked the next day to teach the Dutch English in Holland. The wind was fair, our voyage short; and after having paid my passage with half my moveables, I found myself, fallen as from the skies, a stranger in one of the principal streets of Amsterdam. In this situation I was unwilling to let any time pass unemployed in teaching. I addressed myself, therefore, to two or three of those I met whose appearance seemed most promising; but it was impossible to make ourselves mutually understood. It was not till this very moment I recollected, that in order to teach the Dutchmen English, it was necessary that they should first teach me Dutch. How I came to overlook so obvious an objection is to me amazing: but certain it is I overlooked it.

"This scheme thus blown up, I had some thoughts of fairly shipping back to England again, but falling into company with an Irish student, who was returning from Louvain, our conversation turning upon topics of literature, (for, by the way, it may be observed that I always forgot the meanness of my circumstances when I could converse upon such subjects,) from him I learned that there were not two men in his whole university who understood Greek. This amazed me. I instantly resolved to travel to Louvain, and there live by teaching Greek: and in this design I was heartened by my brother student, who threw out some hints that a fortune might be got by it.

"I set boldly forward the next morning. Every day lessened the burden of my moveables, like Æsop and his basket of bread; for I paid them for my lodgings to the Dutch, as I travelled on. When I came to Louvain, I was resolved not to go sneaking to the lower professors, but openly tendered my talents to the Principal himself. I went, had admittance, and offered him my service as a master of the Greek language, which I had been told was a desideratum in his university. The Principal seemed at first to doubt of my abilities; but of these I offered to convince him, by turning a part of any Greek author he should fix upon into Latin. Finding me perfectly earnest in my proposal, he addressed me thus: 'You see me, young man; I never learned Greek, and I don't find that I have ever missed it. I have had a Doctor's cap and gown without Greek; I have ten thousand florins a year without Greek; I eat heartily without Greek; and, in short,' continued he, 'as I don't know Greek, I do not believe there is any good in it.'

"I was now too far from home to think of returning; so I resolved to go forward. I had some knowledge of music, with a tolerable voice, and now turned what was my amusement into a present means of subsistence. I passed among the harmless peasants of Flanders, and among such of the French as were poor enough to be very merry; for I ever found them sprightly in proportion to their wants. Whenever I approached a peasant's house towards nightfall, I played one of my most merry tunes, and that procured me not only a lodging, but subsistence for the next day. I once or twice attempted to play for people of fashion, but they always thought my performance odious, and never rewarded me even with a trifle. This was to me the more extraordinary, as, whenever I used, in better days, to play for company, when playing was my amusement, my music never failed to throw them into raptures, and the ladies especially; but as it was now my only means, it was received with contempt—a proof how ready the world is to underrate those talents by which a man is supported.

"In this manner I proceeded to Paris, with no design but just to look about me, and then to go forward. The people of Paris are much fonder of strangers that have money, than those that have wit. As I could not boast much of either, I was no great favourite. After walking about the town four or five days, and seeing the outsides of the best houses, I was preparing to leave this retreat of venal hospitality, when passing through one of the principal streets, whom should I meet but our cousin, to whom you first recommended me. This meeting was very agreeable to me, and I believe not displeasing to him. He inquired into the nature of my journey to Paris, and informed me of his own business there, which was to collect pictures, medals, intaglios, and antiques of all kinds, for a gentleman in London who had just stepped into taste and a large fortune. I was the more surprised at seeing our cousin pitched upon for this office, as he himself had often assured me he knew nothing of the matter. Upon asking how he had been taught the art of a cognoscento so very suddenly, he assured me that nothing was more easy. The whole secret consisted in a strict adherence to two rules: the one, always to observe the picture might have been better if the painter had taken more pains; and the other, to praise the works of Pietro Perugino. 'But,' says he, 'as I once taught you how to be an author in London, I'll now undertake to instruct you in the art of picture-buying at Paris.'

"With this proposal I very readily closed, as it was a living, and now all my ambition was to live. I went therefore to his lodgings, improved my dress by his assistance; and, after some time, accompanied him to auctions of pictures, where the English gentry were expected to be purchasers. I was not a little surprised at his intimacy with people of the best of fashion, who referred themselves to his judgment upon every picture or medal, as to an unerring standard of taste. He made very good use of my assistance upon these occasions; for, when asked his opinion, he would gravely take me aside and ask mine, shrug, look wise, return, and assure the company that he could give no opinion upon an affair of so much importance. Yet there was sometimes an occasion for a more important assurance. I remember to have seen him, after giving his opinion that the colouring of a picture was not mellow enough, very deliberately take a brush with brown varnish, that was accidentally lying by, and rub it over the piece with great composure before all the company, and then ask if he had not improved the tints.

"When he had finished his commission in Paris, he left me strongly recommended to several men of distinction, as a person very proper for a travelling tutor; and after some time, I was employed in that capacity by a gentleman who brought his ward to Paris, in order to set him forward on his tour through Europe. I was to be the young gentleman's governor; but with a proviso, that he should always be permitted to govern himself. My pupil, in fact, understood the art of guiding in money concerns much better than I. He was heir to a fortune of about two hundred thousand pounds, left him by an uncle in the West Indies; and his guardians, to qualify him for the management of it, had bound him apprentice to an attorney. Thus avarice was his prevailing passion: all his questions on the road were, how money might be saved; which was the least expensive course of travel; whether anything could be bought that would turn to account when disposed of again in London? Such curiosities on the way as could be seen for nothing, he was ready enough to look at; but if the sight of them was to be paid for, he usually asserted that he had been told they were not worth seeing. He never paid a bill that he would not observe how amazingly expensive travelling was! and all this though he was not yet twenty-one. When arrived at Leghorn, as we took a walk to look at the port and shipping, he inquired the expense of the passage by sea home to England. This he was informed was but a trifle compared to his returning by land; he was therefore unable to withstand the temptation; so paying me the small part of my salary that was due, he took leave, and embarked with only one attendant for London.

"I now therefore was left once more upon the world at large; but then, it was a thing I was used to. However, my skill in music could avail me nothing in a country where every peasant was a better musician than I: but by this time I had acquired another talent, which answered my purpose as well, and this was a skill in disputation. In all the foreign universities and convents there are, upon certain days, philosophical theses maintained against every adventitious disputant; for which, if the champion opposes with any dexterity, he can claim a gratuity in money, a dinner, and a bed for one night. In this manner, therefore, I fought my way towards England; walked along from city to city; examined mankind more nearly; and, if I may so express it, saw both sides of the picture. My remarks, however, are but few: I found that monarchy was the best government for the poor to live in, and commonwealths for the rich. I found that riches in general were in every country another name for freedom; and that no man is so fond of liberty himself, as not to be desirous of subjecting the will of some individuals in society to his own.

"Upon my arrival in England, I resolved to pay my respects first to you, and then to enlist as a volunteer in the first expedition that was going forward; but on my journey down, my resolutions were changed by meeting an old acquaintance, who I found belonged to a company of comedians that were going to make a summer campaign in the country. The company seemed not much to disapprove of me for an associate. They all, however, apprised me of the importance of the task at which I aimed; that the public was a many-headed monster, and that only such as had very good heads could please it: that acting was not to be learned in a day; and that without some traditional shrugs, which had been on the stage, and only on the stage, these hundred years, I could never pretend to please. The next difficulty was in fitting me with parts, as almost every character was in keeping. I was driven for some time from one character to another, till at last Horatio was fixed upon, which the presence of the present company has happily hindered me from acting."

CHAPTER XXI.

The short continuance of friendship amongst the vicious, which is coeval only with mutual satisfaction.

My son's account was too long to be delivered at once; the first part of it was begun that night, and he was concluding the rest after dinner the next day, when the appearance of Mr. Thornhill's equipage at the door seemed to make a pause in the general satisfaction. The butler, who was now become my friend in the family, informed me, with a whisper, that the Squire had already made some overtures to Miss Wilmot, and that her aunt and uncle seemed highly to approve the match. Upon Mr. Thornhill's entering, he seemed, at seeing my son and me, to start back; but I readily imputed that to surprise, and not displeasure. However, upon our advancing to salute him, he returned our greeting with the most apparent candour; and after a short time his presence served only to increase the general good humour.

After tea he called me aside to inquire after my daughter: but upon my informing him that my inquiry was unsuccessful, he seemed greatly surprised; adding that he had been since frequently at my house in order to comfort the rest of my family, whom he left perfectly well. He then asked if I communicated her misfortune to Miss Wilmot or my son; and upon my replying that I had not told them as yet, he greatly approved my prudence and precaution, desiring me by all means to keep it a secret: "For at best," cried he, "it is but divulging one's own infamy; and perhaps Miss Livy may not be so guilty as we all imagine." We were here interrupted by a servant who came to ask the Squire in, to stand up at country-dances: so that he left me quite pleased with the interest he seemed to take in my concerns. His addresses, however, to Miss Wilmot were too obvious to be mistaken: and yet, she seemed not perfectly pleased, but bore them rather in compliance to the will of her aunt than from real inclination. I had even the satisfaction to see her lavish some kind looks upon my unfortunate son, which the other could neither extort by his fortune nor assiduity. Mr. Thornhill's seeming composure, however, not a little surprised me: we had now continued here a week at the pressing instances of Mr. Arnold; but each day the more tenderness Miss Wilmot showed my son, Mr. Thornhill's friendship seemed proportionably to increase for him.

He had formerly made us the most kind assurances of using his interest to serve the family; but now his generosity was not confined to promises alone. The morning I designed for my departure, Mr. Thornhill came to me with looks of real pleasure, to inform me of a piece of service he had done for his friend George. This was nothing less than his having procured him an ensign's commission in one of the regiments that was going to the West Indies, for which he had promised but one hundred pounds, his interest having been sufficient to get an abatement of the other two. "As for this trifling piece of service," continued the young gentleman, "I desire no other reward but the pleasure of having served my friend; and as for the hundred pounds to be paid, if you are unable to raise it yourselves, I will advance it, and you shall repay me at your leisure." This was a favour we wanted words to express our sense of: I readily, therefore, gave my bond for the money, and testified as much gratitude as if I never intended to pay.

George was to depart for town the next day, to secure his commission, in pursuance of his generous patron's directions, who judged it highly expedient to use dispatch, lest in the meantime another should step in with more advantageous proposals. The next morning, therefore, our young soldier was early prepared for his departure, and seemed the only person among us that was not affected by it. Neither the fatigues and dangers he was going to encounter, nor the friends and mistress—for Miss Wilmot actually loved him—he was leaving behind, any way damped his spirits. After he had taken leave of the rest of the company, I gave him all I had, my blessing. "And now, my boy," cried I, "thou art going to fight for thy country: remember how thy brave grandfather fought for his sacred king, when loyalty among Britons was a virtue. Go, my boy, and imitate him in all but his misfortunes, if it was a misfortune to die with Lord Falkland. Go, my boy, and if you fall, though distant, exposed, and unwept by those that love you, the most precious tears are those with which Heaven bedews the unburied head of a soldier."

The next morning I took leave of the good family, that had been kind enough to entertain me so long, not without several expressions of gratitude to Mr. Thornhill for his late bounty. I left them in the enjoyment of all that happiness which affluence and good breeding procure, and returned towards home, despairing of ever finding my daughter more, but sending a sigh to Heaven to spare and to forgive her.

I was now come within about twenty miles of home, having hired an horse to carry me, as I was yet but weak, and comforted myself with the hopes of soon seeing all I held dearest upon earth. But the night coming on, I put up at a little public-house by the road-side, and asked for the landlord's company over a pint of wine. We sat beside his kitchen fire, which was the best room in the house, and chatted on politics and the news of the country. We happened, among other topics, to talk of young Squire Thornhill, who, the host assured me, was hated as much as his uncle Sir William, who sometimes came down to the country, was loved. He went on to observe, that he made it his whole study to betray the daughters of such as received him to their houses, and, after a fortnight or three weeks' possession, turned them out unrewarded and abandoned to the world. As we continued our discourse in this manner, his wife, who had been out to get change, returned, and perceiving that her husband was enjoying a pleasure in which she was not a sharer, she asked him, in an angry tone, what he did there? to which he only replied, in an ironical way, by drinking her health. "Mr. Symonds," cried she, "you use me very ill, and I'll bear it no longer. Here three parts of the business is left for me to do, and the fourth left unfinished, while you do nothing but soak with the guests all day long; whereas, if a spoonful of liquor were to cure me of a fever, I never touch a drop." I now found what she would be at, and immediately poured her out a glass, which she received with a courtesy; and, drinking towards my good health, "Sir," resumed she, "it is not so much for the value of the liquor I am angry, but one cannot help it when the house is going out of the windows. If the customers or guests are to be dunned, all the burden lies upon my back: he'd as lief eat that glass as budge after them himself. There, now, above stairs, we have a young woman who has come to take up her lodging here, and I don't believe she has got any money, by her over-civility. I am certain she is very slow of payment, and I wish she were put in mind of it."—"What signifies minding her?" cried the host; "if she be slow, she is sure."—"I don't know that," replied the wife; "but I know that I am sure she has been here a fortnight, and we have not yet seen the cross of her money."—"I suppose, my dear," cried he, "we shall have it all in a lump."—"In a lump!" cried the other: "I hope we may get it any way; and that I am resolved we will this very night, or out she tramps, bag and baggage."—"Consider, my dear," cried the husband, "she is a gentlewoman, and deserves more respect."—"As for the matter of that," returned the hostess, "gentle or simple, out she shall pack with a sussarara. Gentry may be good things where they take; but, for my part, I never saw much good of them at the sign of the Harrow." Thus saying, she ran up a narrow flight of stairs that went from the kitchen to a room overhead; and I soon perceived, by the loudness of her voice, and the bitterness of her reproaches, that no money was to be had from her lodger. I could hear her remonstrances very distinctly: "Out, I say; pack out this moment! tramp, thou infamous strumpet, or I'll give thee a mark thou won't be the better for this three months. What! you trumpery, to come and take up an honest house without cross or coin to bless yourself with! Come along, I say!"—"Oh, dear madam," cried the stranger, "pity me—pity a poor abandoned creature, for one night, and death will soon do the rest!" I instantly knew the voice of my poor ruined child Olivia. I flew to her rescue, while the woman was dragging her along by her hair, and I caught the dear forlorn wretch in my arms. "Welcome, any way welcome, my dearest lost one—my treasure—to your poor old father's bosom! Though the vicious forsake thee, there is yet one in the world that will never forsake thee; though thou hadst ten thousand crimes to answer for, he will forget them all!"—"Oh, my own dear—" for minutes she could say no more—"my own dearest good papa! Could angels be kinder? How do I deserve so much? The villain, I hate him and myself, to be a reproach to so much goodness! You can't forgive me, I know you cannot."—"Yes, my child, from my heart I do forgive thee: only repent, and we both shall yet be happy. We shall see many pleasant days yet, my Olivia."—"Ah! never, sir, never. The rest of my wretched life must be infamy abroad. and shame at home. But, alas!

papa, you look much paler than you used to do. Could such a thing as I am give you so much uneasiness? Surely you have too much wisdom to take the miseries of my guilt upon yourself."—"Our wisdom, young woman," replied I.—"Ah, why so cold a name, papa?" cried she. "This is the first time you ever called me by so cold a name."—"I ask pardon, my darling," returned I; "but I was going to observe, that wisdom makes but a slow defence against trouble, though at last a sure one." The landlady now returned, to know if we did not choose a more genteel apartment; to which assenting, we were shown a room where we could converse more freely. After we had talked ourselves into some degree of tranquillity, I could not avoid desiring some account of the gradations that led her to her present wretched situation. "That villain, sir," said she, "from the first day of our meeting, made me honourable, though private proposals."

"Villain, indeed!" cried I: "and yet it in some measure surprises me, how a person of Mr. Burchell's good sense and seeming honour could be guilty of such deliberate baseness, and thus step into a family to undo it."

"My dear papa," returned my daughter, "you labour under a strange mistake. Mr. Burchell never attempted to deceive me: instead of that, he took every opportunity of privately admonishing me against the artifices of Mr. Thornhill, who, I now find, was even worse than he represented him."—"Mr. Thornhill!" interrupted I; "can it be?"—"Yes, sir," returned she, "it was Mr. Thornhill who seduced me; who employed the two ladies, as he called them, but who in fact were abandoned women of the town, without breeding or pity, to decoy us up to London. Their artifices, you may remember, would have certainly succeeded, but for Mr. Burchell's letter, who directed those reproaches at them which we all applied to ourselves. How he came to have so much influence as to defeat their intentions still remains a secret to me; but I am convinced he was ever our warmest, sincerest friend."

"You amaze me, my dear," cried I; "but now I find my first suspicions of Mr. Thornhill's baseness were too well grounded: but he can triumph in security; for he is rich, and we are poor. But tell me, my child, sure it was no small temptation that could thus obliterate all the impressions of such an education and so virtuous a disposition as thine?"

"Indeed, sir," replied she, "he owes all his triumph to the desire I had of making him, and not myself, happy. I knew that the ceremony of our marriage, which was privately performed by a popish priest, was no way binding, and that I had nothing to trust to but his honour."—"What!" interrupted I, "and were you indeed married by a priest in orders?"—"Indeed, sir, we were," replied she, "though we were both sworn to conceal his name."—"Why then, my child, come to my arms again; and now you are a thousand times more welcome than before; for you are now his wife to all intents and purposes; nor can all the laws of man, though written upon tables of adamant, lessen the force of that sacred connexion."

"Alas, papa!" replied she, "you are but little acquainted with his villanies: he has been married already by the same priest to six or eight wives more, whom, like me, he has deceived and abandoned."

"Has he so?" cried I; "then we must hang the priest, and you shall inform against him to-morrow."—"But, sir," returned she, "will that be right, when I am sworn to secresy?"—"My dear," I replied, "if you have made such a promise, I cannot, nor will I tempt you to break it. Even though it may benefit the public, you must not inform against him. In all human institutions a smaller evil is allowed to procure a greater good; as, in politics, a province may be given away to secure a kingdom; in medicine, a limb may be lopped off to preserve the body: but in religion, the law is written, and inflexible, *never* to do evil. And this law, my child, is right; for otherwise, if we commit a smaller evil to procure a greater good, certain guilt would be thus incurred, in expectation of contingent advantage. And though the advantage should certainly follow, yet the interval between commission and advantage, which is allowed to be guilty, may be that in which we are called away to answer for the things we have done, and the volume of human actions is closed for ever. But I interrupt you, my dear; go on."

"The very next morning," continued she, "I found what little expectation I was to have from his sincerity. That very morning he introduced me to two unhappy women more, whom, like me, he had deceived, but who lived in contented prostitution. I loved him too tenderly to bear such rivals in his affections, and strove to forget my infamy in a tumult of pleasures. With this view I danced, dressed, and talked; but still was unhappy. The gentlemen who visited there told me every moment of the power of my charms, and this only contributed to increase my melancholy, as I had thrown all their power quite away. Thus each day I grew more pensive, and he more insolent, till at last the monster had the assurance to offer me to a young baronet of his acquaintance. Need I describe, sir, how his ingratitude stung me? My answer to this proposal was almost madness. I desired to part. As I was going, he offered me a purse; but I flung it at him with indignation, and burst from him in a rage, that for a while kept me insensible of the miseries of my situation. But I soon looked round me, and saw myself a vile, abject, guilty thing, without one friend in the world to apply to. Just in that interval, a stage coach happening to pass by, I took a place, it being my only aim to be driven at a distance from a wretch I despised and detested. I was set down here, where, since my arrival, my own anxiety and this woman's unkindness have been my only companions. The hours of pleasure that I have passed with my mamma and sister now grow painful to me. Their sorrows are much; but mine are greater than theirs, for mine are mixed with guilt and infamy."

"Have patience, my child," cried I, "and I hope things will yet be better. Take some repose to-night, and to-morrow I'll carry you home to your mother and the rest of the family, from whom you will receive a kind reception. Poor woman! this has gone to her heart; but she loves you still, Olivia, and will forget it."

CHAPTER XXII.

Offences are easily pardoned, where there is Love at bottom.

THE next morning I took my daughter behind me, and set out on my return home. As we travelled along, I strove, by every persuasion, to calm her sorrows and fears, and to arm her with resolution to bear the presence of her offended mother. I took every opportunity, from the prospect of a fine country, through which we passed, to observe how much kinder Heaven was to us than we to each other; and that the misfortunes of Nature's making were very few. I assured her, that she should never perceive any change in my affections, and that, during my life, which yet might be long, she might depend upon a guardian and an instructor. I armed her against the censure of the world, showed her that books were sweet unreproaching companions to the miserable, and that, if they could not bring us to enjoy life, they would at least teach us to endure it.

The hired horse that we rode was to be put up that night at an inn by the way, within about five miles from my house; and as I was willing to prepare my family for my daughter's reception, I determined to leave her that night at the inn, and to return for her, accompanied by my daughter Sophia, early the next morning. It was night before we reached our appointed stage; however, after seeing her provided with a decent apartment, and having ordered the hostess to prepare proper refreshments, I kissed her, and proceeded towards home. And now my heart caught new sensations of pleasure, the nearer I approached that peaceful mansion. As a bird that had been frighted from its nest, my affections outwent my haste, and hovered round my little fireside with all the rapture of expectation. I called up the many fond things I had to say, and anticipated the welcome I was to receive. I already felt my wife's tender embrace, and smiled at the joy of my little ones. As I walked but slowly, the night waned apace. The labourers of the day were all retired to rest; the lights were out in every cottage; no sounds were heard but of the shrilling cock, and the deep-mouthed watch-dog, at hollow distance. I approached my little abode of pleasure, and, before I was within a furlong of the place, our honest mastiff came running to welcome me.

It was now near midnight that I came to knock at my door: all was still and silent: my heart dilated with unutterable happiness, when, to my amazement, I saw the house bursting out in a blaze of fire, and every aperture red with conflagration. I gave a loud convulsive outcry, and fell upon the pavement, insensible. This alarmed my son, who had, till this, been asleep; and he, perceiving the flames, instantly waked my wife and daughter; and all running out, naked, and wild with apprehension, recalled me to life with their anguish. But it was only to objects of new terror; for the flames had, by this time, caught the roof of our dwelling, part after part continuing to fall in, while the family stood, with silent agony, looking on, as if they enjoyed the blaze. I gazed upon them and upon it by turns, and then looked round me for my two little ones; but they were not to be seen. O misery! "Where," cried I, "where are my little ones?"—"They are burnt to death in the flames," said my wife, calmly, "and I will die with them." That moment I heard the cry of the babes within, who were just awaked by the fire, and nothing could have stopped me. "Where, where are my children?" cried I, rushing through the flames, and bursting the door of the chamber in which they were confined!—"Where are my little ones?"—"Here, dear papa, here we are," cried they together, while the flames were just catching the bed where they lay. I caught them both in my arms, and snatched them through the fire as fast as possible, while, just as I was got out, the roof sunk in. "Now," cried I, holding up my children, "now let the flames burn on, and all my possessions perish. Here they are; I have saved my treasure. Here, my dearest, here are our treasures, and we shall yet be happy." We kissed our little darlings a thousand times; they clasped us round the neck, and seemed to share our transports, while their mother laughed and wept by turns.

I now stood a calm spectator of the flames; and, after some time, began to perceive that my arm to the shoulder was scorched in a terrible manner. It was, therefore, out of my power to give my son any assistance, either in attempting to save our goods, or preventing the flames spreading to our corn. By this time the neighbours were alarmed, and came running to our assistance; but all they could do was to stand, like us—spectators of the calamity.

My goods, among which were the notes I had reserved for my daughters' fortunes, were entirely consumed, except a box with some papers that stood in the kitchen, and two or three things more of little consequence, which my son brought away in the beginning. The neighbours contributed, however, what they could to lighten our distress. They brought us clothes, and furnished one of our outhouses with kitchen utensils; so that by daylight we had another, though a wretched dwelling to retire to. My honest next neighbour and his children were not the least assiduous in providing us with everything necessary, and offering whatever consolation untutored benevolence could suggest.

When the fears of my family had subsided, curiosity to know the cause of my long stay began to take place: having therefore informed them of every particular, I proceeded to prepare them for the reception of our lost one; and though we had nothing but wretchedness now to impart, I was willing to procure her a welcome to what we had. This task would have been more difficult but for our recent calamity, which had humbled my wife's pride, and blunted it by more poignant afflictions. Being unable to go for my poor child myself, as my arm grew very painful, I sent my son and daughter, who soon returned, supporting the wretched delinquent, who had not the courage to look up at her mother, whom no instructions of mine could persuade to a perfect reconciliation; for women have a much stronger sense of female error than men. "Ah, madam," cried her mother, "this is but a poor place you are come to after so much finery. My daughter Sophy and I can afford but little entertainment to persons who have kept company only with people of distinction. Yes, Miss Livy, your poor father and I have suffered very much of late; but I hope Heaven will forgive you." During this reception, the unhappy victim stood pale and trembling, unable to weep or to reply: but I could not continue a silent spectator of her distress; wherefore, assuming a degree of severity in my voice and manner, which was ever followed with instant submission, "I entreat, woman, that my words may be now marked once for all: I have here brought you back a poor deluded wanderer; her return to duty demands the revival of our tenderness. The real hardships of life are now coming fast upon us; let us not, therefore, increase them by dissension among each other. If we live harmoniously together, we may yet be contented, as there are enough of us to shut out the censuring world, and keep each other in countenance. The kindness of Heaven is promised to the penitent, and let ours be directed by the example. Heaven, we are assured, is much more pleased to view a repentant sinner, than ninety-nine persons who have supported a course of undeviating rectitude. And this is right; for that single effort by which we stop short in the down-hill path to perdition, is itself a greater exertion of virtue than a hundred acts of justice."

CHAPTER XXIII.

None but the Guilty can be long and completely miserable.

SOME assiduity was now required to make our present abode as convenient as possible, and we were soon again qualified to enjoy our former serenity. Being disabled myself from assisting my son in our usual occupations, I read to my family from the few books that were saved, and particularly from such as, by amusing the imagination, contributed to ease the heart. Our good neighbours, too, came every day, with the kindest condolence, and fixed a time in which they were all to assist at repairing my former dwelling. Honest Farmer Williams was not last among these visitors; but heartily offered his friendship. He would even have renewed his addresses to my daughter; but she rejected him in such a manner, as totally repressed his future solicitations. Her grief seemed formed for continuing, and she was the only person of our little society that a week did not restore to cheerfulness. She now lost that unblushing innocence which once taught her to respect herself, and to seek pleasure by pleasing. Anxiety now had taken strong possession of her mind; her beauty began to be impaired with her constitution, and neglect still more contributed to diminish it. Every tender epithet bestowed on her sister brought a pang to her heart, and a tear to her eye; and as one vice, though cured, ever plants others where it has been, so her former guilt, though driven out by repentance, left jealousy and envy behind. I strove a thousand ways to lessen her care, and even forgot my own pain in a concern for hers, collecting such amusing passages of history as a strong memory and some reading could suggest. "Our happiness, my dear," I would say, "is in the power of One who can bring it about a thousand unforeseen ways, that mock our foresight. If example be necessary to prove this, I'll give you a story, my child, told us by a grave though sometimes a romancing historian.

"Matilda was married very young to a Neapolitan nobleman of the first quality, and found herself a widow and a mother at the age of fifteen. As she stood one day caressing her infant son in the open window of an apartment which hung over the river Volturna, the child with a sudden spring leaped from her arms into the flood below, and disappeared in a moment. The mother, struck with instant surprise, and making an effort to save him, plunged in after; but far from being able to assist the infant, she herself with great difficulty escaped to the opposite shore, just when some French soldiers were plundering the country on that side, who immediately made her their prisoner.

"As the war was then carried on between the French and Italians with the utmost inhumanity, they were going at once to perpetrate those two extremes suggested by appetite and cruelty. This base resolution, however, was opposed by a young officer, who, though their retreat required the utmost expedition, placed her behind him, and brought her in safety to his native city. Her beauty at first caught his eye;

her merit, soon after, his heart. They were married: he rose to the highest posts; they lived long together, and were happy. But the felicity of a soldier can never be called permanent: after an interval of several years, the troops which he commanded having met with a repulse, he was obliged to take shelter in the city where he had lived with his wife. Here they suffered a siege, and the city at length was taken. Few histories can produce more various instances of cruelty than those which the French and Italians at that time exercised upon each other. It was resolved by the victors, upon this occasion, to put all the French prisoners to death; but particularly the husband of the unfortunate Matilda, as he was principally instrumental in protracting the siege. Their determinations were, in general, executed almost as soon as resolved upon. The captive soldier was led forth, and the executioner with his sword stood ready, while the spectators in gloomy silence awaited the fatal blow, which was only suspended till the general who presided as judge should give the signal. It was in this interval of anguish and expectation that Matilda came to take her last farewell of her husband and deliverer, deploring her wretched situation, and the cruelty of fate, that had saved her from perishing by a premature death in the river Volturna, to be the spectator of still greater calamities. The general, who was a young man, was struck with surprise at her beauty, and pity at her distress; but with still stronger emotions when he heard her mention her former dangers. He was her son, the infant for whom she had encountered so much danger. He acknowledged her at once as his mother, and fell at her feet. The rest may be easily supposed: the captive was set free, and all the happiness that love, friendship, and duty, could confer on each, were united."

In this manner I would attempt to amuse my daughter: but she listened with divided attention; for her own misfortunes engrossed all the pity she once had for those of another, and nothing gave her ease. In company she dreaded contempt; and in solitude she only found anxiety. Such was the colour of her wretchedness, when we received certain information that Mr. Thornhill was going to be married to Miss Wilmot, for whom I always suspected he had a real passion, though he took every opportunity before me to express his contempt both of her person and fortune. This news only served to increase poor Olivia's affliction: such a flagrant breach of fidelity was more than her courage could support. I was resolved, however, to get more certain information, and to defeat, if possible, the completion of his designs, by sending my son to old Mr. Wilmot's, with instructions to know the truth of the report, and to deliver Miss Wilmot a letter, intimating Mr. Thornhill's conduct in my family. My son went in pursuance of my directions, and in three days returned, assuring us of the truth of the account; but that he had found it impossible to deliver the letter, which he was therefore obliged to leave, as Mr. Thornhill and Miss Wilmot were visiting round the country. They were to be married, he said, in a few days, having appeared together at church the Sunday before he was there, in great splendour, the bride attended by six young ladies, and he by as many gentlemen. Their approaching nuptials filled the whole country with rejoicing, and they usually rode out together in the grandest equipage that had been seen in the country for many years. All the friends of both families, he said, were there, particularly the Squire's uncle, Sir William Thornhill, who bore so good a character. He added, that nothing but mirth and feasting were going forward; that all the country praised the young bride's beauty, and the bridegroom's fine person, and that they were immensely fond of each other; concluding, that he could not help thinking Mr. Thornhill one of the most happy men in the world.

"Why, let him, if he can," returned I: "but, my son, observe this bed of straw and unsheltering roof; those mouldering walls and humid floor; my wretched body thus disabled by fire, and my children weeping round me for bread: you have come home, my child, to all this; yet here, even here, you see a man that would not for a thousand worlds exchange situations. Oh, my children, if you could but learn to commune with your own hearts, and know what noble company you can make them, you would little regard the elegance and splendour of the worthless. Almost all men have been taught to call life a passage, and themselves the travellers. The similitude still may be improved, when we observe that the good are joyful and serene, like travellers that are going towards home; the wicked but by intervals happy, like travellers that are going into exile."

My compassion for my poor daughter, overpowered by this new disaster, interrupted what I had further to observe. I bade her mother support her, and after a short time she recovered. She appeared from that time more calm, and I imagined had gained a new degree of resolution; but appearances deceived me: for her tranquillity was the languor of over-wrought resentment. A supply of provisions, charitably sent us by my kind parishioners, seemed to diffuse new cheerfulness among the rest of the family, nor was I displeased at seeing them once more sprightly and at ease. It would have been unjust to damp their satisfactions, merely to condole with resolute melancholy, or to burden them with a sadness they did not feel. Thus, once more the tale went round, and the song was demanded, and cheerfulness condescended to hover round our little habitation.

CHAPTER XXIV.

Fresh Calamities.

THE next morning the sun arose with peculiar warmth for the season, so that we agreed to breakfast together on the honeysuckle bank; where, while we sat, my youngest daughter at my request joined her voice to the concert on the trees about us. It was in this place my poor Olivia first met her seducer, and every object served to recall her sadness. But that melancholy which is excited by objects of pleasure, or inspired by sounds of harmony, soothes the heart instead of corroding it. Her mother, too, upon this occasion, felt a pleasing distress, and wept, and loved her daughter as before. "Do, my pretty Olivia," cried she, "let us have that little melancholy air your papa was so fond of; your sister Sophy has already obliged us. Do, child; it will please your old father." She complied in a manner so exquisitely pathetic as moved me:

When lovely woman stoops to folly,
  And finds too late that men betray,
What charm can soothe her melancholy?
  What art can wash her guilt away?

The only art her guilt to cover,
  To hide her shame from every eye,
To give repentance to her lover,
  And wring his bosom, is—to die.

As she was concluding the last stanza, to which an interruption in her voice from sorrow gave peculiar softness, the appearance of Mr. Thornhill's equipage at a distance alarmed us all, but particularly increased the uneasiness of my eldest daughter, who, desirous of shunning her betrayer, returned to the house with her sister. In a few minutes he was alighted from his chariot, and making up to the place where I was still sitting, inquired after my health with his usual air of familiarity. "Sir," replied I, "your present assurance only serves to aggravate the baseness of your character; and there was a time when I would have chastised your insolence for presuming thus to appear before me. But now you are safe; for age has cooled my passions, and my calling restrains them."

"I vow, my dear sir," returned he, "I am amazed at all this; nor can I understand what it means! I hope you don't think your daughter's late excursion with me had anything criminal in it?"

"Go," cried I; "thou art a wretch, a poor, pitiful wretch, and every way a liar: but your meanness secures you from my anger! Yet, sir, I am descended from a family that would not have borne this!—And so, thou vile thing, to gratify a momentary passion, thou hast made one poor creature wretched for life, and polluted a family that had nothing but honour for their portion!"

"If she or you," returned he, "are resolved to be miserable, I cannot help it. But you may still be happy; and whatever opinion you may have formed of me, you shall ever find me ready to contribute to it. We can marry her to another in a short time; and, what is more, she may keep her lover beside; for I protest I shall ever continue to have a true regard for her."

I found all my passions alarmed at this new degrading proposal; for though the mind may often be calm under great injuries, little villany can at any time get within the soul, and sting it into rage.—"Avoid my sight, thou reptile!" cried I, "nor continue to insult me with thy presence. Were my brave son at home, he would not suffer this; but I am old and disabled, and every way undone."

"I find," cried he, "you are bent upon obliging me to talk in a harsher manner than I intended. But as I have shown you what may be hoped from my friendship, it may not be improper to represent what may be the consequences of my resentment. My attorney, to whom your late bond has been transferred, threatens hard; nor do I know how to prevent the course of justice, except by paying the money myself; which, as I have been at some expenses lately previous to my intended marriage, is not so easy to be done. And then my steward talks of driving for the rent: it is certain he knows his duty; for I never trouble myself with affairs of that nature. Yet still I could wish to serve you, and even to have you and your daughter present at my marriage, which is shortly to be solemnized with Miss Wilmot; it is even the request of my charming Arabella herself, whom I hope you will not refuse."

"Mr. Thornhill," replied I, "hear me once for all: as to your marriage with any but my daughter, that I never will consent to; and though your friendship could raise me to a throne, or your resentment sink me to the grave, yet would I despise both. Thou hast once wofully, irreparably deceived me. I reposed my heart upon thine honour, and have found its baseness. Never more, therefore, expect friendship from me. Go, and possess what fortune has given thee—beauty, riches, health, and pleasure. Go, and leave me to want, infamy, disease, and sorrow. Yet, humbled as I am, shall my heart still vindicate its dignity; and though thou hast my forgiveness, thou shalt ever have my contempt."

"If so," returned he, "depend upon it you shall feel the effects of this insolence; and we shall shortly see which is the fittest object of scorn, you or me."—Upon which he departed abruptly.

My wife and son, who were present at this interview, seemed terrified with apprehension. My daughters also, finding that he was gone, came out to be informed of the result of our conference, which, when known, alarmed them not less than the rest. But as to myself, I disregarded the utmost stretch of his malevolence: he had already struck the blow, and now I stood prepared to repel every new effort, like one of those instruments used in the art of war, which, however thrown, still presents a point to receive the enemy.

We soon, however, found that he had not threatened in vain; for the very next morning his steward came to demand my annual rent, which, by the train of accidents already related, I was unable to pay. The consequence of my incapacity was his driving my cattle that evening, and their being appraised and sold the next day for less than half their value. My wife and children now therefore entreated me to comply upon any terms, rather than incur certain destruction. They even begged of me to admit his visits once more, and used all their little eloquence to paint the calamities I was going to endure,—the terrors of a prison in so rigorous a season as the present, with the danger that threatened my health from the late accident that happened by the fire. But I continued inflexible.

"Why, my treasures," cried I, "why will you thus attempt to persuade me to the thing that is not right? My duty has taught me to forgive him; but my conscience will not permit me to approve. Would you have me applaud to the world what my heart must internally condemn? Would you have me tamely sit down and flatter our infamous betrayer; and, to avoid a prison, continually suffer the more galling bonds of mental confinement? No, never! If we are to be taken from this abode, only let us hold to the right; and wherever we are thrown, we can still retire to a charming apartment, when we can look round our own hearts with intrepidity and with pleasure!"

In this manner we spent that evening. Early the next morning, as the snow had fallen in great abundance in the night, my son was employed in clearing it away, and opening a passage before the door. He had not been thus engaged long, when he came running in, with looks all pale, to tell us that two strangers, whom he knew to be officers of justice, were making towards the house.

Just as he spoke they came in, and approaching the bed where I lay, after previously informing me of their employment and business, made me their prisoner, bidding me prepare to go with them to the county gaol, which was eleven miles off.

"My friends," said I, "this is severe weather in which you have come to take me to a prison; and it is particularly unfortunate at this time, as one of my arms has lately been burnt in a terrible manner, and it has thrown me into a slight fever, and I want clothes to cover me, and I am now too weak and old to walk far in such deep snow; but, if it must be so——"

I then turned to my wife and children, and directed them to get together what few things were left us, and to prepare immediately for leaving this place. I entreated them to be expeditious; and desired my son to assist his eldest sister, who, from a consciousness that she was the cause of all our calamities, was fallen, and had lost anguish in insensibility. I encouraged my wife, who, pale and trembling, clasped our affrighted little ones in her arms, that clung to her bosom in silence, dreading to look round at the strangers. In the meantime my youngest daughter prepared for our departure, and as she received several hints to use dispatch, in about an hour we were ready to depart.

CHAPTER XXV.

No situation, however wretched it seems, but has some sort of comfort attending it.

WE set forward from this peaceful neighbourhood, and walked on slowly. My eldest daughter being enfeebled by a slow fever, which had begun for some days to undermine her constitution, one of the officers who had a horse kindly took her behind him; for even these men cannot entirely divest themselves of humanity. My son led one of the little ones by the hand, and my wife the other, while I leaned upon my youngest girl, whose tears fell, not for her own, but my distresses.

We were now got from my late dwelling about two miles, when we saw a crowd, running and shouting behind us, consisting of about fifty of my poorest parishioners. These, with dreadful imprecations, soon seized upon the two officers of justice, and swearing they would never see their minister go to gaol while they had a drop of blood to shed in his defence, were going to use them with great severity. The consequence might have been fatal, had I not immediately interposed, and with some difficulty rescued the officers from the hands of the enraged multitude. My children, who looked upon my delivery now as certain, appeared transported with joy, and were incapable of containing their raptures. But they were soon undeceived, upon hearing me address the poor deluded people, who came, as they imagined, to do me service.

"What! my friends," cried I, "and is this the way you love me? Is this the manner you obey the instructions I have given you from the pulpit? Thus to fly in the face of justice, and bring down ruin on yourselves and me? Which is your ringleader? Show me the man that has thus seduced you. As sure as he lives he shall feel my resentment. Alas! my dear deluded flock, return back to the duty you owe to God, to your country, and to me. I shall yet perhaps one day see you in greater felicity here, and contribute to make your lives more happy. But, let it at least be my comfort, when I pen my fold for immortality, that not one here shall be wanting."

They now seemed all repentance, and, melting into tears, came one after the other to bid me farewell. I shook each tenderly by the hand, and leaving them my blessing, proceeded forward without meeting any further interruption. Some hours before night, we reached the town, or rather village, for it consisted but of a few mean houses, having lost all its former opulence, and retaining no marks of its ancient superiority but the gaol.

Upon entering, we put up at an inn, where we had such refreshments as could most readily be procured, and I supped with my family with my usual cheerfulness. After seeing them properly accommodated for that night, I next attended the sheriff's officers to the prison, which had formerly been built for the purposes of war, and consisted of one large apartment, strongly grated, and paved with stone, common to both felons and debtors at certain hours in the four-and-twenty. Besides this, every prisoner had a separate cell, where he was locked in for the night.

I expected, upon my entrance, to find nothing but lamentations and various sounds of misery; but it was very different. The prisoners seemed all employed in one common design, that of forgetting thought in merriment or clamour. I was apprised of the usual perquisites required upon these occasions, and immediately complied with the demand, though the little money I had was very near being all exhausted. This was immediately sent away for liquor, and the whole prison was soon filled with riot, laughter, and profaneness.

"How," cried I to myself, "shall men so very wicked be cheerful, and shall I be melancholy? I feel only the same confinement with them, and I think I have more reason to be happy."

With such reflections I laboured to become cheerful; but cheerfulness was never yet produced by effort, which is itself painful. As I was sitting, therefore, in a corner of the gaol, in a pensive posture, one of my fellow-prisoners came up, and, sitting by me, entered into conversation. It was my constant rule in life never to avoid the conversation of any man who seemed to desire it: for if good, I might profit by his instruction; if bad, he might be assisted by mine. I found this to be a knowing man, of strong unlettered sense, but a thorough knowledge of the world, as it is called, or, more properly speaking, of human nature on the wrong side. He asked me if I had taken care to provide myself with a bed, which was a circumstance I had never once attended to.

"That's unfortunate," cried he, "as you are allowed here nothing but straw, and your apartment is very large and cold. However, you seem to be something of a gentleman, and, as I have been one myself in my time, part of my bed-clothes are heartily at your service."

I thanked him, professing my surprise at finding such humanity in a gaol in misfortunes; adding, to let him see that I was a scholar, "That the sage ancient seemed to understand the value of company in affliction, when he said *Ton kosmon aire, ei dos ton etairon;* and, in fact," continued I, "what is the world if it affords only solitude?"

"You talk of the world, sir," returned my fellow-prisoner; "the world is in its dotage; and yet the cosmogony or creation of the world has puzzled the philosophers of every age. What a medley of opinions have they not broached upon the creation of the world! Sanchoniathon, Manetho, Berosus, and Ocellus Lucanus, have all attempted it in vain. The latter has these words, *Anarchon ara kai atelutaion to pan*, which implies"—"I ask pardon, sir," cried I, "for interrupting so much learning; but I think I have heard all this before. Have I not had the pleasure of once seeing you at Wellbridge fair, and is not your name Ephraim Jenkinson?" At this demand he only sighed. "I suppose you must recollect," resumed I, "one Doctor Primrose, from whom you bought a horse?"

He now at once recollected me; for the gloominess of the place and the approaching night had prevented his distinguishing my features before. "Yes, sir," returned Mr. Jenkinson, "I remember you perfectly well; I bought a horse, but forgot to pay for him. Your neighbour Flamborough is the only prosecutor I am any way afraid of at the next assizes; for he intends to swear positively against me as a coiner. I am heartily sorry, sir, I ever deceived you, or indeed any man; for you see," continued he, showing his shackles, "what my tricks have brought me to."

"Well, sir," replied I, "your kindness in offering me assistance when you could expect no return shall be repaid with my endeavours to soften, or totally suppress

Mr. Flamborough's evidence, and I will send my son to him for that purpose the first opportunity; nor do I in the least doubt but he will comply with my request; and as to my own evidence, you need be under no uneasiness about that."

"Well, sir," cried he, "all the return I can make shall be yours. You shall have more than half my bed-clothes to-night, and I'll take care to stand your friend in the prison, where I think I have some influence."

I thanked him, and could not avoid being surprised at the present youthful change in his aspect; for at the time I had seen him before, he appeared at least sixty. "Sir," answered he, "you are little acquainted with the world; I had, at that time, false hair, and have learnt the art of counterfeiting every age from seventeen to seventy. Ah, sir! had I but bestowed half the pains in learning a trade that I have in learning to be a scoundrel, I might have been a rich man at this day. But, rogue as I am, still I may be your friend, and that, perhaps, when you least expect it."

We were now prevented from further conversation by the arrival of the gaoler's servants, who came to call over the prisoners' names, and lock up for the night. A fellow also, with a bundle of straw for my bed, attended, who led me along a dark narrow passage, into a room paved like the common prison, and in one corner of this I spread my bed, and the clothes given me by my fellow-prisoner; which done, my conductor, who was civil enough, bade me a good night. After my usual meditations, and having praised my Heavenly Corrector, I laid myself down, and slept with the utmost tranquillity till morning.

CHAPTER XXVI.

A Reformation in the Gaol: to make laws complete, they should reward as well as punish.

THE next morning early, I was awakened by my family, whom I found in tears at my bedside. The gloomy strength of every thing about us, it seems, had daunted them. I gently rebuked their sorrow, assuring them I had never slept with greater tranquillity; and next inquired after my eldest daughter, who was not among them. They informed me that yesterday's uneasiness and fatigue had increased her fever, and it was judged proper to leave her behind. My next care was to send my son to procure a room or two to lodge the family in, as near the prison as conveniently could be found. He obeyed; but could only find one apartment, which was hired at a small expense for his mother and sisters, the gaoler, with humanity, consenting to let him and his two little brothers lie in the prison with me. A bed was therefore prepared for them in a corner of the room, which I thought answered very conveniently. I was willing, however, previously to know whether my little children chose to lie in a place which seemed to fright them upon entrance.

"Well," cried I, "my good boys, how do you like your bed? I hope you are not afraid to lie in this room, dark as it appears?"

"No, papa," says Dick, "I am not afraid to lie anywhere, where you are."

"And I," says Bill, who was yet but four years old, "love every place best that my papa is in."

After this I allotted to each of the family what they were to do. My daughter was particularly directed to watch her declining sister's health; my wife was to attend me; my little boys were to read to me: "And as for you, my son," continued I, "it is by the labour of your hands we must all hope to be supported. Your wages as a day-labourer will be fully sufficient, with proper frugality, to maintain us all, and comfortably too. Thou art now sixteen years old, and hast strength; and it was given thee, my son, for very useful purposes; for it must save from famine your helpless parents and family. Prepare then, this evening, to look out for work against to-morrow, and bring home every night what money you earn for our support."

Having thus instructed him, and settled the rest, I walked down to the common prison, where I could enjoy more air and room. But I was not long there when the execrations, lewdness, and brutality that invaded me on every side, drove me back to my apartment again. Here I sat for some time pondering upon the strange infatuation of wretches, who, finding all mankind in open arms against them, were labouring to make themselves a future and a tremendous enemy.

Their insensibility excited my highest compassion, and blotted my own uneasiness from my mind. It even appeared a duty incumbent upon me to attempt to reclaim them. I resolved, therefore, once more to return, and, in spite of their contempt, to give them my advice, and conquer them by my perseverance. Going, therefore, among them again, I informed Mr. Jenkinson of my design, at which he laughed heartily, but communicated it to the rest. The proposal was received with the greatest good humour, as it promised to afford a new fund of entertainment to persons who had now no other resource for mirth but what could be derived from ridicule or debauchery.

I therefore read them a portion of the service with a loud, unaffected voice, and found my audience perfectly merry upon the occasion. Lewd whispers, groans of contrition burlesqued, winking and coughing, alternately excited laughter. However, I continued with my natural solemnity to read on, sensible that what I did might mend some, but could itself receive no contamination from any.

After reading, I entered upon my exhortation, which was rather calculated at first to amuse them than to reprove. I previously observed, that no other motive but their welfare could induce me to this; that I was their fellow-prisoner, and now got nothing by preaching. I was sorry, I said, to hear them so very profane; because they got nothing by it, but might lose a great deal: "For be assured, my friends," cried I,—"for you are my friends, however the world may disclaim your friendship,—though you swore twelve thousand oaths in a day, it would not put one penny in your purse. Then what signifies calling every moment upon the devil, and courting his friendship, since you find how scurvily he uses you? He has given you nothing here, you find, but a mouthful of oaths and an empty belly; and, by the best accounts I have of him, he will give you nothing that's good hereafter.

"If used ill in our dealings with one man, we naturally go elsewhere. Were it not worth your while, then, just to try how you may like the usage of another master, who gives you fair promises at least to come to him? Surely, my friends, of all stupidity in the world, his must be the greatest, who, after robbing a house, runs to the thief-takers for protection. And yet, how are you more wise? You are all seeking comfort from one that has already betrayed you, applying to a more malicious being than any thief-taker of them all; for they only decoy and then hang you; but he decoys and hangs, and, what is worst of all, will not let you loose after the hangman has done."

When I had concluded, I received the compliments of my audience, some of whom came and shook me by the hand, swearing that I was a very honest fellow, and that they desired my further acquaintance. I therefore promised to repeat my lecture next day, and actually conceived some hopes of making a reformation here; for it had ever been my opinion, that no man was past the hour of amendment, every heart lying open to the shafts of reproof, if the archer could but take a proper aim. When I had thus satisfied my mind, I went back to my apartment, where my wife prepared a frugal meal, while Mr. Jenkinson begged leave to add his dinner to ours, and partake of the pleasure, as he was kind enough to express it, of my conversation. He had not yet seen my family; for as they came to my apartment by a door in the narrow passage already described, by this means they avoided the common prison. Jenkinson at the first interview, therefore, seemed not a little struck with the beauty of my youngest daughter, which her pensive air contributed to heighten; and my little ones did not pass unnoticed.

"Alas, Doctor," cried he, "these children are too handsome and too good for such a place as this!"

"Why, Mr. Jenkinson," replied I, "thank Heaven, my children are pretty tolerable in morals; and if they be good, it matters little for the rest."

"I fancy, sir," returned my fellow-prisoner, "that it must give you great comfort to have all this little family about you."

"A comfort, Mr. Jenkinson!" replied I; "yes, it is indeed a comfort, and I would not be without them for all the world; for they can make a dungeon seem a palace. There is but one way in this life of wounding my happiness, and that is by injuring them."

"I am afraid then, sir," cried he, "that I am in some measure culpable; for I think I see here (looking at my son Moses) one that I have injured, and by whom I wish to be forgiven."

My son immediately recollected his voice and features, though he had before seen him in disguise, and taking him by the hand, with a smile, forgave him. "Yet," continued he, "I can't help wondering at what you could see in my face, to think me a proper mark for deception."

"My dear sir," returned the other, "it was not your face, but your white stockings, and the black ribbon in your hair, that allured me. But, no disparagement to your parts, I have deceived wiser men than you in my time; and yet, with all my tricks, the blockheads have been too many for me at last."

"I suppose," cried my son, "that the narrative of such a life as yours must be extremely instructive and amusing."

"Not much of either," returned Mr. Jenkinson. "Those relations which describe the tricks and vices only of mankind, by increasing our suspicion in life, retard our success. The traveller that distrusts every person he meets, and turns back upon the appearance of every man that looks like a robber, seldom arrives in time at his journey's end.

"Indeed, I think, from my own experience, that the knowing one is the silliest fellow under the sun. I was thought cunning from my very childhood: when but seven years old, the ladies would say that I was a perfect little man; at fourteen, I knew the world, cocked my hat, and loved the ladies; at twenty, though I was perfectly honest, yet every one thought me so cunning, that not one would trust me. Thus I was at last obliged to turn sharper in my own defence, and have lived ever since, my head throbbing with schemes to deceive, and my heart palpitating with fears of detection. I used often to laugh at your honest simple neighbour Flamborough, and, one way or another, generally cheated him once a year. Yet still the honest man went forward without suspicion, and grew rich, while I still continued tricksy and cunning, and was poor, without the consolation of being honest. However," continued he, "let me know your case, and what has brought you here; perhaps, though I have not skill to avoid a gaol myself, I may extricate my friends."

In compliance with his curiosity, I informed him of the whole train of accidents and follies that had plunged me into my present troubles, and my utter inability to get free.

After hearing my story, and pausing some minutes, he slapped his forehead, as if he had hit upon something material, and took his leave, saying, he would try what could be done.

CHAPTER XXVII.

The same subject continued.

THE next morning I communicated to my wife and children the scheme I had planned of reforming the prisoners, which they received with universal disapprobation, alleging the impossibility and impropriety of it; adding that my endeavours would no way contribute to their amendment, but might probably disgrace my calling.

"Excuse me," returned I; "these people, however fallen, are still men; and that is a very good title to my affections. Good counsel rejected, returns to enrich the giver's bosom; and though the instruction I communicate may not mend them, yet it will assuredly mend myself. If these wretches, my children, were princes, there would be thousands ready to offer their ministry; but, in my opinion, the heart that is buried in a dungeon is as precious as that seated upon a throne. Yes, my treasures, if I can mend them, I will: perhaps they will not all despise me. Perhaps I may catch up even one from the gulf, and that will be great gain; for is there upon earth a gem so precious as the human soul?"

Thus saying, I left them, and descended to the common prison, where I found the prisoners very merry, expecting my arrival; and each prepared with some gaol trick to play upon the Doctor. Thus, as I was going to begin, one turned my wig awry, as if by accident, and then asked my pardon. A second, who stood at some distance, had a knack of spitting through his teeth, which fell in showers upon my book. A third would cry Amen in such an affected tone, as gave the rest great delight. A fourth had slyly picked my pocket of my spectacles. But there was one whose trick gave more universal pleasure than all the rest; for, observing the manner in which I had disposed my books on the table before me, he very dexterously displaced one of them, and put an obscene jest-book of his own in the place. However, I took no notice of all that this mischievous group of little beings could do, but went on, perfectly sensible that what was ridiculous in my attempt would excite mirth only the first or second time, while what was serious would be permanent. My design succeeded, and in less than six days some were penitent, and all attentive.

It was now that I applauded my perseverance and address, at thus giving sensibility to wretches divested of every moral feeling, and now began to think of doing them temporal services also, by rendering their situation somewhat more comfortable. Their time had hitherto been divided between famine and excess, tumultuous riot and bitter repining. Their only employment was quarrelling among each other, playing at cribbage, and cutting tobacco-stoppers. From this last mode of idle industry I took the hint of setting such as chose to work at cutting pegs for tobacconists and shoemakers, the proper wood being bought by a general subscription, and, when manufactured, sold by my appointment; so that each earned something every day—a trifle indeed, but sufficient to maintain him.

I did not stop here, but instituted fines for the punishment of immorality, and rewards for peculiar industry. Thus, in less than a fortnight I had formed them into something social and humane, and had the pleasure of regarding myself as a legislator, who had brought men from their native ferocity into friendship and obedience.

And it were highly to be wished, that legislative power would thus direct the law rather to reformation than severity; that it would seem convinced that the work of eradicating crimes is not by making punishments familiar, but formidable. Then, instead of our present prisons, which find or make men guilty, which enclose wretches for the commission of one crime, and return them, if returned alive, fitted for the perpetration of thousands; we should see, as in other parts of Europe, places of penitence and solitude, where the accused might be attended by such as could give them repentance, if guilty, or new motives to virtue, if innocent. And this, but not the increasing punishments, is the way to mend a State. Nor can I avoid even questioning the validity of that right which social combinations have assumed, of capitally punishing offences of a slight nature. In cases of murder, their right is obvious, as it is the duty of us all, from the law of self-defence, to cut off that man who has shown a disregard for the life of another. Against such, all nature rises in arms; but it is not so against him who steals my property. Natural law gives me no right to take away his life, as, by that, the horse he steals is as much his property as mine. If, then, I have any right, it must be from a compact made between us, that he who deprives the other of his horse shall die. But this is a false compact; because no man has a right to barter his life any more than to take it away, as it is not his own. And besides, the compact is inadequate, and would be set aside, even in a court of modern equity, as there is a great penalty for a very trifling convenience, since it is far better that two men should live than that one man should ride. But a compact that is false between two men, is equally so between a hundred, or a hundred thousand; for as ten millions of circles can never make a square, so the united voice of myriads cannot lend the smallest foundation to falsehood. It is thus that reason speaks, and untutored nature says the same thing. Savages, that are directed by natural law alone, are very tender of the lives of each other; they seldom shed blood but to retaliate former cruelty.

Our Saxon ancestors, fierce as they were

in war, had but few executions in times of peace; and, in all commencing governments that have the print of nature still strong upon them, scarce any crime is held capital.

It is among the citizens of a refined community that penal laws, which are in the hands of the rich, are laid upon the poor. Government, while it grows older, seems to acquire the moroseness of age; and, as if our property were become dearer in proportion as it increased—as if the more enormous our wealth the more extensive our fears—all our possessions are paled up with new edicts every day, and hung round with gibbets to scare every invader.

I cannot tell whether it is from the number of our penal laws, or the licentiousness of our people, that this country should show more convicts in a year than half the dominions of Europe united. Perhaps it is owing to both; for they mutually produce each other. When, by indiscriminate penal laws, a nation beholds the same punishment affixed to dissimilar degrees of guilt, from perceiving no distinction in the penalty, the people are led to lose all sense of distinction in the crime, and this distinction is the bulwark of all morality: thus the multitude of laws produce new vices, and new vices call for fresh restraints.

It were to be wished, then, that power, instead of contriving new laws to punish vice; instead of drawing hard the cords of society till a convulsion come to burst them; instead of cutting away wretches as useless before we have tried their utility; instead of converting correction into vengeance,—it were to be wished that we tried the restrictive arts of government, and made law the protector, but not the tyrant of the people. We should then find that creatures, whose souls are held as dross, only wanted the hand of a refiner: we should then find that creatures, now stuck up for long tortures, lest luxury should feel a momentary pang, might, if properly treated, serve to sinew the state in times of danger; that as their faces are like ours, their hearts are so too; that few minds are so base as that perseverance cannot amend; that a man may see his last crime without dying for it; and that very little blood will serve to cement our security.

CHAPTER XXVIII.

Happiness and Misery rather the result of Prudence than of Virtue in this life; temporal evils or felicities being regarded by Heaven as things merely in themselves trifling, and unworthy its care in the distribution.

I HAD now been confined more than a fortnight, but had not since my arrival been visited by my dear Olivia, and I greatly longed to see her. Having communicated my wishes to my wife, the next morning the poor girl entered my apartment, leaning on her sister's arm. The change which I saw in her countenance struck me. The numberless graces that once resided there were now fled, and the hand of death seemed to have moulded every feature to alarm me. Her temples were sunk, her forehead was tense, and a fatal paleness sat upon her cheek.

"I am glad to see thee, my dear," cried I; "but why this dejection, Livy? I hope, my love, you have too great a regard for me to permit disappointment thus to undermine a life which I prize as my own. Be cheerful, child, and we may yet see happier days."

"You have ever, sir," replied she, "been kind to me, and it adds to my pain that I shall never have an opportunity of sharing that happiness you promise. Happiness, I fear, is no longer reserved for me here; and I long to be rid of a place where I have only found distress. Indeed, sir, I wish you would make a proper submission to Mr. Thornhill; it may in some measure induce him to pity you, and it will give me relief in dying."

"Never, child," replied I; "never will I be brought to acknowledge my daughter a prostitute; for though the world may look upon your offence with scorn, let it be mine to regard it as a mark of credulity, not of guilt. My dear, I am no way miserable in this place, however dismal it may seem; and be assured, that while you continue to bless me by living, he shall never have my consent to make you more wretched by marrying another."

After the departure of my daughter, my fellow-prisoner, who was by at this interview, sensibly enough expostulated on my obstinacy in refusing a submission which promised to give me freedom. He observed, that the rest of my family was not to be sacrificed to the peace of one child alone, and she the only one who had offended me. "Besides," added he, "I don't know if it be just thus to obstruct the union of man and wife, which you do at present, by refusing to consent to a match you cannot hinder, but may render unhappy."

"Sir," replied I, "you are unacquainted with the man that oppresses us. I am very sensible that no submission I can make could procure me liberty even for an hour. I am told that even in this very room a debtor of his, no later than last year, died for want. But though my submission and approbation could transfer me from hence to the most beautiful apartment he is possessed of, yet I would grant neither, as something whispers me that it would be giving a sanction to adultery. While my daughter lives, no other marriage of his shall ever be legal in my eye. Were she removed, indeed, I should be the basest of men, from any resentment of my own, to attempt putting asunder those who wish for a union. No, villain as he is, I should then wish him married, to prevent the consequences of his future debaucheries. But now, should I not be the most cruel of all fathers to sign an instrument which must send my child to the grave, merely to avoid a prison myself; and thus, to escape one pang, break my child's heart with a thousand?"

He acquiesced in the justice of this answer, but could not avoid observing, that he feared my daughter's life was already too much wasted to keep me long a prisoner. "However," continued he, "though you refuse to submit to the nephew, I hope you have no objections to laying your case before the uncle, who has the first character in the kingdom for everything that is just and good. I would advise you to send him a letter by the post, intimating all his nephew's ill usage; and my life for it, that in three days you shall have an answer." I thanked him for the hint, and instantly set about complying; but I wanted paper, and unluckily all our money had been laid out that morning in provisions: however, he supplied me.

For the three ensuing days I was in a state of anxiety to know what reception my letter might meet with; but in the meantime was frequently solicited by my wife to submit to any conditions rather than remain here, and every hour received repeated accounts of the decline of my daughter's health. The third day and the fourth arrived, but I received no answer to my letter: the complaints of a stranger against a favourite nephew were no way likely to succeed; so that these hopes soon vanished like all my former. My mind, however, still supported itself, though confinement and bad air began to make a visible alteration in my health, and my arm that had suffered in the fire grew worse. My children, however, sat by me, and while I was stretched on my straw, read to me by turns, or listened and wept at my instructions. But my daughter's health declined faster than mine: every message from her contributed to increase my apprehensions and pain. The fifth morning after I had written the letter which was sent to Sir William Thornhill, I was alarmed with an account that she was speechless. Now it was that confinement was truly painful to me; my soul was bursting from its prison to be near the pillow of my child, to comfort, to strengthen her, to receive her last wishes, and teach her soul the way to Heaven! Another account came: she was expiring, and yet I was debarred the small comfort of weeping by her. My fellow-prisoner, some time after, came with the last account. He bade me be patient: she was dead!—— The next morning he returned, and found me with my two little ones, now my only companions, who were using all their innocent efforts to comfort me. They entreated to read to me, and bade me not to cry, for I was now too old to weep. "And is not my sister an angel, now, papa?" cried the eldest; "and why, then, are you sorry for her? I wish I were an angel out of this frightful place, if my papa were with me."—"Yes," added my youngest darling, "Heaven, where my sister is, is a finer place than this, and there are none but good people there, and the people here are very bad."

Mr. Jenkinson interrupted their harmless

prattle by observing, that, now my daughter was no more, I should seriously think of the rest of my family, and attempt to save my own life, which was every day declining for want of necessaries and wholesome air. He added, that it was now incumbent on me to sacrifice any pride or resentment of my own to the welfare of those who depended on me for support; and that I was now, both by reason and justice, obliged to try to reconcile my landlord.

"Heaven be praised," replied I, "there is no pride left me now: I should detest my own heart if I saw either pride or resentment lurking there. On the contrary, as my oppressor has been once my parishioner, I hope one day to present him up an unpolluted soul at the eternal tribunal. No, sir, I have no resentment now; and though he has taken from me what I held dearer than all his treasures, though he has wrung my heart,—for I am sick almost to fainting, very sick, my fellow-prisoner, —yet that shall never inspire me with vengeance. I am now willing to approve his marriage: and, if this submission can do him any pleasure, let him know that if I have done him any injury I am sorry for it."

Mr. Jenkinson took pen and ink, and wrote down my submission nearly as I have expressed it, to which I signed my name. My son was employed to carry the letter to Mr. Thornhill, who was then at his seat in the country. He went, and, in about six hours, returned with a verbal answer. He had some difficulty, he said, to get a sight of his landlord, as the servants were insolent and suspicious: but he accidentally saw him as he was going out upon business, preparing for his marriage, which was to be in three days. He continued to inform us, that he stept up in the humblest manner, and delivered the letter, which, when Mr. Thornhill had read, he said that all submission was now too late and unnecessary; that he had heard of our application to his uncle, which met with the contempt it deserved; and, as for the rest, that all future applications should be directed to his attorney, not to him. He observed, however, that as he had a very good opinion of the discretion of the two young ladies, they might have been the most agreeable intercessors.

"Well, sir," said I to my fellow-prisoner, "you now discover the temper of the man that oppresses me. He can at once be facetious and cruel: but, let him use me as he will, I shall soon be free, in spite of all his bolts to restrain me. I am now drawing towards an abode that looks brighter as I approach it: this expectation cheers my afflictions, and though I leave an helpless family of orphans behind me, yet they will not be utterly forsaken: some friend, perhaps, will be found to assist them for the sake of their poor father, and some may charitably relieve them for the sake of their heavenly Father."

Just as I spoke, my wife, whom I had not seen that day before, appeared with looks of terror, and making efforts, but unable, to speak. "Why, my love," cried I, "why will you thus increase my afflictions by your own? What though no submissions can turn our severe master, though he has doomed me to die in this place of wretchedness, and though we have lost a darling child, yet still you will find comfort in your other children when I shall be no more."—"We have indeed lost," returned she, "a darling child. My Sophia, my dearest is gone; snatched from us, carried off by ruffians!"—"How, madam," cried my fellow-prisoner, "Miss Sophia carried off by villains! sure it cannot be?"

She could only answer by a fixed look, and a flood of tears. But one of the prisoners' wives who was present, and came in with her, gave us a more distinct account: she informed us, that as my wife, my daughter, and herself were taking a walk together on the great road, a little way out of the village, a post-chaise and pair drove up to them, and instantly stopped; upon which a well-dressed man, but not Mr. Thornhill, stepping out, clasped my daughter round the waist, and forcing her in, bade the postilion drive on, so that they were out of sight in a moment.

"Now," cried I, "the sum of my miseries is made up, nor is it in the power of anything on earth to give me another pang. What! not one left!—not to leave me one! —The monster!—The child that was next my heart!—she had the beauty of an angel, and almost the wisdom of an angel.—But support that woman, nor let her fall.—Not to leave me one!"

"Alas! my husband," said my wife, "you seem to want comfort even more than I. Our distresses are great, but I could bear this and more, if I saw you but easy. They may take away my children, and all the world, if they leave me but you."

My son, who was present, endeavoured to moderate our grief; he bade us take comfort, for he hoped that we might still have reason to be thankful. "My child," cried I, "look round the world, and see if there be any happiness left me now. Is not every ray of comfort shut out, while all our bright prospects only lie beyond the grave?"—"My dear father," returned he, "I hope there is still something that will give you an interval of satisfaction; for I have a letter from my brother George."—"What of him, child?" interrupted I; "does he know our misery? I hope my boy is exempt from any part of what his wretched family suffers?"—"Yes, sir," returned he, "he is perfectly gay, cheerful, and happy. His letter brings nothing but good news; he is the favourite of his colonel, who promises to procure him the very next lieutenancy that becomes vacant."

"And are you sure of all this?" cried my wife; "are you sure that nothing ill has befallen my boy?"—"Nothing, indeed, madam," returned my son; "you shall see the letter, which will give you the highest pleasure; and if anything can procure you comfort, I am sure that will."—"But are you sure," still repeated she, "that the letter is from himself, and that he is really so happy?"—"Yes, madam," replied he, "it is certainly his, and he will one day be the credit and support of our family."—"Then, I thank Providence," cried she, "that my last letter to him has miscarried. Yes, my dear," continued she, turning to me, "I will now confess, that though the hand of Heaven is sore upon us in other instances, it has been favourable here. By the last letter I wrote my son, which was in the bitterness of anger, I desired him, upon his mother's blessing, and if he had the heart of a man, to see justice done his father and sister, and avenge our cause. But, thanks be to Him that directs all things, it has miscarried, and I am at rest."—"Woman!" cried I, "thou hast done very ill, and, at another time, my reproaches might have been more severe. Oh! what a tremendous gulf hast thou escaped, that would have buried both thee and him in endless ruin! Providence, indeed, has here been kinder to us than we to ourselves. It has reserved that son to be the father and protector of my children when I shall be away. How unjustly did I complain of being stripped of every comfort, when still I hear that he is happy, and insensible of our afflictions; still kept in reserve to support his widowed mother, and to protect his brothers and sisters! But what sisters has he left? He has no sisters now: they are all gone, robbed from me, and I am undone."—"Father," interrupted my son, "I beg you will give me leave to read this letter—I know it will please you." Upon which, with my permission, he read as follows:

Honoured Sir,—I have called off my imagination a few moments from the pleasures that surround me, to fix it upon objects that are still more pleasing,—the dear little fireside at home. My fancy draws that harmless group, as listening to every line of this with great composure. I view those faces with delight, which never felt the deforming hand of ambition or distress! But, whatever your happiness may be at home, I am sure it will be some addition to it to hear, that I am perfectly pleased with my situation, and every way happy here.

Our regiment is countermanded, and is not to leave the kingdom. The colonel, who professes himself my friend, takes me with him to all companies where he is acquainted, and, after my first visit, I generally find myself received with increased respect upon repeating it. I danced last night with Lady G——, and, could I forget you know whom, I might be perhaps successful. But it is my fate still to remember others, while I am myself forgotten by most of my absent friends; and in this number, I fear, sir, that I must consider you; for I have long expected the pleasure of a letter from home, to no purpose. Olivia and Sophia too promised to write, but seem to have forgotten me. Tell them they are two arrant little baggages, and that I am, at this moment, in a most violent passion with them; yet still, I know not how, though I want to bluster a little, my heart is respondent only to softer emotions. Then, tell them, sir, that, after all, I love them affectionately; and be assured of my ever remaining

Your dutiful Son.

"In all our miseries," cried I, "what thanks have we not to return, that one at least of our family is exempted from what we suffer? Heaven be his guard, and keep my boy thus happy, to be the support of his widowed mother, and the father of these two babes, which is all the patrimony I can now bequeath him! May he keep their innocence from the temptations of want, and be their conductor in the paths of honour!" I had scarce said these words, when a noise like that of a tumult seemed to proceed from the prison below: it died away soon after, and a clanking of fetters was heard along the passage that led to my apartment. The keeper of the prison entered, holding a man all bloody, wounded, and fettered with the heaviest irons. I looked with compassion on the wretch as he approached me, but with horror, when I found it was my own son. "My George! my George! and do I behold thee thus? Wounded—fettered! Is this thy happiness? is this the manner you return to me? Oh that this sight could break my heart at once, and let me die!"

"Where, sir, is your fortitude?" returned my son, with an intrepid voice. "I must suffer; my life is forfeited, and let them take it."

I tried to restrain my passions for a few minutes in silence, but I thought I should have died with the effort.—"Oh, my boy, my heart weeps to behold thee thus, and I cannot, cannot help it. In the moment that I thought thee blest, and prayed for thy safety, to behold thee thus again! Chained—wounded; and yet the death of the youthful is happy. But I am old, a very old man, and have lived to see this day! To see my children all untimely falling about me, while I continue a wretched survivor in the midst of ruin! May all the curses that ever sunk a soul fall heavy upon the murderer of my children! May he live, like me, to see——"

"Hold, sir!" replied my son, "or I shall blush for thee. How, sir! forgetful of your age, your holy calling, thus to arrogate the justice of Heaven, and fling those curses upward that must soon descend to crush thy own grey head with destruction! No, sir, let it be your care now to fit me for that vile death I must shortly suffer; to arm me with hope and resolution; to give me courage to drink of that bitterness which must shortly be my portion."

"My child, you must not die: I am sure no offence of thine can deserve so vile a punishment. My George could never be guilty of any crime to make his ancestors ashamed of him."

"Mine, sir," returned my son, "is, I fear, an unpardonable one. When I received my mother's letter from home, I immediately came down, determined to punish the betrayer of our honour, and sent him an order to meet me, which he answered, not in person, but by despatching four of his domestics to seize me. I wounded one who first assaulted me, and I fear desperately; but the rest made me their prisoner. The coward is determined to put the law in execution against me; the proofs are undeniable: I have sent a challenge, and as I am the first transgressor upon the statute, I see no hopes of pardon. But you have often charmed me with your lessons of fortitude; let me now, sir, find them in your example."

"And, my son, you shall find them. I am now raised above this world, and all the pleasures it can produce. From this moment I break from my heart all the ties that held it down to earth, and will prepare to fit us both for eternity. Yes, my son, I will point out the way, and my soul shall guide yours in the ascent, for we will take our flight together. I now see, and am convinced, you can expect no pardon here; and I can only exhort you to seek it at that greatest tribunal where we both shall shortly answer. But, let us not be niggardly in our exhortation, but let all our fellow-prisoners have a share:—Good gaoler, let them be permitted to stand here while I attempt to improve them." Thus saying, I made an effort to rise from my straw, but wanted strength, and was able only to recline against the wall. The prisoners assembled themselves according to my directions, for they loved to hear my counsel: my son and his mother supported me on either side; I looked and saw that none were wanting, and then addressed them with the following exhortation.

CHAPTER XXIX.

The equal dealings of Providence demonstrated with regard to the Happy and the Miserable here below. That, from the nature of Pleasure and Pain, the wretched must be repaid the balance of their sufferings in the life hereafter.

"My friends, my children, and fellow-sufferers, when I reflect on the distribution of good and evil here below, I find that much has been given man to enjoy, yet still more to suffer. Though we should examine the whole world, we shall not find one man so happy as to have nothing left to wish for; but we daily see thousands who by suicide show us they have nothing left to hope. In this life, then, it appears that we cannot be entirely blest, but yet we may be completely miserable.

"Why man should thus feel pain; why our wretchedness should be requisite in the formation of universal felicity; why, when all other systems are made perfect by the perfection of their subordinate parts, the great system should require for its perfection parts that are not only subordinate to others, but imperfect in themselves—these are questions that never can be explained, and might be useless if known. On this subject, Providence has thought fit to elude our curiosity, satisfied with granting us motives to consolation.

"In this situation man has called in the friendly assistance of philosophy; and Heaven, seeing the incapacity of that to console him, has given him the aid of religion. The consolations of philosophy are very amusing, but often fallacious: it tells us, that life is filled with comforts, if we will but enjoy them; and, on the other hand, that though we unavoidably have miseries here, life is short and they will soon be over. Thus do these consolations destroy each other; for, if life is a place of comfort, its shortness must be misery, and if it be long, our griefs are protracted. Thus philosophy is weak; but religion comforts in a higher strain. Man is here, it tells us, fitting up his mind, and preparing it for another abode. When the good man leaves the body, and is all a glorious mind, he will find he has been making himself a heaven of happiness here; while the wretch that has been maimed and contaminated by his vices, shrinks from his body with terror, and finds that he has anticipated the vengeance of Heaven. To religion, then, we must hold, in every circumstance of life, for our truest comfort: for if already we are happy, it is a pleasure to think that we can make that happiness unending; and if we are miserable, it is very consoling to think that there is a place of rest. Thus, to the fortunate, religion holds out a continuance of bliss; to the wretched, a change from pain.

"But though religion is very kind to all men, it has promised peculiar rewards to the unhappy: the sick, the naked, the houseless, the heavy laden, and the prisoner, have ever most frequent promises in our sacred law. The Author of our religion everywhere professes himself the wretch's friend, and, unlike the false ones of this world, bestows all his caresses upon the forlorn. The unthinking have censured this as partiality, as a preference without merit to deserve it. But they never reflect, that it is not in the power even of Heaven itself to make the offer of unceasing felicity as great a gift to the happy as to the miserable. To the first, eternity is but a single blessing, since at most it but increases what they already possess. To the latter, it is a double advantage; for it diminishes their pain here, and rewards them with heavenly bliss hereafter.

"But Providence is in another respect kinder to the poor than to the rich; for as it thus makes the life after death more desirable, so it smoothes the passage there. The wretched have had a long familiarity with every face of terror. The man of sorrows lays himself quietly down, without possessions to regret, and but few ties to stop his departure: he feels only nature's pang in the final separation, and this is no way greater than he has often fainted under before; for, after a certain degree of pain, every new breach that death opens in the constitution nature kindly covers with insensibility.

"Thus Providence has given the wretched two advantages over the happy in this life,—greater felicity in dying, and in heaven all that superiority of pleasure which arises from contrasted enjoyment. And this superiority, my friends, is no small advantage, and seems to be one of the pleasures of the poor man in the parable; for though he was already in heaven, and felt all the raptures it could give, yet it was mentioned as an addition to his happiness, that he had once been wretched, and now was comforted; that he had known what it was to be miserable, and now felt what it was to be happy.

"Thus, my friends, you see religion does what philosophy could never do: it shows the equal dealings of Heaven to the happy and the unhappy, and levels all human enjoyments to nearly the same standard. It gives to both rich and poor the same happiness hereafter, and equal hopes to aspire after it; but, if the rich have the advantage of enjoying pleasure here, the poor have the endless satisfaction of knowing what it was once to be miserable, when crowned with endless felicity hereafter; and even though this should be called a small advantage, yet, being an eternal one, it must make up by duration what the temporal happiness of the great may have exceeded by intenseness.

"These are, therefore, the consolations which the wretched have peculiar to themselves, and in which they are above the rest of mankind: in other respects, they are below them. They who would know the miseries of the poor, must see life and endure it. To declaim on the temporal advantages they enjoy, is only repeating what none either believe or practise. The men who have the necessaries of living, are not poor; and they who want them, must be miserable. Yes, my friends, we must be miserable. No vain efforts of a refined imagination can soothe the wants of nature, can give elastic sweetness to the dank vapour of a dungeon, or ease to the throbbings of a broken heart. Let the philosopher, from his couch of softness tell us that we can resist all these: alas! the effort by which we resist them is still the greatest pain. Death is slight, and any man may sustain it; but torments are dreadful, and these no man can endure.

"To us then, my friends, the promises of happiness in heaven should be peculiarly dear; for if our reward be in this life alone, we are then, indeed, of all men the most miserable. When I look round these gloomy walls, made to terrify as well as to confine us; this light, that only serves to show the horrors of the place; those shackles, that tyranny has imposed, or crime made necessary; when I survey these emaciated looks, and hear those groans—oh, my friends, what a glorious exchange would heaven be for these! To fly through regions unconfined as air—to bask in the sunshine of eternal bliss—to carol over endless hymns of praise—to have no master to threaten or insult us, but the form of Goodness himself for ever in our eyes!—when I think of these things, death becomes the messenger of very glad tidings; when I think of these things, his sharpest arrow becomes the staff of my support; when I think of these things, what is there in life worth having; when I think of these things, what is there that should not be spurned away: kings in their palaces should groan for such advantages; but we, humbled as we are, should yearn for them.

"And shall these things be ours? Ours they will certainly be, if we but try for them; and, what is a comfort, we are shut out from many temptations that would retard our pursuit. Only let us try for them, and they will certainly be ours; and, what is still a comfort, shortly too: for if we look back on a past life, it appears but a very short span, and whatever we may think of the rest of life, it will yet be found of less duration; as we grow older, the days seem to grow shorter, and our intimacy with Time ever lessens the perception of his stay. Then let us take comfort now, for we shall soon be at our journey's end; we shall soon lay down the heavy burden laid by Heaven upon us; and though death, the only friend of the wretched, for a little while mocks the weary traveller with the view, and like his horizon still flies before him; yet the time will certainly and shortly come, when we shall cease from our toil; when the luxuriant great ones of the world shall no more tread us to the earth; when we shall think with pleasure of our sufferings below; when we shall be surrounded with all our friends, or such as deserved our friendship; when our bliss shall be unutterable, and still, to crown all, unending."

CHAPTER XXX.

Happier Prospects begin to appear. Let us be inflexible, and Fortune will at last change in our favour.

WHEN I had thus finished, and my audience was retired, the gaoler, who was one of the most humane of his profession, hoped I would not be displeased, as what he did was but his duty, observing, that he must be obliged to remove my son into a stronger cell, but that he should be permitted to revisit me every morning. I thanked him for his clemency, and grasping my boy's hand, bade him farewell, and be mindful of the great duty that was before him.

I again therefore laid me down, and one of my little ones sat by my bedside reading, when Mr. Jenkinson entering, informed me that there was news of my daughter; for that she was seen by a person about two hours before in a strange gentleman's company, and that they had stopped at a neighbouring village for refreshment, and seemed as if returning to town. He had scarcely delivered this news when the gaoler came, with looks of haste and pleasure, to inform me that my daughter was found. Moses came running in a moment after, crying out that his sister Sophia was below, and coming up with our old friend Mr. Burchell.

Just as he delivered this news, my dearest girl entered, and, with looks almost wild with pleasure, ran to kiss me, in a transport of affection. Her mother's tears and silence also showed her pleasure. "Here, papa," cried the charming girl, "here is the brave man to whom I owe my delivery; to this gentleman's intrepidity I am indebted for my happiness and safety——" A kiss from Mr. Burchell, whose pleasure seemed even greater than hers, interrupted what she was going to add.

"Ah! Mr. Burchell," cried I, "this is but a wretched habitation you now find us in; and we are now very different from what you last saw us. You were ever our friend: we have long discovered our errors with regard to you, and repented of our ingratitude. After the vile usage you then received at my hands, I am almost ashamed to behold your face; yet I hope you'll forgive me, as I was deceived by a base ungenerous wretch, who, under the mask of friendship, has undone me."

"It is impossible," cried Mr. Burchell, "that I should forgive you, as you never deserved my resentment. I partly saw your delusion then, and as it was out of my power to restrain, I could only pity it."

"It was ever my conjecture," cried I, "that your mind was noble; but now I find it so.—But tell me, my dear child, how thou hast been relieved, or who the ruffians were who carried thee away?"

"Indeed, sir," replied she, "as to the villain who carried me off, I am yet ignorant. For, as my mamma and I were walking out, he came behind us, and, almost before I could call for help, forced me into the post-chaise, and in an instant the horses drove away. I met several on the road, to whom I cried out for assistance, but they disregarded my entreaties. In the meantime, the ruffian himself used every art to hinder me from crying out: he flattered and threatened by turns, and swore that, if I continued but silent, he intended no harm. In the meantime I had broken the canvas that he had drawn up, and whom should I perceive at some distance but your old friend Mr. Burchell, walking along with his usual swiftness, with the great stick for which we used so much to ridicule him. As soon as we came within hearing, I called out to him by name, and entreated his help. I repeated my exclamations several times, upon which, with a very loud voice, he bid the postilion stop; but the boy took no notice, but drove on with still greater speed. I now thought he could never overtake us, when, in less than a minute, I saw Mr. Burchell come running up by the side of the horses, and, with one blow, knock the postilion to the ground. The horses, when he was fallen, soon stopped of themselves, and the ruffian, stepping out, with oaths and menaces, drew his sword, and ordered him, at his peril, to retire; but Mr. Burchell, running up, shivered his sword to pieces, and then pursued him for near a quarter of a mile; but he made his escape. I was at this time come out myself, willing to assist my deliverer; but he soon returned to me in triumph. The postilion, who was recovered, was going to make his escape too; but Mr. Burchell ordered him at his peril to mount again and drive back to town. Finding it impossible to resist, he reluctantly complied, though the wound he had received seemed, to me at least, to be dangerous. He continued to complain of the pain as we drove along, so that he at last excited Mr. Burchell's compassion, who, at my request, exchanged him for another, at an inn where we called on our return."

"Welcome, then," cried I, "my child! and thou, her gallant deliverer, a thousand welcomes! Though our cheer is but wretched, yet our hearts are ready to receive you. And now, Mr. Burchell, as you have delivered my girl, if you think her a recompense, she is yours: if you can stoop to an alliance with a family so poor as mine, take her; obtain her consent,—as I know you have her heart,—and you have mine. And let me tell you, sir, that I give you no small treasure: she has been celebrated for beauty, it is true, but that is not my meaning,—I give you up a treasure in her mind."

"But I suppose, sir," cried Mr. Burchell, "that you are apprised of my circumstances, and of my incapacity to support her as she deserves?"

"If your present objection," replied I, "be meant as an evasion of my offer, I desist: but I know no man so worthy to deserve her as you; and if I could give her thousands, and thousands sought her from me, yet my honest brave Burchell should be my dearest choice."

To all this his silence alone seemed to give a mortifying refusal: and, without the least reply to my offer, he demanded if he could not be furnished with refreshments from the next inn; to which being answered in the affirmative, he ordered them to send in the best dinner that could be provided upon such short notice. He bespoke also a dozen of their best wine, and some cordials for me; adding, with a smile, that he would stretch a little for once, and, though in a prison, asserted he was never better disposed to be merry. The waiter soon made his appearance with preparations for dinner; a table was lent us by the gaoler, who seemed remarkably assiduous; the wine was disposed in order, and two very well dressed dishes were brought in.

My daughter had not yet heard of her poor brother's melancholy situation, and we all seemed unwilling to damp her cheerfulness by the relation. But it was in vain that I attempted to appear cheerful: the circumstances of my unfortunate son broke through all efforts to dissemble; so that I was at last obliged to damp our mirth by relating his misfortunes, and wishing that he might be permitted to share with us in this little interval of satisfaction. After my guests were recovered from the consternation my account had produced, I requested also that Mr. Jenkinson, a fellow-prisoner, might be admitted, and the gaoler granted my request with an air of unusual submission. The clanking of my son's irons was no sooner heard along the passage, than his sister ran impatiently to meet him, while Mr. Burchell, in the meantime, asked me if my son's name was George; to which replying in the affirmative, he still continued silent. As soon as my boy entered the room, I could perceive he regarded Mr. Burchell with a look of astonishment and reverence. "Come on," cried I, "my son; though we are fallen very low, yet Providence has been pleased to grant us some small relaxation from pain. Thy sister is restored to us, and there is her deliverer: to that brave man it is that I am indebted for yet having a daughter: give him, my boy, the hand of friendship; he deserves our warmest gratitude."

My son seemed all this while regardless of what I said, and still continued fixed at a respectful distance. "My dear brother," cried his sister, "why don't you thank my good deliverer? the brave should ever love each other."

He still continued his silence and astonishment, till our guest at last perceived himself to be known, and, assuming all his native dignity, desired my son to come forward. Never before had I seen anything so truly majestic as the air he assumed on this occasion. The greatest object in the universe, says a certain philosopher, is a good man struggling with adversity; yet there is still a greater, which is the good man that comes to relieve it. After he had regarded my son for some time with a superior air, "I again find," said he, "unthinking boy, that the same crime——" But here he was interrupted by one of the gaoler's servants, who came to inform us that a person of distinction, who had driven into town with a chariot and several attendants, sent his respects to the gentleman that was with us, and begged to know when he should think proper to be waited upon. "Bid the fellow wait," cried our guest, "till I shall have leisure to receive him:" and then turning to my son, "I again find, sir," proceeded he, "that you are guilty of the same offence for which you once had my reproof, and for which the law is now preparing its justest punishments. You imagine, perhaps, that a contempt for your own life gives you a right to take that of another: but where, sir, is the difference between a duellist, who hazards a life of no value, and the murderer who acts with greater security? Is it any diminution of the gamester's fraud, when he alleges that he has staked a counter?"

"Alas, sir," cried I, "whoever you are, pity the poor misguided creature; for what he has done was in obedience to a deluded mother, who, in the bitterness of her resentment, required him, upon her blessing, to avenge her quarrel. Here, sir, is the letter, which will serve to convince you of her imprudence, and diminish his guilt."

He took the letter, and hastily read it over. "This," says he, "though not a perfect excuse, is such a palliation of his fault as induces me to forgive him. And now, sir," continued he, kindly taking my son by the hand, "I see you are surprised at finding me here; but I have often visited prisons upon occasions less interesting. I am now come to see justice done a worthy man, for whom I have the most sincere esteem. I have long been a disguised spectator of thy father's benevolence. I have, at his little dwelling, enjoyed respect uncontaminated by flattery; and have received that happiness that courts could not give, from the amusing simplicity around his fire-side. My nephew has been apprised of my intentions of coming here, and, I find, is arrived. It would be wronging him and you to condemn him without examination: if there be injury, there shall be redress; and this I may say, without boasting, that none have ever taxed the injustice of Sir William Thornhill."

We now found the personage whom we had so long entertained as an harmless amusing companion, was no other than the celebrated Sir William Thornhill, to whose virtues and singularities scarce any were strangers. The poor Mr. Burchell was in reality a man of large fortune and great interest, to whom senates listened with applause, and whom party heard with conviction; who was the friend of his country, but loyal to his king. My poor wife, recollecting her former familiarity, seemed to shrink with apprehension; but Sophia, who a few moments before thought him her own, now perceiving the immense distance to which he was removed by fortune, was unable to conceal her tears.

"Ah! sir," cried my wife, with a piteous aspect, "how is it possible that I can ever have your forgiveness? The slights you received from me the last time I had the honour of seeing you at our house, and the jokes which I audaciously threw out—these, sir, I fear, can never be forgiven."

"My dear good lady," returned he with a smile, "if you had your joke, I had my answer: I'll leave it to all the company if mine were not as good as yours. To say the truth, I know nobody whom I am disposed to be angry with at present, but the fellow who so frighted my little girl here. I had not even time to examine the rascal's person so as to describe him in an advertisement. Can you tell me, Sophia, my dear, whether you should know him again?"

"Indeed, sir," replied she, "I can't be positive; yet now I recollect, he had a large mark over one of his eyebrows."—"I ask pardon, madam," interrupted Jenkinson, who was by, "but be so good as to inform me if the fellow wore his own red hair?"—"Yes, I think so," cried Sophia. "And did your honour," continued he, turning to Sir William, "observe the length of his legs?"—"I can't be sure of their length," cried the Baronet, "but I am convinced of their swiftness; for he outran me, which is what I thought few men in the kingdom could have done."—"Please your honour," cried Jenkinson, "I know the man: it is certainly the same; the best runner in England; he has beaten Pinwire of Newcastle: Timothy Baxter is his name; I know him perfectly, and the very place of his retreat this moment. If your honour will bid Mr. Gaoler let two of his men go with me, I'll engage to produce him to you in an hour at farthest." Upon this the gaoler was called, who instantly appearing, Sir William demanded if he knew him. "Yes, please your honour," replied the gaoler, "I know Sir William Thornhill well, and everybody that knows anything of him will desire to know more of him."—"Well, then," said the Baronet, "my request is, that you will permit this man and two of your servants to go upon a message by my authority; and as I am in the commission of the peace, I undertake to secure you."—"Your promise is sufficient," replied the other, "and you may, at a minute's warning, send them over England whenever your honour thinks fit."

In pursuance of the gaoler's compliance, Jenkinson was despatched in search of Timothy Baxter, while we were amused with the assiduity of our youngest boy Bill, who had just come in and climbed up Sir William's neck, in order to kiss him. His mother was immediately going to chastise his familiarity, but the worthy man prevented her; and taking the child, all ragged as he was, upon his knee, "What, Bill, you chubby rogue," cried he, "do you remember your old friend Burchell? and Dick, too, my honest veteran, are you here? you shall find I have not forgot you." So saying, he gave each a large piece of gingerbread, which the poor fellows ate very heartily, as they had got that morning a very scanty breakfast.

We now sat down to dinner, which was almost cold; but previously, my arm still continuing painful, Sir William wrote a prescription, for he had made the study of physic his amusement, and was more than moderately skilled in the profession: this being sent to an apothecary who lived in the place, my arm was dressed, and I found almost instantaneous relief. We were waited upon at dinner by the gaoler himself, who was willing to do our guest all the honour in his power. But before we had well dined, another message was brought from his nephew, desiring permission to appear in order to vindicate his innocence and honour; with which request the Baronet complied, and desired Mr. Thornhill to be introduced.

CHAPTER XXXI.

Former Benevolence now repaid with unexpected Interest.

MR. THORNHILL made his appearance with a smile, which he seldom wanted, and was going to embrace his uncle, which the other repulsed with an air of disdain. "No fawning, sir, at present," cried the Baronet, with a look of severity; "the only way to my heart is by the road of honour; but here I only see complicated instances of falsehood, cowardice, and oppression. How is it, sir, that this poor man, for whom I know you professed a friendship, is used thus hardly? His daughter vilely seduced as a recompense for his hospitality, and he himself thrown into prison, perhaps for resenting the insult? His son, too, whom you feared to face as a man——"

"Is it possible, sir," interrupted his nephew, "that my uncle should object that as a crime, which his repeated instructions alone have persuaded me to avoid?"

"Your rebuke," cried Sir William, "is just; you have acted, in this instance, prudently and well, though not quite as your father would have done: my brother, indeed, was the soul of honour; but thou—— Yes, you have acted, in this intance, perfectly right, and it has my warmest approbation."

"And I hope," said his nephew, "that the rest of my conduct will not be found to deserve censure. I appeared, sir, with this gentleman's daughter at some places of public amusement: thus, what was levity, scandal called by a harsher name, and it was reported I had debauched her. I waited on her father in person, willing to clear the thing to his satisfaction, and he received me only with insult and abuse. As for the rest, with regard to his being here, my attorney and steward can best inform you, as I commit the management of business entirely to them. If he has contracted debts, and is unwilling, or even unable to pay them, it is their business to proceed in this manner: and I see no hardship or injustice in pursuing the most legal means of redress."

"If this," cried Sir William "be as you have stated it, there is nothing unpardonable in your offence; and though your conduct might have been more generous in not suffering this gentleman to be oppressed by subordinate tyranny, yet it has been at least equitable."

"He cannot contradict a single particular," replied the Squire; "I defy him to do so; and several of my servants are ready to attest what I say. Thus, sir," continued he, finding that I was silent, for in fact I could not contradict him—"thus, sir, my own innocence is vindicated: but though at your entreaty I am ready to forgive this gentleman every other offence, yet his attempts to lessen me in your esteem excite a resentment that I cannot govern; and this, too, at a time when his son was actually preparing to take away my life,—this, I say, was such guilt, that I am determined to let the law take its course. I have here the challenge that was sent me, and two witnesses to prove it: one of my servants has been wounded dangerously; and even though my uncle himself should dissuade me, which I know he will not, yet I will see public justice done, and he shall suffer for it."

"Thou monster!" cried my wife, "hast thou not had vengeance enough already, but must my poor boy feel thy cruelty? I hope that good Sir William will protect us; for my son is as innocent as a child: I am sure he is, and never did harm to man."

"Madam," replied the good man, "your wishes for his safety are not greater than mine; but I am sorry to find his guilt too plain; and if my nephew persists——" But the appearance of Jenkinson and the gaoler's two servants now called off our attention, who entered, hauling in a tall man, very genteelly dressed, and answering the description already given of the ruffian who had carried off my daughter. "Here," cried Jenkinson, pulling him in, "here we have him; and if ever there was a candidate for Tyburn, this is one."

The moment Mr. Thornhill perceived the prisoner, and Jenkinson who had him in custody, he seemed to shrink back with terror. His face became pale with conscious guilt, and he would have withdrawn, but Jenkinson, who perceived his design, stopped him. "What, Squire," cried he, "are you ashamed of your two old acquaintances, Jenkinson and Baxter? But this is the way that all great men forget their friends, though I am resolved we will not forget you. Our prisoner, please your honour," continued he, turning to Sir William, "has already confessed all. This is the gentleman reported to be so dangerously wounded. He declares that it was Mr. Thornhill who first put him upon this affair; that he gave him the clothes he now wears, to appear like a gentleman, and furnished him with the post-chaise. The plan was laid between them, that he should carry off the young lady to a place of safety, and that there he should threaten and terrify her; but Mr. Thornhill was to come in, in the meantime, as if by accident, to her rescue; and that they should fight a while, and then he was to run off,—by which Mr. Thornhill would have the better opportunity of gaining her affections himself, under the character of her defender."

Sir William remembered the coat to have been worn by his nephew, and all the rest the prisoner himself confirmed by a more circumstantial account; concluding, that Mr. Thornhill had often declared to him that he was in love with both sisters at the same time.

"Heavens!" cried Sir William, "what a viper have I been fostering in my bosom! And so fond of public justice, too, as he seemed to be! But he shall have it: secure him, Mr. Gaoler—Yet, hold! I fear there is not legal evidence to detain him."

Upon this Mr. Thornhill, with the

utmost humility, entreated that two such abandoned wretches might not be admitted as evidences against him, but that his servants should be examined. "Your servants!" replied Sir William. "Wretch! call them yours no longer: but come, let us hear what those fellows have to say; let his butler be called."

When the butler was introduced, he soon perceived by his former master's looks that all his power was now over. "Tell me," cried Sir William, sternly, "have you ever seen your master, and that fellow dressed up in his clothes, in company together?"—"Yes, please your honour," cried the butler, "a thousand times: he was the man that always brought him his ladies."—"How!" interrupted young Mr. Thornhill, "this to my face?" "Yes," replied the butler, "or to any man's face. To tell you a truth, Master Thornhill, I never either loved you or liked you, and I don't care if I tell you now a piece of my mind."—"Now, then," cried Jenkinson, "tell his honour whether you know anything of me."—"I can't say," replied the butler, "that I know much good of you. The night that gentleman's daughter was deluded to our house, you were one of them."—"So then," cried Sir William, "I find you have brought a very fine witness to prove your innocence: thou stain to humanity! to associate with such wretches! But," continuing his examination, "you tell me, Mr. Butler, that this was the person who brought him this old gentleman's daughter."—"No, please your honour," replied the butler, "he did not bring her, for the Squire himself undertook that business; but he brought the priest that pretended to marry them."—"It is but too true," cried Jenkinson; "I cannot deny it; that was the employment assigned me, and I confess it to my confusion."

"Good heavens!" exclaimed the Baronet, "how every new discovery of his villany alarms me! All his guilt is now too plain, and I find his prosecution was dictated by tyranny, cowardice, and revenge. At my request, Mr. Gaoler, set this young officer, now your prisoner, free, and trust to me for the consequences. I'll make it my business to set the affair in a proper light to my friend the magistrate, who has committed him. But where is the unfortunate young lady herself? Let her appear to confront this wretch: I long to know by what arts he has seduced her. Entreat her to come in. Where is she?"

"Ah! sir," said I, "that question stings me to the heart: I was once indeed happy in a daughter, but her miseries——" Another interruption here prevented me; for who should make her appearance but Miss Arabella Wilmot, who was next day to have been married to Mr. Thornhill. Nothing could equal her surprise at seeing Sir William and his nephew here before her; for her arrival was quite accidental. It happened that she and the old gentleman, her father, were passing through the town, on the way to her aunt's, who had insisted that her nuptials with Mr. Thornhill should be consummated at her house; but stopping for refreshment, they put up at an inn at the other end of the town. It was there, from the window, that the young lady happened to observe one of my little boys playing in the street, and instantly sending a footman to bring the child to her, she learned from him some account of our misfortunes; but was still kept ignorant of young Mr. Thornhill's being the cause. Though her father made several remonstrances on the impropriety of going to a prison to visit us, yet they were ineffectual; she desired the child to conduct her, which he did, and it was thus she surprised us at a juncture so unexpected.

Nor can I go on without a reflection on those accidental meetings, which, though they happen every day, seldom excite our surprise but upon some extraordinary occasion. To what a fortuitous concurrence do we not owe every pleasure and convenience of our lives! How many seeming accidents must unite before we can be clothed or fed! The peasant must be disposed to labour, the shower must fall, the wind fill the merchant's sail, or numbers must want the usual supply.

We all continued silent for some moments, while my charming pupil, which was the name I generally gave this young lady, united in her looks compassion and astonishment, which gave new finishing to her beauty.—"Indeed, my dear Mr. Thornhill," cried she to the Squire, who she supposed was come here to succour, and not to oppress us, "I take it a little unkindly that you should come here without me, or never inform me of the situation of a family so dear to us both: you know I should take as much pleasure in contributing to the relief of my reverend old master here, whom I shall ever esteem, as you can. But I find that, like your uncle, you take a pleasure in doing good in secret."

"He find pleasure in doing good!" cried Sir William, interrupting her. "No, my dear, his pleasures are as base as he is. You see in him, madam, as complete a villain as ever disgraced humanity. A wretch, who, after having deluded this poor man's daughter, after plotting against the innocence of her sister, has thrown the father into prison, and the eldest son into fetters because he had the courage to face her betrayer. And give me leave, madam, now to congratulate you upon an escape from the embraces of such a monster."

"O goodness!" cried the lovely girl, "how have I been deceived! Mr. Thornhill informed me for certain that this gentleman's eldest son, Captain Primrose, was gone off to America with his new-married lady."

"My sweetest Miss," cried my wife, "he has told you nothing but falsehoods. My son George never left the kingdom, nor ever was married. Though you have forsaken him, he has always loved you too well to think of anybody else; and I have heard him say, he would die a bachelor for your sake." She then proceeded to expatiate upon the sincerity of her son's passion: she set his duel with Mr. Thornhill in a proper light; from thence she made a rapid digression to the Squire's debaucheries, his pretended marriages, and ended with a most insulting picture of his cowardice.

"Good heavens!" cried Miss Wilmot, "how very near have I been to the brink of ruin! Ten thousand falsehoods has this gentleman told me! He had at last art enough to persuade me, that my promise to the only man I esteemed was no longer binding, since he had been unfaithful. By his falsehoods I was taught to detest one equally brave and generous."

But by this time my son was freed from the encumbrances of justice, as the person supposed to be wounded was detected to be an impostor. Mr. Jenkinson, also, who had acted as his valet-de-chambre, had dressed up his hair, and furnished him with whatever was necessary to make a genteel appearance. He now therefore entered handsomely dressed in his regimentals; and, without vanity (for I am above it), he appeared as handsome a fellow as ever wore a military dress. As he entered, he made Miss Wilmot a modest and distant bow, for he was not as yet acquainted with the change which the eloquence of his mother had wrought in his favour. But no decorums could restrain the impatience of his blushing mistress to be forgiven. Her tears, her looks, all contributed to discover the real sensations of her heart, for having forgotten her former promise, and having suffered herself to be deluded by an impostor. My son appeared amazed at her condescension, and could scarce believe it real.—"Sure, madam," cried he, "this is but delusion! I can never have merited this! To be blessed thus is to be too happy."—"No, sir," replied she; "I have been deceived, basely deceived, else nothing could have ever made me unjust to my promise. You know my friendship—you have long known it—but forget what I have done, and as you once had my warmest vows of constancy, you shall now have them repeated; and be assured, that if your Arabella cannot be yours, she shall never be another's."—"And no other's you shall be," cried Sir William, "if I have any influence with your father."

This hint was sufficient for my son Moses, who immediately flew to the inn where the old gentleman was, to inform him of every circumstance that had happened. But, in the meantime, the Squire, perceiving that he was on every side undone, now finding that no hopes were left from flattery or dissimulation, concluded that his wisest way would be to turn and face his pursuers. Thus, laying aside all shame, he appeared the open, hardy villain. "I find, then," cried he, "that I am to expect no justice here; but I am resolved it shall be done me. You shall know, sir," turning to Sir William, "I am no longer a poor dependent upon your favours. I scorn them. Nothing can keep Miss Wilmot's fortune from me, which, I thank her father's assiduity, is pretty large. The articles and a bond for her fortune are signed, and safe in my possession. It was her fortune, not her person, that induced me to wish for this match; and, possessed of the one, let who will take the other."

This was an alarming blow. Sir William was sensible of the justice of his claims, for he had been instrumental in drawing up the marriage articles himself. Miss Wilmot, therefore, perceiving that her fortune was irretrievably lost, turning to my son, asked if the loss of fortune could lessen her value to him? "Though fortune," said she, "is out of my power, at least I have my hand to give."

"And that, madam," cried her real lover, "was indeed all that you ever had to give; at least all that I ever thought worth the acceptance. And I now protest, my Arabella, by all that's happy, your want of fortune this moment increases my pleasure, as it serves to convince my sweet girl of my sincerity."

Mr. Wilmot now entering, he seemed not a little pleased at the danger his daughter had just escaped, and readily consented to a dissolution of the match. But finding that her fortune, which was secured to Mr. Thornhill by bond, would not be given up, nothing could exceed his disappointment. He now saw that his money must all go to enrich one who had no fortune of his own. He could bear his being a rascal, but to want an equivalent to his daughter's fortune was wormwood. He sat, therefore, for some minutes employed in the most mortifying speculations, till Sir William attempted to lessen his anxiety. "I must confess, sir," cried he, "that your present disappointment does not entirely displease me. Your immoderate passion for wealth is now justly punished. But though the young lady cannot be rich, she has still a competence sufficient to give content. Here you see an honest young soldier, who is willing to take her without fortune: they have long loved each other; and, for the friendship I bear his father, my interest shall not be wanting in his promotion. Leave, then, that ambition which disappoints you, and for once admit that happiness which courts your acceptance."

"Sir William," replied the old gentleman, "be assured I never yet forced her inclinations, nor will I now. If she still continues to love this young gentleman, let her have him, with all my heart. There is still, thank Heaven, some fortune left, and your promise will make it something more. Only let my old friend here" (meaning me) "give me a promise of settling six thousand pounds upon my girl if ever he should come to his fortune, and I am ready, this night, to be the first to join them together."

As it now remained with me to make the young couple happy, I readily gave a promise of making the settlement he required; which, to one who had such little expectations as I, was no great favour. We had now, therefore, the satisfaction of seeing them fly into each other's arms in a transport. "After all my misfortunes," cried my son George, "to be thus rewarded! Sure this is more than I could ever have presumed to hope for. To be possessed of all that's good, and after such an interval of pain! My warmest wishes could never rise so high!"

"Yes, my George," returned his lovely bride, "now let the wretch take my fortune; since you are happy without it, so am I. Oh, what an exchange have I made, —from the basest of men to the dearest, best! Let him enjoy our fortune, I can now be happy even in indigence."—"And I promise you," cried the Squire, with a malicious grin, "that I shall be very happy with what you despise."—"Hold, hold, sir," cried Jenkinson, "there are two words to that bargain. As for that lady's fortune, sir, you shall never touch a single stiver of it. Pray, your honour," continued he to Sir William, "can the Squire have this lady's fortune if he be married to another?" —"How can you make such a simple demand?" replied the Baronet: "undoubtedly he cannot."—"I am sorry for that," cried Jenkinson; "for as this gentleman and I have been old fellow-sporters, I have a friendship for him. But I must declare, well as I love him, that this contract is not worth a tobacco-stopper, for he is married already."—"You lie, like a rascal!" returned the Squire, who seemed roused by this insult; "I never was legally married to any woman."

"Indeed, begging your honour's pardon," replied the other, "you were: and I hope you will show a proper return of friendship to your own honest Jenkinson, who brings you a wife; and if the company restrain their curiosity a few minutes, they shall see her." So saying, he went off, with his usual celerity, and left us all unable to form any probable conjecture as to his design. "Ay, let him go," cried the Squire; "whatever else I may have done, I defy him there. I am too old now to be frightened with squibs."

"I am surprised," said the Baronet, "what the fellow can intend by this. Some low piece of humour, I suppose."—"Perhaps, sir," replied I, "he may have a more serious meaning. For when we reflect on the various schemes this gentleman has laid to seduce innocence, perhaps some one more artful than the rest has been found able to deceive him. When we consider what numbers he has ruined, how many parents now feel, with anguish, the infamy and the contamination which he has brought into their families, it would not surprise me if some one of them—— Amazement! Do I see my lost daughter? Do I hold her? It is, it is my life, my happiness! I thought thee lost, my Olivia, yet still I hold thee—and still thou shalt live to bless me." The warmest transports of the fondest lover were not greater than mine, when I saw him introduce my child, and held my daughter in my arms, whose silence only spoke her raptures.

"And art thou returned to me, my darling," cried I, "to be my comfort in age!" —"That she is," cried Jenkinson; "and make much of her, for she is your own honourable child, and as honest a woman as any in the whole room, let the other be who she will. And as for you, Squire, as sure as you stand there, this young lady is your lawful wedded wife: and to convince you that I speak nothing but the truth, here is the licence by which you were married together." So saying, he put the licence into the Baronet's hands, who read it, and found it perfect in every respect. "And now, gentlemen," continued he, "I find you are surprised at all this; but a few words will explain the difficulty. That there Squire of renown, for whom I have a great friendship (but that's between ourselves), has often employed me in doing odd little things for him. Among the rest, he commissioned me to procure him a false licence and a false priest, in order to deceive this young lady. But as I was very much his friend, what did I do, but went and got a true licence and a true priest, and married them both as fast as the cloth could make them. Perhaps you'll think it was generosity that made me do all this: but no: to my shame I confess it, my only design was to keep the licence, and let the Squire know that I could prove it upon him whenever I thought proper, and so make him come down whenever I wanted money." A burst of pleasure now seemed to fill the whole apartment; our joy reached even to the common room, where the prisoners themselves sympathised,

——And shook their chains
In transport and rude harmony.

Happiness was expanded upon every face, and even Olivia's cheek seemed flushed with pleasure. To be thus restored to reputation, to friends, and fortune at once, was a rapture sufficient to stop the progress of decay, and restore former health and vivacity. But, perhaps, among all, there was not one who felt sincerer pleasure than I. Still holding the dear loved child in my arms, I asked my heart if these transports were not delusion. "How could you," cried I, turning to Mr. Jenkinson, "how could you add to my miseries by the story of her death? But it matters not; my pleasure at finding her again is more than a recompense for the pain."

"As to your question," replied Jenkinson, "that is easily answered. I thought the only probable means of freeing you from prison was by submitting to the Squire, and consenting to his marriage with the other young lady. But these you had vowed never to grant while your daughter was living: there was therefore no other method to bring things to bear, but by persuading you that she was dead,

I prevailed on your wife to join in the deceit, and we have not had a fit opportunity of undeceiving you till now.

In the whole assembly now there appeared only two faces that did not glow with transport. Mr. Thornhill's assurance had entirely forsaken him: he now saw the gulf of infamy and want before him, and trembled to take the plunge. He therefore fell on his knees before his uncle, and in a voice of piercing misery implored compassion. Sir William was going to spurn him away, but at my request he raised him, and, after pausing a few moments, "Thy vices, crimes, and ingratitude," cried he, "deserve no tenderness; yet thou shalt not be entirely forsaken,—a bare competence shall be supplied to support the wants of life, but not its follies. This young lady, thy wife, shall be put in possession of a third part of that fortune which once was thine, and from her tenderness alone thou art to expect any extraordinary supplies for the future." He was going to express his gratitude for such kindness in a set speech; but the Baronet prevented him, by bidding him not aggravate his meanness, which was already but too apparent. He ordered him at the same time to be gone, and from all his former domestics to choose one, such as he should think proper, which was all that should be granted to attend him.

As soon as he left us, Sir William very politely stepped up to his new niece with a smile, and wished her joy. His example was followed by Miss Wilmot and her father. My wife, too, kissed her daughter with much affection; as, to use her own expression, she was now made an honest woman of. Sophia and Moses followed in turn; and even our benefactor Jenkinson desired to be admitted to that honour. Our satisfaction seemed scarcely capable of increase. Sir William, whose greatest pleasure was in doing good, now looked round with a countenance open as the sun, and saw nothing but joy in the looks of all except that of my daughter Sophia, who, for some reasons we could not comprehend, did not seem perfectly satisfied. "I think now," cried he, with a smile, "that all the company except one or two seem perfectly happy. There only remains an act of justice for me to do. You are sensible, sir," continued he, turning to me, "of the obligations we both owe to Mr. Jenkinson; and it is but just we should both reward him for it. Miss Sophia will, I am sure, make him very happy, and he shall have from me five hundred pounds as her fortune; and upon this I am sure they can live very comfortably together. Come, Miss Sophia, what say you to this match of my making? Will you have him?" My poor girl seemed almost sinking into her mother's arms at the hideous proposal. "Have him, sir!" cried she faintly: "No, sir, never!"—"What!" cried he again, "not have Mr. Jenkinson, your benefactor, a handsome young fellow, with five hundred pounds, and good expectations?"—"I beg, sir," returned she, scarce able to speak, "that you'll desist, and not make me so very wretched."—"Was ever such obstinacy known?" cried he again, "to refuse a man whom the family have such infinite obligations to, who has preserved your sister, and who has five hundred pounds! What! not have him!"—"No, sir, never!" replied she, angrily; "I'd sooner die first."—"If that be the case, then," cried he, "if you will not have him—I think I must have you myself." And, so saying, he caught her to his breast with ardour. "My loveliest, my most sensible of girls," cried he, "how could you ever think your own Burchell could deceive you, or that Sir William Thornhill could ever cease to admire a mistress that loved him for himself alone? I have for some years sought for a woman, who, a stranger to my fortune, could think that I had merit as a man. After having tried in vain, even amongst the pert and the ugly, how great at last must be my rapture to have made a conquest over such sense and such heavenly beauty." Then turning to Jenkinson: "As I cannot, sir, part with this young lady myself, for she has taken a fancy to the cut of my face, all the recompense I can make is to give you her fortune; and you may call upon my steward to-morrow for five hundred pounds." Thus we had all our compliments to repeat, and Lady Thornhill underwent the same round of ceremony that her sister had done before.

In the meantime Sir William's gentleman appeared to tell us that the equipages were ready to carry us to the inn, where every thing was prepared for our reception. My wife and I led the van, and left those gloomy mansions of sorrow. The generous Baronet ordered forty pounds to be distributed among the prisoners, and Mr. Wilmot, induced by his example, gave half that sum. We were received below by the shouts of the villagers, and I saw and shook by the hand two or three of my honest parishioners, who were among the number. They attended us to our inn, where a sumptuous entertainment was provided, and coarser provisions were distributed in great quantities among the populace.

After supper, as my spirits were exhausted by the alternation of pleasure and pain which they had sustained during the day, I asked permission to withdraw; and, leaving the company in the midst of their mirth, as soon as I found myself alone, I poured out my heart in gratitude to the Giver of joy as well as of sorrow, and then slept undisturbed till morning.

CHAPTER XXXII.

The Conclusion.

THE next morning, as soon as I awaked, I found my eldest son sitting by my bedside, who came to increase my joy with another turn of fortune in my favour. First having released me from the settlement that I had made the day before in his favour, he let me know that my merchant, who had failed in town, was arrested at Antwerp, and there had given up effects to a much greater amount than what was due to his creditors. My boy's generosity pleased me almost as much as this unlooked-for good fortune; but I had some doubts whether I ought, in justice, to accept his offer. While I was pondering upon this Sir William entered the room, to whom I communicated my doubts. His opinion was that, as my son was already possessed of a very affluent fortune by his marriage, I might accept his offer without any hesitation. His business, however, was to inform me, that as he had the night before sent for the licences, and expected them every hour, he hoped that I would not refuse my assistance in making all the company happy that morning. A footman entered while we were speaking, to tell us that the messenger was returned; and as I was by this time ready, I went down, where I found the whole company as merry as affluence and innocence could make them. However, as they were now preparing for a very solemn ceremony, their laughter entirely displeased me. I told them of the grave, becoming, and sublime deportment they should assume upon this mystical occasion, and read them two homilies, and a thesis of my own composing, in order to prepare them. Yet they still seemed perfectly refractory and ungovernable. Even as we were going along to church, to which I led the way, all gravity had quite forsaken them, and I was often tempted to turn back in indignation. In church a new dilemma arose, which promised no easy solution. This was, which couple should be married first: my son's bride warmly insisted that Lady Thornhill (that was to be) should take the lead; but this the other refused with equal ardour, protesting she would not be guilty of such rudeness for the world. The argument was supported for some time between both, with equal obstinacy and good breeding. But, as I stood all this time with my book ready, I was at last quite tired of the contest; and, shutting it, "I perceive," cried I, "that none of you have a mind to be married, and I think we had as good go back again; for I suppose there will be no business done here to-day." This at once reduced them to reason. The Baronet and his lady were first married, and then my son and his lovely partner.

I had previously, that morning, given orders that a coach should be sent for my honest neighbour Flamborough and his family; by which means, upon our return to the inn, we had the pleasure of finding the two Miss Flamboroughs alighted before us. Mr. Jenkinson gave his hand to the eldest, and my son Moses led up the other (and I have since found, that he has taken a real liking to the girl, and my consent and bounty he shall have, whenever he thinks proper to demand them). We were no sooner returned to the inn, but numbers of my parishioners, hearing of my success, came to congratulate me; but, among the rest, were those who rose to rescue me, and whom I formerly rebuked with such sharpness. I told the story to Sir William, my son-in-law, who went out and reproved them with great severity; but finding them quite disheartened by his harsh reproof, he gave them half a guinea apiece to drink his health, and raise their dejected spirits.

Soon after this we were called to a very genteel entertainment, which was dressed by Mr. Thornhill's cook.—And it may not be improper to observe with respect to that gentleman, that he now resides, in quality of companion, at a relation's house, being very well liked, and seldom sitting at the side-table, except when there is no room at the other; for they make no stranger of him. His time is pretty much taken up in keeping his relation, who is a little melancholy, in spirits, and in learning to blow the French horn. My eldest daughter, however, still remembers him with regret; and she has even told me, though I make a great secret of it, that when he reforms, she may be brought to relent.—But to return, for I am not apt to digress thus: when we were to sit down to dinner our ceremonies were going to be renewed. The question was, whether my eldest daughter, as being a matron, should not sit above the two young brides; but the debate was cut short by my son George, who proposed that the company should sit indiscriminately, every gentleman by his lady. This was received with great approbation by all, excepting my wife, who, I could perceive, was not perfectly satisfied, as she expected to have had the pleasure of sitting at the head of the table, and carving all the meat for all the company. But, notwithstanding this, it is impossible to describe our good humour. I can't say whether we had more wit among us now than usual; but I am certain we had more laughing, which answered the end as well. One jest I particularly remember: old Mr. Wilmot drinking to Moses, whose head was turned another way, my son replied, "Madam, I thank you." Upon which the old gentleman, winking upon the rest of the company, observed that he was thinking of his mistress. At which jest I thought the two Miss Flamboroughs would have died with laughing. As soon as dinner was over, according to my old custom, I requested that the table might be taken away to have the pleasure of seeing all my family assembled once more by a cheerful fire-side. My two little ones sat upon each knee, the rest of the company by their partners. I had nothing now on this side of the grave to wish for: all my cares were over; my pleasure was unspeakable. It now only remained, that my gratitude in good fortune should exceed my former submission in adversity.

END OF THE VICAR OF WAKEFIELD.

THE

CITIZEN OF THE WORLD.

THE CITIZEN OF THE WORLD.

THE EDITOR'S PREFACE.

The schoolmen had formerly a very exact way of computing the abilities of their saints or authors. Escobar, for instance, was said to have learning as five, genius as four, and gravity as seven. Caramuel was greater than he. His learning was as eight, his genius as six, and his gravity as thirteen. Were I to estimate the merits of our Chinese Philosopher by the same scale, I would not hesitate to state his genius still higher; but as to his learning and gravity, these, I think, might safely be marked as nine hundred and ninety-nine, within one degree of absolute frigidity.

Yet, upon his first appearance here, many were angry not to find him as ignorant as a Tripoline ambassador or an envoy from Mujac. They were surprised to find a man born so far from London, that school of prudence and wisdom, endued even with a moderate capacity. They expressed the same surprise at his knowledge that the Chinese do at ours. "How comes it," said they, "that the Europeans, so remote from China, think with so much justice and precision? They have never read our books, they scarcely know even our letters, and yet they talk and reason just as we do." The truth is, the Chinese and we are pretty much alike. Different degrees of refinement, and not of distance, mark the distinctions among mankind. Savages of the most opposite climates have all but one character of improvidence and rapacity; and tutored nations, however separate, make use of the very same methods to procure refined enjoyment.

The distinctions of polite nations are few; but such as are peculiar to the Chinese appear in every page of the following correspondence. The metaphors and allusions are all drawn from the East. Their formality our author carefully preserves. Many of their favourite tenets in morals are illustrated. The Chinese are always concise; so is he. Simple; so is he. The Chinese are grave and sententious; so is he. But in one particular the resemblance is peculiarly striking: the Chinese are often dull; and so is he. Nor has my assistance been wanting. We are told in an old romance of a certain knight-errant and his horse who contracted an intimate friendship. The horse most usually bore the knight; but, in cases of extraordinary dispatch, the knight returned the favour, and carried his horse. Thus, in the intimacy between my author and me, he has usually given me a lift of his eastern sublimity, and I have sometimes given him a return of my colloquial ease.

Yet it appears strange, in this season of panegyric, when scarcely an author passes unpraised either by his friends or himself, that such merit as our Philosopher's should be forgotten. While the epithets of ingenious, copious, elaborate, and refined are lavished among the mob, like medals at a coronation, the lucky prizes fall on every side, but not one on him. I could on this occasion make myself melancholy, by considering the capriciousness of public taste, or the mutability of fortune; but during this fit of morality, lest my reader should sleep, I'll take a nap myself, and when I awake tell him my dream.

I imagined the Thames was frozen over, and I stood by its side. Several booths were erected upon the ice, and I was told by one of the spectators, that Fashion Fair was going to begin. He added, that every author who would carry his works there might probably find a very good reception. I was resolved, however, to observe the humours of the place in safety from the shore; sensible that ice was at best precarious, and having been always a little cowardly in my sleep.

Several of my acquaintance seemed much more hardy than I, and went over the ice with intrepidity. Some carried their works to the fair on sledges, some on carts, and those which were more voluminous were conveyed in waggons. Their temerity astonished me. I knew their cargoes were heavy, and expected every moment they would have gone to the bottom. They all entered the fair, however, in safety, and each soon after returned, to my great surprise, highly satisfied with his entertainment and the bargains he had brought away.

The success of such numbers at last began to operate upon me. If these, cried I, meet with favour and safety, some luck may, perhaps, for once attend the unfortunate. I am resolved to make a new adventure. The furniture, frippery, and fireworks of China have long been fashionably bought up. I'll try the fair with a small cargo of Chinese morality. If the Chinese have contributed to vitiate our taste, I'll try how far they can help to improve our understanding. But, as others have driven into the market in waggons, I'll cautiously begin by venturing with a wheelbarrow. Thus resolved, I baled up my goods, and fairly ventured; when, upon just entering the fair, I fancied the ice, that had supported an hundred waggons before, cracked under me, and wheel-barrow and all went to the bottom.

Upon awaking from my reverie with the fright, I cannot help wishing that the pains taken in giving this correspondence an English dress had been employed in contriving new political systems, or new plots for farces. I might then have taken my station in the world, either as a poet or a philosopher, and made one in those little societies where men club to raise each other's reputation. But at present I belong to no particular class. I resemble one of those animals that has been forced from its forest to gratify human curiosity. My earliest wish was to escape unheeded through life; but I have been set up for half-pence, to fret and scamper at the end of my chain. Though none are injured by my rage, I am naturally too savage to court any friends by fawning, too obstinate to be taught new tricks, and too improvident to mind what may happen. I am appeased, though not contented. Too indolent for intrigue, and too timid to push for favour, I am—But what signifies what am I?

'Ελπὶς καὶ σὺ τύχη μέγα χαίρετε· τὸν λιμέν' εὗρον.
Οὐδὲν ἐμοί χ' ὑμῖν· παίζετε τούς μετ' ἐμὲ.

[1760—62.]

LETTER I.

To Mr. ——, Merchant in London.

Amsterdam.

SIR,—Yours of the 13th instant, covering two bills, one on Messrs R. and D., value £478 10s., and the other on Mr——, value £285, duly came to hand, the former of which met with honour, but the other has been trifled with, and I am afraid will be returned protested.

The bearer of this is my friend, therefore let him be yours. He is a native of Honan in China, and one who did me signal services, when he was a mandarine, and I a factor, at Canton. By frequently conversing with the English there he has learned the language, though entirely a stranger to their manners and customs. I am told he is a philosopher; I am sure he is an honest man: that to you will be his best recommendation, next to the consideration of his being the friend of, sir, yours, &c.

LETTER II.

From Lien Chi Altangi to ——, Merchant in Amsterdam.

London.

FRIEND OF MY HEART,—May the wings of peace rest upon thy dwelling, and the shield of conscience preserve thee from vice and misery! For all thy favours accept my gratitude and esteem. the only tributes a poor philosophic wanderer can return. Sure, fortune is resolved to make me unhappy, when she gives others a power of testifying their friendship by actions, and leaves me only words to express the sincerity of mine.

I am perfectly sensible of the delicacy with which you endeavour to lessen your own merit and my obligations. By calling your late instances of friendship only a return for former favours you would induce me to impute to your justice what I owe to your generosity.

The services I did you at Canton justice, humanity, and my office bade me perform; those you have done me since my arrival at Amsterdam no laws obliged you to, no justice required. Even half your favours would have been greater than my most sanguine expectations.

The sum of money, therefore, which you privately conveyed into my baggage, when I was leaving Holland, and which I was ignorant of till my arrival in London, I must beg leave to return. You have been bred a merchant, and I a scholar; you consequently love money better than I. You can find pleasure in superfluity; I am perfectly content with what is sufficient. Take therefore what is yours: it may give you some pleasure, even though you have no occasion to use it; my happiness it cannot improve, for I have already all that I want.

My passage by sea from Rotterdam to England was more painful to me than all the journeys I ever made on land. I have traversed the immeasurable wilds of Mogul Tartary; felt all the rigours of Siberian skies: I have had my repose a hundred times disturbed by invading savages, and have seen, without shrinking, the desert sands rise like a troubled ocean all around me. Against these calamities I was armed with resolution; but in my passage to England, though nothing occurred that gave the mariners any uneasiness, to one who was never at sea before all was a subject of astonishment and terror. To find the land disappear—to see our ship mount the waves, swift as an arrow from the Tartar bow—to hear the wind howling through the cordage—to feel a sickness which depresses even the spirits of the brave, —these were unexpected distresses, and consequently assaulted me, unprepared to receive them.

You men of Europe think nothing of a voyage by sea. With us of China a man who has been from sight of land is regarded upon his return with admiration. I have known some provinces where there is not even a name for the ocean. What a strange people, therefore, am I got amongst, who have founded an empire on this unstable element, who build cities upon billows that rise higher than the mountains of Tipartala, and make the deep more formidable than the wildest tempest!

Such accounts as these, I must confess, were my first motives for seeing England. These induced me to undertake a journey of seven hundred painful days, in order to examine its opulence, buildings, sciences, arts, and manufactures, on the spot. Judge, then, my disappointment on entering London, to see no signs of that opulence so much talked of abroad: wherever I turn I am presented with a gloomy solemnity in the houses, the streets, and the inhabitants; none of that beautiful gilding which makes a principal ornament in Chinese architecture. The streets of Nankin are sometimes strewed with gold leaf: very different are those of London: in the midst of their pavement a great lazy puddle moves muddily along; heavy-laden machines, with wheels of unwieldy thickness, crowd up every passage: so that a stranger, instead of finding time for observation, is often happy if he has time to escape from being crushed to pieces.

The houses borrow very few ornaments from architecture; their chief decoration seems to be a paltry piece of painting hung out at their doors or windows, at once a proof of their indigence and vanity: their vanity, in each having one of those pictures exposed to public view; and their indigence, in being unable to get them better painted. In this respect the fancy of their painters is also deplorable. Could you believe it? I have seen five black lions and three blue boars in less than the circuit of half a mile; and yet you know that animals of these colours are nowhere to be found, except in the wild imaginations of Europe.

From these circumstances in their buildings, and from the dismal looks of the inhabitants, I am induced to conclude that the nation is actually poor; and that, like the Persians, they make a splendid figure everywhere but at home. The proverb of Xixofou is, that a man's riches may be seen in his eyes: if we judge of the English by this rule, there is not a poorer nation under the sun.

I have been here but two days, so will not be hasty in my decisions. Such letters as I shall write to Fipsihi in Moscow I beg you'll endeavour to forward with all diligence; I shall send them open, in order that you may take copies or translations, as you are equally versed in the Dutch and Chinese languages. Dear friend, think of my absence with regret, as I sincerely regret yours; even while I write, I lament our separation.—Farewell.

LETTER III.

From Lien Chi Altangi to the care of Fipsihi, resident in Moscow, to be forwarded by the Russian caravan to Fum Hoam, First President of the Ceremonial Academy at Pekin, in China.

THINK not, O thou guide of my youth! that absence can impair my respect, or interposing trackless deserts blot your reverend figure from my memory. The farther I travel I feel the pain of separation with stronger force; those ties that bind me to my native country and you are still unbroken. By every remove I only drag a greater length of chain.

Could I find ought worth transmitting from so remote a region as this to which I have wandered, I should gladly send it; but, instead of this, you must be content with a renewal of my former professions, and an imperfect account of a people with whom I am as yet but superficially acquainted. The remarks of a man who has been but three days in the country can only be those obvious circumstances which force themselves upon the imagination. I consider myself here as a newly created being introduced into a new world. Every object strikes with wonder and surprise. The imagination, still unsated, seems the only active principle of the mind. The most trifling occurrences give pleasure, till the gloss of novelty is worn away. When I have ceased to wonder, I may possibly grow wise; I may then call the reasoning principle to my aid, and compare those objects with each other, which were before examined without reflection.

Behold me, then, in London, gazing at the strangers, and they at me. It seems they find somewhat absurd in my figure; and had I never been from home, it is possible I might find an infinite fund of ridicule in theirs: but by long travelling I am taught to laugh at folly alone, and to find nothing truly ridiculous but villainy and vice.

When I had just quitted my native country, and crossed the Chinese wall, I fancied every deviation from the customs and manners of China was a departing from nature. I smiled at the blue lips and red foreheads of the Tonguese; and could hardly contain when I saw the Daures dress their heads with horns: the Ostiacs powdered with red earth; and the Calmuck beauties, tricked out in all the finery of sheepskin, appeared highly ridiculous. But I soon perceived that the ridicule lay not in them, but in me; that I falsely condemned others for absurdity, because they happened to differ from a standard originally founded in prejudice or partiality.

I find no pleasure, therefore, in taxing the English with departing from nature in their external appearance, which is all I yet know of their character: it is possible they only endeavour to improve her simple plan, since every extravagance in dress proceeds from a desire of becoming more beautiful than nature made us; and this is so harmless a vanity, that I not only pardon, but approve it. A desire to be more excellent than others is what actually makes us so; and as thousands find a livelihood in society by such appetites, none but the ignorant inveigh against them.

You are not insensible, most reverend Fum Hoam, what numberless trades, even among the Chinese, subsist by the harmless pride of each other. Your nose-borers, feet-swathers, teeth-stainers, eyebrow-pluckers, would all want bread, should their neighbours want vanity. These vanities, however, employ much fewer hands in China than in England; and a fine gentleman or a fine lady here, dressed up to the fashion, seems scarcely to have a single limb that does not suffer some distortions from art.

To make a fine gentleman several trades are required, but chiefly a barber. You have undoubtedly heard of the Jewish champion, whose strength lay in his hair. One would think that the English were for placing all wisdom there. To appear wise nothing more is requisite here than for a man to borrow hair from the heads of all his neighbours, and clap it like a bush on his own. The distributors of law and physic stick on such quantities, that it is almost impossible, even in idea, to distinguish between the head and the hair.

Those whom I have now been describing affect the gravity of the lion; those I am going to describe more resemble the pert vivacity of smaller animals. The barber, who is still master of the ceremonies, cuts their hair close to the crown; and then, with a composition of meal and hog's-lard, plasters the whole in such a manner as to make it impossible to distinguish whether the patient wears a cap or a plaster: but, to make the picture more perfectly striking, conceive the tail of some beast, a greyhound's tail, or a pig's tail, for instance, appended to the back of the head, and reaching down to the place where tails in other animals are generally seen to begin: thus betailed and bepowdered, the man of taste fancies he improves in beauty, dresses up his hard-featured face in smiles, and attempts to look hideously tender. Thus equipped, he is qualified to make love, and hopes for success more from the powder on the outside of his head than the sentiments within.

Yet when I consider what sort of a creature the fine lady is to whom he is supposed to pay his addresses, it is not strange to find him thus equipped in order to please. She is herself every whit as fond of powder, and tails, and hog's-lard, as he. To speak my secret sentiments, most reverend Fum, the ladies here are horribly ugly; I can hardly endure the sight of them; they no way resemble the beauties of China: the Europeans have a quite different idea of beauty from us. When I reflect on the small-footed perfections of an Eastern beauty, how is it possible I should have eyes for a woman whose feet are ten inches long? I shall never forget the beauties of my native city of Nangfew. How very broad their faces! how very short their noses! how very little their eyes! how very thin their lips! how very black their teeth! the snow on the tops of Bao is not fairer than their cheeks; and their eyebrows are small as the line by the pencil of Quamsi. Here a lady with such perfections would be frightful. Dutch and Chinese beauties, indeed, have some resemblance, but English women are entirely different: red cheeks, big eyes, and teeth of a most odious whiteness, are not only seen here, but wished for; and then they have such masculine feet, as actually serve *some* for walking!

Yet, uncivil as nature has been, they seem resolved to outdo her in unkindness: they use white powder, blue powder, and black powder for their hair, and a red powder for the face on some particular occasions.

They like to have the face of various colours, as among the Tartars of Koreki, frequently sticking on, with spittle, little black patches on every part of it, except on the tip of the nose, which I have never seen with a patch. You'll have a better idea of their manner of placing these spots when I have finished a map of an English face patched up to the fashion, which shall shortly be sent to increase your curious collection of paintings, medals, and monsters.

But what surprises more than all the rest is what I have just now been credibly informed of by one of this country. "Most ladies here," says he, "have two faces; one face to sleep in, and another to show in company. The first is generally reserved for the husband and family at home; the other put on to please strangers abroad: the family face is often indifferent enough, but the out-door one looks something better; this is always made at the toilet, where the looking-glass and toad-eater sit in council, and settle the complexion of the day."

I cannot ascertain the truth of this remark: however, it is actually certain, that they wear more clothes within doors than without; and I have seen a lady, who seemed to shudder at a breeze in her own apartment, appear half naked in the streets.—Farewell.

LETTER IV.

To the same.

The English seem as silent as the Japanese, yet vainer than the inhabitants of Siam. Upon my arrival I attributed that reserve to modesty, which, I now find, has its origin in pride. Condescend to address them first, and you are sure of their acquaintance; stoop to flattery, and you conciliate their friendship and esteem. They bear hunger, cold, fatigue, and all the miseries of life, without shrinking; danger only calls forth their fortitude; they even exult in calamity: but contempt is what they cannot bear. An Englishman fears contempt more than death; he often flies to death as a refuge from its pressure; and dies when he fancies the world has ceased to esteem him.

Pride seems the source not only of their national vices, but of their national virtues also. An Englishman is taught to love his king as his friend, but to acknowledge no other master than the laws which himself has contributed to enact. He despises those nations who, that one may be free, are all content to be slaves; who first lift a tyrant into terror, and then shrink under his power as if delegated from Heaven. Liberty is echoed in all their assemblies: and thousands might be found ready to offer up their lives for the sound, though perhaps not one of all the number understands its meaning. The lowest mechanic, however, looks upon it as his duty to be a watchful guardian of his country's freedom, and often uses a language that might seem haughty even in the mouth of the great emperor who traces his ancestry to the Moon.

A few days ago, passing by one of their prisons, I could not avoid stopping, in order to listen to a dialogue which I thought might afford me some entertainment. The conversation was carried on between a debtor through the grate of his prison, a porter, who had stopped to rest his burden, and a soldier at the window. The subject was upon a threatened invasion from France, and each seemed extremely anxious to rescue his country from the impending danger. "For my part," cries the prisoner, "the greatest of my apprehensions is for our freedom; if the French should conquer, what would become of English liberty? My dear friends, liberty is the Englishman's prerogative; we must preserve that at the expense of our lives; of that the French shall never deprive us. It is not to be expected that men who are slaves themselves would preserve our freedom should they happen to conquer."—"Ay, slaves," cries the porter, "they are all slaves, fit only to carry burdens, every one of them. Before I would stoop to slavery may this be my poison! (and he held the goblet in his hand,) may this be my poison!—but I would sooner list for a soldier."

The soldier, taking the goblet from his friend with much awe, fervently cried out, "It is not so much our liberties, as our religion, that would suffer by such a change: ay, our religion, my lads. May the devil sink me into flames, (such was the solemnity of his adjuration,) if the French should come over, but our religion would be utterly undone!"—So saying, instead of a libation, he applied the goblet to his lips, and confirmed his sentiments with a ceremony of the most persevering devotion.

In short, every man here pretends to be a politician; even the fair sex are sometimes found to mix the severity of national altercation with the blandishments of love, and often become conquerors by more weapons of destruction than their eyes.

This universal passion for politics is gratified by daily gazettes, as with us in China. But as in ours the emperor endeavours to instruct his people, in theirs the people endeavour to instruct the administration. You must not, however, imagine, that they who compile these papers have any actual knowledge of the politics, or the government, of a state; they only collect their materials from the oracle of some coffeehouse, which oracle has himself gathered them the night before from a beau at a gaming-table, who has pillaged his knowledge from a great man's porter, who has had his information from the great man's gentleman, who has invented the whole story for his own amusement the night preceding.

The English, in general, seem fonder of gaining the esteem than the love of those they converse with. This gives a formality to their amusements: their gayest conversations have something too wise for innocent relaxation: though in company you are seldom disgusted with the absurdity of a fool, you are seldom lifted into rapture by those strokes of vivacity, which give instant, though not permanent, pleasure.

What they want, however, in gaiety, they make up in politeness. You smile at hearing me praise the English for their politeness; you who have heard very different accounts from the missionaries at Pekin, who have seen such a different behaviour in their merchants and seamen at home. But I must still repeat it, the English seem more polite than any of their neighbours: their great art in this respect lies in endeavouring, while they oblige, to lessen the force of the favour. Other countries are fond of obliging a stranger; but seem desirous that he should be sensible of the obligation. The English confer their kindness with an appearance of indifference, and give away benefits with an air as if they despised them.

Walking, a few days ago, between an English and a French man, into the suburbs of the city, we were overtaken by a heavy shower of rain. I was unprepared; but they had each large coats, which defended them from what seemed to me a perfect inundation. The Englishman, seeing me shrink from the weather, accosted me thus: "Psha, man, what dost shrink at? Here, take this coat; I don't want it; I find it no way useful to me; I had as lief be without it." The Frenchman began to show his politeness in turn. "My dear friend," cries he, "why won't you oblige me by making use of my coat? you see how well it defends me from the rain; I should not choose to part with it to others, but to such a friend as you I could even part with my skin to do him service."

From such minute instances as these, most reverend Fum Hoam, I am sensible your sagacity will collect instruction. The volume of nature is the book of knowledge; and he becomes most wise who makes the most judicious selection. —Farewell.

LETTER V.

To the same.

I HAVE already informed you of the singular passion of this nation for politics. An Englishman, not satisfied with finding, by his own prosperity, the contending powers of Europe properly balanced, desires also to know the precise value of every weight in either scale. To gratify this curiosity, a leaf of political instruction is served up every morning with tea: when our politician has feasted upon this, he repairs to a coffeehouse, in order to ruminate upon what he has read, and increase his collection; from thence he proceeds to the ordinary, inquires what news, and treasuring up every acquisition there, hunts about all the evening in quest of more, and carefully adds it to the rest. Thus at night he retires home, full of the important advices of the day: when lo! awaking next morning, he finds the instructions of yesterday a collection of absurdity or palpable falsehood. This one would think a mortifying repulse in the pursuit of wisdom; yet our politician, no way discouraged, hunts on, in order to collect fresh materials, and in order to be again disappointed.

I have often admired the commercial spirit which prevails over Europe; have been surprised to see them carry on a traffic with productions that an Asiatic stranger would deem entirely useless. It is a proverb in China that an European suffers not even his spittle to be lost; the maxim, however, is not sufficiently strong, since they sell even their lies to great advantage. Every nation drives a considerable trade in this commodity with their neighbours.

An English dealer in this way, for instance, has only to ascend to his workhouse, and manufacture a turbulent speech averred to be spoken in the senate; or a report supposed to be dropped at court; a piece of scandal that strikes at a popular mandarine; or a secret treaty between two neighbouring powers. When finished, these goods are baled up, and consigned to a factor abroad, who sends in return two battles, three sieges, and a shrewd letter filled with dashes ——, blanks , and stars * * * of great importance.

Thus you perceive that a single gazette is the joint manufacture of Europe; and he who would peruse it with a philosophical eye might perceive in every paragraph something characteristic of the nation to which it belongs. A map does not exhibit a more distinct view of the boundaries and situation of every country, than its news does a picture of the genius and the morals of its inhabitants. The superstition and erroneous delicacy of Italy, the formality of Spain, the cruelty of Portugal, the fears of Austria, the confidence of Prussia, the levity of France, the avarice of Holland, the pride of England, the absurdity of Ireland, and the national partiality of Scotland, are all conspicuous in every page.

But, perhaps, you may find more satisfaction in a real newspaper, than in my description of one; I therefore send a specimen, which may serve to exhibit the manner of their being written, and distinguish the characters of the various nations which are united in its composition.

NAPLES.—We have lately dug up here a curious Etruscan monument, broke in two in the raising. The characters are scarce visible; but Nugosi, the learned antiquary, supposes it to have been erected in honour of Picus, a Latin king, as one of the lines may be plainly distinguished to begin with a P. It is hoped this discovery will produce something valuable, as the literati of our twelve academies are deeply engaged in the disquisition.

PISA.—Since Father Fudgi, prior of St. Gilbert's, has gone to reside at Rome, no miracles have been performed at the shrine of St. Gilbert: the devout begin to grow uneasy, and some begin actually to fear that St. Gilbert has forsaken them with the reverend father.

LUCCA.—The administrators of our serene republic have frequent conferences upon the part they shall take in the present commotions of Europe. Some are for sending a body of their troops, consisting of one company of foot and six horsemen, to make a diversion in favour of the empress-queen; others are as strenuous assertors of the Prussian interest: what turn these debates may take time only can discover. However, certain it is, we shall be able to bring into the field, at the opening of the next campaign, seventy-five armed men, a commander-in-chief, and two drummers of great experience.

SPAIN.—Yesterday the new king showed himself to his subjects, and, after having stayed half an hour in his balcony, retired to the royal apartment. The night concluded, on this extraordinary occasion, with illuminations and other demonstrations of joy.

The queen is more beautiful than the rising sun, and reckoned one of the first wits in Europe. She had a glorious opportunity of displaying the readiness of her invention and her skill in repartee lately at court. The Duke of Lerma coming up to her with a low bow and a smile, and presenting a nosegay set with diamonds, "Madam," cries he, "I am your most obedient humble servant."—"O sir," replies the queen, without any prompter, or the least hesitation, "I'm very proud of the very great honour you do me." Upon which she made a low courtesy, and all the courtiers fell a-laughing at the readiness and the smartness of her reply.

LISBON.—Yesterday we had an *auto da fé*, at which were burned three young women accused of heresy, one of them of exquisite beauty, two Jews, and an old woman, convicted of being a witch: one of the friars who attended this last reports, that he saw the devil fly out of her at the stake in the shape of a flame of fire. The populace behaved on this occasion with great good-humour, joy, and sincere devotion.

Our merciful sovereign has been for some time past recovered of his fright: though so atrocious an attempt deserved to exterminate half the nation, yet he has been graciously pleased to spare the lives of his subjects, and not above five hundred have been broke upon the wheel, or otherwise executed, upon this horrid occasion.

VIENNA.—We have received certain advices that a party of twenty thousand Austrians, having attacked a much superior body of Prussians, put them all to flight, and took the rest prisoners of war.

BERLIN.—We have received certain advices that a party of twenty thousand Prussians, having attacked a much superior body of Austrians, put them to flight, and took a great number of prisoners, with their military chest, cannon, and baggage.

Though we have not succeeded this campaign to our wishes, yet, when we think of him who commands us, we rest in security: while we sleep, our king is watchful for our safety.

PARIS.—We shall soon strike a signal blow. We have seventeen flat-bottomed boats at Havre. The people are in excellent spirits, and our ministers make no difficulty in raising the supplies.

We are all undone; the people are discontented to the last degree; the ministers are obliged to have recourse to the most rigorous methods to raise the expenses of the war.

Our distresses are great; but Madame Pompadour continues to supply our king, who is now growing old, with a fresh lady every night. His health, thank Heaven, is still pretty well; nor is he in the least unfit, as was reported, for any kind of royal exercitation. He was so frightened at the affair of Damiens, that his physicians were apprehensive lest his reason should suffer; but that wretch's tortures soon composed the kingly terrors of his breast.

ENGLAND.—Wanted an usher to an academy.—N. B. He must be able to read, dress hair, and must have had the small-pox.

DUBLIN.—We hear that there is a benevolent subscription on foot among the nobility and gentry of this kingdom, who are great patrons of merit, in order to assist Black and All Black, in his contest with the Paddereen mare.

We hear from Germany that Prince Ferdinand has gained a complete victory, and taken twelve kettle-drums, five standards, and four waggons of ammunition, prisoners of war.

EDINBURGH.—We are positive when we say that Saunders M'Gregor, who was lately executed for horse-stealing, is not a Scotsman, but born in Carrickfergus.—Farewell.

LETTER VI.

Fum Hoam, First President of the Ceremonial Academy at Pekin, to Lien Chi Altangi, the discontented Wanderer; by the way of Moscow.

WHETHER sporting on the flowery banks of the river Irtis, or scaling the steepy mountains of Douchenour; whether traversing the black deserts of Kobi, or giving lessons of politeness to the savage inhabitants of Europe; in whatever country, whatever climate, and whatever circumstances, all hail! May Tien, the Universal Soul, take you under his protection, and inspire you with a superior portion of himself!

How long, my friend, shall an enthusiasm for knowledge continue to obstruct your happiness, and tear you from all the connexions that make life pleasing? How long will you continue to rove from climate to climate, circled by thousands, and yet without a friend, feeling all the inconveniences of a crowd, and all the anxiety of being alone?

I know you will reply, that the refined pleasure of growing every day wiser is a sufficient recompense for every inconvenience. I know you will talk of the vulgar satisfaction of soliciting happiness from sensual enjoyment only; and probably enlarge upon the exquisite raptures of sentimental bliss. Yet, believe me, friend, you are deceived; all our pleasures, though seemingly never so remote from sense, derive their origin from some one of the senses. The most exquisite demonstration in mathematics, or the most pleasing disquisition in metaphysics, if it does not ultimately tend to increase some sensual satisfaction, is delightful only to fools, or to men who have by long habit contracted a false idea of pleasure; and he who separates sensual and sentimental enjoyments, seeking happiness from mind alone, is in fact as wretched as the naked inhabitant of the forest, who places all happiness in the first, regardless of the latter. There are two extremes in this respect: the savage, who swallows down the draught of pleasure without staying to reflect on his happiness; and the sage, who passeth the cup while he reflects on the conveniences of drinking.

It is with a heart full of sorrow, my dear Altangi, that I must inform you, that what the world calls happiness must now be yours no longer. Our great emperor's displeasure at your leaving China, contrary to the rules of our government and the immemorial custom of the empire, has produced the most terrible effects. Your wife, daughter, and the rest of your family, have been seized by his order, and appropriated to his use; all, except your son, are now the peculiar property of him who possesses all: him I have hidden from the officers employed for this purpose; and even at the hazard of my life I have concealed him. The youth seems obstinately bent on finding you out, wherever you are; he is determined to face every danger that opposes his pursuit. Though yet but fifteen, all his father's virtues and obstinacy sparkle in his eyes, and mark him as one destined to no mediocrity of fortune.

You see, my dearest friend, what imprudence has brought thee to: from opulence, a tender family, surrounding friends, and your master's esteem, it has reduced thee to want, persecution, and, still worse, to our mighty monarch's displeasure. Want of prudence is too frequently the want of virtue; nor is there on earth a more powerful advocate for vice than poverty. As I shall endeavour to guard thee from the one, so guard thyself from the other; and still think of me with affection and esteem.—Farewell.

LETTER VII.

From Lien Chi Altangi to Fum Hoam, First President of the Ceremonial Academy in China.

[The Editor thinks proper to acquaint the reader, that the greatest part of the following Letter seems to him to be little more than a rhapsody of sentences borrowed from Confucius, the Chinese philosopher.]

A WIFE, a daughter, carried into captivity to expiate my offence—a son, scarce yet arrived at maturity, resolving to encounter every danger in the pious pursuit of one who has undone him,—these indeed are circumstances of distress: though my tears were more precious than the gem of Golconda, yet would they fall upon such an occasion.

But I submit to the stroke of Heaven: I hold the volume of Confucius in my hand, and, as I read, grow humble, and patient, and wise. We should feel sorrow, says he, but not sink under its oppression. The heart of a wise man should resemble a mirror, which reflects every object without being sullied by any. The wheel of fortune turns incessantly round; and who can say within himself, I shall to-day be uppermost? We should hold the immutable mean that lies between insensibility and anguish; our attempts should not be to extinguish nature, but to repress it; not to stand unmoved at distress, but endeavour to turn every disaster to our own advantage. Our greatest glory is, not in never falling, but in rising every time we fall.

I fancy myself at present, O thou reverend disciple of Tao, more than a match for all that can happen. The chief business of my life has been to procure wisdom, and the chief object of that wisdom was to be happy. My attendance on your lectures, my conferences with the missionaries of Europe, and all my subsequent adventures upon quitting China, were calculated to increase the sphere of my happiness, not my curiosity. Let European travellers cross seas and deserts merely to measure the height of a mountain, to describe the cataract of a river, or tell the commodities which every country may produce: merchants or geographers, perhaps, may find profit by such discoveries; but what advantage can accrue to a philosopher from such accounts, who is desirous of understanding the human heart, who seeks to know the *men* of every country, who desires to discover those differences which result from climate, religion, education, prejudice, and partiality.

I should think my time very ill bestowed, were the only fruits of my adventures to consist in being able to tell, that a tradesman of London lives in a house three times as high as that of our great Emperor; that the ladies wear longer clothes than the men; that the priests are dressed in colours which we are taught to detest; and that their soldiers wear scarlet, which is with us the symbol of peace and innocence. How many travellers are there who confine their relations to such minute and useless particulars! For one who enters into the genius of those nations with whom he has conversed,—who discloses their morals, their opinions, the ideas which they entertain of religious worship, the intrigues of their ministers, and their skill in sciences,—there are twenty who only mention some idle particulars, which can be of no real use to a true philosopher. All their remarks tend neither to make themselves nor others more happy; they no way contribute to control their passions, to bear adversity, to inspire true virtue, or raise a detestation of vice.

Men may be very learned, and yet very miserable; it is easy to be a deep geometrician, or a sublime astronomer, but very difficult to be a good man. I esteem, therefore, the traveller who instructs the heart, but despise him who only indulges the imagination. A man who leaves home to mend himself and others, is a philosopher; but he who goes from country to country, guided by the blind impulse of curiosity, is only a vagabond. From Zerdusht down to him of Tyana, I honour all those great names who endeavoured to unite the world by their travels: such men grew wiser as well as better the farther they departed from home, and seemed like rivers, whose streams are not only increased, but refined, as they travel from their source.

For my own part, my greatest glory is, that travelling has not more steeled my constitution against all the vicissitudes of climate, and all the depressions of fatigue, than it has my mind against the accidents of fortune, or the accesses of despair.—Farewell.

LETTER VIII.

To the same.

How insupportable, O thou possessor of heavenly wisdom, would be this separation, this immeasurable distance from my friend, were I not able thus to delineate my heart upon paper, and to send thee daily a map of my mind!

I am every day better reconciled to the people among whom I reside, and begin to fancy, that in time I shall find them more opulent, more charitable, and more hospitable, than I at first imagined. I begin to learn somewhat of their manners and customs, and to see reasons for several deviations which they make from us, from whom all other nations derive their politeness, as well as their original.

In spite of taste, in spite of prejudice, I now begin to think their women tolerable. I can now look on a languishing blue eye without disgust, and pardon a set of teeth, even though whiter than ivory. I now begin to fancy there is no universal standard for beauty. The truth is, the manners of the ladies in this city are so very open, and so vastly engaging, that I am inclined to pass over the more glaring defects of their persons, since compensated by the more solid yet latent beauties of the mind. What though they want black teeth, or are deprived of the allurements of feet no bigger than their thumbs, yet still they have souls, my friend; such souls—so free, so pressing, so hospitable, and so engaging! I have received more invitations in the streets of London from the sex in one night, than I have met with at Pekin in twelve revolutions of the moon.

Every evening, as I return home from my usual solitary excursions, I am met by several of these well-disposed daughters of hospitality, at different times, and in different streets, richly dressed, and with minds not less noble than their appearance. You know that nature has indulged me with a person by no means agreeable; yet are they too generous to object to my homely appearance; they feel no repugnance at my broad face and flat nose; they perceive me to be a stranger, and that alone is a sufficient recommendation. They even seem to think it their duty to do the honours of the country by every act of complaisance in their power. One takes me under the arm, and in a manner forces me along; another catches me round the neck, and desires to partake in this office of hospitality; while a third, kinder still, invites me to refresh my spirits with wine. Wine is, in England, reserved only for the rich; yet here even wine is given away to the stranger.

A few nights ago, one of these generous creatures, dressed all in white, and flaunting like a meteor by my side, forcibly attended me home to my own apartment. She seemed charmed with the elegance of the furniture, and the convenience of my situation; and well indeed she might, for I have hired an apartment for not less than two shillings of their money every week. But her civility did not rest here; for, at parting, being desirous to know the hour, and perceiving my watch out of order, she kindly took it to be repaired by a relation of her own, which, you may imagine, will save some expense; and she assures me that it will cost her nothing. I shall have it back in a few days, when mended, and am preparing a proper speech, expressive of my gratitude on the occasion: "Celestial excellence!" I intend to say, "happy I am in having found out, after many painful adventures, a land of innocence, and a people of humanity: I may rove into other climes, and converse with nations yet unknown; but where shall I meet a soul of such purity as that which resides in thy breast! Sure thou hast been nurtured by the bill of the Shin Shin, or sucked the breasts of the provident Gin Hiung. The melody of thy voice could rob the Chong Fou of her whelps, or inveigle the Boh that lives in the midst of the waters. Thy servant shall ever retain a sense of thy favours; and one day boast of thy virtue, sincerity, and truth, among the daughters of China."—Adieu.

LETTER IX.

To the same.

I HAVE been deceived! She whom I fancied a daughter of paradise, has proved to be one of the infamous disciples of Han! I have lost a trifle; I have gained the consolation of having discovered a deceiver. I once more, therefore, relax into my former indifference with regard to the English ladies; they once more begin to appear disagreeable in my eyes. Thus is my whole time passed in forming conclusions which the next minute's experience may probably destroy; the present moment becomes a comment on the past, and I improve rather in humility than wisdom.

Their laws and religion forbid the English to keep more than one woman; I therefore concluded, that prostitutes were banished from society. I was deceived; every man here keeps as many wives as he can maintain: the laws are cemented with blood, praised and disregarded. The very Chinese, whose religion allows him two wives, takes not half the liberties of the English in this particular. Their laws may be compared to the books of the Sybils,—they are held in great veneration, but seldom read, or seldomer understood; even those who pretend to be their guardians, dispute about the meaning of many of them, and confess their ignorance of others. The law, therefore, which commands them to have but one wife, is strictly observed only by those for whom one is more than sufficient, or by such as have not money to buy two. As for the rest, they violate it publicly, and some glory in its violation. They seem to think, like the Persians, that they give evident marks of manhood by increasing their seraglio. A mandarine, therefore, here generally keeps four wives, a gentleman three, and a stage-player two. As for the magistrates, the country justices and squires, they are employed first in debauching young virgins, and then punishing the transgression.

From such a picture you will be apt to conclude, that he who employs four ladies for his amusement has four times as much constitution to spare as he who is contented with one; that a mandarine is much cleverer than a gentleman, and a gentleman than a player; and yet it is quite the reverse: a mandarine is frequently supported on spindle shanks, appears emaciated by luxury, and is obliged to have recourse to variety, merely from the weakness, not the vigour, of his constitution, the number of his wives being the most equivocal symptom of his virility.

Besides the country squire, there is also another set of men whose whole employment consists in corrupting beauty: these the silly part of the fair sex call amiable; the more sensible part of them, however, give them the title of abominable. You will probably demand, what are the talents of a man thus caressed by the majority of the opposite sex? what talents or what beauty is he possessed of, superior to the rest of his fellows? To answer you directly, he has neither talents nor beauty; but then he is possessed of impudence and assiduity. With assiduity and impudence, men of all ages, and all figures, may commence admirers. I have even been told of some who made professions of expiring for love, when all the world could perceive they were going to die of old age: and, what is more surprising still, such battered beaux are generally most infamously successful.

A fellow of this kind employs three hours every morning in dressing his head, by which is understood only his hair.

He is a professed admirer, not of any particular lady, but of the whole sex.

He is to suppose every lady has caught cold every night, which gives him an opportunity of calling to see how she does the next morning.

He is, upon all occasions, to show himself in very great pain for the ladies: if a lady drops even a pin, he is to fly in order to present it.

He never speaks to a lady without advancing his mouth to her ear, by which he frequently addresses more senses than one.

Upon proper occasions, he looks excessively tender. This is performed by laying his hand upon his heart, shutting his eyes, and showing his teeth.

He is excessively fond of dancing a minuet with the ladies, by which is only meant walking round the floor eight or ten times with his hat on, affecting great gravity, and sometimes looking tenderly on his partner.

He never affronts any man himself, and never resents an affront from another.

He has an infinite variety of small talk upon all occasions, and laughs when he has nothing more to say.

Such is the killing creature who prostrates himself to the sex till he has undone them; all whose submissions are the effects of design, and who, to please the ladies, almost becomes himself a lady.

LETTER X.

To the same.

I HAVE hitherto given you no account of my journey from China to Europe—of my travels through countries where nature sports in primeval rudeness, where she pours forth her wonders in solitude—countries from whence the rigorous climate, the sweeping inundation, the drifted desert, the howling forest, and mountains of immeasurable height, banish the husbandman and spread extensive desolation—countries where the brown Tartar wanders for a precarious subsistence, with an heart that never felt pity, himself more hideous than the wilderness he makes.

You will easily conceive the fatigue of crossing vast tracts of land, either desolate, or still more dangerous by its inhabitants,—the retreat of men who seem driven from society, in order to make war upon all the human race; nominally professing a subjection to Muscovy or China, but without any resemblance to the countries on which they depend.

After I had crossed the Great Wall, the first objects that presented themselves were the remains of desolated cities, and all the magnificence of venerable ruin. There were to be seen temples of beautiful structure, statues wrought by the hand of a master, and around, a country of luxuriant plenty; but not one single inhabitant to reap the bounties of nature. These were prospects that might humble the pride of kings, and repress human vanity. I asked my guide the cause of such desolation. These countries, says he, were once the dominions of a Tartar prince; and these ruins, the seat of arts, elegance, and ease. This prince waged an unsuccessful war with one of the emperors of China; he was conquered, his cities plundered, and all his subjects carried into captivity. Such are the effects of the ambition of kings! Ten dervises, says the Indian proverb, shall sleep in peace upon a single carpet, while two kings shall quarrel, though they have kingdoms to divide them. Sure, my friend, the cruelty and the pride of man have made more deserts than Nature ever made: she is kind, but man is ungrateful!

Proceeding in my journey through this pensive scene of desolated beauty, in a few days I arrived among the Daures, a nation still dependent on China. Xaizigar is their principal city, which, compared with those of Europe, scarcely deserves the name. The governors, and other officers, who are sent yearly from Pekin, abuse their authority, and often take the wives and daughters of the inhabitants to themselves. The Daures, accustomed to base submission, feel no resentment at these injuries, or stifle what they feel. Custom and necessity teach even barbarians the same art of dissimulation that ambition and intrigue inspire in the breasts of the polite. Upon beholding such unlicensed stretches of power, alas! thought I, how little does our wise and good emperor know of these intolerable exactions! These provinces are too distant for complaint, and too insignificant to expect redress. The more distant the government, the honester should be the governor to whom it is intrusted; for hope of impunity is a strong inducement to violation.

The religion of the Daures is more absurd than even that of the sectaries of Fohi. How would you be surprised, O sage disciple and follower of Confucius! you who believe one eternal intelligent cause of all, should you be present at the barbarous ceremonies of this infatuated people! How would you deplore the blindness and folly of mankind! His boasted reason seems only to light him astray, and brutal instinct more regularly points out the path to happiness. Could you think it? they adore a wicked divinity; they fear him and they worship him; they imagine him a malicious Being, ready to injure and ready to be appeased. The men and women assemble at midnight in a hut, which serves for a temple. A priest stretches himself on the ground, and all the people pour forth the most horrid cries, while drums and timbrels swell the infernal concert. After this dissonance, miscalled music, has continued about two hours, the priest rises from the ground, assumes an air of inspiration, grows big with the inspiring demon, and pretends to a skill in futurity.

In every country, my friend, the bonzes, the brahmins, and the priests deceive the people: all reformations begin from the laity; the priests point us out the way to heaven with their fingers, but stand still themselves, nor seem to travel towards the country in view.

The customs of this people correspond to their religion; they keep their dead for three days on the same bed where the person died; after which they bury him in a grave moderately deep, but with the head still uncovered. Here for several days they present him different sorts of meats; which, when they perceive he does not consume, they fill up the grave, and desist from desiring him to eat for the future. How, how can mankind be guilty of such strange absurdity? to entreat a dead body, already putrid, to partake of the banquet! Where, I again repeat it, is human reason? not only some men, but whole nations, seem divested of its illumination. Here we observe a whole country adoring a divinity through fear, and attempting to feed the dead. These are their most serious and most religious occupations. Are these men rational, or are not the apes of Borneo more wise?

Certain I am, O thou instructor of my youth! that without philosophers—without some few virtuous men, who seem to be of a different nature from the rest of mankind—without such as these, the worship of a wicked divinity would surely be established over every part of the earth. Fear guides more to their duty than gratitude: for one man who is virtuous from the love of virtue, from the obligation which he thinks he lies under to the Giver of all, there are ten thousand who are good only from the apprehensions of punishment. Could these last be persuaded, as the Epicureans were, that heaven had no thunders in store for the villain, they would no longer continue to acknowledge subordination, or thank that Being who gave them existence.—Adieu.

LETTER XI.

To the same.

FROM such a picture of nature in primeval simplicity, tell me, my much respected friend, are you in love with fatigue and solitude? Do you sigh for the severe frugality of the wandering Tartar, or regret being born amidst the luxury and dissimulation of the polite? Rather tell me, has not every kind of life vices peculiarly its own? Is it not a truth, that refined countries have more vices, but those not so terrible; barbarous nations few, and they of the most hideous complexion? Perfidy and fraud are the vices of civilized nations, credulity and violence those of the inhabitants of the desert.

Does the luxury of the one produce half the evils of the inhumanity of the other? Certainly, those philosophers who declaim against luxury have but little understood its benefits; they seem insensible, that to luxury we owe not only the greatest part of our knowledge, but even of our virtues.

It may sound fine in the mouth of a declaimer, when he talks of subduing our appetites, of teaching every sense to be content with a bare sufficiency, and of supplying only the wants of nature; but is there not more satisfaction in indulging those appetites, if with innocence and safety, than in restraining them? Am not I better pleased in enjoyment than in the sullen satisfaction of thinking that I can live without enjoyment? The more various our artificial necessities, the wider is our circle of pleasure; for all pleasures consist in obviating necessities as they rise: luxury, therefore, as it increases our wants, increases our capacity for happiness.

Examine the history of any country remarkable for opulence and wisdom, you will find they would never have been wise had they not been first luxurious; you will find poets, philosophers, and even patriots, marching in luxury's train. The reason is obvious: we then only are curious after knowledge, when we find it connected with sensual happiness. The senses ever point out the way, and reflection comments upon the discovery. Inform a native of the desert of Kobi of the exact measure of the parallax of the moon, he finds no satisfaction at all in the information; he wonders how any could take such pains, and lay out such treasures, in order to solve so useless a difficulty: but connect it with his happiness, by showing that it improves navigation—that by such an investigation he may have a warmer coat, a better gun, or a finer knife,—and he is instantly in raptures at so great an improvement. In short, we only desire to know what we desire to possess; and whatever we may talk against it, luxury adds the spur to curiosity, and gives us a desire of becoming more wise.

But not our knowledge only, but our virtues are improved by luxury. Observe the brown savage of Thibet, to whom the fruits of the spreading pomegranate supply food, and its branches an habitation. Such a character has few vices, I grant, but those he has are of the most hideous nature: rapine and cruelty are scarcely crimes in his eye; neither pity nor tenderness, which ennoble every virtue, have any place in his heart; he hates his enemies, and kills those he subdues. On the other hand, the polite Chinese and civilized European seem even to love their enemies. I have just now seen an instance, where the English have succoured those enemies whom their own countrymen actually refused to relieve.

The greater the luxuries of every country, the more closely, politically speaking, is that country united. Luxury is the child of society alone; the luxurious man stands in need of a thousand different artists to furnish out his happiness: it is more likely, therefore, that he should be a good citizen who is connected by motives of self-interest with so many, than the abstemious man who is united to none.

In whatsoever light, therefore, we consider luxury, whether as employing a number of hands, naturally too feeble for more laborious employment; as finding a variety of occupation for others who might be totally idle; or as furnishing out new inlets to happiness, without encroaching on mutual property; in whatever light we regard it, we shall have reason to stand up in its defence, and the sentiment of Confucius still remains unshaken: "That we should enjoy as many of the luxuries of life as are consistent with our own safety and the prosperity of others; and that he who finds out a new pleasure, is one of the most useful members of society."

LETTER XII.

To the same.

From the funeral solemnities of the Daures, who think themselves the politest people in the world, I must make a transition to the funeral solemnities of the English, who think themselves as polite as they. The numberless ceremonies which are used here when a person is sick appear to me so many evident marks of fear and apprehension. Ask an Englishman, however, whether he is afraid of death, and he boldly answers in the negative; but observe his behaviour in circumstances of approaching sickness, and you will find his actions give his assertions the lie.

The Chinese are very sincere in this respect; they hate to die, and they confess their terrors: a great part of their life is spent in preparing things proper for their funeral. A poor artisan shall spend half his income in providing himself a tomb twenty years before he wants it; and denies himself the necessaries of life that he may be amply provided for when he shall want them no more.

But people of distinction in England really deserve pity, for they die in circumstances of the most extreme distress. It is an established rule, never to let a man know that he is dying: physicians are sent for, the clergy are called, and everything passes in silent solemnity round the sick-bed. The patient is in agonies, looks round for pity, yet not a single creature will say that he is dying. If he is possessed of fortune, his relations entreat him to make his will, as it may restore the tranquillity of his mind. He is desired to undergo the rites of the Church, for decency requires it. His friends take their leave only because they do not care to see him in pain. In short, an hundred stratagems are used to make him do what he might have been induced to perform only by being told, "Sir, you are past all hopes, and had as good think decently of dying."

Besides all this, the chamber is darkened, the whole house echoes to the cries of the wife, the lamentations of the children, the grief of the servants, and the sighs of friends. The bed is surrounded with priests and doctors in black, and only flambeaux emit a yellow gloom. Where is the man, how intrepid soever, that would not shrink at such a hideous solemnity? For fear of affrighting their expiring friends, the English practise all that can fill them with terror. Strange effect of human prejudice, thus to torture, merely from mistaken tenderness!

You see, my friend, what contradictions there are in the tempers of these islanders: when prompted by ambition, revenge, or disappointment, they meet death with the utmost resolution: the very man who in his bed would have trembled at the aspect of a doctor, shall go with intrepidity to attack a bastion, or deliberately noose himself up in his garters.

The passion of the Europeans for magnificent interments is equally strong with that of the Chinese. When a tradesman dies, his frightful face is painted up by an undertaker, and placed in a proper situation to receive company: this is called lying in state. To this disagreeable spectacle all the idlers in town flock, and learn to loath the wretch dead whom they despised when living. In this manner, you see some who would have refused a shilling to save the life of their dearest friend, bestow thousands on adorning their putrid corpse. I have been told of a fellow, who, grown rich by the price of blood, left it in his will that he should lie in state; and thus unknowingly gibbeted himself into infamy, when he might have otherwise quietly retired into oblivion.

When the person is buried, the next care is to make his epitaph: they are generally reckoned best which flatter most; such relations, therefore, as have received most benefits from the defunct, discharge this friendly office, and generally flatter in proportion to their joy. When we read these monumental histories of the dead, it may be justly said, that all men are equal in the dust; for they all appear equally remarkable for being the most sincere Christians, the most benevolent neighbours, and the honestest men of their time. To go through an European cemetery, one would be apt to wonder how mankind could have so basely degenerated from such excellent ancestors. Every tomb pretends to claim your reverence and regret; some are praised for piety, in those inscriptions, who never entered the temple until they were dead; some are praised for being excellent poets, who were never mentioned except for their dulness when living; others for sublime orators, who were never noted except for their impudence; and others still, for military achievements, who were never in any other skirmishes but with the watch. Some even make epitaphs for themselves, and bespeak the reader's good-will. It were indeed to be wished, that every man would early learn in this manner to make his own; that he would draw it up in terms as flattering as possible, and that he would make it the employment of his whole life to deserve it.

I have not yet been in a place called Westminster Abbey, but soon intend to visit it. There, I am told, I shall see justice done to deceased merit: none, I am told, are permitted to be buried there, but such as have adorned as well as improved mankind. There, no intruders, by the influence of friends or fortune, presume to mix their unhallowed ashes with philosophers, heroes, and poets. Nothing but true merit has a place in that awful sanctuary. The guardianship of the tombs is committed to several reverend priests, who are never guilty, for a superior reward, of taking down the names of good men, to make room for others of equivocal character, nor ever profane the sacred walls with pageants that posterity cannot know, or shall blush to own.

I always was of opinion, that sepulchral honours of this kind should be considered as a national concern, and not trusted to the care of the priests of any country, how respectable soever: but from the conduct of the reverend personages, whose disinterested patriotism I shall shortly be able to discover, I am taught to retract my former sentiments. It is true, the Spartans and the Persians made a fine political use of sepulchral vanity: they permitted none to be thus interred who had not fallen in the vindication of their country. A monument thus became a real mark of distinction; it nerved the hero's arm with tenfold vigour, and he fought without fear who only fought for a grave.—Farewell.

LETTER XIII.

To the same.

I AM just returned from Westminster Abbey, the place of sepulture for the philosophers, heroes, and kings of England. What a gloom do monumental inscriptions and all the venerable remains of deceased merit inspire! Imagine a temple marked with the hand of antiquity, solemn as religious awe, adorned with all the magnificence of barbarous profusion, dim windows, fretted pillars, long colonnades, and dark ceilings. Think, then, what were my sensations at being introduced to such a scene. I stood in the midst of the temple, and threw my eyes round on the walls, filled with the statues, the inscriptions, and the monuments of the dead.

Alas! I said to myself, how does pride attend the puny child of dust even to the grave! Even humble as I am, I possess more consequence in the present scene than the greatest hero of them all: they have toiled for an hour to gain a transient immortality, and are at length retired to the grave, where they have no attendant but the worm, none to flatter but the epitaph.

As I was indulging such reflections, a gentleman dressed in black, perceiving me to be a stranger, came up, entered into conversation, and politely offered to be my instructor and guide through the temple. "If any monument," said he, "should particularly excite your curiosity, I shall endeavour to satisfy your demands." I accepted, with thanks, the gentleman's offer, adding, that "I was come to observe the policy, the wisdom, and the justice of the English, in conferring rewards upon deceased merit. If adulation like this," continued I, "be properly conducted, as it can no ways injure those who are flattered, so it may be a glorious incentive to those who are now capable of enjoying it. It is the duty of every good government to turn this monumental pride to its own advantage; to become strong in the aggregate from the weakness of the individual. If none but the truly great have a place in this awful repository, a temple like this will give the finest lessons of morality, and be a strong incentive to true ambition. I am told, that none have a place here but characters of the most distinguished merit." The Man in Black seemed impatient at my observations, so I discontinued my remarks, and we walked on together to take a view of every particular monument in order as it lay.

As the eye is naturally caught by the finest objects, I could not avoid being particularly curious about one monument, which appeared more beautiful than the rest. "That," said I to my guide, "I take to be the tomb of some very great man.

By the peculiar excellence of the workmanship, and the magnificence of the design, this must be a trophy raised to the memory of some king who has saved his country from ruin, or lawgiver who has reduced his fellow-citizens from anarchy into just subjection."—"It is not requisite," replied my companion, smiling, "to have such qualifications in order to have a very fine monument here: more humble abilities will suffice."—"What! I suppose, then, the gaining two or three battles, or the taking half a score of towns, is thought a sufficient qualification?"—"Gaining battles, or taking towns," replied the Man in Black, "may be of service; but a gentleman may have a very fine monument here without ever seeing a battle or a siege."—"This, then, is the monument of some poet, I presume—of one whose wit has gained him immortality?"—"No, sir," replied my guide, "the gentleman who lies here never made verses; and as for wit, he despised it in others, because he had none himself."—"Pray tell me, then, in a word," said I, peevishly, "what is the great man who lies here particularly remarkable for?"—"Remarkable, sir!" said my companion; "why, sir, the gentleman that lies here is remarkable, very remarkable—for a tomb in Westminister Abbey."—"But, head of my ancestors! how has he got here? I fancy he could never bribe the guardians of the temple to give him a place. Should he not be ashamed to be seen among company where even moderate merit would look like infamy?"—"I suppose," replied the Man in Black, "the gentleman was rich, and his friends, as is usual in such a case, told him he was great. He readily believed them; the guardians of the temple, as they got by the self-delusion, were ready to believe him too; so he paid his money for a fine monument; and the workman, as you see, has made him one of the most beautiful. Think not, however, that this gentleman is singular in his desire of being buried among the great; there are several others in the temple, who, hated and shunned by the great while alive, have come here fully resolved to keep them company now they are dead."

As we walked along to a particular part of the temple, "There," says the gentleman, pointing with his finger, "that is the Poet's Corner; there you see the monuments of Shakspeare, and Milton, and Prior, and Drayton."—"Drayton!" I replied; "I never heard of him before; but I have been told of one Pope—is he there?"—"It is time enough," replied my guide, "these hundred years; he is not long dead; people have not done hating him yet."—"Strange," cried I; "can any be found to hate a man whose life was wholly spent in entertaining and instructing his fellow-creatures?"—"Yes," says my guide, "they hate him for that very reason. There are a set of men called answerers of books, who take upon them to watch the republic of letters, and distribute reputation by the sheet; they somewhat resemble the eunuchs in a seraglio, who are incapable of giving pleasure themselves, and hinder those that would. These answerers have no other employment but to cry out Dunce and Scribbler; to praise the dead and revile the living; to grant a man of confessed abilities some small share of merit; to applaud twenty blockheads in order to gain the reputation of candour; and to revile the moral character of the man whose writings they cannot injure. Such wretches are kept in pay by some mercenary bookseller, or more frequently the bookseller himself takes this dirty work off their hands, as all that is required is to be very abusive and very dull. Every poet of any genius is sure to find such enemies; he feels, though he seems to despise, their malice; they make him miserable here, and in the pursuit of empty fame, at last he gains solid anxiety."

"Has this been the case with every poet I see here?" cried I.—"Yes, with every mother's son of them," replied he, "except he happened to be born a mandarine. If he has much money, he may buy reputation from your book-answerers, as well as a monument from the guardians of the temple."

"But are there not some men of distinguished taste, as in China, who are willing to patronize men of merit, and soften the rancour of malevolent dulness."

"I own there are many," replied the Man in Black; "but, alas! sir, the book-answerers crowd about them, and call themselves the writers of books; and the patron is too indolent to distinguish: thus poets are kept at a distance, while their enemies eat up all their rewards at the mandarine's table."

Leaving this part of the temple, we made up to an iron gate, through which my companion told me we were to pass, in order to see the monuments of the kings. Accordingly, I marched up without further ceremony, and was going to enter, when a person who held the gate in his hand told me I must pay first. I was surprised at such a demand; and asked the man, whether the people of England kept a show?—whether the paltry sum he demanded was not a national reproach?—whether it was not more to the honour of the country to let their magnificence or their antiquities be openly seen, than thus meanly to tax a curiosity which tended to their own honour?—"As for your questions," replied the gate-keeper, "to be sure they may be very right, because I don't understand them; but, as for that there threepence, I farm it from one—who rents it from another—who hires it from a third—who leases it from the guardians of the temple: and we all must live." I expected, upon paying here, to see something extraordinary, since what I had seen for nothing filled me with so much surprise: but in this I was disappointed; there was little more within than black coffins, rusty armour, tattered standards, and some few slovenly figures in wax. I was sorry I had paid, but I comforted myself by considering it would be my last payment. A person attended us who without once blushing told an hundred lies: he talked of a lady who died by pricking her finger; of a king with a golden head, and twenty such pieces of absurdity. "Look ye there, gentlemen," says he, pointing to an old oak chair, "there's a curiosity for ye; in that chair the kings of England were crowned: you see also a stone underneath, and that stone is Jacob's pillow." I could see no curiosity either in the oak chair or the stone: could I, indeed, behold one of the old kings of England seated in this, or Jacob's head laid upon the other, there might be something curious in the sight; but in the present case, there was no more reason for my surprise, than if I should pick a stone from their streets, and call it a curiosity, merely because one of the kings happened to tread upon it as he passed in a procession.

From hence our conductor led us through several dark walks and winding ways, uttering lies, talking to himself, and flourishing a wand which he held in his hand. He reminded me of the black magicians of Kobi. After we had been almost fatigued with a variety of objects, he at last desired me to consider attentively a certain suit of armour, which seemed to show nothing remarkable. "This armour," said he, "belonged to General Monk."—"Very surprising that a general should wear armour!"—"And pray," added he, "observe this cap; this is General Monk's cap."—"Very strange indeed, very strange, that a general should have a cap also! Pray, friend, what might this cap have cost originally?"—"That, sir," says he, "I don't know; but this cap is all the wages I have for my trouble."—"A very small recompense, truly," said I.—"Not so very small," replied he, "for every gentleman puts some money into it, and I spend the money."—"What, more money! still more money!"—"Every gentleman gives something, sir."—"I'll give thee nothing," returned I; "the guardians of the temple should pay you your wages, friend, and not permit you to squeeze thus from every spectator. When we pay our money at the door to see a show, we never give more as we are going out. Sure, the guardians of the temple can never think they get enough. Show me the gate; if I stay longer, I may probably meet with more of those ecclesiastical beggars."

Thus leaving the temple precipitately, I returned to my lodgings, in order to ruminate over what was great, and to despise what was mean, in the occurrences of the day.

LETTER XIV.

To the same.

I WAS some days ago agreeably surprised by a message from a lady of distinction, who sent me word, that she most passionately desired the pleasure of my acquaintance, and with the utmost impatience expected an interview. I will not deny, my dear Fum Hoam, but that my vanity was raised at such an invitation: I flattered myself that she had seen me in some public place, and had conceived an affection for my person, which thus induced her to deviate from the usual decorums of the sex. My imagination painted her in all the bloom of youth and beauty. I fancied her attended by the Loves and Graces; and I set out with the most pleasing expectations of seeing the conquest I had made.

When I was introduced into her apartment, my expectations were quickly at an end: I perceived a little shrivelled figure indolently reclined on a sofa, who nodded, by way of approbation, at my approach. This, as I was afterwards informed, was the lady herself,—a woman equally distinguished for rank, politeness, taste, and understanding. As I was dressed after the fashion of Europe, she had taken me for an Englishman, and consequently saluted me in her ordinary manner: but when the footman informed her grace that I was the gentleman from China, she instantly lifted herself from the couch, while her eyes sparkled with unusual vivacity. "Bless me! can this be the gentleman that was born so far from home? What an unusual share of *somethingness* in his whole appearance! Lord, how I am charmed with the outlandish cut of his face! how bewitching the exotic breadth of his forehead! I would give the world to see him in his own country dress. Pray, turn about, sir, and let me see you behind. There, there's a travelled air for you! You that attend there, bring up a plate of beef cut into small pieces; I have a violent passion to see him eat. Pray, sir, have you got your chopsticks about you? It will be so pretty to see the meat carried to the mouth with a jerk. Pray, speak a little Chinese: I have learned some of the language myself. Lord! have you nothing pretty from China about you; something that one does not know what to do with? I have got twenty things from China that are of no use in the world. Look at those jars; they are of the right pea-green: these are the furniture!"—"Dear madam," said I, "these, though they may appear fine in your eyes, are but paltry to a Chinese; but as they are useful utensils, it is proper they should have a place in every apartment."—"Useful, sir!" replied the lady; "sure you mistake; they are of no use in the world."—"What! are they not filled with an infusion of tea, as in China?" replied I. "Quite empty and useless, upon my honour, sir."—"Then they are the most cumbrous and clumsy furniture in the world, as nothing is truly elegant but what unites use with beauty."—"I protest," says the lady, "I shall begin to suspect thee of being an actual barbarian. I suppose you hold my two beautiful pagods in contempt."—"What!" cried I, "has Fohi spread his gross superstitions here also! Pagods of all kinds are my aversion."—"A Chinese, a traveller, and want taste! It surprises me. Pray, sir, examine the beauties of that Chinese temple which you see at the end of the garden. Is there anything in China more beautiful?"—"Where I stand, I see nothing, madam, at the end of the garden, that may not as well be called an Egyptian pyramid as a Chinese temple; for that little building in view is as like the one as t'other."—"What, sir! is not that a Chinese temple? you must surely be mistaken. Mr. Freeze, who designed it, calls it one, and nobody disputes his pretensions to taste." I now found it vain to contradict the lady in anything she thought fit to advance; so was resolved rather to act the disciple than the instructor. She took me through several rooms, all furnished, as she told me, in the Chinese manner; sprawling dragons, squatting pagods, and clumsy mandarines were stuck upon every shelf: in turning round, one must have used caution not to demolish a part of the precarious furniture.

In a house like this, thought I, one must live continually upon the watch; the inhabitant must resemble a knight in an enchanted castle, who expects to meet an adventure at every turning. "But, madam," said I, "do not accidents ever happen to all this finery?"—"Man, sir," replied the lady, "is born to misfortunes; and it is but fit I should have a share. Three weeks ago, a careless servant snapped off the head of a favourite mandarine: I had scarce done grieving for that, when a monkey broke a beautiful jar; this I took the more to heart, as the injury was done me by a friend! However, I survived the calamity; when yesterday crash went half a dozen dragons upon the marble hearthstone: and yet I live; I survive it all: you can't conceive what comfort I find under afflictions from philosophy. There is Seneca, and Bolingbroke, and some others, who guide me through life, and teach me to support its calamities." I could not but smile at a woman who makes her own misfortunes, and then deplores the miseries of her situation. Wherefore, tired of acting with dissimulation, and willing to indulge my meditations in solitude, I took leave just as the servant was bringing in a plate of beef, pursuant to the directions of his mistress.—Adieu.

LETTER XV.

To the same.

THE better sort here pretend to the utmost compassion for animals of every kind: to hear them speak, a stranger would be apt to imagine they could hardly hurt the gnat that stung them; they seem so tender, and so full of pity, that one would take them for the harmless friends of the whole creation, the protectors of the meanest insect or reptile that was privileged with existence. And yet (would you believe it?) I have seen the very men who have thus boasted of their tenderness, at the same time devouring the flesh of six different animals tossed up in a fricassee. Strange contrariety of conduct! they pity, and they eat the objects of their compassion! The lion roars with terror over its captive; the tiger sends forth its hideous shriek to intimidate its prey; no creature shows any fondness for its short-lived prisoner, except a man and a cat.

Man was born to live with innocence and simplicity, but he has deviated from nature; he was born to share the bounties of Heaven, but he has monopolized them; he was born to govern the brute creation, but he is become their tyrant. If an epicure now shall happen to surfeit on his last night's feast, twenty animals the next day are to undergo the most exquisite tortures, in order to provoke his appetite to another guilty meal. Hail, O ye simple, honest brahmins of the East! ye inoffensive friends of all that were born to happiness as well as you! You never sought a short-lived pleasure from the miseries of other creatures! You never studied the tormenting arts of ingenious refinement; you never surfeited upon a guilty meal! How much more purified and refined are all your sensations than ours! You distinguish every element with the utmost precision: a stream untasted before is a new luxury, a change of air is a new banquet, too refined for Western imaginations to conceive.

Though the Europeans do not hold the transmigration of souls, yet one of their doctors has, with great force of argument and great plausibility of reasoning, endeavoured to prove that the bodies of animals are the habitations of demons and wicked spirits, which are obliged to reside in these prisons till the resurrection pronounces their everlasting punishment; but are previously condemned to suffer all the pains and hardships inflicted upon them by man, or by each other, here. If this be the case, it may frequently happen, that while we whip pigs to death, or boil live lobsters, we are putting some old acquaintance, some near relation, to excruciating tortures, and are serving him up to the very same table where he was once the most welcome companion.

"Kabul," says the Zendavesta, "was born on the rushy banks of the river Mawra; his possessions were great, and his luxuries kept pace with the affluence of his fortune; he hated the harmless brahmins, and despised their holy religion; every day his table was decked out with the flesh of an hundred different animals, and his cooks had an hundred different ways of dressing it, to solicit even satiety.

"Notwithstanding all his eating, he did not arrive at old age; he died of a surfeit caused by intemperance: upon this his soul was carried off, in order to take its trial before a select assembly of the souls of those animals which his gluttony had caused to be slain, and who were now appointed his judges.

"He trembled before a tribunal, to every member of which he had formerly acted as an unmerciful tyrant: he sought for pity, but found none disposed to grant it. 'Does he not remember,' cries the angry boar, 'to what agonies I was put, not to satisfy his hunger, but his vanity? I was first hunted to death, and my flesh scarce thought worthy of coming once to his table. Were my advice followed, he should do penance in the shape of an hog, which in life he most resembled.'

"'I am rather,' cries a sheep upon the bench, 'for having him suffer under the appearance of a lamb; we may then send him through four or five transmigrations in the space of a month.'—'Were my voice of any weight in the assembly,' cries a calf, 'he should rather assume such a form as mine; I was bled every day, in order to make my flesh white, and at last killed without mercy.'—'Would it not be wiser,' cries a hen, 'to cram him in the shape of a fowl, and then smother him in his own blood, as I was served?' The majority of the assembly were pleased with this punishment, and were going to condemn him without further delay, when the ox rose up to give his opinion,—'I am informed,' says this counsellor, 'that the prisoner at the bar has left a wife with child behind him. By my knowledge in divination, I foresee that this child will be a son, decrepit, feeble, sickly, a plague to himself and all about him. What say you, then, my companions, if we condemn the father to animate the body of his own son; and by this means make him feel in himself those miseries his intemperance must otherwise have entailed upon his posterity?' The whole court applauded the ingenuity of his torture: they thanked him for his advice. Kabul was driven once more to revisit the earth; and his soul, in the body of his own son, passed a period of thirty years, loaded with misery, anxiety, and disease."

LETTER XVI.

To the same.

I KNOW not whether I am more obliged to the Chinese missionaries for the instruction I have received from them, or prejudiced by the falsehoods they have made me believe. By them I was told that the Pope was universally allowed to be a man, and placed at the head of the church; in England, however, they plainly prove him to be a whore in man's clothes, and often burn him in effigy as an impostor. A thousand books have been written on either side of the question: priests are eternally disputing against each other; and those mouths that want argument are filled with abuse. Which party must I believe? or shall I give credit to neither? When I survey the absurdities and falsehoods with which the books of the Europeans are filled, I thank Heaven for having been born in China, and that I have sagacity enough to detect imposture.

The Europeans reproach us with false history and fabulous chronology: how should they blush to see their own books, many of which are written by the doctors of their religion, filled with the most monstrous fables, and attested with the utmost solemnity! The bounds of a letter do not permit me to mention all the absurdities of this kind which, in my reading, I have met with. I shall confine myself to the accounts which some of their lettered men give of the persons of some of the inhabitants on our globe: and, not satisfied with the most solemn asseverations, they sometimes pretend to have been eye-witnesses of what they describe.

A Christian doctor, in one of his principal performances, says, that it was not impossible for a whole nation to have but one eye in the middle of the forehead. He is not satisfied with leaving it in doubt; but, in another work, assures us, that the fact was certain, and that he himself was an eye-witness of it. "When," says he, "I took a journey into Ethiopia, in company with several other servants of Christ, in order to preach the Gospel, there I beheld, in the southern provinces of that country, a nation which had only one eye in the midst of their foreheads."

You will no doubt be surprised, reverend Fum, with this author's effrontery; but, alas! he is not alone in this story; he has only borrowed it from several others who wrote before him. Solinus creates another nation of Cyclops, the Arimaspians, who inhabit those countries that border on the Caspian Sea. This author goes on to tell us of a people of India who have but one leg and one eye, and yet are extremely active, run with great swiftness, and live by hunting. These people we scarce know how to pity or admire: but the men whom Pliny calls Cynamolci, who have got the heads of dogs, really deserve our compassion: instead of language, they express their sentiments by barking. Solinus confirms what Pliny mentions; and Simon Mayole, a French bishop, talks of them as of particular and familiar acquaintances. "After passing the deserts of Egypt," says he, "we met with the Kunokephaloi, who inhabit those regions that border on Ethiopia: they live by hunting; they cannot speak, but whistle; their chins resemble a serpent's head; their hands are armed with long sharp claws; their breast resembles that of a greyhound; and they excel in swiftness and agility." Would you think it, my friend, that these odd kind of people are, notwithstanding their figure, excessively delicate? not even an alderman's wife, or Chinese mandarine, can excel them in this particular. "These people," continues our faithful bishop, "never refuse wine; love roast and boiled meat: they are particularly curious in having their meat well dressed, and spurn at it if in the least tainted." "When the Ptolemies reigned in Egypt," says he, a little farther on, "these men with dogs' heads taught grammar and music." For men who had no voices to teach music, and who could not speak, to teach grammar, is, I confess, a little extraordinary. Did ever the disciples of Fohi broach anything more ridiculous?

Hitherto we have seen men with heads strangely deformed, and with dogs' heads; but what would you say if you heard of men without any heads at all? Pomponius Mela, Solinus, and Aulus Gellius describe them to our hand: "The Blemiæ have a nose, eyes, and mouth on their breast; or, as others will have it, placed on their shoulders."

One would think that these authors had an antipathy to the human form, and were resolved to make a new figure of their own; but let us do them justice. Though they sometimes deprive us of a leg, an arm, a head, or some such trifling part of the body, they often as liberally bestow upon us something that we wanted before. Simon Mayole seems our particular friend in this respect; if he has denied heads to one part of mankind, he has given tails to another. He describes many of the English of his time, which is more than an hundred years ago, as having tails. His own words are as follow: "In England there are some families which have tails, as a punishment for deriding an Augustin friar sent by St. Gregory, and who preached in Dorsetshire. They sewed the tails of different animals to his clothes; but soon they found those tails entailed upon them and their posterity for ever." It is certain that the author had some ground for this description. Many of the English wear tails to their wigs to this very day; as a mark, I suppose, of the antiquity of their families, and perhaps as a symbol of those tails with which they were formerly distinguished by nature.

You see, my friend, there is nothing so ridiculous that has not at some time been said by some philosopher. The writers of books in Europe seem to think themselves authorized to say what they please; and an ingenious philosopher among them has openly asserted, that he would undertake to persuade the whole republic of readers to believe, that the sun was neither the cause of light nor heat, if he could only get six philosophers on his side.—Farewell.

LETTER XVII.

To the same.

Were an Asiatic politician to read the treaties of peace and friendship that have been annually making for more than an hundred years among the inhabitants of Europe, he would probably be surprised how it should ever happen that Christian princes could quarrel among each other. Their compacts for peace are drawn up with the utmost precision, and ratified with the greatest solemnity: to these each party promises a sincere and inviolable obedience, and all wears the appearance of open friendship and unreserved reconciliation.

Yet, notwithstanding those treaties, the people of Europe are almost continually at war. There is nothing more easy than to break a treaty ratified in all the usual forms, and yet neither party be the aggressor. One side, for instance, breaks a trifling article by mistake; the opposite party, upon this, makes a small but premeditated reprisal; this brings on a return of greater from the other; both sides complain of injuries and infractions; war is declared; they beat—are beaten; some two or three hundred thousand men are killed; they grow tired; leave off just where they began; and so sit coolly down to make new treaties.

The English and French seem to place themselves foremost among the champion states of Europe. Though parted by a narrow sea, yet are they entirely of opposite characters; and, from their vicinity, are taught to fear and admire each other. They are at present engaged in a very destructive war, have already spilled much blood, are excessively irritated, and all upon account of one side's desiring to wear greater quantities of *furs* than the other.

The pretext of the war is about some lands a thousand leagues off,—a country cold, desolate, and hideous—a country belonging to a people who were in possession for time immemorial. The savages of Canada claim a property in the country in dispute; they have all the pretensions which long possession can confer. Here they had reigned for ages without rivals in dominion, and knew no enemies but the prowling bear or insidious tiger; their native forests produced all the necessaries of life, and they found ample luxury in the enjoyment. In this manner they might have continued to live to eternity, had not the English been informed that those countries produced furs in great abundance. From that moment the country became an object of desire: it was found that furs were things very much wanted in England; the ladies edged some of their clothes with furs, and muffs were worn both by gentlemen and ladies. In short, furs were found indispensably necessary for the happiness of the state; and the king was consequently petitioned to grant, not only the country of Canada, but all the savages belonging to it, to the subjects of England, in order to have the people supplied with proper quantities of this necessary commodity.

So very reasonable a request was immediately complied with, and large colonies were sent abroad to procure furs, and take possession. The French, who were equally in want of furs, (for they were as fond of muffs and tippets as the English,) made the very same request to their monarch, and met with the same gracious reception from their king, who generously granted what was not his to give. Wherever the French landed, they called the country their own; and the English took possession wherever they came, upon the same equitable pretensions. The harmless savages made no opposition; and, could the intruders have agreed together, they might peaceably have shared this desolate country between them; but they quarrelled about the boundaries of their settlements, about grounds and rivers to which neither side could show any other right than that of power, and which neither could occupy but by usurpation. Such is the contest, that no honest man can heartily wish success to either party.

The war has continued for some time with various success. At first the French seemed victorious; but the English have of late dispossessed them of the whole country in dispute. Think not, however, that success on one side is the harbinger of peace; on the contrary, both parties must be heartily tired, to effect even a temporary reconciliation. It should seem the business of the victorious party to offer terms of peace: but there are many in England who, encouraged by success, are for still protracting the war.

The best English politicians, however, are sensible, that to keep their present conquests would be rather a burden than an advantage to them; rather a diminution of their strength than an increase of power. It is in the politic as in the human constitution: if the limbs grow too large for the body, their size, instead of improving, will diminish the vigour of the whole. The colonies should always bear an exact proportion to the mother country: when they grow populous, they grow powerful, and, by becoming powerful, they become independent also: thus subordination is destroyed, and a country swallowed up in the extent of its own dominions. The Turkish empire would be more formidable, were it less extensive—were it not for those countries which it can neither command nor give entirely away, which it is obliged to protect, but from which it has no power to exact obedience.

Yet, obvious as these truths are, there are many Englishmen who are for transplanting new colonies into this late acquisition, for peopling the deserts of America with the refuse of their countrymen, and (as they express it) with the waste of an exuberant nation. But who are those unhappy creatures who are to be thus drained away? Not the sickly, for they are unwelcome guests abroad as well as at home; nor the idle, for they would starve as well behind the Apalachian mountains as in the streets of London. This refuse is composed of the laborious and enterprising—of such men as can be serviceable to their country at home—of men who ought to be regarded as the sinews of the people, and cherished with every degree of political indulgence. And what are the commodities which this colony, when established, is to produce in return? Why, raw silk, hemp, and tobacco. England, therefore, must make an exchange of her best and bravest subjects for raw silk, hemp, and tobacco; her hardy veterans and honest tradesmen must be trucked for a box of snuff or a silk petticoat. Strange absurdity! Surely the politics of the Daures are not more strange, who sell their religion, their wives, and their liberty, for a glass bead or a paltry penknife.—Farewell.

LETTER XVIII.

To the same.

THE English love their wives with much passion, the Hollanders with much prudence: the English, when they give their hands, frequently give their hearts; the Dutch give the hand, but keep the heart wisely in their own possession. The English love with violence, and expect violent love in return; the Dutch are satisfied with the slightest acknowledgment, for they give little away. The English expend many of the matrimonial comforts in the first year; the Dutch frugally husband out their pleasures, and are always constant, because they are always indifferent.

There seems very little difference between a Dutch bridegroom and a Dutch husband. Both are equally possessed of the same cool unexpecting serenity; they can see neither Elysium nor Paradise behind the curtain; and Yiffrow is not more a goddess on the wedding-night than after twenty years matrimonial acquaintance. On the other hand, many of the English marry in order to have one happy month in their lives; they seem incapable of looking beyond that period; they unite in hopes of finding rapture, and, disappointed in that, disdain ever to accept of happiness. From hence we see open hatred ensue; or, what is worse, concealed disgust under the appearance of fulsome endearment. Much formality, great civility, and studied compliments are exhibited in public; cross looks, sulky silence, or open recrimination, fill up their hours of private entertainment.

Hence I am taught, whenever I see a new married couple more than ordinarily fond before faces, to consider them as attempting to impose upon the company or themselves; either hating each other heartily, or consuming that stock of love in the beginning of their course which should serve them through their whole journey. Neither side should expect those instances of kindness which are inconsistent with true freedom or happiness to bestow. Love, when founded in the heart, will show itself in a thousand unpremeditated sallies of fondness; but every cool deliberate exhibition of the passion only argues little understanding, or great insincerity.

Choang was the fondest husband, and Hansi the most endearing wife, in all the kingdom of Korea: they were a pattern of conjugal bliss; the inhabitants of the country around saw, and envied their felicity: wherever Choang came, Hansi was sure to follow: and in all the pleasures of Hansi, Choang was admitted a partner. They walked hand in hand wherever they appeared, showing every mark of mutual satisfaction, embracing, kissing—their mouths were for ever joined; and, to speak in the language of anatomy, it was with them one perpetual anastomosis.

Their love was so great, that it was thought nothing could interrupt their mutual peace, when an accident happened, which, in some measure, diminished the husband's assurance of his wife's fidelity; for love so refined as his was subject to a thousand little disquietudes.

Happening to go one day alone among the tombs that lay at some distance from his house, he there perceived a lady dressed in the deepest mourning, (being clothed all over in white,) fanning the wet clay that was raised over one of the graves with a large fan which she held in her hand. Choang, who had early been taught wisdom in the school of Tao, was unable to assign a cause for her present employment; and coming up, civilly demanded the reason. "Alas," replied the lady, her eyes bathed in tears, "how is it possible to survive the loss of my husband, who lies buried in this grave! He was the best of men, the tenderest of husbands: with his dying breath he bid me never marry again till the earth over his grave should be dry; and here you see me steadily resolving to obey his will, and endeavouring to dry it with my fan. I have employed two whole days in fulfilling his commands, and am determined not to marry till they are punctually obeyed, even though his grave should take up four days in drying."

Choang, who was struck with the widow's beauty, could not, however, avoid smiling at her haste to be married; but, concealing the cause of his mirth, civilly invited her home, adding, that he had a wife who might be capable of giving her some consolation. As soon as he and his guest were returned, he imparted to Hansi in private what he had seen, and could not avoid expressing his uneasiness that such might be his own case if his dearest wife should one day happen to survive him.

It is impossible to describe Hansi's resentment at so unkind a suspicion. As her passion for him was not only great, but extremely delicate, she employed tears, anger, frowns, and exclamations, to chide his suspicions: the widow herself was inveighed against; and Hansi declared, she was resolved never to sleep under the same roof with a wretch, who, like her, could be guilty of such barefaced inconstancy. The night was cold and stormy; however, the stranger was obliged to seek another lodging, for Choang was not disposed to resist, and Hansi would have her way.

The widow had scarce been gone an hour, when an old disciple of Choang's, whom he had not seen for many years, came to pay him a visit. He was received with the utmost ceremony, placed in the most honourable seat at supper, and the wine began to circulate with great freedom. Choang and Hansi exhibited open marks of mutual tenderness and unfeigned reconciliation: nothing could equal their apparent happiness; so fond a husband, so obedient a wife, few could behold without regretting their own infelicity; when, lo! their happiness was at once disturbed by a most fatal accident. Choang fell lifeless in an apoplectic fit upon the floor. Every method was used, but in vain, for his recovery. Hansi was at first inconsolable for his death: after some hours, however, she found spirits to read his last will. The ensuing day, she began to moralize and talk wisdom; the next day, she was able to comfort the young disciple; and on the third, to shorten a long story, they both agreed to be married.

There was now no longer mourning in the apartments: the body of Choang was now thrust into an old coffin, and placed in one of the meanest rooms, there to lie unattended until the time prescribed by law for his interment. In the meantime, Hansi and the young disciple were arrayed in the most magnificent habits; the bride wore in her nose a jewel of immense price, and her lover was dressed in all the finery of his former master, together with a pair of artificial whiskers that reached down to his toes. The hour of their nuptials was arrived; the whole family sympathised with their approaching happiness; the apartments were brightened up with lights that diffused the most exquisite perfume, and a lustre more bright than noon-day. The lady expected her youthful lover in an inner apartment with impatience; when his servant, approaching with terror in his countenance, informed her, that his master was fallen into a fit which would certainly be mortal, unless the heart of a man lately dead could be obtained, and applied to his breast. She scarcely waited to hear the end of his story, when, tucking up her clothes, she ran with a mattock in her hand to the coffin where Choang lay, resolving to apply the heart of her dead husband as a cure for the living. She therefore struck the lid with the utmost violence. In a few blows the coffin flew open, when the body, which to all appearance had been dead, began to move. Terrified at the sight, Hansi dropped the mattock, and Choang walked out, astonished at his own situation, his wife's unusual magnificence, and her more amazing surprise. He went among the apartments, unable to conceive the cause of so much splendour. He was not long in suspense before his domestics informed him of every transaction since he first became insensible. He could scarce believe what they told him, and went in pursuit of Hansi herself, in order to receive more certain information, or to reproach her infidelity. But she prevented his reproaches: he found her weltering in blood; for she had stabbed herself to the heart, being unable to survive her shame and disappointment.

Choang, being a philosopher, was too wise to make any loud lamentations: he thought it best to bear his loss with serenity; so, mending up the old coffin where he had lain himself, he placed his faithless spouse in his room; and unwilling that so many nuptial preparations should be expended in vain, he the same night married the widow with the large fan.

As they both were apprised of the foibles of each other beforehand, they knew how to excuse them after marriage. They lived together for many years in great tranquillity, and not expecting rapture, made a shift to find contentment. —Farewell.

LETTER XIX.

To the same.

THE gentleman dressed in black, who was my companion through Westminster Abbey, came yesterday to pay me a visit; and, after drinking tea, we both resolved to take a walk together, in order to enjoy the freshness of the country, which now begins to resume its verdure. Before we got out of the suburbs, however, we were stopped in one of the streets by a crowd of people, gathered in a circle round a man and his wife, who seemed too loud and too angry to be understood. The people were highly pleased with the dispute, which, upon inquiry, we found to be between Dr. Cacafogo, an apothecary, and his wife. The doctor, it seems, coming unexpectedly into his wife's apartment, found a gentleman there, in circumstances not in the least equivocal.

The doctor, who was a person of nice honour, resolving to revenge the flagrant insult, immediately flew to the chimney-piece, and, taking down a rusty blunderbuss, drew the trigger upon the defiler of his bed: the delinquent would certainly have been shot through the head, but that the piece had not been charged for many years. The gallant made a shift to escape through the window, but the lady still remained; and, as she well knew her husband's temper, undertook to manage the quarrel without a second. He was furious, and she loud; their noise had gathered all the mob, who charitably assembled on the occasion, not to prevent, but to enjoy the quarrel.

"Alas!" said I to my companion, "what will become of this unhappy creature thus caught in adultery? Believe me, I pity her from my heart; her husband, I suppose, will show her no mercy. Will they burn her, as in India, or behead her, as in Persia? Will they load her with stripes, as in Turkey, or keep her in perpetual imprisonment, as with us in China? Prithee, what is the wife's punishment in England for such offences?"

—"When a lady is thus caught tripping," replied my companion, "they never punish her, but the husband."—"You surely jest," interrupted I; "I am a foreigner, and you would abuse my ignorance!"—"I am really serious," returned he: "Dr. Cacafogo has caught his wife in the act; but, as he had no witnesses, his small testimony goes for nothing: the consequence, therefore, of his discovery will be, that she will be packed off to live among her relations, and the doctor must be obliged to allow her a separate maintenance."—"Amazing!" cried I; "is it not enough that she is permitted to live separate from the object she detests, but must he give her money to keep her in spirits too?"—"That he must," said my guide, "and be called a cuckold by all his neighbours into the bargain. The men will laugh at him, the ladies will pity him; and all that his warmest friends can say in his favour will be that 'the poor good soul has never had any harm in him.'"—"I want patience," interrupted I. "What! are there no private chastisements for the wife—no schools of penitence to show her folly—no rods for such delinquents?"—"Pshaw, man," replied he, smiling, "if every delinquent among us were to be treated in your manner, one half of the kingdom would flog the other." I must confess, my dear Fum, that if I were an English husband, of all things I would take care not to be jealous, nor busily pry into those secrets my wife was pleased to keep from me. Should I detect her infidelity, what is the consequence? If I calmly pocket the abuse, I am laughed at by her and her gallant: if I talk my griefs aloud, like a tragedy hero, I am laughed at by the whole world. The course, then, I would take would be, whenever I went out, to tell my wife where I was going, lest I should unexpectedly meet her abroad in company with some dear deceiver. Whenever I returned, I would use a peculiar rap at the door, and give four loud hems as I walked deliberately up the staircase. I would never inquisitively peep under her bed, or look behind the curtains. And even though I knew the captain was there, I would calmly take a dish of my wife's cool tea, and talk of the army with reverence.

Of all nations, the Russians seem to me to behave most wisely in such circumstances. The wife promises her husband never to let him see her transgressions of this nature; and he as punctually promises, whenever she is so detected, without the least anger, to beat her without mercy: so they both know what each has to expect; the lady transgresses, is beaten, taken again into favour, and all goes on as before.

When a Russian young lady, therefore, is to be married, her father, with a cudgel in his hand, asks the bridegroom, whether he chooses this virgin for his bride? to which the other replies in the affirmative. Upon this, the father, turning the lady three times round, and giving her three strokes with his cudgel on the back,—"My dear," cries he, "these are the last blows you are ever to receive from your tender father: I resign my authority, and my cudgel, to your husband; he knows better than me the use of either." The bridegroom knows decorum too well to accept of the cudgel abruptly; he assures the father that the lady will never want it, and that he would not for the world make any use of it: but the father, who knows what the lady may want better than he, insists upon his acceptance; upon this there follows a scene of Russian politeness, while one refuses, and the other offers, the cudgel. The whole, however, ends with the bridegroom's taking it; upon which the lady drops a curtsey in token of obedience, and the ceremony proceeds as usual.

There is something excessively fair and open in this method of courtship: by this both sides are prepared for all the matrimonial adventures that are to follow. Marriage has been compared to a game of skill for life: it is generous thus in both parties to declare they are sharpers in the beginning. In England, I am told, both sides use every art to conceal their defects from each other before marriage, and the rest of their lives may be regarded as doing penance for their former dissimulation.—Farewell.

LETTER XX.

To the same.

THE *Republic of Letters* is a very common expression among the Europeans; and yet when applied to the learned of Europe is the most absurd that can be imagined; since nothing is more unlike a republic than the society which goes by that name. From this expression one would be apt to imagine that the learned were united into a single body, joining their interests, and concurring in the same design. From this one might be apt to compare them to our literary societies in China, where each acknowledges a just subordination, and all contribute to build the temple of science, without attempting, from ignorance or envy, to obstruct each other.

But very different is the state of learning here: every member of this fancied republic is desirous of governing, and none willing to obey; each looks upon his fellow as a rival, not an assistant in the same pursuit. They calumniate, they injure, they despise, they ridicule each other; if one man writes a book that pleases, others shall write books to show that he might have given still greater pleasure, or should not have pleased. If one happens to hit upon something new, there are numbers ready to assure the public that all this was no novelty to them or the learned; that Cardanus, or Brunus, or some other author too dull to be generally read, had anticipated the discovery. Thus, instead of uniting like the members of a commonwealth, they are divided into almost as many factions as there are men; and their jarring constitution, instead of being styled a republic of letters, should be entitled an anarchy of literature.

It is true, there are some of superior abilities, who reverence and esteem each other; but their mutual admiration is not sufficient to shield off the contempt of the crowd. The wise are but few, and they praise with a feeble voice; the vulgar are many, and roar in reproaches. The truly great seldom unite in societies; have few meetings, no cabals; the dunces hunt in full cry, till they have run down a reputation, and then snarl and fight with each other about dividing the spoil. Here you may see the compilers and the book-answerers of every month, when they have cut up some respectable name, most frequently reproaching each other with stupidity and dulness; resembling the wolves of the Russian forest, who prey upon venison, or horse-flesh, when they can get it; but in cases of necessity, lying in wait to devour each other. While they have new books to cut up, they make a hearty meal; but if this resource should unhappily fail, then it is that critics eat up critics, and compilers rob from compilations.

Confucius observes, that it is the duty of the learned to unite society more closely, and to persuade men to become citizens of the world; but the authors I refer to are not only for disuniting society, but kingdoms also: if the English are at war with France, the dunces of France think it their duty to be at war with those of England. Thus Fréron, one of their first-rate scribblers, thinks proper to characterise all the English writers in the gross: "Their whole merit," says he, "consists in exaggeration, and often in extravagance: correct their pieces as you please, there still remains a leaven which corrupts the whole. They sometimes discover genius, but not the smallest share of taste: England is not a soil for the plants of genius to thrive in." This is open enough, with not the least adulation in the picture: but hear what a Frenchman of acknowledged abilities says upon the same subject: "I am at a loss to determine in what we excel the English, or where they excel us; when I compare the merits of both in any one species of literary composition, so many reputable and pleasing writers present themselves from either country, that my judgment rests in suspense: I am pleased with the disquisition, without finding the object of my inquiry." But lest you should think the French alone are faulty in this respect, hear how an English journalist delivers his sentiments of them: "We are amazed," says he, "to find so many works translated from the French, while we have such numbers neglected of our own. In our opinion, notwithstanding their fame throughout the rest of Europe, the French are the most contemptible reasoners (we had almost said writers) that can be imagined. However, nevertheless, excepting," &c. Another English writer, Shaftesbury, if I remember, on the contrary, says that the French authors are pleasing and judicious, more clear, more methodical and entertaining, than those of his own country.

From these opposite pictures you perceive that the good authors of either country praise, and the bad revile, each other; and yet, perhaps, you will be surprised that indifferent writers should thus be the most apt to censure, as they have the most to apprehend from recrimination: you may, perhaps, imagine, that such as are possessed of fame themselves should be most ready to declare their opinions, since what they say might pass for decision. But the truth happens to be, that the great are solicitous only of raising their own reputations, while the opposite class, alas! are solicitous of bringing every reputation down to a level with their own.

But let us acquit them of malice and envy. A critic is often guided by the same motives that direct his author: the author endeavours to persuade us, that he has written a good book; the critic is equally solicitous to show that he could write a better had he thought proper. A critic is a being possessed of all the vanity, but not the genius, of a scholar: incapable, from his native weakness, of lifting himself from the ground, he applies to contiguous merit for support; makes the sportive sallies of another's imagination his serious employment; pretends to take our feelings under his care; teaches where to condemn, where to lay the emphasis of praise; and may with as much justice be called a man of taste as the Chinese who measures his wisdom by the length of his nails.

If, then, a book, spirited or humorous, happens to appear in the republic of letters, several critics are in waiting to bid the public not to laugh at a single line of it; for themselves had read it, and they know what is proper to excite laughter. Other critics contradict the fulminations of this tribunal, call them all spiders, and assure the public, that they ought to laugh without restraint. Another set are in the meantime quietly employed in writing notes to the book, intended to show the particular passages to be laughed at: when these are out, others still there are who write notes upon notes: thus a single new book employs not only the paper-makers, the printers, the pressmen, the bookbinders, the hawkers, but twenty critics, and as many compilers. In short, the body of the learned may be compared to a Persian army, where there are many pioneers, several sutlers, numberless servants, women and children in abundance, and but few soldiers.—Adieu.

LETTER XXI.

To the same.

THE English are as fond of seeing plays acted as the Chinese; but there is a vast difference in the manner of conducting them. We play our pieces in the open air, the English theirs under cover; we act by daylight, they by the blaze of torches. One of our plays continues eight or ten days successively; an English piece seldom takes up above four hours in the representation.

My companion in black, with whom I am now beginning to contract an intimacy, introduced me a few nights ago to the playhouse, where we placed ourselves conveniently at the foot of the stage. As the curtain was not drawn before my arrival, I had an opportunity of observing the behaviour of the spectators, and indulging those reflections which novelty generally inspires.

The richest in general were placed in the lowest seats, and the poor rose above them in degrees proportioned to their poverty. The order of precedence seemed here inverted; those who were undermost all the day, now enjoyed a temporary eminence, and became masters of the ceremonies. It was they who called for the music, indulging every noisy freedom, and testifying all the insolence of beggary in exaltation.

They who held the middle region seemed not so riotous as those above them, nor yet so tame as those below: to judge by their looks, many of them seemed strangers there as well as myself; they were chiefly employed, during this period of expectation, in eating oranges, reading the story of the play, or making assignations.

Those who sat in the lowest rows, which are called the pit, seemed to consider themselves as judges of the merit of the poet and the performers; they were assembled partly to be amused, and partly to show their taste; appearing to labour under that restraint which an affectation of superior discernment generally produces. My companion, however, informed me, that not one in a hundred of them knew even the first principles of criticism; that they assumed the right of being censors because there was none to contradict their pretensions; and that every man who now called himself a connoisseur, became such to all intents and purposes.

Those who sat in the boxes appeared in the most unhappy situation of all. The rest of the audience came merely for their own amusement; these, rather to furnish out a part of the entertainment themselves. I could not avoid considering them as acting parts in dumb show—not a curtsey or nod that was not the result of art; not a look nor a smile that was not designed for murder. Gentlemen and ladies ogled each other through spectacles; for my companion observed, that blindness was of late become fashionable; all affected indifference and ease, while their hearts at the same time burned for conquest. Upon the whole, the lights, the music, the ladies in their gayest dresses, the men with cheerfulness and expectation in their looks, all conspired to make a most agreeable picture, and to fill a heart that sympathises at human happiness with inexpressible serenity.

The expected time for the play to begin at last arrived; the curtain was drawn, and the actors came on. A woman, who personated a queen, came in curtseying to the audience, who clapped their hands upon her appearance. Clapping of hands is, it seems, the manner of applauding in England; the manner is absurd, but every country, you know, has its peculiar absurdities. I was equally surprised, however, at the submission of the actress, who should have considered herself as a queen, as at the little discernment of the audience who gave her such marks of applause before she attempted to deserve them. Preliminaries between her and the audience being thus adjusted, the dialogue was supported between her and a most hopeful youth, who acted the part of her confidant. They both appeared in extreme distress, for it seems the queen had lost a child some fifteen years before, and still kept its dear resemblance next her heart, while her kind companion bore a part in her sorrows.

Her lamentations grew loud; comfort is offered, but she detests the very sound: she bids them preach comfort to the winds. Upon this her husband comes in, who, seeing the queen so much afflicted, can himself hardly refrain from tears, or avoid partaking in the soft distress. After thus grieving through three scenes, the curtain dropped for the first act.

"Truly," said I to my companion, "these kings and queens are very much disturbed at no very great misfortune: certain I am, were people of humbler stations to act in this manner, they would be thought divested of common sense." I had scarce finished this observation, when the curtain rose, and the king came on in a violent passion. His wife had, it seems, refused his proffered tenderness, had spurned his royal embrace, and he seemed resolved not to survive her fierce disdain. After he had thus fretted, and the queen had fretted through the second act, the curtain was let down once more.

"Now," says my companion, "you perceive the king to be a man of spirit; he feels at every pore: one of your phlegmatic sons of clay would have given the queen her own way, and let her come to herself by degrees; but the king is for immediate tenderness, or instant death: death and tenderness are leading passions of every modern buskined hero; this moment they embrace, and the next stab, mixing daggers and kisses in every period."

I was going to second his remarks, when my attention was engrossed by a new object; a man came in balancing a straw upon his nose, and the audience were clapping their hands in all the raptures of applause. "To what purpose," cried I, "does this unmeaning figure make his appearance? is he a part of the plot?"—"Unmeaning do you call him?" replied my friend in black; "this is one of the most important characters of the whole play; nothing pleases the people more than seeing a straw balanced: there is a great deal of meaning in a straw: there is something suited to every apprehension in the sight; and a fellow possessed of talents like these is sure of making his fortune."

The third act now began with an actor who came to inform us that he was the villain of the play, and intended to show strange things before all was over. He was joined by another who seemed as much disposed for mischief as he; their intrigues continued through this whole division. "If that be a villain," said I, "he must be a very stupid one to tell his secrets without being asked; such soliloquies of late are never admitted in China."

The noise of clapping interrupted me once more; a child of six years old was learning to dance on the stage, which gave the ladies and mandarines infinite satisfaction. "I am sorry," said I, "to see the pretty creature so early learning so bad a trade; dancing being, I presume, as contemptible here as in China."—"Quite the reverse," interrupted my companion; "dancing is a very reputable and genteel employment here; men have a greater chance for encouragement from the merit of their heels than their heads. One who jumps up and flourishes his toes three times before he comes to the ground, may have three hundred a year: he who flourishes them four times, gets four hundred; but he who arrives at five is inestimable, and may demand what salary he thinks proper. The female dancers, too, are valued for this sort of jumping and crossing; and it is a cant word amongst them, that she deserves most who shows highest. But the fourth act is begun; let us be attentive."

In the fourth act the queen finds her long lost child, now grown up into a youth of smart parts and great qualifications; wherefore she wisely considers that the crown will fit his head better than that of her husband, whom she knows to be a driveller. The king discovers her design, and here comes on the deep distress; he loves the queen, and he loves the kingdom; he resolves, therefore, in order to possess both, that her son must die. The queen exclaims at his barbarity, is frantic with rage, and at length, overcome with sorrow, falls into a fit; upon which the curtain drops, and the act is concluded.

"Observe the art of the poet," cries my companion. "When the queen can say no more, she falls into a fit. While thus her eyes are shut, while she is supported in the arms of her Abigail, what horrors do we not fancy! We feel it in every nerve: take my word for it, that fits are the true *aposiopesis* of modern tragedy."

The fifth act began, and a busy piece it was. Scenes shifting, trumpets sounding, mobs hallooing, carpets spreading, guards bustling from one door to another; gods, demons, daggers, racks, and ratsbane. But whether the king was killed, or the queen was drowned, or the son was poisoned, I have absolutely forgotten.

When the play was over, I could not avoid observing, that the persons of the drama appeared in as much distress in the first act as the last. "How is it possible," said I, "to sympathise with them through five long acts! Pity is but a short-lived passion. I hate to hear an actor mouthing trifles: neither startings, strainings, nor attitudes, affect me, unless there be cause: after I have been once or twice deceived by those unmeaning alarms, my heart sleeps in peace, probably unaffected by the principal distress. There should be one great passion aimed at by the actor as well as the poet; all the rest should be subordinate, and only contribute to make that the greater; if the actor, therefore, exclaims upon every occasion, in tones of despair, he attempts to move us too soon; he anticipates the blow, he ceases to affect, though he gains our applause."

I scarce perceived that the audience were almost all departed; wherefore, mixing with the crowd, my companion and I got into the street, where, essaying an hundred obstacles from coach-wheels and palanquin poles, like birds in their flight through the branches of a forest, after various turnings, we both at length got home in safety.—Adieu.

LETTER XXII.

From the same.

THE letter which came by the way of Smyrna, and which you sent me unopened, was from my son. As I have permitted you to take copies of all those I sent to China, you might have made no ceremony in opening those directed to me. Either in joy or sorrow, my friend should participate in my feelings. It would give pleasure to see a good man pleased at my success; it would give almost equal pleasure to see him sympathise at my disappointment.

Every account I receive from the East seems to come loaded with some new affliction. My wife and daughter were taken from me, and yet I sustained the loss with intrepidity; my son is made a slave among the barbarians, which was the only blow that could have reached my heart: yes, I will indulge the transports of nature for a little, in order to show I can overcome them in the end. True magnanimity consists not in never falling, but in rising every time we fall.

When our mighty emperor had published his displeasure at my departure, and seized upon all that was mine, my son was privately secreted from his resentment. Under the protection and guardianship of Fum Hoam, the best and the wisest of all the inhabitants of China, he was for some time instructed in the learning of the missionaries, and the wisdom of the East. But hearing of my adventures, and incited by filial piety, he was resolved to follow my fortunes, and share my distress.

He passed the confines of China in disguise, hired himself as a camel-driver to a caravan that was crossing the deserts of Thibet, and was within one day's journey of the river Laur, which divides that country from India, when a body of wandering Tartars falling unexpectedly upon the caravan, plundered it, and made those who escaped their first fury slaves. By those he was led into the extensive and desolate regions that border on the shores of the Aral lake.

Here he lived by hunting; and was obliged to supply every day a certain proportion of the spoil, to regale his savage masters. His learning, his virtues, and even his beauty, were qualifications that no way served to recommend him; they knew no merit, but that of providing large quantities of milk and raw flesh; and were sensible of no happiness but that of rioting on the undressed meal.

Some merchants from Mesched, however, coming to trade with the Tartars for slaves, he was sold among the number, and led into the kingdom of Persia, where he is now detained. He is there obliged to watch the looks of a voluptuous and cruel master, a man fond of pleasure, yet incapable of refinement, whom many years' service in war has taught pride, but not bravery.

That treasure which I still keep within my bosom—my child, my all that was left to me—is now a slave. Good heavens! why was this? Why have I been introduced into this mortal apartment, to be a spectator of my own misfortunes, and the misfortunes of my fellow-creatures? Wherever I turn, what a labyrinth of doubt, error, and disappointment appears! Why was I brought into being? for what purposes made? from whence have I come? whither strayed? or to what regions am I hastening? Reason cannot resolve. It lends a ray to show the horrors of my prison, but not a light to guide me to escape them. Ye boasted revelations of the earth, how little do you aid the inquiry! How am I surprised at the inconsistency of the Magi! Their two principles of good and evil affright me. The Indian who bathes his visage in urine, and calls it piety, strikes me with astonishment. The Christian who believes in three Gods is highly absurd. The Jews, who pretend that Deity is pleased with the effusion of blood, are not less displeasing. I am equally surprised, that rational beings can come from the extremities of the earth, in order to kiss a stone, or scatter pebbles. How contrary to reason are those! and yet all pretend to teach me to be happy.

Surely all men are blind and ignorant of truth. Mankind wanders, unknowing his way, from morning till evening. Where shall we turn after happiness; or is it wisest to desist from the pursuit?—Like reptiles in a corner of some stupendous palace, we peep from our holes, look about us, wonder at all we see, but are ignorant of the great architect's design. Oh for a revelation of Himself, for a plan of His universal system! Oh for the reasons of our creation; or why were we created to be thus unhappy! If we are to experience no other felicity but what this life affords, then are we miserable indeed; if we are born only to look about us, repine and die, then has Heaven been guilty of injustice. If this life terminates my existence, I despise the blessings of Providence, and the wisdom of the giver; if this life be my all, let the following epitaph be written on the tomb of Altangi:—BY MY FATHER'S CRIMES I RECEIVED THIS; BY MY OWN CRIMES I BEQUEATH IT TO POSTERITY!

LETTER XXIII.

To the same.

YET, while I sometimes lament the case of humanity, and the depravity of human nature, there now and then appear gleams of greatness that serve to relieve the eye oppressed with the hideous prospect, and resemble those cultivated spots that are sometimes found in the midst of an Asiatic wilderness. I see many superior excellences among the English, which it is not in the power of all their follies to hide: I see virtues, which in other countries are known only to a few, practised here by every rank of people.

I know not whether it proceeds from their superior opulence that the English are more charitable than the rest of mankind; whether by being possessed of all the conveniences of life themselves, they have more leisure to perceive the uneasy situation of the distressed; whatever be the motive, they are not only the most charitable of any other nation, but most judicious in distinguishing the properest objects of compassion.

In other countries, the giver is generally influenced by the immediate impulse of pity; his generosity is exerted as much to relieve his own uneasy sensations as to comfort the object in distress. In England, benefactions are of a more general nature. Some men of fortune and universal benevolence propose the proper objects; the wants and the merits of the petitioners are canvassed by the people; neither passion nor pity find a place in the cool discussion; and charity is then only exerted when it has received the approbation of reason.

A late instance of this finely directed benevolence forces itself so strongly on my imagination, that it in a manner reconciles me to pleasure, and once more makes me the universal friend of man.

The English and French have not only political reasons to induce them to mutual hatred, but often the more prevailing motive of private interest to widen the breach. A war between other countries is carried on collectively; army fights against army, and a man's own private resentment is lost in that of the community: but in England and France, the individuals of each country plunder each other at sea without redress, and consequently feel that animosity against each other which passengers do at a robber. They have for some time carried on an expensive war; and several captives have been taken on both sides: those made prisoners by the French have been used with cruelty, and guarded with unnecessary caution: those taken by the English, being much more numerous, were confined in the ordinary manner; and not being released by their countrymen, began to feel all those inconveniences which arise from want of covering and long confinement.

Their countrymen were informed of their deplorable situation; but they, more intent on annoying their enemies than relieving their friends, refused the least assistance. The English now saw thousands of their fellow-creatures starving in every prison, forsaken by those whose duty it was to protect them, labouring with disease, and without clothes to keep off the severity of the season. National benevolence prevailed over national animosity; their prisoners were indeed enemies, but they were enemies in distress; they ceased to be hateful when they no longer continued to be formidable: forgetting, therefore, their national hatred, the men who were brave enough to conquer, were generous enough to forgive; and they whom all the world seemed to have disclaimed, at last found pity and redress from those they attempted to subdue. A subscription was opened, ample charities collected, proper necessaries procured, and the poor gay sons of a merry nation were once more taught to resume their former gaiety.

When I cast my eye over the list of those who contributed on this occasion, I find the names almost entirely English; scarce one foreigner appears among the number. It was for Englishmen alone to be capable of such exalted virtue. I own I cannot look over this catalogue of good men and philosophers, without thinking better of myself, because it makes me entertain a more favourable opinion of mankind. I am particularly struck with one who writes these words upon the paper that enclosed his benefaction: "The mite of an Englishman, a citizen of the world, to Frenchmen, prisoners of war, and naked." I only wish that he may find as much pleasure from his virtues as I have done in reflecting upon them; that alone will amply reward him. Such a one, my friend, is an honour to human nature; he makes no private distinctions of party; all that are stamped with the divine image of their Creator are friends to him: he is a native of the world; and the Emperor of China may be proud that he has such a countryman.

To rejoice at the destruction of our enemies is a foible grafted upon human nature, and we must be permitted to indulge it: the true way of atoning for such an ill-founded pleasure, is thus to turn our triumph into an act of benevolence, and to testify our own joy by endeavouring to banish anxiety from others.

Hamti, the best and wisest emperor that ever filled the throne, after having gained three signal victories over the Tartars, who had invaded his dominions, returned to Nankin, in order to enjoy the glory of his conquest. After he had rested for some days, the people, who are naturally fond of processions, impatiently expected the triumphant entry which emperors upon such occasions were accustomed to make: their murmurs came to the emperor's ear; he loved his people, and was willing to do all in his power to satisfy their just desires. He therefore assured them, that he intended, upon the next feast of the Lanterns, to exhibit one of the most glorious triumphs that had ever been seen in China.

The people were in raptures at his condescension; and, on the appointed day, assembled at the gates of the palace with the most eager expectations. Here they waited for some time, without seeing any of those preparations which usually precede a pageant. The lantern, with ten thousand tapers, was not yet brought forth; the fireworks, which usually covered the city walls, were not yet lighted: the people once more began to murmur at this delay, when, in the midst of their impatience, the palace-gates flew open, and the emperor himself appeared, not in splendour or magnificence, but in an ordinary habit, followed by the blind, the maimed, and the strangers of the city, all in new clothes, and each carrying in his hand money enough to supply his necessities for the year. The people were at first amazed, but soon perceived the wisdom of their king, who taught them, that to make one man happy, was more truly great than having ten thousand captives groaning at the wheels of his chariot.—Adieu.

LETTER XXIV.

To the same.

WHATEVER may be the merits of the English in other sciences, they seem peculiarly excellent in the art of healing. There is scarcely a disorder incident to humanity, against which they are not possessed with a most infallible antidote. The professors of other arts confess the inevitable intricacy of things; talk with doubt, and decide with hesitation: but doubting is entirely unknown in medicine; the advertising professors here delight in cases of difficulty. Be the disorder never so desperate or radical, you will find numbers in every street, who, by levelling a pill at the part affected, promise a certain cure, without loss of time, knowledge of a bedfellow, or hindrance of business.

When I consider the assiduity of this profession, their benevolence amazes me. They not only in general give their medicines for half value, but use the most persuasive remonstrances to induce the sick to come and be cured. Sure, there must be something strangely obstinate in an English patient who refuses so much health upon such easy terms. Does he take a pride in being bloated with a dropsy? does he find pleasure in the alternations of an intermittent fever? or feel as much satisfaction in nursing up his gout, as he found pleasure in acquiring it? He must, otherwise he would not reject such repeated assurances of instant relief. What can be more convincing than the manner in which the sick are invited to be well? The doctor first begs the most earnest attention of the public to what he is going to propose: he solemnly affirms the pill was never found to want success; he produces a list of those who have been rescued from the grave by taking it: yet, notwithstanding all this, there are many here who now and then think proper to be sick. Only sick, did I say? there are some who even think proper to die! Yes, by the head of Confucius! they die; though they might have purchased the health-restoring specific for half-a-crown at every corner.

I am amazed, my dear Fum Hoam, that these doctors, who know what an obstinate set of people they have to deal with, have never thought of attempting to revive the dead. When the living are found to reject their prescriptions, they ought in conscience to apply to the dead, from whom they can expect no such mortifying repulses: they would find in the dead the most complying patients imaginable; and what gratitude might they not expect from the patient's son, now no longer an heir, and his wife, now no longer a widow!

Think not, my friend, that there is any thing chimerical in such an attempt; they already perform cures equally strange. What can be more truly astonishing, than to see old age restored to youth, and vigour to the most feeble constitutions? Yet this is performed here every day: a simple electuary effects these wonders, even without the bungling ceremonies of having the patient boiled up in a kettle, or ground down in a mill.

Few physicians here go through the ordinary courses of education, but receive all their knowledge of medicine by immediate inspiration from Heaven. Some are thus inspired even in the womb; and, what is very remarkable, understand their profession as well at three years old, as at threescore. Others have spent a great part of their lives unconscious of any latent excellence, till a bankruptcy, or residence in gaol, have called their miraculous powers into exertion. And others still there are indebted to their superlative ignorance alone for success; the more ignorant the practitioner, the less capable is he thought of deceiving. The people here judge as they do in the East, where it is thought absolutely requisite that a man should be an idiot, before he pretend to be either a conjurer or a doctor.

When a physician by inspiration is sent for, he never perplexes the patient by previous examination; he asks very few questions, and those only for form sake. He knows every disorder by intuition; he adminsters the pill or drop for every distemper; nor is more inquisitive than the farrier while he drenches an horse. If the patient lives, then has he one more to add to the surviving list; if he dies, then it may be justly said of the patient's disorder, that, as it was not cured, the disorder was incurable.

LETTER XXV.

To the same.

I WAS some days ago in company with a politician, who very pathetically declaimed upon the miserable situation of his country: he assured me, that the whole political machine was moving in a wrong track, and that scarce even abilities like his own could ever set it right again. "What have we," said he, "to do with the wars on the Continent? We are a commercial nation; we have only to cultivate commerce, like our neighbours the Dutch; it is our business to increase trade by settling new colonies; riches are the strength of a nation; and for the rest, our ships, our ships alone, will protect us." I found it vain to oppose my feeble arguments to those of a man who thought himself wise enough to direct even the ministry. I fancied, however, that I saw with more certainty, because I reasoned without prejudice: I therefore begged leave, instead of argument, to relate a short history. He gave me a smile at once of condescension and contempt; and I proceeded as follows to describe "THE RISE AND DECLENSION OF THE KINGDOM OF LAO."

Northward of China, and in one of the doublings of the Great Wall, the fruitful province of Lao enjoyed its liberty, and a peculiar government of its own. As the inhabitants were on all sides surrounded by the wall, they feared no sudden invasion from the Tartars; and being each possessed of property, they were zealous in its defence.

The natural consequence of security and affluence in any country is a love of pleasure; when the wants of nature are supplied, we seek after the conveniences; when possessed of these, we desire the luxuries of life; and when every luxury is provided, it is then ambition takes up the man, and leaves him still something to wish for. The inhabitants of the country, from primitive simplicity, soon began to aim at elegance, and from elegance proceeded to refinement. It was now found absolutely requisite, for the good of the state, that the people should be divided. Formerly, the same hand that was employed in tilling the ground, or in dressing up the manufactures, was also, in time of need, a soldier; but the custom was now changed; for it was perceived, that a man bred up from childhood to the arts of either peace or war, became more eminent by this means in his respective profession. The inhabitants were, therefore, now distinguished into artisans and soldiers; and while those improved the luxuries of life, these watched for the security of the people.

A country possessed of freedom has always two sorts of enemies to fear,—foreign foes, who attack its existence from without, and internal miscreants, who betray its liberties within. The inhabitants of Lao were to guard against both. A country of artisans were most likely to preserve internal liberty; and a nation of soldiers were fittest to repel a foreign invasion. Hence naturally arose a division of opinion between the artisans and soldiers of the kingdom. The artisans, ever complaining that freedom was threatened by an armed internal force, were for disbanding the soldiers, and insisted that their walls, their walls alone, were sufficient to repel the most formidable invasion: the warriors, on the contrary, represented the power of the neighbouring kings, the combinations formed against their state, and the weakness of the wall, which every earthquake might overturn. While this altercation continued, the kingdom might be justly said to enjoy its greatest share of vigour: every order in the state, by being watchful over each other, contributed to diffuse happiness equally, and balanced the state. The arts of peace flourished, nor were those of war neglected: the neighbouring powers, who had nothing to apprehend from the ambition of men whom they only saw solicitous, not for riches, but freedom, were contented to traffic with them: they sent their goods to be manufactured in Lao, and paid a large price for them upon their return.

By these means, this people at length became moderately rich, and their opulence naturally invited the invader: a Tartar prince led an immense army against them, and they as bravely stood up in their own defence; they were still inspired with a love of their country; they fought the barbarous enemy with fortitude, and gained a complete victory.

From this moment, which they regarded as the completion of their glory, historians date their downfall. They had risen in strength by a love of their country, and fell by indulging ambition. The country possessed by the invading Tartars seemed to them a prize that would not only render them more formidable for the future, but which would increase their opulence for the present; it was unanimously resolved, therefore, both by soldiers and artisans, that those desolate regions should be peopled by colonies from Lao. When a trading nation begins to act the conqueror, it is then perfectly undone. It subsists in some measure by the support of its neighbours: while they continue to regard it without envy or apprehension, trade may flourish; but when once it presumes to assert as its right what is only enjoyed as a favour, each country reclaims that part of commerce which it has power to take back, and turns it into some other channel more honourable, though perhaps less convenient.

Every neighbour now began to regard with jealous eyes this ambitious commonwealth, and forbade their subjects any future intercourse with them. The inhabitants of Lao, however, still pursued the same ambitious maxims: it was from their colonies alone they expected riches; and riches, said they, are strength, and strength is security. Numberless were the migrations of the desperate and enterprising of this country to people the desolate dominions lately possessed by the Tartar. Between these colonies and the mother country a very advantageous traffic was at first carried on: the republic sent their colonies large quantities of the manufactures of the country, and they in return provided the republic with an equivalent in ivory and ginseng. By this means the inhabitants became immensely rich, and this produced an equal degree of voluptuousness; for men who have much money will always find some fantastical modes of enjoyment. How shall I mark the steps by which they declined? Every colony in process of time spreads over the whole country where it first was planted. As it grows more populous, it becomes more polite; and those manufactures for which it was in the beginning obliged to others, it learns to dress up itself. Such was the case with the colonies of Lao: they, in less than a century, became a powerful and a polite people, and the more polite they grew, the less advantageous was the commerce which still subsisted between them and others. By this means the mother country, being abridged in its commerce, grew poorer, but not less luxurious. Their former wealth had introduced luxury; and wherever luxury once fixes, no art can either lessen or remove it. Their commerce with their neighbours was totally destroyed, and that with their colonies was every day naturally and necessarily declining; they still, however, preserved the insolence of wealth, without a power to support it, and persevered in being luxurious, while contemptible from poverty. In short, the state resembled one of those bodies bloated with disease, whose bulk is only a symptom of its wretchedness.

Their former opulence only rendered them more impotent, as those individuals who are reduced from riches to poverty are of all men the most unfortunate and helpless. They had imagined, because their colonies tended to make them rich upon the first acquisition, they would still continue to do so; they now found, however, that on themselves alone they should have depended for support; that colonies ever afforded but temporary affluence; and when cultivated and polite, are no longer useful. From such a concurrence of circumstances they soon became contemptible. The Emperor Honti invaded them with a powerful army. Historians do not say whether their colonies were too remote to lend assistance, or else were desirous of shaking off their dependence; but certain it is, they scarce made any resistance: their walls were now found but a weak defence, and they at length were obliged to acknowledge subjection to the empire of China.

Happy, very happy might they have been, had they known when to bound their riches and their glory; had they known that extending empire is often diminishing power; that countries are ever strongest which are internally powerful: that colonies, by draining away the brave and enterprising, leave the country in the hands of the timid and avaricious; that walls give little protection, unless manned with resolution; that too much commerce may injure a nation as well as too little; and that there is a wide difference between a conquering and a flourishing empire.—Adieu.

LETTER XXVI.

To the same.

THOUGH fond of many acquaintances, I desire an intimacy only with a few. The Man in Black, whom I have often mentioned, is one whose friendship I could wish to acquire, because he possesses my esteem. His manners, it is true, are tinctured with some strange inconsistencies; and he may be justly termed a humorist in a nation of humorists. Though he is generous even to profusion, he affects to be thought a prodigy of parsimony and prudence; though his conversation be replete with the most sordid and selfish maxims, his heart is dilated with the most unbounded love. I have known him profess himself a man-hater, while his cheek was glowing with compassion; and, while his looks were softened into pity, I have heard him use the language of the most unbounded ill-nature. Some affect humanity and tenderness, others boast of having such dispositions from nature; but he is the only man I ever knew who seemed ashamed of his natural benevolence. He takes as much pains to hide his feelings, as any hypocrite would to conceal his indifference; but on every unguarded moment the mask drops off, and reveals him to the most superficial observer.

In one of our late excursions into the country, happening to discourse upon the provision that was made for the poor in England, he seemed amazed how any of his countrymen could be so foolishly weak as to relieve occasional objects of charity, when the laws had made such ample provision for their support. "In every parish-house," says he, "the poor are supplied with food, clothes, fire, and a bed to lie on; they want no more, I desire no more myself; yet still they seem discontented. I am surprised at the inactivity of our magistrates, in not taking up such vagrants, who are only a weight upon the industrious; I am surprised that the people are found to relieve them, when they must be at the same time sensible that it in some measure encourages idleness, extravagance, and imposture. Were I to advise any man for whom I had the least regard, I would caution him by all means not to be imposed upon by their false pretences: let me assure you, sir, they are impostors, every one of them, and rather merit a prison than relief."

He was proceeding in this strain, earnestly to dissuade me from an imprudence of which I am seldom guilty, when an old man, who still had about him the remnants of tattered finery, implored our compassion. He assured us that he was no common beggar, but forced into the shameful profession to support a dying wife and five hungry children. Being prepossessed against such falsehoods, his story had not the least influence upon me; but it was quite otherwise with the Man in Black: I could see it visibly operate upon his countenance, and effectually interrupt his harangue. I could easily perceive, that his heart burned to relieve the five starving children, but he seemed ashamed to discover his weakness to me. While he thus hesitated between compassion and pride, I pretended to look another way, and he seized this opportunity of giving the poor petitioner a piece of silver, bidding him at the same time, in order that I should hear, go work for his bread, and not tease passengers with such impertinent falsehoods for the future.

As he had fancied himself quite unperceived, he continued, as we proceeded, to rail against beggars with as much animosity as before: he threw in some episodes on his own amazing prudence and economy, with his profound skill in discovering impostors; he explained the manner in which he would deal with beggars were he a magistrate, hinted at enlarging some of the prisons for their reception, and told two stories of ladies that were robbed by beggar-men. He was beginning a third to the same purpose, when a sailor with a wooden leg once more crossed our walks, desiring our pity, and blessing our limbs. I was for going on without taking any notice, but my friend, looking wistfully upon the poor petitioner, bid me stop, and he would show me with how much ease he could at any time detect an impostor.

He now, therefore, assumed a look of importance, and in an angry tone began to examine the sailor, demanding in what engagement he was thus disabled and rendered unfit for service. The sailor replied, in a tone as angrily as he, that he had been an officer on board a private ship of war, and that he had lost his leg abroad, in defence of those who did nothing at home. At this reply, all my friend's importance vanished in a moment; he had not a single question more to ask; he now only studied what method he should take to relieve him unobserved. He had, however, no easy part to act, as he was obliged to preserve the appearance of ill-nature before me, and yet relieve himself by relieving the sailor. Casting, therefore, a furious look upon some bundles of chips which the fellow carried in a string at his back, my friend demanded how he sold his matches; but, not waiting for a reply, desired, in a surly tone, to have a shilling's worth. The sailor seemed at first surprised at his demand, but soon recollecting himself, and presenting his whole bundle, "Here, master," says he, "take all my cargo, and a blessing into the bargain."

It is impossible to describe with what an air of triumph my friend marched off with his new purchase: he assured me, that he was firmly of opinion that those fellows must have stolen their goods, who could thus afford to sell them for half value. He informed me of several different uses to which those chips might be applied; he expatiated largely upon the savings that would result from lighting candles with a match, instead of thrusting them into the fire. He averred, that he would as soon have parted with a tooth as his money to those vagabonds, unless for some valuable consideration. I cannot tell how long this panegyric upon frugality and matches might have continued, had not his attention been called off by another object more distressful than either of the former. A woman in rags, with one child in her arms, and another on her back, was attempting to sing ballads, but with such a mournful voice, that it was difficult to determine whether she was singing or crying. A wretch, who in the deepest distress still aimed at good-humour, was an object my friend was by no means capable of withstanding: his vivacity and his discourse were instantly interrupted; upon this occasion, his very dissimulation had forsaken him. Even in my presence he immediately applied his hands to his pockets, in order to relieve her; but guess his confusion when he found he had already given away all the money he carried about him to former objects. The misery painted in the woman's visage was not half so strongly expressed as the agony in his. He continued to search for some time, but to no purpose, till, at length recollecting himself, with a face of ineffable good-nature, as he had no money, he put into her hands his shilling's worth of matches.

LETTER XXVII.

To the same.

As there appeared something reluctantly good in the character of my companion, I must own it surprised me what could be his motives for thus concealing virtues which others take such pains to display. I was unable to repress my desire of knowing the history of a man who thus seemed to act under continual restraint, and whose benevolence was rather the effect of appetite than reason.

It was not, however, till after repeated solicitations he thought proper to gratify my curiosity. "If you are fond," says he, "of hearing hairbreadth 'scapes, my history must certainly please; for I have been for twenty years upon the very verge of starving, without ever being starved.

"My father, the younger son of a good family, was possessed of a small living in the church. His education was above his fortune, and his generosity greater than his education. Poor as he was, he had his flatterers, still poorer than himself; for every dinner he gave them they returned an equivalent in praise, and this was all he wanted. The same ambition that actuates a monarch at the head of an army influenced my father at the head of his table: he told the story of the ivy-tree, and that was laughed at; he repeated the jest of the two scholars and one pair of breeches, and the company laughed at that; but the story of Taffy in the sedan-chair was sure to set the table in a roar: thus his pleasure increased in proportion to the pleasure he gave; he loved all the world, and he fancied all the world loved him.

"As his fortune was but small, he lived up to the very extent of it; he had no intentions of leaving his children money, for that was dross; he was resolved they should have learning; for learning, he used to observe, was better than silver or gold. For this purpose, he undertook to instruct us himself; and took as much pains to form our morals as to improve our understanding. We were told, that universal benevolence was what first cemented society: we were taught to consider all the wants of mankind as our own; to regard the human face divine with affection and esteem; he wound us up to be mere machines of pity, and rendered us incapable of withstanding the slightest impulse made either by real or fictitious distress: in a word, we were perfectly instructed in the art of giving away thousands, before we were taught the more necessary qualifications of getting a farthing.

"I cannot avoid imagining, that thus refined by his lessons out of all my suspicion, and divested of even all the little cunning which nature had given me, I resembled, upon my first entrance into the busy and insidious world, one of those gladiators who were exposed without armour in the amphitheatre at Rome. My father, however, who had only seen the world on one side, seemed to triumph in my superior discernment; though my whole stock of wisdom consisted in being able to talk like himself upon subjects that once were useful, because they were then topics of the busy world, but that now were utterly useless, because connected with the busy world no longer.

"The first opportunity he had of finding his expectations disappointed was in the very middling figure I made in the university; he had flattered himself that he should soon see me rising into the foremost rank in literary reputation, but was mortified to find me utterly unnoticed and unknown. His disappointment might have been partly ascribed to his having overrated my talents, and partly to my dislike of mathematical reasonings, at a time when my imagination and memory, yet unsatisfied, were more eager after new objects than desirous of reasoning upon those I knew. This did not, however, please my tutor, who observed, indeed, that I was a little dull; but at the same time allowed, that I seemed to be very good-natured, and had no harm in me.

"After I had resided at college seven years, my father died, and left me—his blessing. Thus shoved from shore without ill-nature to protect, or cunning to guide, or proper stores to subsist me in so dangerous a voyage, I was obliged to embark in the wide world at twenty-two. But, in order to settle in life, my friends advised (for they always advise when they begin to despise us), they advised me, I say, to go into orders.

"To be obliged to wear a long wig, when I liked a short one, or a black coat, when I generally dressed in brown, I thought was such a restraint upon my liberty, that I absolutely rejected the proposal. A priest in England is not the same mortified creature with a bonze in China: with us, not he that fasts best, but eats best, is reckoned the best liver; yet I rejected a life of luxury, indolence, and ease, from no other consideration but that boyish one of dress. So that my friends were now perfectly satisfied I was undone; and yet they thought it a pity for one who had not the least harm in him and was so very good-natured.

"Poverty naturally begets dependence, and I was admitted as flatterer to a great man. At first, I was surprised that the situation of a flatterer at a great man's table could be thought disagreeable: there was no great trouble in listening attentively when his lordship spoke, and laughing when he looked round for applause. This even good manners might have obliged me to perform. I found, however, too soon, that his lordship was a greater dunce than myself; and from that very moment my power of flattery was at an end. I now rather aimed at setting him right, than at receiving his absurdities with submission: to flatter those we do not know is an easy task; but to flatter our intimate acquaintances, all whose foibles are strongly in our eye, is drudgery insupportable. Every time I now opened my lips in praise, my falsehood went to my conscience; his lordship soon perceived me to be unfit for service; I was therefore discharged; my patron at the same time being graciously pleased to observe, that he believed I was tolerably good-natured, and had not the least harm in me.

"Disappointed in ambition, I had recourse to love. A young lady, who lived with her aunt, and was possessed of a pretty fortune in her own disposal, had given me, as I fancied, some reason to expect success. The symptoms by which I was guided were striking. She had always laughed with me at her awkward acquaintance, and at her aunt among the number; she always observed, that a man of sense would make a better husband than a fool, and I as constantly applied the observation in my own favour. She continually talked, in my company, of friendship and the beauties of the mind, and spoke of Mr. Shrimp my rival's high-heeled shoes with detestation. These were circumstances which I thought strongly in my favour; so, after resolving and resolving, I had courage enough to tell her my mind. Miss heard my proposal with serenity, seeming at the same time to study the figures of her fan. Out at last it came. There was but one small objection to complete our happiness, which was no more than——that she was married three months before to Mr. Shrimp, with high-heeled shoes! By way of consolation, however, she observed, that, though I was disappointed in her, my addresses to her aunt would probably kindle her into sensibility; as the old lady always allowed me to be very good-natured, and not to have the least share of harm in me.

"Yet still I had friends, numerous friends, and to them I was resolved to apply. O friendship! thou fond soother of the human breast, to thee we fly in every calamity; to thee the wretched seek for succour; on thee the care-tired son of misery fondly relies: from thy kind assistance the unfortunate always hopes relief, and may be ever sure of—disappointment. My first application was to a city scrivener, who had frequently offered to lend me money, when he knew I did not want it. I informed him, that now was the time to put his friendship to the test; that I wanted to borrow a couple of hundred for a certain occasion, and was resolved to take it up from him. 'And pray, sir,' cried my friend, 'do you want all this money?'—'Indeed, I never wanted it more,' returned I.—'I am sorry for that,' cries the scrivener, 'with all my heart; for they who want money when they come to borrow, will always want money when they should come to pay.'

"From him I flew, with indignation, to one of the best friends I had in the world, and made the same request. 'Indeed, Mr. Drybone,' cries my friend, 'I always thought it would come to this. You know, sir, I would not advise you but for your own good; but your conduct has hitherto been ridiculous in the highest degree, and some of your acquaintance always thought you a very silly fellow. Let me see—you want two hundred pounds. Do you only want two hundred, sir, exactly?'—'To confess a truth,' returned I, 'I shall want three hundred; but then, I have another friend, from whom I can borrow the rest.'—'Why, then,' replied my friend, 'if you would take my advice, (and you know I should not presume to advise you but for your own good,) I would recommend it to you to borrow the whole sum from that other friend; and then one note will serve for all, you know.'

"Poverty now began to come fast upon me; yet instead of growing more provident or cautious as I grew poor, I became every day more indolent and simple. A friend was arrested for fifty pounds; I was unable to extricate him, except by becoming his bail. When at liberty, he fled from his creditors, and left me to take his place. In prison I expected greater satisfactions than I enjoyed at large. I hoped to converse with men in this new world, simple and believing like myself; but I found them as cunning and as cautious as those in the world I had left behind. They spunged up my money while it lasted, borrowed my coals and never paid for them, and cheated me when I played at cribbage. All this was done because they believed me to be very good-natured, and knew that I had no harm in me.

"Upon my first entrance into this mansion, which is to some the abode of despair, I felt no sensations different from those I experienced abroad. I was now on one side the door, and those who were unconfined were on the other: this was all the difference between us. At first, indeed, I felt some uneasiness, in considering how I should be able to provide this week for the wants of the week ensuing; but after some time, if I found myself sure of eating one day, I never troubled my head how I was to be supplied another. I seized every precarious meal with the utmost good-humour; indulged no rants of spleen at my situation; never called down Heaven and all the stars to behold me dining upon a halfpenny-worth of radishes; my very companions were taught to believe that I liked salad better than mutton. I contented myself with thinking, that all my life I should either eat white bread or brown; considered that all that happened was best; laughed when I was not in pain, took the world as it went, and read Tacitus often for want of more books and company.

"How long I might have continued in this torpid state of simplicity I cannot tell, had I not been roused by seeing an old acquaintance, whom I knew to be a prudent blockhead, preferred to a place in the government. I now found that I had pursued a wrong track, and that the true way of being able to relieve others was first to aim at independence myself: my immediate care, therefore, was to leave my present habitation and make an entire reformation in my conduct and behaviour. For a free, open, undesigning deportment, I put on that of closeness, prudence, and economy. One of the most heroic actions I ever performed, and for which I shall praise myself as long as I live, was the refusing half-a-crown to an old acquaintance, at the time when he wanted it, and I had it to spare: for this alone I deserve to be decreed an ovation.

"I now therefore pursued a course of uninterrupted frugality, seldom wanted a dinner, and was consequently invited to twenty. I soon began to get the character of a saving hunks that had money, and insensibly grew into esteem. Neighbours have asked my advice in the disposal of their daughters; and I have always taken care not to give any. I have contracted a friendship with an alderman, only by observing, that if we take a farthing from a thousand pounds, it will be a thousand pounds no longer. I have been invited to a pawnbroker's table, by pretending to hate gravy; and am now actually upon treaty of marriage with a rich widow, for only having observed that the bread was rising. If ever I am asked a question, whether I know it or not, instead of answering, I only smile and look wise. If a charity is proposed, I go about with the hat, but put nothing in myself. If a wretch solicits my pity, I observe that the world is filled with impostors, and take a certain method of not being deceived by never relieving. In short, I now find the truest way of finding esteem, even from the indigent, is to give away nothing, and thus have much in our power to give."

LETTER XXVIII.

To the same.

LATELY, in company with my friend in black, whose conversation is now both my amusement and instruction, I could not avoid observing the great numbers of old bachelors and maiden ladies with which this city seems to be overrun. "Sure, marriage," said I, "is not sufficiently encouraged, or we should never behold such crowds of battered beaux and decayed coquettes, still attempting to drive a trade they have been so long unfit for, and swarming upon the gaiety of the age. I behold an old bachelor in the most contemptible light, as an animal that lives upon the common stock without contributing his share: he is a beast of prey, and the laws should make use of as many stratagems, and as much force, to drive the reluctant savage into the toils, as the Indians when they hunt the hyæna or the rhinoceros. The mob should be permitted after him, boys might play tricks on him with impunity, every well-bred company should laugh at him; and if, when turned of sixty, he offered to make love, his mistress might spit in his face, or, what would be perhaps a greater punishment, should fairly grant the favour.

"As for old maids," continued I, "they should not be treated with so much severity, because I suppose none would be so if they could. No lady in her senses would choose to make a subordinate figure at christenings or lyings-in, when she might be the principal herself; nor curry favour with a sister-in-law, when she might command a husband; nor toil in preparing custards, when she might lie a-bed, and give directions how they ought to be made; nor stifle all her sensations in demure formality, when she might, with matrimonial freedom, shake her acquaintance by the hand, and wink at a *double entendre.* No lady could be so very silly as to live single, if she could help it. I consider an unmarried lady, declining into the vale of years, as one of those charming countries bordering on China, that lies waste for want of proper inhabitants. We are not to accuse the country, but the ignorance of its neighbours, who are insensible of its beauties, though at liberty to enter and cultivate the soil."

"Indeed, sir," replied my companion, "you are very little acquainted with the English ladies, to think they are old maids against their will. I dare venture to affirm, that you can hardly select one of them all, but has had frequent offers of marriage, which either pride or avarice has not made her reject. Instead of thinking it a disgrace, they take every occasion to boast of their former cruelty: a soldier does not exult more when he counts over the wounds he has received, than a female veteran when she relates the wounds she has formerly given: exhaustless when she begins a narrative of the former death-dealing power of her eyes. She tells of the knight in gold lace, who died with a single frown, and never rose again till—he was married to his maid; of the squire who, being cruelly denied, in a rage flew to the window, and lifting up the sash, threw himself, in an agony—into his arm-chair; of the parson, who, crossed in love, resolutely swallowed opium, which banished the stings of despised love by—making him sleep. In short, she talks over her former losses with pleasure, and, like some tradesmen, finds consolation in the many bankruptcies she has suffered.

"For this reason, whenever I see a superannuated beauty still unmarried, I tacitly accuse her either of pride, avarice, coquetry, or affectation. There's Miss Jenny Tinderbox, I once remember her to have had some beauty and a moderate fortune. Her elder sister happened to marry a man of quality, and this seemed as a statute of virginity against poor Jane. Because there was one lucky hit in the family, she was resolved not to disgrace it by introducing a tradesman. By thus rejecting her equals, and neglected or despised by her superiors, she now acts in the capacity of tutoress to her sister's children, and undergoes the drudgery of three servants, without receiving the wages of one.

"Miss Squeeze was a pawnbroker's daughter; her father had early taught her that money was a very good thing, and left her a moderate fortune at his death. She was so perfectly sensible of the value of what she had got, that she was resolved never to part with a farthing without an equality on the part of her suitor: she thus refused several offers made her by people who wanted to better themselves, as the saying is, and grew old and ill-natured, without ever considering that she should have made an abatement in her pretensions, from her face being pale, and marked with the small-pox.

"Lady Betty Tempest, on the contrary, had beauty, with fortune and family. But, fond of conquest, she passed from triumph to triumph: she had read plays and romances, and there had learned, that a plain man of common sense was no better than a fool; such she refused, and sighed only for the gay, giddy, inconstant, and thoughtless. After she had thus rejected hundreds who liked her, and sighed for hundreds who despised her, she found herself insensibly deserted: at present she is company only for her aunts and cousins, and sometimes makes one in a country-dance, with only one of the chairs for a partner, casts off round a joint-stool, and sets to a corner cupboard. In a word, she is treated with civil contempt from every quarter, and placed, like a piece of old-fashioned lumber, merely to fill up a corner.

"But Sophronia, the sagacious Sophronia, how shall I mention her? She was taught to love Greek and hate the men from her very infancy; she has rejected fine gentlemen because they were not pedants, and pedants because they were not fine gentlemen; her exquisite sensibility has taught her to discover every fault in every lover, and her inflexible justice has prevented her pardoning them: thus she rejected several offers, till the wrinkles of age had overtaken her; and now, without one good feature in her face, she talks incessantly of the beauties of the mind."—Farewell.

LETTER XXIX.

To the same.

WERE we to estimate the learning of the English by the number of books that are every day published among them, perhaps no country, not even China itself, could equal them in this particular. I have reckoned not less than twenty-three new books published in one day, which, upon computation, makes eight thousand three hundred and ninety-five in one year. Most of these are not confined to one single science, but embrace the whole circle. History, politics, poetry, mathematics, metaphysics, and the philosophy of nature, are all comprised in a manual not larger than that in which our children are taught the letters. If, then, we suppose the learned of England to read but an eighth part of the works which daily come from the press, (and sure none can pretend to learning upon less easy terms,) at this rate every scholar will read a thousand books in one year. From such a calculation you may conjecture what an amazing fund of literature a man must be possessed of. who thus reads three new books every day, not one of which but contains all the good things that ever were said or written.

And yet I know not how it happens, but the English are not, in reality, so learned as would seem from this calculation. We meet but few who know all arts and sciences to perfection; whether it is that the generality are incapable of such extensive knowledge, or that the authors of those books are not adequate instructors. In China the emperor himself takes cognizance of all the doctors in the kingdom who profess authorship. In England every man may be an author that can write; for they have by law a liberty, not only of saying what they please, but of being also as dull as they please.

Yesterday I testified my surprise to the Man in Black, where writers could be found in sufficient number to throw off the books I daily saw crowding from the press. I at first imagined that their learned seminaries might take this method of instructing the world. But, to obviate this objection, my companion assured me, that the doctors of colleges never wrote, and that some of them had actually forgot their reading; "but if you desire," continued he, "to see a collection of authors, I fancy I can introduce you this evening to a club, which assembles every Saturday at seven, at the sign of the Broom, near Islington, to talk over the business of the last and the entertainment of the week ensuing." I accepted his invitation: we walked together, and entered the house some time before the usual hour for the company assembling.

My friend took this opportunity of letting me into the characters of the principal members of the club, not even the host excepted, who, it seems, was once an author himself, but preferred by a bookseller to this situation as a reward for his former services.

"The first person," said he, "of our society is Doctor Nonentity, a metaphysician. Most people think him a profound scholar; but, as he seldom speaks, I cannot be positive in that particular: he generally spreads himself before the fire, sucks his pipe, talks little, drinks much, and is reckoned very good company. I'm told he writes indexes to perfection; he makes essays on the origin of evil, philosophical inquiries upon any subject, and draws up an answer to any book upon twenty-four hours' warning. You may distinguish him from the rest of the company by his long gray wig and the blue handkerchief round his neck.

"The next to him in merit and esteem is Tim Syllabub, a droll creature: he sometimes shines as a star of the first magnitude among the choice spirits of the age; he is reckoned equally excellent at a rebus, a riddle, a bawdy song, and an hymn for the Tabernacle. You will know him by his shabby finery, his powdered wig, dirty shirt, and broken silk stockings.

"After him succeeds Mr. Tibbs, a very useful hand: he writes receipts for the bite of a mad dog, and throws off an Eastern tale to perfection; he understands the business of an author as well as any man, for no bookseller alive can cheat him. You may distinguish him by the peculiar clumsiness of his figure and the coarseness of his coat; however, though it be coarse, (as he frequently tells the company,) he has paid for it.

"Lawyer Squint is the politician of the society: he makes speeches for Parliament, writes addresses to his fellow-subjects, and letters to noble commanders; he gives the history of every new play, and finds seasonable thoughts upon every occasion." My companion was proceeding in his description, when the host came running in, with terror on his countenance, to tell us that the door was beset with bailiffs. "If that be the case, then," says my companion, "we had as good be going; for I am positive we shall not see one of the company this night." Wherefore, disappointed, we were both obliged to return home—he to enjoy the oddities which compose his character alone, and I to write as usual to my friend the occurrences of the day.—Adieu.

LETTER XXX.

To the same.

BY my last advices from Moscow I find the caravan has not yet departed for China: I still continue to write, expecting that you may receive a large number of letters at once. In them you will find rather a minute detail of English peculiarities, than a general picture of their manners or dispositions. Happy it were for mankind, if all travellers would thus, instead of characterising a people in general terms, lead us into a detail of those minute circumstances which first influenced their opinion. The genius of a country should be investigated with a kind of experimental inquiry: by this means we should have more precise and just notions of foreign nations, and detect travellers themselves when they happened to form wrong conclusions.

My friend and I repeated our visit to the club of authors; where, upon our entrance, we found the members all assembled, and engaged in a loud debate.

The poet in shabby finery, holding a manuscript in his hand, was earnestly endeavouring to persuade the company to hear him read the first book of an heroic poem, which he had composed the day before. But against this all the members very warmly objected. They knew no reason why any member of the club should be indulged with a particular hearing, when many of them had published whole volumes which had never been looked in. They insisted that the law should be observed, where reading in company was expressly noticed. It was in vain that the poet pleaded the peculiar merit of his piece; he spoke to an assembly insensible to all his remonstrances: the book of laws was opened, and read by the secretary, where it was expressly enacted, "That whatsoever poet, speech-maker, critic, or historian, should presume to engage the company by reading his own works, he was to lay down sixpence previous to opening the manuscript, and should be charged one shilling an hour while he continued reading: the said shilling to be equally distributed among the company, as a recompense for their trouble."

Our poet seemed at first to shrink at the penalty, hesitating for some time whether he should deposit the fine or shut up the poem; but, looking round, and perceiving two strangers in the room, his love of fame outweighed his prudence, and laying down the sum by law established, he insisted on his prerogative.

A profound silence ensuing, he began by explaining his design. "Gentlemen," says he, "the present piece is not one of your common epic poems, which come from the press like paper-kites in summer: there are none of your Turnuses or Didos in it; it is an heroical description of nature. I only beg you'll endeavour to make your souls unison with mine, and hear with the same enthusiasm with which I have written. The poem begins with the description of an author's bedchamber: the picture was sketched in my own apartment; for you must know, gentlemen, that I am myself the hero." Then, putting himself into the attitude of an orator, with all the emphasis of voice and action he proceeded:

Where the Red Lion, flaring o'er the way,
Invites each passing stranger that can pay;
Where Calvert's butt and Parson's black champagne
Regale the drabs and bloods of Drury Lane:
There, in a lonely room, from bailiffs snug,
The Muse found Scroggen stretched beneath a rug.
A window, patched with paper, lent a ray,
That dimly showed the state in which he lay;
The sanded floor, that grits beneath the tread;
The humid wall, with paltry pictures spread;
The royal game of goose was there in view,
And the twelve rules the Royal Martyr drew;
The Seasons, framed with listing, found a place,
And brave Prince William showed his lamp-black face.
The morn was cold; he views with keen desire
The rusty grate, unconscious of a fire:
With beer and milk arrears the frieze was scored,
And five cracked teacups dressed the chimney board.
A night-cap decked his brows instead of bay;
A cap by night—a stocking all the day!

With this last line he seemed so much elated, that he was unable to proceed. "There, gentlemen!" cries he, "there is a description for you; Rabelais' bedchamber is but a fool to it.

A cap by night—a stocking all the day!

There is sound, and sense, and truth, and nature in the trifling compass of ten little syllables."

He was too much employed in self-admiration to observe the company, who by nods, winks, shrugs, and stifled laughter, testified every mark of contempt. He turned severally to each for their opinion, and found all, however, ready to applaud. One swore it was inimitable, another said it was damned fine, and a third cried out in a rapture, *Carissimo!* At last, addressing himself to the president, "And pray, Mr. Squint," says he, "let us have your opinion."—"Mine!" answered the president, taking the manuscript out of the author's hand, "may this glass suffocate me, but I think it equal to anything I have seen: and I fancy," continued he, doubling up the poem and forcing it into the author's pocket, "that you will get great honour when it comes out; so I shall beg leave to put it in. We will not intrude upon your good-nature, in desiring to hear more of it at present; *ex ungue Herculem*, we are satisfied, perfectly satisfied." The author made two or three attempts to pull it out a second time, and the president made as many to prevent him. Thus, though with reluctance, he was at last obliged to sit down, contented with the commendations for which he had paid.

When this tempest of poetry and praise was blown over, one of the company changed the subject, by wondering how any man could be so dull as to write poetry at present, since prose itself would hardly pay. "Would you think it, gentlemen," continued he, "I have actually written last week sixteen prayers, twelve bawdy jests, and three sermons, all at the rate of sixpence a-piece; and, what is still more extraordinary, the bookseller has lost by the bargain. Such sermons would once have gained me a prebend's stall; but now, alas! we have neither piety, taste, nor humour among us. Positively, if this season does not turn out better than it has begun, unless the ministry commit some blunders to furnish us with a new topic of abuse, I shall resume my old business of working at the press, instead of finding it employment."

The whole club seemed to join in condemning the season, as one of the worst that had come for some time: a gentleman particularly observed that the nobility were never known to subscribe worse than at present. "I know not how it happens," said he, "though I follow them up as close as possible, yet I can hardly get a single subscription in a week. The houses of the great are as inaccessible as a frontier garrison at midnight. I never see a nobleman's door half opened, that some surly porter or footman does not stand full in the breach. I was yesterday to wait with a subscription proposal upon my Lord Squash, the Creolian. I had posted myself at his door the whole morning, and just as he was getting into his coach, thrust my proposal snug into his hand, folded up in the form of a letter from myself. He just glanced at the superscription, and, not knowing the hand, consigned it to his valet-de-chambre; this respectable personage treated it as his master, and put it into the hands of the porter; the porter grasped my proposal frowning; and, measuring my figure from top to toe, put it back into my own hands unopened."

"To the devil I pitch all the nobility," cries a little man, in a peculiar accent; "I am sure they have of late used me most scurvily. You must know, gentlemen, some time ago, upon the arrival of a certain noble duke from his travels, I sat myself down, and vamped up a fine flaunting poetical panegyric, which I had written in such a strain, that I fancied it would have even wheedled milk from a mouse. In this I represented the whole kingdom welcoming his grace to his native soil, not forgetting the loss France and Italy would sustain in their arts by his departure. I expected to touch for a bank-bill at least; so, folding up my verses in gilt paper, I gave my last half-crown to a genteel servant to be the bearer. My letter was safely conveyed to his grace, and the servant, after four hours' absence, during which time I led the life of a fiend, returned with a letter four times as big as mine. Guess my extasy at the prospect of so fine a return. I eagerly took the packet into my hands, that trembled to receive it. I kept it some time unopened before me, brooding over the expected treasure it contained; when opening it, as I hope to be saved, gentlemen, his grace had sent me, in payment for my poem, no bank-bills, but six copies of verses, each longer than mine, addressed to him upon the same occasion."

"A nobleman," cries a member who had hitherto been silent, "is created as much for the confusion of us authors as the catch-pole. I'll tell you a story, gentlemen, which is as true as that this pipe is made of clay:—When I was delivered of my first book, I owed my tailor for a suit of clothes; but that is nothing new, you know, and may be any man's case as well as mine. Well, owing him for a suit of clothes, and hearing that my book took very well, he sent for his money, and insisted upon being paid immediately. Though I was at that time rich in fame—for my book ran like wild-fire—yet I was very short in money, and, being unable to satisfy his demand, prudently resolved to keep my chamber, preferring a prison of my own choosing at home to one of my tailor's choosing abroad. In vain the bailiffs used all their arts to decoy me from my citadel; in vain they sent to let me know that a gentleman wanted to speak with me at the next tavern; in vain they came with an urgent message from my aunt in the country; in vain I was told that a particular friend was at the point of death, and desired to take his last farewell: I was deaf, insensible, rock, adamant; the bailiffs could make no impression on my hard heart, for I effectually kept my liberty by never stirring out of the room.

"This was very well for a fortnight; when one morning I received a most splendid message from the Earl of Doomsday, importing, that he had read my book, and was in raptures with every line of it; he impatiently longed to see the author, and had some designs which might turn out greatly to my advantage. I paused upon the contents of this message, and found there could be no deceit, for the card was gilt at the edges, and the bearer, I was told, had quite the looks of a gentleman. Witness, ye powers, how my heart triumphed at my own importance! I saw a long perspective of felicity before me; I applauded the taste of the times which never saw genius forsaken: I had prepared a set introductory speech for the occasion; five glaring compliments for his lordship, and two more modest for myself. The next morning, therefore, in order to be punctual to my appointment, I took coach, and ordered the fellow to drive to the street and house mentioned in his lordship's address. I had the precaution to pull up the window as I went along, to keep off the busy part of mankind, and, big with expectation, fancied the coach never went fast enough. At length, however, the wished-for moment of its stopping arrived: this for some time I impatiently expected, and letting down the window in a transport, in order to take a previous view of his lordship's magnificent palace and situation, I found—poison to my sight!—I found myself not in an elegant street, but a paltry lane; not at a nobleman's door, but the door of a spunging-house: I found the coachman had all this while been driving me to gaol; and I saw the bailiff, with a devil's face, coming out to secure me."

To a philosopher no circumstance, however trifling, is too minute; he finds instruction and entertainment in occurrences which are passed over by the rest of mankind as low, trite, and indifferent; it is from the number of these particulars, which to many appear insignificant, that he is at last enabled to form general conclusions: this, therefore, must be my excuse for sending so far as China accounts of manners and follies, which, though minute in their own nature, serve more truly to characterise this people, than histories of their public treaties, courts, ministers, negotiations, and ambassadors. —Adieu.

LETTER XXXI.

To the same.

THE English have not yet brought the art of gardening to the same perfection with the Chinese, but have lately begun to imitate them. Nature is now followed with greater assiduity than formerly: the trees are suffered to shoot out into the utmost luxuriance; the streams, no longer forced from their native beds, are permitted to wind along the valleys; spontaneous flowers take place of the finished parterre, and the enamelled meadow of the shaven green.

Yet still the English are far behind us in this charming art: their designers have not yet attained the power of uniting instruction with beauty. An European will scarcely conceive my meaning, when I say that there is scarce a garden in China which does not contain some fine moral, couched under the general design, where one is taught wisdom as he walks, and feels the force of some noble truth, or delicate precept, resulting from the disposition of the groves, streams, or grottos. Permit me to illustrate what I mean by a description of my gardens at Quamsi. My heart still hovers round those scenes of former happiness with pleasure; and I find a satisfaction in enjoying them at this distance, though but in imagination.

You descended from the house between two groves of trees, planted in such a manner, that they were impenetrable to the eye; while on each hand the way was adorned with all that was beautiful in porcelain, statuary, and painting. This passage from the house opened into an area surrounded with rocks, flowers, trees, and shrubs, but all so disposed as if each was the spontaneous production of nature. As you proceeded forward on this lawn, to your right and left hand were two gates, opposite each other, of very different architecture and design; and before you lay a temple, built rather with minute elegance than ostentation.

The right hand gate was planned with the utmost simplicity, or rather rudeness: ivy clasped round the pillars, the baleful cypress hung over it; time seemed to have destroyed all the smoothness and regularity of the stone; two champions, with lifted clubs, appeared in the act of guarding its access; dragons and serpents were seen in the most hideous attitudes, to deter the spectator from approaching; and the perspective view that lay behind seemed dark and gloomy to the last degree; the stranger was tempted to enter only from the motto,—PERVIA VIRTUTI.

The opposite gate was formed in a very different manner: the architecture was light, elegant, and inviting; flowers hung in wreaths round the pillars; all was finished in the most exact and masterly manner; the very stone of which it was built still preserved its polish; nymphs, wrought by the hand of a master, in the most alluring attitudes, beckoned the stranger to approach; while all that lay behind, as far as the eye could reach, seemed gay, luxuriant, and capable of affording endless pleasure. The motto itself contributed to invite him; for over the gate were written these words,—FACILIS DESCENSUS.

By this time I fancy you begin to perceive that the gloomy gate was designed to represent the road to Virtue, the opposite the more agreeable passage to Vice. It is but natural to suppose, that the spectator was always tempted to enter by the gate which offered him so many allurements. I always in these cases left him to his choice; but generally found that he took to the left, which promised most entertainment.

Immediately upon his entering the gate of Vice the trees and flowers were disposed in such a manner as to make the most pleasing impression; but, as he walked farther on, he insensibly found the garden assume the air of a wilderness,—the landscapes began to darken—the paths grew more intricate—he appeared to go downwards—frightful rocks seemed to hang over his head—gloomy caverns, unexpected precipices, awful ruins, heaps of unburied bones, and terrifying sounds, caused by unseen waters, began to take place of what at first appeared so lovely: it was in vain to attempt returning; the labyrinth was too much perplexed for any but myself to find the way back. In short, when sufficiently impressed with the horrors of what he saw, and the imprudence of his choice, I brought him by a hidden door a shorter way back into the area from whence at first he had strayed.

The gloomy gate now presented itself before the stranger; and though there seemed little in its appearance to tempt his curiosity, yet, encouraged by the motto, he gradually proceeded. The darkness of the entrance, the frightful figures that seemed to obstruct his way, the trees of a mournful green, conspired at first to disgust him: as he went forward, however, all began to open and wear a more pleasing appearance; beautiful cascades, beds of flowers, trees loaded with fruit or blossoms, and unexpected brooks, improved the scene; he now found that he was ascending, and as he proceeded all nature grew more beautiful; the prospect widened as he went higher; even the air itself seemed to become more pure. Thus, pleased and happy from unexpected beauties, I at last led him to an arbour, from whence he could view the garden and the whole country around, and where he might own, that the road to Virtue terminated in Happiness.

Though from this description you may imagine that a vast tract of ground was necessary to exhibit such a pleasing variety in, yet, be assured, I have seen several gardens in England take up ten times the space which mine did, without half the beauty. A very small extent of ground is enough for an elegant taste; the greater room is required if magnificence is in view. There is no spot, though ever so little, which a skilful designer might not thus improve, so as to convey a delicate allegory, and impress the mind with truths the most useful and necessary.—Adieu.

LETTER XXXII.

To the same.

IN a late excursion with my friend into the country, a gentleman with a blue riband tied round his shoulder, and in a chariot drawn by six horses, passed swiftly by us, attended with a numerous train of captains, lackeys, and coaches filled with women. When we were recovered from the dust raised by this cavalcade, and could continue our discourse without danger of suffocation, I observed to my companion, that all this state and equipage, which he seemed to despise, would in China be regarded with the utmost reverence, because such distinctions were always the reward of merit; the greatness of a mandarine's retinue being a most certain mark of the superiority of his abilities or virtue.

"The gentleman who has now passed us," replied my companion, "has no claims from his own merit to distinction; he is possessed neither of abilities nor virtue; it is enough for him that one of his ancestors was possessed of these qualities two hundred years before him. There was a time, indeed, when his family deserved their title; but they are long since degenerated, and his ancestors, for more than a century, have been more and more solicitous to keep up the breed of their dogs and horses, than that of their children. This very nobleman, simple as he seems, is descended from a race of statesmen and heroes; but unluckily, his great-grandfather marrying a cook-maid, and she having a trifling passion for his lordship's groom, they somehow crossed the strain, and produced an heir, who took after his mother in his great love to good eating, and his father in a violent affection for horse-flesh. These passions have for some generations passed on from father to son, and are now become the characteristics of the family, his present lordship being equally remarkable for his kitchen and his stable."

"But such a nobleman," cried I, "deserves our pity, thus placed in so high a sphere of life, which only the more exposes to contempt. A king may confer titles, but it is personal merit alone that ensures respect. I suppose," added I, "that such men are despised by their equals, neglected by their inferiors, and condemned to live among involuntary dependants in irksome solitude."

"You are still under a mistake," replied my companion, "for, though this nobleman is a stranger to generosity; though he takes twenty opportunities in a day of letting his guests know how much he despises them; though he is possessed neither of taste, wit, nor wisdom; though incapable of improving others by his conversation, and never known to enrich any by his bounty; yet, for all this, his company is eagerly sought after: he is a lord, and that is as much as most people desire in a companion. Quality and title have such allurements, that hundreds are ready to give up all their own importance, to cringe, to flatter, to look little, and to pall every pleasure in constraint, merely to be among the great, though without the least hopes of improving their understanding, or sharing their generosity: they might be happy among their equals, but those are despised for company where they are despised in turn. You saw what a crowd of humble cousins, card-ruined beaux, and captains on half-pay, were willing to make up this great man's retinue down to his country seat. Not one of all these that could not lead a more comfortable life at home, in their little lodging of three shillings a week, with their lukewarm dinner, served up between two pewter plates from a cook's shop. Yet, poor devils! they are willing to undergo the impertinence and pride of their entertainer, merely to be thought to live among the great; they are willing to pass the summer in bondage, though conscious they are taken down only to approve his lordship's taste upon every occasion, to tag all his stupid observations with a 'very true,' to praise his stable, and descant upon his claret and cookery."

"The pitiful humiliations of the gentlemen you are now describing," said I, "put me in mind of a custom among the Tartars of Koreki, not entirely dissimilar to this we are now considering. The Russians, who trade with them, carry thither a kind of mushrooms, which they exchange for furs of squirrels, ermines, sables, and foxes. These mushrooms the rich Tartars lay up in large quantities for the winter; and when a nobleman makes a mushroom feast, all the neighbours around are invited. The mushrooms are prepared by boiling, by which the water acquires an intoxicating quality, and is a sort of drink which the Tartars prize beyond all other. When the nobility and ladies are assembled, and the ceremonies usual between people of distinction over, the mushroom broth goes freely round; they laugh, talk *double entendre*, grow fuddled, and become excellent company. The poorer sort, who love mushroom broth to distraction as well as the rich, but cannot afford it at the first hand, post themselves on these occasions round the huts of the rich, and watch the opportunity of the ladies and gentlemen as they come down to pass their liquor; and holding a wooden bowl, catch the delicious fluid, very little altered by filtration, being still strongly tinctured with the intoxicating quality. Of this they drink with the utmost satisfaction, and thus they get as drunk and as jovial as their betters."

"Happy nobility!" cries my companion, "who can fear no diminution of respect, unless by being seized with strangury, and who when most drunk are most useful! Though we have not this custom among us, I foresee, that if it were introduced we might have many a toad-eater in England ready to drink from the wooden bowl on these occasions, and to praise the flavour of his lordship's liquor. As we have different classes of gentry, who knows but we may see a lord holding the bowl to a minister, a knight holding it to his lordship, and a simple squire drinking it double distilled from the loins of the knighthood? For my part, I shall never for the future hear a great man's flatterers haranguing in his praise, that I shall not fancy I behold the wooden bowl; for I can see no reason why a man, who can live easily and happily at home, should bear the drudgery of decorum and the impertinence of his entertainer, unless intoxicated with a passion for all that was quality; unless he thought that whatever came from the great was delicious, and had the tincture of the mushroom in it."—Adieu.

LETTER XXXIII.

To the same.

I AM disgusted, O Fum Hoam! even to sickness disgusted! Is it possible to bear the presumption of these Islanders, when they pretend to instruct me in the ceremonies of China? They lay it down as a maxim, that every person who comes from thence must express himself in metaphor, swear by Alla, rail against wine, and behave, and talk, and write, like a Turk or Persian. They make no distinction between our elegant manners and the voluptuous barbarities of our Eastern neighbours. Wherever I come, I raise either diffidence or astonishment: some fancy me no Chinese, because I am formed more like a man than a monster; and others wonder to find one born five thousand miles from England endued with common sense. "Strange," say they, "that a man who has received his education at such a distance from London should have common sense; to be born out of England, and yet have common sense! Impossible! He must be some Englishman in disguise; his very visage has nothing of the true exotic barbarity."

I yesterday received an invitation from a lady of distinction, who, it seems, had collected all her knowledge of Eastern manners from fictions every day propagated here, under the titles of Eastern tales and Oriental histories. She received me very politely, but seemed to wonder that I neglected bringing opium and a tobacco box: when chairs were drawn for the rest of the company, I was assigned my place on a cushion on the floor. It was in vain that I protested the Chinese used chairs, as in Europe; she understood decorum too well to entertain me with the ordinary civilities.

I had scarcely been seated according to her directions, when the footman was ordered to pin a napkin under my chin: this I protested against, as being no way Chinese; however, the whole company, who, it seems, were a club of connoisseurs, gave it unanimously against me, and the napkin was pinned accordingly.

It was impossible to be angry with people who seemed to err only from an excess of politeness, and I sat contented, expecting their importunities were now at an end; but, as soon as ever dinner was served, the lady demanded whether I was for a plate of bear's claws, or a slice of birds' nests. As these were dishes with which I was utterly unacquainted, I was desirous of eating only what I knew, and therefore begged to be helped from a piece of beef that lay on the side table: my request at once disconcerted the whole company. A Chinese eat beef! that could never be: there was no local propriety in Chinese beef, whatever there might be in Chinese pheasant. "Sir," said my entertainer, "I think I have some reason to fancy myself a judge of these matters; in short, the Chinese never eat beef; so that I must be permitted to recommend the pilaw. There was never better dressed at Pekin; the saffron and rice are well boiled, and the spices in perfection."

I had no sooner begun to eat what was laid before me, than I found the whole company as much astonished as before; it seems I made no use of my chop-sticks. A grave gentleman, whom I take to be an author, harangued very learnedly (as the company seemed to think) upon the use which was made of them in China. He entered into a long argument with himself about their first introduction, without once appealing to me, who might be supposed best capable of silencing the inquiry. As the gentleman therefore took my silence for a mark of his own superior sagacity, he was resolved to pursue the triumph: he talked of our cities, mountains, and animals as familiarly as if he had been born in Quamsi, but as erroneously as if a native of the moon. He attempted to prove that I had nothing of the true Chinese cut in my visage; showed that my high cheekbones should have been higher, and my forehead broader. In short, he almost reasoned me out of my country, and effectually persuaded the rest of the company to be of his opinion.

I was going to expose his mistakes, when it was insisted, that I had nothing of the true Eastern manner in my delivery. "This gentleman's conversation," says one of the ladies, who was a great reader, "is like our own,—mere chit-chat and common sense: there is nothing like sense in the true Eastern style, where nothing more is required but sublimity. Oh! for a history of Aboulfaouris, the grand voyager, of genii, magicians, rocks, bags of bullets, giants, and enchanters, where all is great, obscure, magnificent, and unintelligible."—"I have written many a sheet of Eastern tale myself," interrupts the author, "and I defy the severest critic to say but that I have stuck close to the true manner. I have compared a lady's chin to the snow upon the mountains of Bomek; a soldier's sword to the clouds that obscure the face of heaven. If riches are mentioned, I compare them to the flocks that graze the verdant Tefflis; if poverty, to the mists that veil the brow of Mount Baku. I have used *thee* and *thou* upon all occasions; I have described fallen stars and splitting mountains, not forgetting the little houris, who make a pretty figure in every description. But you shall hear how I generally begin—'Eben-benbolo, who was the son of Ban, was born on the foggy summits of Benderabassi. His beard was whiter than the feathers which veil the breast of the penguin; his eyes were like the eyes of doves when washed by the dews of the morning; his hair, which hung like the willow weeping over the glossy stream, was so beautiful that it seemed to reflect its own brightness; and his feet were as the feet of a wild deer which fleeth to the tops of the mountains.' There, there is the true Eastern taste for you; every advance made towards sense is only a deviation from sound. Eastern tales should always be sonorous, lofty, musical, and unmeaning."

I could not avoid smiling, to hear a native of England attempt to instruct me in the true Eastern idiom; and after he looked round some time for applause, I presumed to ask him, whether he had ever travelled into the East; to which he replied in the negative. I demanded whether he understood Chinese or Arabic; to which also he answered as before. "Then how, sir," said I, "can you pretend to determine upon the Eastern style, who are entirely unacquainted with the Eastern writings? Take, sir, the word of one who is professedly a Chinese, and who is actually acquainted with the Arabian writers, that what is palmed upon you daily for an imitation of Eastern writing no way resembles their manner, either in sentiment or diction. In the East similes are seldom used, and metaphors almost wholly unknown; but in China particularly, the very reverse of what you allude to takes place: a cool phlegmatic method of writing prevails there. The writers of that country, ever more assiduous to instruct than to please, address rather the judgment than the fancy. Unlike many authors of Europe, who have no consideration of the reader's time, they generally leave more to be understood than they express.

"Besides, sir, you must not expect from an inhabitant of China the same ignorance, the same unlettered simplicity, that you find in a Turk, Persian, or native of Peru. The Chinese are versed in the sciences as well as you, and are masters of several arts unknown to the people of Europe. Many of them are instructed not only in their own national learning, but are perfectly well acquainted with the languages and learning of the West. If my word in such a case is not to be taken, consult your own travellers on this head, who affirm, that the scholars of Pekin and Siam sustain theological theses in Latin. 'The college of Masprend, which is but a league from Siam,' says one of your travellers, 'came in a body to salute our ambassador. Nothing gave me more sincere pleasure, than to behold a number of priests, venerable both from age and modesty, followed by a number of youths of all nations, Chinese, Japanese, Tonquinese, of Cochin China, Pegu, and Siam, all willing to pay their respects in the most polite manner imaginable. A Cochin Chinese made an excellent Latin oration upon this occasion; he was succeeded, and even outdone, by a student of Tonquin, who was as well skilled in the Western learning as any scholar of Paris.' Now, sir, if youths who never stirred from home are so perfectly skilled in your laws and learning, surely more must be expected from one like me, who have travelled so many thousand miles; who have conversed familiarly for several years with the English factors established at Canton and the missionaries sent us from every part of Europe. The unaffected of every country nearly resemble each other, and a page of our Confucius and of your Tillotson have scarce any material difference. Paltry affectation, strained allusions, and disgusting finery are easily attained by those who choose to wear them: and they are but too frequently the badges of ignorance or of stupidity, whenever it would endeavour to please."

I was proceeding in my discourse, when, looking round, I perceived the company no way attentive to what I attempted, with so much earnestness, to enforce. One lady was whispering her that sat next, another was studying the merits of a fan, a third began to yawn, and the author himself fell fast asleep. I thought it, therefore, high time to make a retreat; nor did the company seem to show any regret at my preparations for departure: even the lady who had invited me, with the most mortifying insensibility, saw me seize my hat, and rise from my cushion; nor was I invited to repeat my visit, because it was found that I aimed at appearing rather a reasonable creature, than an outlandish idiot.—Adieu.

LETTER XXXIV.

To the same.

THE polite arts are in this country subject to as many revolutions as its laws or politics: not only the objects of fancy and dress, but even of delicacy and taste, are directed by the capricious influence of fashion. I am told there has been a time when poetry was universally encouraged by the great; when men of the first rank not only patronised the poet, but produced the finest models for his imitation. It was then the English sent forth those glowing rhapsodies, which we have so often read over together with rapture; poems big with all the sublimity of Mencius, and supported by reasoning as strong as that of Zimpo.

The nobility are fond of wisdom, but they are also fond of having it without study; to read poetry required thought; and the English nobility were not fond of thinking: they soon therefore placed their affections upon music, because in this they might indulge a happy vacancy, and yet still have pretensions to delicacy and taste as before. They soon brought their numerous dependants into an approbation of their pleasures; who, in turn, led their thousand imitators to feel or feign similitude of passion. Colonies of singers were now imported from abroad at a vast expense; and it was expected the English would soon be able to set examples to Europe. All these expectations, however, were soon dissipated. In spite of the zeal which fired the great, the ignorant vulgar refused to be taught to sing; refused to undergo the ceremonies which were to initiate them in the singing fraternity: thus the colony from abroad dwindled by degrees; for they were of themselves unfortunately incapable of propagating the breed.

Music having thus lost its splendour, painting is now become the sole object of fashionable care. The title of connoisseur in that art is at present the safest passport in every fashionable society; a well-timed shrug, an admiring attitude, and one or two exotic tones of exclamation, are sufficient qualifications for men of low circumstances to curry favour. Even some of the young nobility are themselves early instructed in handling the pencil, while their happy parents, big with expectation, foresee the walls of every apartment covered with the manufactures of their posterity.

But many of the English are not content with giving all their time to this art at home; some young men of distinction are found to travel through Europe, with no other intent than that of understanding and collecting pictures, studying seals, and describing statues. On they travel from this cabinet of curiosities to that gallery of pictures; waste the prime of life in wonder; skilful in pictures, ignorant in men; yet impossible to be reclaimed, because their follies take shelter under the names of delicacy and taste.

It is true, painting should have due encouragement; as the painter can undoubtedly fit up our apartments in a much more elegant manner than the upholsterer: but I should think a man of fashion makes but an indifferent exchange, who lays out all that time in furnishing his house, which he should have employed in the furniture of his head. A person who shows no other symptoms of taste than his cabinet or gallery, might as well boast to me of the furniture of his kitchen.

I know no other motive but vanity, that induces the great to testify such an inordinate passion for pictures. After the piece is bought, and gazed at eight or ten days successively, the purchaser's pleasure must surely be over; all the satisfaction he can then have is to show it to others; he may be considered as the guardian of a treasure of which he makes no manner of use; his gallery is furnished, not for himself, but the connoisseur, who is generally some humble flatterer, ready to feign a rapture he does not feel, and as necessary to the happiness of a picture buyer, as gazers are to the magnificence of an Asiatic procession.

I have enclosed a letter from a youth of distinction, on his travels, to his father in England; in which he appears addicted to no vice, seems obedient to his governor, of a good natural disposition, and fond of improvement; but, at the same time, early taught to regard cabinets and galleries as the only proper schools of improvement, and to consider a skill in pictures as the properest knowledge for a man of quality.

"MY LORD,—We have been but two days at Antwerp; wherefore I have sat down, as soon as possible, to give you some account of what we have seen since our arrival, desirous of letting no opportunity pass without writing to so good a father. Immediately upon alighting from our Rotterdam machine, my governor, who is immoderately fond of paintings, and at the same time an excellent judge, would let no time pass till we paid our respects to the church of the Virgin Mother, which contains treasure beyond estimation. We took an infinity of pains in knowing its exact dimensions, and differed half a foot in our calculation; so I leave that to some succeeding information. I really believe my governor and I could have lived and died there. There is scarce a pillar in the whole church that is not adorned by a Rubens, a Vander Meuylen, a Vandyke, or a Wouverman. What attitudes, carnations, and draperies! I am almost induced to pity the English, who have none of those exquisite pieces among them. As we were willing to let slip no opportunity of doing business, we immediately after went to wait on Mr. Hogendorp, whom you have so frequently commended for his judicious collection. His cameos are indeed beyond price; his intaglios not so good. He showed us one of an officiating Flamen, which he thought to be an antique; but my governor, who is not to be deceived in these particulars, soon found it out to be an arrant *cinque cento*. I could not, however, sufficiently admire the genius of Mr. Hogendorp, who has been able to collect, from all parts of the world, a thousand things which nobody knows the use of. Except your Lordship and my governor, I do not know anybody I admire so much. He is, indeed, a surprising genius. The next morning early, as we were resolved to take the whole day before us, we sent our compliments to Mr. Van Sprockken, desiring to see his gallery, which request he very politely complied with. His gallery measures fifty feet by twenty, and is well filled; but what surprised me most of all was to see a Holy Family just like your Lordship's, which this ingenious gentleman assures me is the true original. I own this gave me inexpressible uneasiness, and I fear it will to your Lordship, as I had flattered myself that the only original was in your Lordship's possession. I would advise you, however, to take yours down, till its merit can be ascertained, my governor assuring me, that he intends to write a long dissertation to prove its originality. One might study in this city for ages, and still find something new. We went from this to view the cardinal's statues, which are really very fine; there were three spintria executed in a very masterly manner, all arm in arm: the torse which I heard you talk so much of is at last discovered to be a Hercules spinning, and not a Cleopatra bathing, as your Lordship had conjectured: there has been a treatise written to prove it.

"My Lord Firmly is certainly a Goth, a Vandal; no taste in the world for painting. I wonder how any call him a man of taste. Passing through the streets of Antwerp a few days ago, and observing the nakedness of the inhabitants, he was so barbarous as to observe that he thought the best method the Flemings could take was to sell their pictures, and buy clothes. Ah, Coglione! We shall go to-morrow to Mr. Carwarden's cabinet, and the next day we shall see the curiosities collected by Van Ran, and the day after we shall pay a visit to Mount Calvary, and after that—but I find my paper finished; so, with the most sincere wishes for your Lordship's happiness, and with hopes, after having seen Italy, that centre of pleasure, to return home worthy the care and expense which has been generously laid out in my improvement, I remain, my Lord, yours," &c.

LETTER XXXV.

From Hingpo, a Slave in Persia, to Altangi, a travelling Philosopher of China, by the way of Moscow.

FORTUNE has made me the slave of another, but nature and inclination render me entirely subservient to you: a tyrant commands my body, but you are master of my heart. And yet let not thy inflexible nature condemn me when I confess, that I find my soul shrink with my circumstances. I feel my mind, not less than my body, bend beneath the rigours of servitude; the master whom I serve grows every day more formidable. In spite of reason, which should teach me to despise him, his hideous image fills even my dreams with horror.

A few days ago a Christian slave, who wrought in the gardens, happening to enter an arbour where the tyrant was entertaining the ladies of his harem with coffee, the unhappy captive was instantly stabbed to the heart for his intrusion. I have been preferred to his place, which, though less laborious than my former station, is yet more ungrateful, as it brings me nearer him whose presence excites sensations at once of disgust and apprehension.

Into what a state of misery are the modern Persians fallen! A nation famous for setting the world an example of freedom is now become a land of tyrants, and a den of slaves. The houseless Tartar of Kamschatka, who enjoys his herbs and his fish in unmolested freedom, may be envied, if compared to the thousands who pine here in hopeless servitude, and curse the day that gave them being. Is this just dealing, Heaven! to render millions wretched to swell up the happiness of a few? cannot the powerful of this earth be happy without our sighs and tears? must every luxury of the great be woven from the calamities of the poor? It must, it must surely, be that this jarring discordant life is but the prelude to some future harmony: the soul, attuned to virtue here, shall go from hence to fill up the universal choir where Tien presides in person, where there shall be no tyrants to frown, no shackles to bind, nor no whips to threaten; where I shall once more meet my father with rapture, and give a loose to filial piety; where I shall hang on his neck, and hear the wisdom of his lips, and thank him for all the happiness to which he has introduced me.

The wretch whom fortune has made my master has lately purchased several slaves of both sexes; among the rest, I hear, a Christian captive talked of with admiration. The eunuch who bought her, and who is accustomed to survey beauty with indifference, speaks of her with emotion. Her pride, however, astonishes her attendant slaves not less than her beauty. It is reported that she refuses the warmest solicitations of her haughty lord: he has even offered to make her one of his four wives upon changing her religion, and conforming to his. It is probable she cannot refuse such extraordinary offers, and her delay is perhaps intended to enhance her favours.

I have just now seen her; she inadvertently approached the place, without a veil, where I sat writing. She seemed to regard the heavens alone with fixed attention: there her most ardent gaze was directed. Genius of the sun! what unexpected softness! what animated grace! her beauty seemed the transparent covering of virtue. Celestial beings could not wear a look of more perfection, while sorrow humanized her form, and mixed my admiration with pity. I rose from the bank on which I sat, and she retired: happy that none observed us; for such an interview might have been fatal.

I have regarded, till now, the opulence and the power of my tyrant without envy. I saw him with a mind incapable of enjoying the gifts of fortune, and consequently regarded him as one loaded, rather than enriched, with its favours; but at present, when I think that so much beauty is reserved only for him; that so many charms should be lavished on a wretch incapable of feeling the greatness of the blessing,—I own I feel a reluctance to which I have hitherto been a stranger.

But let not my father impute those uneasy sensations to so trifling a cause as love. No; never let it be thought that your son, and the pupil of the wise Fum Hoam, could stoop to so degrading a passion: I am only displeased at seeing so much excellence so unjustly disposed of.

The uneasiness which I feel is not for myself, but for the beautiful Christian. When I reflect on the barbarity of him for whom she is designed, I pity, indeed I pity her: when I think that she must only share one heart, who deserves to command a thousand, excuse me if I feel an emotion, which universal benevolence extorts from me. As I am convinced that you take a pleasure in those sallies of humanity, and are particularly pleased with compassion, I could not avoid discovering the sensibility with which I felt this beautiful stranger's distress. I have for a while forgot, in hers, the miseries of my own hopeless situation: the tyrant grows every day more severe; and love, which softens all other minds into tenderness, seems only to have increased his severity.—Adieu.

LETTER XXXVI.

From the same.

THE whole harem is filled with a tumultuous joy; Zelis, the beautiful captive, has consented to embrace the religion of Mahomet, and become one of the wives of the fastidious Persian. It is impossible to describe the transport that sits on every face on this occasion. Music and feasting fill every apartment; the most miserable slave seems to forget his chains, and sympathises with the happiness of Mostadad. The herb we tread beneath our feet is not made more for our use than every slave around him for their imperious master; mere machines of obedience, they wait with silent assiduity, feel his pains, and rejoice in his exultation. Heavens! how much is requisite to make one man happy!

Twelve of the most beautiful slaves, and I among the number, have got orders to prepare for carrying him in triumph to the bridal apartment. The blaze of perfumed torches are to imitate the day: the dancers and singers are hired at a vast expense. The nuptials are to be celebrated on the approaching feast of Barboura, when an hundred taels in gold are to be distributed among the barren wives, in order to pray for fertility from the approaching union.

What will not riches procure? An hundred domestics, who curse the tyrant in their souls, are commanded to wear a face of joy, and they are joyful. An hundred flatterers are ordered to attend, and they fill his ears with praise. Beauty, all-commanding beauty, sues for admittance, and scarcely receives an answer; even love itself seems to wait upon fortune; or though the passion be only feigned, yet it wears every appearance of sincerity; and what greater pleasure can even true sincerity confer, or what would the rich have more?

Nothing can exceed the intended magnificence of the bridegroom but the costly dresses of the bride: six eunuchs in the most sumptuous habits are to conduct him to the nuptial couch, and wait his orders. Six ladies, in all the magnificence of Persia, are directed to undress the bride. Their business is to assist, to encourage her, to divest her of every encumbering part of her dress, all but the last covering, which, by an artful complication of ribands, is purposely made difficult to unloose, and with which she is to part reluctantly even to the joyful possessor of her beauty.

Mostadad, O my father, is no philosopher; and yet he seems perfectly contented with ignorance. Possessed of numberless slaves, camels, and women, he desires no greater possession. He never opened the page of Mencius, and yet all the slaves tell me that he is happy.

Forgive the weakness of my nature, if I sometimes feel my heart rebellious to the dictates of wisdom, and eager for happiness like his. Yet why wish for his wealth, with his ignorance? to be, like him, incapable of sentimental pleasures, incapable of feeling the happiness of making others happy, incapable of teaching the beautiful Zelis philosophy?

What! shall I in a transport of passion give up the golden mean, the universal harmony, the unchanging essence, for the possession of an hundred camels, as many slaves, thirty-five beautiful horses, and seventy-three fine women. First blast me to the centre! degrade me beneath the most degraded! pare my nails, ye powers of Heaven! ere I would stoop to such an exchange. What! part with philosophy, which teaches me to suppress my passions, instead of gratifying them, which teaches me even to divest my soul of passion, which teaches serenity in the midst of tortures; philosophy, by which even now I am so very serene, and so very much at ease, to be persuaded to part with it for any other enjoyment! Never, never, even though persuasion spoke in the accents of Zelis!

A female slave informs me that the bride is to be arrayed in a tissue of silver, and her hair adorned with the largest pearls of Ormus. But why tease you with particulars, in which we both are so little concerned? The pain I feel in separation throws a gloom over my mind, which in this scene of universal joy I fear may be attributed to some other cause: how wretched are those who are, like me, denied even the last resource of misery,—their tears!—Adieu.

LETTER XXXVII.

From the same.

I BEGIN to have doubts whether wisdom be alone sufficient to make us happy: whether every step we make in refinement is not an inlet into new disquietudes. A mind too vigorous and active serves only to consume the body to which it is joined, as the richest jewels are soonest found to wear their settings.

When we rise in knowledge, as the prospect widens, the objects of our regard become more obscure: and the unlettered peasant, whose views are only directed to the narrow sphere around him, beholds Nature with a finer relish, and tastes her blessings with a keener appetite, than the philosopher whose mind attempts to grasp an universal system.

As I was some days ago pursuing this subject among a circle of my fellow-slaves, an ancient Guebre of the number, equally remarkable for his piety and wisdom, seemed touched with my conversation, and desired to illustrate what I had been saying with an allegory taken from the Zendavesta of Zoroaster: "By this we shall be taught," says he, "that they who travel in pursuit of wisdom walk only in a circle; and after all their labour, at last return to their pristine ignorance: and in this also we shall see, that enthusiastic confidence or unsatisfying doubts terminate all our inquiries.

"In early times, before myriads of nations covered the earth, the whole human race lived together in one valley. The simple inhabitants, surrounded on every side by lofty mountains, knew no other world but the little spot to which they were confined. They fancied the heavens bent down to meet the mountain tops, and formed an impenetrable wall to surround them. None had ever yet ventured to climb the steepy cliff, in order to explore those regions that lay beyond it; they knew the nature of the skies only from a tradition, which mentioned their being made of adamant: traditions make up the reasonings of the simple, and serve to silence every inquiry.

"In this sequestered vale, blessed with all the spontaneous productions of Nature, the honeyed blossom, the refreshing breeze, the gliding brook, and golden fruitage, the simple inhabitants seemed happy in themselves, in each other; they desired no greater pleasure, for they knew of none greater; ambition, pride, and envy, were vices unknown among them; and from this peculiar simplicity of its possessors the country was called THE VALLEY OF IGNORANCE.

"At length, however, an unhappy youth, more aspiring than the rest, undertook to climb the mountain's side, and examine the summits which were hitherto deemed inaccessible. The inhabitants from below gazed with wonder at his intrepidity; some applauded his courage, others censured his folly: still, however, he proceeded towards the place where the earth and heavens seemed to unite, and at length arrived at the wished-for height with extreme labour and assiduity.

"His first surprise was to find the skies not, as he expected, within his reach, but still as far off as before. His amazement increased when he saw a wide-extended region lying on the opposite side of the mountain; but it rose to astonishment when he beheld a country, at a distance, more beautiful and alluring than even that he had just left behind.

"As he continued to gaze with wonder, a Genius with a look of infinite modesty, approaching, offered to be his guide and instructor. 'The distant country which you so much admire,' says the angelic being, 'is called the LAND OF CERTAINTY: in that charming retreat sentiment contributes to refine every sensual banquet; the inhabitants are blessed with every solid enjoyment, and still more blessed in a perfect consciousness of their own felicity: ignorance in that country is wholly unknown; all there is satisfaction without alloy, for every pleasure first undergoes the examination of reason. As for me, I am called the Genius of Demonstration, and am stationed here in order to conduct every adventurer to that land of happiness, through those intervening regions you see overhung with fogs and darkness, and horrid with forests, cataracts, caverns, and various other shapes of danger. But follow me, and in time I may lead you to that distant desirable land of tranquillity.

"The intrepid traveller immediately put himself under the direction of the Genius, and both journeying on together with a slow but agreeable pace, deceived the tediousness of the way by conversation. The beginning of the journey seemed to promise true satisfaction, but, as they proceeded forward, the skies became more gloomy and the way more intricate; they often inadvertently approached the brow of some frightful precipice, or the brink of a torrent, and were obliged to measure back their former way: the gloom increasing as they proceeded, their pace became more slow; they paused at every step, frequently stumbled, and their distrust and timidity increased. The Genius of Demonstration now therefore advised his pupil to grope upon hands and feet, as a method, though more slow, yet less liable to error.

"In this manner they attempted to pursue their journey for some time, when they were overtaken by another Genius, who with a precipitate pace seemed travelling the same way. He was instantly known by the other to be the Genius of Probability. He wore two wide-extended wings at his back, which incessantly waved, without increasing the rapidity of his motion; his countenance betrayed a confidence that the ignorant might mistake for sincerity, and he had but one eye, which was fixed in the middle of his forehead.

"'Servant of Hormizda,' cried he, approaching the mortal pilgrim, 'if thou art travelling to the LAND OF CERTAINTY, how is it possible to arrive there under the guidance of a Genius, who proceeds forward so slowly, and is so little acquainted with the way? Follow me, we shall soon perform the journey to where every pleasure waits our arrival.'

"The peremptory tone in which this Genius spoke, and the speed with which he moved forward, induced the traveller to change his conductor, and leaving his modest companion behind, he proceeded forward with his more confident director, seeming not a little pleased at the increased velocity of his motion.

"But soon he found reason to repent. Whenever a torrent crossed their way, his guide taught him to despise the obstacle by plunging him in; whenever a precipice presented, he was directed to fling himself forward. Thus each moment miraculously escaping, his repeated escapes only served to increase his guide's temerity. He led him, therefore, forward, amidst infinite difficulties, till they arrived at the borders of an ocean, which appeared unnavigable from the black mists that lay upon its surface. Its unquiet waves were of the darkest hue, and gave a lively representation of the various agitations of the human mind.

"The Genius of Probability now confessed his temerity; owned his being an improper guide to the LAND OF CERTAINTY, a country where no mortal had ever been permitted to arrive; but, at the same time, offered to supply the traveller with another conductor, who should carry him to the LAND OF CONFIDENCE, a region where the inhabitants lived with the utmost tranquillity, and tasted almost as much satisfaction as if in the LAND OF CERTAINTY. Not waiting for a reply, he stamped three times on the ground, and called forth the Demon of Error, a gloomy fiend of the servants of Arimanes. The yawning earth gave up the reluctant savage, who seemed unable to bear the light of the day. His stature was enormous, his colour black and hideous, his aspect betrayed a thousand varying passions, and he spread forth pinions that were fitted for the most rapid flight. The traveller at first was shocked at the spectre; but, finding him obedient to a superior power, he assumed his former tranquillity.

"'I have called you to duty,' cries the Genius to the Demon; 'to bear on your back a son of mortality over the OCEAN OF DOUBTS, into the LAND OF CONFIDENCE; I expect you will perform your commission with punctuality. And as for you,' continued the Genius, addressing the traveller, 'when once I have bound this fillet round your eyes, let no voice of persuasion, nor threats the most terrifying, induce you to unbind it, in order to look round; keep the fillet fast, look not at the ocean below, and you may certainly expect to arrive at a region of pleasure.'

"Thus saying, and the traveller's eyes being covered, the Demon, muttering curses, raised him on his back, and instantly, upborne by his strong pinions, directed his flight among the clouds. Neither the loudest thunder, nor the most angry tempest, could persuade the traveller to unbind his eyes. The Demon directed his flight downwards, and skimmed the surface of the ocean; a thousand voices, some with loud invectives, others in the sarcastic tones of contempt, vainly endeavoured to persuade him to look round; but he still continued to keep his eyes covered, and would in all probability have arrived at the happy land, had not flattery effected what other means could not perform. For now he heard himself welcomed on every side to the promised land, and an universal shout of joy was sent forth at his safe arrival. The wearied traveller, desirous of seeing the long wished for country, at length pulled the fillet from his eyes, and ventured to look round him. But he had unloosed the band too soon; he was not yet above half way over. The Demon, who was still hovering in the air, and had produced those sounds only in order to deceive, was now freed from his commission; wherefore, throwing the astonished traveller from his back, the unhappy youth fell headlong into the subjacent OCEAN OF DOUBTS, from whence he never after was seen to rise."

LETTER XXXVIII.

From Lien Chi Altangi to Fum Hoam, First President of the Ceremonial Academy at Pekin in China.

WHEN Parmenio, the Grecian, had done something which excited a universal shout from the surrounding multitude, he was instantly struck with the doubt, that what had their approbation must certainly be wrong; and turning to a philosopher who stood near him, "Pray, sir," says he, "pardon me; I fear I have been guilty of some absurdity."

You know that I am, not less than him, a despiser of the multitude; you know that I equally detest flattery to the great: yet so many circumstances have concurred to give a lustre to the latter part of the present English monarch's reign, that I cannot withhold my contribution of praise; I cannot avoid acknowledging the crowd, for once, just in their unanimous approbation.

Yet think not that battles gained, dominion extended, or enemies brought to submission, are the virtues which at present claim my admiration. Were the reigning monarch only famous for his victories, I should regard his character with indifference: the boast of heroism in this enlightened age is justly regarded as a qualification of a very subordinate rank, and mankind now begin to look with becoming horror on these foes to man. The virtue in this aged monarch which I have at present in view is one of a much more exalted nature, is one of the most difficult attainment, is the least praised of all kingly virtues, and yet deserves the greatest praise; the virtue I mean is JUSTICE,—a strict administration of justice, without severity and without favour.

Of all virtues this is the most difficult to be practised by a king who has a power to pardon. All men, even tyrants themselves, lean to mercy when unbiassed by passions or interest; the heart naturally persuades to forgiveness, and pursuing the dictates of this pleasing deceiver, we are led to prefer our private satisfaction to public utility. What a thorough love for the public, what a strong command over the passions, what a finely-conducted judgment, must he possess, who opposes the dictates of reason to those of his heart, and prefers the future interest of his people to his own immediate satisfaction!

If still to a man's own natural bias for tenderness we add the numerous solicitations made by a criminal's friends for mercy; if we survey a king not only opposing his own feelings, but reluctantly refusing those he regards, and this to satisfy the public, whose cries he may never hear, whose gratitude he may never receive; this surely is true greatness! Let us fancy ourselves for a moment in this just old man's place; surrounded by numbers, all soliciting the same favour—a favour that nature disposes us to grant, where the inducements to pity are laid before us in the strongest light, suppliants at our feet, some ready to resent a refusal, none opposing a compliance; let us, I say, suppose ourselves in such a situation, and I fancy we should find ourselves more apt to act the character of good-natured men than of upright magistrates.

What contributes to raise justice above all other kingly virtues is, that it is seldom attended with a due share of applause, and those who practise it must be influenced by greater motives than empty fame: the people are generally well pleased with a remission of punishment, and all that wears the appearance of humanity; it is the wise alone who are capable of discerning that impartial justice is the truest mercy: they know it to be very difficult at once to compassionate, and yet condemn, an object that pleads for tenderness.

I have been led into this commonplace train of thought by a late striking instance in this country of the impartiality of justice, and of the king's inflexible resolution of inflicting punishment where it was justly due. A man of the first quality, in a fit either of passion, melancholy, or madness, murdered his servant: it was expected that his station in life would have lessened the ignominy of his punishment; however, he was arraigned, condemned, and underwent the same degrading death with the meanest malefactor. It was well considered that virtue alone is true nobility; and that he, whose actions sink him even beneath the vulgar, has no right to those distinctions which should be the rewards only of merit: it was perhaps considered that crimes were more heinous among the higher classes of people, as necessity exposes them to fewer temptations.

Over all the East, even China not excepted, a person of the same quality, guilty of such a crime, might, by giving up a share of his fortune to the judge, buy off his sentence. There are several countries, even in Europe, where the servant is entirely the property of his master: if a slave kills his lord, he dies by the most excruciating tortures; but if the circumstances are reversed, a small fine buys off the punishment of the offender. Happy the country where all are equal, and where those who sit as judges have too much integrity to receive a bribe, and too much honour to pity, from a similitude of the prisoner's title or circumstances with their own! Such is England: yet think not that it was always equally famed for this strict impartiality. There was a time, even here, when title softened the rigours of the law, when dignified wretches were suffered to live, and continue for years an equal disgrace to justice and nobility.

To this day, in a neighbouring country, the great are often most scandalously pardoned for the most scandalous offences. A person is still alive among them who has more than once deserved the most ignominious severity of justice. His being of the blood royal, however, was thought a sufficient atonement for his being a disgrace to humanity. This remarkable personage took pleasure in shooting at the passengers below from the top of his palace; and in this most princely amusement he usually spent some time every day. He was at length arraigned by the friends of a person whom in this manner he had killed, was found guilty of the charge, and condemned to die. His merciful monarch pardoned him, in consideration of his rank and quality. The unrepenting criminal soon after renewed his usual entertainment, and in the same manner killed another man. He was a second time condemned; and, strange to think, a second time received his majesty's pardon! Would you believe it? A third time the very same man was guilty of the very same offence: a third time, therefore, the laws of his country found him guilty—I wish, for the honour of humanity, I could suppress the rest—a third time he was pardoned! Will you not think such a story too extraordinary for belief? will you not think me describing the savage inhabitants of Congo? Alas! the story is but too true; and the country where it was transacted regards itself as the politest in Europe!—Adieu.

LETTER XXXIX.

From Lien Chi Altangi to ——, Merchant in Amsterdam.

CEREMONIES are different in every country; but true politeness is everywhere the same. Ceremonies, which take up so much of our attention, are only artificial helps which ignorance assumes in order to imitate politeness, which is the result of good sense and good nature. A person possessed of those qualities, though he had never seen a court, is truly agreeable; and if without them, would continue a clown, though he had been all his life a gentleman usher.

How would a Chinese, bred up in the formalities of an Eastern court, be regarded should he carry all his good manners beyond the Great Wall? How would an Englishman, skilled in all the decorums of Western good breeding, appear at an Eastern entertainment? Would he not be reckoned more fantastically savage than even his unbred footman?

Ceremony resembles that base coin which circulates through a country by the royal mandate; it serves every purpose of real money at home, but is entirely useless if carried abroad: a person who should attempt to circulate his native trash in another country would be thought either ridiculous or culpable. He is truly well-bred, who knows when to value and when to despise those national peculiarities, which are regarded by some with so much observance; a traveller of taste at once perceives that the wise are polite all the world over, but that fools are polite only at home.

I have now before me two very fashionable letters upon the same subject, both written by ladies of distinction; one of whom leads the fashion in England, and the other sets the ceremonies of China: they are both regarded in their respective countries by all the *beau monde*, as standards of taste and models of true politeness, and both give us a true idea of what they imagine elegant in their admirers: which of them understands true politeness, or whether either, you shall be at liberty to determine. The English lady writes thus to her female confidant :—

"As I live, my dear Charlotte, I believe the Colonel will carry it at last; he is a most irresistible fellow, that is flat. So well dressed, so neat, so sprightly, and plays about one so agreeably, that I vow he has as much spirits as the Marquis of Monkeyman's Italian greyhound. I first saw him at Ranelagh; he shines there: he is nothing without Ranelagh, and Ranelagh nothing without him. The next day he sent a card and compliments, desiring to wait on mamma and me to the music subscription. He looked all the time with such irresistible impudence, that positively he had something in his face gave me as much pleasure as a pair-royal of naturals in my own hand. He waited on mamma and me the next morning to know how we got home: you must know the insidious devil makes love to us both. Rap went the footman at the door; bounce went my heart: I thought he would have rattled the house down. Chariot drove up to the window, with his footmen in the prettiest liveries; he has infinite taste, that is flat. Mamma had spent all the morning at her head; but, for my part, I was in an undress to receive him; quite easy, mind that; no way disturbed at his approach: mamma pretended to be as *degagée* as I; and yet I saw her blush in spite of her. Positively he is a most killing devil! We did nothing but laugh all the time he staid with us; I never heard so many very good things before: at first he mistook mamma for my sister, at which she laughed; then he mistook my natural complexion for paint, at which I laughed; and then he shewed us a picture in the lid of his snuff-box, at which we all laughed. He plays picquet so very ill, and is so very fond of cards, and loses with such a grace, that positively he has won me; I have got a cool hundred, but have lost my heart. I need not tell you that he is only a colonel of the train-bands. I am, dear Charlotte, yours for ever, BELINDA."

The Chinese lady addresses her confidant, a poor relation of the family, upon the same occasion; in which she seems to understand decorums even better than the Western beauty. You who have resided so long in China will readily acknowledge the picture to be taken from nature; and, by being acquainted with the Chinese customs, will better apprehend the lady's meaning.

FROM YAOUA TO YAYA.

"Papa insists upon one, two, three, four hundred taels from the colonel, my lover, before he parts with a lock of my hair. Oh how I wish the dear creature may be able to produce the money, and pay papa my fortune! The colonel is reckoned the politest man in all Shensi. The first visit he paid at our house—mercy, what stooping, and cringing, and stopping, and fidgeting, and going back, and creeping forward, there was between him and papa! one would have thought he had got the seventeen books of ceremonies all by heart. When he was come into the hall, he flourished his hands three times in a very graceful manner. Papa, who would not be outdone, flourished his four times; upon this the colonel began again, and both thus continued flourishing for some minutes in the politest manner imaginable. I was posted in the usual place behind the screen, where I saw the whole ceremony through a slit. Of this the colonel was sensible, for papa informed him. I would have given the world to have shewn him my little shoes, but had no opportunity. It was the first time I had ever the happiness of seeing any man but papa, and I vow, my dear Yaya, I thought my three souls would actually have fled from my lips. Ho! but he looked most charmingly: he is reckoned the best shaped man in the whole province, for he is very fat and very short; but even those natural advantages are improved by his dress, which is fashionable past description. His head was close shaven, all but the crown, and the hair of that was braided into a most beautiful tail, that reached down to his heels, and was terminated by a bunch of yellow roses. Upon his first entering the room, I could easily perceive he had been highly perfumed with assafœtida. But then his looks—his looks, my dear Yaya, were irresistible. He kept his eyes steadfastly fixed on the wall during the whole ceremony, and I sincerely believe no accident could have discomposed his gravity, or drawn his eyes away. After a polite silence of two hours, he gallantly begged to have the singing women introduced, purely for my amusement. After one of them had for some time entertained us with her voice, the colonel and she retired for some minutes together. I thought they would never have come back: I must own he is a most agreeable creature. Upon his return they again renewed the concert, and he continued to gaze upon the wall as usual, when, in less than half an hour more, ho! but he retired out of the room with another. He is, indeed, a most agreeable creature.

"When he came to take his leave, the whole ceremony began afresh: papa would see him to the door; but the colonel swore he would rather see the earth turned upside down than permit him to stir a single step, and papa was at last obliged to comply. As soon as he was got to the door, papa went out to see him on horseback: here they continued half an hour bowing and cringing, before one would mount or the other go in; but the colonel was at last victorious. He had scarce gone an hundred paces from the house, when papa running out hallooed after him, 'A good journey;' upon which the colonel returned, and would see papa into his house before ever he would depart. He was no sooner got home than he sent me a very fine present of duck eggs painted of twenty different colours. His generosity, I own, has won me. I have ever since been trying over the eight letters of good fortune, and have great hopes. All I have to apprehend is, that after he has married me, and that I am carried to his house close shut up in my chair, when he comes to have the first sight of my face, he may shut me up a second time, and send me back to papa. However, I shall appear as fine as possible: mamma and I have been to buy the clothes for my wedding. I am to have a new *foong hoang* in my hair, the beak of which will reach down to my nose; the milliner from whom we bought that and our ribands cheated us as if she had no conscience, and so, to quiet mine, I cheated her. All this is fair, you know. I remain, my dear Yaya, your ever faithful "YAOUA."

LETTER XL.

From Lien Chi Altangi to Fum Hoam, First President of the Ceremonial Academy at Pekin in China.

YOU have always testified the highest esteem for the English poets, and thought them not inferior to the Greeks, Romans, or even the Chinese, in the art. But it is now thought, even by the English themselves, that the race of their poets is extinct; every day produces some pathetic exclamation upon the decadence of taste and genius. "Pegasus," say they, "has slipped the bridle from his mouth, and our modern bards attempt to direct his flight by catching him by the tail."

Yet, my friend, it is only among the ignorant that such discourses prevail; men of true discernment can see several poets still among the English, some of whom equal, if not surpass, their predecessors. The ignorant term that alone poetry which is couched in a certain number of syllables in every line, where a vapid thought is drawn out into a number of verses of equal length, and perhaps pointed with rhymes at the end. But glowing sentiment, striking imagery, concise expression, natural description, and modulated periods, are fully sufficient entirely to fill up my idea of this art, and make way to every passion.

If my idea of poetry, therefore, be just, the English are not at present so destitute of poetical merit as they seem to imagine. I can see several poets in disguise among them,—men furnished with the strength of soul, sublimity of sentiment, and grandeur of expression, which constitutes the character. Many of the writers of their modern odes, sonnets, tragedies, or rebusses, it is true, deserve not the name, though they have done nothing but clink rhymes and measure syllables for years together: their Johnsons and Smolletts are truly poets; though, for aught I know, they never made a single verse in their whole lives.

In every incipient language the poet

and the prose writer are very distinct in their qualifications: the poet ever proceeds first; treading unbeaten paths, enriching his native funds, and employed in new adventures. The other follows with more cautious steps, and though slow in his motions, treasures up every useful or pleasing discovery. But when once all the extent and the force of the language is known, the poet then seems to rest from his labour, and is at length overtaken by his assiduous pursuer. Both characters are then blended into one: the historian and orator catch all the poet's fire, and leave him no real mark of distinction, except the iteration of numbers regularly returning. Thus, in the decline of ancient European learning, Seneca, though he wrote in prose, is as much a poet as Lucan; and Longinus, though but a critic, more sublime than Apollonius.

From this then it appears that poetry is not discontinued, but altered among the English at present; the outward form seems different from what it was, but poetry still continues internally the same: the only question remains, whether the metric feet used by the good writers of the last age or the prosaic numbers employed by the good writers of this be preferable? And here the practice of the last age appears to me superior: they submitted to the restraint of numbers and similar sounds; and this restraint, instead of diminishing, augmented the force of their sentiment and style. Fancy restrained may be compared to a fountain, which plays highest by diminishing the aperture. Of the truth of this maxim in every language every fine writer is perfectly sensible from his own experience, and yet to explain the reason would be perhaps as difficult as to make a frigid genius profit by the discovery.

There is still another reason in favour of the practice of the last age, to be drawn from the variety of modulation. The musical period in prose is confined to a very few changes; the numbers in verse are capable of infinite variation. I speak not now from the practice of modern verse writers, few of whom have any idea of musical variety, but run on in the same monotonous flow through the whole poem; but rather from the example of their former poets, who were tolerable masters of this variety, and also from a capacity in the language of still admitting various unanticipated music.

Several rules have been drawn up for varying the poetic measure, and critics have elaborately talked of accents and syllables; but good sense and a fine ear, which rules can never teach, are what alone can in such a case determine. The rapturous flowings of joy, or the interruptions of indignation, require accents placed entirely different, and a structure consonant to the emotions they would express. Changing passions, and numbers changing with those passions, make the whole secret of Western as well as Eastern poetry. In a word, the great faults of the modern professed English poets are, that they seem to want numbers which should vary with the passion, and are more employed in describing to the imagination than striking at the heart.—Adieu.

LETTER XLI.

To the same.

SOME time since I sent thee, O holy disciple of Confucius, an account of the grand abbey, or mausoleum, of the kings and heroes of this nation: I have since been introduced to a temple, not so ancient, but far superior in beauty and magnificence. In this, which is the most considerable of the empire, there are no pompous inscriptions, no flattery paid the dead, but all is elegant and awfully simple. There are, however, a few rags hung round the walls, which have, at a vast expense, been taken from the enemy in the present war. The silk of which they are composed, when new, might be valued at half a string of copper money in China; yet this wise people fitted out a fleet and an army in order to seize them, though now grown old, and scarcely capable of being patched up into a handkerchief. By this conquest the English are said to have gained, and the French to have lost, much honour. Is the honour of European nations placed only in tattered silk?

In this temple I was permitted to remain during the whole service; and were you not already acquainted with the religion of the English, you might from my description be inclined to believe them as grossly idolatrous as the disciples of Lao. The idol which they seem to address strides like a colossus over the door of the inner temple, which here, as with the Jews, is esteemed the most sacred part of the building. Its oracles are delivered in an hundred various tones, which seem to inspire the worshippers with enthusiasm and awe: an old woman, who appeared to be the priestess, was employed in various attitudes as she felt the inspiration. When it began to speak, all the people remained fixed in silent attention, nodding assent, looking approbation, appearing highly edified by those sounds which to a stranger might seem inarticulate and unmeaning.

When the idol had done speaking, and the priestess had locked up its lungs with a key, observing almost all the company leaving the temple, I concluded the service was over, and taking my hat, was going to walk away with the crowd, when I was stopped by the Man in Black, who assured me that the ceremony had scarcely yet begun. "What!" cried I, "do I not see almost the whole body of the worshippers leaving the church? Would you persuade me that such numbers who profess religion and morality would, in this shameless manner, quit the temple before the service was concluded? You surely mistake: not even the Kalmucks would be guilty of such an indecency, though all the object of their worship was but a joint-stool." My friend seemed to blush for his countrymen, assuring me that those whom I saw running away were only a parcel of musical blockheads, whose passion was merely for sounds, and whose heads are as empty as a fiddle-case: those who remain behind, says he, are the true religious; they make use of music to warm their hearts, and to lift them to a proper pitch of rapture: examine their behaviour, and you will confess there are some among us who practise true devotion.

I now looked round me as directed, but saw nothing of that fervent devotion which he had promised: one of the worshippers appeared to be ogling the company through a glass: another was fervent, not in addresses to Heaven, but to his mistress; a third whispered; a fourth took snuff; and the priest himself, in a drowsy tone, read over the *duties* of the day.

"Bless my eyes!" cried I, as I happened to look towards the door, "what do I see? one of the worshippers fallen fast asleep, and actually sunk down on his cushion! He is now enjoying the benefit of a trance, or does he receive the influence of some mysterious vision?"—"Alas! alas!" replied my companion, "no such thing; he has only had the misfortune of eating too hearty a dinner, and finds it impossible to keep his eyes open." Turning to another part of the temple, I perceived a young lady just in the same circumstances and attitude: "Strange," cried I; "can she, too, have over-eaten herself?"—"Oh, fie!" replied my friend, "you now grow censorious. She grow drowsy from eating too much! that would be profanation. She only sleeps now from having sat up all night at a brag party." "Turn me where I will, then," says I, "I can perceive no single symptom of devotion among the worshippers, except from that old woman in the corner, who sits groaning behind the long sticks of a mourning fan; she indeed seems greatly edified with what she hears."—"Ay," replied my friend, "I knew we should find some to catch you: I know her; that is the deaf lady who lives in the cloisters."

In short, the remissness of behaviour in almost all the worshippers, and some even of the guardians, struck me with surprise. I had been taught to believe that none were ever promoted to offices in the temple, but men remarkable for their superior sanctity, learning, and rectitude; that there was no such thing heard of as persons being introduced into the church merely to oblige a senator, or provide for the younger branch of a noble family: I expected, as their minds were continually set upon heavenly things, to see their eyes directed there also; and hoped from their behaviour to perceive their inclinations corresponding with their duty. But I am since informed, that some are appointed to preside over temples they never visit; and, while they receive all the money, are contented with letting others do all the good.—Adieu.

LETTER XLII.

From Fum Hoam to Lien Chi Altangi, the Discontented Wanderer, by the way of Moscow.

MUST I ever continue to condemn thy perseverance, and blame that curiosity which destroys thy happiness? What yet untasted banquet, what luxury yet unknown, has rewarded thy painful adventures? Name a pleasure which thy native country could not amply procure: frame a wish that might not have been satisfied in China. Why then such toil, and such danger, in pursuit of raptures within your reach at home?

The Europeans, you will say, excel us in sciences and in arts,—those sciences which bound the aspiring wish, and those arts which tend to gratify even unrestrained desire. They may perhaps outdo us in the arts of building ships, casting cannon, or measuring mountains; but are they superior in the greatest of all arts—the art of governing kingdoms and ourselves?

When I compare the history of China with that of Europe, how do I exult in being a native of that kingdom which derives its original from the sun. Upon opening the Chinese history, I there behold an ancient extended empire, established by laws which nature and reason seem to have dictated. The duty of children to their parents—a duty which nature implants in every breast—forms the strength of that government which has subsisted for time immemorial. Filial obedience is the first and greatest requisite of a state: by this we become good subjects to our emperors, capable of behaving with just subordination to our superiors, and grateful dependants on Heaven; by this we become fonder of marriage, in order to be capable of exacting obedience from others in our turn; by this we become good magistrates, for early submission is the truest lesson to those who would learn to rule; by this the whole state may be said to resemble one family, of which the emperor is the protector, father, and friend.

In this happy region, sequestered from the rest of mankind, I see a succession of princes who in general considered themselves as the fathers of their people; a race of philosophers who bravely combated idolatry, prejudice, and tyranny, at the expense of their private happiness and immediate reputation. Whenever an usurper or a tyrant intruded into the administration, how have all the good and great been united against him! Can European history produce an instance like that of the twelve mandarines, who all resolved to apprise the vicious emperor Tisiang of the irregularity of his conduct? He who first undertook the dangerous task was cut in two by the emperor's order; the second was ordered to be tormented, and then put to a cruel death; the third undertook the task with intrepidity, and was instantly stabbed by the tyrant's hand: in this manner they all suffered, except one. But, not to be turned from his purpose, the brave survivor, entering the palace with the instruments of torture in his hand, "Here," cried he, addressing himself to the throne, "here, O Tisiang, are the marks your faithful subjects receive for their loyalty; I am wearied with serving a tyrant, and now come for my reward." The emperor, struck with his intrepidity, instantly forgave the boldness of his conduct, and reformed his own. What European annals can boast of a tyrant thus reclaimed to lenity?

When five brethren had set upon the great Emperor Ginsong alone, with his sabre he slew four of them; he was struggling with the fifth, when his guards coming up were going to cut the conspirator into a thousand pieces. "No, no," cried the emperor, with a calm and placid countenance, "of all his brothers he is the only one remaining; at least let one of the family be suffered to live, that his aged parents may have somebody left to feed and comfort them."

When Haitong, the last emperor of the house of Ming, saw himself besieged in his own city by the usurper, he was resolved to issue from his palace with six hundred of his guards, and give the enemy battle; but they forsook him. Being thus without hopes, and choosing death rather than to fall alive into the hands of a rebel, he retired to his garden, conducting his little daughter, an only child, in his hand; there in a private arbour, unsheathing his sword, he stabbed the young innocent to the heart, and then despatched himself, leaving the following words written with his blood on the border of his vest: "Forsaken by my subjects, abandoned by my friends, use my body as you will, but spare, O spare, my people!"

An empire which has thus continued invariably the same for such a long succession of ages; which, though at last conquered by the Tartars, still preserves its ancient laws and learning, and may more properly be said to annex the dominions of Tartary to its empire, than to admit a foreign conqueror; an empire as large as Europe, governed by one law, ackowledging subjection to one prince, and experiencing but one revolution of any continuance in the space of four thousand years: this is something so peculiarly great, that I am naturally led to despise all other nations on the comparison. Here we see no religious persecutions, no enmity between mankind for difference in opinion. The disciples of Lao Keun, the idolatrous sectaries of Fohi, and the philosophical children of Confucius, only strive to show by their actions the truth of their doctrines.

Now turn from this happy, peaceful scene to Europe, the theatre of intrigue, avarice, and ambition. How many revolutions does it not experience in the compass even of one age! and to what do these revolutions tend but the destruction of thousands? Every great event is replete with some new calamity. The seasons of serenity are passed over in silence; their histories seem to speak only of the storm.

There we see the Romans extending their power over barbarous nations, and in turn becoming a prey to those whom they had conquered. We see those barbarians, when become Christians, engaged in continual war with the followers of Mahomet; or, more dreadful still, destroying each other. We see councils in the earlier ages authorizing every iniquity—crusades spreading desolation in the country left, as well as that to be conquered—excommunications freeing subjects from natural allegiance, and persuading to sedition—blood flowing in the fields and on scaffolds—tortures used as arguments to convince the recusant: to heighten the horror of the piece, behold it shaded with wars, rebellions, treasons, plots, politics, and poison.

And what advantage has any country of Europe obtained from such calamities? Scarce any. Their dissensions, for more than a thousand years, have served to make each other unhappy, but have enriched none. All the great nations still nearly preserve their ancient limits; none have been able to subdue the other, and so terminate the dispute. France, in spite of the conquests of Edward the Third and Henry the Fifth, notwithstanding the efforts of Charles the Fifth and Philip the Second, still remains within its ancient limits. Spain, Germany, Great Britain, Poland, the States of the North, are nearly still the same. What effect, then, has the blood of so many thousands, the destruction of so many cities, produced? Nothing either great or considerable. The Christian princes have lost, indeed, much from the enemies of Christendom, but they have gained nothing from each other. Their princes, because they preferred ambition to justice, deserve the character of enemies to mankind; and their priests, by neglecting morality for opinion, have mistaken the interests of society.

On whatever side we regard the history of Europe, we shall perceive it to be a tissue of crimes, follies, and misfortunes—of politics without design, and wars without consequences: in this long list of human infirmity a great character, or a shining virtue, may sometimes happen to arise, as we often meet a cottage or a cultivated spot in the most hideous wilderness. But for an Alfred, an Alphonso, a Frederick, or an Alexander III., we meet a thousand princes who have disgraced humanity.

LETTER XLIII.

From Lien Chi Altangi to Fum Hoam, First President of the Ceremonial Academy at Pekin, in China.

We have just received accounts here, that Voltaire, the poet and philosopher of

Europe, is dead! He is now beyond the reach of the thousand enemies who, while living, degraded his writings, and branded his character. Scarce a page of his latter productions that does not betray the agonies of a heart bleeding under the scourge of unmerited reproach. Happy, therefore, at last in escaping from calumny! happy in leaving a world that was unworthy of him and his writings!

Let others, my friend, bestrew the hearses of the great with panegyric; but such a loss as the world has now suffered affects me with stronger emotions. When a philosopher dies, I consider myself as losing a patron, an instructor, and a friend. I consider the world as losing one who might serve to console her amidst the desolations of war and ambition. Nature every day produces in abundance men capable of filling all the requisite duties of authority; but she is niggard in the birth of an exalted mind, scarcely producing in a century a single genius to bless and enlighten a degenerate age. Prodigal in the production of kings, governors, mandarines, chams, and courtiers, she seems to have forgotten, for more than three thousand years, the manner in which she once formed the brain of a Confucius; and well it is she has forgotten, when a bad world gave him so very bad a reception.

Whence, my friend, this malevolence, which has ever pursued the great, even to the tomb? whence this more than fiend-like disposition of embittering the lives of those who would make us more wise and more happy?

When I cast my eye over the fates of several philosophers, who have at different periods enlightened mankind, I must confess it inspires me with the most degrading reflections on humanity. When I read of the stripes of Mencius, the tortures of Tchin, the bowl of Socrates, and the bath of Seneca; when I hear of the persecutions of Dante, the imprisonment of Galileo, the indignities suffered by Montaigne, the banishment of Cartesius, the infamy of Bacon, and that even Locke himself escaped not without reproach: when I think on such subjects, I hesitate whether most to blame the ignorance or the villainy of my fellow-creatures.

Should you look for the character of Voltaire among the journalists and illiterate writers of the age, you will there find him characterised as a monster, with a head turned to wisdom and a heart inclining to vice; the powers of his mind and the baseness of his principles forming a detestable contrast. But seek for his character among writers like himself, and you find him very differently described. You perceive him, in their accounts, possessed of good-nature, humanity, greatness of soul, fortitude, and almost every virtue; in this description those who might be supposed best acquainted with his character are unanimous. The Royal Prussian, D'Argens, Diderot, D'Alembert, and Fontenelle, conspire in drawing the picture, in describing the friend of man, and the patron of every rising genius.

An inflexible perseverance in what he thought was right and a generous detestation of flattery formed the groundwork of this great man's character. From these principles many strong virtues and few faults arose: as he was warm in his friendship, and severe in his resentment, all that mention him seem possessed of the same qualities, and speak of him with rapture or detestation. A person of his eminence can have few indifferent as to his character: every reader must be an enemy or an admirer.

This poet began the course of glory so early as the age of eighteen, and even then was author of a tragedy which deserves applause. Possessed of a small patrimony, he preserved his independence in an age of venality; and supported the dignity of learning, by teaching his contemporary writers to live like him, above the favours of the great. He was banished his native country for a satire upon the royal concubine. He had accepted the place of historian to the French king, but refused to keep it, when he found it was presented only in order that he should be the first flatterer of the state.

The great Prussian received him as an ornament to his kingdom, and had sense enough to value his friendship, and profit by his instructions. In this court he continued, till an intrigue, with which the world seems hitherto unacquainted, obliged him to quit that country. His own happiness, the happiness of the monarch, of his sister, of a part of the court, rendered his departure necessary.

Tired at length of courts and all the follies of the great, he retired to Switzerland, a country of liberty, where he enjoyed tranquillity and the muse. Here, though without any taste for magnificence himself, he usually entertained at his table the learned and polite of Europe, who were attracted by a desire of seeing a person from whom they had received so much satisfaction. The entertainment was conducted with the utmost elegance, and the conversation was that of philosophers. Every country that at once united liberty and science were his peculiar favourites. The being an Englishman was to him a character that claimed admiration and respect.

Between Voltaire and the disciples of Confucius there are many differences; however, being of a different opinion does not in the least diminish my esteem: I am not displeased with my brother, because he happens to ask our father for favours in a different manner from me. Let his errors rest in peace; his excellencies deserve admiration: let me with the wise admire his wisdom; let the envious and the ignorant ridicule his foibles: the folly of others is ever most ridiculous to those who are themselves most foolish. —Adieu.

LETTER XLIV.

From Lien Chi Altangi to Hingpo, a Slave in Persia.

It is impossible to form a philosophic system of happiness which is adapted to every condition in life, since every person who travels in this great pursuit takes a separate road. The differing colours which suit different complexions are not more various than the different pleasures appropriated to particular minds. The various sects who have pretended to give lessons to instruct men in happiness have described their own particular sensations, without considering ours; have only loaded their disciples with constraint, without adding to their real felicity.

If I find pleasure in dancing, how ridiculous would it be in me to prescribe such an amusement for the entertainment of a cripple: should he, on the other hand, place his chief delight in painting, yet would he be absurd in recommending the same relish to one who had lost the power of distinguishing colours. General directions are, therefore, commonly useless: and to be particular would exhaust volumes, since each individual may require a particular system of precepts to direct his choice.

Every mind seems capable of entertaining a certain quantity of happiness, which no institutions can increase, no circumstances alter, and entirely independent of fortune. Let any man compare his present fortune with the past, and he will probably find himself, upon the whole, neither better nor worse than formerly.

Gratified ambition, or irreparable calamity, may produce transient sensations of pleasure or distress. Those storms may discompose in proportion as they are strong, or the mind is pliant to their impression. But the soul, though at first lifted up by the event, is every day operated upon with diminished influence, and at length subsides into the level of its usual tranquillity. Should some unexpected turn of fortune take thee from fetters, and place thee on a throne, exultation would be natural upon the change; but the temper, like the face, would soon resume its native serenity.

Every wish, therefore, which leads us to expect happiness somewhere else but where we are, every institution which teaches us that we should be better by being possessed of something new, which promises to lift us a step higher than we are, only lays a foundation for uneasiness, because it contracts debts which we cannot repay; it calls that a good, which, when we have found it, will in fact add nothing to our happiness.

To enjoy the present, without regret for the past, or solicitude for the future, has been the advice rather of poets than philosophers. And yet the precept seems more rational than is generally imagined.

It is the only general precept respecting the pursuit of happiness, that can be applied with propriety to every condition of life. The man of pleasure, the man of business, and the philosopher, are equally interested in its disquisition. If we do not find happiness in the present moment, in what shall we find it? either in reflecting on the past, or prognosticating the future. But let us see how these are capable of producing satisfaction.

A remembrance of what is past and an anticipation of what is to come seem to be the two faculties by which man differs most from other animals. Though brutes enjoy them in a limited degree, yet their whole life seems taken up in the present, regardless of the past and the future. Man, on the contrary, endeavours to derive his happiness, and experiences most of his miseries, from these two sources.

Is this superiority of reflection a prerogative of which we should boast, and for which we should thank nature? or is it a misfortune of which we should complain, and be humble? Either from the abuse, or from the nature of things, it certainly makes our condition more miserable.

Had we a privilege of calling up, by the power of memory, only such passages as were pleasing, unmixed with such as were disagreeable, we might then excite, at pleasure, an ideal happiness, perhaps more poignant than actual sensation. But this is not the case: the past is never represented without some disagreeable circumstance, which tarnishes all its beauty; the remembrance of an evil carries in it nothing agreeable, and to remember a good is always accompanied with regret. Thus we lose more than we gain by the remembrance.

And we shall find our expectation of the future to be a gift more distressful even than the former. To fear an approaching evil is certainly a most disagreeable sensation; and in expecting an approaching good we experience the inquietude of wanting actual possession.

Thus, whichever way we look, the prospect is disagreeable. Behind, we have left pleasures we shall never more enjoy, and therefore regret; and before, we see pleasures which we languish to possess, and are consequently uneasy till we possess them. Was there any method of seizing the present, unembittered by such reflections, then would our state be tolerably easy.

This, indeed, is the endeavour of all mankind, who, untutored by philosophy, pursue as much as they can a life of amusement and dissipation. Every rank in life, and every size of understanding, seems to follow this alone; or not pursuing it, deviates from happiness. The man of pleasure pursues dissipation by profession; the man of business pursues it not less, as every voluntary labour he undergoes is only dissipation in disguise. The philosopher himself, even while he reasons upon the subject, does it unknowingly, with a view of dissipating the thoughts of what he was, or what he must be.

The subject, therefore, comes to this: Which is the most perfect sort of dissipation,—pleasure, business, or philosophy? Which best serves to exclude those uneasy sensations which *memory* or *anticipation* produce?

The enthusiasm of pleasure charms only by intervals. The highest rapture lasts only for a moment; and all the senses seem so combined, as to be soon tired into languor by the gratification of any one of them. It is only among the poets we hear of men changing to one delight, when satiated with another. In nature it is very different: the glutton, when sated with the full meal, is unqualified to feel the real pleasure of drinking; the drunkard, in turn, finds few of those transports which lovers boast in enjoyment; and the lover, when cloyed, finds a diminution of every other appetite. Thus, after a full indulgence of any one sense, the man of pleasure finds a languor in all, is placed in a chasm between past and expected enjoyment, perceives an interval which must be filled up. The present can give no satisfaction, because he has already robbed it of every charm: a mind thus left without immediate employment naturally recurs to the past or future; the reflector finds that he was happy, and knows that he cannot be so now; he sees that he may yet be happy, and wishes the hour was come: thus every period of his continuance is miserable, except that very short one of immediate gratification. Instead of a life of dissipation, none has more frequent conversations with disagreeable *self* than he: his enthusiasms are but few and transient; his appetites, like angry creditors, continually making fruitless demands for what he is unable to pay; and the greater his former pleasures, the more strong his regret, the more impatient his expectations. A life of pleasure is therefore the most unpleasing life in the world.

Habit has rendered the man of business more cool in his desires; he finds less regret for past pleasures, and less solicitude for those to come. The life he now leads, though tainted in some measure with hope, is yet not afflicted so strongly with regret, and is less divided between short-lived rapture and lasting anguish. The pleasures he has enjoyed are not so vivid, and those he has to expect cannot consequently create so much anxiety.

The philosopher, who extends his regard to all mankind, must still have a smaller concern for what has already affected, or may hereafter affect, himself: the concerns of others make his whole study, and that study is his pleasure; and this pleasure is continuing in its nature, because it can be changed at will, leaving but few of these anxious intervals which are employed in remembrance or anticipation. The philosopher by this means leads a life of almost continued dissipation; and reflection, which makes the uneasiness and misery of others, serves as a companion and instructor to him.

In a word, positive happiness is constitutional, and incapable of increase; misery is artificial, and generally proceeds from our folly. Philosophy can add to our happiness in no other manner but by diminishing our misery: it should not pretend to increase our present stock, but make us economists of what we are possessed of. The great source of calamity lies in regret or anticipation: he, therefore, is most wise who thinks of the present alone, regardless of the past or the future. This is impossible to the man of pleasure; it is difficult to the man of business; and is in some measure attainable by the philosopher. Happy were we all born philosophers, all born with a talent of thus dissipating our own cares, by spreading them upon all mankind!—Adieu.

LETTER XLV.

From Lien Chi Altangi to Fum Hoam, First President of the Ceremonial Academy at Pekin, in China.

THOUGH the frequent invitations I receive from men of distinction here might excite the vanity of some, I am quite mortified, however, when I consider the motives that inspire their civility. I am sent for not to be treated as a friend, but to satisfy curiosity; not to be entertained so much as wondered at; the same earnestness which excites them to see a Chinese would have made them equally proud of a visit from the rhinoceros.

From the highest to the lowest, this people seem fond of sights and monsters. I am told of a person here who gets a very comfortable livelihood by making wonders, and then selling or showing them to the people for money: no matter how insignificant they were in the beginning, by locking them up close, and showing for money, they soon become prodigies! His first essay in this way was to exhibit himself as a wax-work figure behind a glass door at a puppet show. Thus, keeping the spectators at a proper distance, and having his head adorned with a copper crown, he looked extremely "natural, and very like the life itself." He continued this exhibition with success, till an involuntary fit of sneezing brought him to life before all the spectators, and consequently rendered him for that time as entirely useless as the peaceable inhabitant of a catacomb.

Determined to act the statue no more, he next levied contributions under the figure of an Indian king; and by painting his face, and counterfeiting the savage howl, he frighted several ladies and children with amazing success: in this manner, therefore, he might have lived very comfortably, had he not been arrested for a debt that was contracted when he was the figure in wax-work: thus his face underwent an involuntary ablution, and he found himself reduced to his primitive complexion and indigence.

After some time, being freed from gaol, he was now grown wiser, and instead of making himself a wonder, was resolved only to make wonders. He learned the art of pasting up mummies; was never at a loss for an artificial *lusus naturæ*: nay, it has been reported, that he has sold seven petrified lobsters of his own manufacture to a noted collector of rarities: but this the learned Cracovius Putridus has undertaken to refute in a very elaborate dissertation.

His last wonder was nothing more than an halter; yet by this halter he gained more than by all his former exhibitions. The people, it seems, had got it in their heads, that a certain noble criminal was to be hanged with a silken rope. Now there was nothing they so much wished to see as this very rope; and he was resolved to gratify their curiosity: he therefore got one made, not only of silk, but to render it more striking, several threads of gold were intermixed. The people paid their money only to see silk, but were highly satisfied when they found it was mixed with gold into the bargain. It is scarce necessary to mention, that the projector sold his silken rope for almost what it had cost him, as soon as the criminal was known to be hanged in hempen materials.

By their fondness of sights one would be apt to imagine that, instead of desiring to see things as they should be, they are rather solicitous of seeing them as they ought not to be. A cat with four legs is disregarded, though never so useful; but if it has but two, and is consequently incapable of catching mice, it is reckoned inestimable, and every man of taste is ready to raise the auction. A man, though in his person faultless as an aërial genius, might starve; but if stuck over with hideous warts like a porcupine, his fortune is made for ever, and he may propagate the breed with impunity and applause.

A good woman in my neighbourhood, who was bred a habit-maker, though she handled her needle tolerably well, could scarcely get employment. But being obliged, by an accident, to have both her hands cut off from the elbows, what would in another country have been her ruin made her fortune here: she was now thought more fit for her trade than before; business flowed in apace, and all people paid for seeing the mantua-maker who wrought without hands.

A gentleman, showing me his collection of pictures, stopped at one with peculiar admiration: "There," cries he, "is an inestimable piece." I gazed at the picture for some time, but could see none of those graces with which he seemed enraptured; it appeared to me the most paltry piece of the whole collection: I therefore demanded where those beauties lay, of which I was yet insensible. "Sir," cries he, "the merit does not consist in the piece, but in the manner in which it was done. The painter drew the whole with his foot, and held the pencil between his toes: I bought it at a very great price; for peculiar merit should ever be rewarded."

But these people are not more fond of wonders, than liberal in rewarding those who show them. From the wonderful dog of knowledge, at present under the patronage of the nobility, down to the man with the box, who professes to show "the best imitation of Nature that was ever seen," they all live in luxury. A singing woman shall collect subscriptions in her own coach and six; a fellow shall make a fortune by tossing a straw from his toe to his nose; one in particular has found that eating fire was the most ready way to live; and another, who jingles several bells fixed to his cap, is the only man that I know of who has received emolument from the labours of his head.

A young author, a man of good-nature and learning, was complaining to me some nights ago of this misplaced generosity of the times. "Here," says he, "have I spent part of my youth in attempting to instruct and amuse my fellow-creatures, and all my reward has been solitude, poverty, and reproach; while a fellow, possessed of even the smallest share of fiddling merit, or who has perhaps learned to whistle double, is rewarded, applauded, and caressed!"—"Prithee, young man," says I to him, "are you ignorant, that in so large a city as this it is better to be an amusing than a useful member of society? Can you leap up, and touch your feet four times before you come to the ground?"—"No, sir."—"Can you pimp for a man of quality?"—"No, sir."—"Can you stand upon two horses at full speed?"—"No, sir."—"Can you swallow a penknife?"—"I can do none of these tricks."—"Why then," cried I, "there is no other prudent means of subsistence left, but to apprise the town that you speedily intend to eat up your own nose by subscription."

I have frequently regretted that none of our Eastern posture-masters, or showmen, have ever ventured to England. I should be pleased to see that money circulate in Asia, which is now sent to Italy and France, in order to bring their vagabonds hither. Several of our tricks would undoubtedly give the English high satisfaction. Men of fashion would be greatly pleased with the postures as well as the condescension of our dancing girls; and the ladies would equally admire the conductors of our fireworks. What an agreeable surprise would it be to see a huge fellow with whiskers flash a charged blunderbuss full in a lady's face, without singeing her hair, or melting her pomatum. Perhaps, when the first surprise was over, she might then grow familiar with danger; and the ladies might vie with each other in standing fire with intrepidity.

But of all the wonders of the East, the most useful, and I should fancy the most pleasing, would be the looking-glass of Lao, which reflects the mind as well as the body. It is said that the Emperor Chusi used to make his concubines dress their heads and their hearts in one of these glasses every morning: while the lady was at her toilet, he would frequently look over her shoulder; and it is recorded that, among the three hundred which composed his seraglio, not one was found whose mind was not even more beautiful than her person.

I make no doubt but a glass in this country would have the very same effect. The English ladies, concubines and all, would undoubtedly cut very pretty figures in so faithful a monitor. There, should we happen to peep over a lady's shoulder while dressing, we might be able to see neither gaming nor ill-nature; neither pride, debauchery, nor a love of gadding. We should find her, if any sensible defect appeared in the mind, more careful in rectifying it, than plastering up the irreparable decays of the person; nay, I am even apt to fancy, that ladies would find more real pleasure in this utensil in private, than in any other bauble imported from China, though never so expensive or amusing.

LETTER XLVI.

To the same.

UPON finishing my last letter I retired to rest, reflecting upon the wonders of the glass of Lao, wishing to be possessed of one here, and resolved in such case to oblige every lady with a sight of it for nothing. What fortune denied me waking, fancy supplied in a dream: the glass, I know not how, was put into my possession, and I could perceive several ladies approaching, some voluntarily, others driven forward against their wills, by a set of discontented genii, whom by intuition I knew were their husbands.

The apartment in which I was to show away was filled with several gaming-tables, as if just forsaken; the candles were burnt to the socket, and the hour was five o'clock in the morning. Placed at one end of the room, which was of prodigious length, I could more easily distinguish every female figure as she marched up from the door; but, guess my surprise, when I could scarce perceive one blooming or agreeable face among the number. This, however, I attributed to the early hour, and kindly considered that the face of a lady just risen from bed ought always to find a compassionate advocate.

The first person who came up in order to view her intellectual face was a commoner's wife, who, as I afterwards found, being bred up during her virginity in a pawnbroker's shop, now attempted to make up the defects of breeding and sentiment by the magnificence of her dress and the expensiveness of her amusements. "Mr. Showman," cried she, approaching, "I am told you has something to show in that there sort of magic lanthorn, by which folks can see themselves on the inside: I protest, as my Lord Beetle says, I am sure it will be vastly pretty, for I have never seen any thing like it before. But how,—Are we to strip off our clothes, and be turned inside out? if so, as Lord Beetle says, I absolutely declare off; for I would not strip for the world before a man's face, and so I tells his Lordship almost every night of my life." I informed the lady that I would dispense with the ceremony of stripping, and immediately presented my glass to her view.

As when a first-rate beauty, after having with difficulty escaped the small-pox, revisits her favourite mirror—that mirror which had repeated the flattery of every lover, and even added force to the compliment—expecting to see what had so often given her pleasure, she no longer beholds the cherry lip, the polished forehead, and speaking blush, but a hateful phiz, quilted into a thousand seams by the hand of deformity; grief, resentment, and rage fill her bosom by turns—she blames the fates and the stars, but, most of all, the unhappy glass feels her resentment: so it was with the lady in question; she had never seen her own mind before, and was now shocked at its deformity. One single look was sufficient to satisfy her curiosity: I held up the glass to her face, and she shut her eyes; no entreaties could prevail upon her to gaze once more. She was even going to snatch it from my hands, and break it in a thousand pieces. I found it was time, therefore, to dismiss her as incorrigible, and show away to the next that offered.

This was an unmarried lady, who continued in a state of virginity till thirty-six, and then admitted a lover when she despaired of a husband. No woman was louder at a revel than she, perfectly freehearted, and almost, in every respect, a man; she understood ridicule to perfection, and was known even to sally out in order to beat the watch. "Here, you, my dear, with the outlandish face," said she, addressing me, "let me take a single peep. Not that I care three damns what figure I may cut in the glass of such an old-fashioned creature: if I am allowed the beauties of the face by people of fashion, I know the world will be complaisant enough to toss me the beauties of the mind into the bargain." I held my glass before her as she desired, and, must confess, was shocked with the reflection. The lady, however, gazed for some time with the utmost complacency; and, at last, turning to me with the most satisfied smile, said she never could think she had been half so handsome.

Upon her dismission, a lady of distinction was reluctantly hauled along to the glass by her husband. In bringing her forward, as he came first to the glass himself, his mind appeared tinctured with immoderate jealousy, and I was going to reproach him for using her with such severity; but when the lady came to present herself, I immediately retracted: for, alas! it was seen that he had but too much reason for his suspicions.

The next was a lady who usually teased all her acquaintance in desiring to be told of her faults, and then never mended any. Upon approaching the glass, I could readily perceive vanity, affectation, and some other ill-looking blots on her mind; wherefore, by my advice, she immediately set about mending. But I could easily find she was not earnest in the work; for as she repaired them on one side, they generally broke out on another. Thus, after three or four attempts, she began to make the ordinary use of the glass in setting her hair.

The company now made room for a woman of learning, who approached with a slow pace and a solemn countenance, which, for her own sake, I could wish had been cleaner. "Sir," cried the lady, flourishing her hand, which held a pinch of snuff, "I shall be enraptured by having presented to my view a mind with which I have so long studied to be acquainted; but, in order to give the sex a proper example, I must insist that all the company may be permitted to look over my shoulder." I bowed assent, and, presenting the glass, showed the lady a mind by no means so fair as she had expected to see. Ill-nature, ill-placed pride, and spleen were too legible to be mistaken. Nothing could be more amusing than the mirth of her female companions who had looked over.

They had hated her from the beginning, and now the apartment echoed with a universal laugh. Nothing but a fortitude like hers could have withstood their raillery: she stood it, however; and when the burst was exhausted, with great tranquillity she assured the company, that the whole was a *deceptio visus*, and that she was too well acquainted with her own mind, to believe any false representations from another. Thus saying, she retired with a sullen satisfaction, resolved not to mend her faults, but to write a criticism on the mental reflector.

I must own, by this time I began myself to suspect the fidelity of my mirror; for as the ladies appeared at least to have the merit of rising early, since they were up at five, I was amazed to find nothing of this good quality pictured upon their minds in the reflection: I was resolved, therefore, to communicate my suspicions to a lady whose intellectual countenance appeared more fair than any of the rest, not having above seventy-nine spots in all, besides slips and foibles. "I own, young woman," said I, "that there are some virtues upon that mind of yours; but there is still one which I do not see represented, —I mean that of rising betimes in the morning; I fancy the glass false in that particular." The young lady smiled at my simplicity; and, with a blush, confessed, that she and the whole company had been up all night gaming.

By this time all the ladies, except one, had seen themselves successively, and disliked the show or scolded the showman: I was resolved, however, that she who seemed to neglect herself, and was neglected by the rest, should take a view; and, going up to a corner of the room where she still continued sitting, I presented my glass full in her face. Here it was that I exulted in my success; no blot, no stain appeared on any part of the faithful mirror. As when the large unwritten page presents its snowy spotless bosom to the writer's hand, so appeared the glass to my view. "Here, O ye daughters of English ancestors!" cried I, "turn hither, and behold an object worthy imitation! Look upon the mirror now, and acknowledge its justice, and this woman's pre-eminence!" The ladies, obeying the summons, came up ir a group, and looking on, acknowledgec there was some truth in the picture, as the person now represented had been deaf, dumb, and a fool from her cradle!

This much of my dream I distinctly re member; the rest was filled with chimeras enchanted castles, and flying dragons, a usual. As you, my dear Fum Hoam are particularly versed in the interpretatio of those midnight warnings, what pleasur should I find in your explanation! Bu that, our distance prevents: I make n doubt, however, but that, from my descrip tion, you will very much venerate the goo qualities of the English ladies in genera since dreams, you know, go always b contraries.—Adieu.

LETTER XLVII.

From Lien Chi Altangi to Hingpo, a Slave in Persia.

YOUR last letters betray a mind seemingl fond of wisdom, yet tempested up by thousand various passions. You woul fondly persuade me, that my former lessor still influence your conduct, and yet you mind seems not less enslaved than you body. Knowledge, wisdom, eruditior arts, and elegance, what are they but th mere trappings of the mind, if they do nc serve to increase the happiness of the pos sessor? A mind rightly instituted in th school of philosophy acquires at once th stability of the oak and the flexibility c the osier. The truest manner of lessenin our agonies is to shrink from their pressure is to confess that we feel them.

The fortitude of European sages is bu a dream; for where lies the merit in bein insensible to the strokes of fortune, or i dissembling our sensibility? If we ar insensible, that arises only from a happ constitution; that is a blessing previousl granted by Heaven, and which no art ca procure, no institutions improve.

If we dissemble our feelings, we onl artificially endeavour to persuade other that we enjoy privileges which we actuall do not possess. Thus, while we endea vour to appear happy, we feel at onc all the pangs of eternal misery and a the self-reproaching consciousness of er deavouring to deceive.

I know but of two sects of philosophers in the world that have endeavoured to inculcate that fortitude is but an imaginary virtue,—I mean the followers of Confucius, and those who profess the doctrines of Christ. All other sects teach pride under misfortunes; they alone teach humility. Night, says our Chinese philosopher, not more surely follows the day, than groans and tears grow out of pain; when misfortunes therefore oppress, when tyrants threaten, it is our interest, it is our duty, to fly even to dissipation for support, to seek redress from friendship, or from that best of friends who loved us into being.

Philosophers, my son, have long declaimed against the passions, as being the source of all our miseries: they are the source of all our misfortunes, I own; but they are the source of our pleasures too; and every endeavour of our lives, and all the institutions of philosophy, should tend to this, not to dissemble an absence of passion, but to repel those which lead to vice, by those which direct to virtue.

The soul may be compared to a field of battle, where two armies are ready every moment to encounter: not a single vice but has a more powerful opponent, and not one virtue but may be overborne by a combination of vices. Reason guides the bands of either host; nor can it subdue one passion but by the assistance of another. Thus as a bark on every side beset with storms, enjoys a state of rest, so does the mind, when influenced by a just equipoise of the passions, enjoy tranquillity.

I have used such means as my little fortune would admit to procure your freedom. I have lately written to the governor of Argun to pay your ransom, though at the expense of all the wealth I brought with me from China. If we become poor, we shall at least have the pleasure of bearing poverty together; for what is fatigue or famine, when weighed against friendship and freedom?—Adieu.

LETTER XLVIII.

From Lien Chi Altangi to ——, Merchant in Amsterdam.

HAPPENING some days ago to call at a painter's to amuse myself in examining some pictures (I had no design to buy), it surprised me to see a young prince in the working room, dressed in a painter's apron, and assiduously learning the trade. We instantly remembered to have seen each other; and, after the usual compliments, I stood by while he continued to paint on. As everything done by the rich is praised; as princes here, as well as in China, are never without followers; three or four persons, who had the appearance of gentlemen, were placed behind to comfort and applaud him at every stroke. Need I tell, that it struck me with very disagreeable sensations, to see a youth, who by his station in life had it in his power to be useful to thousands, thus letting his mind run to waste upon canvas, and at the same time fancying himself improving in taste, and filling his rank with proper decorum?

As seeing an error and attempting to redress it are only one and the same with me, I took occasion, upon his lordship's desiring my opinion of a Chinese scroll, intended for the frame of a picture, to assure him, that a mandarin of China thought a minute acquaintance with such mechanical trifles below his dignity.

This reply raised the indignation of some, and the contempt of others: I could hear the names of Vandal, Goth, taste, polite arts, delicacy, and fire, repeated in tones of ridicule or resentment. But considering that it was in vain to argue against people who had so much to say, without contradicting them, I begged leave to repeat a fairy tale. This request redoubled their laughter; but, not easily abashed at the raillery of boys, I persisted, observing, that it would set the absurdity of placing our affections upon trifles in the strongest point of view; and adding, that it was hoped the moral would compensate for its stupidity. "For Heaven's sake," cried the great man, washing his brush in water, "let us have no morality at present; if we must have a story, let it be without any moral." I pretended not to hear; and, while he handled the brush, proceeded as follows:—

"In the kingdom of Bonbobbin, which, by the Chinese annals, appears to have flourished twenty thousand years ago, there reigned a prince endowed with every accomplishment which generally distinguishes the sons of kings. His beauty was brighter than the sun. The sun, to which he was nearly related, would sometimes stop his course, in order to look down and admire him.

"His mind was not less perfect than his body: he knew all things, without having ever read: philosophers, poets, and historians submitted their works to his decision; and so penetrating was he, that he could tell you the merit of a book by looking on the cover. He made epic poems, tragedies, and pastorals with surprising facility; song, epigram, or rebus, was all one to him, though it was observed he could never finish an acrostic. In short, the fairy who presided at his birth had endowed him with almost every perfection, or, what was just the same, his subjects were ready to acknowledge he possessed them all; and, for his own part, he knew nothing to the contrary. A prince so accomplished received a name suitable to his merit; and he was called Bonbennin bonbobbin-bonbobbinet, which signifies, *Enlightener of the Sun.*

"As he was very powerful, and yet unmarried, all the neighbouring kings earnestly sought his alliance. Each sent his daughter, dressed out in the most magnificent manner, and with the most sumptuous retinue imaginable, in order to allure the prince; so that at one time there were seen at his court not less than seven hundred foreign princesses, of exquisite sentiment and beauty, each alone sufficient to make seven hundred ordinary men happy.

"Distracted in such a variety, the generous Bonbennin, had he not been obliged by the laws of the empire to make choice of one, would very willingly have married them all, for none understood gallantry better. He spent numberless hours of solicitude in endeavouring to determine whom he should choose: one lady was possessed of every perfection, but he disliked her eyebrows; another was brighter than the morning star, but he disapproved her fong-whang; a third did not lay white enough on her cheek; and a fourth did not sufficiently blacken her nails. At last, after numberless disappointments o the one side and the other, he made choic of the incomparable Nanhoa, Queen c the Scarlet Dragons.

"The preparations for the royal nuptials, or the envy of the disappointe ladies, need no description; both the on and the other were as great as they coul be: the beautiful princess was conducte amidst admiring multitudes to the roya couch, where, after being divested of ever encumbering ornament, she was placed in expectance of the youthful bridegroom who did not keep her long in expectation He came more cheerful than the morning and printing on her lips a burning kiss the attendants took this as a proper signa to withdraw.

"Perhaps I ought to have mentione in the beginning that, among several othe qualifications, the prince was fond of collecting and breeding mice, which being harmless pastime, none of his counsellor thought proper to dissuade him from: h therefore kept a great variety of thes pretty little animals, in the most beautifu cages, enriched with diamonds, rubies emeralds, pearls, and other precious stones thus he innocently spent four hours eac day in contemplating their innocent littl pastimes.

"But to proceed: the prince and princess were now in bed; one with all th love and expectation, the other with al the modesty and fear, which is natural t suppose; both willing, yet afraid to begin when the prince, happening to look towards the outside of the bed, perceive one of the most beautiful animals in th world, a white mouse with green eyes playing about the floor, and performing hundred pretty tricks. He was alread master of blue mice, red mice, and eve white mice with yellow eyes; but white mouse with green eyes was what h had long endeavoured to possess: wherefore, leaping from bed with the utmos impatience and agility, the youthful princ attempted to seize the little charmer but it was fled in a moment; for, alas the mouse was sent by a discontente princess, and was itself a fairy.

"It is impossible to describe the agon of the prince upon this occasion; h sought round and round every part of the room; even the bed where the princess lay was not exempt from the inquiry: he turned the princess on one side and the other, stripped her quite naked, but no mouse was to be found; the princess herself was kind enough to assist, but still to no purpose.

"'Alas!' cried the young prince in agony, 'how unhappy am I to be thus disappointed! never, sure, was so beautiful an animal seen: I would give half my kingdom, and my princess, to him that would find it.' The princess, though not much pleased with the latter part of his offer, endeavoured to comfort him as well as she could: she let him know that he had an hundred mice already, which ought to be at least sufficient to satisfy any philosopher like him. Though none of them had green eyes, yet he should learn to thank Heaven that they had eyes. She told him (for she was a profound moralist) that incurable evils must be borne, and that useless lamentations were vain, and that man was born to misfortunes; she even entreated him to return to bed, and she would endeavour to lull him on her bosom to repose: but still the prince continued inconsolable; and regarding her with a stern air, for which his family was remarkable, he vowed never to sleep in the royal palace, or indulge himself in the innocent pleasures of matrimony, till he had found the white mouse with the green eyes."

"Prythee, Colonel Leech," cried his Lordship, interrupting me, "how do you like that nose? don't you think there is something of the manner of Rembrandt in it?—A prince in all this agony for a white mouse, oh, ridiculous!—Don't you think, Major Vampyre, that eyebrow stippled very prettily?—But pray, what are the green eyes to the purpose, except to amuse children?—I would give a thousand guineas to lay on the colouring of his cheek more smoothly. But I ask pardon; pray, sir, proceed."

LETTER XLIX.

To the same.

"KINGS," continued I, "at that time were different from what they are now; they then never engaged their word for anything which they did not rigorously intend to perform. This was the case of Bonbennin, who continued all night to lament his misfortunes to the princess, who echoed groan for groan. When morning came, he published an edict, offering half his kingdom, and his princess, to the person who should catch and bring him the white mouse with the green eyes.

"The edict was scarcely published, when all the traps in the kingdom were baited with cheese; numberless mice were taken and destroyed; but still the much-wished-for mouse was not among the number. The privy council was assembled more than once to give their advice; but all their deliberations came to nothing, even though there were two complete vermin-killers and three professed rat-catchers of the number. Frequent addresses, as is usual on extraordinary occasions, were sent from all parts of the empire; but though these promised well, though in them he received an assurance that his faithful subjects would assist in his search with their lives and fortunes, yet, with all their loyalty, they failed when the time came that the mouse was to be caught.

"The prince, therefore, was resolved to go himself in search, determined never to lie two nights in one place, till he had found what he sought for. Thus, quitting his palace without attendants, he set out upon his journey, and travelled through many a desert, and crossed many a river, over high hills, and down long vales, still restless, still inquiring wherever he came; but no white mouse was to be found.

"As one day, fatigued with his journey, he was shading himself from the heat of the mid-day sun, under the arching branches of a banana-tree, meditating on the object of his pursuit, he perceived an old woman, hideously deformed, approaching him; by her stoop, and the wrinkles of her visage, she seemed at least five hundred years old; and the spotted toad was not more freckled than was her skin. 'Ah! Prince Bonbennin-bonbobbin-bonbobbinet,' cried the creature, 'what has led you so many thousand miles from your own kingdom? what is it you look for? and what induces you to travel into the kingdom of the Emmets?' The prince, who was excessively complaisant, told her the whole story three times over; for she was hard of hearing. 'Well,' says the old fairy, for such she was, 'I promise to put you in possession of the white mouse with green eyes, and that immediately too, upon one condition.'—'One condition,' cried the prince in a rapture; 'name a thousand: I shall undergo them all with pleasure.'—'Nay,' interrupted the old fairy, 'I ask but one, and that not very mortifying neither; it is only that you instantly consent to marry me.'

"It is impossible to express the prince's confusion at this demand; he loved the mouse, but he detested the bride: he hesitated; he desired time to think upon the proposal; he would have been glad to consult his friends on such an occasion. 'Nay, nay,' cried the odious fairy, 'if you demur, I retract my promise; I do not desire to force my favours on any man. Here, you my attendants,' cried she, stamping with her foot, 'let my machine be driven up; Barbacela, Queen of Emmets, is not used to contemptuous treatment.' She had no sooner spoken than her fiery chariot appeared in the air, drawn by two snails; and she was just going to step in, when the prince reflected, that now or never was the time to be possessed of the white mouse; and quite forgetting his lawful princess Nanhoa, falling on his knees, he implored forgiveness for having rashly rejected so much beauty. This well-timed compliment instantly appeased the angry fairy. She affected a hideous leer of approbation, and taking the young prince by the hand, conducted him to a neighbouring church, where they were married together in a moment. As soon as the ceremony was performed, the prince, who was to the last degree desirous of seeing his favourite mouse, reminded the bride of her promise. 'To confess a truth, my prince,' cried she, 'I myself am that very white mouse you saw on your wedding-night in the royal apartment. I now, therefore, give you the choice, whether you would have me a mouse by day and a woman by night, or a mouse by night and a woman by day?' Though the prince was an excellent casuist, he was quite at a loss how to determine; but at last thought it most prudent to have recourse to a blue cat that had followed him from his own dominions, and frequently amused him with its conversation, and assisted him with its advice: in fact, this cat was no other than the faithful princess Nanhoa herself, who had shared with him all his hardships in this disguise.

"By her instructions he was determined in his choice, and returning to the old fairy, prudently observed, that as she must have been sensible he had married her 'only for the sake of what she had,' and not for her personal qualifications, he thought it would, for several reasons, be most convenient if she continued a woman by day, and appeared a mouse by night.

"The old fairy was a good deal mortified at her husband's want of gallantry, though she was reluctantly obliged to comply: the day was therefore spent in the most polite amusements; the gentlemen talked smut, the ladies laughed, and were angry. At last the happy night drew near, the blue cat still stuck by the side of its master, and even followed him to the bridal apartment. Barbacela entered the chamber, wearing a train fifteen yards long, supported by porcupines, and all over beset with jewels, which served to render her more detestable. She was just stepping into bed to the prince, forgetting her promise, when he insisted upon seeing her in the shape of a mouse. She had promised, and no fairy can break her word; wherefore, assuming the figure of the most beautiful mouse in the world, she skipped and played about with an infinity of amusement. The prince, in an agony of rapture, was desirous of seeing his pretty playfellow move a slow dance about the floor to his own singing; he began to sing, and the mouse immediately to perform with the most perfect knowledge of time, and the finest grace and greatest gravity imaginable. It only began; for Nanhoa, who had long waited for the opportunity in the shape of a cat, flew upon it instantly without remorse, and eating it up in the hundredth part of a moment, broke the charm, and then resumed her natural figure.

"The prince now found that he had all

along been under the power of enchantment, that his passion for the white mouse was entirely fictitious, and not the genuine complexion of his soul; he now saw that his earnestness after mice was an illiberal amusement, and much more becoming a rat-catcher than a prince. All his meannesses now stared him in the face; he begged the discreet princess's pardon a hundred times. The princess very readily forgave him; and both returning to their palace in Bonbobbin, lived very happily together, and reigned many years, with all that wisdom which, by the story, they appear to have been possessed of; perfectly convinced by their former adventures, that they who place their affections on trifles at first for amusement, will find those trifles at last become their most serious concern."—Adieu.

LETTER L.

From Lien Chi Altangi to Fum Hoam, First President of the Ceremonial Academy at Pekin in China.

Ask an Englishman what nation in the world enjoys most freedom, and he immediately answers, his own. Ask him in what that freedom principally consists, and he is instantly silent. This happy pre-eminence does not arise from the people's enjoying a larger share in legislation than elsewhere, for in this particular several states in Europe excel them; nor does it arise from a greater exemption from taxes, for few countries pay more; it does not proceed from their being restrained by fewer laws, for no people are burdened with so many; nor does it particularly consist in the security of their property, for property is pretty well secured in every polite state in Europe.

How, then, are the English more free—for more free they certainly are—than the people of any other country, or under any other form of government whatever? Their freedom consists in their enjoying all the advantages of democracy, with this superior prerogative borrowed from monarchy, that the severity of their laws may be relaxed without endangering the constitution.

In a monarchical state, in which the constitution is strongest, the laws may be relaxed without danger; for though the people should be unanimous in the breach of any one in particular, yet still there is an effective power superior to the people, capable of enforcing obedience, whenever it may be proper to inculcate the law either towards the support or welfare of the community.

But in all those governments where laws derive their sanction from the people alone, transgressions cannot be overlooked without bringing the constitution into danger. They who transgress the law in such a case are those who prescribe it, by which means it loses not only its influence, but its sanction. In every republic the laws must be strong, because the constitution is feeble; they must resemble an Asiatic husband, who is justly jealous, because he knows himself impotent. Thus, in Holland, Switzerland, and Genoa, new laws are not frequently enacted, but the old ones are observed with unremitting severity. In such republics, therefore, the people are slaves to laws of their own making, little less than in unmixed monarchies, where they are slaves to the will of one subject to frailties like themselves.

In England, from a variety of happy accidents, their constitution is just strong enough, or, if you will, monarchical enough, to permit a relaxation of the severity of laws, and yet those laws still to remain sufficiently strong to govern the people. This is the most perfect state of civil liberty of which we can form any idea: here we see a greater number of laws than in any other country, while the people at the same time obey only such as are immediately conducive to the interests of society; several are unnoticed, many unknown; some kept to be revived and enforced upon proper occasions; others left to grow obsolete, even without the necessity of abrogation.

There is scarcely an Englishman who does not almost every day of his life offend with impunity against some express law, and for which, in a certain conjuncture of circumstances, he would not receive punishment. Gaming-houses, preaching at prohibited places, assembled crowds, nocturnal amusements, public shows, and a hundred other instances, are forbid and frequented. These prohibitions are useful; though it be prudent in their magistrates, and happy for the people, that they are not enforced, and none but the venal or mercenary attempt to enforce them.

The law in this case, like an indulgent parent, still keeps the rod, though the child is seldom corrected. Were those pardoned offences to rise into enormity, were they likely to obstruct the happiness of society, or endanger the state, it is then that justice would resume her terrors, and punish those faults she had so often overlooked with indulgence. It is to this ductility of the laws that an Englishman owes the freedom he enjoys superior to others in a more popular government: every step, therefore, the constitution takes towards a democratic form, every diminution of the regal authority, is, in fact, a diminution of the subject's freedom; but every attempt to render the government more popular not only impairs natural liberty, but even will at last dissolve the political constitution.

Every popular government seems calculated to last only for a time: it grows rigid with age; new laws are multiplying, and the old continue in force; the subjects are oppressed, burdened with a multiplicity of legal injunctions; there are none from whom to expect redress, and nothing but a strong convulsion in the state can vindicate them into former liberty: thus the people of Rome, a few great ones excepted, found more real freedom under their emperors, though tyrants, than they had experienced in the old age of the commonwealth, in which their laws were become numerous and painful, in which new laws were every day enacting, and the old ones executed with rigour. They even refused to be reinstated in their former prerogatives, upon an offer made them to this purpose; for they actually found emperors the only means of softening the rigours of their constitution.

The constitution of England is at present possessed of the strength of its native oak and the flexibility of the bending tamarisk; but should the people at any time, with a mistaken zeal, pant after an imaginary freedom, and fancy that abridging monarchy was increasing their privileges, they would be very much mistaken, since every jewel plucked from the crown of majesty would only be made use of as a bribe to corruption: it might enrich the few who shared it among them, but would in fact impoverish the public.

As the Roman senators, by slow and imperceptible degrees, became masters of the people, yet still flattered them with a show of freedom, while themselves only were free: so it is possible for a body of men, while they stand up for privileges, to grow into an exuberance of power themselves; and the public become actually dependent, while some of its individuals only govern.

If then, my friend, there should in this country ever be on the throne a king who, through good nature or age, should give up the smallest part of his prerogative to the people; if there should come a minister of merit and popularity—but I have room for no more.—Adieu.

LETTER LI.

To the same.

As I was yesterday seated at breakfast over a pensive dish of tea, my meditations were interrupted by my old friend and companion, who introduced a stranger, dressed pretty much like himself. The gentleman made several apologies for his visit, begged of me to impute his intrusion to the sincerity of his respect and the warmth of his curiosity.

As I am very suspicious of my company when I find them very civil without any apparent reason, I answered the stranger's caresses at first with reserve; which my friend perceiving, instantly let me into my visitant's trade and character, asking Mr. Fudge, whether he had lately published anything new? I now conjectured that my guest was no other than a bookseller, and his answer confirmed my suspicions.

"Excuse me, sir," says he, "it is not the season; books have their time as well as cucumbers. I would no more bring out a new work in summer, than I would sell pork in the dog days. Nothing in my way goes off in summer, except very light goods indeed. A review, a magazine, or a sessions' paper, may amuse a summer reader; but all our stock of value we reserve for a spring and winter trade."—"I must confess, sir," says I, "a curiosity to know what you call a valuable stock, which can only bear a winter perusal."—"Sir," replied the bookseller, "it is not my way to cry up my own goods; but, without exaggeration, I will venture to show with any of the trade: my books at least have the peculiar advantage of being always new; and it is my way to clear off my old to the trunk-makers every season. I have ten new title-pages now about me, which only want books to be added to make them the finest things in nature. Others may pretend to direct the vulgar; but that is not my way; I always let the vulgar direct me; wherever popular clamour arises, I always echo the million. For instance, should the people in general say that such a man is a rogue, I instantly give orders to set him down in print a villain; thus every man buys the book, not to learn new sentiments, but to have the pleasure of seeing his own reflected."—"But, sir," interrupted I, "you speak as if you yourself wrote the books you published; may I be so bold as to ask a sight of some of those intended publications which are shortly to surprise the world?"—"As to that, sir," replied the talkative bookseller, "I only draw out the plans myself; and though I am very cautious of communicating them to any, yet, as in the end I have a favour to ask, you shall see a few of them. Here, sir, here they are; diamonds of the first water, I assure you. *Imprimis*, a translation of several medical precepts for the use of such physicians as do not understand Latin. *Item*, the young clergyman's art of placing patches regularly, with a dissertation on the different manners of smiling without distorting the face. *Item*, the whole art of love made perfectly easy, by a broker of Change Alley. *Item*, the proper manner of cutting blacklead pencils, and making crayons, by the Right Hon. the Earl of ——. *Item*, the muster-master-general, or the review of reviews."—"Sir," cried I, interrupting him, "my curiosity with regard to title-pages is satisfied; I should be glad to see some longer manuscript, a history or an epic poem."—"Bless me," cries the man of industry, "now you speak of an epic poem, you shall see an excellent farce. Here it is; dip into it where you will, it will be found replete with true modern humour. Strokes, sir; it is filled with strokes of wit and satire in every line."—"Do you call these dashes of the pen strokes?" replied I; "for I must confess I can see no other."—"And pray, sir," returned he, "what do you call them? Do you see anything good now-a-days, that is not filled with strokes—and dashes?—Sir, a well-placed dash makes half the wit of our writers of modern humour. I bought a piece last season that had no other merit upon earth than nine hundred and ninety-five breaks, seventy-two ha-ha's, three good things, and a garter. And yet it played off, and bounced, and cracked, and made more sport than a firework."—"I fancy, then, sir, you were a considerable gainer?"—"It must be owned the piece did pay; but, upon the whole, I cannot much boast of last winter's success: I gained by two murders; but then I lost by an ill-timed charity sermon. I was a considerable sufferer by my Direct Road to an Estate, but the Infernal Guide brought me up again. Ah, sir, that was a piece touched off by the hand of a master; filled with good things from one end to the other. The author had nothing but the jest in view; no dull moral lurking beneath, nor ill-natured satire to sour the reader's good-humour; he wisely considered, that moral and humour at the same time were quite overdoing the business."—"To what purpose was the book then published?" cried I.—"Sir, the book was published in order to be sold; and no book sold better, except the criticisms upon it, which came out soon after: of all kinds of writing, that goes off best at present; and I generally fasten a criticism upon every selling book that is published.

"I once had an author who never left the least opening for the critics: close was the word, always very right and very dull, ever on the safe side of an argument; yet, with all his qualifications, incapable of coming into favour. I soon perceived that his bent was for criticism; and, as he was good for nothing else, supplied him with pens and paper, and planted him, at the beginning of every month, as a censor on the works of others. In short, I found him a treasure; no merit could escape him: but what is most remarkable of all, he ever wrote best and bitterest when drunk."—"But are there not some works," interrupted I, "that, from the very manner of their composition, must be exempt from criticism; particularly such as profess to disregard its laws?"—"There is no work whatsoever but he can criticise," replied the bookseller; "even though you wrote in Chinese, he would have a pluck at you. Suppose you should take it into your head to publish a book, let it be a volume of Chinese letters, for instance; write how you will, he shall show the world you could have written better. Should you, with the most local exactness, stick to the manners and customs of the country from whence you come; should you confine yourself to the narrow limits of Eastern knowledge, and be perfectly simple and perfectly natural, he has then the strongest reason to exclaim. He may, with a sneer, send you back to China for readers. He may observe that, after the first or second letter, the iteration of the same simplicity is insupportably tedious; but the worst of all is, the public, in such a case, will anticipate his censures, and leave you, with all your uninstructive simplicity, to be mauled at discretion."

"Yes," cried I, "but in order to avoid his indignation, and, what I should fear more, that of the public, I would, in such a case, write with all the knowledge I was master of. As I am not possessed of much learning, at least I would not suppress what little I had; nor would I appear more stupid than nature has made me."—"Here, then," cries the bookseller, "we should have you entirely in our power: unnatural, un-Eastern, quite out of character, erroneously sensible, would be the whole cry. Sir, we should then hunt you down like a rat."—"Head of my father!" said I, "sure there are but two ways; the door must either be shut or it must be open. I must either be natural or unnatural."—"Be what you will, we shall criticise you," returned the bookseller, "and prove you a dunce in spite of your teeth. But, sir, it is time that I should come to business. I have just now in the press a history of China; and if you will but put your name to it as the author, I shall repay the obligation with gratitude."—"What, sir!" replied I, "put my name to a work which I have not written? Never! while I retain a proper respect for the public and myself." The bluntness of my reply quite abated the ardour of the bookseller's conversation; and, after about half an hour's disagreeable reserve, he, with some ceremony, took his leave and withdrew.—Adieu.

LETTER LII.

To the same.

In all other countries, my dear Fum Hoam, the rich are distinguished by their dress. In Persia, China, and most parts of Europe, those who are possessed of much gold or silver put some of it upon their clothes; but in England those who carry much upon their clothes are remarked for having but little in their pockets. A tawdry outside is regarded as a badge of poverty; and those who can sit at home, and gloat over their thousands in silent satisfaction, are generally found to do it in plain clothes.

This diversity of thinking from the rest of the world which prevails here I was at first at a loss to account for: but am since informed, that it was introduced by an intercourse between them and their neighbours, the French, who, whenever they came in order to pay these islanders a visit, were generally very well dressed, and very poor, daubed with lace, but all the gilding on the outside. By this means laced clothes have been brought so much into contempt, that, at present, even their mandarines are ashamed of finery.

I must own myself a convert to English simplicity; I am no more for ostentation of wealth than of learning: the person who in company should pretend to be wiser than others, I am apt to regard as illiterate and ill-bred; the person whose clothes are extremely fine, I am too apt to consider as not being possessed of any superiority of fortune, but resembling those Indians who are found to wear all the gold they have in the world in a bob at the nose.

I was lately introduced into a company of the best dressed men I have seen since my arrival. Upon entering the room, I was struck with awe at the grandeur of the different dresses. That personage, thought I, in blue and gold must be some emperor's son; that in green and silver a prince of the blood; he in embroidered scarlet a prime minister; all first-rate noblemen, I suppose, and well-looking noblemen too. I sat for some time with that uneasiness which conscious inferiority produces in the ingenuous mind, all attention to their discourse. However, I found their conversation more vulgar than I could have expected from personages of such distinction. If these, thought I to myself, be princes, they are the most stupid princes I have ever conversed with: yet still I continued to venerate their dress! for dress has a kind of mechanical influence on the mind.

My friend in black, indeed, did not behave with the same deference, but contradicted the finest of them all in the most peremptory tones of contempt. But I had scarcely time to wonder at the imprudence of his conduct, when I found occasion to be equally surprised at the absurdity of theirs; for upon the entrance of a middle-aged man, dressed in a cap, dirty shirt, and boots, the whole circle seemed diminished of their former importance, and contended who should be first to pay their obeisance to the stranger. They somewhat resembled a circle of Kalmucks offering incense to a bear.

Eager to know the cause of so much seeming contradiction, I whispered my friend out of the room, and found that the august company consisted of no other than a dancing master, two fiddlers, and a third-rate actor, all assembled in order to make a set at country dances; and the middle-aged gentleman whom I saw enter was a squire from the country, and desirous of learning the new manner of footing, and smoothing up the rudiments of his rural minuet.

I was no longer surprised at the authority which my friend assumed among them; nay, was even displeased, (pardon my Eastern education,) that he had not kicked every creature of them down stairs. "What," said I, "shall a set of such paltry fellows dress themselves up like sons of kings, and claim even the transitory respect of half an hour? There should be some law to restrain so manifest a breach of privilege; they should go from house to house, as in China, with the instruments of their profession strung round their necks; by this means we might be able to distinguish and treat them in a style of becoming contempt."—"Hold, my friend," replied my companion, "were your reformation to take place, as dancing masters and fiddlers now mimic gentlemen in appearance, we should then find our fine gentlemen conforming to theirs. A beau might be introduced to a lady of fashion, with a fiddle-case hanging at his neck by a red riband; and, instead of a cane, might carry a fiddlestick. Though to be as dull as a first-rate dancing master might be used with proverbial justice: yet, dull as he is, many a fine gentleman sets him up as the proper standard of politeness; copies not only the pert vivacity of his air, but the flat insipidity of his conversation. In short, if you make a law against dancing masters imitating the fine gentleman, you should with as much reason enact, that no fine gentleman shall imitate the dancing master."

After I had left my friend, I made towards home, reflecting as I went upon the difficulty of distinguishing men by their appearance. Invited, however, by the freshness of the evening, I did not return directly, but went to ruminate on what had passed in a public garden belonging to the city. Here, as I sat upon one of the benches, and felt the pleasing sympathy which nature in bloom inspires, a disconsolate figure who sat on the other end of the seat seemed no way to enjoy the serenity of the season.

His dress was miserable beyond description: a threadbare coat, of the rudest materials; a shirt, though clean, yet extremely coarse; hair that seemed to have been long unconscious of the comb; and all the rest of his equipage impressed with the marks of genuine poverty.

As he continued to sigh and testify every symptom of despair, I was naturally led, from a motive of humanity, to offer comfort and assistance. You know my heart; and that all who are miserable may claim a place there. The pensive stranger at first declined my conversation; but at last perceiving a peculiarity in my accent and manner of thinking, he began to unfold himself by degrees.

I now found that he was not so very miserable as he at first appeared; upon my offering him a small piece of money, he refused my favour, yet without appearing displeased at my intended generosity. It is true, he sometimes interrupted the conversation with a sigh, and talked pathetically of neglected merit; yet still I could perceive a serenity in his countenance, that, upon a closer inspection, bespoke inward content.

Upon a pause in the conversation I was going to take my leave, when he begged I would favour him with my company home to supper. I was surprised at such a demand from a person of his appearance, but, willing to indulge curiosity, I accepted his invitation; and, though I felt some repugnance at being seen with one who appeared so very wretched, went along with seeming alacrity.

Still, as he approached nearer home, his good humour proportionably seemed to increase. At last he stopped, not at the gate of a hovel, but of a magnificent palace! When I cast my eyes upon all the sumptuous elegance which everywhere presented upon entering, and then when I looked at my seeming miserable conductor, I could scarcely think that all this finery belonged to him; yet in fact it did. Numerous servants ran through the apartments with silent assiduity; several ladies of beauty, and magnificently dressed, came to welcome his return; a most elegant supper was provided: in short, I found the person whom a little before I had sincerely pitied to be in reality a most refined epicure,—one who courted contempt abroad, in order to feel with keener gust the pleasure of pre-eminence at home.—Adieu.

LETTER LIII.

From the same.

How often have we admired the eloquence of Europe! that strength of thinking, that delicacy of imagination, even beyond the efforts of the Chinese themselves. How were we enraptured with those bold figures which sent every sentiment with force to the heart! How have we spent whole days together, in learning those arts by which European writers got within the passions, and led the reader as if by enchantment!

But though we have learned most of the rhetorical figures of the last age, yet there seems to be one or two of great use here, which have not yet travelled to China. The figures I mean are called Bawdry and Pertness: none are more fashionable, none so sure of admirers; they are of such a nature, that the merest blockhead, by a proper use of them, shall have the reputation of a wit; they lie level to the meanest capacities, and address those passions which all have, or would be ashamed to disown.

It has been observed, and I believe with some truth, that it is very difficult for a dunce to obtain the reputation of a wit; yet, by the assistance of the figure Bawdry, this may be easily affected, and a bawdy blockhead often passes for a fellow of smart parts and pretensions. Every object in nature helps the jokes forward, without scarce any effort of the imagination. If a lady stands, something very good may be said upon that; if she happens to fall, with the help of a little fashionable pruriency, there are forty sly things ready on the occasion. But a prurient jest has always been found to give most pleasure to a few very old gentlemen, who, being in some measure dead to other sensations, feel the force of the allusion with double violence on the organs of risibility.

An author who writes in this manner is generally sure, therefore, of having the very old and the impotent among his admirers; for these he may properly be said to write, and from these he ought to expect his reward; his works being often a very proper succedaneum to cantharides or an asafœtida pill. His pen should be considered in the same light as the squirt of an apothecary, both being directed to the same generous end.

But though this manner of writing be perfectly adapted to the taste of gentlemen and ladies of fashion here, yet still it deserves greater praise in being equally suited to the most vulgar apprehensions. The very ladies and gentlemen of Benin or Caffraria are in this respect tolerably polite, and might relish a prurient joke of this kind with critical propriety; probably, too, with higher gust, as they wear neither breeches nor petticoats to intercept the application.

It is certain I never could have thought the ladies here, biassed as they are by education, capable at once of bravely throwing off their prejudices, and not only applauding books in which this figure makes the only merit, but even adopting it in their own conversation. Yet so it is; the pretty innocents now carry those books openly in their hands, which formerly were hid under the cushion; they now lisp their double meanings with so much grace, and talk over the raptures they bestow with such little reserve, that I am sometimes reminded of a custom among the entertainers in China, who think it a piece of necessary breeding to whet the appetites of their guests, by letting them smell dinner in the kitchen, before it is served up to table.

The veneration we have for many things entirely proceeds from their being carefully concealed. Were the idolatrous Tartar permitted to lift the veil which keeps his idol from view, it might be a certain method to cure his future superstition: with what a noble spirit of freedom, therefore, must that writer be possessed, who bravely paints things as they are, who lifts the veil of modesty, who displays the most hidden recesses of the temple, and shows the erring people that the object of their vows is either, perhaps, a mouse or a monkey!

However, though this figure be at present so much in fashion; though the professors of it are so much caressed by the great, those perfect judges of literary excellence; yet it is confessed to be only a revival of what was once fashionable here before. There was a time when, by this very manner of writing, the gentle Tom D'Urfey, as I read in English authors, acquired his great reputation, and became the favourite of a king.

The works of this original genius, though they never travelled abroad to China, and scarcely have reached posterity at home, were once found upon every fashionable toilet, and made the subject of polite, I mean very polite, conversation. "Has your grace seen Mr. D'Urfey's last new thing, the *Oylet Hole?*—a most facetious piece!"—"Sure, my lord, all the world must have seen it; D'Urfey is certainly the most comical creature alive. It is impossible to read his things and live. Was there ever anything so natural and pretty, as when the Squire and Bridget meet in the cellar? And then the difficulties they both find in broaching the beer barrel are so arch and so ingenious! We have certainly nothing of this kind in the language." In this manner they spoke then, and in this manner they speak now; for though the successor of D'Urfey does not excel him in wit, the world must confess he outdoes him in obscenity.

There are several very dull fellows, who, by a few mechanical helps, sometimes learn to become extremely brilliant and pleasing; with a little dexterity in the management of the eyebrows, fingers, and nose. By imitating a cat, a sow and pigs,—by a loud laugh, and a slap on the shoulder,—the most ignorant are furnished out for conversation. But the writer finds it impossible to throw his winks, his shrugs, or his attitudes upon paper; he may borrow some assistance, indeed, by printing his face at the title-page; but, without wit, to pass for a man of ingenuity, no other mechanical help but downright obscenity will suffice. By speaking of some peculiar sensations we are always sure of exciting laughter, for the jest does not lie in the writer, but in the subject.

But Bawdry is often helped on by

another figure, called Pertness; and few indeed are found to excel in one, that are not possessed of the other.

As in common conversation the best way to make the audience laugh is by first laughing yourself; so in writing the properest manner is to show an attempt at humour, which will pass upon most for humour in reality. To effect this, readers must be treated with the most perfect familiarity: in one page the author is to make them a low bow, and in the next to pull them by the nose; he must talk in riddles, and then send them to bed, in order to dream for the solution. He must speak of himself, and his chapters, and his manner, and what he would be at, and his own importance, and his mother's importance, with the most unpitying prolixity; now and then testifying his contempt for all but himself, smiling without a jest, and without wit professing vivacity. —Adieu.

LETTER LIV.

From the same.

THOUGH naturally pensive, yet I am fond of gay company, and take every opportunity of thus dismissing the mind from duty. From this motive I am often found in the centre of a crowd; and wherever pleasure is to be sold, am always a purchaser. In those places, without being remarked by any, I join in whatever goes forward; work my passions into a similitude of frivolous earnestness, shout as they shout, and condemn as they happen to disapprove. A mind thus sunk for a while below its natural standard is qualified for stronger flights, as those first retire who would spring forward with greater vigour.

Attracted by the serenity of the evening, my friend and I lately went to gaze upon the company in one of the public walks near the city. Here we sauntered together for some time, either praising the beauty of such as were handsome, or the dresses of such as had nothing else to recommend them. We had gone thus deliberately forward for some time, when, stopping on a sudden, my friend caught me by the elbow, and led me out of the public walk. I could perceive by the quickness of his pace, and by his frequently looking behind, that he was attempting to avoid somebody who followed: we now turned to the right, then to the left; as we went forward, he still went faster; but in vain: the person whom he attempted to escape hunted us through every doubling, and gained upon us each moment, so that at last we fairly stood still, resolving to face what we could not avoid.

Our pursuer soon came up, and joined us with all the familiarity of an old acquaintance. "My dear Drybone," cries he, shaking my friend's hand, "where have you been hiding this half a century? Positively I had fancied you were gone to cultivate matrimony and your estate in the country." During the reply I had an opportunity of surveying the appearance of our new companion: his hat was pinched up with peculiar smartness; his looks were pale, thin, and sharp; round his neck he wore a broad black riband, and in his bosom a buckle studded with glass; his coat was trimmed with tarnished twist; he wore by his side a sword with a black hilt; and his stockings of silk, though newly washed, were grown yellow by long service. I was so much engaged with the peculiarity of his dress, that I attended only to the latter part of my friend's reply, in which he complimented Mr. Tibbs on the taste of his clothes, and the bloom in his countenance. "Pshaw, pshaw, Will," cried the figure, "no more of that, if you love me: you know I hate flattery,—on my soul I do; and yet, to be sure, an intimacy with the great will improve one's appearance, and a course of venison will fatten; and yet, faith, I despise the great as much as you do; but there are a great many damn'd honest fellows among them, and we must not quarrel with one half, because the other wants weeding. If they were all such as my Lord Mudler, one of the most good-natured creatures that ever squeezed a lemon, I should myself be among the number of their admirers. I was yesterday to dine at the Duchess of Piccadilly's. My lord was there. 'Ned,' says he to me, 'Ned,' says he, 'I'll hold gold to silver I can tell where you were poaching last night.' 'Poaching, my lord?' says I: 'faith, you have missed already; for I staid at home, and let the girls poach for me. That's my way: I take a fine woman as some animals do their prey—stand still, and, swoop, they fall into my mouth.'"

"Ah, Tibbs, thou art a happy fellow," cried my companion, with looks of infinite pity; "I hope your fortune is as much improved as your understanding in such company?"—"Improved!" replied the other: "you shall know,—but let it go no farther—a great secret—five hundred a year to begin with—my lord's word of honour for it. His lordship took me down in his own chariot yesterday, and we had a *tête-à-tête* dinner in the country, where we talked of nothing else."—"I fancy you forget, sir," cried I; "you told us but this moment of your dining yesterday in town."—"Did I say so?" replied he coolly; "to be sure, if I said so, it was so. Dined in town! egad, now I do remember, I did dine in town; but I dined in the country too; for you must know, my boys, I eat two dinners. By the by, I am grown as nice as the devil in my eating. I'll tell you a pleasant affair about that: we were a select party of us to dine at Lady Grogram's,—an affected piece, but let it go no farther—a secret.—Well, there happened to be no asafœtida in the sauce to a turkey, upon which, says I, I'll hold a thousand guineas, and say done first, that—But, dear Drybone, you are an honest creature; lend me half-a-crown for a minute or two, or so, just till——; but hearkee, ask me for it the next time we meet, or it may be twenty to one but I forget to pay you."

When he left us, our conversation naturally turned upon so extraordinary a character. "His very dress," cries my friend, "is not less extraordinary than his conduct. If you meet him this day, you find him in rags; if the next, in embroidery. With those persons of distinction of whom he talks so familiarly he has scarcely a coffeehouse acquaintance. However, both for the interests of society, and perhaps for his own, Heaven has made him poor; and while all the world perceives his wants, he fancies them concealed from every eye. An agreeable companion, because he understands flattery; and all must be pleased with the first part of his conversation, though all are sure of its ending with a demand on their purse. While his youth countenances the levity of his conduct, he may thus earn a precarious subsistence; but when age comes on, the gravity of which is incompatible with buffoonery, then will he find himself forsaken by all; condemned in the decline of life to hang upon some rich family whom he once despised, there to undergo all the ingenuity of studied contempt, to be employed only as a spy upon the servants, or a bugbear to fright the children into obedience."—Adieu.

LETTER LV.

To the same.

I AM apt to fancy I have contracted a new acquaintance whom it will be no easy matter to shake off. My little beau yesterday overtook me again in one of the public walks, and slapping me on the shoulder, saluted me with an air of the most perfect familiarity. His dress was the same as usual, except that he had more powder in his hair, wore a dirtier shirt, a pair of temple spectacles, and his hat under his arm.

As I knew him to be a harmless, amusing little thing, I could not return his smiles with any degree of severity: so we walked forward on terms of the utmost intimacy, and in a few minutes discussed all the usual topics preliminary to particular conversation. The oddities that marked his character, however, soon began to appear; he bowed to several well-dressed persons, who, by their manner of returning the compliment, appeared perfect strangers. At intervals he drew out a pocket-book, seeming to take memorandums, before all the company, with much importance and assiduity. In this manner he led me through the length of the whole walk, fretting at his absurdities, and fancying myself laughed at not less than him by every spectator.

When we were got to the end of our procession, "Blast me," cries he, with an air of vivacity, "I never saw the Park so thin in my life before! There's no company at all to-day; not a single face to be seen."—"No company!" interrupted I peevishly; "no company, where there is such a crowd? why, man, there's too much. What are the thousands that have been laughing at us but company?"—"Lord, my dear," returned he, with the utmost good humour, "you seem immensely chagrined; but, blast me, when the world laughs at me, I laugh at the world, and so we are even. My Lord Trip, Bill Squash the Creolian, and I, sometimes make a party at being ridiculous; and so we say and do a thousand things for the joke's sake. But I see you are grave, and if you are for a fine grave sentimental companion, you shall dine with me and my wife to-day; I must insist on't. I'll introduce you to Mrs. Tibbs, a lady of as elegant qualifications as any in nature; she was bred, but that's between ourselves, under the inspection of the Countess of All-night. A charming body of voice; but no more of that,—she will give us a song. You shall see my little girl too, Carolina Wilhelmina Amelia Tibbs, a sweet pretty creature! I design her for my Lord Drumstick's eldest son; but that's in friendship, let it go no farther: she's but six years old, and yet she walks a minuet, and plays on the guitar immensely already. I intend she shall be as perfect as possible in every accomplishment. In the first place, I'll make her a scholar: I'll teach her Greek myself, and learn that language purposely to instruct her; but let that be a secret."

Thus saying, without waiting for a reply, he took me by the arm, and hauled me along. We passed through many dark alleys and winding ways; for, from some motives to me unknown, he seemed to have a particular aversion to every frequented street: at last, however, we got to the door of a dismal-looking house in the outlets of the town, where he informed me he chose to reside for the benefit of the air.

We entered the lower door, which ever seemed to lie most hospitably open; and I began to ascend an old and creaking staircase, when, as he mounted to show me the way, he demanded whether I delighted in prospects; to which answering in the affirmative, "Then," says he, "I shall show you one of the most charming in the world out of my window; we shall see the ships sailing, and the whole country for twenty miles round, tip top, quite high. My Lord Swamp would give ten thousand guineas for such a one; but, as I sometimes pleasantly tell him, I always love to keep my prospects at home, that my friends may visit me the oftener."

By this time we were arrived as high as the stairs would permit us to ascend, till we came to what he was facetiously pleased to call the first floor down the chimney; and knocking at the door, a voice from within demanded, "Who's there?" My conductor answered that it was him. But this not satisfying the querist, the voice again repeated the demand; to which he answered louder than before; and now the door was opened by an old woman with cautious reluctance.

When we were got in, he welcomed me to his house with great ceremony, and turning to the old woman, asked where was her lady? "Good troth," replied she, in a peculiar dialect, "she's washing your twa shirts at the next door, because they have taken an oath against lending out the tub any longer."—"My two shirts!" cried he in a tone that faltered with confusion; "what does the idiot mean?"—"I ken what I mean weel enough," replied the other; "she's washing your twa shirts at the next door, because——."—"Fire and fury, no more of thy stupid explanations!" cried he; "go and inform her we have got company. Were that Scotch hag," continued he, turning to me, "to be for ever in my family, she would never learn politeness, nor forget that absurd poisonous accent of hers, or testify the smallest specimen of breeding or high life; and yet it is very surprising too, as I had her from a parliament man, a friend of mine from the Highlands, one of the politest men in the world; but that's a secret."

We waited some time for Mrs. Tibbs' arrival, during which interval I had a full opportunity of surveying the chamber and all its furniture, which consisted of four chairs with old wrought bottoms, that he assured me were his wife's embroidery; a square table that had been once japanned; a cradle in one corner, a lumbering cabinet in the other; a broken shepherdess.

and a mandarine without a head, were stuck over the chimney; and round the walls several paltry unframed pictures, which, he observed, were all his own drawing. "What do you think, sir, of that head in the corner, done in the manner of Grisoni? There's the true keeping in it; it is my own face, and though there happens to be no likeness, a Countess offered me an hundred for its fellow. I refused her, for, hang it, that would be mechanical, you know."

The wife at last made her appearance, at once a slattern and a coquette; much emaciated, but still carrying the remains of beauty. She made twenty apologies for being seen in such odious dishabille, but hoped to be excused, as she had staid out all night at the gardens with the Countess, who was excessively fond of the horns. "And, indeed, my dear," added she, turning to her husband, "his lordship drank your health in a bumper."—"Poor Jack!" cries he; "a dear good-natured creature, I know he loves me. But I hope, my dear, you have given orders for dinner; you need make no great preparations neither, there are but three of us; something elegant and little will do,—a turbot, an ortolan, a——."—"Or what do you think, my dear," interrupts the wife, "of a nice pretty bit of ox-cheek, piping hot, and dressed with a little of my own sauce?"—"The very thing!" replies he; "it will eat best with some smart bottled beer: but be sure to let us have the sauce his Grace was so fond of. I hate your immense loads of meat; that is country all over; extreme disgusting to those who are in the least acquainted with high life."

By this time my curiosity began to abate, and my appetite to increase: the company of fools may at first make us smile, but at last never fails of rendering us melancholy; I therefore pretended to recollect a prior engagement, and, after having shown my respect to the house, according to the fashion of the English, by giving the old servant a piece of money at the door, I took my leave; Mrs. Tibbs assuring me that dinner, if I stayed, would be ready at least in less than two hours.

LETTER LVI.

From Fum Hoam to Altangi, the Discontented Wanderer.

THE distant sounds of music, that catch new sweetness as they vibrate through the long-drawn valley, are not more pleasing to the ear than the tidings of a far distant friend.

I have just received two hundred of thy letters by the Russian caravan, descriptive of the manners of Europe. You have left it to geographers to determine the site of their mountains and extent of their lakes, seeming only employed in discovering the genius, the government, and disposition of the people.

In those letters I perceive a journal of the operations of your mind upon whatever occurs, rather than a detail of your travels from one building to another; of your taking a draft of this ruin, or that obelisk; of paying so many *tomans* for this commodity, or laying up a proper store for the passage of some new wilderness.

From your accounts of Russia, I learn that this nation is again relaxing into pristine barbarity; that its great emperor wanted a life of an hundred years more to bring about his vast designs. A savage people may be resembled to their own forests; a few years are sufficient to clear away the obstructions to agriculture, but it requires many ere the ground acquires a proper degree of fertility: the Russians, attached to their ancient prejudices, again renew their hatred to strangers, and indulge every former brutal excess. So true it is, that the revolutions of wisdom are slow and difficult; the revolutions of folly or ambition precipitate and easy. "We are not to be astonished," says Confucius, "that the wise walk more slowly in their road to virtue, than fools in their passage to vice; since passion drags us along, while wisdom only points out the way."

The German empire, that remnant of the majesty of ancient Rome, appears, from your accounts, on the eve of dissolution. The members of its vast body want every tie of government to unite them, and seem feebly held together only by their respect for ancient institutions. The very name of country and countrymen, which in other nations makes one of the strongest bonds of government, has been here for some time laid aside; each of its inhabitants seeming more proud of being called from the petty state which gives him birth, than by the more well-known title of German.

This government may be regarded in the light of a severe master and a feeble opponent. The states which are now subject to the laws of the empire, are only watching a proper occasion to fling off the yoke; and those which are become too powerful to be compelled to obedience, now begin to think of dictating in their turn. The struggles in this state are, therefore, not in order to preserve, but to destroy, the ancient constitution: if one side succeeds, the government must become despotic; if the other, several states will subsist without even nominal subordination; but in either case the Germanic constitution will be no more.

Sweden, on the contrary, though now seemingly a strenuous assertor of its liberties, is probably only hastening on to despotism. Their senators, while they pretend to vindicate the freedom of the people, are only establishing their own independence. The deluded people will, however, at last perceive the miseries of an aristocratical government; they will perceive that the administration of a society of men is ever more painful than that of one only. They will fly from this most oppressive of all forms, where one single member is capable of controlling the whole, to take refuge under the throne, which will ever be attentive to their complaints. No people long endure an aristocratical government, when they can apply elsewhere for redress. The lower orders of people may be enslaved for a time by a number of tyrants, but, upon the first opportunity, they will ever take a refuge in despotism or democracy.

As the Swedes are making concealed approaches to despotism, the French, on the other hand, are imperceptibly vindicating themselves into freedom. When I consider that those parliaments (the members of which are all created by the court, the presidents of which can act only by immediate direction) presume even to mention privileges and freedom, who, till of late, received directions from the throne with implicit humility; when this is considered, I cannot help fancying that the genius of freedom has entered that kingdom in disguise. If they have but three weak monarchs more successively on the throne, the mask will be laid aside, and the country will certainly once more be free.

When I compare the figure which the Dutch make in Europe with that they assume in Asia, I am struck with surprise. In Asia, I find them the great lords of all the Indian seas; in Europe, the timid inhabitants of a paltry state. No longer the sons of freedom, but of avarice; no longer assertors of their rights by courage, but by negotiations, fawning on those who insult them, and crouching under the rod of every neighbouring power. Without a friend to save them in distress, and without virtue to save themselves, their government is poor, and their private wealth will serve but to invite some neighbouring invader.

I long with impatience for your letters from England, Denmark, Holland, and Italy; yet why wish for relations which only describe new calamities, which show that ambition and avarice are equally terrible in every region!—Adieu.

LETTER LVII.

From Lien Chi Altangi to Fum Hoam, First President of the Ceremonial Academy at Pekin in China.

I HAVE frequently admired the manner of criticising in China, where the learned are assembled in a body to judge of every new publication; to examine the merits of the work, without knowing the circumstances of the author; and then to usher it into the world with proper marks of respect or reprobation.

In England there are no such tribunals erected; but if a man thinks proper to be a judge of genius, few will be at the pains to contradict his pretensions. If any choose to be critics, it is but saying they are critics, and from that time forward they become invested with full power and authority over every caitiff who aims at their instruction or entertainment.

As almost every member of society has, by this means, a vote in literary transactions, it is no way surprising to find the rich leading the way here, as in other common concerns of life; to see them either bribing the numerous herd of voters by their interest, or browbeating them by their authority.

A great man says, at his table, that such a book *is no bad thing*. Immediately the praise is carried off by five flatterers, to be dispersed at twelve different coffee-houses, from whence it circulates, still improving as it proceeds, through forty-five houses where cheaper liquors are sold; from thence it is carried away by the honest tradesman to his own fireside, where the applause is eagerly caught up by his wife and children, who have been long taught to regard his judgment as the standard of perfection. Thus, when we have traced a wide-extended literary reputation up to its original source, we shall find it derived from some great man, who has perhaps received all his education and English from a tutor of Berne or a dancing master of Picardy.

The English are a people of good sense, and I am the more surprised to find them swayed in their opinions by men who often from their very education are incompetent judges. Men who, being always bred in affluence, see the world only on one side, are surely improper judges of human nature. They may, indeed, describe a ceremony, a pageant, or a ball; but how can they pretend to dive into the secrets of the human heart, who have been nursed up only in forms, and daily behold nothing but the same insipid adulation smiling upon every face? Few of them have been bred in that best of schools, the school of adversity; and, by what I can learn, fewer still have been bred in any school at all.

From such a description one would think that a droning duke, or a dowager duchess, was not possessed of more just pretensions to taste than persons of less quality; and yet whatever the one or the other may write or praise shall pass for perfection, without farther examination. A nobleman has but to take a pen, ink, and paper, write away through three large volumes, and then sign his name to the title-page; though the whole might have been before more disgusting than his own rent-roll, yet signing his name and title gives value to the deed, title being alone equivalent to taste, imagination, and genius.

As soon as a piece, therefore, is published, the first questions are, Who is the author? Does he keep a coach? Where lies his estate? What sort of a table does he keep? If he happens to be poor and unqualified for such a scrutiny, he and his works sink into irremediable obscurity, and too late he finds, that having fed upon turtle is a more ready way to fame, than having digested Tully.

The poor devil against whom fashion has set its face vainly alleges that he has been bred in every part of Europe where knowledge was to be sold; that he has grown pale in the study of nature and himself. His works may please upon the perusal, but his pretensions to fame are entirely disregarded. He is treated like a fiddler, whose music, though liked, is not much praised, because he lives by it; while a gentleman performer, though the most wretched scraper alive, throws the audience into raptures. The fiddler, indeed, may in such a case console himself by thinking, that while the other goes off with all the praise, he runs away with all the money. But here the parallel drops; for while the nobleman triumphs in unmerited applause, the author by profession steals off with—nothing.

The poor, therefore, here, who draw their pens auxiliary to the laws of their country, must think themselves very happy if they find, not fame, but forgiveness: and yet they are hardly treated; for as every country grows more polite, the press becomes more useful, and writers become more necessary as readers are supposed to increase. In a polished society, that man, though in rags, who has the power of enforcing virtue from the press, is of more real use than forty stupid brahmins, or bonzes, or guebres, though they preached never so often, never so loud, or never so long. That man, though in rags, who is capable of deceiving even indolence into wisdom, and who professes amusement, while he aims at reformation, is more useful in refined society than twenty cardinals, with all their scarlet, and tricked out in all the fopperies of scholastic finery.

LETTER LVIII.

To the same.

As the Man in Black takes every opportunity of introducing me to such company as may serve to indulge my speculative temper, or gratify my curiosity, I was by his influence lately invited to a *visitation* dinner. To understand this term, you must know that it was formerly the custom here for the principal priests to go about the country once a year, and examine upon the spot whether those of subordinate orders did their duty, or were qualified for the task; whether their temples were kept in proper repair, or the laity pleased with their administration.

Though a visitation of this nature was very useful, yet it was found to be exceedingly troublesome, and for many reasons utterly inconvenient; for as the principal priests were obliged to attend at court, in order to solicit preferment, it was impossible they could at the same time attend in the country, which was quite out of the road to promotion. If we add to this the gout, which has been, time immemorial, a clerical disorder here, together with the bad wine and ill-dressed provisions that must infallibly be served up by the way, it was not strange that the custom has been long discontinued. At present, therefore, every head of the church, instead of going about to visit his priests, is satisfied if his priests come in a body once a year to visit him; by this means the duty of half a year is despatched in a day. When assembled, he asks each in turn how they have behaved, and are liked, upon which those who have neglected their duty, or are disagreeable to their congregation, no doubt accuse themselves, and tell him all their faults, for which he reprimands them most severely.

The thoughts of being introduced into a company of philosophers and learned men (for as such I conceived them) gave me no small pleasure. I expected our entertainment would resemble those sentimental banquets so finely described by Xenophon and Plato; I was hoping some Socrates would be brought in from the door, in order to harangue upon divine love: but as for eating and drinking, I had prepared myself to be disappointed in that particular. I was apprised that fasting and temperance were tenets strongly recommended to the professors of Christianity, and I had seen the frugality and mortification of the priests of the East; so that I expected an entertainment where we should have much reasoning and little meat.

Upon being introduced, I confess I found no great signs of mortification in the faces or persons of the company. However, I imputed their florid looks to temperance, and their corpulency to a sedentary way of living. I saw several preparations, indeed, for dinner, but none for philosophy. The company seemed to gaze upon the table with silent expectation; but this I easily excused. Men of wisdom, thought I, are ever slow of speech; they deliver nothing unadvisedly. "Silence," says Confucius, "is a friend that will never betray." They are now probably inventing maxims or hard sayings for their mutual instruction, when some one shall think proper to begin.

My curiosity was now wrought up to the highest pitch. I impatiently looked round to see if any were going to interrupt the mighty pause, when at last one of the company declared that there was a sow in his neighbourhood that farrowed fifteen pigs at a litter. This I thought a very preposterous beginning; but just as another was going to second the remark, dinner was served, which interrupted the conversation for that time.

The appearance of dinner, which consisted of a variety of dishes, seemed to diffuse new cheerfulness upon every face, so that I now expected the philosophical conversation to begin, as they improved in good humour. The principal priest, however, opened his mouth with only observing, that the venison had not been kept enough, though he had given strict orders for having it killed ten days before. "I fear," continued he, "it will be found to want the true heathy flavour; you will find nothing of the original wildness in it." A priest who sat next him having smelt it, and wiped his nose, "Ah, my good lord," cries he, "you are too modest; it is perfectly fine: everybody knows that nobody understands keeping venison with your lordship."—"Ay, and partridges, too," interrupted another; "I never find them right anywhere else." His lordship was going to reply, when a third took off the attention of the company, by recommending the pig as inimitable. "I fancy, my lord," continues he, "it has been smothered in its own blood."—"If it has been smothered in its blood," cried a facetious member, helping himself, "we'll now smother it in egg sauce." This poignant piece of humour produced a long loud laugh, which the facetious brother observing, and now that he was in luck, willing to second his blow, assured the company he would tell them a good story about that. "As good a story," cries he, bursting into a violent fit of laughter himself, "as ever you heard in your lives. There was a farmer in my parish who used to sup upon wild ducks and flummery; so this farmer——" —"Doctor Marrowfat," cries his lordship, interrupting him, "give me leave to drink your health." "So being fond of wild ducks and flummery,——" —"Doctor," adds a gentleman who sat next to him, "let me advise you to a wing of this turkey." "So this farmer being fond ——"—"Hob and nob, Doctor; which do you choose, white or red?" "So, being fond of wild ducks and flummery; ——" —"Take care of your band, sir, it may dip in the gravy." The Doctor, now looking round, found not a single *eye* disposed to listen; wherefore, calling for a glass of wine, he gulped down the disappointment and the tale in a bumper.

The conversation now began to be little more than a rhapsody of exclamations: as each had pretty well satisfied his own appetite, he now found sufficient time to press others. "Excellent! the very thing! let me recommend the pig. Do but taste the bacon! never ate a better thing in my life: exquisite! delicious!" This edifying discourse continued through three courses, which lasted as many hours, till every one of the company was unable to swallow or utter anything more.

It is very natural for men who are abridged in one excess to break into some other. The clergy here, particularly those who are advanced in years, think, if they are abstemious with regard to women and wine, they may indulge their other appetites without censure. Thus some are found to rise in the morning only to a consultation with their cook about dinner, and, when that has been swallowed, make no other use of their faculties (if they have any) but to ruminate on the succeeding meal.

A debauch of wine is even more pardonable than this, since one glass insensibly leads on to another, and, instead of sating, whets the appetite. The progressive steps to it are cheerful and seducing; the grave are animated, the melancholy relieved, and there is even classic authority to countenance the excess. But in eating, after nature is once satisfied, every additional morsel brings stupidity and distempers with it, and, as one of their own poets expresses it,—

> The soul subsides, and wickedly inclines
> To seem but mortal, e'en in sound divines.

Let me suppose, after such a meal as this I have been describing, while all the company are sitting in lethargic silence round the table, groaning under a load of soup, pig, pork, and bacon; let me suppose, I say, some hungry beggar, with looks of want, peeping through one of the windows, and thus addressing the assembly: "Prithee, pluck those napkins from your chins; after nature is satisfied, all that you eat extraordinary is my property, and I claim it as mine. It was given you in order to relieve me, and not to oppress yourselves. How can they comfort or instruct others, who can scarce feel their own existence, except from the unsavoury returns of an ill-digested meal? But though neither you nor the cushions you sit upon will hear me, yet the world regards the excesses of its teachers with a prying eye, and notes their conduct with double severity." I know no other answer any one of the company could make to such an expostulation but this: "Friend, you talk of our losing a character, and being disliked by the world; well, and supposing all this to be true, what then! who cares for the world? We'll preach for the world, and the world shall pay us for preaching, whether we like each other or not."

LETTER LIX.

From Hingpo to Lien Chi Altangi, by the way of Moscow.

YOU will probably be pleased to see my letter dated from Terki, a city which lies beyond the bounds of the Persian empire: here, blessed with security, with all that is dear, I double my raptures by communicating them to you: the mind sympathising with the freedom of the body, my whole soul is dilated in gratitude, love, and praise.

Yet, were my own happiness all that inspired my present joy, my raptures might justly merit the imputation of self-interest; but when I think that the beautiful Zelis is also free, forgive my triumph when I boast of having rescued from captivity the most deserving object upon earth.

You remember the reluctance she testified at being obliged to marry the tyrant she hated. Her compliance at last was only feigned, in order to gain time to try some future means of escape. During the interval between her promise and the intended performance of it she came, undiscovered, one evening to the place where I generally retired after the fatigues of the day: her appearance was like that of an aërial genius, when it descends to minister comfort to undeserved distress; the mild lustre of her eye served to banish my timidity; her accents were sweeter than the echo of some distant symphony. "Unhappy stranger," said she, in the Persian language, "you here perceive one more wretched than thyself! All this solemnity of preparation, this elegance of dress, and the number of my attendants, serve but to increase my miseries: if you have courage to rescue an unhappy woman from approaching ruin, and our detested tyrant, you may depend upon my future gratitude." I bowed to the ground, and she left me filled with rapture and astonishment. Night brought me no rest, nor could the ensuing morning calm the anxieties of my mind. I projected a thousand methods for her delivery; but each, when strictly examined, appeared impracticable: in this uncertainty the evening again arrived, and I placed myself on my former station, in hopes of a repeated visit. After some short expectation, the bright perfection again appeared: I bowed, as before, to the ground; when, raising me up, she observed that the time was not to be spent in useless ceremony; she observed that the day following was appointed for the celebration of her nuptials, and that something was to be done that very night for our mutual deliverance. I offered with the utmost humility to pursue whatever scheme she should direct: upon which she proposed that instant to scale the garden wall, adding that she had prevailed upon a female slave, who was now waiting at the appointed place, to assist her with a ladder.

Pursuant to this information, I led her trembling to the place appointed; but, instead of the slave we expected to see, Mostadad himself was there awaiting our arrival: the wretch in whom we had confided, it seems, had betrayed our design to her master, and he now saw the most convincing proofs of her information. He was just going to draw his sabre, when a principle of avarice repressed his fury; and he resolved, after a severe chastisement, to dispose of me to another master; in the meantime he ordered me to be confined in the strictest manner, and the next day to receive a hundred blows on the soles of my feet.

When the morning came, I was led out in order to receive the punishment, which, from the severity with which it is generally inflicted upon slaves, is worse even than death.

A trumpet was to be the signal for the solemnization of the nuptials of Zelis, and for the infliction of my punishment. Each ceremony, to me equally dreadful, was just going to begin, when we were informed that a large body of Circassian Tartars had invaded the town, and were laying all in ruin. Every person now thought only of saving himself: I instantly unloosed the cords with which I was bound, and seizing a scimitar from one of the slaves, who had not courage to resist me, flew to the women's apartment, where Zelis was confined, dressed out for the intended nuptials. I bade her follow me without delay, and, going forward, cut my way through the eunuchs, who made but a faint resistance. The whole city was now a scene of conflagration and terror; every person was willing to save himself, unmindful of others. In this confusion, seizing upon two of the fleetest coursers in the stables of Mostadad, we fled northward towards the kingdom of Circassia. As there were several others flying in the same manner, we passed without notice, and in three days arrived at Terki, a city that lies in a valley within the bosom of the frowning mountains of Caucasus. Here, free from every apprehension of danger, we enjoy all those satisfactions which are consistent with virtue: though I find my heart at intervals give way to unusual passions, yet such is my admiration for my fair companion, that I lose even tenderness in distant respect. Though her person demands particular regard even among the beauties of Circassia, yet is her mind far more lovely. How very different is a woman who thus has cultivated her understanding, and been refined into delicacy of sentiment, from the daughters of the East, whose education is only formed to improve the person, and make them more tempting objects of prostitution.—Adieu.

LETTER LX.

From the same.

WHEN sufficiently refreshed after the fatigues of our precipitate flight, my curiosity, which had been restrained by the appearance of immediate danger, now began to revive: I longed to know by what distressful accident my fair fugitive became a captive, and could not avoid testifying a surprise how so much beauty could be involved in the calamities from whence she had been so lately rescued.

"Talk not of personal charms," cried she, with emotion, "since to them I owe every misfortune. Look round on the numberless beauties of the country where we are, and see how Nature has poured its charms upon every face; and yet, by this profusion, Heaven would seem to show how little it regards such a blessing, since the gift is lavished upon a nation of prostitutes.

"I perceive you desire to know my story, and your curiosity is not so great as my impatience to gratify it: I find a pleasure in telling past misfortunes to any; but when my deliverer is pleased with the relation, my pleasure is prompted by duty.

"I was born in a country far to the west, where the men are braver, and the women more fair, than those of Circassia; where the valour of the hero is guided by wisdom, and where delicacy of sentiment points the shafts of female beauty. I was the only daughter of an officer in the army, the child of his age, and, as he used fondly to express it, the only chain that bound him to the world, or made his life pleasing. His station procured him an acquaintance with men of greater rank and fortune than himself, and his regard for me induced him to bring me into every family where he was acquainted. Thus I was early taught all the elegancies and fashionable foibles of such as the world calls polite, and, though without fortune myself, was taught to despise those who lived as if they were poor.

"My intercourse with the great, and my affectation of grandeur, procured me many lovers; but want of fortune deterred them all from any other views than those of passing the present moment agreeably, or of meditating my future ruin. In every company I found myself addressed in a warmer strain of passion than other ladies who were superior in point of rank and beauty; and this I imputed to an excess of respect, which in reality proceeded from very different motives.

"Among the number of such as paid me their addresses was a gentleman, a friend of my father, rather in the decline of life, with nothing remarkable either in his person or address to commend him. His age, which was about forty; his fortune, which was moderate, and barely sufficient to support him, served to throw me off my guard: so that I considered him as the only sincere admirer I had.

"Designing lovers in the decline of life are ever most dangerous. Skilled in all the weaknesses of the sex, they seize each favourable opportunity; and by having less passion than youthful admirers, have less real respect, and therefore less timidity. This insidious wretch used a thousand arts to succeed in his base designs, all which I saw, but imputed to different views, because I thought it absurd to believe the real motives.

"As he continued to frequent my father's, the friendship between them became every day greater; and at last, from the intimacy with which he was received, I was taught to look upon him as a guardian and a friend. Though I never loved, yet I esteemed him; and this was enough to make me wish for an union, for which he seemed desirous, but to which he feigned several delays; while, in the meantime, from a false report of our being married, every other admirer forsook me.

"I was at last, however, awakened from the delusion, by an account of his being just married to another young lady with a considerable fortune. This was no great mortification to me, as I had always regarded him merely from prudential motives; but it had a very different effect upon my father, who, rash and passionate by nature, and, besides, stimulated by a mistaken notion of military honour, upbraided his friend in such terms, that a challenge was soon given and accepted.

"It was about midnight when I was awakened by a message from my father, who desired to see me that moment. I rose with some surprise, and following the messenger, attended only by another servant, came to a field not far from the house, where I found him—the assertor of my honour, my only friend and supporter, the tutor and companion of my youth—lying on one side, covered over with blood, and just expiring. No tears streamed down my cheeks, nor sigh escaped from my breast, at an object of such terror. I sat down, and supporting his aged head in my lap, gazed upon the ghastly visage with an agony more poignant even than despairing madness. The servants were gone for more assistance. In this gloomy stillness of the night no sounds were heard but his agonizing respirations; no object was presented but his wounds, which still continued to stream. With silent anguish I hung over his dear face, and with my hands strove to stop the blood as it flowed from his wounds: he seemed at first insensible, but at last, turning his dying eyes upon me, 'My dear, dear child,' cried he; 'dear, though you have forgotten your own honour and stained mine, I will yet forgive you: by abandoning virtue you have undone me and yourself; yet take my forgiveness with the same compassion I wish Heaven may pity me.' He expired. All my succeeding happiness fled with him. Reflecting that I was the cause of his death, whom only I loved upon earth—accused of betraying the honour of his family with his latest breath—conscious of my own innocence, yet without even a possibility of vindicating it—without fortune or friends to relieve or pity me—abandoned to infamy and the wide censuring world,—I called out upon the dead body that lay stretched before me, and in the agony of my heart asked, why he could have left me thus?—'Why, my dear, my only papa, why could you ruin me thus and yourself for ever? Oh, pity and return, since there is none but you to comfort me!'

"I soon found that I had real cause for sorrow; that I was to expect no compassion from my own sex, nor assistance from the other; and that reputation was much more useful in our commerce with mankind, than really to deserve it. Wherever I came, I perceived myself received either with contempt or detestation; or whenever I was civilly treated, it was from the most base and ungenerous motives.

"Thus driven from the society of the virtuous, I was at last, in order to dispel the anxieties of insupportable solitude, obliged to take up with the company of those whose characters were blasted like my own; but who perhaps deserved their infamy. Among this number was a lady of the first distinction, whose character the public thought proper to brand even with greater infamy than mine. A similitude of distress soon united us; I knew that general reproach had made her miserable; and I had learned to regard misery as an excuse for guilt. Though this lady had not virtue enough to avoid reproach, yet she had too much delicate sensibility not to feel it. She therefore proposed our leaving the country where we were born, and going to live in Italy, where our characters and misfortunes would be unknown. With this I eagerly complied, and we soon found ourselves in one of the most charming retreats in the most beautiful province of that enchanting country.

"Had my companion chosen this as a retreat for injured virtue, an harbour where we might look with tranquillity on the distant angry world, I should have been happy: but very different was her design; she had pitched upon this situation only to enjoy those pleasures in private, which she had not sufficient effrontery to satisfy in a more open manner. A nearer acquaintance soon showed me the vicious part of her character; her mind, as well as her body, seemed formed only for pleasure: she was sentimental only as it served to protract the immediate enjoyment. Formed for society alone, she spoke infinitely better than she wrote, and wrote infinitely better than she lived. A person devoted to pleasure often leads the most miserable life imaginable; such was her case; she considered the natural moments of languor as insupportable, passed all her hours between rapture and anxiety; ever in an extreme of agony or of bliss. She felt a pain as severe for want of appetite as the starving wretch who wants a meal. In those intervals she usually kept her bed, and rose only when in expectation of some new enjoyment. The luxuriant air of the country, the romantic situation of her palace, and the genius of a people whose only happiness lies in sensual refinement, all contributed to banish the remembrance of her native country.

"But though such a life gave her pleasure, it had a very different effect upon me; I grew every day more pensive, and my melancholy was regarded as an insult upon her good humour. I now perceived myself entirely unfit for all society; discarded from the good, and detesting the infamous, I seemed in a state of war with every rank of people; that virtue, which should have been my protection in the world, was here my crime; in short, detesting life, I was determined to become a recluse, to leave a world where I found no pleasure that could allure me to stay. Thus determined, I embarked in order to go by sea to Rome, where I intended to take the veil: but even in so short a passage my hard fortune still attended me; our ship was taken by a Barbary corsair; the whole crew, and I among the number, being made slaves. It carries too much the air of romance to inform you of my distresses or obstinacy in this miserable state; it is enough to observe, that I have been bought by several masters, each of whom, perceiving my reluctance, rather than use violence, sold me to another, till it was my happiness to be at last rescued by you."

Thus ended her relation, which I have abridged; but as soon as we are arrived at Moscow, for which we intend to set out shortly, you shall be informed of all more particularly. In the meantime, the greatest addition to my happiness will be to hear of yours.—Adieu.

LETTER LXI.

From Lien Chi Altangi to Hingpo.

THE news of your freedom lifts the load of former anxiety from my mind; I can now think of my son without regret, applaud his resignation under calamities, and his conduct in extricating himself from them.

You are now free, just let loose from the bondage of a hard master: this is the crisis of your fate; and as you now manage fortune, succeeding life will be marked with happiness or misery. A few years' perseverance in prudence, which at your age is but another name for virtue, will ensure comfort, pleasure, tranquillity, esteem; too eager an enjoyment of every good that now offers, will reverse the medal, and present you with poverty, anxiety, remorse, contempt.

As it has been observed, that none are better qualified to give others advice, than those who have taken the least of it themselves; so in this respect I find myself perfectly authorized to offer mine, even though I should waive my paternal authority upon this occasion.

The most usual way among young men who have no resolution of their own is, first to ask one friend's advice, and follow it for some time; then to ask advice of another, and turn to that; so of a third: still unsteady, always changing. However, be assured, that every change of this nature is for the worse: people may tell you of your being unfit for some peculiar occupations in life; but heed them not; whatever employment you follow with perseverance and assiduity will be found fit for you; it will be your support in youth, and comfort in age. In learning the useful part of every profession very moderate abilities will suffice; even if the mind be a little balanced with stupidity, it may in this case be useful. Great abilities have always been less serviceable to the possessors than moderate ones. Life has been compared to a race; but the allusion still improves by observing, that the most swift are ever the least manageable.

To know one profession only, is enough for one man to know; and this (whatever the professors may tell you to the contrary) is soon learned. Be contented, therefore, with one good employment; for if you understand two at a time, people will give you business in neither.

A conjurer and a tailor once happened to converse together. "Alas!" cries the tailor, "what an unhappy poor creature am I; if people should ever take it in their heads to live without clothes, I am undone; I have no other trade to have recourse to."—"Indeed, friend, I pity you sincerely," replies the conjurer; "but, thank Heaven, things are not quite so bad with me; for if one trick should fail, I have a hundred tricks more for them yet. However, if at any time you are reduced to beggary, apply to me, and I will relieve you." A famine overspread the land; the tailor made a shift to live, because his customers could not be without clothes; but the poor conjurer, with all his hundred tricks, could find none that had money to throw away: it was in vain that he promised to eat fire, or to vomit pins; no single creature would relieve him, till he was at last obliged to beg from the very tailor whose calling he had formerly despised.

There are no obstructions more fatal to fortune than pride and resentment. If you must resent injuries at all, at least suppress your indignation until you become rich, and then show away: the resentment of a poor man is like the efforts of a harmless insect to sting; it may get him crushed, but cannot defend him. Who values that anger which is consumed only in empty menaces?

Once upon a time, a goose fed its young by a pond side; and a goose, in such circumstances, is always extremely proud, and excessively punctilious. If any other animal, without the least design to offend, happened to pass that way, the goose was immediately at him. The pond, she said, was hers, and she would maintain a right in it, and support her honour, while she had a bill to hiss, or a wing to flutter. In this manner she drove away ducks, pigs, and chickens; nay, even the insidious cat was seen to scamper. A lounging mastiff, however, happened to pass by, and thought it no harm if he should lap a little of the water, as he was thirsty. The guardian goose flew at him like a fury, pecked at him with her beak, and flapped him with her feathers. The dog grew angry, and had twenty times a good mind to give her a sly snap; but suppressing his indignation, because his master was nigh, "A pox take thee," cries he, "for a fool! sure those who have neither strength nor weapons to fight, at least should be civil: that fluttering and hissing of thine may one day get thine head snapped off, but it can neither injure thy enemies, nor ever protect thee." So saying, he went forward to the pond, quenched his thirst in spite of the goose, and followed his master.

Another obstruction to the fortune of youth is, that while they are willing to take offence from none, they are also equally desirous of giving nobody offence. From hence they endeavour to please all, comply with every request, attempt to suit themselves to every company, have no will of their own, but, like wax, catch every contiguous impression. By thus attempting to give universal satisfaction, they at last find themselves miserably disappointed: to bring the generality of admirers on our side, it is sufficient to attempt pleasing a very few.

A painter of eminence was once resolved to finish a piece which should please the whole world. When, therefore, he had drawn a picture, in which his utmost skill was exhausted, it was exposed in the public market-place, with directions at the bottom for every spectator to mark with a brush, which lay by, every limb and feature which seemed erroneous. The spectators came, and in general applauded; but each, willing to show his talent at criticism, marked whatever he thought proper. At evening, when the painter came, he was mortified to find the whole picture one universal blot—not a single stroke that was not stigmatized with marks of disapprobation: not satisfied with this trial, the next day he was resolved to try them in a different manner, and, exposing his picture as before, desired that every spectator would mark those beauties he approved or admired. The people complied; and the artist returning, found his picture replete with the marks of beauty: every stroke that had been yesterday condemned, now received the character of approbation. "Well," cries the painter, "I now find that the best way to please one half of the world, is not to mind what the other half says; since what are faults in the eyes of these, shall be by those regarded as beauties."—Adieu.

LETTER LXII.

To the same.

A CHARACTER, such as you have represented that of your fair companion, which continues virtuous, though loaded with infamy, is truly great. Many regard virtue because it is attended with applause; your favourite only for the internal pleasure it confers. I have often wished that ladies like her were proposed as models for female imitation, and not such as have acquired fame by qualities repugnant to the natural softness of the sex.

Women famed for their valour, their skill in politics, or their learning, leave the duties of their own sex, in order to invade the privileges of ours. I can no more pardon a fair one for endeavouring to wield the club of Hercules, than I could him for attempting to twirl her distaff.

The modest virgin, the prudent wife, or the careful matron, are much more serviceable in life than petticoated philosophers, blustering heroines, or virago queens. She who makes her husband and her children happy, who reclaims the one from vice, and trains up the other to virtue, is a much greater character than ladies described in romance, whose whole occupation is to murder mankind with shafts from their quiver or their eyes.

Women, it has been observed, are not naturally formed for great cares themselves, but to soften ours. Their tenderness is the proper reward for the dangers we undergo for their preservation; and the ease and cheerfulness of their conversation, our desirable retreat from the fatigues of intense application. They are confined within the narrow limits of domestic assiduity: and, when they stray beyond them, they move beyond their sphere, and consequently without grace.

Fame, therefore, has been very unjustly dispensed among the female sex. Those who least deserved to be remembered, meet our admiration and applause; while many, who have been an honour to humanity, are passed over in silence. Perhaps no age has produced a stronger instance of misplaced fame than the present: the Semiramis and the Thalestris of antiquity are talked of, while a modern character, infinitely greater than either, is unnoticed and unknown.

Catharina Alexowna, born near Derpat, a little city in Livonia, was heir to no other inheritance than the virtues and frugality of her parents. Her father being dead, she lived with her aged mother in their cottage covered with straw; and both, though very poor, were very contented. Here, retired from the gaze of the world, by the labour of her hands she supported her parent, who was now incapable of supporting herself. While Catharina spun, the old woman would sit by and read some book of devotion; thus, when the fatigues of the day were over, both would sit down contentedly by their fireside, and enjoy the frugal meal with vacant festivity.

Though her face and person were models of perfection, yet her whole attention seemed bestowed upon her mind; her mother taught her to read, and an old Lutheran minister instructed her in the maxims and duties of religion. Nature had furnished her, not only with a ready, but a solid turn of thought, not only with a strong, but a right understanding. Such truly female accomplishments procured her several solicitations of marriage from the peasants of the country; but their offers were refused; for she loved her mother too tenderly to think of a separation.

Catharina was fifteen when her mother died; she now therefore left her cottage, and went to live with the Lutheran minister, by whom she had been instructed from her childhood. In his house she resided in quality of governess to his children, at once reconciling in her character unerring prudence with surprising vivacity.

The old man, who regarded her as one of his own children, had her instructed in dancing and music by the masters who attended the rest of his family; thus she continued to improve till he died, by which accident she was once more reduced to pristine poverty. The country of Livonia was at this time wasted by war, and lay in a most miserable state of desolation. Those calamities are ever most heavy upon the poor; wherefore Catharina, though possessed of so many accomplishments, experienced all the miseries of hopeless indigence. Provisions becoming every day more scarce, and her private stock being entirely exhausted, she resolved at last to travel to Marienburgh, a city of greater plenty.

With her scanty wardrobe packed up in a wallet, she set out on her journey on foot: she was to walk through a region miserable by nature, but rendered still more hideous by the Swedes and Russians, who, as each happened to become masters, plundered it at discretion: but hunger had taught her to despise the dangers and fatigues of the way.

One evening upon her journey, as she had entered a cottage by the wayside, to take up her lodging for the night, she was insulted by two Swedish soldiers, who insisted upon qualifying her, as they termed it, "to follow the camp." They might probably have carried their insults into violence, had not a subaltern officer, accidentally passing by, come in to her assistance: upon his appearing, the soldiers immediately desisted; but her thankfulness was hardly greater than her surprise, when she instantly recollected in her deliverer, the son of the Lutheran minister, her former instructor, benefactor, and friend.

This was an happy interview for Catharina: the little stock of money she had brought from home was by this time quite exhausted; her clothes were gone, piece by piece, in order to satisfy those who had entertained her in their houses: her generous countryman, therefore, parted with what he could spare, to buy her clothes, furnished her with a horse, and gave her letters of recommendation to Mr. Gluck, a faithful friend of his father's, and superintendent at Marienburgh.

Our beautiful stranger had only to appear to be well received; she was immediately admitted into the superintendent's family, as governess to his two daughters; and though yet but seventeen, showed herself capable of instructing her sex, not only in virtue, but politeness. Such was her good sense and beauty, that her master himself in a short time offered her his hand, which, to his great surprise, she thought proper to refuse. Actuated by a principle of gratitude, she was resolved to marry her deliverer only, even though he had lost an arm, and was otherwise disfigured by wounds in the service.

In order, therefore, to prevent further solicitations from others, as soon as the officer came to town upon duty, she offered him her person, which he accepted with transport, and their nuptials were solemnized as usual. But all the lines of her fortune were to be striking: the very day on which they were married, the Russians laid siege to Marienburgh. The unhappy soldier had now no time to enjoy the well-earned pleasures of matrimony; he was called off, before consummation, to an attack, from which he was never after seen to return.

In the meantime the siege went on with fury, aggravated on one side by obstinacy, on the other by revenge. This war between the two northern powers at that time was truly barbarous; the innocent peasant, and the harmless virgin, often shared the fate of the soldier in arms. Marienburgh was taken by assault; and such was the fury of the assailants, that not only the garrison, but almost all the inhabitants, men, women, and children, were put to the sword: at length, when the carnage was pretty well over, Catharina was found hid in an oven.

She had been hitherto poor, but still was free; she was now to conform to her hard fate, and learn what it was to be a slave: in this situation, however, she behaved with piety and humility; and though misfortunes had abated her vivacity, yet she was cheerful. The fame of her merit and resignation reached even Prince Menzikoff, the Russian general; he desired to see her, was struck with her beauty, bought her from the soldier her master, and placed her under the direction of his own sister. Here she was treated with all the respect which her merit deserved, while her beauty every day improved with her good fortune.

She had not been long in this situation, when Peter the Great, paying the Prince a visit, Catharina happened to come in with some dry fruits, which she served round with peculiar modesty. The mighty monarch saw, and was struck with her beauty. He returned the next day, called for the beautiful slave, asked her several questions, and found her understanding even more perfect than her person.

He had been forced, when young, to marry from motives of interest; he was now resolved to marry pursuant to his own inclinations. He immediately inquired the history of the fair Livonian, who was not yet eighteen. He traced her through the vale of obscurity, through all the vicissitudes of her fortune, and found her truly great in them all. The meanness of her birth was no obstruction to his design; their nuptials were solemnized in private; the Prince assuring his courtiers that virtue alone was the properest ladder to a throne.

We now see Catharina, from the low mud-walled cottage, empress of the greatest kingdom upon earth. The poor solitary wanderer is now surrounded by thousands, who find happiness in her smile. She, who formerly wanted a meal, is now capable of diffusing plenty upon whole nations. To her fortune she owed a part of this pre-eminence, but to her virtues more.

She ever after retained those great qualities which first placed her on a throne; and while the extraordinary prince, her husband, laboured for the reformation of his male subjects, she studied in her turn the improvement of her own sex. She altered their dresses, introduced mixed assemblies, instituted an order of female knighthood; and at length, when she had greatly filled all the stations of empress, friend, wife, and mother, bravely died without regret, regretted by all.—Adieu.

LETTER LXIII.

From Lien Chi Altangi to Fum Hoam, First President of the Ceremonial Academy at Pekin in China.

In every letter I expect accounts of some new revolutions in China, some strange occurrence in the state, or disaster among my private acquaintance. I open every packet with tremulous expectation, and am agreeably disappointed when I find my friends and my country continuing in felicity. I wander, but they are at rest; they suffer few changes but what pass in my own restless imagination: it is only the rapidity of my own motion gives an imaginary swiftness to objects which are in some measure immoveable.

Yet believe me, my friend, that even China itself is imperceptibly degenerating from her ancient greatness: her laws are now more venal, and her merchants are more deceitful than formerly; the very arts and sciences have run to decay. Observe the carvings on our ancient bridges, figures that add grace even to nature: there is not an artist now in all the empire that can imitate their beauty. Our manufacturers in porcelain, too, are inferior to what we once were famous for; and even Europe now begins to excel us. There was a time when China was the receptacle of strangers; when all were welcome who either came to improve the state, or admire its greatness: now the empire is shut up from every foreign improvement, and the very inhabitants discourage each other from prosecuting their own internal advantages.

Whence this degeneracy in a state so little subject to external revolutions? how happens it that China, which is now more powerful than ever, which is less subject to foreign invasions, and even assisted in some discoveries by her connexions with Europe; whence comes it, I say, that the empire is thus declining so fast into barbarity?

This decay is surely from nature, and not the result of voluntary degeneracy. In a period of two or three thousand years she seems at proper intervals to produce great minds, with an effort resembling that which introduces the vicissitudes of seasons. They rise up at once, continue for an age, enlighten the world, fall like ripened corn, and mankind again gradually relapse into pristine barbarity. We little ones look around, are amazed at the decline, seek after the causes of this invisible decay, attribute to want of encouragement what really proceeds from want of power, are astonished to find every art and every science in the decline, not considering that autumn is over, and fatigued nature again begins to repose for some succeeding effort.

Some periods have been remarkable for the production of men of extraordinary stature; others for producing some particular animals in great abundance; some for excessive plenty; and others again for seemingly causeless famine. Nature, which shows herself so very different in her visible productions, must surely differ also from herself in the production of minds; and while she astonishes one age with the strength and stature of a Milo or a Maximin, may bless another with the wisdom of a Plato, or the goodness of an Antonine.

Let us not, then, attribute to accident the falling off of every nation, but to the natural revolution of things. Often in the darkest ages there has appeared some one man of surprising abilities, who, with all his understanding, failed to bring his barbarous age into refinement: all mankind seemed to sleep, till nature gave the general call, and then the whole world seemed at once roused at the voice; science triumphed in every country, and the brightness of a single genius seemed lost in a galaxy of contiguous glory.

Thus the enlightened periods in every age have been universal. At the time when China first began to emerge from barbarity, the Western world was equally rising into refinement; when we had our Yaou, they had their Sesostris. In succeeding ages, Confucius and Pythagoras seem born nearly together, and a train of philosophers then sprung up as well in Greece as in China. The period of renewed barbarity began to have an universal spread much about the same time, and continued for several centuries, till, in the year of the Christian era, 1400, the Emperor Yonglo arose to revive the learning of the East; while about the same time the Medicean family laboured in Italy to raise infant genius from the cradle. Thus we see politeness spreading over every part of the world in one age, and barbarity succeeding in another; at one period a blaze of light diffusing itself over the whole world, and at another all mankind wrapped up in the profoundest ignorance.

Such has been the situation of things in times past, and such probably it will ever be. China, I have observed, has evidently begun to degenerate from its former politeness; and were the learning of the Europeans at present candidly considered, the decline would perhaps appear to have already taken place. We should find among the natives of the West, the study of morality displaced for mathematical disquisition, or metaphysical subtleties; we should find learning begin to separate from the useful duties and concerns of life, while none ventured to aspire after that character, but they who know much more than is truly amusing or useful. We should find every great attempt suppressed by prudence, and the rapturous sublimity in writing cooled by a cautious fear of offence. We should find few of those daring spirits who bravely venture to be wrong, and who are willing to hazard much for the sake of great acquisitions. Providence has indulged the world with a period of almost four hundred years' refinement; does it not now by degrees sink us into our former ignorance, leaving us only the love of wisdom, while it deprives us of its advantages?—Adieu.

LETTER LXIV.

To the same.

THE princes of Europe have found out a manner of rewarding their subjects who have behaved well, by presenting them with about two yards of blue riband, which is worn about the shoulder. They who are honoured with this mark of distinction are called knights, and the king himself is always the head of the order. This is a very frugal method of recompensing the most important services; and it is very fortunate for kings that their subjects are satisfied with such trifling rewards. Should a nobleman happen to lose his leg in a battle, the king presents him with two yards of riband, and he is paid for the loss of his limb. Should an ambassador spend all his paternal fortune in supporting the honour of his country abroad, the king presents him with two yards of riband, which is to be considered as an equivalent to his estate. In short, while an European king has a yard of blue or green riband left, he need be under no apprehensions of wanting statesmen, generals, and soldiers.

I cannot sufficiently admire those kingdoms in which men with large patrimonial estates are willing thus to undergo real hardships for empty favours. A person, already possessed of a competent fortune, who undertakes to enter the career of ambition, feels many real inconveniences from his station, while it procures him no real happiness that he was not possessed of before. He could eat, drink, and sleep, before he became a courtier, as well, perhaps better, than when invested with his authority. He could command flatterers in a private station, as well as in his public capacity, and indulge at home every favourite inclination, uncensured and unseen by the people.

What real good, then, does an addition to a fortune already sufficient procure? Not any. Could the great man, by having his fortune increased, increase also his appetites, then precedence might be attended with real amusement.

Was he, by having his one thousand made two, thus enabled to enjoy two wives, or eat two dinners, then indeed he might be excused for undergoing some pain in order to extend the sphere of his enjoyments. But, on the contrary, he finds his desire for pleasure often lessen, as he takes pains to be able to improve it; and his capacity of enjoyment diminishes as his fortune happens to increase.

Instead, therefore, of regarding the great with envy, I generally consider them with some share of compassion. I look upon them as a set of good-natured, misguided people, who are indebted to us, and not to themselves, for all the happiness they enjoy. For our pleasure, and not their own, they sweat under a cumbrous heap of finery; for our pleasure, the lacquied train, the slow-parading pageant, with all the gravity of grandeur, moves in review: a single coat, or a single footman, answers all the purposes of the most indolent refinement as well; and those who have twenty, may be said to keep one for their own pleasure, and the other nineteen merely for ours. So true is the observation of Confucius, "That we take greater pains to persuade others that we are happy, than in endeavouring to think so ourselves."

But though this desire of being seen, of being made the subject of discourse, and of supporting the dignities of an exalted station, be troublesome enough to the ambitious, yet it is well for society that there are men thus willing to exchange ease and safety for danger and a riband. We lose nothing by their vanity, and it would be unkind to endeavour to deprive a child of its rattle. If a duke or a duchess are willing to carry a long train for our entertainment, so much the worse for themselves; if they choose to exhibit in public, with a hundred lacquies and mamelukes in their equipage, for our entertainment, still so much the worse for themselves; it is the spectators alone who give and receive the pleasure; they only are the sweating figures that swell the pageant.

A mandarine, who took much pride in appearing with a number of jewels on every part of his robe, was once accosted by an old sly bonze, who, following him through several streets, and bowing often to the ground, thanked him for his jewels. "What does the man mean?" cried the mandarine. "Friend, I never gave thee any of my jewels."—"No," replied the other; "but you have let me look at them, and that is all the use you can make of them yourself; so there is no difference between us, except that you have the trouble of watching them, and that is an employment I don't much desire."—Adieu.

LETTER LXV.

To the same.

THOUGH not very fond of seeing a pageant myself, yet I am generally pleased with being in the crowd which sees it: it is amusing to observe the effect which such a spectacle has upon the variety of faces; the pleasure it excites in some, the envy in others, and the wishes it raises in all. With this design I lately went to see the entry of a foreign ambassador, resolved to make one in the mob, to shout as they shouted, to fix with earnestness upon the same frivolous objects, and participate for a while the pleasures and the wishes of the vulgar.

Struggling here for some time, in order to be first to see the cavalcade as it passed, some one of the crowd unluckily happened to tread upon my shoe, and tore it in such a manner, that I was utterly unqualified to march forward with the main body, and obliged to fall back in the rear. Thus rendered incapable of being a spectator of the show myself, I was at least willing to observe the spectators, and limped behind like one of the invalids which follow the march of an army.

In this plight, as I was considering the eagerness that appeared on every face, how some bustled to get foremost, and others contented themselves with taking a transient peep when they could; how some praised the four black servants that were stuck behind one of the equipages, and some the ribands that decorated the horses' necks in another, my attention was called off to an object more extraordinary than any I had yet seen. A poor cobbler sat in his stall by the wayside, and continued to work, while the crowd passed by, without testifying the smallest share of curiosity. I own his want of attention excited mine; and as I stood in need of his assistance, I thought it best to employ a philosophic cobbler on this occasion. Perceiving my business, therefore, he desired me to enter and sit down, took my shoe in his lap, and began to mend it with his usual indifference and taciturnity.

"How, my friend," said I to him, "can you continue to work, while all those fine things are passing by your door?" "Very fine they are, master," returned the cobbler, "for those that like them, to be sure; but what are all those fine things to me? You don't know what it is to be a cobbler, and so much the better for yourself. Your bread is baked: you may go and see sights the whole day, and eat a warm supper when you come home at night; but for me, if I should run hunting after all these fine folk, what should I get by my journey but an appetite, and, God help me! I have too much of that at home already, without stirring out for it. Your people, who may eat four meals a day and a supper at night, are but a bad example to such a one as I. No, master, as God has called me into this world in order to mend old shoes, I have no business with fine folk, and they no business with me." I here interrupted him with a smile. "See this last, master," continues he, "and this hammer; this last and hammer are the two best friends I have in this world; nobody else will be my friend, because I want a friend. The great folks you saw pass by just now have five hundred friends, because they have no occasion for them: now, while I stick to my good friends here, I am very contented; but when I ever so little run after sights and fine things, I begin to hate my work; I grow sad, and have no heart to mend shoes any longer."

This discourse only served to raise my curiosity to know more of a man whom nature had thus formed into a philosopher. I therefore insensibly led him into a history of his adventures. "I have lived," said he, "a wandering sort of a life now five and fifty years, here to-day, and gone to-morrow; for it was my misfortune, when I was young, to be fond of changing."—"You have been a traveller, then, I presume," interrupted I.—"I cannot boast much of travelling," continued he, "for I have never left the parish in which I was born but three times in my life, that I can remember; but then there is not a street in the whole neighbourhood that I have not lived in, at some time or another. When I began to settle and to take to my business in one street, some unforeseen misfortune, or a desire of trying my luck elsewhere, has removed me, perhaps a whole mile away from my former customers, while some more lucky cobbler would come into my place, and make a handsome fortune among friends of my making: there was one who actually died in a stall that I had left worth seven pounds seven shillings, all in hard gold, which he had quilted into the waistband of his breeches."

I could not but smile at these migrations of a man by the fireside, and continued to ask if he had ever been married. "Ay, that I have, master," replied he, "for sixteen long years; and a weary life I had of it, Heaven knows. My wife took it into her head, that the only way to thrive in this world was to save money; so, though our comings-in were but about three shillings a week, all that ever she could lay her hands upon she used to hide away from me, though we were obliged to starve the whole week after for it.

"The first three years we used to quarrel about this every day, and I always got the better; but she had a hard spirit, and still continued to hide as usual: so that I was at last tired of quarrelling and getting the better, and she scraped and scraped at pleasure, till I was almost starved to death. Her conduct drove me at last in despair to the alehouse; here I used to sit with people who hated home like myself, drank while I had money left, and ran in score when anybody would trust me; till at last the landlady coming one day with a long bill when I was from home, and putting it into my wife's hands, the length of it effectually broke her heart. I searched the whole stall, after she was dead, for money; but she had hidden it so effectually, that, with all my pains, I could never find a farthing."

By this time my shoe was mended, and satisfying the poor artist for his trouble, and rewarding him besides for his information, I took my leave, and returned home to lengthen out the amusement his conversation afforded, by communicating it to my friend.—Adieu.

LETTER LXVI.

From Lien Chi Altangi to Hingpo, by the way of Moscow.

GENEROSITY, properly applied, will supply every other external advantage in life, but the love of those we converse with; it will procure esteem, and a conduct resembling real affection; but actual love is the spontaneous production of the mind; no generosity can purchase, no rewards increase, nor no liberality continue it: the very person who is obliged has it not in his power to force his lingering affections upon the object he should love, and voluntarily mix passion with gratitude.

Imparted fortune and well-placed liberality may procure the benefactor good-will, may load the person obliged with the sense of the duty he lies under to retaliate; this is gratitude, and simple gratitude, untinctured with love, is all the return an ingenuous mind can bestow for former benefits.

But gratitude and love are almost opposite affections. Love is often an involuntary passion placed upon our companions without our consent, and frequently conferred without our previous esteem. We love some men, we know not why; our tenderness is naturally excited in all their concerns; we excuse their faults with the same indulgence, and approve their virtues with the same applause, with which we consider our own. While we entertain the passion, it pleases us; we cherish it with delight, and give it up with reluctance; and love for love is all the reward we expect or desire.

Gratitude, on the contrary, is never conferred but where there have been previous endeavours to excite it. We consider it as a debt, and our spirits wear a load till we have discharged the obligation. Every acknowledgment of gratitude is a circumstance of humiliation, and some are found to submit to frequent mortifications of this kind, proclaiming what obligations they owe, merely because they think it in some measure cancels the debt.

Thus love is the most easy and agreeable, and gratitude the most humiliating, affection of the mind. We never reflect on the man we love without exulting in our choice, while he who has bound us to him by benefits alone rises to our idea as a person to whom we have in some measure forfeited our freedom. Love and gratitude are seldom, therefore, found in the same breast without impairing each other. We may tender the one or the other singly to those we converse with, but cannot command both together. By attempting to increase, we diminish them; the mind becomes bankrupt under too large obligations; all additional benefits lessen every hope of future return, and shut up every avenue that leads to tenderness.

In all our connections with society, therefore, it is not only generous, but prudent, to appear insensible of the value of those favours we bestow, and endeavour to make the obligation seem as slight as possible. Love must be taken by stratagem, and not by open force. We should seem ignorant that we oblige, and leave the mind at full liberty to give or refuse its affections; for constraint may indeed leave the receiver still grateful, but it will certainly produce disgust.

If to procure gratitude be our only aim, there is no great art in making the acquisition; a benefit conferred demands a just acknowledgment, and we have a right to insist upon our due.

But it were much more prudent to forego our right on such an occasion, and exchange it, if we can, for love. We receive but little advantage from repeated protestations of gratitude, but they cost him very much from whom we exact them in return. Exacting a grateful acknowledgment is demanding a debt by which the creditor is not advantaged, and the debtor pays with reluctance.

As Mencius, the philosopher, was travelling in pursuit of wisdom, night overtook him at the foot of a gloomy mountain, remote from the habitations of men. Here, as he was straying, while rain and thunder conspired to make solitude still more hideous, he perceived a hermit's cell, and approaching, asked for shelter. "Enter," cries the hermit in a severe tone; "men deserve not to be obliged, but it would be imitating their ingratitude to treat them as they deserve. Come in; examples of vice may sometimes strengthen us in the ways of virtue."

After a frugal meal, which consisted of roots and tea, Mencius could not repress his curiosity to know why the hermit had retired from mankind, the actions of whom taught the truest lessons of wisdom. "Mention not the name of man," cries the hermit with indignation; "here let me live retired from a base ungrateful world; here among the beasts of the forest I shall find no flatterers. The lion is a generous enemy, and the dog a faithful friend; but man, base man, can poison the bowl, and smile while he presents it." —"You have been used ill by mankind?" interrupted the philosopher shrewdly. "Yes," returned the hermit, "on mankind I have exhausted my whole fortune; and this staff, and that cup, and those roots, are all that I have in return."—"Did you bestow your fortune, or did you only lend it?" returned Mencius.—"I bestowed it undoubtedly," replied the other; "for where were the merit of being a money-lender?"—"Did they ever own that they received it?" still adds the philosopher.—"A thousand times," cries the hermit; "they every day loaded me with professions of gratitude for obligations received, and solicitations for future favours."—"If, then," says Mencius, smiling, "you did not lend your fortune in order to have it returned, it is unjust to accuse them of ingratitude; they owned themselves obliged; you expected no more, and they certainly earned each favour by frequently acknowledging the obligation." The hermit was struck with the reply, and surveying his guest with emotion,—"I have heard of the great Mencius, and you certainly are the man. I am now fourscore years old, but still a child in wisdom. Take me back to the school of man, and educate me as one of the most ignorant and the youngest of your disciples."

Indeed, my son, it is better to have friends in our passage through life, than grateful dependants; and as love is a more willing, so it is a more lasting, tribute than extorted obligation. As we are uneasy when greatly obliged, gratitude once refused can never after be recovered. The mind that is base enough to disallow the just return, instead of feeling any uneasiness upon recollection, triumphs in its new acquired freedom, and in some measure is pleased with conscious baseness.

Very different is the situation of disagreeing friends. Their separation produces mutual uneasiness. Like that divided being in fabulous creation, their sympathetic souls once more desire their former union; the joys of both are imperfect; their gayest moments tinctured with uneasiness; each seeks for the smallest concessions to clear the way to a wished-for explanation; the most trifling acknowledgment, the slightest accident, serves to effect a mutual reconciliation.

But instead of pursuing the thought, permit me to soften the severity of advice by an European story, which will fully illustrate my meaning.

A fiddler and his wife, who had rubbed through life, as most couples usually do, sometimes good friends, at others not quite so well, one day happened to have a dispute, which was conducted with becoming spirit on both sides. The wife was sure she was right, and the husband was resolved to have his own way. What was to be done in such a case? The quarrel grew worse by explanations, and at last the fury of both rose to such a pitch, that they made a vow never to sleep together in the same bed for the future. This was the most rash vow that could be imagined, for they were still friends at bottom, and, besides, they had but one bed in the house. However, resolved they were to go through with it, and at night the fiddle-case was laid in the bed between them, in order to make a separation. In this manner they continued for three weeks; every night the fiddle-case being placed as a barrier to divide them.

By this time, however, each heartily repented of their vow; their resentment was at an end, and their love began to return; they wished the fiddle-case away, but both had too much spirit to begin. One night, however, as they were both lying awake, with the detested fiddle-case between them, the husband happened to sneeze, to which the wife, as is usual in such cases, bid God bless him. "Ay, but," returns the husband, "woman, do you say that from your heart?"—"Indeed I do, my poor Nicholas," cries his wife; "I say it with all my heart."—"If so, then," says the husband, "we had as good remove the fiddle-case."

LETTER LXVII.

To the same.

BOOKS, my son, while they teach us to respect the interests of others, often make us unmindful of our own; while they instruct the youthful reader to grasp at social happiness, he grows miserable in detail, and, attentive to universal harmony, often forgets that he himself has a part to sustain in the concert. I dislike, therefore, the philosopher who describes the inconveniences of life in such pleasing colours that the pupil grows enamoured of distress, longs to try the charms of poverty, meets it without dread, nor fears its inconveniences till he severely feels them.

A youth who has thus spent his life among books, new to the world, and unacquainted with man but by philosophic information, may be considered as a being whose mind is filled with the vulgar errors of the wise; utterly unqualified for a journey through life, yet confident of his own skill in the direction, he sets out with confidence, blunders on with vanity, and finds himself at last undone.

He first has learned from books, and then lays it down as a maxim, that all mankind are virtuous or vicious in excess; and he has been long taught to detest vice, and love virtue. Warm, therefore, in attachments, and steadfast in enmity, he treats every creature as a friend or foe; expects from those he loves unerring integrity, and consigns his enemies to the reproach of wanting every virtue. On this principle he proceeds; and here begin his disappointments. Upon a closer inspection of human nature he perceives that he should have moderated his friendship, and softened his severity; for he often finds the excellencies of one part of mankind clouded with vice, and the faults of the other brightened with virtue; he finds no character so sanctified that has not its failings, none so infamous but has somewhat to attract our esteem; he beholds impiety in lawn, and fidelity in fetters.

He now, therefore, but too late, perceives that his regards should have been more cool, and his hatred less violent; that the truly wise seldom court romantic friendships with the good, and avoid, if possible, the resentment even of the wicked: every moment gives him fresh instances that the bonds of friendship are broken, if drawn too closely, and that those whom he has treated with disrespect more than retaliate the injury; at length, therefore, he is obliged to confess, that he has declared war upon the vicious half of mankind, without being able to form an alliance among the virtuous to espouse his quarrel.

Our book-taught philosopher, however, is now too far advanced to recede; and though poverty be the just consequence of the many enemies his conduct has created, yet he is resolved to meet it without shrinking. Philosophers have described poverty in most charming colours, and even his vanity is touched in thinking that he shall show the world, in himself, one more example of patience, fortitude, and resignation. "Come, then, O Poverty! for what is there in thee dreadful to the WISE? Temperance, Health, and Frugality walk in thy train; Cheerfulness and Liberty are ever thy companions. Shall any be ashamed of thee, of whom Cincinnatus was not ashamed? The running brook, the herbs of the field, can amply satisfy nature; man wants but little, nor that little long. Come, then, O Poverty, while kings stand by and gaze with admiration at the true philosopher's resignation."

The goddess appears; for Poverty ever comes at the call: but, alas! he finds her by no means the charming figure books and his warm imagination had painted. As when an Eastern bride, whom her friends and relations had long described as a model of perfection, pays her first visit, the longing bridegroom lifts the veil to see a face he had never seen before; but instead of a countenance blazing with beauty like the sun, he beholds deformity shooting icicles to his heart: such appears Poverty to her new entertainer; all the fabric of enthusiasm is at once demolished, and a thousand miseries rise up on its ruins, while Contempt, with pointing finger, is foremost in the hideous procession.

The poor man now finds that he can get no kings to look at him while he is eating; he finds that, in proportion as he grows poor, the world turns its back upon him, and gives him leave to act the philosopher in all the majesty of solitude. It might be agreeable enough to play the philosopher while we are conscious that mankind are spectators; but what signifies wearing the mask of sturdy contentment, and mounting the stage of restraint, when not one creature will assist at the exhibition? Thus is he forsaken of men, while his fortitude wants the satisfaction even of self-applause: for either he does not feel his present calamities, and that is natural insensibility; or he disguises his feelings, and that is dissimulation.

Spleen now begins to take up the man: not distinguishing in his resentments, he regards all mankind with detestation, and commencing man-hater, seeks solitude to be at liberty to rail.

It has been said, that he who retires to solitude is either a beast or an angel. The censure is too severe, and the praise unmerited; the discontented being who retires from society is generally some good-natured man, who has begun life without experience, and knew not how to gain it in his intercourse with mankind.—Adieu.

LETTER LXVIII.

From Lien Chi Altangi to Fum Hoam, First President of the Ceremonial Academy at Pekin in China.

I FORMERLY acquainted thee, most grave Fum, with the excellence of the English in the art of healing. The Chinese boast their skill in pulses, the Siamese their botanical knowledge, but the English advertising physicians alone of being the great restorers of health, the dispensers of youth, and the insurers of longevity. I can never enough admire the sagacity of this country, for the encouragement given to the professors of this art: with what indulgence does she foster up those of her own growth, and kindly cherish those that come from abroad! Like a skilful gardener, she invites them from every foreign climate to herself. Here every great exotic strikes root as soon as imported, and feels the genial beam of favour; while the mighty metropolis, like one vast magnificent dunghill, receives them indiscriminately to her breast, and supplies each with more than native nourishment.

In other countries the physician pretends to cure disorders in the lump: the same doctor who combats the gout in the toe, shall pretend to prescribe for a pain in the head; and he who at one time cures a consumption, shall at another give drugs for a dropsy. How absurd and ridiculous! this is being a mere jack-of-all-trades. Is the animal machine less complicated than a brass pin? Not less than ten different hands are required to make a pin; and shall the body be set right by one single operator?

The English are sensible of the force of this reasoning: they have, therefore, one doctor for the eyes, another for the toes; they have their sciatica doctors, and inoculating doctors; they have one doctor who is modestly content with securing them from bug-bites, and five hundred who prescribe for the bite of mad dogs.

The learned are not here retired, with vicious modesty, from public view; for every dead wall is covered with their names, their abilities, their amazing cures, and places of abode. Few patients can escape falling into their hands, unless blasted by lightning, or struck dead with some sudden disorder. It may sometimes happen, that a stranger who does not understand English, or a countryman who cannot read, dies, without ever hearing of the vivifying drops or restorative electuary; but, for my part, before I was a week in town, I had learned to bid the whole catalogue of disorders defiance, and was perfectly acquainted with the names and the medicines of every great man, or great woman, of them all.

But as nothing pleases curiosity more than anecdotes of the great, however minute or trifling, I must present you, inadequate as my abilities are to the subject, with some account of those personages who lead in this honourable profession.

The first upon the list of glory is Doctor Richard Rock, F.U.N. This great man, short of stature, is fat, and waddles as he walks. He always wears a white three-tailed wig nicely combed, and frizzed upon each cheek; sometimes he carries a cane, but an hat never. It is indeed very remarkable, that this extraordinary personage should never wear an hat; but so it is, he never wears an hat. He is usually drawn at the top of his own bills, sitting in his arm-chair, holding a little bottle between his finger and thumb, and surrounded with rotten teeth, nippers, pills, packets, and gallipots. No man can promise fairer nor better than he; for, as he observes, "Be your disorder never so far gone, be under no uneasiness, make yourself quite easy: I can cure you."

The next in fame, though by some reckoned of equal pretensions, is Doctor Timothy Franks, F.O.G.H., living in a place called the Old Bailey. As Rock is remarkably squab, his great rival, Franks, is as remarkably tall. He was born in the year of the Christian era 1692, and is, while I now write, exactly sixty-eight years, three months, and four days old. Age, however, has no ways impaired his usual health and vivacity: I am told he generally walks with his breast open. This gentleman, who is of a mixed reputation, is particularly remarkable for a becoming assurance, which carries him gently through life; for, except Doctor Rock, none are more blessed with the advantages of face than Doctor Franks.

And yet the great have their foibles as well as the little. I am almost ashamed to mention it: let the foibles of the great rest in peace: yet I must impart the whole to my friend. These two great men are actually now at variance: yes, my dear Fum Hoam, by the head of our grandfather, they are now at variance like mere men, mere common mortals! The champion Rock advises the world to beware of bog-trotting quacks, while Franks retorts the wit and the sarcasm (for they have both a world of wit) by fixing on his rival the odious appellation of Dumplin Dick. He calls the serious Doctor Rock Dumplin Dick! Head of Confucius, what profanation! Dumplin Dick! What a pity, ye powers, that the learned, who were born mutually to assist in enlightening the world, should thus differ among themselves, and make even the profession ridiculous! Sure the world is wide enough, at least for two great personages to figure in: men of science should leave controversy to the little world below them; and then we might see Rock and Franks walking together hand in hand, smiling onward to immortality.

Next to these is Doctor Walker, preparator of his own medicines. This gentleman is remarkable for an aversion to quacks; frequently cautioning the public to be careful into what hands they commit their safety; by which he would insinuate, that if they do not employ him alone, they must be undone. His public spirit is equal to his success. Not for himself, but his country, is the gallipot prepared, and the drops sealed up, with proper directions for any part of the town or country: all this is for his country's good; so that he is now grown old in the practice of physic and virtue; and, to use his own elegance of expression, "There is not such another medicine as his in the world again."

This, my friend, is a formidable triumvirate; and yet, formidable as they are, I am resolved to defend the honour of Chinese physic against them all. I have made a vow to summon Doctor Rock to a solemn disputation in all the mysteries of the profession, before the face of every Philomath student in astrology, and member of the learned societies. I adhere to and venerate the doctrines of old Wang-shu-ho. In the very teeth of opposition I will maintain, "That the heart is the son of the liver, which has the kidneys for its mother, and the stomach for its wife." I have, therefore, drawn up a disputation challenge, which is to be sent speedily, to this effect:—

"I, Lien Chi Altangi, D. N. R. H., native of Honan in China, to Richard Rock, F. U. N., native of Garbage Alley, in Wapping, defiance. Though, sir, I am perfectly sensible of your importance, though no stranger to your studies in the paths of nature, yet there may be many things in the art of physic with which you are yet unacquainted. I know full well a doctor thou art, great Rock, and so am I. Wherefore I challenge, and do hereby invite, you to a trial of learning upon hard problems and knotty physical points. In this debate we will calmly investigate the whole theory and practice of medicine, botany, and chemistry; and I invite all the Philomaths, with many of the lecturers in medicine, to be present at the dispute, which, I hope, will be carried on with due decorum, with proper gravity, and as befits men of erudition and science, among each other. But before we meet face to face, I would thus publicly, and in the face of the whole world, desire you to answer me one question; I ask it with the same earnestness with which you have often solicited the public; answer me, I say, at once, without having recourse to your physical dictionary,—Which of those three disorders incident to the human body is the most fatal, the *syncope*, *parenthesis*, or *apoplexy?* I beg your reply may be as public as this my demand. I am, as hereafter may be, your admirer or your rival."—Adieu.

LETTER LXIX.

To the same.

INDULGENT Nature seems to have exempted this island from many of those epidemic evils which are so fatal in other parts of the world. A want of rain but for a few days beyond the expected season in China spreads famine, desolation, and terror over the whole country; the winds that blow from the brown bosom of the western desert are impregnated with death in every gale; but in this fortunate land of Britain the inhabitant courts health in every breeze, and the husbandman ever sows in joyful expectation.

But though the nation be exempt from real evils, think not, my friend, that it is more happy on this account than others. They are afflicted, it is true, with neither famine nor pestilence, but then there is a disorder peculiar to the country, which every season makes strange ravages among them; it spreads with pestilential rapidity, and infects almost every rank of people; what is still more strange, the natives have no name for this peculiar malady, though well known to foreign physicians by the appellation of epidemic terror.

A season is never known to pass in which the people are not visited by this cruel calamity in one shape or another; seemingly different, though ever the same: one year it issues from a baker's shop in the shape of a sixpenny loaf; the next, it takes the appearance of a comet with a fiery tail; a third, it threatens like a flat-bottomed boat; and a fourth, it carries consternation at the bite of a mad dog. The people, when once infected, lose their relish for happiness, saunter about with looks of despondence, ask after the calamities of the day, and receive no comfort but in heightening each other's distress. It is insignificant how remote or near, how weak or powerful, the objects of terror may be; when once they resolve to fright and be frighted, the merest trifles sow consternation and dismay: each proportions his fears, not to the object, but to the dread he discovers in the countenance of others; for when once the fermentation is begun, it goes on of itself, though the original cause be discontinued which first set it in motion.

A dread of mad dogs is the epidemic terror which now prevails; and the whole nation is at present actually groaning under the malignity of its influence. The people sally from their houses with that circumspection which is prudent in such as expect a mad dog at every turning. The physician publishes his prescription, the beadle prepares his halter, and a few of unusual bravery arm themselves with boots and buff gloves, in order to face the enemy if he should offer to attack them. In short, the whole people stand bravely upon their defence, and seem, by their present spirit, to show a resolution of not being tamely bit by mad dogs any longer.

Their manner of knowing whether a dog be mad or no somewhat resembles the ancient European custom of trying witches. The old woman suspected was tied hand and foot, and thrown into the water. If she swam, then she was instantly carried off to be burnt for a witch; if she sunk, then indeed she was acquitted of the charge, but drowned in the experiment. In the same manner, a crowd gather round a dog suspected of madness, and they begin by teasing the devoted animal on every side: if he attempts to stand upon the defensive and bite, then he is unanimously found guilty, for "a mad dog always snaps at everything;" if, on the contrary, he strives to escape by running away, then he can expect no compassion, for "mad dogs always run straight forward before them."

It is pleasant enough for a neutral being like me, who have no share in these ideal calamities, to mark the stages of this national disease. The terror at first feebly enters with a disregarded story of a little dog, that had gone through a neighbouring village, that was thought to be mad by several that had seen him. The next account comes, that a mastiff ran through a certain town, and had bit five geese, which immediately ran mad, foamed at the bill, and died in great agonies soon after. Then comes an affecting history of a little boy bit in the leg, and gone down to be dipt in the salt water. When the people have sufficiently shuddered at that, they are next congealed with a frightful account of a man who was said lately to have died from a bite he had received some years before. This relation only prepares the way for another still more hideous, as how the master of a family, with seven small children, were all bit by a mad lapdog; and how the poor father first perceived the infection by calling for a draught of water, where he saw the lapdog swimming in the cup.

When epidemic terror is thus once excited, every morning comes loaded with some new disaster: as in stories of ghosts each loves to hear the account, though it only serves to make him uneasy, so here each listens with eagerness, and adds to the tidings new circumstances of peculiar horror. A lady, for instance, in the country, of very weak nerves, has been frighted by the barking of a dog; and this, alas! too frequently happens. The story soon is improved and spreads, that a mad dog had frighted a lady of distinction. These circumstances begin to grow terrible before they have reached the neighbouring village, and there the report is, that a lady of quality was bit by a mad mastiff. This account every moment gathers new strength, and grows more dismal as it approaches the capital; and by the time it has arrived in town the lady is described, with wild eyes, foaming mouth, running mad upon all-fours, barking like a dog, biting her servants, and at last smothered between two beds by the advice of her doctors; while the mad mastiff is in the meantime ranging the whole country over, slavering at the mouth, and seeking whom he may devour.

My landlady, a good-natured woman, but a little credulous, waked me some mornings ago before her usual hour, with horror and astonishment in her looks: she desired me, if I had any regard for my safety, to keep within; for a few days ago so dismal an accident had happened, as to put all the world upon their guard. A mad dog down in the country, she assured me, had bit a farmer, who soon becoming mad, ran into his own yard, and bit a fine brindled cow; the cow quickly became as mad as the man, began to foam at the mouth, and raising herself up, walked about on her hind legs, sometimes barking like a dog, and sometimes attempting to talk like the farmer. Upon examining the grounds of this story, I found my landlady had it from one neighbour, who had it from another neighbour, who heard it from very good authority.

Were most stories of this nature thoroughly examined, it would be found that numbers of such as have been said to suffer were no way injured; and that of those who have been actually bitten, not one in an hundred was bit by a mad dog. Such accounts in general, therefore, only serve to make the people miserable by false terrors, and sometimes fright the patient into actual phrenzy by creating those very symptoms they pretended to deplore.

But even allowing three or four to die in a season of this terrible death (and four is probably too large a concession), yet still it is not considered, how many are preserved in their health and in their property by this devoted animal's services. The midnight robber is kept at a distance; the insidious thief is often detected; the healthful chase repairs many a worn constitution; and the poor man finds in his dog a willing assistant, eager to lessen his toil, and content with the smallest retribution.

"A dog," says one of the English poets, "is an honest creature, and I am a friend to dogs." Of all the beasts that graze the lawn or hunt the forest, a dog is the only animal that, leaving his fellows, attempts to cultivate the friendship of man: to man he looks in all his necessities with a speaking eye for assistance; exerts for him all the little service in his power with cheerfulness and pleasure; for him bears famine and fatigue with patience and resignation; no injuries can abate his fidelity; no distress induce him to forsake his benefactor: studious to please, and fearing to offend, he is still an humble steadfast dependant; and in him alone fawning is not flattery. How unkind, then, to torture this faithful creature, who has left the forest to claim the protection of man! how ungrateful a return to the trusty animal for all his services! —Adieu.

LETTER LXX.

From Lien Chi Altangi to Hingpo, by the way of Moscow.

THE Europeans are themselves blind, who describe Fortune without sight. No first-rate beauty ever had finer eyes, or saw more clearly: they who have no other trade but seeking their fortune, need never hope to find her; coquette-like, she flies from her close pursuers, and at last fixes on the plodding mechanic, who stays at home, and minds his business.

I am amazed how men call her blind, when, by the company she keeps, she seems so very discerning. Wherever you see a gaming-table, be very sure Fortune is not there; wherever you see an house with the doors open, be very sure Fortune is not there; when you see a man whose pocket-holes are laced with gold, be satisfied Fortune is not there; wherever you see a beautiful woman good-natured and obliging, be convinced Fortune is never there. In short, she is ever seen accompanying industry, and as often trundling a wheelbarrow as lolling in a coach and six.

If you would make Fortune your friend, or, to personize her no longer, if you desire, my son, to be rich, and have money, be more eager to save than acquire: when people say, Money is to be got here, and money is to be got there, take no notice; mind your own business; stay where you are, and secure all you can get without stirring. When you hear that your neighbour has picked up a purse of gold in the street, never run out into the same street, looking about you in order to pick up such another; or when you are informed that he has made a fortune in one branch of business, never change your own in order to be his rival. Do not desire to be rich all at once; but patiently add farthing to farthing. Perhaps you despise the petty sum; and yet they who want a farthing, and have no friend that will lend them it, think farthings very good things. Whang, the foolish miller, when he wanted a farthing in his distress, found that no friend would lend, because they knew he wanted. Did you ever read the story of Whang in our books of Chinese learning? he who, despising small sums, and grasping at all, lost even what he had.

Whang, the miller, was naturally avaricious; nobody loved money better than he, or more respected those that had it. When people would talk of a rich man in company, Whang would say, I know him very well; he and I have been long acquainted; he and I are intimate; he stood for a child of mine: but if ever a poor man was mentioned, he had not the least knowledge of the man; he might be very well for aught he knew; but he was not fond of many acquaintances, and loved to choose his company.

Whang, however, with all his eagerness for riches, was in reality poor; he had nothing but the profits of his mill to support him; but though these were small, they were certain: while his mill stood and went, he was sure of eating; and his frugality was such, that he every day laid some money by, which he would at intervals count and contemplate with much satisfaction. Yet still his acquisitions were not equal to his desires; he only found himself above want, whereas he desired to be possessed of affluence.

One day, as he was indulging these wishes, he was informed that a neighbour of his had found a pan of money under ground, having dreamed of it three nights running before. These tidings were daggers to the heart of poor Whang. "Here am I," says he, "toiling and moiling from morning till night for a few paltry farthings, while neighbour Hunks only goes quietly to bed, and dreams himself into thousands before morning. Oh that I could dream like him! with what pleasure would I dig round the pan; how slily would I carry it home; not even my wife should see me; and then, oh, the pleasure of thrusting one's hand into a heap of gold up to the elbow!"

Such reflections only served to make the miller unhappy; he discontinued his former assiduity; he was quite disgusted with small gains, and his customers began to forsake him. Every day he repeated the wish, and every night laid himself down in order to dream. Fortune, that was for a long time unkind, at last, however, seemed to smile upon his distresses, and indulged him with the wished-for vision. He dreamed, that under a certain part of the foundation of his mill there was concealed a monstrous pan of gold and diamonds, buried deep in the ground, and covered with a large flat stone. He rose up, thanked the stars that were at last pleased to take pity on his sufferings, and concealed his good luck from every person, as is usual in money dreams, in order to have the vision repeated the two succeeding nights, by which he should be certain of its veracity. His wishes in this also were answered; he still dreamed of the same pan of money, in the very same place.

Now, therefore, it was past a doubt; so, getting up early the third morning, he repairs alone, with a mattock in his hand, to the mill, and began to undermine that part of the wall which the vision directed. The first omen of success that he met was a broken mug; digging still deeper, he turns up a house tile, quite new and entire. At last, after much digging, he came to the broad flat stone, but then so large, that it was beyond one man's strength to remove it. "Here," cried he, in raptures, to himself, "here it is! under this stone there is room for a very large pan of diamonds indeed! I must e'en go home to my wife, and tell her the whole affair, and get her to assist me in turning it up." Away therefore he goes, and acquaints his wife with every circumstance of their good fortune. Her raptures on this occasion may easily be imagined; she flew round his neck, and embraced him in an agony of joy: but those transports, however, did not delay their eagerness to know the exact sum; returning, therefore, speedily together to the place where Whang had been digging, there they found—not indeed the expected treasure, but the mill, their only support, undermined and fallen.—Adieu.

LETTER LXXI.

From Lien Chi Altangi to Fum Hoam, First President of the Ceremonial Academy at Pekin in China.

THE people of London are as fond of walking as our friends at Pekin of riding; one of the principal entertainments of the citizens here in summer is to repair about nightfall to a garden not far from town, where they walk about, show their best clothes and best faces, and listen to a concert provided for the occasion.

I accepted an invitation a few evenings ago from my old friend, the Man in Black, to be one of a party that was to sup there; and at the appointed hour waited upon him at his lodgings. There I found the company assembled, and expecting my arrival. Our party consisted of my friend, in superlative finery, his stockings rolled, a black velvet waistcoat, which was formerly new, and a gray wig combed down in imitation of hair; a pawnbroker's widow, of whom, by the by, my friend was a professed admirer, dressed out in green damask, with three gold rings on every finger; Mr. Tibbs, the second-rate beau I have formerly described; together with his lady, in flimsy silk, dirty gauze instead of linen, and an hat as big as an umbrella.

Our first difficulty was in settling how we should set out. Mrs. Tibbs had a natural aversion to the water, and the widow, being a little in flesh, as warmly protested against walking; a coach was therefore agreed upon; which being too small to carry five, Mr. Tibbs consented to sit in his wife's lap.

In this manner, therefore, we set forward, being entertained by the way with the bodings of Mr. Tibbs, who assured us he did not expect to see a single creature for the evening above the degree of a cheesemonger; that this was the last night of the gardens, and that consequently we should be pestered with the nobility and gentry from Thames Street and Crooked Lane; with several other prophetic ejaculations, probably inspired by the uneasiness of his situation.

The illuminations began before we arrived, and I must confess, that upon entering the gardens I found every sense overpaid with more than expected pleasure: the lights everywhere glimmering through the scarcely moving trees—the full-bodied concert bursting on the stillness of the night—the natural concert of the birds, in the more retired part of the grove, vying with that which was formed by art—the company gaily dressed, looking satisfaction—and the tables spread with various delicacies,—all conspired to fill my imagination with the visionary happiness of the Arabian lawgiver, and lifted me into an ecstasy of admiration. "Head of Confucius," cried I to my friend, "this is fine! this unites rural beauty with courtly magnificence! if we except the virgins of immortality, that hang on every tree, and may be plucked at every desire, I do not see how this falls short of Mahomet's Paradise!"—"As for virgins," cries my friend, "it is true they are a fruit that do not much abound in our gardens here; but if ladies, as plenty as apples in autumn, and as complying as any Houri of them all, can content you, I fancy we have no need to go to heaven for Paradise."

I was going to second his remarks, when we were called to a consultation by Mr. Tibbs and the rest of the company, to know in what manner we were to lay out the evening to the greatest advantage.

Mrs. Tibbs was for keeping the genteel walk of the garden, where, she observed, there was always the very best company; the widow, on the contrary, who came but once a season, was for securing a good standing place to see the waterworks, which she assured us would begin in less than an hour at farthest: a dispute therefore began, and as it was managed between two of very opposite characters, it threatened to grow more bitter at every reply. Mrs. Tibbs wondered how people could pretend to know the polite world, who had received all their rudiments of breeding behind a counter: to which the other replied, that though some people sat behind counters, yet they could sit at the head of their own tables too, and carve three good dishes of hot meat whenever they thought proper; which was more than some people could say for themselves, that hardly knew a rabbit and onions from a green goose and gooseberries.

It is hard to say where this might have ended, had not the husband, who probably knew the impetuosity of his wife's disposition, proposed to end the dispute by adjourning to a box, and try if there was anything to be had for supper that was supportable. To this we all consented; but here a new distress arose: Mr. and Mrs. Tibbs would sit in none but a genteel box—a box where they might see and be seen—one, as they expressed it, in the very focus of public view; but such a box was not easy to be obtained, for though we were perfectly convinced of our own gentility, and the gentility of our appearance, yet we found it a difficult matter to persuade the keepers of the boxes to be of our opinion; they chose to reserve genteel boxes for what they judged more genteel company.

At last, however, we were fixed, though somewhat obscurely, and supplied with the usual entertainment of the place. The widow found the supper excellent, but Mrs. Tibbs thought everything detestable. "Come, come, my dear," cries the husband, by way of consolation, "to be sure we can't find such dressing here as we have at Lord Crump's or Lady Crimp's; but, for Vauxhall dressing, it is pretty good: it is not their victuals, indeed, I find fault with, but their wine; their wine," cries he, drinking off a glass, "indeed, is most abominable."

By this last contradiction the widow was fairly conquered in point of politeness. She perceived now that she had no pretensions in the world to taste; her very senses were vulgar, since she had praised detestable custard, and smacked at wretched wine; she was therefore content to yield the victory, and for the rest of the night to listen and improve. It is true, she would now and then forget herself, and confess she was pleased; but they soon brought her back again to miserable refinement. She once praised the painting of the box in which we were sitting, but was soon convinced that such paltry pieces ought rather to excite horror than satisfaction: she ventured again to commend one of the singers, but Mrs. Tibbs soon let her know, in the style of a connoisseur, that the singer in question had neither ear, voice, nor judgment.

Mr. Tibbs, now willing to prove that his wife's pretensions to music were just, entreated her to favour the company with a song; but to this she gave a positive denial—"for you know very well, my dear," says she, "that I am not in voice to-day, and when one's voice is not equal to one's judgment, what signifies singing? besides, as there is no accompaniment, it would be but spoiling music." All these excuses, however, were overruled by the rest of the company, who, though one would think they already had music enough, joined in the entreaty. But particularly the widow, now willing to convince the company of her breeding, pressed so warmly, that she seemed determined to take no refusal. At last, then, the lady complied, and after humming for some minutes, began with such a voice, and such affectation, as, I could perceive, gave but little satisfaction to any except her husband. He sat with rapture in his eye, and beat time with his hand on the table.

You must observe, my friend, that it is the custom of this country, when a lady or gentleman happens to sing, for the company to sit as mute and motionless as statues. Every feature, every limb, must seem to correspond in fixed attention; and while the song continues, they are to remain in a state of universal petrifaction. In this mortifying situation we had continued for some time, listening to the song, and looking with tranquillity, when the master of the box came to inform us, that the waterworks were going to begin. At this information I could instantly perceive the widow bounce from her seat; but correcting herself, she sat down again, repressed by motives of good breeding. Mrs. Tibbs, who had seen the waterworks an hundred times, resolving not to be interrupted, continued her song without any share of mercy, nor had the smallest pity on our impatience. The widow's face, I own, gave me high entertainment; in it I could plainly read the struggle she felt between good breeding and curiosity: she talked of the waterworks the whole evening before, and seemed to have come merely in order to see them; but then she could not bounce out in the very middle of a song, for that would be forfeiting all pretensions to high life, or high-lived company, ever after. Mrs. Tibbs, therefore, kept on singing, and we continued to listen, till at last, when the song was just concluded, the waiter came to inform us that the water-works were over.

"The waterworks over!" cried the widow; "the waterworks over already! that's impossible! they can't be over so soon!"—"It is not my business," replied the fellow, "to contradict your ladyship; I'll run again and see." He went, and soon returned with a confirmation of the dismal tidings. No ceremony could now bind my friend's disappointed mistress. She testified her displeasure in the openest manner; in short, she now began to find fault in turn, and at last insisted upon going home, just at the time that Mr. and Mrs. Tibbs assured the company that the polite hours were going to begin, and that the ladies would instantaneously be entertained with the horns.—Adieu.

LETTER LXXII.

To the same.

Not far from this city lives a poor tinker, who has educated seven sons, all at this very time in arms, and fighting for their country; and what reward do you think has the tinker from the state for such important services? None in the world. His sons, when the war is over, may probably be whipped from parish to parish as vagabonds, and the old man, when past labour, may die a prisoner in some house of correction.

Such a worthy subject in China would be held in universal reverence; his services would be rewarded, if not with dignities, at least with an exemption from labour; he would take the left hand at feasts, and mandarines themselves would be proud to show their submission. The English laws punish vice; the Chinese laws do more,—they reward virtue.

Considering the little encouragement given to matrimony here, I am not surprised at the discouragement given to propagation. Would you believe it, my dear Fum Hoam, there are laws made which even forbid the people's marrying each other! By the head of Confucius, I jest not; there are such laws in being here; and yet their lawgivers have never been instructed among the Hottentots, nor imbibed their principles of equity from the natives of Anamaboo.

There are laws which ordain, that no man shall marry a woman against her own consent. This, though contrary to what we are taught in Asia, and though in some measure a clog upon matrimony, I have no great objection to. There are laws which ordain, that no woman shall marry against her father and mother's consent, unless arrived at an age of maturity; by which is understood, those years when women with us are generally past child-bearing. This must be a clog upon matrimony, as it is more difficult for the lover to please three than one, and much more difficult to please old people than young ones. The laws ordain, that the consenting couple shall take a long time to consider before they marry: this is a very great clog, because people love to have all rash actions done in a hurry. It is ordained, that all marriages shall be proclaimed before celebration: this is a severe clog, as many are ashamed to have their marriage made public, from motives of vicious modesty, and many afraid, from views of temporal interest. It is ordained, that there is nothing sacred in the ceremony, but that it may be dissolved, to all intents and purposes, by the authority of any civil magistrate. And yet, opposite to this, it is ordained, that the priest shall be paid a large sum of money for granting his sacred permission.

Thus you see, my friend, that matrimony here is hedged round with so many obstructions, that those who are willing to break through or surmount them must be contented if at last they find it a bed of thorns. The laws are not to blame, for they have deterred the people from engaging as much as they could. It is, indeed, become a very serious affair in England, and none but serious people are generally found willing to engage. The young, the gay, and the beautiful, who have motives of passion only to induce them, are seldom found to embark, as those inducements are taken away; and none but the old, the ugly, and the mercenary, are seen to unite, who, if they have any posterity at all, will probably be an ill-favoured race like themselves.

What gave rise to those laws might have been some such accidents as these. It sometimes happened that a miser, who had spent all his youth in scraping up money to give his daughter such a fortune as might get her a mandarine husband, found his expectations disappointed at last, by her running away with his footman: this must have been a sad shock to the poor disconsolate parent, to see his poor daughter in a one-horse chaise, when he had designed her for a coach and six. What a stroke from Providence! to see his dear money go to enrich a beggar; all nature cried out at the profanation.

It sometimes happened, also, that a lady, who had inherited all the titles and all the nervous complaints of nobility, thought fit to impair her dignity, and mend her constitution, by marrying a farmer: this must have been a sad shock to her inconsolable relations, to see so fine a flower snatched from a flourishing family, and planted in a dunghill; this was an absolute inversion of the first principles of things.

In order, therefore, to prevent the great from being thus contaminated by vulgar alliances, the obstacles to matrimony have been so contrived, that the rich only can marry amongst the rich; and the poor, who would leave celibacy, must be content to increase their poverty with a wife. Thus have their laws fairly inverted the inducements to matrimony. Nature tells us, that beauty is the proper allurement of those who are rich, and money of those who are poor; but things here are so contrived, that the rich are invited to marry by that fortune which they do not want, and the poor have no inducement but that beauty which they do not feel.

An equal diffusion of riches through any country ever constitutes its happiness. Great wealth in the possession of one stagnates, and extreme poverty with another keeps him in unambitious indigence; but the moderately rich are generally active: not too far removed from poverty to fear its calamities, nor too near extreme wealth to slacken the nerve of labour, they remain still between both in a state of continual fluctuation. How impolitic, therefore, are those laws which promote the accumulation of wealth among the rich; more impolitic still, in attempting to increase the depression on poverty.

Bacon, the English philosopher, compares money to manure. "If gathered in heaps," says he, "it does no good; on the contrary, it becomes offensive. But being spread, though never so thinly, over the surface of the earth, it enriches the whole country." Thus the wealth a nation possesses must expatiate, or it is of no benefit to the public; it becomes rather a grievance, where matrimonial laws thus confine it to a few.

But this restraint upon matrimonial community, even considered in a physical light, is injurious. As those who rear up animals take all possible pains to cross the strain, in order to improve the breed; so in those countries where marriage is most free the inhabitants are found every age to improve in stature and in beauty; on the contrary, where it is confined to a *caste*, a *tribe*, or an *horde*, as among the Gaours, the Jews, or the Tartars, each division soon assumes a family likeness, and every tribe degenerates into peculiar deformity. Hence it may be easily inferred, that if the mandarines here are resolved only to marry among each other, they will soon produce a posterity with mandarine faces; and we shall see the heir of some honourable family scarce equal to the abortion of a country farmer.

These are a few of the obstacles to marriage here, and it is certain they have, in some measure, answered the end, for celibacy is both frequent and fashionable. Old bachelors appear abroad without a mask, and old maids, my dear Fum Hoam, have been absolutely known to ogle. To confess in friendship, if I were an Englishman I fancy I should be an old bachelor myself; I should never find courage to run through all the adventures prescribed by the law. I could submit to court my mistress herself upon reasonable terms, but to court her father, her mother, and a long tribe of cousins, aunts, and relations, and then stand the butt of a whole country church,—I would as soon turn tail, and make love to her grandmother.

I can conceive no other reason for thus loading matrimony with so many prohibitions, unless it be that the country was thought already too populous, and this was found to be the most effectual means of thinning it. If this was the motive, I cannot but congratulate the wise projectors on the success of their scheme. "Hail, O ye dim-sighted politicians, ye weeders of men! 'Tis yours to clip the wing of industry, and convert Hymen to a broker. 'Tis yours to behold small objects with a microscopic eye, but to be blind to those which require an extent of vision. 'Tis yours, O ye discerners of mankind! to lay the line between society, and weaken that force by dividing, which should bind with united vigour. 'Tis yours to introduce national real distress, in order to avoid the imaginary distresses of a few. Your actions can be justified by an hundred reasons like truth; they can be opposed by but a few reasons, and those reasons are true."—Farewell.

LETTER LXXIII.

From Lien Chi Altangi to Hingpo, by the way of Moscow.

Age, that lessens the enjoyment of life, increases our desire of living. Those dangers which, in the vigour of youth, we had learned to despise, assume new terrors as we grow old. Our caution increasing as our years increase, fear becomes at last the prevailing passion of the mind; and the small remainder of life is taken up in useless efforts to keep off our end, or provide for a continued existence.

Strange contradiction in our nature, and to which even the wise are liable! If I should judge of that part of life which lies before me by that which I have already seen, the prospect is hideous. Experience tells me, that my past enjoyments have brought no real felicity; and sensation assures me, that those I have felt are stronger than those which are yet to come. Yet experience and sensation in vain persuade; hope, more powerful than either, dresses out the distant prospect in fancied beauty; some happiness in long perspective still beckons me to pursue; and, like a losing gamester, every new disappointment increases my ardour to continue the game.

Whence, my friend, this increased love of life, which grows upon us with our years? whence comes it, that we thus make greater efforts to preserve our existence at a period when it becomes scarcely worth the keeping? Is it that nature, attentive to the preservation of mankind, increases our wishes to live, while she lessens our enjoyments; and, as she robs the senses of every pleasure, equips imagination in the spoil? Life would be insupportable to an old man, who, loaded with infirmities, feared death no more than in the vigour of manhood: the numberless calamities of decaying nature, and the consciousness of surviving every pleasure, would at once induce him, with his own hand, to terminate the scene of misery: but, happily, the contempt of death forsakes him at a time when only it could be prejudicial; and life acquires an imaginary value, in proportion as its real value is no more.

Our attachment to every object around

us increases, in general, from the length of our acquaintance with it. "I would not choose," says a French philosopher, "to see an old post pulled up, with which I had been long acquainted." A mind long habituated to a certain set of objects insensibly becomes fond of seeing them, visits them from habit, and parts from them with reluctance; from hence proceeds the avarice of the old in every kind of possession. They love the world and all that it produces; they love life and all its advantages; not because it gives them pleasure, but because they have known it long.

Chinvang the Chaste, ascending the throne of China, commanded that all who were unjustly detained in prison during the preceding reigns should be set free. Among the number who came to thank their deliverer on this occasion there appeared a majestic old man, who, falling at the emperor's feet, addressed him as follows:—"Great father of China, behold a wretch, now eighty-five years old, who was shut up in a dungeon at the age of twenty-two. I was imprisoned, though a stranger to crime, or without being even confronted by my accusers. I have now lived in solitude and darkness for more than fifty years, and am grown familiar with distress. As yet, dazzled with the splendour of that sun to which you have restored me, I have been wandering the streets to find some friend that would assist, or relieve, or remember me; but my friends, my family, and relations are all dead, and I am forgotten. Permit me, then, O Chinvang, to wear out the wretched remains of life in my former prison: the walls of my dungeon are to me more pleasing than the most splendid palace; I have not long to live, and shall be unhappy except I spend the rest of my days where my youth was passed,—in that prison from which you were pleased to release me."

The old man's passion for confinement is similar to that we all have for life. We are habituated to the prison, we look round with discontent, are displeased with the abode, and yet the length of our captivity only increases our fondness for the cell. The trees we have planted, the houses we have built, or the posterity we have begotten, all serve to bind us closer to earth, and embitter our parting. Life sues the young like a new acquaintance; the companion, as yet unexhausted, is at once instructive and amusing: its company pleases; yet, for all this, it is but little regarded. To us who are declined in years life appears like an old friend; its jests have been anticipated in former conversation; it has no new story to make us smile, no new improvement with which to surprise, yet still we love it; destitute of every enjoyment, still we love it, husband the wasting treasure with increased frugality, and feel all the poignancy of anguish in the fatal separation.

Sir Philip Mordaunt was young, beautiful, sincere, brave, an Englishman. He had a complete fortune of his own, and the love of the king his master, which was equivalent to riches. Life opened all her treasure before him, and promised a long succession of future happiness. He came, tasted of the entertainment, but was disgusted even in the beginning. He professed an aversion to living; was tired of walking round the same circle; had tried every enjoyment, and found them all grow weaker at every repetition. "If life be in youth so displeasing," cried he to himself, "what will it appear when age comes on? if it be at present indifferent, sure it will then be execrable." This thought embittered every reflection; till at last, with all the serenity of perverted reason, he ended the debate with a pistol! Had this self-deluded man been apprised, that existence grows more desirable to us the longer we exist, he would have then faced old age without shrinking, he would have boldly dared to live, and served that society by his future assiduity, which he basely injured by his desertion.—Adieu.

LETTER LXXIV.

From Lien Chi Altangi to Fum Hoam, First President of the Ceremonial Academy at Pekin in China.

In reading the newspapers here I have reckoned up not less than twenty-five great men, seventeen very great men, and nine very extraordinary men, in less than the compass of half a year. "These," said the gazettes, "are the men that posterity are to gaze at with admiration; these the names that fame will be employed in holding up for the astonishment of succeeding ages." Let me see—forty-six great men in half a year amount to just ninety-two in a year. I wonder how posterity will be able to remember them all, or whether the people, in future times, will have any other business to mind, but that of getting the catalogue by heart.

Does the mayor of a corporation make a speech? he is instantly set down for a great man. Does a pedant digest his commonplace book into a folio? he quickly becomes great. Does a poet string up trite sentiments in rhyme? he also becomes the great man of the hour. How diminutive soever the object of admiration, each is followed by a crowd of still more diminutive admirers. The shout begins in his train; onward he marches to immortality; looks back at the pursuing crowd with self-satisfaction; catching all the oddities, the whimsies, the absurdities, and the littlenesses of conscious greatness, by the way.

I was yesterday invited by a gentleman to dinner, who promised that our entertainment should consist of a haunch of venison, a turtle, and a great man. I came according to appointment. The venison was fine, the turtle good, but the great man insupportable. The moment I ventured to speak, I was at once contradicted with a snap. I attempted, by a second and a third assault, to retrieve my lost reputation, but was still beat back with confusion. I was resolved to attack him once more from entrenchment, and turned the conversation upon the government of China: but even here he asserted, snapped, and contradicted as before. "Heavens," thought I, "this man pretends to know China even better than myself!" I looked round to see who was on my side; but every eye was fixed in admiration on the great man: I therefore at last thought proper to sit silent, and act the pretty gentleman during the ensuing conversation.

When a man has once secured a circle of admirers, he may be as ridiculous here as he thinks proper; and it all passes for elevation of sentiment or learned absence. If he transgresses the common forms of breeding, mistakes even a teapot for a tobacco-box, it is said that his thoughts are fixed on more important objects: to speak and to act like the rest of mankind, is to be no greater than they. There is something of oddity in the very idea of greatness; for we are seldom astonished at a thing very much resembling ourselves.

When the Tartars make a Lama, their first care is to place him in a dark corner of the temple: here he is to sit half concealed from view, to regulate the motion of his hands, lips, and eyes; but, above all, he is enjoined gravity and silence. This, however, is but the prelude to his apotheosis: a set of emissaries are despatched among the people, to cry up his piety, gravity, and love of raw flesh; the people take them at their word, approach the Lama, now become an idol, with the most humble prostration; he receives their addresses without motion, commences a god, and is ever after fed by his priests with the spoon of immortality. The same receipt in this country serves to make a great man. The idol only keeps close, sends out his little emissaries to be hearty in his praise; and straight, whether statesman or author, he is set down in the list of fame, continuing to be praised while it is fashionable to praise, or while he prudently keeps his minuteness concealed from the public.

I have visited many countries, and have been in cities without number, yet never did I enter a town which could not produce ten or twelve of those little great men; all fancying themselves known to the rest of the world, and complimenting each other upon their extensive reputation. It is amusing enough when two of these domestic prodigies of learning mount the stage of ceremony, and give and take praise from each other. I have been present when a German doctor, for having pronounced a panegyric upon a certain monk, was thought the most ingenious man in the world; till the monk soon after divided this reputation by returning the compliment; by which means they both marched off with universal applause.

The same degree of undeserved adulation that attends our great man while living, often also follows him to the tomb. It frequently happens that one of his little admirers sits down, big with the important subject, and is delivered of the history of his life and writings. This may probably be called the revolutions of a life between the fireside and the easy chair. In this we learn the year in which he was born, at what an early age he gave symptoms of uncommon genius and application, together with some of his smart sayings, collected by his aunt and mother while yet but a boy. The next book introduces him to the university, where we are informed of his amazing progress in learning, his excellent skill in darning stockings, and his new invention for papering books, to save the covers. He next makes his appearance in the republic of letters, and publishes his folio. Now the colossus is reared; his works are eagerly bought up by all the purchasers of scarce books. The learned societies invite him to become a member: he disputes against some foreigner with a long Latin name, conquers in the controversy, is complimented by several authors of gravity and importance, is excessively fond of egg-sauce with his pig, becomes president of a literary club, and dies in the meridian of his glory. Happy they who thus have some little faithful attendant, who never forsakes them, but prepares to wrangle and to praise against every opposer; at once ready to increase their pride while living, and their character when dead! For you and I, my friend, who have no humble admirer thus to attend us; we, who neither are, nor never will be, great men, and who do not much care whether we are great men or no; at least let us strive to be honest men, and to have common sense.—Adieu.

LETTER LXXV.

To the same.

THERE are numbers in this city who live by writing new books; and yet there are thousands of volumes in every large library unread and forgotten. This, upon my arrival, was one of those contradictions which I was unable to account for. "Is it possible," said I, "that there should be any demand for new books, before those already published are read? Can there be so many employed in producing a commodity with which the market is already overstocked—and with goods also better than any of modern manufacture?"

What at first view appeared an inconsistence, is a proof at once of this people's wisdom and refinement. Even allowing the works of their ancestors better written than theirs, yet those of the moderns acquire a real value, by being marked with the impression of the times. Antiquity has been in the possession of others; the present is our own: let us first, therefore, learn to know what belongs to ourselves, and then, if we have leisure, cast our reflections back to the reign of Shonou, who governed twenty thousand years before the creation of the moon.

The volumes of antiquity, like medals, may very well serve to amuse the curious; but the works of the moderns, like the current coin of a kingdom, are much better for immediate use: the former are often prized above their intrinsic value, and kept with care; the latter seldom pass for more than they are worth, and are often subject to the merciless hands of sweating critics and clipping compilers: the works of antiquity are ever praised, those of the moderns read: the treasures of our ancestors have our esteem, and we boast the passion; those of contemporary genius engage our heart, although we blush to own it. The visits we pay the former resemble those we pay the great,—the ceremony is troublesome, and yet such as we would not choose to forego: our acquaintance with modern books is like sitting with a friend,—our pride is not flattered in the interview, but it gives more internal satisfaction.

In proportion as society refines, new books must ever become more necessary. Savage rusticity is reclaimed by oral admonition alone; but the elegant excesses of refinement are best corrected by the still voice of studious inquiry. In a polite age almost every person becomes a reader, and receives more instruction from the press than the pulpit. The preaching bonze may instruct the illiterate peasant; but nothing less than the insinuating address of a fine writer can win its way to an heart already relaxed in all the effeminacy of refinement. Books are necessary to correct the vices of the polite; but those vices are ever changing, and the antidote should be changed accordingly—should still be new.

Instead, therefore, of thinking the number of new publications here too great, I could wish it still greater, as they are the most useful instruments of reformation. Every country must be instructed either by writers or preachers: but as the number of readers increases, the number of hearers is proportionally diminished; the writer becomes more useful, and the preaching bonze less necessary.

Instead, therefore, of complaining that writers are overpaid, when their works procure them a bare subsistence, I should imagine it the duty of a state, not only to encourage their numbers, but their industry. A bonze is rewarded with immense riches for instructing only a few, even of the most ignorant of the people; and sure the poor scholar should not beg his bread, who is capable of instructing a million.

Of all rewards, I grant, the most pleasing to a man of real merit is fame; but a polite age, of all times, is that in which scarcely any share of merit can acquire it. What numbers of fine writers in the latter empire of Rome, when refinement was carried to the highest pitch, have missed that fame and immortality which they had fondly arrogated to themselves! How many Greek authors, who wrote at that period when Constantinople was the refined mistress of the empire, now rest, either not printed or not read, in the libraries of Europe! Those who came first, while either state as yet was barbarous, carried all the reputation away. Authors, as the age refined, became more numerous, and their numbers destroyed their fame. It is but natural, therefore, for the writer, when conscious that his works will not procure him fame hereafter, to endeavour to make them turn out to his temporal interest here.

Whatever be the motives which induce men to write, whether avarice or fame, the country becomes most wise and happy in which they most serve for instructors. The countries where sacerdotal instruction alone is permitted remain in ignorance, superstition, and hopeless slavery. In England, where there are as many new books published as in all the rest of Europe together, a spirit of freedom and reason reigns among the people: they have been often known to act like fools; they are generally found to think like men.

The only danger that attends a multiplicity of publications is, that some of them may be calculated to injure rather than benefit society. But where writers are numerous, they also serve as a check upon each other; and perhaps a literary inquisition is the most terrible punishment that can be conceived to a literary transgressor.

But, to do the English justice, there are but few offenders of this kind; their publications, in general, aim either at mending the heart, or improving the common weal. The dullest writer talks of virtue, and liberty, and benevolence, with esteem; tells his true story, filled with good and wholesome advice; warns against slavery, bribery, or the bite of a mad dog; and dresses up his little useful magazine of knowledge and entertainment at least with a good intention. The dunces of France, on the other hand, who have less encouragement, are more vicious. Tender hearts, languishing eyes, Leonora in love at thirteen, ecstatic transports, stolen blisses, are the frivolous subjects of their frivolous memoirs. In England, if a bawdy blockhead thus breaks in on the community, he sets his whole fraternity in a roar; nor can he escape, even though he should fly to nobility for shelter.

Thus, even dunces, my friend, may make themselves useful. But there are others, whom nature has blessed with talents above the rest of mankind; men capable of thinking with precision, and impressing their thought with rapidity; beings who diffuse those regards upon mankind, which others contract and settle upon themselves. These deserve every honour from that community of which they are more peculiarly the children; to such I would give my heart, since to them I am indebted for its humanity.—Adieu.

LETTER LXXVI.

From Hingpo to Lien Chi Altangi, by the way of Moscow.

I STILL remain at Terki, where I have received that money which was remitted here in order to release me from captivity. My fair companion still improves in my esteem; the more I know her mind, her beauty becomes more poignant: she appears charming, even among the daughters of Circassia.

Yet, were I to examine her beauty with the art of a statuary, I should find numbers here that far surpass her; nature has not granted her all the boasted Circassian regularity of feature, and yet she greatly exceeds the fairest of the country in the art of seizing the affections. "Whence," have I often said to myself, "this resistless magic that attends even moderate charms? Though I regard the beauties of the country with admiration, every interview weakens the impression; but the form of Zelis grows upon my imagination—I never behold her without an increase of tenderness and respect. Whence this injustice of the mind, in preferring imperfect beauty to that which nature seems to have finished with care? Whence the infatuation that he whom a comet could not amaze, should be astonished at a meteor?" When reason was thus fatigued to find an answer, my imagination pursued the subject, and this was the result.

I fancied myself placed between two landscapes, this called the Region of Beauty, and that the Valley of the Graces: the one adorned with all that luxuriant nature could bestow; the fruits of various climates adorned the trees—the grove resounded with music—the gale breathed perfume—every charm that could arise from symmetry and exact distribution were here conspicuous,—the whole offering a prospect of pleasure without end. The Valley of the Graces, on the other hand, seemed by no means so inviting; the streams and the groves appeared just as they usually do in frequented countries: no magnificent parterres, no concert in the grove, the rivulet was edged with weeds, and the rook joined its voice to that of the nightingale. All was simplicity and nature.

The most striking objects ever first allure the traveller. I entered the Region of Beauty with increased curiosity, and promised myself endless satisfaction in being introduced to the presiding goddess. I perceived several strangers, who entered with the same design; and what surprised me not a little was, to see several others hastening to leave this abode of seeming felicity.

After some fatigue, I had at last the honour of being introduced to the goddess who represented Beauty in person. She was seated on a throne, at the foot of which stood several strangers, lately introduced like me, all regarding her form in ecstasy.

"Ah, what eyes! what lips! how clear her complexion! how perfect her shape!" At these exclamations Beauty, with downcast eyes, would endeavour to counterfeit modesty, but soon again looking round as if to confirm every spectator in his favourable sentiments: sometimes she would attempt to allure us by smiles; and at intervals would bridle back, in order to inspire us with respect as well as tenderness.

This ceremony lasted for some time, and had so much employed our eyes that we had forgot all this while that the goddess was silent. We soon, however, began to perceive the defect. "What," said we, among each other, "are we to have nothing but languishing airs, soft looks, and inclinations of the head? Will the goddess only deign to satisfy our eyes?" Upon this, one of the company stepped up to present her with some fruits he had gathered by the way. She received the present most sweetly smiling, and with one of the whitest hands in the world, but still not a word escaped her lips.

I now found that my companions grew weary of their homage; they went off one by one, and resolving not to be left behind, I offered to go in my turn, when, just at the door of the temple, I was called back by a female whose name was Pride, and who seemed displeased at the behaviour of the company. "Where are you hastening?" said she to me with an angry air; "the goddess of Beauty is here."—"I have been to visit her, madam," replied I, "and find her more beautiful even than report had made her."—"And why then will you leave her?" added the female.—"I have seen her long enough," returned I; "I have got all her features by heart. Her eyes are still the same. Her nose is a very fine one, but it is still just such a nose now as it was half an hour ago: could she throw a little more mind into her face, perhaps I should be for wishing to have more of her company."—"What signifies," replied my female, "whether she has a mind or not? has she any occasion for a mind, so formed as she is by nature? If she had a common face, indeed, there might be some reason for thinking to improve it; but when features are already perfect, every alteration would but impair them. A fine face is already at the point of perfection, and a fine lady should endeavour to keep it so: the impression it would receive from thought would but disturb its whole economy."

To this speech I gave no reply, but made the best of my way to the Valley of the Graces. Here I found all those who before had been my companions in the Region of Beauty, now upon the same errand.

As we entered the valley, the prospect insensibly seemed to improve; we found everything so natural, so domestic, and pleasing, that our minds, which before were congealed in admiration, now relaxed into gaiety and good-humour. We had designed to pay our respects to the presiding goddess, but she was nowhere to be found. One of our companions asserted that her temple lay to the right, another to the left, a third insisted that it was straight before us, and a fourth, that we had left it behind. In short, we found everything familiar and charming, but could not determine where to seek for the Grace in person.

In this agreeable incertitude we passed several hours, and though very desirous of finding the goddess, by no means impatient of the delay. Every part of the valley presented some minute beauty, which, without offering itself, at once stole upon the soul, and captivated us with the charms of our retreat. Still, however, we continued to search, and might still have continued, had we not been interrupted by a voice, which, though we could not see from whence it came, addressed us in this manner:—"If you would find the goddess of Grace, seek her not under one form, for she assumes a thousand. Ever changing under the eye of inspection, her variety, rather than her figure, is pleasing. In contemplating her beauty, the eye glides over every perfection with giddy delight, and capable of fixing nowhere, is charmed with the whole. She is now Contemplation with solemn look, again Compassion with humid eye; she now sparkles with joy, soon every feature speaks distress; her looks at times invite our approach, at others repress our presumption: the goddess cannot be properly called beautiful under any one of these forms, but by combining them all she becomes irresistibly pleasing."—Adieu.

LETTER LXXVII.

From Lien Chi Altangi to Fum Hoam, First President of the Ceremonial Academy at Pekin in China.

THE shops of London are as well furnished as those of Pekin. Those of London have a picture hung at their door, informing the passengers what they have to sell, as those at Pekin have a board to assure the buyer that they have no intent to cheat him.

I was this morning to buy silk for a nightcap. Immediately upon entering the mercer's shop, the master and his two men, with wigs plastered with powder, appeared to ask my commands. They were certainly the civillest people alive; if I but looked, they flew to the place where I cast my eye; every motion of mine sent them running round the whole shop for my satisfaction. I informed them that I wanted what was good, and they showed me not less than forty pieces, and each was better than the former, the prettiest pattern in nature, and the fittest in the world for nightcaps. "My very good friend," said I to the mercer, "you must not pretend to instruct me in silks;

I know these in particular to be no better than your mere flimsy bungees."—"That may be," cried the mercer, who, I afterwards found, had never contradicted a man in his life: "I cannot pretend to say but they may; but I can assure you, my Lady Trail has had a sack from this piece this very morning."—"But, friend," said I, "though my lady has chosen a sack from it, I see no necessity that I should wear it for a nightcap."—"That may be," returned he again; "yet what becomes a pretty lady, will at any time look well on a handsome gentleman." This short compliment was thrown in so very seasonably upon my ugly face, that even though I disliked the silk, I desired him to cut me off the pattern of a nightcap.

While this business was consigned to his journeymen, the master himself took down some pieces of silk still finer than any I had yet seen, and spreading them before me, "There," cries he, "there's beauty; my Lord Snakeskin has bespoke the fellow to this for the birthnight this very morning; it would look charmingly in waistcoats."—"But I don't want a waistcoat," replied I. "Not want a waistcoat!" returned the mercer: "then I would advise you to buy one; when waistcoats are wanted, you may depend upon it they will come dear. Always buy before you want, and you are sure to be well used, as they say in Cheapside." There was so much justice in his advice, that I could not refuse taking it; besides, the silk, which was really a good one, increased the temptation; so I gave orders for that too.

As I was waiting to have my bargains measured and cut, which, I know not how, they executed but slowly, during the interval the mercer entertained me with the modern manner of some of the nobility receiving company in their morning gowns. "Perhaps, sir," adds he, "you have a mind to see what kind of silk is universally worn." Without waiting for my reply, he spreads a piece before me, which might be reckoned beautiful even in China. "If the nobility," continues he, "were to know I sold this to any under a Right Honourable, I should certainly lose their custom; you see, my lord, it is at once rich, tasty, and quite the thing."—"I am no lord," interrupted I.—"I beg pardon," cried he; "but be pleased to remember, when you intend buying a morning gown, that you had an offer from me of something worth money. Conscience, sir, conscience is my way of dealing; you may buy a morning gown now, or you may stay till they become dearer and less fashionable; but it is not my business to advise." In short, most reverend Fum, he persuaded me to buy a morning gown also, and would probably have persuaded me to have bought half the goods in his shop, if I had stayed long enough, or was furnished with sufficient money.

Upon returning home, I could not help reflecting, with some astonishment, how this very man, with such a confined education and capacity, was yet capable of turning me as he thought proper, and moulding me to his inclinations. I knew he was only answering his own purposes, even while he attempted to appear solicitous about mine: yet, by a voluntary infatuation, a sort of passion, compounded of vanity and good-nature, I walked into the snare with my eyes open, and put myself to future pain in order to give him immediate pleasure. The wisdom of the ignorant somewhat resembles the instinct of animals; it is diffused in but a very narrow sphere, but within that circle it acts with vigour, uniformity, and success.—Adieu.

LETTER LXXVIII.

To the same.

FROM my former accounts you may be apt to fancy the English the most ridiculous people under the sun. They are indeed ridiculous; yet every other nation in Europe is equally so; each laughs at each, and the Asiatic at all.

I may upon another occasion point out what is most strikingly absurd in other countries; I shall at present confine myself only to France. The first national peculiarity a traveller meets upon entering that kingdom is an odd sort of staring vivacity in every eye, not excepting even the children; the people, it seems, have got it into their heads, that they have more wit than others, and so stare, in order to look smart.

I know not how it happens, but there appears a sickly delicacy in the faces of their finest women. This may have introduced the use of paint, and paint produces wrinkles; so that a fine lady shall look like a hag at twenty-three. But as, in some measure, they never appear young, so it may be equally asserted, that they actually think themselves never old; a gentle miss shall prepare for new conquests at sixty, shall hobble a rigadoon when she can scarce walk out without a crutch; she shall affect the girl, play her fan and her eyes, and talk of sentiments, bleeding hearts, and expiring for love, when actually dying with age. Like a departing philosopher, she attempts to make her last moments the most brilliant of her life.

Their civility to strangers is what they are chiefly proud of; and, to confess sincerely, their beggars are the very politest beggars I ever knew: in other places a traveller is addressed with a piteous whine, or a sturdy solemnity, but a French beggar shall ask your charity with a very genteel bow, and thank you for it with a smile and shrug.

Another instance of this people's breeding I must not forget. An Englishman would not speak his native language in a company of foreigners, where he was sure that none understood him; a travelling Hottentot himself would be silent if acquainted only with the language of his country; but a Frenchman shall talk to you whether you understand his language or not; never troubling his head whether you have learned French, still he keeps up the conversation, fixes his eye full in your face, and asks a thousand questions, which he answers himself, for want of a more satisfactory reply.

But their civility to foreigners is not half so great as their admiration of themselves. Everything that belongs to them and their nation is great, magnificent beyond expression, quite romantic! every garden is a paradise, every hovel a palace, and every woman an angel. They shut their eyes close, throw their mouths wide open, and cry out in a rapture, "*Sacre!* what beauty! *O Ciel!* what taste! *Mort de ma vie!* what grandeur! was ever any people like ourselves? we are the nation of men, and all the rest no better than two-legged barbarians."

I fancy the French would make the best cooks in the world if they had but meat; as it is, they can dress you out five different dishes from a nettle-top, seven from a dock-leaf, and twice as many from a frog's haunches: these eat prettily enough when one is a little used to them, are easy of digestion, and seldom overload the stomach with crudities. They seldom dine under seven hot dishes: it is true, indeed, with all this magnificence, they seldom spread a cloth before the guests; but in that I cannot be angry with them, since those who have got no linen on their backs may very well be excused for wanting it upon their tables.

Even religion itself loses its solemnity among them. Upon their roads, at about every five miles distance, you see an image of the Virgin Mary, dressed up in grim head-cloths, painted cheeks, and an old red petticoat; before her a lamp is often kept burning, at which, with the saint's permission, I have frequently lighted my pipe. Instead of the Virgin, you are sometimes presented with a crucifix, at other times with a wooden Saviour, fitted out in complete garniture, with sponge, spear, nails, pincers, hammer, bees'-wax, and vinegar-bottle. Some of these images, I have been told, came down from heaven; if so, in heaven they have but bungling workmen.

In passing through their towns you frequently see the men sitting at the doors knitting stockings, while the care of cultivating the ground and pruning the vines falls to the women. This is, perhaps, the reason why the fair sex are granted some peculiar privileges in this country; particularly, when they can get horses, of riding without a side-saddle.

But I begin to think you may find this description pert and dull enough; perhaps it is so; yet, in general, it is the manner in which the French usually describe foreigners; and it is but just to force a part of that ridicule back upon them, which they attempt to lavish on others.—Adieu.

LETTER LXXIX.

To the same.

THE two theatres which serve to amuse the citizens here are again opened for the winter. The mimetic troops, different from those of the state, begin their campaign when all the others quit the field; and at a time when the Europeans cease to destroy each other in reality, they are entertained with mock battles upon the stage.

The dancing master once more shakes his quivering feet; the carpenter prepares his paradise of pasteboard; the hero resolves to cover his forehead with brass, and the heroine begins to scour up her copper tail, preparative to future operations; in short, all are in motion, from the theatrical letter carrier, in yellow clothes, to Alexander the Great that stands on a stool.

Both houses have already commenced hostilities. War, open war, and no quarter received or given! Two singing women, like heralds, have begun the contest; the whole town is divided on this solemn occasion; one has the finest pipe, the other the finest manner; one curtsies to the ground, the other salutes the audience with a smile; one comes on with modesty which asks, the other with boldness which extorts, applause; one wears powder, the other has none; one has the longest waist, but the other appears most easy: all, all is important and serious; the town as yet perseveres in its neutrality; a cause of such moment demands the most mature deliberation; they continue to exhibit, and it is very possible this contest may continue to please to the end of the season.

But the generals of either army have, as I am told, several reinforcements to lend occasional assistance. If they produce a pair of diamond buckles at one house, we have a pair of eyebrows that can match them at the other. If we outdo them in our attitude, they can overcome us by a shrug; if we can bring more children on the stage, they can bring more guards in red clothes, who strut and shoulder their swords to the astonishment of every spectator.

They tell me here, that people frequent the theatre in order to be instructed as well as amused. I smile to hear the assertion. If I ever go to one of their playhouses, what with trumpets, hallooing behind the stage, and bawling upon it, I am quite dizzy before the performance is over. If I enter the house with any sentiments in my head, I am sure to have none going away, the whole mind being filled with a dead march, a funeral procession, a cat-call, a jig, or a tempest.

There is, perhaps, nothing more easy than to write properly for the English theatre; I am amazed that none are apprenticed to the trade. The author, when well acquainted with the value of thunder and lightning; when versed in all the mystery of scene-shifting and trapdoors; when skilled in the proper periods to introduce a wire-walker or a waterfall; when instructed in every actor's peculiar talent, and capable of adapting his speeches to the supposed excellence; when thus instructed, he knows all that can give a modern audience pleasure. One player shines in an exclamation, another in a groan, a third in a horror, a fourth in a start, a fifth in a smile, a sixth faints, and a seventh fidgets round the stage with peculiar vivacity; that piece, therefore, will succeed best, where each has a proper opportunity of shining: the actor's business is not so much to adapt himself to the poet, as the poet's to adapt himself to the actor.

The great secret, therefore, of tragedy-writing at present is a perfect acquaintance with theatrical ah's and oh's; a certain number of these, interspersed with gods! tortures! racks! and damnation! shall distort every actor almost into convulsions, and draw tears from every spectator; a proper use of these will infallibly fill the whole house with applause. But, above all, a whining scene must strike most forcibly. I would advise, from my present knowledge of the audience, the two favourite players of the town to introduce a scene of this sort in every play. Towards the middle of the last act I would have them enter with wild looks and outspread arms: there is no necessity for speaking, they are only to groan at each other; they must vary the tones of exclamation and despair through the whole theatrical gamut, wring their figures into every shape of distress, and, when their calamities have drawn a proper quantity of tears from the sympathetic spectators, they may go off in dumb solemnity at different doors, clapping their hands, or slapping their pocket-holes: this, which may be called a tragic pantomime, will answer every purpose of moving the passions as well as words could have done, and it must save those expenses which go to reward an author.

All modern plays that would keep the audience alive must be conceived in this manner; and, indeed, many a modern play is made up on no other plan. This is the merit that lifts up the heart, like opium, into a rapture of insensibility, and can dismiss the mind from all the fatigue of thinking: this is the eloquence that shines in many a long-forgotten scene, which has been reckoned excessively fine upon acting; this the lightning that flashes no less in the hyperbolical tyrant, who breakfasts on the wind, than in little Norval, as harmless as the babe unborn. —Adieu.

LETTER LXXX.

To the same.

I HAVE always regarded the spirit of mercy which appears in the Chinese laws with admiration. An order for the execution of a criminal is carried from court by slow journeys of six miles a day, but a pardon is sent down with the most rapid dispatch. If five sons of the same father be guilty of the same offence, one of them is forgiven, in order to continue the family, and comfort his aged parents in their decline.

Similar to this, there is a spirit of mercy breathes through the laws of England, which some erroneously endeavour to suppress; the laws, however, seem unwilling to punish the offender, or to furnish the officers of justice with every means of acting with severity. Those who arrest debtors are denied the use of arms; the nightly watch is permitted to repress the disorders of the drunken citizens only with clubs; justice, in such a case, seems to hide her terrors, and permits some offenders to escape rather than load any with a punishment disproportioned to the crime.

Thus it is the glory of an Englishman, that he is not only governed by laws, but that these are also tempered by mercy; a country restrained by severe laws, and those, too, executed with severity (as in Japan), is under the most terrible species of tyranny; a royal tyrant is generally dreadful to the great, but numerous penal laws grind every rank of people, and chiefly those least able to resist oppression,—the poor.

It is very possible thus for a people to become slaves to laws of their own enacting, as the Athenians were to those of Draco. "It might first happen," says the historian, "that men with peculiar talents for villainy attempted to evade the ordinances already established; their practices, therefore, soon brought on a new law levelled against them; but the same degree of cunning which had taught the knave to evade the former statutes, taught him to evade the latter also; he flew to new shifts, while justice pursued with new ordinances; still, however, he kept his proper distance, and whenever one crime was judged penal by the state, he left committing it, in order to practise some unforbidden species of villainy. Thus the criminal against whom the threatenings were denounced always escaped free, while the simple rogue alone felt the rigour of justice. In the meantime, penal laws became numerous; almost every person in the state, unknowingly, at different times offended, and was every moment subject to a malicious prosecution." In fact, penal laws, instead of preventing crimes, are generally enacted after the commission; instead of repressing the growth of ingenious villainy, only multiply deceit, by putting it upon new shifts and expedients of practising with impunity.

Such laws, therefore, resemble the guards which are sometimes imposed upon tributary princes, apparently, indeed, to secure them from danger, but, in reality, to confirm their captivity.

Penal laws, it must be allowed, secure property in a state, but they also diminish personal security in the same proportion: there is no positive law, how equitable soever, that may not be sometimes capable of injustice. When a law enacted to make theft punishable with death happens to be equitably executed, it can at best only guard our possessions; but when, by favour or ignorance, justice pronounces a wrong verdict, it then attacks our lives, since, in such a case, the whole community suffers with the innocent victim: if, therefore, in order to secure the effects of one man, I should make a law which should take away the life of another, in such a case, to attain a smaller good, I am guilty of a greater evil; to secure society in the possession of a bauble, I render a real and valuable possession precarious. And indeed the experience of every age may serve to vindicate the assertion. No law could be more just than that called *lesæ majestatis*, when Rome was governed by emperors: it was but reasonable, that every conspiracy against the administration should be detected and punished: yet what terrible slaughters succeeded in consequence of its enactment! proscriptions, stranglings, poisonings, in almost every family of distinction; yet all done in a legal way,—every criminal had his trial, and lost his life by a majority of witnesses.

And such will ever be the case, where punishments are numerous, and where a weak, vicious, but above all, where a mercenary magistrate is concerned in their execution: such a man desires to see penal laws increased, since he too frequently has it in his power to turn them into instruments of extortion; in such hands, the more laws, the wider means, not of satisfying justice, but of satiating avarice.

A mercenary magistrate, who is rewarded in proportion, not to his integrity, but to the number he convicts, must be a person of the most unblemished character, or he will lean on the side of cruelty; and when once the work of injustice is begun, it is impossible to tell how far it will proceed. It is said of the hyæna, that, naturally, it is no way ravenous; but when once it has tasted human flesh, it becomes the most voracious animal of the forest, and continues to persecute mankind ever after. A corrupt magistrate may be considered as a human hyæna: he begins, perhaps, by a private snap, he goes on to a morsel among friends, he proceeds to a meal in public, from a meal he advances to a surfeit, and at last sucks blood like a vampire.

Not into such hands should the administration of justice be entrusted, but to those who know how to reward as well as to punish. It was a fine saying of Nangfu the emperor, who, being told that his enemies had raised an insurrection in one of the distant provinces, "Come, then, my friends," said he, "follow me, and I promise you that we shall quickly destroy them." He marched forward, and the rebels submitted upon his approach. All now thought that he would take the most signal revenge, but were surprised to see the captives treated with mildness and humanity. "How!" cries his first minister, "is this the manner in which you fulfil your promise? your royal word was given that your enemies should be destroyed, and behold you have pardoned all, and even caressed some!"—"I promised," replied the emperor with a generous air, "to *destroy* my enemies; I have fulfilled my word, for see they are enemies no longer; I have made *friends* of them."

This, could it always succeed, were the true method of destroying the enemies of a state; well it were, if rewards and mercy alone could regulate the commonwealth: but since punishments are sometimes necessary, let them at least be rendered terrible, by being executed but seldom; and let Justice lift her sword rather to terrify than revenge.—Adieu.

LETTER LXXXI.

To the same.

I HAVE as yet given you but a short and imperfect description of the ladies of England. Woman, my friend, is a subject not easily understood, even in China; what, therefore, can be expected from my knowledge of the sex, in a country where they are universally allowed to be riddles, and I but a stranger?

To confess a truth, I was afraid to begin the description, lest the sex should undergo some new revolution before it was finished; and my picture should thus become old before it could well be said to have ever been new. To-day they are lifted upon stilts; to-morrow they lower their heels, and raise their heads: their clothes at one time are bloated out with whalebone; at present they have laid their hoops aside, and are become as slim as mermaids. All, all is in a state of continual fluctuation, from the mandarine's wife who rattles through the street in her chariot, to the humble sempstress who clatters over the pavement in iron-shod pattens.

What chiefly distinguishes the sex at present is the train. As a lady's quality or fashion was once determined here by the circumference of her hoop, both are now measured by the length of her tail. Women of moderate fortunes are contented with tails moderately long; but ladies of true taste and distinction set no bounds to their ambition in this particular. I am told the lady mayoress, on days of ceremony, carries one longer than a bell-wether of Bantam, whose tail, you know, is trundled along in a wheelbarrow.

Sun of China, what contradictions do we find in this strange world! not only the people of different countries think in opposition to each other, but the inhabitants of a single island are often found inconsistent with themselves. Would you believe it? this very people, my Fum, who are so fond of seeing their women with long tails, at the same time dock their horses to the very rump!

But you may easily guess, that I am no ways displeased with a fashion which tends to increase a demand for the commodities of the East, and is so very beneficial to the country in which I was born. Nothing can be better calculated to increase the price of silk than the present manner of dressing. A lady's train is not bought but at some expense, and after it has swept the public walks for a very few evenings, is fit to be worn no longer: more silk must be bought in order to repair the breach, and some ladies of peculiar economy are thus found to patch up their tails eight or ten times in a season. This unnecessary consumption may introduce poverty here, but then we shall be the richer for it in China.

The Man in Black, who is a professed enemy to this manner of ornamenting the tail, assures me there are numberless inconveniences attending it, and that a lady dressed up to the fashion is as much a cripple as any in Nankin. But his chief indignation is levelled at those who dress in this manner, without a proper fortune to support it. He assures me, that he has known some who would have a tail though they wanted a petticoat; and others, who, without any other pretensions, fancied they became ladies merely from the addition of three superfluous yards of ragged silk. "I know a thrifty good woman," continues he, "who, thinking herself obliged to carry a train like her betters, never walks from home without the uneasy apprehension of wearing it out too soon: every excursion she makes gives her new anxiety; and her train is every bit as importunate, and wounds her peace as much, as the bladder we sometimes see tied to the tail of a cat."

Nay, he ventures to affirm, that a train may often bring a lady into the most critical circumstances: "for, should a rude fellow," says he, "offer to come up to ravish a kiss, and the lady attempt to avoid it, in retiring she must necessarily tread upon her train, and thus fall fairly upon her back; by which means, every one knows—her clothes may be spoiled."

The ladies here make no scruple to laugh at the smallness of a Chinese slipper; but I fancy our wives in China would have a more real cause of laughter, could they but see the immoderate length of an European train. Head of Confucius! to view a human being crippling herself with a great unwieldy tail for our diversion. Backward she cannot go, forward she must move but slowly; and if ever she attempts to turn round, it must be in a circle not smaller than that described by the wheeling crocodile, when it would face an assailant. And yet to think that all this confers importance and majesty! to think that a lady acquires additional respect from fifteen yards of trailing taffety! I cannot contain—ha! ha! ha! this is certainly a remnant of European barbarity: the female Tartar, dressed in sheep skins, is in far more convenient drapery. Their own writers have sometimes inveighed against the absurdity of this fashion; but perhaps it has never been ridiculed so well as upon the Italian theatre, where Pasquariello being engaged to attend on the Countess of Fernambroco, having one of his hands employed in carrying her muff, and the other her lapdog, he bears her train majestically along, by sticking it in the waistband of his breeches.—Adieu.

LETTER LXXXII.

To the same.

A DISPUTE has for some time divided the philosophers of Europe: it is debated whether arts and sciences are more serviceable or prejudicial to mankind? They who maintain the cause of literature endeavour to prove their usefulness from the impossibility of a large number of men subsisting in a small tract of country without them; from the pleasure which attends the acquisition; and from the influence of knowledge in promoting practical morality.

They who maintain the opposite opinion display the happiness and innocence of those uncultivated nations who live without learning; urge the numerous vices which are to be found only in polished society; enlarge upon the oppression, the cruelty, and the blood which must necessarily be shed, in order to cement civil society; and insist upon the happy equality of conditions in a barbarous state, preferable to the unnatural subordination of a more refined constitution.

This dispute, which has already given so much employment to speculative indolence, has been managed with much ardour, and (not to suppress our sentiments) with but little sagacity. They who insist that the sciences are useful in refined society are certainly right, and they who maintain that barbarous nations are more happy without them are right also: but when one side, for this reason, attempts to prove them as universally useful to the solitary barbarian as to the native of a crowded commonwealth; or when the other endeavours to banish them as prejudicial to all society, even from populous states as well as from the inhabitants of the wilderness, they are both wrong; since that knowledge which makes the happiness of a refined European, would be a torment to the precarious tenant of an Asiatic wild.

Let me, to prove this, transport the imagination for a moment to the midst of a forest in Siberia. There we behold the inhabitant, poor indeed, but equally fond of happiness with the most refined philosopher of China. The earth lies uncultivated and uninhabited for miles around him: his little family and he the sole and undisputed possessors. In such circumstances nature and reason will induce him to prefer a hunter's life to that of cultivating the earth. He will certainly adhere to that manner of living which is carried on at the smallest expense of labour, and that food which is most agreeable to the appetite; he will prefer indolent, though precarious, luxury to a laborious, though permanent, competence; and a knowledge of his own happiness will determine him to persevere in native barbarity.

In like manner, his happiness will incline him to bind himself by no law: laws are made in order to secure present property; but he is possessed of no property which he is afraid to lose, and desires no more than will be sufficient to sustain him; to enter into compacts with others, would be undergoing a voluntary obligation without the expectance of any reward. He and his countrymen are tenants, not rivals, in the same inexhaustible forest; the increased possessions of one by no means diminish the expectations arising from equal assiduity in another; there is no need of laws, therefore, to repress ambition, where there can be no mischief attending its most boundless gratification.

Our solitary Siberian will, in like manner, find the sciences not only entirely useless in directing his practice, but disgusting even in speculation. In every contemplation our curiosity must be first excited by the appearances of things, before our reason undergoes the fatigue of investigating the causes. Some of those appearances are produced by experiment, others by minute inquiry; some arise from a knowledge of foreign climates, and others from an intimate study of our own. But there are few objects, in comparison, which present themselves to the inhabitant of a barbarous country; the game he hunts, or the transient cottage he builds, make up the chief objects of his concern; his curiosity, therefore, must be proportionably less; and if that is diminished, the reasoning faculty will be diminished in proportion.

Besides, sensual enjoyment adds wings to curiosity. We consider few objects with ardent attention, but those which have some connexion with our wishes, our pleasures, or our necessities. A desire of enjoyment first interests our passions in the pursuit, points out the object of investigation, and reason then comments where sense has led the way. An increase in the number of our enjoyments, therefore, necessarily produces an increase of scientific research: but in countries where almost every enjoyment is wanting, reason there seems destitute of its great inspirer, and speculation is the business of fools when it becomes its own reward.

The barbarous Siberian is too wise, therefore, to exhaust his time in quest of knowledge, which neither curiosity prompts nor pleasure impels him to pursue. When told of the exact admeasurement of a degree upon the equator at Quito, he feels no pleasure in the account; when informed that such a discovery tends to promote navigation and commerce, he finds himself no way interested in either. A discovery which some have pursued at the hazard of their lives, affects him with neither astonishment nor pleasure. He is satisfied with thoroughly understanding the few objects which contribute to his own felicity; he knows the properest places where to lay the snare for the sable, and discerns the value of furs with more than European sagacity. More extended knowledge would only serve to render him unhappy; it might lend a ray to show him the misery of his situation, but could not guide him in his efforts to avoid it. Ignorance is the happiness of the poor.

The misery of being endowed with sentiments above its capacity of fruition is most admirably described in one of the fables of Lokman, the Indian moralist. "An elephant that had been peculiarly serviceable in fighting the battles of Wistnow was ordered by the god to wish for whatever he thought proper, and the desire should be attended with immediate gratification. The elephant thanked his benefactor on bended knees, and desired to be endowed with the reason and the faculties of a man. Wistnow was sorry to hear the foolish request, and endeavoured to dissuade him from his misplaced ambition; but finding it to no purpose, gave him at last such a portion of wisdom, as could correct even the Zendavesta of Zoroaster. The reasoning elephant went away rejoicing in his new acquisition; and though his body still retained its ancient form, he found his appetites and passions entirely altered. He first considered, that it would not only be more comfortable, but also more becoming, to wear clothes; but unhappily he had no method of making them himself, nor had he the use of speech to demand them from others; and this was the first time he felt real anxiety. He soon perceived how much more elegantly men were fed than he; therefore he began to loathe his usual food, and longed for those delicacies which adorn the tables of princes: but here again he found it impossible to be satisfied, for though he could easily obtain flesh, yet he found it impossible to dress it in any degree of perfection. In short, every pleasure that contributed to the felicity of mankind served only to render him more miserable, as he found himself utterly deprived of the power of enjoyment. In this manner he led a repining, discontented life, detesting himself, and displeased with his ill-judged ambition; till at last his benefactor, Wistnow, taking compassion on his forlorn situation, restored him to the ignorance and the happiness which he was originally formed to enjoy."

No, my friend, to attempt to introduce the sciences into a nation of wandering barbarians, is only to render them more miserable than ever nature designed they should be. A life of simplicity is best fitted to a state of solitude.

The great lawgiver of Russia attempted to improve the desolate inhabitants of Siberia, by sending among them some of the politest men of Europe. The consequence has shown, that the country was as yet unfit to receive them; they languished for a time, with a sort of exotic malady; every day degenerated from themselves, and at last, instead of rendering the country more polite, they conformed to the soil, and put on barbarity.

No, my friend, in order to make the sciences useful in any country, it must first become populous; the inhabitant must go through the different stages of hunter, shepherd, and husbandman; then, when property becomes valuable, and consequently gives cause for injustice—then, when laws are appointed to repress injury, and secure possession—when men, by the sanction of those laws, become possessed of superfluity—when luxury is thus introduced, and demands its continual supply, —then it is that the sciences become necessary and useful; the state then cannot subsist without them; they must then be introduced, at once to teach men to draw the greatest possible quantity of pleasure from circumscribed possession, and to restrain them within the bounds of moderate enjoyment.

The sciences are not the cause of luxury, but its consequence; and this destroyer thus brings with it an antidote which resists the virulence of its own poison. By asserting that luxury introduces the sciences, we assert a truth; but if, with those who reject the utility of learning, we assert that the sciences also introduce luxury, we shall be at once false, absurd, and ridiculous.—Adieu.

LETTER LXXXIII.

From Lien Chi Altangi to Hingpo, by the way of Moscow.

YOU are now arrived at an age, my son, when pleasure dissuades from application; but rob not, by present gratification, all the succeeding period of life of its happiness. Sacrifice a little pleasure at first to the expectance of greater. The study of a few years will make the rest of life completely easy.

But instead of continuing the subject myself, take the following instructions, borrowed from a modern philosopher of China. "He who has begun his fortune by study, will certainly confirm it by perseverance. The love of books damps the passion for pleasure; and when this passion is once extinguished, life is then cheaply supported: thus a man being possessed of more than he wants, can never be subject to great disappointments, and avoids all those meannesses which indigence sometimes unavoidably produces.

"There is unspeakable pleasure attending the life of a voluntary student. The first time I read an excellent book, it is to me just as if I had gained a new friend: when I read over a book I have perused before, it resembles the meeting with an old one. We ought to lay hold of every incident in life for improvement, the trifling as well as the important. It is not one diamond alone which gives lustre to another; a common coarse stone is also employed for that purpose. Thus I ought to draw advantage from the insults and contempt I meet with from a worthless fellow. His brutality ought to induce me to self-examination, and correct every blemish that may have given rise to his calumny.

"Yet with all the pleasures and profits which are generally produced by learning, parents often find it difficult to induce their children to study. They often seem dragged to what wears the appearance of application. Thus, being dilatory in the beginning, all future hopes of eminence are entirely cut off. If they find themselves obliged to write two lines more polite than ordinary, their pencil then seems as heavy as a mill-stone, and they spend ten years in turning two or three periods with propriety.

"These persons are most at a loss when a banquet is almost over; the plate and the dice go round, that the number of little verses, which each is obliged to repeat, may be determined by chance. The booby, when it comes to his turn, appears quite stupid and insensible. The company divert themselves with his confusion; and sneers, winks, and whispers are circulated at his expense. As for him, he opens a pair of large heavy eyes, stares at all about him, and even offers to join in the laugh, without ever considering himself as the burden of all their good humour.

"But it is of no importance to read much, except you be regular in your reading. If it be interrupted for any considerable time, it can never be attended with proper improvement. There are some who study for one day with intense application, and repose themselves for ten days after. But wisdom is a coquette, and must be courted with unabating assiduity.

"It was a saying of the ancients, that a man never opens a book without reaping some advantage by it. I say with them, that every book can serve to make us more expert, except romances, and these are no better than instruments of debauchery. They are dangerous fictions, where love is the ruling passion.

"The most indecent strokes there pass for turns of wit; intrigue and criminal liberties for gallantry and politeness. Assignations, and even villainy, are put in such strong lights, as may inspire even grown men with the strongest passion; how much more, therefore, ought the youth of either sex to dread them, whose reason is so weak, and whose hearts are so susceptible of passion?

"To slip in by a back-door, or leap a wall, are accomplishments that, when handsomely set off, enchant a young heart. It is true, the plot is commonly wound up by a marriage, concluded with the consent of parents, and adjusted by every ceremony prescribed by law. But as in the body of the work there are many passages that offend good morals, overthrow laudable customs, violate the laws, and destroy the duties most essential to society, virtue is thereby exposed to the most dangerous attacks.

"But, say some, the authors of these romances have nothing in view, but to represent vice punished, and virtue rewarded. Granted. But will the greater number of readers take notice of these punishments and rewards? Are not their minds carried to something else? Can it be imagined that the art with which the author inspires the love of virtue can overcome that crowd of thoughts which sway them to licentiousness? To be able to inculcate virtue by so leaky a vehicle the author must be a philosopher of the first rank. But in our age we can find but few first-rate philosophers.

"Avoid such performances where vice assumes the face of virtue: seek wisdom and knowledge, without ever thinking you have found them. A man is wise, while he continues in the pursuit of wisdom; but when he once fancies that he has found the object of his inquiry, he then becomes a fool. Learn to pursue virtue from the man that is blind, who never makes a step without first examining the ground with his staff.

"The world is like a vast sea; mankind like a vessel sailing on its tempestuous bosom. Our prudence is its sails, the sciences serve us for oars, good or bad fortune are the favourable or contrary winds, and judgment is the rudder; without this last the vessel is tossed by every billow, and will find shipwreck in every breeze. In a word, obscurity and indigence are the parents of vigilance and economy; vigilance and economy of riches and honour; riches and honour of pride and luxury; pride and luxury of impurity and idleness; and impurity and idleness again produce indigence and obscurity. Such are the revolutions of life."—Adieu.

LETTER LXXXIV.

From Lien Chi Altangi to Fum Hoam, First President of the Ceremonial Academy at Pekin in China.

I FANCY the character of a poet is in every country the same: fond of enjoying the present, careless of the future; his conversation that of a man of sense, his actions those of a fool; of fortitude able to stand unmoved at the bursting of an earthquake, yet of sensibility to be affected by the breaking of a teacup. Such is his character, which, considered in every light, is the very opposite of that which leads to riches.

The poets of the West are as remarkable for their indigence as their genius, and yet, among the numerous hospitals designed to relieve the poor, I have heard of but one erected for the benefit of decayed authors. This was founded by Pope

Urban VIII., and called THE RETREAT OF THE INCURABLES; intimating, that it was equally impossible to reclaim the patients who sued for reception from poverty or from poetry. To be sincere, were I to send you an account of the lives of the Western poets, either ancient or modern, I fancy you would think me employed in collecting materials for a history of human wretchedness.

Homer is the first poet and beggar of note among the ancients: he was blind, and sung his ballads about the streets; but it is observed, that his mouth was more frequently filled with verses than with bread. Plautus, the comic poet, was better off,—he had two trades; he was a poet for his diversion, and helped to turn a mill in order to gain a livelihood. Terence was a slave; and Boethius died in a gaol.

Among the Italians, Paulo Borghese, almost as good a poet as Tasso, knew fourteen different trades, and yet died because he could get employment in none. Tasso himself, who had the most amiable character of all poets, has often been obliged to borrow a crown from some friend, in order to pay for a month's subsistence: he has left us a pretty sonnet, addressed to his cat, in which he begs the light of her eyes to write by, being too poor to afford himself a candle. But Bentivoglio, poor Bentivoglio! chiefly demands our pity. His comedies will last with the Italian language: he dissipated a noble fortune in acts of charity and benevolence; but, falling into misery in his old age, was refused to be admitted into an hospital which he himself had erected.

In Spain, it is said, the great Cervantes died of hunger; and it is certain that the famous Camoens ended his days in an hospital.

If we turn to France, we shall there find even stronger instances of the ingratitude of the public. Vaugelas, one of the politest writers and one of the honestest men of his time, was surnamed the Owl, from his being obliged to keep within all day, and venture out only by night, through fear of his creditors. His last will is very remarkable. After having bequeathed all his worldly substance to the discharging his debts, he goes on thus: "But, as there still may remain some creditors unpaid, even after all that I have shall be disposed of, in such a case it is my last will, that my body should be sold to the surgeons to the best advantage, and that the purchase should go to the discharging those debts which I owe to society; so that if I could not, while living, at least when dead I may be useful."

Cassandre was one of the greatest geniuses of his time, yet all his merit could not procure him a bare subsistence. Being by degrees driven into an hatred of all mankind, from the little pity he found amongst them, he even ventured at last ungratefully to impute his calamities to Providence. In his last agonies, when the priest entreated him to rely on the justice of Heaven, and ask mercy from him that made him,—"If God," replies he, "has shown me no justice here, what reason have I to expect any from him hereafter?" But being answered, that a suspension of justice was no argument that should induce us to doubt of its reality,—"Let me entreat you," continued his confessor, "by all that is dear, to be reconciled to God, your father, your maker, and friend."—"No," replied the exasperated wretch, "you know the manner in which he left me to live; and," pointing to the straw on which he was stretched, "you see the manner in which he leaves me to die!"

But the sufferings of the poet in other countries is nothing when compared to his distresses here; the names of Spenser and Otway, Butler and Dryden, are every day mentioned as a national reproach: some of them lived in a state of precarious indigence, and others literally died of hunger.

At present the few poets of England no longer depend on the great for subsistence; they have now no other patrons but the public, and the public, collectively considered, is a good and a generous master. It is, indeed, too frequently mistaken as to the merits of every candidate for favour; but to make amends, it is never mistaken long. A performance, indeed, may be forced for a time into reputation, but, destitute of real merit, it soon sinks; time, the touchstone of what is truly valuable, will soon discover the fraud, and an author should never arrogate to himself any share of success, till his works have been read at least ten years with satisfaction.

A man of letters at present, whose works are valuable, is perfectly sensible of their value. Every polite member of the community, by buying what he writes, contributes to reward him. The ridicule, therefore, of living in a garret might have been wit in the last age, but continues such no longer, because no longer true. A writer of real merit now may easily be rich, if his heart be set only on fortune; and for those who have no merit, it is but fit that such should remain in merited obscurity. He may now refuse an invitation to dinner, without fearing to incur his patron's displeasure, or to starve by remaining at home. He may now venture to appear in company with just such clothes as other men generally wear, and talk even to princes with all the conscious superiority of wisdom. Though he cannot boast of fortune here, yet he can bravely assert the dignity of independence.—Adieu.

LETTER LXXXV.

To the same.

I HAVE interested myself so long in all the concerns of this people, that I am almost become an Englishman; I now begin to read with pleasure of their taking towns or gaining battles, and secretly wish disappointment to all the enemies of Britain. Yet still my regard to mankind fills me with concern for their contentions. I could wish to see the disturbances of Europe once more amicably adjusted: I am an enemy to nothing in this good world but war; I hate fighting between rival states; I hate it between man and man; I hate fighting even between women!

I already informed you that, while Europe was at variance, we were also threatened from the stage with an irreconcilable opposition, and that our singing women were resolved to sing at each other to the end of the season. O my friend, those fears were just! They are not only determined to sing at each other to the end of the season, but, what is worse, to sing the same song; and, what is still more insupportable, to make us pay for hearing.

If they be for war, for my part, I should advise them to have a public congress, and there fairly squall at each other. What signifies sounding the trumpet of defiance at a distance, and calling in the town to fight their battles? I would have them come boldly into one of the most open and frequented streets, face to face, and there try their skill in quavering.

However this may be, resolved I am that they shall not touch one single piece of silver more of mine. Though I have ears for music, thanks be to Heaven, they are not altogether ass's ears. What! Polly and the Pickpocket to-night, Polly and the Pickpocket to-morrow night, and Polly and the Pickpocket again! I want patience. I'll hear no more. My soul is out of tune; all jarring discord and confusion. Rest, rest, ye dear three clinking shillings in my pocket's bottom; the music you make is more harmonious to my spirit, than catgut, rosin, or all the nightingales that ever chirruped in petticoats!

But what raises my indignation to the greatest degree is, that this piping does not only pester me on the stage, but is my punishment in private conversation. What is it to me, whether the "fine pipe" of the one or the "great manner" of the other be preferable? what care I, if one has a better top or the other a nobler bottom? how am I concerned, if one sings from the stomach or the other sings with a snap? Yet, paltry as these matters are, they make a subject of debate wherever I go; and this musical dispute, especially among the fair sex, almost always ends in a very unmusical altercation.

Sure the spirit of contention is mixed with the very constitution of the people! Divisions among the inhabitants of other countries arise only from their higher concerns, but subjects the most contemptible are made an affair of party here; the spirit is carried even into their amusements. The very ladies, whose duty should seem to allay the impetuosity of the opposite sex, become themselves party champions, engage in the thickest of the fight, scold at each other, and show their courage, even at the expense of their lovers and their beauty.

There are even a numerous set of poets who help to keep up the contention, and write for the stage. Mistake me not; I do not mean pieces to be acted upon it, but panegyrical verses on the performers,—for that is the most universal method of writing for the stage at present. It is the business of the stage poet, therefore, to watch the appearance of every new player at his own house, and so come out next day with a flaunting copy of newspaper verses. In these, nature and the actor may be set to run races, the player always coming off victorious; or nature may mistake him for herself; or old Shakespeare may put on his winding-sheet, and pay him a visit; or the tuneful Nine may strike up their harps in his praise; or, should it happen to be an actress, Venus, the beauteous queen of love, and the naked Graces, are ever in waiting: the lady must be herself a goddess bred and born; she must—but you shall have a specimen of one of these poems, which may convey a more precise idea.

On seeing Mrs. —— perform in the character of ——.

To you, bright fair, the Nine address their lays,
And tune my feeble voice to sing thy praise.
The heartfelt power of every charm divine,
Who can withstand their all-commanding shine?
See how she moves along with every grace,
While soul-brought tears steal down each shining face!
She speaks,—'tis rapture all and nameless bliss!
Ye gods! what transport e'er compared to this!
As when in Paphian groves the Queen of Love,
With fond complaint, addressed the listening Jove,
'Twas joy and endless blisses all around,
And rocks forgot their hardness at the sound.
Then, first, at last e'en Jove was taken in,
And felt her charms, without disguise, within.

And yet think not, my friend, that I have any particular animosity against the champions who are at the head of the present commotion; on the contrary, I could find pleasure in the music, if served up at proper intervals; if I heard it only on proper occasions, and not about it wherever I go. In fact, I could patronize them both; and as an instance of my condescension in this particular, they may come and give me a song at my lodgings, on any evening when I am at leisure, provided they keep a becoming distance, and stand, while they continue to entertain me, with decent humility at the door.

You perceive I have not read the seventeen books of Chinese ceremonies to no purpose. I know the proper share of respect due to every rank in society. Stage-players, fire-eaters, singing women, dancing dogs, wild beasts, and wire-walkers, as their efforts are exerted for our amusement, ought not entirely to be despised. The laws of every country should allow them to play their tricks at least with impunity. They should not be branded with the ignominious appellation of vagabonds; at least they deserve a rank in society equal to the mystery of barbers or undertakers, and, could my influence extend so far, they should be allowed to earn even forty or fifty pounds a year, if eminent in their profession.

I am sensible, however, that you will censure me for profusion in this respect, bred up as you are in the narrow prejudices of Eastern frugality. You will undoubtedly assert, that such a stipend is too great for so useless an employment. Yet how will your surprise increase, when told that, though the law holds them as vagabonds, many of them earn more than a thousand a year! You are amazed. There is cause for amazement. A vagabond with a thousand a year is indeed a curiosity in nature; a wonder far surpassing the flying fish, petrified crab, or travelling lobster. However, from my great love to the profession, I would willingly have them divested of their contempt, and part of their finery: the law should kindly take them under the wing of protection; fix them into a corporation, like that of the barbers; and abridge their ignominy and their pensions. As to their abilities in other respects, I would leave that entirely to the public, who are certainly, in this case, the properest judges—whether they despise them or no.

Yes, my Fum, I would abridge their pensions. A theatrical warrior, who conducts the battles of the stage, should be cooped up with the same caution as a bantam cock that is kept for fighting. When one of those animals is taken from its native dunghill, we retrench it both in the quantity of its food and the number of its seraglio: players should in the same manner be fed, not fattened; they should be permitted to get their bread, but not eat the people's bread into the bargain; and, instead of being permitted to keep four mistresses, in conscience they should be contented only with two.

Were stage-players thus brought into bounds, perhaps we should find their admirers less sanguine, and consequently less ridiculous, in patronising them. We should be no longer struck with the absurdity of seeing the same people, whose valour makes such a figure abroad, apostrophizing in the praise of a bouncing blockhead, and wrangling in the defence of a copper-tailed actress at home.

I shall conclude my letter with the sensible admonition of Mé the philosopher: "You love harmony," says he, "and are charmed with music. I do not blame you for hearing a fine voice when you are in your closet, with a lovely parterre under your eye, or in the night time, while perhaps the moon diffuses her silver rays. But is a man to carry this passion so far as to let a company of comedians, musicians, and singers, grow rich upon his exhausted fortune? If so, he resembles one of those dead bodies, whose brains the embalmer has picked out through its ears."—Adieu.

LETTER LXXXVI.

To the same.

Of all the places of amusement where gentlemen and ladies are entertained, I have not been yet to visit Newmarket. This, I am told, is a large field, where, upon certain occasions, three or four horses are brought together, then set a-running, and that horse which runs swiftest wins the wager.

This is reckoned a very polite and fashionable amusement here, much more followed by the nobility than partridge fighting at Java, or paper kites in Madagascar: several of the great here, I am told, understand as much of farriery as their grooms; and a horse with any share of merit can never want a patron among the nobility.

We have a description of this entertainment almost every day in some of the gazettes, as for instance: "On such a day the Give and Take Plate was run for between his Grace's Crab, his Lordship's Periwinkle, and Squire Smackem's Slamerkin. All rode their own horses. There was the greatest concourse of nobility that has been known here for several seasons. The odds were in favour of Crab in the beginning; but Slamerkin, after the first heat, seemed to have the match hollow: however, it was soon seen that Periwinkle improved in wind, which at last turned out accordingly; Crab was run to a standstill, Slamerkin was knocked up, and Periwinkle was brought in with universal applause." Thus, you see, Periwinkle received universal applause, and, no doubt, his Lordship came in for some share of that praise which was so liberally bestowed upon Periwinkle. Sun of China! how glorious must the senator appear in his cap and leather breeches, his whip crossed in his mouth, and thus coming to the goal, amongst the shouts of grooms, jockeys, pimps, stable-bred dukes, and degraded generals!

From the description of this princely amusement now transcribed, and from the great veneration I have for the characters of its principal promoters, I make no doubt but I shall look upon a horse-race with becoming reverence, predisposed as I am by a similar amusement, of which I have lately been a spectator; for just now I happened to have an opportunity of being present at a cart race.

Whether this contention between three carts of different parishes was promoted by a subscription among the nobility, or whether the grand jury, in council assembled, had gloriously combined to encourage plaustral merit, I cannot take upon me to determine; but certain it is, the whole was conducted with the utmost regularity and decorum, and the company, which made a brilliant appearance, were universally of opinion, that the sport was high, the running fine, and the riders influenced by no bribe.

It was run on the road from London to a village called Brentford, between a turnip-cart, a dust-cart, and a dung-cart; each of the owners condescending to mount, and be his own driver. The odds at starting were, Dust against Dung, five to four; but, after half a mile's going, the knowing ones found themselves all on the wrong side, and it was Turnip against the field, brass to silver.

Soon, however, the contest became more doubtful; Turnip indeed kept the way, but it was perceived that Dung had better bottom. The road re-echoed with the shouts of the spectators. "Dung against Turnip! Turnip against Dung!" was now the universal cry; neck and neck; one rode lighter, but the other had more judgment. I could not but particularly observe the ardour with which the fair sex espoused the cause of the different riders on this occasion: one was charmed with the unwashed beauties of Dung; another was captivated with the patibulary aspect of Turnip; while, in the meantime, unfortunate gloomy Dust, who came whipping behind, was cheered by the encouragement of some, and pity of all.

The contention now continued for some time, without a possibility of determining to whom victory designed the prize. The winning post appeared in view, and he who drove the turnip-cart assured himself of success; and successful he might have been, had his horse been as ambitious as he; but upon approaching a turn from the road, which led homewards, the horse fairly stood still, and refused to move a foot farther. The dung-cart had scarce time to enjoy this temporary triumph, when it was pitched headlong into a ditch by the way-side, and the rider left to wallow in congenial mud. Dust, in the meantime, soon came up, and not being far from the post, came in, amidst the shouts and acclamations of all the spectators, and greatly caressed by all the quality of Brentford. Fortune was kind only to one, who ought to have been favourable to all; each had peculiar merit, each laboured hard to earn the prize, and each richly deserved the cart he drove.

I do not know whether this description may not have anticipated that which I intended giving of Newmarket. I am told, there is little else to be seen even there. There may be some minute differences in the dress of the spectators, but none at all in their understandings: the quality of Brentford are as remarkable for politeness and delicacy as the breeders of Newmarket. The quality of Brentford drive their own carts, and the honourable fraternity at Newmarket ride their own horses. In short, the matches in one place are as rational as those in the other; and it is more than probable, that turnips, dust, and dung are all that can be found to furnish out description in either.

Forgive me, my friend; but a person like me, bred up in a philosophic seclusion, is apt to regard perhaps with too much asperity those occurrences which sink man below his station in nature, and diminish the intrinsic value of humanity. —Adieu.

LETTER LXXXVII.

From Fum Hoam to Lien Chi Altangi.

YOU tell me the people of Europe are wise; but where lies their wisdom? You say they are valiant too; yet I have some reasons to doubt of their valour. They are engaged in war among each other, yet apply to the Russians, their neighbours and ours, for assistance. Cultivating such an alliance argues at once imprudence and timidity. All subsidies paid for such an aid, is strengthening the Russians, already too powerful, and weakening the employers, already exhausted by intestine commotions.

I cannot avoid beholding the Russian empire as the natural enemy of the more western parts of Europe; as an enemy already possessed of great strength, and, from the nature of the government, every day threatening to become more powerful. This extensive empire, which, both in Europe and Asia, occupies almost a third of the old world, was, about two centuries ago, divided into separate kingdoms and dukedoms, and, from such a division, consequently feeble. Since the times, however, of Johan Basilides it has increased in strength and extent; and those untrodden forests, those innumerable savage animals, which formerly covered the face of the country, are now removed, and colonies of mankind planted in their room. A kingdom thus enjoying peace internally, possessed of an unbounded extent of dominion, and learning the military art at the expense of others abroad, must every day grow more powerful: and it is probable we shall hear Russia, in future times, as formerly, called the *Officina Gentium.*

It was long the wish of Peter, their great monarch, to have a fort in some of the western parts of Europe: many of his schemes and treaties were directed to this end, but, happily for Europe, he failed in them all. A fort in the power of this people would be like the possession of a floodgate; and whenever ambition, interest, or necessity prompted, they might then be able to deluge the whole western world with a barbarous inundation.

Believe me, my friend, I cannot sufficiently contemn the politicians of Europe, who thus make this powerful people arbitrators in their quarrel. The Russians are now at that period between refinement and barbarity, which seems most adapted to military achievement; and if once they happen to get footing in the western parts of Europe, it is not the feeble efforts of the sons of effeminacy and dissension that can serve to remove them. The fertile valley and soft climate will ever be sufficient inducements to draw whole myriads from their native deserts, the trackless wild, or snowy mountain.

History, experience, reason, nature, expand the book of wisdom before the eyes of mankind, but they will not read. We have seen with terror a winged phalanx of famished locusts, each singly contemptible, but from multitude become hideous, cover like clouds the face of day, and threaten the whole world with ruin. We have seen them settling on the fertile plains of India and Egypt, destroying in an instant the labours and the hopes of nations; sparing neither the fruit of the earth nor the verdure of the fields, and changing into a frightful desert landscapes of once luxuriant beauty. We have seen myriads of ants issuing together from the southern desert, like a torrent whose source was inexhaustible, succeeding each other without end, and renewing their destroyed forces with unwearied perseverance, bringing desolation wherever they came, banishing men and animals, and, when destitute of all subsistence, in heaps infecting the wilderness which they had made! Like these have been the migrations of men. When as yet savage, and almost resembling their brute partners in the forest, subject like them only to the instincts of nature, and directed by hunger alone in the choice of an abode, how have we seen whole armies starting wild at once from their forests and their dens! Goths, Huns, Vandals, Saracens, Turks, Tartars, myriads of men, animals in human form, without country, without name, without laws, overpowering by numbers all opposition, ravaging cities, overturning empires, and, after having destroyed whole nations, and spread extensive desolation, how have we seen them sink oppressed by some new enemy more barbarous and even more unknown than they!—Adieu.

LETTER LXXXVIII.

From Lien Chi Altangi to Fum Hoam, First President of the Ceremonial Academy at Pekin in China.

As the instruction of the fair sex in this country is entirely committed to the care of foreigners; as their language masters, music masters, hair frizzers, and governesses, are all from abroad, I had some intentions of opening a female academy myself, and made no doubt, as I was quite a foreigner, of meeting a favourable reception.

In this I intended to instruct the ladies in all the conjugal mysteries; wives should be taught the art of managing husbands, and maids the skill of properly choosing them; I would teach a wife how far she might venture to be sick, without giving disgust; she should be acquainted with the great benefits of the cholic in the stomach, and all the thorough-bred insolence of fashion; maids should learn the secret of nicely distinguishing every competitor; they should be able to know the difference between a pedant and a scholar, a citizen and a prig, a squire and his horse, a beau and his monkey; but chiefly, they should be taught the art of managing their smiles, from the contemptuous simper to the long laborious laugh.

But I have discontinued the project; for what would signify teaching ladies the manner of governing or choosing husbands, when marriage is at present so much out of fashion, that a lady is very well off who can get any husband at all? Celibacy now prevails in every rank of life; the streets are crowded with old bachelors, and the houses with ladies who have refused good offers, and are never likely to receive any for the future.

The only advice, therefore, I could give the fair sex, as things stand at present, is to get husbands as fast as they can. There is certainly nothing in the whole creation, not even Babylon in ruins, more truly deplorable than a lady in the virgin bloom of sixty-three, or a battered unmarried beau, who squibs about from place to place, showing his pigtail wig and his ears. The one appears to my imagination in the form of a double nightcap or a roll of pomatum, the other in the shape of an electuary or a box of pills.

I would once more, therefore, advise the ladies to get husbands. I would desire them not to discard an old lover without very sufficient reasons, nor treat the new with ill-nature till they know him false; let not prudes allege the falseness of the sex, coquettes the pleasures of long courtship, or parents the necessary preliminaries of penny for penny. I have reasons that would silence even a casuist in this particular. In the first place, therefore, I divide the subject into fifteen heads, and then *sic argumentor*, ——But not to give you and myself the spleen, be contented at present with an Indian tale.

"In a winding of the river Amidar, just before it falls into the Caspian Sea, there lies an island unfrequented by the inhabitants of the continent. In this seclusion, blest with all that wild uncultivated nature could bestow, lived a princess and her two daughters. She had been wrecked upon the coast while her children as yet were infants, who, of consequence, though grown up, were entirely unacquainted with man. Yet, inexperienced as the young ladies were in the opposite sex, both early discovered symptoms, the one of prudery, the other of being a coquette. The eldest was ever learning maxims of wisdom and discretion from her mamma, while the youngest employed all her hours in gazing at her own face in a neighbouring fountain.

"Their usual amusement in this solitude was fishing: their mother had taught them all the secrets of the art; she showed them which were the most likely places to throw out the line, what baits were most proper for the various seasons, and the best manner to draw up the finny prey, when they had hooked it. In this manner they spent their time, easy and innocent, till one day the princess, being indisposed, desired them to go and catch her a sturgeon or a shark for supper, which she fancied might sit easy on her stomach. The daughters obeyed, and clapping on a gold fish, the usual bait on those occasions, went and sat upon one of the rocks, letting the gilded hook glide down with the stream.

"On the opposite shore, farther down, at the mouth of the river, lived a diver for pearls, a youth who, by long habit in his trade, was almost grown amphibious; so that he could remain whole hours at the bottom of the water, without ever fetching breath. He happened to be at that very instant diving when the ladies were fishing with the gilded hook. Seeing therefore the bait, which to him had the appearance of real gold, he was resolved to seize the prize; but both his hands being already filled with pearl oysters, he found himself obliged to snap at it with his mouth: the consequence is easily imagined; the hook, before unperceived, was instantly fastened in his jaw, nor could he, with all his efforts or his floundering, get free.

"'Sister,' cries the youngest princess, 'I have certainly caught a monstrous fish; I never perceived anything struggle so at the end of my line before; come and help me to draw it in.' They both now, therefore, assisted in fishing up the diver on shore; but nothing could equal their surprise on seeing him. 'Bless my eyes!' cries the prude, 'what have we got here? this is a very odd fish, to be sure; I never saw anything in my life look so queer: what eyes, what terrible claws, what a monstrous snout! I have read of this monster somewhere before—it certainly must be a *tanlang*, that eats women; let us throw it back again into the sea where we found it.'

"The diver, in the meantime, stood upon the beach at the end of the line, with the hook in his mouth, using every art that he thought could best excite pity, and particularly looking extremely tender, which is usual in such circumstances. The coquette, therefore, in some measure influenced by the innocence of his looks, ventured to contradict her companion. 'Upon my word, sister,' says she, 'I see nothing in the animal so very terrible as you are pleased to apprehend; I think it may serve well enough for a change. Always sharks, and sturgeons, and lobsters, and crawfish, make me quite sick. I fancy a slice of this, nicely grilled, and dressed up with shrimp sauce, would be very pretty eating. I fancy mamma would like a bit with pickles above all things in the world; and if it should not sit easy on her stomach, it will be time enough to discontinue it when found disagreeable, you know.'—'Horrid!' cries the prude; 'would the girl be poisoned? I tell you it is a *tanlang;* I have read of it in twenty places. It is everywhere described as being the most pernicious animal that ever infested the ocean. I am certain it is the most insidious ravenous creature in the world, and is certain destruction if taken internally.' The youngest sister was now therefore obliged to submit: both assisted in drawing the hook with some violence from the diver's jaw; and he, finding himself at liberty, bent his breast against the broad wave, and disappeared in an instant.

"Just at this juncture the mother came down to the beach to know the cause of her daughters' delay; they told her every circumstance, describing the monster they had caught. The old lady was one of the most discreet women in the world; she was called the black-eyed princess, from two black eyes she had received in her youth, being a little addicted to boxing in her liquor. 'Alas, my children,' cries she, 'what have you done! the fish you caught was a man-fish; one of the most tame domestic animals in the world. We could have let him run and play about the garden, and he would have been twenty times more entertaining than our squirrel or monkey.'—'If that be all,' says the young coquette, 'we will fish for him again. If that be all, I'll hold three toothpicks to one pound of snuff, I catch him whenever I please.' Accordingly they threw in their line once more, but with all their gilding, and paddling, and assiduity, they could never after catch the diver. In this state of solitude and disappointment they continued for many years, still fishing, but without success; till at last the Genius of the place, in pity to their distresses, changed the prude into a shrimp, and the coquette into an oyster."—Adieu.

LETTER LXXXIX.

To the same.

I AM amused, my dear Fum, with the labours of some of the learned here. One shall write you a whole folio on the dissection of a caterpillar; another shall swell his works with a description of the plumage on the wing of a butterfly; a third shall see a little world on a peach leaf, and publish a book to describe what his readers might see more clearly in two minutes, only by being furnished with eyes and a microscope.

I have frequently compared the understandings of such men to their own glasses. Their field of vision is too contracted to take in the whole of any but minute objects; they view all nature bit by bit; now the proboscis, now the antennæ, now the pinnæ of—a flea. Now the polypus comes to breakfast upon a worm; now it is kept up, to see how long it will live without eating; now it is turned inside outward, and now it sickens and dies. Thus they proceed, laborious in trifles, constant in experiment, without one single abstraction, by which alone knowledge may be properly said to increase; till at last their ideas, ever employed upon minute things, contract to the size of the diminutive object, and a single mite shall fill the whole mind's capacity.

Yet believe me, my friend, ridiculous as

these men are to the world, they are set up as objects of esteem for each other. They have particular places appointed for their meetings: in which one shows his cockle-shell, and is praised by all the society; another produces his powder, makes some experiments that result in nothing, and comes off with admiration and applause; a third comes out with the important discovery of some new process in the skeleton of a mole, and is set down as the accurate and sensible; while one, still more fortunate than the rest, by pickling, potting, and preserving monsters, rises into unbounded reputation.

The labours of such men, instead of being calculated to amuse the public, are laid out only in diverting each other. The world becomes very little the better, or the wiser, for knowing what is the peculiar food of an insect, that is itself the food of another, which in its turn is eaten by a third; but there are men who have studied themselves into a habit of investigating and admiring such minutiæ. To these such subjects are pleasing, as there are some who contentedly spend whole days in endeavouring to solve enigmas, or disentangle the puzzling sticks of children.

But of all the learned, those who pretend to investigate remote antiquity have least to plead in their own defence, when they carry this passion to a faulty excess. They are generally found to supply by conjecture the want of record, and then by perseverance are wrought up into a confidence of the truth of opinions which, even to themselves, at first appeared founded only in imagination.

The Europeans have heard much of the kingdom of China: its politeness, arts, commerce, laws, and morals are, however, but very imperfectly known among them. They have even now in their Indian warehouses numberless utensils, plants, minerals, and machines, of the use of which they are entirely ignorant; nor can any among them even make a probable guess for what they might have been designed. Yet, though this people be so ignorant of the present real state of China, the philosophers I am describing have entered into long, learned, laborious disputes about what China was two thousand years ago. China and European happiness are but little connected even at this day; but European happiness and China two thousand years ago have certainly no connexion at all. However, the learned have written on, and pursued the subject through all the labyrinths of antiquity; though the early dews and the tainted gale be passed away, though no footsteps remain to direct the doubtful chase, yet still they run forward, open upon the uncertain scent, and though in fact they follow nothing, are earnest in the pursuit. In this chase, however, they all take different ways. One, for example, confidently assures us, that China was peopled by a colony from Egypt. Sesostris, he observes, led his army as far as the Ganges; therefore, if he went so far, he might still have gone as far as China, which is but about a thousand miles from thence; therefore he did go to China; therefore China was not peopled before he went there; therefore it was peopled by him. Besides, the Egyptians have pyramids; the Chinese have, in like manner, their porcelain tower: the Egyptians used to light up candles upon every rejoicing; the Chinese have lanterns upon the same occasion: the Egyptians had their great river; so have the Chinese. But what serves to put the matter past a doubt is, that the ancient kings of China and those of Egypt were called by the same names. The Emperor Ki is certainly the same with King Atoes; for, if we only change *K* into *A*, and *i* into *toes*, we shall have the name Atoes: and, with equal ease, Menes may be proved to be the same with the Emperor Yu; therefore the Chinese are a colony from Egypt.

But another of the learned is entirely different from the last; and he will have the Chinese to be a colony planted by Noah, just after the Deluge. First, from the vast similitude there is between the name of Fohi, the founder of the Chinese monarchy, and that of Noah, the preserver of the human race: Noah, Fohi, —very like each other truly; they have each but four letters, and only two of the four happen to differ. But, to strengthen the argument, Fohi, as the Chinese chronicle asserts, had no father. Noah, it is true, had a father, as the European Bible tells us; but then, as this father was probably drowned in the flood, it is just the same as if he had no father at all; therefore Noah and Fohi are the same. Just after the flood the earth was covered with mud; if it was covered with mud, it must have been incrustated mud; if it was incrustated, it was clothed with verdure: this was a fine unembarrassed road for Noah to fly from his wicked children; he therefore did fly from them, and took a journey of two thousand miles for his own amusement; therefore Noah and Fohi are the same.

Another sect of literati—for they all pass among the vulgar for very great scholars—assert, that the Chinese came neither from the colony of Sesostris, nor from Noah, but are descended from Magog, Meshec, and Tubal, and therefore neither Sesostris, nor Noah, nor Fohi, are the same.

It is thus, my friend, that indolence assumes the airs of wisdom, and while it tosses the cup and ball with infantine folly, desires the world to look on, and calls the stupid pastime philosophy and learning.—Adieu.

LETTER XC.

To the same.

WHEN the men of this country are once turned of thirty, they regularly retire every year, at proper intervals, to lie in of the spleen. The vulgar, unfurnished with the luxurious comforts of the soft cushion, down bed, and easy chair, are obliged, when the fit is on them, to nurse it up by drinking, idleness, and ill humour. In such dispositions unhappy is the foreigner who happens to cross them; his long chin, tarnished coat, or pinched hat, are sure to receive no quarter. If they meet no foreigner, however, to fight with, they are, in such cases, generally content with beating each other.

The rich, as they have more sensibility, are operated upon with greater violence by this disorder. Different from the poor, instead of becoming more insolent, they grow totally unfit for opposition. A general here, who would have faced a culverin when well, if the fit be on him, shall hardly find courage to snuff a candle. An admiral, who could have opposed a broadside without shrinking, shall sit whole days in his chamber, mobbed up in double nightcaps, shuddering at the intrusive breeze, and distinguishable from his wife only by his black beard and heavy eyebrows.

In the country this disorder mostly attacks the fair sex; in town it is most unfavourable to the men. A lady who has pined whole years amidst cooing doves and complaining nightingales, in rural retirement, shall resume all her vivacity in one night at a city gaming-table; her husband, who roared, hunted, and got drunk at home, shall grow splenetic in town in proportion to his wife's good humour. Upon their arrival in London, they exchange their disorders. In consequence of her parties and excursions, he puts on the furred cap and scarlet stomacher, and perfectly resembles an Indian husband, who, when his wife is safely delivered, permits her to transact business abroad, while he undergoes all the formality of keeping his bed, and receiving all the condolence in her place.

But those who reside constantly in town, owe this disorder mostly to the influence of the weather. It is impossible to describe what a variety of transmutations an east wind shall produce; it has been known to change a lady of fashion into a parlour couch; an alderman into a plate of custards; and a dispenser of justice into a rat-trap. Even philosophers themselves are not exempt from its influence; it has often converted a poet into a coral and bells, and a patriot senator into a dumb waiter.

Some days ago I went to visit the Man in Black, and entered his house with that cheerfulness which the certainty of a favourable reception always inspires. Upon opening the door of his apartment, I found him with the most rueful face imaginable, in a morning gown and flannel nightcap, earnestly employed in learning to blow the German flute. Struck with the absurdity of a man in the decline of life thus blowing away all his constitution and spirits, even without the consolation of being musical, I ventured to ask what could induce him to attempt learning so difficult an instrument so late in life? To this he made no reply, but groaning, and still holding the flute to his lips, continued to gaze at me for some moments very angrily, and then proceeded to practise his gamut as before. After having produced a variety of the most hideous tones in nature, at last turning to me, he demanded, whether I did not think he had made a surprising progress in two days? "You see," continues he, "I have got the *ambusheer* already; and as for fingering, my master tells me, I shall have that in a few lessons more." I was so much astonished with this instance of inverted ambition, that I knew not what to reply; but soon discerned the cause of all his absurdities: my friend was under a metamorphosis by the power of spleen, and flute-blowing was unluckily become his adventitious passion.

In order, therefore, to banish his anxiety imperceptibly, by seeming to indulge it, I began to descant on those gloomy topics by which philosophers often get rid of their own spleen, by communicating it: the wretchedness of a man in this life; the happiness of some wrought out of the miseries of others; the necessity that wretches should expire under punishment, that rogues might enjoy affluence in tranquillity: I led him on from the inhumanity of the rich to the ingratitude of the beggar; from the insincerity of refinement to the fierceness of rusticity; and at last had the good fortune to restore him to his usual serenity of temper, by permitting him to expatiate upon all the modes of human misery.

"Some nights ago," says my friend, "sitting alone by my fire, I happened to look into an account of the detection of a set of men called the thief-takers. I read over the many hideous cruelties of those haters of mankind, of their pretended friendship to wretches they meant to betray, of their sending men out to rob, and then hanging them. I could not avoid sometimes interrupting the narrative, by crying out, 'Yet these are men!' As I went on, I was informed that they had lived by this practice several years, and had been enriched by the price of blood: 'And yet,' cried I, 'I have been sent into this world, and am desired to call these men my brothers!' I read, that the very man who led the condemned wretch to the gallows, was he who falsely swore his life away: 'And yet,' continued I, 'that perjurer had just such a nose, such lips, such hands, and such eyes, as Newton.' I at last came to the account of the wretch that was searched after robbing one of the thief-takers of half-a-crown. Those of the confederacy knew that he had got but that single half-crown in the world; after a long search, therefore, which they knew would be fruitless, and taking from him the half-crown, which they knew was all he had, one of the gang compassionately cried out, 'Alas! poor creature, let him keep all the rest he has got; it will do him service in Newgate, where we are sending him.' This was an instance of such complicated guilt and hypocrisy, that I threw down the book in an agony of rage, and began to think with malice of all the human kind. I sat silent for some minutes, and soon perceiving the ticking of my watch beginning to grow noisy and troublesome, I quickly placed it out of hearing, and strove to resume my serenity. But the watchman soon gave me a second alarm. I had scarcely recovered from this, when my peace was assaulted by the wind at my window; and when that ceased to blow, I listened for death-watches in the wainscot. I now found my whole system discomposed. I strove to find a resource in philosophy and reason; but what could I oppose, or where direct my blow, when I could see no enemy to combat? I saw no misery approaching, nor knew any I had to fear, yet still I was miserable. Morning came; I sought for tranquillity in dissipation, sauntered from one place of public resort to another, but found myself disagreeable to my acquaintance, and ridiculous to others. I tried at different times dancing, fencing, and riding; I solved geometrical problems, shaped tobacco-stoppers, wrote verses, and cut paper. At last I placed my affections on music, and find, that earnest employment, if it cannot cure, at least will palliate every anxiety."—Adieu.

LETTER XCI.

To the same.

It is no unpleasing contemplation, to consider the influence which soil and climate have upon the disposition of the inhabitants, the animals, and vegetables of different countries. That among the brute creation is much more visible than in man, and that in vegetables more than either. In some places those plants which are entirely poisonous at home lose their deleterious quality by being carried abroad: there are serpents in Macedonia so harmless as to be used as playthings for children; and we are told that, in some parts of Fez, there are lions so very timorous as to be scared, though coming in herds, by the cries of women.

I know of no country where the influence of climate and soil is more visible than in England; the same hidden cause which gives courage to their dogs and cocks, gives also a fierceness to their men. But chiefly this ferocity appears among the vulgar. The polite of every country pretty nearly resemble each other. But as, in simpling, it is among the uncultivated productions of nature we are to examine the characteristic differences of climate and soil, so in an estimate of the genius of the people we must look among the sons of unpolished rusticity. The vulgar English, therefore, may be easily distinguished from all the rest of the world, by superior pride, impatience, and a peculiar hardiness of soul.

Perhaps no qualities in the world are more susceptible of a finer polish than these; artificial complaisance and easy deference being superinduced over these, generally form a great character: something at once elegant and majestic; affable, yet sincere. Such in general are the better sort; but they who are left in primitive rudeness are the least disposed for society with others, or comfort internally, of any people under the sun.

The poor, indeed, of every country, are but little prone to treat each other with tenderness; their own miseries are too apt to engross all their pity; and perhaps, too, they give but little commiseration, as they find but little from others. But in England the poor treat each other upon every occasion with more than savage animosity, and as if they were in a state of open war by nature. In China, if two porters should meet in a narrow street, they would lay down their burdens, make a thousand excuses to each other for the accidental interruption, and beg pardon on their knees; if two men of the same occupation should meet here, they would first begin to scold, and at last to beat each other. One would think they had miseries enough resulting from penury and labour, not to increase them by ill-nature among themselves, and subjection to new penalties; but such considerations never weigh with them.

But to recompense this strange absurdity, they are in the main generous, brave, and enterprising. They feel the slightest injuries with a degree of ungoverned impatience, but resist the greatest calamities with surprising fortitude. Those miseries under which any other people in the world would sink, they have often showed they were capable of enduring; if accidentally cast upon some desolate coast, their perseverance is beyond what any other nation is capable of sustaining; if imprisoned for crimes, their efforts to escape are greater than among others. The peculiar strength of their prisons, when compared to those elsewhere, argues their hardiness; even the strongest prisons I have ever seen in other countries would be very insufficient to confine the untameable spirit of an Englishman. In short, what man dares do in circumstances of danger, an Englishman will. His virtues seem to sleep in the calm, and are called out only to combat the kindred storm.

But the greatest eulogy of this people is the generosity of their miscreants; the tenderness, in general, of their robbers and highwaymen. Perhaps no people can produce instances of the same kind, where the desperate mix pity with injustice; still show that they understand a distinction in crimes, and even in acts of violence, have still some tincture of remaining virtue. In every other country robbery and murder go almost always together; here it seldom happens, except upon ill-judged resistance or pursuit. The banditti of other countries are unmerciful to a supreme degree; the highwayman and robber here are generous, at least in their intercourse among each other. Taking, therefore, my opinion of the English from the virtues and vices practised among the vulgar, they at once present to a stranger all their faults, and keep their virtues up only for the inquiring eye of a philosopher.

Foreigners are generally shocked at their insolence upon first coming among them: they find themselves ridiculed and insulted in every street; they meet with none of those trifling civilities, so frequent elsewhere, which are instances of mutual good-will, without previous acquaintance; they travel through the country, either too ignorant or too obstinate to cultivate a closer acquaintance; meet every moment something to excite their disgust, and return home to characterise this as the region of spleen, insolence, and ill-nature. In short England would be the last place in the world I would travel to by way of amusement, but the first for instruction. I would choose to have others for my acquaintance, but Englishmen for my friends.

LETTER XCII.

To the same.

THE mind is ever ingenious in making its own distress. The wandering beggar, who has none to protect, or feed, or to shelter him, fancies complete happiness in labour and a full meal; take him from rags and want, feed, clothe, and employ him, his wishes now rise one step above his station; he could be happy were he possessed of raiment, food, and ease. Suppose his wishes gratified even in these, his prospects widen as he ascends; he finds himself in affluence and tranquillity, indeed, but indolence soon breeds anxiety, and he desires not only to be freed from pain, but to be possessed of pleasure: pleasure is granted him, and this but opens his soul to ambition; and ambition will be sure to taint his future happiness, either with jealousy, disappointment, or fatigue.

But of all the arts of distress found out by man for his own torment, perhaps that of philosophic misery is most truly ridiculous; a passion nowhere carried to so extravagant an excess as in the country where I now reside. It is not enough to engage all the compassion of a philosopher here, that his own globe is harassed with wars, pestilence, or barbarity; he shall grieve for the inhabitants of the moon, if the situation of her imaginary mountains happens to alter; and dread the extinction of the sun, if the spots on his surface happen to increase. One should imagine, that philosophy was introduced to make men happy; but here it serves to make hundreds miserable.

My landlady, some days ago, brought me the diary of a philosopher of this desponding sort who had lodged in the apartment before me. It contains the history of a life which seems to be one continued tissue of sorrow, apprehension, and distress. A single week will serve as a specimen of the whole:—

"MONDAY.—In what a transient decaying situation are we placed; and what various reasons does philosophy furnish to make mankind unhappy! A single grain of mustard shall continue to produce its similitude through numberless successions; yet what has been granted to this little seed, has been denied to our planetary system: the mustard seed is still unaltered, but the system is growing old, and must quickly fall to decay. How terrible will it be, when the motions of all the planets have at last become so irregular as to need repairing; when the moon shall fall into frightful paroxysms of alteration; when the earth, deviating from its ancient track, and with every other planet forgetting its circular revolutions, shall become so eccentric, that unconfined by the laws of system, it shall fly off into boundless space, to knock against some distant world, or fall in upon the sun, either extinguishing his light, or burned up by his flames in a moment! Perhaps, while I write, this dreadful change has begun. Shield me from universal ruin! Yet idiot man laughs, sings, and rejoices, in the very face of the sun, and seems no way touched with his situation.

"TUESDAY.—Went to bed in great distress, awaked and was comforted by considering that this change was to happen at some indefinite time; and therefore, like death, the thoughts of it might easily be borne. But there is a revolution, a fixed determined revolution, which must certainly come to pass; yet which, by good fortune, I shall never feel, except in my posterity. The obliquity of the equator with the ecliptic is now twenty minutes less than when it was observed two thousand years ago by Piteas. If this be the case, in six thousand the obliquity will be still less by an whole degree. This being supposed, it is evident that our earth, as Louville has clearly proved, has a motion, by which the climates must necessarily change place, and in the space of one million of years England shall actually travel to the Antarctic pole. I shudder at the change! How shall our unhappy grandchildren endure the hideous climate! A million of years will soon be accomplished; they are but a moment when compared to eternity; then shall our charming country, as I may say, in a moment of time, resemble the hideous wilderness of Nova Zembla.

"WEDNESDAY.—To-night, by my calculation, the long predicted comet is to make its first appearance. Heavens! what terrors are impending over our little dim speck of earth! Dreadful visitation! Are we to be scorched in its fires, or only smothered in the vapour of its tail? That is the question! Thoughtless mortals, go build houses, plant orchards, purchase estates, for to-morrow you die. But what if the comet should not come? That would be equally fatal. Comets are servants which periodically return to supply the sun with fuel. If our sun, therefore, should be disappointed of the expected supply, and all his fuel be in the meantime burnt out, he must expire like an exhausted taper. What a miserable situation must our earth be in without his enlivening rays! Have we not seen several neighbouring suns entirely disappear? Has not a fixed star, near the tail of the Ram, lately been quite extinguished?

"THURSDAY.—The comet has not yet appeared; I am sorry for it: first, sorry because my calculation is false; secondly, sorry lest the sun should want fuel; thirdly, sorry lest the wits should laugh at our erroneous predictions; and, fourthly, sorry because, if it appears to-night, it must necessarily come within the sphere of the earth's attraction; and Heaven help the unhappy country on which it happens to fall!

"FRIDAY.—Our whole society have been out, all eager in search of the comet. We have seen not less than sixteen comets in different parts of the heavens. However, we are unanimously resolved to fix upon one only to be the comet expected. That near Virgo wants nothing but a tail to fit it out completely for terrestrial admiration.

"SATURDAY.—The moon is, I find, at her old pranks. Her appulses, librations, and other irregularities, indeed amaze me. My daughter, too, is this morning gone off with a grenadier. No way surprising; I was never able to give her a relish for wisdom. She ever promised to be a mere expletive in the creation. But the moon, the moon gives me real uneainess; I fondly fancied I had fixed her. I had thought her constant, and constant only to me; but every night discovers her infidelity, and proves me a desolate and abandoned lover."—Adieu.

LETTER XCIII.

To the same.

IT is surprising what an influence titles shall have upon the mind, even though these titles be of our own making. Like children, we dress up the puppets in finery, and then stand in astonishment at the plastic wonder. I have been told of a rat-catcher here, who strolled for a long time about the villages near town, without finding any employment; at last, however, he thought proper to take the title of his Majesty's Rat-catcher in ordinary, and thus succeeded beyond his expectations: when it was known that he caught rats at court, all were ready to give him countenance and employment.

But of all the people, they who make books seem most perfectly sensible of the advantages of titular dignity. All seem convinced, that a book written by vulgar hands can neither instruct nor improve; none but kings, chams, and mandarines can write with any probability of success. If the titles inform me right, not only kings and courtiers, but emperors themselves, in this country, periodically supply the press.

A man here who should write, and honestly confess that he wrote, for bread, might as well send his manuscript to fire the baker's oven ; not one creature will read him : all must be court-bred poets, or pretend at least to be court-bred, who can expect to please. Should the caitiff fairly avow a design of emptying our pockets and filling his own, every reader would instantly forsake him : even those who write for bread themselves would combine to worry him, perfectly sensible that his attempts only served to take the bread out of their mouths.

And yet this silly prepossession the more amazes me, when I consider, that almost all the excellent productions in wit that have appeared here were purely the offspring of necessity ; their Drydens, Butlers, Otways, and Farquhars, were all writers for bread. Believe me, my friend, hunger has a most amazing faculty of sharpening the genius ; and he who, with a full belly, can think like a hero, after a course of fasting, shall rise to the sublimity of a demi-god.

But what will most amaze is, that this very set of men, who are now so much depreciated by fools, are, however, the very best writers they have among them at present. For my own part, were I to buy a hat, I would not have it from a stocking-maker, but a hatter ; were I to buy shoes, I should not go to the tailor's for that purpose. It is just so with regard to wit : did I, for my life, desire to be well served, I would apply only to those who made it their trade, and lived by it. You smile at the oddity of my opinion : but be assured, my friend, that wit is in some measure mechanical ; and that a man long habituated to catch at even its resemblance, will at last be happy enough to possess the substance. By a long habit of writing he acquires a justness of thinking, and a mastery of manner, which holiday writers, even with ten times his genius, may vainly attempt to equal.

How then are they deceived who expect from title, dignity, and exterior circumstance, an excellence, which is in some measure acquired by habit, and sharpened by necessity ! You have seen, like me, many literary reputations, promoted by the influence of fashion, which have scarce survived the possessor ; you have seen the poor hardly earn the little reputation they acquired, and their merit only acknowledged when they were incapable of enjoying the pleasures of popularity : such, however, is the reputation worth possessing ; that which is hardly earned is hardly lost.—Adieu.

LETTER XCIV.

From Hingpo, in Moscow, to Lien Chi Altangi, in London.

WHERE will my disappointments end? Must I still be doomed to accuse the severity of my fortune, and show my constancy in distress, rather than moderation in prosperity? I had at least hopes of conveying my charming companion safe from the reach of every enemy, and of again restoring her to her native soil. But those hopes are now no more.

Upon leaving Terki, we took the nearest road to the dominions of Russia. We passed the Ural mountains, covered with eternal snow, and traversed the forests of Ufa, where the prowling bear and shrieking hyæna keep an undisputed possession. We next embarked upon the rapid river Bulija, and made the best of our way to the banks of the Wolga, where it waters the fruitful valleys of Casan.

There were two vessels in company, properly equipped and armed, in order to oppose the Wolga pirates, who, we were informed, infested this river. Of all mankind these pirates are the most terrible. They are composed of the criminals and outlawed peasants of Russia, who fly to the forests that lie along the banks of the Wolga for protection. Here they join in parties, lead a savage life, and have no other subsistence but plunder. Being deprived of houses, friends, or a fixed habitation, they become more terrible even than the tiger, and as insensible to all the feelings of humanity. They neither give quarter to those they conquer, nor receive it when overpowered themselves. The severity of the laws against them serves to increase their barbarity, and seems to make them a neutral species of beings, between the wildness of the lion and the subtlety of the man. When taken alive, their punishment is hideous. A floating gibbet is erected, which is let run down with the stream; here, upon an iron hook stuck under their ribs, and upon which the whole weight of their body depends, they are left to expire in the most terrible agonies, some being thus found to linger several days successively.

We were but three days' voyage from the confluence of this river into the Wolga, when we perceived at a distance behind us an armed bark coming up, with the assistance of sails and oars, in order to attack us. The dreadful signal of death was hung upon the mast, and our captain with his glass could easily discern them to be pirates. It is impossible to express our consternation on this occasion; the whole crew instantly came together to consult the properest means of safety. It was, therefore, soon determined to send off our women and valuable commodities in one of our vessels, and that the men should stay in the other, and boldly oppose the enemy. This resolution was soon put into execution, and I now reluctantly parted from the beautiful Zelis, for the first time since our retreat from Persia. The vessel in which she was disappeared to my longing eyes, in proportion as that of the pirates approached us. They soon came up; but, upon examining our strength, and perhaps sensible of the manner in which we had sent off our most valuable effects, they seemed more eager to pursue the vessel we had sent away, than attack us. In this manner they continued to harass us for three days, still endeavouring to pass us without fighting. But, on the fourth day, finding it entirely impossible, and despairing to seize the expected booty, they desisted from their endeavours, and left us to pursue our voyage without interruption.

Our joy on this occasion was great; but soon a disappointment more terrible, because unexpected, succeeded. The bark in which our women and treasure were sent off was wrecked upon the banks of the Wolga, for want of a proper number of hands to manage her, and the whole crew carried by the peasants up the country. Of this, however, we were not sensible till our arrival at Moscow; where, expecting to meet our separated bark, we were informed of its misfortune, and our loss. Need I paint the situation of my mind on this occasion? Need I describe all I feel, when I despair of beholding the beautiful Zelis more? Fancy had dressed the future prospect of my life in the gayest colouring; but one unexpected stroke of fortune has robbed it of every charm. Her dear idea mixes with every scene of pleasure, and without her presence to enliven it, the whole becomes tedious, insipid, insupportable. I will confess—now that she is lost, I will confess I loved her; nor is it in the power of time or of reason to erase her image from my heart. —Adieu.

LETTER XCV.

From Lien Chi Altangi to Hingpo, at Moscow.

YOUR misfortunes are mine; but, as every period of life is marked with its own, you must learn to endure them. Disappointed love makes the misery of youth; disappointed ambition, that of manhood; and successless avarice, that of age. These three attack us through life; and it is our duty to stand upon our guard. To love we ought to oppose dissipation, and endeavour to change the object of the affections; to ambition, the happiness of indolence and obscurity; and to avarice, the fear of soon dying. These are the shields with which we should arm ourselves; and thus make every scene of life, if not pleasing, at least supportable.

Men complain of not finding a place of repose. They are in the wrong: they have it for seeking. What they should indeed complain of, is that the heart is an enemy to that very repose they seek. To themselves alone should they impute their discontent. They seek within the short span of life to satisfy a thousand desires, each of which alone is insatiable. One month passes, and another comes on; the year ends, and then begins; but man is still unchanging in folly, still blindly continuing in prejudice. To the wise man every climate and every soil is pleasing; to him a parterre of flowers is the famous valley of gold; to him a little brook the fountain of the young peach-trees; to such a man the melody of birds is more ravishing than the harmony of a full concert; and the tincture of the cloud preferable to the touch of the finest pencil.

The life of man is a journey; a journey that must be travelled, however bad the roads or the accommodation. If in the beginning it is found dangerous, narrow, and difficult, it must either grow better in the end, or we shall by custom learn to bear its inequality.

But, though I see you incapable of penetrating into grand principles, attend at least to a simile, adapted to every apprehension. I am mounted upon a wretched ass, I see another man before me upon a sprightly horse, at which I find some uneasiness. I look behind me, and see numbers on foot, stooping under heavy burdens; let me learn to pity their estate, and thank Heaven for my own.

Shingfu, when under misfortunes, would in the beginning weep like a child; but he soon recovered his former tranquillity. After indulging grief for a few days, he would become, as usual, the most merry old man in all the province of Shansi. About the time that his wife died, his possessions were all consumed by fire, and his only son sold into captivity; Shingfu grieved for one day, and the next went to dance at a mandarine's door for his dinner. The company were surprised to see the old man so merry, when suffering such great losses; and the mandarine himself coming out, asked him, how he, who had grieved so much, and given way to calamity the day before, could now be so cheerful? "You ask me one question," cries the old man; "let me answer by asking another: Which is the most durable, a hard thing, or a soft thing; that which resists, or that which makes no resistance?"—"A hard thing, to be sure," replied the mandarine.—"There you are wrong," returned Shingfu. "I am now four score years old; and, it you look in my mouth, you will find that I have lost all my teeth, but not a bit of my tongue."—Adieu.

LETTER XCVI.

From Lien Chi Altangi to Fum Hoam, First President of the Ceremonial Academy at Pekin, in China.

THE manner of grieving for our departed friends in China is very different from that of Europe. The mourning colour of Europe is black; that of China white. When a parent or relation dies here—for they seldom mourn for friends—it is only clapping on a suit of sables, grimacing it for a few days, and all, soon forgotten, goes on as before; not a single creature missing the deceased, except perhaps a favourite housekeeper or a favourite cat.

On the contrary, with us in China it is a very serious affair. The piety with which I have seen you behave, on one of these occasions, should never be forgotten. I remember it was upon the death of thy grandmother's maiden sister. The coffin was exposed in the principal hall, in public view. Before it were placed the figures of eunuchs, horses, tortoises, and other animals, in attitudes of grief and respect. The more distant relations of the old lady, and I among the number, came to pay our compliments of condolence, and to salute the deceased after the manner of our country. We had scarce presented our wax candles and perfumes, and given the howl of departure, when, crawling on his belly from under a curtain, out came the reverend Fum Hoam himself, in all the dismal solemnity of distress. Your looks were set for sorrow; your clothing consisted in a hempen bag tied round the neck with a string. For two long months did this mourning continue. By night you lay stretched on a single mat, and sat on the stool of discontent by day. Pious man! who could thus set an example of sorrow and decorum to our country. Pious country! where, if we do not grieve at the departure of our friends for their sakes, at least we are taught to regret them for our own.

All is very different here; amazement all! What sort of people am I got amongst? Fum, thou son of Fo, what sort of people am I got amongst? No crawling round the coffin; no dressing up in hempen bags; no lying on mats, or sitting on stools! Gentlemen here shall put on first mourning with as sprightly an air as if preparing for a birthnight; and widows shall actually dress for another husband in their weeds for the former. The best jest of all is, that our merry mourners clap bits of muslin on their sleeves, and these are called *weepers*. Weeping muslin! alas, alas, very sorrowful truly! These weepers, then, it seems, are to bear the whole burden of the distress.

But I have had the strongest instance of this contrast, this tragi-comical behaviour in distress, upon a recent occasion. Their king, whose departure though sudden was not unexpected, died after a reign of many years. His age and uncertain state of health served, in some measure, to diminish the sorrow of his subjects; and their expectations from his successor seemed to balance their minds between uneasiness and satisfaction. But how ought they to have behaved on such an occasion? Surely, they ought rather to have endeavoured to testify their *gratitude* to their deceased friend, than to proclaim their *hopes* of the future! Sure, even the successor must suppose their love to wear the face of adulation, which so quickly changed the object! However, the very same day on which the old king died they made rejoicings for the new.

For my part, I have no conception of this new manner of mourning and rejoicing in a breath; of being merry and sad; of mixing a funeral procession with a jig and a bonfire. At least, it would have been just, that they who flattered the king while living for virtues which he had not should lament him dead for those he really had.

In this universal cause for national distress, as I had no interest myself, so it is but natural to suppose I felt no real affliction. "In all the losses of our friends," says an European philosopher, "we first consider how much our own welfare is affected by their departure, and moderate our real grief just in the same proportion." Now, as I had neither received, nor expected to receive, favours from kings or their flatterers; as I had no acquaintance in particular with their late monarch; as I know that the place of a king is soon supplied; and as the Chinese proverb has it, that though the world may sometimes want cobblers to mend their shoes, there is no danger of its wanting emperors to rule their kingdoms: from such considerations, I could bear the loss of a king with the most philosophic resignation. However, I thought it my duty at least to appear sorrowful, to put on a melancholy aspect, or to set my face by that of the people.

The first company I came amongst, after the news became general, was a set of jolly companions, who were drinking prosperity to the ensuing reign. I entered the room with looks of despair, and even expected applause for the superlative misery of my countenance. Instead of that, I was universally condemned by the company for a grimacing son of a whore, and desired to take away my penitential phiz to some other quarter. I now corrected my former mistake, and, with the most sprightly air imaginable, entered a company where they were talking over the ceremonies of the approaching funeral. Here I sat for some time with an air of pert vivacity; when one of the chief mourners immediately observing my good humour, desired me, if I pleased, to go and grin somewhere else; they wanted no disaffected scoundrels there. Leaving this company, therefore, I was resolved to assume a look perfectly neutral; and have ever since been studying the fashionable air; something between jest and earnest: a complete virginity of face, uncontaminated with the smallest symptom of meaning.

But though grief be a very slight affair here, the mourning, my friend, is a very important concern. When an emperor dies in China, the whole expense of the solemnities is defrayed from the royal coffers. When the great die here, mandarines are ready enough to order mourning; but I do not see they are so ready to pay for it. If they send me down from court the gray undress frock, or the black coat without pocket-holes, I am willing enough to comply with their commands, and wear both; but, by the head of Confucius! to be obliged to wear black, and buy it into the bargain, is more than my tranquillity of temper can bear. What! order me to wear mourning before they know whether I can buy it or no! Fum, thou son of Fo, what sort of a people am I got amongst; where being out of black is a certain symptom of poverty; where those who have miserable faces cannot have mourning, and those who have mourning will not wear a miserable face!

LETTER XCVII.

To the same.

It is usual for the booksellers here, when a book has given universal pleasure upon one subject, to bring out several more upon the same plan; which are sure to have purchasers and readers, from that desire which all men have to view a pleasing object on every side. The first performance serves rather to awaken than satisfy attention; and when that is once moved, the slightest effort serves to continue its progression; the merit of the first diffuses a light sufficient to illuminate the succeeding efforts; and no other subject can be relished, till that is exhausted. A stupid work coming thus immediately in the train of an applauded performance weans the mind from the object of its pleasure, and resembles the sponge thrust into the mouth of a discharged culverin, in order to adapt it for a new explosion.

This manner, however, of drawing off a subject, or a peculiar mode of writing to the dregs, effectually precludes a revival of that subject or manner for some time for the future; the sated reader turns from it with a kind of literary nausea; and, though the titles of books are the part of them most read, yet he has scarce perseverance enough to wade through the title-page.

Of this number I own myself one: I am now grown callous to several subjects, and different kinds of composition. Whether such originally pleased I will not take upon me to determine; but at present I spurn a new book, merely upon seeing its name in an advertisement; nor have the smallest curiosity to look beyond the first leaf, even though in the second the author promises his own face neatly engraved on copper.

I am become a perfect epicure in reading; plain beef or solid mutton will never do. I am for a Chinese dish of bears' claws and birds' nests. I am for sauce strong with asafœtida, or fuming with garlic. For this reason there are a hundred very wise, learned, virtuous, well-intended productions, that have no charms for me. Thus, for the soul of me, I could never find courage nor grace enough to wade above two pages deep into "Thoughts upon God and Nature;" or "Thoughts upon Providence;" or "Thoughts upon Free Grace;" or, indeed, into thoughts upon anything at all. I can no longer meditate with meditations for every day in the year. Essays upon divers subjects cannot allure me, though never so interesting; and as for funeral sermons, or even thanksgiving sermons, I can neither weep with the one nor rejoice with the other.

But it is chiefly in gentle poetry, where I seldom look farther than the title. The truth is, I take up books to be told something new; but here, as it is now managed, the reader is told nothing. He opens the book, and there finds very good words truly, and much exactness of rhyme, but no information. A parcel of gaudy images pass on before his imagination like the figures in a dream; but curiosity, induction, reason, and the whole train of affections, are fast asleep. The *jucunda et idonea vitæ*—those sallies which mend the heart, while they amuse the fancy—are quite forgotten; so that a reader who would take up some modern applauded performances of this kind must, in order to be pleased, first leave his good sense behind him, take for his recompense and guide bloated and compound epithet, and dwell on paintings, just indeed, because laboured with minute exactness.

If we examine, however, our internal sensations, we shall find ourselves but little pleased with such laboured vanities; we shall find that our applause rather proceeds from a kind of contagion caught up from others, and which we contribute to diffuse, than from what we privately feel. There are some subjects of which almost all the world perceive the futility; yet all combine in imposing them upon each other, as worthy of praise. But chiefly this imposition obtains in literature, where men publicly contemn what they relish with rapture in private, and approve abroad what has given disgust at home. The truth is, we deliver those criticisms in public which are supposed to be best calculated, not to do justice to the author, but to impress others with an opinion of our superior discernment. But let works of this kind, which have already come off with such applause, enjoy it all. It is not my wish to diminish, as I was never considerable enough to add to, their fame; but, for the future, I fear there are many poems of which I shall find spirits to read but the title. In the first place, all odes upon Winter, or Summer, or Autumn; in short, all odes, epodes, and monodies whatsoever, shall hereafter be deemed too polite, classical, obscure, and refined, to be read, and entirely above human comprehension. Pastorals are pretty enough—for those that like them: but to me Thyrsis is one of the most insipid fellows I ever conversed with; and as for Corydon, I do not choose his company. Elegies and epistles are very fine—to those to whom they are addressed; and as for epic poems, I am generally able to discover the whole plan in reading the two first pages.

Tragedies, however, as they are now made, are good instructive moral sermons enough; and it would be a fault not to be pleased with good things. There I learn several great truths: as, that it is impossible to see into the ways of futurity; that punishment always attends the villain; that love is the fond soother of the human breast; that we should not resist Heaven's will,—for in resisting Heaven's will, Heaven's will is resisted; with several other sentiments equally new, delicate, and striking. Every new tragedy, therefore, I shall go to see; for reflections of this nature make a tolerable harmony, when mixed up with a proper quantity of drum, trumpet, thunder, lightning, or the scene-shifter's whistle.—Adieu.

LETTER XCVIII.

To the same.

I HAD some intentions lately of going to visit Bedlam, the place where those who go mad are confined. I went to wait upon the Man in Black to be my conductor, but I found him preparing to go to Westminster Hall, where the English hold their courts of justice. It gave me some surprise to find my friend engaged in a lawsuit, but more so when he informed me that it had been depending for several years. "How is it possible," cried I, "for a man who knows the world to go to law? I am well acquainted with the courts of justice in China: they resemble rat-traps every one of them; nothing more easy than to get in, but to get out again is attended with some difficulty, and more cunning than rats are generally found to possess!"

"Faith," replied my friend, "I should not have gone to law but that I was assured of success before I began; things were presented to me in so alluring a light, that I thought by barely declaring myself a candidate for the prize, I had nothing more to do but to enjoy the fruits of the victory. Thus have I been upon the eve of an imaginary triumph every term these ten years; have travelled forward with victory ever in my view, but ever out of reach; however, at present I fancy we have hampered our antagonist in such a manner, that, without some unforeseen demur, we shall this very day lay him fairly on his back."

"If things be so situated," said I, "I don't care if I attend you to the courts, and partake in the pleasure of your success. But prithee," continued I, as we set forward, "what reasons have you to think an affair at last concluded, which has given you so many former disappointments?"—"My lawyer tells me," returned he, "that I have Salkeld and Ventris strong in my favour, and that there are no less than fifteen cases in point."—"I understand," said I; "those are two of your judges who have already declared their opinions."—"Pardon me," replied my friend, "Salkeld and Ventris are lawyers who some hundred years ago gave their opinions on cases similar to mine: these opinions which make for me, my lawyer is to cite; and those opinions which look another way are cited by the lawyer employed by my antagonist: as I observed, I have Salkeld and Ventris for me; he has Coke and Hale for him; and he that has most opinions is most likely to carry his cause."—"But where is the necessity," cried I, "of prolonging a suit by citing the opinions and reports of others, since the same good sense which determined lawyers in former ages, may serve to guide your judges at this day? They at that time gave their opinions only from the light of reason; your judges have the same light at present to direct them; let me even add, a greater, as in former ages there were many prejudices from which the present is happily free. If arguing from authorities be exploded from every other branch of learning, why should it be particularly adhered to in this? I plainly foresee how such a method of investigation must embarrass every suit, and even perplex the student; ceremonies will be multiplied, formalities must increase, and more time will thus be spent in learning the arts of litigation, than in the discovery of right."

"I see," cries my friend, "that you are for a speedy administration of justice; but all the world will grant, that the more time that is taken up in considering any subject, the better it will be understood. Besides, it is the boast of an Englishman, that his property is secure, and all the world will grant, that a deliberate administration of justice is the best way to secure his property. Why have we so many lawyers, but to secure our property? Why so many formalities, but to secure our property? Not less than one hundred thousand families live in opulence, elegance, and ease, merely by securing our property."

"To embarrass justice," returned I, "by a multiplicity of laws, or to hazard it by a confidence in our judges, are, I grant, the opposite rocks on which legislative wisdom has ever split. In one case, the client resembles that emperor who is said to have been suffocated with the bedclothes which were only designed to keep him warm; in the other, to that town which let the enemy take possession of its walls, in order to show the world how little they depended upon aught but courage for safety. But, bless me! what numbers do I see here—all in black!—how is it possible that half this multitude can find employment?"—"Nothing so easily conceived," returned my companion; "they live by watching each other. For instance, the catchpole watches the man in debt, the attorney watches the catchpole, the counsellor watches the attorney, the solicitor the counsellor, and all find sufficient employment."—"I conceive you," interrupted I; "they watch each other, but it is the client that pays them all for watching: it puts me in mind of a Chinese fable, which is entitled, FIVE ANIMALS AT A MEAL.

"A grasshopper, filled with dew, was merrily singing under a shade; a whangam, that eats grasshoppers, had marked it for its prey, and was just stretching forth to devour it; a serpent, that had for a long time fed only on whangams, was coiled up to fasten on the whangam; a yellow bird was just upon the wing to dart upon the serpent; a hawk had just stooped from above to seize the yellow bird; all were intent on their prey, and unmindful of their danger: so the whangam ate the grasshopper, the serpent ate the whangam, the yellow bird the serpent, and the hawk the yellow bird; when, sousing from on high, a vulture gobbled up the hawk, grasshopper, whangam, and all in a moment."

I had scarcely finished my fable, when the lawyer came to inform my friend, that his cause was put off till another term, that money was wanting to retain, and that all the world was of opinion, that the very next hearing would bring him off victorious. "If so, then," cries my friend, "I believe it will be my wisest way to continue the cause for another term; and, in the meantime, my friend here and I will go and see Bedlam."—Adieu.

LETTER XCIX.

To the same.

I LATELY received a visit from the little Beau, who I found had assumed a new flow of spirits with a new suit of clothes. Our discourse happened to turn upon the different treatment of the fair sex here and in Asia, with the influence of beauty in refining our manners, and improving our conversation.

I soon perceived he was strongly prejudiced in favour of the Asiatic method of treating the sex, and that it was impossible to persuade him, but that a man was happier who had four wives at his command, than he who had only one. "It is true," cries he, "your men of fashion in the East are slaves, and under some terrors of having their throats squeezed by a bowstring; but what then? they can find ample consolation in a seraglio; they make, indeed, an indifferent figure in conversation abroad, but then they have a seraglio to console them at home. I am told they have no balls, drums, nor operas, but then they have got a seraglio; they may be deprived of wine and French cookery, but they have a seraglio: a seraglio—a seraglio, my dear creature, wipes off every inconvenience in the world!

"Besides, I am told your Asiatic beauties are the most convenient women alive; for they have no souls: positively there is nothing in nature I should like so much as ladies without souls; soul here, is the utter ruin of half the sex. A girl of eighteen shall have soul enough to spend a hundred pounds in the turning of a trump; her mother shall have soul enough to ride a sweepstake match at a horse-race; her maiden aunt shall have soul enough to purchase the furniture of a whole toy-shop; and others shall have soul enough to behave as if they had no souls at all."

"With respect to the soul," interrupted I, "the Asiatics are much kinder to the fair sex than you imagine: instead of one soul, Fohi, the idol of China, gives every woman three; the Brahmins give them fifteen; and even Mahomet himself nowhere excludes the sex from Paradise. Abulfeda reports, that an old woman one day importuning him to know what she ought to do in order to gain Paradise—'My good lady,' answered the prophet, 'old women never get there.'—'What! never get to Paradise?' returned the matron, in a fury. 'Never,' says he; 'for they always grow young by the way.' No, sir," continued I; "the men of Asia behave with more deference to the sex than you seem to imagine. As you of Europe say grace upon sitting down to dinner, so it is the custom in China to say grace when a man goes to bed to his wife."—"And may I die," returned my companion, "but it is a very pretty ceremony; for, seriously, sir, I see no reason why a man should not be as grateful in one situation as in the other. Upon honour, I always find myself much more disposed to gratitude on the couch of a fine woman, than upon sitting down to a sirloin of beef."

"Another ceremony," said I, resuming the conversation, "in favour of the sex, amongst us, is the bride's being allowed after marriage *her three days of freedom.* During this interval a thousand extravagances are practised by either sex. The lady is placed upon the nuptial bed, and numberless monkey tricks are played round to divert her. One gentleman smells her perfumed handkerchief, another attempts to untie her garters, a third pulls off her shoe to play hunt the slipper, another pretends to be an idiot, and endeavours to raise a laugh by grimacing; in the meantime the glass goes briskly about, till ladies, gentlemen, wife, husband, and all, are mixed together in one inundation of arrack punch."

"Strike me dumb, deaf, and blind," cried my companion, "but that's very pretty! there's some sense in your Chinese ladies' condescensions; but among us, you shall scarce find one of the whole sex that shall hold her good-humour for three days together. No later than yesterday, I happened to say some civil things to a citizen's wife of my acquaintance, not because I loved her, but because I had charity; and what do you think was the tender creature's reply? Only that she detested my pig-tail wig, high-heeled shoes, and sallow complexion! That is all! Nothing more!—Yes, by the Heavens, though she was more ugly than an unpainted actress, I found her more insolent than a thoroughbred woman of quality!"

He was proceeding in this wild manner, when his invective was interrupted by the Man in Black, who entered the apartment, introducing his niece, a young lady of exquisite beauty. Her very appearance was sufficient to silence the severest satirist of the sex; easy without pride, and free without impudence, she seemed capable of supplying every sense with pleasure. Her looks, her conversation, were natural and unconstrained; she had neither been taught to languish nor ogle, to laugh without a jest, or sigh without sorrow. I found that she had just returned from abroad, and had been conversant in the manners of the world. Curiosity prompted me to ask several questions, but she declined them all. I own I never found myself so strongly prejudiced in favour of apparent merit before, and could willingly have prolonged our conversation; but the company after some time withdrew. Just, however, before the little Beau took his leave, he called me aside, and requested I would change him a twenty pound bill; which as I was incapable of doing, he was contented with borrowing half-a-crown. —Adieu.

LETTER C.

From Lien Chi Altangi to Hingpo, by the way of Moscow.

FEW virtues have been more praised by moralists than generosity; every practical treatise of ethics tends to increase our sensibility of the distresses of others, and to relax the grasp of frugality. Philosophers that are poor praise it, because they are gainers by its effects; and the opulent Seneca himself has written a treatise on benefits, though he was known to give nothing away.

But among many who have enforced the duty of giving, I am surprised there are none to inculcate the ignominy of receiving; to show that by every favour we accept we in some measure forfeit our native freedom; and that a state of continual dependence on the generosity of others is a life of gradual debasement.

Were men taught to despise the receiving obligations with the same force of reasoning and declamation that they are instructed to confer them, we might then see every person in society filling up the requisite duties of his station with cheerful industry, neither relaxed by hope, nor sullen from disappointment.

Every favour a man receives in some measure sinks him below his dignity; and, in proportion to the value of the benefit, or the frequency of its acceptance, he gives up so much of his natural independence. He, therefore, who thrives upon the unmerited bounty of another, if he has any sensibility, suffers the worst of servitude: the shackled slave may murmur without reproach, but the humble dependant is taxed with ingratitude upon every symptom of discontent; the one may rave round the walls of his cell, but the other lingers in all the silence of mental confinement. To increase his distress, every new obligation but adds to the former load, which kept the vigorous mind from rising; till at last, elastic no longer, it shapes itself to constraint, and puts on habitual servility.

It is thus with a feeling mind: but there are some who, born without any share of sensibility, receive favour after favour, and still cringe for more; who accept the offer of generosity with as little reluctance as the wages of merit, and even make thanks for past benefits an indirect petition for new: such, I grant, can suffer no debasement from dependence, since they were originally as vile as was possible to be; dependence degrades only the ingenuous, but leaves the sordid mind in pristine meanness. In this manner, therefore, long continued generosity is misplaced, or it is injurious; it either finds a man worthless, or it makes him so; and true it is, that the person who is contented to be often obliged, ought not to have been obliged at all.

Yet, while I describe the meanness of a life of continued dependence, I would not be thought to include those natural or political subordinations which subsist in every society; for in such, though dependence is exacted from the inferior, yet the obligation on either side is mutual. The son must rely upon his parent for support, but the parent lies under the same obligations to give that the other has to expect; the subordinate officer must receive the commands of his superior, but for this obedience the former has a right to demand an intercourse of favour. Such is not the dependence I would deprecate, but that where every expected favour must be the result of mere benevolence in the giver, where the benefit can be kept without remorse, or transferred without injustice. The character of a legacy hunter, for instance, is detestable in some countries, and despicable in all; this universal con tempt of a man who infringes upon none of the laws of society some moralists have arraigned as a popular and unjust prejudice; never considering the necessary degradations a wretch must undergo, who previously expects to grow rich by benefits, without having either natural or social claims to enforce his petitions.

But this intercourse of benefaction and acknowledgment is often injurious even to the giver, as well as the receiver. A man can gain but little knowledge of himself, or of the world, amidst a circle of those whom hope or gratitude has gathered round him; their unceasing humiliations must necessarily increase his comparative magnitude, for all men measure their own abilities by those of their company: thus being taught to overrate his merit, he in reality lessens it; increasing in confidence, but not in power, his professions end in empty boast, his undertakings in shameful disappointment.

It is perhaps one of the severest misfortunes of the great, that they are, in general, obliged to live among men whose real value is lessened by dependence, and whose minds are enslaved by obligation. The humble companion may have at first accepted patronage with generous views; but soon he feels the mortifying influence of conscious inferiority, by degrees sinks into a flatterer, and from flattery at last degenerates into stupid veneration. To remedy this, the great often dismiss their old dependants and take new. Such changes are falsely imputed to levity, falsehood, or caprice in the patron, since they may be more justly ascribed to the client's deterioration.

No, my son, a life of independence is generally a life of virtue. It is that which fits the soul for every generous flight of humanity, freedom, and friendship. To give should be our pleasure, but to receive, our shame: serenity, health, and affluence attend the desire of rising by labour; misery, repentance, and disrespect, that of succeeding by extorted benevolence: the man who can thank himself alone for the happiness he enjoys is truly blest; and lovely, far more lovely, the sturdy gloom of laborious indigence, than the fawning simper of thriving adulation.—Adieu.

LETTER CI.

From Lien Chi Altangi to Fum Hoam, First President of the Ceremonial Academy at Pekin in China.

In every society some men are born to teach, and others to receive instruction; some to work, and others to enjoy in idleness the fruits of their industry; some to govern, and others to obey. Every people, how free soever, must be contented to give up part of their liberty and judgment to those who govern, in exchange for their hopes of security; and the motives which first influenced their choice in the election of their governors should ever be weighed against the succeeding apparent inconsistencies of their conduct. All cannot be rulers, and men are generally best governed by a few. In making way through the intricacies of business, the smallest obstacles are apt to retard the execution of what is to be planned by a multiplicity of counsels; the judgment of one alone being always fittest for winding through the labyrinths of intrigue, and the obstructions of disappointment. A serpent which, as the fable observes, is furnished with one head and many tails, is much more capable of subsistence and expedition than another which is furnished with but one tail and many heads.

Obvious as these truths are, the people of this country seem insensible of their force. Not satisfied with the advantages of internal peace and opulence, they still murmur at their governors, and interfere in the execution of their designs, as if they wanted to be something more than happy. But as the Europeans instruct by argument, and the Asiatics mostly by narration, were I to address them, I should convey my sentiments in the following story:—

"Takupi had long been prime minister of Tipartala, a fertile country that stretches along the western confines of China. During his administration whatever advantages could be derived from arts, learning and commerce, were seen to bless the people; nor were the necessary precautions of providing for the security of the state forgotten. It often happens, however, that when men are possessed of all they want, they then begin to find torment from imaginary afflictions, and lessen their present enjoyments, by foreboding that those enjoyments are to have an end. The people now, therefore, endeavoured to find out grievances; and, after some search, actually began to think themselves aggrieved. A petition against the enormities of Takupi was carried to the throne in due form; and the Queen who governed the country, willing to satisfy her subjects, appointed a day in which his accusers should be heard, and the minister should stand upon his defence.

"The day being arrived, and the minister brought before the tribunal, a carrier, who supplied the city with fish, appeared among the number of his accusers. He exclaimed, that it was the custom, time immemorial, for carriers to bring their fish upon a horse in a hamper; which being placed on one side, and balanced by a stone on the other, was thus conveyed with ease and safety; but that the prisoner, moved either by a spirit of innovation, or perhaps bribed by the hamper makers, had obliged all carriers to use the stone no longer, but balance one hamper with another; an order entirely repugnant to the customs of all antiquity, and those of the kingdom of Tipartala in particular.

"The carrier finished, and the whole court shook their heads at the innovating minister; when a second witness appeared. He was inspector of the city buildings, and accused the disgraced favourite of having given orders for the demolition of an ancient ruin, which obstructed the passage through one of the principal streets. He observed, that such buildings were noble monuments of barbarous antiquity; contributed finely to show how little their ancestors understood of architecture; and for that reason such monuments should be held sacred, and suffered gradually to decay.

"The last witness now appeared. This was a widow, who had laudably attempted to burn herself upon her husband's funeral pile. But the innovating minister had prevented the execution of her design, and was insensible to her tears, protestations, and entreaties.

"The Queen could have pardoned the two former offences; but this last was considered as so gross an injury to the sex, and so directly contrary to all the customs of antiquity, that it called for immediate justice. 'What!' cried the Queen, 'not suffer a woman to burn herself when she thinks proper? The sex are to be prettily tutored, no doubt, if they must be restrained from entertaining their female friends now and then with a fried wife, or roasted acquaintance. I sentence the criminal to be banished my presence for ever, for his injurious treatment of the sex.'

"Takupi had been hitherto silent, and spoke only to show the sincerity of his resignation. 'Great Queen,' cried he, 'I acknowledge my crime; and since I am to be banished, I beg it may be to some ruined town, or desolate village, in the country I have governed. I shall find some pleasure in improving the soil, and bringing back a spirit of industry among the inhabitants.' His request appearing reasonable, it was immediately complied with; and a courtier had orders to fix upon a place of banishment answering the minister's description. After some months' search, however, the inquiry proved fruitless; neither a desolate village nor a ruined town was found in the whole kingdom. 'Alas,' said Takupi then to the Queen, 'how can that country be ill governed which has neither a desolate village nor a ruined town in it?' The Queen perceived the justice of his expostulation, and the minister was received into more than former favour."

LETTER CII.

To the same.

THE ladies here are by no means such ardent gamesters as the women of Asia. In this respect I must do the English justice; for I love to praise where applause is justly merited. Nothing is more common in China than to see two women of fashion continue gaming till one has won all the other's clothes, and stripped her quite naked; the winner thus marching off in a double suit of finery, and the loser shrinking behind in the primitive simplicity of nature.

No doubt you remember when Shang,

our maiden aunt, played with a sharper. First her money went; then her trinkets were produced; her clothes followed piece by piece soon after; when she had thus played herself quite naked, being a woman of spirit, and willing to pursue her own, she staked her teeth: fortune was against her even here, and her teeth followed her clothes. At last she played for her left eye, and, oh! hard fate, this too she lost: however, she had the consolation of biting the sharper, for he never perceived that it was made of glass till it became his own.

How happy, my friend, are the English ladies, who never rise to such an inordinance of passion! Though the sex here are generally fond of games of chance, and are taught to manage games of skill from their infancy, yet they never pursue ill fortune with such amazing intrepidity. Indeed, I may entirely acquit them of ever playing—I mean of playing for their eyes or their teeth.

It is true they often stake their fortune, their beauty, health, and reputation, at a gaming table. It even sometimes happens, that they play their husbands into a gaol; yet still they preserve a decorum unknown to our wives and daughters of China. I have been present at a rout in this country, where a woman of fashion, after losing her money, has sat writhing in all the agonies of bad luck, and yet, after all, never once attempted to strip a single petticoat, or cover the board, as her last stake, with her head-clothes.

However, though I praise their moderation at play, I must not conceal their assiduity. In China our women, except upon some great days, are never permitted to finger a dice-box; but here every day seems to be a festival, and night itself, which gives others rest, only serves to increase the female gamester's industry. I have been told of an old lady in the country who, being given over by the physicians, played with the curate of her parish to pass the time away: having won all his money, she next proposed playing for her funeral charges: her proposal was accepted; but unfortunately the lady expired just as she had taken in her game.

There are some passions which, though differently pursued, are attended with equal consequences in every country: here they game with more perseverance, there with greater fury; here they strip their families, there they strip themselves naked. A lady in China who indulges a passion for gaming, often becomes a drunkard; and by flourishing a dice-box in one hand, she generally comes to brandish a dram-cup in the other. Far be it from me to say there are any who drink drams in England; but it is natural to suppose, that when a lady has lost everything else but her honour, she will be apt to toss that into the bargain, and grown insensible to nicer feelings, behave like the Spaniard, who, when all his money was gone, endeavoured to borrow more by offering to pawn his whiskers.—Adieu.

LETTER CIII.

From Lien Chi Altangi to ——, Merchant in Amsterdam.

I HAVE just received a letter from my son, in which he informs me of the fruitlessness of his endeavours to recover the lady with whom he fled from Persia. He strives to cover, under the appearance of fortitude, a heart torn with anxiety and disappointment. I have offered little consolation, since that but too frequently feeds the sorrow which it pretends to deplore, and strengthens the impression which nothing but the external rubs of time and accident can thoroughly efface.

He informs me of his intentions of quitting Moscow the first opportunity, and travelling by land to Amsterdam. I must, therefore, upon his arrival, entreat the continuance of your friendship, and beg of you to provide him with proper directions for finding me in London. You can scarcely be sensible of the joy I expect upon seeing him once more: the ties between the father and the son among us of China are much more closely drawn than with you of Europe.

The remittances sent me from Argun to Moscow came in safety. I cannot sufficiently admire that spirit of honesty which prevails through the whole country of Siberia: perhaps the savages of that desolate region are the only untutored people of the globe that cultivate the moral virtues, even without knowing that their actions merit praise. I have been told surprising things of their goodness, benevolence, and generosity; and the uninterrupted commerce between China and Russia serves as a collateral confirmation.

"Let us," says the Chinese lawgiver, "admire the rude virtues of the ignorant, but rather imitate the delicate morals of the polite." In the country where I reside, though honesty and benevolence be not so congenial, yet art supplies the place of nature. Though here every vice is carried to excess, yet every virtue is practised also with unexampled superiority. A city like this is the soil for great virtues and great vices: the villain can soon improve himself in the deepest mysteries of deceiving; and the practical philosopher can every day meet new incitements to mend his honest intentions. There are no pleasures, sensual or sentimental, which this city does not produce; yet, I know not how, I could not be content to reside here for life. There is something so seducing in that spot in which we first had existence, that nothing but it can please. Whatever vicissitudes we experience in life, however we toil, or wheresoever we wander, our fatigued wishes still recur to home for tranquillity: we long to die in that spot which gave us birth, and in that pleasing expectation find an opiate for every calamity.

You now, therefore, perceive that I have some intentions of leaving this country; and yet my designed departure fills me with reluctance and regret. Though the friendships of travellers are generally more transient than vernal snows, still I feel an uneasiness at breaking the connexions I have formed since my arrival; particularly, I shall have no small pain in leaving my usual companion, guide, and instructor.

I shall wait for the arrival of my son before I set out. He shall be my companion in every intended journey for the future; in his company I can support the fatigues of the way with redoubled ardour, pleased at once with conveying instruction, and exacting obedience.—Adieu.

LETTER CIV.

From Lien Chi Altangi to Fum Hoam, First President of the Ceremonial Academy at Pekin in China.

Our scholars in China have a most profound veneration for forms. A first-rate beauty never studied the decorums of dress with more assiduity; they may properly enough be said to be clothed with wisdom from head to foot: they have their philosophical caps, and philosophical whiskers; their philosophical slippers, and philosophical fans; there is even a philosophical standard for measuring the nails; and yet, with all this seeming wisdom, they are often found to be mere empty pretenders.

A philosophical beau is not so frequent in Europe; yet I am told that such characters are found here. I mean such as punctually support all the decorums of learning without being really very profound, or naturally possessed of a fine understanding; who labour hard to obtain the titular honours attending literary merit, who flatter others in order to be flattered in turn, and only study to be thought students.

A character of this kind generally receives company in his study, in all the pensive formality of slippers, night-gown, and easy chair. The table is covered with a large book, which is always kept open, and never read; his solitary hours being dedicated to dozing, mending pens, feeling his pulse, peeping through the microscope, and sometimes reading amusing books, which he condemns in company. His library is preserved with the most religious neatness, and is generally a repository of scarce books, which bear a high price, because too dull or useless to become common by the ordinary methods of publication.

Such men are generally candidates for admittance into literary clubs, academies, and institutions, where they regularly meet to give and receive a little instruction, and a great deal of praise. In conversation they never betray ignorance, because they never seem to receive information. Offer a new observation, they have heard it before; pinch them in argument, and they reply with a sneer.

Yet, how trifling soever these little arts may appear, they answer one valuable purpose,—of gaining the practisers the esteem they wish for. The bounds of a man's knowledge are easily concealed, if he has but prudence; but all can readily see and admire a gilt library, a set of long nails, a silver standish, or a well-combed whisker, who are incapable of distinguishing a dunce.

When Father Matthew, the first European missionary, entered China, the court was informed that he possessed great skill in astronomy; he was therefore sent for, and examined. The established astronomers of state undertook this task, and made their report to the Emperor that his skill was but very superficial, and no way comparable to their own. The missionary, however, appealed from their judgment to experience, and challenged them to calculate an eclipse of the moon that was to happen a few nights following. "What!" said some, "shall a barbarian without nails pretend to vie with men in astronomy who have made it the study of their lives; with men who know half the knowable characters of words, who wear scientifical caps and slippers, and who have gone through every literary degree with applause?" They accepted the challenge, confident of success. The eclipse began: the Chinese produced a most splendid apparatus, and were fifteen minutes wrong; the missionary, with a single instrument, was exact to a second. This was convincing: but the court astronomers were not to be convinced; instead of acknowledging their error, they assured the Emperor that their calculations were certainly exact, but that the stranger without nails had actually bewitched the moon. "Well, then," cries the good Emperor, smiling at their ignorance, "you shall still continue to be servants of the moon, but I constitute this man her controller."

China is thus replete with men whose only pretensions to knowledge arise from external circumstances; and in Europe every country abounds with them in proportion to its ignorance. Spain and Flanders, who are behind the rest of Europe in learning at least three centuries, have twenty literary titles and marks of distinction unknown in France or England. They have their *Clarissimi* and *Præclarissimi*, their *Accuratissimi* and *Minutissimi*. A round cap entitles one student to argue, and a square cap permits another to teach, while a cap with a tassel almost sanctifies the head it happens to cover. But where true knowledge is cultivated, these formalities begin to disappear. The ermine cowl, the solemn beard, and sweeping train, are laid aside; philosophers dress, and talk, and think, like other men; and lamb-skin dressers, and cap-makers, and tail-carriers, now deplore a literary age.

For my own part, my friend, I have seen enough of presuming ignorance, never to venerate wisdom but where it actually appears. I have received literary titles and distinctions myself; and, by the quantity of my own wisdom, know how very little wisdom they can confer.—Adieu.

LETTER CV.

To the same.

THE time for the young king's coronation approaches. The great and the little world look forward with impatience. A knight from the country, who has brought up his family to see and be seen on this occasion, has taken all the lower part of the house where I lodge. His wife is laying in a large quantity of silks, which the mercer tells her are to be fashionable next season; and miss, her daughter, has actually had her ears bored previous to the ceremony. In all this bustle of preparation, I am considered as mere lumber, and have been shoved up two stories higher, to make room for others my landlady seems perfectly convinced are my betters; but whom, before me, she is contented with only calling very good company.

The little Beau, who has now forced himself into my intimacy, was yesterday giving me a most minute detail of the intended procession. All men are eloquent upon their favourite topic; and this seemed peculiarly adapted to the size and turn of his understanding. His whole mind was blazoned over with a variety of glittering images,—coronets, escutcheons, lace, fringe, tassels, stones, bugles, and spun glass. "Here," cried he, "Garter is to walk; and there Rouge Dragon marches with the escutcheons on his back. Here Clarencieux moves forward; and there Blue Mantle disdains to be left behind. Here the Aldermen march two and two; and there the undaunted Champion of England, no way terrified at the very numerous appearance of gentlemen and ladies, rides forward in complete armour, and with an intrepid air throws down his glove. Ah!" continued he, "should any be so hardy as to take up that fatal glove, and so accept the challenge, we should see fine sport; the Champion would show him no mercy; he would soon teach him all his passes, with a witness. However, I am afraid we shall have none willing to try it with him upon the approaching occasion, for two reasons,—first, because his antagonist would stand a chance of being killed in the single combat; and, secondly, because if he escapes the champion's arm, he would certainly be hanged for treason. No, no; I fancy none will be so hardy as to dispute it with a champion like him, inured to arms; and we shall probably see him prancing unmolested away, holding his bridle thus in one hand, and brandishing his dram-cup in the other."

Some men have a manner of describing which only wraps the subject in more than former obscurity; thus I was unable, with all my companion's volubility, to form a distinct idea of the intended procession. I was certain that the inauguration of a king should be conducted with solemnity and religious awe; and I could not be persuaded that there was much solemnity in this description. "If this be true," cried I to myself, "the people of Europe surely have a strange manner of mixing solemn and fantastic images together; pictures at once replete with burlesque and the sublime. At a time when the king enters into the most solemn compact with his people, nothing surely should be admitted to diminish from the real majesty of the ceremony. A ludicrous image brought in at such a time throws an air of ridicule upon the whole. It someway resembles a picture I have seen, designed by Albert Durer, where, amidst all the solemnity of that awful scene, a deity judging, and a trembling world awaiting the decree, he has introduced a merry mortal trundling a scolding wife to hell in a wheelbarrow."

My companion, who mistook my silence, during this interval of reflection, for the rapture of astonishment, proceeded to describe those frivolous parts of the show that most struck his imagination; and to assure me, that if I stayed in this country some months longer, I should see fine things. "For my own part," continued he, "I know already of fifteen suits of clothes that would stand on one end with gold lace, all designed to be first shown there; and as for diamonds, rubies, emeralds, and pearls, we shall see them as thick as brass nails in a sedan chair. And then we are all to walk so majestically, thus; this foot always behind the foot before. The ladies are to fling nosegays; the court poets to scatter verses; the spectators are to be all in full dress; Mrs. Tibbs in a new sack, ruffles, and Frenched hair: look where you will, one thing finer than another; Mrs. Tibbs curtsies to the Duchess; her Grace returns the compliment with a bow. 'Largess!' cries the herald. 'Make room!' cries the gentleman usher. 'Knock him down!' cries the guard. Ah!" continued he, amazed at his own description, "what an astonishing scene of grandeur can art produce from the smallest circumstance, when it thus actually turns to wonder one man putting on another man's hat!"

I now found his mind was entirely set upon the fopperies of the pageant, and quite regardless of the real meaning of such costly preparations. "Pageants," says Bacon, "are pretty things; but we should rather study to make them elegant than expensive." Processions, cavalcades, and all that fund of gay frippery furnished out by tailors, barbers, and tirewomen, mechanically influence the mind into veneration. An emperor in his nightcap would not meet with half the respect of an emperor with a glittering crown. Politics resemble religion; attempting to divest either of ceremony is the most certain method of bringing either into contempt. The weak must have their inducements to admiration as well as the wise; and it is the business of a sensible government to impress all ranks with a sense of subordination, whether this be effected by a diamond buckle or a virtuous edict, a sumptuary law or a glass necklace.

This interval of reflection only gave my companion spirits to begin his description afresh; and, as a greater inducement to raise my curiosity, he informed me of the vast sums that were given by the spectators for places. "That the ceremony must be fine," cries he, "is very evident from the fine price that is paid for seeing it. Several ladies have assured me, they would willingly part with one eye rather than be prevented from looking on with the other. Come, come," continues he, "I have a friend, who, for my sake, will supply us with places at the most reasonable rates; I'll take care you shall not be imposed upon; and he will inform you of the use, finery, rapture, splendour, and enchantment of the whole ceremony, better than I."

Follies often repeated lose their absurdity, and assume the appearance of reason. His arguments were so often and so strongly enforced, that I had actually some thoughts of becoming a spectator. We accordingly went together to bespeak a place; but guess my surprise when the man demanded a purse of gold for a single seat! I could hardly believe him serious upon making the demand. "Prithee, friend," cried I, "after I have paid twenty pounds for sitting here an hour or two, can I bring a part of the coronation back?"—"No, sir."—"How long can I live upon it, after I have come away?"—"Not long, sir."—"Can a coronation clothe, feed, or fatten me?"—"Sir," replied the man, "you seem to be under a mistake; all that you can bring away is the pleasure of having it to say, that you saw the coronation."—"Blast me!" cries Tibbs, "if that be all, there is no need of paying for that; since I am resolved to have that pleasure, whether I am there or no!"

I am conscious, my friend, that this is but a very confused description of the intended ceremony. You may object, that I neither settle rank, precedency, nor place; that I seem ignorant whether Gules walks before or behind Garter; that I have neither mentioned the dimensions of a lord's cap, nor measured the length of a lady's tail. I know your delight is in minute description: and this I am unhappily disqualified from furnishing; yet, upon the whole, I fancy it will be no way comparable to the magnificence of our late Emperor Whangti's procession, when he was married to the moon, at which Fum Hoam himself presided in person.—Adieu.

LETTER CVI.

To the same.

It was formerly the custom here, when men of distinction died, for their surviving acquaintance to throw each a slight present into the grave. Several things of little value were made use of for that purpose,—perfumes, relics, spices, bitter herbs, camomile, wormwood, and verses. This custom, however, is almost discontinued, and nothing but verses alone are now lavished on such occasions; an oblation which they suppose may be interred with the dead, without any injury to the living.

Upon the death of the great, therefore, the poets and undertakers are sure of employment. While one provides the long cloak, black staff, and mourning coach, the other produces the pastoral or elegy, the monody or apotheosis. The nobility need be under no apprehensions, but die as fast as they think proper,—the poet and undertaker are ready to supply them; these can find metaphorical tears and family escutcheons at an hour's warning; and when the one has soberly laid the body in the grave, the other is ready to fix it figuratively among the stars.

There are several ways of being poetically sorrowful on such occasions. The bard is now some pensive youth of science, who sits deploring among the tombs; again, he is Thyrsis complaining in a circle of harmless sheep. Now Britannia sits upon her own shore, and gives a loose to maternal tenderness; at another time Parnassus, even the mountain Parnassus, gives way to sorrow, and is bathed in tears of distress.

But the most usual manner is this: Damon meets Menalcas, who has got a most gloomy countenance. The shepherd asks his friend, whence that look of distress? To which the other replies, that Pollio is no more. "If that be the case, then," cries Damon, "let us retire to yonder bower at some distance off, where the cypress and the jessamine add fragrance to the breeze; and let us weep alternately for Pollio, the friend of shepherds, and the patron of every muse."—"Ah!" returns his fellow shepherd, "what think you rather of that grotto by the fountain side? the murmuring stream will help to assist our complaints, and a nightingale on a neighbouring tree will join her voice to the concert!" When the place is thus settled, they begin; the brook stands still to hear their lamentations; the cows forget to graze; and the very tigers start from the forest with sympathetic concern. By the tombs of our ancestors, my dear Fum, I am quite unaffected in all this distress: the whole is liquid laudanum to my spirits; and a tiger of common sensibility has twenty times more tenderness than I.

But though I could never weep with the complaining shepherd, yet I am sometimes induced to pity the poet, whose trade is thus to make demigods and heroes for a dinner. There is not in nature a more dismal figure than a man who sits down to premeditated flattery: every stanza he writes tacitly reproaches the meanness of his occupation, till at last his stupidity becomes more stupid, and his dulness more diminutive.

I am amazed, therefore, that none have yet found out the secret of flattering the worthless, and yet of preserving a safe conscience. I have often wished for some method, by which a man might do himself and his deceased patron justice, without being under the hateful reproach of self-conviction. After long lucubration, I have hit upon such an expedient: and send you the specimen of a poem upon the decease of a great man, in which the flattery is perfectly fine, and yet the poet perfectly innocent.

On the Death of the Right Honourable ——.

Ye Muses, pour the pitying tear
  For Pollio snatched away;
Oh, had he lived another year—
  He had not died to-day.

Oh, were he born to bless mankind
  In virtuous times of yore,
Heroes themselves had fall'n behind—
  Whene'er he went before.

How sad the groves and plains appear,
  And sympathetic sheep;
E'en pitying hills would drop a tear—
  If hills could learn to weep.

His bounty in exalted strain
  Each bard may well display;
Since none implored relief in vain—
  That went relieved away.

And hark! I hear the tuneful throng
  His obsequies forbid:
He still shall live, shall live as long—
  As ever dead man did.

LETTER CVII.

To the same.

It is the most usual method in every report, first to examine its probability, and then act as the conjuncture may require. The English, however, exert a different spirit in such circumstances: they first act, and when too late, begin to examine. From a knowledge of this disposition, there are several here, who make it their business to frame new reports at every convenient interval, all tending to denounce ruin both on their contemporaries and their posterity. This denunciation is eagerly caught up by the public: away they fling to propagate the distress; sell out at one place, buy in at another, grumble at their governors, shout in mobs, and, when they have thus for some time behaved like fools, sit down coolly to argue and talk wisdom, to puzzle each other with syllogism, and prepare for the next report that prevails, which is always attended with the same success.

Thus are they ever rising above one report, only to sink into another. They resemble a dog in a well, pawing to get free. When he has raised his upper parts above water, and every spectator imagines him disengaged, his lower parts drag him down again, and sink him to the nose; he makes new efforts to emerge, and every effort increasing his weakness, only tends to sink him the deeper.

There are some here who, I am told, make a tolerable subsistence by the credulity of their countrymen. As they find the people fond of blood, wounds, and death, they contrive political ruins suited to every month in the year. This month the people are to be eaten up by the French in flat-bottomed boats; the next, by the soldiers designed to beat the French back. Now the people are going to jump down the gulf of luxury; and now nothing but a herring subscription can fish them up again. Time passes on; the report proves false; new circumstances produce new changes; but the people never change,—they are persevering in folly.

In other countries those boding politicians would be left to fret over their own schemes alone, and grow splenetic without hopes of infecting others; but England seems to be the very region where spleen delights to dwell: a man not only can give an unbounded scope to the disorder in himself, but may, if he pleases, propagate it over the whole kingdom, with a certainty of success. He has only to cry out that the government, the government is all wrong; that their schemes are leading to ruin; that Britons are no more; every good member of the commonwealth thinks it his duty, in such a case, to deplore the universal decadence with sympathetic sorrow, and, by fancying the constitution in a decay, absolutely to impair its vigour.

This people would laugh at my simplicity, should I advise them to be less sanguine in harbouring gloomy predictions, and examine coolly before they attempted to complain. I have just heard a story which, though transacted in a private family, serves very well to describe the behaviour of the whole nation, in cases of threatened calamity. As there are public, so there are private incendiaries here. One of the last, either for the amusement of his friends, or to divert a fit of the spleen, lately sent a threatening letter to a worthy family in my neighbourhood, to this effect:—

"SIR,—Knowing you to be very rich, and finding myself to be very poor, I think proper to inform you, that I have learned the secret of poisoning man, woman, and child, without danger of detection. Don't be uneasy, sir; you may take your choice of being poisoned in a fortnight, or poisoned in a month, or poisoned in six weeks; you shall have full time to settle all your affairs. Though I am poor, I love to do things like a gentleman. But, sir, you must die; I have determined it within my own breast that you must die. Blood, sir! blood is my trade! so I could wish you would, this day six weeks, take leave of your friends, wife, and family, for I cannot possibly allow you longer time. To convince you more certainly of the power of my art, by which you may know I speak truth, take this letter; when you have read it, tear off the seal, fold it up, and give it to your favourite Dutch mastiff that sits by the fire; he will swallow it, sir, like a buttered toast: in three hours four minutes after he has eaten it he will attempt to bite off his own tongue, and, half an hour after, burst asunder in twenty pieces. Blood, blood, blood! So no more at present from, sir, your most obedient, most devoted humble servant to command, till death."

You may easily imagine the consternation into which this letter threw the whole good-natured family. The poor man to whom it was addressed was the more surprised, as not knowing how he could merit such inveterate malice. All the friends of the family were convened; it was universally agreed that it was a most terrible affair, and that the government should be solicited to offer a reward and a pardon: a fellow of this kind would go on poisoning family after family; and it was impossible to say where the destruction would end. In pursuance of these determinations, the government was applied to; strict search was made after the incendiary, but all in vain. At last, therefore, they recollected that the experiment was not yet tried upon the dog; the Dutch mastiff was brought up and placed in the midst of the friends and relations, the seal was torn off, the packet folded up with care, and soon they found, to the great surprise of all, that the dog would not eat the letter.—Adieu.

LETTER CVIII.

To the same.

I HAVE frequently been amazed at the ignorance of almost all the European travellers who have penetrated any considerable way eastward into Asia. They have been influenced either by motives of commerce or piety; and their accounts are such as might reasonably be expected from men of very narrow or very prejudiced education,—the dictates of superstition, or the result of ignorance. Is it not surprising, that in such a variety of adventurers not one single philosopher should be found? for, as to the travels of Gemelli, the learned are long agreed that the whole is but an imposture.

There is scarcely any country, how rude or uncultivated soever, where the inhabitants are not possessed of some peculiar secrets, either in nature or art, which might be transplanted with success. In Siberian Tartary, for instance, the natives extract a strong spirit from milk, which is a secret probably unknown to the chemists of Europe. In the most savage parts of India they are possessed of the secret of dyeing vegetable substances scarlet, and of refining lead into a metal which, for hardness and colour, is little inferior to silver: not one of which secrets but would, in Europe, make a man's fortune. The power of the Asiatics in producing winds, or bringing down rain, the Europeans are apt to treat as fabulous, because they have no instances of the like nature among themselves; but they would have treated the secrets of gunpowder and the mariner's compass in the same manner, had they been told the Chinese used such arts before the invention was common with themselves at home.

Of all the English philosophers I most reverence Bacon, that great and hardy genius. He it is who allows of secrets yet unknown; who, undaunted by the seeming difficulties that oppose, prompts human curiosity to examine every part of nature, and even exhorts man to try whether he cannot subject the tempest, the thunder, and even earthquakes, to human control! Oh, did a man of his daring spirit, of his genius, penetration, and learning, travel to those countries which have been visited only by the superstitious and the mercenary, what might not mankind expect! How would he enlighten the regions to which he travelled! and what a variety of knowledge and useful improvement would he not bring back in exchange!

There is, probably, no country so barbarous, that would not disclose all it knew, if it received from the traveller equivalent information; and I am apt to think, that a person who was ready to give more knowledge than he received would be welcome wherever he came. All his care in travelling should only be to suit his intellectual banquet to the people with whom he conversed; he should not attempt to teach the unlettered Tartar astronomy, nor yet instruct the polite Chinese in the ruder arts of subsistence. He should endeavour to improve the barbarian in the secrets of living comfortably; and the inhabitant of a more refined country in the speculative pleasures of science. How much more nobly would a philosopher thus employed spend his time, than by sitting at home, earnestly intent upon adding one star more to his catalogue, or one monster more to his collection; or still, if possible, more triflingly sedulous in the incatenation of fleas, or the sculpture of a cherry-stone!

I never consider this subject without being surprised, that none of those societies so laudably established in England for the promotion of arts and learning have ever thought of sending one of their members into the most eastern parts of Asia, to make what discoveries he was able. To be convinced of the utility of such an undertaking, let them but read the relations of their own travellers. It will be there found, that they are as often deceived themselves, as they attempt to deceive others. The merchant tells us, perhaps, the price of different commodities, the methods of baling them up, and the properest manner for an European to preserve his health in the country. The missionary, on the other hand, informs us, with what pleasure the country to which he was sent embraced Christianity, and the numbers he converted; what methods he took to keep Lent in a region where there was no fish, or the shifts he made to celebrate the rites of his religion in places where there was neither bread nor wine! Such accounts, with the usual appendage of marriages and funerals, inscriptions, rivers, and mountains, make up the whole of an European traveller's diary: but as to all the secrets of which the inhabitants are possessed, those are universally attributed to magic; and when the traveller can give no other account of the wonders he sees performed, very contentedly ascribes them to the power of the devil.

It was a usual observation of Boyle, the English chemist, "That if every artist would but discover what new observations occurred to him in the exercise of his trade, philosophy would thence gain innumerable improvements." It may be observed, with still greater justice, that if the useful knowledge of every country, howsoever barbarous, was gleaned by a judicious observer, the advantages would be inestimable. Are there not even in Europe many useful inventions known or practised but in one place? The instrument, as an example, for cutting down corn in Germany is much more handy and expeditious, in my opinion, than the sickle used in England. The cheap and expeditious manner of making vinegar, without previous fermentation, is known only in a part of France. If such discoveries, therefore, remain still to be known at home, what funds of knowledge might not be collected in countries yet unexplored, or only passed through by ignorant travellers in hasty caravans?

The caution with which foreigners are received in Asia may be alleged as an objection to such a design. But how readily have several European merchants found admission into regions the most suspecting, under the character of *Sanjapins*, or northern pilgrims. To such not even China itself denies access.

To send out a traveller properly qualified for these purposes might be an object of national concern; it would in some measure repair the breaches made by ambition; and might show that there were still some who boasted a greater name than that of patriots, who professed themselves lovers of men. The only difficulty would remain in choosing a proper person for so arduous an enterprise. He should be a man of philosophical turn; one apt to deduce consequences of general utility from particular occurrences; neither swollen with pride, nor hardened by prejudice; neither wedded to one particular system, nor instructed only in one particular science; neither wholly a botanist, nor quite an antiquarian; his mind should be tinctured with miscellaneous knowledge, and his manner humanized by an intercourse with men. He should be in some measure an enthusiast in the design; fond of travelling, from a rapid imagination and an innate love of change; furnished with a body capable of sustaining every fatigue, and a heart not easily terrified at danger.—Adieu.

LETTER CIX.

To the same.

ONE of the principal tasks I had proposed to myself on my arrival here was, to become acquainted with the names and characters of those now living who, as scholars or wits, had acquired the greatest share of reputation. In order to succeed in this design, I fancied the surest method would be to begin my inquiry among the ignorant, judging that his fame would be greatest, which was loud enough to be heard by the vulgar. Thus predisposed, I began to search, but only went in quest of disappointment and perplexity. I found every district had a peculiar famous man of its own. Here the story-telling shoemaker had engrossed the admiration on one side of the street, while the bellman, who excelleth at a catch, was in quiet possession of the other. At one end of a lane the sexton was regarded as the greatest man alive; but I had not travelled half its length, till I found an enthusiastic teacher had divided his reputation. My landlady, perceiving my design, was kind enough to offer me her advice in this affair. It was true, she observed, that she was no judge, but she knew what pleased herself, and if I would rest upon her judgment, I should set down Tom Collins as the most ingenious man in the world; for Tom was able to take off all mankind, and imitate besides a sow and pigs to perfection.

I now perceived, that taking my standard of reputation among the vulgar would swell my catalogue of great names above the size of a court calendar; I therefore discontinued this method of pursuit, and resolved to prosecute my inquiry in that usual residence of fame, a bookseller's shop. In consequence of this I entreated the bookseller to let me know who were they who now made the greatest figure, either in morals, wit, or learning. Without giving me a direct answer, he pulled a pamphlet from the shelf, *The Young Attorney's Guide.* "There, sir," cries he, "there is a touch for you; fifteen hundred of these moved off in a day: I take the author of this pamphlet, either for title, preface, plan, body, or index, to be the completest hand in England." I found it was vain to prosecute my inquiry, where my informer appeared so incompetent a judge of merit; so, paying for the *Young Attorney's Guide*, which good manners obliged me to buy, I walked off.

My pursuit after famous men now brought me into a print-shop. "Here," thought I, "the painter only reflects the public voice. As every man who deserved it had formerly his statue placed up in the Roman forum, so here, probably, the pictures of none but such as merit a place in our affections are held up for public sale." But guess my surprise, when I came to examine this repository of noted faces; all distinctions were levelled here, as in the grave, and I could not but regard it as the catacomb of real merit: the brick-dust man took up as much room as the truncheoned hero, and the judge was elbowed by the thief-taker; quacks, pimps, and buffoons increased the group, and noted stallions only made room for more noted strumpets. I had read the works of some of the moderns previous to my coming to England with delight and approbation; but I found their faces had no place here: the walls were covered with the names of authors I had never known, or had endeavoured to forget,—with the little self-advertising things of a day, who had forced themselves into fashion, but not into fame. I could read at the bottom of some pictures the names of **, and***, and****, all equally candidates for the vulgar shout, and foremost to propagate their unblushing faces upon brass. My uneasiness, therefore, at not finding my few favourite names among the number was now changed into congratulation. I could not avoid reflecting on the fine observation of Tacitus on a similar occasion. "In this cavalcade of flattery," cries the historian, "neither the pictures of Brutus, Cassius, nor Cato, were to be seen; *eo clariores quia imagines eorum non deferebantur;*" their absence being the strongest proof of their merit.

"It is in vain," cried I, "to seek for true greatness among these monuments of the unburied dead: let me go among the tombs of those who are confessedly famous, and see if any have been lately deposited there who deserve the attention of posterity, and whose names may be transmitted to my distant friend, as an honour to the present age." Determined in my pursuit, I paid a second visit to Westminster Abbey. There I found several new monuments, erected to the memory of several great men; the names of the great men I absolutely forget, but I well remember that Roubiliac was the statuary who carved them. I could not help smiling at two modern epitaphs in particular, one of which praised the deceased for being *ortus ex antiquâ stirpe:* the other commended the dead because *hanc ædem suis sumptibus reædificavit.* The greatest merit of one consisted in his being descended from an illustrious house; the chief distinction of the other, that he had propped up an old house that was falling. "Alas! alas!" cried I, "such monuments as these confer honour, not upon the great men, but upon little Roubiliac."

Hitherto disappointed in my inquiry after the great of the present age, I was resolved to mix in company, and try what I could learn among critics in coffee-houses; and here it was that I heard my favourite names talked of even with inverted fame. A gentleman of exalted merit as a writer was branded in general terms as a bad man; another of exquisite delicacy as a poet was reproached for wanting good nature; a third was accused of free-thinking; and a fourth of having once been a player. "Strange," cried I; "how unjust are mankind in the distribution of fame! the ignorant, among whom I sought at first, were willing to grant, but incapable of distinguishing, the virtues of those who deserved it; among those I now converse with, they know the proper objects of admiration, but mix envy with applause."

Disappointed so often, I was now resolved to examine those characters in person, of whom the world talked so freely. By conversing with men of real merit, I began to find out those characters which really deserved, though they strove to avoid, applause. I found the vulgar admiration entirely misplaced, and malevolence without its sting. The truly great, possessed of numerous small faults and shining virtues, preserve a sublime in morals as in writing. They who have attained an excellence in either commit numberless transgressions, observable to the meanest understanding. The ignorant critic and dull remarker can readily spy blemishes in eloquence or morals, whose sentiments are not sufficiently elevated to observe a beauty. But such are judges neither of books nor of life; they can diminish no solid reputation by their censure, nor bestow a lasting character by their applause. In short, I found by my search, that such only can confer real fame upon others, who have merit themselves to deserve it. —Adieu.

LETTER CX.

To the same.

THERE are numberless employments in the courts of the Eastern monarchs utterly unpractised and unknown in Europe. They have no such officers, for instance, as the emperor's ear-tickler or tooth-picker; they have never introduced at the courts the mandarine appointed to bear the royal tobacco-box, or the grave director of the imperial exercitations in the seraglio. Yet I am surprised that the English have imitated us in none of these particulars, as they are generally pleased with everything that comes from China, and excessively fond of creating new and useless employments. They have filled their houses with our furniture, their public gardens with our fireworks, and their very ponds with our fish. Our courtiers, my friend, are the fish and the furniture they should have imported; our courtiers would fill up the necessary ceremonies of a court better than those of Europe; would be contented with receiving large salaries for doing little; whereas some of this country are at present discontented, though they receive large salaries for doing nothing.

I lately, therefore, had thoughts of publishing a proposal here, for the admission of some new Eastern offices and titles into their Court Register. As I consider myself in the light of a cosmopolite, I find as much satisfaction in scheming for the countries in which I happen to reside, as for that in which I was born.

The finest apartments in the palace of Pegu are frequently infested with rats. These the religion of the country strictly forbids the people to kill. In such circumstances, therefore, they are obliged to have recourse to some great man of the court, who is willing to free the royal apartment even at the hazard of his salvation. After a weak monarch's reign, the quantity of court vermin in every part of the palace is surprising; but a prudent king, and a vigilant officer, soon drive them from their sanctuaries behind the mats and tapestry, and effectually free the court. Such an officer in England would, in my opinion, be serviceable at this juncture; for if, as I am told, the palace be old, much vermin must undoubtedly have taken refuge behind the wainscot and hangings. A minister should therefore be invested with the title and dignities of court vermin-killer; he should have full power either to banish, take, poison, or destroy them, with enchantments, traps, ferrets, or ratsbane. He might be permitted to brandish his besom without remorse, and brush down every part of the furniture, without sparing a single cobweb, however sacred by long prescription. I communicated this proposal some days ago in a company of the first distinction, and enjoying the most honourable offices of the state. Among the number were the inspector of Great Britain, Mr. Henriquez the director of the ministry, Ben. Victor the treasurer, John Lockman the secretary, and the conductor of the Imperial Magazine. They all acquiesced in the utility of my proposal, but were apprehensive it might meet with some obstruction from court upholsterers and chambermaids, who would object to it from the demolition of the furniture, and the dangerous use of ferrets and ratsbane.

My next proposal is rather more general than the former, and might probably meet with less opposition. Though no people in the world flatter each other more than the English, I know none who understand the art less, and flatter with such little refinement. Their panegyric, like a Tartar feast, is indeed served up with profusion, but their cookery is insupportable. A client here shall dress up a fricassee for his patron, that shall offend an ordinary nose before it enters the room. A town shall send up their address to a great minister, which shall prove at once a satire on the minister and themselves. If the favourite of the day sits, or stands, or sleeps, there are poets to put it into verse, and priests to preach it in the pulpit. In order, therefore, to free both those who praise and those who are praised from a duty probably disagreeable to both, I would constitute professed flatterers here, as in several courts of India. These are appointed in the courts of their princes, to instruct the people where to exclaim with admiration, and where to lay an emphasis of praise. But an officer of this kind is always in waiting when the emperor converses in a familiar manner among his rajahs and other nobility. At every sentence, when the monarch pauses, and smiles at what he has been saying, the Karamatman, as this officer is called, is to take it for granted that his majesty has said a good thing. Upon which he cries out—"Karamat! Karamat!—a miracle! a miracle!" and throws up his hands and his eyes in ecstasy. This is echoed by the courtiers around, while the emperor sits all this time in sullen satisfaction, enjoying the triumph of his joke, or studying a new repartee.

I would have such an officer placed at every great man's table in England. By frequent practice he might soon become a perfect master of the art, and in time would turn out pleasing to his patron, no way troublesome to himself, and might prevent the nauseous attempts of many more ignorant pretenders. The clergy here, I am convinced, would relish this proposal. It would provide places for several of them. And, indeed, by some of their late productions many appear to have qualified themselves as candidates for this office already.

But my last proposal I take to be of the utmost importance. Our neighbour, the empress of Russia, has, you may remember, instituted an order of female knighthood; the empress of Germany has also instituted another; the Chinese have had such an order time immemorial. I am amazed the English have never come into such an institution. When I consider what kind of men are made knights here, it appears strange that they have never conferred this honour upon women. They make cheesemongers and pastrycooks knights; then, why not their wives? They have called up tallow chandlers to maintain the hardy profession of chivalry and arms; then, why not their wives? Haberdashers are sworn, as I suppose all knights must be sworn, NEVER TO FLY IN TIME OF MELLAY OR BATTLE, TO MAINTAIN AND UPHOLD THE NOBLE ESTATE OF CHIVALRY, WITH HORSE, HARNISHE, AND OTHER KNIGHTLYE HABILIMENTS. Haberdashers, I say, are sworn to all this; then, why not their wives? Certain I am, their wives understand fighting and feats of mellay and battle better than they; and as for knightlye horse and harnishe, it is probable both know nothing more than the harness of a one-horse chaise. No, no, my friend, instead of conferring any order upon the husbands, I would knight their wives. However, the state should not be troubled with a new institution upon this occasion. Some ancient exploded order might be revived, which would furnish both a motto and a name,—the ladies might be permitted to choose for themselves. There are, for instance, the obsolete orders of the Dragon in Germany, of the Rue in Scotland, and the Porcupine in France,—all well-sounding names, and very applicable to my intended female institution.—Adieu.

LETTER CXI.

To the same.

RELIGIOUS sects in England are far more numerous than in China. Every man who has interest enough to hire a conventicle here may set up for himself, and sell off a new religion. The sellers of the newest pattern at present give extreme good bargains, and let their disciples have a great deal of confidence for very little money.

Their shops are much frequented, and their customers every day increasing; for people are naturally fond of going to Paradise at as small expense as possible.

Yet you must not conceive this modern sect as differing in opinion from those of the established religion; difference of opinion, indeed, formerly divided their sectaries, and sometimes drew their armies to the field. White gowns and black mantles, flapped hats and cross pocket-holes, were once the obvious causes of quarrel; men then had some reason for fighting; they knew what they fought about: but at present they are arrived to such refinement in religion-making, that they have actually formed a new sect without a new opinion; they quarrel for opinions they both equally defend; they hate each other, and that is all the difference between them.

But though their principles are the same, their practice is somewhat different. Those of the established religion laugh when they are pleased, and their groans are seldom extorted but by pain or danger. The new sect, on the contrary, weep for their amusement, and use little music, except a chorus of sighs and groans, or tunes that are made to imitate groaning. Laughter is their aversion; lovers court each other from the Lamentations; the bridegroom approaches the nuptial couch in sorrowful solemnity, and the bride looks more dismal than an undertaker's shop. Dancing round the room is with them running in a direct line to the devil; and as for gaming, though but in jest, they would sooner play with a rattlesnake's tail than finger a dice-box.

By this time you perceive that I am describing a sect of enthusiasts, and you have already compared them with the Faquirs, Brahmins, and Talapoins of the East. Among these, you know, are generations that have never been known to smile, and voluntary affliction makes up all the merit they can boast of. Enthusiasm in every country produces the same effects: stick the Faquir with pins, or confine the Brahmin to a vermin hospital; spread the Talapoin on the ground, or load the sectary's brow with contrition—those worshippers who discard the light of reason are ever gloomy; their fears increase in proportion to their ignorance, as men are continually under apprehensions who walk in darkness.

Yet there is still a stronger reason for the enthusiast's being an enemy to laughter; namely, his being himself so proper an object of ridicule. It is remarkable, that the propagators of false doctrines have ever been averse to mirth, and always begin by recommending gravity, when they intended to disseminate imposture. Fohi, the idol of China, is represented as having never laughed; Zoroaster, the leader of the Brahmins, is said to have laughed but twice,—upon his coming into the world, and upon his leaving it; and Mahomet himself, though a lover of pleasure, was a professed opposer of gaiety. Upon a certain occasion, telling his followers that they would appear all naked at the resurrection, his favourite wife represented such an assembly as immodest and unbecoming. —"Foolish woman!" cried the grave prophet, "though the whole assembly be naked on that day, they shall have forgotten to laugh." Men like him opposed ridicule, because they knew it to be a most formidable antagonist, and preached up gravity, to conceal their own want of importance.

Ridicule has ever been the most powerful enemy of enthusiasm, and, properly, the only antagonist that can be opposed to it with success. Persecution only serves to propagate new religions: they acquire fresh vigour beneath the executioner and the axe, and, like some vivacious insects, multiply by dissection. It is also impossible to combat enthusiasm with reason; for, though it makes a show of resistance, it soon eludes the pressure, refers you to distinctions not to be understood, and feelings which it cannot explain. A man who would endeavour to fix an enthusiast by argument might as well attempt to spread quicksilver with his fingers. The only way to conquer a visionary is to despise him; the stake, the faggot, and the disputing doctor, in some measure ennoble the opinions they are brought to oppose: they are harmless against innovating pride; contempt alone is truly dreadful. Hunters generally know the most vulnerable part of the beasts they pursue, by the care which every animal takes to defend the side which is weakest: on what side the enthusiast is most vulnerable may be known by the care which he takes in the beginning to work his disciples into gravity, and guard them against the power of ridicule.

When Philip the Second was king of Spain, there was a contest in Salamanca between two orders of friars for superiority. The legend of one side contained more extraordinary miracles, but the legend of the other was reckoned most authentic. They reviled each other, as is usual in disputes of divinity, the people were divided into factions, and a civil war appeared unavoidable. In order to prevent such an imminent calamity, the combatants were prevailed upon to submit their legends to the fiery trial, and that which came forth untouched by the fire was to have the victory, and to be honoured with a double share of reverence. Whenever the people flock to see a miracle, it is a hundred to one but that they see a miracle; incredible, therefore, were the numbers that were gathered round upon this occasion. The friars on each side approached, and confidently threw their respective legends into the flames, when, lo! to the utter disappointment of all the assembly, instead of a miracle, both legends were consumed. Nothing but this turning both parties into contempt could have prevented the effusion of blood. The people now laughed at their former folly, and wondered why they fell out.—Adieu.

LETTER CXII.

To the same.

THE English are at present employed in celebrating a feast, which becomes general every seventh year; the parliament of the nation being then dissolved, and another appointed to be chosen. This solemnity falls infinitely short of our Feast of the Lanterns in magnificence and splendour; it is also surpassed by others of the East in unanimity and pure devotion; but no festival in the world can compare with it for eating. Their eating, indeed, amazes me; had I five hundred heads, and were each head furnished with brains, yet would they all be insufficient to compute the number of cows, pigs, geese, and turkeys, which, upon this occasion, die for the good of their country.

To say the truth, eating seems to make a grand ingredient in all English parties of zeal, business, or amusement. When a church is to be built, or an hospital endowed, the directors assemble, and instead of consulting upon it, they eat upon it, by which means the business goes forward with success. When the poor are to be relieved, the officers appointed to dole out public charity assemble and eat upon it. Nor has it ever been known that they filled the bellies of the poor, till they had previously satisfied their own. But in the election of magistrates the people seem to exceed all bounds: the merits of a candidate are often measured by the number of his treats; his constituents assemble, eat upon him, and lend their applause, not to his integrity or sense, but to the quantities of his beef and brandy.

And yet I could forgive this people their plentiful meals on this occasion, as it is extremely natural for every man to eat a great deal when he gets it for nothing; but what amazes me is, that all this good living no way contributes to improve their good humour. On the contrary, they seem to lose their temper as they lose their appetites; every morsel they swallow, and every glass they pour down, serves to increase their animosity. Many an honest man, before as harmless as a tame rabbit, when loaded with a single election dinner, has become more dangerous than a charged culverin. Upon one of these occasions I have actually seen a bloody-minded man-milliner sally forth at the head of a mob, determined to face a desperate pastrycook, who was general of the opposite party.

But you must not suppose they are without a pretext for thus beating each other. On the contrary, no man here is so uncivilized as to beat his neighbour without producing very sufficient reasons. One candidate, for instance, treats with gin, a spirit of their own manufacture; another always drinks brandy, imported from abroad. Brandy is a wholesome liquor; gin, a liquor wholly their own. This, then, furnishes an obvious cause of quarrel,—Whether it be most reasonable to get drunk with gin, or get drunk with brandy? The mob meet upon the debate, fight themselves sober, and then draw off to get drunk again, and charge for another encounter. So that the English may now properly be said to be engaged in war; since, while they are subduing their enemies abroad, they are breaking each other's heads at home.

I lately made an excursion to a neighbouring village, in order to be a spectator of the ceremonies practised upon this occasion. I left town in company with three fiddlers, nine dozen of hams, and a corporation poet, which were designed as reinforcements to the gin-drinking party. We entered the town with a very good face; the fiddlers, no way intimidated by the enemy, kept handling their arms up the principal street. By this prudent manœuvre, they took peaceable possession of their head-quarters, amidst the shouts of multitudes, who seemed perfectly rejoiced at hearing their music, but above all at seeing their bacon.

I must own, I could not avoid being pleased to see all ranks of people, on this occasion, levelled into an equality, and the poor, in some measure, enjoying the primitive privileges of nature. If there was any distinction shown, the lowest of the people seemed to receive it from the rich. I could perceive a cobbler with a levee at his door, and a haberdasher giving audience from behind his counter.

But my reflections were soon interrupted by a mob, who demanded whether I was for the distillery or the brewery? As these were terms with which I was totally unacquainted, I chose at first to be silent; however, I know not what might have been the consequence of my reserve, had not the attention of the mob been called off to a skirmish between a brandy-drinker's cow and a gin-drinker's mastiff, which turned out, greatly to the satisfaction of the mob, in favour of the mastiff.

This spectacle, which afforded high entertainment, was at last ended by the appearance of one of the candidates, who came to harangue the mob: he made a very pathetic speech upon the late excessive importation of foreign drams, and the downfall of the distillery; I could see some of the audience shed tears. He was accompanied in his procession by Mrs. Deputy and Mrs. Mayoress. Mrs. Deputy was not in the least in liquor; and as for Mrs. Mayoress, one of the spectators assured me in my ear, that—she was a very fine woman before she had the small-pox.

Mixing with the crowd, I was now conducted to the hall where the magistrates are chosen: but what tongue can describe this scene of confusion! the whole crowd seemed equally inspired with anger, jealousy, politics, patriotism, and punch. I remarked one figure that was carried up by two men upon this occasion. I at first began to pity his infirmities as natural, but soon found the fellow so drunk that he could not stand; another made his appearance to give his vote, but though he could stand, he actually lost the use of his tongue, and remained silent; a third, who, though excessively drunk, could both stand and speak, being asked the candidate's name for whom he voted, could be prevailed upon to make no other answer but "Tobacco and brandy." In short, an election hall seems to be a theatre, where every passion is seen without disguise; a school where fools may readily become worse, and where philosophers may gather wisdom.—Adieu.

LETTER CXIII.

To the same.

THE disputes among the learned here are now carried on in a much more compendious manner than formerly. There was a time when folio was brought to oppose folio, and a champion was often listed for life under the banners of a single sorites. At present the controversy is decided in a summary way; an epigram or an acrostic finishes the debate, and the combatant, like the incursive Tartar, advances and retires with a single blow.

An important literary debate at present engrosses the attention of the town. It is carried on with sharpness, and a proper share of this epigrammatical fury. An author, it seems, has taken an aversion to the faces of several players, and has written verses to prove his dislike; the players fall upon the author, and assure the town he must be dull, and their faces must be good, because he wants a dinner: a critic comes to the poet's assistance, asserting that the verses were perfectly original, and so smart, that he could never have written them without the assistance of friends; the friends, upon this, arraign the critic, and plainly prove the verses to be all the author's own. So at it they are, all four together by the ears; the friends at the critic, the critic at the players, the players at the author, and the author at the players again. It is impossible to determine how this many-sided contest will end, or which party to adhere to. The town, without siding with any, views the combat in suspense, like the fabled hero of antiquity, who beheld the earth-born brothers give and receive mutual wounds, and fall by indiscriminate destruction.

This is, in some measure, the state of the present dispute; but the combatants here differ in one respect from the champions of the fable. Every new wound only gives vigour for another blow; though they appear to strike, they are in fact mutually swelling themselves into consideration, and thus advertising each other into fame. "To-day," says one, "my name shall be in the Gazette, the next day my rival's; people will naturally inquire about us; thus we shall at least make a noise in the streets, though we have got nothing to sell." I have read of a dispute of a similar nature, which was managed here about twenty years ago. Hildebrand Jacob, as I think he was called, and Charles Johnson were poets, both at that time possessed of great reputation; for Johnson had written eleven plays, acted with great success; and Jacob, though he had written but five, had five times thanked the town for their unmerited applause. They soon became mutually enamoured of each other's talents; they wrote, they felt, they challenged the town for each other. Johnson assured the public, that no poet alive had the easy simplicity of Jacob, and Jacob exhibited Johnson as a masterpiece in the pathetic. Their mutual praise was not without effect; the town saw their plays, were in raptures, read, and, without censuring them, forgot them. So formidable an union, however, was soon opposed by Tibbald. Tibbald asserted that the tragedies of the one had faults, and the comedies of the other substituted wit for vivacity: the combined champions flew at him like tigers, arraigned the censurer's judgment, and impeached his sincerity. It was a long time a dispute among the learned, which was in fact the greatest man, Jacob, Johnson, or Tibbald; they had all written for the stage with great success, their names were seen in almost every paper, and their works in every coffee-house. However, in the hottest of the dispute, a fourth combatant made his appearance, and swept away the three combatants, tragedy, comedy, and all, into undistinguished ruin.

From this time they seemed consigned into the hands of criticism; scarce a day passed in which they were not arraigned as detested writers. The critics, those enemies of Dryden and Pope, were their enemies. So Jacob and Johnson, instead of mending by criticism, called it envy; and because Dryden and Pope were censured, they compared themselves to Dryden and Pope.

But to return. The weapon chiefly used in the present controversy is epigram; and certainly never was a keener made use of. They have discovered surprising sharpness on both sides. The first that came out upon this occasion was a new kind of composition in this way, and might more properly be called an epigrammatic thesis, than an epigram. It consists, first, of an argument in prose; next follows a motto from Roscommon; then comes the epigram; and, lastly, notes serving to explain the epigram. But you shall have it with all its decorations.

AN EPIGRAM,

ADDRESSED TO THE GENTLEMAN REFLECTED ON IN THE ROSCIAD, A POEM, BY THE AUTHOR.

Worried with debts, and past all hopes of bail,
His pen he prostitutes, t' avoid a jail.—ROSCOMMON.

Let not the *hungry* Bavius' angry stroke
Awake resentment, or your rage provoke;
But pitying his distress, let virtue shine,
And giving each your bounty, *let him dine;*
For, thus retained, as learned counsel can,
Each case, however bad, he'll new japan,
And, by a quick transition, plainly show
'Twas no defect of yours, but *pocket low,*
That caused his *putrid kennel* to o'erflow.

The last lines are certainly executed in a very masterly manner. It is of that species of argumentation, called the perplexing. It effectually flings the antagonist into a mist; there is no answering it: the laugh is raised against him, while he is endeavouring to find out the jest. At once he shows, that the author has a kennel, and that his kennel is putrid, and that his putrid kennel overflows. But why does it overflow? It overflows, because the author happens to have low pockets!

There was also another new attempt in this way; a prosaic epigram which came out upon this occasion. This is so full of matter, that a critic might split it into fifteen epigrams, each properly fitted with its sting. You shall see it.

TO G. C. AND R. L.

'Twas you, or I, or he, or all together;
'Twas one, both, three of them, they know not whether.
This I believe, between us great or small,
You, I, he, wrote it not—'twas Churchill's all.

There, there's a perplex! I could have wished, to make it quite perfect, the author, as in the case before, had added notes. Almost every word admits a scholium, and a long one too. I, YOU, HE! Suppose a stranger should ask, "and who are you?" Here are three obscure persons spoken of, that may in a short time be utterly forgotten. Their names should have consequently been mentioned in notes at the bottom. But when the reader comes to the words *great* and *small,* the maze is inextricable. Here the stranger may dive for a mystery, without ever reaching the bottom. Let him know, then, that *small* is a word purely introduced to make good rhyme, and *great* was a very proper word to keep *small* company.

Yet, by being thus a spectator of others' dangers, I must own I begin to tremble in this literary contest for my own. I begin to fear that my challenge to Dr. Rock was unadvised, and has procured me more antagonists than I had at first expected. I have received private letters from several of the literati here, that fill my soul with apprehension. I may safely aver, that I never gave any creature in this good city offence, except only my rival Dr. Rock; yet by the letters I every day receive, and by some I have seen printed, I am arraigned at one time as being a dull fellow, at another as being pert; I am here petulant, there I am heavy. By the head of my ancestors, they treat me with more inhumanity than a flying fish. If I dive and run my nose to the bottom, there a devouring shark is ready to swallow me up; if I skim the surface, a pack of dolphins are at my tail to snap me; but when I take wing, and attempt to escape them by flight, I become a prey to every ravenous bird that winnows the bosom of the deep.—Adieu.

LETTER CXIV.

To the same.

THE formalities, delays, and disappointments that precede a treaty of marriage here are usually as numerous as those previous to a treaty of peace. The laws of this country are finely calculated to promote all commerce but the commerce between the sexes. Their encouragements for propagating hemp, madder, and tobacco, are indeed admirable: marriages are the only commodity that meets with none.

Yet from the vernal softness of the air, the verdure of the fields, the transparency of the streams, and the beauty of the women, I know few countries more proper to invite to courtship. Here Love might sport among painted lawns and warbling groves, and revel upon gales, wafting at once both fragrance and harmony. Yet it seems he has forsaken the island; and, when a couple are now to be married, mutual love, or an union of minds, is the last and most trifling consideration. If their goods and chattels can be brought to unite, their sympathetic souls are ever ready to guarantee the treaty. The gentleman's mortgaged lawn becomes enamoured of the lady's marriageable grove: the match is struck up, and both parties are piously in love—according to act of parliament.

Thus they who have fortune are possessed at least of something that is lovely; but I actually pity those that have none. I am told there was a time when ladies, with no other merit but youth, virtue, and beauty, had a chance for husbands, at least among the ministers of the church, or the officers of the army. The blush and innocence of sixteen was said to have a powerful influence over these two professions. But of late all the little traffic of blushing, ogling, dimpling, and smiling, has been forbidden by an act in that case wisely made and provided. A lady's whole cargo of smiles, sighs, and whispers, is declared utterly contraband, till she arrives in the warm latitudes of twenty-two, where commodities of this nature are too often found to decay. She is then permitted to dimple and smile when the dimples and smiles begin to forsake her; and, when perhaps grown ugly, is charitably entrusted with an unlimited use of her charms. Her lovers, however, by this time have forsaken her: the captain has changed for another mistress; the priest himself leaves her in solitude to bewail her virginity; and she dies even without benefit of clergy.

Thus you find the Europeans discouraging Love with as much earnestness as the rudest savage of Sofala. The Genius is surely now no more. In every region I find enemies in arms to oppress him. Avarice in Europe, jealousy in Persia, ceremony in China, poverty among the Tartars, and lust in Circassia, are all prepared to oppose his power. The Genius is certainly banished from earth, though once adored under such a variety of forms. He is nowhere to be found; and all that the ladies in each country can produce are but a few trifling relics, as instances of his former residence and favour.

"The Genius of Love," says the Eastern apologue, "had long resided in the happy plains of Abra, where every breeze was health, and every sound produced tranquillity. His temple at first was crowded, but every age lessened the number of his votaries, or cooled their devotion. Perceiving, therefore, his altars at length quite deserted, he was resolved to remove to some more propitious region, and he apprised the fair sex of every country where he could hope for a proper reception, to assert their right to his presence among them. In return to this proclamation embassies were sent from the ladies of every part of the world to invite him, and to display the superiority of their claims.

"And first the beauties of China appeared. No country could compare with them for modesty, either of look, dress, or behaviour: their eyes were never lifted from the ground; their robes of the most beautiful silk hid their hands, bosom, and neck, while their faces only were left uncovered. They indulged no airs that might express loose desire, and they seemed to study only the graces of inanimate beauty. Their black teeth and plucked eyebrows were, however, alleged by the Genius against them, and he set them entirely aside when he came to examine their little feet.

"The beauties of Circassia next made their appearance. They advanced hand-in-hand, singing the most immodest airs, and leading up a dance in the most luxurious attitudes. Their dress was but half a covering; the neck, the left breast, and all the limbs, were exposed to view, which, after some time, seemed rather to satiate than inflame desire. The lily and the rose contended in forming their complexions; and a soft sleepiness of eye added irresistible poignancy to their charms: but their beauties were obtruded, not offered, to their admirers; they seemed to give, rather than receive, courtship; and the Genius of Love dismissed them as unworthy his regard, since they exchanged the duties of love, and made themselves not the pursued, but the pursuing sex.

"The kingdom of Cashmire next produced its charming deputies. This happy region seemed peculiarly sequestered by nature for his abode. Shady mountains fenced it on one side from the scorching sun, and sea-borne breezes on the other gave peculiar luxuriance to the air. Their complexions were of a bright yellow, that appeared almost transparent, while the crimson tulip seemed to blossom on their cheeks. Their features and limbs were delicate beyond the statuary's power to express, and their teeth whiter than their own ivory. He was almost persuaded to reside among them, when unfortunately one of the ladies talked of appointing his seraglio.

"In this procession the naked inhabitants of Southern America would not be left behind; their charms were found to surpass whatever the warmest imagination could conceive, and served to show, that beauty could be perfect, even with the seeming disadvantage of a brown complexion. But their savage education rendered them utterly unqualified to make the proper use of their power, and they were rejected as being incapable of uniting mental with sensual satisfaction. In this manner the deputies of other kingdoms had their suits rejected: the black beauties of Benin, and the tawny daughters of Borneo; the women of Wida, with well-scarred faces, and the hideous virgins of Caffraria; the squab ladies of Lapland, three feet high, and the giant fair ones of Patagonia.

"The beauties of Europe at last appeared: grace was in their steps, and sensibility sat smiling in every eye. It was the universal opinion while they were approaching, that they would prevail; and the Genius seemed to lend them his most favourable attention. They opened their pretensions with the utmost modesty; but unfortunately, as their orator proceeded, she happened to let fall the words, 'house in town, settlement, and pin-money.' These seemingly harmless terms had instantly a surprising effect: the Genius with ungovernable rage burst from amidst the circle; and, waving his youthful pinions, left this earth, and flew back to those ethereal mansions from whence he descended.

"The whole assembly was struck with amazement; they now justly apprehended, that female power would be no more, since Love had forsaken them. They continued some time thus in a state of torpid despair, when it was proposed by one of the number, that since the real Genius had left them, in order to continue their power, they should set up an idol in his stead; and that the ladies of every country should furnish him with what each liked best. This proposal was instantly relished and agreed to. An idol was formed by uniting the capricious gifts of all the assembly, though no way resembling the departed Genius. The ladies of China furnished the monster with wings; those of Cashmire supplied him with horns; the dames of Europe clapped a purse in his hand; and the virgins of Congo furnished him with a tail. Since that time all the vows addressed to Love are in reality paid to the idol; but, as in other false religions, the adoration seems most fervent where the heart is least sincere."—Adieu.

LETTER CXV.

To the same.

MANKIND have ever been prone to expatiate in the praise of human nature. The dignity of man is a subject that has always been the favourite theme of humanity: they have declaimed with that ostentation which usually acompanies such as are sure of having a partial audience; they have obtained victories because there were none to oppose. Yet, from all I have ever read or seen, men appear more apt to err by having too high, than by having too despicable an opinion of their nature; and, by attempting to exalt their original place in creation, depress their real value in society.

The most ignorant nations have always been found to think most highly of themselves. The Deity has ever been thought peculiarly concerned in their glory and preservation; to have fought their battles, and inspired their teachers: their wizards are said to be familiar with heaven; and every hero has a guard of angels, as well as men, to attend him. When the Portuguese first came among the wretched inhabitants of the coast of Africa, these savage nations readily allowed the strangers more skill in navigation and war; yet still considered them at best but as useful servants, brought to their coast by their guardian serpent, to supply them with luxuries they could have lived without. Though they could grant the Portuguese more riches, they could never allow them to have such a king as their Tottimondelem, who wore a bracelet of shells round his neck, and whose legs were covered with ivory.

In this manner, examine a savage in the history of his country and predecessors, you ever find his warriors able to conquer armies, and his sages acquainted with more than possible knowledge. Human nature is to him an unknown country: he thinks it capable of great things, because he is ignorant of its boundaries; whatever can be conceived to be done, he allows to be possible, and whatever is possible, he conjectures must have been done. He never measures the actions and powers of others by what himself is able to perform; nor makes a proper estimate of the greatness of his fellows, by bringing it to the standard of his own incapacity. He is satisfied to be one of a country where mighty things have been; and imagines the fancied powers of others reflect a lustre on himself. Thus, by degrees, he loses the idea of his own insignificance in a confused notion of the extraordinary powers of humanity, and is willing to grant extraordinary gifts to every pretender, because unacquainted with their claims.

This is the reason why demigods and heroes have ever been erected in times or countries of ignorance and barbarity: they addressed a people who had high opinions of human nature, because they were ignorant how far it could extend; they addressed a people who were willing to allow that men should be gods, because they were yet imperfectly acquainted with God and with man. These impostors knew, that all men are naturally fond of seeing something very great made from little materials of humanity; that ignorant nations are not more proud of building a tower to reach heaven, or a pyramid to last for ages, than of raising up a demigod of their own country and creation. The same pride that erects a colossus or a pyramid instals a god or an hero; but though the adoring savage can raise his colossus to the clouds, he can exalt the hero not one inch above the standard of humanity: incapable, therefore, of exalting the idol, he debases himself, and falls prostrate before him.

When man has thus acquired an erroneous idea of the dignity of his species, he and the gods become perfectly intimate; men are but angels, angels are but men—nay, but servants, that stand in waiting to execute human commands. The Persians, for instance, thus address their prophet Haly: "I salute thee, glorious Creator, of whom the sun is but the shadow. Masterpiece of the Lord of human creatures, great star of justice and religion! The sea is not rich and liberal but by the gifts of thy munificent hands. The angel treasurer of heaven reaps his harvest in the fertile gardens of the purity of thy nature. The *primum mobile* would never dart the ball of the sun through the trunk of heaven, were it not to serve the morning, out of the extreme love she has for thee. The angel Gabriel, messenger of truth, every day kisses the groundsel of thy gate. Were there a place more exalted than the most high throne of God, I would affirm it to be thy place, O master of the faithful! Gabriel, with all his art and knowledge, is but a mere scholar to thee." Thus, my friend, men think proper to treat angels; but if indeed there be such an order of beings, with what a degree of satirical contempt must they listen to the songs of little mortals thus flattering each other: thus to see creatures, wiser indeed than the monkey, and more active than the oyster, claiming to themselves the mastery of heaven! minims, the tenants of an atom, thus arrogating a partnership in the creation of universal nature! Sure Heaven is kind, that launches no thunder at those guilty heads: but it is kind, and regards their follies with pity, nor will destroy creatures that it loved into being.

But whatever success this practice of making demigods might have been attended with in barbarous nations, I do not know that any man became a god in a country where the inhabitants were refined. Such countries generally have too close an inspection into human weakness, to think it invested with celestial power. They sometimes indeed admit the gods of strangers, or of their ancestors, which had their existence in times of obscurity; their weakness being forgotten, while nothing but their power and their miracles were remembered. The Chinese, for instance, never had a god of their own country: the idols which the vulgar worship at this day were brought from the barbarous nations around them. The Roman emperors who pretended to divinity were generally taught by a poniard that they were mortal; and Alexander, though he passed among barbarous countries for a real god, could never persuade his polite countrymen into a similitude of thinking. The Lacedemonians shrewdly complied with his commands by the following sarcastic edict:—

Εἰ Ἀλέξανδρος βούλεται εἶναι θεὸς, θεὸς ἔστω.

Adieu.

LETTER CXVI.

To the same.

THERE is something irresistibly pleasing in the conversation of a fine woman; even though her tongue be silent, the eloquence of her eyes teaches wisdom. The mind sympathises with the regularity of the object in view, and, struck with external grace, vibrates into respondent harmony. In this agreeable disposition, I lately found myself in company with my friend and his niece. Our conversation turned upon love, which she seemed equally capable of defending and inspiring. We were each of different opinions upon this subject: the lady insisted that it was a natural and universal passion, and produced the happiness of those who cultivated it with proper precaution; my friend denied it to be the work of nature, but allowed it to have a real existence, and affirmed, that it was of infinite service in refining society; while I, to keep up the dispute, affirmed it to be merely a name, first used by the cunning part of the fair sex, and admitted by the silly part of ours; therefore no way more natural than taking snuff, or chewing opium.

"How is it possible," cried I, "that such a passion can be natural, when our opinions even of beauty, which inspires it, are entirely the result of fashion and caprice? The ancients, who pretended to be connoisseurs in the art, have praised narrow foreheads, red hair, and eyebrows that joined each other above the nose. Such were the charms that once captivated Catullus, Ovid, and Anacreon. Ladies would at present be out of humour, if their lovers praised them for such graces; and should an antique beauty now revive, her face would certainly be put under the discipline of the tweezer, forehead-cloth, and lead comb, before it could be seen in public company.

"But the difference between the ancients and moderns is not so great as between the different countries of the present world. A lover of Gongora, for instance, sighs for thick lips: a Chinese lover is poetical in praise of thin. In Circassia a straight nose is thought most consistent with beauty: cross but a mountain which separates it from the Tartars, and there flat noses, tawny skins, and eyes three inches asunder, are all the fashion. In Persia, and some other countries, a man, when he marries, chooses to have his bride a maid: in the Philippine Islands, if a bridegroom happens to perceive, on the first night, that he is put off with a virgin, the marriage is declared void to all intents and purposes, and the bride sent back with disgrace. In some parts of the East a woman of beauty, properly fed up for sale, often amounts to one hundred crowns: in the kingdom of Loango ladies of the very best fashion are sold for a pig; queens, however, sell better, and sometimes amount to a cow. In short, turn even to England, don't I there see the beautiful part of the sex neglected; and none now marrying or making love, but old men and old women that have saved money? Don't I see beauty from fifteen to twenty-one rendered null and void to all intents and purposes, and those six precious years of womanhood put under a statute of virginity? What! shall I call that rancid passion love, which passes between an old bachelor of fifty-six and a widow lady of forty-nine? Never, never! what advantage is society to reap from an intercourse, where the big belly is oftenest on the man's side? Would any persuade me that such a passion was natural, unless the human race were more fit for love as they approached the decline, and, like silk worms, became breeders just before they expired?"

"Whether love be natural or no," replied

my friend gravely, "it contributes to the happiness of every society into which it is introduced. All our pleasures are short, and can only charm at intervals; love is a method of protracting our greatest pleasure; and surely that gamester who plays the greatest stake to the best advantage, will, at the end of life, rise victorious. This was the opinion of Vanini, who affirmed, that every hour was lost which was not spent in love. His accusers were unable to comprehend his meaning, and the poor advocate for love was burned in flames—alas! no way metaphorical. But whatever advantages the individual may reap from this passion, society will certainly be refined and improved by its introduction: all laws calculated to discourage it tend to imbrute the species and weaken the state. Though it cannot plant morals in the human breast, it cultivates them when there: pity, generosity, and honour receive a brighter polish from its assistance; and a single amour is sufficient entirely to brush off the clown.

"But it is an exotic of the most delicate constitution: it requires the greatest art to introduce it into a state, and the smallest discouragement is sufficient to repress it again. Let us only consider with what ease it was formerly extinguished in Rome, and with what difficulty it was lately revived in Europe; it seemed to sleep for ages, and at last fought its way among us, through tilts, tournaments, dragons, and all the dreams of chivalry. The rest of the world, China only excepted, are, and have ever been, utter strangers to its delights and advantages. In other countries, as men find themselves stronger than women, they lay claim to a rigorous superiority; this is natural, and love, which gives up this natural advantage, must certainly be the effect of art—an art calculated to lengthen out our happier moments, and add new graces to society."

"I entirely acquiesce in your sentiments," says the lady, "with regard to the advantages of this passion, but cannot avoid giving it a nobler origin than you have been pleased to assign. I must think, that those countries where it is rejected are obliged to have recourse to art, to stifle so natural a production: and those nations where it is cultivated, only make nearer advances to nature. The same efforts that are used in some places to suppress pity, and other natural passions, may have been employed to extinguish love. No nation, however unpolished, is remarkable for innocence, that is not famous for passion; it has flourished in the coldest, as well as in the warmest regions. Even in the sultry wilds of Southern America the lover is not satisfied with possessing his mistress's person, without having her mind:

In all my Enna's beauties blest,
Amidst profusion still I pine;
For though she gives me up her breast,
Its panting tenant is not mine.

"But the effects of love are too violent to be the result of an artificial passion. Nor is it in the power of fashion to force the constitution into those changes which we every day observe. Several have died of it. Few lovers are unacquainted with the fate of the two Italian lovers, Da Corsin and Julia Bellamano, who, after a long separation, expired with pleasure in each other's arms. Such instances are too strong confirmations of the reality of the passion, and serve to show that suppressing it is but opposing the natural dictates of the heart."—Adieu.

LETTER CXVII.

To the same.

THE clock just struck two, the expiring taper rises and sinks in the socket, the watchman forgets the hour in slumber, the laborious and the happy are at rest, and nothing wakes but meditation, guilt, revelry, and despair. The drunkard once more fills the destroying bowl, the robber walks his midnight round, and the suicide lifts his guilty arm against his own sacred person.

Let me no longer waste the night over the page of antiquity, or the sallies of contemporary genius, but pursue the solitary walk, where vanity, ever changing, but a few hours past walked before me; where she kept up the pageant, and now, like a froward child, seems hushed with her own importunities.

What a gloom hangs all around! The dying lamp feebly emits a yellow gleam;

no sound is heard but of the chiming clock, or the distant watch-dog. All the bustle of human pride is forgotten ; an hour like this may well display the emptiness of human vanity.

There will come a time, when this temporary solitude may be made continual, and the city itself, like its inhabitants, fade away, and leave a desert in its room.

What cities as great as this have once triumphed in existence, had their victories as great, joy as just, and as unbounded ; and, with short-sighted presumption, promised themselves immortality ! Posterity can hardly trace the situation of some ; the sorrowful traveller wanders over the awful ruins of others ; and, as he beholds, he learns wisdom, and feels the transience of every sublunary possession.

"Here," he cries, "stood their citadel, now grown over with weeds ; there their senate house, but now the haunt of every noxious reptile ; temples and theatres stood here, now only an undistinguished heap of ruin. They are fallen, for luxury and avarice first made them feeble. The rewards of the state were conferred on amusing and not on useful members of society. Their riches and opulence invited the invaders, who, though at first repulsed, returned again, conquered by perseverance, and at last swept the defendants into undistinguished destruction."

How few appear in those streets which but some few hours ago were crowded ! and those who appear now no longer wear their daily mask, nor attempt to hide their lewdness or their misery.

But who are those who make the streets their couch, and find a short repose from wretchedness at the doors of the opulent? These are strangers, wanderers, and orphans, whose circumstances are too humble to expect redress, and whose distresses are too great even for pity. Their wretchedness excites rather horror than pity. Some are without the covering even of rags, and others emaciated with disease ; the world has disclaimed them ; society turns its back upon their distress, and has given them up to nakedness and hunger. These poor shivering females have once seen happier days, and been flattered into beauty. They have been prostituted to the gay luxurious villain, and are now turned out to meet the severity of winter. Perhaps, now lying at the doors of their betrayers, they sue to wretches whose hearts are insensible, or debauchees who may curse, but will not relieve them.

Why, why was I born a man, and yet see the sufferings of wretches I cannot relieve? Poor houseless creatures ! the world will give you reproaches, but will not give you relief. The slightest misfortunes of the great, the most imaginary uneasiness of the rich, are aggravated with all the power of eloquence, and held up to engage our attention and sympathetic sorrow. The poor weep unheeded, persecuted by every subordinate species of tyranny ; and every law which gives others security, becomes an enemy to them.

Why was this heart of mine formed with so much sensibility? or why was not my fortune adapted to its impulse? Tenderness, without a capacity of relieving, only makes the man who feels it more wretched than the object which sues for assistance. —Adieu.

LETTER CXVIII.

From Fum Hoam to Lien Chi Altangi, the Discontented Wanderer, by the way of Moscow.

I HAVE been just sent upon an embassy to Japan ; my commission is to be despatched in four days, and you can hardly conceive the pleasure I shall find upon revisiting my native country. I shall leave with joy this proud, barbarous, inhospitable region, where every object conspires to diminish my satisfaction, and increase my patriotism.

But though I find the inhabitants savage, yet the Dutch merchants who are permitted to trade hither seem still more detestable. They have raised my dislike to Europe in general : by them I learn how low avarice can degrade human nature ; how many indignities an European will suffer for gain.

I was present at an audience given by the emperor to the Dutch envoy, who had sent several presents to all the courtiers, some days previous to his admission ; but he was obliged to attend those designed for the emperor himself. From the accounts I had heard of this ceremony, my curiosity prompted me to be a spectator of the whole.

First went the presents, set out on beautiful enamelled tables, adorned with flowers, borne on men's shoulders, and followed by Japanese music and dancers. From so great respect paid to the gifts themselves, I had fancied the donors must have received almost divine honours. But, about a quarter of an hour after the presents had been carried in triumph, the envoy and his train were brought forward. They were covered from head to foot with long black veils, which prevented their seeing, each led by a conductor, chosen from the meanest of the people. In this dishonourable manner, having traversed the city of Jeddo, they at length arrived at the palace gate; and, after waiting half an hour, were admitted into the guard-room. Here their eyes were uncovered, and in about an hour the gentleman usher introduced them into the hall of audience. The emperor was at length shown, sitting in a kind of alcove at the upper end of the room, and the Dutch envoy was conducted towards the throne.

As soon as he had approached within a certain distance, the gentleman usher cried out with a loud voice, "Holanda Capitan;" upon these words the envoy fell flat upon the ground, and crept upon his hands and feet towards the throne. Still approaching, he reared himself upon his knees, and then bowed his forehead to the ground. These ceremonies being over, he was directed to withdraw, still grovelling on his belly, and going backward like a lobster.

Men must be excessively fond of riches, when they are earned with such circumstances of abject submission. Do the Europeans worship Heaven itself with marks of more profound respect? Do they confer those honours on the Supreme of Beings, which they pay to a barbarous king, who gives them a permission to purchase trinkets and porcelain? What a glorious exchange, to forfeit their national honour, and even their title to humanity, for a screen or a snuff-box!

If these ceremonies essayed in the first audience appeared mortifying, those which were practised in the second were infinitely more so. In the second audience the emperor and the ladies of the court were placed behind lattices, in such a manner as to see, without being seen. Here all the Europeans were directed to pass in review, and grovel and act the serpent as before: with this spectacle the whole court seemed highly delighted. The strangers were asked a thousand ridiculous questions, as their names, and their ages; they were ordered to write, to stand upright, to sit, to stoop, to compliment each other, to be drunk, to speak the Japanese language, to talk Dutch, to sing, to eat; in short, they were ordered to do all that could satisfy the curiosity of woman.

Imagine, my dear Altangi, a set of grave men thus transformed into buffoons, and acting a part every whit as honourable as that of those instructed animals which are shown in the streets of Pekin to the mob on a holiday. Yet the ceremony did not end here, for every great lord of the court was to be visited in the same manner; and their ladies, who took the whim from their husbands, were all equally fond of seeing the strangers perform, even the children seeming highly diverted with the dancing Dutchmen.

"Alas!" cried I to myself, upon returning from such a spectacle, "is this the nation which assumes such dignity at the court of Pekin? Is this the people that appear so proud at home, and in every country where they have the least authority? How does a love of gain transform the gravest of mankind into the most contemptible and ridiculous! I had rather continue poor all my life, than become rich at such a rate. Perish those riches which are acquired at the expense of my honour or my humanity! Let me quit," said I, "a country where there are none but such as treat all others like slaves, and more detestable still, in suffering such treatment. I have seen enough of this nation to desire to see more of others. Let me leave a people suspicious to excess, whose morals are corrupted, and equally debased by superstition and vice; where the sciences are left uncultivated, where the great are slaves to the prince, and tyrants to the people; where the women are chaste only when debarred of the power of transgression; where the true disciples of Confucius are not less persecuted than those of Christianity; in a word, a country where men are forbidden to think, and consequently labour under the most miserable slavery,—that of mental servitude.—Adieu.

LETTER CXIX.

From Lien Chi Altangi to Fum Hoam, First President of the Ceremonial Academy at Pekin in China.

THE misfortunes of the great, my friend, are held up to engage our attention, are enlarged upon in tones of declamation, and the world is called upon to gaze at the noble sufferers: they have at once the comfort of admiration and pity.

Yet, where is the magnanimity of bearing misfortunes when the whole world is looking on? Men in such circumstances can act bravely even from motives of vanity. He only who in the vale of obscurity can brave adversity—who, without friends to encourage, acquaintances to pity, or even without hope to alleviate his distresses, can behave with tranquillity and indifference, is truly great: whether peasant or courtier, he deserves admiration, and should be held up for our imitation and respect.

The miseries of the poor are, however, entirely disregarded; though some undergo more real hardships in one day, than the great in their whole lives. It is indeed inconceivable what difficulties the meanest English sailor or soldier endures without murmuring or regret. Every day to him is a day of misery, and yet he bears his hard fate without repining.

With what indignation do I hear the heroes of tragedy complain of misfortunes and hardships, whose greatest calamity is founded in arrogance and pride! Their severest distresses are pleasures compared to what many of the adventuring poor every day sustain, without murmuring. These may eat, drink, and sleep; have slaves to attend them, and are sure of subsistence for life; while many of their fellow-creatures are obliged to wander, without a friend to comfort or to assist them, find enmity in every law, and are too poor to obtain even justice.

I have been led into these reflections from accidentally meeting, some days ago, a poor fellow begging at one of the outlets of this town, with a wooden leg. I was curious to learn what had reduced him to his present situation; and, after giving him what I thought proper, desired to know the history of his life and misfortunes, and the manner in which he was reduced to his present distress. The disabled soldier, for such he was, with an intrepidity truly British, leaning on his crutch, put himself into an attitude to comply with my request, and gave me his history as follows:—

"As for misfortunes, sir, I cannot pretend to have gone through more than others. Except the loss of my limb, and my being obliged to beg, I don't know any reason, thank Heaven, that I have to complain: there are some who have lost both legs and an eye; but, thank Heaven, it is not quite so bad with me.

"My father was a labourer in the country, and died when I was five years old; so I was put upon the parish. As he had been a wandering sort of a man, the parishioners were not able to tell to what parish I belonged, or where I was born; so they sent me to another parish, and that parish sent me to a third: till at last it was thought I belonged to no parish at all. At length, however, they fixed me. I had some disposition to be a scholar, and had actually learned my letters; but the master of the workhouse put me to business as soon as I was able to handle a mallet.

"Here I lived an easy kind of a life for five years. I only wrought ten hours in the day, and had my meat and drink provided for my labour. It is true, I was not suffered to stir far from the house, for fear I should run away: but what of that? I had the liberty of the whole house, and the yard before the door, and that was enough for me.

"I was next bound out to a farmer, where I was up both early and late; but I ate and drank well, and liked my business well enough, till he died. Being then obliged to provide for myself, I was resolved to go and seek my fortune. Thus I lived, and went from town to town, working when I could get employment, and starving when I could get none, and might have lived so still; but happening one day to go through a field belonging to a magistrate, I spied a hare crossing the path just before me. I believe the devil put it in my head to fling my stick at it: well, what will you have on't? I killed the hare, and was bringing it away in triumph, when the Justice himself met me: he called me a villain, and collaring me, desired I would give an account of myself. I began immediately to give a full account of all that I knew of my breed, seed, and generation; but though I gave a very long account, the Justice said I could give no account of myself; so I was indicted, and found guilty of being poor, and sent to Newgate, in order to be transported to the plantations.

"People may say this and that of being in gaol; but, for my part, I found Newgate as agreeable a place as ever I was in in all my life. I had my bellyful to eat and drink, and did no work; but, alas! this kind of life was too good to last for ever. I was taken out of prison, after five months, put on board of a ship, and sent off with two hundred more. Our passage was but indifferent, for we were all confined in the hold, and died very fast, for want of sweet air and provisions: but, for my part, I did not want meat, because I had a fever all the way: Providence was kind; when provisions grew short, it took away my desire of eating. When we came ashore, we were sold to the planters. I was bound for seven years, and as I was no scholar—for I had forgot my letters—I was obliged to work among the negroes; and served out my time, as in duty bound to do.

"When my time was expired, I worked my passage home, and glad I was to see old England again, because I loved my country. O liberty! liberty! liberty! that is the property of every Englishman, and I will die in its defence. I was afraid, however, that I should be indicted for a vagabond once more; so I did not much care to go into the country, but kept about town; and did little jobs when I could get them. I was very happy in this manner for some time; till one evening, coming home from work, two men knocked me down, and then desired me to stand still. They belonged to a press-gang: I was carried before the Justice, and as I could give no account of myself (that was the thing that always hobbled me), I had my choice left, whether to go on board a man-of-war, or list for a soldier. I chose to be a soldier; and in this post of a gentleman I served two campaigns in Flanders, was at the battles of Val and Fontenoy, and received but one wound through the breast, which is troublesome to this day.

"When the peace came on, I was discharged; and as I could not work, because my wound was sometimes painful, I listed for a landman in the East India Company's service. I here fought the French in six pitched battles; and verily believe, that if I could read and write, our captain would have given me promotion, and made me a corporal. But that was not my good fortune; I soon fell sick, and when I became good for nothing, got leave to return home again with forty pounds in my pocket, which I saved in the service. This was at the beginning of the present war, so I hoped to be set on shore, and to have the pleasure of spending my money; but the government wanted men, and I was pressed again, before ever I could set foot on shore.

"The boatswain found me, as he said, an obstinate fellow: he swore that I understood my business perfectly well, but that I shammed Abraham merely to be idle. God knows, I knew nothing of sea business: he beat me without considering what he was about. But still my forty pounds was some comfort to me under every beating: the money was my comfort, and the money I might have had to this day, but that our ship was taken by the French, and so I lost it all.

"Our crew was carried into a French prison, and many of them died, because they were not used to live in a gaol; but, for my part, it was nothing to me, for I was seasoned. One night, however, as I was sleeping on a bed of boards, with a warm blanket about me, (for I always loved to lie well,) I was awakened by the boatswain, who had a dark lantern in his hand. 'Jack,' says he to me, 'will you knock out the French sentry's brains?'—'I don't care,' says I, striving to keep myself awake, 'if I lend a hand.'—'Then follow me,' says he, 'and I hope we shall do business.' So up I got, and tied my blanket, which was all the clothes I had, about my middle, and went with him to fight the Frenchmen. We had no arms; but one Englishman is able to beat five Frenchmen at any time; so we went down to the door, where both the sentries were posted, and, rushing upon them, seized their arms in a moment, and knocked them down. From thence nine of us ran together to the quay, and seizing the first boat we met, got out of the harbour, and put to sea. We had not been here three days before we were taken up by an English privateer, who was glad of so many good hands; and we consented to run our chance. However, we had not so much luck as we expected. In three days we fell in with a French man-of-war, of forty guns, while we had but twenty-three; so to it we went. The fight lasted for three hours, and I verily believe we should have taken the Frenchman, but unfortunately we lost almost all our men, just as we were going to get the victory. I was once more in the power of the French, and I believe it would have gone hard with me, had I been brought back to my old gaol in Brest; but, by good fortune, we were retaken, and carried to England once more.

"I had almost forgot to tell you, that in this last engagement I was wounded in two places,—I lost four fingers of the left hand, and my leg was shot off. Had I had the good fortune to have lost my leg and use of my hand on board a king's ship, and not a privateer, I should have been entitled to clothing and maintenance during the rest of my life; but that was not my chance: one man is born with a silver spoon in his mouth, and another with a wooden ladle. However, blessed be God, I enjoy good health, and have no enemy in this world that I know of, but the French and the Justice of Peace."

Thus saying, he limped off, leaving my friend and me in admiration of his intrepidity and content; nor could we avoid acknowledging, that an habitual acquaintance with misery is the truest school of fortitude and philosophy.—Adieu.

LETTER CXX.

To the same.

THE titles of European princes are rather more numerous than ours of Asia, but by no means so sublime. The king of Visapour or Pegu, not satisfied with claiming the globe and all its appurtenances to him and his heirs, asserts a property even in the firmament, and extends his orders to the milky way. The monarchs of Europe, with more modesty, confine their titles to earth, but make up by number what is wanting in their sublimity. Such is their passion for a long list of these splendid trifles, that I have known a German prince with more titles than subjects, and a Spanish nobleman with more names than shirts.

Contrary to this, "the English monarchs," says a writer of the last century, "disdain to accept of such titles, which tend only to increase their pride, without improving their glory; they are above depending on the feeble helps of heraldry for respect, perfectly satisfied with the consciousness of acknowledged power." At present, however, these maxims are laid aside; the English monarchs have of late assumed new titles, and have impressed their coins with the names and arms of obscure dukedoms, petty states, and subordinate employments. Their design in this, I make no doubt, was laudably to add new lustre to the British throne; but, in reality, paltry claims only serve to diminish that respect they are designed to secure.

There is in the honours assumed by kings, as in the decorations of architecture, a majestic simplicity, which best conduces to inspire our reverence and respect; numerous and trifling ornaments in either are strong indications of meanness in the designer, or of concealed deformity. Should, for instance, the emperor of China, among other titles, assume that of deputy mandarine of Maccau; or the monarch of Great Britain, France, and Ireland, desire to be acknowledged as Duke of Brentford, Lunenburg, or Lincoln; the observer revolts at this mixture of important and paltry claims, and forgets the emperor in his familiarity with the duke or the deputy.

I remember a similar instance of this inverted ambition in the illustrious king of Manacabo, upon his first treaty with the Portuguese. Among the presents that were made him by the ambassador of that nation was a sword, with a brass hilt, which he seemed to set a peculiar value upon. This he thought too great an acquisition to his glory to be forgotten among the number of his titles. He therefore gave orders, that his subjects should style him for the future, Talipot, the immortal Potentate of Manacabo, Messenger of the Morning, Enlightener of the Sun, Possessor of the whole Earth, and mighty Monarch of the Brass-handled Sword.

This method of mixing majestic and paltry titles, of quartering the arms of a great empire and an obscure province upon the same medal here, had its rise in the virtuous partiality of their late monarchs. Willing to testify an affection to their native country, they gave its name and ensigns a place upon their coins, and thus in some measure ennobled its obscurity. It was, indeed, but just, that a people which had given England up their king, should receive some honorary equivalent in return; but at present these motives are no more: England has now a monarch wholly British; and it has some reason to hope for British titles upon British coins.

However, were the money of England designed to circulate in Germany, there would be no flagrant impropriety in impressing it with German names and arms; but though this might have been so upon former occasions, I am told there is no danger of it for the future. As England, therefore, designs to keep back its gold, I candidly think, Lunenburg, Oldenburg, and the rest of them, may very well keep back their titles.

It is a mistaken prejudice in princes to think that a number of loud-sounding names can give new claims to respect. The truly great have ever disdained them. When Timur the Lame had conquered Asia, an orator by profession came to compliment him upon the occasion. He began his harangue by styling him the most omnipotent and the most glorious object of the creation. The emperor seemed displeased with his paltry adulation; yet still he went on, complimenting him as the most mighty, the most valiant, and the most perfect of beings. "Hold there, my friend," cries the lame emperor, "hold there, till I have got another leg." In fact, the feeble or the despotic alone find pleasure in multiplying these pageants of vanity; but strength and freedom have nobler aims, and often find the finest adulation in majestic simplicity.

The young monarch of this country has already testified a proper contempt for several unmeaning appendages on royalty; cooks and scullions have been obliged to quit their fires; gentlemen's gentlemen, and the whole tribe of necessary people who did nothing, have been dismissed from farther services. A youth who can thus bring back simplicity and frugality to a court, will soon probably have a true respect for his own glory; and while he has dismissed all useless employments, may disdain to accept of empty or degrading titles.—Adieu.

LETTER CXXI.

To the same.

WHENEVER I attempt to characterise the English in general, some unforeseen difficulties constantly occur to disconcert my design; I hesitate between censure and praise. When I consider them as a reasoning, philosophical people, they have my applause; but when I reverse the medal, and observe their inconstancy and irresolution, I can scarcely persuade myself that I am observing the same people.

Yet, upon examination, this very inconstancy, so remarkable here, flows from no other source than their love of reasoning. The man who examines a complicated subject on every side, and calls in reason to his assistance, will frequently change; will find himself distracted by opposing improbabilities and contending proofs; every alteration of place will diversify the prospect, will give some latent argument new force, and contribute to maintain an anarchy in the mind.

On the contrary, they who never examine with their own reason act with more simplicity. Ignorance is positive, instinct perseveres, and the human being moves in safety within the narrow circle of brutal uniformity. What is true with regard to individuals, is not less so when applied to states. A reasoning government like this is in continual fluctuation, while those kingdoms where men are taught not to controvert, but obey, continue always the same. In Asia, for instance, where the monarch's authority is supported by force, and acknowledged through fear, a change of government is entirely unknown. All the inhabitants seem to wear the same mental complexion, and remain contented with hereditary oppression. The sovereign's pleasure is the ultimate rule of duty; every branch of the administration is a perfect epitome of the whole; and if one tyrant is deposed, another starts up in his room to govern as his predecessor. The English, on the contrary, instead of being led by power, endeavour to guide themselves by reason: instead of appealing to the pleasure of the prince, appeal to the original rights of mankind. What one rank of men assert, is denied by others, as the reasons on opposite sides happen to come home with greater or less conviction. The people of Asia are directed by precedent, which never alters; the English by reason, which is ever changing its appearance.

The disadvantages of an Asiatic government, acting in this manner by precedent, are evident: original errors are thus continued, without hopes of redress; and all marks of genius are levelled down to one standard, since no superiority of thinking can be allowed its exertion in mending obvious defects. But to recompense those defects, their governments undergo no new alterations; they have no new evils to fear, nor no fermentations in the constitution that continue; the struggle for power is soon over, and all becomes tranquil as before; they are habituated to subordination, and men are taught to form no other desires than those which they are allowed to satisfy.

The disadvantages of a government acting from the immediate influence of reason, like that of England, are not less than those of the former. It is extremely difficult to induce a number of free beings to co-operate for their mutual benefit; every possible advantage will necessarily be sought, and every attempt to procure it must be attended with a new fermentation; various reasons will lead different ways, and equity and advantage will often be outbalanced by a combination of clamour and prejudice. But though such a people may be thus in the wrong, they have been influenced by a happy delusion; their errors are seldom seen till they are felt; each man is himself the tyrant he has obeyed, and such a master he can easily forgive. The disadvantages he feels may, in reality, be equal to what is felt in the most despotic government; but man will bear every calamity with patience when he knows himself to be the author of his own misfortunes.—Adieu.

LETTER CXXII.

To the same.

My long residence here begins to fatigue me. As every object ceases to be new, it no longer continues to be pleasing: some minds are so fond of variety, that pleasure itself, if permanent, would be insupportable, and we are thus obliged to solicit new happiness even by courting distress. I only, therefore, wait the arrival of my son to vary this trifling scene, and borrow new pleasure from danger and fatigue. A life, I own, thus spent in wandering from place to place is at best but empty dissipation. But to pursue trifles is the lot of humanity: and whether we bustle in a pantomime, or strut at a coronation; whether we shout at a bonfire, or harangue in a senate-house; whatever object we follow, it will at last surely conduct us to futility and disappointment. The wise bustle and laugh as they walk in the pageant, but fools bustle and are important; and this probably is all the difference between them.

This may be an apology for the levity of my former correspondence; I talked of trifles, and I knew that they were trifles: to make the things of this life ridiculous, it is only sufficient to call them by their names.

In other respects, I have omitted several striking circumstances in the description of this country, as supposing them either already known to you, or as not being thoroughly known to myself; but there is one omission for which I expect no forgiveness, namely, my being totally silent upon their buildings, roads, rivers, and mountains. This is a branch of science on which all other travellers are so very prolix, that my deficiency will appear the more glaring. With what pleasure, for instance, do some read of a traveller in Egypt measuring a fallen column with his cane, and finding it exactly five feet nine inches long; of his creeping through the mouth of a catacomb, and coming out by a different hole from that he entered; of his stealing the finger of an antique statue, in spite of the janizary that watched him; or his adding a new conjecture to the hundred and fourteen conjectures already published upon the names of Osiris and Isis.

Methinks I hear some of my friends in China demanding a similar account of London and the adjacent villages; and if I remain here much longer, it is probable I may gratify their curiosity. I intend, when run dry on other topics, to take a serious survey of the city wall; to describe that beautiful building the mansion-house; I will enumerate the magnificent squares in which the nobility chiefly reside, and the royal palaces appointed for the reception of the English monarch; nor will I forget the beauties of Shoe Lane, in which I myself have resided since my arrival. You shall find me no way inferior to many of my brother travellers in the arts of description. At present, however, as a specimen of this way of writing, I send you a few hasty remarks, collected in a late journey I made to Kentish Town, and this in the manner of modern voyagers.

"Having heard much of Kentish Town, I conceived a strong desire to see that celebrated place. I could have wished, indeed, to satisfy my curiosity without going thither; but that was impracticable, and therefore I resolved to go. Travellers have two methods of going to Kentish Town,—they take coach, which costs ninepence, or they may go afoot, which costs nothing: in my opinion, a coach is by far the most eligible convenience, but I was resolved to go on foot, having considered with myself, that going in that manner would be the cheapest way.

"As you set out from Dog-house bar, you enter upon a fine level road railed in on both sides, commanding on the right a small prospect of groves and fields, enamelled with flowers, which would wonderfully charm the sense of smelling, were it not for a dunghill on the left, which mixes its effluvia with their odours. This dunghill is of much greater antiquity than the road; and I must not omit a piece of injustice I was going to commit upon this occasion. My indignation was levelled against the makers of the dunghill, for having brought it so near the road; whereas, it should have fallen upon the makers of the road, for having brought that so near the dunghill.

"After proceeding in this manner for some time, a building, resembling somewhat a triumphal arch, salutes the traveller's view. This structure, however, is peculiar to this country, and vulgarly called a turnpike-gate: I could perceive a long inscription, in large characters, on the front, probably upon the occasion of some triumph, but, being in haste, I left it to be made out by some subsequent adventurer who may happen to travel this way; so, continuing my course to the west, I soon arrived at an unwalled town, called Islington.

"Islington is a pretty neat town, mostly built of brick, with a church and bells; it has a small lake, or rather pond, in the midst, though at present very much neglected. I am told it is dry in summer: if this be the case, it can be no very proper receptacle for fish; of which the inhabitants themselves seem sensible, by bringing all that is eaten there from London.

"After having surveyed the curiosities of this fair and beautiful town, I proceeded forward, leaving a fair stone building, called the White Conduit House, on my right. Here the inhabitants of London often assemble to celebrate a feast of hot rolls and butter: seeing such numbers, each with their little tables before them, employed on this occasion, must, no doubt, be a very amusing sight to the looker-on, but still more so to those who perform in the solemnity.

"From hence I parted with reluctance to Pancras, as it is written, or Pancridge, as it is pronounced; but which should be both pronounced and written Pangrace: this emendation I will venture *meo arbitrio*: *παν*, in the Greek language, signifies *all*, which, added to the English word *grace*, maketh *all grace*, or *Pangrace;* and, indeed, this is a very proper appellation to a place of so much sanctity as Pangrace is universally esteemed. However this be, if you except the parish church and its fine bells, there is little in Pangrace worth the attention of the curious observer.

"From Pangrace to Kentish Town is an easy journey of one mile and a quarter: the road lies through a fine champaign country, well watered with beautiful drains, and enamelled with flowers of all kinds, which might contribute to charm every sense, were it not that the odoriferous gales are often more impregnated with dust than perfume.

"As you enter Kentish Town, the eye is at once presented with the shops of artificers, such as venders of candles, small coal, and hair brooms; there are also several august buildings of red brick, with numberless sign posts, or rather pillars, in a peculiar order of architecture. I send you a drawing of several—*vide* A B C. This pretty town probably borrows its name from its vicinity to the county of Kent; and, indeed, it is not unnatural that it should, as there are only London and the adjacent villages that lie between them. Be this as it will, perceiving night approach, I made a hasty repast on roasted mutton and a certain dried fruit called potatoes, resolving to protract my remarks upon my return; and this I would very willingly have done, but was prevented by a circumstance which, in truth, I had for some time foreseen, for night coming on, it was impossible to take a proper survey of the country, as I was obliged to return home in the dark."—Adieu.

LETTER CXXIII.

To the same.

After a variety of disappointments, my wishes are at length fully satisfied. My son, so long expected, is arrived; at once, by his presence, banishing my anxiety, and opening a new scene of unexpected pleasure. His improvements in mind and person have far surpassed even the sanguine expectations of a father. I left him a boy, but he is returned a man; pleasing in his person, hardened by travel, and polished by adversity. His disappointment in love, however, had infused an air of melancholy into his conversation, which seemed at intervals to interrupt our mutual satisfaction. I expected that this could find a cure only from time; but fortune, as if willing to load us with her favours, has, in a moment, repaid every uneasiness with rapture.

Two days after his arrival the Man in Black, with his beautiful niece, came to congratulate us upon this pleasing occasion; but guess our surprise, when my friend's lovely kinswoman was found to be the very captive my son had rescued from Persia, and who had been wrecked on the Wolga, and was carried by the Russian peasants to the port of Archangel. Were I to hold the pen of a novelist, I might be prolix in describing their feelings at so unexpected an interview; but you may conceive their joy without my assistance: words were unable to express their transports; then how can words describe it?

When two young persons are sincerely enamoured of each other, nothing can give me such pleasure as seeing them married: whether I know the parties or not, I am happy at thus binding one link more in the universal chain. Nature has, in some measure, formed me for a match-maker, and given me a soul to sympathise with every mode of human felicity. I instantly, therefore, consulted the Man in Black, whether we might not crown their mutual wishes by marriage: his soul seems formed of similar materials with mine; he instantly gave his consent, and the next day was appointed for the solemnization of their nuptials.

All the acquaintances which I had made since my arrival were present at this gay solemnity. The little Beau was constituted master of the ceremonies, and his wife, Mrs. Tibbs, conducted the entertainment with proper decorum. The Man in Black and the pawnbroker's widow were very sprightly and tender upon this occasion. The widow was dressed up under the direction of Mrs. Tibbs; and as for her lover, his face was set off by the assistance of a pig-tail wig, which was lent by the little Beau, to fit him for making love with proper formality. The whole company easily perceived that it would be a double wedding before all was over, and, indeed, my friend and the widow seemed to make no secret of their passion; he even called me aside, in order to know my candid opinion, whether I did not think him a little too old to be married. "As for my own part," continued he, "I know I am going to play the fool; but all my friends will praise my wisdom, and produce me as the very pattern of discretion to others."

At dinner everything seemed to run on with good humour, harmony, and satisfaction. Every creature in company thought themselves pretty, and every jest was laughed at. The Man in Black sat next his mistress, helped her plate, chimed her glass, and jogging her knees and her elbow, he whispered something arch in her ear, on which she patted his cheek: never was antiquated passion so playful, so harmless, and amusing, as between this reverend couple.

The second course was now called for, and, among a variety of other dishes, a fine turkey was placed before the widow. The Europeans, you know, carve as they eat; my friend, therefore, begged his mistress to help him to a part of the turkey. The widow, pleased with an opportunity of showing her skill in carving, (an art upon which it seems she piqued herself,) began to cut it up by first taking off the leg. "Madam," cries my friend, "if I might be permitted to advise, I would begin by cutting off the wing, and then the leg will come off more easily."—"Sir," replies the widow, "give me leave to understand cutting up a fowl: I always begin with the leg."—"Yes, madam," replies the lover; "but if the wing be the most convenient manner, I would begin with the wing."—"Sir," interrupts the lady, "when you have fowls of your own, begin with the wing if you please, but give me leave to take off the leg; I hope I am not to be taught at this time of day."—"Madam," interrupts he, "we are never too old to be instructed."—"Old, sir!" interrupts the other; "who is old, sir? when I die of age, I know of some that will quake for fear. If the leg does not come off, take the turkey to yourself."—"Madam," replied the Man in Black, "I don't care a farthing whether the leg or the wing comes off; if you are for the leg first, why, you shall have the argument, even though it be as I say."—"As for the matter of that," cries the widow, "I don't care a fig whether you are for the leg off or on: and, friend, for the future keep your distance."—"Oh," replied the other, "that is easily done; it is only removing to the other end of the table; and so, madam, your most obedient humble servant."

Thus was this courtship of an age destroyed in one moment; for this dialogue effectually broke off the match between this respectable couple, that had been but just concluded. The smallest accidents disappoint the most important treaties. However, though it in some measure interrupted the general satisfaction, it no ways lessened the happiness of the youthful couple; and, by the young lady's looks, I could perceive she was not entirely displeased with this interruption.

In a few hours the whole transaction seemed entirely forgotten, and we have all since enjoyed those satisfactions which result from a consciousness of making each other happy. My son and his fair partner are fixed here for life: the Man in Black has given them up a small estate in the country, which, added to what I was able to bestow, will be capable of supplying all the real, but not the fictitious, demands of happiness. As for myself, the world being but one city to me, I do not much care in which of the streets I happen to reside: I shall, therefore, spend the remainder of my days in examining the manners of different countries, and have prevailed upon the Man in Black to be my companion. "They must often change," says Confucius, "who would be constant in happiness or wisdom."—Adieu.

END OF THE CITIZEN OF THE WORLD.

ESSAYS.

ESSAYS.

THE PREFACE.

The following Essays have already appeared at different times, and in different publications. The pamphlets in which they were inserted being generally unsuccessful, these shared the common fate, without assisting the bookseller's aims, or extending the writer's reputation. The public were too strenuously employed with their own follies to be assiduous in estimating mine, so that many of my best attempts in this way have fallen victims to the transient topic of the times—the Ghost in Cock Lane, or the siege of Ticonderoga.

But though they have passed pretty silently into the world, I can by no means complain of their circulation. The magazines and papers of the day have indeed been liberal enough in this respect. Most of these Essays have been regularly reprinted twice or thrice a year, and conveyed to the public through the kennel of some engaging compilation. If there be a pride in multiplied editions, I have seen some of my labours sixteen times reprinted, and claimed by different parents as their own. I have seen them flourished at the beginning with praise, and signed at the end with the names of Philautos, Philalethes, Philaleutheros, and Philanthropos. These gentlemen have kindly stood sponsors to my productions, and to flatter me more, have always taken my errors on themselves.

It is time, however, at last, to vindicate my claims; and as these entertainers of the public, as they call themselves, have partly lived upon me for some years, let me now try if I cannot live a little upon myself. I would desire, in this case, to imitate that fat man whom I have somewhere heard of in a shipwreck, who when the sailors, pressed by famine, were taking slices from his posteriors to satisfy their hunger, insisted, with great justice, on having the first cut for himself.

Yet, after all, I cannot be angry with any who have taken it into their heads to think that whatever I write is worth reprinting, particularly when I consider how great a majority will think it scarcely worth reading. Trifling *and* superficial *are terms of reproach that are easily objected, and that carry an air of penetration in the observer. These faults have been objected to the following Essays; and it must be owned, in some measure, that the charge is true. However, I could have made them more metaphysical, had I thought fit; but I would ask, whether in a short Essay it is not necessary to be superficial? Before we have prepared to enter into the depths of a subject in the usual forms, we have got to the bottom of our scanty page, and thus lose the honours of a victory by too tedious a preparation for the combat.*

There is another fault in this collection of trifles, which, I fear, will not be so easily pardoned. It will be alleged, that the humour of them (if any be found) is stale and hackneyed. This may be true enough, as matters now stand; but I may with great truth assert, that the humour was new when I wrote it. Since that time, indeed, many of the topics which were first started here have been hunted down, and many of the thoughts blown upon. In fact, these Essays were considered as quietly laid in the grave of oblivion; and our modern compilers, like sextons and executioners, think it their undoubted right to pillage the dead.

However, whatever right I have to complain of the public, they can, as yet, have no just reason to complain of me. If I have written dull Essays, they have hitherto treated them as dull Essays. Thus far we are at least upon par, and until they think fit to make me their humble debtor by praise, I am resolved not to lose a single inch of my self-importance. Instead, therefore, of attempting to establish a credit amongst them, it will perhaps be wiser to apply to some more distant correspondent; and as my drafts are in some danger of being protested at home, it may not be imprudent, upon this occasion, to draw my bills upon Posterity.

MR. POSTERITY,

SIR,—*Nine hundred and ninety-nine years after sight hereof pay the bearer, or order, a thousand pounds worth of praise, free from all deductions whatsoever, it being a commodity that will then be very serviceable to him, and place it to the account of, &c.*

[1758—1765.]

ESSAY I.

Description of various Clubs.

I REMEMBER to have read in some philosopher (I believe in Tom Brown's works), that, let a man's character, sentiments, or complexion, be what they will, he can find company in London to match them. If he be splenetic, he may every day meet companions on the seats in St. James's Park, with whose groans he may mix his own, and pathetically talk of the weather. If he be passionate, he may vent his rage among the old orators at Slaughter's Coffee-house, and damn the nation, because it keeps him from starving. If he be phlegmatic, he may sit in silence at the Humdrum Club in Ivy Lane; and, if actually mad, he may find very good company in Moorfields, either at Bedlam or the Foundery, ready to cultivate a nearer acquaintance.

But, although such as have a knowledge of the town may easily class themselves with tempers congenial to their own, a countryman who comes to live in London finds nothing more difficult. With regard to myself, none ever tried with more assiduity, or came off with such indifferent success. I spent a whole season in the search, during which time my name has been enrolled in societies, lodges, convocations, and meetings, without number. To some I was introduced by a friend, to others invited by an advertisement: to these I introduced myself, and to those I changed my name to gain admittance. In short, no coquette was ever more solicitous to match her ribbons to her complexion, than I to suit my club to my temper; for I was too obstinate to bring my temper to conform to it.

The first club I entered, upon coming to town, was that of the Choice Spirits. The name was entirely suited to my taste,—I was a lover of mirth, good-humour, and even sometimes of fun, from my childhood.

As no other passport was requisite but the payment of two shillings at the door, I introduced myself without farther ceremony to the members, who were already assembled, and had for some time begun upon business. The Grand, with a mallet in his hand, presided at the head of the table. I could not avoid, upon my entrance, making use of all my skill in physiognomy, in order to discover that superiority of genius in men who had taken a title so superior to the rest of mankind. I expected to see the lines of every face marked with strong thinking; but though I had some skill in this science, I could for my life discover nothing but a pert simper, fat, or profound stupidity.

My speculations were soon interrupted by the Grand, who had knocked down Mr. Spriggins for a song. I was upon this whispered by one of the company who sat next me, that I should now see something touched off to a nicety, for Mr. Spriggins was going to give us "Mad Tom" in all its glory. Mr. Spriggins endeavoured to excuse himself; for as he was to act a madman and a king, it was impossible to go through the part properly without a crown and chains. His excuses were overruled by a great majority, and with much vociferation. The president ordered up the jack-chain, and, instead of a crown, our performer covered his brows with an inverted jordan. After he had rattled his chain and shook his head, to the great delight of the whole company, he began his song. As I have heard few young fellows offer to sing in company that did not expose themselves, it was no great disappointment to me to find Mr. Spriggins among the number; however, not to seem an odd fish, I rose from my seat in rapture, cried out "Bravo! Encore!" and slapped the table as loud as any of the rest.

The gentleman who sat next me seemed highly pleased with my taste and the ardour of my approbation; and whispering, told me that I had suffered an immense loss, for had I come a few minutes sooner, I might have heard "Gee-ho Dobbin" sung in a tip-top manner by the pimple-nosed spirit at the president's right elbow; but he was evaporated before I came.

As I was expressing my uneasiness at this disappointment, I found the attention of the company employed upon a fat figure, who, with a voice more rough than the Staffordshire giant's, was giving us the "Softly sweet in Lydian measure" of Alexander's Feast. After a short pause of admiration, to this succeeded a Welsh dialogue, with the humours of Teague and Taffy; after that came on "Old Jackson," with a story between every stanza: next was sung the "Dust Cart," and then "Solomon's Song." The glass begun now to circulate pretty freely; those who were silent when sober, would now be heard in their turn; every man had his song, and he saw no reason why he should not be heard as well as any of the rest: one begged to be heard while he gave "Death and the Lady" in high taste; another sang to a plate which he kept trundling on the edges. Nothing was now heard but singing; voice rose above voice, and the whole became one universal shout, when the landlord came to acquaint the company that the reckoning was drunk out. Rabelais calls the moments in which a reckoning is mentioned the most melancholy of our lives: never was so much noise so quickly quelled, as by this short but pathetic oration of our landlord. "Drunk out!" was echoed in a tone of discontent round the table: "drunk out already! that was very odd! that so much punch could be drunk out already—impossible!" The landlord, however, seeming resolved not to retreat from his first assurances, the company was dissolved, and a president chosen for the night ensuing.

A friend of mine, to whom I was complaining some time after the entertainment I have been describing, proposed to bring me to the club that he frequented, which he fancied would suit the gravity of my temper exactly. "We have at the Muzzy Club," says he, "no riotous mirth nor awkward ribaldry; no confusion or bawling; all is conducted with wisdom and decency: besides, some of our members are worth forty thousand pounds—men of prudence and foresight every one of them: these are the proper acquaintance, and to such I will to-night introduce you." I was charmed at the proposal: to be acquainted with men worth forty thousand pounds, and to talk wisdom the whole night, were offers that threw me into rapture.

At seven o'clock I was accordingly introduced by my friend, not indeed to the company—for though I made my best bow, they seemed insensible of my approach—but to the table at which they were sitting. Upon my entering the room, I could not avoid feeling a secret veneration from the solemnity of the scene before me; the members kept a profound silence, each with a pipe in his mouth, and a pewter pot in his hand, and with faces that might easily be construed into absolute wisdom. Happy society, thought I to myself, where the members think before they speak, deliver nothing rashly, but convey their thoughts to each other pregnant with meaning, and matured by reflection!

In this pleasing speculation I continued

a full half-hour, expecting each moment that somebody would begin to open his mouth: every time the pipe was laid down I expected it was to speak; but it was only to spit. At length, resolving to break the charm myself, and overcome their extreme diffidence—for to this I imputed their silence—I rubbed my hands, and, looking as wise as possible, observed that the nights began to grow a little coolish at this time of the year. This, as it was directed to none of the company in particular, none thought himself obliged to answer; wherefore I continued still to rub my hands and look wise. My next effort was addressed to a gentleman who sat next me; to whom I observed, that the beer was extremely good: my neighbour made no reply, but by a large puff of tobacco smoke.

I now began to be uneasy in this dumb society, till one of them a little relieved me, by observing, that bread had not risen these three weeks. "Ay," says another, still keeping the pipe in his mouth, "that puts me in mind of a pleasant story about that—hem—very well; you must know—but before I begin—sir, my service to you—where was I?"

My next club goes by the name of the Harmonical Society; probably from that love of order and friendship which every person commends in institutions of this nature. The landlord was himself the founder. The money spent is fourpence each; and they sometimes whip for a double reckoning. To this club few recommendations are requisite, except the introductory fourpence, and my landlord's good word, which, as he gains by it, he never refuses.

We all here talked and behaved as everybody else usually does on his club night; we discussed the topic of the day, drank each other's healths, snuffed the candles with our fingers, and filled our pipes from the same plate of tobacco. The company saluted each other in the common manner: Mr. Bellows-mender hoped Mr. Currycomb-maker had not caught cold going home the last club night; and he returned the compliment by hoping that young Master Bellows-mender had got well again of the chin-cough. Dr. Twist told us a story of a parliament-man with whom he was intimately acquainted; while the bag-man, at the same time, was telling a better story of a noble lord with whom he could do anything. A gentleman in a black wig and leather breeches, at t'other end of the table, was engaged in a long narrative of the Ghost in Cock Lane: he had read it in the papers of the day, and was telling it to some that sat next him, who could not read. Near him, Mr. Dibbins was disputing on the old subject of religion with a Jew pedlar, over the table; while the president vainly knocked down Mr. Leathersides for a song. Besides the combinations of these voices, which I could hear altogether, and which formed an upper part to the concert, there were several others playing under parts by themselves, and endeavouring to fasten on some luckless neighbour's ear, who was himself bent upon the same design against some other.

We have often heard of the speech of a corporation, and this induced me to transcribe a speech of this club, taken in short-hand, word for word, as it was spoken by every member of the company. It may be necessary to observe, that the man who told of the ghost had the loudest voice, and the longest story to tell, so that his continuing narrative filled every chasm in the conversation.

"So, sir, d'ye perceive me, the ghost giving three loud raps at the bed-post—Says my lord to me, my dear Smokeum, you know there is no man upon the face of the yearth for whom I have so high—A damnable false heretical opinion of all sound doctrine and good learning; for I'll tell it aloud, and spare not, that—Silence for a song; Mr. Leathersides for a song—'As I was a-walking upon the highway, I met a young damsel'—Then what brings you here? says the parson to the ghost—Sanconiathon, Manetho, and Berosus—The whole way from Islington turnpike to Dog-house bar—Dam—As for Abel Drugger, sir, he's damned low in it: my 'prentice boy has more of the gentleman than he—For murder will out one time or another; and none but a ghost, you know, gentlemen, can —— Damme, if I don't;

for my friend, whom you know, gentlemen, and who is a parliament-man, a man of consequence, a dear honest creature, to be sure; we were laughing last night at —Death and damnation upon all his posterity, by simple barely tasting—Sour grapes, as the fox said once when he could not reach them: and I'll, I'll tell you a story about that that will make you burst your sides with laughing: a fox once—Will nobody listen to the song—'As I was a-walking upon the highway, I met a young damsel both buxom and gay,'—No ghost, gentlemen, can be murdered; nor did I ever hear but of one ghost killed in all my life, and that was stabbed in the belly with a—My blood and soul if I don't —Mr. Bellows-mender, I have the honour of drinking your very good health—Blast me if I do—dam—blood—bugs—fire—whiz—blid—tit—rat—trip"——The rest all riot, nonsense, and rapid confusion.

Were I to be angry at men for being fools, I could here find ample room for declamation; but, alas! I have been a fool myself; and why should I be angry with them for being something so natural to every child of humanity?

Fatigued with this society, I was introduced the following night to a club of fashion. On taking my place, I found the conversation sufficiently easy, and tolerably good-natured: for my Lord and Sir Paul were not yet arrived. I now thought myself completely fitted, and resolving to seek no farther, determined to take up my residence here for the winter; while my temper began to open insensibly to the cheerfulness I saw diffused on every face in the room: but the delusion soon vanished, when the waiter came to apprise us that his Lordship and Sir Paul were just arrived.

From this moment all our felicity was at an end; our new guests bustled into the room, and took their seats at the head of the table. Adieu, now, all confidence! every creature strove who should most recommend himself to our members of distinction. Each seemed quite regardless of pleasing any but our new guests; and what before wore the appearance of friendship, was now turned into rivalry.

Yet I could not observe that, amidst all this flattery and obsequious attention, our great men took any notice of the rest of the company. Their whole discourse was addressed to each other. Sir Paul told his Lordship a long story of Moravia the Jew; and his Lordship gave Sir Paul a very long account of his new method of managing silk-worms: he led him, and consequently the rest of the company, through all the stages of feeding, sunning, and hatching; with an episode on mulberry-trees, a digression upon grass seeds, and a long parenthesis about his new postilion. In this manner we travelled on, wishing every story to be the last; but all in vain:

Hills over hills, and Alps on Alps arose.

The last club in which I was enrolled a member was a society of moral philosophers, as they called themselves, who assembled twice a week, in order to show the absurdity of the present mode of religion, and establish a new one in its stead.

I found the members very warmly disputing when I arrived, not indeed about religion or ethics, but about who had neglected to lay down his preliminary sixpence upon entering the room. The president swore that he had laid his own down, and so swore all the company.

During this contest I had an opportunity of observing the laws, and also the members, of the society. The president, who had been, as I was told, lately a bankrupt, was a tall pale figure, with a long black wig; the next to him was dressed in a large white wig and a black cravat; a third, by the brownness of complexion, seemed a native of Jamaica; and a fourth, by his hue, appeared to be a blacksmith. But their rules will give the most just idea of their learning and principles.

I. We, being a laudable society of moral philosophers, intends to dispute twice a week about religion and priestcraft; leaving behind us old wives' tales, and following good learning and sound sense: and if so be, that any other persons has a mind to be of the society, they shall be entitled so to do, upon paying the sum of three shillings, to be spent by the company in punch.

II. That no member get drunk before nine of the clock, upon pain of forfeiting threepence, to be spent by the company in punch.

III. That, as members are sometimes apt to go way without paying, every person shall pay sixpence upon his entering the room; and all disputes shall be settled by a majority; and all fines shall be paid in punch.

IV. That sixpence shall be every night given to the president, in order to buy books of learning for the good of the society: the president has already put himself to a good deal of expense in buying books for the club; particularly, the works of Tully, Socrates, and Cicero, which he will soon read to the society.

V. All them who brings a new argument against religion, and who being a philosopher and a man of learning, as the rest of us is, shall be admitted to the freedom of the society, upon paying sixpence only, to be spent in punch.

VI. Whenever we are to have an extraordinary meeting, it shall be advertised by some outlandish name in the newspapers.

SAUNDERS MACWILD, *President.*
ANTHONY BLEWIT, *Vice-President,*
his ✠ mark.
WILLIAM TURPIN, *Secretary.*

ESSAY II.

Specimen of a Magazine in Miniature.

WE essayists, who are allowed but one subject at a time, are by no means so fortunate as the writers of magazines, who write upon several. If a magaziner be dull upon the Spanish war, he soon has us up again with the Ghost in Cock Lane; if the reader begins to doze upon that, he is quickly roused by an Eastern tale: tales prepare us for poetry, and poetry for the meteorological history of the weather. It is the life and soul of a magazine never to be long dull upon one subject; and the reader, like the sailor's horse, has at least the comfortable refreshment of having the spur often changed.

As I see no reason why these should carry off all the rewards of genius, I have some thoughts for the future of making my Essays a magazine in miniature: I shall hop from subject to subject, and if properly encouraged, I intend in time to adorn my *feuille volant* with pictures. But to begin in the usual form with

A modest Address to the Public.

The public has been so often imposed upon by the unperforming promises of others, that it is with the utmost modesty we assure them of our inviolable design of giving the very best collection that ever astonished society. The public we honour and regard, and, therefore, to instruct and entertain them is our highest ambition, with labours calculated as well for the head as the heart. If four extraordinary pages of letter-press be any recommendation of our wit, we may at least boast the honour of vindicating our own abilities. To say more in favour of the INFERNAL MAGAZINE would be unworthy the public; to say less, would be injurious to ourselves. As we have no interested motives for this undertaking, being a society of gentlemen of distinction, we disdain to eat or write like hirelings: we are all gentlemen, resolved to sell our magazine for sixpence merely for our own amusement.

N.B.—*Be careful to ask for the Infernal Magazine.*

Dedication to that most ingenious of all Patrons, the Tripoline Ambassador.

May it please your Excellency,—As your taste in the fine arts is universally allowed and admired, permit the authors of the Infernal Magazine to lay the following sheets humbly at your Excellency's toe; and should our labours ever have the happiness of one day adorning the courts of Fez, we doubt not that the influence wherewith we are honoured, shall be ever retained with the most warm ardour by,

May it please your Excellency,
Your most devoted humble servants,
The Authors of the
INFERNAL MAGAZINE.

Speech spoken by the Indigent Philosopher, to persuade his Club at Cateaton to declare War against Spain.

My honest friends and brother politicians,—I perceive that the intended war with Spain makes many of you uneasy. Yesterday, as we were told, the stocks rose, and you were glad; to-day they fall, and you are again miserable. But, my dear friends, what is the rising or the falling of the stocks to us, who have no money? Let Nathan Ben Funk, the Dutch Jew, be glad or sorry for this; but, my good Mr. Bellows-mender, what is all this to you or me? You must mend broken bellows, and I write bad prose, as long as we live, whether we like a Spanish war or not. Believe me, my honest friends, whatever you may talk of liberty and your own reason, both that liberty and reason are conditionally resigned by every poor man in every society; and as we are born to work, so others are born to watch over us while we are working. In the name of common sense then, my good friends, let the great keep watch over us, and let us mind our business, and perhaps we may at last get money ourselves, and set beggars at work in our turn. I have a Latin sentence that is worth its weight in gold, and which I shall beg leave to translate for your instruction. An author, called Lilly's Grammar, finely observes, that "Æs in præsenti perfectum format;" that is, "Ready money makes a perfect man." Let us then get ready money, and let them that will spend theirs by going to war with Spain.

Rules for Behaviour, drawn up by the Indigent Philosopher.

If you be a rich man, you may enter the room with three loud hems, march deliberately up to the chimney, and turn your back to the fire. If you be a poor man, I would advise you to shrink into the room as fast as you can, and place yourself as usual upon the corner of a chair in a remote corner.

When you are desired to sing in company, I would advise you to refuse; for it is a thousand to one but that you torment us with affectation or a bad voice.

If you be young, and live with an old man, I would advise you not to like gravy: I was disinherited myself for liking gravy.

Don't laugh much in public; the spectators that are not as merry as you will hate you, either because they envy your happiness, or fancy themselves the subject of your mirth.

Rules for raising the Devil. Translated from the Latin of Danæus de Sortiariis, a writer contemporary with Calvin, and one of the reformers of our Church.

The person who desires to raise the devil is to sacrifice a dog, a cat, and a hen, all of his own property, to Beelzebub. He is to swear an eternal obedience, and then to receive a mark in some unseen place, either under the eye-lid, or in the roof of the mouth, inflicted by the devil himself. Upon this he has power given him over three spirits; one for earth, another for air, and a third for the sea. Upon certain times the devil holds an assembly of magicians, in which each is to give an account of what evil he has done, and what he wishes to do. At this assembly he appears in the shape of an old man, or often like a goat with large horns. They, upon this occasion, renew their vows of obedience; and then form a grand dance in honour of their false deity. The devil instructs them in every method of injuring mankind, in gathering poisons, and of riding, upon occasion, through the air. He shows them the whole method, upon examination, of giving evasive answers; his spirits have power to assume the form of angels of light, and there is but one method of detecting them, viz. to ask them, in proper form, What method is the most certain to propagate the faith over all the world? To this they are not permitted by the Superior Power to make a false reply, nor are they willing to give the true one; wherefore they continue silent, and are thus detected.

ESSAY III.

Asem, an Eastern Tale; or a Vindication of the Wisdom of Providence in the Moral Government of the World.

WHERE Tauris lifts its head above the storm, and presents nothing to the sight of the distant traveller but a prospect of nodding rocks, falling torrents, and all the variety of tremendous nature; on the bleak bosom of this frightful mountain, secluded from society, and detesting the ways of men, lived Asem the Man-hater.

Asem had spent his youth with men, had shared in their amusements, and had been taught to love his fellow-creatures with the most ardent affection; but, from the tenderness of his disposition, he exhausted all his fortune in relieving the wants of the distressed. The petitioner never sued in vain; the weary traveller never passed his door; he only desisted from doing good when he had no longer the power of relieving.

For a fortune thus spent in benevolence he expected a grateful return from those he had formerly relieved, and made his application with confidence of redress: the ungrateful world soon grew weary of his importunity; for pity is but a short-lived passion. He soon, therefore, began to view mankind in a very different light from that in which he had before beheld them: he perceived a thousand vices he had never before suspected to exist; wherever he turned, ingratitude, dissimulation, and treachery, contributed to increase his detestation of them. Resolved, therefore, to continue no longer in a world which he hated, and which repaid his detestation with contempt, he retired to this region of sterility, in order to brood over his resentment in solitude, and converse with the only honest heart he knew,—namely, with his own.

A cave was his only shelter from the inclemency of the weather; fruits, gathered with difficulty from the mountain's side, his only food; and his drink was fetched, with danger and toil, from the headlong torrent. In this manner he lived, sequestered from society, passing the hours in meditation, and sometimes exulting that he was able to live independent of his fellow creatures.

At the foot of the mountain an extensive lake displayed its glassy bosom, reflecting on its broad surface the impending horrors of the mountain. To this capacious mirror he would sometimes descend, and, reclining on its steep banks, cast an eager look on the smooth expanse that lay before him. "How beautiful," he often cried, "is Nature! how lovely even in her wildest scenes! How finely contrasted is the level plain that lies beneath me with yon awful pile that hides its tremendous head in clouds! But the beauty of these scenes is no way comparable with their utility; hence an hundred rivers are supplied, which distribute health and verdure to the various countries through which they flow. Every part of the universe is beautiful, just, and wise; but man, vile man, is a solecism in nature, the only monster in the creation. Tempests and whirlwinds have their use; but vicious, ungrateful, man is a blot in the fair page of universal beauty. Why was I born of that detested species, whose vices are almost a reproach to the wisdom of the divine Creator? Were men entirely free from vice, all would be uniformity, harmony, and order. A world of moral rectitude should be the result of a perfect moral agent. Why, why then, O Alla! must I be thus confined in darkness, doubt, and despair?"

Just as he uttered the word despair, he was going to plunge into the lake beneath him, at once to satisfy his doubts, and put a period to his anxiety, when he perceived a most majestic being walking on the surface of the water, and approaching the bank on which he stood. So unexpected an object at once checked his purpose; he stopped, contemplated, and fancied he saw something awful and divine in his aspect.

"Son of Adam," cried the Genius, "stop thy rash purpose; the Father of the Faithful has seen thy justice, thy integrity, thy miseries, and hath sent me to afford and administer relief. Give me thine hand, and follow without trembling wherever I shall lead: in me behold the Genius of Conviction, kept by the great Prophet, to turn from their errors those who go astray, not from curiosity, but a rectitude of intention. Follow me and be wise."

Asem immediately descended upon the lake, and his guide conducted him along the surface of the water, till, coming near the centre of the lake, they both began to sink; the waters closed over their heads; they descended several hundred fathoms, till Asem, just ready to give up his life as inevitably lost, found himself, with his celestial guide, in another world, at the bottom of the waters, where human foot had never trod before. His astonishment was beyond description, when he saw a sun like that he had left, a serene sky over his head, and blooming verdure under his feet.

"I plainly perceive your amazement," said the Genius; "but suspend it for a while. This world was formed by Alla, at the request, and under the inspection, of our great Prophet, who once entertained the same doubts which filled your mind when I found you, and from the consequence of which you were so lately rescued. The rational inhabitants of this world are formed agreeable to your own ideas; they are absolutely without vice. In other respects it resembles your earth, but differs from it in being wholly inhabited by men who never do wrong. If you find this world more agreeable than that you so lately left, you have free permission to spend the remainder of your days in it; but permit me for some time to attend you, that I may silence your doubts, and make you better acquainted with your company and your new habitation."

"A world without vice! Rational beings without immorality!" cried Asem, in a rapture; "I thank thee, O Alla! who hast at length heard my petitions: this, this indeed will produce happiness, ecstasy, and ease. Oh, for an immortality, to spend it among men who are incapable of ingratitude, injustice, fraud, violence, and a thousand other crimes that render society miserable!"

"Cease thine exclamations," replied the Genius. "Look around thee: reflect on every object and action before us, and communicate to me the result of thine observations. Lead wherever you think proper, I shall be your attendant and instructor." Asem and his companion travelled on in silence for some time, the former being entirely lost in astonishment; but at last recovering his former serenity, he could not help observing, that the face of the country bore a near resemblance to that he had left, except that this subterranean world still seemed to retain its primeval wildness.

"Here," cried Asem, "I perceive animals of prey and others that seem only designed for their subsistence; it is the very same in the world over our heads. But had I been permitted to instruct our Prophet, I would have removed this defect, and formed no voracious or destructive animals, which only prey on the other parts of the creation."—"Your tenderness for inferior animals is, I find, remarkable," said the Genius, smiling. "But, with regard to meaner creatures, this world exactly resembles the other, and, indeed, for obvious reasons; for the earth can support a more considerable number of animals by their thus becoming food for each other, than if they had lived entirely on her vegetable productions. So that animals of different natures thus formed, instead of lessening their multitude, subsist in the greatest number possible. But let us hasten on to the inhabited country before us, and see what that offers for instruction."

They soon gained the utmost verge of the forest, and entered the country inhabited by men without vice; and Asem anticipated in idea the rational delight he hoped to experience in such an innocent society. But they had scarcely left the confines of the wood, when they beheld one of the inhabitants flying with hasty steps, and terror in his countenance, from an army of squirrels, that closely pursued him. "Heavens!" cried Asem, "why does he fly? What can he fear from animals so contemptible?" He had scarcely spoken, when he perceived two dogs pursuing another of the human species, who with equal terror and haste attempted to avoid them. "This," cried Asem to his guide, "is truly surprising; nor can I conceive the reason for so strange an action."—"Every species of animals," replied the Genius, "has of late grown very powerful in this country; for the inhabitants, at first, thinking it unjust to use either fraud or force in destroying them, they have insensibly increased, and now frequently ravage their harmless frontiers."—"But they should have been destroyed," cried Asem; "you see the consequence of such neglect."—"Where is, then, that tenderness you so lately expressed for subordinate animals?" replied the Genius, smiling; "you seem to have forgot that branch of justice."—"I must acknowledge my mistake," returned Asem; "I am now convinced that we must be guilty of tyranny and injustice to the brute creation, if we would enjoy the world ourselves. But let us no longer observe the duty of man to these irrational creatures, but survey their connections with one another."

As they walked farther up the country, the more he was surprised to see no vestiges of handsome houses, no cities, nor any mark of elegant design. His conductor, perceiving his surprise, observed, that the inhabitants of this new world were perfectly content with their ancient simplicity; each had a house, which, though homely, was sufficient to lodge his little family; they were too good to build houses, which could only increase their own pride, and the envy of the spectator: what they built was for convenience, and not for show. "At least, then," said Asem, "they have neither architects, painters, nor statuaries, in their society; but these are idle arts, and may be spared. However, before I spend much more time here, you should have my thanks for introducing me into the society of some of their wisest men: there is scarce any pleasure to me equal to a refined conversation; there is nothing of which I am so much enamoured as wisdom."—"Wisdom!" replied his instructor; "how ridiculous! We have no wisdom here, for we have no occasion for it; true wisdom is only a knowledge of our own duty, and the duty of others to us; but of what use is such wisdom here? each intuitively performs what is right in himself, and expects the same from others. If by wisdom you should mean vain curiosity and empty speculation, as such pleasures have their origin in vanity, luxury, or avarice, we are too good to pursue them."—"All this may be right," says Asem: "but methinks I observe a solitary disposition prevail among the people; each family keeps separately within their own precincts, without society, or without intercourse."—"That indeed is true," replied the other; "here is no established society, nor should there be any; all societies are made either through fear or friendship: the people we are among are too good to fear each other; and there are no motives to private friendship, where all are equally meritorious."—"Well, then," said the sceptic, "as I am to spend my time here, if I am to have neither the polite arts, nor wisdom, nor friendship, in such a world, I should be glad at least of an easy companion, who may tell me his thoughts, and to whom I may communicate mine."—"And to what purpose should either do this?" says the Genius: "flattery or curiosity are vicious motives, and never allowed of here; and wisdom is out of the question."

"Still, however," said Asem, "the inhabitants must be happy; each is contented with his own possessions, nor avariciously endeavours to heap up more than is necessary for his own subsistence; each has therefore leisure for pitying those that stand in need of his compassion." He had scarce spoken, when his ears were assaulted with the lamentations of a wretch who sat by the way-side, and in the most deplorable distress seemed gently to murmur at his own misery. Asem immediately ran to his relief, and found him in the last stage of a consumption. "Strange," cried the son of Adam, "that men who are free from vice should thus suffer so much misery without relief!"—"Be not surprised," said the wretch who was dying: "would it not be the utmost injustice for beings who have only just sufficient to support themselves, and are content with a bare subsistence, to take it from their own mouths to put it into mine? They never are possessed of a single meal more than is necessary, and what is barely necessary cannot be dispensed with."—"They should have been supplied with more than is necessary," cried Asem—"and yet I contradict my own opinion but a moment before—all is doubt, perplexity, and confusion. Even the want of ingratitude is no virtue here, since they never received a favour. They have, however, another excellence yet behind; the love of their country is still, I hope, one of their darling virtues."—"Peace, Asem," replied the Guardian, with a countenance not less severe than beautiful; "nor forfeit all thy pretensions to wisdom: the same selfish motives by which we prefer our own interests to that of others, induce us to regard our country preferably to that of another. Nothing less than universal benevolence is free from vice, and that you see is practised here."—"Strange!" cries the disappointed pilgrim, in an agony of distress; "what sort of a world am I now introduced to? There is scarce a single virtue, but that of temperance, which they practise: and in that they are no way superior to the very brute creation. There is scarce an amusement which they enjoy; fortitude, liberality, friendship, wisdom, conversation, and love of country, all are virtues entirely unknown here: thus it seems that to be unacquainted with vice is not to know virtue. Take me, O my Genius, back to that very world which I have despised: a world which has Alla for its contriver is much more wisely formed than that which has been projected by Mahomet. Ingratitude, contempt, and hatred, I can now suffer, for perhaps I have deserved them. When I arraigned the wisdom of Providence, I only showed my own ignorance; henceforth let me keep from vice myself, and pity it in others."

He had scarce ended, when the Genius, assuming an air of terrible complacency, called all his thunders around him, and vanished in a whirlwind. Asem, astonished at the terror of the scene, looked for his imaginary world; when, casting his eyes around, he perceived himself in the very situation, and in the very place, where he first began to repine and despair; his right foot had been just advanced to take the fatal plunge, nor had it been yet withdrawn; so instantly did Providence strike the series of truths just imprinted on his soul. He now departed from the water side in tranquillity; and leaving his horrid mansion, travelled to Segestan, his native city, where he diligently applied himself to commerce, and put in practice that wisdom he had learned in solitude. The frugality of a few years soon produced opulence; the number of his domestics increased; his friends came to him from every part of the city; nor did he receive them with disdain; and a youth of misery was concluded with an old age of elegance, affluence, and ease.

ESSAY IV.

On the English Clergy and popular Preachers.

It is allowed on all hands, that our English divines receive a more liberal education, and improve that education by frequent study more than any others of this reverend profession in Europe. In general, also, it may be observed, that a greater degree of gentility is affixed to the character of a student in England than elsewhere; by which means our clergy have an opportunity of seeing better company while young, and of sooner wearing off those prejudices which they are apt to imbibe even in the best regulated universities, and which may be justly termed the vulgar errors of the wise.

Yet, with all these advantages, it is very obvious that the clergy are nowhere so little thought of by the populace as here; and though our divines are foremost with respect to abilities, yet they are found last in the effects of their ministry; the vulgar in general appearing no way impressed with a sense of religious duty. I am not for whining at the depravity of the times, or for endeavouring to paint a prospect more gloomy than in nature; but certain it is, no person who has travelled will contradict me when I aver, that the lower orders of mankind in other countries testify on every occasion the profoundest awe of religion; while in England they are scarcely awakened into a sense of its duties, even in circumstances of the greatest distress.

This dissolute and fearless conduct foreigners are apt to attribute to climate and constitution. May not the vulgar being pretty much neglected in our exhortations from the pulpit be a conspiring cause? Our divines seldom stoop to their mean capacities; and they who want instruction most, find least in our religious assemblies.

Whatever may become of the higher orders of mankind, who are generally possessed of collateral motives to virtue, the vulgar should be particularly regarded, whose behaviour in civil life is totally hinged upon their hopes and fears. Those who constitute the basis of the great fabric of society should be particularly regarded; for in policy, as in architecture, ruin is most fatal when it begins from the bottom.

Men of real sense and understanding prefer a prudent mediocrity to a precarious popularity; and fearing to outdo their duty, leave it half done. Their discourses from the pulpit are generally dry, methodical, and unaffecting; delivered with the most insipid calmness; insomuch, that should the peaceful preacher lift his head over the cushion, which alone he seems to address, he might discover his audience, instead of being awakened to remorse, actually sleeping over his methodical and laboured composition.

This method of preaching is, however, by some called an address to reason, and not to the passions; this is styled the making of converts from conviction: but such are indifferently acquainted with human nature, who are not sensible, that men seldom reason about their debaucheries till they are committed. Reason is but a weak antagonist when headlong passion dictates; in all such cases we should arm one passion against another: it is with the human mind as in nature, from the mixture of two opposites the result is most frequently neutral tranquillity. Those who attempt to reason us out of our follies begin at the wrong end, since the attempt naturally presupposes us capable of reason; but to be made capable of this is one great point of the cure.

There are but few talents requisite to become a popular preacher; for the people are easily pleased, if they perceive any endeavours in the orator to please them; the meanest qualifications will work this effect, if the preacher sincerely sets about it. Perhaps little, indeed very little, more is required than sincerity and assurance; and a becoming sincerity is always certain of producing a becoming assurance. "Si vis me flere, dolendum est primum tibi ipsi" is so trite a quotation, that it almost demands an apology to repeat it; yet, though all allow the justice of the remark, how few do we find put it in practice! Our orators, with the most faulty bashfulness, seem impressed rather with an awe of their audience, than with a just respect for the truths they are about to deliver; they, of all professions, seem the most bashful, who have the greatest right to glory in their commission.

The French preachers generally assume all that dignity which becomes men who are ambassadors from Christ: the English divines, like erroneous envoys, seem more solicitous not to offend the court to which they are sent, than to drive home the interests of their employer. Massillon, bishop of Clermont, in the first sermon he ever preached, found the whole audience, upon his getting into the pulpit, in a disposition no way favourable to his intentions; their nods, whispers, or drowsy behaviour, showed him that there was no great profit to be expected from his sowing in a soil so improper; however, he soon changed the disposition of his audience by his manner of beginning. "If," says he, "a cause, the most important that could be conceived, were to be tried at the bar before qualified judges—if this cause interested ourselves in particular—if the eyes of the whole kingdom were fixed upon the event—if the most eminent counsel were employed on both sides—and if we had heard from our infancy of this yet undetermined trial,—would you not all sit with due attention, and warm expectation, to the pleadings on each side? would not all your hopes and fears be hinged upon the final decision? And yet, let me tell you, you have this moment a cause of much greater importance before you—a cause where not one nation, but all the world are spectators; tried not before a fallible tribunal, but the awful throne of Heaven; where not your temporal and transitory interests are the subject of debate, but your eternal happiness or misery; where the cause is still undetermined, but, perhaps, the very moment I am speaking may fix the irrevocable decree that shall last for ever; and yet, notwithstanding all this, you can hardly sit with patience to hear the tidings of your own salvation: I plead the cause of Heaven, and yet I am scarcely attended to," &c.

The style, the abruptness of a beginning like this, in the closet would appear absurd; but in the pulpit it is attended with the most lasting impressions: that style which in the closet might justly be called flimsy, seems the true mode of eloquence here. I never read a fine composition, under the title of a sermon, that I do not think the author has miscalled his piece;

for the talents to be used in writing well entirely differ from those of speaking well. The qualifications for speaking, as has been already observed, are easily acquired; they are accomplishments which may be taken up by every candidate who will be at the pains of stooping. Impressed with a sense of the truths he is about to deliver, a preacher disregards the applause or the contempt of his audience, and he insensibly assumes a just and manly sincerity. With this talent alone, we see what crowds are drawn around enthusiasts, even destitute of common sense; what numbers converted to Christianity. Folly may sometimes set an example for wisdom to practise; and our regular divines may borrow instruction from even Methodists, who go their circuits and preach prizes among the populace. Even Whitfield may be placed as a model to some of our young divines: let them join to their own good sense his earnest manner of delivery.

It will be perhaps objected, that by confining the excellencies of a preacher to proper assurance, earnestness, and openness of style, I make the qualifications too trifling for estimation: there will be something called oratory brought up on this occasion; action, attitude, grace, elocution, may be repeated as absolutely necessary to complete the character. But let us not be deceived; common sense is seldom swayed by fine tones, musical periods, just attitudes, or the display of a white handkerchief: oratorial behaviour, except in very able hands indeed, generally sinks into awkward and paltry affectation.

It must be observed, however, that these rules are calculated only for him who would instruct the vulgar, who stand in most need of instruction; to address philosophers, and to obtain the character of a polite preacher among the polite—a much more useless, though more sought for character—requires a different method of proceeding. All I shall observe on this head is, to entreat the polemic divine, in his controversy with the deists, to act rather offensively than to defend; to push home the grounds of his belief, and the impracticability of theirs, rather than to spend time in solving the objections of every opponent. "It is ten to one," says a late writer on the art of war, "but that the assailant who attacks the enemy in his trenches is always victorious."

Yet, upon the whole, our clergy might employ themselves more to the benefit of society by declining all controversy, than by exhibiting even the profoundest skill in polemic disputes. Their contests with each other often turn on speculative trifles; and their disputes with the deists are almost at an end, since they can have no more than victory; and that they are already possessed of, as their antagonists have been driven into a confession of the necessity of revelation, or an open avowal of atheism. To continue the dispute longer would only endanger it: the sceptic is ever expert at puzzling a debate which he finds himself unable to continue; "and, like an Olympic boxer, generally fights best when undermost."

ESSAY V.

A Reverie at the Boar's-Head Tavern, Eastcheap.

THE improvements we make in mental acquirements only render us each day more sensible of the defects of our constitution: with this in view, therefore, let us often recur to the amusements of youth, endeavour to forget age and wisdom, and, as far as innocence goes, be as much a boy as the best of them.

Let idle declaimers mourn over the degeneracy of the age: but in my opinion every age is the same. This I am sure of, that man in every season is a poor fretful being, with no other means to escape the calamities of the times but by endeavouring to forget them; for if he attempts to resist, he is certainly undone. If I feel poverty and pain, I am not so hardy as to quarrel with the executioner, even while under correction: I find myself no way disposed to make fine speeches while I am making wry faces. In a word, let me drink when the fit is on, to make me insensible; and drink when it is over, for joy that I feel pain no longer.

The character of old Falstaff, even with all his faults, gives me more consolation than the most studied efforts of wisdom;

I here behold an agreeable old fellow forgetting age, and showing me the way to be young at sixty-five. Sure I am well able to be as merry, though not so comical, as he. Is it not in my power to have, though not so much wit, at least as much vivacity?—Age, care, wisdom, reflection, begone—I give you to the winds! Let's have t'other bottle: here's to the memory of Shakespeare, Falstaff, and all the merry men of Eastcheap!

Such were the reflections that naturally arose while I sat at the Boar's-Head Tavern, still kept at Eastcheap. Here, by a pleasant fire, in the very room where old Sir John Falstaff cracked his jokes, in the very chair which was sometimes honoured by Prince Henry, and sometimes polluted by his immoral merry companions, I sat and ruminated on the follies of youth; wished to be young again, but was resolved to make the best of life while it lasted; and now and then compared past and present times together. I considered myself as the only living representative of the old knight, and transported my imagination back to the times when the Prince and he gave life to the revel, and made even debauchery not disgusting. The room also conspired to throw my reflections back into antiquity: the oak floor, the Gothic windows, and the ponderous chimney-piece, had long withstood the tooth of time; the watchman had gone twelve; my companions had all stolen off; and none now remained with me but the landlord. From him I could have wished to know the history of a tavern that had such a long succession of customers; I could not help thinking that an account of this kind would be a pleasing contrast of the manners of different ages: but my landlord could give me no information. He continued to doze and sot, and tell a tedious story, as most other landlords usually do, and though he said nothing, yet was never silent; one good joke followed another good joke; and the best joke of all was generally begun towards the end of a bottle. I found at last, however, his wine and his conversation operate by degrees: he insensibly began to alter his appearance; his cravat seemed quilled into a ruff, and his breeches swelled out into a fardingale. I now fancied him changing sexes; and as my eyes began to close in slumber, I imagined my fat landlord actually converted into as fat a landlady. However, sleep made but few changes in my situation: the tavern, the apartment, and the table, continued as before: nothing suffered mutation but my host, who was fairly altered into a gentle-woman, whom I knew to be Dame Quickly, mistress of this tavern in the days of Sir John; and the liquor we were drinking seemed converted into sack and sugar.

"My dear Mrs. Quickly," cried I, (for I knew her perfectly well at first sight,) "I am heartily glad to see you. How have you left Falstaff, Pistol, and the rest of our friends below stairs? Brave and hearty, I hope?"—"In good sooth," replied she, "he did deserve to live for ever; but he maketh foul work on't where he hath flitted. Queen Proserpine and he have quarrelled for his attempting a rape upon her divinity; and were it not that she still had bowels of compassion, it more than seems probable he might have been now sprawling in Tartarus."

I now found that spirits still preserve the frailties of the flesh; and that, according to the laws of criticism and dreaming, ghosts have been known to be guilty of even more than platonic affection: wherefore, as I found her too much moved on such a topic to proceed, I was resolved to change the subject, and desiring she would pledge me in a bumper, observed with a sigh, that our sack was nothing now to what it was in former days. "Ah, Mrs. Quickly, those were merry times when you drew sack for Prince Henry: men were twice as strong, and twice as wise, and much braver, and ten thousand times more charitable, than now. Those were the times! The battle of Agincourt was a victory indeed! Ever since that we have only been degenerating; and I have lived to see the day when drinking is no longer fashionable, when men wear clean shirts, and women show their necks and arms. All are degenerated, Mrs. Quickly; and we shall probably, in another century, be frittered away into beaux or monkeys. Had you been on earth to see what I have seen, it would congeal all the blood in your body—your soul, I mean. Why, our very nobility now have the intolerable arrogance, in spite of what is every day remonstrated from the press—our very nobility, I say, have the assurance to frequent assemblies, and presume to be as merry as the vulgar. See, my very friends have scarcely manhood enough to sit to it till eleven; and I only am left to make a night on't. Prithee do me the favour to console me a little for their absence by the story of your own adventures, or the history of the tavern where we are now sitting: I fancy the narrative may have something singular."

"Observe this apartment," interrupted my companion; "of neat device, and excellent workmanship: in this room I have lived, child, woman, and ghost, more than three hundred years. I am ordered by Pluto to keep an annual register of every transaction that passed here; and I have whilome compiled three hundred tomes, which eftsoons may be submitted to thy regards."—"None of your whilomes or eftsoons, Mrs. Quickly, if you please," I replied: "I know you can talk every whit as well as I can; for, as you have lived here so long, it is but natural to suppose you should learn the conversation of the company. Believe me, dame, at best you have neither too much sense nor too much language to spare; so give me both as well as you can: but first, my service to you; old women should water their clay a little now and then; and now to your story."

"The story of my own adventures," replied the vision, "is but short and unsatisfactory; for, believe me, Mr. Rigmarole, believe me, a woman with a butt of sack at her elbow is never long-lived. Sir John's death afflicted me to such a degree, that I sincerely believe, to drown sorrow, I drank more liquor myself than I drew for my customers: my grief was sincere, and the sack was excellent. The prior of a neighbouring convent, (for our priors then had as much power as a Middlesex Justice now,) he, I say, it was who gave me a licence for keeping a disorderly house, upon condition that I should never make hard bargains with the clergy, that he should have a bottle of sack every morning, and the liberty of confessing which of my girls he thought proper in private every night. I had continued for several years to pay this tribute; and he, it must be confessed, continued as rigorously to exact it. I grew old insensibly; my customers continued, however, to compliment my looks while I was by, but I could hear them say I was wearing when my back was turned. The prior, however, still was constant, and so were half his convent; but one fatal morning he missed the usual beverage, for I had incautiously drunk over-night the last bottle myself. What will you have on't? The very next day Doll Tearsheet and I were sent to the house of correction, and accused of keeping a low bawdy-house. In short, we were so well purified there with stripes, mortification, and penance, that we were afterwards utterly unfit for worldly conversation: though sack would have killed me, had I stuck to it, yet I soon died for want of a drop of something comfortable, and fairly left my body to the care of the beadle.

"Such is my own history; but that of the tavern, where I have ever since been stationed, affords greater variety. In the history of this, which is one of the oldest in London, you may view the different manners, pleasures, and follies of men at different periods. You will find mankind neither better nor worse now than formerly; the vices of an uncivilized people are generally more detestable, though not so frequent as those in polite society. It is the same luxury which formerly stuffed your alderman with plum-porridge, and now crams him with turtle: it is the same low ambition that formerly induced a courtier to give up his religion to please his king, and now persuades him to give up his conscience to please his minister: it is the same vanity that formerly stained our ladies' cheeks and necks with woad, and now paints them with carmine. Your ancient Briton formerly powdered his hair with red earth like brick-dust, in order to appear frightful: your modern Briton cuts his hair on the crown, and plasters it with hog's lard and flour; and this to make him look killing. It is the same vanity, the same folly, and the same vice, only appearing different, as viewed through the glass of fashion. In a word, all mankind are a ——"

"Sure the woman is dreaming," interrupted I. "None of your reflections, Mrs. Quickly, if you love me; they only give me the spleen. Tell me your history at once. I love stories, but hate reasoning."

"If you please, then, sir," returned my companion, "I'll read you an abstract which I made of the three hundred volumes I mentioned just now.

"My body was no sooner laid in the dust, than the prior and several of his convent came to purify the tavern from the pollutions with which they said I had filled it. Masses were said in every room, relics were exposed upon every piece of furniture, and the whole house washed with a deluge of holy water. My habitation was soon converted into a monastery; instead of customers now applying for sack and sugar, my rooms were crowded with images, relics, saints, whores, and friars; instead of being a scene of occasional debauchery, it was now filled with continual lewdness. The prior led the fashion, and the whole convent imitated his pious example. Matrons came hither to confess their sins, and to commit new: virgins came hither who seldom went virgins away. Nor was this a convent peculiarly wicked; every convent at that period was equally fond of pleasure, and gave a boundless loose to appetite. The laws allowed it; each priest had a right to a favourite companion, and a power of discarding her as often as he pleased. The laity grumbled, quarrelled with their wives and daughters, hated their confessors—and maintained them in opulence and ease.—These, these were happy times, Mr. Rigmarole! these were times of piety, bravery, and simplicity."—"Not so very happy, neither, good madam; pretty much like the present,—those that labour starve, and those that do nothing wear fine clothes, and live in luxury."

"In this manner the fathers lived for some years without molestation; they transgressed, confessed themselves to each other, and were forgiven. One evening, however, our prior keeping a lady of distinction somewhat too long at confession, her husband unexpectedly came upon them, and testified all the indignation which was natural upon such an occasion. The prior assured the gentleman that it was the devil who put it into his heart; and the lady was very certain that she was under the influence of magic, or she could never have behaved in so unfaithful a manner. The husband, however, was not to be put off by such evasions, but summoned both before the tribunal of justice. His proofs were flagrant, and he expected large damages. Such, indeed, he had a right to expect, were the tribunals of those days constituted in the same manner as they are now. The cause of the priest was to be tried before an assembly of priests; and a layman was to expect redress only from their impartiality and candour. What plea, then, do you think the prior made to obviate this accusation? He denied the fact, and challenged the plaintiff to try the merits of their cause by single combat. It was a little hard, you may be sure, upon the poor gentleman, not only to be made a cuckold, but to be obliged to fight a duel into the bargain; yet such was the justice of the times. The prior threw down his glove, and the injured husband was obliged to take it up, in token of his accepting the challenge. Upon this the priest supplied his champion, for it was not lawful for the clergy to fight; and the defendant and plaintiff, according to custom, were put in prison; both ordered to fast and pray, every method being previously used to induce both to a confession of the truth. After a month's imprisonment, the hair of each was cut, their bodies anointed with oil, the field of battle appointed and guarded by soldiers, while his majesty presided over the whole in person. Both the champions were sworn not to seek victory either by fraud or magic. They prayed and confessed upon their knees; and after these ceremonies, the rest was left to the courage and conduct of the combatants. As the champion whom the prior had pitched upon had fought six or eight times upon similar occasions, it was no way extraordinary to find him victorious in the present combat. In short, the husband was discomfited; he was taken from the field of battle, stripped to his shirt, and after one of his legs had been cut off, as justice ordained in such cases, he was hanged as a terror to future offenders.—These, these were the times, Mr. Rigmarole! you see how much more just, and wise, and valiant, our ancestors were than us."—"I rather fancy, madam, that the times then were pretty much like our own; where a multiplicity of laws give a judge as much power as a want of law, since he is ever sure to find among the number some to countenance his partiality."

"Our convent, victorious over their enemies, now gave a loose to every demonstration of joy. The lady became a nun, the prior was made a bishop, and three Wickliffites were burned in the illuminations and fireworks that were made on the present occasion. Our convent now began to enjoy a very high degree of reputation. There was not one in London that had the character of hating heretics so much as ours. Ladies of the first distinction chose from our convent their confessors. In short, it flourished, and might have flourished to this hour, but for a fatal accident which terminated in its overthrow. The lady, whom the prior had placed in a nunnery, and whom he continued to visit for some time with great punctuality, began at last to perceive that she was quite forsaken. Secluded from conversation, as usual, she now entertained the visions of a devotee; found herself strangely disturbed; but hesitated in determining whether she was possessed by an angel or a demon. She was not long in suspense; for upon vomiting a large quantity of crooked pins, and finding the palms of her hands turned outward, she quickly concluded that she was possessed by the devil. She soon lost entirely the use of speech; and when she seemed to speak, everybody that was present perceived that her voice was not her own, but that of the devil within her. In short, she was bewitched; and all the difficulty lay in determining who it could be that bewitched her. The nuns and the monks all demanded the magician's name, but the devil made no reply; for he knew they had no authority to ask questions. By the rules of witchcraft, when an evil spirit has taken possession, he may refuse to answer any questions asked him, unless they are put by a bishop, and to these he is obliged to reply. A bishop, therefore, was sent for, and now the whole secret came out: the devil reluctantly owned that he was a servant of the prior; that by his command he resided in his present habitation, and that without his command he was resolved to keep in possession. The bishop was an able exorcist; he drove the devil out by force of mystical arms: the prior was arraigned for witchcraft; the witnesses were strong and numerous against him, not less than fourteen persons being by, who heard the devil talk Latin. There was no resisting such a cloud of witnesses: the prior was condemned; and he who had assisted at so many burnings, was burned himself in turn.—These were times, Mr. Rigmarole! the people of those times were not infidels, as now, but sincere believers." —"Equally faulty with ourselves; they believed what the devil was pleased to tell them, and we seem resolved at last to believe neither God nor devil."

"After such a stain upon the convent, it was not to be supposed it could subsist any longer; the fathers were ordered to decamp, and the house was once again converted into a tavern. The king conferred it on one of his cast mistresses; she was constituted landlady by royal authority; and as the tavern was in the neighbourhood of the court, and the mistress a very polite woman, it began to have more business than ever, and sometimes took not less than four shillings a day.

"But perhaps you are desirous of knowing what were the peculiar qualifications of a woman of fashion at that period; and in a description of the present landlady you will have a tolerable idea of all the rest. This lady was the daughter of a nobleman, and received such an education in the country as became her quality, beauty, and great expectations. She could make shifts and hose for herself and all the servants of the family when she was twelve years old. She knew the names of the four-and-twenty letters, so that it was impossible to bewitch her; and this was a greater piece of learning than any lady in the whole country could pretend to.

She was always up early, and saw breakfast served in the great hall by six o'clock. At this scene of festivity she generally improved good humour by telling her dreams, relating stories of spirits, several of which she herself had seen, and one of which she was reported to have killed with a black-hafted knife. From hence she usually went to make pastry in the larder, and here she was followed by her sweethearts, who were much helped on in conversation by struggling with her for kisses. About ten Miss generally went to play at hot-cockles and blind-man's-buff in the parlour; and when the young folks (for they seldom played at hot-cockles when grown old) were tired of such amusements, the gentlemen entertained Miss with the history of their greyhounds, bear-baitings, and victories at cudgel-playing. If the weather was fine, they ran at the ring, and shot at butts; while Miss held in her hand a ribbon, with which she adorned the conqueror. Her mental qualifications were exactly fitted to her external accomplishments. Before she was fifteen she could tell the story of Jack the Giant Killer, could name every mountain that was inhabited by fairies, knew a witch at first sight, and could repeat four Latin prayers without a prompter. Her dress was perfectly fashionable; her arms and her hair were completely covered; a monstrous ruff was put round her neck, so that her head seemed like that of John the Baptist placed in a charger. In short, when completely equipped, her appearance was so very modest, that she discovered little more than her nose.—These were the times, Mr. Rigmarole! when every lady that had a good nose might set up for a beauty; when every woman that could tell stories might be cried up for a wit."—"I am as much displeased at those dresses which conceal too much as at those which discover too much: I am equally an enemy to a female dunce or a female pedant."

"You may be sure that Miss chose a husband with qualifications resembling her own: she pitched upon a courtier equally remarkable for hunting and drinking, who had given several proofs of his great virility among the daughters of his tenants and domestics. They fell in love at first sight (for such was the gallantry of the times), were married, came to court, and madam appeared with superior qualifications. The king was struck with her beauty. All property was at the king's command: the husband was obliged to resign all pretensions in his wife to the sovereign, whom God had anointed to commit adultery where he thought proper. The king loved her for some time; but at length, repenting of his misdeeds, and instigated by his father-confessor, from a principle of conscience removed her from his levee to the bar of this tavern, and took a new mistress in her stead. Let it not surprise you to behold the mistress of a king degraded to so humble an office. As the ladies had no mental accomplishments, a good face was enough to raise them to the royal couch; and she who was this day a royal mistress, might the next, when her beauty palled upon enjoyment, be doomed to infamy and want.

"Under the care of this lady the tavern grew into great reputation; the courtiers had not yet learned to game, but they paid it off by drinking: drunkenness is ever the vice of a barbarous, and gaming of a luxurious age. They had not such frequent entertainments as the moderns have, but were more expensive and more luxurious in those they had. All their fooleries were more elaborate, and more admired by the great and the vulgar, than now. A courtier has been known to spend his whole fortune at a single feast, a king to mortgage his dominions to furnish out the frippery of a tournament. There were certain days appointed for riot and debauchery, and to be sober at such times was reputed a crime. Kings themselves set the example; and I have seen monarchs, in this room, drunk before the entertainment was half concluded.—These were the times, sir, when kings kept mistresses, and got drunk in public; they were too plain and simple in those happy times to hide their vices, and act the hypocrite, as now." —"Lord! Mrs. Quickly," interrupting her, "I expected to have heard a story, and here you are going to tell me I know not what of times and vices: prithee let me entreat thee once more to wave reflections, and give thy history without deviation."

"No lady upon earth," continued my visionary correspondent, "knew how to put off her damaged wine or women with more art than she. When these grew flat, or those paltry, it was but changing the names; the wine became excellent, and the girls agreeable. She was also possessed of the engaging leer, the chuck under the chin, winked at a *double entendre,* could nick the opportunity of calling for something comfortable, and perfectly understood the discreet moments when to withdraw. The gallants of those times pretty much resembled the bloods of ours; they were fond of pleasure, but quite ignorant of the art of refining upon it: thus a court bawd of those times resembled the common low-lived harridan of a modern bagnio. Witness, ye powers of debauchery, how often I have been present at the various appearances of drunkenness, riot, guilt, and brutality! A tavern is the true picture of human infirmity: in history we find only one side of the age exhibited to our view; but in the accounts of a tavern we see every age equally absurd and equally vicious.

"Upon this lady's decease, the tavern was successively occupied by adventurers, bullies, pimps, and gamesters. Towards the conclusion of the reign of Henry VII. gaming was more universally practised in England than even now. Kings themselves have been known to play off at Primero, not only all the money and jewels they could part with, but the very images in churches. The last Henry played away, in this very room, not only the four great bells of St. Paul's Cathedral, but the fine image of St. Paul, which stood upon the top of the spire, to Sir Miles Partridge, who took them down the next day, and sold them by auction. Have you, then, any cause to regret being born in the times you now live? or do you still believe that human nature continues to run on, declining every age? If we observe the actions of the busy part of mankind, your ancestors will be found infinitely more gross, servile, and even dishonest, than you. If, forsaking history, we only trace them in their hours of amusement and dissipation, we shall find them more sensual, more entirely devoted to pleasure, and infinitely more selfish.

"The last hostess of note I find upon record was Jane Rouse. She was born among the lower ranks of the people, and by frugality and extreme complaisance contrived to acquire a moderate fortune: this she might have enjoyed for many years, had she not unfortunately quarrelled with one of her neighbours, a woman who was in high repute for sanctity through the whole parish. In the times of which I speak two women seldom quarrelled, that one did not accuse the other of witchcraft, and she who first contrived to vomit crooked pins was sure to come off victorious. The scandal of a modern tea-table differs widely from the scandal of former times: the fascination of a lady's eyes at present is regarded as a compliment; but if a lady formerly should be accused of having witchcraft in her eyes, it were much better, both for her soul and body, that she had no eyes at all.

"In short, Jane Rouse was accused of witchcraft, and though she made the best defence she could, it was all to no purpose: she was taken from her own bar to the bar of the Old Bailey, condemned, and executed accordingly.—These were times, indeed, when even women could not scold in safety.

"Since her time the tavern underwent several revolutions, according to the spirit of the times, or the disposition of the reigning monarch. It was this day a brothel, and the next a conventicle for enthusiasts. It was one year noted for harbouring Whigs, and the next infamous for a retreat to Tories. Some years ago it was in high vogue, but at present it seems declining. This only may be remarked, in general, that whenever taverns flourish most, the times are then most extravagant and luxurious."—"Lord! Mrs. Quickly!" interrupted I, "you have really deceived me; I expected a romance, and here you have been this half hour giving me only a description of the spirit of the times: if you have nothing but tedious remarks to communicate, seek some other hearer; I am determined to hearken only to stories."

I had scarcely concluded, when my eyes and ears seemed open to my landlord, who had been all this while giving me an account of the repairs he had made in the house, and was now got into the story of the cracked glass in the dining-room.

ESSAY VI.

Adventures of a strolling Player.

I AM fond of amusement, in whatever company it is to be found; and wit, though dressed in rags, is ever pleasing to me. I went some days ago to take a walk in St. James's Park, about the hour in which company leave it to go to dinner. There were but few in the walks, and those who stayed seemed, by their looks, rather more willing to forget that they had an appetite than gain one. I sat down on one of the benches, at the other end of which was seated a man in very shabby clothes.

We continued to groan, to hem, and to cough, as usual upon such occasions; and at last ventured upon conversation. "I beg pardon, sir," cried I, "but I think I have seen you before; your face is familiar to me."—"Yes, sir," replied he, "I have a good familiar face, as my friends tell me. I am as well known in every town in England as the dromedary or live crocodile. You must understand, sir, that I have been these sixteen years Merry Andrew to a puppet-show; last Bartholomew Fair my master and I quarrelled, beat each other, and parted; he to sell his puppets to the pincushion-makers in Rosemary Lane, and I to starve in St. James's Park."

"I am sorry, sir, that a person of your appearance should labour under any difficulties." "Oh, sir," returned he, "my appearance is very much at your service; but though I cannot boast of eating much, yet there are few that are merrier: if I had twenty thousand a year, I should be very merry; and, thank the Fates, though not worth a groat, I am very merry still. If I have threepence in my pocket, I never refuse to be my three-halfpence; and if I have no money, I never scorn to be treated by any that are kind enough to pay my reckoning. What think you, sir, of a steak and a tankard? You shall treat me now; and I will treat you again, when I find you in the Park in love with eating, and without money to pay for a dinner."

As I never refuse a small expense for the sake of a merry companion, we instantly adjourned to a neighbouring ale house, and in a few moments had a frothing tankard and a smoking steak spread on the table before us. It is impossible to express how much the sight of such good cheer improved my companion's vivacity. "I like this dinner, sir," says he, "for three reasons: first, because I am naturally fond of beef; secondly, because I am hungry; and, thirdly and lastly, because I get it for nothing: no meat eats so sweet as that for which we do not pay."

He therefore now fell to, and his appetite seemed to correspond with his inclination. After dinner was over, he observed that the steak was tough: "and yet, sir," returns he, "bad as it was, it seemed a rump-steak to me. Oh, the delights of poverty and a good appetite! We beggars are the very fondlings of Nature; the rich she treats like an arrant stepmother; they are pleased with nothing: cut a steak from what part you will, and it is insupportably tough; dress it up with pickles, and even pickles cannot procure them an appetite. But the whole creation is filled with good things for the beggar; Calvert's butt outtastes Champagne, and Sedgeley's home-brewed excels Tokay. Joy, joy, my blood! though our estates lie nowhere, we have fortunes wherever we go. If an inundation sweeps away half the grounds of Cornwall, I am content—I have no lands there; if the stocks sink, that gives me no uneasiness—I am no Jew." The fellow's vivacity, joined to his poverty, I own, raised my curiosity to know something of his life and circumstances; and I entreated that he would indulge my desire. "That I will, sir," said he, "and welcome; only let us drink to prevent our sleeping: let us have another tankard while we are awake—let us have another tankard; for, ah, how charming a tankard looks when full!

"You must know, then, that I am very well descended: my ancestors have made some noise in the world; for my mother cried oysters, and my father beat a drum: I am told we have even had some trumpeters in our family. Many a nobleman cannot show so respectable a genealogy; but that is neither here nor there. As I was their only child, my father designed to breed me up to his own employment, which was that of a drummer to a puppet-show. Thus the whole employment of my younger years was that of interpreter to Punch and King Solomon in all his glory. But though my father was very fond of instructing me in beating all the marches and points of war, I made no very great progress, because I naturally had no ear for music; so at the age of fifteen I went and listed for a soldier. As I had ever hated beating a drum, so I soon found that I disliked carrying a musket also; neither the one trade nor the other was to my taste, for I was by nature fond of being a gentleman: besides, I was obliged to obey my captain: he has his will, I have mine, and you have yours; now I very reasonably concluded, that it was much more comfortable for a man to obey his own will than another's.

"The life of a soldier soon, therefore, gave me the spleen. I asked leave to quit the service; but as I was tall and strong, my captain thanked me for my kind intention, and said, because he had a regard for me, we should not part. I wrote to my father a very dismal penitent letter, and desired that he would raise money to pay for my discharge; but the good man was as fond of drinking as I was,—sir, my service to you,—and those who are fond of drinking never pay for other people's discharges; in short, he never answered my letter. What could be done? If I have not money, said I to myself, to pay for my discharge, I must find an equivalent some other way; and that must be by running away. I deserted, and that answered my purpose every bit as well as if I had bought my discharge.

"Well, I was now fairly rid of my military employment; I sold my soldier's clothes, bought worse, and, in order not to be overtaken, took the most unfrequented roads possible. One evening, as I was entering a village, I perceived a man, whom I afterwards found to be the curate of the parish, thrown from his horse in a miry road, and almost smothered in the mud. He desired my assistance; I gave it, and drew him out with some difficulty. He thanked me for my trouble, and was going off; but I followed him home, for I loved always to have a man thank me at his own door. The curate asked an hundred questions: as, whose son I was; from whence I came; and whether I would be faithful. I answered him greatly to his satisfaction, and gave myself one of the best characters in the world for sobriety,—sir, I have the honour of drinking your health,—discretion, and fidelity. To make a long story short, he wanted a servant, and hired me. With him I lived but two months; we did not much like each other: I was fond of eating, and he gave me but little to eat; I loved a pretty girl, and the old woman, my fellow-servant, was ill-natured and ugly. As they endeavoured to starve me between them, I made a pious resolution to prevent their committing murder: I stole the eggs as soon as they were laid; I emptied every unfinished bottle that I could lay my hands on; whatever eatable came in my way was sure to disappear,—in short, they found I would not do; so I was discharged one morning, and paid three shillings and sixpence for two months' wages.

"While my money was getting ready, I employed myself in making preparations for my departure. Two hens were hatching in an outhouse—I went and took the eggs from habit; and not to separate the parents from the children, I lodged hens and all in my knapsack. After this piece of frugality, I returned to receive my money, and with my knapsack on my back, and a staff in my hand, I bade adieu, with tears in my eyes, to my old benefactor. I had not gone far from the house when I heard behind me the cry of 'Stop thief!' but this only increased my despatch: it would have been foolish to stop, as I knew the voice could not be levelled at me—But hold, I think I passed those two months at the curate's without drinking. Come, the times are dry, and may this be my poison, if ever I spent two more pious, stupid months in all my life!

"Well, after travelling some days, whom should I light upon but a company of strolling players! The moment I saw them at a distance my heart warmed to them; I had a sort of natural love for everything of the vagabond order. They were employed in settling their baggage, which had been overturned in a narrow way; I offered my assistance, which they accepted; and we soon became so well acquainted, that they took me as a servant. This was a paradise to me; they sang, danced, drank, eat, and travelled, all at the same time. By the blood of the Mirabels, I thought I had never lived till then; I grew as merry as a grig, and laughed at every word that was spoken. They liked me as much as I liked them: I was a very good figure, as you may see; and though I was poor, I was not modest.

"I love a straggling life above all things in the world; sometimes good, sometimes bad; to be warm to-day, and cold to-morrow; to eat when one can get it, and drink when—the tankard is out—it stands before me. We arrived that evening at Tenterden, and took a large room at the Greyhound, where we resolved to exhibit Romeo and Juliet, with the funeral procession, the grave, and the garden scene. Romeo was to be performed by a gentleman from the Theatre Royal in Drury Lane; Juliet by a lady who had never appeared on any stage before; and I was to snuff the candles; all excellent in our way. We had figures enough, but the difficulty was to dress them. The same coat that served Romeo, turned with the blue lining outwards, served for his friend Mercutio; a large piece of crape sufficed at once for Juliet's petticoat and pall; a pestle and mortar, from a neighbouring apothecary's, answered all the purposes of a bell; and our landlord's own family, wrapped in white sheets, served to fill up the procession. In short, there were but three figures among us that might be said to be dressed with any propriety,—I mean the nurse, the starved apothecary, and myself. Our performance gave universal satisfaction: the whole audience were enchanted with our powers.

"There is one rule by which a strolling player may be ever secure of success; that is, in our theatrical way of expressing it, to make a great deal of the character. To speak and act as in common life is not playing, nor is it what people come to see: natural speaking, like sweet wine, runs glibly over the palate, and scarce leaves any taste behind it; but being high in a part resembles vinegar, which grates upon the taste, and one feels it while he is drinking. To please in town or country the way is to cry, wring, cringe into attitudes, mark the emphasis, slap the pockets, and labour like one in the falling sickness: that is the way to work for applause—that is the way to gain it.

"As we received much reputation for our skill on this first exhibition, it was but natural for me to ascribe part of the success to myself: I snuffed the candles, and let me tell you, that without a candle-snuffer the piece would lose half its embellishments. In this manner we continued a fortnight, and drew tolerable houses; but the evening before our intended departure we gave out our very best piece, in which all our strength was to be exerted. We had great expectations from this, and even doubled our prices, when, behold, one of the principal actors fell ill of a violent fever. This was a stroke like thunder to our little company: they were resolved to go in a body, to scold the man for falling sick at so inconvenient a time, and that, too, of a disorder that threatened to be expensive: I seized the moment, and offered to act the part myself in his stead. The case was desperate: they accepted my offer: and I accordingly sat down, with the part in my hand, and a tankard before me,—sir, your health,—and studied the character, which was to be rehearsed the next day, and played soon after.

"I found my memory excessively helped by drinking: I learned my part with astonishing rapidity, and bade adieu to snuffing candles ever after. I found that Nature had designed me for more noble employments, and I was resolved to take her when in the humour. We got together, in order to rehearse; and I informed my companions—masters now no longer—of the surprising change I felt within me.

'Let the sick man,' said I, 'be under no uneasiness to get well again; I'll fill his place to universal satisfaction: he may even die if he thinks proper; I'll engage that he shall never be missed.' I rehearsed before them, strutted, ranted, and received applause. They soon gave out that a new actor of eminence was to appear, and immediately all the genteel places were bespoke. Before I ascended the stage, however, I concluded within myself, that as I brought money to the house I ought to have my share in the profits. 'Gentlemen,' said I, addressing our company, 'I don't pretend to direct you; far be it from me to treat you with so much ingratitude: you have published my name in the bills with the utmost good nature, and, as affairs stand, cannot act without me: so, gentlemen, to show you my gratitude, I expect to be paid for my acting as much as any of you; otherwise I declare off; I'll brandish my snuffers and clip candles as usual.' This was a very disagreeable proposal, but they found it was impossible to refuse it; it was irresistible,—it was adamant; they consented, and I went on in King Bajazet—my frowning brows bound with a stocking stuffed into a turban, while on my captived arms I brandished a jack-chain. Nature seemed to have fitted me for the part; I was tall, and had a loud voice; my very entrance excited universal applause; I looked round on the audience with a smile, and made a most low and graceful bow, for that is the rule among us. As it was a very passionate part, I invigorated my spirits with three full glasses—the tankard is almost out—of brandy. By Alla! it is almost inconceivable how I went through it; Tamerlane was but a fool to me; though he was sometimes loud enough too, yet I was still louder than he; but then, besides, I had attitudes in abundance: in general I kept my arms folded up thus, upon the pit of my stomach; it is the way at Drury-lane, and has always a fine effect. The tankard would sink to the bottom before I could get through the whole of my merits: in short, I came off like a prodigy; and such was my success, that I could ravish the laurels even from a sirloin of beef. The principal gentlemen and ladies of the town came to me, after the play was over, to compliment me upon my success: one praised my voice, another my person. 'Upon my word,' says the Squire's lady, 'he will make one of the finest actors in Europe; I say it, and I think I am something of a judge.' Praise in the beginning is agreeable enough, and we receive it as a favour; but when it comes in great quantities, we regard it only as a debt, which nothing but our merit could extort: instead of thanking them, I internally applauded myself. We were desired to give our piece a second time: we obeyed: and I was applauded even more than before.

"At last we left the town, in order to be at a horse-race at some distance from thence. I shall never think of Tenterden without tears of gratitude and respect. The ladies and gentlemen there, take my word for it, are very good judges of plays and actors.—Come, let us drink their healths, if you please, sir. We quitted the town, I say; and there was a wide difference between my coming in and going out: I entered the town a candle-snuffer, and I quitted it an hero!—Such is the world: little to-day, and great to-morrow. I could say a great deal more upon that subject—something truly sublime, upon the ups and downs of fortune; but it would give us both the spleen, and so I shall pass it over.

"The races were ended before we arrived at the next town, which was no small disappointment to our company; however, we were resolved to take all we could get. I played capital characters there too, and came off with my usual brilliancy. I sincerely believe I should have been the first actor in Europe, had my growing merit been properly cultivated; but there came an unkindly frost, which nipped me in the bud, and levelled me once more down to the common standard of humanity. I played Sir Harry Wildair; all the country ladies were charmed: if I but drew out my snuff-box, the whole house was in a roar of rapture; when I exercised my cudgel, I thought they would have fallen into convulsions.

"There was here a lady who had received an education of nine months in

London, and this gave her pretensions to taste, which rendered her the indisputable mistress of the ceremonies wherever she came. She was informed of my merits; everybody praised me, yet she refused at first going to see me perform. She could not conceive, she said, anything but stuff from a stroller; talked something in praise of Garrick, and amazed the ladies with her skill in enunciations, tones, and cadences. She was at last, however, prevailed upon to go; and it was privately intimated to me what a judge was to be present at my next exhibition. However, no way intimidated, I came on in Sir Harry, one hand stuck in my breeches, and the other in my bosom, as usual at Drury-lane; but instead of looking at me, I perceived the whole audience had their eyes turned upon the lady who had been nine months in London; from her they expected the decision which was to secure the general's truncheon in my hand, or sink me down into a theatrical letter-carrier. I opened my snuff-box, took snuff; the lady was solemn, and so were the rest: I broke my cudgel on Alderman Smuggler's back; still gloomy, melancholy all—the lady groaned and shrugged her shoulders: I attempted, by laughing myself, to excite at least a smile; but the devil a cheek could I perceive wrinkled into sympathy: I found it would not do. All my good-humour now became forced; my laughter was converted into hysteric grinning; and while I pretended spirits, my eye showed the agony of my heart: in short, the lady came with an intention to be displeased, and displeased she was; my fame expired; I am here, and—the tankard is no more!"

ESSAY VII.

Rules enjoined to be observed at a Russian Assembly.

WHEN Catharina Alexowna was made Empress of Russia, the women were in an actual state of bondage; but she undertook to introduce mixed assemblies, as in other parts of Europe. She altered the women's dress by substituting the fashions of England; instead of furs, she brought in the use of taffeta and damask, and cornets and commodes instead of caps of sable. The women now found themselves no longer shut up in separate apartments, but saw company, visited each other, and were present at every entertainment.

But as the laws to this effect were directed to a savage people, it is amusing enough to see the manner in which the ordinances ran. Assemblies were quite unknown among them; the Czarina was satisfied with introducing them, for she found it impossible to render them polite. An ordinance was therefore published, according to their notions of breeding; which, as it is a curiosity, and has never before been printed, that we know of, we shall give our readers:

"I. The person at whose house the assembly is to be kept shall signify the same by hanging out a bill, or by giving some other public notice, by way of advertisement to persons of both sexes.

"II. The assembly shall not be open sooner than four or five o'clock in the afternoon, nor continue longer than ten at night.

"III. The master of the house shall not be obliged to meet his guests, or conduct them out, or keep them company; but, though he is exempt from all this, he is to find them chairs, candles, liquors, and all other necessaries that company may ask for: he is likewise to provide them with cards, dice, and every necessary for gaming.

"IV. There shall be no fixed hour for coming or going away; it is enough for a person to appear in the assembly.

"V. Every one shall be free to sit, walk, or game, as he pleases; nor shall any one go about to hinder him, or take exceptions at what he does, upon pain of emptying the great eagle (a pint bowl full of brandy): it shall likewise be sufficient, at entering or retiring, to salute the company.

"VI. Persons of distinction, noblemen, superior officers, merchants, and tradesmen of note, head workmen, especially carpenters, and persons employed in chancery, are to have liberty to enter the assemblies; as likewise their wives and children.

"VII. A particular place shall be

assigned the footmen, except those of the house, that there may be room enough in the apartments designed for the assembly.

"VIII. No ladies are to get drunk upon any pretence whatsoever; nor shall gentlemen be drunk before nine.

"IX. Ladies who play at forfeitures, questions and commands, &c. shall not be riotous: no gentleman shall attempt to force a kiss, and no person shall offer to strike a woman in the assembly, under pain of future exclusion."

Such are the statutes upon this occasion, which, in their very appearance, carry an air of ridicule and satire. But politeness must enter every country by degrees; and these rules resemble the breeding of a clown, awkward but sincere.

ESSAY VIII.

Biographical Memoir, supposed to be written by the Ordinary of Newgate.

Man is a most frail being, incapable of directing his steps, unacquainted with what is to happen in this life; and perhaps no man is a more manifest instance of the truth of this maxim than Mr. The. Cibber, just now gone out of the world. Such a variety of turns of fortune, yet such a persevering uniformity of conduct, appears in all that happened in his short span, that the whole may be looked upon as one regular confusion: every action of his life was matter of wonder and surprise, and his death was an astonishment.

This gentleman was born of creditable parents, who gave him a very good education and a great deal of good learning, so that he could read and write before he was sixteen. However, he early discovered an inclination to follow lewd courses: he refused to take the advice of his parents, and pursued the bent of his inclination; he played at cards on Sundays; called himself a gentleman; fell out with his mother and laundress; and, even in these early days, his father was frequently heard to observe, that young The. would be hanged.

As he advanced in years, he grew more fond of pleasure; would eat an ortolan for dinner, though he begged the guinea that bought it; and was once known to give three pounds for a plate of green peas, which he had collected over-night as charity for a friend in distress: he ran into debt with everybody that would trust him, and none could build a sconce better than he; so that at last his creditors swore, with one accord, that The. would be hanged.

But as getting into debt by a man who had no visible means but impudence for a subsistence is a thing that every reader is not acquainted with, I must explain that point a little, and that to his satisfaction.

There are three ways of getting into debt: first, by pushing a face; as thus: "You, Mr. Lutestring, send me home six yards of that paduasoy, damme; but, harkee, don't think I ever intend to pay you for it, damme." At this the mercer laughs heartily; cuts off the paduasoy, and sends it home; nor is he, till too late, surprised to find the gentleman had said nothing but the truth, and kept his word.

The second method of running into debt is called fineering; which is getting goods made in such a fashion as to be unfit for every other purchaser, and if the tradesman refuses to give them on credit, then threaten to leave them upon his hands.

But the third and best method is called "being the good customer." The gentleman first buys some trifle, and pays for it in ready money; he comes a few days after with nothing about him but bank bills, and buys, we will suppose, a sixpenny tweezer-case; the bills are too great to be changed, so he promises to return punctually the day after, and pay for what he has bought. In this promise he is punctual, and this is repeated for eight or ten times, till his face is well known, and he has got at last the character of a good customer: by this means he gets credit for something considerable, and then never pays for it.

In all this the young man who is the unhappy subject of our present reflections was very expert, and could face, fineer, and bring custom to a shop with any man in England: none of his companions could exceed him in this; and his very companions at last said that The. would be hanged.

As he grew old, he grew never the better: he loved ortolans and green peas as before; he drank gravy soup when he could get it, and always thought his oysters tasted best when he got them for nothing, or, which was just the same, when he bought them upon tick: thus the old man kept up the vices of youth, and what he wanted in power, he made up by inclination; so that all the world thought that old The. would be hanged.

And now, reader, I have brought him to his last scene, where, perhaps, my duty should have obliged me to assist. You expect, perhaps, his dying words, and the tender farewell he took of his wife and children; you expect an account of his coffin and white gloves, his pious ejaculations, and the papers he left behind him. In this I cannot indulge your curiosity; for, oh! the mysteries of Fate, The.—was drowned!

"Reader," as Hervey saith, "pause and ponder, and ponder and pause; who knows what thy own end may be!"

ESSAY IX.

National Concord.

I TAKE the liberty to communicate to the public a few loose thoughts upon a subject which, though often handled, has not yet in my opinion been fully discussed,—I mean national concord, or unanimity, which in this kingdom has been generally considered as a bare possibility, that existed nowhere but in speculation. Such an union is perhaps neither to be expected nor wished for in a country whose liberty depends rather upon the genius of the people than upon any precautions which they have taken in a constitutional way for the guard and preservation of this inestimable blessing.

There is a very honest gentleman with whom I have been acquainted these thirty years, during which there has not been one speech uttered against the ministry in parliament, nor struggle at an election for a burgess to serve in the House of Commons, nor a pamphlet published in opposition to any measure of the administration, nor even a private censure passed in his hearing upon the misconduct of any person concerned in public affairs, but he is immediately alarmed, and loudly exclaims against such factious doings, in order to set the people by the ears together at such a delicate juncture. "At any other time," says he, "such opposition might not be improper, and I don't question the facts that are alleged; but at this crisis, sir, to inflame the nation—the man deserves to be punished as a traitor to his country." In a word, according to this gentleman's opinion, the nation has been in a violent crisis at any time these thirty years; and were it possible for him to live another century, he would never find any period at which a man might with safety impugn the infallibility of a minister.

The case is no more than this: my honest friend has invested his whole fortune in the stocks, on Government security, and trembles at every whiff of popular discontent. Were every British subject of the same tame and timid disposition, Magna Charta (to use the coarse phrase of Oliver Cromwell) would be no more regarded by an ambitious prince than Magna F—ta, and the liberties of England expire without a groan. Opposition, when restrained within due bounds, is the salubrious gale that ventilates the opinions of the people, which might otherwise stagnate into the most abject submission. It may be said to purify the atmosphere of politics; to dispel the gross vapours raised by the influence of ministerial artifice and corruption, until the constitution, like a mighty rock, stands full disclosed to the view of every individual who dwells within the shade of its protection. Even when this gale blows with augmented violence, it generally tends to the advantage of the commonwealth: it awakes the apprehension, and consequently arouses all the faculties of the pilot at the helm, who redoubles his vigilance and caution, exerts his utmost skill, and, becoming acquainted with the nature of the navigation, in a little time learns to suit his canvas to the roughness of the sea and the trim of the vessel. Without these intervening storms of opposition to exercise his faculties, he would become enervated, negligent, and presumptuous; and in the wantonness of his power, trusting to some deceitful calm, perhaps hazard a step that would wreck the constitution. Yet there is a measure in all things. A moderate frost will fertilize the glebe with nitrous particles, and destroy the eggs of pernicious insects that prey upon the fancy of the year: but if this frost increases in severity and duration, it will chill the seeds, and even freeze up the roots of vegetables; it will check the bloom, nip the buds, and blast all the promise of the spring. The vernal breeze that drives the fogs before it, that brushes the cobwebs from the boughs, that fans the air, and fosters vegetation, if augmented to a tempest, will strip the leaves, overthrow the tree, and desolate the garden. The auspicious gale before which the trim vessel ploughs the bosom of the sea, while the mariners are kept alert in duty and in spirits, if converted into a hurricane, overwhelms the crew with terror and confusion. The sails are rent, the cordage cracked, the masts give way; the master eyes the havoc with mute despair, and the vessel founders in the storm. Opposition, when confined within its proper channels, sweeps away those beds of soil and banks of sand which corruptive power had gathered; but when it overflows its banks, and deluges the plain, its course is marked by ruin and devastation.

The opposition necessary in a free state, like that of Great Britain, is not at all incompatible with that national concord which ought to unite the people on all emergencies in which the general safety is at stake. It is the jealousy of patriotism, not the rancour of party—the warmth of candour, not the virulence of hate—a transient dispute among friends, not an implacable feud that admits of no reconciliation. The history of all ages teems with the fatal effects of internal discord; and were history and tradition annihilated, common sense would plainly point out the mischiefs that must arise from want of harmony and national union. Every schoolboy can have recourse to the fable of the rods, which, when united in a bundle, no strength could bend, but when separated into single twigs, a child could break with ease.

ESSAY X.

Female Warriors.

I HAVE spent the greater part of my life in making observations on men and things, and in projecting schemes for the advantage of my country; and though my labours have met with an ungrateful return, I will still persist in my endeavours for its service, like that venerable, unshaken, and neglected patriot, Mr. Jacob Henriquez, who, though of the Hebrew nation, hath exhibited a shining example of Christian fortitude and perseverance. And here my conscience urges me to confess, that the hint upon which the following proposals are built was taken from an advertisement of the said patriot Henriquez, in which he gave the public to understand, that Heaven had indulged him with "seven blessed daughters." Blessed they are, no doubt, on account of their own and their father's virtues; but more blessed may they be, if the scheme I offer should be adopted by the legislature.

The proportion which the number of females born in these kingdoms bears to the male children is, I think, supposed to be as thirteen to fourteen; but as women are not so subject as the other sex to accidents and intemperance, in numbering adults we shall find the balance on the female side. If, in calculating the numbers of the people, we take in the multitudes that emigrate to the plantations, whence they never return; those that die at sea, and make their exit at Tyburn; together with the consumption of the present war, by sea and land, in the Atlantic, Mediterranean, in the German and Indian Oceans, in Old France, New France, North America, the Leeward Islands, Germany, Africa, and Asia, we may fairly state the loss of men during the war at one hundred thousand. If this be the case, there must be a superplus of the other sex, amounting to the same number, and this superplus will consist of women able to bear arms; as I take it for granted, that all those who are fit to bear children are likewise fit to bear arms. Now, as we have seen the nation governed by old women, I hope to make it appear, that it may be defended by young women: and surely this scheme will not be rejected as unnecessary at such a juncture (1762), when our armies, in the four quarters of the globe, are in want of recruits; when we find ourselves entangled in a new war with Spain, on the eve of a rupture in Italy, and, indeed, in a fair way of being obliged to make head against all the great potentates of Europe.

But, before I unfold my design, it may be necessary to obviate, from experience, as well as argument, the objections which may be made to the delicate frame and tender disposition of the female sex, rendering them incapable of the toils, and insuperably averse to the horrors, of war. All the world has heard of the nation of Amazons, who inhabited the banks of the river Thermodon in Cappadocia, who expelled their men by force of arms, defended themselves by their own prowess, managed the reins of government, prosecuted the operations in war, and held the other sex in the utmost contempt. We are informed by Homer that Penthesilea, queen of the Amazons, acted as auxiliary to Priam, and fell, valiantly fighting in his cause, before the walls of Troy. Quintus Curtius tells us, that Thalestris brought one hundred armed Amazons in a present to Alexander the Great. Diodorus Siculus expressly says there was a nation of female warriors in Africa, who fought against the Libyan Hercules. We read in the voyages of Columbus, that one of the Caribbee Islands was possessed by a tribe of female warriors, who kept all the neighbouring Indians in awe. But we need not go farther than our own age and country to prove, that the spirit and constitution of the fair sex are equal to the dangers and fatigues of war. Every novice who has read the authentic and important History of the Pirates is well acquainted with the exploits of two heroines, called Mary Read and Anne Bonny. I myself have had the honour to drink with Anne Cassier, alias Mother Wade, who had distinguished herself among the Buccaneers of America, and in her old age kept a punch-house, in Port-Royal of Jamaica. I have likewise conversed with Moll Davis, who had served as a dragoon in all Queen Anne's wars, and was admitted on the pension of Chelsea. The late war with Spain, and even the present, hath produced instances of females enlisting both in the land and sea service, and behaving with remarkable bravery in the disguise of the other sex. And who has not heard of the celebrated Jenny Cameron, and some other enterprising ladies of North Britain, who attended a certain Adventurer in all his expeditions, and headed their respective clans in a military character? That strength of body is often equal to the courage of mind implanted in the fair sex will not be denied by those who have seen the waterwomen of Plymouth; the female drudges of Ireland, Wales, and Scotland; the fishwomen of Billingsgate; the weeders, podders, and hoppers who swarm in the fields; and the bunters who swagger in the streets of London; not to mention the indefatigable trulls who follow the camp, and keep up with the line of march, though loaded with bantlings and other baggage.

There is scarcely a street in this metropolis without one or more viragos, who discipline their husbands and domineer over the whole neighbourhood. Many months are not elapsed since I was witness to a pitched battle between two athletic females, who fought with equal skill and fury until one of them gave out, after having sustained seven falls on the hard stones. They were both stripped to the under petticoat; their breasts were carefully swathed with handkerchiefs; and as no vestiges of features were to be seen in either when I came up, I imagined the combatants were of the other sex, until a bystander assured me of the contrary, giving me to understand, that the conqueror had lain in about five weeks of twin-bastards, begot by her second, who was an Irish chairman. When I see the avenues of the Strand beset every night with troops of fierce Amazons, who, with dreadful imprecations, stop, and beat, and plunder passengers, I cannot help wishing that such martial talents were converted to the benefit of the public; and that those who were so loaded with temporal fire, and so little afraid of eternal fire, should, instead of ruining the souls and bodies of their fellow-citizens, be put in a way of turning their destructive qualities against the enemies of the nation.

Having thus demonstrated that the fair sex are not deficient in strength and resolution, I would humbly propose, that as there is an excess on their side in quantity to the amount of one hundred thousand, part of that number may be employed in recruiting the army, as well as in raising thirty new Amazonian regiments, to be commanded by females, and serve in regimentals adapted to their sex. The Amazons of old appeared with the left breast bare, an open jacket, and trowsers that descended no farther than the knee; the right breast was destroyed, that it might not impede them in bending the bow, or darting the javelin: but there is no occasion for this cruel excision in the present discipline, as we have seen instances of women who handle the musket, without finding any inconvenience from that protuberance.

As the sex love gaiety, they may be clothed in vests of pink satin, and open drawers of the same, with buskins on their feet and legs, their hair tied behind, and floating on their shoulders, and their hats adorned with white feathers: they may be armed with light carbines and long bayonets, without the encumbrance of swords or shoulder-belts. I make no doubt but many young ladies of figure and fashion will undertake to raise companies at their own expense, provided they like their colonels; but I must insist upon it, if this scheme should be embraced, that Mr. Henriquez's seven blessed daughters may be provided with commissions, as the project is in some measure owing to the hints of that venerable patriot. I, moreover, give it as my opinion, that Mrs. Kitty Fisher shall have the command of a battalion, and the nomination of her own officers, provided she will warrant them all sound, and be content to wear proper badges of distinction.

A female brigade, properly disciplined and accoutred, would not, I am persuaded, be afraid to charge a numerous body of the enemy, over whom they would have a manifest advantage; for if the barbarous Scythians were ashamed to fight with the Amazons who invaded them, surely the French, who pique themselves on their sensibility and devotion to the fair sex, would not act upon the offensive against a band of female warriors, arrayed in all the charms of youth and beauty.

ESSAY XI.

National Prejudices.

As I am one of that sauntering tribe of mortals who spend the greatest part of their time in taverns, coffee-houses, and other places of public resort, I have thereby an opportunity of observing an infinite variety of characters, which to a person of a contemplative turn is a much higher entertainment than a view of all the curiosities of art or nature. In one of these my late rambles I accidentally fell into a company of half a dozen gentlemen, who were engaged in a warm dispute about some political affair, the decision of which, as they were equally divided in their sentiments, they thought proper to refer to me, which naturally drew me in for a share of the conversation.

Amongst a multiplicity of other topics, we took occasion to talk of the different characters of the several nations of Europe; when one of the gentlemen, cocking his hat, and assuming such an air of importance as if he had possessed all the merit of the English nation in his own person, declared, that the Dutch were a parcel of avaricious wretches; the French a set of flattering sycophants; that the Germans were drunken sots, and beastly gluttons; and the Spaniards proud, haughty, and surly tyrants; but that in bravery, generosity, clemency, and in every other virtue, the English excelled all the world.

This very learned and judicious remark was received with a general smile of approbation by all the company—all, I mean, but your humble servant, who, endeavouring to keep my gravity as well as I could, and reclining my head upon my arm, continued for some time in a posture of affected thoughtfulness, as if I had been musing on something else, and did not seem to attend to the subject of conversation; hoping by this means to avoid the disagreeable necessity of explaining myself, and thereby depriving the gentleman of his imaginary happiness.

But my pseudo-patriot had no mind to let me escape so easily. Not satisfied that his opinion should pass without contradiction, he was determined to have it ratified by the suffrage of every one in the company; for which purpose, addressing himself to me with an air of inexpressible confidence, he asked me if I was not of the same way of thinking. As I am never forward in giving my opinion, especially when I have reason to believe that it will not be agreeable; so, when I am obliged to give it, I always hold it for a maxim to speak my real sentiments. I therefore told him that, for my own part, I should not have ventured to talk in such a peremptory strain unless I had made the tour of Europe, and examined the manners of these several nations with great care and accuracy: that perhaps a more impartial judge would not scruple to affirm, that the Dutch were more frugal and industrious, the French more temperate and polite, the Germans more hardy and patient of labour and fatigue, and the Spaniards more staid and sedate, than the English; who, though undoubtedly brave and generous, were at the same time rash, headstrong, and impetuous; too apt to be elated with prosperity, and to despond in adversity.

I could easily perceive, that all the company began to regard me with a jealous eye before I had finished my answer, which I had no sooner done, than the patriotic gentleman observed, with a contemptuous sneer, that he was greatly surprised how some people could have the conscience to live in a country which they did not love, and to enjoy the protection of a government to which in their hearts they were inveterate enemies. Finding that by this modest declaration of my sentiments I had forfeited the good opinion of my companions, and given them occasion to call my political principles in question, and well knowing that it was in vain to argue with men who were so very full of themselves, I threw down my reckoning and retired to my own lodgings, reflecting on the absurd and ridiculous nature of national prejudice and prepossession.

Among all the famous sayings of antiquity, there is none that does greater honour to the author, or affords greater pleasure to the reader, (at least if he be a person of a generous and benevolent heart,) than that of the philosopher who, being asked what countryman he was, replied, that he was "a citizen of the world." How few are there to be found in modern times who can say the same, or whose conduct is consistent with such a profession! We are now become so much Englishmen, Frenchmen, Dutchmen, Spaniards, or Germans, that we are no longer citizens of the world; so much the natives of one particular spot, or members of one petty society, that we no longer consider ourselves as the general inhabitants of the globe, or members of that grand society which comprehends the whole human kind.

Did these prejudices prevail only among the meanest and lowest of the people, perhaps they might be excused, as they have few, if any, opportunities of correcting them by reading, travelling, or conversing with foreigners: but the misfortune is, that they infect the minds, and influence the conduct, even of our gentlemen; of those, I mean, who have every title to this appellation but an exemption from prejudice, which, however, in my opinion, ought to be regarded as the characteristical mark of a gentleman; for let a man's birth be ever so high, his station ever so exalted, or his fortune ever so large, yet if he is not free from national and other prejudices, I should make bold to tell him, that he had a low and vulgar mind, and had no just claim to the character of a gentleman. And, in fact, you will always find that those are most apt to boast of national merit, who have little or no merit of their own to depend on; than which, to be sure, nothing is more natural: the slender vine twists around the sturdy oak, for no other reason in the world but because it has not strength sufficient to support itself.

Should it be alleged in defence of national prejudice, that it is the natural and necessary growth of love to our country, and that therefore the former cannot be destroyed without hurting the latter, I answer that this is a gross fallacy and delusion. That it is the growth of love to our country, I will allow; but that it is the natural and necessary growth of it, I absolutely deny. Superstition and enthusiasm, too, are the growth of religion; but who ever took it in his head to affirm, that they are the necessary growth of this noble principle? They are, if you will, the bastard sprouts of this heavenly plant, but not its natural and genuine branches, and may safely enough be lopped off, without doing any harm to the parent stock: nay, perhaps, till once they are lopped off, this goodly tree can never flourish in perfect health and vigour.

Is it not very possible that I may love my own country, without hating the natives of other countries? that I may exert the most heroic bravery, the most undaunted resolution, in defending its laws and liberty, without despising all the rest of the world as cowards and poltroons? Most certainly it is; and if it were not—But why need I suppose what is absolutely impossible?—But if it were not, I must own I should prefer the title of the ancient philosopher, viz. a citizen of the world, to that of an Englishman, a Frenchman, an European, or to any other appellation whatever.

ESSAY XII.

Taste.

AMIDST the frivolous pursuits and pernicious dissipations of the present age a respect for the qualities of the understanding still prevails to such a degree, that almost every individual pretends to have a taste for the Belles Lettres. The spruce apprentice sets up for a critic, and the puny beau piques himself upon being a connoisseur. Without assigning causes for this universal presumption, we shall proceed to observe, that if it was attended with no other inconvenience than that of exposing the pretender to the ridicule of those few who can sift his pretensions, it might be unnecessary to undeceive the public, or to endeavour at the reformation of innocent folly, productive of no evil to the commonwealth. But in reality this folly is productive of manifold evils to the community. If the reputation of taste can be acquired, without the least assistance of literature, by reading modern poems and seeing modern plays, what person will deny himself the pleasure of such an easy qualification? Hence the youth of both sexes are debauched to diversion, and seduced from much more profitable occupations into idle endeavours after literary fame; and a superficial, false taste, founded on ignorance and conceit, takes possession of the public. The acquisition of learning, the study of nature, is neglected as superfluous labour; and the best faculties of the mind remain unexercised, and indeed unopened, by the power of thought and reflection. False taste will not only diffuse itself through all our amusements, but even influence our moral and political conduct; for what is false taste but want of perception to discern propriety and distinguish beauty?

It has often been alleged, that taste is a natural talent, as independent of art as strong eyes or a delicate sense of smelling; and, without all doubt, the principal ingredient in the composition of taste is a natural sensibility, without which it cannot exist: but it differs from the senses in this particular, that they are finished by nature, whereas taste cannot be brought to perfection without proper cultivation; for taste pretends to judge, not only of nature, but also of art; and that judgment is founded upon observation and comparison.

What Horace has said of genius is still more applicable to taste:

> Naturâ fieret laudabile carmen, an arte,
> Quæsitum est. Ego nec studium sine divite venâ,
> Nec rude quid prosit video ingenium: alterius sic
> Altera poscit opem res, et conjurat amicè.
>
> HOR. *Art. Poet.*

> 'Tis long disputed, whether poets claim
> From *art* or *nature* their best right to fame.
> But *art*, if not enriched by nature's vein,
> And a rude *genius* of uncultured strain,
> Are useless both; but when in friendship joined,
> A mutual succour in each other find.
>
> FRANCIS.

We have seen *genius* shine without the help of *art*, but *taste* must be cultivated by art before it will produce agreeable fruit. This, however, we must still inculcate with

Quintilian, that study, precept, and observation will nought avail, without the assistance of nature:

Illud tamen imprimis testandum est, nihil præcepta atque artes valere, nisi adjuvante naturâ.

Yet even though nature has done her part, by implanting the seeds of taste, great pains must be taken, and great skill exerted, in raising them to a proper pitch of vegetation. The judicious tutor must gradually and tenderly unfold the mental faculties of the youth committed to his charge. He must cherish his delicate perception; store his mind with proper ideas; point out the different channels of observation; teach him to compare objects; to establish the limits of right and wrong, of truth and falsehood; to distinguish beauty from tinsel, and grace from affectation: in a word, to strengthen and improve by culture, experience, and instruction those natural powers of feeling and sagacity which constitute the faculty called taste, and enable the professor to enjoy the delights of the Belles Lettres.

We cannot agree in opinion with those who imagine, that nature has been equally favourable to all men, in conferring upon them a fundamental capacity, which may be improved to all the refinement of taste and criticism. Every day's experience convinces us of the contrary. Of two youths educated under the same preceptor, instructed with the same care, and cultivated with the same assiduity, one shall not only comprehend, but even anticipate, the lessons of his master, by dint of natural discernment, while the other toils in vain to imbibe the least tincture of instruction. Such, indeed, is the distinction between genius and stupidity, which every man has an opportunity of seeing among his friends and acquaintance. Not that we ought too hastily to decide upon the natural capacities of children, before we have maturely considered the peculiarity of disposition, and the bias by which genius may be strangely warped from the common path of education. A youth incapable of retaining one rule of grammar, or of acquiring the least knowledge of the classics, may nevertheless make great progress in mathematics —nay, he may have a strong genius for the mathematics, without being able to comprehend a demonstration of Euclid; because his mind conceives in a peculiar manner, and is so intent upon contemplating the object in one particular point of view, that it cannot perceive it in any other. We have known an instance of a boy, who, while his master complained that he had not capacity to comprehend the properties of a right-angled triangle, had actually, in private, by the power of his genius, formed a mathematical system of his own, discovered a series of curious theorems, and even applied his deductions to practical machines of surprising construction. Besides, in the education of youth we ought to remember, that some capacities are like the *pyra præcocia*,—they soon blow, and soon attain to all the degree of maturity which they are capable of acquiring; while, on the other hand, there are geniuses of slow growth, that are late in bursting the bud, and long in ripening. Yet the first shall yield a faint blossom and insipid fruit; whereas the produce of the other shall be distinguished and admired for its well concocted juice and exquisite flavour. We have known a boy of five years of age surprise everybody by playing on the violin in such a manner as seemed to promise a prodigy in music. He had all the assistance that art could afford; by the age of ten his genius was at the ἀκμή; yet after that period, notwithstanding the most intense application, he never gave the least signs of improvement. At six he was admired as a miracle of music; at six-and-twenty he was neglected as an ordinary fiddler. The celebrated Dean Swift was a remarkable instance in the other extreme. He was long considered as an incorrigible dunce, and did not obtain his degree at the University but *ex speciali gratia;* yet when his powers began to unfold, he signalized himself by a very remarkable superiority of genius. When a youth therefore appears dull of apprehension, and seems to derive no advantage from study and instruction, the tutor must exercise his sagacity in discovering whether the soil be absolutely barren, or sown with seed repugnant to its nature, or of such a quality as requires repeated culture and length of time to set its juices in fermentation. These observations, however, relate to capacity in general, which we ought carefully to distinguish from taste. Capacity implies the power of retaining what is received; taste is the power of relishing or rejecting whatever is offered for the entertainment of the imagination. A man may have capacity to acquire what is called learning and philosophy; but he must have also sensibility before he feels those emotions with which taste receives the impressions of beauty.

Natural taste is apt to be seduced and debauched by vicious precept and bad example. There is a dangerous tinsel in false taste, by which the unwary mind and young imagination are often fascinated. Nothing has been so often explained, and yet so little understood, as simplicity in writing. Simplicity, in this acceptation, has a larger signification than either the ἁπλόον of the Greeks or the *simplex* of the Latins; for it implies beauty. It is the ἁπλόον καὶ ἡδύν of Demetrius Phalereus, the *simplex munditiis* of Horace, and expressed by one word, *naïveté*, in the French language. It is, in fact, no other than beautiful nature, without affectation or extraneous ornament. In statuary it is the Venus of Medicis; in architecture the Pantheon. It would be an endless task to enumerate all the instances of this natural simplicity that occur in poetry and painting, among the ancients and moderns. We shall only mention two examples of it, the beauty of which consists in the pathetic.

Anaxagoras the philosopher, and preceptor of Pericles, being told that both his sons were dead, laid his hand upon his heart, and, after a short pause, consoled himself with a reflection couched in three words, ᾔδειν θνητοὺς γεγεννηκώς, "I knew they were mortal." The other instance we select from the tragedy of Macbeth. The gallant Macduff, being informed that his wife and children were murdered by order of the tyrant, pulls his hat over his eyes, and his internal agony bursts out into an exclamation of four words, the most expressive perhaps that ever were uttered: "He has no children." This is the energetic language of simple nature, which is now grown into disrepute. By the present mode of education we are forcibly warped from the bias of nature, and all simplicity in manners is rejected. We are taught to disguise and distort our sentiments, until the faculty of thinking is diverted into an unnatural channel; and we not only relinquish and forget, but also become incapable of, our original dispositions. We are totally changed into creatures of art and affectation. Our perception is abused, and even our senses are perverted. Our minds lose their native force and flavour. The imagination, sweated by artificial fire, produces nought but vapid bloom. The genius, instead of growing like a vigorous tree, extending its branches on every side, and bearing delicious fruit, resembles a stunted yew, tortured into some wretched form, projecting no shade, displaying no flower, diffusing no fragrance, yielding no fruit, and affording nothing but a barren conceit for the amusement of the idle spectator.

Thus debauched from nature, how can we relish her genuine productions? As well might a man distinguish objects through a prism, that presents nothing but a variety of colours to the eye; or a maid pining in the green sickness prefer a biscuit to a cinder. It has been often alleged, that the passions can never be wholly deposited, and that by appealing to these a good writer will always be able to force himself into the hearts of his readers: but even the strongest passions are weakened—nay, sometimes totally extinguished—by mutual opposition, dissipation, and acquired insensibility. How often at the theatre is the tear of sympathy and the burst of laughter repressed by a ridiculous species of pride, refusing approbation to the author and actor, and renouncing society with the audience! This seeming insensibility is not owing to any original defect. Nature has stretched the string, though it has long ceased to vibrate. It may have been displaced and distracted by the violence of pride; it may have lost its tone through long disuse, or be so twisted or overstrained as to produce the most jarring discords.

If so little regard is paid to nature when she knocks so powerfully at the breast, she must be altogether neglected and despised in her calmer mood of serene tranquillity, when nothing appears to recommend her but simplicity, propriety, and innocence. A person must have delicate feelings that can taste the celebrated repartee in Terence: "Homo sum; nihil humani a me alienum puto,"—"I am a man; therefore think I have an interest in every thing that concerns humanity." A clear blue sky, spangled with stars, will prove an insipid object to eyes accustomed to the glare of torches and tapers, gilding and glitter; eyes that will turn with disgust from the green mantle of the spring, so gorgeously adorned with buds and foliage, flowers and blossoms, to contemplate a gaudy silken robe, striped and intersected with unfriendly tints, that fritter the masses of light, and distract the vision, pinked into the most fantastic forms, flounced, and furbelowed, and fringed with all the littleness of art unknown to elegance.

Those ears that are offended by the notes of the thrush, the blackbird, and the nightingale will be regaled and ravished by the squeaking fiddle, touched by a musician who has no other genius than that which lies in his fingers: they will even be entertained with the rattling of coaches, and the alarming knock by which the doors of fashionable people are so loudly distinguished. The sense of smelling that delights in the scent of excrementitious animal juices, such as musk, civet, and urinous salts, will loathe the fragrance of new mown hay, the sweetbrier, the honeysuckle, and the rose. The organs that are gratified with the taste of sickly veal bled into a palsy, crammed fowls, and dropsical brawn, peas without substance, peaches without taste, and pine-apples without flavour, will certainly nauseate the native, genuine, and salutary taste of Welch beef, Banstead mutton, and barn-door fowls, whose juices are concocted by a natural digestion, and whose flesh is consolidated by free air and exercise. In such a total perversion of the senses the ideas must be misrepresented, the powers of the imagination disordered, and the judgment, of consequence, unsound. The disease is attended with a false appetite, which the natural food of the mind will not satisfy. It will prefer Ovid to Tibullus, and the rant of Lee to the tenderness of Otway. The soul sinks into a kind of sleepy idiotism, and is diverted by toys and baubles, which can only be pleasing to the most superficial curiosity. It is enlivened by a quick succession of trivial objects, that glisten and dance before the eye, and, like an infant, is kept awake and inspirited by the sound of a rattle. It must not only be dazzled and aroused, but also cheated, hurried, and perplexed, by the artifice of deception, business, intricacy, and intrigue,—a kind of low juggle, which may be termed the legerdemain of genius.

In this state of depravity the mind cannot enjoy, nor indeed distinguish, the charms of natural and moral beauty and decorum. The ingenuous blush of native innocence, the plain language of ancient faith and sincerity, the cheerful resignation to the will of Heaven, the mutual affection of the charities, the voluntary respect paid to superior dignity or station, the virtue of beneficence, extended even to the brute creation—nay, the very crimson glow of health, and swelling lines of beauty, are despised, detested, scorned, and ridiculed, as ignorance, rudeness, rusticity, and superstition. Thus we see how moral and natural beauty are connected, and of what importance it is, even to the formation of taste, that the manners should be severely superintended. This is a task which ought to take the lead of science: for we will venture to say, that virtue is the foundation of taste; or rather, that virtue and taste are built upon the same foundation of sensibility, and cannot be disjoined without offering violence to both. But virtue must be informed, and taste instructed; otherwise they will both remain imperfect and ineffectual:

Qui didicit patriæ quid debeat, et quid amicis;
Quo sit amore parens, quo frater amandus, et hospes;
Quod sit conscripti, quod judicis officium, quæ
Partes in bellum missi ducis; ille profecto
Reddere personæ scit convenientia cuique.
HOR.

The critic who with nice discernment knows
What to his country and his friends he owes;

How various nature warms the human breast,
To love the parent, brother, friend, or guest;
What the great functions of our judges are,
Of senators, and generals sent to war;
He can distinguish, with unerring art,
The strokes peculiar to each different part.
FRANCIS.

Thus we see taste is composed of nature improved by art, of feeling tutored by instruction.

ESSAY XIII.

Cultivation of Taste.

HAVING explained what we conceive to be true taste, and in some measure accounted for the prevalence of vitiated taste, we should proceed to point out the most effectual manner in which a natural capacity may be improved into a delicacy of judgment, and an intimate acquaintance with the Belles Lettres. We shall take it for granted that proper means have been used to form the manners, and attach the mind to virtue. The heart, cultivated by precept, and warned by example, improves in sensibility, which is the foundation of taste. By distinguishing the influence and scope of morality, and cherishing the ideas of benevolence, it acquires a habit of sympathy, which tenderly feels responsive, like the vibration of unisons, every touch of moral beauty. Hence it is that a man of a social heart, entendered by the practice of virtue, is awakened to the most pathetic emotions by every uncommon instance of generosity, compassion, and greatness of soul. Is there any man so dead to sentiment, so lost to humanity, as to read unmoved the generous behaviour of the Romans to the states of Greece, as it is recounted by Livy, or embellished by Thomson in his poem of Liberty? Speaking of Greece in the decline of her power, when her freedom no longer existed, he says:

As at her Isthmian games—a fading pomp—
Her full assembled youth innumerous swarmed,
On a tribunal raised FLAMINIUS sat:
A victor he, from the deep phalanx pierced
Of iron-coated Macedon, and back
The Grecian tyrant to his bounds repelled.
In the high thoughtless gaiety of game,
While sport alone their unambitious hearts
Possessed, the sudden trumpet, sounding hoarse,
Bade silence o'er the bright assembly reign.
Then thus a herald,—"To the states of Greece
The Roman people unconfined restore
Their countries, cities, liberties, and laws;
Taxes remit, and garrisons withdraw."
The crowd, astonished half, and half informed,
Stared dubious round; some questioned, some exclaimed,
(Like one who, dreaming between hope and fear,
Is lost in anxious joy,) "Be that again—
Be that again proclaimed distinct and loud!
Loud and distinct it was again proclaimed;
And, still as midnight in the rural shade,
When the gale slumbers, they the words devoured.
Awhile severe amazement held them mute,
Then, bursting broad, the boundless shout to heaven
From many a thousand hearts ecstatic sprung!
On every hand rebellowed to their joy
The swelling sea, the rocks, and vocal hills.——
————Like Bacchanals they flew,
Each other straining in a strict embrace;
Nor strained a slave: and loud acclaims till night
Round the proconsul's tent repeated rung.

To one acquainted with the genius of Greece, the character and disposition of that polished people, admired for science, renowned for an inextinguishable love of freedom, nothing can be more affecting than this instance of generous magnanimity of the Roman people, in restoring them unasked to the full fruition of those liberties which they had so unfortunately lost.

The mind of sensibility is equally struck by the generous confidence of Alexander, who drinks without hesitation the potion presented by his physician Philip, even after he had received intimation that poison was contained in the cup: a noble and pathetic scene, which hath acquired new dignity and expression under the inimitable pencil of a Le Sueur. Humanity is melted into tears of tender admiration by the deportment of Henry IV. of France, while his rebellious subjects compelled him to form the blockade of his capital. In chastising his enemies, he could not but remember they were his people; and knowing they were reduced to the extremity of famine, he generously connived at the methods practised to supply them with provision. Chancing one day to meet two peasants who had been detected in these practices as they were led to execution, they implored his clemency, declaring, in the sight of Heaven, they had no other way to procure subsistence for their wives and children; he pardoned them on the spot, and giving them all the money that was in his purse, "Henry of Bearne is poor," said he; "had he more money to afford, you should have it: go home to your families in peace; and remember your duty to God and your allegiance to your sovereign." Innumerable examples of the same kind may be selected from history both ancient and modern, the study of which we would therefore strenuously recommend.

Historical knowledge, indeed, becomes necessary on many other accounts, which in its place we will explain: but as the formation of the heart is of the first consequence, and should precede the cultivation of the understanding, such striking instances of superior virtue ought to be culled for the perusal of the young pupil, who will read them with eagerness, and revolve them with pleasure. Thus the young mind becomes enamoured of moral beauty, and the passions are listed on the side of humanity. Meanwhile, knowledge of a different species will go hand in hand with the advances of morality, and the understanding be gradually extended. Virtue and sentiment reciprocally assist each other, and both conduce to the improvement of perception. While the scholar's chief attention is employed in learning the Latin and Greek languages, and this is generally the task of childhood and early youth, it is even then the business of the preceptor to give his mind a turn for observation, to direct his powers of discernment, to point out the distinguishing marks of character, and dwell upon the charms of moral and intellectual beauty, as they may chance to occur in the classics that are used for his instruction. In reading Cornelius Nepos and Plutarch's Lives, even with a view to grammatical improvement only, he will insensibly imbibe, and learn to compare, ideas of great importance. He will become enamoured of virtue and patriotism, and acquire a detestation for vice, cruelty, and corruption. The perusal of the Roman story in the works of Florus, Sallust, Livy, and Tacitus will irresistibly engage his attention, expand his conception, cherish his memory, exercise his judgment, and warm him with a noble spirit of emulation. He will contemplate with love and admiration the disinterested candour of Aristides, surnamed the Just, whom the guilty cabals of his rival Themistocles exiled from his ungrateful country by a sentence of ostracism. He will be surprised to learn, that one of his fellow-citizens, an illiterate artisan, bribed by his enemies, chancing to meet him in the street without knowing his person, desired he would write Aristides on his shell (which was the method those plebeians used to vote against delinquents), when the innocent patriot wrote his own name without complaint or expostulation. He will with equal astonishment applaud the inflexible integrity of Fabricius, who preferred the poverty of innocence to all the pomp of affluence with which Pyrrhus endeavoured to seduce him from the arms of his country. He will approve with transport the noble generosity of his soul in rejecting the proposal of that Prince's physician, who offered to take him off by poison; and in sending the caitiff bound to his sovereign, whom he would have so basely and cruelly betrayed.

In reading the ancient authors, even for the purposes of school education, the unformed taste will begin to relish the irresistible energy, greatness, and sublimity of Homer; the serene majesty, the melody, and pathos of Virgil; the tenderness of Sappho and Tibullus; the elegance and propriety of Terence; the grace, vivacity, satire, and sentiment of Horace.

Nothing will more conduce to the improvement of the scholar in his knowledge of the languages, as well as in taste and morality, than his being obliged to translate choice parts and passages of the most approved classics, both poetry and prose, especially the latter: such as the orations of Demosthenes and Isocrates, the treatise of Longinus on the Sublime, the Commentaries of Cæsar, the Epistles of Cicero aud the younger Pliny, and the two celebrated speeches in the Catilinarian conspiracy by Sallust. By this practice he will become more intimate with the beauties of the writing and the idioms of the language from which he translates; at the same time, it will form his style, and, by exercising his talent of expression, make him a more perfect master of his mother tongue. Cicero tells us, that in translating two orations which the most celebrated orators of Greece pronounced against each other, he performed this task, not as a servile interpreter, but as an orator; preserving the sentiments, forms, and figures of the original, but adapting the expression to the taste and manners of the Romans: "In quibus non verbum pro verbo necesse habui reddere, sed genus omnium verborum vimque servavi,"—"in which I did not think it was necessary to translate literally word for word, but I preserved the natural and full scope of the whole." Of the same opinion was Horace, who says, in his Art of Poetry:

Nec verbum verbo curabis reddere fidus
Interpres——

Nor word for word translate with painful care.

Nevertheless, in taking the liberty here granted, we are apt to run into the other extreme, and substitute equivalent thoughts and phrases, till hardly any features of the original remain. The metaphors of figures, especially in poetry, ought to be as religiously preserved as the images of painting, which we cannot alter or exchange without destroying, or injuring at least, the character and style of the original.

In this manner the preceptor will sow the seeds of that taste which will soon germinate, rise, blossom, and produce perfect fruit by dint of future care and cultivation. In order to restrain the luxuriancy of the young imagination, which is apt to run riot, to enlarge the stock of ideas, exercise the reason, and ripen the judgment, the pupil must be engaged in the severer study of science. He must learn geometry, which Plato recommends for strengthening the mind, and enabling it to think with precision. He must be made acquainted with geography and chronology, and trace philosophy through all her branches. Without geography and chronology he will not be able to acquire a distinct idea of history; nor judge of the propriety of many interesting scenes, and a thousand allusions, that present themselves in the works of genius. Nothing opens the mind so much as the researches of philosophy: they inspire us with sublime conceptions of the Creator, and subject, as it were, all nature to our command. These bestow that liberal turn of thinking, and in a great measure contribute to that universality in learning, by which a man of taste ought to be eminently distinguished. But history is the inexhaustible source from which he will derive his most useful knowledge respecting the progress of the human mind, the constitution of government, the rise and decline of empires, the revolution of arts, the variety of character, and the vicissitudes of fortune.

The knowledge of history enables the poet not only to paint characters, but also to describe magnificent and interesting scenes of battle and adventure. Not that the poet or painter ought to be restrained to the letter of historical truth. History represents what has really happened in nature; the other arts exhibit what might have happened, with such exaggeration of circumstance and feature as may be deemed an improvement on nature: but this exaggeration must not be carried beyond the bounds of probability; and these, generally speaking, the knowledge of history will ascertain. It would be extremely difficult, if not impossible, to find a man actually existing, whose proportions should answer to those of the Greek statue distinguished by the name of the Apollo of Belvedere, or to produce a woman similar in proportion of parts to the other celebrated piece called the Venus de Medicis; therefore it may be truly affirmed, that they are not conformable to the real standard of nature: nevertheless, every artist will own, that they are the very archetypes of grace, elegance, and symmetry; and every judging eye must behold them with admiration, as improvements on the lines and lineaments of nature. The truth is, the sculptor or statuary composed the various proportions in nature from a great number of different subjects, every individual of which he found imperfect or defective in some one particular, though beautiful in all the rest; and from these observations, corroborated by taste and judgment, he formed an ideal pattern, according to which his idea was modelled, and produced in execution.

Everybody knows the story of Zeuxis, the famous painter of Heraclea, who, according to Pliny, invented the *chiaro oscuro*, or disposition of light and shade, among the ancients, and excelled all his contemporaries in the chromatique, or art of colouring. This great artist being employed to draw a perfect beauty in the character of Helen, to be placed in the temple of Juno, culled out five of the most beautiful damsels the city could produce, and selecting what was excellent in each, combined them in one picture according to the predisposition of his fancy, so that it shone forth an amazing model of perfection. In like manner every man of genius, regulated by true taste, entertains in his imagination an ideal beauty, conceived and cultivated as an improvement upon nature: and this we refer to the article of invention.

It is the business of art to imitate nature, but not with a servile pencil; and to choose those attitudes and dispositions only which are beautiful and engaging. With this view, we must avoid all disagreeable prospects of nature, which excite the ideas of abhorrence and disgust. For example, a painter would not find his account in exhibiting the resemblance of a dead carcase half consumed by vermin, or of swine wallowing in ordure, or of a beggar lousing himself on a dunghill, though these scenes should be painted never so naturally, and all the world must allow that the scenes were taken from nature, because the merit of the imitation would be greatly overbalanced by the vile choice of the artist. There are nevertheless many scenes of horror which please in the representation, from a certain interesting greatness, which we shall endeavour to explain when we come to consider the sublime.

Were we to judge every production by the rigorous rules of nature, we should reject the Iliad of Homer, the Æneid of Virgil, and every celebrated tragedy of antiquity and the present times, because there is no such thing in nature as a Hector or Turnus talking in hexameter, or an Othello in blank verse: we should condemn the Hercules of Sophocles, and the Miser of Molière, because we never knew a hero so strong as the one, or a wretch so sordid as the other. But if we consider poetry as an elevation of natural dialogue, as a delightful vehicle for conveying the noblest sentiments of heroism and patriot virtue, to regale the sense with the sounds of musical expression, while the fancy is ravished with enchanting images, and the heart warmed to rapture and ecstasy, we must allow that poetry is a perfection to which nature would gladly aspire; and that, though it surpasses, it does not deviate from her, provided the characters are marked with propriety, and sustained by genius. Characters, therefore, both in poetry and painting, may be a little overcharged, or exaggerated, without offering violence to nature; nay, they must be exaggerated in order to be striking, and to preserve the idea of imitation, whence the reader and spectator derive, in many instances, their chief delight. If we meet a common acquaintance in the street, we see him without emotion; but should we chance to spy his portrait well executed, we are struck with pleasing admiration. In this case the pleasure arises entirely from the imitation. We every day hear unmoved the natives of Ireland and Scotland speaking their own dialects; but should an Englishman mimic either, we are apt to burst out into a loud laugh of applause, being surprised and tickled by the imitation alone; though, at the same time, we cannot but allow that the imitation is imperfect. We are more affected by reading Shakespeare's description of Dover Cliff, and Otway's picture of the Old Hag, than we should be were we actually placed on the summit of the one, or met in reality with such a beldame as the other; because in reading these descriptions we refer to our own experience, and perceive, with surprise, the justness of the imitations. But if it is so close as to be mistaken for nature, the pleasure then will cease, because the *μίμησις*, or imitation, no longer appears.

Aristotle says, that all poetry and music is imitation, whether epic, tragic, or comic, whether vocal or instrumental, from the pipe or the lyre. He observes, that in man there is a propensity to imitate, even from his infancy; that the first perceptions of the mind are acquired by imitation; and seems to think, that the pleasure derived from imitation is the gratification of an appetite implanted by nature. We should rather think the pleasure it gives arises from the mind's contemplating that excellency of art, which thus rivals nature, and seems to vie with her in creating such a striking resemblance of her works. Thus the arts may be justly termed imitative, even in the article of invention: for, in forming a character, contriving an incident, and describing a scene, he must still keep nature in view, and refer every particular of his invention to her standard; otherwise his production will be destitute of truth and probability, without which the beauties of imitation cannot subsist. It will be a monster of incongruity, such as Horace alludes to in the beginning of his Epistle to the Pisos:

Humano capiti cervicem pictor equinam
Jungere si velit, et varias inducere plumas
Undique collatis membris, ut turpiter atrum
Desinat in piscem mulier formosa superne;
Spectatum admissi risum teneatis amici?

Suppose a painter to a human head
Should join a horse's neck, and wildly spread
The various plumage of the feather'd kind
O'er limbs of different beasts, absurdly join'd;
Or if he gave to view a beauteous maid,
Above the waist with every charm array'd,
Should a foul fish her lower parts unfold,
Would you not laugh such pictures to behold?

The magazine of nature supplies all those images which compose the most beautiful imitations. This the artist examines occasionally, as he would consult a collection of masterly sketches; and selecting particulars for his purpose, mingles the ideas with a kind of enthusiasm, or τὸ θεῖον, which is that gift of Heaven we call genius, and finally produces such a whole as commands admiration and applause.

ESSAY XIV.

Origin of Poetry.

THE study of polite literature is generally supposed to include all the liberal arts of poetry, painting, sculpture, music, eloquence, and architecture. All these are founded on imitation; and all of them mutually assist and illustrate each other. But as painting, sculpture, music, and architecture cannot be perfectly attained without long practice of manual operation, we shall distinguish them from poetry and eloquence, which depend entirely on the faculties of the mind; and on these last, as on the arts which immediately constitute the Belles Lettres, employ our attention in the present inquiry: or, if it should run to a greater length than we propose, it shall be confined to poetry alone; a subject that comprehends in its full extent the province of taste, or what is called polite literature; and differs essentially from eloquence, both in its end and origin.

Poetry sprang from ease, and was consecrated to pleasure; whereas eloquence arose from necessity, and aims at conviction. When we say poetry sprang from ease, perhaps we ought to except that species of it which owed its rise to inspiration and enthusiasm, and properly belonged to the culture of religion. In the first ages of mankind, and even in the original state of nature, the unlettered mind must have been struck with sublime conceptions, with admiration and awe, by those great phenomena which, though every day repeated, can never be viewed without internal emotion. Those would break forth in exclamations expressive of the passion produced, whether surprise or gratitude, terror or exultation. The rising, the apparent course, the setting, and seeming renovation of the sun; the revolution of light and darkness; the splendour, change, and circuit of the moon, and the canopy of heaven bespangled with stars, must have produced expressions of wonder and adoration. "O glorious luminary! great eye of the world! source of that light which guides my steps! of that heat which warms me when chilled with cold! of that influence which cheers the face of nature! whither dost thou retire every evening with the shades? Whence dost thou spring every morning with renovated lustre and never-fading glory? Art not thou the ruler, the creator, the god of all that I behold? I adore thee, as thy child, thy slave, thy suppliant! I crave thy protection, and the continuance of thy goodness! Leave me not to perish with cold, or to wander solitary in utter darkness! Return, return, after thy wonted absence: drive before thee the gloomy clouds that would obscure the face of nature. The birds begin to warble, and every animal is filled with gladness at thy approach: even the trees, the herbs, and the flowers seem to rejoice with fresher beauties, and send forth a grateful incense to thy power, whence their origin is derived!" A number of individuals, inspired with the same ideas, would join in these orisons, which would be accompanied with corresponding gesticulations of the body. They would be improved by practice, and grow regular from repetition. The sounds and gestures would naturally fall into measured cadence. Thus the song and dance would be produced; and a system of worship being formed, the muse would be consecrated to the purposes of religion.

Hence those forms of thanksgivings and litanies of supplication with which the religious rites of all nations, even the most barbarous, are at this day celebrated in every quarter of the known world. Indeed, this is a circumstance in which all nations surprisingly agree, how much soever they may differ in every other article of laws, customs, manners, and religion. The ancient Egyptians celebrated the festivals of their god Apis with hymns and dances. The superstition of the Greeks, partly derived from the Egyptians, abounded with poetical ceremonies, such as choruses and hymns, sung and danced at their apotheoses, sacrifices, games, and divinations. The Romans had their *Carmen Seculare* and Salian priests, who on certain festivals sung and danced through the streets of Rome. The Israelites were famous for this kind of exultation: "And Miriam, the prophetess, the sister of Aaron, took a timbrel in her hand, and all the women went out after her, with timbrels and with dances, and Miriam answered them, Sing ye to the Lord," &c.—"And David danced before the Lord with all his might." The psalms composed by this monarch, the songs of Deborah and Isaiah, are farther confirmations of what we have advanced.

From the Phœnicians the Greeks borrowed the cursed Orthyan song, when they sacrificed their children to Diana. The poetry of the bards constituted great part of the religious ceremonies among the Gauls and Britons; and the carousals of the Goths were religious institutions, celebrated with songs of triumph. The Mahometan Dervise dances to the sound of the flute, and whirls himself round until he grows giddy, and falls into a trance. The Marabous compose hymns in praise of Alla. The Chinese celebrate their grand festivals with processions of idols, songs, and instrumental music. The Tartars, Samoiedes, Laplanders, Negroes, even the Caffres called Hottentots, solemnize their worship (such as it is) with songs and dancing; so that we may venture to say poetry is the universal vehicle in which all nations have expressed their most sublime conceptions.

Poetry was, in all appearance, previous to any concerted plan of worship, and to every established system of legislation. When certain individuals, by dint ot superior prowess or understanding, had acquired the veneration of their fellow savages, and erected themselves into divinities on the ignorance and superstition of mankind; then mythology took place, and such a swarm of deities arose, as produced a religion replete with the most shocking absurdities. Those whom their superior talents had deified were found to be still actuated by the most brutal passions of human nature; and, in all probability, their votaries were glad to find such examples, to countenance their own vicious inclinations. Thus fornication, incest, rape, and even bestiality, were sanctified by the amours of Jupiter, Pan, Mars, Venus, and Apollo. Theft was patronized by Mercury, drunkenness by Bacchus, and cruelty by Diana. The same heroes and legislators, those who delivered their country, founded cities, established societies, invented useful arts, or contributed in any eminent degree to the security and happiness of their fellow-creatures, were inspired by the same lusts and appetites which domineered among the inferior classes of mankind; therefore every vice incident to human nature was celebrated in the worship of one or other of these divinities, and every infirmity consecrated by public feast and solemn sacrifice. In these institutions the Poet bore a principal share. It was his genius that contrived the plan, that executed the form of worship, and recorded in verse the origin and adventures of their gods and demigods. Hence the impurities and horrors of certain rites; the groves of Paphos and Baal-

Peor; the orgies of Bacchus; the human sacrifices to Moloch and Diana. Hence the theogony of Hesiod; the theology of Homer; and those innumerable maxims scattered through the ancient poets, inviting mankind to gratify their sensual appetites, in imitation of the gods, who were certainly the best judges of happiness. It is well known that Plato expelled Homer from his commonwealth on account of the infamous characters by which he has distinguished his deities, as well as for some depraved sentiments which he found diffused through the course of the Iliad and Odyssey. Cicero enters into the spirit of Plato, and exclaims, in his first book *De Natura Deorum*:—"Nec multa absurdiora sunt ea quæ, poetarum vocibus fusa, ipsa suavitate nocuerunt: qui et ira inflammatos et libidine furentes induxerunt Deos, feceruntque ut eorum bella, pugnas, prælia, vulnera videremus; odia præterea, dissidia, discordias, ortus, interritus, querelas, lamentationes, effusas in omni intemperantiâ libidines, adulteria, vincula, cum humano genere concubitus, mortalesque ex immortali procreatos."—"Nor are those things much more absurd which, flowing from the poet's tongue, have done mischief even by the sweetness of his expression. The poets have introduced gods inflamed with anger and enraged with lust; and even produced before our eyes their wars, their wrangling, their duels, and their wounds. They have exposed, besides, their antipathies, animosities, and dissensions; their origin and death; their complaints and lamentations; their appetites indulged to all manner of excess, their adulteries, their fetters, their amorous commerce with the human species, and from immortal parents derived a mortal offspring."

As the festivals of the gods necessarily produced good cheer, which often carried to riot and debauchery, mirth of consequence prevailed; and this was always attended with buffoonery. Taunts and jokes, and raillery and repartee, would necessarily ensue; and individuals would contend for the victory in wit and genius. These contests would in time be reduced to some regulations, for the entertainment of the people thus assembled, and some prize would be decreed to him who was judged to excel his rivals. The candidates for fame and profit being thus stimulated, would task their talents, and naturally recommend these alternate recriminations to the audience by clothing them with a kind of poetical measure, which should bear a near resemblance to prose. Thus, as the solemn service of the day was composed in the most sublime species of poetry, such as the ode or hymn, the subsequent altercation was carried on in iambics, and gave rise to satire. We are told by the Stagirite, that the highest species of poetry was employed in celebrating great actions, but the humbler sort used in this kind of contention; and that in the ages of antiquity there were some bards that professed heroics, and some that pretended to iambics only.

Οἱ μὲν ἡροϊκῶν, οἱ δὲ ἰάμβων ποιηταί.

To these rude beginnings we not only owe the birth of satire, but likewise the origin of dramatic poetry. Tragedy herself, which afterwards attained to such dignity as to rival the epic muse, was at first no other than a trial of crambo, or iambics, between two peasants, and a goat was the prize, as Horace calls it, *vile certamen ob hircum*, "a mean contest for a he-goat." Hence the name τραγῳδία, signifying the goat-song, from τράγος, *hircus*, and ᾠδή, *carmen*.

Carmine qui tragico vilem certavit ob hircum,
Mox etiam agrestes satyros nudavit, et asper
Incolumi gravitate jocum tentavit eo, quod
Illecebris erat et gratâ novitate morandus
Spectator, functusque sacris, et potus et exlex.

HORACE.

The tragic bard, a goat his humble prize,
Bade satyrs naked and uncouth arise;
His muse severe, secure and undismay'd,
The rustic joke in solemn strain convey'd;
For novelty alone he knew could charm
A lawless crowd, with wine and feasting warm.

Satire, then, was originally a clownish dialogue in loose iambics, so called because the actors were disguised like satyrs, who not only recited the praises of Bacchus, or some other deity, but interspersed their hymns with sarcastic jokes and altercation. Of this kind is the *Cyclop* of Euripides, in which Ulysses is the principal actor. The Romans also had their *Atellanæ*, or interludes, of the same nature, so called from the city of *Atella*, where they were first acted; but these were highly polished in comparison of the original entertainment, which was altogether rude and innocent. Indeed the *Cyclop* itself, though composed by the accomplished Euripides, abounds with such impurity as ought not to appear on the stage of any civilized nation.

It is very remarkable that the *Atellanæ*, which were in effect tragi-comedies, grew into such esteem among the Romans, that the performers in these pieces enjoyed several privileges which were refused to the ordinary actors. They were not obliged to unmask, like the other players, when their action was disagreeable to the audience. They were admitted into the army, and enjoyed the privileges of free citizens, without incurring that disgrace which was affixed to the characters of other actors. The poet Laberius, who was of equestrian order, being pressed by Julius Cæsar to act a part in his own performance, complied with great reluctance, and complained of the dishonour he had incurred in his prologue, preserved by Macrobius, which is one of the most elegant morsels of antiquity.

Tragedy and comedy flowed from the same fountain, though their streams were soon divided. The same entertainment which, under the name of tragedy, was rudely exhibited by clowns, for the prize of a goat, near some rural altar of Bacchus, assumed the appellation of comedy when it was transferred into cities, and represented with a little more decorum in a cart or waggon that strolled from street to street, as the name κωμῳδία implies, being derived from κώμη, a street, and ῳδή, a poem. To this origin Horace alludes in these lines:

> Dicitur et plaustris vexisse poemata Thespis,
> Quæ canerent agerentque peruncti fæcibus ora.

> Thespis, inventor of dramatic art,
> Convey'd his vagrant actors in a cart:
> High o'er the crowd the mimic tribe appear'd,
> And play'd and sung, with lees of wine besmear'd.

Thespis is called the inventor of the dramatic art, because he raised the subject from clownish altercation to the character and exploits of some hero: he improved the language and versification, and relieved the chorus by the dialogue of two actors. This was the first advance towards that consummation of genius and art, which constitutes what is now called a perfect tragedy. The next great improver was Æschylus, of whom the same critic says:

> Post hunc personæ pallæque repertor honestæ
> Æschylus, et modicis instravit pulpita tignis:
> Et docuit magnumque loqui nitique cothurno.

> Then Æschylus a decent vizard used,
> Built a low stage, the flowing robe diffused:
> In language more sublime the actors rage,
> And in the graceful buskin tread the stage.

The dialogue which Thespis introduced was called the Episode, because it was an addition to the former subject, namely, the praises of Bacchus; so that now tragedy consisted of two distinct parts, independent of each other; the old *recitative*, which was the *chorus*, sung in honour of the gods; and the *episode*, which turned upon the adventures of some hero. This episode being found very agreeable to the people, Æschylus, who lived about half a century after Thespis, still improved the drama, united the chorus to the episode, so as to make them both parts or members of one fable, multiplied the actors, contrived the stage, and introduced the decorations of the theatre; so that Sophocles, who succeeded Æschylus, had but one step to surmount in order to bring the drama to perfection. Thus tragedy was gradually detached from its original institution, which was entirely religious. The priests of Bacchus loudly complained of this innovation by means of the episode, which was foreign to the intention of the chorus; and hence arose the proverb of *Nihil ad Dionysium*, "Nothing to the purpose." Plutarch himself mentions the episode as a perversion of tragedy from the honour of the gods to the passions of men. But notwithstanding all opposition, the new tragedy succeeded to admiration; because it was found the most pleasing vehicle of conveying moral truths, of meliorating the heart, and extending the interests of humanity.

Comedy, according to Aristotle, is the younger sister of Tragedy. As the first originally turned upon the praises of the gods, the latter dwelt on the follies and vices of mankind. Such, we mean, was the scope of that species of poetry which acquired the name of comedy, in contradiction to the tragic muse; for in the beginning they were the same. The foundation upon which comedy was built we have already explained to be the practice of satirical repartee or altercation, in which individuals exposed the follies and frailties of each other on public occasions of worship and festivity.

The first regular plan of comedy is said to have been the *Margites* of Homer, exposing the idleness and folly of a worthless character; but of this performance we have no remains. That division which is termed the *Ancient Comedy* belongs to the labours of Eupolis, Cratinus, and Aristophanes, who were contemporaries, and flourished at Athens about four hundred and thirty years before the Christian era. Such was the licence of the muse at this period, that, far from lashing vice in general characters, she boldly exhibited the exact portrait of every individual who had rendered himself remarkable or notorious by his crimes, folly, or debauchery. She assumed every circumstance of his external appearance, his very attire, air, manner, and even his name; according to the observation of Horace,

————————Poetæ
————quorum comœdia prisca virorum est;
Si quis erat dignus describi, quod malus, aut fur,
Quod mœchus foret, aut sicarius, aut alioqui
Famosus, multa cum libertate notabant.

The comic poets, in its earliest age,
Who form'd the manners of the Grecian stage—
Was there a villain who might justly claim
A better right of being damn'd to fame,
Rake, cut-throat, thief, whatever was his crime,
They boldly stigmatized the wretch in rhyme.

Eupolis is said to have satirized Alcibiades in this manner, and to have fallen a sacrifice to the resentment of that powerful Athenian: but others say he was drowned in the Hellespont, during a war against the Lacedemonians; and that in consequence of this accident the Athenians passed a decree, that no poet should ever bear arms.

The comedies of Cratinus are recommended by Quintilian for their eloquence; and Plutarch tells us, that even Pericles himself could not escape the censure of this poet.

Aristophanes, of whom there are eleven comedies still extant, enjoyed such a pre-eminence of reputation, that the Athenians, by a public decree, honoured him with a crown made of a consecrated olive tree, which grew in the citadel, for his care and success in detecting and exposing the vices of those who governed the commonwealth. Yet this poet, whether impelled by mere wantonness of genius, or actuated by malice and envy, could not refrain from employing the shafts of his ridicule against Socrates, the most venerable character of Pagan antiquity. In the comedy of The Clouds this virtuous philosopher was exhibited on the stage, under his own name, in a cloak exactly resembling that which Socrates wore, in a mask modelled from his features, disputing publicly on the nature of right and wrong. This was undoubtedly an instance of the most flagrant licentiousness; and what renders it the more extraordinary, the audience received it with great applause, even while Socrates himself sat publicly in the theatre. The truth is, the Athenians were so fond of ridicule, that they relished it even when employed against the gods themselves, some of whose characters were very roughly handled by Aristophanes and his rivals in reputation.

We might here draw a parallel between the inhabitants of Athens and the natives of England in point of constitution, genius, and disposition. Athens was a free state like England, that piqued itself upon the influence of the democracy. Like England, its wealth and strength depended upon its maritime power; and it generally acted as umpire in the disputes that arose among its neighbours. The people of Athens, like those of England, were remarkably ingenious, and made great progress in the arts and sciences. They excelled in poetry, history, philosophy, mechanics, and manufactures; they were acute, discerning, disputatious, fickle, wavering, rash, and combustible, and, above all other nations in Europe, addicted to ridicule; a character which the English inherit in a very remarkable degree.

If we may judge from the writings of Aristophanes, his chief aim was to gratify the spleen and excite the mirth of his audience; of an audience, too, that would seem to have been uninformed by taste, and altogether ignorant of decorum; for his pieces are replete with the most extravagant absurdities, virulent slander, impiety, impurities, and low buffoonery. The comic muse, not contented with being allowed to make free with the gods and philosophers, applied her scourge so severely to the magistrates of the commonwealth, that it was thought proper to restrain her within bounds by a law, enacting, that no person should be stigmatized under his real name; and thus the chorus was silenced. In order to elude the penalty of this law, and gratify the taste of the people, the poets began to substitute fictitious names, under which they exhibited particular characters in such lively colours, that the resemblance could not possibly be mistaken or overlooked. This practice gave rise to what is called the *Middle Comedy,* which was but of short duration; for the legislature, perceiving that the first law had not removed the grievance against which it was provided, issued a second ordinance, forbidding, under severe penalties, any real or family occurrences to be represented. This restriction was the immediate cause of improving comedy into a general mirror, held forth to reflect the various follies and foibles incident to human nature; a species of writing called the *New Comedy,* introduced by Diphilus and Menander, of whose works nothing but a few fragments remain.

ESSAY XV.

Poetry distinguished from other Writing.

HAVING communicated our sentiments touching the origin of poetry, by tracing tragedy and comedy to their common source, we shall now endeavour to point out the criteria by which poetry is distinguished from every other species of writing. In common with other arts, such as statuary and painting, it comprehends imitation, invention, composition, and enthusiasm. Imitation is indeed the basis of all the liberal arts; invention and enthusiasm constitute genius, in whatever manner it may be displayed. Eloquence of all sorts admits of enthusiasm. Tully says an orator should be "vehemens ut procella, excitatus ut torrens, incensus ut fulmen: tonat, fulgurat, et rapidis eloquentiæ fluctibus cuncta proruit et proturbat."—"Violent as a tempest, impetuous as a torrent, and glowing intense like the red bolt of heaven, he thunders, lightens, overthrows, and bears down all before him, by the irresistible tide of eloquence." This is the *mens divinior atque os magna sonaturum* of Horace. This is the talent,

——— Meum qui pectus inaniter angit,
Irritat, mulcet, falsis terroribus implet,
Ut magus.

With passions not my own who fires my heart;
Who with unreal terrors fills my breast,
As with a magic influence possess'd.

We are told that Michael Angelo Buonaroti used to work at his statues in a fit of enthusiasm, during which he made the fragments of the stone fly about him with surprising violence. The celebrated Lully being one day blamed for setting nothing to music but the languid verses of Quinault, was animated with the reproach, and running in a fit of enthusiasm to his harpsichord, sung in recitative and accompanied four pathetic lines from the Iphigenia of Racine, with such expression as filled the hearers with astonishment and horror.

Though versification be one of the criteria that distinguish poetry from prose, yet it is not the sole mark of distinction. Were the histories of Polybius and Livy simply turned into verse, they would not become poems; because they would be destitute of those figures, embellishments, and flights of imagination, which display the poet's art and invention. On the other hand, we have many productions that justly lay claim to the title of poetry, without having the advantage of versification; witness the Psalms of David, the Song of Solomon, with many beautiful hymns, descriptions, and rhapsodies, to be found in different parts of the Old Testament, some of them the immediate production of divine inspiration; witness the Celtic fragments which have lately appeared in the English language, and are certainly replete with poetical merit. But though good versification alone will not constitute poetry, bad versification alone will certainly degrade and render disgustful the sublimest sentiments and finest flowers of imagination. This humiliating power of bad verse appears in many translations of the ancient poets; in Ogilby's Homer, Trapp's Virgil, and frequently in Creech's Horace. This last indeed is not wholly devoid of spirit; but it seldom rises above mediocrity, and, as Horace says,

—— Mediocribus esse poetis
Non homines, non Di, non concessere columnæ.

But God, and man, and letter'd post denies,
That Poets ever are of middling size.

How is that beautiful ode beginning with *Justum et tenacem propositi virum* chilled and tamed by the following translation:

He who by principle is sway'd,
In truth and justice still the same,
Is neither of the crowd afraid,
Though civil broils the state inflame;
Nor to a haughty tyrant's frown will stoop,
Nor to a raging storm, when all the winds are up.

Should nature with convulsions shake,
Struck with the fiery bolts of Jove,
The final doom and dreadful crack
Cannot his constant courage move.

That long Alexandrine—"Nor to a raging storm, when all the winds are up," is drawling, feeble, swoln with a pleonasm or tautology, as well as deficient in the rhyme; and as for the "dreadful crack," in the next stanza, instead of exciting terror, it conveys a low and ludicrous idea. How much more elegant and energetic is this paraphrase of the same ode, inserted in one of the volumes of Hume's *History of England*:

The man whose mind, on virtue bent,
Pursues some greatly good intent
With undiverted aim,
Serene beholds the angry crowd;
Nor can their clamours fierce and loud
His stubborn honour tame.

Nor the proud tyrant's fiercest threat,
Nor storms that from their dark retreat
The lawless surges wake;
Nor Jove's dread bolt, that shakes the pole,
The firmer purpose of his soul
With all its powers can shake.

Should nature's frame in ruins fall,
And chaos o'er the sinking ball
Resume primeval sway,
His courage chance and fate defies,
Nor feels the wreck of earth and skies
Obstruct its destined way.

If poetry exists independent of versification, it will naturally be asked, how then is it to be distinguished? Undoubtedly by its own peculiar expression: it has a language of its own, which speaks so feelingly to the heart, and so pleasingly to the imagination, that its meaning cannot possibly be misunderstood by any person of delicate sensations. It is a species of painting with words, in which the figures are happily conceived, ingeniously arranged, affectingly expressed, and recommended with all the warmth and harmony of colouring: it consists of imagery, description, metaphors, similes, and sentiments, adapted with propriety to the subject, so contrived and executed as to soothe the ear, surprise and delight the fancy, mend and melt the heart, elevate the mind, and please the understanding. According to Flaccus:

Aut prodesse volunt, aut delectare poetæ;
Aut simul et jucunda et idonea dicere vitæ.

Poets would profit or delight mankind,
And with th' amusing show th' instructive join'd.

Omne tulit punctum, qui miscuit utile dulci,
Lectorem delectando pariterque monendo.

Profit and pleasure mingled thus with art,
To soothe the fancy and improve the heart.

Tropes and figures are likewise liberally used in rhetoric; and some of the most celebrated orators have owned themselves much indebted to the poets. Theophrastus expressly recommends the poets for this purpose. From their source the spirit and energy of the pathetic, the sublime, and the beautiful, are derived. But these figures must be more sparingly used in rhetoric than in poetry, and even then mingled with argumentation, and a detail of facts, altogether different from poetical narration. The poet, instead of simply relating the incident, strikes off a glowing picture of the scene, and exhibits it in the most lively colours to the eye of the imagination. "It is reported that Homer was blind," says Tully in his Tusculan Questions; "yet his poetry is no other than painting. What country, what climate, what ideas, battles, commotions, and contests of men, as well as of wild beasts, has he not painted in such a manner, as to bring before our eyes those very scenes which he himself could not behold?" We cannot, therefore, subscribe to the opinion of some ingenious critics, who have blamed Mr. Pope for deviating in some instances from the simplicity of Homer, in his translation of the Iliad and Odyssey. For example, the Grecian bard says simply "the sun rose;" and his translator gives us a beautiful picture of the sun rising. Homer mentions a person who played upon the lyre; the translator sets him before us warbling to the silver strings. If this be a deviation, it is at the same time an improvement. Homer himself, as Cicero observes above, is full of this kind of painting, and particularly fond of description, even in situations where the action seems to require haste. Neptune, observing from Samothrace the discomfiture of the Grecians before Troy, flies to their assistance, and might have been wafted thither in half a line; but the bard describes him, first, descending the mountain on which he sat; secondly, striding towards his palace at Ægæ, and yoking his horses; thirdly, he describes him putting on his armour; and, lastly, ascending his car, and driving along the surface of the sea. Far from being disgusted by these delays, we are delighted with the particulars of the description. Nothing can be more sublime than the circumstance of the mountain's trembling beneath the footsteps of an immortal:

———Τρέμε δ' οὐρέα μακρὰ καὶ ὕλη
Ποσσὶν ὑπ' ἀθανάτοισι Ποσειδάωνος ἰόντος.

But his passage to the Grecian fleet is altogether transporting:

Βῆ δ' ἐλάαν ἐπὶ κύματ, κ. τ. λ.

He mounts the car, the golden scourge applies,
He sits superior, and the chariot flies;
His whirling wheels the glassy surface sweep;
Th' enormous monsters, rolling o'er the deep,
Gambol around him on the watery way,
And heavy whales in awkward measures play:
The sea subsiding spreads a level plain,
Exults and crowns the monarch of the main;
The parting waves before his coursers fly;
The wond'ring waters leave his axle dry.

With great veneration for the memory of Mr. Pope, we cannot help objecting to some lines of this translation. We have no idea of the sea's exulting and crowning Neptune, after it had subsided into a level plain. There is no such image in the original. Homer says, the whales exulted, and knew, or owned their king; and that the sea parted with joy: γηθοσύνη δὲ θαλάσσα διΐσατο. Neither is there a word of the wondering waters: we therefore think the lines might be thus altered to advantage:

They knew and own'd the monarch of the main:
The sea subsiding spreads a level plain;
The curling waves before his coursers fly;
The parting surface leaves his brazen axle dry.

Besides the metaphors, similes, and allusions of poetry, there is an infinite variety of tropes, or turns of expression, occasionally disseminated through works of genius, which serve to animate the whole, and distinguish the glowing effusions of real inspiration from the cold efforts of mere science. These tropes consist of a certain happy choice and arrangement of words, by which ideas are artfully disclosed in a great variety of attitudes; of epithets, and compound epithets; of sounds collected in order to echo the sense conveyed; of apostrophes; and, above all, the enchanting use of the prosopopœia, which is a kind of magic, by which the poet gives life and motion to every inanimate part of nature. Homer, describing the wrath of Agamemnon, in the first book of the Iliad, strikes off a glowing image in two words:

———ὄσσε δ' οἱ πυρὶ λαμπετόωντι ἐΐκτην.

—and from his eyeballs *flash'd the living fire.*

This indeed is a figure which has been copied by Virgil, and almost all the poets of every age,—*oculis* micat *acribus ignis* —ignescunt iræ: *auris dolor ossibus* ardet. Milton, describing Satan in hell, says,

With head uplift above the wave, and eye
That *sparkling blazed*—

—He spake: and to confirm his words out flew
Millions of flaming swords, drawn from the thighs
Of mighty cherubim. The sudden *blaze*
Far round *illumined* hell—

There are certain words in every language particularly adapted to the poetical expression; some from the image or idea they convey to the imagination, and some from the effect they have upon the ear. The first are truly *figurative;* the others may be called *emphatical.* Rollin observes that Virgil has, upon many occasions, poetized (if we may be allowed the expression) a whole sentence by means of the same word, which is *pendere.*

Ite meæ, felix quondam pecus, ite capellæ;
Non ego vos posthac, viridi projectus in antro,
Dumosa pendere procul de rupe videbo.

At ease reclined beneath the verdant shade,
No more shall I behold my happy flock
Aloft *hang* browsing on the tufted rock.

Here the word *pendere* wonderfully improves the landscape, and renders the whole passage beautifully picturesque. The same figurative verb we meet with in many different parts of the Æneid.

Hi summo fluctu *pendent*, his unda *dehiscens*
Terram inter fluctus aperit.

These on the mountain billow *hung;* to those
The *yawning waves* the yellow sand disclose.

In this instance the words *pendent* and *dehiscens*, *hung* and *yawning*, are equally poetical. Addison seems to have had this passage in his eye when he wrote his Hymn, which is inserted in the Spectator:

—For though in dreadful worlds we *hung*,
High on the broken wave.

And in another piece of a like nature in the same collection:

Thy providence my life sustain'd,
And all my wants redress'd,
When in the silent womb I lay,
And *hung* upon the breast.

Shakespeare, in his admired description of Dover cliff, uses the same expression:

——half way down
Hangs one that gathers samphire—dreadful trade!

Nothing can be more beautiful than the following picture, in which Milton has introduced the same expressive tint:

——he, on his side
Leaning, half raised, with looks of cordial love
Hung over her enamour'd.

We shall give one example more from Virgil, to show in what a variety of scenes it may appear with propriety and effect. In describing the progress of Dido's passion for Æneas the poet says:

Iliacos iterum demens audire labores
Exposcit, *pendetque* iterum narrantis ab ore

The woes of Troy once more she begg'd to hear;
Once more the mournful tale employ'd his tongue,
While in fond rapture on his lips she *hung*.

The reader will perceive, in all these instances, that no other word could be substituted with equal energy; indeed, no other word could be used, without degrading the sense and defacing the image.

There are many other verbs of poetical import, fetched from nature and from art, which the Poet uses to advantage, both in a literal and metaphorical sense; and these have been always translated for the same purpose from one language to another; such as *quasso*, *concutio*, *cio*, *suscito*, *lenio*, *sævio*, *mano*, *fluo*, *ardeo*, *mico*, *aro*, to shake, to wake, to rouse, to soothe, to rage, to flow, to shine or blaze, to plough.—Quassantia *tectum limina—Æneas casu* concussus *acerbo—Ære* ciere *viros*, *Martemque accendere cantu—Æneas acuit Martem et se* suscitat *ira—Impium* lenite *clamorem*—Lenibant *curas*—*Ne* sævi *magne sacerdos—Sudor ad imos* manabat *solos—Suspensæque diu lachrymæ* fluxere *per ora—Juvenali* ardebat *amore*—Micat *æreus ensis—Nullum maris æquor* arandum. It will be unnecessary to insert examples of the same nature from the English poets.

The words we term *emphatical* are such as by their sound express the sense they are intended to convey; and with these the Greek abounds, above all other languages, not only from its natural copiousness, flexibility, and significance, but also from the variety of its dialects, which enables a writer to vary his terminations occasionally as the nature of the subject requires, without offending the most delicate ear, or incurring the imputation of adopting vulgar provincial expressions. Every smatterer in Greek can repeat

Βῆ δ' ἀκέων παρὰ θῖνα πολυφλοισβοῖο θαλάσσης,

in which the two last words wonderfully echo to the sense, conveying the idea of the sea dashing on the shore. How much more significant in sound than that beautiful image of Shakespeare—

The sea that on the unnumber'd pebbles beats!

And yet, if we consider the strictness of propriety, this last expression would seem to have been selected on purpose to concur with the other circumstances, which are brought together to ascertain the vast height of Dover cliff; for the poet adds, "cannot be heard so high." The place where Glo'ster stood was so high above the surface of the sea that the φλοῖσβος, or *dashing*, could not be heard; and therefore an enthusiastic admirer of Shakespeare might, with some plausibility, affirm the poet had chosen an expression in which that sound is not at all conveyed.

In the very same page of Homer's Iliad we meet with two other striking instances of the same sort of beauty. Apollo, incensed at the insults his priest had sustained, descends from the top of Olympus with his bow and quiver rattling on his shoulder as he moved along:

Ἔκλαγξαν δ' ἄρ' ὀϊστω ἐπ' ὤμων.

Here the sound of the word ἔκλαγξαν admirably expresses the clanking of armour; as the third line after this surprisingly imitates the twanging of a bow.

Δεινὴ δὲ κλαγγὴ γένετ' ἀργυρέοιο βιοῖο.

In shrill-toned murmurs sang the twanging bow.

Many beauties of the same kind are scattered through Homer, Pindar, and Theocritus, such as the βομβεῦσα μέλισσα, *susurrans apicula;* the ἁδὺ ψιθύρισμα, *dulcem susurrum;* and the μελίσδεται, for the sighing of the pine.

The Latin language teems with sounds adapted to every situation, and the English is not destitute of this significant energy. We have the *cooing* turtle, the *sighing* reed, the *warbling* rivulet, the *gliding* stream, the *whispering* breeze, the glance, the gleam, the flash, the *bickering* flame, the *dashing* wave, the *gushing* spring, the *howling* blast, the *rattling* storm, the *pattering* shower, the *crimp* earth, the *mouldering* tower, the *twanging* bowstring, the *clanging* arms, the *clanking* chains, the *twinkling* stars, the *tinkling* chords, the *trickling* drops, the *twittering* swallow, the *cawing* rook, the *screeching* owl; and a thousand other words and epithets, wonderfully suited to the sense they imply.

Among the select passages of poetry which we shall insert by way of illustration, the reader will find instances of all the different tropes and figures which the best authors have adopted in the variety of their poetical works, as well as of the apostrophe, abrupt transition, repetition, and prosopopœia.

In the meantime it will be necessary still farther to analyse those principles which constitute the essence of poetical merit; to display those delightful parterres that teem with the fairest flowers of imagination; and distinguish between the gaudy offspring of a cold insipid fancy and the glowing progeny, diffusing sweets, produced and invigorated by the sun of genius.

ESSAY XVI.

Metaphor.

Of all the implements of Poetry, the metaphor is the most generally and successfully used, and indeed may be termed the Muse's caduceus, by the power of which she enchants all nature. The metaphor is a shorter simile, or rather a kind of magical coat, by which the same idea assumes a thousand different appearances. Thus the word *plough*, which originally belongs to agriculture, being metaphorically used, represents the motion of a ship at sea and the effects of old age upon the human countenance:

——Plough'd the bosom of the deep—
And time had plough'd his venerable front.

Almost every verb, noun substantive, or term of art in any language, may be in this manner applied to a variety of subjects with admirable effect; but the danger is in sowing metaphors too thick, so as to distract the imagination of the reader, and incur the imputation of deserting nature, in order to hunt after conceits. Every day produces poems of all kinds so inflated with metaphor, that they may be compared to the gaudy bubbles blown up from a solution of soap. Longinus is of opinion, that a multitude of metaphors is never excusable, except in those cases when the passions are roused, and, like a winter torrent, rush down impetuous, sweeping them with collective force along. He brings an instance of the following quotation from Demosthenes: "Men," says he, "profligates, miscreants, and flatterers, who having severally preyed upon the bowels of their country, at length betrayed her liberty, first to Philip, and now again to Alexander; who, placing the chief felicity of life in the indulgence of infamous lusts and appetites, overturned in the dust that freedom and independence which was the chief aim and end of all our worthy ancestors."

Aristotle and Theophrastus seem to think it is rather too bold and hazardous to use metaphors so freely, without interposing some mitigating phrase, such as, "if I may be allowed the expression," or some equivalent excuse. At the same time, Longinus finds fault with Plato for hazarding some metaphors, which, indeed, appear to be equally affected and extravagant; when he says, "The government of a state should not resemble a bowl of hot fermenting wine, but a cool and moderate beverage *chastised by the sober deity*,"—a metaphor that signifies nothing more than "mixed or lowered with water." Demetrius Phalereus justly observes, that though a judicious use of metaphors wonderfully raises, sublimes, and adorns oratory or elocution, yet they should seem to flow naturally from the subject; and too great a redundancy of them inflates the discourse to a mere rhapsody. The same observation will hold in poetry; and the more liberal or sparing use of them will depend, in a great measure, on the nature of the subject.

Passion itself is very figurative, and often bursts out into metaphors; but, in touching the pathos, the poet must be perfectly well acquainted with the emotions of the human soul, and carefully distinguish between those metaphors which rise glowing from the heart, and those cold conceits which are engendered in the fancy. Should one of these last unfortunately intervene, it will be apt to destroy the whole effect of the most pathetical incident or situation. Indeed, it requires the most delicate taste, and a consummate knowledge of propriety, to employ metaphors in such a manner as to avoid what the ancients call the τὸ ψυχρόν, the *frigid*, or false sublime. Instances of this kind were frequent even among the correct ancients. Sappho herself is blamed for using the hyperbole λευκοτέροι χιόνος, *whiter than snow*. Demetrius is so nice as to be disgusted at the simile of *swift as the wind;* though, in speaking of a race-horse, we know from experience that this is not even a hyperbole. He would have had more reason to censure that kind of metaphor which Aristotle styles κατ' ἐνέργειαν, exhibiting things inanimate as endued with sense and reason; such as that of the sharp pointed arrow, *eager* to take wing among the crowd: ὀξυβελὴς καθ' ὅμιλον ἐπιπτέσθαι μενεαίνων. Not but that, in descriptive poetry, this figure is often allowed and admired. The *cruel* sword, the *ruthless* dagger, the *ruffian* blast, are epithets which frequently occur. The *faithful* bosom of the earth, the *joyous* boughs, the trees that *admire their images* reflected in the stream, and many other examples of this kind, are found disseminated through the works of our best modern poets: yet still they must be sheltered under the privilege of the *poetica licentia;* and, except in poetry, they would give offence.

More chaste metaphors are freely used in all kinds of writing; more sparingly in history, and more abundantly in rhetoric: we have seen that Plato indulges in them even to excess. The orations of Demosthenes are animated, and even inflamed with metaphors, some of them so bold as even to entail upon him the censure of the critics. Τότε τῷ Πύθωνι τῷ ῥήτορι ῥέοντι καθ' ὑμῶν.—"Then I did not yield to Python the orator, when he *overflowed* you with a tide of eloquence." Cicero is still more liberal in the use of them; he ransacks all nature, and pours forth a redundancy of figures even with a lavish hand. Even the chaste Xenophon, who generally illustrates his subject by way of simile, sometimes ventures to produce an expressive metaphor, such as "Part of the phalanx *fluctuated* in the march;" and, indeed, nothing can be more significant than this word ἐξεκύμηνε, to represent a body of men staggered, and on the point of giving way. Armstrong has used the word *fluctuate* with admirable efficacy, in his philosophical poem, entitled *The Art of Preserving Health.*

> Oh! when the growling winds contend, and all
> The sounding forest *fluctuates* in the storm,
> To sink in warm repose, and hear the din
> Howl o'er the steady battlements——

The word *fluctuate* on this occasion not only exhibits an idea of struggling, but also echoes to the sense like the ἔφριξεν δὲ μαχή of Homer; which, by the by, it is impossible to render into English, for the verb φρίσσω signifies not only to stand erect like prickles, as a grove of lances, but also to make a noise like the crashing of armour, the hissing of javelins, and the splinters of spears.

Over and above an excess of figures, a young author is apt to run into a confusion of mixed metaphors, which leave the sense disjointed, and distract the imagination: Shakespeare himself is often guilty of these irregularities. The soliloquy in Hamlet, which we have so often heard extolled in terms of admiration, is, in our opinion, a heap of absurdities, whether we consider the situation, the sentiment, the argumentation, or the poetry. Hamlet is informed by the Ghost, that his father was murdered, and therefore he is tempted to murder himself, even after he had promised to take vengeance on the usurper, and expressed the utmost eagerness to achieve this enterprise. It does not appear that he had the least reason to wish for death; but every motive which may be supposed to influence the mind of a young prince concurred to render life desirable,—revenge towards the usurper, love for the fair Ophelia, and the ambition of reigning. Besides, when he had an opportunity of dying without being accessory to his own death—when he had nothing to do but, in obedience to his uncle's command, to allow himself to be conveyed quietly to England, where he was sure of suffering death,—instead of amusing himself with meditations on mortality, he very wisely consulted the means of self-preservation, turned the tables upon his attendants, and returned to Denmark. But granting him to have been reduced to the lowest state of despondency, surrounded with nothing but horror and despair, sick of this life, and eager to tempt futurity, we shall see how far he argues like a philosopher.

In order to support this general charge against an author so universally held in veneration, whose very errors have helped to sanctify his character among the multitude, we will descend to particulars, and analyse this famous soliloquy.

Hamlet, having assumed the disguise of madness, as a cloak under which he might the more effectually revenge his father's death upon the murderer and usurper, appears alone upon the stage, in a pensive and melancholy attitude, and communes with himself in these words:

To be, or not to be? that is the question:—
Whether 'tis nobler in the mind, to suffer
The slings and arrows of outrageous fortune,
Or to take arms against a sea of troubles,
And, by opposing, end them?—To die—to sleep—
No more: and, by a sleep, to say we end
The heartache, and the thousand natural shocks
That flesh is heir to,—'tis a consummation
Devoutly to be wish'd. To die—to sleep:
To sleep! perchance to dream!—ay, there's the rub!
For in that sleep of death what dreams may come,
When we have shuffled off this mortal coil,
Must give us pause. There's the respect
That makes calamity of so long life:
For who would bear the whips and scorns of time,
The oppressor's wrong, the proud man's contumely,
The pangs of despised love, the law's delay,
The insolence of office, and the spurns
That patient merit of the unworthy takes,
When he himself might his quietus make
With a bare bodkin? Who would fardels bear,
To groan and sweat under a weary life,
But that the dread of something after death,—
That undiscovered country, from whose bourne
No traveller returns,—puzzles the will,
And makes us rather bear those ills we have,
Than fly to others that we know not of?
Thus conscience does make cowards of us all;
And thus the native hue of resolution
Is sicklied o'er with the pale cast of thought;
And enterprises of great pith and moment,
With this regard, their currents turn awry,
And lose the name of action.

We have already observed, that there is not any apparent circumstance in the fate or situation of Hamlet that should prompt him to harbour one thought of self-murder; and therefore these expressions of despair imply an impropriety in point of character. But supposing his condition was truly desperate, and he saw no possibility of repose but in the uncertain harbour of death, let us see in what manner he argues on that subject. The question is, "To be, or not to be;" to die by my own hand, or live and suffer the miseries of life. He proceeds to explain the alternative in these terms, "Whether 'tis nobler in the mind to suffer, or endure, the frowns of fortune, or to take arms, and, by opposing, end them." Here he deviates from his first proposition, and death is no longer the question. The only doubt is, whether he will stoop to misfortune, or exert his faculties in order to surmount it. This surely is the obvious meaning, and indeed the only meaning that can be implied in these words,—

> Whether 'tis nobler in the mind, to suffer
> The slings and arrows of outrageous fortune,
> Or to take arms against a sea of troubles,
> And, by opposing, end them.

He now drops this idea, and reverts to his reasoning on death, in the course of which he owns himself deterred from suicide by the thoughts of what may follow death:

> ——the dread of something after death,—
> That undiscovered country, from whose bourne
> No traveller returns.

This might be a good argument in a Heathen or Pagan, and such indeed Hamlet really was; but Shakespeare has already represented him as a good Catholic, who must have been acquainted with the truths of revealed religion, and says expressly in this very play,

> ——had not the Everlasting fix'd
> His canon 'gainst self-murder.

Moreover, he had just been conversing with his father's spirit piping hot from purgatory, which we presume is not within the bourne of this world. The dread of what may happen after death, says he,

> Makes us rather bear those ills we have,
> Than fly to others that we know not of.

This declaration at least implies some knowledge of the other world, and expressly asserts, that there must be ills in that world, though what kind of ills they are we do not know. The argument, therefore, may be reduced to this lemma: this world abounds with ills which I feel; the other world abounds with ills, the nature of which I do not know; therefore, I will rather bear those ills I have, "than fly to others which I know not of:" a deduction amounting to a certainty, with respect to the only circumstance that could create a doubt, namely, whether in death he should rest from his misery; and if he was certain there were evils in the next world, as well as in this, he had no room to reason at all about the matter. What alone could justify his thinking on this subject would have been the hope of flying from the ills of this world, without encountering any others in the next.

Nor is Hamlet more accurate in the following reflection:

> Thus conscience does make cowards of us all.

A bad conscience will make us cowards; but a good conscience will make us brave. It does not appear that any thing lay heavy on his conscience; and from the premises we cannot help inferring, that conscience in this case was entirely out of the question. Hamlet was deterred from suicide by a full conviction, that, in flying from one sea of troubles which he did know, he should fall into another which he did not know.

His whole chain of reasoning, therefore, seems inconsistent and incongruous. "I am doubtful whether I should live or do violence upon my own life; for I know not whether it is more honourable to bear misfortune patiently than to exert myself in opposing misfortune, and, by opposing, end it." Let us throw it into the form of a syllogism, it will stand thus: "I am oppressed with ills; I know not whether it is more honourable to bear those ills patiently, or to end them by taking arms against them: *ergo*, I am doubtful whether I should slay myself or live. To die is no more than to sleep; and to say that by a sleep we end the heartache," &c. "'tis a consummation devoutly to be wished." Now to *say* it was of no consequence, unless it had been true. "I am afraid of the dreams that may happen in that sleep of death! and I choose rather to bear those ills I have in this life, than to fly to other ills in that undiscovered country, from whose bourne no traveller ever returns. I have ills that are almost insupportable in this life. I know not what is in the next, because it is an undiscovered country: *ergo*, I'd rather bear those ills I have, than fly to others which I know not of." Here the conclusion is by no means warranted by the premises. "I am sore afflicted in this life; but I would rather bear the afflictions of this life, than plunge myself in the afflictions of another life: *ergo*, conscience makes cowards of us all." But this conclusion would justify the logician in saying, *negatur consequens;* for it is entirely detached both from the major and minor proposition.

This soliloquy is not less exceptionable in the propriety of expression, than in the chain of argumentation. "To die—to sleep —no more," contains an ambiguity, which all the art of punctuation cannot remove; for it may signify that "to die" is to sleep no more; or the expression "no more" may be considered as an abrupt apostrophe in thinking, as if he meant to say "no more of that reflection."

"Ay, there's the rub," is a vulgarism beneath the dignity of Hamlet's character, and the words that follow leave the sense imperfect:

> For in that sleep of death what dreams may come,
> When we have shuffled off this mortal coil,
> Must give us pause.

Not the dreams that might come, but the fear of what dreams might come, occasioned the pause or hesitation. *Respect* in the same line may be allowed to pass for consideration: but

> The oppressor's wrong, the proud man's contumely,

according to the invariable acceptation of the words *wrong* and *contumely*, can signify nothing but the wrongs sustained by the oppressor, and the contumely or abuse thrown upon the proud man; though it is plain that Shakespeare used them in a different sense: neither is the word *spurn* a substantive, yet as such he has inserted it in these lines:

> The insolence of office, and the spurns
> That patient merit of th' unworthy takes.

If we consider the metaphors of the soliloquy, we shall find them jumbled together in a strange confusion.

If the metaphors were reduced to painting, we should find it a very difficult task, if not altogether impracticable, to represent with any propriety outrageous fortune using her slings and arrows, between which, indeed, there is no sort of analogy in nature. Neither can any figure be more ridiculously absurd than that of a man taking arms against a sea, exclusive of the incongruous medley of slings, arrows, and seas, justled within the compass of one reflection. What follows is a strange rhapsody of broken images of sleeping, dreaming, and shifting off a *coil*, which last conveys no idea that can be represented on canvas. A man may be exhibited shuffling off his garments, or his chains; but how he should shuffle off a *coil*, which is another term for noise and tumult, we cannot comprehend. Then we have "long-lived calamity," and "time armed with whips and scorns;" and "patient merit spurned at by unworthiness;" and "misery with a bare bodkin going to make his own *quietus*," which at best is but a mean metaphor. These are followed by figures, "sweating under fardels of burdens," "puzzled with doubts," "shaking with fears," and "flying from evils." Finally, we see "resolution sicklied o'er with pale thought," a conception like that of representing health by sickness; and a "current of pith turned awry, so as to lose the name of action," which is both an error in fancy, and a solecism in sense. In a word, the soliloquy may be compared to the *Ægri somnia* and the *Tabula, cujus vanæ finguntur species.*

But while we censure the chaos of broken, incongruous metaphors, we ought also to caution the young poet against the opposite extreme of pursuing a metaphor, until the spirit is quite exhausted in a succession of cold conceits; such as we see in the following letter, said to be sent by Tamerlane to the Turkish Emperor Bajazet. "Where is the monarch that dares oppose our arms? Where is the potentate who doth not glory in being numbered among our vassals? As for thee, descended from a Turcoman mariner, since the vessel of thy unbounded ambition hath been wrecked in the gulf of thy self-love, it would be proper that thou shouldst furl the sails of thy temerity, and cast the anchor of repentance in the port of sincerity and justice, which is the harbour of safety; lest the tempest of our vengeance make thee perish in the sea of that punishment thou hast deserved."

But if these laboured conceits are ridiculous in poetry, they are still more inexcusable in prose: such as we find them frequently occur in Strada's *Bellum Belgicum:* "Vix descenderat à prætoria navi Cæsar, cùm fœda ilico exorta in portu tempestas; classem impetu disjecit, prætoriam hausit, quasi non vecturam amplius Cæsarem Cæsarisque fortunam."—"Cæsar had scarcely set his feet on shore, when a terrible tempest arising, shattered the fleet even in the harbour, and sent to the bottom the prætorian ship, as if he resolved it should no longer carry Cæsar and his fortunes."

Yet this is modest in comparison of the following flowers: "Alii, pulsis è tormento catenis discerpti sectique, dimidiato corpore pugnabant sibi superstites, ac peremptæ partis ultores."—"Others, dissevered and cut in twain by chain-shot, fought with one half of their bodies that remained, in revenge of the other half that was slain."

Homer, Horace, and even the chaste Virgil, is not free from conceits. The latter, speaking of a man's hand cut off in battle, says,

> Te decisa suum, Laride, dextera quærit:
> Semianimesque micant digiti, ferrumque retractant:

thus enduing the amputated hand with sense and volition. This, to be sure, is a violent figure, and hath been justly condemned by some accurate critics; but we think they are too severe in extending the same censure to some other passages in the most admired authors.

Virgil, in his sixth Eclogue, says:

> Omnia quæ, Phœbo quondam meditante, beatus
> Audiit Eurotas, jussitque ediscere lauros,
> Ille canit.

> Whate'er, when Phœbus bless'd the Arcadian plain,
> Eurotas heard and taught his bays the strain,
> The senior sung—

And Pope has copied the conceit in his Pastorals:

> Thames heard the numbers as he flow'd along,
> And bade his willows learn the moving song.

Vida thus begins his first Eclogue:

> Dicite, vos musæ, et juvenum memorate querelas:
> Dicite; nam motas ipsas ad carmina cautes,
> Et requiêsse suos perhibent vaga flumina cursus.

> Say, heavenly muse, their youthful frays rehearse;
> Begin, ye daughters of immortal verse:
> Exulting rocks have own'd the power of song,
> And rivers listen'd as they flow'd along.

Racine adopts the same bold figure in his Phædra:

> Le flot qui l'apporta recule épouvanté.

> The wave that bore him backwards shrunk appall'd.

Even Milton has indulged himself in the same license of expression:

> ——As when to them who sail
> Beyond the Cape of Hope, and now are past
> Mozambic, off at sea north-east winds blow
> Sabæan odour from the spicy shore
> Of Araby the blest; with such delay
> Well pleased, they slack their course, and many a league,
> Cheer'd with the grateful smell, old Ocean smiles.

Shakespeare says,

> ——I've seen
> Th' ambitious ocean swell, and rage, and foam,
> To be exalted with the threat'ning clouds.

And indeed more correct writers, both ancient and modern, abound with the same kind of figure, which is reconciled to propriety, and even invested with beauty, by the efficacy of the prosopopœia, which personifies the object. Thus, when Virgil says Enipeus heard the songs of Apollo, he raises up, as by enchantment, the idea of a river god crowned with sedges, his head raised above the stream, and in his countenance the expression of pleased attention. By the same magic we see, in the couplet quoted from Pope's Pastorals, old father Thames leaning upon his urn, and listening to the poet's strain.

Thus in the regions of poetry all nature, even the passions and affections of the mind, may be personified into picturesque figures for the entertainment of the reader. Ocean smiles or frowns, as the sea is calm or tempestuous; a Triton rules on every angry billow; every mountain has its Nymph; every stream its Naiad; every tree its Hamadryad; and every art its Genius. We cannot, therefore, assent to those who censure Thomson as licentious for using the following figure:

> O vale of bliss! O softly swelling hills!
> On which the power of cultivation lies,
> And joys to see the wonders of his toil.

We cannot conceive a more beautiful image than that of the Genius of Agriculture, distinguished by the implements of his art, imbrowned with labour, glowing with health, crowned with a garland of foliage, flowers, and fruit, lying stretched at his ease on the brow of a gentle swelling hill, and contemplating with pleasure the happy effects of his own industry.

Neither can we join issue against Shakespeare for this comparison, which hath likewise incurred the censure of the critics:

——The noble sister of Poplicola,
The moon of Rome; chaste as the icicle
That's curdled by the frost from purest snow,
And hangs on Dian's temple——

This is no more than illustrating a quality of the mind, by comparing it with a sensible object. If there is no impropriety in saying such a man is true as steel, firm as a rock, inflexible as an oak, unsteady as the ocean; or in describing a disposition cold as ice, or fickle as the wind—and these expressions are justified by constant practice—we shall hazard an assertion, that the comparison of a chaste woman to an icicle is proper and picturesque, as it obtains only in the circumstances of cold and purity; but that the addition of its being curdled from the purest snow, and hanging on the temple of Diana, the patroness of virginity, heightens the whole into a most beautiful simile, that gives a very respectable and amiable idea of the character in question.

The simile is no more than an extended metaphor, introduced to illustrate and beautify the subject; it ought to be apt, striking, properly pursued, and adorned with all the graces of poetical melody. But a simile of this kind ought never to proceed from the mouth of a person under any great agitation of spirit; such as a tragic character overwhelmed with grief, distracted by contending cares, or agonising in the pangs of death. The language of passion will not admit simile, which is always the result of study and deliberation. We will not allow a hero the privilege of a dying swan, which is said to chant its approaching fate in the most melodious strain; and therefore nothing can be more ridiculously unnatural than the representation of a lover dying upon the stage with a laboured simile in his mouth.

The Orientals, whose language was extremely figurative, have been very careless in the choice of their similes; provided the resemblance obtained in one circumstance, they minded not whether they disagreed with the subject in every other respect. Many instances of this defect in congruity may be culled from the most sublime parts of Scripture.

Homer has been blamed for the bad choice of his similes on some particular occasions. He compares Ajax to an ass, in the Iliad, and Ulysses to a steak broiling on the coals, in the Odyssey. His admirers have endeavoured to excuse him, by reminding us of the simplicity of the age in which he wrote; but they have not been able to prove that any ideas of dignity or importance were, even in those days, affixed to the character of an ass, or the quality of a beef collop; therefore they were very improper illustrations for any situation in which a hero ought to be represented.

Virgil has degraded the wife of King Latinus, by comparing her, when she was actuated by the Fury, to a top which the boys lash for diversion. This, doubtless, is a low image, though in other respects the comparison is not destitute of propriety: but he is much more justly censured for the following simile, which has no sort of reference to the subject. Speaking of Turnus, he says:

——medio dux agmine Turnus
Vertitur arma tenens, et toto vertice supra est:
Ceu septem surgens sedatis amnibus altus
Per tacitum Ganges; aut pingui flumine Nilus
Cum refluit campis, et jam se condidit alveo.

But Turnus, chief amidst the warrior train,
In armour towers the tallest on the plain.
The Ganges, thus by seven rich streams supplied,
A mighty mass devolves in silent pride;
Thus Nilus pours from his prolific urn,
When from the fields o'erflow'd his vagrant streams return.

These, no doubt, are majestic images: but they bear no sort of resemblance to a hero glittering in armour at the head of his forces.

Horace has been ridiculed by some shrewd critics for this comparison, which, however, we think is more defensible than the former. Addressing himself to Munatius Plancus, he says:

Albus ut obscuro deterget nubila cœlo
Sæpe Notus, neque parturit imbres
Perpetuos: sic tu sapiens finire memento
Tristitiam, vitæque labores
Molli, Plance, mero.——

As Notus often, when the welkin lowers,
Sweeps off the clouds, nor teems perpetual showers,
So let thy wisdom, free from anxious strife,
In mellow wine dissolve the cares of life.
DUNKIN.

The analogy, it must be confessed, is not very striking; but, nevertheless, it is not altogether void of propriety. The poet reasons thus: as the south wind, though generally attended with rain, is often known to dispel the clouds, and render the weather serene; so do you, though generally on the rack of thought, remember to relax sometimes, and drown your cares in wine. As the south wind is not always moist, so you ought not always to be dry. A few instances of inaccuracy, or mediocrity, can never derogate from the superlative merit of Homer and Virgil, whose poems are the great magazines, replete with every species of beauty and magnificence, particularly abounding with similes, which astonish, delight, and transport the reader.

Every simile ought not only to be well adapted to the subject, but also to include every excellence of description, and to be coloured with the warmest tints of poetry. Nothing can be more happily hit off than the following in the Georgics, to which the poet compares Orpheus lamenting his lost Eurydice:—

Qualis populeâ mœrens Philomela sub umbrâ
Amissos queritur fœtus, quos durus arator
Observans nido implumes detraxit; at illa
Flet noctem, ramoque sedens miserabile carmen
Integrat, et mœstis late loca questibus implet.

So Philomela, from th' umbrageous wood,
In strains melodious mourns her tender brood,
Snatched from the nest by some rude ploughman's hand:
On some lone bough the warbler takes her stand;
The live-long night she mourns the cruel wrong,
And hill and dale resound the plaintive song.

Here we not only find the most scrupulous propriety, and the happiest choice, in comparing the Thracian bard to Philomel, the poet of the grove; but also the most beautiful description, containing a fine touch of the pathos—in which last particular, indeed, Virgil, in our opinion, excels all other poets, whether ancient or modern.

One would imagine that nature had exhausted itself, in order to embellish the poems of Homer, Virgil, and Milton, with similes and metaphors. The first of these very often uses the comparison of the wind, the whirlwind, the hail, the torrent, to express the rapidity of his combatants; but when he comes to describe the velocity of the immortal horses that drew the chariot of Juno, he raises his ideas to the subject, and, as Longinus observes, measures every leap by the whole breadth of the horizon.

Ὅσσον δ' ἠεροειδὲς ἀνὴρ ἴδεν ὀφθαλμοῖσιν
Ἥμενος ἐν σκοπιῇ, λεύσσων ἐπὶ οἴνοπα πόντον,
Τόσσον ἐπιθρώσκουσι θεῶν ὑψηχέες ἵπποι.

For, as a watchman, from some rock on high,
O'er the wide main extends his boundless eye;
Through such a space of air, with thund'ring sound,
At every leap th' immortal coursers bound.

The celerity of this goddess seems to be a favourite idea with the poet; for in another place he compares it to the thought of a traveller revolving in his mind the different places he had seen, and passing through them, in imagination, more swift than the lightning flies from east to west.

Homer's best similes have been copied by Virgil and almost every succeeding poet, howsoever they may have varied in the manner of expression. In the third book of the Iliad, Menelaus seeing Paris is compared to a hungry lion espying a hind or goat:

Ὥστε λέων ἐχάρη μεγάλῳ ἐπὶ σώματι κύρσας
Εὑρὼν ἢ ἔλαφον κεραὸν, ἢ ἄγριον αἶγα, κ. τ. λ.

So joys the lion, if a branching deer
Or mountain goat his bulky prize appear;
In vain the youths oppose, the mastiffs bay—
The lordly savage rends the panting prey.
Thus, fond of vengeance, with a furious bound,
In clanging arms he leaps upon the ground.

The Mantuan bard, in the tenth book of the Æneid, applies the same simile to Mezentius, when he beholds Acron in the battle:

Impastus stabula alta leo ceu sæpe peragrans
(Suadet enim vesana fames) si forte fugacem
Conspexit capream, aut surgentem in cornua cervum;
Gaudet hians immane, comasque arrexit, et hæret
Visceribus super accumbens: lavit improba teter
Ora cruor.——

Then, as a hungry lion, who beholds
A gamesome goat who frisks about the folds,
Or beamy stag that grazes on the plain;
He runs, he roars, he shakes his rising mane:
He grins, and opens wide his greedy jaws—
The prey lies panting underneath his paws;
He fills his famish'd maw; his mouth runs o'er
With unchew'd morsels, while he churns the gore.—DRYDEN.

The reader will perceive that Virgil has improved the simile in one particular, and in another fallen short of his original. The description of the lion shaking his mane, opening his hideous jaws distained with the blood of his prey, is great and picturesque; but, on the other hand, he has omitted the circumstance of devouring it without being intimidated or restrained by the dogs and youths that surround him—a circumstance that adds greatly to our idea of his strength, intrepidity, and importance.

ESSAY XVII.

Hyperbole.

OF all the figures in poetry, that called the *hyperbole* is managed with the greatest difficulty. The hyperbole is an exaggeration with which the Muse is indulged for the better illustration of her subject, when she is warmed into enthusiasm. Quintilian calls it an ornament of the bolder kind. Demetrius Phalereus is still more severe. He says the hyperbole is of all forms of speech the most frigid; Μάλιστα δὲ ἡ ὑπερβολὴ ψυχρότατον πάντων: but this must be understood with some grains of allowance. Poetry is animated by the passions; and all the passions exaggerate. Passion itself is a magnifying medium. There are beautiful instances of the hyperbole in the Scripture, which a reader of sensibility cannot read without being strongly affected. The difficulty lies in choosing such hyperboles as the subject will admit of; for, according to the definition of Theophrastus, the frigid in style is that which exceeds the expression suitable to the subject. The judgment does not revolt against Homer for representing the horses of Ericthonius running over the standing corn without breaking off the heads, because the whole is considered as a fable, and the north wind is represented as their sire; but the imagination is a little startled, when Virgil, in imitation of this hyperbole, exhibits Camilla as flying over it without even touching the tops:

Illa vel intactæ segetis per summa volaret
Gramina.

This elegant author, we are afraid, has, upon some other occasions, degenerated into the frigid, in straining to improve upon his great master.

Homer, in the Odyssey, a work which Longinus does not scruple to charge with bearing the marks of old age, describes a storm in which all the four winds were concerned together:

Σὺν δ' Εὐρός τε, Νοτός τ' ἔπεσε, Ζεφυρός τε δυσαής,
Καὶ Βορέης αἰθρηγενέτης μέγα λῦμα κυλίνδων.

We know that such a contention of contrary blasts could not possibly exist in nature; for, even in hurricanes, the winds blow alternately from different points of the compass. Nevertheless, Virgil adopts the description, and adds to its extravagance:

Incubuere mari, totumque à sedibus imis
Una Eurusque Notusque ruunt, creberque procellis
Africus.

Here the winds not only blow together, but they turn the whole body of the ocean topsy-turvy:

East, west, and south, engage with furious sweep,
And from its lowest bed upturn the foaming deep.

The north wind, however, is still more mischievous:

——Stridens aquilone procella
Velum adversa ferit, fluctusque ad sidera tollit.

The sail then Boreas rends with hideous cry,
And whirls the madd'ning billows to the sky.

The motion of the sea between Scylla and Charybdis is still more magnified; and Ætna is exhibited as throwing out volumes of flame which brush the stars. Such expressions as these are not intended as a real representation of the thing specified: they are designed to strike the reader's imagination; but they generally serve as marks of the author's sinking under his own ideas, who, apprehensive of injuring the greatness of his own conception, is hurried into excess and extravagance.

Quintilian allows the use of hyperbole when words are wanting to express anything in its just strength or due energy: then, he says, it is better to exceed in expression than fall short of the conception; but he likewise observes, that there is no figure or form of speech so apt to run into fustian: "Nec alia magis via in κακοζηλίαν itur."

If the chaste Virgil has thus trespassed upon poetical probability, what can we expect from Lucan but hyperboles even more ridiculously extravagant? He represents the winds in contest, the sea in suspense, doubting to which it shall give way. He affirms, that its motion would have been so violent as to produce a second deluge, had not Jupiter kept it under by the clouds; and as to the ship during this dreadful uproar, the sails touch the clouds, while the keel strikes the ground:

> Nubila tanguntur velis, et terra carina.

This image of dashing water at the stars Sir Richard Blackmore has produced in colours truly ridiculous. Describing spouting whales in his Prince Arthur, he makes the following comparison:—

> Like some prodigious water-engine made
> To play on heaven, if fire should heaven invade.

The great fault in all these instances is a deviation from propriety, owing to the erroneous judgment of the writer, who, endeavouring to captivate the admiration with novelty, very often shocks the understanding with extravagance. Of this nature is the whole description of the Cyclops, both in the Odyssey of Homer and in the Æneid of Virgil. It must be owned, however, that the Latin poet, with all his merit, is more apt than his great original to dazzle us with false fire, and practise upon the imagination with gay conceits, that will not bear the critic's examination. There is not in any of Homer's works now subsisting such an example of the false sublime as Virgil's description of the thunderbolts forging under the hammers of the Cyclops:

> Tres imbris torti radios, tres nubis aquosæ
> Addiderant, rutili tres ignis et alitis Austri.

> Three rays of writhen rain, of fire three more,
> Of winged southern winds and cloudy store
> As many parts, the dreadful mixture frame.
> DRYDEN.

This is altogether a fantastic piece of affectation, of which we can form no sensible image, and serves to chill the fancy, rather than warm the admiration, of a judging reader.

Extravagant hyperbole is a weed that grows in great plenty through the works of our admired Shakespeare. In the following description, which hath been much celebrated, one sees he has had an eye to Virgil's thunderbolts:—

> Oh, then, I see Queen Mab hath been with you.
> She is the fairy's midwife; and she comes,
> In shape no bigger than an agate-stone
> On the fore-finger of an alderman,
> Drawn with a team of little atomies
> Athwart men's noses as they lie asleep:
> Her wagon-spokes made of long spinner's legs;
> The cover, of the wings of grasshoppers;
> The traces, of the smallest spider's web;
> The collars, of the *moonshine's watery beams*,
> &c.

Even in describing fantastic beings there is a propriety to be observed; but surely nothing can be more revolting to common sense, than this numbering of the *moonbeams* among the other implements of Queen Mab's harness, which, though extremely slender and diminutive, are nevertheless objects of the touch, and may be conceived capable of use.

The Ode and Satire admit of the boldest hyperboles: such exaggerations suit the impetuous warmth of the one; and in the other have a good effect in exposing folly, and exciting horror against vice. They may be likewise successfully used in Comedy, for moving and managing the powers of ridicule.

ESSAY XVIII.

Versification.

VERSE is an harmonious arrangement of long and short syllables, adapted to different kinds of poetry, and owes its origin entirely to the measured cadence, or music, which was used when the first songs and hymns were recited. This music, divided into different parts, required a regular return of the same measure, and thus every *strophe*, *antistrophe*, *stanza*, contained the same number of feet. To know what constituted the different kinds of rhythmical feet among the ancients, with respect to the number and quantity of their syllables, we have nothing to do but to consult those who have written on grammar and prosody: it is the business of a schoolmaster, rather than the accomplishment of a man of taste.

Various essays have been made in different countries to compare the characters of ancient and modern versification, and to point out the difference beyond any possibility of mistake. But they have made distinctions where, in fact, there was no difference, and left the criterion unobserved. They have transferred the name of rhyme to a regular repetition of the same sound at the end of the line, and set up this vile monotony as the characteristic of modern verse, in contradistinction to the feet of the ancients, which they pretend the poetry of modern language will not admit.

Rhyme, from the Greek word *ῥυθμός*, is nothing else but number, which was essential to the ancient as well as to the modern versification. As to the jingle of similar sounds, though it was never used by the ancients in any regular return in the middle or at the end of the line, and was by no means deemed essential to the versification, yet they did not reject it as a blemish, where it occurred without the appearance of constraint. We meet with it often in the epithets of Homer—*ἀργυρέοιο βιοῖο*, *Ἄναξ ἀνδρῶν Ἀγαμέμνων*: almost the whole first ode of Anacreon is what we call rhyme. The following line of Virgil has been admired for the similitude of sound in the first two words:

*Ore Are*thusa tuo Siculis confunditur undis.

Rhythmus, or number, is certainly essential to verse, whether in the dead or living languages; and the real difference between the two is this: the number in ancient verse relates to the feet, and in modern poetry to the syllables; for to assert that modern poetry has no feet is a ridiculous absurdity. The feet that principally enter into the composition of Greek and Latin verses are either of two or three syllables. Those of two syllables are either both long, as the spondee; or both short, as the pyrrhic; or one short and the other long, as the iambic; or one long, and the other short, as the trochee. Those of three syllables are the dactyl, of one long and two short syllables; the anapest, of two short and one long; the tribrachium, of three short; and the molossus, of three long.

From the different combinations of these feet, restricted to certain numbers, the ancients formed their different kinds of verses, such as the hexameter, or heroic, distinguished by six feet, dactyls and spondees, the fifth being always a dactyl, and the last a spondee. *Exempli gratiâ:*

1 2 3 4 5 6
Principi-is ob-sta, se-ro medi-cina pa-ratur.

The pentameter of five feet, dactyls and spondees, or of six, reckoning two cæsuras:

1 2 3 4 5 6
Cum mala per lon-gas invalu-ere mo-ras.

They had likewise the iambic of three sorts—the dimeter, the trimeter, and the tetrameter—and all the different kinds of lyric verse specified in the odes of Sappho, Alcæus, Anacreon, and Horace. Each of these was distinguished by the number as well as by the species of their feet; so that they were doubly restricted. Now all the feet of the ancient poetry are still found in the versification of living languages; for as cadence was regulated by the ear, it was impossible for a man to write melodious verse without naturally falling into the use of ancient feet, though perhaps he neither knows their measure nor denomination. Thus Spenser, Shakespeare, Milton, Dryden, Pope, and all our poets, abound with dactyls, spondees, trochees, anapests, &c. which they use indiscriminately in all kinds of composition, whether tragic, epic, pastoral, or ode, having in this particular greatly the advantage of the ancients, who were restricted to particular kinds of feet in particular kinds of verse. If we, then, are confined with the fetters of what is called rhyme, they were restricted to particular species of feet; so that the advantages and disadvantages are pretty equally balanced: but indeed the English are more free in this particular than any other modern nation. They not only use blank verse in tragedy and the epic, but even in lyric poetry. Milton's translation of Horace's ode to Pyrrha is universally known and generally admired, in our opinion much above its merit. There is an ode extant without rhyme addressed to Evening, by the late Mr. Collins, much more beautiful; and Mr. Warton, with some others, has happily succeeded in divers occasional pieces, that are free of this restraint: but the number in all of these depends upon the syllables, and not upon the feet, which are unlimited.

It is generally supposed that the genius of the English language will not admit of Greek or Latin measure; but this, we apprehend, is a mistake, owing to the prejudice of education. It is impossible that the same measure, composed of the same times, should have a good effect upon the ear in one language and a bad effect in another. The truth is, we have been accustomed from our infancy to the numbers of English poetry, and the very sound and signification of the words dispose the ear to receive them in a certain manner; so that its disappointment must be attended with a disagreeable sensation. In imbibing the first rudiments of education, we acquire, as it were, another ear for the numbers of Greek and Latin poetry; and this being reserved entirely for the sounds and significations of the words that constitute those dead languages, will not easily accommodate itself to the sounds of our vernacular tongue, though conveyed in the same time and measure. In a word, Latin and Greek have annexed to them the ideas of the ancient measure, from which they are not easily disjoined. But we will venture to say this difficulty might be surmounted by an effort of attention and a little practice; and in that case we should in time be as well pleased with English as with Latin hexameters.

Sir Philip Sydney is said to have miscarried in his essays; but his miscarriage was no more than that of failing in an attempt to introduce a new fashion. The failure was not owing to any defect or imperfection in the scheme, but to the want of taste, to the irresolution and ignorance of the public. Without all doubt the ancient measure, so different from that of modern poetry, must have appeared remarkably uncouth to people in general, who were ignorant of the classics; and nothing but the countenance and perseverance of the learned could reconcile them to the alteration. We have seen several late specimens of English hexameters and sapphics so happily composed that, by attaching them to the idea of ancient measure, we found them in all respects as melodious and agreeable to the ear as the works of Virgil and Anacreon, or Horace.

Though the number of syllables distinguishes the nature of the English verse from that of the Greek and Latin, it constitutes neither harmony, grace, nor expression. These must depend upon the choice of words, the seat of the accent, the pause, and the cadence. The accent or tone is understood to be an elevation or sinking of the voice in reciting: the pause is a rest that divides the verse into two parts, each of them called an hemistich. The pause and accent in English poetry vary occasionally, according to the meaning of the words; so that the hemistich does not always consist of an equal number of syllables; and this variety is agreeable, as it prevents a dull repetition of regular stops, like those in the French versification, every line of which is divided by a pause exactly in the middle. The cadence comprehends that poetical style which animates every line, that propriety which gives strength and expression, that numerosity which renders the verse smooth, flowing, and harmonious, that significancy which marks the passions, and in many cases makes the sound an echo of the sense. The Greek and Latin languages, in being copious and ductile, are susceptible of a vast variety of cadences which the living languages will not admit; and of these a reader of any ear will judge for himself.

ESSAY XIX.

Schools of Music.

A SCHOOL, in the polite arts, properly signifies that succession of artists which has learned the principles of the art from some eminent master, either by hearing his lessons or studying his works, and consequently who imitate his manner either through design or from habit. Musicians seem agreed in making only three principal schools in music; namely, the school of Pergolese in Italy, of Lully in France and of Handel in England; though some are for making Rameau the founder of a new school, different from those of the former, as he is the inventor of beauties peculiarly his own.

Without all doubt Pergolese's music deserves the first rank; though excelling neither in variety of movements, number of parts, nor unexpected flights, yet he is universally allowed to be the musical Raphael of Italy. This great master's principal art consisted in knowing how to excite our passions by sounds which seem frequently opposite to the passion they would express: by slow solemn sounds he is sometimes known to throw us into all the rage of battle; and even by faster movements he excites melancholy in every heart that sounds are capable of affecting. This is a talent which seems born with the artist. We are unable to tell why such sounds affect us: they seem no way imitative of the passion they would express, but operate upon us by an inexpressible sympathy; the original of which is as inscrutable as the secret springs of life itself. To this excellence he adds another, in which he is superior to every other artist of the profession,—the happy transition from one passion to another. No dramatic poet better knows to prepare his incidents than he; the audience are pleased in those intervals of passion with the delicate, the simple harmony, if I may so express it, in which the parts are all thrown into fugues, or often are barely unison. His melodies also, where no passion is expressed, give equal pleasure from this delicate simplicity; and I need only instance that song in the *Serva Padrona* which begins "Lo conosco a quegl' occelli," as one of the finest instances of excellence in the duo.

The Italian artists in general have followed his manner, yet seem fond of embellishing the delicate simplicity of the original. Their style in music seems somewhat to resemble that of Seneca in writing, where there are some beautiful starts of thought; but the whole is filled with studied elegance and unaffecting affectation.

Lully in France first attempted the improvement of their music, which in general resembled that of our old solemn chants in churches. It is worthy of remark, in general, that the music in every country is solemn in proportion as the inhabitants are merry; or, in other words, the merriest and sprightliest nations are remarked for having the slowest music; and those whose character it is to be melancholy are pleased with the most brisk and airy movements. Thus, in France, Poland, Ireland, and Switzerland, the national music is slow, melancholy, and solemn; in Italy, England, Spain, and Germany, it is faster, proportionably as the people are grave. Lully only changed a bad manner, which he found, for a bad one of his own. His drowsy pieces are played still to the most sprightly audience that can be conceived; and even though Rameau, who is at once a musician and a philosopher, has shown, both by precept and example, what improvements French music may still admit of, yet his countrymen seem little convinced by his reasonings; and the Pont-Neuf taste, as it is called, still prevails in their best performances.

The English school was first planned by Purcell: he attempted to unite the Italian manner that prevailed in his time with the ancient Celtic carol and the Scottish ballad, which probably had also its origin in Italy; for some of the best Scottish ballads,—"The Broom of Cowdenknows," for instance,—are still ascribed to David Rizzio. But be that as it will, his manner was something peculiar to the English; and he might have continued as head of the English school, had not his merits been entirely eclipsed by Handel. Handel, though originally a German, yet adopted the English manner: he had long laboured to please by Italian composition, but without success; and though his English oratorios are accounted inimitable, yet his Italian operas are fallen into oblivion. Pergolese excelled in passionate simplicity: Lully was remarkable for creating a new species of music, where all is elegant, but nothing passionate or sublime. Handel's true characteristic is sublimity; he has employed all the variety of sounds and parts in all his pieces: the performances of the rest may be pleasing, though executed by few performers; his require the full band. The attention is awakened, the soul is roused up at his pieces; but distinct passion is seldom expressed. In this particular he has seldom found success; he has been obliged, in order to express passion, to imitate words by sounds, which, though it gives the pleasure which imitation always produces, yet it fails of exciting those lasting affections which it is in the power of sounds to produce. In a word, no man ever understood harmony so well as he; but in melody he has been exceeded by several.

ESSAY XX.

Carolan, the Irish Bard.

THERE can be perhaps no greater entertainment than to compare the rude Celtic simplicity with modern refinement. Books, however, seem incapable of furnishing the parallel; and to be acquainted with the ancient manners of our own ancestors, we should endeavour to look for their remains in those countries which, being in some measure retired from an intercourse with other nations, are still untinctured with foreign refinement, language, or breeding.

The Irish will satisfy curiosity in this respect preferably to all other nations I have seen. They, in several parts of that country, still adhere to their ancient language, dress, furniture, and superstitions; several customs exist among them that still speak their original; and, in some respects, Cæsar's description of the ancient Britons is applicable to these.

Their bards, in particular, are still held in great veneration among them; those traditional heralds are invited to every funeral, in order to fill up the intervals of the howl with their songs and harps. In these they rehearse the actions of the ancestors of the deceased, bewail the bondage of their country under the English government, and generally conclude with advising the young men and maidens to make the best use of their time; for they will soon, for all their present bloom, be stretched under the table, like the dead body before them.

Of all the bards this country ever produced, the last and the greatest was CAROLAN THE BLIND. He was at once a poet, a musician, a composer, and sung his own verses to his harp. The original natives never mention his name without rapture; both his poetry and music they have by heart; and even some of the English themselves, who have been transplanted there, find his music extremely pleasing. A song beginning,

O'Rourke's noble fare will ne'er be forgot,

translated by Dean Swift, is of his composition; which, though perhaps by this means the best known of his pieces, is yet by no means the most deserving. His songs in general may be compared to those of Pindar, as they have frequently the same flights of imagination; and are composed (I do not say written, for he could not write) merely to flatter some man of fortune upon some excellence of the same kind. In these one man is praised for the excellence of his stable, as in Pindar, another for his hospitality, a third for the beauty of his wife and children, and a fourth for the antiquity of his family. Whenever any of the original natives of distinction were assembled at feasting or revelling, Carolan was generally there, where he was always ready with his harp to celebrate their praises. He seemed by nature formed for his profession; for as he was born blind, so also he was possessed of a most astonishing memory, and a facetious turn of thinking, which gave his entertainers infinite satisfaction. Being once at the house of an Irish nobleman, where there was a musician present who was eminent in the profession, Carolan immediately challenged him to a trial of skill. To carry the jest forward, his lordship persuaded the musician to accept the challenge, and he accordingly played over on his fiddle the fifth concerto of Vivaldi. Carolan, immediately taking his harp, played over the whole piece after him, without missing a note, though he had never heard it before, which produced some surprise; but their astonishment increased, when he assured them he could make a concerto in the same taste himself, which he instantly composed; and that with such spirit and elegance, that it may compare (for we have it still) with the finest compositions of Italy.

His death was not less remarkable than his life. Homer was never more fond of a glass than he; he would drink whole pints of usquebaugh, and, as he used to think, without any ill consequence. His intemperance, however, in this respect, at length brought on an incurable disorder; and when just at the point of death, he called for a cup of his beloved liquor. Those who were standing round him, surprised at the demand, endeavoured to persuade him to the contrary; but he persisted, and when the bowl was brought to him, attempted to drink, but could not; wherefore, giving away the bowl, he observed, with a smile, that it would be hard if two such friends as he and the cup should part at least without kissing, and then expired.

ESSAY XXI.

On the Tenants of the Leasowes.

Of all men who form gay illusions of distant happiness, perhaps a poet is the most sanguine. Such is the ardour of his hopes, that they often are equal to actual enjoyment; and he feels more in expectance than actual fruition. I have often regarded a character of this kind with some degree of envy. A man possessed of such warm imagination commands all nature, and arrogates possessions of which the owner has a blunter relish. While life continues, the alluring prospect lies before him; he travels in the pursuit with confidence, and resigns it only with his last breath.

It is this happy confidence which gives life its true relish, and keeps up our spirits amidst every distress and disappointment. How much less would be done, if a man knew how little he can do! How wretched a creature would he be if he saw the end as well as the beginning of his projects! He would have nothing left but to sit down in torpid despair, and exchange employment for actual calamity.

I was led into this train of thinking upon lately visiting the beautiful gardens of the late Mr. Shenstone, who was himself a poet, and possessed of that warm imagination which made him ever foremost in the pursuit of flying happiness. Could he but have foreseen the end of all his schemes, for whom he was improving, and what changes his designs were to undergo, he would have scarcely amused his innocent life with what, for several years, employed him in a most harmless manner, and abridged his scanty fortune. As the progress of this improvement is a true picture of sublunary vicissitude, I could not help calling up my imagination, which, while I walked pensively along, suggested the following Reverie.

As I was turning my back upon a beautiful piece of water, enlivened with cascades and rock-work, and entering a dark walk, by which ran a prattling brook, the Genius of the place appeared before me, but more resembling the God of Time, than him more peculiarly appointed to the care of gardens. Instead of shears he bore a scythe; and he appeared rather with the implements of husbandry than those of a modern gardener. Having remembered this place in its pristine beauty, I could not help condoling with him on its present ruinous situation. I spoke to him of the many alterations which had been made, and all for the worse; of the many shades which had been taken away, of the bowers that were destroyed by neglect, and the hedge-rows that were spoiled by clipping. The Genius, with a sigh, received my condolement, and assured me that he was equally a martyr to ignorance and taste, to refinement and rusticity. Seeing me desirous of knowing farther, he went on:

"You see, in the place before you, the paternal inheritance of a poet; and, to a man content with little, fully sufficient for his subsistence: but a strong imagination, and a long acquaintance with the rich, are dangerous foes to contentment. Our poet, instead of sitting down to enjoy life, resolved to prepare for its future enjoyment, and set about converting a place of profit into a scene of pleasure. This he at first supposed could be accomplished at a small expense; and he was willing for a while to stint his income, to have an opportunity of displaying his taste. The improvement in this manner went forward; one beauty attained led him to wish for some other; but he still hoped that every emendation would be the last. It was now therefore found, that the Improvement exceeded the subsidy—that the place was grown too large and too fine for the inhabitant. But that pride which was once exhibited could not retire; the garden was made for the owner, and though it was become unfit for him, he could not willingly resign it to another. Thus the first idea, of its beauties contributing to the happiness of his life, was found unfaithful; so that, instead of looking within for satisfaction, he began to think of having recourse to the praises of those who came to visit his Improvement.

"In consequence of this hope, which now took possession of his mind, the gardens were opened to the visits of every stranger; and the country flocked round to walk, to criticize, to admire, and to do mischief. He soon found that the admirers of his taste left by no means such strong marks of their applause, as the envious did of their malignity. All the windows of his temples and the walls of his retreats were impressed with the characters of profaneness, ignorance, and obscenity; his hedges were broken, his statues and urns defaced, and his lawns worn bare. It was now, therefore, necessary to shut up the gardens once more, and to deprive the public of that happiness which had before ceased to be his own.

"In this situation the poet continued for a time, in the character of a jealous lover, fond of the beauty he keeps, but unable to supply the extravagance of every demand. The garden by this time was completely grown and finished; the marks of art were covered up by the luxuriance of nature; the winding walks were grown dark; the brook assumed a natural sylvage; and the rocks were covered with moss. Nothing now remained but to enjoy the beauties of the place, when the poor poet died, and his garden was obliged to be sold for the benefit of those who had contributed to its embellishment.

"The beauties of the place had now for some time been celebrated as well in prose as in verse; and all men of taste wished for so envied a spot, where every turn was marked with the poet's pencil, and every walk awakened genius and meditation. The first purchaser was one Mr. Truepenny, a button maker, who was possessed of three thousand pounds, and was willing also to be possessed of taste and genius.

"As the poet's ideas were for the natural wildness of the landscape, the button maker's were for the more regular productions of art. He conceived, perhaps, that as it is a beauty in a button to be of a regular pattern, so the same regularity ought to obtain in a landscape. Be this as it will, he employed the shears to some purpose; he clipped up the hedges, cut down the gloomy walks, made vistas upon the stables and hog-sties, and showed his friends that a man of taste should always be doing.

"The next candidate for taste and genius was a captain of a ship, who bought the garden because the former possessor could find nothing more to mend: but unfortunately he had taste too. His great passion lay in building, in making Chinese temples and cage-work summer-houses. As the place before had an appearance of retirement and inspired meditation, he gave it a more peopled air; every turning presented a cottage, or ice-house, or a temple; the Improvement was converted into a little city, and it only wanted inhabitants to give it the air of a village in the East Indies.

"In this manner, in less than ten years, the Improvement has gone through the hands of as many proprietors, who were all willing to have taste, and to show their taste too. As the place had received its best finishing from the hand of the first possessor, so every innovator only lent a hand to do mischief. Those parts which were obscure, have been enlightened; those walks which led naturally, have been twisted into serpentine windings. The colour of the flowers of the field is not more various than the variety of tastes that have been employed here, and all in direct contradiction to the original aim of the first improver. Could the original possessor but revive, with what a sorrowful heart would he look upon his favourite spot again! He would scarcely recollect a Dryad or a Wood-nymph of his former acquaintance, and might perhaps find himself as much a stranger in his own plantation as in the deserts of Siberia."

ESSAY XXII.

Sentimental Comedy.

THE theatre, like all other amusements, has its fashions and its prejudices; and when satiated with its excellence, mankind begin to mistake change for improvement. For some years tragedy was the reigning entertainment; but of late it has entirely given way to comedy, and our best efforts are now exerted in these lighter kinds of composition. The pompous train, the swelling phrase, and the unnatural rant are displaced for that natural portrait of human folly and frailty, of which all are judges, because all have sat for the picture.

But as in describing nature it is presented with a double face, either of mirth or sadness, our modern writers find themselves at a loss which chiefly to copy from; and it is now debated, whether the exhibition of human distress is likely to afford the mind more entertainment than that of human absurdity?

Comedy is defined by Aristotle to be a picture of the frailties of the lower part of mankind, to distinguish it from tragedy, which is an exhibition of the misfortunes of the great. When comedy, therefore, ascends to produce the characters of princes or generals upon the stage, it is out of its walk, since low life and middle life are entirely its object. The principal question therefore is, whether, in describing low or middle life, an exhibition of its follies be not preferable to a detail of its calamities? Or, in other words, which deserves the preference,—the weeping sentimental comedy so much in fashion at present, or the laughing and even low comedy which seems to have been last exhibited by Vanbrugh and Cibber?

If we apply to authorities, all the great masters in the dramatic art have but one opinion. Their rule is, that as tragedy displays the calamities of the great, so comedy should excite our laughter by ridiculously exhibiting the follies of the lower part of mankind. Boileau, one of the best modern critics, asserts that comedy will not admit of tragic distress:

> Le comique, ennemi des soupirs et des pleurs,
> N'admet point dans ses vers de tragiques douleurs

Nor is this rule without the strongest foundation in nature, as the distresses of the mean by no means affect us so strongly as the calamities of the great. When tragedy exhibits to us some great man fallen from his height, and struggling with want and adversity, we feel his situation in the same manner as we suppose he himself must feel, and our pity is increased in proportion to the height from which he fell. On the contrary, we do not so strongly sympathise with one born in humbler circumstances, and encountering accidental distress; so that while we melt for Belisarius, we scarce give halfpence to the beggar who accosts us in the street. The one has our pity; the other our contempt. Distress, therefore, is the proper object of tragedy, since the great excite our pity by their fall; but not equally so of comedy, since the actors employed in it are originally so mean, that they sink but little by their fall.

Since the first origin of the stage, tragedy and comedy have run in distinct channels, and never till of late encroached upon the provinces of each other. Terence, who seems to have made the nearest approaches, always judiciously stops short before he comes to the downright pathetic; and yet he is even reproached by Cæsar for wanting the *vis comica*. All the other comic writers of antiquity aim only at rendering folly or vice ridiculous, but never exalt their characters into buskined pomp, or make what Voltaire humorously calls *a tradesman's tragedy*.

Yet notwithstanding this weight of authority, and the universal practice of former ages, a new species of dramatic composition has been introduced, under the name of sentimental comedy, in which the virtues of private life are exhibited, rather than the vices exposed; and the distresses rather than the faults of mankind make our interest in the piece. These comedies have had of late great success, perhaps from their novelty, and also from their flattering every man in his favourite foible. In these plays almost all the characters are good, and exceedingly generous; they are lavish enough of their tin money on the stage; and though they want humour, have abundance of sentiment and feeling. If they happen to have faults or foibles, the spectator is taught, not only to pardon, but to applaud them, in consideration of the goodness of their hearts; so that folly, instead of being ridiculed, is commended, and the comedy aims at touching our passions without the power of being truly pathetic. In this manner we are likely to lose one great source of entertainment on the stage; for while the comic poet is invading the province of the tragic muse, he leaves her lovely sister quite neglected. Of this, however, he is no way solicitous, as he measures his fame by his profits.

But it will be said that the theatre is formed to amuse mankind, and that it matters little, if this end be answered, by what means it is obtained. If mankind find delight in weeping at comedy, it would be cruel to abridge them in that or any other innocent pleasure. If those pieces are denied the name of comedies, yet call them by any other name, and if they are delightful, they are good. Their success, it will be said, is a mark of their merit, and it is only abridging our happiness to deny us an inlet to amusement.

These objections, however, are rather specious than solid. It is true that amusement is a great object of the theatre, and it will be allowed that these sentimental pieces do often amuse us; but the question is, whether the true comedy would not amuse us more? The question is, whether a character supported throughout a piece with its ridicule still attending, would not give us more delight than this species of bastard tragedy, which only is applauded because it is new?

A friend of mine, who was sitting unmoved at one of these sentimental pieces, was asked how he could be so indifferent? "Why, truly," says he, "as the hero is but a tradesman, it is indifferent to me whether he be turned out of his counting-house on Fish-street Hill, since he will still have enough left to open shop in St. Giles's."

The other objection is as ill-grounded; for though we should give these pieces another name, it will not mend their efficacy. It will continue a kind of mulish production, with all the defects of its opposite parents, and marked with sterility. If we are permitted to make comedy weep, we have an equal right to make tragedy laugh, and to set down in blank verse the jests and repartees of all the attendants in a funeral procession.

But there is one argument in favour of sentimental comedy, which will keep it on the stage, in spite of all that can be said against it. It is, of all others, the most easily written. Those abilities that can hammer out a novel are fully sufficient for the production of a sentimental comedy. It is only sufficient to raise the characters a little; to deck out the hero with a ribbon, or give the heroine a title; then to put an insipid dialogue, without character or humour, into their mouths, give them mighty good hearts, very fine clothes, furnish a new set of scenes, make a pathetic scene or two, with a sprinkling of tender melancholy conversation through the whole, and there is no doubt but all the ladies will cry, and all the gentlemen applaud.

Humour at present seems to be departing from the stage, and it will soon happen that our comic players will have nothing left for it but a fine coat and a song. It depends upon the audience whether they will actually drive those poor merry creatures from the stage, or sit at a play as gloomy as at the tabernacle. It is not easy to recover an art when once lost; and it will be but a just punishment, that when, by our being too fastidious, we have banished humour from the stage, we should ourselves be deprived of the art of laughing.

ESSAY XXIII.

Scottish Marriages.

As I see you are fond of gallantry, and seem willing to set young people together as soon as you can, I cannot help lending my assistance to your endeavours, as I am greatly concerned in the attempt. You must know, sir, that I am landlady of one of the most noted inns on the road to Scotland, and have seldom less than eight or ten couples a week, who go down rapturous lovers, and return man and wife.

If there be in this world an agreeable situation, it must be that in which a young couple find themselves, when just let loose from confinement, and whirling off to the land of promise. When the post-chaise is driving off, and the blinds are drawn up, sure nothing can equal it. And yet, I do not know how, what with the fears of being pursued, or the wishes for greater happiness, not one of my customers but seems gloomy and out of temper. The gentlemen are all sullen, and the ladies discontented.

But if it be so going down, how is it with them coming back? Having been for a fortnight together, they are then mighty good company to be sure. It is then the young lady's indiscretion stares her in the face, and the gentleman himself finds that much is to be done before the money comes in.

For my own part, sir, I was married in the usual way; all my friends were at the wedding; I was conducted with great ceremony from the table to the bed; and I do not find that it any ways diminished my happiness with my husband, while, poor man! he continued with me. For my part, I am entirely for doing things in the old family way; I hate your new-fashioned manners, and never loved an outlandish marriage in my life.

As I have had numbers call at my house, you may be sure I was not idle in inquiring who they were, and how they did in the world after they left me. I cannot say that I ever heard much good come of them: and of an history of twenty-five that I noted down in my ledger, I do not know a single couple that would not have been full as happy if they had gone the plain way to work, and asked the consent of their parents. To convince you of it, I will mention the names of a few, and refer the rest to some fitter opportunity.

Imprimis, Miss Jenny Hastings went down to Scotland with a tailor, who, to be sure, for a tailor, was a very agreeable sort of a man. But, I do not know how, he did not take proper measure of the young lady's disposition: they quarrelled at my house on their return; so she left him for a cornet of dragoons, and he went back to his shop-board.

Miss Rachel Runfort went off with a grenadier. They spent all their money going down; so that he carried her down in a post-chaise, and coming back, she helped to carry his knapsack.

Miss Racket went down with her lover in their own phaeton; but upon their return, being very fond of driving, she would be every now and then for holding the whip. This bred a dispute; and before they were a fortnight together, she felt that he could exercise the whip on somebody else besides the horses.

Miss Meekly, though all compliance to the will of her lover, could never reconcile him to the change of his situation. It seems he married her supposing she had a large fortune; but being deceived in their expectations, they parted; and they now keep separate garrets in Rosemary Lane.

The next couple of whom I have any account actually lived together in great harmony and uncloying kindness for no less than a month; but the lady, who was a little in years, having parted with her fortune to her dearest life, he left her to make love to that better part of her which he valued more.

The next pair consisted of an Irish fortune-hunter and one of the prettiest, modestest ladies that ever my eyes beheld. As he was a well-looking gentleman, all dressed in lace, and as she seemed very fond of him, I thought they were blest for life. Yet I was quickly mistaken. The lady was no better than a common woman of the town, and he was no better than a sharper; so they agreed upon a mutual divorce: he now dresses at the York Ball, and she is in keeping by the member for our borough in Parliament.

In this manner we see that all those marriages, in which there is interest on one side, and disobedience on the other, are not likely to promise a long harvest of delights. If our fortune-hunting gentlemen would but speak out, the young lady, instead of a lover, would often find a sneaking rogue, that only wanted the lady's purse, and not her heart. For my own part, I never saw anything but design and falsehood in every one of them; and my blood has boiled in my veins when I saw a young fellow of twenty kneeling at the feet of a twenty-thousand pounder, professing his passion, while he was taking aim at her money. I do not deny but there may be love in a Scottish marriage, but it is generally all on one side.

Of all the sincere admirers I ever knew, a man of my acquaintance, who however did not run away with his mistress to Scotland, was the most so. An old exciseman of our town, who, as you may guess, was not very rich, had a daughter who, as you shall see, was not very handsome. It was the opinion of everybody that this young woman would not soon be married, as she wanted two main articles, beauty and fortune. But, for all this, a very well-looking man, that happened to be travelling those parts, came and asked the exciseman for his daughter in marriage. The exciseman, willing to deal openly by him, asked if he had seen the girl; "for," says he, "she is humpbacked."—"Very well," cried the stranger, "that will do for me."—"Ay," says the exciseman, "but my daughter is as brown as a berry."—"So much the better," cried the stranger; "such skins wear well."—"But she is bandy-legged," says the exciseman.—"No matter," cries the other; "her petticoats will hide that defect."—"But then she is very poor, and wants an eye."—"Your description delights me," cries the stranger: "I have been looking out for one of her make; for I keep an exhibition of wild beasts, and intend to show her off for a chimpanzee."

END OF ESSAYS.

THE BEE:

A SELECT COLLECTION OF ESSAYS ON THE MOST INTERESTING AND ENTERTAINING SUBJECTS.

[1759.]

THE BEE.

No. I.—*Saturday, October* 6, 1759.

THERE is not, perhaps, a more whimsically dismal figure in nature than a man of real modesty, who assumes an air of impudence—who, while his heart beats with anxiety, studies ease, and affects good-humour. In this situation, however, a periodical writer often finds himself upon his first attempt to address the public in form. All his power of pleasing is damped by solicitude, and his cheerfulness dashed with apprehension. Impressed with the terrors of the tribunal before which he is going to appear, his natural humour turns to pertness, and for real wit he is obliged to substitute vivacity. His first publication draws a crowd; they part dissatisfied; and the author, never more to be indulged with a favourable hearing, is left to condemn the indelicacy of his own address or their want of discernment.

For my part, as I was never distinguished for address, and have often even blundered in making my bow, such bodings as these had like to have totally repressed my ambition. I was at a loss whether to give the public specious promises, or give none; whether to be merry or sad on this solemn occasion. If I should decline all merit, it was too probable the hasty reader might have taken me at my word. If, on the other hand, like labourers in the magazine trade, I had, with modest impudence, humbly presumed to promise an epitome of all the good things that ever were said or written, this might have disgusted those readers I most desire to please. Had I been merry, I might have been censured as vastly low; and had I been sorrowful, I might have been left to mourn in solitude and silence; in short, whichever way I turned, nothing presented but prospects of terror, despair, chandlers' shops, and waste paper.

In this debate between fear and ambition my publisher happening to arrive, interrupted for a while my anxiety. Perceiving my embarrassment about making my first appearance, he instantly offered his assistance and advice. "You must know, sir," says he, "that the republic of letters is at present divided into three classes. One writer, for instance, excels at a plan or a title-page, another works away the body of the book, and a third is a dab at an index. Thus a magazine is not the result of any single man's industry, but goes through as many hands as a new pin, before it is fit for the public. I fancy, sir," continues he, "I can provide an eminent hand, and upon moderate terms, to draw up a promising plan to smooth up our readers a little, and pay them as Colonel Charteris paid his seraglio, at the rate of three halfpence in hand, and three shillings more in promises."

He was proceeding in his advice, which however I thought proper to decline, by assuring him, that as I intended to pursue no fixed method, so it was impossible to form any regular plan; determined never to be tedious in order to be logical, wherever pleasure presented, I was resolved to follow. Like the Bee, which I had taken for the title of my paper, I would rove from flower to flower, with seeming inattention, but concealed choice, expatiate over all the beauties of the season, and make my industry my amusement.

This reply may also serve as an apology to the reader, who expects, before he sits down, a bill of his future entertainment. It would be improper to pall his curiosity by lessening his surprise, or anticipate any pleasure I am able to procure him by saying what shall come next. Thus much, however, he may be assured of, that neither war nor scandal shall make any part of it.

Homer finely imagines his deity turning away with horror from the prospect of a field of battle, and seeking tranquillity among a nation noted for peace and simplicity. Happy could any effort of mine, but for a moment, repress that savage pleasure some men find in the daily accounts of human misery! How gladly would I lead them from scenes of blood and altercation to prospects of innocence and ease, where every breeze breathes health, and every sound is but the echo of tranquillity.

But whatever the merit of his intentions may be, every writer is now convinced, that he must be chiefly indebted to good fortune for finding readers willing to allow him any degree of reputation. It has been remarked, that almost every character which has excited either attention or praise has owed part of its success to merit, and part to an happy concurrence of circumstances in its favour. Had Cæsar or Cromwell exchanged countries, the one might have been a sergeant, and the other an exciseman. So it is with wit, which generally succeeds more from being happily addressed, than from its native poignancy. A *bon mot*, for instance, that might be relished at White's may lose all its flavour when delivered at the Cat and Bagpipes in St. Giles's. A jest calculated to spread at a gaming table may be received with a perfect neutrality of face should it happen to drop in a mackerel boat. We have all seen dunces triumph in such companies, when men of real humour were disregarded, by a general combination in favour of stupidity. To drive the observation as far as it will go, should the labours of a writer who designs his performances for readers of a more refined appetite fall into the hands of a devourer of compilations, what can he expect but contempt and confusion? If his merits are to be determined by judges who estimate the value of a book from its bulk or its frontispiece, every rival must acquire an easy superiority who, with persuasive eloquence, promises four extraordinary pages of letter-press or three beautiful prints, curiously coloured from nature.

But to proceed: though I cannot promise as much entertainment, or as much elegance, as others have done, yet the reader may be assured, he shall have as much of both as I can. He shall, at least, find me alive while I study his entertainment; for I solemnly assure him, I was never yet possessed of the secret at once of writing and sleeping.

During the course of this paper, therefore, all the wit and learning I have are heartily at his service; which if, after so candid a confession, he should, notwithstanding, still find intolerably dull, low, or sad stuff, this, I protest, is more than I know. I have a clear conscience, and am entirely out of the secret.

Yet I would not have him, upon the perusal of a single paper, pronounce me incorrigible; he may try a second, which, as there is a studied difference in subject and style, may be more suited to his taste: if this also fails, I must refer him to a third, or even to a fourth, in case of extremity. If he should still continue to be refractory, and find me dull to the last, I must inform him, with Bayes, in the Rehearsal, that I think him a very odd kind of a fellow, and desire no more of his acquaintance.

It is with such reflections as these I endeavour to fortify myself against the future contempt or neglect of some readers, and am prepared for their dislike by mutual recrimination. If such should impute dealing neither in battles nor scandal to me as a fault, instead of acquiescing in their censure, I must beg leave to tell them a story.

"A traveller, in his way to Italy, happening to pass at the foot of the Alps, found himself at last in a country where the inhabitants had each a large excrescence depending from the chin, like the pouch of a monkey. This deformity, as it was endemic, and the people little used to strangers, it had been the custom, time immemorial, to look upon as the greatest ornament of the human visage. Ladies grew toasts from the size of their chins, and none were regarded as pretty fellows but such whose faces were broadest at the bottom. — It was Sunday; a country church was at hand, and our traveller was willing to perform the duties of the day. Upon his first appearance at the church door the eyes of all were naturally fixed upon the stranger; but what was their amazement, when they found that he actually wanted that emblem of beauty, a pursed chin! This was a defect that not a single creature had sufficient gravity (though they were noted for being grave) to withstand. Stifled bursts of laughter, winks, and whispers circulated from visage to visage, and the prismatic figure of the stranger's face was a fund of infinite gaiety; even the parson, equally remarkable for his gravity and chin, could hardly refrain joining in the good humour. Our traveller could no longer patiently continue an object for deformity to point at. 'Good folks,' said he, 'I perceive that I am the unfortunate cause of all this good humour. It is true I may have faults in abundance; but I shall never be induced to reckon my want of a swelled face among the number.'"

ON A BEAUTIFUL YOUTH STRUCK BLIND WITH LIGHTNING.

IMITATED FROM THE SPANISH.

LUMINE Acon dextro capta est Leonida sinistro,
Et poterat forma vincere uterque Deos.
Parve puer, lumen quod habes concede puellæ;
Sic tu cæcus amor, sic erit illa Venus.

REMARKS ON OUR THEATRES.

OUR theatres are now opened, and all Grub Street is preparing its advice to the managers. We shall undoubtedly hear learned disquisitions on the structure of one actor's legs and another's eyebrows. We shall be told much of enunciations, tones, and attitudes; and shall have our lightest pleasures commented upon by didactic dulness. We shall, it is feared, be told that Garrick is a fine actor, but then, as a manager, so avaricious! That Palmer is a most surprising genius, and Holland likely to do well in a particular caste of character. We shall have them giving Shuter instructions to amuse us by rule, and deploring over the ruins of desolated majesty at Covent Garden. As I love to be advising too—for advice is easily given, and bears a show of wisdom and superiority—I must be permitted to offer a few observations upon our theatres and actors, without, on this trivial occasion, throwing my thoughts into the formality of method.

There is something in the deportment of all our players infinitely more stiff and formal than among the actors of other nations. Their action sits uneasy upon them; for as the English use very little gesture in ordinary conversation, our English bred actors are obliged to supply stage gestures by their imagination alone. A French comedian finds proper models of action in every company and in every coffee-house he enters. An Englishman is obliged to take his models from the stage itself; he is obliged to imitate nature from an imitation of nature. I know of no set of men more likely to be improved by travelling than those of the theatrical profession. The inhabitants of the Continent are less reserved than here; they may be seen through upon a first acquaintance: such are the proper models to draw from; they are at once striking, and are found in great abundance.

Though it would be inexcusable in a comedian to add anything of his own to the poet's dialogue, yet, as to action, he is entirely at liberty. By this he may show the fertility of his genius, the poignancy of his humour, and the exactness of his judgment. We scarcely see a coxcomb or a fool in common life that has not some peculiar oddity in his action. These peculiarities it is not in the power of words to represent, and depend solely upon the actor. They give a relish to the humour of the poet, and make the appearance of nature more illusive. The Italians, it is true, mask some characters, and endeavour to preserve the peculiar humour by the make of the mask; but I have seen others still preserve a great fund of humour in the face without a mask; one actor, particularly, by a squint which he threw into some characters of low life, assumed a look of infinite solidity. This, though upon reflection we might condemn, yet immediately upon representation we could not avoid being pleased with. To illustrate what I have been saying by the plays which I have of late gone to see: in the Miser, which was played a few nights ago at Covent Garden, Lovegold appears through the whole in circumstances of exaggerated avarice; all the player's action, therefore, should conspire with the poet's design, and represent him as an epitome of penury. The French comedian in this character, in the midst of one of his most violent passions, while he appears in an ungovernable rage, feels the demon of avarice still upon him, and stoops down to pick up a pin, which he quilts into the flap of his coat pocket with great assiduity. Two candles are lighted up for his wedding; he flies and turns one of them into the socket: it is, however, lighted up again; he then steals to it, and privately crams it into his pocket. The Mock Doctor was lately played at the other house. Here again the comedian had an opportunity of heightening the ridicule by action. The French player sits in a chair with a high back, and then begins to show away by talking nonsense, which he would have thought Latin by those he knows do not understand a syllable of the matter. At last he grows enthusiastic, enjoys the admiration of the company, tosses his legs and arms about, and, in the midst of his raptures and vociferation, he and the chair fall back together. All this appears dull enough in the recital, but the gravity of Cato could not stand it in the representation. In short, there is hardly a character in comedy to which a player of any real humour might not add strokes of vivacity that could not fail of applause. But, instead of this, we too often see our fine gentlemen do nothing, through a whole part, but strut and open their snuff-box; our pretty fellows sit indecently with their legs across; and our clowns pull up their breeches. These, if once, or even twice, repeated, might do well enough; but to see them served up in every scene argues the actor almost as barren as the character he would expose.

The magnificence of our theatres is far superior to any others in Europe, where plays only are acted. The great care our performers take in painting for a part, their exactness in all the minutiæ of dress, and other little scenical proprieties, have been taken notice of by Ricoboni, a gentleman of Italy, who travelled Europe with no other design but to remark upon the stage; but there are several improprieties still continued, or lately come into fashion. As, for instance, spreading a carpet punctually at the beginning of the death scene, in order to prevent our actors from spoiling their clothes: this immediately apprises us of the tragedy to follow; for laying the cloth is not a more sure indication of dinner, than laying the carpet of bloody work at Drury Lane. Our little pages, also, with unmeaning faces, that bear up the train of a weeping princess, and our awkward lords in waiting, take off much from her distress. Mutes of every kind divide our attention, and lessen our sensibility; but here it is entirely ridiculous, as we see them seriously employed in doing nothing. If we must have dirty-shirted guards upon the theatres, they should be taught to keep their eyes fixed on the actors, and not roll them round upon the audience, as if they were ogling the boxes.

Beauty, methinks, seems a requisite qualification in an actress. This seems scrupulously observed elsewhere, and, for my part, I could wish to see it observed at home. I can never conceive an hero dying for love of a lady totally destitute of beauty. I must think the part unnatural; for I cannot bear to hear him call that face angelic, where even paint cannot hide its wrinkles. I must condemn him of stupidity; and the person whom I can accuse for want of taste will seldom become the object of my affections or admiration. But if this be a defect, what must be the entire perversion of scenical decorum, when, for instance, we see an actress that might act the Wapping landlady without a bolster, pining in the character of Jane Shore, and, while unwieldy with fat, endeavouring to convince the audience that she is dying with hunger!

For the future, then, I could wish that the parts of the young or beautiful were given to performers of suitable figures; for I must own I could rather see the stage filled with agreeable objects, though they might sometimes bungle a little, than see it crowded with withered or misshapen figures, be their emphasis, as I think it is called, ever so proper. The first may have the awkward appearance of new raised troops; but in viewing the last I cannot avoid the mortification of fancying myself placed in an hospital of invalids.

THE STORY OF ALCANDER AND SEPTIMIUS,

Translated from a Byzantine Historian.

ATHENS, even long after the decline of the Roman empire, still continued the seat of learning, politeness, and wisdom. The emperors and generals, who in these periods of approaching ignorance still felt a passion for science, from time to time added to its buildings, or increased its professorships. Theodoric, the Ostrogoth, was of the number: he repaired those schools which barbarity was suffering to fall into decay, and continued those pensions to men of learning which avaricious governors had monopolized to themselves.

In this city, and about this period, Alcander and Septimius were fellow-students together: the one the most subtle reasoner of all the Lyceum, the other the most eloquent speaker in the Academic grove. Mutual admiration soon begot an acquaintance, and a similitude of disposition made them perfect friends. Their fortunes were nearly equal, their studies the same, and they were natives of the two most celebrated cities in the world; for Alcander was of Athens, Septimius came from Rome.

In this mutual harmony they lived for some time together, when Alcander, after passing the first part of his youth in the indolence of philosophy, thought at length of entering into the busy world, and, as a step previous to this, placed his affections on Hypatia, a lady of exquisite beauty. Hypatia showed no dislike to his addresses. The day of their intended nuptials was fixed, the previous ceremonies were performed, and nothing now remained but her being conducted in triumph to the apartment of the intended bridegroom.

An exultation in his own happiness, or his being unable to enjoy any satisfaction without making his friend Septimius a partner, prevailed upon him to introduce his mistress to his fellow-student, which he did with all the gaiety of a man who found himself equally happy in friendship and love. But this was an interview fatal to the peace of both; for Septimius no sooner saw her, but he was smit with an involuntary passion. He used every effort, but in vain, to suppress desires at once so imprudent and unjust. He retired to his apartment in inexpressible agony; and the emotions of his mind in a short time became so strong, that they brought on a fever, which the physicians judged incurable.

During this illness Alcander watched him with all the anxiety of fondness, and brought his mistress to join in those amiable offices of friendship. The sagacity of the physicians, by this means, soon discovered the cause of their patient's disorder; and Alcander, being apprised of their discovery, at length extorted a confession from the reluctant dying lover.

It would but delay the narrative to describe the conflict between love and friendship in the breast of Alcander on this occasion; it is enough to say, that the Athenians were at this time arrived at such refinement in morals, that every virtue was carried to excess. In short, forgetful of his own felicity, he gave up his intended bride, in all her charms, to the young Roman. They were married privately by his connivance; and this unlooked-for change of fortune wrought as unexpected a change in the constitution of the now happy Septimius. In a few days he was perfectly recovered, and set out with his fair partner for Rome. Here, by an exertion of those talents of which he was so eminently possessed, he in a few years arrived at the highest dignities of the state, and was constituted the city judge, or prætor.

Meanwhile Alcander not only felt the pain of being separated from his friend and mistress, but a prosecution was also commenced against him by the relations of Hypatia, for his having basely given her up, as was suggested, for money. Neither his innocence of the crime laid to his charge, nor his eloquence in his own defence, was able to withstand the influence of a powerful party. He was cast, and condemned to pay an enormous fine. Unable to raise so large a sum at the time appointed, his possessions were confiscated, himself stripped of the habit of freedom, exposed in the market-place, and sold as a slave to the highest bidder.

A merchant of Thrace becoming his purchaser, Alcander, with some other companions of distress, was carried into that region of desolation and sterility. His stated employment was to follow the herds of an imperious master; and his skill in hunting was all that was allowed him to supply a precarious subsistence. Condemned to hopeless servitude, every morning waked him to a renewal of famine or toil, and every change of season served but to aggravate his unsheltered distress. Nothing but death or flight was left him, and almost certain death was the consequence of his attempting to fly. After some years of bondage, however, an opportunity of escaping offered; he embraced it with ardour, and travelling by night, and lodging in caverns by day, to shorten a long story, he at last arrived in Rome. The day of Alcander's arrival Septimius sat in the forum administering justice; and hither our wanderer came, expecting to be instantly known and publicly acknowledged. Here he stood the whole day among the crowd, watching the eyes of the judge, and expecting to be taken notice of; but so much was he altered by a long succession of hardships, that he passed entirely without notice; and in the evening, when he was going up to the prætor's chair, he was brutally repulsed by the attending lictors. The attention of the poor is generally driven from one ungrateful object to another; night coming on, he now found himself under a necessity of seeking a place to lie in, and yet knew not where to apply. All emaciated and in rags as he was, none of the citizens would harbour so much wretchedness, and sleeping in the streets might be attended with interruption or danger: in short, he was obliged to take up his lodging in one of the tombs without the city, the usual retreat of guilt, poverty, or despair.

In this mansion of horror, laying his head upon an inverted urn, he forgot his miseries for a while in sleep; and virtue found on this flinty couch more ease than down can supply to the guilty.

It was midnight when two robbers came to make this cave their retreat; but happening to disagree about the division of their plunder, one of them stabbed the other to the heart, and left him weltering in blood at the entrance. In these circumstances he was found next morning, and this naturally induced a farther inquiry. The alarm was spread, the cave was examined, Alcander was found sleeping, and immediately apprehended and accused of robbery and murder. The circumstances against him were strong, and the wretchedness of his appearance confirmed suspicion. Misfortune and he were now so long acquainted, that he at last became regardless of life. He detested a world where he had found only ingratitude, falsehood, and cruelty, and was determined to make no defence. Thus, lowering with resolution, he was dragged, bound with cords, before the tribunal of Septimius. The proofs were positive against him, and he offered nothing in his own vindication; the judge, therefore, was proceeding to doom him to a most cruel and ignominious death, when, as if illumined by a ray from Heaven, he discovered, through all his misery, the features, though dim with sorrow, of his long lost, loved Alcander. It is impossible to describe his joy and his pain on this strange occasion; happy in once more seeing the person he most loved on earth, distressed at finding him in such circumstances. Thus agitated by contending passions, he flew from his tribunal, and, falling on the neck of his dear benefactor, burst into an agony of distress. The attention of the multitude was soon, however, divided by another object. The robber who had been really guilty was apprehended selling his plunder, and, struck with a panic, confessed his crime. He was brought bound to the same tribunal, and acquitted every other person of any partnership in his guilt. Need the sequel be related? Alcander was acquitted, shared the friendship and the honours of his friend Septimius, lived afterwards in happiness and ease, and left it to be engraved on his tomb, that "no circumstances are so desperate which Providence may not relieve."

A LETTER FROM A TRAVELLER.

CRACOW, *August 2, 1758.*

MY DEAR WILL,—You see, by the date of my letter, that I am arrived in Poland. When will my wanderings be at an end? When will my restless disposition give me leave to enjoy the present hour? When at Lyons, I thought all happiness lay beyond the Alps; when in Italy, I found myself still in want of something, and expected to leave solicitude behind me by going into Romelia; and now you find me turning back, still expecting ease everywhere but where I am. It is now seven years since I saw the face of a single creature who cared a farthing whether I was dead or alive. Secluded from all the comforts of confidence, friendship, or society, I feel the solitude of a hermit, but not his ease.

The Prince of —— has taken me in his train, so that I am in no danger of starving for this bout. The prince's governor is a rude ignorant pedant, and his tutor a battered rake; thus, between two such characters, you may imagine he is finely instructed. I made some attempts to display all the little knowledge I had acquired by reading or observation; but I find myself regarded as an ignorant intruder. The truth is, I shall never be able to acquire a power of expressing myself with ease in any language but my own; and, out of my own country, the highest character I can ever acquire is that of being a philosophic vagabond.

When I consider myself in the country which was once so formidable in war, and spread terror and desolation over the whole Roman empire, I can hardly account for the present wretchedness and pusillanimity of its inhabitants: a prey to every invader; their cities plundered without an enemy; their magistrates seeking redress by complaints, and not by vigour. Everything conspires to raise my compassion for their miseries, were not my thoughts too busily engaged by my own. The whole kingdom is in a strange disorder: when our equipage, which consists of the prince and thirteen attendants, had arrived at some towns, there were no conveniences to be found, and we were obliged to have girls to conduct us to the next. I have seen a woman travel thus on horseback before us for thirty miles, and think herself highly paid, and make twenty reverences, upon receiving, with ecstasy, about twopence for her trouble. In general, we were better served by the women than the men on these occasions. The men seemed directed by a low sordid interest alone: they seemed mere machines, and all their thoughts were employed in the care of their horses. If we gently desired them to make more speed, they took not the least notice: kind language was what they had by no means been used to. It was proper to speak to them in the tones of anger, and sometimes it was even necessary to use blows, to excite them to their duty. How different these from the common people of England, whom a blow might induce to return the affront sevenfold! These poor people, however, from being brought up to vile usage, lose all the respect which they should have for themselves. They have contracted a habit of regarding constraint as the great rule of their duty. When they were treated with mildness, they no longer continued to perceive a superiority. They fancied themselves our equals, and a continuance of our humanity might probably have rendered them insolent: but the imperious tone, menaces, and blows, at once changed their sensations and their ideas; their ears and shoulders taught their souls to shrink back into servitude, from which they had for some moments fancied themselves disengaged.

The enthusiasm of liberty an Englishman feels is never so strong as when presented by such prospects as these. I must own, in all my indigence, it is one of my comforts, (perhaps, indeed, it is my only boast,) that I am of that happy country; though I scorn to starve there; though I do not choose to lead a life of wretched dependence, or be an object for my former acquaintance to point at. While you enjoy all the ease and elegance of prudence and virtue, your old friend wanders over the world, without a single anchor to hold by, or a friend, except you, to confide in.

Yours, &c.

A SHORT ACCOUNT OF THE LATE MR. MAUPERTUIS.

MR. MAUPERTUIS, lately deceased, was the first to whom the English philosophers owed their being particularly admired by the rest of Europe. The romantic system of Des Cartes was adapted to the taste of the superficial and the indolent; the foreign universities had embraced it with ardour, and such are seldom convinced of their errors till all others give up such false opinions as untenable. The philosophy of Newton and the metaphysics of Locke appeared; but, like all new truths, they were at once received with opposition and contempt. The English, it is true, studied, understood, and, consequently, admired them: it was very different on the Continent. Fontenelle, who seemed to preside over the republic of letters, unwilling to acknowledge that all his life had been spent in erroneous philosophy, joined in the universal disapprobation, and the English philosophers seemed entirely unknown.

Maupertuis, however, made them his study: he thought he might oppose the physics of his country, and yet still be a good citizen; he defended our countrymen, wrote in their favour, and, at last, as he had truth on his side, carried his cause. Almost all the learning of the English, till very lately, was conveyed in the language of France. The writings of Maupertuis spread the reputation of his master, Newton, and by a happy fortune have united his fame with that of our human prodigy.

The first of his performances, openly in vindication of the Newtonian system, is his treatise entitled "Sur la Figure des Astres," if I remember right; a work at once expressive of a deep geometrical knowledge and the most happy manner of delivering abstruse science with ease. This met with violent opposition from a people, though fond of novelty in everything else, yet, however, in matters of science, attached to ancient opinions with bigotry. As the old and obstinate fell away, the youth of France embraced the new opinions, and now seem more eager to defend Newton than even his countrymen.

The oddity of character which great men are sometimes remarkable for, Maupertuis was not entirely free from. If we can believe Voltaire, he once attempted to castrate himself; but whether this be true or no, it is certain he was extremely whimsical. Though born to a large fortune, when employed in mathematical inquiries he disregarded his person to such a degree, and loved retirement so much, that he has been more than once put on the list of modest beggars by the curates of Paris, when he retired to some private quarter of the town, in order to enjoy his meditations without interruption. The character given of him by one of Voltaire's antagonists, if it can be depended upon, is much to his honour. "You," says this writer to Mr. Voltaire, "were entertained by the King of Prussia as a buffoon, but Maupertuis as a philosopher." It is certain that the preference which this royal scholar gave to Maupertuis was the cause of Voltaire's disagreement with him. Voltaire could not bear to see a man whose talents he had no great opinion of preferred before him as president of the Royal Academy. His "Micromegas" was designed to ridicule Maupertuis; and, probably, it has brought more disgrace on the author than the subject. Whatever absurdities men of letters have indulged, and how fantastical soever the modes of science have been, their anger is still more subject to ridicule.

No. II.—*Saturday, October* 13, 1759.

ON DRESS.

FOREIGNERS observe that there are no ladies in the world more beautiful, or more ill dressed, than those of England. Our countrywomen have been compared to those pictures where the face is the work of a Raphael, but the draperies thrown out by some empty pretender, destitute of taste, and entirely unacquainted with design.

If I were a poet, I might observe on this occasion, that so much beauty set off with all the advantages of dress would be too powerful an antagonist for the opposite sex; and, therefore, it was wisely ordered that our ladies should want taste, lest their admirers should entirely want reason.

But, to confess a truth, I do not find they have a greater aversion to fine clothes than the women of any other country whatsoever. I cannot fancy that a shopkeeper's wife in Cheapside has a greater tenderness for the fortune of her husband than a citizen's wife in Paris, or that Miss in a boarding-school is more an economist in dress than Mademoiselle in a nunnery.

Although Paris may be accounted the soil in which almost every fashion takes its rise, its influence is never so general there as with us. They study there the happy method of uniting grace and fashion, and never excuse a woman for being awkwardly dressed by saying her clothes are made in the mode. A French woman is a perfect architect in dress: she never, with Gothic ignorance, mixes the order; she never tricks out a squabby Doric shape with Corinthian finery; or, to speak without metaphor, she conforms to general fashion only when it happens not to be repugnant to private beauty.

Our ladies, on the contrary, seem to have no other standard for grace but the run of the town. If fashion gives the word, every distinction of beauty, complexion, or stature ceases. Sweeping trains, Prussian bonnets, and trollopees, as like each other as if cut from the same piece, level all to one standard. The Mall, the gardens, and the playhouses are filled with ladies in uniform, and their whole appearance shows as little variety or taste as if their clothes were bespoke by the colonel of a marching regiment, or fancied by the same artist who dresses the three battalions of Guards.

But not only ladies of every shape and complexion, but of every age too, are possessed of this unaccountable passion of dressing in the same manner. A lady of no quality can be distinguished from a lady of some quality only by the redness of her hands; and a woman of sixty, masked, might easily pass for her granddaughter. I remember, a few days ago, to have walked behind a damsel, tossed out in all the gaiety of fifteen; her dress was loose, unstudied, and seemed the result of conscious beauty. I called up all my poetry on this occasion, and fancied twenty Cupids prepared for execution in every folding of her white negligee. I had prepared my imagination for an angel's face; but what was my mortification to find that the imaginary goddess was no other than my cousin Hannah, four years older than myself, and I shall be sixty-two the twelfth of next November.

After the transports of our first salute were over, I could not avoid running my eye over her whole appearance. Her gown was of cambric, cut short before, in order to discover a high-heeled shoe, which was buckled almost at the toe. Her cap, if cap it might be called that cap was none, consisted of a few bits of cambric, and flowers of painted paper stuck on one side of her head. Her bosom, that had felt no hand but the hand of time these twenty years, rose suing, but in vain, to be pressed. I could, indeed, have wished her more than a handkerchief of Paris net to shade her beauties; for, as Tasso says of the rosebud, "Quanto si mostra men tanto e piu bella," I should think hers most pleasing when least discovered.

As my cousin had not put on all this finery for nothing, she was at that time sallying out to the Park, when I had overtaken her. Perceiving, however, that I had on my best wig, she offered, if I would squire her there, to send home the footman. Though I trembled for our reception in public, yet I could not with any civility refuse; so, to be as gallant as possible, I took her hand in my arm, and thus we marched on together.

When we made our entry at the Park, two antiquated figures, so polite and so tender as we seemed to be, soon attracted the eyes of the company. As we made our way among crowds who were out to show their finery as well as we, wherever we came I perceived we brought good humour in our train. The polite could not forbear smiling, and the vulgar burst out into a horse-laugh at our grotesque figures. Cousin Hannah, who was perfectly conscious of the rectitude of her own appearance, attributed all this mirth to the oddity of mine, while I as cordially placed the whole to her account. Thus, from being two of the best-natured creatures alive, before we got half-way up the Mall, we both began to grow peevish, and, like two mice on a string, endeavoured to revenge the impertinence of others upon ourselves. "I am amazed, cousin Jeffrey," says Miss, "that I can never get you to dress like a Christian. I knew we should have the eyes of the Park upon us, with your great wig so frizzed, and yet so beggarly, and your monstrous muff. I hate those odious muffs." I could have patiently borne a criticism on all the rest of my equipage; but as I had always a peculiar veneration for my muff, I could not forbear being piqued a little; and, throwing my eyes with a spiteful air on her bosom, "I could heartily wish, madam," replied I, "that for your sake my muff was cut into a tippet."

As my cousin, by this time, was grown heartily ashamed of her gentleman usher, and as I was never very fond of any kind of exhibition myself, it was mutually agreed to retire for a while to one of the seats, and from that retreat remark on others as freely as they had remarked on us.

When seated, we continued silent for some time, employed in very different speculations. I regarded the whole company, now passing in review before me, as drawn out merely for my amusement. For my entertainment the beauty had all that morning been improving her charms; the beau had put on lace, and the young doctor a big-wig, merely to please me. But quite different were the sentiments of cousin Hannah; she regarded every well-dressed woman as a victorious rival, hated every face that seemed dressed in good humour, or wore the appearance of greater happiness than her own. I perceived her uneasiness, and attempted to lessen it by observing that there was no company in the Park to-day. To this she readily assented; "and yet," says she, "it is full enough of scrubs of one kind or another." My smiling at this observation gave her spirits to pursue the bent of her inclination, and now she began to exhibit her skill in secret history, as she found me disposed to listen. "Observe," says she to me, "that old woman in tawdry silk, and dressed out even beyond the fashion. That is Miss Biddy Evergreen. Miss Biddy, it seems, has money; and as she considers that money was never so scarce as it is now, she seems resolved to keep what she has to herself. She is ugly enough you see; yet I assure you she has refused several offers, to my own knowledge, within this twelvemonth. Let me see, three gentlemen from Ireland who study the law, two waiting captains, a doctor, and a Scotch preacher, who had like to have carried her off. All her time is passed between sickness and finery. Thus she spends the whole week in a close chamber, with no other company but her monkey, her apothecary, and cat; and comes dressed out to the Park every Sunday, to show her airs, to get new lovers, to catch a new cold, and to make new work for the doctor.

"There goes Mrs. Roundabout—I mean the fat lady in the lutestring trollopee. Between you and I, she is but a cutler's wife. See how she's dressed, as fine as hands and pins can make her, while her two marriageable daughters, like bunters in stuff gowns, are now taking sixpenny worth of tea at the White Conduit House. Odious puss! how she waddles along, with her train two yards behind her! She puts me in mind of my Lord Bantam's Indian sheep, which are obliged to have their monstrous tails trundled along in a go-cart. For all her airs, it goes to her husband's heart to see four yards of good lutestring wearing against the ground, like one of his knives on a grindstone. To speak my mind, cousin Jeffrey, I never liked tails; for suppose a young fellow should be rude, and the lady should offer to step back in a fright, instead of retiring, she treads upon her train, and falls fairly on her back; and then, you know, cousin—her clothes may be spoiled.

"Ah, Miss Mazzard! I knew we should not miss her in the Park; she in the monstrous Prussian bonnet. Miss, though so very fine, was bred a milliner, and might have had some custom if she had minded her business; but the girl was fond of finery, and instead of dressing her customers, laid out all her goods in adorning herself. Every new gown she put on impaired her credit: she still, however, went on improving her appearance, and lessening her little fortune, and is now, you see, become a belle and a bankrupt."

My cousin was proceeding in her remarks, which were interrupted by the approach of the very lady she had been so freely describing. Miss had perceived her at a distance, and approached to salute her. I found, by the warmth of the two ladies' protestations, that they had been long intimate esteemed friends and acquaintance. Both were so pleased at this happy rencounter, that they were resolved not to part for the day. So we all crossed the Park together, and I saw them into a hackney coach at the gate of St. James's. I could not, however, help observing, That they are generally most ridiculous themselves, who are apt to see most ridicule in others.

SOME PARTICULARS RELATIVE TO CHARLES XII.

NOT COMMONLY KNOWN.

STOCKHOLM.

SIR,—I cannot resist your solicitations, though it is possible I shall be unable to satisfy your curiosity. The polite of every country seem to have but one character. A gentleman of Sweden differs but little, except in trifles, from one of any other country. It is among the vulgar we are to find those distinctions which characterise a people, and from them it is that I take my picture of the Swedes.

Though the Swedes, in general, appear to languish under oppression, which often renders others wicked or of malignant dispositions, it has not, however, the same influence upon them, as they are faithful, civil, and incapable of atrocious crimes. Would you believe that, in Sweden, highway robberies are not so much as heard of? For my part, I have not in the whole country seen a gibbet or a gallows. They pay an infinite respect to their ecclesiastics, whom they suppose to be the privy councillors of Providence, who, on their part, turn this credulity to their own advantage, and manage their parishioners as they please. In general, however, they seldom abuse their sovereign authority. Hearkened to as oracles, regarded as the dispensers of eternal rewards and punishments, they readily influence their hearers into justice, and make them practical philosophers without the pains of study.

As to their persons, they are perfectly well made, and the men particularly have a very engaging air. The greatest part of the boys whom I saw in the country had very white hair. They were as beautiful as Cupids, and there was something open and entirely happy in their little chubby faces. The girls, on the contrary, have neither such fair nor such even complexions, and their features are much less delicate, which is a circumstance different from that of almost every other country. Besides this, it is observed that the women are generally afflicted with the itch, for which Scania is particularly remarkable. I had an instance of this in one of the inns on the road. The hostess was one of the most beautiful women I have ever seen: she had so fine a complexion, that I could not avoid admiring it. But what was my surprise, when she opened her bosom in order to suckle her child, to perceive that seat of delight all covered with this disagreeable distemper. The careless manner in which she exposed to our eyes so disgusting an object sufficiently testifies that they regard it as no very extraordinary malady, and seem to take no pains to conceal it. Such are the remarks, which probably you may think trifling enough, I have made in my journey to Stockholm, which, to take it all together, is a large, beautiful, and even a populous city.

The arsenal appears to me one of its greatest curiosities: it is a handsome, spacious building, but, however, scantily supplied with the implements of war. To recompense this defect, they have almost filled it with trophies and other marks of their former military glory. I saw there several chambers filled with Danish, Saxon, Polish, and Russian standards. There was at least enough to suffice half a dozen armies; but new standards are more easily made than new armies can be enlisted. I saw, besides, some very rich furniture, and some of the crown jewels, of great value; but what principally engaged my attention, and touched me with passing melancholy, were the bloody, yet precious, spoils of the two greatest heroes the North ever produced. What I mean are the clothes in which the great Gustavus Adolphus and the intrepid Charles XII. died by a fate not unusual to kings. The first, if I remember, is a sort of a buff waistcoat, made antique fashion, very plain, and without the least ornaments; the second, which was even more remarkable, consisted only of a coarse blue cloth coat, a large hat of less value, a shirt of coarse linen, large boots, and buff gloves made to cover a great part of the arm. His saddle, his pistols, and his sword have nothing in them remarkable: the meanest soldier was in this respect no way inferior to his gallant monarch. I shall use this opportunity to give you some particulars of the life of a man already so well known, which I had from persons who knew him when a child, and who now, by a fate not unusual to courtiers, spend a life of poverty and retirement, and talk over in raptures all the actions of their old victorious king, companion, and master.

Courage and inflexible constancy formed the basis of this monarch's character. In his tenderest years he gave instances of both. When he was yet scarcely seven years old, being at dinner with the queen his mother, intending to give a bit of bread to a great dog he was fond of, this hungry animal snapt too greedily at the morsel, and bit his hand in a terrible manner. The wound bled copiously; but our young hero, without offering to cry, or taking the least notice of his misfortune, endeavoured to conceal what had happened, lest his dog should be brought into trouble, and wrapped his bloody hand in the napkin. The queen, perceiving that he did not eat, asked him the reason. He contented himself with replying, that he thanked her, he was not hungry. They thought he was taken ill, and so repeated their solicitations; but all was in vain, though the poor child was already grown pale with the loss of blood. An officer who attended at table at last perceived it; for Charles would sooner have died than betrayed his dog, who, he knew, intended no injury.

At another time, when in the small-pox, and his case appeared dangerous, he grew one day very uneasy in his bed, and a gentleman who watched him, desirous of covering him up close, received from the patient a violent box on his ear. Some hours after, observing the prince more calm, he entreated to know how he had incurred his displeasure, or what he had done to have merited a blow. "A blow?" replied Charles; "I don't remember anything of it: I remember, indeed, that I thought myself in the battle of Arbela, fighting for Darius, where I gave Alexander a blow which brought him to the ground."

What great effects might not these two qualities of courage and constancy have produced, had they at first received a just direction! Charles, with proper instructions, thus naturally disposed, would have been the delight and the glory of his age. Happy those princes who are educated by men who are at once virtuous and wise, and have been for some time in the school of affliction; who weigh happiness against glory, and teach their royal pupils the real value of fame; who are ever showing the superior dignity of man to that of royalty—that a peasant who does his duty is a nobler character than a king of even middling reputation! Happy, I say, were princes, could such men be found to instruct them; but those to whom such an education is generally intrusted are men who themselves have acted in a sphere too high to know mankind. Puffed up themselves with the ideas of false grandeur, and measuring merit by adventitious circumstances of greatness, they generally communicate those fatal prejudices to their pupils, confirm their pride by adulation, or increase their ignorance by teaching them to despise that wisdom which is found among the poor.

But not to moralize when I only intend a story,—what is related of the journeys of this prince is no less astonishing. He has sometimes been on horseback for four-and-twenty hours successively, and thus traversed the greatest part of his kingdom. At last none of his officers were found capable of following him; he thus consequently rode the greatest part of his journeys quite alone, without taking a moment's repose, and without any other subsistence but a bit of bread. In one of these rapid courses he underwent an adventure singular enough. Riding thus post one day, all alone, he had the misfortune to have his horse fall dead under him. This might have embarrassed an ordinary man, but it gave Charles no sort of uneasiness. Sure of finding another horse, but not equally so of meeting with a good saddle and pistols, he ungirths his horse, claps the whole equipage on his own back, and, thus accoutred, marches on to the next inn, which by good fortune was not far off. Entering the stable, he here found an horse entirely to his mind; so, without farther ceremony, he clapped on his saddle and housing with great composure, and was just going to mount, when the gentleman who owned the horse was apprised of a stranger's going to steal his property out of the stable. Upon asking the king, whom he had never seen, bluntly how he presumed to meddle with his horse, Charles coolly replied, squeezing in his lips, which was his usual custom, that he took the horse because he wanted one; "for you see," continued he, "if I have none, I shall be obliged to carry the saddle myself." This answer did not seem at all satisfactory to the gentleman, who instantly drew his sword. In this the king was not much behindhand with him, and to it they were going, when the guards by this time came up, and testified that surprise which was natural to see arms in the hand of a subject against his king. Imagine whether the gentleman was less surprised than they at his unpremeditated disobedience. His astonishment, however, was soon dissipated by the king, who, taking him by the hand, assured him he was a brave fellow, and himself would take care he should be provided for. This promise was afterwards fulfilled, and I have been assured the king made him a captain.

HAPPINESS IN A GREAT MEASURE DEPENDENT ON CONSTITUTION.

When I reflect on the unambitious retirement in which I passed the earlier part of my life in the country, I cannot avoid feeling some pain in thinking that those happy days are never to return. In that retreat all nature seemed capable of affording pleasure: I then made no refinements on happiness, but could be pleased with the most awkward efforts of rustic mirth; thought cross purposes the highest stretch of human wit, and questions and commands the most rational amusement for spending the evening. Happy could so charming an illusion still continue. I find age and knowledge only contribute to sour our dispositions. My present enjoyments may be more refined, but they are infinitely less pleasing. The pleasure Garrick gives can no way compare to that I have received from a country wag, who imitated a Quaker's sermon. The music of Mattei is dissonance to what I felt when our old dairymaid sang me into tears with Johnny Armstrong's Last Good Night, or the cruelty of Barbara Allen.

Writers of every age have endeavoured to show that pleasure is in us, and not in the objects offered for our amusement. If the soul be happily disposed, everything becomes a subject of entertainment, and distress will almost want a name. Every occurrence passes in review like the figures of a procession: some may be awkward, others ill dressed; but none but a fool is for this enraged with the master of the ceremonies.

I remember to have once seen a slave in a fortification in Flanders, who appeared no way touched with his situation. He was maimed, deformed, and chained; obliged to toil from the appearance of day till nightfall, and condemned to this for life; yet with all these circumstances of apparent wretchedness, he sang, would have danced, but that he wanted a leg, and appeared the merriest, happiest man of all the garrison. What a practical philosopher was here! an happy constitution supplied philosophy, and though seemingly destitute of wisdom, he was really wise. No reading or study had contributed to disenchant the fairy-land around him. Everything furnished him with an opportunity of mirth; and though some thought him, from his insensibility, a fool, he was such an idiot as philosophers might wish in vain to imitate.

They who, like him, can place themselves on that side of the world in which everything appears in a ridiculous or pleasing light, will find something in every occurrence to excite their good humour. The most calamitous events, either to themselves or others, can bring no new affliction: the whole world is to them a theatre, on which comedies only are acted. All the bustle of heroism or the rants of ambition serve only to heighten the absurdity of the scene, and make the humour more poignant. They feel, in short, as little anguish at their own distress, or the complaints of others, as the undertaker, though dressed in black, feels sorrow at a funeral.

Of all the men I ever read of, the famous Cardinal de Retz possessed this happiness of temper in the highest degree. As he was a man of gallantry, and despised all that wore the pedantic appearance of philosophy, wherever pleasure was to be sold he was generally foremost to raise the auction. Being an universal admirer of the fair sex, when he found one lady cruel, he generally fell in love with another, from whom he expected a more favourable reception; if she too rejected his addresses, he never thought of retiring into deserts, or pining in hopeless distress: he persuaded himself that, instead of loving the lady, he only fancied he had loved her, and so all was well again. When Fortune wore her angriest look, when he at last fell into the power of his most deadly enemy, Cardinal Mazarine, and was confined a close prisoner in the Castle of Valenciennes, he never attempted to support his distress by wisdom or philosophy, for he pretended to neither. He laughed at himself and his persecutor, and seemed infinitely pleased at his new situation. In this mansion of distress, though secluded from his friends, though denied all the amusements, and even the conveniences, of life, teased every hour by the impertinence of wretches who were employed to guard him, he still retained his good humour, laughed at all their little spite, and carried the jest so far as to be revenged, by writing the life of his gaoler.

All that philosophy can teach is to be stubborn or sullen under misfortunes. The Cardinal's example will instruct us to be merry in circumstances of the highest affliction. It matters not whether our good humour be construed by others into insensibility, or even idiotism: it is happiness to ourselves; and none but a fool would measure his satisfaction by what the world thinks of it.

Dick Wildgoose was one of the happiest silly fellows I ever knew. He was of the number of those good-natured creatures that are said to do no harm to any but themselves. Whenever Dick fell into any misery, he usually called it "seeing life." If his head was broke by a chairman, or his pocket picked by a sharper, he comforted himself by imitating the Hibernian dialect of the one, or the more fashionable cant of the other. Nothing came amiss to Dick. His inattention to money matters had incensed his father to such a degree, that all the intercession of friends in his favour was fruitless. The old gentleman was on his deathbed. The whole family, and Dick among the number, gathered round him. "I leave my second son Andrew," said the expiring miser, "my whole estate, and desire him to be frugal." Andrew in a sorrowful tone, as is usual on these occasions, "prayed Heaven to prolong his life and health to enjoy it himself."—"I recommend Simon, my third son, to the care of his elder brother, and leave him beside four thousand pounds."—"Ah, father!" cried Simon, (in great affliction to be sure,) "may Heaven give you life and health to enjoy it yourself!" At last, turning to poor Dick, "As for you, you have always been a sad dog—you'll never come to good, you'll never be rich; I'll leave you a shilling to buy an halter."—"Ah, father!" cries Dick, without any emotion, "may Heaven give you life and health to enjoy it yourself!" This was all the trouble the loss of fortune gave this thoughtless imprudent creature. However, the tenderness of an uncle recompensed the neglect of a father; and Dick is not only excessively good-humoured, but competently rich.

The world, in short, may cry out at a bankrupt who appears at a ball; at an author who laughs at the public which pronounces him a dunce; at a general who smiles at the reproach of the vulgar; or the lady who keeps her good humour in spite of scandal: but such is the wisest behaviour they can possibly assume. It is certainly a better way to oppose calamity by dissipation, than to take up the arms of reason or resolution to oppose it: by the first method we forget our miseries, by the last we only conceal them from others. By struggling with misfortunes we are sure to receive some wounds in the conflict: the only method to come off victorious is by running away.

ON OUR THEATRES.

MADEMOISELLE CLAIRON, a celebrated actress at Paris, seems to me the most perfect female figure I have ever seen upon any stage. Not perhaps that nature has been more liberal of personal beauty to her, than some to be seen upon our theatres at home. There are actresses here who have as much of what connoisseurs call statuary grace, by which is meant elegance unconnected with motion, as she; but they all fall infinitely short of her when the soul comes to give expression to the limbs, and animates every feature.

Her first appearance is excessively engaging: she never comes in staring round upon the company, as if she intended to count the benefits of the house, or at least to see, as well as be seen. Her eyes are always, at first, intently fixed upon the persons of the drama, and she lifts them, by degrees, with enchanting diffidence, upon the spectators. Her first speech, or at least the first part of it, is delivered with scarce any motion of the arm: her hands and her tongue never set out together; but the one prepares us for the other. She sometimes begins with a mute eloquent attitude; but never goes forward all at once with hands, eyes, head, and voice. This observation, though it may appear of no importance, should certainly be adverted to; nor do I see any one performer (Garrick only excepted) among us, that is not in this particular apt to offend. By this simple beginning she gives herself a power of rising in the passion of the scene. As she proceeds every gesture, every look, acquires new violence, till at last, transported, she fills the whole vehemence of the part, and all the idea of the poet.

Her hands are not alternately stretched out, and then drawn in again, as with the singing women at Sadlers' Wells: they are employed with graceful variety, and every moment please with new and unexpected eloquence. Add to this, that their motion is generally from the shoulder; she never flourishes her hands while the upper part of her arm is motionless, nor has she the ridiculous appearance as if her elbows were pinned to her hips.

But of all the cautions to be given to our rising actresses, I would particularly recommend it to them never to take notice of the audience upon any occasion whatsoever; let the spectators applaud never so loudly, their praises should pass, except at the end of the epilogue, with seeming inattention. I can never pardon a lady on the stage who, when she draws the admiration of the whole audience, turns about to make them a low courtesy for their applause. Such a figure no longer continues Belvidera, but at once drops into Mrs. Cibber. Suppose a sober tradesman, who once a year takes his shilling's worth at Drury Lane, in order to be delighted with the figure of a queen—the Queen of Sheba, for instance, or any other queen—this honest man has no other idea of the great but from their superior pride and impertinence: suppose such a man placed among the spectators, the first figure that appears on the stage is the queen herself, courtesying and cringing to all the company; how can he fancy her the haughty favourite of King Solomon the wise, who appears actually more submissive than the wife of his bosom? We are all tradesmen of a nicer relish in this respect, and such conduct must disgust every spectator who loves to have the illusion of nature strong upon him.

Yet, while I recommend to our actresses a skilful attention to gesture, I would not have them study it in the looking-glass. This, without some precaution, will render their action formal; by too great an intimacy with this they become stiff and affected. People seldom improve when they have no other model but themselves to copy after. I remember to have known a notable performer of the other sex, who made great use of this flattering monitor, and yet was one of the stiffest figures I ever saw. I am told his apartment was hung round with looking-glasses, that he might see his person twenty times reflected upon entering the room; and I will make bold to say, he saw twenty very ugly fellows whenever he did so.

No. III.—*Saturday, October* 20, 1759.

ON THE USE OF LANGUAGE.

THE manner in which most writers begin their treatises on the use of language is generally thus:—"Language has been granted to man, in order to discover his wants and necessities, so as to have them relieved by society. Whatever we desire, whatever we wish, it is but to clothe those desires or wishes in words, in order to fruition. The principal use of language, therefore," say they, "is to express our wants, so as to receive a speedy redress."

Such an account as this may serve to satisfy grammarians and rhetoricians well enough, but men who know the world maintain very contrary maxims; they hold, and I think with some show of reason, that he who best knows how to conceal his necessity and desires is the most likely person to find redress, and that the true use of speech is not so much to express our wants, as to conceal them.

When we reflect on the manner in which mankind generally confer their favours, we shall find that they who seem to want them least are the very persons who most liberally share them. There is something so attractive in riches, that the large heap generally collects from the smaller; and the poor find as much pleasure in increasing the enormous mass, as the miser who owns it sees happiness in its increase. Nor is there in this anything repugnant to the laws of true morality. Seneca himself allows that, in conferring benefits, the present should always be suited to the dignity of the receiver. Thus the rich receive large presents, and are thanked for accepting them; men of middling stations are obliged to be content with presents something less; while the beggar, who may be truly said to want indeed, is well paid if a farthing rewards his warmest solicitations.

Every man who has seen the world, and has had his ups and downs in life, as the expression is, must have frequently experienced the truth of this doctrine, and must know, that to have much, or to seem to have it, is the only way to have more. Ovid finely compares a man of broken fortune to a falling column; the lower it sinks, the greater weight it is obliged to sustain. Thus, when a man has no occasion to borrow, he finds numbers willing to lend him. Should he ask his friend to lend him a hundred pounds, it is possible, from the largeness of his demand, he may find credit for twenty; but should he humbly only sue for a trifle, it is two to one whether he might be trusted for twopence. A certain young fellow at George's, whenever he had occasion to ask his friend for a guinea, used to prelude his request as if he wanted two hundred, and talked so familiarly of large sums, that none could ever think he wanted a small one. The same gentleman, whenever he wanted credit for a new suit from his tailor, always made a proposal in laced clothes: for he found by experience that if he appeared shabby on these occasions, Mr. Lynch had taken an oath against trusting; or, what was every bit as bad, his foreman was out of the way, and would not be at home these two days.

There can be no inducement to reveal our wants, except to find pity, and by this means relief; but before a poor man opens his mind in such circumstances, he should first consider whether he is contented to lose the esteem of the person he solicits, and whether he is willing to give up friendship only to excite compassion. Pity and friendship are passions incompatible with each other, and it is impossible that both can reside in any breast for the smallest space, without impairing each other. Friendship is made up of esteem and pleasure; pity is composed of sorrow and contempt: the mind may for some time fluctuate between them, but it never can entertain both together.

Yet let it not be thought that I would exclude pity from the human mind. There are scarcely any who are not, in some degree, possessed of this pleasing softness; but it is at best but a short-lived passion, and seldom affords distress more than transitory assistance: with some it scarcely lasts from the first impulse till the hand can be put into the pocket; with others it may continue for twice that space, and on some of extraordinary sensibility I have seen it operate for half an hour. But, however, last as it will, it generally produces but beggarly effects; and where, from this motive, we give a halfpenny, from others we give always pounds. In great distress we sometimes, it is true, feel the influence of tenderness strongly; when the same distress solicits a second time, we then feel with diminished sensibility; but, like the repetition of an echo, every new impulse becomes weaker, till at last our sensations lose every mixture of sorrow, and degenerate into downright contempt.

Jack Spindle and I were old acquaintance; but he's gone. Jack was bred in a compting-house, and his father dying just as he was out of his time, left him a handsome fortune, and many friends to advise with. The restraint in which he had been brought up had thrown a gloom upon his temper, which some regarded as habitual prudence, and from such considerations he had every day repeated offers of friendship. Those who had money were ready to offer him their assistance that way; and they who had daughters frequently, in the warmth of affection, advised him to marry. Jack, however, was in good circumstances; he wanted neither money, friends, nor a wife, and therefore modestly declined their proposals.

Some errors in the management of his affairs and several losses in trade soon brought Jack to a different way of thinking; and he at last thought it his best way to let his friends know, that their offers were at length acceptable. His first address was, therefore, to a scrivener who had formerly made him frequent offers of money and friendship at a time when, perhaps, he knew those offers would have been refused.

Jack, therefore, thought he might use his old friend without any ceremony; and, as a man confident of not being refused, requested the use of an hundred guineas for a few days, as he just then had an occasion for money. "And pray, Mr. Spindle," replied the scrivener, "do you want all this money?"—"Want it, sir," says the other; "if I did not want it, I should not have asked it."—"I am sorry for that," says the friend; "for those who want money when they come to borrow, will want money when they should come to pay. To say the truth, Mr. Spindle, money is money now-a-days. I believe it is all sunk in the bottom of the sea, for my part; and he that has got a little is a fool if he does not keep what he has got."

Not quite disconcerted by this refusal, our adventurer was resolved to apply to another, whom he knew to be the very best friend he had in the world. The gentleman whom he now addressed received his proposal with all the affability that could be expected from generous friendship. "Let me see,—you want an hundred guineas; and pray, dear Jack, would not fifty answer?"—"If you have but fifty to spare, sir, I must be contented." —"Fifty to spare! I do not say that, for I believe I have but twenty about me."—"Then I must borrow the other thirty from some other friend."—"And pray," replied the friend, "would it not be the best way to borrow the whole money from that other friend? then one note will serve for all, you know? Lord, Mr. Spindle, make no ceremony with me at any time; you know I'm your friend, when you choose a bit of dinner or so. You, Tom, see the gentleman down. You won't forget to dine with us now and then? Your very humble servant."

Distressed, but not discouraged at this treatment, he was at last resolved to find that assistance from love which he could not have from friendship. Miss Jenny Dismal had a fortune in her own hands, and she had already made all the advances that her sex's modesty would permit. He made his proposal, therefore, with confidence, but soon perceived "No bankrupt ever found the fair one kind." Miss Jenny and Master Billy Galoon were lately fallen deeply in love with each other, and the whole neighbourhood thought it would soon be a match.

Every day now began to strip Jack of his former finery: his clothes flew piece by piece to the pawnbrokers; and he seemed at length equipped in the genuine mourning of antiquity. But still he thought himself secure from starving; the numberless invitations he had received to dine, even after his losses, were yet unanswered: he was, therefore, now resolved to accept of a dinner, because he wanted one; and in this manner he actually lived among his friends a whole week without being openly affronted. The last place I saw poor Jack was at the Reverend Dr. Gosling's. He had, as he fancied, just nicked the time, for he came in just as the cloth was laying. He took a chair without being desired, and talked for some time without being attended to. He assured the company, that nothing procured so good an appetite as a walk to White Conduit House, where he had been that morning. He looked at the tablecloth, and praised the figure of the damask; talked of a feast where he had been the day before, but that the venison was overdone. All this, however, procured the poor creature no invitation, and he was not yet sufficiently hardened to stay without being asked; wherefore, finding the gentleman of the house insensible to all his fetches, he thought proper at last to retire, and mend his appetite by a walk in the Park.

You then, O ye beggars of my acquaintance, whether in rags or lace—whether in Kent Street or the Mall—whether at Smyrna or St. Giles's,—might I advise you as a friend, never seem in want of the favour which you solicit. Apply to every passion but pity for redress. You may find relief from vanity, from self-interest, or from avarice, but seldom from compassion. The very eloquence of a poor man is disgusting; and that mouth which is opened, even for flattery, is seldom expected to close without a petition.

If, then, you would ward off the gripe of poverty, pretend to be a stranger to her, and she will at least use you with ceremony. Hear not my advice, but that of Ofellus. If you be caught dining upon a halfpenny porringer of pease soup and potatoes, praise the wholesomeness of your frugal repast. You may observe that Dr. Cheyne has prescribed pease broth for the gravel; hint that you are not one of those who are always making a god of your belly. If you are obliged to wear a flimsy stuff in the midst of winter, be the first to remark that stuffs are very much worn at Paris. If there be found some irreparable defects in any part of your equipage, which cannot be concealed by all the arts of sitting cross-legged, coaxing, or darning, say that neither you nor Sampson Gideon were ever very fond of dress. Or if you be a philosopher, hint that Plato and Seneca are the tailors you choose to employ; assure the company, that men ought to be content with a bare covering, since what is now so much the pride of some, was formerly our shame. Horace will give you a Latin sentence fit for the occasion,—

Toga defendere frigus,
Quamvis crassa, queat.

In short, however caught, do not give up, but ascribe to the frugality of your disposition what others might be apt to attribute to the narrowness of your circumstances, and appear rather to be a miser than a beggar. To be poor, and to seem poor, is a certain method never to rise. Pride in the great is hateful, in the wise it is ridiculous; beggarly pride is the only sort of vanity I can excuse.

THE HISTORY OF HYPATIA.

MAN, when secluded from society, is not a more solitary being than the woman who leaves the duties of her own sex to invade the privileges of ours. She seems, in such circumstances, like one in banishment; she appears like a neutral being between the sexes; and, though she may have the admiration of both, she finds true happiness from neither.

Of all the ladies of antiquity I have read of, none was ever more justly celebrated than the beautiful Hypatia, the daughter of Theon the philosopher. This most accomplished of women was born at Alexandria, in the reign of Theodosius the Younger. Nature was never more lavish of its gifts than it had been to her, endued as she was with the most exalted understanding and the happiest turn to science. Education completed what nature had begun, and made her the prodigy not only of her age, but the glory of her sex.

From her father she learned geometry and astronomy; she collected from the conversation and schools of the other philosophers, for which Alexandria was at that time famous, the principles of the rest of the sciences.

What cannot be conquered by natural penetration and a passion of study? The boundless knowledge which, at that period of time, was required to form the character of a philosopher no way discouraged her; she delivered herself up to the study of Aristotle and Plato, and soon not one in all Alexandria understood so perfectly as she all the difficulties of these two philosophers.

But not their systems alone, but those of every other sect, were quite familiar to her; and to this knowledge she added that of polite learning and the art of oratory. All the learning which it was possible for the human mind to contain, being joined to a most enchanting eloquence, rendered this lady the wonder not only of the populace, who easily admire, but of philosophers themselves, who are seldom fond of admiration.

The city of Alexandria was every day crowded with strangers, who came from all parts of Greece and Asia to see and hear her. As for the charms of her person, they might not probably have been mentioned, did she not join to a beauty the most striking a virtue that might repress the most assuming: and though in the whole capital, famed for charms, there was not one who could equal her in beauty; though in a city, the resort of all the learning then existing in the world, there was not one who could equal her in knowledge; yet, with such accomplishments, Hypatia was the most modest of her sex. Her reputation for virtue was not less than her virtues; and, though in a city divided between two factions, though visited by the wits and the philosophers of the age, calumny never dared to suspect her morals, or attempt her character. Both the Christians and the Heathens who have transmitted her history and her misfortunes have but one voice, when they speak of her beauty, her knowledge, and her virtue. Nay, so much harmony reigns in their accounts of this prodigy of perfection, that, in spite of the opposition of their faith, we should never have been able to judge of what religion was Hypatia, were we not informed, from other circumstances, that she was an heathen. Providence had taken so much pains in forming her, that we are almost induced to complain of its not having endeavoured to make her a Christian; but from this complaint we are deterred by a thousand contrary observations, which lead us to reverence its inscrutable mysteries.

This great reputation, of which she so justly was possessed, was, at last, however, the occasion of her ruin.

The person who then possessed the patriarchate of Alexandria was equally remarkable for his violence, cruelty, and pride. Conducted by an ill-grounded zeal for the Christian religion, or, perhaps, desirous of augmenting his authority in the city, he had long meditated the banishment of the Jews. A difference arising between them and the Christians, with respect to some public games, seemed to him a proper juncture for putting his ambitious designs into execution. He found no difficulty in exciting the people, naturally disposed to revolt. The prefect who at that time commanded the city interposed on this occasion, and thought it just to put one of the chief creatures of the patriarch to the torture, in order to discover the first promoter of the conspiracy. The patriarch, enraged at the injustice he thought offered to his character and dignity, and piqued at the protection which was offered to the Jews, sent for the chiefs of the synagogue, and enjoined them to renounce their designs, upon pain of incurring his highest displeasure.

The Jews, far from fearing his menaces, excited new tumults, in which several citizens had the misfortune to fall. The patriarch could no longer contain: at the head of a numerous body of Christians, he flew to the synagogues, which he demolished, and drove the Jews from a city of which they had been possessed since the times of Alexander the Great. It may be easily imagined that the prefect could not behold, without pain, his jurisdiction thus insulted, and the city deprived of a number of its most industrious inhabitants.

The affair was, therefore, brought before the emperor. The patriarch complained of the excesses of the Jews, and the prefect of the outrages of the patriarch. At this very juncture five hundred monks of Mount Nitria, imagining the life of their chief to be in danger, and that their religion was threatened in his fall, flew into the city with ungovernable rage, attacked the prefect in the streets, and, not content with loading him with reproaches, wounded him in several places.

The citizens had by this time notice of the fury of the monks; they therefore assembled in a body, put the monks to flight, seized on him who had been found throwing a stone, and delivered him to the prefect, who caused him to be put to death without farther delay.

The patriarch immediately ordered the dead body, which had been exposed to view, to be taken down, procured for it all the pomp and rites of burial, and went even so far as himself to pronounce the funeral oration, in which he classed a seditious monk among the martyrs. This conduct was by no means generally approved of; the most moderate even among the Christians perceived and blamed his indiscretion; but he was now too far advanced to retire. He had made several overtures towards a reconciliation with the prefect, which not succeeding, he bore all those an implacable hatred whom he imagined to have had any hand in traversing his designs; but Hypatia was particularly destined to ruin. She could not find pardon, as she was known to have a most refined friendship for the prefect; wherefore the populace were incited against her. Peter, a reader of the principal church, one of those vile slaves by whom men in power are too frequently attended —wretches ever ready to commit any crime which they hope may render them agreeable to their employer,—this fellow, I say, attended by a crowd of villains, waited for Hypatia, as she was returning from a visit, at her own door, seized her as she was going in, and dragged her to one of the churches called Cesarea, where, stripping her in a most inhuman manner, they exercised the most horrible cruelties upon her, cut her into pieces, and burnt her remains to ashes. Such was the end of Hypatia, the glory of her own sex, and the astonishment of ours.

ON JUSTICE AND GENEROSITY.

LYSIPPUS is a man whose greatness of soul the whole world admires. His generosity is such that it prevents a demand, and saves the receiver the trouble and the confusion of a request. His liberality also does not oblige more by its greatness than by his inimitable grace in giving. Sometimes he even distributes his bounties to strangers, and has been known to do good offices to those who professed themselves his enemies. All the world are unanimous in the praise of his generosity: there is only one sort of people who complain of his conduct,—Lysippus does not pay his debts.

It is no difficult matter to account for a conduct so seemingly incompatible with itself. There is greatness in being generous, and there is only simple justice in satisfying his creditors. Generosity is the part of a soul raised above the vulgar. There is in it something of what we admire in heroes, and praise with a degree of rapture. Justice, on the contrary, is a mere mechanic virtue, fit only for tradesmen, and what is practised by every broker in Change Alley.

In paying his debts a man barely does his duty, and it is an action attended with no sort of glory. Should Lysippus satisfy his creditors, who would be at the pains of telling it to the world? Generosity is a virtue of a very different complexion. It is raised above duty, and, from its elevation, attracts the attention and the praises of us little mortals below.

In this manner do men generally reason upon justice and generosity. The first is despised, though a virtue essential to the good of society; and the other attracts our esteem, which too frequently proceeds from an impetuosity of temper, rather directed by vanity than reason. Lysippus is told that his banker asks a debt of forty pounds, and that a distressed acquaintance petitions for the same sum. He gives it without hesitating to the latter; for he demands as a favour what the former requires as a debt.

Mankind in general are not sufficiently acquainted with the import of the word *justice:* it is commonly believed to consist only in a performance of those duties to which the laws of society can oblige us. This, I allow, is sometimes the import of the word, and in this sense justice is distinguished from equity; but there is a justice still more extensive, and which can be shown to embrace all the virtues united.

Justice may be defined to be that virtue which impels us to give to every person what is his due. In this extended sense of the word, it comprehends the practice of every virtue which reason prescribes or society should expect. Our duty to our Maker, to each other, and to ourselves, are fully answered, if we give them what we owe them. Thus justice, properly speaking, is the only virtue, and all the rest have their origin in it.

The qualities of candour, fortitude, charity, and generosity, for instance, are not, in their own nature, virtues; and if ever they deserve the title, it is owing only to justice, which impels and directs them. Without such a moderator candour might become indiscretion, fortitude obstinacy, charity imprudence, and generosity mistaken profusion.

A disinterested action, if it be not conducted by justice, is at best indifferent in its nature, and not unfrequently even turns to vice. The expenses of society, of presents, of entertainments, and the other helps to cheerfulness, are actions merely indifferent, when not repugnant to a better method of disposing of our superfluities; but they become vicious when they obstruct or exhaust our abilities from a more virtuous disposition of our circumstances.

True generosity is a duty as indispensably necessary as those imposed upon us by law. It is a rule imposed upon us by reason, which should be the sovereign law of a rational being. But this generosity does not consist in obeying every impulse of humanity, in following blind passion for our guide, and impairing our circumstances by present benefactions, so as to render us incapable of future ones.

Misers are generally characterised as men without honour or without humanity, who live only to accumulate, and to this passion sacrifice every other happiness. They have been described as madmen, who, in the midst of abundance, banish every pleasure, and make from imaginary wants real necessities. But few, very few, correspond to this exaggerated picture; and perhaps there is not one in whom all these circumstances are found united. Instead of this, we find the sober and the industrious branded by the vain and the idle with this odious appellation; men who, by frugality and labour, raise themselves above their equals, and contribute their share of industry to the common stock.

Whatever the vain or the ignorant may say, well were it for society had we more of this character among us. In general, these close men are found at last the true benefactors of society. With an avaricious man we seldom lose in our dealings; but too frequently in our commerce with prodigality.

A French priest, whose name was Godinot, went for a long time by the name of the Griper. He refused to relieve the most apparent wretchedness, and, by a skilful management of his vineyard, had the good fortune to acquire immense sums of money. The inhabitants of Rheims, who were his fellow-citizens, detested him; and the populace, who seldom love a miser, wherever he went received him with contempt. He still, however, continued his former simplicity of life, his amazing and unremitted frugality. This good man had long perceived the wants of the poor in the city, particularly in having no water but what they were obliged to buy at an advanced price; wherefore that whole fortune which he had been amassing he laid out in an aqueduct, by which he did the poor more useful and lasting service than if he had distributed his whole income in charity every day at his door.

Among men long conversant with books we too frequently find those misplaced virtues of which I have been now complaining. We find the studious animated with a strong passion for the great virtues, as they are mistakenly called, and utterly forgetful of the ordinary ones. The declamations of philosophy are generally rather exhausted on these supererogatory duties, than on such as are indispensably necessary. A man, therefore, who has taken his ideas of mankind from study alone, generally comes into the world with a heart melting at every fictitious distress. Thus he is induced, by misplaced liberality, to put himself into the indigent circumstances of the person he relieves.

I shall conclude this paper with the advice of one of the ancients to a young man whom he saw giving away all his substance to pretended distress. "It is possible that the person you relieve may be an honest man; and I know that you who relieve him are such. You see, then, by your generosity, you only rob a man who is certainly deserving, to bestow it on one who may possibly be a rogue; and, while you are unjust in rewarding uncertain merit, you are doubly guilty by stripping yourself."

SOME PARTICULARS RELATING TO FATHER FEYJOO.

Primus mortales tollere contra
Est oculos ausus, primusque assurgere contra.
LUCR.

THE Spanish nation has, for many centuries past, been remarkable for the grossest ignorance in polite literature, especially in point of natural philosophy—a science so useful to mankind, that her neighbours have ever esteemed it a matter of the greatest importance to endeavour, by repeated experiments, to strike a light out of the chaos in which truth seemed to be confounded. Their curiosity in this respect was so indifferent, that though they had discovered new worlds, they were at a loss to explain the phenomena of their own, and their pride so unaccountable, that they disdained to borrow from others that instruction which their natural indolence permitted them not to acquire.

It gives me, however, a secret satisfaction to behold an extraordinary genius now existing in that nation, whose studious endeavours seem calculated to undeceive the superstitious and instruct the ignorant, —I mean the celebrated Padre Feyjoo. In unravelling the mysteries of nature, and explaining physical experiments, he takes an opportunity of displaying the concurrence of second causes, in those very wonders which the vulgar ascribe to supernatural influence.

An example of this kind happened a few years ago in a small town of the kingdom of Valencia. Passing through at the hour of mass, he alighted from his mule, and proceeded to the parish church, which he found extremely crowded, and there appeared on the faces of the faithful a more than usual alacrity. The sun, it seems, which had been for some minutes under a cloud, had begun to shine on a large crucifix, that stood on the middle of the altar, studded with several precious stones. The reflection from these, and from the diamond eyes of some silver saints, so dazzled the multitude, that they unanimously cried out, "A miracle! a miracle!" whilst the priest at the altar, with seeming consternation, continued his heavenly conversation. Padre Feyjoo soon dissipated the charm, by tying his handkerchief round the head of one of the statues, for which he was arraigned by the Inquisition; whose flames, however, he has had the good fortune hitherto to escape.

No. IV.—*Saturday, October 27, 1759.*

MISCELLANEOUS.

WERE I to measure the merit of my present undertaking by its success or the rapidity of its sale, I might be led to form conclusions by no means favourable to the pride of an author. Should I estimate my fame by its extent, every newspaper and magazine would leave me far behind. Their fame is diffused in a very wide circle—that of some as far as Islington, and some yet farther still; while mine, I sincerely believe, has hardly travelled beyond the sound of Bow-Bell; and while the works of others fly like unpinioned swans, I find my own move as heavily as a new-plucked goose.

Still, however, I have as much pride

as they who have ten times as many readers. It is impossible to repeat all the agreeable delusions in which a disappointed author is apt to find comfort. I conclude, that what my reputation wants in extent, is made up by its solidity. *Minus juvat gloria lata quam magna.* I have great satisfaction in considering the delicacy and discernment of those readers I have, and in ascribing my want of popularity to the ignorance or inattention of those I have not. All the world may forsake an author, but vanity will never forsake him.

Yet, notwithstanding so sincere a confession, I was once induced to show my indignation against the public, by discontinuing my endeavours to please; and was bravely resolved, like Raleigh, to vex them by burning my manuscript in a passion. Upon recollection, however, I considered what set or body of people would be displeased at my rashness. The sun, after so sad an accident, might shine next morning as bright as usual; men might laugh and sing the next day, and transact business as before, and not a single creature feel any regret but myself.

I reflected upon the story of a minister who, in the reign of Charles II., upon a certain occasion resigned all his posts, and retired into the country in a fit o resentment. But as he had not given the world entirely up with his ambition, he sent a messenger to town, to see how the courtiers would bear his resignation. Upon the messenger's return he was asked, whether there appeared any commotion at court? To which he replied, there were very great ones. "Ay," says the minister, "I knew my friends would make a bustle; all petitioning the king for my restoration, I presume?"—"No, sir," replied the messenger; "they are only petitioning his majesty to be put in your place." In the same manner, should I retire in indignation, instead of having Apollo in mourning, or the Muses in a fit of the spleen; instead of having the learned world apostrophizing at my untimely decease; perhaps all Grub Street might laugh at my fall, and self-approving dignity might never be able to shield me from ridicule. In short, I am resolved to write on, if it were only to spite them. If the present generation will not hear my voice, hearken, O Posterity,—to you I call, and from you I expect redress! What rapture will it not give to have the Scaligers, Daciers, and Warburtons of future times commenting with admiration upon every line I now write, working away those ignorant creatures who offer to arraign my merit with all the virulence of learned reproach. Ay, my friends, let them feel it: call names, never spare them; they deserve it all, and ten times more. I have been told of a critic who was crucified at the command of another to the reputation of Homer. That, no doubt, was more than poetical justice, and I shall be perfectly content if those who criticise me are only clapped in the pillory, kept fifteen days upon bread and water, and obliged to run the gauntlet through Paternoster Row. The truth is, I can expect happiness from Posterity either way. If I write ill, happy in being forgotten; if well, happy in being remembered with respect.

Yet, considering things in a prudential light, perhaps I was mistaken in designing my paper as an agreeable relaxation to the studious, or an help to conversation among the gay; instead of addressing it to such, I should have written down to the taste and apprehension of the many, and sought for reputation on the broad road. Literary fame, I now find, like religious, generally begins among the vulgar. As for the polite, they are so very polite as never to applaud upon any account. One of these, with a face screwed up into affectation, tells you, that fools may *admire*, but men of sense only *approve*. Thus, lest he should rise in rapture at anything new, he keeps down every passion but pride and self-importance; approves with phlegm; and the poor author is damned in the taking a pinch of snuff. Another has written a book himself, and being condemned for a dunce, he turns a sort of king's evidence in criticism, and now becomes the terror of every offender. A third, possessed of full-grown reputation, shades off every beam of favour from those who endeavour to grow beneath him, and keeps down that merit which, but for his influence, might rise into equal eminence. While others, still worse, peruse old books for their amusement, and new books only to condemn; so that the public seem heartily sick of all but the business of the day, and read everything now with as little attention as they examine the faces of the passing crowd.

From these considerations, I was once determined to throw off all connexions with taste, and fairly address my countrymen in the same engaging style and manner with other periodical pamphlets much more in vogue than probably mine shall ever be. To effect this, I had thoughts of changing the title into that of the ROYAL BEE, the ANTIGALLICAN BEE, or the BEE'S MAGAZINE. I had laid in a proper stock of popular topics, such as encomiums on the King of Prussia, invectives against the Queen of Hungary and the French, the necessity of a militia, our undoubted sovereignty of the seas, reflections upon the present state of affairs, a dissertation upon liberty, some seasonable thoughts upon the intended bridge of Blackfriars, and an address to Britons; the history of an old woman, whose teeth grew three inches long, an ode upon our victories, a rebus, an acrostic upon Miss Peggy P., and a journal of the weather. All this, together with four extraordinary pages of letter-press, a beautiful map of England, and two prints curiously coloured from nature, I fancied might touch their very souls. I was actually beginning an address to the people, when my pride at last overcame my prudence, and determined me to endeavour to please by the goodness of my entertainment, rather than by the magnificence of my sign.

The Spectator and many succeeding essayists frequently inform us of the numerous compliments paid them in the course of their lucubrations—of the frequent encouragements they meet to inspire them with ardour, and increase their eagerness to please. I have received *my letters* as well as they; but, alas! not congratulatory ones—not assuring me of success and favour—but pregnant with bodings that might shake even fortitude itself.

One gentleman assures me, he intends to throw away no more threepences in purchasing the BEE; and what is still more dismal, he will not recommend me as a poor author wanting encouragement to his neighbourhood, which, it seems, is very numerous. Were my soul set upon threepences, what anxiety might not such a denunciation produce! But such does not happen to be the present motive of publication: I write partly to show my good nature, and partly to show my vanity; nor will I lay down the pen till I am satisfied one way or another.

Others have disliked the title and the motto of my paper; point out a mistake in the one, and assure me the other has been consigned to dulness by anticipation. All this may be true; but what is that to me? Titles and mottoes to books are like escutcheons and dignities in the hands of a king: the wise sometimes condescend to accept of them, but none but a fool will imagine them of any real importance. We ought to depend upon intrinsic merit, and not the slender helps of title. *Nam quæ non fecimus ipsi, vix ea nostra voco.*

For my part, I am ever ready to mistrust a promising title, and have, at some expense, been instructed not to hearken to the voice of an advertisement, let it plead never so loudly or never so long. A countryman coming one day to Smithfield, in order to take a slice of Bartholomew Fair, found a perfect show before every booth. The drummer, the fire-eater, the wire-walker, and the salt-box, were all employed to invite him in. "Just a-going; the court of the King of Prussia in all his glory; pray, gentlemen, walk in and see." From people who generously gave so much away the clown expected a monstrous bargain for his money when he got in. He steps up, pays his sixpence, the curtain is drawn; when, too late, he finds that he had the best part of the show for nothing at the door.

A FLEMISH TRADITION.

EVERY country has its traditions, which, either too minute or not sufficiently authentic to receive historical sanction, are handed down among the vulgar, and serve at once to instruct and amuse them.

Of this number the adventures of Robin Hood, the hunting of Chevy Chase, and the bravery of Johnny Armstrong, among the English; of Kaul Dereg, among the Irish; and Creichton, among the Scots, are instances. Of all the traditions, however, I remember to have heard, I do not recollect any more remarkable than one still current in Flanders; a story generally the first the peasants tell their children, when they bid them behave like Bidderman the wise. It is by no means, however, a model to be set before a polite people for imitation; since if, on the one hand, we perceive in it the steady influence of patriotism, we, on the other, find as strong a desire of revenge. But, to waive introduction, let us to the story.

When the Saracens overran Europe with their armies, and penetrated as far even as Antwerp, Bidderman was lord of a city which time has since swept into destruction. As the inhabitants of this country were divided under separate leaders, the Saracens found an easy conquest, and the city of Bidderman, among the rest, became a prey to the victors.

Thus dispossessed of his paternal city, our unfortunate governor was obliged to seek refuge from the neighbouring princes, who were as yet unsubdued, and he for some time lived in a state of wretched dependence among them.

Soon, however, his love to his native country brought him back to his own city, resolved to rescue it from the enemy, or fall in the attempt: thus in disguise he went among the inhabitants, and endeavoured, but in vain, to excite them to a revolt. Former misfortunes lay so heavily on their minds, that they rather chose to suffer the most cruel bondage, than attempt to vindicate their former freedom.

As he was thus one day employed, whether by information or from suspicion is not known, he was apprehended by a Saracen soldier as a spy, and brought before the very tribunal at which he once presided. The account he gave of himself was by no means satisfactory. He could produce no friends to vindicate his character; wherefore, as the Saracens knew not their prisoner, and as they had no direct proofs against him, they were content with condemning him to be publicly whipped as a vagabond.

The execution of this sentence was accordingly performed with the utmost rigour. Bidderman was bound to the post, the executioner seeming disposed to add to the cruelty of the sentence, as he received no bribe for lenity. Whenever Bidderman groaned under the scourge, the other, redoubling his blows, cried out, "Does the villain murmur?" If Bidderman entreated but a moment's respite from torture, the other only repeated his former exclamation, "Does the villain murmur?"

From this period revenge, as well as patriotism, took entire possession of his soul. His fury stooped so low as to follow the executioner with unremitting resentment. But, conceiving that the best method to attain these ends was to acquire some eminence in the city, he laid himself out to oblige its new masters, studied every art, and practised every meanness, that serve to promote the needy or render the poor pleasing; and by these means, in a few years, he came to be of some note in the city, which justly belonged entirely to him.

The executioner was, therefore, the first object of his resentment, and he even practised the lowest fraud to gratify the revenge he owed him. A piece of plate, which Bidderman had previously stolen from the Saracen governor, he privately conveyed into the executioner's house, and then gave information of the theft. They who are any way acquainted with the rigour of the Arabian laws know that theft is punished with immediate death. The proof was direct in this case; the executioner had nothing to offer in his own defence; and he was therefore condemned to be beheaded upon a scaffold in the public market-place. As there was no executioner in the city but the very man who was now to suffer, Bidderman himself undertook this, to him, most agreeable office. The criminal was conducted from the judgment seat, bound with cords: the scaffold was erected, and he placed in such a manner as he might lie most convenient for the blow.

But his death alone was not sufficient

to satisfy the resentment of this extraordinary man, unless it was aggravated with every circumstance of cruelty. Wherefore, coming up the scaffold, and disposing everything in readiness for the intended blow, with the sword in his hand he approached the criminal, and, whispering in a low voice, assured him that he himself was the person that had once been used with so much cruelty; that, to his knowledge, he died very innocently, for the plate had been stolen by himself, and privately conveyed into the house of the other.

"Oh, my countrymen!" cried the criminal, "do you hear what this man says?"—"Does the villain murmur?" replied Bidderman, and immediately, at one blow, severed his head from his body.

Still, however, he was not content, till he had ample vengeance of the governors of the city, who condemned him. To effect this, he hired a small house adjoining to the town wall, under which he every day dug, and carried out the earth in a basket. In this unremitting labour he continued several years, every day digging a little, and carrying the earth unsuspected away. By this means he at last made a secret communication from the country into the city, and only wanted the appearance of an enemy in order to betray it. This opportunity at length offered: the French army came into the neighbourhood, but had no thoughts of sitting down before a town which they considered as impregnable. Bidderman, however, soon altered their resolutions, and upon communicating his plan to the general, he embraced it with ardour. Through the private passage above mentioned he introduced a large body of the most resolute soldiers, who soon opened the gates for the rest, and the whole army rushing in, put every Saracen that was found to the sword.

THE SAGACITY OF SOME INSECTS.

To the Author of the Bee.

SIR,—Animals, in general, are sagacious in proportion as they cultivate society. The elephant and the beaver show the greatest signs of this when united; but when man intrudes into their communities, they lose all their spirit of industry, and testify but a very small share of that sagacity for which, when in a social state, they are so remarkable.

Among insects, the labours of the bee and the ant have employed the attention and admiration of the naturalist; but their whole sagacity is lost upon separation, and a single bee or ant seems destitute of every degree of industry, is the most stupid insect imaginable, languishes for a time in solitude, and soon dies.

Of all the solitary insects I have ever remarked, the spider is the most sagacious; and its actions, to me who have attentively considered them, seem almost to exceed belief. This insect is formed by nature for a state of war, not only upon other insects, but upon each other. For this state nature seems perfectly well to have formed it. Its head and breast are covered with a strong natural coat of mail, which is impenetrable to the attempts of every other insect, and its belly is enveloped in a soft pliant skin, which eludes the sting even of a wasp. Its legs are terminated by strong claws, not unlike those of a lobster; and their vast length, like spears, serves to keep every assailant at a distance.

Not worse furnished for observation than for an attack or a defence, it has several eyes, large, transparent, and covered with a horny substance, which, however, does not impede its vision. Besides this, it is furnished with a forceps above the mouth, which serves to kill or secure the prey already caught in its claws or its net.

Such are the implements of war with which the body is immediately furnished; but its net to entangle the enemy seems what it chiefly trusts to, and what it takes most pains to render as complete as possible. Nature has furnished the body of this little creature with a glutinous liquid, which, proceeding from the anus, it spins into thread, coarser or finer as it chooses to contract or dilate its sphincter. In order to fix its thread, when it begins to weave it emits a small drop of its liquid against the wall, which, hardening by degrees, serves to hold the thread very firmly; then receding from the first point, as it recedes the thread lengthens; and, when the spider has come to the place where the other end of the thread should be fixed, gathering up with its claws the thread, which would otherwise be too slack, it is stretched tightly, and fixed in the same manner to the wall as before.

In this manner it spins and fixes several threads parallel to each other, which, so to speak, serve as the warp to the intended web. To form the woof, it spins in the same manner its thread, transversely fixing one end to the first thread that was spun, and which is always the strongest of the whole web, and the other to the wall. All these threads, being newly spun, are glutinous, and therefore stick to each other wherever they happen to touch; and, in those parts of the web most exposed to be torn, our natural artist strengthens them, by doubling the threads sometimes sixfold.

Thus far naturalists have gone in the description of this animal; what follows is the result of my own observation upon that species of the insect called a house spider. I perceived, about four years ago, a large spider in one corner of my room, making its web; and, though the maid frequently levelled her fatal broom against the labours of the little animal, I had the good fortune then to prevent its destruction; and, I may say, it more than paid me by the entertainment it afforded.

In three days the web was, with incredible diligence, completed; nor could I avoid thinking, that the insect seemed to exult in its new abode. It frequently traversed it round, examined the strength of every part of it, retired into its hole, and came out very frequently. The first enemy, however, it had to encounter, was another and a much larger spider, which, having no web of its own, and having probably exhausted all its stock in former labours of this kind, came to invade the property of its neighbour. Soon, then, a terrible encounter ensued, in which the invader seemed to have the victory, and the laborious spider was obliged to take refuge in its hole. Upon this I perceived the victor using every art to draw the enemy from his stronghold. He seemed to go off, but quickly returned; and when he found all arts in vain, began to demolish the new web without mercy. This brought on another battle, and, contrary to my expectations, the laborious spider became conqueror, and fairly killed his antagonist.

Now, then, in peaceable possession of what was justly its own, it waited three days with the utmost impatience, repairing the breaches of its web, and taking no sustenance that I could perceive. At last, however, a large blue fly fell into the snare, and struggled hard to get loose. The spider gave it leave to entangle itself as much as possible, but it seemed to be too strong for the cobweb. I must own I was greatly surprised when I saw the spider immediately sally out, and in less than a minute weave a new net round its captive, by which the motion of its wings was stopped; and when it was fairly hampered in this manner, it was seized and dragged into the hole.

In this manner it lived, in a precarious state; and nature seemed to have fitted it for such a life, for upon a single fly it subsisted for more than a week. I once put a wasp into the net; but when the spider came out in order to seize it as usual, upon perceiving what kind of an enemy it had to deal with, it instantly broke all the bands that held it fast, and contributed all that lay in its power to disengage so formidable an antagonist. When the wasp was at liberty, I expected the spider would have set about repairing the breaches that were made in its net; but those, it seems, were irreparable; wherefore the cobweb was now entirely forsaken, and a new one begun, which was completed in the usual time.

I had now a mind to try how many cobwebs a single spider could furnish; wherefore I destroyed this, and the insect set about another. When I destroyed the other also, its whole stock seemed entirely exhausted, and it could spin no more. The arts it made use of to support itself, now deprived of its great means of subsistence, were indeed surprising. I have seen it roll up its legs like a ball, and lie motionless for hours together, but cautiously watching all the time: when a fly happened to approach sufficiently near, it would dart out all at once, and often seize its prey.

Of this life, however, it soon began to grow weary, and resolved to invade the possession of some other spider, since it could not make a web of its own. It formed an attack upon a neighbouring fortification with great vigour, and at first was as vigorously repulsed. Not daunted, however, with one defeat, in this manner it continued to lay siege to another's web for three days, and at length, having killed the defendant, actually took possession. When smaller flies happen to fall into the snare, the spider does not sally out at once, but very patiently waits till it is sure of them; for, upon his immediately approaching, the terror of his appearance might give the captive strength sufficient to get loose: the manner then is to wait patiently till, by ineffectual and impotent struggles, the captive has wasted all its strength, and then he becomes a certain and easy conquest.

The insect I am now describing lived three years; every year it changed its skin, and got a new set of legs. I have sometimes plucked off a leg, which grew again in two or three days. At first it dreaded my approach to its web, but at last it became so familiar as to take a fly out of my hand; and upon my touching any part of the web, would immediately leave its hole, prepared either for a defence or an attack.

To complete this description, it may be observed, that the male spiders are much less than the female, and that the latter are oviparous. When they come to lay, they spread a part of their web under the eggs, and then roll them up carefully, as we roll up things in a cloth, and thus hatch them in their hole. If disturbed in their holes, they never attempt to escape without carrying this young brood in their forceps away with them, and thus frequently are sacrificed to their parental affection.

As soon as ever the young ones leave their artificial covering, they begin to spin, and almost sensibly seem to grow bigger. If they have the good fortune, when even but a day old, to catch a fly, they fall to with good appetites; but they live sometimes three or four days without any sort of sustenance, and yet still continue to grow larger, so as every day to double their former size. As they grow old, however, they do not still continue to increase, but their legs only continue to grow longer; and when a spider becomes entirely stiff with age, and unable to seize its prey, it dies at length of hunger.

THE CHARACTERISTICS OF GREATNESS.

In every duty, in every science in which we would wish to arrive at perfection, we should propose for the object of our pursuit some certain station even beyond our abilities—some imaginary excellence, which may amuse and serve to animate our inquiry. In deviating from others, in following an unbeaten road, though we perhaps may never arrive at the wished-for object, yet it is possible we may meet several discoveries by the way; and the certainty of small advantages, even while we travel with security, is not so amusing as the hopes of great rewards, which inspire the adventurer. "Evenit nonnunquam," says Quintilian, "ut aliquid grande inveniat qui semper quærit quod nimium est."

This enterprising spirit is, however, by no means the character of the present age; every person who should now leave received opinions, who should attempt to be more than a commentator upon philosophy, or an imitator in polite learning, might be regarded as a chimerical projector. Hundreds would be ready not only to point out his errors, but to load him with reproach. Our probable opinions are now regarded as certainties; the difficulties hitherto undiscovered as utterly inscrutable; and the writers of the last age inimitable, and therefore the properest models of imitation.

One might be almost induced to deplore the philosophic spirit of the age, which, in proportion as it enlightens the mind, increases its timidity, and represses the vigour of every undertaking. Men are now content with being prudently in the right; which, though not the way to make new acquisitions, it must be owned is the best method of securing what we have. Yet this is certain, that the writer who never deviates, who never hazards a new thought or a new expression, though his friends may compliment him upon his sagacity, though criticism lifts her feeble voice in his praise, will seldom arrive at any degree of perfection. The way to acquire lasting esteem is not by the fewness of a writer's faults, but the greatness of his beauties; and our noblest works are generally most replete with both.

An author who would be sublime, often runs his thought into burlesque; yet I can readily pardon his mistaking ten times for once succeeding. True genius walks along a line; and perhaps our greatest pleasure is in seeing it so often near falling, without being ever actually down.

Every science has its hitherto undiscovered mysteries, after which men should travel, undiscouraged by the failure of former adventurers. Every new attempt serves perhaps to facilitate its future invention. We may not find the philosopher's stone, but we shall probably hit upon new inventions in pursuing it. We shall perhaps never be able to discover the longitude, yet perhaps we may arrive at new truths in the investigation.

Were any of those sagacious minds among us,—and surely no nation, or no period, could ever compare with us in this particular,—were any of those minds, I say, who now sit down contented with exploring the intricacies of another's system, bravely to shake off admiration, and, undazzled with the splendour of another's reputation, to chalk out a path to fame for themselves, and boldly cultivate untried experiment, what might not be the result of their inquiries, should the same study that has made them wise make them enterprising also? What could not such qualities united produce? But such is not the character of the English: while our neighbours of the Continent launch out into the ocean of science without proper store for the voyage, we fear shipwreck in every breeze, and consume in port those powers which might probably have weathered every storm.

Projectors in a state are generally rewarded above their deserts; projectors in the republic of letters never. If wrong, every inferior dunce thinks himself entitled to laugh at their disappointment; if right, men of superior talents think their honour engaged to oppose, since every new discovery is a tacit diminution of their own pre-eminence.

To aim at excellence our reputation, our friends, and our all must be ventured; by aiming only at mediocrity we run no risk, and we do little service. Prudence and greatness are ever persuading us to contrary pursuits. The one instructs us to be content with our station, and to find happiness in bounding every wish; the other impels us to superiority, and calls nothing happiness but rapture. The one directs us to follow mankind, and to act and think with the rest of the world; the other drives us from the crowd, and exposes us as a mark to all the shafts of envy or ignorance:

> Nec minus periculum ex magna fama quam ex mala.—TACIT.

The rewards of mediocrity are immediately paid, those attending excellence generally paid in reversion. In a word, the little mind who loves itself will write and think with the vulgar; but the great mind will be bravely eccentric, and scorn the beaten road, from universal benevolence.

A CITY NIGHT PIECE.

> Ille dolet vere, qui sine teste dolet.—MART.

THE clock has just struck two, the expiring taper rises and sinks in the socket, the watchman forgets the hour in slumber, the laborious and the happy are at rest, and nothing wakes but meditation, guilt, revelry, and despair. The drunkard once more fills the destroying bowl, the robber walks his midnight round, and the suicide lifts his guilty arm against his own sacred person.

Let me no longer waste the night over the page of antiquity or the sallies of contemporary genius, but pursue the solitary walk, where Vanity, ever changing, but a few hours past walked before me—where she kept up the pageant, and now, like a froward child, seems hushed with her own importunities.

What a gloom hangs all around! The dying lamp feebly emits a yellow gleam; no sound is heard but of the chiming clock, or the distant watch-dog. All the bustle of human pride is forgotten: an hour like this may well display the emptiness of human vanity.

There will come a time, when this temporary solitude may be made continual, and the city itself, like its inhabitants, fade away, and leave a desert in its room.

What cities, as great as this, have once triumphed in existence, had their victories as great, joy as just and as unbounded; and, with short-sighted presumption, promised themselves immortality. Posterity can hardly trace the situation of some: the sorrowful traveller wanders over the awful ruins of others; and, as he beholds, he learns wisdom, and feels the transience of every sublunary possession.

"Here," he cries, "stood their citadel, now grown over with weeds; there their senate-house, but now the haunt of every noxious reptile; temples and theatres stood here, now only an undistinguished heap of ruin. They are fallen, for luxury and avarice first made them feeble. The rewards of the state were conferred on amusing, and not on useful, members of society. Their riches and opulence invited the invaders, who, though at first repulsed, returned again, conquered by perseverance, and at last swept the defendants into undistinguished destruction."

How few appear in those streets which but some few hours ago were crowded; and those who appear, now no longer wear their daily mask, nor attempt to hide their lewdness or their misery.

But who are those who make the streets their couch, and find a short repose from wretchedness at the doors of the opulent? These are strangers, wanderers, and orphans, whose circumstances are too humble to expect redress, and their distresses are too great even for pity. Their wretchedness excites rather horror. Some are without the covering even of rags, and others emaciated with disease; the world has disclaimed them; society turns its back upon their distress, and has given them up to nakedness and hunger. These poor shivering females have once seen happier days, and been flattered into beauty. They have been prostituted to the gay luxurious villain, and are now turned out to meet the severity of winter. Perhaps, now lying at the doors of their betrayers, they sue to wretches whose hearts are insensible, or debauchees who may curse, but will not relieve them.

Why, why was I born a man, and yet see the sufferings of wretches I cannot relieve! Poor houseless creatures! the world will give you reproaches, but will not give you relief. The slightest misfortunes of the great, the most imaginary uneasiness of the rich, are aggravated with all the power of eloquence, and held up to engage our attention and sympathetic sorrow. The poor weep unheeded, persecuted by every subordinate species of tyranny; and every law which gives others security, becomes an enemy to them.

Why was this heart of mine formed with so much sensibility? or why was not my fortune adapted to its impulse? Tenderness, without a capacity of relieving, only makes the man who feels it more wretched than the object which sues for assistance.

But let me turn from a scene of such distress to the sanctified hypocrite, who has been talking of virtue till the time of bed, and now steals out, to give a loose to his vices under the protection of midnight—vices more atrocious because he attempts to conceal them. See how he pants down the dark alley, and, with hastening steps, fears an acquaintance in every face! He has passed the whole day in company he hates, and now goes to prolong the night among company that as heartily hate him. May his vices be detected: may the morning rise upon his shame! Yet I wish to no purpose: villany, when detected, never gives up, but boldly adds impudence to imposture.

No. V.—*Saturday, November* 3, 1759.

UPON POLITICAL FRUGALITY.

FRUGALITY has ever been esteemed a virtue as well among Pagans as Christians: there have been even heroes who have practised it. However, we must acknowledge, that it is too modest a virtue, or, if you will, too obscure a one, to be essential to heroism; few heroes have been able to attain to such an height. Frugality agrees much better with politics; it seems to be the base and support, and, in a word, the inseparable companion of a just administration.

However this be, there is not, perhaps, in the world a people less fond of this virtue than the English; and of consequence there is not a nation more restless, more exposed to the uneasiness of life, or less capable of providing for particular happiness. We are taught to despise this virtue from our childhood; our education is improperly directed, and a man who has gone through the politest institutions is generally the person who is least acquainted with the wholesome precepts of frugality. We every day hear the elegance of taste, the magnificence of some, and the generosity of others, made the subject of our admiration and applause. All this we see represented, not as the end and recompense of labour and desert, but as the actual result of genius, as the mark of a noble and exalted mind.

In the midst of these praises bestowed on luxury, for which elegance and taste are but another name, perhaps it may be thought improper to plead the cause of frugality. It may be thought low, or vainly declamatory, to exhort our youth, from the follies of dress and of every other superfluity, to accustom themselves, even with mechanic meanness, to the simple necessaries of life. Such sort of instructions may appear antiquated; yet, however, they seem the foundations of all our virtues, and the most efficacious method of making mankind useful members of society. Unhappily, however, such discourses are not fashionable among us, and the fashion seems every day growing still more obsolete, since the press, and every other method of exhortation, seems disposed to talk of the luxuries of life as harmless enjoyments I remember, when a boy, to have remarked, that those who in school wore the finest clothes were pointed at as being conceited and proud. At present our little masters are taught to consider dress betimes, and they are regarded, even at school, with contempt, who do not appear as genteel as the rest. Education should teach us to become useful, sober, disinterested, and laborious members of society; but does it not at present point out a different path? It teaches us to multiply our wants, by which means we become more eager to possess, in order to dissipate; a greater charge to ourselves, and more useless or obnoxious to society.

If a youth happens to be possessed of more genius than fortune, he is early informed, that he ought to think of his advancement in the world—that he should labour to make himself pleasing to his superiors—that he should shun low company (by which is meant the company of his equals)—that he should rather live a little above than below his fortune—that he should think of becoming great: but he finds none to admonish him to become frugal—to persevere in one single design—to avoid every pleasure and all flattery, which, however seeming to conciliate the favour of his superiors, never conciliate their esteem. There are none to teach him, that the best way of becoming happy in himself, and useful to others, is to continue in the state in which fortune at first placed him, without making too hasty strides to advancement; that greatness may be attained, but should not be expected; and that they who most impatiently expect advancement, are seldom possessed of their wishes. He has few, I say, to teach him this lesson, or to moderate his youthful passions; yet this experience may say, that a young man, who but for six years of the early part of his life could seem divested of all his passions, would certainly make, or considerably increase, his fortune, and might indulge several of his favourite inclinations in manhood with the utmost security.

The efficaciousness of these means is sufficiently known and acknowledged; but as we are apt to connect a low idea with all our notions of frugality, the person who would persuade us to it might be accused of preaching up avarice.

Of all vices, however, against which morality dissuades, there is not one more undetermined than this of avarice. Misers are described by some as men divested of honour, sentiment, or humanity; but this is only an ideal picture, or the resemblance at least is found but in a few. In truth, they who are generally called misers are some of the very best members of society. The sober, the laborious, the attentive, the frugal, are thus styled by the gay, giddy, thoughtless, and extravagant. The first set of men do society all the good, and the latter all the evil, that is felt. Even the excesses of the first no way injure the commonwealth; those of the latter are the most injurious that can be conceived.

The ancient Romans, more rational than we in this particular, were very far from thus misplacing their admiration or praise: instead of regarding the practice of parsimony as low or vicious, they made it synonymous even with probity. They esteemed those virtues so inseparable, that the known expression of *Vir frugi* signified, at one and the same time, a sober and managing man, an honest man, and a man of substance.

The Scriptures, in a thousand places, praise economy; and it is everywhere distinguished from avarice. But, in spite of all its sacred dictates, a taste for vain pleasures and foolish expense is the ruling passion of the present times. Passion, did I call it? rather the madness which at once possesses the great and the little, the rich and the poor: even some are so intent upon acquiring the superfluities of life, that they sacrifice its necessaries in this foolish pursuit.

To attempt the entire abolition of luxury, as it would be impossible, so it is not my intent. The generality of mankind are too weak, too much slaves to custom and opinion, to resist the torrent of bad example. But if it be impossible to convert the multitude, those who have received a more extended education, who are enlightened and judicious, may find some hints on this subject useful. They may see some abuses, the suppression of which would by no means endanger public liberty; they may be directed to the abolition of some unnecessary expenses, which have no tendency to promote happiness or virtue, and which might be directed to better purposes. Our fireworks, our public feasts and entertainments, our entries of ambassadors, &c.—what mummery all this! what childish pageants! what millions are sacrificed in paying tribute to custom! what an unnecessary charge at times when we are pressed with real want, which cannot be satisfied without burdening the poor!

Were such suppressed entirely, not a single creature in the state would have the least cause to mourn their suppression, and many might be eased of a load they now feel lying heavily upon them. If this were put in practice, it would agree with the advice of a sensible writer of Sweden, who, in the *Gazette de France*, 1753, thus expressed himself on that subject: "It were sincerely to be wished," says he, "that the custom were established amongst us, that in all events which cause a public joy we made our exultations conspicuous only by acts useful to society. We should then quickly see many useful monuments of our reason, which would much better perpetuate the memory of things worthy of being transmitted to posterity, and would be much more glorious to humanity, than all those tumultuous preparations of feasts, entertainments, and other rejoicings used upon such occasions."

The same proposal was long before confirmed by a Chinese emperor, who lived in the last century, who, upon an occasion of extraordinary joy, forbade his subjects to make the usual illuminations, either with a design of sparing their substance, or of turning them to some more durable indications of joy, more glorious for him and more advantageous to his people.

After such instances of political frugality, can we then continue to blame the Dutch ambassador at a certain court, who receiving at his departure the portrait of the king, enriched with diamonds, asked what this fine thing might be worth? Being told that it might amount to about two thousand pounds,—"And why," cries he, cannot his majesty keep the picture and give me the money?" The simplicity may be ridiculed at first; but when we come to examine it more closely, men of sense will at once confess that he had reason in what he said, and that a purse of two thousand guineas is much more serviceable than a picture.

Should we follow the same method of state frugality in other respects, what numberless savings might not be the result! How many possibilities of saving in the administration of justice, which now burdens the subject, and enriches some members of society, who are useful only from its corruption!

It were to be wished, that they who govern kingdoms would imitate artisans. When at London a new stuff has been invented, it is immediately counterfeited in France. How happy were it for society if a first minister would be equally solicitous to transplant the useful laws of other countries into his own. We are arrived at a perfect imitation of porcelain; let us endeavour to imitate the good to society that our neighbours are found to practise, and let our neighbours also imitate those parts of duty in which we excel.

There are some men who, in their garden, attempt to raise those fruits which nature has adapted only to the sultry climates beneath the Line. We have at our very doors a thousand laws and customs infinitely useful: these are the fruits we should endeavour to transplant—these the exotics that would speedily become naturalized to the soil. They might grow in every climate, and benefit every possessor.

The best and the most useful laws I have ever seen are generally practised in Holland. When two men are determined to go to law with each other, they are first obliged to go before the reconciling judges, called the peace-makers. If the parties come attended with an advocate, or a solicitor, they are obliged to retire, as we take fuel from the fire we are desirous of extinguishing.

The peace-makers then begin advising the parties, by assuring them, that it is the height of folly to waste their substance, and make themselves mutually miserable, by having recourse to the tribunals of justice; "follow but our direction, and we will accommodate matters without any expense to either." If the rage of debate is too strong upon either party, they are remitted back for another day, in order that time may soften their tempers, and produce a reconciliation. They are thus sent for twice or thrice: if their folly happens to be incurable, they are permitted to go to law, and, as we give up to amputation such members as cannot be cured by art, justice is permitted to take its course.

It is unnecessary to make here long declamations, or calculate what society would save were this law adopted. I am sensible that the man who advises any reformation only serves to make himself ridiculous. What! mankind will be apt to say, adopt the customs of countries that have not so much real liberty as our own? our present customs, what are they to any man? we are very happy under them: this must be a very pleasant fellow, who attempts to make us happier than we already are! Does he not know that abuses are the patrimony of a great part of the nation? Why deprive us of a malady by which such numbers find their account? This, I must own, is an argument to which I have nothing to reply.

What numberless savings might there not be made in both arts and commerce, particularly in the liberty of exercising trade, without the necessary prerequisites of freedom! Such useless obstructions have crept into every state, from a spirit of monopoly, a narrow selfish spirit of gain, without the least attention to general society. Such a clog upon industry frequently drives the poor from labour, and reduces them by degrees to a state of hopeless indigence. We have already a more than sufficient repugnance to labour; we should by no means increase the obstacles, or make excuses in a state for idleness. Such faults have ever crept into a state under wrong or needy administrations.

Exclusive of the masters, there are numberless faulty expenses among the workmen,—clubs, garnishes, freedoms, and such like impositions, which are not too minute even for law to take notice of, and which should be abolished without mercy, since they are ever the inlets to excess and idleness, and are the parent of all those outrages which naturally fall upon the more useful part of society. In the towns and countries I have seen I never saw a city or village yet, whose miseries were not in proportion to the number of its public-houses. In Rotterdam, you may go through eight or ten streets without finding a public-house. In Antwerp almost every second house seems an alehouse. In the one city, all wears the appearance of happiness and warm affluence; in the other, the young fellows walk about the streets in shabby finery, their fathers sit at the door darning or knitting stockings while their ports are filled with dunghills.

Alehouses are ever an occasion of debauchery and excess, and, either in a religious or political light, it would be our highest interest to have the greatest part of them suppressed. They should be put under laws of not continuing open beyond a certain hour, and harbouring only proper persons. These rules, it may be said, will diminish the necessary taxes; but this is false reasoning, since what was consumed in debauchery abroad would, if such a regulation took place, be more justly, and perhaps more equitably for the workman's family, spent at home; and this cheaper to them, and without loss of time. On the other hand, our alehouses being ever open, interrupt business; the workman is never certain who frequents them, nor can the master be sure of having what was begun finished at a convenient time.

An habit of frugality among the lower orders of mankind is much more beneficial to society than the unreflecting might imagine. The pawnbroker, the attorney, and other pests of society, might, by proper management, be turned into serviceable members; and were these trades abolished, it is possible the same avarice that conducts the one, or the same chicanery that characterises the other, might, by proper regulations, be converted into frugality and commendable prudence.

But some who have made the eulogium of luxury have represented it as the natural consequence of every country that is become rich. Did we not employ our extraordinary wealth in superfluities, say they, what other means would there be to employ it in? To which it may be answered, if frugality were established in the state, if our expenses were laid out rather in the necessaries than the superfluities of life, there might be fewer wants, and even fewer pleasures, but infinitely more happiness. The rich and the great would be better able to satisfy their creditors; they would be better able to marry their children, and, instead of one marriage at present, there might be two, if such regulations took place.

The imaginary calls of vanity, which in reality contribute nothing to our real felicity, would not then be attended to, while the real calls of nature might be always and universally supplied. The difference of employment in the subject what, in reality, produces the good of society. If the subject be engaged in providing only the luxuries, the necessaries must be deficient in proportion. If, neglecting the produce of our own country, our minds are set upon the productions of another, we increase our wants, but not our means; and every new imported delicacy for our tables, or ornament in our equipage, is a tax upon the poor.

The true interest of every government is to cultivate the necessaries, by which is always meant every happiness our own country can produce; and suppress all the luxuries, by which is meant, on the other hand, every happiness imported from abroad. Commerce has, therefore, its bounds; and every new import, instead of receiving encouragement, should be first examined whether it be conducive to the interest of society.

Among the many publications with which the press is every day burdened, I have often wondered why we never had, as in other countries, an Economical Journal, which might at once direct to all the useful discoveries in other countries, and spread those of our own. As other journals serve to amuse the learned, or, what is more often the case, to make them quarrel—while they only serve to give us the history of the mischievous world, for so I call our warriors, or the idle world, for so may the learned be called,—they never trouble their heads about the most useful part of mankind, our peasants and our artisans. Were such a work carried into execution, with proper management and just direction, it might serve as a repository for every useful improvement, and increase that knowledge which learning often serves to confound.

Sweden seems the only country where the science of economy appears to have fixed its empire. In other countries it is cultivated only by a few admirers, or by societies which have not received sufficient sanction to become completely useful; but here there is founded a royal academy destined to this purpose only, composed of the most learned and powerful members of the state—an academy which declines every thing which only terminates in amusement, erudition, or curiosity; and admits only of observations tending to illustrate husbandry, agriculture, and every real physical improvement. In this country nothing is left to private rapacity; but every improvement is immediately diffused, and its inventor immediately recompensed by the state. Happy were it so in other countries! By this means every impostor would be prevented from ruining or deceiving the public with pretended discoveries or nostrums; and every real inventor would not, by this means, suffer the inconveniences of suspicion.

In short, the economy equally unknown to the prodigal and avaricious seems to be a just mean between both extremes; and to a transgression of this at present decried virtue it is that we are to attribute a great part of the evils which infest society. A taste for superfluity, amusement, and pleasure bring effeminacy, idleness, and expense in their train. But a thirst of riches is always proportioned to our debauchery, and the greatest prodigal is too frequently found to be the greatest miser: so that the vices which seem the most opposite are frequently found to produce each other; and, to avoid both, it is only necessary to be frugal.

Virtus est medium vitiorum et utrinque reductum.—HOR.

A REVERIE.

SCARCELY a day passes in which we do not hear compliments paid to Dryden, Pope, and other writers of the last age, while not a month comes forward that is not loaded with invectives against the writers of this. Strange, that our critics should be fond of giving their favours to those who are insensible of the obligation, and their dislike to those who, of all mankind, are most apt to retaliate the injury.

Even though our present writers had not equal merit with their predecessors, it would be politic to use them with ceremony. Every compliment paid them would be more agreeable, in proportion as they least deserved it. Tell a lady with a handsome face that she is pretty, she only thinks it her due; it is what she has heard a thousand times before from others, and disregards the compliment: but assure a lady the cut of whose visage is something more plain that she looks killing to-day, she instantly bridles up, and feels the force of the well-timed flattery the whole day after. Compliments which we think are deserved, we accept only as debts, with indifference; but those which conscience informs us we do not merit, we receive with the same gratitude that we do favours given away.

Our gentlemen, however, who preside at the distribution of literary fame, seem resolved to part with praise neither from motives of justice or generosity: one would think, when they take pen in hand, that it was only to blot reputations, and to put their seals to the packet which consigns every new-born effort to oblivion.

Yet, notwithstanding the republic of letters hangs at present so feebly together—though those friendships which once promoted literary fame seem now to be discontinued—though every writer who now draws the quill seems to aim at profit, as well as applause,—many among them are probably laying in stores for immortality, and are provided with a sufficient stock of reputation to last the whole journey.

As I was indulging these reflections, in order to eke out the present page, I could not avoid pursuing the metaphor of going a journey in my imagination, and formed the following Reverie, too wild for allegory, and too regular for a dream.

I fancied myself placed in the yard of a large inn, in which there were an infinite number of waggons and stage-coaches, attended by fellows who either invited the company to take their places, or were busied in packing their baggage. Each vehicle had its inscription, showing the place of its destination. On one I could read, The Pleasure Stage Coach; on another, The Waggon of Industry; on a third, The Vanity Whim; and on a fourth, The Landau of Riches. I had some inclination to step into each of these, one after another; but, I know not by what means, I passed them by, and at last fixed my eye upon a small carriage, Berlin fashion, which seemed the most convenient vehicle at a distance in the world; and upon my nearer approach found it to be The Fame Machine.

I instantly made up to the coachman, whom I found to be an affable and seemingly good-natured fellow. He informed me, that he had but a few days ago returned from the Temple of Fame, to which he had been carrying Addison, Swift, Pope, Steele, Congreve, and Colley Cibber; that they made but indifferent company by the way; and that he once or twice was going to empty his berlin of the whole cargo: "However," says he, "I got them all safe home, with no other damage than a black eye, which Colley gave Mr. Pope, and am now returned for another coachful."—"If that be all, friend," said I, "and if you are in want of company, I'll make one with all my heart. Open the door: I hope the machine rides easy."—"Oh, for that, sir, extremely easy." But still keeping the door shut, and measuring me with his eye, "Pray, sir, have you no luggage? You seem to be a good-natured sort of a gentleman; but I don't find you have got any luggage, and I never permit any to travel with me but such as have something valuable to pay for coach-hire." Examining my pockets, I own I was not a little disconcerted at this unexpected rebuff; but considering that I carried a number of the BEE under my arm, I was resolved to open it in his eyes, and dazzle him with the splendour of the page. He read the title and contents, however, without any emotion, and assured me he had never heard of it before. "In short, friend," said he, now losing all his former respect, "you must not come in: I expect better passengers; but as you seem a harmless creature, perhaps, if there be room left, I may let you ride a while for charity."

I now took my stand by the coachman at the door; and since I could not command a seat, was resolved to be as useful as possible, and earn by my assiduity what I could not by my merit.

The next that presented for a place was a most whimsical figure indeed. He was hung round with papers of his own composing, not unlike those who sing ballads in the streets, and came dancing up to the door with all the confidence of instant admittance. The volubility of his motion and address prevented my being able to read more of his cargo than the word Inspector, which was written in great letters at the top of some of the papers. He opened the coach-door himself without any ceremony, and was just slipping in, when the coachman, with as little ceremony, pulled him back. Our figure seemed perfectly angry at this repulse, and demanded gentleman's satisfaction. "Lord, sir!" replied the coachman, "instead of proper luggage, by your bulk you seem loaded for a West India voyage. You are big enough, with all your papers, to crack twenty stage-coaches. Excuse me, indeed, sir, for you must not enter." Our figure now began to expostulate: he assured the coachman, that though his baggage seemed so bulky, it was perfectly light, and that he would be contented with the smallest corner of room. But Jehu was inflexible, and the carrier of the Inspectors was sent to dance back again, with all his papers fluttering in the wind. We expected to have no more trouble from this quarter, when, in a few minutes, the same figure changed his appearance, like harlequin upon the stage, and with the same confidence again made his approaches, dressed in lace, and carrying nothing but a nosegay. Upon coming nearer, he thrust the nosegay to the coachman's nose, grasped the brass, and seemed now resolved to enter by violence. I found the struggle soon begin to grow hot, and the coachman, who was a little old, unable to continue the contest; so, in order to ingratiate myself, I stepped in to his assistance, and our united efforts sent our literary Proteus, though worsted, unconquered still. clear oft, dancing a rigadoon, and smelling to his own nosegay.

The person who after him appeared as candidate for a place in the stage came up with an air not quite so confident, but somewhat, however, theatrical; and, instead of entering, made the coachman a very low bow, which the other returned, and desired to see his baggage; upon which he instantly produced some farces, a tragedy, and other miscellany productions. The coachman, casting his eye upon the cargo, assured him, at present he could not possibly have a place, but hoped in time he might aspire to one, as he seemed to have read in the book of nature, without a careful perusal of which none ever found entrance at the Temple of Fame. "What!" replied the disappointed poet, "shall my tragedy, in which I have vindicated the cause of liberty and virtue ——"—"Follow nature," returned the other, "and never expect to find lasting fame by topics which only please from their popularity. Had you been first in the cause of freedom, or praised in virtue more than an empty name, it is possible you might have gained admittance; but at present I beg, sir, you will stand aside for another gentleman whom I see approaching."

This was a very grave personage, whom at some distance I took for one of the most reserved, and even disagreeable, figures I had seen; but as he approached his appearance improved, and when I could distinguish him thoroughly, I perceived that, in spite of the severity of his brow, he had one of the most good-natured countenances that could be imagined. Upon coming to open the stage-door, he lifted a parcel of folios into the seat before him, but our inquisitorial coachman at once shoved them out again. "What! not take in my Dictionary?" exclaimed the other in a rage. "Be patient, sir," replied the coachman: "I have drove a coach, man and boy, these two thousand years; but I do not remember to have carried above one dictionary during the whole time. That little book which I perceive peeping from one of your pockets, may I presume to ask what it contains?"—"A mere trifle," replied the author; "it is called the Rambler."—"The Rambler!" says the coachman: "I beg, sir, you'll take your place; I have heard our ladies in the court of Apollo frequently mention it with rapture; and Clio, who happens to be a little grave, has been heard to prefer it to the Spectator; though others have observed, that the reflections, by being refined, sometimes become minute."

This grave gentleman was scarcely seated, when another, whose appearance was something more modern, seemed willing to enter, yet afraid to ask. He carried in his hand a bundle of essays, of which the coachman was curious enough to inquire the contents. "These," replied the gentleman, "are rhapsodies against the religion of my country."—"And how can you expect to come into my coach, after thus choosing the wrong side of the question?"—"Ay, but I am right," replied the other; "and if you give me leave, I shall, in a few minutes, state the argument."—"Right or wrong," said the coachman, "he who disturbs religion is a blockhead, and he shall never travel in a coach of mine."—"If, then," said the gentleman, mustering up all his courage, "if I am not to have admittance as an essayist, I hope I shall not be repulsed as an historian; the last volume of my history met with applause."—"Yes," replied the coachman, "but I have heard only the first approved at the Temple of Fame; and as I see you have it about you, enter, without farther ceremony." My attention was now diverted to a crowd who were pushing forward a person that seemed more inclined to the Stage-coach of Riches; but by their means he was driven forward to the same machine, which he, however, seemed heartily to despise. Impelled, however, by their solicitations, he steps up, flourishing a voluminous history, and demanding admittance. "Sir, I have formerly heard your name mentioned," says the coachman, "but never as an historian. Is there no other work upon which you may claim a place?"—"None," replied the other, "except a romance; but this is a work of too trifling a nature to claim future attention."—"You mistake," says the inquisitor; "a well-written romance is no such easy task as is generally imagined. I remember formerly to have carried Cervantes and Segrais; and if you think fit, you may enter."

Upon our three literary travellers coming into the same coach, I listened attentively to hear what might be the conversation that passed upon this extraordinary occasion; when, instead of agreeable or entertaining dialogue, I found them grumbling at each other, and each seemed discontented with his companions. Strange! thought I to myself, that they who are thus born to enlighten the world, should still preserve the narrow prejudices of childhood, and, by disagreeing, make even the highest merit ridiculous. Were the learned and the wise to unite against the dunces of society, instead of sometimes siding into opposite parties with them, they might throw a lustre upon each other's reputation, and teach every rank of subordinate merit, if not to admire, at least not to avow dislike.

In the midst of these reflections I perceived the coachman, unmindful of me, had now mounted the box. Several were approaching to be taken in whose pretensions I was sensible were very just; I therefore desired him to stop, and take in more passengers: but he replied, as he had now mounted the box, it would be improper to come down; but that he should take them all, one after the other, when he should return. So he drove away; and for myself, as I could not get in, I mounted behind, in order to hear the conversation on the way.

(*To be continued.*)

A WORD OR TWO ON THE LATE FARCE CALLED "HIGH LIFE BELOW STAIRS."

JUST as I had expected before I saw this farce, I found it formed on too narrow a plan to afford a pleasing variety. The sameness of the humour in every scene could not at last fail of being disagreeable. The poor affecting the manners of the rich might be carried on through one character, or two at the most, with great propriety; but to have almost every personage on the scene almost of the same character, and reflecting the follies of each other, was unartful in the poet to the last degree.

The scene was also almost a continuation of the same absurdity, and my Lord Duke and Sir Harry (two footmen who assume these characters) have nothing else to do but to talk like their masters, and are only introduced to speak and to show themselves. Thus, as there is a sameness of character, there is a barrenness of incident, which, by a very small share of address, the poet might have easily avoided.

From a conformity to critic rules, which perhaps on the whole have done more harm than good, our author has sacrificed all the vivacity of the dialogue to nature; and though he makes his characters talk like servants, they are seldom absurd enough, or lively enough, to make us merry. Though he is always natural, he happens seldom to be humorous.

The satire was well intended, if we regard it as being masters ourselves; but probably a philosopher would rejoice in that liberty which Englishmen give their domestics; and for my own part, I cannot avoid being pleased at the happiness of those poor creatures, who in some measure contribute to mine. The Athenians, the politest and best-natured people upon earth, were the kindest to their slaves; and if a person may judge who has seen the world, our English servants are the best treated, because the generality of our English gentlemen are the politest under the sun.

But not to lift my feeble voice among the pack of critics, who probably have no other occupation but that of cutting up everything new, I must own there are one or two scenes that are fine satire, and sufficiently humorous; particularly the first interview between the two footmen, which at once ridicules the manners of the great, and the absurdity of their imitators.

Whatever defects there might be in the composition, there were none in the action; in this the performers showed more humour than I had fancied them capable of. Mr. Palmer and Mr. King were entirely what they desired to represent; and Mrs. Clive—(but what need I talk of her, since, without the least exaggeration, she has more true humour than any other actor or actress upon the English or any other stage I have seen)—

she, I say, did the part all the justice it was capable of. And, upon the whole, a farce which has only this to recommend it, that the author took his plan from the volume of nature, by the sprightly manner in which it was performed, was, for one night, a tolerable entertainment. This much may be said in its vindication, that people of fashion seemed more pleased in the representation than the subordinate ranks of people.

UPON UNFORTUNATE MERIT.

EVERY age seems to have its favourite pursuits, which serve to amuse the idle and to relieve the attention of the industrious. Happy the man who is born excellent in the pursuit in vogue, and whose genius seems adapted to the times in which he lives. How many do we see who might have excelled in arts or sciences, and who seem furnished with talents equal to the greatest discoveries, had the road not been already beaten by their predecessors, and nothing left for them except trifles to discover, while others of very moderate abilities become famous, because happening to be first in the reigning pursuit!

Thus, at the renewal of letters in Europe the taste was not to compose new books, but to comment on the old ones. It was not to be expected that new books should be written, when there were so many of the ancients either not known or not understood. It was not reasonable to attempt new conquests, while they had such an extensive region lying waste for want of cultivation. At that period criticism and erudition were the reigning studies of the times, and he who had only an inventive genius might have languished in hopeless obscurity. When the writers of antiquity were sufficiently explained and known, the learned set about imitating them: hence proceeded the number of Latin orators, poets, and historians, in the reigns of Clement the Seventh and Alexander the Sixth. This passion for antiquity lasted for many years, to the utter exclusion of every other pursuit, till some began to find, that those works which were imitated from nature were more like the writings of antiquity, than even those written in express imitation. It was then modern language began to be cultivated with assiduity, and our poets and orators poured forth their wonders upon the world.

As writers become more numerous, it is natural for readers to become more indolent; whence must necessarily arise a desire of attaining knowledge with the greatest possible ease. No science or art offers its instruction and amusement in so obvious a manner as statuary and painting. Hence we see that a desire of cultivating those arts generally attends the decline of science. Thus the finest statues and the most beautiful paintings of antiquity preceded but a little the absolute decay of every other science. The statues of Antoninus, Commodus, and their contemporaries are the finest productions of the chisel, and appeared but just before learning was destroyed by comment, criticism, and barbarous invasions.

What happened in Rome may probably be the case with us at home. Our nobility are now more solicitous in patronising painters and sculptors than those of any other polite profession; and from the lord, who has his gallery, down to the apprentice, who has his twopenny copperplate, all are admirers of this art. The great, by their caresses, seem insensible to all other merit but that of the pencil; and the vulgar buy every book rather from the excellence of the sculptor than the writer.

How happy were it now, if men of real excellence in that profession were to arise! Were the painters of Italy now to appear, who once wandered like beggars from one city to another, and produce their almost breathing figures, what rewards might they not expect! But many of them lived without rewards, and therefore rewards alone will never produce their equals. We have often found the great exert themselves, not only without promotion, but in spite of opposition. We have often found them flourishing, like medical plants, in a region of savageness and barbarity, their excellence unknown, and their virtues unheeded.

They who have seen the paintings of

Caravagio are sensible of the surprising impression they make,—bold, swelling, terrible to the last degree; all seems animated, and speaks him among the foremost of his profession; yet this man's fortune and his fame seemed ever in opposition to each other.

Unknowing how to flatter the great, he was driven from city to city in the utmost indigence, and might truly be said to paint for his bread.

Having one day insulted a person of distinction, who refused to pay him all the respect which he thought his due, he was obliged to leave Rome and travel on foot, his usual method of going his journeys, down into the country, without either money or friends to subsist him.

After he had travelled in this manner as long as his strength would permit, faint with famine and fatigue, he at last called at an obscure inn by the wayside. The host knew, by the appearance of his guest, his indifferent circumstances, and refused to furnish him a dinner without previous payment.

As Caravagio was entirely destitute of money, he took down the innkeeper's sign, and painted it anew for his dinner.

Thus refreshed, he proceeded on his journey, and left the innkeeper not quite satisfied with this method of payment. Some company of distinction, however, coming soon after, and struck with the beauty of the new sign, bought it at an advanced price, and astonished the innkeeper with their generosity: he was resolved, therefore, to get as many signs as possible drawn by the same artist, as he found he could sell them to good advantage; and accordingly set out after Caravagio, in order to bring him back. It was nightfall before he came up to the place where the unfortunate Caravagio lay dead by the roadside, overcome by fatigue, resentment, and despair.

No. VI.—*Saturday, November* 10, 1759.

ON EDUCATION.

To the Author of the Bee.

SIR,—As few subjects are more interesting to society, so few have been more frequently written upon, than the education of youth. Yet is it not a little surprising, that it should have been treated almost by all in a declamatory manner? They have insisted largely on the advantages that result from it, both to the individual and to society, and have expatiated in the praise of what no one has ever been so hardy as to call in question.

Instead of giving us fine but empty harangues upon this subject, instead of indulging each his particular and whimsical system, it had been much better if the writers on this subject had treated it in a more scientific manner, repressed all the sallies of imagination, and given us the result of their observations with didactic simplicity. Upon this subject the smallest errors are of the most dangerous consequence; and the author should venture the imputation of stupidity upon a topic, where his slightest deviations may tend to injure the rising generation.

I shall, therefore, throw out a few thoughts upon this subject, which have not been attended to by others, and shall dismiss all attempts to please, while I study only instruction.

The manner in which our youth of London are at present educated is, some in free schools in the city, but the far greater number in boarding schools about town. The parent justly consults the health of his child, and finds that an education in the country tends to promote this much more than a continuance in the town. Thus far they are right: if there were a possibility of having even our free schools kept a little out of town, it would certainly conduce to the health and vigour of perhaps the mind as well as of the body. It may be thought whimsical, but it is truth,—I have found by experience, that they who have spent all their lives in cities contract not only an effeminacy of habit, but even of thinking.

But when I have said that the boarding schools are preferable to free schools, as being in the country, this is certainly the only advantage I can allow them; otherwise it is impossible to conceive the ignorance of those who take upon them the important trust of education. Is any man unfit for any of the professions? he finds his last resource in setting up school.

Do any become bankrupts in trade? they still set up a boarding school, and drive a trade this way, when all others fail: nay, I have been told of butchers and barbers who have turned schoolmasters; and, more surprising still, made fortunes in their new professions.

Could we think ourselves in a country of civilized people—could it be conceived that we have any regard for posterity—when such are permitted to take the charge of the morals, genius, and health of those dear little pledges, who may one day be the guardians of the liberties of Europe, and who may serve as the honour and bulwark of their aged parents? The care of our children, is it below the state? is it fit to indulge the caprice of the ignorant with the disposal of their children in this particular? For the state to take the charge of all its children, as in Persia or Sparta, might at present be inconvenient; but surely with great ease it might cast an eye to their instructors. Of all members of society, I do not know a more useful or a more honourable one than a schoolmaster; at the same time that I do not see any more generally despised, or whose talents are so ill rewarded.

Were the salaries of schoolmasters to be augmented from a diminution of useless sinecures, how might it turn to the advantage of this people—a people whom, without flattery, I may in other respects term the wisest and greatest upon earth! But, while I would reward the deserving, I would dismiss those utterly unqualified for their employment: in short, I would make the business of a schoolmaster every way more respectable, by increasing their salaries, and admitting only men of proper abilities.

There are already schoolmasters appointed, and they have some small salaries; but where at present there is but one schoolmaster appointed, there should at least be two; and wherever the salary is at present twenty pounds, it should be an hundred. Do we give immoderate benefices to those who instruct ourselves, and shall we deny even subsistence to those who instruct our children? Every member of society should be paid in proportion as he is necessary: and I will be bold enough to say, that schoolmasters in a state are more necessary than clergymen, as children stand in more need of instruction than their parents.

But instead of this, as I have already observed, we send them to board in the country to the most ignorant set of men that can be imagined. But lest the ignorance of the master be not sufficient, the child is generally consigned to the usher. This is generally some poor needy animal, little superior to a footman either in learning or spirit, invited to his place by an advertisement, and kept there merely from his being of a complying disposition, and making the children fond of him. "You give your child to be educated to a slave," says a philosopher to a rich man: "instead of one slave, you will then have two."

It were well, however, if parents, upon fixing their children in one of these houses, would examine the abilities of the usher as well as of the master; for, whatever they are told to the contrary, the usher is generally the person most employed in their education. If, then, a gentleman upon putting out his son to one of these houses, sees the usher disregarded by the master, he may depend upon it, that he is equally disregarded by the boys; the truth is, in spite of all their endeavours to please, they are generally the laughing-stock of the school. Every trick is played upon the usher; the oddity of his manners, his dress, or his language, is a fund of eternal ridicule; the master himself now and then cannot avoid joining in the laugh, and the poor wretch, eternally resenting this ill usage, seems to live in a state of war with all the family. This is a very proper person, is it not, to give children a relish for learning? They must esteem learning very much when they see its professors used with such ceremony. If the usher be despised, the father may be assured his child will never be properly instructed.

But let me suppose that there are some schools without these inconveniences,—where the master and ushers are men of learning, reputation, and assiduity. If there are to be found such, they cannot be prized in a state sufficiently. A boy will learn more true wisdom in a public school in a year, than by private education in five. It is not from masters, but from their equals, youth learn a knowledge of the world: the little tricks they play each other, the punishment that frequently attends the commission, is a just picture of the great world, and all the ways of men are practised in a public school in miniature. It is true a child is early made acquainted with some vices in a school; but it is better to know these when a boy, than be first taught them when a man, for their novelty then may have irresistible charms.

In a public education boys early learn temperance; and if the parents and friends would give them less money upon their usual visits, it would be much to their advantage, since it may justly be said, that a great part of their disorders arise from surfeit,—*plus occidit gula quam gladius.* And now I am come to the article of health, it may not be amiss to observe, that Mr. Locke and some others have advised, that children should be inured to cold, to fatigue, and hardship, from their youth; but Mr. Locke was but an indifferent physician. Habit, I grant, has great influence over our constitutions; but we have not precise ideas upon this subject.

We know that among savages, and even among our peasants, there are found children born with such constitutions, that they cross rivers by swimming, endure cold, thirst, hunger, and want of sleep, to a surprising degree; that when they happen to fall sick, they are cured, without the help of medicine, by nature alone. Such examples are adduced, to persuade us to imitate their manner of education, and accustom ourselves betimes to support the same fatigues. But had these gentlemen considered, first, that those savages and peasants are generally not so long lived as they who have led a more indolent life; secondly, that the more laborious the life is, the less populous is the country: had they considered that what physicians call the *stamina vitæ* by fatigue and labour become rigid, and thus anticipate old age; that the number who survive those rude trials bears no proportion to those who die in the experiment: had these things been properly considered, they would not have thus extolled an education begun in fatigue and hardships. Peter the Great, willing to inure the children of his seamen to a life of hardship, ordered that they should drink only sea-water; but they unfortunately all died under the experiment.

But while I would exclude all unnecessary labours, yet still I would recommend temperance in the highest degree. No luxurious dishes with high seasoning, nothing given children to force an appetite, as little sugared or salted provisions as possible, though never so pleasing; but milk, morning and night, should be their constant food. This diet would make them more healthy than any of those slops that are usually cooked by the mistress of a boarding school; besides, it corrects any consumptive habits, not unfrequently found amongst the children of city parents.

As boys should be educated with temperance, so the first, greatest lesson that should be taught them is, to admire frugality. It is by the exercise of this virtue alone they can ever expect to be useful members of society. It is true lectures continually repeated upon this subject may make some boys, when they grow up, run into an extreme, and become misers; but it were well had we more misers than we have among us. I know few characters more useful in society; for a man's having a larger or smaller share of money lying useless by him no way injures the commonwealth: since, should every miser now exhaust his stores, this might make gold more plenty, but it would not increase the commodities or pleasures of life; they would still remain as they are at present: it matters not, therefore, whether men are misers or not, if they be only frugal, laborious, and fill the station they have chosen. If they deny themselves the necessaries of life, society is no way injured by their folly.

Instead, therefore, of romances, which praise young men of spirit, who go through a variety of adventures, and, at last, conclude a life of dissipation, folly, and extravagance, in riches and matrimony, there should be some men of wit employed to compose books that might equally interest the passions of our youth; where such an one might be praised for having resisted allurements when young, and how he, at last, became lord mayor—how he was married to a lady of great sense, fortune, and beauty: to be as explicit as possible, the old story of Whittington, were his cat left out, might be more serviceable to the tender mind than either Tom Jones, Joseph Andrews, or an hundred others, where frugality is the only good quality the hero is not possessed of. Were our schoolmasters, if any of them had sense enough to draw up such a work, thus employed, it would be much more serviceable to their pupils than all the grammars and dictionaries they may publish these ten years.

Children should early be instructed in the arts from which they would afterwards draw the greatest advantages. When the wonders of nature are never exposed to our view, we have no great desire to become acquainted with those parts of learning which pretend to account for the phenomena. One of the ancients complains, that as soon as young men have left school, and are obliged to converse in the world, they fancy themselves transported into a new region: "Ut cum in forum venerint existiment se in aliam terrarum orbem delatos." We should early, therefore, instruct them in the experiments, if I may so express it, of knowledge, and leave to maturer age the accounting for the causes. But instead of that, when boys begin natural philosophy in colleges, they have not the least curiosity for those parts of the science which are proposed for their instruction; they have never before seen the phenomena, and consequently have no curiosity to learn the reasons. Might natural philosophy, therefore, be made their pastime in school, by this means it would in college become their amusement.

In several of the machines now in use there would be ample field both for instruction and amusement: the different sorts of the phosphorus, the artificial pyrites, magnetism, electricity, the experiments upon the rarefaction and weight of the air, and those upon elastic bodies, might employ their idle hours, and none should be called from play to see such experiments but such as thought proper. At first, then, it would be sufficient if the instruments, and the effects of their combination, were only shown; the causes should be deferred to a maturer age, or to those times when natural curiosity prompts us to discover the wonders of nature. Man is placed in this world as a spectator; when he is tired with wondering at all the novelties about him, and not till then, does he desire to be made acquainted with the causes that create those wonders.

What I have observed with regard to natural philosophy, I would extend to every other science whatsoever. We should teach them as many of the facts as were possible, and defer the causes until they seemed of themselves desirous of knowing them. A mind thus leaving school stored with all the simple experiences of science, would be the fittest in the world for the college course; and though such a youth might not appear so bright, or so talkative, as those who had learned the real principles and causes of some of the sciences, yet he would make a wiser man, and would retain a more lasting passion for letters, than he who was early burdened with the disagreeable institution of effect and cause.

In history, such stories alone should be laid before them as might catch the imagination: instead of this, they are too frequently obliged to toil through the four empires, as they are called, where their memories are burdened by a number of disgusting names, that destroy all their future relish for our best historians, who may be termed the truest teachers of wisdom.

Every species of flattery should be carefully avoided: a boy who happens to say a sprightly thing is generally applauded so much, that he happens to continue a coxcomb sometimes all his life after. He is reputed a wit at fourteen, and becomes a blockhead at twenty. Nurses, footmen, and such, should therefore be driven away as much as possible. I was even going to add, that the mother herself should stifle her pleasure or her vanity, when little master happens to say a good or smart thing. Those modest lubberly boys who seem to want spirit generally go through their business with more ease to themselves and more satisfaction to their instructors.

There has of late a gentleman appeared, who thinks the study of rhetoric essential to a perfect education. That bold male eloquence, which often without pleasing convinces, is generally destroyed by such institutions. Convincing eloquence, however, is infinitely more serviceable to its possessor than the most florid harangue or the most pathetic tones that can be imagined; and the man who is thoroughly convinced himself, who understands his subject and the language he speaks in, will be more apt to silence opposition, than he who studies the force of his periods, and fills our ears with sounds, while our minds are destitute of conviction.

It was reckoned the fault of the orators at the decline of the Roman empire, when they had been long instructed by rhetoricians, that their periods were so harmonious, as that they could be sung as well as spoken. What a ridiculous figure must one of these gentlemen cut, thus measuring syllables, and weighing words, when he should plead the cause of his client! Two architects were once candidates for the building a certain temple at Athens: the first harangued the crowd very learnedly upon the different orders of architecture, and showed them in what manner the temple should be built; the other, who got up to speak after him, only observed, that what his brother had spoken he could do; and thus he at once gained his cause.

To teach men to be orators, is little less than to teach them to be poets; and for my part, I should have too great a regard for my child, to wish him a manor only in a bookseller's shop.

Another passion which the present age is apt to run into is to make children learn all things,—the languages, the sciences, music, the exercises, and painting. Thus the child soon becomes a *talker* in all, but a *master* in none. He thus acquires a superficial fondness for everything, and only shows his ignorance when he attempts to exhibit his skill.

As I deliver my thoughts without method or connexion, so the reader must not be surprised to find me once more addressing schoolmasters on the present method of teaching the learned languages, which is commonly by literal translations. I would ask such, if they were to travel a journey, whether those parts of the road in which they found the greatest difficulties would not be most strongly remembered? Boys who, if I may continue the allusion, gallop through one of the ancients with the assistance of a translation can have but a very slight acquaintance either with the author or his language. It is by the exercise of the mind alone that a language is learned; but a literal translation, on the opposite page, leaves no exercise for the memory at all. The boy will not be at the fatigue of remembering, when his doubts are at once satisfied by a glance of the eye; whereas, were every word to be sought from a dictionary, the learner would attempt to remember, in order to save him the trouble of looking out for it for the future.

To continue in the same pedantic strain, though no schoolmaster, of all the various grammars now taught in schools about town I would recommend only the old common one; I have forgot whether Lilly's, or an emendation of him. The others may be improvements; but such improvements seem to me only mere grammatical niceties, no way influencing the learner, but perhaps loading him with trifling subtleties, which at a proper age he must be at some pains to forget.

Whatever pains a master may take to make the learning of the languages agreeable to his pupil, he may depend upon it, it will be at first extremely unpleasant. The rudiments of every language, therefore, must be given as a task, not as an amusement. Attempting to deceive children into instruction of this kind is only deceiving ourselves; and I know no passion capable of conquering a child's natural laziness but fear. Solomon has said it before me; nor is there any more certain, though perhaps more disagreeable truth, than the proverb in verse, too well known to repeat on the present occasion. It is very probable that parents are told of some masters who never use the rod, and consequently are thought the properest instructors for their children; but though tenderness is a requisite quality in an instructor, yet there is too often the truest tenderness in well-timed correction.

Some have justly observed, that all passion should be banished on this terrible occasion; but, I know not how, there is a frailty attending human nature, that few masters are able to keep their temper whilst they correct. I knew a good-natured man, who was sensible of his own weakness in this respect, and consequently had recourse to the following expedient to prevent his passions from being engaged, yet at the same time administer justice with impartiality:—Whenever any of his pupils committed a fault, he summoned a jury of his peers,—I mean of the boys of his own or the next classes to him; his accusers stood forth; he had a liberty of pleading in his own defence, and one or two more had a liberty of pleading against him: when found guilty by the panel, he was consigned to the footman who attended in the house, who had previous orders to punish, but with lenity. By this means the master took off the odium of punishment from himself; and the footman, between whom and the boys there could not be even the slightest intimacy, was placed in such a light as to be shunned by every boy in the school.

And now I have gone thus far, perhaps you will think me some pedagogue, willing, by a well-timed puff, to increase the reputation of his own school; but such is not the case. The regard I have for society, for those tender minds who are the objects of the present essay, is the only motive I have for offering those thoughts, calculated not to surprise by their novelty or the elegance of composition, but merely to remedy some defects which have crept into the present system of school education. If this letter should be inserted, perhaps I may trouble you in my next with some thoughts upon a university education, not with an intent to exhaust the subject, but to amend some few abuses. I am, &c.

ON THE INSTABILITY OF WORLDLY GRANDEUR.

An alehouse keeper near Islington, who had long lived at the sign of the French King, upon the commencement of the last war with France pulled down his old sign, and put up the Queen of Hungary. Under the influence of her red face and golden sceptre, he continued to sell ale till she was no longer the favourite of his customers; he changed her therefore, some time ago, for the King of Prussia, who may probably be changed in turn for the next great man that shall be set up for vulgar admiration.

Our publican in this imitates the great exactly, who deal out their figures, one after the other, to the gazing crowd beneath them. When we have sufficiently wondered at one, that is taken in, and another exhibited in its room, which seldom holds its station long, for the mob are ever pleased with variety.

I must own I have such an indifferent opinion of the vulgar, that I am ever led to suspect that merit which raises their shout; at least I am certain to find those great and sometimes good men, who find satisfaction in such acclamations, made worse by it; and history has too frequently taught me, that the head which has grown this day giddy with the roar of the million has the very next been fixed upon a pole.

As Alexander VI. was entering a little town in the neighbourhood of Rome, which had just been evacuated by the enemy, he perceived the townsmen busy in the market-place in pulling down from a gibbet a figure which had been designed to represent himself. There were also some knocking down a neighbouring statue of one of the Orsini family, with whom he was at war, in order to put Alexander's effigy, when taken down, in its place. It is possible a man who knew less of the world would have condemned the adulation of those barefaced flatterers; but Alexander seemed pleased at their zeal, and, turning to Borgia his son, said with a smile, *Vides, mi fili, quam leve discrimen patibulum inter et statuam.*—"You see, my son, the small difference between a gibbet and a statue." If the great could be taught any lesson, this might serve to teach them upon how weak a foundation their glory stands, which is built upon popular applause; for as such praise what seems like merit, they as quickly condemn what has only the appearance of guilt.

Popular glory is a perfect coquette: her lovers must toil, feel every inquietude, indulge every caprice, and perhaps at last be jilted into the bargain. True glory, on the other hand, resembles a woman of sense: her admirers must play no tricks; they feel no great anxiety, for they are sure in the end of being rewarded in proportion to their merit. When Swift used to appear in public, he generally had the mob shouting in his train. "Pox take these fools!" he would say: "how much joy might all this bawling give my Lord Mayor!"

We have seen those virtues which have, while living, retired from the public eye, generally transmitted to posterity as the truest objects of admiration and praise. Perhaps the character of the late Duke of Marlborough may one day be set up, even above that of his more talked of predecessor; since an assemblage of all the mild and amiable virtues is far superior to those vulgarly called the great ones. I must be pardoned for this short tribute to the memory of a man who, while living, would as much detest to receive anything that wore the appearance of flattery, as I should to offer it.

I know not how to turn so trite a subject out of the beaten road of commonplace, except by illustrating it rather by the assistance of my memory than my judgment, and, instead of making reflections, by telling a story.

A Chinese who had long studied the works of Confucius, who knew the characters of fourteen thousand words, and could read a great part of every book that came in his way, once took it into his head to travel into Europe, and observe the customs of a people whom he thought not very much inferior even to his own countrymen in the arts of refining upon every pleasure. Upon his arrival at Amsterdam, his passion for letters naturally led him to a bookseller's shop; and, as he could speak a little Dutch, he civilly asked the bookseller for the works of the immortal Ilixofou. The bookseller assured him he had never heard the book mentioned before. "What! have you never heard of that immortal poet?" returned the other, much surprised; "that light of the eyes, that favourite of kings, that rose of perfection! I suppose you know nothing of the immortal Fipsihihi, second cousin to the moon?"—"Nothing at all, indeed, sir," returned the other.—"Alas!" cries our traveller, "to what purpose, then, has one of these fasted to death, and the other offered himself up as a sacrifice to the Tartarean enemy, to gain a renown which has never travelled beyond the precincts of China!"

There is scarcely a village in Europe, and not one university, that is not thus furnished with its little great men. The head of a petty corporation, who opposes the designs of a prince who would tyrannically force his subjects to save their best clothes for Sundays—the puny pedant who finds one undiscovered property in the polype, describes an unheeded process in the skeleton of a mole and whose mind, like his microscope, perceives nature only in detail—the rhymer who makes smooth verses, and paints to our imagination when he should only speak to our hearts,—all equally fancy themselves walking forward to immortality, and desire the crowd behind them to look on. The crowd takes them at their word. Patriot, philosopher, and poet are shouted in their train. Where was there ever so much merit seen? no times so important as our own! ages yet unborn shall gaze with wonder and applause! To such music the important pigmy moves forward, bustling and swelling, and aptly compared to a puddle in a storm.

I have lived to see generals who once had crowds hallooing after them wherever they went, who were bepraised by newspapers and magazines, those echoes of the voice of the vulgar, and yet they have long sunk into merited obscurity, with scarcely even an epitaph left to flatter. A few years ago the herring fishery employed all Grub Street; it was the topic in every coffeehouse, and the burden of every ballad. We were to drag up oceans of gold from the bottom of the sea; we were to supply all Europe with herrings upon our own terms. At present we hear no more of all this. We have fished up very little gold that I can learn; nor do we furnish the world with herrings, as was expected.

Let us wait but a few years longer, and we shall find all our expectations an herring fishery.

SOME ACCOUNT OF THE ACADEMIES OF ITALY.

THERE is not, perhaps, a country in Europe in which learning is so fast upon the decline as in Italy; yet not one in which there are such a number of academies instituted for its support. There is scarce a considerable town in the whole country which has not one or two institutions of this nature, where the learned, as they are pleased to call themselves, meet to harangue, to compliment each other, and praise the utility of their institution.

Jarchius has taken the trouble to give us a list of those clubs or academies, which amount to five hundred and fifty, each distinguished by somewhat whimsical in the name. The academies of Bologna, for instance, are divided into the Abbandonati, the Ausiosi, the Ociosi, Arcadi, Confusi, Dubbiosi, &c. There are few of these who have not published their transactions, and scarce a member who is not looked upon as the most famous man in the world, at home.

Of all those societies, I know of none whose works are worth being known out of the precincts of the city in which they were written except the Cicalata Academia (or, as we might express it, the Tickling Society) of Florence. I have just now before me a manuscript oration, spoken by the late Tomaso Crudeli at that society, which will at once serve to give a better picture of the manner in which men of wit amuse themselves in that country than anything I can say upon the occasion. The oration is this:

"The younger the nymph, my dear companions, the more happy the lover. From fourteen to seventeen you are sure of finding love for love; from seventeen to twenty-one there is always a mixture of interest and affection. But when that period is passed, no longer expect to receive, but to buy—no longer expect a nymph who gives, but who sells, her favours. At this age every glance is taught its duty; not a look, not a sigh, without design; the lady, like a skilful warrior, aims at the heart of another, while she shields her own from danger.

"On the contrary, at fifteen you may expect nothing but simplicity, innocence, and nature. The passions are then sincere; the soul seems seated in the lips; the dear object feels present happiness, without being anxious for the future; her eyes brighten if her lover approaches; her smiles are borrowed from the Graces, and her very mistakes seem to complete her desires.

"Lucretia was just sixteen. The rose and lily took possession of her face, and her bosom, by its hue and its coldness, seemed covered with snow. So much beauty and so much virtue seldom want admirers. Orlandino, a youth of sense and merit, was among the number. He had long languished for an opportunity of declaring his passion, when Cupid, as if willing to indulge his happiness, brought the charming young couple by mere accident to an arbour, where every prying eye but love was absent. Orlandino talked of the sincerity of his passion, and mixed flattery with his addresses; but it was all in vain. The nymph was pre-engaged, and had long devoted to Heaven those charms for which he sued. 'My dear Orlandino,' said she, 'you know I have been long dedicated to St. Catherine, and to her belongs all that lies below my girdle; all that is above you may freely possess, but farther I cannot, must not, comply. The vow is passed; I wish it were undone, but now it is impossible.' You may conceive, my companions, the embarrassment our young lovers felt upon this occasion. They kneeled to St. Catherine, and though both despaired, both implored her assistance. Their tutelar saint was entreated to show some expedient by which both might continue to love, and yet both be happy. Their petition was sincere. St. Catherine was touched with compassion; for lo, a miracle! Lucretia's girdle unloosed, as if without hands; and though before bound round her middle, fell spontaneously down to her feet, and gave Orlandino the possession of all those beauties which lay above it."

No. VII.—*Saturday, November* 17, 1759.

OF ELOQUENCE.

OF all kinds of success, that of an orator is the most pleasing. Upon other occasions the applause we deserve is conferred in our absence, and we are insensible of the pleasure we have given; but in eloquence the victory and the triumph are inseparable. We read our own glory in the face of every spectator; the audience is moved; the antagonist is defeated; and the whole circle bursts into unsolicited applause.

The rewards which attend excellence in this way are so pleasing, that numbers have written professed treatises to teach us the art; schools have been established with no other intent; rhetoric has taken place among the institutions; and pedants have ranged under proper heads, and distinguished with long learned names, some of the strokes of nature, or of passion, which orators have used. I say only some; for a folio volume could not contain all the figures which have been used by the truly eloquent; and scarce a good speaker or writer but makes use of some that are peculiar or new.

Eloquence has preceded the rules of rhetoric, as languages have been formed before grammar. Nature renders men eloquent in great interests or great passions. He that is sensibly touched sees things with a very different eye from the rest of mankind. All nature to him becomes an object of comparison and metaphor, without attending to it; he throws life into all, and inspires his audience with a part of his own enthusiasm.

It has been remarked, that the lower parts of mankind generally express themselves most figuratively, and that tropes are found in the most ordinary forms of conversation. Thus, in every language the heart burns; the courage is roused; the eyes sparkle; the spirits are cast down; passion inflames, pride swells, and pity sinks the soul. Nature everywhere speaks in those strong images, which, from their frequency, pass unnoticed.

Nature it is which inspires those rapturous enthusiasms, those irresistible turns; a strong passion, a pressing danger, calls up all the imagination, and gives the orator irresistible force. Thus a captain of the first caliphs, seeing his soldiers fly, cried out, "Whither do you run? the enemy are not there! You have been told that the caliph is dead; but God is still living. He regards the brave, and will reward the courageous. Advance!"

A man, therefore, may be called eloquent, who transfers the passion or sentiment with which he is moved himself into the breast of another; and this definition appears the more just, as it comprehends the graces of silence and of action. An intimate persuasion of the truth to be proved is the sentiment and passion to be transferred; and who effects this is truly possessed of the talent of eloquence.

I have called eloquence a talent, and not an art, as so many rhetoricians have done, as art is acquired by exercise and study, and eloquence is the gift of nature. Rules will never make either a work or a discourse eloquent; they only serve to prevent faults, but not to introduce beauties; to prevent those passages which are truly eloquent and dictated by nature from being blended with others which might disgust, or at least abate our passion.

What we clearly conceive, says Boileau, we can clearly express. I may add, that what is felt with emotion is expressed also with the same movements; the words rise as readily to paint our emotions as to express our thoughts with perspicuity. The cool care an orator takes to express passions which he does not feel, only prevents his rising into that passion he would seem to feel. In a word, to feel your subject thoroughly, and to speak without fear, are the only rules of eloquence, properly so called, which I can offer. Examine a writer of genius on the most beautiful parts of his work, and he will always assure you, that such passages are generally those which have given him the least trouble, for they came as if by inspiration. To pretend that cold and didactic precepts will make a man eloquent is only to prove that he is incapable of eloquence.

But, as in being perspicuous it is necessary to have a full idea of the subject, so in being eloquent it is not sufficient, if I may so express it, to feel by halves. The orator should be strongly impressed, which is generally the effect of a fine and exquisite sensibility, and not that transient and superficial emotion which he excites in the greatest part of his audience. It is even impossible to affect the hearers in any great degree without being affected ourselves. In vain it will be objected, that many writers have had the art to inspire their readers with a passion for virtue without being virtuous themselves, since it may be answered, that sentiments of virtue filled their minds at the time they were writing. They felt the inspiration strongly, while they praised justice, generosity, or good nature; but, unhappily for them, these passions might have been discontinued when they laid down the pen. In vain will it be objected again, that we can move without being moved, as we can convince without being convinced. It is much easier to deceive our reason than ourselves: a trifling defect in reasoning may be overseen, and lead a man astray, for it requires reason and time to detect the falsehood; but our passions are not easily imposed upon,—our eyes, our ears, and every sense are watchful to detect the imposture.

No discourse can be eloquent that does not elevate the mind. Pathetic eloquence, it is true, has for its only object to affect; but I appeal to men of sensibility, whether their pathetic feelings are not accompanied with some degree of elevation. We may then call eloquence and sublimity the same thing, since it is impossible to be one without feeling the other. Hence it follows, that we may be eloquent in any language, since no language refuses to paint those sentiments with which we are thoroughly impressed. What is usually called sublimity of style seems to be only an error. Eloquence is not in the words, but in the subject; and in great concerns, the more simply anything is expressed, it is generally the more sublime. True eloquence does not consist, as the rhetoricians assure us, in saying great things in a sublime style, but in a simple style: for there is, properly speaking, no such thing as a sublime style; the sublimity lies only in the things; and when they are not so, the language may be turgid, affected, and metaphorical,—but not affecting.

What can be more simply expressed than the following extract from a celebrated preacher, and yet what was ever more sublime? Speaking of the small number of the elect, he breaks out thus among his audience:—"Let me suppose that this was the last hour of us all—that the heavens were opening over our heads—that time was past and eternity begun—that Jesus Christ in all His glory, that man of sorrows, in all His glory, appeared on the tribunal, and that we were assembled here to receive our final decree of life or death eternal! Let me ask, impressed with terror like you, and not separating my lot from yours, but putting myself in the same situation in which we must all one day appear before God, our Judge,—let me ask, if Jesus Christ should now appear to make the terrible separation of the just from the unjust, do you think the greatest number would be saved? Do you think the number of the elect would even be equal to that of the sinners? Do you think, if all our works were examined with justice, would He find ten just persons in this great assembly? Monsters of ingratitude! would He find one?" Such passages as these are sublime in every language. The expression may be less striking, or more indistinct, but the greatness of the idea still remains. In a word, we may be eloquent in every language and in every style, since elocution is only an assistant, but not a constituter, of eloquence.

Of what use, then, will it be said, are all the precepts given us upon this head both by the ancients and moderns? I answer, that they cannot make us eloquent, but they will certainly prevent us from becoming ridiculous. They can seldom procure a single beauty, but they may banish a thousand faults. The true method of an orator is not to attempt always to move, always to affect, to be continually sublime, but at proper intervals to give rest both to his own and the passions of his audience. In these periods of relaxation, or of preparation rather, rules may teach him to avoid anything low, trivial, or disgusting. Thus criticism, properly speaking, is intended not to assist those parts which are sublime, but those which are naturally mean and humble, which are composed with coolness and caution, and where the orator rather endeavours not to offend than attempts to please.

I have hitherto insisted more strenuously on that eloquence which speaks to the passions, as it is a species of oratory almost unknown in England. At the bar it is quite discontinued, and I think with justice. In the senate it is used but sparingly, as the orator speaks to enlightened judges. But in the pulpit, in which the orator should chiefly address the vulgar, it seems strange that it should be entirely laid aside.

The vulgar of England are, without exception, the most barbarous and the most unknowing of any in Europe. A great part of their ignorance may be chiefly ascribed to their teachers, who, with the most pretty, gentlemanlike serenity, deliver their cool discourses, and address the reason of men who have never reasoned in all their lives. They are told of cause and effect, of beings self-existent, and the universal scale of beings. They are informed of the excellence of the Bangorian controversy, and the absurdity of an intermediate state. The spruce preacher reads his lucubration without lifting his nose from the text, and never ventures to earn the shame of an enthusiast.

By this means, though his audience feel not one word of all he says, he earns, however, among his acquaintance, the character of a man of sense: among his acquaintance only, did I say? nay, even with his bishop.

The polite of every country have several motives to induce them to a rectitude of action,—the love of virtue for its own sake, the shame of offending, and the desire of pleasing. The vulgar have but one,—the enforcements of religion; and yet those who should push this motive home to their hearts are basely found to desert their post. They speak to the Squire, the philosopher, and the pedant; but the poor, those who really want instruction, are left uninstructed.

I have attended most of our pulpit orators, who, it must be owned, write extremely well upon the text they assume. To give them their due also, they read their sermons with elegance and propriety; but this goes but a very short way in true eloquence. The speaker must be moved. In this, in this alone, our English divines are deficient. Were they to speak to a few calm, dispassionate hearers, they certainly use the properest methods of address; but their audience is chiefly composed of the poor, who must be influenced by motives of reward and punishment, and whose only virtues lie in self-interest or fear.

How, then, are such to be addressed? not by studied periods or cold disquisitions; not by the labours of the head, but the honest spontaneous dictates of the heart. Neither writing a sermon with regular periods, and all the harmony of elegant expression—neither reading it with emphasis, propriety, and deliberation—neither pleasing with metaphor, simile, or rhetorical fustian—neither arguing coolly, and untying consequences united in *à priori*, nor bundling up inductions *à posteriori*—neither pedantic jargon, nor academical trifling, can persuade the poor. Writing a discourse coolly in the closet, then getting it by memory, and delivering it on Sundays, even that will not do. What then is to be done? I know of no expedient to speak—to speak at once intelligibly and feelingly—except to understand the language—to be convinced of the truth of the object—to be perfectly acquainted with the subject in view—to prepossess yourself with a low opinion of your audience—and to do the rest extempore: by this means strong expressions, new thoughts, rising passions, and the true declamatory style, will naturally ensue.

Fine declamation does not consist in flowery periods, delicate allusions, or musical cadences, but in a plain, open, loose style, where the periods are long and obvious; where the same thought is often exhibited in several points of view: all this strong sense, a good memory, and a small share of experience will furnish to every orator: and without these a clergyman may be called a fine preacher, a judicious preacher, and a man of good sense; he may make his hearers admire his understanding, but will seldom enlighten theirs.

When I think of the Methodist preachers among us, how seldom they are endued with common sense, and yet how often and how justly they affect their hearers; I cannot avoid saying within myself, Had these been bred gentlemen and been endued with even the meanest share of understanding, what might they not effect! Did our bishops, who can add dignity to their expostulations, testify the same fervour, and entreat their hearers, as well as argue, what might not be the consequence! The vulgar, by which I mean the bulk of mankind, would then have a double motive to love religion; first, from seeing its professors honoured here, and next, from the consequences hereafter. At present the enthusiasms of the poor are opposed to law; did law conspire with their enthusiasms, we should not only be the happiest nation upon earth, but the wisest also.

Enthusiasm in religion, which prevails only among the vulgar, should be the chief object of politics. A society of enthusiasts, governed by reason, among the great, is the most indissoluble, the most virtuous, and the most efficient of its own decrees that can be imagined. Every country possessed of any degree of strength have had their enthusiasms, which ever serve as laws among the people. The Greeks had their καλοκἀγαθία, the Romans their *Amor Patriæ*, and we the truer and firmer bond of the Protestant Religion. The principle is the same in all: how much, then, is it the duty of those whom the law has appointed teachers of this religion, to enforce its obligations, and to raise those enthusiasms among people, by which alone political society can subsist?

From eloquence, therefore, the morals of our people are to expect emendation: but how little can they be improved by men who get into the pulpit rather to show their parts than convince us of the truth of what they deliver; who are painfully correct in their style, musical in their tones; where every sentiment, every expression, seems the result of meditation and deep study.

Tillotson has been commended as the model of pulpit eloquence: thus far he should be imitated, where he generally strives to convince rather than to please; but to adopt his long, dry, and sometimes tedious discussions, which serve to amuse only divines, and are utterly neglected by the generality of mankind—to praise the intricacy of his periods, which are too long to be spoken—to continue his cool phlegmatic manner of enforcing every truth,—is certainly erroneous. As I said before, the good preacher should adopt no model, write no sermons, study no periods; let him but understand his subject, the language he speaks, and be convinced of the truths he delivers. It is amazing to what heights eloquence of this kind may reach! This is that eloquence the ancients represented as lightning, bearing down every opposer; this the power which has turned whole assemblies into astonishment, admiration, and awe; that is described by the torrent, the flame, and every other instance of irresistible impetuosity.

But to attempt such noble heights belongs only to the truly great or the truly good. To discard the lazy manner of reading sermons, or speaking sermons by rote; to set up singly against the opposition of men who are attached to their own errors, and to endeavour to be great, instead of being prudent, are qualities we seldom see united. A minister of the Church of England, who may be possessed of good sense and some hopes of preferment, will seldom give up such substantial advantages for the empty pleasure of improving society. By his present method he is liked by his friends, admired by his dependants, not displeasing to his bishop; he lives as well, eats and sleeps as well, as if a real orator, and an eager assertor of his mission: he will hardly, therefore, venture all this to be called, perhaps, an enthusiast; nor will he depart from customs established by the brotherhood, when, by such a conduct, he only singles himself out for their contempt.

CUSTOM AND LAWS COMPARED.

WHAT, say some, can give us a more contemptible idea of a large state, than to find it mostly governed by custom; to have few written laws, and no boundaries to mark the jurisdiction between the senate and the people? Among the number who speak in this manner is the great Montesquieu, who asserts that every nation is free in proportion to the number of its written laws, and seems to hint at a despotic and arbitrary conduct in the present King of Prussia, who has abridged the laws of his country into a very short compass.

As Tacitus and Montesquieu happen to differ in sentiment upon a subject of so much importance, (for the Roman expressly asserts that the state is generally vicious in proportion to the number of its laws,) it will not be amiss to examine it a little more minutely, and see whether a state which, like England, is burdened with a multiplicity of written laws, or which, like Switzerland, Geneva, and some other republics, is governed by custom and the determination of the judge, is best.

And to prove the superiority of custom to written law we shall at least find history conspiring. Custom, or the traditional observance of the practice of their forefathers, was what directed the Romans as well in their public as private determinations. Custom was appealed to in pronouncing sentence against a criminal, where part of the formulary was *more majorum*. So Sallust, speaking of the expulsion of Tarquin, says *mutato more*, and not *lege mutatâ;* and Virgil, *pacisque imponere morem*. So that, in those times of the empire in which the people retained their liberty, they were governed by custom; when they sank into oppression and tyranny, they were restrained by new laws, and the laws of tradition abolished.

As getting the ancients on our side is half a victory, it will not be amiss to fortify the argument with an observation of Chrysostom's: "That the enslaved are the fittest to be governed by laws, and free men by custom." Custom partakes of the nature of parental injunction; it is kept by the people themselves, and observed with a willing obedience. The observance of it must, therefore, be a mark of freedom; and coming originally to a state from the reverenced founders of its liberty, will be an encouragement and assistance to it in the defence of that blessing: but a conquered people, a nation of slaves, must pretend to none of this freedom, or these happy distinctions; having, by degeneracy, lost all right to their brave forefathers' free institutions, their masters will in policy take the forfeiture; and the fixing a conquest must be done by giving laws, which may every moment serve to remind the people enslaved of their conquerors; nothing being more dangerous than to trust a late subdued people with old customs, that presently upbraid their degeneracy, and provoke them to revolt.

The wisdom of the Roman republic in their veneration for custom, and backwardness to introduce a new law, was perhaps the cause of their long continuance, and of the virtues of which they have set the world so many examples. But to show in what that wisdom consists, it may be proper to observe, that the benefit of new written laws is merely confined to the consequences of their observance; but customary laws, keeping up a veneration for the founders, engage men in the imitation of their virtues as well as policy. To this may be ascribed the religious regard the Romans paid to their forefathers' memory, and their adhering for so many ages to the practice of the same virtues, which nothing contributed more to efface than the introduction of a voluminous body of new laws over the neck of venerable custom.

The simplicity, conciseness, and antiquity of custom gives an air of majesty and immutability that inspires awe and veneration; but new laws are too apt to be voluminous, perplexed, and indeterminate, whence must necessarily arise neglect, contempt, and ignorance.

As every human institution is subject to gross imperfections, so laws must necessarily be liable to the same inconveniences, and their defects soon discovered. Thus, through the weakness of one part all the rest are liable to be brought into contempt.

But such weaknesses in a custom, for very obvious reasons, evade an examination; besides, a friendly prejudice always stands up in their favour.

But let us suppose a new law to be perfectly equitable and necessary; yet, if the procurers of it have betrayed a conduct that confesses by-ends and private motives, the disgust to the circumstances disposes us, unreasonably indeed, to an irreverence of the law itself; but we are indulgently blind to the most visible imperfections of an old custom. Though we perceive the defects ourselves, yet we remain persuaded that our wise forefathers had good reason for what they did; and though such motives no longer continue, the benefit will still go along with the observance, though we do not know how. It is thus the Roman lawyers speak: "Non omnium quæ a majoribus constituta sunt ratio reddi potest, et ideo rationes eorum quæ constituuntur inquiri non oportet, alioquin multa ex his quæ certa sunt subvertuntur."

Those laws which preserve to themselves the greatest love and observance must needs be best; but custom, as it executes itself, must be necessarily superior to written laws in this respect, which are to be executed by another. Thus, nothing can be more certain than that numerous written laws are a sign of a degenerate community, and are frequently not the consequences of vicious morals in a state, but the causes.

Hence we see how much greater benefit it would be to the state rather to abridge than increase its laws. We every day find them increasing; acts and reports, which may be termed the acts of judges, are every day becoming more voluminous, and loading the subject with new penalties.

Laws ever increase in number and severity, until they at length are strained so tight as to break themselves. Such was the case of the latter empire, whose laws were at length become so strict, that the barbarous invaders did not bring servitude but liberty.

OF THE PRIDE AND LUXURY OF THE MIDDLING CLASS OF PEOPLE.

Of all the follies and absurdities under which this great metropolis labours, there is not one, I believe, that at present appears in a more glaring and ridiculous light, than the pride and luxury of the middling class of people. Their eager desire of being seen in a sphere far above their capacities and circumstances is daily —nay, hourly—instanced by the prodigious numbers of mechanics who flock to the races, gaming tables, brothels, and all public diversions this fashionable town affords.

You shall see a grocer or a tallow-chandler sneak from behind the counter, clap on a laced coat and a bag, fly to the E O table, throw away fifty pieces with some sharping man of quality; while his industrious wife is selling a pennyworth of sugar, or a pound of candles, to support her fashionable spouse in his extravagances.

I was led into this reflection by an odd adventure which happened to me the other day at Epsom races, whither I went, not through any desire, I do assure you, of laying bets or winning thousands, but at the earnest request of a friend, who had long indulged the curiosity of seeing the sport, very natural for an Englishman. When we had arrived at the course, and had taken several turns to observe the different objects that made up this whimsical group, a figure suddenly darted by us, mounted and dressed in all the elegance of those polite gentry who come to show you they have a little money, and rather than pay their just debts at home, generously come abroad to bestow it on gamblers and pickpockets. As I had not an opportunity of viewing his face till his return, I gently walked after him, and met him as he came back, when, to my no small surprise, I beheld in this gay Narcissus the visage of Jack Varnish, an humble vendor of prints. Disgusted at the sight, I pulled my friend by the sleeve, pressed him to return home, telling him all the way, that I was so enraged at the fellow's impudence, that I was resolved never to lay out another penny with him.

And now, pray, sir, let me beg of you to give this a place in your paper, that Mr. Varnish may understand he mistakes the thing quite, if he imagines horse-racing commendable in a tradesman; and that he who is revelling every night in the arms of a common strumpet (though blessed with an indulgent wife), when he ought to be minding his business, will never thrive in this world. He will find himself soon mistaken, his finances decrease, his friends shun him, customers fall off, and himself thrown into a gaol. I would earnestly recommend this adage to every mechanic in London, "Keep your shop, and your shop will keep you." A strict observance of these words will, I am sure, in time gain them estates. Industry is the road to wealth, and honesty to happiness; and he who strenuously endeavours to pursue them both may never fear the critic's lash or the sharp cries of penury and want.

SABINUS AND OLINDA.

In a fair, rich, and flourishing country, whose cliffs are washed by the German ocean, lived Sabinus, a youth formed by nature to make a conquest wherever he thought proper; but the constancy of his disposition fixed him only with Olinda. He was indeed superior to her in fortune; but that defect on her side was so amply supplied by her merit, that none was thought more worthy of his regards than she. He loved her—he was beloved by her; and in a short time, by joining hands publicly, they avowed the union of their hearts. But, alas! none, however fortunate, however happy, are exempt from the shafts of envy and the malignant effects of ungoverned appetite. How unsafe, how detestable, are they who have this fury for their guide! How certainly will it lead them from themselves, and plunge them in errors they would have shuddered at, even in apprehension! Ariana, a lady of many amiable qualities, very nearly allied to Sabinus, and highly esteemed by him, imagined herself slighted and injuriously treated since his marriage with Olinda. By incautiously suffering this jealousy to corrode in her breast, she began to give a loose to passion; she forgot those many virtues for which she had been so long and so justly applauded. Causeless suspicion and mistaken resentment betrayed her into all the gloom of discontent; she sighed without ceasing; the happiness of others gave her intolerable pain; she thought of nothing but revenge. How unlike what she was,—the cheerful, the prudent, the compassionate Ariana.

She continually laboured to disturb an union so firmly, so affectionately founded, and planned every scheme which she thought most likely to disturb it.

Fortune seemed willing to promote her unjust intentions: the circumstances of Sabinus had been long embarrassed by a tedious lawsuit, and the court determining the cause unexpectedly in favour of his opponent, it sank his fortune to the lowest pitch of penury from the highest affluence. From the nearness of relationship, Sabinus expected from Ariana those assistances his present situation required; but she was insensible to all his entreaties and the justice of every remonstrance, unless he first separated from Olinda, whom she regarded with detestation. Upon a compliance with her desires in this respect, she promised that her fortune, her interest, and her all should be at his command. Sabinus was shocked at the proposal; he loved his wife with inexpressible tenderness, and refused those offers with indignation which were to be purchased at so high a price. Ariana was no less displeased to find her offers rejected, and gave a loose to all that warmth which she had long endeavoured to suppress. Reproach generally produces recrimination; the quarrel rose to such a height, that Sabinus was marked for destruction, and the very next day, upon the strength of an old family debt, he was sent to gaol, with none but Olinda to comfort him in his miseries. In this mansion of distress they lived together with resignation, and even with comfort. She provided the frugal meal, and he read to her while employed in the little offices of domestic concern. Their fellow-prisoners admired their contentment, and whenever they had a desire of relaxing into mirth, and enjoying those little comforts that a prison affords, Sabinus and Olinda were sure to be of the party. Instead of reproaching each other for their mutual wretchedness, they both lightened it, by bearing each a share of the load imposed by Providence. Whenever Sabinus showed the least concern on his dear partner's account, she conjured him by the love he bore her, by those tender ties which now united them for ever, not to discompose himself; that so long as his affection lasted, she defied all the ills of fortune and every loss of fame or friendship; that nothing could make her miserable but his seeming to want happiness; nothing pleased but his sympathising with her pleasure. A continuance in prison soon robbed them of the little they had left, and famine began to make its horrid appearance; yet still was neither found to murmur: they both looked upon their little boy, who, insensible of their or his own distress, was playing about the room, with inexpressible yet silent anguish, when a messenger came to inform them that Ariana was dead, and that her will in favour of a very distant relation, who was now in another country, might easily be procured and burnt, in which case all her large fortune would revert to him, as being the next heir at law.

A proposal of so base a nature filled our unhappy couple with horror; they ordered the messenger immediately out of the room, and, falling upon each other's neck, indulged an agony of sorrow, for now even all hopes of relief were banished. The messenger who made the proposal, however, was only a spy sent by Ariana to sound the dispositions of a man she at once loved and persecuted. This lady, though warped by wrong passions, was naturally kind, judicious, and friendly. She found that all her attempts to shake the constancy or the integrity of Sabinus were ineffectual; she had therefore begun to reflect, and to wonder how she could so long and so unprovoked injure such uncommon fortitude and affection.

She had, from the next room, herself heard the reception given to the messenger, and could not avoid feeling all the force of superior virtue: she therefore reassumed her former goodness of heart; she came into the room with tears in her eyes, and acknowledged the severity of her former treatment. She bestowed her first care in providing them all the necessary supplies, and acknowledged them as the most deserving heirs of her fortune. From this moment Sabinus enjoyed an uninterrupted happiness with Olinda, and both were happy in the friendship and assistance of Ariana, who, dying soon after, left them in possession of a large estate, and in her last moments confessed, that virtue was the only path to true glory; and that, however innocence may for a time be depressed, a steady perseverance will in time lead it to a certain victory.

THE SENTIMENTS OF A FRENCHMAN ON THE TEMPER OF THE ENGLISH.

NOTHING is so uncommon among the English as that easy affability, that instant method of acquaintance, or that cheerfulness of disposition, which make in France the charm of every society. Yet in this gloomy reserve they seem to pride themselves, and think themselves less happy if obliged to be more social. One may assert, without wronging them, that they do not study the method of going through life with pleasure and tranquillity like the French. Might not this be a proof that they are not so much philosophers as they imagine? Philosophy is no more than the art of making ourselves happy; that is, of seeking pleasure in regularity, and reconciling what we owe to society with what is due to ourselves.

This cheerfulness, which is the characteristic of our nation, in the eye of an Englishman passes almost for folly. But is their gloominess a greater mark of their wisdom? and, folly against folly, is not the most cheerful sort the best? If our gaiety makes them sad, they ought not to find it strange if their seriousness makes us laugh.

As this disposition to levity is not familiar to them, and as they look on everything as a fault which they do not find at home, the English who live among us are hurt by it. Several of their authors reproach us with it as a vice, or at least as a ridicule.

Mr. Addison styles us a comic nation. In my opinion, it is not acting the philosopher on this point, to regard as a fault that quality which contributes most to the pleasure of society and happiness of life. Plato, convinced that whatever makes men happier makes them better, advises to neglect nothing that may excite and convert to an early habit this sense of joy in children. Seneca places it in the first rank of good things. Certain it is, at least, that gaiety may be a concomitant of all sorts of virtue, but that there are some vices with which it is incompatible.

As to him who laughs at everything, and him who laughs at nothing, neither of them has sound judgment. All the difference I find between them is, that the last is constantly the most unhappy. Those who speak against cheerfulness prove nothing else but that they were born melancholic, and that, in their hearts, they rather envy than condemn that levity they affect to despise.

The Spectator, whose constant object was the good of mankind in general, and of his own nation in particular, should, according to his own principles, place cheerfulness among the most desirable qualities; and, probably, whenever he contradicts himself in this particular, it is only to conform to the tempers of the people whom he addresses. He asserts that gaiety is one great obstacle to the prudent conduct of women. But are those of a melancholy temper, as the English women generally are, less subject to the foibles of love? I am acquainted with some doctors in this science, to whose judgment I would more willingly refer than to his. And perhaps, in reality, persons naturally of a gay temper are too easily taken off by different objects to give themselves up to all the excesses of this passion.

Mr. Hobbes, a celebrated philosopher of his nation, maintains that laughing proceeds from our pride alone. This is only a paradox, if asserted of laughing in general, and only argues that misanthropical disposition for which he was remarkable.

To bring the causes he assigns for laughing under suspicion it is sufficient to remark, that proud people are commonly those who laugh least. Gravity is the inseparable companion of pride. To say that a man is vain, because the humour of a writer, or the buffooneries of an harlequin, excite his laughter, would be advancing a great absurdity. We should distinguish between laughter inspired by joy and that which arises from mockery. The malicious sneer is improperly called laughter. It must be owned, that pride is the parent of such laughter as this: but this is, in itself, vicious; whereas the other sort has nothing in its principles or effects that deserves condemnation. We find this amiable in others, and is it unhappiness to feel a disposition towards it in ourselves?

When I see an Englishman laugh, I fancy I rather see him hunting after joy than having caught it; and this is more particularly remarkable in their women, whose tempers are inclined to melancholy. A laugh leaves no more traces on their countenance than a flash of lightning on the face of the heavens. The most laughing air is instantly succeeded by the most gloomy. One would be apt to think that their souls open with difficulty to joy, or, at least, that joy is not pleased with its habitation there.

In regard to fine raillery, it must be allowed that it is not natural to the English, and, therefore, those who endeavour at it make but an ill figure. Some of their authors have candidly confessed, that pleasantry is quite foreign to their character; but, according to the reason they give, they lose nothing by this confession. Bishop Sprat gives the following one: "The English," says he, "have too much bravery to submit to be derided, and too much virtue and honour to mock others."

No. VIII.—*Saturday, November 24, 1759.*

ON DECEIT AND FALSEHOOD.

THE following account is so judiciously conceived, that I am convinced the reader will be more pleased with it than with anything of mine; so I shall make no apology for this new publication:—

To the Author of the Bee.

SIR,—Deceit and falsehood have ever been an overmatch for truth, and followed and admired by the majority of mankind. If we inquire after the reason of this, we shall find it in our own imaginations, which are amused and entertained with the perpetual novelty and variety that fiction affords, but find no manner of delight in the uniform simplicity of homely truth, which still sues them under the same appearance.

He, therefore, that would gain our hearts, must make his court to our fancy, which, being sovereign controller of the passions, lets them loose, and inflames them more or less, in proportion to the force and efficacy of the first cause, which is ever the more powerful the more new it is. Thus, in mathematical demonstrations themselves, though they seem to aim at pure truth and instruction, and to be addressed to our reason alone, yet I think it is pretty plain, that our understanding is only made a drudge to gratify our invention and curiosity, and we are pleased, not so much because our discoveries are certain, as because they are new.

I do not deny but the world is still pleased with things that pleased it many ages ago, but it should at the same time be considered, that man is naturally so much a logician, as to distinguish between matters that are plain and easy, and others that are hard and inconceivable. What we understand we overlook and despise, and what we know nothing of we hug and delight in. Thus there are such things as perpetual novelties; for we are pleased no longer than we are amazed, and nothing so much contents us as that which confounds us.

This weakness in human nature gave occasion to a party of men to make such gainful markets as they have done of our credulity. All objects and facts whatever now ceased to be what they had been for ever before, and received what make and meaning it was found convenient to put upon them: what people eat, and drank, and saw, was not what they eat, and drank, and saw, but something farther, which they were fond of because they were ignorant of it. In short, nothing was itself, but something beyond itself; and by these artifices and amusements the heads of the world were so turned and intoxicated, that at last there was scarce a sound set of brains left in it.

In this state of giddiness and infatuation it was no very hard task to persuade the already deluded that there was an actual society and communion between human creatures and spiritual demons. And when they had thus put people into the power and clutches of the devil, none but they alone could have either skill or strength to bring the prisoners back again.

But so far did they carry this dreadful drollery, and so fond were they of it, that to maintain it and themselves in profitable repute they literally sacrificed for it, and made impious victims of, numberless old women and other miserable persons, who either through ignorance could not say what they were bid to say, or through madness said what they should not have said. Fear and stupidity made them incapable of defending themselves, and frenzy and infatuation made them confess guilty impossibilities, which produced cruel sentences, and then inhuman executions.

Some of these wretched mortals, finding themselves either hateful or terrible to all, and befriended by none, and perhaps wanting the common necessaries of life, came at last to abhor themselves as much as they were abhorred by others, and grew willing to be burned or hanged out of a world which was no other to them than a scene of persecution and anguish.

Others of strong imaginations and little understandings were, by positive and repeated charges against them of committing mischievous and supernatural facts and villanies, deluded to judge of themselves by the judgment of their enemies, whose weakness or malice prompted them to be accusers. And many have been condemned as witches and dealers with the devil for no other reason but their knowing more than those who accused, tried, and passed sentence upon them.

In these cases credulity is a much greater error than infidelity, and it is safer to believe nothing than too much. A man that believes little or nothing of witchcraft will destroy nobody for being under the imputation of it; and so far he certainly acts with humanity to others and safety to himself; but he that credits all or too much, upon that article, is obliged, if he acts consistently with his persuasion, to kill all those whom he takes to be the killers of mankind; and such are witches. It would be a jest and a contradiction to say that he is for sparing them who are harmless of that tribe, since the received notion of their supposed contract with the devil implies, that they are engaged, by covenant and inclination, to do all the mischief they possibly can.

I have heard many stories of witches, and read many accusations against them; but I do not remember any that would have induced me to have consigned over to the halter or the flame any of those deplorable wretches, who, as they share our likeness and nature, ought to share our compassion, as persons cruelly accused of impossibilities.

But we love to delude ourselves, and often fancy or forge an effect, and then set ourselves as gravely as ridiculously to find out the cause. Thus, for example, when a dream or the hyp has given us false terrors or imaginary pains, we immediately conclude that the infernal tyrant owes us a spite, and inflicts his wrath and stripes upon us by the hands of some of his sworn servants among us. For this end an old woman is promoted to a seat in Satan's privy-council, and appointed his executioner in chief within her district. So ready and civil are we to allow the devil the dominion over us, and even to provide him with butchers and hangmen of our own make and nature.

I have often wondered why we did not, in choosing our proper officers for Beelzebub, lay the lot rather upon men than women, the former being more bold and robust, and more equal to that bloody service; but, upon inquiry, I find it has been so ordered for two reasons: first, the men, having the whole direction of this affair, are wise enough to slip their own necks out of the collar; and, secondly, an old woman is grown by custom the most avoided and most unpitied creature under the sun, the very name carrying contempt and satire in it. And so far, indeed, we pay but an uncourtly sort of respect to Satan, in sacrificing to him nothing but the dry sticks of human nature.

We have a wondering quality within us, which finds huge gratification when we see strange feats done, and cannot at the same time see the doer or the cause. Such actions are sure to be attributed to some witch or demon; for if we come to find they are slily performed by artists of our own species, and by causes purely natural, our delight dies with our amazement.

It is, therefore, one of the most unthankful offices in the world, to go about to expose the mistaken notions of witchcraft and spirits; it is robbing mankind of a valuable imagination, and of the privilege of being deceived. Those who at any time undertook the task have always met with rough treatment and ill language for their pains, and seldom escaped the imputation of atheism, because they would not allow the devil to be too powerful for the Almighty. For my part, I am so much a heretic as to believe that God Almighty, and not the devil, governs the world.

If we inquire what are the common marks and symptoms by which witches are discovered to be such, we shall see how reasonably and mercifully those poor creatures were burned and hanged who unhappily fell under that name.

In the first place, the old woman must be prodigiously ugly; her eyes hollow and red, her face shrivelled; she goes double, and her voice trembles. It frequently happens that this rueful figure frightens a child into the palpitation of the heart: home he runs, and tells his mamma that Goody Such-a-one looked at him, and he is very ill. The good woman cries out her dear baby is bewitched, and sends for the parson and the constable.

It is moreover necessary that she be very poor. It is true her master, Satan, has mines and hidden treasures in his gift; but no matter, she is, for all that, very poor, and lives on alms. She goes to Sisly the cook-maid for a dish of broth, or the heel of a loaf, and Sisly denies them to her. The old woman goes away muttering, and perhaps in less than a month's time Sisly hears the voice of a cat, and strains her ankles, which are certain signs that she is bewitched.

A farmer sees his cattle die of the murrain, and his sheep of the rot, and poor Goody is forced to be the cause of their death, because she was seen talking to herself the evening before such a ewe departed, and had been gathering sticks at the side of the wood where such a cow run mad.

The old woman has always for her companion an old grey cat, which is a disguised devil too, and confederate with Goody in works of darkness. They frequently go journeys into Egypt upon a broom-staff in half an hour's time, and now and then Goody and her cat change shapes. The neighbours often overhear them in deep and solemn discourse together, plotting some dreadful mischief, you may be sure.

There is a famous way of trying witches, recommended by King James I. The old woman is tied hand and foot, and thrown into the river; and if she swims, she is guilty, and taken out and burned; but if she is innocent, she sinks, and is only drowned.

The witches are said to meet their master frequently in churches and churchyards. I wonder at the boldness of Satan and his congregation, in revelling and playing mountebank farces on consecrated ground; and I have as often wondered at the oversight and ill policy of some people in allowing it possible.

It would have been both dangerous and impious to have treated this subject at one certain time in this ludicrous manner. It used to be managed with all possible gravity, and even terror: and indeed it was made a tragedy in all its parts, and thousands were sacrificed, or rather murdered, by such evidence and colours as, God be thanked! we are this day ashamed of. An old woman may be miserable now, and not be hanged for it.

AN ACCOUNT OF THE AUGUSTAN AGE OF ENGLAND.

THE history of the rise of language and learning is calculated to gratify curiosity rather than to satisfy the understanding. An account of that period only when language and learning arrived at its highest perfection is the most conducive to real improvement, since it at once raises emulation and directs to the proper objects. The age of Leo X. in Italy is confessed to be the Augustan age with them: the French writers seem agreed to give the same appellation to that of Louis XIV.: but the English are yet undetermined with respect to themselves.

Some have looked upon the writers in the times of Queen Elizabeth as the true standard for future imitation; others have descended to the reign of James I.; and others still lower, to that of Charles II. Were I to be permitted to offer an opinion upon this subject, I should readily give my vote for the reign of Queen Anne, or some years before that period. It was then that taste was united to genius; and as before our writers charmed with their strength of thinking, so then they pleased with strength and grace united. In that period of British glory, though no writer attracts our attention singly, yet, like stars lost in each other's brightness, they have cast such a lustre upon the age in which they lived that their minutest transactions will be attended to by posterity with a greater eagerness than the most important occurrences of even empires which have been transacted in greater obscurity.

At that period there seemed to be a just balance between patronage and the press. Before it, men were little esteemed whose only merit was genius; and since, men who can prudently be content to catch the public, are certain of living without dependence. But the writers of the period of which I am speaking, were sufficiently esteemed by the great, and not rewarded enough by booksellers to set them above dependence. Fame, consequently, then was the truest road to happiness; a sedulous attention to the mechanical business of the day makes the present never-failing resource.

The age of Charles II., which our countrymen term the age of wit and immorality, produced some writers that at once served to improve our language and corrupt our hearts. The king himself had a large share of knowledge and some wit; and his courtiers were generally men who had been brought up in the school of affliction and experience. For this reason, when the sunshine of their fortune returned, they gave too great a loose to pleasure, and language was by them cultivated only as a mode of elegance. Hence it became more enervated, and was dashed with quaintnesses, which gave the public writings of those times a very illiberal air.

L'Estrange, who was by no means so bad a writer as some have represented him, was sunk in party faction; and having generally the worst side of the argument, often had recourse to scolding, pertness, and, consequently, a vulgarity that discovers itself even in his more liberal compositions. He was the first writer who regularly enlisted himself under the banners of a party for pay, and fought for it, through right and wrong, for upwards of forty literary campaigns. This intrepidity gained him the esteem of Cromwell himself; and the papers he wrote even just before the Revolution, almost with the rope about his neck, have his usual characters of impudence and perseverance. That he was a standard writer cannot be disowned, because a great many very eminent authors formed their style by his. But his standard was far from being a just one; though, when party considerations are set aside, he certainly was possessed of elegance, ease, and perspicuity.

Dryden, though a great and undisputed genius, had the same cast as L'Estrange. Even his plays discover him to be a party man, and the same principle infects his style in subjects of the lightest nature; but the English tongue, as it stands at present, is greatly his debtor. He first gave it regular harmony, and discovered its latent powers. It was his pen that formed the Congreves, the Priors, and the Addisons, who succeeded him; and had it not been for Dryden, we never should have known a Pope, at least in the meridian lustre he now displays. But Dryden's excellences as a writer were not confined to poetry alone. There is in his prose writings an ease and elegance that have never yet been so well united in works of taste or criticism.

The English language owes very little to Otway, though, next to Shakespeare, the greatest genius England ever produced in tragedy. His excellences lay in painting directly from nature, in catching every emotion just as it rises from the soul, and in all the powers of the moving and pathetic. He appears to have had no learning, no critical knowledge, and to have lived in great distress. When he died (which he did in an obscure house near the Minories) he had about him the copy of a tragedy, which, it seems, he had sold for a trifle to Bentley the bookseller. I have seen an advertisement at the end of one of L'Estrange's political papers, offering a reward to any one who should bring it to his shop. What an invaluable treasure was there irretrievably lost by the ignorance and neglect of the age he lived in.

Lee had a great command of language and vast force of expression, both which the best of our succeeding dramatic poets thought proper to take for their models. Rowe, in particular, seems to have caught that manner, though in all other respects inferior. The other poets of that reign contributed but little towards improving the English tongue, and it is not certain whether they did not injure rather than improve it. Immorality has its cant as well as party, and many shocking expressions now crept into the language, and became the transient fashion of the day. The upper galleries, by the prevalence of party spirit, were courted with great assiduity, and a horse-laugh following ribaldry was the highest instance of applause, the chastity as well as energy of diction being overlooked or neglected.

Virtuous sentiment was recovered, but energy of style never was. This, though disregarded in plays and party writings, still prevailed amongst men of character and business. The despatches of Sir Richard Fanshaw, Sir William Godolphin, Lord Arlington, and many other ministers of state, are all of them, with respect to diction, manly, bold, and nervous. Sir William Temple, though a man of no learning, had great knowledge and experience. He wrote always like a man of sense and a gentleman; and his style is the model by which the best prose writers in the reign of Queen Anne formed theirs. The beauties of Mr. Locke's style, though not so much celebrated, are as striking as that of his understanding. He never says more nor less than he ought, and never makes use of a word that he could have changed for a better. The same observation holds good of Dr. Samuel Clarke.

Mr. Locke was a philosopher; his antagonist, Stillingfleet, Bishop of Worcester, was a man of learning; and therefore the contest between them was unequal. The clearness of Mr. Locke's head renders his language perspicuous, the learning of Stillingfleet's clouds his. This is an instance of the superiority of good sense over learning, towards the improvement of every language.

There is nothing peculiar to the language of Archbishop Tillotson, but his manner of writing is inimitable; for one who reads him wonders why he himself did not think and speak it in that very manner. The turn of his periods is agreeable though artless, and everything he says seems to flow spontaneously from inward conviction. Barrow, though greatly his superior in learning, falls short of him in other respects.

The time seems to be at hand when justice will be done to Mr. Cowley's prose as well as poetical writings; and though his friend Dr. Sprat, Bishop of Rochester, in his diction falls far short of the abilities for which he has been celebrated, yet there is sometimes a happy flow in his periods, something that looks like eloquence. The style of his successor, Atterbury, has been much commended by his friends, which always happens when a man distinguishes himself in party; but there is in it nothing extraordinary. Even the speech which he made for himself at the bar of the House of Lords, before he was sent into exile, is void of eloquence, though it has been cried up by his friends to such a degree that his enemies have suffered it to pass uncensured.

The philosophic manner of Lord Shaftesbury's writing is nearer to that of Cicero than any English author has yet arrived at; but perhaps had Cicero written in English, his composition would have greatly exceeded that of our countryman. The diction of the latter is beautiful, but such beauty as upon nearer inspection carries with it evident symptoms of affectation. This has been attended with very disagreeable consequences. Nothing is so easy to copy as affectation, and his Lordship's rank and fame have procured him more imitators in Britain than any other writer I know; all faithfully preserving his blemishes, but unhappily not one of his beauties.

Mr. Trenchard and Dr. Davenant were political writers of great abilities in diction, and their pamphlets are now standards in that way of writing. They were followed by Dean Swift, who, though in other respects far their superior, never could arise to that manliness and clearness of diction in political writing for which they were so justly famous.

They were all of them exceeded by the late Lord Bolingbroke, whose strength lay in that province; for as a philosopher and a critic he was ill qualified, being destitute of virtue for the one, and of learning for the other. His writings against Sir Robert Walpole are incomparably the best part of his works. The personal and perpetual antipathy he had for that family, to whose places he thought his own abilities had a right, gave a glow to his style, and an edge to his manner, that never yet have been equalled in political writing. His misfortunes and disappointments gave his mind a turn which his friends mistook for philosophy, and at one time of his life he had the art to impose the same belief upon some of his enemies. His idea of a patriot king, which I reckon (as indeed it was) amongst his writings against Sir Robert Walpole, is a masterpiece of diction. Even in his other works his style is excellent; but where a man either does not or will not understand the subject he writes on, there must always be a deficiency. In politics, he was generally master of what he undertook; in morals, never.

Mr. Addison, for a happy and natural style, will be always an honour to British literature. His diction, indeed, wants strength; but it is equal to all the subjects he undertakes to handle, as he never (at least in his finished works) attempts anything either in the argumentative or demonstrative way.

Though Sir Richard Steele's reputation as a public writer was owing to his connexions with Mr. Addison, yet after their intimacy was formed, Steele sank in his merit as an author. This was not owing so much to the evident superiority on the part of Addison, as to the unnatural efforts which Steele made to equal or eclipse him. This emulation destroyed that genuine flow of diction which is discoverable in all his former compositions.

Whilst their writings engaged attention and the favour of the public, reiterated but unsuccessful endeavours were made towards forming a grammar of the English language. The authors of those efforts went upon wrong principles. Instead of endeavouring to retrench the absurdities of our language, and bringing it to a certain criterion, their grammars were no other than a collection of rules attempting to naturalize those absurdities, and bring them under a regular system.

Somewhat effectual, however, might have been done towards fixing the standard of the English language, had it not been for the spirit of party. For both Whigs and Tories being ambitious to stand at the head of so great a design, the Queen's death happened before any plan of an academy could be resolved on.

Meanwhile, the necessity of such an institution became every day more apparent. The periodical and political writers, who then swarmed, adopted the very worst manner of L'Estrange, till not only all decency, but all propriety, of language was lost in the nation. Leslie, a pert writer, with some wit and learning, insulted the government every week with the grossest abuse. His style and manner, both of which were illiberal, were imitated by Ridpath, Defoe, Dunton, and others of the opposite party; and Toland pleaded the cause of atheism and immorality in much the same strain: his subject seemed to debase his diction, and he ever failed most in one, when he grew most licentious in the other.

Towards the end of Queen Anne's reign some of the greatest men in England devoted their time to party, and then a much better manner obtained in political writing. Mr. Walpole, Mr. Addison, Mr. Mainwaring, Mr. Steele, and many members of both houses of Parliament, drew their pens for the Whigs; but they seem to have been overmatched, though not in argument, yet in writing, by Bolingbroke, Prior, Swift, Arbuthnot, and the other friends of the opposite party. They who oppose a ministry have always a better field for ridicule and reproof than they who defend it.

Since that period our writers have either been encouraged above their merits or below them. Some who were possessed of the meanest abilities acquired the highest preferments, while others who seemed born to reflect a lustre upon their age perished by want or neglect. More, Savage, and Amherst were possessed of great abilities, yet they were suffered to feel all the miseries that usually attend the ingenious and the imprudent—that attend men of strong passions, and no phlegmatic reserve in their command.

At present, were a man to attempt to improve his fortune or increase his friendship by poetry, he would soon feel the anxiety of disappointment. The press lies open, and is a benefactor to every sort of literature but that alone.

I am at a loss whether to ascribe this falling off of the public to a vicious taste in the poet or in them. Perhaps both are to be reprehended. The poet, either drily didactive, gives us rules which might appear abstruse even in a system of ethics, or, triflingly volatile, writes upon the most unworthy subjects; content, if he can give music instead of sense; content, if he can paint to the imagination without any desires or endeavours to affect: the public, therefore, with justice, discard such empty sound, which has nothing but a jingle, or, what is worse, the unmusical flow of blank verse, to recommend it. The late method, also, into which our newspapers have fallen, of giving an epitome of every new publication, must greatly damp the writer's genius. He finds himself, in this case, at the mercy of men who have neither abilities nor learning to distinguish his merit. He finds his own composition mixed with the sordid trash of every daily scribbler. There is a sufficient specimen given of his work to abate curiosity, and yet so mutilated as to render him contemptible. His first, and perhaps his second, work by these means sink, among the crudities of the age, into oblivion. Fame, he finds, begins to turn her back: he therefore flies to profit, which invites him, and he enrols himself in the lists of dulness and of avarice for life.

Yet there are still among us men of the greatest abilities, and who, in some parts of learning, have surpassed their predecessors. Justice and friendship might here impel me to speak of names which will shine out to all posterity, but prudence restrains me from what I should otherwise eagerly embrace. Envy might rise against every honoured name I should mention, since scarcely one of them has not those who are his enemies, or those who despise him, &c.

OF THE OPERA IN ENGLAND.

THE rise and fall of our amusements pretty much resemble that of empire. They this day flourish without any visible cause for such vigour; the next they decay without any reason that can be assigned for their downfall. Some years ago the Italian opera was the only fashionable amusement among our nobility. The managers of the play-houses dreaded it as a mortal enemy, and our very poets listed themselves in the opposition: at present the house seems deserted; the *castrati* sing to empty benches; even Prince Vologese himself, a youth of great expectations, sings himself out of breath, and rattles his chain to no purpose.

To say the truth, the opera, as it is conducted among us, is but a very humdrum amusement: in other countries the decorations are entirely magnificent, the singers all excellent, and the burlettas, or interludes, quite entertaining; the best poets compose the words, and the best masters the music; but with us it is otherwise: the decorations are but trifling and cheap; the singers, Mattei only excepted, but indifferent. Instead of interlude, we have those sorts of skipping dances which are calculated for the galleries of the theatre. Every performer sings his favourite song, and the music is only a medley of old Italian airs or some meagre modern capricio.

When such is the case, it is not much to be wondered if the opera is pretty much neglected. The lower orders of people have neither taste nor fortune to relish such an entertainment; they would find more satisfaction in the "Roast Beef of Old England" than in the finest closes of an eunuch; they sleep amidst all the agony of recitative. On the other hand, people of fortune or taste can hardly be pleased where there is a visible poverty in the decorations, and an entire want of taste in the composition.

Would it not surprise one, that when Metastasio is so well known in England, and so universally admired, the manager or the composer should have recourse to any other operas than those written by him? I might venture to say, that "written by Metastasio," put up in the bills of the day, would alone be sufficient to fill a house, since thus the admirers of sense as well as sound might find entertainment.

The performers also should be entreated to sing only their parts, without clapping in any of their own favourite airs. I must own, that such songs are generally to me the most disagreeable in the world. Every singer generally chooses a favourite air, not from the excellency of the music, but from difficulty; such songs are generally chosen as surprise rather than please, where the performer may show his compass, his breath, and his volubility.

Hence proceed those unnatural startings, those unmusical closings, and shakes lengthened out to a painful continuance: such, indeed, may show a voice, but it must give a truly delicate ear the utmost uneasiness. Such tricks are not music; neither Corelli nor Pergolesi ever permitted them, and they begin even to be discontinued in Italy, where they first had their rise.

And now I am upon the subject; our composers also should affect greater simplicity: let their bass clef have all the variety they can give it,—let the body of the music (if I may so express it) be as various as they please; but let them avoid ornamenting a barren groundwork; let them not attempt by flourishing to cheat us of solid harmony.

The works of Mr. Rameau are never heard without a surprising effect. I can attribute it only to the simplicity he everywhere observes, insomuch that some of his finest harmonies are often only octave and unison. This simple manner has greater powers than is generally imagined; and were not such a demonstration misplaced, I think, from the principles of music, it might be proved to be most agreeable.

But to leave general reflection, with the present set of performers the operas, if the conductor thinks proper, may be carried on with some success, since they have all some merit, if not as actors, at least as singers. Signora Mattei is at once both a perfect actress and a very fine singer. She is possessed of a fine sensibility in her manner, and seldom indulges those extravagant and unmusical flights of voice complained of before. Cornacini, on the other hand, is a very indifferent actor—has a most unmeaning face—seems not to feel his part—is infected with a passion of showing his compass; but, to recompense all these defects, his voice is melodious—he has vast compass and great volubility—his swell and shake are perfectly fine, unless that he continues the latter too long. In short, whatever the defects of his action may be, they are amply recompensed by his excellency as a singer; nor can I avoid fancying that he might make a much greater figure in an oratorio than upon the stage.

However, upon the whole, I know not whether ever operas can be kept up in England; they seem to be entirely exotic, and require the nicest management and care. Instead of this, the care of them is assigned to men unacquainted with the genius and disposition of the people they would amuse, and whose only motives are immediate gain. Whether a discontinuance of such entertainments would be more to the loss or to the advantage of the nation, I will not take upon me to determine, since it is as much our interest to induce foreigners of taste among us on the one hand, as it is to discourage those trifling members of society who generally compose the operatical *dramatis personæ* on the other.

END OF THE BEE.

AN INQUIRY INTO THE PRESENT STATE

OF

POLITE LEARNING.

[1759.]

Ἐμοὶ πρὸς φιλοσόφους ἔστι φιλία· πρὸς μὲν σοφιστὰς ἢ γραμματιστὰς οὔτε νῦν ἔστι φιλία μήτε ὕστερον πότε γένοιτο.

Tolerabile si ædificia nostra diruerent ædificandi capaces.

AN INQUIRY INTO THE PRESENT STATE OF

POLITE LEARNING.

INTRODUCTION.

It has been so long the practice to represent literature as declining, that every renewal of this complaint now comes with diminished influence. The public has been so often excited by a false alarm, that at present the nearer we approach the threatened period of decay, the more our security increases.

It will now probably be said, that taking the decay of genius for granted, as I do, argues either resentment or partiality. The writer possessed of fame, it may be asserted, is willing to enjoy it without a rival, by lessening every competitor: or, if unsuccessful, he is desirous to turn upon others the contempt which is levelled at himself; and being convicted at the bar of literary justice, hopes for pardon by accusing every brother of the same profession.

Sensible of this, I am at a loss where to find an apology for persisting to arraign the merit of the age; for joining in a cry which the judicious have long since left to be kept up by the vulgar; and for adopting the sentiments of the multitude in a performance that at best can please only a few.

Complaints of our degeneracy in literature, as well as in morals, I own, have been frequently exhibited of late, but seem to be enforced more with the ardour of devious declamation than the calmness of deliberate inquiry. The dullest critic, who strives at a reputation for delicacy by showing he cannot be pleased, may pathetically assure us, that our taste is upon the decline; may consign every modern performance to oblivion, and bequeath nothing to posterity, except the labours of our ancestors, or his own. Such general invective, however, conveys no instruction: all it teaches is, that the writer dislikes an age by which he is probably disregarded. The manner of being useful on the subject would be, to point out the symptoms, to investigate the causes, and direct to the remedies, of the approaching decay. This is a subject hitherto unattempted in criticism,—perhaps it is the only subject in which criticism can be useful.

How far the writer is equal to such an undertaking the reader must determine; yet perhaps his observations may be just, though his manner of expressing them should only serve as an example of the errors he undertakes to reprove.

Novelty, however, is not permitted to usurp the place of reason; it may attend, but shall not conduct the inquiry. But it should be observed, that the more original any performance is, the more it is liable to deviate; for cautious stupidity is always in the right.

CHAPTER I.

The Causes which contribute to the Decline of Learning.

If we consider the revolutions which have happened in the commonwealth of letters, survey the rapid progress of learning in one period of antiquity, or its amazing decline in another, we shall be almost induced to accuse Nature of partiality; as if she had exhausted all her efforts in adorning one age, while she left the succeeding entirely neglected. It is not to Nature, however, but to ourselves alone, that this partiality must be ascribed; the seeds of excellence are sown in every age, and it is wholly owing to a wrong direction in the passions or pursuits of mankind that they have not received the proper cultivation.

As in the best regulated societies the very laws which at first give the government solidity may in the end contribute to its dissolution, so the efforts which might have promoted learning in its feeble commencement may, if continued, retard its progress. The paths of science, which were at first intricate, because untrodden, may at last grow toilsome, because too much frequented. As learning advances, the candidates for its honours become more numerous, and the acquisition of fame more uncertain: the modest may despair of attaining it, and the opulent think it too precarious to pursue. Thus the task of supporting the honour of the times may at last devolve on indigence and effrontery; while learning must partake of the contempt of its professors.

To illustrate these assertions, it may be proper to take a slight review of the decline of ancient learning; to consider how far its depravation was owing to the impossibility of supporting continued perfection; in what respects it proceeded from voluntary corruption; and how far it was hastened on by accident. If modern learning be compared with ancient in these different lights, a parallel between both, which has hitherto produced only vain dispute, may contribute to amusement, perhaps to instruction. We shall thus be enabled to perceive what period of antiquity the present age most resembles; whether we are making advances towards excellence, or retiring again to primeval obscurity: we shall thus be taught to acquiesce in those defects which it is impossible to prevent, and reject all faulty innovations, though offered under the specious titles of improvement.

Learning, when planted in any country, is transient and fading, nor does it flourish till slow gradations of improvement have naturalized it to the soil. It makes feeble advances, begins among the vulgar, and rises into reputation among the great. It cannot be established in a state at once, by introducing the learned of other countries; these may grace a court, but seldom enlighten a kingdom. Ptolemy Philadelphus, Constantine Porphyrogeneta, Alfred, or Charlemagne, might have invited learned foreigners into their dominions, but could not establish learning. While in the radiance of royal favour, every art and science seemed to flourish; but when that was withdrawn, they quickly felt the rigours of a strange climate, and with exotic constitutions perished by neglect.

As the arts and sciences are slow in coming to maturity, it is requisite, in order to their perfection, that the state should be permanent which gives them reception. There are numberless attempts without success, and experiments without conclusion, between the first rudiments of an art and its utmost perfection; between the outlines of a shadow and the picture of an Apelles. Leisure is required to go through the tedious interval, to join the experience of predecessors to our own, or enlarge our views by building on the ruined attempts of former adventurers. All this may be performed in a society of long continuance; but if the kingdom be but of short duration, as was the case of Arabia, learning seems coeval, sympathises with its political struggles, and is annihilated in its dissolution.

But permanence in a state is not alone sufficient; it is requisite, also, for this end, that it should be free. Naturalists assure us, that all animals are sagacious in proportion as they are removed from the tyranny of others. In native liberty the elephant is a citizen, and the beaver an architect; but whenever the tyrant man intrudes upon their community, their spirit is broken, they seem anxious only for safety, and their intellects suffer an equal diminution with their prosperity. The parallel will hold with regard to mankind. Fear naturally represses invention—benevolence, ambition; for in a nation of slaves, as in the despotic governments of the East, to labour after fame is to be a candidate for danger.

To attain literary excellence also it is requisite that the soil and climate should, as much as possible, conduce to happiness. The earth must supply man with the necessaries of life, before he has leisure or inclination to pursue more refined enjoyments. The climate also must be equally indulgent; for, in too warm a region, the mind is relaxed into languor, and by the opposite excess is chilled into torpid inactivity.

These are the principal advantages which tend to the improvement of learning; and all these were united in the states of Greece and Rome.

We must now examine what hastens, or prevents, its decline.

Those who behold the phenomena of nature, and content themselves with the view, without inquiring into their causes, are perhaps wiser than is generally imagined. In this manner our rude ancestors were acquainted with facts; and poetry, which helped the imagination and the memory, was thought the most proper vehicle for conveying their knowledge to posterity. It was the poet who harmonized the ungrateful accents of his native dialect, who lifted it above common conversation, and shaped its rude combinations into order. From him the orator formed a style; and, though poetry first rose out of prose, in turn it gave birth to every prosaic excellence. Musical period, concise expression, and delicacy of sentiment, were all excellencies derived from the poet; in short, he not only preceded, but formed the orator, philosopher, and historian.

When the observations of past ages were collected, philosophy next began to examine their causes. She had numberless facts from which to draw proper inferences, and poetry had taught her the strongest expression to enforce them. Thus, the Greek philosophers, for instance, exerted all their happy talents in the investigation of truth and the production of beauty. They saw that there was more excellence in captivating the judgment, than in raising a momentary astonishment. In their arts, they imitated only such parts of nature as might please in the representation in the sciences; they cultivated such parts of knowledge as it was every man's duty to know. Thus learning was encouraged, protected, honoured, and, in its turn, it adorned, strengthened and harmonized the community.

But, as the mind is vigorous and active, and experiment is dilatory and painful, the spirit of philosophy being excited, the reasoner, when destitute of experiment, had recourse to theory, and gave up what was useful for refinement.

Critics, sophists, grammarians, rhetoricians, and commentators, now began to figure in the literary commonwealth. In the dawn of science such are generally modest, and not entirely useless. Their performances serve to mark the progress of learning, though they seldom contribute to its improvement. But as nothing but speculation was required in making proficients in their respective departments, so neither the satire nor the contempt of the wise, though Socrates was of the number, nor the laws levelled at them by the state, though Cato was in the legislature, could prevent their approaches. Possessed of all the advantages of unfeeling dulness, laborious, insensible, and persevering, they still proceeded mending and mending every work of genius, or, to speak without irony, undermining all that was polite and useful. Libraries were loaded, but not enriched, with their labours, while the fatigues of reading their explanatory comments was tenfold that which might suffice for understanding the original; and their works effectually increased our application, by professing to remove it.

Against so obstinate and irrefragable an enemy what could avail the unsupported sallies of genius, or the opposition of transitory resentment? In short, they conquered by persevering, claimed the right of dictating upon every work of taste, sentiment, or genius, and, at last, when destitute of other employment, like the supernumerary domestics of the great, made work for each other.

They now took upon them to teach poetry to those who wanted genius, and the power of disputing to those who knew nothing of the subject in debate. It was observed how some of the most admired poets had copied nature. From these they collected dry rules, dignified with long names, and such were obtruded upon the public for their improvement. Common sense would be apt to suggest, that the art might be studied to more advantage rather by imitation than precept. It might suggest that those rules were collected, not from nature, but a copy of nature, and would consequently give us still fainter resemblances of original beauty. It might still suggest, that explained wit makes but a feeble impression; that the observations of others are soon forgotten, those made by ourselves are permanent and useful. But it seems understandings of every size were to be mechanically instructed in poetry. If the reader was too dull to relish the beauties of Virgil, the comment of Servius was ready to brighten his imagination; if Terence could not raise him to a smile, Evantius was at hand, with a long-winded scholium, to increase his titillation. Such rules are calculated to make blockheads talk, but all the lemmata of the Lyceum are unable to give him feeling.

But it would be endless to recount all the absurdities which were hatched in the schools of those specious idlers; be it sufficient to say, that they increased as learning improved, but swarmed on its decline. It was then that every work of taste was buried in long comments, every useful subject in morals was distinguished away into casuistry, and doubt and subtlety characterised the learning of the age. Metrodorus, Valerius Probus, Aulus Gellius, Pedianus, Boethius, and an hundred others, to be acquainted with whom might show much reading and but little judgment; these, I say, made choice each of an author, and delivered all their load of learning on his back. Shame to our ancestors! many of their works have reached our times entire, while Tacitus himself has suffered mutilation.

In a word, the commonwealth of literature was at last wholly overrun by these studious triflers. Men of real genius were lost in the multitude, or, as in a world of fools it were folly to aim at being an only exception, obliged to conform to every prevailing absurdity of the times. Original productions seldom appeared, and learning, as if grown superannuated, bestowed all its panegyric upon the vigour of its youth, and turned encomiast upon its former achievements.

It is to these, then, that the depravation of ancient polite learning is principally to be ascribed. By them it was separated from common sense, and made the proper employment of speculative idlers. Men bred up among books, and seeing nature only by reflection, could do little except hunt after perplexity and confusion. The public, therefore, with reason rejected learning, when thus rendered barren, though voluminous; for we may be assured, that the generality of mankind never lose a passion for letters, while they continue to be either amusing or useful.

It was such writers as these that rendered learning unfit for uniting and strengthening civil society, or for promoting the views of ambition. True philosophy had kept the Grecian states cemented into one effective body, more than any law for that purpose; and the Etrurian philosophy, which prevailed in the first ages of Rome, inspired those patriot virtues which paved the way to universal empire. But by the labours of commentators, when philosophy became abstruse or triflingly minute—when doubt was presented instead of knowledge—when the orator was taught to charm the multitude with the music of his periods, and pronounced a declamation that might be sung as well as spoken, and often upon subjects wholly fictitious,—in such circumstances, learning was entirely unsuited to all the purposes of government, or the designs of the ambitious. As long as the sciences could influence the state, and its politics were strengthened by them, so long did the community give them countenance and protection. But the wiser part of mankind would not be imposed upon by unintelligible jargon, nor, like the knight in Pantagruel, swallow a chimera for a breakfast, though even cooked by Aristotle. As the philosopher grew useless in the state, he also became contemptible. In the times of Lucian he was chiefly remarkable for his avarice, his impudence, and his beard.

Under the auspicious influence of genius, arts and sciences grew up together, and mutually illustrated each other. But when once pedants became lawgivers, the sciences began to want grace, and the polite arts solidity; these grew crabbed and sour, those meretricious and gaudy; the philosopher became disgustingly precise, and the poet, ever straining after grace, caught only finery.

These men also contributed to obstruct the progress of wisdom, by addicting their readers to one particular sect, or some favourite science. They generally carried on a petty traffic in some little creek: within that they busily plied about, and drove an insignificant trade; but never ventured out into the great ocean of knowledge, nor went beyond the bounds that chance, conceit, or laziness, had first prescribed their inquiries. Their disciples, instead of aiming at being originals themselves, became imitators of that merit alone which was constantly proposed for their admiration. In exercises of this kind the most stupid are generally most successful; for there is not in nature a more imitative animal than a dunce.

Hence ancient learning may be distinguished into three periods,—its commencement, or the age of poets; its maturity, or the age of philosophers; and its decline, or the age of critics. In the poetical age commentators were very few, but might have in some respects been useful. In its philosophical, their assistance must necessarily become obnoxious; yet, as if the nearer we approached perfection, the more we stood in need of their directions, in this period they began to grow numerous. But when polite learning was no more, then it was those literary lawgivers made the most formidable appearance. *Corruptissima republica, plurimæ leges.*

But let us take a more distinct view of those ages of ignorance in which false refinement had involved mankind, and see how far they resemble our own.

CHAPTER II.

A View of the Obscure Ages.

WHATEVER the skill of any country may be in sciences, it is from its excellence in polite learning alone that it must expect a character from posterity. The poet and the historian are they who diffuse a lustre upon the age, and the philosopher scarcely acquires any applause, unless his character be introduced to the vulgar by their mediation.

The obscure ages which succeeded the decline of the Roman empire, are a striking instance of the truth of this assertion. Whatever period of those ill-fated times we happen to turn to, we shall perceive more skill in the sciences among the professors of them, more abstruse and deeper inquiry into every philosophical subject, and a greater show of subtlety and close reasoning, than in the most enlightened ages of all antiquity. But their writings were mere speculative amusements, and all their researches exhausted upon trifles. Unskilled in the arts of adorning their knowledge, or adapting it to common sense, their voluminous productions rest peacefully in our libraries, or, at best, are inquired after from motives of curiosity, not by the scholar, but the virtuoso.

I am not insensible that several late French historians have exhibited the obscure ages in a very different light. They have represented them as utterly ignorant both of arts and sciences, buried in the profoundest darkness, or only illuminated with a feeble gleam, which, like an expiring taper, rose and sunk by intervals. Such assertions, however, though they serve to help out the declaimer, should be cautiously admitted by the historian. For instance, the tenth century is particularly distinguished by posterity with the appellation of obscure. Yet even in this the reader's memory may possibly suggest the names of some whose works, still preserved, discover a most extensive erudition, though rendered almost useless by affectation and obscurity. A few of their names and writings may be mentioned, which will serve at once to confirm what I assert, and give the reader an idea of what kind of learning an age declining into obscurity chiefly chooses to cultivate.

About the tenth century flourished Leo the philosopher. We have seven volumes folio of his collections of laws, published at Paris, 1647. He wrote upon the art military, and understood also astronomy and judicial astrology. He was seven times more voluminous than Plato.

Solomon, the German, wrote a most elegant dictionary of the Latin tongue, still preserved in the university of Louvain: Pantaleon, in the lives of his illustrious countrymen, speaks of it in the warmest strains of rapture. Dictionary writing was at that time much in fashion.

Constantine Porphyrogeneta was a man universally skilled in the sciences. His tracts on the administration of an empire, on tactics, and on laws, were published some years since at Leyden. His court—for he was emperor of the East—was resorted to by the learned from all parts of the world.

Luitprandus was a most voluminous historian, and particularly famous for the history of his own times. The compliments paid him as a writer are said to exceed even his own voluminous productions. I cannot pass over one of a later date made him by a German divine: "Luitprandus nunquam Luitprando dissimilis."

Alfric composed several grammars and dictionaries still preserved among the curious.

Pope Sylvester the Second wrote a treatise on the sphere, on arithmetic and geometry, published some years since at Paris.

Michael Psellus lived in this age, whose books on the sciences, I will not scruple to assert, contain more learning than those of any one of the earlier ages. His erudition was indeed amazing; and he was as voluminous as he was learned. The character given him by Allatius has, perhaps, more truth in it than will be granted by those who have seen none of his productions. There was, says he, no science with which he was unacquainted, none which he did not write something upon, and none which he did not leave better than he found it. To mention his works would be endless. His commentaries on Aristotle alone amount to three folios.

Bertholdus Teutonicus, a very voluminous historian, was a politician, and wrote against the government under which he lived; but most of his writings, though not all, are lost.

Constantius Afer was a philosopher and physician. We have remaining but two volumes folio of his philological performances. However, the historian who prefixes the life of the author to his work says that he wrote many more, as he kept on writing during the course of a long life.

Lambertus published an universal history about this time, which has been printed at Frankfort in folio. An universal history in one folio! If he had consulted with his bookseller, he would have spun it out to ten at least; but Lambertus might have had too much modesty.

By this time the reader perceives the spirit of learning which at that time prevailed. The ignorance of the age was not owing to a dislike of knowledge, but a false standard of taste was erected, and a wrong direction given to philosophical inquiry. It was the fashion of the day to write dictionaries, commentaries, and compilations, and to evaporate in a folio the spirit that could scarcely have sufficed for an epigram. The most barbarous times had men of learning, if commentators, compilers, polemic divines, and intricate metaphysicians deserved the title.

I have mentioned but a very inconsiderable number of the writers in this age of obscurity. The multiplicity of their publications will at least equal those of any similar period of the most polite antiquity. As, therefore, the writers of those times are almost entirely forgotten, we may infer that the number of publications alone will never secure any age whatsoever from oblivion. Nor can printing, contrary to what Mr. Beumelle has remarked, prevent literary decline for the future, since it only increases the number of books, without advancing their intrinsic merit.

CHAPTER III.

Of the present State of Polite Learning in Italy.

FROM ancient we are now come to modern times, and, in running over Europe, we shall find that wherever learning has been cultivated, it has flourished by the same advantages as in Greece and Rome; and that, wherever it has declined, it sinks by the same causes of decay.

Dante, the poet of Italy, who wrote in

the thirteenth century, was the first who attempted to bring learning from the cloister into the community, and paint human nature in a language adapted to modern manners. He addressed a barbarous people in a method suited to their apprehensions; united purgatory and the river Styx, St. Peter and Virgil, heaven and hell, together, and shows a strange mixture of good sense and absurdity. The truth is, he owes most of his reputation to the obscurity of the times in which he lived. As in the land of Benin a man may pass for a prodigy of parts who can read, so in an age of barbarity a small degree of excellence ensures success. But it was great merit in him to have lifted up the standard of nature, in spite of all the opposition and the persecution he received from contemporary criticism. To this standard every succeeding genius resorted; the germ of every art and science began to unfold; and to imitate nature was found to be the surest way of imitating antiquity. In a century or two after, modern Italy might justly boast of rivalling ancient Rome; equal in some branches of polite learning, and not far surpassed in others.

They soon, however, fell from emulating the wonders of antiquity into simple admiration. As if the word had been given, when Vida and Tasso wrote on the arts of poetry, the whole swarm of critics was up. The Speronis of the age attempted to be awkwardly merry; and the Virtuosi and the Nascotti sat upon the merits of every contemporary performance. After the age of Clement VII. the Italians seemed to think that there was more merit in praising or censuring well, than in writing well; almost every subsequent performance since their time being designed rather to show the excellence of the critic's taste than his genius. One or two poets, indeed, seem at present born to redeem the honour of their country. Metastasio has restored nature in all her simplicity, and Maffei is the first that has introduced a tragedy among his countrymen without a love-plot. Perhaps the Samson of Milton and the Athalia of Racine might have been his guides in such an attempt. But two poets in an age are not sufficient to revive the splendour of decaying genius; nor should we consider them as the standard by which to characterise a nation. Our measures of literary reputation must be taken rather from that numerous class of men who, placed above the vulgar, are yet beneath the great, and who confer fame on others without receiving any portion of it themselves.

In Italy, then, we shall nowhere find a stronger passion for the arts of taste, yet no country making more feeble efforts to promote either. The Virtuosi and Filosofi seem to have divided the Encyclopedia between each other. Both inviolably attached to their respective pursuits; and, from an opposition of character, each holding the other in the most sovereign contempt. The Virtuosi, professed critics of beauty in the works of art, judge of medals by the smell, and pictures by feeling: in statuary, hang over a fragment with the most ardent gaze of admiration; though wanting the head and the other extremities, if dug from a ruin, the *Torso* becomes inestimable. An unintelligible monument of Etruscan barbarity cannot be sufficiently prized; and anything from Herculaneum excites rapture. When the intellectual taste is thus decayed, its relishes become false, and, like that of sense, nothing will satisfy but what is best suited to feed the disease.

Poetry is no longer among them an imitation of what we see, but of what a visionary might wish. The zephyr breathes the most exquisite perfume, the trees wear eternal verdure; fawns, and dryads, and hamadryads, stand ready to fan the sultry shepherdess, who has forgot, indeed, the prettiness with which Guarini's shepherdesses have been reproached, but is so simple and innocent as often to have no meaning. Happy country, where the pastoral age begins to revive!—where the wits even of Rome are united into a rural group of nymphs and swains, under the appellation of modern Arcadians!—where in the midst of porticoes, processions, and cavalcades, abbés turned shepherds, and shepherdesses without sheep indulge their innocent *divertimenti!*

The Filosofi are entirely different from

the former. As those pretend to have got their knowledge from conversing with the living and polite, so these boast of having theirs from books and study. Bred up all their lives in colleges, they have there learned to think in track, servilely to follow the leader of their sect, and only to adopt such opinions as their universities, or the inquisition, are pleased to allow. By these means they are behind the rest of Europe in several modern improvements; afraid to think for themselves; and their universities seldom admit opinions as true, till universally received among the rest of mankind. In short, were I to personize my ideas of learning in this country, I would represent it in the tawdry habits of the stage, or else in the more homely guise of bearded school philosophy.

CHAPTER IV.

Of Polite Learning in Germany.

If we examine the state of learning in Germany, we shall find that the Germans early discovered a passion for polite literature; but unhappily, like conquerors who, invading the dominions of others, leave their own to desolation, instead of studying the German tongue, they continue to write in Latin. Thus, while they cultivated an obsolete language, and vainly laboured to apply it to modern manners, they neglected their own.

At the same time, also, they began at the wrong end,—I mean by being commentators; and though they have given many instances of their industry, they have scarcely afforded any of genius. If criticism could have improved the taste of a people, the Germans would have been the most polite nation alive. We shall nowhere behold the learned wear a more important appearance than here; nowhere more dignified with professorships, or dressed out in the fopperies of scholastic finery. However, they seem to earn all the honour of this kind which they enjoy. Their assiduity is unparalleled and did they employ half those hours on study which they bestow on reading, we might be induced to pity as well as praise their painful pre-eminence. But, guilty of a fault too common to great readers, they write through volumes, while they do not think through a page. Never fatigued themselves, they think the reader can never be weary; so they drone on, saying all that can be said on the subject, not selecting what may be advanced to the purpose. Were angels to write books, they would never write folios.

But let the Germans have their due: if they are dull, no nation alive assumes a more laudable solemnity, or better understands all the decorums of stupidity. Let the discourse of a professor run on ever so heavily, it cannot be irksome to his dozing pupils, who frequently lend him sympathetic nods of approbation. I have sometimes attended their disputes at graduation. On this occasion they often dispense with their gravity, and seem really all alive. The disputes are managed between the followers of Cartesius, whose exploded system they continue to call the new philosophy, and those of Aristotle. Though both parties are in the wrong, they argue with an obstinacy worthy the cause of truth; Nego, Probo, and Distinguo grow loud; the disputants become warm, the moderator cannot be heard, the audience take part in the debate, till at last the whole hall buzzes with sophistry and error.

There are, it is true, several societies in this country which are chiefly calculated to promote knowledge. His late majesty, as Elector of Hanover, has established one at Gottingen, at an expense of not less than a hundred thousand pounds. This university has already pickled monsters, and dissected live puppies without number. Their transactions have been published in the learned world at proper intervals since their institution, and will, it is hoped, one day give them just reputation. But had the fourth part of the immense sum above mentioned been given in proper rewards to genius, in some neighbouring countries, it would have rendered the name of the donor immortal, and added to the real interests of society.

Yet it ought to be observed, that, of late, learning has been patronized here by a prince who, in the humblest station, would have been the first of mankind. The society established by the King of Prussia at Berlin is one of the finest literary institutions that any age or nation has produced. This academy comprehends all the sciences under four different classes; and although the object of each is different, and admits of being separately treated, yet these classes mutually influence the progress of each other, and concur in the same general design. Experimental philosophy, mathematics, metaphysics, and polite literature, are here carried on together. The members are not collected from among the students of some obscure seminary or the wits of a metropolis, but chosen from all the literati of Europe, supported by the bounty, and ornamented by the productions, of their royal founder. We can easily discern how much such an institution excels any other now subsisting. One fundamental error among societies of this kind is their addicting themselves to one branch of science, or some particular part of polite learning. Thus, in Germany, there are nowhere so many establishments of this nature; but as they generally profess the promotion of natural or medical knowledge, he who reads their Acta will only find an obscure farago of experiment, most frequently terminated by no resulting phenomena. To make experiments is, I own, the only way to promote natural knowledge; but to treasure up every unsuccessful inquiry into nature, or to communicate every experiment without conclusion, is not to promote science, but to oppress it. Had the members of these societies enlarged their plans, and taken in art as well as science, one part of knowledge would have repressed any faulty luxuriance in the other, and all would have materially assisted each other's promotion. Besides, the society which, with a contempt of all collateral assistance, admits of members skilled in one science only, whatever their diligence or labour might be, will lose much time in the discovery of such truths as are well known already to the learned in a different line; consequently, their progress must be slow in gaining a proper eminence from which to view their subject, and their strength will be exhausted in attaining the station whence they should have set out. With regard to the Royal Society of London, the greatest, and perhaps the oldest institution of the kind, had it widened the basis of its institution, though they might not have propagated more discoveries, they would probably have delivered them in a more pleasing and compendious form. They would have been free from the contempt of the ill-natured and the raillery of the wit, for which, even candour must allow, there is but too much foundation. But the Berlin academy is subject to none of all these inconveniences; but every one of its individuals is in a capacity of deriving more from the common stock than he contributes to it, while each academician serves as a check upon the rest of his fellows.

Yet very probably even this fine institution will soon decay. As it rose, so it will decline with its great encourager. The society, if I may so speak, is artificially supported. The introduction of foreigners of learning was right; but in adopting a foreign language also—I mean the French—in which all the transactions are to be published, and questions debated, in this there was an error. As I have already hinted, the language of the natives of every country should be also the language of its polite learning. To figure in polite learning, every country should make their own language from their own manners; nor will they ever succeed by introducing that of another, which has been formed from manners which are different. Besides, any academy composed of foreigners must still be recruited from abroad, unless all the natives of the country to which it belongs are in a capacity of becoming candidates for its honours or rewards. While France, therefore, continues to supply Berlin, polite learning will flourish: but when royal favour is withdrawn, learning will return to its natural country.

CHAPTER V.

Of Polite Learning in Holland and some other Countries of Europe.

HOLLAND, at first view, appears to have some pretensions to polite learning. It may be regarded as the great emporium not less of literature than of every other commodity. Here, though destitute of what may be properly called a language of their own, all the languages are understood, cultivated, and spoken. All useful inventions in arts, and new discoveries in science, are published here almost as soon as at the places which first produced them. Its individuals have the same faults, however, with the Germans, of making more use of their memory than their judgment. The chief employment of their literati is to criticise or answer the new performance which appear elsewhere.

A dearth of wit in France or England naturally produces a scarcity in Holland. What Ovid says of Echo may be applied here: "Nec loqui prius ipsa didicit nec reticere loquenti." They wait till something new comes out from others; examine its merits, and reject it, or make it reverberate through the rest of Europe.

After all, I know not whether they should be allowed any national character for polite learning. All their taste is derived to them from neighbouring nations, and that in a language not their own. They somewhat resemble their brokers, who trade for immense sums without having any capital.

The other countries of Europe may be considered as immersed in ignorance, or making but feeble efforts to rise. Spain has long fallen from amazing Europe with her wit, to amusing them with the greatness of her catholic credulity. Rome considers her as the most favourite of all her children, and school divinity still reigns there in triumph. In spite of all attempts of the Marquis D'Ensenada, who saw with regret the barbarity of his countrymen, and bravely offered to oppose it by introducing new systems of learning, and suppressing the seminaries of monastic ignorance—in spite of the ingenuity of Padre Feio, whose book of vulgar errors so finely exposes the monkish stupidity of the times,—the religious have prevailed. Ensenada has been banished, and now lives in exile. Feio has incurred the hatred and contempt of every bigot whose errors he has attempted to oppose, and feels, no doubt, the unremitting displeasure of the priesthood. Persecution is a tribute the great must ever pay for pre-eminence.

It is a little extraordinary, however, how Spain, whose genius is naturally fine, should be so much behind the rest of Europe in this particular; or why school divinity should hold its ground there for nearly six hundred years. The reason must be, that philosophical opinions, which are otherwise transient, acquire stability in proportion as they are connected with the laws of the country; and philosophy and law have nowhere been so closely united as here.

Sweden has of late made some attempts in polite learning in its own language. Count Tessin's instructions to the prince, his pupil, are no bad beginning. If the Muses can fix their residence so far northward, perhaps no country bids so fair for their reception. They have, I am told, a language rude but energetic; if so, it will bear a polish. They have also a jealous sense of liberty, and that strength of thinking peculiar to northern climates, without its attendant ferocity. They will certainly in time produce somewhat great, if their intestine divisions do not unhappily prevent them.

The history of polite learning in Denmark may be comprised in the life of one single man: it rose and fell with the late famous Baron Holberg. This was, perhaps, one of the most extraordinary personages that has done honour to the present century. His being the son of a private sentinel did not abate the ardour of his ambition, for he learned to read though without a master. Upon the death of his father, being left entirely destitute, he was involved in all that distress which is common among the poor, and of which the great have scarcely any idea. However, though only a boy of nine years old, he still persisted in pursuing his studies, travelled about from school to school, and begged his learning and his bread. When at the age of seventeen, instead of applying himself to any of the lower occupations, which seem best adapted to such circumstances, he was resolved to travel for improvement from Norway, the place of his birth, to Copenhagen, the capital city of Denmark. He lived there by teaching French, at the same time avoiding no opportunity of improvement that his scanty funds could permit. But his ambition was not to be restrained, or his thirst of knowledge satisfied, until he had seen the world. Without money, recommendations, or friends, he undertook to set out upon his travels, and make the tour of Europe on foot. A good voice and a trifling skill in music, were the only finances he had to support an undertaking so extensive; so he travelled by day, and at night sung at the doors of peasants' houses to get himself a lodging. In this manner, while yet very young, Holberg passed through France, Germany, and Holland; and coming over to England, took up his residence for two years in the university of Oxford. Here he subsisted by teaching French and music, and wrote his universal history, his earliest, but worst, performance. Furnished with all the learning of Europe, he at last thought proper to return to Copenhagen, where his ingenious productions quickly gained him that favour he deserved. He composed not less than eighteen comedies. Those in his own language are said to excel, and those which are translated into French have peculiar merit. He was honoured with nobility, and enriched by the bounty of the king; so that a life begun in contempt and penury ended in opulence and esteem.

Thus we see in what a low state polite learning is in the countries I have mentioned,—either past its prime, or not yet arrived at maturity. And though the sketch I have drawn be general, yet it was for the most part taken on the spot. I am sensible, however, of the impropriety of national reflection; and did not truth bias me more than inclination in this particular, I should, instead of the account already given, have presented the reader with a panegyric on many of the individuals of every country whose merits deserve the warmest strains of praise. Apostol Zeno, Algarotti, Goldoni, Muratori, and Stay, in Italy—Haller, Klopstock, and Rabner, in Germany—Muschenbrook and Gaubius, in Holland,—all deserve the highest applause. Men like these, united by one bond, pursuing one design, spend their labour and their lives in making their fellow-creatures happy, and in repairing the breaches caused by ambition. In this light, the meanest philosopher, though all his possessions are his lamp or his cell, is more truly valuable than he whose name echoes to the shout of the million, and who stands in all the glare of admiration. In this light, though poverty and contemptuous neglect are all the wages of his good will from mankind, yet the rectitude of his intention is an ample recompense; and self-applause for the present, and the alluring prospect of fame for futurity, reward his labours. The perspective of life brightens upon us, when terminated by an object so charming. Every intermediate image of want, banishment, or sorrow, receives a lustre from its distant influence. With this in view, the patriot, philosopher, and poet have often looked with calmness on disgrace and famine, and rested on their straw with cheerful serenity. Even the last terrors of departing nature abate of their severity, and look kindly on him who considers his sufferings as a passport to immortality, and lays his sorrows on the bed of fame.

CHAPTER VI.

Of Polite Learning in France.

WE have hitherto seen, that wherever the poet was permitted to begin by improving his native language, polite learning flourished; but where the critic undertook the same task, it has never risen to any degree of perfection. Let us now examine the merits of modern learning in France and England; where, though it may be on the decline, yet it is still capable of retrieving much of its former splendour. In other places learning has not yet been planted, or has suffered a total decay. To attempt amendment there would be only like the application of remedies to an insensible or a mortified part; but here there is still life, and there is hope. And indeed the French themselves are so far from giving in to any despondence of this kind that, on the contrary, they admire the progress they are daily making in every science. That levity for which we are apt to despise this nation is probably the principal source of their happiness. An agreeable oblivion of past pleasures, a freedom from solicitude about future ones, and a poignant zest of every present enjoyment, if they be not philosophy, are at least excellent substitutes. By this they are taught to regard the period in which they live with admiration. The present manners and the present conversation surpass all that preceded. A similar enthusiasm as strongly tinctures their learning and their taste. While we, with a despondence characteristic of our nature, are for removing back British excellence to the reign of Queen Elizabeth, our most happy rivals of the Continent cry up the writers of the present times with rapture, and regard the age of Louis XV. as the true Augustan age of France.

The truth is, their present writers have not fallen so far short of the merits of their ancestors as ours have done. That self-sufficiency now mentioned may have been of service to them in this particular. By fancying themselves superior to their ancestors, they have been encouraged to enter the lists with confidence; and by not being dazzled at the splendour of another's reputation, have sometimes had sagacity to mark out an unbeaten path to fame for themselves.

Other causes also may be assigned, that their second growth of genius is still more vigorous than ours. Their encouragements to merit are more skilfully directed; the link of patronage and learning still continues unbroken. The French nobility have certainly a most pleasing way of satisfying the vanity of an author, without indulging his avarice. A man of literary merit is sure of being caressed by the great, though seldom enriched. His pension from the crown just supplies half a competence, and the sale of his labours makes some small addition to his circumstances. Thus the author leads a life of splendid poverty, and seldom becomes wealthy or indolent enough to discontinue an exertion of those abilities by which he rose. With the English it is different. Our writers of rising merit are generally neglected, while the few of an established reputation are overpaid by luxurious affluence. The young encounter every hardship which generally attends upon aspiring indigence; the old enjoy the vulgar, and perhaps the more prudent, satisfaction of putting riches in competition with fame. Those are often seen to spend their youth in want and obscurity; these are sometimes found to lead an old age of indolence and avarice. But such treatment must naturally be expected from Englishmen, whose national character it is to be slow and cautious in making friends, but violent in friendships once contracted. The English nobility, in short, are often known to give greater rewards to genius than the French, who, however, are much more judicious in the application of their empty favours.

The fair sex in France have also not a little contributed to prevent the decline of taste and literature, by expecting such qualifications in their admirers. A man of fashion at Paris, however contemptible we may think him here, must be acquainted with the reigning modes of philosophy as well as of dress, to be able to entertain his mistress agreeably. The sprightly pedants are not to be caught by dumb show, by the squeeze of the hand, or the ogling of a broad eye; but must be pursued at once through all the labyrinths of the Newtonian system or the metaphysics of Locke. I have seen as bright a circle of beauty at the chemical lectures of Rouelle as gracing the court of Versailles. And indeed wisdom never appears so charming, as when graced and protected by beauty.

To these advantages may be added the reception of their language in the different courts of Europe. An author who excels is sure of having all the polite for admirers, and is encouraged to write by the pleasing expectation of universal fame. Add to this, that those countries who can make nothing good from their own language have lately begun to write in this, some of whose productions contribute to support the present literary reputation of France.

There are, therefore, many among the French who do honour to the present age, and whose writings will be transmitted to posterity with an ample share of fame. Some of the most celebrated are as follow:—

Voltaire, whose voluminous yet spirited productions are too well known to require an eulogy. Does he not resemble the champion mentioned by Xenophon, of great reputation in all the gymnastic exercises united, but inferior to each champion singly, who excels only in one?

Montesquieu, a name equally deserving

fame with the former. The Spirit of Laws is an instance how much genius is able to lead learning. His system has been adopted by the literati; and yet, is it not possible for opinions equally plausible to be formed upon opposite principles, if a genius like his could be found to attempt such an undertaking? He seems more a poet than a philosopher.

Rousseau of Geneva, a professed man-hater, or, more properly speaking, a philosopher enraged with one half of mankind, because they unavoidably make the other half unhappy. Such sentiments are generally the result of much good-nature and little experience.

Piron, an author possessed of as much wit as any man alive, yet with as little prudence to turn it to his own advantage. A comedy of his, called *La Metromanie*, is the best theatrical production that has appeared of late in Europe. But I know not whether I should most commend his genius or censure his obscenity. His *Ode à Priape* has justly excluded him from a place in the academy of Belles Lettres. However, the good-natured Montesquieu, by his interest, procured the starving bard a trifling pension. His own epitaph was all the revenge he took upon the academy for being repulsed :

> Cy git Piron ; qui ne fut jamais rien,
> Pas même Academicien.

Crébillon, junior, a writer of real merit, but guilty of the same indelicate faults with the former. Wit employed in dressing up obscenity is like the art used in painting a corpse: it may be thus rendered tolerable to one sense, but fails not quickly to offend some other.

Gresset, agreeable and easy. His comedy called the Méchant, and a humorous poem entitled Vert-Vert, have original merit. He was bred a Jesuit; but his wit procured his dismission from the society. This last work particularly could expect no pardon from the Convent, being a satire against nunneries.

D'Alembert has united an extensive skill in scientifical learning with the most refined taste for the polite arts. His excellence in both has procured him a seat in each academy.

Diderot is an elegant writer and subtile reasoner. He is the supposed author of the famous Thesis which the Abbé Prade sustained before the doctors of the Sorbonne. It was levelled against Christianity, and the Sorbonne too hastily gave it their sanction. They perceived its purport, however, when it was too late. The college was brought into some contempt, and the Abbé obliged to take refuge at the court of Berlin.

The Marquis D'Argens attempts to add the character of a philosopher to the vices of a debauchee.

The catalogue might be increased with several other authors of merit, such as Marivaux, Le Franc, Saint Foix, Destouches, and Modonville; but let it suffice to say, that by these the character of the present age is tolerably supported. Though their poets seldom rise to fine enthusiasm, they never sink into absurdity; though they fail to astonish, they are generally possessed of talents to please.

The age of Louis XIV., notwithstanding these respectable names, is still vastly superior. For, beside the general tendency of critical corruption, which shall be spoken of by and by, there are other symptoms which indicate a decline. There is, for instance, a fondness of scepticism, which runs through the works of some of their most applauded writers, and which the numerous class of their imitators have contributed to diffuse. Nothing can be a more certain sign that genius is in the wane, than its being obliged to fly to paradox for support, and attempting to be erroneously agreeable. A man who, with all the impotence of wit, and all the eager desires of infidelity, writes against the religion of his country, may raise doubts, but will never give conviction; all he can do is to render society less happy than he found it. It was a good manner which the father of the late poet Saint Foix took to reclaim his son from this juvenile error. The young poet had shut himself up for some time in his study; and his father, willing to know what had engaged his attention so closely, upon entering, found him busied in drawing up a new system of religion, and endeavouring to show the absurdity of that already established. The old man knew by experience that it was useless to endeavour to convince a vain young man by right reason, so only desired his company up stairs. When come into the father's apartment, he takes his son by the hand, and, drawing back a curtain at one end of the room, discovered a crucifix exquisitely painted. "My son," says he, "you desire to change the religion of your country,—behold the fate of a reformer!" The truth is, vanity is more apt to misguide men than false reasoning. As some would rather be conspicuous in a mob, than unnoticed even in a privy-council, so others choose rather to be foremost in the retinue of error, than follow in the train of truth. What influence the conduct of such writers may have on the morals of a people is not my business here to determine. Certain I am, that it has a manifest tendency to subvert the literary merits of the country in view. The change of religion in every nation has hitherto produced barbarism and ignorance; and such will be probably its consequences in every future period. For when the laws and opinions of society are made to clash, harmony is dissolved, and all the parts of peace unavoidably crushed in the encounter.

The writers of this country have also of late fallen into a method of considering every part of art and science as arising from simple principles. The success of Montesquieu and one or two more has induced all the subordinate ranks of genius into vicious imitation. To this end they turn to our view that side of the subject which contributes to support their hypothesis, while the objections are generally passed over in silence. Thus an universal system rises from a partial representation of the question, a whole is concluded from a part, a book appears entirely new, and the fancy-built fabric is styled for a short time very ingenious. In this manner we have seen of late almost every subject in morals, natural history, politics, economy, and commerce treated. Subjects naturally proceeding on many principles, and some even opposite to each other, are all taught to proceed along the line of systematic simplicity, and continue, like other agreeable falsehoods, extremely pleasing till they are detected.

I must still add another fault, of a nature somewhat similar to the former. As those above mentioned are for contracting a single science into system, so those I am going to speak of are for drawing up a system of all the sciences united. Such undertakings as these are carried on by different writers cemented into one body, and concurring in the same design by the mediation of a bookseller. From these inauspicious combinations proceed those monsters of learning, the Trevoux, Encyclopédies, and Bibliothèques of the age. In making these, men of every rank in literature are employed, wits and dunces contribute their share, and Diderot, as well as Desmaretz, are candidates for oblivion. The genius of the first supplies the gale of favour, and the latter adds the useful ballast of stupidity. By such means the enormous mass heavily makes its way among the public, and, to borrow a bookseller's phrase, the whole impression moves off. These great collections of learning may serve to make us inwardly repine at our own ignorance; may serve, when gilt and lettered, to adorn the lower shelves of a regular library; but woe to the reader who, not daunted at the immense distance between one great pasteboard and the other, opens the volume, and explores his way through a region so extensive, but barren of entertainment. No unexpected landscape there to delight the imagination; no diversity of prospect to cheat the painful journey. He sees the wide extended desert lie before him: what is past only increases his terror of what is to come. His course is not half finished; he looks behind him with affright, and forward with despair. Perseverance is at last overcome, and a night of oblivion lends its friendly aid to terminate the perplexity.

CHAPTER VII.

Of Learning in Great Britain.

To acquire a character for learning among the English at present it is necessary to know much more than is either important or useful. It seems the spirit of the times for men here to exhaust their natural sagacity in exploring the intricacies of another man's thought, and thus never to have leisure to think for themselves. Others have carried on learning from that stage, where the good sense of our ancestors have thought it too minute, or too speculative, to instruct or amuse. By the industry of such, the sciences, which in themselves are easy of access, affright the learner with the severity of their appearance. He sees them surrounded with speculation and subtlety, placed there by their professors as if with a view of deterring his approach. Hence it happens that the generality of readers fly from the scholar to the compiler, who offers them a more safe and speedy conveyance.

From this fault also arises that mutual contempt between the scholar and the man of the world, of which every day's experience furnisheth instances.

The man of taste, however, stands neutral in this controversy. He seems placed in a middle station, between the world and the cell, between learning and common sense. He teaches the vulgar on what part of a character to lay the emphasis of praise, and the scholar where to point his application so as to deserve it. By his means even the philosopher acquires popular applause, and all that are truly great the admiration of posterity. By means of polite learning alone the patriot and the hero, the man who praiseth virtue and he who practises it, who fights successfully for his country or who dies in its defence, becomes immortal. But this taste now seems cultivated with less ardour than formerly, and consequently the public must one day expect to see the advantages arising from it, and the exquisite pleasures it affords our leisure, entirely annihilated. For if, as it should seem, the rewards of genius are improperly directed; if those who are capable of supporting the honour of the times by their writings prefer opulence to fame; if the stage should be shut to writers of merit, and open only to interest or intrigue; if such should happen to be the vile complexion of the times (and that it is nearly so we shall shortly see), the very virtue of the age will be forgotten by posterity, and nothing remembered, except our filling a chasm in the registers of time, or having served to continue the species.

CHAPTER VIII.

Of rewarding Genius in England.

THERE is nothing authors are more apt to lament, than want of encouragement from the age. Whatever their differences in other respects, they are all ready to unite in this complaint, and each indirectly offers himself as an instance of the truth of his assertion.

The beneficed divine, whose wants are only imaginary, expostulates as bitterly as the poorest author. Should interest or good fortune advance the divine to a bishopric, or the poor son of Parnassus into that place which the other has resigned, both are authors no longer: the one goes to prayers once a day, kneels upon cushions of velvet, and thanks gracious Heaven for having made the circumstances of all mankind so extremely happy; the other battens on all the delicacies of life, enjoys his wife and his easy chair, and sometimes, for the sake of conversation, deplores the luxury of these degenerate days.

All encouragements to merit are therefore misapplied which make the author too rich to continue his profession. There can be nothing more just than the old observation, that authors, like running horses, should be fed, but not fattened. If we would continue them in our service, we should reward them with a little money and a great deal of praise, still keeping their avarice subservient to their ambition. Not that I think a writer incapable of filling an employment with dignity: I would only insinuate, that when made a bishop or statesman he will continue to please us as a writer no longer; as, to resume a former allusion, the running horse, when fattened, will still be fit for very useful purposes, though unqualified for a courser.

No nation gives greater encouragements to learning than we do; yet, at the same time, none are so injudicious in the application. We seem to confer them with the same view that statesmen have been known to grant employments at court, rather as bribes to silence than incentives to emulation.

Upon this principle, all our magnificent endowments of colleges are erroneous; and, at best, more frequently enrich the prudent than reward the ingenious. A lad whose passions are not strong enough in youth to mislead him from that path of science which his tutors, and not his inclinations, have chalked out, by four or five years' perseverance may probably obtain every advantage and honour his college can bestow. I forget whether the simile has been used before, but I would compare the man whose youth has been thus passed in the tranquillity of dispassionate prudence to liquors which never ferment, and, consequently, continue always muddy. Passions may raise a commotion in the youthful breast, but they disturb only to refine it. However this be, mean talents are often rewarded in colleges with an easy subsistence. The candidates for preferments of this kind often regard their admission as a patent for future indolence; so that a life begun in studious labour is often continued in luxurious indolence.

Among the universities abroad I have ever observed their riches and their learning in a reciprocal proportion, their stupidity and pride increasing with their opulence. Happening once, in conversation with Gaubius of Leyden, to mention the college of Edinburgh, he began by complaining, that all the English students which formerly came to his university, now went entirely there; and the fact surprised him more, as Leyden was now as well as ever furnished with masters, excellent in their respective professions. He concluded by asking, if the professors of Edinburgh were rich? I replied, that the salary of a professor there seldom amounted to more than thirty pounds a year. "Poor men," says he, "I heartily wish they were better provided for; until they become rich, we can have no expectation of English students at Leyden."

Premiums, also, proposed for literary excellence, when given as encouragements to boys, may be useful; but when designed as rewards to men, are certainly misapplied. We have seldom seen a performance of any great merit in consequence of rewards proposed in this manner. Who has ever observed a writer of any eminence a candidate in so precarious a contest? The man who knows the real value of his own genius will no more venture it upon an uncertainty, than he who knows the true use of a guinea will stake it with a sharper.

Every encouragement given to stupidity, when known to be such, is also a negative insult upon genius. This appears in nothing more evident, than the undistinguished success of those who solicit subscriptions. When first brought into fashion, subscriptions were conferred upon the ingenious alone, or those who were reputed such. But at present we see them made a resource of indigence, and requested, not as rewards of merit, but as a relief of distress. If tradesmen happen to want skill in conducting their own business, yet they are able to write a book; if mechanics want money, or ladies shame, they write books and solicit subscriptions. Scarcely a morning passes, that proposals of this nature are not thrust into the half-opening doors of the rich, with, perhaps, a paltry petition, showing the author's wants, but not his merits. I would not willingly prevent that pity which is due to indigence; but while the streams of liberality are thus diffused, they must, in the end, become proportionably shallow.

What, then, are the proper encouragements of genius? I answer, subsistence and respect; for these are rewards congenial to its nature. Every animal has an aliment peculiarly suited to its constitution. The heavy ox seeks nourishment from earth; the light chameleon has been supposed to exist on air; a sparer diet even than this will satisfy the man of true genius, for he makes a luxurious banquet upon empty applause. It is this alone which has inspired all that ever was truly great and noble among us. It is, as Cicero finely calls it, the echo of virtue. Avarice is the passion of inferior natures—money the pay of the common herd. The author who draws his quill merely to take a purse no more deserves success than he who presents a pistol.

When the link between patronage and learning was entire, then all who deserved fame were in a capacity of attaining it. When the great Somers was at the helm, patronage was fashionable among our nobility. The middle ranks of mankind, who generally imitate the great, then followed their example, and applauded from fashion, if not from feeling. I have heard an old poet of that glorious age say, that a dinner with his lordship has procured him invitations for the whole week following; that an airing in his patron's chariot has supplied him with a citizen's coach on every future occasion. For who would not be proud to entertain a man who kept so much good company?

But this link now seems entirely broken. Since the days of a certain prime minister of inglorious memory, the learned have been kept pretty much at a distance. A jockey, or a laced player, supplies the place of the scholar, poet, or the man of virtue. Those conversations, once the result of wisdom, wit, and innocence, are now turned to humbler topics, little more being expected from a companion than a laced coat, a pliant bow, and an immoderate friendship for —— a well-served table.

Wit, when neglected by the great, is generally despised by the vulgar. Those who are unacquainted with the world are apt to fancy the man of wit as leading a very agreeable life. They conclude, perhaps, that he is attended to with silent admiration, and dictates to the rest of mankind with all the eloquence of conscious superiority. Very different is his situation. He is called an author, and all know that an author is a thing only to be laughed at. His person, not his jest, becomes the mirth of the company. At his approach the most fat, unthinking face brightens into malicious meaning. Even aldermen laugh, and revenge on him the ridicule which was lavished on their forefathers:

Etiam victis redit in præcordia virtus,
Victoresque cadunt.

It is, indeed, a reflection somewhat mortifying to the author who breaks his ranks, and singles out for public favour, to think that he must combat contempt before he can arrive at glory—that he must expect to have all the fools of society united against him before he can hope for the applause of the judicious. For this, however, he must prepare beforehand; as those who have no idea of the difficulty of his employment will be apt to regard his inactivity as idleness; and not having a notion of the pangs of uncomplying thought in themselves, it is not to be expected they should have any desire of rewarding it in others.

Voltaire has finely described the hardships a man must encounter who writes for the public. I need make no apology for the length of the quotation:

"Your fate, my dear Le Fevre, is too strongly marked to permit your retiring. The bee must toil in making honey, the silkworm must spin, the philosopher must dissect them, and you are born to sing of their labours. You must be a poet and a scholar, even though your inclinations should resist: nature is too strong for inclination. But hope not, my friend, to find tranquillity in the employment you are going to pursue. The route of genius is not less obstructed with disappointment than that of ambition.

"If you have the misfortune not to excel in your profession as a poet, repentance must tincture all your future enjoyments: if you succeed, you make enemies. You tread a narrow path: contempt on one side, and hatred on the other, are ready to seize you upon the slightest deviation.

"But why must I be hated? you will perhaps reply: why must I be persecuted for having written a pleasing poem, for having produced an applauded tragedy, or for otherwise instructing or amusing mankind or myself?

"My dear friend, these very successes shall render you miserable for life. Let me suppose your performance has merit—let me suppose you have surmounted the teasing employments of printing and publishing,—how will you be able to lull the critics, who, like Cerberus, are posted at all the avenues of literature, and who settle the merits of every new performance? How, I say, will you be able to make them open in your favour? There are always three or four literary journals in France, as many in Holland, each supporting opposite interests. The booksellers who guide these periodical compilations find their account in being severe; the authors employed by them have wretchedness to add to their natural malignity. The majority may be in your favour, but you may depend on being torn by the rest. Loaded with unmerited scurrility, perhaps you reply; they rejoin; both plead at the bar of the public, and both are condemned to ridicule.

"But if you write for the stage, your case is still more worthy of compassion. You are there to be judged by men whom the custom of the times has rendered contemptible. Irritated by their own inferiority, they exert all their little tyranny upon you, revenging upon the author the insults they receive from the public. From such men, then, you are to expect your sentence. Suppose your piece admitted, acted: one single ill-natured jest from the pit is sufficient to cancel all your labours. But allowing that it succeeds, there are an hundred squibs flying all abroad to prove that it should not have succeeded. You shall find your brightest scenes burlesqued by the ignorant; and the learned, who know a little Greek, and nothing of their native language, affect to despise you.

"But, perhaps, with a panting heart, you carry your piece before a woman of quality. She gives the labours of your brain to her maid to be cut into shreds for curling her hair; while the laced footman, who carries the gaudy livery of luxury, insults your appearance, who bear the livery of indigence.

"But granting your excellence has at last forced envy to confess that your works have some merit; this, then, is all the reward you can expect while living. However, for this tribute of applause you must expect persecution. You will be reputed the author of scandal which you have never seen, of verses you despise, and of sentiments directly contrary to your own. In short, you must embark in some one party, or all parties will be against you.

"There are among us a number of learned societies, where a lady presides, whose wit begins to twinkle when the splendour of her beauty begins to decline. One or two men of learning compose her ministers of state. These must be flattered, or made enemies by being neglected. Thus, though you had the merit of all antiquity united in your person, you grow old in misery and disgrace. Every place designed for men of letters is filled up by men of intrigue. Some nobleman's private tutor, some court flatterer, shall bear away the prize, and leave you to anguish and to disappointment."

Yet it were well if none but the dunces of society were combined to render the profession of an author ridiculous or unhappy. Men of the first eminence are often found to indulge this illiberal vein of raillery. Two contending writers often by the opposition of their wit render their profession contemptible in the eyes of ignorant persons, who should have been taught to admire. And yet, whatever the reader may think of himself, it is at least two to one but he is a greater blockhead than the most scribbling dunce he affects to despise.

The poet's poverty is a standing topic of contempt. His writing for bread is an unpardonable offence. Perhaps of all mankind an author in these times is used most hardly. We keep him poor, and yet revile his poverty. Like angry parents who correct their children till they cry, and then correct them for crying, we reproach him for living by his wit, and yet allow him no other means to live.

His taking refuge in garrets and cellars has of late been violently objected to him, and that by men who, I dare hope, are more apt to pity than insult his distress. Is poverty the writer's fault? No doubt he knows how to prefer a bottle of champagne to the nectar of the neighbouring alehouse, or a venison pasty to a plate of potatoes. Want of delicacy is not in him, but in us, who deny him the opportunity of making an elegant choice.

Wit certainly is the property of those who have it, nor should we be displeased if it is the only property a man sometimes has. We must not underrate him who uses it for subsistence, and flies from the ingratitude of the age even to a bookseller for redress. If the profession of an author is to be laughed at by the stupid, it is certainly better to be contemptibly rich than contemptibly poor. For all the wit that ever adorned the human mind will at present no more shield the author's poverty from ridicule, than his high-topped gloves conceal the unavoidable omissions of his laundress.

To be more serious: new fashions, follies, and vices make new monitors necessary in every age. An author may be considered as a merciful substitute to the legislature. He acts, not by punishing crimes, but preventing them. However virtuous the present age, there may be still growing employment for ridicule or reproof, for persuasion or satire. If the author be therefore still so necessary among us, let us treat him with proper consideration as a child of the public, not a rent-charge on the community. And indeed a *child* of the public he is in all respects; for while so well able to direct others, how incapable is he frequently found of guiding himself! His simplicity exposes him to all the insidious approaches of cunning; his sensibility to the slightest invasions of contempt. Though possessed of fortitude to stand unmoved the expected bursts of an earthquake, yet of feelings so exquisitely poignant as to agonize under the slightest disappointment. Broken rest, tasteless meals, and causeless anxiety shorten his life, or render it unfit for active employment; prolonged vigils and intense application still farther contract his span, and make his time glide insensibly away. Let us not, then, aggravate those natural inconveniences by neglect; we have had sufficient instances of this kind already. Sale and Moore will suffice for one age at least. But they are dead, and their sorrows are over. The neglected author of the Persian Eclogues, which, however inaccurate, excel any in our language, is still alive. Happy if *insensible* of our neglect, not *raging* at our ingratitude. It is enough that the age has already produced instances of men pressing foremost in the lists of fame, and worthy of better times; schooled by continued adversity into an hatred of their kind, flying from thought to drunkenness, yielding to the united pressure of labour, penury, and sorrow, sinking unheeded, without one friend to drop a tear on their unattended obsequies, and indebted to charity for a grave.

The author, when unpatronized by the great, has naturally recourse to the bookseller. There cannot perhaps be imagined a combination more prejudicial to taste than this. It is the interest of the one to allow as little for writing, and of the other to write as much as possible. Accordingly, tedious compilations and periodical magazines are the result of their joint endeavours. In these circumstances the author bids adieu to fame, writes for bread, and for that only imagination is seldom called in. He sits down to address the venal muse with the most phlegmatic apathy; and, as we are told of the Russian, courts his mistress by falling asleep in her lap. His reputation never spreads in a wider circle than that of the trade, who generally value him, not for the fineness of his compositions, but the quantity he works off in a given time.

A long habit of writing for bread thus turns the ambition of every author at last into avarice. He finds that he has written many years, that the public are scarcely acquainted even with his name; he despairs of applause, and turns to profit, which invites him. He finds that money procures all those advantages, that respect, and that ease which he vainly expected from fame. Thus the man who, under the protection of the great, might have done honour to humanity, when only patronized by the bookseller becomes a thing little superior to the fellow who works at the press.

CHAPTER IX.

Of the Marks of Literary Decay in France and England.

THE faults already mentioned are such as learning is often found to flourish under; but there is one of a much more dangerous nature, which has begun to fix itself among us,—I mean criticism, which may properly be called the natural destroyer of polite learning. We have seen that critics, or those whose only business is to write books upon other books, are always more numerous as learning is more diffused; and experience has shown that, instead of promoting its interest, which they profess to do, they generally injure it. This decay which criticism produces may be deplored, but can scarcely be remedied, as the man who writes against the critics is obliged to add himself to the number. Other depravations in the republic of letters, such as affectation in some popular writer, leading others into vicious imitation; political struggles in the state; a depravity of morals among the people; ill-directed encouragement, or no encouragement, from the great,—these have been often found to co-operate in the decline of literature; and it has sometimes declined, as in modern Italy, without them; but an increase of criticism has always portended a decay. Of all misfortunes, therefore, in the commonwealth of letters, this of judging from rule, and not from feeling, is the most severe. At such a tribunal no work of original merit can please. Sublimity, if carried to an exalted height, approaches burlesque, and humour sinks into vulgarity. The person who cannot feel may ridicule both as such, and bring rules to corroborate his assertion. There is, in short, no excellence in writing that such judges may not place among the neighbouring defects. Rules render the reader more difficult to be pleased, and abridge the author's power of pleasing.

If we turn to either country, we shall perceive evident symptoms of this natural decay beginning to appear. Upon a moderate calculation, there seem to be as many volumes of criticism published in those countries as of all other kinds of polite erudition united. Paris sends forth not less than four literary journals every month: the *Année littéraire* and the *Feuille*, by Fréron; the *Journal Etranger*, by the Chevalier d'Arc; and *Le Mercure*, by Marmontel. We have two literary reviews in London, with critical newspapers and magazines without number. The compilers of these resemble the commoners of Rome; they are all for levelling property, not by increasing their own, but by diminishing that of others. The man who has any good-nature in his disposition must, however, be somewhat displeased to see distinguished reputations often the sport of ignorance,—to see, by one false pleasantry, the future peace of a worthy man's life disturbed, and this only because he has unsuccessfully attempted to instruct or amuse us. Though ill-nature is far from being wit, yet it is generally laughed at as such. The critic enjoys the triumph, and ascribes to his parts what is only due to his effrontery. I fire with indignation, when I see persons wholly destitute of education and genius indent to the press, and thus turn book-makers, adding to the sin of criticism the sin of ignorance also; whose trade is a bad one, and who are bad workmen in the trade.

When I consider those industrious men as indebted to the works of others for a precarious subsistence, when I see them coming down at stated intervals to rummage the bookseller's counter for materials to work upon, it raises a smile, though mixed with pity. It reminds me of an animal called by naturalists the soldier. "This little creature," says the historian, "is passionately fond of a shell; but not being supplied with one by nature, has recourse to the deserted shell of some other. I have seen these harmless reptiles," continues he, "come down once a year from the mountains, rank and file, cover the whole shore, and ply busily about, each in request of a shell to please it. Nothing can be more amusing than their industry upon this occasion. One shell is too big, another too little: they enter and keep possession sometimes for a good while, until one is, at last, found entirely to please. When all are thus properly equipped, they march up again to the mountains, and live in their new acquisition till under a necessity of changing."

There is, indeed, scarcely an error of which our present writers are guilty that does not arise from their opposing systems; there is scarcely an error that criticism cannot be brought to excuse. From this proceeds the affected security of our odes, the tuneless flow of our blank verse, the pompous epithet, laboured diction, and every other deviation from common sense, which procures the poet the applause of the month: he is praised by all, read by a few, and soon forgotten.

There never was an unbeaten path trodden by the poet that the critic did not endeavour to reclaim him, by calling his attempt innovation. This might be instanced in Dante, who first followed nature, and was persecuted by the critics as long as he lived. Thus novelty, one of the greatest beauties in poetry, must be avoided, or the connoisseur be displeased. It is one of the chief privileges, however, of genius, to fly from the herd of imitators by some happy singularity; for, should he stand still, his heavy pursuers will at length certainly come up, and fairly dispute the victory.

The ingenious Mr. Hogarth used to assert, that every one except the connoisseur was a judge of painting. The same may be asserted of writing. The public, in general, set the whole piece in the proper point of view; the critic lays his eye close to all its minuteness, and condemns or approves in detail. And this may be the reason why so many writers at present are apt to appeal from the tribunal of criticism to that of the people.

From a desire in the critic of grafting the spirit of ancient languages upon the English have proceeded of late several disagreeable instances of pedantry. Among the number I think we may reckon blank verse. Nothing but the greatest sublimity of subject can render such a measure pleasing; however, we now see it used upon the most trivial occasions. It has particularly found its way into our didactic poetry, and is likely to bring that species of composition into disrepute, for which the English are deservedly famous.

Those who are acquainted with writing know that our language runs almost naturally into blank verse. The writers of our novels, romances, and all of this class who have no notion of style, naturally hobble into this unharmonious measure. If rhymes, therefore, be more difficult, for that very reason I would have our poets write in rhyme. Such a restriction upon the thought of a good poet, often lifts and increases the vehemence of every sentiment; for fancy, like a fountain, plays highest by diminishing the aperture. But rhymes, it will be said, are a remnant of monkish stupidity, an innovation upon the poetry of the ancients. They are but indifferently acquainted with antiquity who make the assertion. Rhymes are probably of older date than either the Greek or Latin dactyl and spondee. The Celtic, which is allowed to be the first language spoken in Europe, has ever preserved them, as we may find in the Edda of Iceland and the Irish carols, still sung among the original inhabitants of that island. Olaus Wormius gives us some of the Teutonic poetry in this way; and Pantoppidan, bishop of Bergen, some of the Norwegian. In short, this jingle of sounds is almost natural to mankind; at least it is so to our language, if we may judge from many unsuccessful attempts to throw it off.

I should not have employed so much time in opposing this erroneous innovation, if it were not apt to introduce another in its train,—I mean, a disgusting solemnity of manner into our poetry; and, as the prose writer has been ever found to follow the poet, it must consequently banish in both all that agreeable trifling which, if I may so express it, often deceives us into instruction. The finest sentiment and the most weighty truth may put on a pleasant face, and it is even virtuous to jest when serious advice must be disgusting. But, instead of this, the most trifling performance among us now assumes all the didactic stiffness of wisdom. The most diminutive son of fame or of famine has his *we* and his *us*, his *firstlies* and his *secondlies*, as methodical as if bound in cow-hide and closed with clasps of brass. Were these Monthly Reviews and Magazines frothy, pert, or absurd, they might find some pardon; but to be dull and dronish is an encroachment on the prerogative of a folio. These things should be considered as pills to purge melancholy; they should be made up in our splenetic climate to be taken as physic, and not so as to be used when we take it.

However, by the power of one single monosyllable our critics have almost got the victory over humour amongst us. Does the poet paint the absurdities of the vulgar? then he is *low*. Does he exaggerate the features of folly to render it more thoroughly ridiculous? he is then very *low*. In short, they have proscribed the comic or satirical muse from every walk but high life, which, though abounding in fools as well as the humblest station, is by no means so fruitful in absurdity. Among well-bred fools we may despise much, but have little to laugh at; nature seems to present us with a universal blank of silk, ribbons, smiles, and whispers. Absurdity is the poet's game, and good-breeding is the nice concealment of absurdities. The truth is, the critic generally mistakes humour for wit, which is a very different excellence. Wit raises human nature above its level; humour acts a contrary part, and equally depresses it. To expect exalted humour is a contradiction in terms; and the critic, by demanding an impossibility from the comic poet, has, in effect, banished new comedy from the stage. But, to put the same thought in a different light, when an unexpected similitude in two objects strikes the imagination—in other words, when a thing is wittily expressed—all our pleasure turns into admiration of the artist who had fancy enough to draw the picture. When a thing is humorously described, our burst of laughter proceeds from a very different cause: we compare the absurdity of the character represented with our own, and triumph in our conscious superiority. No natural defect can be a cause of laughter, because it is a misfortune to which ourselves are liable. A defect of this kind changes the passion into pity or horror. We only laugh at those instances of moral absurdity, to which we are conscious we ourselves are not liable. For instance, should I describe a man as wanting his nose, there is no humour in this, as it is an accident to which human nature is subject, and may be any man's case; but should I represent this man without his nose as extremely curious in the choice of his snuff-box, we here see him guilty of an absurdity of which we imagine it impossible for ourselves to be guilty, and therefore applaud our own good sense on the comparison. Thus, then, the pleasure we receive from wit turns on the admiration of another; that which we feel from humour centres in the admiration of ourselves. The poet, therefore, must place the object he would have the subject of humour in a state of inferiority; in other words, the subject of humour must be *low*.

The solemnity worn by many of our modern writers is, I fear, often the mask of dulness; for certain it is, it seems to fit every author who pleases to put it on. By the complexion of many of our late publications one might be apt to cry out with Cicero, *Civem, mehercule, non puto esse qui his temporibus ridere possit,*—"On my conscience, I believe we have all forgot to laugh in these days." Such writers probably make no distinction between what is praised and what is pleasing; between those commendations which the reader pays his own discernment, and those which are the genuine result of his sensations. It were to be wished, therefore, that we no longer found pleasure with the inflated style that has for some years been looked upon as fine writing, and which every young writer is now obliged to adopt, if he chooses to be read. We should now dispense with loaded epithet and dressing up trifles with dignity. For, to use an obvious instance, it is not those who make the greatest noise with their wares in the streets that have most to sell. Let us, instead of writing finely, try to write naturally; not hunt after lofty expressions to deliver mean ideas, nor be for ever gaping, when we only mean to deliver a whisper.

CHAPTER X.

Of the Stage.

OUR theatre has been generally confessed to share in this general decline, though partaking of the show and decoration of the Italian opera, with the propriety and declamation of French performance. The stage also is more magnificent with us than any other in Europe, and the people in general fonder of theatrical entertainment. Yet still as our pleasures, as well as more important concerns, are generally managed by party, the stage has felt its influence. The managers, and all who espouse their side, are for decoration and ornament; the critic, and all who have studied French decorum, are for regularity and declamation. Thus it is almost impossible to please both parties: and the poet, by attempting it, finds himself often incapable of pleasing either. If he introduces stage pomp, the critic consigns his performance to the vulgar; if he indulges in recital and simplicity, it is accused of insipidity or dry affectation.

From the nature, therefore, of our theatre, and the genius of our country, it is extremely difficult for a dramatic poet to please his audience. But happy would he be, were these the only difficulties he had to encounter; there are many other more dangerous combinations against the little wit of the age. Our poet's performance must undergo a process truly chemical before it is presented to the public. It must be tried in the manager's fire, strained through a licenser, suffer from repeated corrections, till it may be a mere *caput mortuum* when it arrives before the public.

The success, however, of pieces upon the stage would be of little moment, did it not influence the success of the same piece in the closet. Nay, I think it would be more for the interests of virtue, if stage performances were read, not acted; made rather our companions in the cabinet than on the theatre. While we are readers, every moral sentiment strikes us in all its beauty, but the love scenes are frigid, tawdry, and disgusting. When we are spectators, all the persuasives to vice receive an additional lustre. The love scene is aggravated, the obscenity heightened, the best actors figure in the most debauched characters, while the parts of morality, as they are called, are thrown to some mouthing machine, who puts even virtue out of countenance by his wretched imitation.

But whatever be the incentives to vice which are found at the theatre, public pleasures are generally less guilty than solitary ones. To make our solitary satisfaction truly innocent, the actor is useful, as by his means the poet's work makes its way from the stage to the closet; for all must allow, that the reader receives more benefit by perusing a well-written play than by seeing it acted.

But how is this rule inverted on our theatres at present! Old pieces are revived, and scarcely any new ones admitted. The actor is ever in our eye, and the poet seldom permitted to appear; the public are again obliged to ruminate over those hashes of absurdity, which were disgusting to our ancestors even in an age of ignorance; and the stage, instead of serving the people, is made subservient to the interests of avarice.

We seem to be pretty much in the situation of travellers at a Scotch inn: vile entertainment is served up, complained of, and sent down; up comes worse, and that also is changed; and every change makes our wretched cheer more unsavoury. What must be done? only sit down contented, cry up all that comes before us, and admire even the absurdities of Shakespeare.

Let the reader suspend his censure. I admire the beauties of this great father of our stage as much as they deserve, but could wish, for the honour of our country, and for his honour too, that many of his scenes were forgotten. A man blind of one eye should always be painted in profile. Let the spectator who assists at any of these new revived pieces only ask himself whether he would approve such a performance if written by a modern poet. I fear he will find that much of his applause proceeds merely from the sound of a name, and an empty veneration for antiquity. In fact, the revival of those pieces of forced humour, far-fetched conceit, and unnatural hyperbole, which have been ascribed to Shakespeare, is rather gibbeting than raising a statue to his memory; it is rather a trick of the actor, who thinks it safest acting in exaggerated characters, and who, by outstepping nature, chooses to exhibit the ridiculous *outré* of a harlequin under the sanction of that venerable name.

What strange vamped comedies, farcical tragedies, or what shall I call them, speaking pantomimes, have we not of late seen! No matter what the play may be, it is the actor who draws an audience. He throws life into all; all are in spirits and merry, in at one door and out at another: the spectator, in a fool's paradise, knows not what all this means, till the last act concludes in matrimony. The piece pleases our critics, because it talks old English; and it pleases the galleries, because it has ribaldry. True taste, or even common sense, are out of the question.

But great art must be sometimes used before they can thus impose upon the public. To this purpose a prologue written with some spirit generally precedes the piece, to inform us that it was composed by Shakespeare, or old Ben, or somebody else who took them for his model. A face of iron could not have the assurance to avow dislike; the theatre has its partisans who understand the force of combinations, trained up to vociferation, clapping of hands and clattering of sticks: and though a man might have strength sufficient to overcome a lion in single combat, he may run the risk of being devoured by an army of ants.

I am not insensible that third nights are disagreeable drawbacks upon the annual profits of the stage. I am confident it is much more to the manager's advantage to furbish up all the lumber which the good sense of our ancestors, but for his care, had consigned to oblivion. It is not with him, therefore, but with the public, I would expostulate; they have a right to demand respect, and surely those newly revived plays are no instances of the manager's deference.

I have been informed that no new play can be admitted upon our theatres unless the author chooses to wait some years, or, to use the phrase in fashion, till it comes to be played in turn. A poet thus can never expect to contract a familiarity with the stage, by which alone he can hope to succeed; nor can the most signal success relieve immediate want. Our Saxon ancestors had but one name for a wit and a witch. I will not dispute the propriety of uniting those characters then; but the man who, under the present discouragements, ventures to write for the stage, whatever claim he may have to the appellation of a wit, at least he has no right to be called a conjurer.

From all that has been said upon the state of our theatre we may easily foresee whether it is likely to improve or decline; and whether the freeborn muse can bear to submit to those restrictions which avarice or power would impose. For the future, it is somewhat unlikely that he whose labours are valuable, or who knows their value, will turn to the stage for either fame or subsistence, when he must at once flatter an actor and please an audience.

CHAPTER XI.

On Universities.

INSTEAD of losing myself in a subject of such extent, I shall only offer a few thoughts as they occur, and leave their connexion to the reader.

We seem divided, whether an education formed by travelling or by a sedentary life be preferable. We see more of the world by travel, but more of human nature by remaining at home; as, in an infirmary, the student who only attends to the disorders of a few patients is more likely to understand his profession, than he who indiscriminately examines them all.

A youth just landed at the Brille resembles a clown at a puppet-show; carries his amazement from one miracle to another; from this cabinet of curiosities to that collection of pictures: but wondering is not the way to grow wise.

Whatever resolutions we set ourselves not to keep company with our countrymen abroad, we shall find them broken when once we leave home. Among strangers we consider ourselves as in a solitude, and it is but natural to desire society.

In all the great towns of Europe there are to be found Englishmen residing, either from interest or choice. These generally lead a life of continued debauchery. Such are the countrymen a traveller is likely to meet with.

This may be the reason why Englishmen are all thought to be mad or melancholy by the vulgar abroad. Their money is giddily and merrily spent among sharpers of their own country; and when that is gone, of all nations the English bear worst that disorder called the *maladie du poche*.

Countries wear very different appearances to travellers of different circumstances. A man who is whirled through Europe in a post-chaise, and the pilgrim who walks the grand tour on foot, will form very different conclusions.

To see Europe with advantage, a man should appear in various circumstances of fortune; but the experiment would be too dangerous for young men.

There are many things relative to other countries which can be learned to more advantage at home; their laws and policies are among the number.

The greatest advantages which result to youth from travel are an easy address, the shaking off national prejudices, and the finding nothing ridiculous in national peculiarities.

The time spent in these acquisitions could have been more usefully employed at home. An education in a college seems therefore preferable.

We attribute to universities either too much or too little. Some assert that they are the only proper places to advance learning; while others deny even their utility in forming an education. Both are erroneous.

Learning is most advanced in populous cities, where chance often conspires with industry to promote it; where the members of this large university, if I may so call it, catch manners as they rise; study life, not logic, and have the world for correspondents.

The greatest number of universities have ever been founded in times of the greatest ignorance.

New improvements in learning are seldom adopted in colleges until admitted everywhere else. And this is right: we should always be cautious of teaching the rising generation uncertainties for truth. Thus, though the professors in universities have been too frequently found to oppose the advancement of learning, yet, when once established, they are the properest persons to diffuse it.

There is more knowledge to be acquired from one page of the volume of mankind, if the scholar only knows how to read, than in volumes of antiquity. We grow learned, not wise, by too long continuance at college.

This points out the time in which we should leave the university. Perhaps the age of twenty-one, when at our universities the first degree is generally taken, is the proper period.

The universities of Europe may be divided into three classes. Those upon the old scholastic establishment, where the pupils are immured, talk nothing but Latin, and support every day syllogistical disputations in school philosophy. Would not one be apt to imagine this was the proper education to make a man a fool? Such are the universities of Prague, Louvain, and Padua. The second is, where the pupils are under few restrictions, where all scholastic jargon is banished, where they take a degree when they think proper, and live not in the college, but the city. Such are Edinburgh, Leyden, Gottingen, Geneva. The third is a mixture of the two former, where the pupils are restrained, but not confined; where many, though not all, the absurdities of scholastic philosophy are suppressed, and where the first degree is taken after four years' matriculation. Such are Oxford, Cambridge, and Dublin.

As for the first class, their absurdities are too apparent to admit of a parallel. It is disputed which of the two last are more conducive to national improvement.

Skill in the professions is acquired more by practice than study; two or three years may be sufficient for learning their rudiments. The universities of Edinburgh, &c. grant a licence for practising them when the student thinks proper, which our universities refuse till after a residence of several years.

The dignity of the professions may be supported by this dilatory proceeding; but many men of learning are thus too long excluded from the lucrative advantages which superior skill has a right to expect.

Those universities must certainly be most frequented, which promise to give in two years the advantages which others will not under twelve.

The man who has studied a profession for three years, and practised it for nine more, will certainly know more of his business than he who has only studied it for twelve.

The universities of Edinburgh, &c. must certainly be most proper for the study of those professions in which men choose to turn their learning to profit as soon as possible.

The universities of Oxford, &c. are improper for this, since they keep the student from the world, which, after a certain time, is the only true school of improvement.

When a degree in the professions can be taken only by men of independent fortunes, the number of candidates in learning is lessened, and, consequently, the advancement of learning retarded.

This slowness of conferring degrees is a remnant of scholastic barbarity. Paris, Louvain, and those universities which still retain their ancient institutions, confer the doctor's degree slower even than we.

The statutes of every university should be considered as adapted to the laws of its respective government. Those should alter as these happen to fluctuate.

Four years spent in the arts (as they are called in colleges) is perhaps laying too laborious a foundation: entering a profession without any previous acquisitions of this kind is building too bold a superstructure.

Teaching by lecture, as at Edinburgh, may make men scholars if they think proper; but instructing by examination, as at Oxford, will make them so often against their inclination.

Edinburgh only disposes the student to receive learning; Oxford often makes him actually learned.

In a word, were I poor, I should send my son to Leyden or Edinburgh, though the annual expense in each, particularly in the first, is very great. Were I rich, I would send him to one of our own universities. By an education received in the first, he has the best likelihood of living; by that received in the latter, he has the best chance of becoming great.

We have of late heard much of the necessity of studying oratory. Vespasian was the first who paid professors of rhetoric for publicly instructing youth at Rome. However, those pedants never made an orator.

The best orations that ever were spoken were pronounced in the parliaments of King Charles the First. These men never studied the rules of oratory.

Mathematics are, perhaps, too much studied at our universities. This seems a science to which the meanest intellects are equal. I forget who it is that says, "All men might understand mathematics, if they would."

The most methodical manner of lecturing, whether on morals or nature, is, first rationally to explain, and then produce the experiment. The most instructive method is to show the experiment first; curiosity is then excited, and attention awakened to every subsequent deduction. Hence it is evident, that in a well-formed education a course of history should ever precede a course of ethics.

The sons of our nobility are permitted to enjoy greater liberties in our universities than those of private men. I should blush to ask the men of learning and virtue who preside in our seminaries the reason of such a prejudicial distinction. Our youth should there be inspired with a love of philosophy; and the first maxim among philosophers is, That merit only makes distinction.

Whence has proceeded the vain magnificence of expensive architecture in our colleges? Is it that men study to more advantage in a palace than in a cell? One single performance of taste or genius confers more real honours on its parent university than all the labours of the chisel.

Surely pride itself has dictated to the fellows of our colleges the absurd passion of being attended at meals, and on other public occasions, by those poor men who, willing to be scholars, come in upon some charitable foundation. It implies a contradiction, for men to be at once learning the *liberal* arts and at the same time treated as *slaves;* at once studying freedom and practising servitude.

CHAPTER XII.

The Conclusion.

Every subject acquires an adventitious importance to him who considers it with application. He finds it more closely connected with human happiness than the rest of mankind are apt to allow; he sees consequences resulting from it which do not strike others with equal conviction; and still pursuing speculation beyond the bounds of reason, too frequently becomes ridiculously earnest in trifles or absurdity.

It will perhaps be incurring this imputation, to deduce a universal degeneracy of manners from so slight an origin as the depravation of taste; to assert that, as a nation grows dull, it sinks into debauchery.

Yet such, probably, may be the consequence of literary decay; or, not to stretch the thought beyond what it will bear, vice and stupidity are always mutually productive of each other.

Life, at the greatest and best, has been compared to a froward child, that must be humoured and played with till it falls asleep, and then all the care is over. Our few years are laboured away in varying its pleasures; new amusements are pursued with studious attention; the most childish vanities are dignified with titles of importance; and the proudest boast of the most aspiring philosopher is no more than that he provides his little playfellows the greatest pastime with the greatest innocence.

Thus the mind, ever wandering after amusement, when abridged of happiness on one part, endeavours to find it on another; when intellectual pleasures are disagreeable, those of sense will take the lead. The man who in this age is enamoured of the tranquil joys of study and retirement may in the next, should learning be fashionable no longer, feel an ambition of being foremost at a horse course; or, if such could be the absurdity of the times, of being himself a jockey. Reason and appetite are therefore masters of our revels in turn; and as we incline to the one, or pursue the other, we rival angels or imitate the brutes. In the pursuit of intellectual pleasures lies every virtue; of sensual, every vice.

It is this difference of pursuit which marks the morals and characters of mankind; which lays the line between the enlightened philosopher and the half-taught citizen; between the civil citizen and illiterate peasant; between the law-obeying peasant and the wandering savage of Africa,—an animal less mischievous, indeed, than the tiger, because endued with fewer powers of doing mischief. The man, the nation, must therefore be good, whose chiefest luxuries consist in the refinement of reason; and reason can never be universally cultivated, unless guided by taste, which may be considered as the link between science and common sense, the medium through which learning should ever be seen by society.

Taste will therefore often be a proper standard, when others fail, to judge of a nation's improvement or degeneracy in morals. We have often no permanent characteristics by which to compare the virtues or the vices of our ancestors with our own. A generation may rise and pass away without leaving any traces of what it really was; and all complaints of our deterioration may be only topics of declamation, or the cavillings of disappointment: but in taste we have standing evidence; we can with precision compare the literary performances of our fathers with our own, and from their excellence or defects determine the moral, as well as the literary, merits of either.

If, then, there ever comes a time when taste is so far depraved among us that critics shall load every work of genius with unnecessary comment, and quarter their empty performances with the substantial merits of an author, both for subsistence and applause; if there comes a time when censure shall speak in storms, but praise be whispered in the breeze, while real excellence often finds shipwreck in either; if there be a time when the muse shall seldom be heard, except in plaintive elegy, as if she wept her own decline, while lazy compilations supply the place of original thinking; should there ever be such a time, may succeeding critics, both for the honour of our morals, as well as our learning, say that such a period bears no resemblance to the present age!

END OF AN INQUIRY INTO THE PRESENT STATE OF POLITE LEARNING.

THE LIFE

OF

LORD BOLINGBROKE.

[1770.]

THE LIFE OF LORD BOLINGBROKE.

THERE are some characters that seem formed by nature to take delight in struggling with opposition, and whose most agreeable hours are passed in storms of their own creating. The subject of the present sketch was perhaps, of all others, the most indefatigable in raising himself enemies, to show his power in subduing them; and was not less employed in improving his superior talents, than in finding objects on which to exercise their activity. His life was spent in a continual conflict of politics; and, as if that was too short for the combat, he has left his memory as a subject of lasting contention.

It is, indeed, no easy matter to preserve an acknowledged impartiality in talking of a man so differently regarded on account of his political, as well as his religious, principles. Those whom his politics may please will be sure to condemn him for his religion; and, on the contrary, those most strongly attached to his theological opinions are the most likely to decry his politics. On whatever side he is regarded, he is sure to have opposers; and this was perhaps what he most desired, having, from nature, a mind better pleased with the struggle than the victory.

Henry St. John, Lord Viscount Bolingbroke, was born in the year 1672, at Battersea, in Surrey, at a seat that had been in the possession of his ancestors for ages before. His family was of the first rank, equally conspicuous for its antiquity, dignity, and large possessions. It is found to trace its original as high as Adam de Port, Baron of Basing, in Hampshire, before the Conquest; and in a succession of ages to have produced warriors, patriots, and statesmen, some of whom were conspicuous for their loyalty, and others for their defending the rights of the people. His grandfather, Sir Walter St. John, of Battersea, marrying one of the daughters of Lord Chief Justice St. John, who, as all know, was strongly attached to the republican party, Henry, the subject of the present memoir, was brought up in his family, and, consequently, imbibed the first principles of his education amongst the dissenters. At that time Daniel Burgess, a fanatic of a very peculiar kind, being at once possessed of zeal and humour, and as well known for the archness of his conceits as the furious obstinacy of his principles, was confessor in the presbyterian way to his grandmother, and was appointed to direct our author's first studies. Nothing is so apt to disgust a feeling mind as mistaken zeal; and, perhaps, the absurdity of the first lectures he received might have given him that contempt for all religions which he might have justly conceived against one. Indeed, no task can be more mortifying than what he was condemned to undergo. "I was obliged," says he, in one place, "while yet a boy, to read over the commentaries of Dr. Manton, whose pride it was to have made a hundred and nineteen sermons on the hundred and nineteenth psalm." Dr. Manton and his sermons were not likely to prevail much on one who was, perhaps, the most sharp-sighted in the world at discovering the absurdities of others, however he might have been guilty of establishing many of his own.

But these dreary institutions were of no very long continuance; as soon as it was fit to take him out of the hands of the women, he was sent to Eton School, and removed thence to Christ Church College in Oxford. His genius and understanding were seen and admired in both these seminaries, but his love of pleasure had so much the ascendancy, that he seemed contented rather with the consciousness of his own great powers than their exertion. However, his friends, and those who knew him most intimately, were thoroughly sensible of the extent of his mind; and when he left the university, he was considered as one who had the fairest opportunity of making a shining figure in active life.

Nature seemed not less kind to him in her external embellishments than in adorning his mind. With the graces of a handsome person, and a face in which dignity was happily blended with sweetness, he had a manner of address that was very engaging. His vivacity was always awake, his apprehension was quick, his wit refined, and his memory amazing; his subtlety in thinking and reasoning was profound; and all these talents were adorned with an elocution that was irresistible.

To the assemblage of so many gifts from nature it was expected that art would soon give her finishing hand, and that a youth begun in excellence, would soon arrive at perfection: but such is the perverseness of human nature, that an age which should have been employed in the acquisition of knowledge was dissipated in pleasure; and instead of aiming to excel in praiseworthy pursuits, Bolingbroke seemed more ambitious of being thought the greatest rake about town. This period might have been compared to that of fermentation in liquors, which grow muddy before they brighten; but it must also be confessed, that those liquors which never ferment are seldom clear. In this state of disorder he was not without his lucid intervals; and even while he was noted for keeping Miss Gumley, the most expensive prostitute in the kingdom, and bearing the greatest quantity of wine without intoxication, he even then despised his paltry ambition. "The love of study," says he, "and desire of knowledge, were what I felt all my life: and though my genius, unlike the demon of Socrates, whispered so softly, that very often I heard him not in the hurry of those passions with which I was transported, yet some calmer hours there were, and in them I hearkened to him." These sacred admonitions were indeed very few, since his excesses are remembered to this very day. I have spoken to an old man, who assured me, that he saw him and one of his companions run naked through the Park in a fit of intoxication; but then it was a time when public decency might be transgressed with less danger than at present.

During this period, as all his attachments were to pleasure; so his studies only seemed to lean that way. His first attempts were in poetry, in which he discovers more wit than taste, more labour than harmony in his versification. We have a copy of his verses prefixed to Dryden's Virgil, complimenting the poet, and praising his translation. We have another, not so well known, prefixed to a French work, published in Holland, by the Chevalier de St. Hyacinth, entitled "Le Chef-d'œuvre d'un Inconnu." This performance is a humorous piece of criticism upon a miserable old ballad; and Bolingbroke's compliment, though written in English, is printed in Greek characters, so that at the first glance it may deceive the eye, and be mistaken for real Greek. There are two or three things more of his composition, which have appeared since his death, but which do honour neither to his parts nor memory.

In this mad career of pleasure he continued for some time; but at length, in 1700, when he arrived at the twenty-eighth year of his age, he began to dislike his method of living, and to find that sensual pleasure alone was not sufficient to make the happiness of a reasonable creature. He therefore made his first effort to break from his state of infatuation by marrying the daughter and coheiress of Sir Henry Winchescomb, a descendant from the famous Jack of Newbury, who, though but a clothier in the reign of Henry VIII., was able to entertain the king and all his retinue in the most splendid manner. This lady was possessed of a fortune exceeding forty thousand pounds, and was not deficient in mental accomplishments; but whether he was not yet fully satiated with his former pleasures, or whether her temper was not conformable to his own, it is certain they were far from living happily together. After cohabiting for some time together, they parted by mutual consent, both equally displeased,—he complaining of the obstinacy of her temper, she of the shamelessness of his infidelity. A great part of her fortune some time after, upon his attainder, was given her back; but as her family estates were settled upon him, he enjoyed them after her death, upon the reversal of his attainder.

Having taken a resolution to quit the allurements of pleasure for the stronger attractions of ambition, soon after his marriage he procured a seat in the House of Commons, being elected for the borough of Wotton-Basset in Wiltshire, his father having served several times for the same place. Besides his natural endowments and his large fortune, he had other very considerable advantages that gave him weight in the senate, and seconded his views of preferment. His grandfather, Sir Walter St. John, was still alive; and that gentleman's interest was so great in his own county of Wilts, that he represented it in two Parliaments in a former reign. His father also was then the representative for the same; and the interest of his wife's family in the House was very extensive. Thus Bolingbroke took his seat with many accidental helps; but his chief and great resource lay in his own extensive abilities.

At that time the Whig and the Tory parties were strongly opposed in the House, and pretty nearly balanced. In the latter years of King William, the Tories, who, from every motive, were opposed to the court, had been gaining popularity, and now began to make a public stand against their competitors. Robert Harley, afterwards Earl of Oxford, a stanch and confirmed Tory, was, in the year 1700, chosen Speaker of the House of Commons, and was continued in the same upon the accession of Queen Anne, the year ensuing. Bolingbroke had all along been bred up, as was before observed, among the dissenters, his friends leaned to that persuasion, and all his connexions were in the Whig interest. However, either from principle or from perceiving the Tory party to be then gaining ground, while the Whigs were declining, he soon changed his connexions, and joined himself to Harley, for whom he then had the greatest esteem; nor did he bring him his vote alone, but his opinion, which, even before the end of his first session, he rendered very considerable, the House perceiving even in so young a speaker the greatest eloquence united with the profoundest discernment. The year following he was again chosen anew for the same borough, and persevered in his former attachments, by which he gained such an authority and influence in the House, that it was thought proper to reward his merit; and on the 10th of April, 1704, he was appointed Secretary at War and of the Marine, his friend Harley having a little before been made Secretary of State.

The Tory party being thus established in power, it may easily be supposed that every method would be used to depress the Whig interest, and to prevent it from rising; yet so much justice was done even to merit in an enemy, that the Duke of Marlborough, who might be considered as at the head of the opposite party, was supplied with all the necessaries for carrying on the war in Flanders with vigour: and it is remarkable, that the greatest events of his campaign, such as the battles of Blenheim and Ramilies, and several glorious attempts made by the Duke to shorten the war by some decisive action, fell out while Bolingbroke was Secretary at War. In fact, he was a sincere admirer of that great general, and avowed it upon all occasions to the last moment of his life: he knew his faults, he admired his virtues, and had the boast of being instrumental in giving lustre to those triumphs by which his own power was in a manner overthrown.

As the affairs of the nation were then in as fluctuating a state as at present, Harley, after maintaining the lead for above three years, was in his turn obliged to submit to the Whigs, who once more became the prevailing party, and he was compelled to resign the seals. The friendship between him and Bolingbroke seemed at this time to have been sincere and disinterested; for the latter chose to follow his fortune, and the next day resigned his employments in the administration, following his friend's example, and setting an example at once of integrity and moderation. As an instance of this, when his coadjutors, the Tories, were for carrying a violent measure in the House of Commons, in order to bring the Princess Sophia into England, Bolingbroke so artfully opposed it, that it dropped without a debate. For this his moderation was praised, but perhaps at the expense of his sagacity.

For some time the Whigs seemed to have gained a complete triumph, and upon the election of a new Parliament, in the year 1708, Bolingbroke was not returned. The interval which followed, of above two years, he employed in the severest study; and this recluse period he ever after used to consider as the most active and serviceable of his whole life. But his retirement was soon interrupted by the prevailing of his party once more; for the Whig Parliament being dissolved in the year 1710, he was again chosen; and Harley being made Chancellor and Under Treasurer of the Exchequer, the important post of Secretary of State was given to our author, in which he discovered a degree of genius and assiduity, that perhaps have never been known to be united in one person to the same degree.

The English annals scarcely produce a more trying juncture, or that required such various abilities to regulate. He was then placed in a sphere where he was obliged to conduct the machine of state, struggling with a thousand various calamities; a desperate enraged party, whose characteristic it has ever been to bear none in power but themselves; a war conducted by an able general, his professed opponent, and whose victories only tended to render him every day more formidable; a foreign enemy, possessed of endless resources, and seeming to gather strength from every defeat; an insidious alliance, that wanted only to gain the advantage of victory, without contributing to the expenses of the combat; a weak, declining mistress, that was led by every report, and seemed ready to listen to whatever was said against him; still more, a gloomy, indolent, and suspicious colleague, that envied his power, and hated him for his abilities: these were a part of the difficulties that Bolingbroke had to struggle with in office, and under which he was to conduct the treaty of peace of Utrecht, which was considered as one of the most complicated negotiations that history can afford. But nothing seemed too great for his abilities and industry: he set himself to the undertaking with spirit; he began to pave the way to the intended treaty by making the people discontented at the continuance of the war; for this purpose he employed himself in drawing up accurate computations of the numbers of our own men, and that of foreigners, employed in its destructive progress. He even wrote in the Examiners and other periodical papers of the times, showing how much of the burden rested upon England, and how little was sustained by those who falsely boasted their alliance. By these means, and after much debate in the House of Commons, the Queen received a petition from Parliament, showing the hardships the allies had put upon England in carrying on this war, and consequently how necessary it was to apply relief to so ill-judged a connexion. It may be easily supposed that the Dutch, against whom this petition was chiefly levelled, did all that was in their power to oppose it; many of the foreign courts also, with whom he had any transactions, were continually at work to defeat the minister's intentions. Memorial was delivered after memorial; the people of England, the Parliament, and all Europe were made acquainted with the injustice and the dangers of such a proceeding: however, Bolingbroke went on with steadiness and resolution; and although the attacks of his enemies at home might have been deemed sufficient to employ his attention, yet he was obliged, at the same time that he furnished materials to the press in London, to furnish instructions to all our ministers and ambassadors abroad, who would do nothing but in pursuance of his directions. As an orator in the senate, he exerted all his eloquence: he stated all the great points that were brought before the House; he answered the objections that were made by the leaders of the opposition; and all this with such success, that even his enemies, while they opposed his power, acknowledged his abilities. Indeed, such were the difficulties he had to encounter, that we find him acknowledging himself, some years after, that he never looked back on this great event, passed as it was, without a secret emotion of mind, when he compared the vastness of the undertaking and the importance of the success with the means employed to bring it about, and with those which were employed to frustrate his intentions.

While he was thus industriously employed, he was not without the rewards that deserved to follow such abilities, joined to so much assiduity. In July 1712, he was created Baron St. John of Lidyard-Tregoze in Wiltshire and Viscount Bolingbroke; by the last of which titles he is now generally known, and is likely to be talked of by posterity: he was also the same year appointed Lord Lieutenant of the county of Essex. By the titles of Tregoze and Bolingbroke he united the honours of the elder and younger branch of his family; and thus transmitted into one channel the opposing interests of two races, that had been distinguished, one for their loyalty to King Charles I., the other for their attachment to the Parliament that opposed him. It was afterwards his boast, that he steered clear of the extremes for which his ancestors had been distinguished, having kept the spirit of the one, and acknowledged the subordination that distinguished the other.

Bolingbroke being thus raised very near the summit of power, began to perceive more clearly the defects of him who was placed there. He now began to find that Lord Oxford, whose party he had followed, and whose person he had esteemed, was by no means so able or so industrious as he supposed him to be. He now began from his heart to renounce the friendship which he once had for his coadjutor; he began to imagine him treacherous, mean, indolent, and invidious; he even began to ascribe his own promotion to Oxford's hatred, and to suppose that he was sent up to the House of Lords only to render him contemptible. These suspicions were partly true, and partly suggested by Bolingbroke's own ambition: being sensible of his own superior importance and capacity, he could not bear to see another take the lead in public affairs, when he knew they owed their chief success to his own management. Whatever might have been his motives, whether of contempt, hatred, or ambition, it is certain an irreconcilable breach began between these two leaders of their party; their mutual hatred was so great, that even their own common interest, the vigour of their negotiations, and the safety of their friends were entirely sacrificed to it. It was in vain that Swift, who was admitted into their councils, urged the unreasonable impropriety of their disputes; that while they were thus at variance within the walls, the enemy were making irreparable breaches without. Bolingbroke's antipathy was so great, that even success would have been hateful to him, if Lord Oxford were to be a partner. He abhorred him to that degree, that he could not bear to be joined with him in any case; and even some time after, when the lives of both were aimed at, he could not think of concerting measures with him for their mutual safety, preferring even death itself to the appearance of a temporary friendship.

Nothing could have been more weak and injudicious than their mutual animosities at this juncture; and it may be asserted with truth, that men who were unable to suppress or conceal their resentments upon such a trying occasion were unfit to take the lead in any measures, be their industry or their abilities ever so great. In fact, their dissensions were soon found to involve not only them, but their party in utter ruin: their hopes had for some time been declining, the Whigs were daily gaining ground, and the Queen's death soon after totally destroyed all their schemes with their power.

Upon the accession of George I. to the throne, danger began to threaten the late ministry on every side: whether they had really intentions of bringing in the Pretender, or whether the Whigs made it a pretext for destroying them, is uncertain; but the King very soon began to show that they were to expect neither favour nor mercy at his hands. Upon his landing at Greenwich, when the court came to wait upon him, and Lord Oxford among the number, he studiously avoided taking any notice of him, and testified his resentment by the caresses he bestowed upon the members of the opposite faction. A regency had been some time before appointed to govern the kingdom, and Addison was made secretary. Bolingbroke still maintained his place of State Secretary, but subject to the contempt of the great and the insults of the mean. The first step taken by them to mortify him was to order all letters and packets directed to the Secretary of State to be sent to Mr. Addison; so that Bolingbroke was in fact removed from his office, that is, the execution of it, in two days after the Queen's death. But this was not the worst; for his mortifications were continually heightened by the daily humiliation of waiting at the door of the apartment where the regency sat, with a bag in his hand, and being all the time, as it were, exposed to the insolence of those who were tempted by their natural malevolence, or who expected to make their court to those in power by abusing him.

Upon this sudden turn of fortune, when the seals were taken from him, he went into the country; and having received a message from court to be present when the seal was taken from the door of the Secretary's office, he excused himself, alleging that so trifling a ceremony might as well be performed by one of the under secretaries, but at the same time requested the honour of kissing the King's hand, to whom he testified the utmost submission. This request, however, was rejected with disdain; the King had been taught to regard him as an enemy, and threw himself entirely on the Whigs for safety and protection.

The new Parliament, mostly composed of Whigs, met the 17th of March, and in the King's speech from the throne many inflaming hints were given, and many methods of violence chalked out to the two Houses. "The first steps" (says Lord Bolingbroke, speaking on this occasion) "in both were perfectly answerable; and, to the shame of the peerage be it spoken, I saw at that time several lords concur to condemn in one general vote all that they had approved in a former Parliament by many particular resolutions. Among several bloody resolutions proposed and agitated at this time, the resolution of impeaching me of high treason was taken, and I took that of leaving England, not in a panic terror, improved by the artifices of the Duke of Marlborough, whom I knew even at that time too well to act by his advice or information in any case, but on such grounds as the proceedings which soon followed sufficiently justified, and such as I have never repented building upon. Those who blamed it in the first heat were soon after obliged to change their language: for what other resolution could I take? The method of prosecution designed against me would have put me out of a condition immediately to act for myself, or to serve those who were less exposed than me, but who were, however, in danger. On the other hand, how few were there on whose assistance I could depend, or to whom I would even in these circumstances be obliged? The ferment in the nation was wrought up to a considerable height; but there was at that time no reason to expect that it could influence the proceedings in Parliament, in favour of those who should be accused: left to its own movement, it was much more proper to quicken than slacken the prosecutions; and who was there to guide its motions? The Tories, who had been true to one another to the last, were a handful, and no great vigour could be expected from them; the Whimsicals, disappointed of the figure which they hoped to make, began indeed to join their old friends. One of the principal among them, namely, the Earl of Anglesea, was so very good as to confess to me, that if the court had called the servants of the late Queen to account, and stopped there, he must have considered himself as a judge, and acted according to his conscience on what should have appeared to him; but that war had been declared to the whole Tory party, and that now the state of things was altered. This discourse needed no commentary, and proved to me that I had never erred in the judgment I made of this set of men. Could I then resolve to be obliged to them, or to suffer with Oxford? As much as I still was heated by the disputes in which I had been all my life engaged against the Whigs, I would sooner have chosen to owe my security to their indulgence than to the assistance of the Whimsicals; but I thought banishment, with all her train of evils, preferable to either."

Such was the miserable situation to which he was reduced upon this occasion; of all the number of his former flatterers and dependants, scarcely was one found remaining. Every hour brought fresh reports of his alarming situation and the dangers which threatened him and his party on all sides. Prior, who had been employed in negotiating the treaty of Utrecht, was come over to Dover, and promised to reveal all he knew. The Duke of Marlborough planted his creatures round his lordship, who artfully endeavoured to increase the danger; and an impeachment was actually preparing, in which he was accused of high treason. It argued, therefore, no great degree of timidity in his lordship to take the first opportunity to withdraw from danger, and to suffer the first boilings of popular animosity to quench the flame that had been raised against him; accordingly, having made a gallant show of despising the machinations against him, having appeared in a very unconcerned manner at the playhouse in Drury Lane, and having bespoke another play for the night ensuing—having subscribed to a new opera that was to be acted some time after, and talking of making an elaborate defence,—he went off that same night in disguise to Dover, as a servant to Le Vigne, a messenger belonging to the French king; and there one William Morgan, who had been a captain in General Hill's regiment of dragoons, hired a vessel, and carried him over to Calais, where the governor attended him in his coach, and carried him to his house with all possible distinction.

The news of Lord Bolingbroke's flight was soon known over the whole town; and the next day a letter from him to Lord Lansdowne was handed about in print, to the following effect:

"My Lord,—I left the town so abruptly, that I had no time to take leave of you or any of my friends. You will excuse me when you know that I had certain and repeated informations, from some who are in the secret of affairs, that a resolution was taken, by those who have power to execute it, to pursue me to the scaffold. My blood was to have been the cement of a new alliance, nor could my innocence be any security, after it had once been demanded from abroad, and resolved on at home, that it was necessary to cut me off. Had there been the least reason to hope for a fair and open trial, after having been already prejudged unheard by the two Houses of Parliament, I should not have declined the strictest examination. I challenge the most inveterate of my enemies to produce any one instance of a criminal correspondence, or the least corruption of any part of the administration in which I was concerned. If my zeal for the honour and dignity of my royal mistress and the true interest of my country have anywhere transported me to let slip a warm or unguarded expression, I hope the most favourable interpretation will be put upon it. It is a comfort that will remain with me in all my misfortunes, that I served her Majesty faithfully and dutifully, in that especially which she had most at heart, relieving her people from a bloody and expensive war, and that I have also been too much an Englishman, to sacrifice the interests of my country to any foreign ally; and it is for this crime only that I am now driven from thence. You shall hear more at large from me shortly. Yours," &c.

No sooner was it universally known that he was retired to France, than his flight was construed into a proof of his guilt; and his enemies accordingly set about driving on his impeachment with redoubled alacrity. Mr., afterwards Sir Robert Walpole, who had suffered a good deal by his attachment to the Whig interest during the former reign, now undertook to bring in and conduct the charge against him in the House of Commons. His impeachment consisted of six articles, which Walpole read to the House, in substance as follows:—First, That whereas the Lord Bolingbroke had assured the Dutch ministers that the Queen his mistress would make no peace but in concert with them, yet he had sent Mr. Prior to France that same year, with proposals for a treaty of peace with that monarch, without the consent of the allies. Secondly, That he advised and promoted the making a separate treaty of convention with France, which was signed in September. Thirdly, That he disclosed to M. Mesnager, the French minister at London, this convention, which was the preliminary instructions to her Majesty's Plenipotentiaries at Utrecht. Fourthly, That her Majesty's final instructions to her Plenipotentiaries were disclosed by him to the Abbé Gaultier, who was an emissary of France. Fifthly, That he disclosed to the French the manner how Tournay in Flanders might be gained by them. And lastly, That he advised and promoted the yielding up Spain and the West Indies to the Duke of Anjou, then an enemy to her Majesty. —These were urged by Walpole with great vehemence, and aggravated with all the eloquence of which he was master. He challenged any person in behalf of the accused, and asserted, that to vindicate were in a manner to share his guilt. In this universal consternation of the Tory party, none was for some time seen to stir; but at length General Ross, who had received favours from his lordship, boldly stood up, and said, he wondered that no man more capable was found to appear in defence of the accused. However, in attempting to proceed, he hesitated so much, that he was obliged to sit down, observing, that he would reserve what he had to say to another opportunity. It may easily be supposed that the Whigs found no great difficulty in passing the vote for his impeachment through the House of Commons. It was brought into that House on the 10th of June, 1715; it was sent up to the House of Lords on the 6th of August ensuing, and in consequence of which he was attainted by them of high treason on the 10th of September. Nothing could be more unjust than such a sentence; but justice had been drowned in the spirit of party.

Bolingbroke, thus finding all hopes cut off at home, began to think of improving his wretched fortune upon the Continent. He had left England with a very small fortune, and his attainder totally cut off all resources for the future. In this depressed situation he began to listen to some proposals which were made by the Pretender, who was then residing at Barr, in France, and who was desirous of admitting Bolingbroke into his secret councils. A proposal of this nature had been made him shortly after his arrival at Paris, and before his attainder at home; but while he had yet any hopes of succeeding in England, he absolutely refused, and made the best applications his ruined fortune would permit to prevent the extremity of his prosecution.

He had for some time waited for an opportunity of determining himself, even after he found it vain to think of making peace at home. He let his Jacobite friends in England know that they had but to command him, and he was ready to venture in their service the little all that remained as frankly as he had exposed all that was gone. "At length," says he, talking of himself, "these commands came, and were executed in the following manner. The person who was sent to me arrived in the beginning of July 1715, at the place I had retired to in Dauphiné. He spoke in the name of all his friends whose authority could influence me; and he brought word, that Scotland was not only ready to take arms, but under some sort of dissatisfaction to be withheld from beginning; that in England the people were exasperated against the government to such a degree, that, far from wanting to be encouraged, they could not be restrained from insulting it on every occasion; that the whole Tory party was become avowedly Jacobites; that many officers of the army, and the majority of the soldiers, were well affected to the cause; that the city of London was ready to rise, and that the enterprises for seizing of several places were ripe for execution; in a word, that most of the principal Tories were in concert with the Duke of Ormond; for I had pressed particularly to be informed whether his grace acted alone, or, if not, who were his council; and that the others were so disposed, that there remained no doubt of their joining as soon as the first blow should be struck. He added, that my friends were a little surprised to observe that I lay neuter in such a conjuncture. He represented to me the danger I ran of being prevented by people of all sides from having the merit of engaging early in this enterprise, and how unaccountable it would be for a man impeached and attainted under the present government to take no share in bringing about a revolution so near at hand and so certain. He entreated that I would defer no longer to join the Chevalier, to advise and assist in carrying on his affairs, and to solicit and negotiate at the Court of France, where my friends imagined that I should not fail to meet a favourable reception, and whence they made no doubt of receiving assistance in a situation of affairs so critical, so unexpected, and so promising. He concluded by giving me a letter from the Pretender, whom he had seen in his way to me, in which I was pressed to repair without loss of time to Commercy; and this instance was grounded on the message which the bearer of the letter had brought me from England. In the progress of the conversation with the messenger, he related a number of facts, which satisfied me as to the general disposition of the people; but he gave me little satisfaction as to the measures taken to improve this disposition, for driving the business on with vigour, if it tended to a revolution, or for supporting it to advantage, if it spun into a war. When I questioned him concerning several persons whose disinclination to the government admitted no doubt, and whose names, quality, and experience were very essential to the success of the undertaking, he owned to me that they kept a great reserve, and did at most but encourage others to act, by general and dark expressions. I received this account and this summons ill in my bed; yet, important as the matter was, a few minutes served to determine me. The circumstances wanting to form a reasonable inducement to engage did not excuse me; but the smart of a bill of attainder tingled in every vein, and I looked on my party to be under oppression, and to call for my assistance. Besides which, I considered first that I should be certainly informed, when I conferred with the Chevalier, of many particulars unknown to this gentleman; for I did not imagine that the English could be so near to take up arms as he represented them to be, on no other foundation than that which he exposed."

In this manner, having for some time debated with himself, and taken his resolution, he lost no time in repairing to the Pretender at Commercy, and took the seals of that nominal king, as he had formerly those of his potent mistress. But this was a terrible falling off indeed; and the very first conversation he had with this weak projector gave him the most unfavourable expectations of future success. "He talked to me," says his lordship, "like a man who expected every moment to set out for England or Scotland, but who did not very well know for which: and when he entered into the particulars of his affairs, I found that concerning the former he had nothing more circumstantial or positive to go upon, than what I have already related. But the Duke of Ormond had been for some time, I cannot say how long, engaged with the Chevalier: he had taken the direction of this whole affair, as far as it related to England, upon himself; and had received a commission for this purpose, which contained the most ample powers that could be given. But still, however, all was unsettled, undetermined, and ill understood. The Duke had asked from France a small body of forces, a sum of money, and a quantity of ammunition: but to the first part of the request he received a flat denial, but was made to hope that some arms and some ammunition might be given. This was but a very gloomy prospect; yet hope swelled the depressed party so high, that they talked of nothing less than an instant and ready revolution. It was their interest to be secret and industrious; but, rendered sanguine by their passions, they made no doubt of subverting a government with which they were angry, and gave as great an alarm as would have been imprudent at the eve of a general insurrection."

Such was the state of things when Bolingbroke arrived to take up his new office at Commercy; and although he saw the deplorable state of the party with which he was embarked, yet he resolved to give his affairs the best complexion he was able, and set out for Paris, in order to procure from that court the necessary succours for his new master's invasion of England. But his reception and negotiations at Paris were still more unpromising than those at Commercy; and nothing but absolute infatuation seemed to dictate every measure taken by the party. He there found a multitude of people at work, and every one doing what seemed good in his own eyes; no subordination, no order, no concert. The Jacobites had wrought one another up to look upon the success of the present designs as infallible: every meeting-house which the populace demolished, as he himself says, every little drunken riot which happened, served to confirm them in these sanguine expectations; and there was hardly one among them who would lose the air of contributing by his intrigues to the restoration, which he took for granted would be brought about in a few weeks. Care and hope, says our author very humorously, sat on every busy Irish face; those who could read and write had letters to show, and those who had not arrived to this pitch of erudition had their secrets to whisper. No sex was excluded from this ministry: Fanny Oglethorpe kept her corner in it; and Olive Trant, a woman of the same mixed reputation, was the great wheel of this political machine. The ridiculous correspondence was carried on with England by people of like importance, and who were busy in sounding the alarm in the ears of an enemy whom it was their interest to surprise. By these means, as he himself continues to inform us, the government of England was put on its guard, so that before he came to Paris what was doing had been discovered. The little armament made at Havre de Grace, which furnished the only means to the Pretender of landing on the coasts of Britain, and which had exhausted the treasury of St. Germains, was talked of publicly. The Earl of Stair, the English minister at that city, very soon discovered its destination, and all the particulars of the intended invasion; the names of the persons from whom supplies came, and who were particularly active in the design, were whispered about at tea-tables and coffee-houses. In short, what by the indiscretion of the projectors, what by the private interests and ambitious views of the French, the most private transactions came to light; and such of the more prudent plotters, who supposed that they had trusted their heads to the keeping of one or two friends, were in reality at the mercy of numbers. "Into such company," exclaims our noble writer, "was I fallen for my sins." Still, however, he went on, steering in the wide ocean without a compass, till the death of Louis XIV. and the arrival of the Duke of Ormond at Paris rendered all his endeavours abortive: yet, notwithstanding these unfavourable circumstances, he still continued to despatch several messages and directions for England, to which he received very evasive and ambiguous answers. Among the number of these, he drew up a paper at Chaville, in concert with the Duke of Ormond, Marshal Berwick, and De Torcy, which was sent to England just before the death of the King of France, representing that France could not answer the demands of their memorial, and praying directions what to do. A reply to this came to him through the French Secretary of State, wherein they declared themselves unable to say anything till they saw what turn affairs would take on the death of the King, which had reached their ears. Upon another occasion, a message coming from Scotland to press the Chevalier to hasten their rising, he despatched a messenger to London to the Earl of Mar, to tell him that the concurrence of England in the insurrection was ardently wished and expected: but, instead of that nobleman's waiting for instructions, he had already gone into the Highlands, and there actually put himself at the head of his clans. After this, in concert with the Duke of Ormond, he despatched one Mr. Hamilton, who got all the papers by heart for fear of a miscarriage, to their friends in England, to inform them that though the Chevalier was destitute of succour and all reasonable hopes of it, yet he would land as they pleased in England or Scotland at a minute's warning; and therefore they might rise immediately after they had sent despatches to him. To this message Mr. Hamilton returned very soon with an answer given by Lord Lansdowne, in the name of all the persons privy to the secret, that since affairs grew daily worse, and would not mend by delay, the malcontents in England had resolved to declare immediately, and would be ready to join the Duke of Ormond on his landing; adding, that his person would be as safe in England as in Scotland, and that in every other respect it was better he should land in England; that they had used their utmost endeavours, and hoped the western counties would be in a good posture to receive him; and that he should land as near as possible to Plymouth. With these assurances the Duke embarked, though he had heard before of the seizure of many of his most zealous adherents, of the dispersion of many more, and the consternation of all; so that upon his arrival at Plymouth, finding nothing in readiness, he returned to Brittany. In these circumstances the Pretender himself sent to have a vessel got ready for him at Dunkirk, in which he went to Scotland, leaving Lord Bolingbroke all this while at Paris, to try if by any means some assistance might not be procured, without which all hopes of success were at an end. It was during this negotiation upon this miserable proceeding that he was sent for by Mrs. Trant (a woman who had for some time before ingratiated herself with the Regent of France, by supplying him with mistresses from England), to a little house in the Bois de Boulogne, where she lived with Mademoiselle Chausery, an old superannuated waiting-woman belonging to the Regent. By these he was acquainted with the measures they had taken for the service of the Duke of Ormond; although Bolingbroke, who was actually secretary to the negotiation, had never been admitted to a confidence in their secrets. He was therefore a little surprised at finding such mean agents employed without his privity, and very soon found them utterly unequal to the task. He quickly, therefore, withdrew himself from such wretched auxiliaries, and the Regent himself seemed pleased at his defection.

In the mean time the Pretender set sail from Dunkirk for Scotland; and though Bolingbroke had all along perceived that his cause was hopeless, and his projects ill-designed; although he had met with nothing but opposition and disappointment in his service; yet he considered that this, of all others, was the time he could not be permitted to relax in the cause. He now, therefore, neglected no means, forgot no argument which his understanding could suggest, in applying to the Court of France; but his success was not answerable to his industry. The King of France, not able to furnish the Pretender with money himself, had written some time before his death to his grandson, the King of Spain, and had obtained from him a promise of forty thousand crowns. A small part of this sum had been received by the Queen's treasurer at St. Germains, and had been sent to Scotland, or employed to defray the expenses which were daily making on the coast; at the same time Bolingbroke pressed the Spanish ambassador at Paris, and solicited the minister at the Court of Spain. He took care to have a number of officers picked out of the Irish troops which serve in France, gave them their routes, and sent a ship to receive and transport them to Scotland. Still, however, the money came in so slowly, and in such trifling sums, that it turned to little account, and the officers were on their way to the Pretender. At the same time he formed a design of engaging French privateers in the expedition, that were to have carried whatever should be necessary to send to any part of Britain in their first voyage, and then to cruise under the Pretender's commission. He had actually agreed for some, and had it in his power to have made the same bargain with others: Sweden on the one side, and Scotland on the other, could have afforded them retreats; and if the war had been kept up in any part of the mountains, this armament would have been of the utmost advantage. But all his projects and negotiations failed by the Pretender's precipitate return, who was not above six weeks in his expedition, and flew out of Scotland even before all had been tried in his defence.

The expedition being in this manner totally defeated, Bolingbroke now began to think that it was his duty as well as interest to save the poor remains of the disappointed party. He never had any great opinion of the Pretender's success before he set off; but when this adventurer had taken the last step which it was in his power to make, our secretary then resolved to suffer neither him nor the Scotch to be any longer bubbles of their own credulity and of the scandalous artifices of the French court. In a conversation he had with the Marshal de Huxelles he took occasion to declare, that he would not be the instrument of amusing the Scotch; and since he was able to do them no other service, he would at least inform them of what little dependence they might place upon assistance from France. He added, that he would send them vessels, which, with those already on the coast of Scotland, might serve to bring off the Pretender, the Earl of Mar, and as many others as possible. The Marshal approved his resolution, and advised him to execute it, as the only thing which was left to do; but in the meantime the Pretender landed at Gravelines, and gave orders to stop all vessels bound on his account to Scotland; and Bolingbroke saw him the morning after his arrival at St. Germains, and he received him with open arms.

As it was the secretary's business, as soon as Bolingbroke heard of his return, he went to acquaint the French court with it; when it was recommended to him to advise the Pretender to proceed to Barr with all possible diligence; and in this measure Bolingbroke entirely concurred. But the Pretender himself was in no such haste: he had a mind to stay some time at St. Germains, and in the neighbourhood of Paris, and to have a private meeting with the Regent. He accordingly sent Bolingbroke to solicit this meeting, who exerted all his influence in the negotiation. He wrote and spoke to the Marshal de Huxelles, who answered him by word of mouth, and by letters, refusing him by both, and assuring him that the Regent said the things which were asked were puerilities, and swore he would not see him. The secretary, no ways displeased with his ill success, returned with this answer to his master, who acquiesced in this determination, and declared he would instantly set out for Lorrain, at the same time assuring Bolingbroke of his firm reliance on his integrity.

However, the Pretender, instead of taking post for Lorrain, as he had promised, went to a little house in the Bois de Boulogne, where his female ministers resided, and there continued for several days, seeing the Spanish and Swedish ministers, even the Regent himself. It might have been in these interviews that he was set against his new secretary, and taught to believe that he had been remiss in his duty and false to his trust. Be this as it will, a few days after the Duke of Ormond came to see Bolingbroke, and, having first prepared him for the surprise, put into his hands a note directed to the Duke, and a little scrip of paper directed to the secretary: they were both in the Pretender's handwriting, and dated as if written by him on his way to Lorrain; but in this Bolingbroke was not to be deceived, who knew the place of his present residence. In one of these papers the Pretender declared, that he had no farther occasion for the secretary's service; and the other was an order to him to give up the papers in his office; all which, he observes, might have been contained in a letter-case of a moderate size. He gave the Duke the seals and some papers which he could readily come at; but for some others, in which there were several insinuations, under the Pretender's own hand, reflecting upon the Duke himself, these he took care to convey by a safe hand, since it would have been very improper that the Duke should have seen them. As he thus gave up without scruple all the papers which remained in his hands, because he was determined never to make use of them, so he declares he took a secret pride in never asking for those of his own which were in the Pretender's hands; contenting himself with making the Duke understand, how little need there was to get rid of a man in this manner who only wanted an opportunity to get rid of the Pretender and his cause. In fact, if we survey the measures taken on the one side, and the abilities of the man on the other, it will not appear any way wonderful that he should be disgusted with a party who had neither principle to give a foundation to their hopes, union to advance them, nor abilities to put them in motion.

Bolingbroke being thus dismissed from the Pretender's service, supposed that he had got rid of the trouble and the ignominy of so mean an employment at the same time; but he was mistaken: he was no sooner rejected from the office than articles of impeachment were preferred against him, in the same manner as he had before been impeached in England, though not with such effectual injury to his person and fortune. The articles of his impeachment by the Pretender were branched out into seven heads, in which he was accused of treachery, incapacity, and neglect. The first was, that he was never to be found by those who came to him about business; and if by chance or stratagem they got hold of him, he affected being in a hurry, and by putting them off to another time still avoided giving them any answer. The second was that the Earl of Mar complained by six different messengers at different times, before the Chevalier came from Dunkirk, of his being in want of arms and ammunition, and prayed a speedy relief; and though the things demanded were in my lord's power, there was not so much as one pound of powder in any of the ships which by his lordship's directions parted from France. Thirdly, the Pretender himself, after his arrival, sent General Hamilton to inform him, that his want of arms and ammunition was such, that he should be obliged to leave Scotland, unless he received speedy relief; yet Lord Bolingbroke amused Mr. Hamilton twelve days together, and did not introduce him to any of the French ministers, though he was referred to them for a particular account of affairs; or so much as communicated his letters to the Queen, or anybody else. Fourthly, the Count de Castel Blanco had for several months at Havre a considerable quantity of arms and ammunition, and did daily ask his lordship's orders how to dispose of them, but never got any instructions. Fifthly, the Pretender's friends at the French court had for some time past no very good opinion of his lordship's integrity, and a very bad one of his discretion. Sixthly, at a time when many merchants in France would have carried privately any quantity of arms and ammunition into Scotland, his lordship desired a public order for the embarkation, which being a thing not to be granted, is said to have been done in order to urge a denial. Lastly, the Pretender wrote to his lordship by every occasion after his arrival in Scotland; and though there were many opportunities of writing in return, yet from the time he landed there to the day he left it he never received any letter from his lordship. Such were the articles, by a very extraordinary reverse of fortune, preferred against Lord Bolingbroke, in less than a year after similar articles were drawn up against him by the opposite party at home. It is not easy to find out what he could have done thus to disoblige all sides; but he had learned by this time to make out happiness from the consciousness of his own designs, and to consider all the rest of mankind as uniting in a faction to oppress virtue.

But though it was mortifying to be thus rejected on both sides, yet he was not remiss in vindicating himself from all. Against these articles of impeachment, therefore, he drew up an elaborate answer, in which he vindicates himself with great plausibility. He had long, as he asserts, wished to leave the Pretender's service, but was entirely at a loss how to conduct himself in so difficult a resignation; "but at length," says he, "the Pretender and his council disposed of things better for me than I could have done for myself. I had resolved, on his return from Scotland, to follow him till his residence should be fixed somewhere; after which, having served the Tories in this which I looked upon as their last struggle for power, and having continued to act in the Pretender's affairs till the end of the term for which I embarked with him, I should have esteemed myself to be at liberty, and should, in the civilest manner I was able, have taken my leave of him. Had we parted thus, I should have remained in a very strange situation all the rest of my life; on one side, he would have thought that he had a right on any future occasion to call me out of my retreat; the Tories would probably have thought the same thing; my resolution was taken to refuse them both, and I foresaw that both would condemn me: on the other side, the consideration of his having kept measures with me, joined to that of having once openly declared for him, would have created a point of honour, by which I should have been tied down, not only from ever engaging against him, but also from making my peace at home. The Pretender cut this Gordian knot asunder at one blow: he broke the links of that chain which former engagements had fastened on me, and gave me a right to esteem myself as free from all obligations of keeping measures with him as I should have continued if I had never engaged in his interest."

It is not to be supposed that one so very delicate to preserve his honour would previously have basely betrayed his employer: a man conscious of acting so infamous a part would have undertaken no defence, but let the accusations, which could not materially affect him, blow over, and wait for the calm that was to succeed in tranquillity. He appeals to all the ministers with whom he transacted business, for the integrity of his proceedings at that juncture; and had he been really guilty, when he opposed the ministry here after his return, they would not have failed to brand and detect his duplicity. The truth is, that he perhaps was the most disinterested minister at that time in the Pretender's court; as he had spent great sums of his own money in his service, and never would be obliged to him for a farthing, in which case he believes that he was single. His integrity is much less impeachable on this occasion than his ambition; for all the steps he took may be fairly ascribed to his displeasure at having the Duke of Ormond and the Earl of Mar treated more confidentially than himself. It was his aim always to be foremost in every administration, and he could not bear to act as a subaltern in so paltry a court as that of the Pretender.

At all periods of his exile he still looked towards home with secret regret; and had even taken every opportunity to apply to those in power, either to soften his prosecutions, or lessen the number of his enemies at home. In accepting his office under the Pretender, he made it a condition to be at liberty to quit the post whenever he should think proper; and being now disgracefully dismissed, he turned his mind entirely towards making his peace in England, and employing all the unfortunate experience he had acquired to undeceive his Tory friends, and to promote the union and quiet of his native country. It was not a little favourable to his hopes that about this time, though unknown to him, the Earl of Stair, ambassador to the French court, had received full power to treat with him whilst he was engaged with the Pretender; but yet had never made him any proposals, which might be considered as the grossest outrage. But when the breach with the Pretender was universally known, the Earl sent one Monsieur Saludin, a gentleman of Geneva, to Lord Bolingbroke, to communicate to him his Majesty King George's favourable disposition to grant him a pardon, and his own earnest desire to serve him as far as he was able. This was an offer by much too advantageous for Bolingbroke in his wretched circumstances to refuse; he embraced it, as became him to do, with all possible sense of the King's goodness and of the ambassador's friendship. They had frequent conferences shortly after upon the subject. The turn which the English ministry gave the matter was to enter into a treaty to reverse his attainder, and to stipulate the conditions on which this act of grace should be granted him: but this method of negotiation he would by no means submit to; the notion of a treaty shocked him, and he resolved never to be restored, rather than go that way to work. Accordingly he opened himself without any reserve to Lord Stair, and told him, that he looked upon himself obliged in honour and conscience to undeceive his friends in England, both as to the state of foreign affairs, as to the management of the Jacobite interest abroad, and as to the characters of the persons; in every one of which points he knew them to be most grossly and most dangerously deluded. He observed, that the treatment he had received from the Pretender and his adherents would justify him to the world in doing this; that, if he remained in exile all his life, he might be assured that he would never have more to do with the Jacobite cause; and that, if he were restored, he would give it an effectual blow, in making that apology which the Pretender had put him under a necessity of making; that in doing this he flattered himself that he should contribute something towards the establishment of the King's government, and to the union of his subjects. He added, that if the court thought him sincere in those professions, a treaty with him was unnecessary; and, if they did not believe so, then a treaty would be dangerous to him. The Earl of Stair, who has also confirmed this account of Lord Bolingbroke's in a letter to Mr. Craggs, readily came into his sentiments on this head, and soon after the King approved it upon their representations: he accordingly received a promise of pardon from George I., who on the 2d of July, 1716, created his father Baron of Battersea, in the county of Surrey, and Viscount St. John. This seemed preparatory to his own restoration; and, instead of prosecuting any farther ambitious schemes against the government, he rather began to turn his mind to philosophy; and since he could not gratify his ambition to its full extent, he endeavoured to learn the art of despising it. The variety of distressful events that had hitherto attended all his struggles, at last had thrown him into a state of reflection, and this produced, by way of relief, a *consolatio philosophica*, which he wrote the same year, under the title of "Reflections upon Exile." In this piece, in which he professes to imitate the manner of Seneca, he with some wit draws his own picture, and represents himself as suffering persecution for having served his country with abilities and integrity. A state of exile thus incurred he very justly shows to be rather honourable than distressful; and indeed there are few men who will deny, that the company of strangers to virtue is better than the company of enemies to it. Besides this philosophical tract, he also wrote this year several letters, in answer to the charges laid upon him by the Pretender and his adherents; and the following year he drew up a vindication of his whole conduct with respect to the Tories, in the form of a letter to Sir William Wyndham.

Nor was he so entirely devoted to the fatigues of business, but that he gave pleasure a share in its pursuits. He had never much agreed with the lady he first married, and after a short cohabitation they separated, and lived ever after asunder. She therefore remained in England upon his going into exile, and by proper application to the throne was allowed a sufficient maintenance to support her with becoming dignity: however, she did not long survive his first disgrace; and upon his becoming a widower, he began to think of trying his fortune once more in a state which was at first so unfavourable. For this purpose he cast his eye on the widow of the Marquis of Villette, a niece to the famous Madame Maintenon, a young lady of great merit and understanding, possessed of a very large fortune, but encumbered with a long and troublesome lawsuit. In the company of this very sensible woman he passed his time in France, sometimes in the country, and sometimes at the capital, till the year 1723, in which, after the breaking up of the Parliament, his Majesty was pleased to grant him a pardon as to his personal safety, but neither as yet restoring him to his family inheritance, his title, nor a seat in Parliament.

To obtain this favour had been the governing principle of his politics for some years before; and upon the first notice of his good fortune, he prepared to return to his native country, where, however, his dearest connexions were either dead or declared themselves suspicious of his former conduct in support of their party. It is observable that Bishop Atterbury, who was banished at this time for a supposed treasonable correspondence in favour of the Tories, was set on shore at Calais, just when Lord Bolingbroke arrived there on his return to England. So extraordinary a reverse of fortune could not fail of strongly affecting that good prelate, who observed with some emotion, that he perceived himself to be exchanged: he presently left it to his auditors to imagine whether his country were the loser or the gainer by such an exchange.

Lord Bolingbroke, upon his return to his native country, began to make very vigorous applications for farther favours from the crown: his pardon, without the means of support, was but an empty, or perhaps it might be called a distressful, act of kindness, as it brought him back among his former friends in a state of inferiority his pride could not endure. However, his applications were soon after successful, for in about two years after his return he obtained an act of Parliament to restore him to his family inheritance, which amounted to nearly three thousand pounds a year. He was also enabled by the same to possess any purchase he should make of any other estate in the kingdom; and he accordingly pitched upon a seat of Lord Tankerville's, at Dawley, near Uxbridge in Middlesex, where he settled with his lady, and laid himself out to enjoy the rural pleasures in perfection, since the more glorious ones of ambition were denied him. With this resolution he began to improve his new purchase in a very peculiar style, giving it all the air of a country farm, and adorning even his hall with all the implements of husbandry. We have a sketch of his way of living in this retreat in a letter of Pope to Swift, who omits no opportunity of representing his lordship in the most amiable points of view. This letter is dated from Dawley, the country farm above mentioned, and begins thus: "I now hold the pen for my Lord Bolingbroke, who is reading your letter between two haycocks; but his attention is somewhat diverted by casting his eyes on the clouds, not in the admiration of what you say, but for fear of a shower. He is pleased with your placing him in the triumvirate between yourself and me; though he says he doubts he shall fare like Lepidus, while one of us runs away with all the power, like Augustus, and another with all the pleasure, like Antony. It is upon a foresight of this that he has fitted up his farm, and you will agree that this scheme of retreat is not founded upon weak appearances. Upon his return from Bath he finds all peccant humours are purged out of him; and his great temperance and economy are so signal, that the first is fit for my constitution, and the latter would enable you to lap up so much money as to buy a bishopric in England. As to the return of his health and vigour, were you here, you might inquire of his haymakers; but as to his temperance, I can answer that for one whole day we have had nothing for dinner but mutton broth, beans and bacon, and a barn-door fowl. Now his lordship is run after his cart I have a moment left to myself to tell you, that I overheard him yesterday agree with a painter for two hundred pounds to paint his country hall with trophies of rakes, spades, prongs, &c., merely to countenance his calling this place a farm." What Pope here says of his engagements with a painter was shortly after executed; the hall was painted accordingly in black crayons only, so that at first view it brought to mind the figures often seen scratched with charcoal, or the smoke of a candle, upon the kitchen walls of farmhouses. The whole, however, produced a most striking effect, and over the door at the entrance into it was this motto: *Satis beatus ruris honoribus.* His lordship seemed to be extremely happy in his pursuit of moral tranquillity, and, in the exultation of his heart, could not fail of communicating his satisfactions to his friend Swift. "I am in my own farm," says he, "and here I shoot strong and tenacious roots: I have caught hold of the earth, to use a gardener's phrase, and neither my enemies nor my friends will find it an easy matter to transplant me again."

There is not, perhaps, a stronger instance in the world than his lordship, that an ambitious mind can never be fairly subdued, but will still seek for those gratifications which retirement can never supply. All this time he was mistaken in his passion for solitude, and supposed that to be the child of philosophy which was only the effect of spleen: it was in vain that he attempted to take root in the shade of obscurity; he was originally bred in the glare of public occupation, and he secretly once more wished for transplantation. He was only a titular lord; he had not been thoroughly restored; and, as he was excluded from a seat in the House of Peers, he burned with impatience to play a part in that conspicuous theatre. Impelled by this desire, he could no longer be restrained in obscurity, but once more entered into the bustle of public business, and disavowing all obligations to the minister, he embarked in the opposition against him, in which he had several powerful coadjutors; but previously he had taken care to prefer a petition to the House of Commons, desiring to be reinstated in his former emoluments and capacities. This petition at first occasioned very warm debates: Walpole, who pretended to espouse his cause, alleged that it was very right to admit him to his inheritance; and when Lord William Pawlet moved for a clause to disqualify him from sitting in either House, Walpole rejected the motion, secretly satisfied with a resolution which had been settled in the cabinet, that he should never more be admitted into any share of power. To this artful method of evading his pretensions Bolingbroke was no stranger; and he was now resolved to shake that power which thus endeavoured to obstruct the increase of his own: taking, therefore, his part in the opposition with Pulteney, while the latter engaged to manage the House of Commons, Bolingbroke undertook to enlighten the people. Accordingly, he soon distinguished himself by a multitude of pieces, written during the latter part of George the First's reign, and likewise the beginning of that which succeeded. These were conceived with great vigour and boldness; and now, once more engaged in the service of his country, though disarmed, gagged, and almost bound, as he declared himself to be, yet he resolved not to abandon his cause, as long as he could depend on the firmness and integrity of those coadjutors who did not labour under the same disadvantages with himself. His letters, in a paper called the *Craftsman*, were particularly distinguished in this political contest; and though several of the most expert politicians of the times joined in this paper, his essays were peculiarly relished by the public. However, it is the fate of things written to an occasion seldom to survive that occasion: the *Craftsman*, though written with great spirit and sharpness, is now almost forgotten, although, when it was published as a weekly paper, it sold much more rapidly than even the *Spectator*. Beside this work, he published several other separate pamphlets, which were afterwards reprinted in the second edition of his works, and which were very popular in their day. This political warfare continued for ten years, during which time he laboured with great strength and perseverance, and drew up such a system of politics, as some have supposed to be the most complete now existing. But, as upon all other occasions, he had the mortification once more to see those friends desert him upon whose assistance he most firmly relied, and all that web of fine-spun speculation actually destroyed at once, by the ignorance of some, and the perfidy of others. He then declared that he was perfectly cured of his patriotic frenzy: he fell out not only with Pulteney for his selfish views, but with his old friends the Tories, for abandoning their cause as desperate; averring, that the faint and unsteady exercise of parts on one side was a crime but one degree inferior to the iniquitous misapplication of them on the other. But he could not take leave of a controversy in which he had been so many years engaged, without giving a parting blow, in which he seemed to summon up all his vigour at once, and where, as the poet says,

Animam in vulnere posuit.

This inimitable piece is entitled "A Dissertation on Parties," and of all his masterly pieces it is in general esteemed the best.

Having finished this, which was received with the utmost avidity, he resolved to take leave not only of his enemies and friends, but even of his country; and in this resolution, in the year 1736, he once more retired to France, where he looked to his native country with a mixture of anger and pity, and upon his former professing friends with a share of contempt and indignation. "I expect little," says he, "from the principal actors that tread the stage at present. They are divided not so much as it seemed, and as they would have it believed, about measures: the true division is about their different ends. Whilst the minister was not hard pushed, nor the prospect of succeeding to him near, they appeared to have but one end,—the reformation of the government. The destruction of the minister was pursued only as a preliminary, but of essential and indisputable necessity, to that end; but when his destruction seemed to approach, the object of his succession interposed to the sight of many, and the reformation of the government was no longer their point of view. They had divided the skin, at least in their thought, before they had taken the beast. The common fear of hastening his downfall for others made them all faint in the chase. It was this, and this alone, that saved him, and put off his evil day."

Such were his cooler reflections, after he had laid down his political pen, to employ it in a manner that was much more agreeable to his usual professions and his approaching age. He had long employed the few hours he could spare on subjects of a more general and important nature to the interests of mankind; but as he was frequently interrupted by the alarms of party, he made no great proficiency in his design. Still, however, he kept it in view, and he makes frequent mention, in his letters to Swift, of his intentions to give metaphysics a new and useful turn. "I know," says he, in one of these, "how little regard you pay to writings of this kind; but I imagine that, if you can like any, it must be those that strip metaphysics of all their bombast, keep within the sight of every well-constituted eye, and never bewilder themselves whilst they pretend to guide the reason of others."

Having now arrived at the sixtieth year of his age, and being blessed with a very competent share of fortune, he returned into France, far from the noise and hurry of party, for his seat at Dawley was too near, to devote the rest of his life to retirement and study. Upon his going to that country, as it was generally known that disdain, vexation, and disappointment had driven him there, many of his friends, as well as his enemies, supposed that he was once again gone over to the Pretender. Among the number who entertained this suspicion was Swift, whom Pope, in one of his letters, very roundly chides for harbouring such an unjust opinion. "You should be cautious," says he, "of censuring any motion or action of Lord Bolingbroke, because you hear it only from a shallow, envious, and malicious reporter. What you writ to me about him I find, to my great scandal, repeated in one of yours to another. Whatever you might hint to me, was this for the profane? The thing, if true, should be concealed; but it is, I assure you, absolutely untrue in every circumstance. He has fixed in a very agreeable retirement near Fontainbleau, and makes it his whole business *vacare literis.*"

This reproof from Pope was not more friendly than it was true: Lord Bolingbroke was too well acquainted with the forlorn state of that party, and the folly of its conductors, once more to embark in their desperate concerns. He now saw that he had gone as far towards reinstating himself in the full possession of his former honours as the mere dint of parts and application could go, and was, at length, experimentally convinced, that the decree was absolutely irreversible, and the door of the House of Lords finally shut against him. He, therefore, at Pope's suggestion, retired, merely to be at leisure from the broils of opposition, for the calmer pleasures of philosophy. Thus the decline of his life, though less brilliant, became more amiable; and even his happiness was improved by age, which had rendered his passions more moderate and his wishes more attainable.

But he was far from suffering, even in solitude, his hours to glide away in torpid inactivity. That active, restless disposition still continued to actuate his pursuits; and having lost the season for gaining power over his contemporaries, he was now resolved upon acquiring fame from posterity. He had not been long in his retreat near Fontainbleau when he began a course of letters on the study and use of history for the use of a young nobleman. In these he does not follow the methods of St. Real and others who have treated on this subject, who make history the great fountain of all knowledge; he very wisely confines its benefits, and supposed them rather to consist in deducing general maxims from particular facts, than in illustrating maxims by the application of historical passages. In mentioning ecclesiastical history, he gives his opinion very freely upon the subject of the divine original of the sacred books, which he supposes to have no such foundation. This new system of thinking, which he had always propagated in conversation, and which he now began to adopt in his more laboured compositions, seemed no way supported either by his acuteness or his learning. He began to reflect seriously on these subjects too late in life, and to suppose those objections very new and unanswerable which had been already confuted by thousands. "Lord Bolingbroke," says Pope, in one of his letters, "is above trifling: when he writes of any thing in this world, he is more than mortal. If ever he trifles, it must be when he turns divine."

In the meantime, as it was evident that a man of his active ambition, in choosing retirement when no longer able to lead in public, must be liable to ridicule in resuming a resigned philosophical air, in order to obviate the censure he addressed a letter to Lord Bathurst upon the true use of retirement and study; in which he shows himself still able and willing to undertake the cause of his country, whenever its distresses should require his exertion. "I have," says he, "renounced neither my country nor my friends; and by friends I mean all those, and those alone, who are such to their country. In their prosperity they shall never hear of me; in their distress always. In that retreat wherein the remainder of my days shall be spent I may be of some use to them, since, even thence, I may advise, exhort, and warn them." Bent upon this pursuit only, and having now exchanged the gay statesman for the grave philosopher, he shone forth with distinguished lustre. His conversation took a different turn from what had been usual with him; and, as we are assured by Lord Orrery, who knew him, it united the wisdom of Socrates, the dignity and ease of Pliny, and the wit of Horace.

Yet still, amid his resolutions to turn himself from politics, and to give himself up entirely to the calls of philosophy, he could not resist embarking once more in the debates of his country; and, coming back from France, settled at Battersea, an old seat which was his father's, and had been long in the possession of the family. He supposed he saw an impending calamity, and, though it was not in his power to remove, he thought it his duty to retard its fall. To redeem or save the nation from perdition he thought impossible, since national corruptions were to be purged by national calamities; but he was resolved to lend his feeble assistance to stem the torrent that was pouring in. With this spirit he wrote that excellent piece which is entitled "The Idea of a Patriot King;" in which he describes a monarch uninfluenced by party, leaning to the suggestions neither of Whigs nor Tories, but equally the friend and the father of all. Some time after, in the year 1749, after the conclusion of the peace two years before, the measures taken by the administration seemed not to have been repugnant to his notions of political prudence for that juncture: in that year he wrote his last production, containing reflections on the then state of the nation, principally with regard to her taxes and debts, and on the causes and consequences of them. This undertaking was left unfinished, for death snatched the pen from the hand of the writer.

Having passed the latter part of his life in dignity and splendour, his rational faculties improved by reflection, and his ambition kept under by disappointment, his whole aim seemed to have been to leave the stage of life, on which he had acted such various parts, with applause. He had long wished to fetch his last breath at Battersea, the place where he was born; and fortune, that had through life seemed to traverse all his aims, at last indulged him in this. He had long been troubled with a cancer in his cheek, by which excruciating disease he died, on the verge of fourscore years of age. He was consonant with himself to the last; and those principles which he had all along avowed he confirmed with his dying breath, having given orders that none of the clergy should be permitted to trouble him in his latest moments.

His body was interred in Battersea church with those of his ancestors; and a marble monument erected to his memory, with the following excellent inscription:—

Here lies
HENRY ST. JOHN,
in the reign of Queen Anne
Secretary of War, Secretary of State,
and Viscount Bolingbroke;
in the days of King George I. and
King George II.
something more and better.
His attachment to Queen Anne
exposed him to a long and severe persecution:
he bore it with firmness of mind.
He passed the latter part of his time at home,
the enemy of no national party,
the friend of no faction;
distinguished (under the cloud of a proscription,
which had not been entirely taken off,)
by zeal to maintain the liberty,
and to restore the ancient prosperity,
of Great Britain.
He died the 12th of December, 1751,
aged 79.

In this manner lived and died Lord Bolingbroke, ever active, never depressed, ever pursuing fortune, and as constantly disappointed by her. In whatever light we view his character, we shall find him an object rather properer for our wonder than our imitation, more to be feared than esteemed, and gaining our admiration without our love. His ambition ever aimed at the summit of power, and nothing seemed capable of satisfying his immoderate desires but the liberty of governing all things without a rival. With as much ambition, as great abilities, and more acquired knowledge than Cæsar, he wanted only his courage to be as successful; but the schemes his head dictated his heart often refused to execute; and he lost the ability to perform, just when the great occasion called for all his efforts to engage.

The same ambition that prompted him to be a politician actuated him as a philosopher. His aims were equally great and extensive in both capacities: unwilling to submit to any in the one, or any authority in the other, he entered the fields of science with a thorough contempt of all that had been established before him, and seemed willing to think every thing wrong, that he might show his faculty in the reformation. It might have been better for his quiet, as a man, if he had been content to act a subordinate character in the state; and it had certainly been better for his memory as a writer, if he had aimed at doing less than he attempted. Wisdom in morals, like every other art or science, is an accumulation that numbers have contributed to increase; and it is not for one single man to pretend, that he can add more to the heap than the thousands that have gone before him. Such innovators more frequently retard than promote knowledge; their maxims are more agreeable to the reader, by having the gloss of novelty to recommend them, than those which are trite only because they are true. Such men are, therefore, followed at first with avidity, nor is it till some time that their disciples begin to find their error. They often, though too late, perceive that they have been following a speculative inquiry, while they have been leaving a practical good; and while they have been practising the arts of doubting, they have been losing all firmness of principle, which might tend to establish the rectitude of their private conduct. As a moralist, therefore, Lord Bolingbroke, by having endeavoured at too much, seems to have done nothing; but as a political writer few can equal, and none can exceed, him. As he was a practical politician, his writings are less filled with those speculative illusions, which are the result of solitude and seclusion. He wrote them with a certainty of their being opposed, sifted, examined, and reviled; he therefore took care to build them up of such materials as could not be easily overthrown: they prevailed at the times in which they were written, they still continue to the admiration of the present age, and will probably last for ever.

The last Will and Testament of the late Right Hon. Henry St. John, Lord Viscount Bolingbroke.

In the name of God, whom I humbly adore, to whom I offer up perpetual thanksgiving, and to the order of whose providence I am cheerfully resigned: This is the last Will and Testament of me, Henry St. John, in the reign of Queen Anne, and by her grace and favour, Viscount Bolingbroke. After more than thirty years' proscription, and after the immense losses I have sustained by unexpected events in the course of it; by the injustice and treachery of persons nearest to me; by the negligence of friends, and by the infidelity of servants: as my fortune is so reduced at this time, that it is impossible for me to make such disposition, and to give such ample legacies as I always intended, I content, therefore, to give as follows:—

My debts and the expenses of my burial in a decent and private manner at Battersea, in the vault where my last wife lies, being first paid, I give to William Chetwynd, of Stafford, Esq. and Joseph Taylor, of the Inner Temple, London, Esq., my two assured friends, each of them one hundred guineas, to be laid out by them as to each of them shall seem best in some memorial, as the legacy of their departed friend; and I constitute them executors of this my will. The diamond ring which I wear upon my finger, I give to my old and long approved friend, the Marquis of Matignon, and, after his decease, to his son, the Count de Gace, that I may be kept in the remembrance of a family whom I love and honour above all others.

Item, I give to my said executors the sum of four hundred pounds in trust, to place out the same in some of the public funds, or government securities, or any other securities, as they shall think proper, and to pay the interest or income thereof to Francis Arboneau, my valet-de-chambre, and Ann his wife, and the survivor of them; and after the decease of the survivor of them, if their son, John Arboneau, shall be living, and under the age of eighteen years, to pay the said interest or income to him, until he shall attain his said age, and then to pay the principal money, or assign the securities for the same, to him; but if he shall not be living at the decease of his father and mother, or shall afterwards die before his said age of eighteen years, in either of the said cases the said principal sum of four hundred pounds, and the securities for the same, shall sink into my personal estate, and be accounted part thereof.

Item, I give to my two servants, Marianne Tribon and Remi Charnet, commonly called Picard, each one hundred pounds; and to every other servant living with me at the time of my decease, and who shall have lived with me two years or longer, I give one year's wages more than what shall be due to them at my death.

And whereas I am the author of several books or tracts following, viz.:—

Remarks on the History of England, from the Minutes of Humphrey Oldcastle. In twenty-four letters.

A Dissertation upon Parties. In nineteen letters to Caleb Danvers, Esq.

The Occasional Writer. Numb. 1, 2, 3.

The Vision of Camilick.

An Answer to the London Journal of December 21, 1728, by John Trot.

An Answer to the Defence of the Inquiry into the Reasons of the Conduct of Great Britain.

A Final Answer to the Remarks on the Craftsman's Vindication.

All which books or tracts have been printed and published; and I am also the author of

Four Letters on History, &c.

Which have been privately printed, and not published; but I have not assigned to any person or persons whatsoever the copy, or the liberty of printing or reprinting any of the said books, or tracts, or letters: Now I do hereby, as far as by law I can, give and assign to David Mallet, of Putney, in the county of Surrey, Esquire, the copy and copies of all and each of the before-mentioned books or tracts, and letters, and the liberty of reprinting the same. I also give to the said David Mallet the copy and copies of all the manuscript books, papers, and writings, which I have written or composed, or shall write or compose, and leave at the time of my decease. And I farther give to the said David Mallet all the books which, at the time of my decease, shall be in the room called my library.

All the rest and residue of my personal estate, whatsoever and wheresoever, I give to my said executors; and hereby revoking all former wills, I declare this to be my last will and testament. In witness whereof, I have hereunto set my hand and seal the twenty-second day of November, in the year of our Lord one thousand seven hundred and fifty-one.

HENRY SAINT JOHN BOLINGBROKE.

Signed, sealed, published, and declared by the said testator, as and for his last will and testament, in the presence of
OLIVER PRICE,
THOMAS HALL.

Proved at London, the fifth day of March, 1752, before the worshipful Robert Chapman, doctor of laws and surrogate, by the oaths of William Chetwynd and Joseph Taylor, Esquires, the executors named in the will, to whom administration was granted, being first sworn duly to administer.

March, 1752. WILLIAM LEGARD, PETER ST. ELOY, HENRY STEVENS, } *Deputy Registers.*

In Dr. Matty's Life of Lord Chesterfield, he mentions that he had seen Lord Bolingbroke for several months labouring under a cruel, and, to appearance, incurable disorder. A cancerous humour in his face made a daily progress; and the empirical treatment he submitted to not only hastened his end, but also exposed him to the most excruciating pain. He saw him, for the last time, the day before his tortures began. Though the unhappy patient, as well as his friend, did then expect that he should recover, and accordingly desired him not to come again till his cure was completed, yet he still took leave of him in a manner which showed how much he was affected. He embraced the Earl with tenderness, and said, "God, who placed me here, will do what he pleases with me hereafter,—and He knows best what to do. May He bless you." And in a letter from Chesterfield to a lady of rank at Paris, he says, "I frequently see our friend Bolingbroke, but I see him with great concern. A humour he has long had in his cheek proves to be cancerous, and has made an alarming progress of late. Hitherto it is not attended with pain, which is all he wishes, for as to the rest he is resigned. Truly, a mind like his, so far superior to the generality, would have well deserved that nature should have made an effort in his favour as to the body, and given him an uncommon share of health and duration."

The last scene is thus lamented, in a letter to the same lady:—"Are you not greatly shocked—but I am sure you are—at the dreadful death of our friend Bolingbroke? The remedy has hastened his death, against which there was no remedy, for his cancer was not topical, but universal, and had so infected the whole mass of his blood as to be incurable. What I most lament is, that the medicines put him to exquisite pain—an evil I dread much more than death, both for my friends and myself. I lose a warm, an amiable, and instructive friend. I saw him a fortnight before his death, when he depended upon a cure, and so did I; and he desired I would not come any more till he was quite well, which he expected would be in ten or twelve days. The next day the great pains came on, and never left him till within two days of his death, during which he lay insensible. What a man! what extensive knowledge! what a memory! what eloquence! His passions, which were strong, were injurious to the delicacy of his sentiments; they were apt to be confounded together, and often wilfully. The world will do him more justice now than in his lifetime."

LETTER.

Lord Hyde to David Mallet, Esq.

"PARIS, *March* 7 (N.S.), 1752.

"I LEARN from England, sir, that Lord Bolingbroke has left his manuscripts to you. His friends must see with satisfaction those title-deeds of his reputation in the hands of the author of the life of the great Lord Bacon; and you will have had the distinguished honour of having been guardian to the fame of two of the greatest geniuses which our country, and perhaps humanity, has produced; but with greater honour to you in this last instance, because you are such by the designation and choice of the author himself.

"What works of his you may have for the public I know not. That for which I was solicitous, because I believe it would be most instructive to the world, and might be most for his honour, he told me himself he had laid aside—I mean the history of the great transactions of Europe from the time when he began to consider and know them. There remains of that, I believe, no more than a summary review, which I had the good fortune some time ago to draw from him, upon an application which I made to him to direct me in the study of history. You will probably have seen that summary review, which is in a collection of letters upon history, which he did me the honour to write me. It is but a sketch of the work he had proposed to himself; but it is the sketch of Lord Bolingbroke. He will probably have told you that those letters were by his direction delivered up by me to Mr. Pope, who burnt, as he told me, the manuscripts, and printed off, by a private press, some very few copies, which were to be considered still as manuscripts, one of which Mr. Pope kept, and sent another to Lord Bolingbroke. Sir William Wyndham, Lord Bathurst, Lord Marchmont, Mr. Murray, and Mr. Lyttleton, I think, had each one. I do not remember to have been told of any copies given, except to myself, who have always preserved mine as I would a MS. which was not my own,—observing not only the restrictions which Lord Bolingbroke himself had recommended to me, but securing likewise, as far as I could, even in case of my death, that this work should never become public from that copy which is in my possession. I enlarge upon this, because I think myself particularly obliged, out of regard to Lord Bolingbroke, to give this account of that work to the person whom he has intrusted with all his writings, in case you might not have known this particularity. And at the same time I think it my duty to the memory of Lord Bolingbroke, to myself, and to the world too, to say something more to you in relation to this work.

"It is a work, sir, which will instruct mankind, and do honour to its author; and yet I will take upon me to say, that for the sake of both, you must publish it with caution.

"The greatest men have their faults, and sometimes the greatest faults; but the faults of superior minds are the least indifferent, both to themselves and to society. Humanity is interested in the fame of those who excelled in it; but it is interested, before all, in the good of society, and in the peace of the minds of the individuals that compose it. Lord Bolingbroke's mind embraced all objects, and looked far into all; but not without a strong mixture of passions, which will always necessarily beget some prejudices, and follow more. And on the subject of religion particularly (whatever was the motive that inflamed his passions upon that subject chiefly,) his passions were the most strong; and I will venture to say, (when called upon, as I think, to say what I have said more than once to himself, with the deference due to his age and extraordinary talents,) his passions upon that subject did prevent his otherwise superior reason from seeing, that, even in a political light only, he hurt himself, and wounded society, by striking at establishments, upon which the conduct at least of society depends, and by striving to overturn in men's minds the systems which experience at least has justified, and which authority at least has rendered respectable, as necessary to public order and to private peace, without suggesting to their minds a better, or indeed any, system.

"You will find, sir, what I say to be true in a part of the work I mentioned, where he digresses upon the criticism of church history.

"While this work remained in the hands only of those I have mentioned, (except, as I have been telling you, to himself and to them in private conversation,) I have otherwise been silent upon that subject; but I must now say to you, sir, that, for the world's sake and for his, that part of the work ought by no means to be communicated farther. And you see, that it is a digression not necessary to that work. If this digression should be made public, it will be censured,—it must be censured,—it ought to be censured. It will be criticised, too, by able pens, whose erudition, as well as their reasonings, will not be easily answered. In such a case, I shall owe to myself and to the world to disclaim publicly that part of a work which he did me the honour to address to me; but I owe to the regard which he has sometimes expressed for me to disclaim it rather privately to you, sir, who are intrusted with his writings, and to recommend to you to suppress that part of the work, as a good citizen of the world, for the world's peace, as one intrusted and obliged by Lord Bolingbroke, not to raise new storms to his memory.—I am, sir, your very humble servant, "HYDE."

LETTER.

David Mallet, Esq. to Lord Hyde.

"MY LORD,—I received a very real pleasure, and at the same time a sensible concern, from the letter your lordship has honoured me with. Nothing could be more agreeable to me than the favourable opinion of one whom I have long admired for every quality that enters into an estimable and amiable character; but then nothing can occasion me more uneasiness than not to be able to suppress that part of a work which you would have kept from public view.

"The book was printed off before your lordship's letter reached my hands; but this consideration alone would have appeared trifling to me. I apprehend that I cannot, without being unfaithful to the trust reposed in me, omit or alter any thing in those works which my Lord Bolingbroke had deliberately prepared for the press, and I will publish no other. As to this in particular, his repeated commands to me were, that it should be printed exactly according to the copy he himself, in all the leisure of retirement, had corrected with that view.

"Upon the whole, if your lordship should think it necessary to disclaim the reflections on sacred history, by which I presume is meant some public and authentic declaration, that your notions on this head differ entirely from those of your noble friend; even in this case I am sure you will do it with all the delicacy natural to your own disposition, and with all the tenderness to his memory, that the particular regard he always bore you can deserve. I am, with the greatest respect, my lord," &c.

END OF THE LIFE OF LORD BOLINGBROKE.

THE LIFE

OF

THOMAS PARNELL, D.D.

ARCHDEACON OF CLOGHER.

[1768.]

THE LIFE OF DR. PARNELL.

THE life of a scholar seldom abounds with adventure. His fame is acquired in solitude. And the historian, who only views him at a distance, must be content with a dry detail of actions by which he is scarcely distinguished from the rest of mankind. But we are fond of talking of those who have given us pleasure, not that we have any thing important to say, but because the subject is pleasing.

THOMAS PARNELL, D.D., was descended from an ancient family, that had for some centuries been settled at Congleton in Cheshire. His father, Thomas Parnell, who had been attached to the Commonwealth party, upon the Restoration went over to Ireland; thither he carried a large personal fortune, which he laid out in lands in that kingdom. The estates he purchased there, as also that of which he was possessed in Cheshire, descended to our poet, who was his eldest son, and still remain in the family. Thus want, which has compelled many of our greatest men into the service of the Muses, had no influence upon Parnell: he was a poet by inclination.

He was born in Dublin in the year 1679, and received the first rudiments of his education at the school of Doctor Jones in that city. Surprising things are told us of the greatness of his memory at that early period: as, of his being able to repeat by heart forty lines of any book at the first reading; of his getting the third book of the Iliad in one night's time, which was given in order to confine him for some days. These stories, which are told of almost every celebrated wit, may perhaps be true. But, for my own part, I never found any of those prodigies of parts, although I have known enow that were desirous, among the ignorant, of being thought so.

There is one presumption, however, of the early maturity of his understanding. He was admitted a member of the college of Dublin at the age of thirteen, which is much sooner than usual, as at that university they are a great deal stricter in their examination for entrance than either at Oxford or Cambridge. His progress through the college course of study was probably marked with but little splendour; his imagination might have been too warm to relish the cold logic of Burgersdicius, or the dreary subtleties of Smiglesius; but it is certain that, as a classical scholar, few could equal him. His own compositions show this; and the deference which the most eminent men of his time paid him upon that head, put it beyond a doubt. He took the degree of Master of Arts the 9th of July, 1700; and, in the same year, he was ordained a deacon, by William, Bishop of Derry, having a dispensation from the Primate, as being under twenty-three years of age. He was admitted into priest's orders about three years after, by William, Archbishop of Dublin; and, on the 9th of February, 1705, he was collated by Sir George Ashe, Bishop of Clogher, to the archdeaconry of Clogher. About that time also he married Miss Anne Minchin, a young lady of great merit and beauty, by whom he had two sons, who died young, and one daughter, who is still living. His wife died some time before him; and her death is said to have made so great an impression on his spirits, that it served to hasten his own. On the 31st of May, 1716, he was presented, by his friend and patron Archbishop King, to the vicarage of Finglass, a benefice worth about four hundred pounds a year, in the diocese of Dublin, but he lived to enjoy his preferment a very short time. He died at Chester, in July, 1717, on his way to Ireland, and was buried in Trinity church in that town, without any monument to mark the place of his interment. As he died without male issue, his estate devolved to his only nephew, Sir John Parnell, Baronet, whose father was younger brother to the Archdeacon, and one of the Justices of the King's Bench in Ireland.

Such is the very unpoetical detail of the life of a poet. Some dates, and some few facts scarcely more interesting than those that make the ornaments of a country tombstone, are all that remain of one whose labours now begin to excite universal curiosity. A poet, while living, is seldom an object sufficiently great to attract much attention: his real merits are known but to a few, and these are generally sparing in their praises. When his fame is increased by time, it is then too late to investigate the peculiarities of his disposition: the dews of the morning are past, and we vainly try to continue the chase by the meridian splendour.

There is scarcely any man but might be made the subject of a very interesting and amusing history, if the writer, besides a thorough acquaintance with the character he draws, were able to make those nice distinctions which separate it from all others. The strongest minds have usually the most striking peculiarities, and would consequently afford the richest materials: but in the present instance, from not knowing Dr. Parnell, his peculiarities are gone to the grave with him; and we are obliged to take his character from such as knew but little of him, or who, perhaps, could have given very little information if they had known more.

Parnell, by what I have been able to collect from my father and uncle, who knew him, was the most capable man in the world to make the happiness of those he conversed with, and the least able to secure his own. He wanted that evenness of disposition which bears disappointment with phlegm, and joy with indifference. He was ever very much elated or depressed, and his whole life spent in agony or rapture. But the turbulence of these passions only affected himself, and never those about him: he knew the ridicule of his own character, and very effectually raised the mirth of his companions, as well at his vexations as at his triumphs.

How much his company was desired, appears from the extensiveness of his connections and the number of his friends. Even before he made any figure in the literary world, his friendship was sought by persons of every rank and party. The wits at that time differed a good deal from those who are most eminent for their understanding at present. It would now be thought a very indifferent sign of a writer's good sense, to disclaim his private friends for happening to be of a different party in politics; but it was then otherwise,—the Whig wits held the Tory wits in great contempt, and these retaliated in their turn. At the head of one party were Addison, Steele, and Congreve; at that of the other Pope, Swift, and Arbuthnot. Parnell was a friend to both sides, and, with a liberality becoming a scholar, scorned all those trifling distinctions, that are noisy for the time, and ridiculous to posterity. Nor did he emancipate himself from these without some opposition from home. Having been the son of a Commonwealth's man, his Tory connections on this side of the water gave his friends in Ireland great offence: they were much enraged to see him keep company with Pope, and Swift, and Gay; they blamed his undistinguishing taste, and wondered what pleasure he could find in the conversation of men who approved the treaty of Utrecht, and disliked the Duke of Marlborough. His conversation is said to have been extremely pleasing, but in what its peculiar excellence consisted is now unknown. The letters which were written to him by his friends are full of compliments upon his talents as a companion, and his good-nature as a man. I have several of them now before me. Pope was particularly fond of his company, and seems to regret his absence more than any of the rest.

A letter from him follows thus:

"LONDON, *July* 29.

"DEAR SIR,—I wish it were not as ungenerous as vain to complain too much of a man that forgets me, but I could expostulate with you a whole day upon your inhuman silence: I call it inhuman; nor would you think it less, if you were truly sensible of the uneasiness it gives me. Did I know you so ill as to think you

your company, and our dear friend the Dean's. I am sure the whole entertainment would have been to his relish. Gay has got so much money by his Art of Walking the Streets, that he is ready to set up his equipage; he is just going to the bank to negotiate some exchange bills. Mr. Pope delays his second volume of his Homer till the martial spirit of the rebels is quite quelled, it being judged that the first part did some harm that way. Our love again and again to the dear Dean. *Fuimus Tories*, I can say no more.

"ARBUTHNOT."

"When a man is conscious that he does no good himself, the next thing is to cause others to do some. I may claim some merit this way, in hastening this testimonial from your friends above writing: their love to you indeed wants no spur, their ink wants no pen, their pen wants no hand, their hand wants no heart, and so forth (after the manner of Rabelais, which is betwixt some meaning and no meaning); and yet it may be said, when present thought and opportunity is wanting, their pens want ink, their hands want pens, their hearts want hands, &c. till time, place, and conveniency concur to set them writing, as at present a sociable meeting, a good dinner, warm fire, and an easy situation do, to the joint labour and pleasure of this epistle.

"Wherein if I should say nothing I should say much (much being included in my love), though my love be such, that if I should say much, I should yet say nothing, it being (as Cowley says) equally impossible either to conceal or to express it.

"If I were to tell you the thing I wish above all things, it is to see you again; the next is to see here your treatise of Zoilus, with the Batrachomuomachia, and the Pervigilium Veneris, both which poems are masterpieces in several kinds; and I question not the prose is as excellent in its sort as the Essay on Homer. Nothing can be more glorious to that great author, than that the same hand that raised his best statue, and decked it with its old laurels, should also hang up the scarecrow of his miserable critic, and gibbet up the carcass of Zoilus, to the terror of the witlings of posterity. More, and much more, upon this and a thousand other subjects, will be the matter of my next letter, wherein I must open all the friend to you. At this time I must be content with telling you I am faithfully your most affectionate and humble servant,

"A. POPE."

If we regard this letter with a critical eye, we must find it indifferent enough; if we consider it as a mere effusion of friendship, in which every writer contended in affection, it will appear much to the honour of those who wrote it. To be mindful of an absent friend in the hours of mirth and feasting, when his company is least wanted, shows no slight degree of sincerity. Yet probably there was still another motive for writing thus to him in conjunction. The above-named, together with Swift and Parnell, had some time before formed themselves into a society, called the Scribblerus Club, and I should suppose they commemorated him thus, as being an absent member.

It is past a doubt that they wrote many things in conjunction, and Gay usually held the pen. And yet I do not remember any productions which were the joint effort of this society as doing it honour. There is something feeble and quaint in all their attempts, as if company repressed thought, and genius wanted solitude for its boldest and happiest exertions. Of those productions in which Parnell had a principal share, that of the Origin of the Sciences from the Monkeys in Ethiopia is particularly mentioned by Pope himself, in some manuscript anecdotes which he left behind him. The Life of Homer also, prefixed to the translation of the Iliad, is written by Parnell, and corrected by Pope; and, as that great poet assures us in the same place, this correction was not effected without great labour. "It is still stiff," says he, "and was written still stiffer; as it is, I verily think it cost me more pains in the correcting, than the writing it would have done." All this may be easily credited; for every thing of Parnell's that has appeared in prose is written in a very awkward, inelegant manner. It is true, his productions teem with imagination, and show great learning, but they want that ease and sweetness for which his poetry is so much admired; and the language is also shamefully incorrect. Yet, though all this must be allowed, Pope should have taken care not to leave his errors upon record against him, or put it in the power of envy to tax his friend with faults that do not appear in what he has left to the world. A poet has a right to expect the same secrecy in his friend as in his confessor; the sins he discovers are not divulged for punishment, but pardon. Indeed, Pope is almost inexcusable in this instance, as what he seems to condemn in one place he very much applauds in another. In one of the letters from him to Parnell, above mentioned, he treats the Life of Homer with much greater respect, and seems to say, that the prose is excellent in its kind. It must be confessed, however, that he is by no means inconsistent; what he says in both places may very easily be reconciled to truth; but who can defend his candour and sincerity?

It would be hard, however, to suppose that there was no real friendship between these great men. The benevolence of Parnell's disposition remains unimpeached; and Pope, though subject to starts of passion and envy, yet never missed an opportunity of being truly serviceable to him. The commerce between them was carried on to the common interest of both. When Pope had a Miscellany to publish, he applied to Parnell for poetical assistance, and the latter as implicitly submitted to him for correction. Thus they mutually advanced each other's interest or fame, and grew stronger by conjunction. Nor was Pope the only person to whom Parnell had recourse for assistance. We learn from Swift's letters to Stella that he submitted his pieces to all his friends, and readily adopted their alterations. Swift, among the number, was very useful to him in that particular; and care has been taken that the world should not remain ignorant of the obligation.

But in the connections of wits, interest has generally very little share; they have only pleasure in view, and can seldom find it but among each other. The Scriblerus Club, when the members were in town, were seldom asunder, and they often made excursions together into the country, and generally on foot. Swift was usually the butt of the company, and if a trick was played, he was always the sufferer. The whole party once agreed to walk down to the house of Lord B——, who is still living, and whose seat is about twelve miles from town. As every one agreed to make the best of his way, Swift, who was remarkable for walking, soon left the rest behind him, fully resolved, upon his arrival, to choose the very best bed for himself, for that was his custom. In the meantime Parnell was determined to prevent his intentions, and taking horse, arrived at Lord B——'s by another way, long before him. Having apprized his lordship of Swift's design, it was resolved at any rate to keep him out of the house; but how to effect this was the question. Swift never had the small-pox, and was very much afraid of catching it; as soon, therefore, as he appeared striding along at some distance from the house, one of his lordship's servants was despatched to inform him that the small-pox was then making great ravages in the family, but that there was a summer-house with a field-bed at his service, at the end of the garden. There the disappointed Dean was obliged to retire, and take a cold supper that was sent out to him, while the rest were feasting within. However, at last they took compassion on him; and upon his promising never to choose the best bed again, they permitted him to make one of the company.

There is something satisfactory in these accounts of the follies of the wise: they give a natural air to the picture, and reconcile us to our own. There have been few poetical societies more talked of, or productive of a greater variety of whimsical conceits, than this of the Scribblerus Club, but how long it lasted I cannot exactly determine. The whole of Parnell's poetical existence was not of more than eight or ten years' continuance; his first excursions to England began about the year 1706, and he died in the year 1718;

so that it is probable the club began with him, and his death ended the connection. Indeed, the festivity of his conversation, the benevolence of his heart, and the generosity of his temper, were qualities that might serve to cement any society, and that could hardly be replaced when he was taken away. During the two or three last years of his life he was more fond of company than ever, and could scarcely bear to be alone. The death of his wife, it is said, was a loss to him that he was unable to support or recover. From that time he could never venture to court the Muse in solitude, where he was sure to find the image of her who first inspired his attempts. He began, therefore, to throw himself into every company, and to seek from wine, if not relief, at least insensibility. Those helps that sorrow first called for assistance habit soon rendered necessary, and he died before his fortieth year, in some measure a martyr to conjugal fidelity.

Thus in the space of a very few years Parnell attained a share of fame equal to what most of his contemporaries were a long life in acquiring. He is only to be considered as a poet; and the universal esteem in which his poems are held, and the reiterated pleasure they give in the perusal, are a sufficient test of their merit. He appears to me to be the last of that great school that had modelled itself upon the ancients, and taught English poetry to resemble what the generality of mankind have allowed to excel. A studious and correct observer of antiquity, he sets himself to consider nature with the lights it lent him; and he found that the more aid he borrowed from the one, the more delightfully he resembled the other. To copy nature is a task the most bungling workman is able to execute; to select such parts as contribute to delight is reserved only for those whom accident has blessed with uncommon talents, or such as have read the ancients with indefatigable industry. Parnell is ever happy in the selection of his images, and scrupulously careful in the choice of his subjects. His productions bear no resemblance to those tawdry things, which it has for some time been the fashion to admire; in writing which the poet sits down without any plan, and heaps up splendid images without any selection; where the reader grows dizzy with praise and admiration, and yet soon grows weary, he can scarcely tell why. Our poet, on the contrary, gives out his beauties with a more sparing hand; he is still carrying his reader forward, and just gives him refreshment sufficient to support him to his journey's end. At the end of his course the reader regrets that his way has been so short, he wonders that it gave him so little trouble, and so resolves to go the journey over again.

His poetical language is not less correct than his subjects are pleasing. He found it at that period in which it was brought to its highest pitch of refinement; and ever since his time it has been gradually debasing. It is, indeed, amazing, after what has been done by Dryden, Addison, and Pope, to improve and harmonize our native tongue, that their successors should have taken so much pains to involve it into pristine barbarity. These misguided innovators have not been content with restoring antiquated words and phrases, but have indulged themselves in the most licentious transpositions and the harshest constructions, vainly imagining that the more their writings are unlike prose, the more they resemble poetry. They have adopted a language of their own, and call upon mankind for admiration. All those who do not understand them are silent, and those who make out their meaning are willing to praise, to show they understand. From these follies and affectations the poems of Parnell are entirely free: he has considered the language of poetry as the language of life, and conveys the warmest thoughts in the simplest expression.

Parnell has written several poems besides those published by Pope, and some of them have been made public with very little credit to his reputation. There are still many more that have not yet seen the light in the possession of Sir John Parnell, his nephew, who, from that laudable zeal which he has for his uncle's reputation, will probably be slow in publishing what he may even suspect will do it injury. Of those which are usually inserted in his works, some are indifferent, and some moderately good, but the greater part are excellent. A slight stricture on the most striking shall conclude this account, which I have already drawn out to a disproportionate length.

Hesiod, or the Rise of Woman, is a very fine illustration of a hint from Hesiod. It was one of his earliest productions, and first appeared in a miscellany published by Tonson.

Of the three songs that follow, two of them were written upon the lady he afterwards married: they were the genuine dictates of his passion, but are not excellent in their kind.

The anacreontic beginning with "When spring came on with fresh delight," is taken from a French poet, whose name I forget, and, as far as I am able to judge of the French language, is better than the original. The anacreontic that follows, "Gay Bacchus," &c., is also a translation of a Latin poem by Aurelius Augurellus, an Italian poet, beginning with,

> Invitat olim Bacchus ad cœnam suos
> Comum, Jocum, Cupidinem.

Parnell, when he translated it, applied the characters to some of his friends, and as it was written for their entertainment, it probably gave them more pleasure than it has given the public in the perusal. It seems to have more spirit than the original; but it is extraordinary that it was published as an original, and not as a translation. Pope should have acknowledged it, as he knew.

The Fairy Tale is, incontestably, one of the finest pieces in any language. The old dialect is not perfectly well preserved; but this is a very slight defect, where all the rest is so excellent.

The Pervigilium Veneris (which, by the by, does not belong to Catullus,) is very well versified; and, in general, all Parnell's translations are excellent. The Battle of the Frogs and Mice, which follows, is done as well as the subject would admit; but there is a defect in the translation, which sinks it below the original, and which it was impossible to remedy,—I mean the names of the combatants, which, in the Greek bear a ridiculous allusion to their natures, have no force to the English reader. A Bacon-eater was a good name for a mouse, and Pternotractas in Greek was a very good sounding word, that conveyed that meaning. Puffcheek would sound odiously as a name for a frog, and yet Physignathos does admirably well in the original.

The Letter to Mr. Pope is one of the finest compliments that ever was paid to any poet: the description of his situation at the end of it is very fine, but far from being true. That part of it where he deplores his being far from wit and learning, as being far from Pope, gave particular offence to his friends at home. Mr. Coote, a gentleman in his neighbourhood, who thought that he himself had wit, was very much displeased with Parnell for casting his eyes so far off for a learned friend, when he could so conveniently be supplied at home.

The translation of a part of the Rape of the Lock into monkish verse serves to show what a master Parnell was of the Latin; a copy of verses made in this manner is one of the most difficult trifles that can possibly be imagined. I am assured that it was written upon the following occasion. Before the Rape of the Lock was yet completed, Pope was reading it to his friend Swift, who sat very attentively, while Parnell, who happened to be in the house, went in and out without seeming to take any notice. However, he was very diligently employed in listening, and was able, from the strength of his memory, to bring away the whole description of the Toilet pretty exactly. This he versified in the manner now published in his works; and the next day, when Pope was reading his poem to some friends, Parnell insisted that he had stolen that part of the description from an old monkish manuscript. An old paper with the Latin verses was soon brought forth, and it was not till after some time that Pope was delivered from the confusion which it at first produced.

The Bookworm is another unacknowledged translation from a Latin poem by Beza. It was the fashion with the wits of the last age to conceal the places whence they took their hints or their subjects. A trifling acknowledgment would have made that lawful prize, which may now be considered as plunder.

The Night Piece on Death deserves every praise, and I should suppose, with very little amendment, might be made to surpass all those night pieces and churchyard scenes that have since appeared.

But the poem of Parnell's best known, and on which his best reputation is grounded, is the Hermit. Pope, speaking of this in those manuscript anecdotes already quoted says, "That the poem is very good. The story," continues he, "was written originally in Spanish, whence, probably, Howel had translated it into prose, and inserted it in one of his letters. Addison liked the scheme, and was not disinclined to come into it." However this may be, Dr. Henry Moore, in his Dialogues, has the very same story; and I have been informed by some, that it is originally of Arabian invention.

With respect to the prose works of Parnell, I have mentioned them already; his fame is too well grounded for any defects in them to shake it. I will only add, that the Life of Zoilus was written at the request of his friends, and designed as a satire upon Dennis and Theobald, with whom his club had long been at variance. I shall end this account with a letter to him from Pope and Gay, in which they endeavour to hasten him to finish that production:—

"LONDON, *March* 18.

"DEAR SIR,—I must own I have long owed you a letter, but, you must own, you have owed me one a good deal longer. Besides, I have but two people in the whole kingdom of Ireland to take care of,—the Dean and you; but you have several who complain of your neglect in England. Mr. Gay complains, Mr. Harcourt complains, Mr. Jervas complains, Dr. Arbuthnot complains, my Lord complains, I complain. (Take notice of this figure of iteration when you make your next sermon.) Some say you are in deep discontent at the new turn of affairs; others, that you are so much in the Archbishop's good graces, that you will not correspond with any that have seen the last ministry. Some affirm you have quarreled with Pope (whose friends, they observe, daily fall from him on account of his satirical and comical disposition); others, that you are insinuating yourself into the opinion of the ingenious Mr. What-do-ye-call-him. Some think you are preparing your sermons for the press, and others that you will transform them into essays and moral discourses. But the only excuse that I will allow, is your attention to the life of Zoilus. The frogs already seem to croak for their transportation to England, and are sensible how much that doctor is cursed and hated, who introduced their species into your nation; therefore, as you dread the wrath of St. Patrick, send them hither, and rid the kingdom of those pernicious and loquacious animals.

"I have at length received your poem out of Mr. Addison's hands, which shall be sent as soon as you order it, and in what manner you shall appoint. I shall, in the meantime, give Mr. Tooke a packet for you, consisting of divers merry pieces,—Mr. Gay's new farce, Mr. Burnet's letter to Mr. Pope, Mr. Pope's Temple of Fame, Mr. Thomas Burnet's Grumbler on Mr. Gay, and the Bishop of Ailsbury's Elegy, written either by Mr. Cary or some other hand.

"Mr. Pope is reading a letter, and, in the meantime, I make use of the pen to testify my uneasiness in not hearing from you. I find success, even in the most trivial things, raises the indignation of scribblers: for I, for my what-d'ye-call-it, could neither escape the fury of Mr. Burnet or the German Doctor; then, where will rage end, when Homer is to be translated? Let Zoilus hasten to your friend's assistance, and envious criticism shall be no more. I am in hopes that we may order our affairs so as to meet this summer at the Bath; for Mr. Pope and myself have thoughts of taking a trip thither. You shall preach, and we will write lampoons; for it is esteemed as great an honour to leave the Bath for fear of a broken head, as for a Terræ Filius of Oxford to be expelled. I have no place at court; therefore, that I may not entirely be without one everywhere, show that I have a place in your remembrance.—Your most affectionate, faithful servants, "A. POPE and J. GAY.

"Homer will be published in three weeks."

I cannot finish this trifle without returning my sincerest acknowledgments to Sir John Parnell for the generous assistance he was pleased to give me, in furnishing me with many materials, when he heard I was about writing the life of his uncle; as also to Mr. and Mrs. Hayes, relations of our poet; and to my very good friend Mr. Stevens, who, being an ornament to letters himself, is very ready to assist all the attempts of others.

END OF THE LIFE OF DR. PARNELL.

MEMOIRS

OF

M. DE VOLTAIRE.

[1759.]

MEMOIRS OF M. DE VOLTAIRE.

THAT life which has been wholly employed in the study, is properly seen only in the author's writings; there is no variety to entertain, nor adventure to interest us in the calm anecdotes of such an existence. Cold criticism is all the reader must expect, instead of instructive history.

VOLTAIRE, however, may be justly exempted from the number of those obscure philosophers whose days have been passed between the fireside and the easy chair. It is a doubt whether he appears more remarkable for the busy incidents of his life, or the fine productions of his retirement. If we regard the variety of his adventures, we shall be surprised how he had time to study; and if we look into his voluminous and spirited productions, we shall be apt to conclude that his whole employment was speculation. The truth is, no man can more truly be said to have lived. There is hardly a period of his existence which is not crowded with incidents that characterise either the philosopher or the man of the world. No poet was ever more universally known than he: none more praised or more censured; possessed of more sincere friends or inveterate enemies.

François Marie Arouet de Voltaire was born at Châtenay, near Paris, the 20th of February, 1694. His family was but mean, as his father was the maker of his own fortune. François Arouet was at first an usurer; in which employment, by the most extreme parsimony, he saved as much as entitled him to follow the business of a public notary. Frugality in the lower orders of mankind may be considered as a substitute to ambition: this old man was a miser with no other view; and when his circumstances permitted, he purchased a place under the Government of *greffier du châtelet;* which is equivalent to an under-secretary with us. In this office he acquired a fortune of about 500*l.* a year, and had interest sufficient to get his family ennobled, by having the title of DE added to the name of Voltaire.

Being therefore in easy circumstances, he was resolved to give his son the best education in his power, and accordingly, at the usual age, put him under the care of the celebrated Porée, who at that time professed rhetoric and philosophy in one of the colleges of Paris. Young Voltaire quickly discovered a capacity equal to any task, but at the same time an utter aversion to all that wore the appearance of study—enamoured with poetry and eloquence, yet showing his love by feeble efforts to imitate, rather than by a fondness of reading, the models proposed to his admiration. This dislike of learning the polite arts by precept, the manner in which they are generally taught, made him appear to his fellow-students as if endued but with a very ordinary capacity; nor did any of the assistant-masters view him in a light more advantageous. Porée, however, who was himself a man of genius, perceived in his pupil the sparks of latent fire, and saw with regret—for he loved the boy—that Voltaire was born a poet. To prevent his pursuing an employment that generally points to misfortune, and which, at the greatest and best, is attended with painful pre-eminence, Porée thought proper to change the course of his pupil's studies. He deprived him of his favourite poets, Virgil and Sophocles, and put into his hands Euclid, Tully, and the System of Des Cartes, at that time much in fashion in France. But Voltaire seemed wound up to no other pursuit than that of poetry; he neglected severer studies, and was ridiculed for his backwardness in the sciences, by the whole university. The greatest genius can make no figure in philosophy without application; and application a young poet is ever averse to. The punishments of the academy, and the exhortations of his masters, were insufficient to influence him: anything that wore the face of industry he carefully avoided, and wherever pleasure presented, he was foremost in the pursuit. In conducting a boy of so refractory a disposition, other masters would have redoubled their punishments, or discontinued their care; but Porée, who perceived that all his attempts to thwart nature were to no effect, was at last resolved to indulge the genius of his pupil in his favourite pursuits, and to give that imagination a full liberty of dilating, which all his endeavours could not repress. "I perceive," said he, "that the youth will be miserable, in spite of all my efforts: he must be what nature has made him, a poet; let us then, since we cannot make him happy, endeavour to make him great."

And now the course of Voltaire's studies was changed once more; all the enchanting prospects of poetic ground, and all the invaluable treasures of antiquity, were opened before their youthful admirer. Few equalled, scarcely any excelled Porée in the proper methods of forming a poet. He exhibited to his pupil not only the finest models, but directed his efforts in imitating them; showed him that the true method of copying the ancients was to draw after nature, and instructed him from the copious volume of mankind; of which a long acquaintance with the world had made him a perfect master. The whole college now began to turn their eyes with wonder upon a boy they had before considered in the most despicable light; and Voltaire seemed to glory in his conscious superiority. There were four prizes generally distributed in the year, to the most deserving in the Belles Lettres: he had obtained three, and missed the fourth; however, he was resolved to have all or none. Accordingly, rejecting the three which were offered him, he continued another year at college, until he should obtain the four; which he did with uncommon applause.

When he had passed the usual time at college, his father was resolved to remove him home; by which means he might at once have an opportunity of seeing the world, and finishing his education. The world was too dangerous a scene for a youth of passions as strong as his imagination; in love with pleasure, and as yet seeing human nature only on the pleasing side. But his father, either not considering, or regardless of these precautions, gave him an apartment in his own house, and indulged him, though but a boy of fifteen, in a degree of liberty which others are not allowed till a more advanced age. The truth is, the old man mistook his son's knowledge for prudence, and imagined that a lad so very wise in conversation would be equally so in action. In this he was deceived: Voltaire was a youth of exquisite sensibility, and men of such dispositions generally feel pleasure with a double relish: he had a constitution though not strong, yet delicately pliant, and such a disposition as inclined him to society. His visage, which was thin, might at first view have passed for indifferent; but when he spoke it caught ineffable graces, and his soul seemed beaming through his eyes. His stature was about middle size, and his person, upon the whole, not at all disagreeable. Thus furnished, our young poet launched out into all the excesses of refined debauchery. There are in every great city a set of battered beaus, who, too old for pleasure themselves, introduce every young fellow of spirit into what they call polite company. A kept mistress, an actress, or an opera dancer, generally compose the society. These are all perfectly skilled in the arts of coquetting, teach the young beginner how to make love, set his features, adjust his bow, and—pick his pocket. Into such company as this Voltaire was quickly introduced; and they failed not, according to custom, to flatter him into a high opinion of his parts, and to praise his wit, though incapable of relishing its delicacy. Imagine a youth pleased with himself and everything about him, taking the lead in all conversation, giving a loose to every folly that happened to occur, uttering things which, when spoken, seemed to please, but which, upon reflection, appeared false or trivial:—such was the gay, thoughtless, good-natured Voltaire, in a circle of close, designing beings, who approved his sallies from flattery, and not from their feelings; who despised his efforts to please, or enjoyed his folly with tacit malignity. His father saw with concern the company into which he was fallen: he knew by experience that to be a wit was the surest means of banishing friends and fortune, and saw that his son, by striving after the character of an amusing member of society, was giving up all pretensions of being an useful one. Admonition, he thought, might be serviceable, and accordingly he remonstrated very freely upon Voltaire's behaviour. No youth could receive advice with a better grace than he, or make more faithful promises of amendment. But he was now fallen in love with Mademoiselle G——n, the actress, and lost upon her bosom every domestic concern.

Mademoiselle G——n was extremely pretty, and, though but low in stature, finely shaped. Possessed of a vivacity often more pleasing than true wit, she talked and looked tenderness, and sometimes enlivened conversation with a *double entendre;* which, coming from pretty lips, is generally attended with the desired success. These were qualifications sufficient to captivate a person unacquainted with the world. Voltaire became enamoured, and took every opportunity of indulging the capricious though expensive desires of a woman, since noted for ruining the fortunes of several of her admirers. Wherever pleasure was to be sold, our young poet and his mistress were first to raise the auction. Extravagance, however, soon brings on want, and this threatened a separation. Mademoiselle G——n had no other passion than that general one which women entertain for the opposite sex; any other man equally good-natured, open, and simple, would have been equally agreeable with Voltaire; she therefore felt no pain in the thoughts of separation. But it was quite otherwise with her youthful admirer; he entertained romantic ideas of the sex, considered woman as generally described in books, and looked upon beauty as the transparent covering of virtue. The apprehension, therefore, of being obliged to part gave him no small uneasiness. The more this apprehension increased, the more diligent he was in contriving means to satisfy her rapacity. He had already extorted money from his father by various pretences, but this resource now began to fail him. His mistress had frequently assured him, that it was polite to deceive the old man; that comedy every day afforded instances of this laudable disobedience; and often intimated, that money must be supplied, or love discontinued. What was to be done in such a dilemma? To subdue his passion was a task he was as yet quite unacquainted with; he was resolved, therefore, to add one falsehood more to his former account. In pursuance of this resolution, he gravely assured his father that the Cardinal Polignac, who was employed by the court of France to adjust the plan of pacification at Utrecht, had consented to take him in his retinue; and as it was proper to appear genteelly on such an occasion, our adventurer requested a hundred pounds for his equipment, promising to regulate his future conduct by the strictest prudence. The old man was the more inclined to believe this story, as it w[illegible] a place he had been soliciting for his son some time before; he therefore advanced the money, and Voltaire, rejoicing in the success of his stratagem, flew to share his joy and his acquisition with his charming deluder.

I am not insensible, that by recounting these trifling particulars of a great man's life, I may be accused of being myself a trifler; but such circumstances as these generally best mark a character. These youthful follies, like the fermentation of liquors, often disturb the mind only in order to its future refinement: a life spent in phlegmatic apathy resembles those liquors which never ferment, and are consequently always muddy. Let this, then, be my excuse, if I mention anything that seems derogatory from Voltaire's character, which will be found composed of little vices and great virtues. Besides, it is not here intended either to compose a panegyric or draw up an invective; truth only is my aim: an impartial view of his history may show him guilty of some errors, but it will at last turn the balance greatly in his favour.

But to proceed. In a few days the old man began to testify some uneasiness at seeing his son make no preparations for his intended journey; but lost all patience when he found that the Cardinal had set out, and left him behind. He had for some time known his correspondence with Mademoiselle G——n, and conjectured that her apartment would be the most likely place to find him. He accordingly went to her house, and finding the door by accident open, entered without ceremony; when, unfortunately, the first figure that presented was young Voltaire coming down stairs, pale and emaciated both by his apprehensions and debauchery. The father, being resolved upon the severest correction, with his cane in his hand pursued the delinquent up stairs. Voltaire now saw that a drubbing was inevitable, and therefore thought it the best way, if possible, to divert his father's anger by a jest. Accordingly, when he had run up to the third story, drawing his sword, he cried out to his father, who was not yet got up to the second, "Sir, you must excuse me, if I consider our relationship now at an end; for we are at least three removes asunder."

His father, however, in his present disposition, could by no means relish a jest: he desisted from his pursuit, but went directly away, meditating a much severer punishment. Voltaire, who thought the storm was over, went down to laugh away his fright with his mistress; and the young lovers began to be extremely facetious upon the awkward chagrin of the old man. But their mirth was soon interrupted by a file of musqueteers, who came to conduct our poet to the Bastille, for having drawn his sword upon his father. This was an early initiation into misery: to be snatched from the arms of an alluring mistress, and be confined in a gloomy prison, without fire, candle, pen, or ink, was a reverse of fortune which might throw a damp upon men of an ordinary degree of fortitude; but Voltaire bore it with an air that showed the utmost resolution; he entered his prison with the most cheerful serenity, repeating from his favourite poets such passages as were applicable to his circumstances. On such occasions of distress, the poet, perhaps, has the advantage of all others; when forsaken by society, the Muse administers her friendly consolation, and softens even the horrors of confinement. A bit of red chalk was all that Voltaire had to serve instead of a pen, and the white walls of his prison supplied the place of paper; yet even with these rude materials he sketched out the first canto of his Henriade. The traces of his pencil are, to this day, preserved in the chamber to which he was confined, with as much veneration as the paintings of Raphael in the galleries of the curious.

When he had remained three weeks in prison, his father, who had taken this severe method only in order to his reformation, was appeased, and the delinquent was again admitted into favour. It is a doubt whether the incident of his imprisonment was more fortunate for him, or beneficial to the public. His intrepid behaviour soon gained him the notice of the great; his confinement turned his mind, which was wholly dissipated on pleasure, from debauchery to ambition, and gave the world one of the greatest poets that any age has produced.

He now prepared in good earnest to follow the Cardinal Polignac to Utrecht; and some recommendatory letters which his father's interest had procured, gave him reason to expect a favourable reception from his excellency. Accordingly, without taking leave of the companions of his debauchery, he set out upon his journey, and, arriving at Utrecht, presented his letters of recommendation to the Cardinal. Polignac was one of the deepest scholars and most refined politicians of the age. His Anti-Lucretius is sufficient to establish his character as one of the first in the literary world; and his address at the treaty of Utrecht fully evinces his skill in the business of the cabinet. He was particularly remarkable for reading every man's real character, upon the slightest acquaintance; and, notwithstanding all our young poet's precautions, this penetrating politician quickly perceived his violent attachment to pleasure. Yet he nevertheless had sufficient address to become a favourite, and scarcely a day passed in which the Cardinal did not spend some time in conversation with his gay libertine; for so he was pleased to call him. Madame Dunoyer relates some of the intrigues for which Voltaire was remarkable at Utrecht; but as they contain little more than what every reader may suggest,—namely, his making love, and his addresses being crowned with success, —I shall pass them by, particularly as he himself asserts the falsehood of all that his female biographer has been pleased to say of him.

Upon his return to Paris, he had again an apartment in his father's house: here he united the characters of the man of pleasure and the philosopher; dedicated the morning to study, and the evening to society. His companions now were very different from those he had some time before associated with; he began to have a reputation for genius, and some of the politest of either sex in Paris were pleased to admit him among the number of their intimates.

Our poet had always a desire of thinking differently from other people. He was particularly fond of controversy, and often mistook paradox for refinement. Of this fault he was more guilty in youth than in riper age; for it was about this time that he thought proper to confine himself to his chamber, to draw up a new system of religion, and abolish the old one. He had been employed thus six or seven days; when his father, surprised at his keeping his chamber so closely, thought proper to enter and inquire the reason. When he perceived how the youth was employed, he was almost unable to suppress his astonishment; but recollecting that it was impossible to convince by reason a vain young man, who neither had patience nor perhaps abilities for a slow and painful investigation, he was resolved to work, if possible, upon his passions. Accordingly, taking his son by the hand, he led him into his own apartment, and there, pointing to a large crucifix, exquisitely painted, which hung at one end of the room, "My son," said he, "you would alter the religion of your country,—behold the fate of a reformer!" This seasonable remonstrance had the desired success; he laid by his controversial pieces, and turned to a subject of which he was much more capable. Fired with a love of antiquity, as he himself informs us, he was resolved to modernise the Œdipus Tyrannus of Sophocles, and try how a subject which Aristotle has asserted to be the fittest for tragedy could do upon the French theatre. They had hitherto seen not more than one or two tragedies on their stage without a love plot, and upon that all the other incidents generally turned. It was, therefore, a hardy undertaking in so very young a man, to introduce Grecian severity, and show his countrymen that an instructive and interesting performance, without that effeminating passion, could be adapted even to the stage of a people who made love one of their most serious employments. This play was acted in the beginning of the year 1718: the public received it with the utmost indulgence; it was played several nights without intermission, and still continues to be performed with the highest applause. The author, however, has always been so modest as to attribute its success to the greatness of the subject and the excellence of the performers, rather than to the merit of the poet. The critics were divided in their judgment of this piece; some regarded it as too declamatory, and endeavoured to show, which indeed was no difficult task, how much the Grecian tragedy was superior; others, considering it as the first fruits of a young aspiring genius, were pleased with the harmony and correctness of the versification and the classic propriety which ran through the whole. Among this number was Madame du Châtelet, a lady equally famous for wit and learning; perhaps still more known by her connexion with our poet, and for the variety of beautiful poems which he has addressed to her. Her apartments might have justly been styled the tribunal of criticism; for they were every day frequented by all whose wit or learning gave them any eminence in the literary world. She took the poet under her protection; and those critics whom her wit could not bring over to his interests, became proselytes to her beauty. In short, Voltaire owed his first rise to her; and she perhaps owes to him immortality. However, though the majority of critics were for him, there were still some refractory. Père Folard, and

M. de la Motte of the French Academy, were of the number; the one remarkable for his learning, the other for the fineness of his genius and skill in criticism. They were the reputed authors of several anonymous strictures which were published against the Œdipus of Voltaire; nor did they seem very studious to decline the imputation, though formerly professing themselves among the number of his friends. Men of the first rank in literature often, like the old trees in a forest, keep off those beams of favour from the younger shoots, which are, perhaps, of their own production. De la Motte, either envying the success of our poet, or choosing to enjoy the public favour without a rival, was resolved to show the indifference of Voltaire's performance, rather by example than criticism; and accordingly wrote a tragedy upon the very same subject. From the endeavours of a man of established reputation like him, much was expected; particularly as he had the errors of Voltaire before him to avoid, and his excellences, which he might improve. The town waited with impatience to compare these efforts of contending genius; and their curiosity was at last gratified. La Motte's performance appeared, with a large party to support it; and it accordingly met the fate of all plays which are supported by party: it languished four nights, and then sunk into oblivion. This was a conquest Voltaire's most sanguine hopes could not have suggested: however, such was his ambition, that he was not merely contented with victory, but was resolved to triumph; not satisfied with enjoying the fruits of conquest, but bent upon proclaming himself conqueror. This, indeed, was a fault of which he was always culpable: no person ever gained the victory in literary contentions so often as he has done; but while he pursued his advantages too far, he turned his opponents into enemies, and when they could no longer lessen his reputation as a wit, they often strove to blacken his character as a man. He found the majority now wholly on his side; he saw that none praised the tragedy of La Motte, but such as were attached by private connexions to his person: in order, then, to insure his success, he was determined to show that his rival was his inferior, not only in poetry, but in criticism also; for a skill in which he had, till now, been especially remarkable. La Motte had written an essay against the rules of the drama, in which he endeavoured to show that its laws had been established, not from nature but caprice, from fashion and not from feelings. This Voltaire undertook to answer; which, as it is both a fine piece of criticism, and an instance of the delicacy with which this great man treated his opponent, I shall beg leave to translate:—

"I shall not presume to speak of the tragedies of either Père Folard, or M. de la Motte: my censure or my praise would appear equally suspicious. I am still farther from bestowing anything like panegyric upon my own, being convinced that rules alone never made a genius. Conscious I am, that all the fine reasoning and delicate remark that have been exhausted of late years upon this subject, are not equal to one single scene dictated by a fine imagination. There is more to be learned from reading one of the tragedies of Corneille or Racine, than from all the precepts of the Abbé d'Aubignac. All the books composed by connoisseurs upon the art of painting, convey not half the instructions of a single head, which has come from the pencil of Angelo or Raphael.

"The principles of all arts which depend upon the imagination, are easy and simple, equally founded in nature and in reason. The best and worst poets have composed upon the same; they have both used similar materials, and the difference only lies in their application. The same thing happens in music; and even in painting. Poussin is directed by the very rules which conduct the most wretched dauber. It is as needless, therefore, in a poet to attempt to prejudice the public in favour of his performance by introductory criticism, as it would be in a painter or musician to lay down rules to prove that the spectators or the audience must be pleased with their respective performances.

"However, as M. de la Motte has thought proper to establish rules different from those which have conducted our great masters in the art of poetry, it is but just to defend the laws of antiquity; not indeed because they are ancient, but because they are natural and useful, and also as they are in some danger from so formidable an opponent.

"This gentleman begins with proscribing the unities of action, time, and place. Those are so united with each other, that he who combats one attacks them all. The French were the first among the moderns who revived the laws of the drama: the neighbouring nations were long before they could be brought to submit to a restraint which seemed so severe; but as this restraint proceeded from nature, and reason taught them the justice of the compliance, in time they were brought to submit. At present, even in England, their poets are fond of informing the public in their prefaces, that the time of the action and the representation are equal; and they are even more strict in this particular than us who have been their masters.

"Every country now begins to regard those times as barbarous, when the laws of the stage were either not practised or not known. Shakspeare and Lopez de Vega are admired, but not imitated. All are ready to pay France their acknowledgments for having pointed out this just and natural simplicity. Who would have thought that a Frenchman would be the first again to introduce primeval barbarity?

"Though I had no other answer to make to M. de la Motte, but that Corneille, Racine, Molière, Addison, Congreve, and Maffei have all observed the rules of the drama, this alone might be sufficient to silence my opponent; but M. de la Motte deserves to be opposed with reasons, and not by authorities.

"A tragedy or comedy has been defined the representation of one action. Should it be demanded, why of one only, and not of two or three together, the reasons are obvious. Either because the mind is incapable of attending to two or three objects at once; or because our concern in the events is lessened by being divided; or because we are displeased to see two actions in the same picture. Uniformity is a constituent of beauty, imprinted on our souls by nature; and all the efforts of art excel, in proportion as they imitate the models she draws.

"For these reasons, unity of place is also essential; for one and the same action cannot be transacted in different places at the same time. If the personages whom I behold in the first act are at Athens, how can they be in Persia in the second? Le Brun has not painted Alexander at Arbela and in the Indies on the same canvas. 'But,' says M. de la Motte, 'there is nothing surprising, if a nation which has not studied itself into a fondness for rule should be pleased at the representation of Coriolanus, condemned at Rome in the first act, received among the Volscians in the third, and besieging Rome in the fourth.' Yet, why should a sensible people be so much against those rules, which are made only for their pleasure? Are there not, in a subject thus conducted, three distinct tragedies; and were it put in verse, would it not resemble rather a history or a romance than a theatrical performance? Take away the unity of place, and you necessarily destroy that of action. The unity of time is naturally connected with the two former. Let us then hold to the three unities, as the great Corneille has laid them down: in these we shall find every other rule of the drama contained, resulting from these, or conspiring to assist them.

"M. de la Motte, however, is pleased to call them principles, first invented by fancy, and supported by fashion: he maintains that they may with propriety be dispensed with in our tragedies, since they are entirely neglected in the opera. This method of reasoning somewhat resembles the absurdity of the politician, who would reform a regular government by the example of an anarchy. Absurdity, joined with magnificence, characterise the opera. In this the ears and the eyes find more entertainment than the mind. A subjection of the words to the music, renders the most ridiculous extravagances excusable. Cities are ransacked in recitative: the palaces of Pluto and of the sun, of gods and devils, of magicians and monsters, rise, form a dance, and disappear in the twinkling of an eye. We tolerate, nay, are pleased with these extravagances, because the spectator in such circumstances imagines himself transported into a fairy land; and provided he is entertained with good music, fine dancing, and a few interesting scenes, he is content. It would be as ridiculous to demand unity of action, time, and place in a pleasing opera, as to introduce dancing devils into a regular tragedy.

"Yet, though these regularities may be dispensed with in the opera, the best we have of this kind are those in which the unities are least violated. If I am not mistaken, there are some in which dramatic propriety is inviolably preserved; which serves to prove how necessary, natural, and interesting it is to every spectator. How unjust, therefore, is it to condemn our nation of levity for disapproving in one species of composition, what we approve in another! In tragedy we require perfection; there is in it no music to divert the attention, nor dances to confound; all our pleasure depends upon intellect alone; we there admire the address of the poet, who, in one day and in one place, describes a single action which charms without fatigue, and fills the mind without confusion; where our pleasure rises by just degrees, and terminates with moral propriety. The more difficult this simplicity appears, the more it is cheering; and we find upon examination, that most of our pleasure results from the various uniformity of the representation.

"M. de la Motte is not content with depriving us of theatrical propriety; he would also banish poetry from the stage, and have all our pieces represented in prose. It is a little extraordinary, that an ingenious writer, possessed of an imagination truly poetic, who has seldom written prose, except to vindicate or explain his own poetry, should write against verse, with the same contempt with which he has written against Homer; whom, nevertheless, he has thought proper to translate. Neither Virgil, Tasso, Boileau, Racine, or Pope, ever wrote against poetry, nor Lully against music, nor Newton against astronomy. There are sometimes men found, who fancy themselves superior to their profession—the surest symptoms of their being actually below it; but this is the first time we have seen any attempting to asperse those talents to which they owe all their reputation. There are already too many who, having no acquaintance with the charms of poetry, affect to despise it. Paris abounds with men, otherwise of good understandings, who are naturally destitute of organs capable of relishing harmony; to such music is but noise, and poetry but ingenious trifling. Should these be informed that a person of merit, and who has composed five or six volumes of poetry, is of their opinion, would they not be apt to regard all other poets as fools, and him as the only one of all his brethren who had found the use of his reason? Let me, then, for the honour of our profession, endeavour to answer him; even let me add, for the honour of a country which owes part of its reputation among strangers to a perfection in this very art which he affects to despise.

"It is advanced by this gentleman, that rhyme is a modern invention, and had its rise in times of ignorance and barbarity: yet, notwithstanding this, all nations, except the ancient Greeks and Romans, have rhymed, and continue the custom to this day. The return of similar sounds is so natural to mankind, that we find rhymes obtain even in the most savage regions, as well as in Italy, Spain, France, and England. Montaigne presents us with an American ode, composed in this manner; and in one of the papers of the Spectator, written by Mr. Addison, we are presented with the translation of a Lapland ode, originally composed in rhyme.

"The Greek,—'quibus dedit ore rotundo musa loqui,'—placed in an indulgent climate, and favoured by nature with finer organs than other nations, formed a language which, by the length or shortness of its syllables, expressed the calm or the impetuous dictates of the mind. From this happy variety in the construction of their language, resulted such music in their prose, as well as verse, as no nation but the ancient Italians could ever succeed in imitating.

"It is not, however, rhyme alone, but measure also, which this ingenious gentleman condemns. Before the time of Herodotus, history was written only in verse; this custom the Greeks borrowed from the ancient Egyptians, a people politic, learned, and wise. It was founded in nature; for the end of history being to preserve an account of the actions of a few great personages, which might serve as examples to posterity, as men had not yet attained the art of swelling the transactions of some obscure convent, or insignificant village, into several folios, nothing was transmitted but what was worth remembering; nothing but what was remarkable was generally treasured up in the memory as a guide to action. Verse, therefore, was proper to assist in this particular; accordingly, the first legislators, founders of religion, and historians were poets by profession. On such occasions, however, poetry must necessarily have wanted either harmony or precision. Virgil at last appeared, who united these two excellences which seemed so incompatible. Boileau and Racine had the same success; a person who has read all the three, who knows that they are translated into almost all the European languages, but idly employs his talents in endeavouring to render them contemptible: such censure often reverts upon the accuser.

"I rank Boileau and Racine in the same class with Virgil, in regard to versification; for had the author of the Æneid been born a Frenchman, it is probable he would have written like them; and had they lived in ancient Rome, they would have moulded the Latin language into the same harmonious cadence with the celebrated Mantuan. When, therefore, M. de la Motte censures versification as ridiculous, mechanical, trifling, he not only accuses our poets, but all those of antiquity. Virgil and Horace have been as assiduous as we, in the mechanism of their verses. A happy arrangement of dactyl and spondee was as difficult as our rhyme and metre. Their labour must certainly have been great; since the Æneid, after the corrections of eleven years, was still thought far short of requisite perfection.

"But this ingenious author still asserts, that turning any scene of tragedy into prose diminishes neither its force nor its beauty. To prove this assertion, he transposes the first scene of Mithridates, and has thus rendered it intolerable to even the meanest capacity. 'But still,' continues he, 'our neighbours have rejected rhyme in their tragedies.' This must be granted; but then they are written in verse which, though without rhyme, is, from the nature of their languages, harmonious. Should we attempt to cast off a yoke which was worn by Corneille and Racine, we might, perhaps, be subjected to do it from an inability to imitate rather than a desire to reform. The Italians and the English can dispense with rhyme, since their poetry has several liberties which we want: every language has its particular genius—inflection peculiarly its own: a construction of periods different from all others, and a particular use of the auxiliary verbs: perspicuity and elegance is the genius of ours; we admit of no transpositions in our poetry, but the words must flow in the exact order of our ideas. Hence, therefore, proceeds the unavoidable necessity of rhymes, to make a distinction between our prose and our poetry. He compares our poets—our Corneilles, Racines, and Boileaus—to a juggler who is employed in throwing a grain of corn through the eye of a needle; adding, that all such puerilities have no other merit but that of difficulty surmounted.

"I must confess that bad verses pretty much fall under this censure. They differ from bad prose only by the addition of rhyme; and this advantage alone neither gives merit to the poet, nor pleasure to the reader. What charms us is the harmony which results from this merit. Whoever encounters a difficulty, merely for the sake of overcoming it, without expecting any other advantage, is little better than a fool; but he who brings pleasure from objects which seem incapable of affording any, is certainly meritorious. It is a laborious task to form a fine statue, to paint a striking picture, to compose pleasing music, or good verses. Wherefore, the names of those great men who have surmounted the respective difficulties will last, perhaps, longer than the kingdoms which gave them birth.

"I could continue this dispute to greater length, but it would probably be regarded as proceeding from personal resentment; and my intentions might be branded with a malignity from which I am as remote as from the sentiments of my ingenious adversary. It gives me much greater pleasure to profit by many judicious reflections spread through his book, than to controvert his opinions. Let it be sufficient, then, that I have endeavoured to defend an art I have ever loved; an art which he should have defended also."

This criticism, which conceals a fine satire upon the author it professes to answer, was not published till the year 1730, though written, and communicated to M. Voltaire's friends, long before. M. de la Motte himself pretended to approve it, yet inwardly felt all the resentment of disappointed ambition, and (as if from the time Voltaire had defended poetry, he was no longer to have quarter from his brothers of the profession) he was ever after persecuted by party, and marked as an object of envy and reproach. Père Folard soon after wrote a tragedy upon the same subject, but it was more short-lived than even the former attempt of La Motte; serving only to advance the reputation of the first Œdipus, and to increase the number of the friends and the enemies of M. Voltaire.

There is, perhaps, no situation more uneasy than that of being foremost in the republic of letters. If a man who writes to please the public cannot at the same time stoop to flattery, he is certainly made unhappy for life. There are a hundred writers of inferior merit continually expecting his approbation: these must be all applauded, or made enemies; the public must be deceived by ill-placed praise, or dunces provoked into unremitting persecution. This under-tribe in the literary commonwealth perfectly understand the force of combinations, are liberal in their mutual commendations, and actually enjoy all the pleasures of fame without being so much as known to the public: while the man of eminence is regarded as an outcast of their society, a fit object at which to level all their invective, and every advance he makes towards reputation only lifts his head nearer to the storm; till at last he finds, that, instead of fame, he has been all his life only earning reproach, till he finds himself possessed of professing friends and sincere enemies.

Fontenelle and Voltaire were men of unequal merit; yet how different has been the fate of either! Fontenelle was as passionately fond of adulation as Voltaire was ever averse to flattery. The one kindly told every blockhead that he had wit; the other honestly advised him to discontinue a profession in which he was by no means likely to succeed: the one has received all his fame while living; the other must not expect unmixed applause till dead: the one was prudent, insincere, and happy; the other generous, open, and regarded with detestation.

But though Voltaire was now fairly listed into an open war with all the dunces of society, yet he still had friends of another denomination, who by their power protected him, and by their company made him forget that he had enemies. Madame du Châtelet was of this number. At her house he generally spent the mornings, among the learned of Paris, who composed the levee of this learned lady. The sciences then seemed to triumph when patronised by beauty. Madame du Châtelet had many personal charms; and though a hard student, her complexion never called in assistant red to heighten its colour. She dictated to an admiring circle every morning from Plato, Newton, Clarke, and Leibnitz: and was thought as great an adept in philosophy as the deepest doctor of the Sorbonne. Voltaire soon perceived his deficiency in the sciences; and as he knew that an excellence in them was the only way to secure his mistress, he set about attaining them with the most intense application. As he increased in learning, his intimacy increased in proportion; and at last, an intercourse which began in friendship turned into a passion of a much more masterly nature. His visits became more frequent, his behaviour more submissive, and the philosopher was lost in the gallant. Madame du Châtelet, whose soul knew no other passion but that of science, at first regarded the change in his behaviour with indifference, but soon perceived the real motive, and was not entirely displeased at the discovery. There is a principle of vanity in the sex, which gives them pleasure at the acquisition of a new lover, though they have no intention to accept him. She therefore gave him an opportunity of declaring his regard, and of professing a passion which his actions had before sufficiently indicated. Her answer, however, was very different from what he had expected: she informed him, with an apathy truly stoical, that she neither disliked his addresses, nor entirely approved of them. She had no objection to a lover, provided he was pleased to be content with what she could give. Minds could unite and form a happy intercourse, without indulging any coarser appetites; and she concluded by recommending to him the Banquet of Plato, as containing her system of love—a system which she was determined to act up to; and she found none more fit than M. Voltaire to be the object of so pure a flame.

Our poet now perceived that books had spoiled her for a mistress, and that she was resolved to sacrifice the substance to the shadow. Yet, as she was in some measure beautiful, as she seemed happy in his conversation, and could still be a charming friend, he was resolved to accept of the terms she offered; to be contented with the spare diet which she could afford, and look for more substantial entertainment from others. An opportunity soon offered of this kind.

The Marchioness de Pire, a young widow of exquisite beauty, had taken a fancy to our poet; and, as she was possessed of a large jointure, had some intentions of marrying him. She found means to have Voltaire informed of her inclinations, and took care to have her nobility and fortune placed in the most advantageous point of view. Voltaire, who loved the sex, but hated matrimony, seemed to be happy in her proposal, and begged an interview, in which our lovers seemed mutually pleased with each other. As all his intentions were to please the lady and himself without the previous ceremony, he declined all conversation upon matrimony, but talked of disinterested passion, unconfined rapture, and all the cant of an insidious designer. The marchioness, who was as virtuous as beautiful, quickly perceived the tendency of his discourse, and thought proper to break off a conversation which took a turn not at all to her inclinations. At parting, she gave him hopes, and enjoined him secrecy. He accordingly promised the strictest honour, and, with a heart elated with vanity, he went to communicate his happiness to all his friends. As he unsuspectingly made every person that professed the least regard for him a confidant, among the rest he happened to tell his success to a gentleman who was actually his rival. The consequence of this indiscreet confidence was, that the marchioness was informed of the whole, and proscribed our repentant lover for ever from her presence. In such a disappointment, the muse was his consolation; he worked the adventure into a comedy, which he dedicated to his unforgiving mistress. The dedication, which it is impossible to translate with elegance equal to the original, runs in plain prose thus: "Thou who hast beauty without pride, and vivacity without indiscretion; whom heaven has formed with every gift it could bestow; a mind seriously solid, or rapturously gay; accept this picture of the indiscretion of a lover, who lost a mistress by boasting of her favours. Had the heroine of this piece been possessed of thy beauty, who could blame the lover for mentioning so charming a mistress, either through excess of vanity, or excess of love?"

But one adventure more of this nature. The Platonic passion between Voltaire and Madame du Châtelet was now become a subject of conversation all over Paris. His inconstancy was well known, and it was thought something strange that his attachment to one mistress should have so long a continuance. M. Piron, a man of infinite humour, was resolved to try the sincerity of his passion; not by presenting him with a real, but an imaginary mistress. With this intent he composed a panegyric on Voltaire in the highest strain of flattery, and presented it to him as coming from a lady in one of the provinces, who was enraptured with his poetry, and had almost conceived a passion for his person. Voltaire read the poem, found it inimitable, and fancied a thousand beauties in a lady of so fine discernment. In short, he was actually fallen in love with a creature of his own imagination, and entreated his dear ugly friend—for so he familiarly used to call Piron—to procure him an interview with a lady of so much merit. Piron promised in a few days to gratify his request; and in the meantime came every morning to tell Voltaire that the young lady was upon her journey, and would arrive very shortly; adding many pathetic exclamations on her beauty, and the delicacy of her behaviour. Our poet was at last wound up to the height of expectation; which, when Piron saw, he informed him that the lady was actually arrived, that the chief motive of her journey was to see a man so justly celebrated as M. Voltaire, and that she entreated the honour of his company that very evening. Our poet in raptures prepared himself for the interview, which he expected with the utmost impatience.

The hour at last came, and Voltaire eagerly flew to satisfy at once his love and his curiosity. Upon being introduced into the apartment of his fancied angel, he was at first a little disconcerted to find Madame du Châtelet of the party; but guess his confusion, when he beheld his ugly friend, dressed up in a lappet-head and petticoat, approach to salute him. In short, he was informed that Piron himself was the fair one who wrote the panegyric, and who consequently expected the proper return of gratitude. "Well," said Voltaire, turning his disappointment to a jest, "if Piron had a grain less wit, I could never have forgiven him." This adventure has since served as the groundwork of a comedy called "La Métromanie," infinitely the best modern performance upon the French theatre.

Some disappointments of this kind served to turn our poet from a passion which only tended to obstruct his advancement in more exalted pursuits. His mind, which at that time was pretty well balanced between pleasure and philosophy, quickly began to incline to the latter. He now thirsted after a more comprehensive knowledge of mankind than either books or his own country could possibly bestow.

England, about this time, was coming into repute throughout Europe, as the land of philosophers. Newton, Locke, and others began to attract the attention of the curious, and drew hither a concourse of learned men from every part of Europe. Not our learning alone, but our politics also began to be regarded with admiration: a government in which subordination and liberty were blended in such just proportions, was now generally studied as the finest model of civil society. This was an inducement sufficient to make Voltaire pay a visit to this land of philosophers and of liberty.

Accordingly, in the year 1726, he came over to England. A previous acquaintance with Atterbury, bishop of Rochester, and the Lord Bolingbroke, was sufficient to introduce him among the polite, and his fame as a poet got him the acquaintance of the learned, in a country where foreigners generally find but a cool reception. He only wanted introduction: his own merit was enough to procure the rest. As a companion, no man ever exceeded him when he pleased to lead the conversation; which, however, was not always the case. In company which he either disliked or despised, few could be more reserved than he; but when he was warmed in discourse, and had got over a hesitating manner which sometimes he was subject to, it was rapture to hear him. His meagre visage seemed insensibly to gather beauty; every muscle in it had meaning, and his eye beamed with unusual brightness. The person who writes this Memoir, who had the honour and the pleasure of being his acquaintance, remembers to have seen him in a select company of wits of both sexes at Paris, when the subject happened to turn upon English taste and learning. Fontenelle, who was of the party, and who, being unacquainted with the language or authors of the country he undertook to condemn, with a spirit truly vulgar began to revile both. Diderot, who liked the English, and knew something of their literary pretensions, attempted to vindicate their poetry and learning, but with unequal abilities. The company quickly perceived that Fontenelle was superior in the dispute, and were surprised at the silence which Voltaire had preserved all the former part of the night, particularly as the conversation happened to turn upon one of his favourite topics. Fontenelle continued his triumph till about twelve o'clock, when Voltaire appeared at last roused from his reverie. His whole frame seemed animated. He began his defence with the utmost elegance mixed with spirit, and now and then let fall the finest strokes of raillery upon his antagonist; and his harangue lasted till three in the morning. I must confess, that, whether from national partiality, or from the elegant sensibility of his manner, I never was so much charmed, nor did I ever remember so absolute a victory as he gained in this dispute.

Upon his arrival in England, his first care was to learn so much of the language as might enable him to mix in conversation, and study more thoroughly the genius of the people. Foreigners are unanimous in allowing the English language to be the most difficult to learn of any in Europe. Some have spent years in the study to no purpose; but such was the application, and such the memory of our poet, that in six weeks he was able to speak it with tolerable propriety. In short, his conduct in this particular was such as may serve for a model to future travellers. The French who before visited this island were never at the trouble of attaining our language, but contented with barely describing the buildings and palaces of the kingdom, and transcribing a character of the people from former travellers, who were themselves unacquainted with our national peculiarities. Accordingly, we find few of their books in which the English are not characterised as morose, melancholy, excessive lovers of pudding, and haters of mankind. This stupid account has been continued down from Scaliger to Muralt, while the virtues and vices which were peculiar to the country were wholly unknown. Voltaire quickly perceived that pride seemed to be our characteristic quality; a source from whence we derived our excellences as well as our defects. He perceived that the only way to understand the English was to learn their language, adopt their manners, and even to applaud their oddities. With this view, when sufficiently initiated into our language, he joined in companies of every rank: lords, poets, and artisans were successively visited, and he attained at the same time a proficiency in our language, laws, and government, and thorough insight into our national character. Before him, our reputation for learning had for some time been established in Europe; but, then, we were regarded as entirely destitute of taste, and our men of wit known not even by name among the literati. He was the first foreigner who saw the amazing irregular beauties of Shakspeare, gave Milton the character he deserved, spoke of every English poet with some degree of applause, and opened a new page of beauty to the eyes of his astonished countrymen. It is to him we owe that our language has taken the place of the Italian among the polite, and that even ladies are taught to admire Milton, Pope, and Otway. The greatest part of our poet's time, during a residence of two years in England, was spent at Wandsworth, the seat of his Excellency Sir Everard Falkener. With this gentleman he had contracted an intimacy at Paris; and as Sir Everard had insisted upon his company before he left France, he now could not refuse. Here he spent his time in that tranquillity and learned ease which are so grateful to men of speculation; had leisure to examine the difference between our government and that of which he was born a subject; and to improve by our example his natural passion for liberty.

He was resolved, however, to give some lasting testimony of that love which he had for freedom, and which has ever made one of the strongest features in his character. The elder Brutus, condemning his own son in its cause, seemed a fine subject for this purpose, and naturally suited to the British theatre. The first act of this play he accordingly wrote in English, and communicated it to his friends for their approbation. It was somewhat surprising to find a stranger, who had resided in the country but one year, attempt so arduous an undertaking; but still more so to find him skilled in the beauties and force of our language. The reader may be pleased to see how he wrote in English: he makes Brutus, in the second scene of the first act, thus vindicate the cause of freedom:

"*Brutus.*—Allege not ties; his (Tarquin's) crimes have broke them all. The gods themselves, whom he has offended, have declared against him. Which of our rights has he not trod upon? True, we have sworn to be his subjects, but we have not sworn to be his slaves. You say you've seen our senate in humble suppliance pay him here their vows. Even here himself has sworn to be our father, and make the people happy in his guidance. Broke from his oaths, we are let loose from ours; since he has transgressed our laws, his the rebellion, Rome is free from guilt."

This tragedy he afterwards completed in French; and at Paris it met with the fate he had foreseen. No piece was ever translated into a greater number of foreign languages, more liked by strangers, or more decried at home. He dedicated it to Lord Bolingbroke; and as the dedication contains a fine parallel between the English and French theatres, I shall beg leave to translate some part of it here:

"As it was too venturous an innovation, my lord, to attempt to write a tragedy in French without rhyme, and take such liberties as are allowed in England and Italy, I was at least determined to transplant those beauties from the English stage which I thought not incompatible with French regularity. Certain it is the English theatre is extremely defective. I have heard yourself say there was scarcely a perfect tragedy in the language; but to compensate this, you have several scenes which are admirable. Almost all your tragic writers have been likewise deficient in that regularity and simplicity of plot, that propriety of diction, that elegance of style, and those hidden strokes of art, for which we are remarkable since the times of Corneille. However, your most irregular pieces have a peculiar merit; they excel in action, while ours are frequently tedious declamations, and at best, conversation rather than a picture of passion. Our excessive delicacy often puts us upon making an uninteresting recital of what should rather be represented to the eyes of the spectator. Our poets are afraid to hazard anything new before an audience composed of such as turn all that is not the fashion into ridicule.

"The inconvenience of our theatre also is another cause that our representations frequently appear dry and unentertaining. The spectators being allowed to sit on the stage, destroy almost all propriety of action. For this reason, those decorations which are so much recommended by the ancients can be but very rarely introduced. Thus it happens that the actors can never pass from one apartment into another without being seen by the audience, and all theatrical illusion must consequently be destroyed.

"How could we, for instance, introduce the ghost of Pompey, or the genius of Brutus, into the midst of a parcel of young fellows crowded upon the theatre, and who only stand there to laugh at all that is transacted? How could we, as the late Mr. Addison has done, have the body of Marcus borne in upon the stage before his father? If he should hazard a representation of this nature, the whole pit would rise against the poet, and the ladies themselves would be apt to hide their faces.

"With what pleasure have I seen at London your tragedy of Julius Cæsar, which, though a hundred and fifty years old, still continues the delight of the people! I do not here attempt to defend the barbarous irregularity with which it abounds. What surprises me is, that there are not more in a work written in an age of ignorance, by a man who understood not Latin, and who had no other master but a happy genius. The piece is faulty; but, amidst such a number, still with what rapture do we see Brutus, with his dagger stained with the blood of Cæsar, haranguing the people!

"The French would never suffer a chorus composed of plebeians and artisans to appear upon the theatre; nor would they permit the body of Cæsar to be exposed, or the people excited from the rostrum. Custom, the queen of this world, changes at pleasure the taste of nations, and turns the sources of joy often into objects of disgust.

"The Greeks have exhibited objects upon their stage that would be equally disgusting to a French audience. Hippolitus, bruised by his fall, comes to count his wounds, and to pour forth the most lamentable cries. Philoctetes appears with his wound open, and the black gore streaming from it. Œdipus, covered with the blood which flowed from the sockets of his eyes, complains both of gods and men. In a word, many of the Greek tragedies abound with exaggeration.

"I am not ignorant that both the Greeks and the English have frequently erred, in producing what is shocking, instead of what should be terrible, the disgusting and the incredible for what should have been tragic and marvellous. The art of writing was in its infancy at Athens in the time of Æschylus, and at London in the time of Shakspeare. However, both the one and the other, with all their faults, frequently abound with a fine pathetic, and strike us with beauties beyond the reach of art to imitate. Those Frenchmen who, only acquainted with translations or common report, pretend to censure either, somewhat resemble the blind man who should assert that the rose is destitute of beauty because he perceives the thorns by the touch.

"But, though sometimes the two nations of which I am speaking transcend the bounds of propriety, and present us with objects of affright instead of terror, we, on the other hand, as scrupulous as they are rash, stop short of beauty for fear of being carried beyond it; and seldom arrive at the pathetic for fear of transgressing its bounds.

"I am by no means for having the theatre become a place of carnage, as we often find in Shakspeare and his successors, who, destitute of his genius, have only imitated his faults; but still I insist, that there are numberless incidents which may at present appear shocking to a French spectator, which, if set off with elegance of diction and propriety of representation, would be capable of giving a pleasure beyond what we can at present conceive."

This gives us a tolerably just representation of the state in which Voltaire found the French theatre. His Œdipus was written in this dry manner, where most of the terrible incidents were delivered in cold recitation, and not represented before the spectator. But, by observing our tragedies, like a skilful artist, he joined their fire to French correctness, and formed a manner peculiarly his own.

In studies of this nature he spent his time at Wandsworth, still employed either improving himself in our own language, or borrowing its beauties to transplant into his own. His leisure hours were generally spent in the company of our poets, Congreve, Pope, Young, &c., or among such of our nobility as were remarkable either for arts or arms, as Peterborough, Oxford, and Walpole. He was frequently heard to say, that Peterborough had taught him the art of despising riches, Walpole the art of acquiring them, but Harley alone the secret of being contented.

The first time he visited Mr. Congreve, he met with a reception very different from what he had expected. The English dramatist, grown rich by means of his profession, affected to despise it, and assured Voltaire, that he chose rather to be regarded as a gentleman than a poet. This was a meanness which somewhat disgusted the Frenchman, particularly as he himself owed all his reputation to his excellence in poetry; he therefore informed Mr. Congreve, that his fame as a writer was the only inducement he had to see him, and though he could condescend to desire the acquaintance of a man of wit and learning, he was above soliciting the company of any private gentleman whatsoever. The reflection of another upon this occasion was, that he certainly is below the profession who presumes to think himself above it.

M. Voltaire has often told his friends, that he never observed in himself such a succession of opposite passions as he experienced upon his first interview with Mr. Pope. When he first entered the room, and perceived our poor melancholy

English poet, naturally deformed, and wasted as he was with sickness and study, he could not help regarding him with the utmost compassion. But, when Pope began to speak, and to reason upon moral obligations, and dress the most delicate sentiments in the most charming diction, Voltaire's pity began to be changed into admiration, and at last even into envy. It is not uncommon with him to assert, that no man ever pleased him so much in serious conversation, nor any whose sentiments mended so much upon recollection.

There is a story commonly told of his being in company with Dr. Young and some others, when the conversation happened to turn upon Milton's Paradise Lost. He displayed, as the story goes, all his critical skill in condemning the allegorical personages which Milton has introduced into his poem, and this with the utmost vivacity and unbounded freedom of speech. Upon which Young, regarding him with a fixed eye, spoke the following epigram:

> "So very witty, wicked, and so thin;
> Fit emblem sure of Milton, Death, and Sin."

However, I only mention this to show what trifles are generally ascribed to men when once grown famous. The wretchedness of the epigram will readily convince those who have any pretensions to taste that Dr. Young could never have been the author: probably some blockhead made the verses first, and the story after.

Among the number of those who either patronised him, or enrolled themselves in the list of his friends, was the Duchess of Marlborough. She found infinite pleasure in the agreeable vivacity of his conversation; but mistook his levity for want of principle. Such a man seemed to her the properest person to digest the memoirs of her life; which, even so early as this, she had an inclination of publishing. She proposed the task accordingly to him, and he readily undertook to oblige her. But when she showed him her materials, and began to dictate the use she would have them turned to, Voltaire appeared no longer the good-natured, complying creature which she took him for. He found some characters were to be blackened without just grounds, some of her actions to be vindicated that deserved censure, and a mistress to be exposed to whom she owed infinite obligations. Our poet accordingly remonstrated with her grace, and seemed to intimate the inconsistency of such a conduct with gratitude and justice; he gravely assured her that the publication of secrets which were communicated under the seal of friendship, would give the world no high opinion of her morals. He was thus continuing his discourse, when the Duchess, quite in a passion, snatched the papers out of his hands:—"I thought," said she, "the man had sense; but I find him at bottom either a fool or a philosopher."

He was but two years in England, yet it is somewhat strange to think, how much he either wrote, published, or studied during so short a residence. He gave amongst his friends a criticism he had written in English upon Milton, which he concludes in this manner: "It requires reach of thought to discover the defects of Milton; his excellences lie obvious to every capacity; he atones for a few faults by a thousand beauties; and, like Satan, the hero of his own poem, even when fallen, he wears the appearance of majesty."

But the performance upon which he founds his most lasting share of fame was published in this country. The French language had hitherto been deemed unsusceptible of the true epic dignity. Several unsuccessful attempts by Ronsard, Chapelaine, and others, had made critics despair of ever seeing an heroic poem in the language; and some writers had laid it down as actually impossible. Voltaire, who seemed to be born to encounter difficulty, undertook the task, and that at an age when pleasure is apt to silence the voice of ambition. This poem, the "Henriade," was first published under the title of the "League." He began it in the Bastille, enlarged and corrected it for several years afterwards, and had some thoughts of publishing it in France. Upon showing the manuscript to Fontenelle, his friend, he was by him advised to retrench several passages which seemed to be written with too warm a spirit of liberty, under such a government as theirs; but Voltaire, who considered those very passages as the greatest beauties of his work, was resolved the poem should make its first appearance in a country in love with liberty, and ready to praise every performance written in its defence. With this view, he brought the work over with him to England, and offered it in the usual manner to a bookseller, in order to be published. The bookseller, as some pretend, either unacquainted with its value or willing to impose upon a stranger, offered him but a trifle for the manuscript, and would print only such a number as he thought proper. These were terms with which the author chose not to comply; and, considering the number and the rank of his friends, he was resolved to publish it by subscription. A subscription was opened accordingly, and quickly filled with persons of the first rank and eminence, not only of Great Britain, but of Europe in general. A condition of the proposals was, that the subscribers should have their books a month before it was published in the ordinary manner in London.

In this situation were things, when an unforeseen accident called our poet out of the kingdom, being sent for by M. D'Argenson, prime minister of France, in order to become the king's historiographer. Voltaire was therefore obliged to return with reluctance home, leaving to his bookseller the care of satisfying the subscribers. Voltaire, however, affirms that the bookseller, considering that there was no great difference between reading a book a month sooner or later, was resolved to indulge the curiosity of the public first, and gratify the subscribers after; as by this means, the profits accruing from the sale, which were to be his own, would be greatly increased. The reader may judge for himself whether this is not the true reason why the subscribers to the Henriade had not the work till a month after it was first published in London; and not against the author but his bookseller should their censure be levelled. It cannot be conceived what a number of enemies this raised Voltaire; for all imputed to him that meanness of which those who are of his acquaintance know him to be utterly incapable. A neglect, indeed, he was guilty of, in leaving no friend to see justice done to the public. This may be said of our poet's character in general, that he has frequently been guilty of indiscretions, but never of meanness. A mind employed in the contemplation of great virtues is sometimes guilty of trifling absurdities—

> "——quas aut incuria fudit,
> Aut humana parum cavit natura."—Hor.

An honest man may sometimes unite with such as will render his actions suspected; but then it is the fault of good minds to be too credulous, and instead of condemning such a man of falsehood, we should pity his good nature.

The poem was dedicated to Queen Caroline, for which she made the author a present of her picture, valued at two hundred guineas. The dedication breathes a spirit which at once characterises the poet, the philosopher, and the man of virtue; and some prefer it even to any part of the succeeding performance. It must be confessed the Henriade has its faults: its incidents in general do not sufficiently interest or surprise; it seldom rises to the sublime, though it never falls into flatness. The moral reflections return too frequently, and retard that speed which is one of the greatest beauties of narration. However, with all its faults, the French regard it as the first epic poem in their language, and though (national partiality laid aside) it sinks infinitely below Milton, yet it will be sufficient to gain the author immortality.

Upon his return home, he found his fame greatly increased, the prime minister of France himself being proud of ranking among the number of his friends. Scarcely a country of Europe from which the learned did not send him their acknowledgments, for the pleasure and instruction they had received from his last performance. The King of France used frequently to entreat the pleasure of his company; for he found in him one who had learned from the English to treat monarchs with an honest freedom, and who disdained those mean submissions which at once render kings proud and miserable. Had our poet been inclined to make a large fortune, had he been that avaricious wretch which his enemies have often represented him, he had now an opportunity of gratifying his most sanguine expectations. But he was born free, and had imbibed the privileges of a man and a philosopher. Ambition could not bribe him to forfeit his birthright, and he disdained becoming great at the expense of his liberty. The king would frequently desire his company; but Voltaire came only when he thought proper. Sometimes he would beg of his majesty to excuse his attendance, as he had made an appointment elsewhere; sometimes he would return for answer, that he was detained by Madame du Châtelet, and could not possibly come. These excuses the king generally received with the utmost good humour, and never upon Voltaire's appearance resented his former refusal. The truth is, the king loved a companion who had wit enough to amuse him, and good sense enough not to turn his familiarity into abuse.

But, about this time, there was a still greater honour done to our poet's merit than he had ever yet received, though kings and princes had already conspired to raise his reputation. The house of Brandenburg had been for some ages acquiring strength and power in Germany. At this time Frederick William sat upon the throne of Prussia, a monarch born to be the father and yet the terror of his subjects. All his family, his children as well as his domestics, feared, and sometimes felt the weight of his displeasure. He was arbitrary in all his commands; and though his desires were frequently bent upon trifles, none in all his court were found who were hardy enough to remonstrate, or had courage to lend him advice when he most wanted it. There was however found, at last, one resolved to offer his remonstrances, though the consequence threatened unremitting displeasure. The Prince Royal, his son, took this liberty, and sometimes showed the king, with the utmost deference, the dangers attending an excess of avarice, and the whimsical absurdity of employing soldiers only for show. This conduct was immediately construed into disobedience; and this brought on such severity of treatment, that the prince was resolved to leave the kingdom and fly for protection to England. It is not the business of this memoir to mention the accidents by which his intentions were frustrated, nor the miseries he essayed in seeing his dearest friends, who were partners of his design, sacrificed on the scaffold; be it sufficient to say, that he was now put into close confinement, in which he felt many years of severe captivity. The school of misery is the school of wisdom. Instead of nursing up his mind in indolence, or indulging sorrow, he refined his understanding by books, at first his only companions; and when indulged in greater liberties, the learned of whom he was fond had leave to visit him. Thus did this youth of genius spend his time among philosophers and men of virtue, and learn from them the hardest of all arts—the art of being a king. The Henriade of Voltaire reached our philosophic prince in his retreat. He read it, was charmed with the poem, and wished for the acquaintance of the poet. He had himself already written some metaphysical essays in answer to Horrebow. He had also diverted himself at intervals by translating some of the Latin poets, or composing somewhat of his own; but he wanted a friend whose judgment might be relied on—one to whom he could communicate his productions, and who had a capacity to amend them. He had already several learned men with him in his retreat, but they were rather philosophers than poets: he wanted a companion who could unite both the characters, who had solidity to instruct when he designed to be serious, and vivacity to unbend his mind when fatigued with study. Voltaire seemed to him adapted to both those purposes; he therefore resolved to give him an invitation to Prussia.

But the distinctions paid our poet by majesty, and the endearments he received from friendship, only served, by increasing envy, to increase the number of his enemies. Some years before this, an ecclesiastic, the Abbé des Fontaines, one who had some little reputation for poetry, was accused of a heinous crime, and expelled his convent upon that suspicion. Poor and infamous, he knew not where to apply for succour; from his own order he received only reproaches, and the public paid his merits but small regard. Voltaire saw him an object of compassion; he imagined it doubly his duty to relieve him, since he was in distress, and a poet. He therefore procured his indigent brother all the conveniences of life, made use of his interest to clear his reputation, and at last effectually re-established a character which he imagined had been unjustly injured. There are some obligations too great for gratitude. That is a debt the poor pay as an equivalent for favours; but when those become so great that no gratitude can equal, the mind becomes bankrupt, and pays with envy instead of acknowledgments. Such was the case of the Abbé des Fontaines; and a man whom small obligations might have eternally bound, became an enemy by being too much obliged. I shall not pretend to say, that Des Fontaines was the only person in fault upon this occasion. Voltaire might have required a deference which transcended the bounds of friendship. Des Fontaines could only regard him as an equal, and our poet wanted to be treated as a superior.

Their friendship, as was naturally to be expected, was soon converted into hatred. They mutually taxed each other with pride and ingratitude, and at last pleaded before the bar of the public; where each was more solicitous of injuring his opponent than of defending himself. Des Fontaines wrote a pamphlet, entitled the "Voltairomania," containing all the little levities of Voltaire's youth, some true, others taken up on groundless report; he added also the faults of his father and his family to increase the sum, and exhausted all that malice could suggest upon the occasion. But Des Fontaines did not maintain the unequal combat alone. Rousseau, a man of true genius, whose Odes are perhaps as beautiful as those of Horace, entered into the confederacy, and Ramsay served to complete the triumvirate.

In the republic of letters, he who arrogates superiority is sure to be disappointed: in vain he has the voice of the people, that is lost in idle murmurs; but the press is against him, and that speaks in characters far more lasting. Voltaire found himself attacked in the part he held most dear—his moral character. He appears to have been sensibly wounded by his antagonists; for there is scarcely a subsequent publication of his which does not make mention of the falsehood or the ingratitude of his enemies. The fame he had acquired by the tragedy of Alzira, served to increase their fury, and they only waited an opportunity to renew the assault. That opportunity was soon given. In the year 1736, he published a little poem, intituled "La Défense du Mondain," or an apology for luxury. In this he endeavours to prove that luxuries are rather serviceable than detrimental to an opulent people. This his enemies eagerly caught up. Des Fontaines had interest with one of his brethren, who had an influence on Cardinal Fleury. The piece was represented to this weak minister as a libel containing many shocking impieties, and the author as deserving the severest punishment. Voltaire had scarcely time to make his defence; he was banished France, and thus at last compelled to yield to the vindictive persecution of Des Fontaines, his inveterate enemy. The Prince of Prussia, upon hearing of our poet's situation, repeated his offers of friendship, and invited him into his kingdom. Voltaire, however, declined the invitation, and chose to reside at the chateau of Madame du Châtelet, at Cirey, where he employed his time in instructing her in the polite arts. It was here, and for her use, that he drew up that system of Universal History, which, whatever may be its fidelity, is certainly a fine specimen of the solidity of his judgment, and his intimate acquaintance with human nature.

The banishment of M. Voltaire at this time was but short. His friends were active in defending his innocence, and laid his case before the king in such convincing lights, that he was pleased to recall him from exile and restore him to favour. His good fortune, however, was not of long continuance, and only previous to a new disaster. Among the number of favourites at that time at court was Madame de Pompadour, a lady of as much beauty as ever graced a court, but of as indifferent morals as ever disgraced her sex. She had art enough to gain an entire ascendant over the king, and ambition to convert her power to self-interest. While she and her relations sold places and disposed of employments, the nation became almost bankrupt. Wretches raised without merit from obscurity, place all their ambition in wealth and magnificence. Such were her relations, sacrificing every public consideration to money, and even without a blush avowing their rapacity. I have before mentioned that Voltaire had been constituted historiographer to the king. This post had been usually considered as the reward of flattery and not of truth, and was generally bestowed accordingly. Our poet, however, who despised his predecessors for being no better than first flatterers of state, was resolved to show his integrity, though at the expense of his happiness. He intimated with the utmost humility to his majesty, that he feared he could not give posterity those favourable ideas of Louis XV. which he had done of his predecessor; that a mind filled with love could leave no room for that paternal affection which a king owed his people, and he concluded by praising Madame de Pompadour's beauty, but at the same time insinuating her artifice. This was enough to banish him from court, a disgrace which gave him not the least concern, as he ever preferred the tranquillity of retirement to the glare of pageantry; or perhaps it might be his peculiar temper to dislike all acquaintance with those who presumed to be his superiors.

Among his friends in Paris, he led the life of a man and a philosopher, and professed himself the protector of indigent merit. Every youth whose genius led to poetry found in him an encourager; if poor a supporter, and if rich a friend. He despised the court, and all the honours it could bestow: he laughed at Racine, who was slave enough to die at the frown of a tyrant; vindicated the cause of liberty in a land of slaves; and, by his single example, gave a new mode of thinking to the wits of Paris. However, though he despised the company of courtiers, they did not think proper to overlook him: some sought his conversation with the utmost assiduity, and others pretended tc regard him as a dangerous member of the state.

It has been already observed, that Madame de Pompadour was by no means in his esteem. This dislike he was imprudent enough to publish in a short satire, in which the king is represented as losing the complaints of the kingdom in her society, and preferring the allurements of a mistress to the voice of virtue and fame. Nothing spreads sooner than scandal or satire; this little performance was quickly read at court, and the king was soon apprised of its author. The monarch, weak, indolent, and voluptuous, could not brook any attempt to control his pleasures. He testified the severest displeasure against the poet, but did not think proper to banish him in direct terms, as he had been long the favourite of the public. It was resolved to send him a private hint, that it would be satisfactory if he would quit the kingdom. Cardinal Fleury accordingly acquainted Voltaire with the king's pleasure, and our poet, contrary to his expectations, refused to go, unless his banishment was made public. This was a refusal that quite disconcerted his enemies; however, they were determined to accomplish that by force which he had refused to solicitation. An unexpected accident effected what all their intrigues could not do. In 1749, his friend and pupil, Madame du Châtelet, died. For her conversation, he had formerly withstood all the invitations of the King of Prussia; in her conversation he found a solace against all the calumnies of the envious, and the insults of the powerful. When she was gone, those ties which held him to his country were broken, and he considered himself, in every sense of the word, a citizen of the world. He determined to accept the invitation, and went to acquaint the Cardinal Fleury with his intentions. The Cardinal gave him permission to quit France; and Voltaire prepared, in the year 1750, to set out for Prussia, to grace the court of its philosophic monarch.

Frederick II., who had only been Prince of Prussia when the correspondence between him and Voltaire commenced, had been for some time raised to the throne. There was much expected from him by his subjects while a prince; but, when he came to be invested with regal power, he outdid all their expectations. He had been forced to marry, against his inclinations, a princess of merit and beauty; however, while his father lived, he refused either to cohabit with her, or even to see her. It was generally supposed, that he who had behaved in such a manner while under paternal constraint, would aggravate the lady's misfortunes when he came to the throne. But it was quite otherwise; the day he was crowned she also shared his honours, and though he had not seen her for some years, his treatment of her was now changed into the most assiduous complaisance. Those who had been his favourites in imprisonment expected to enjoy their monarch's bounty without rivals; however, in this they were disappointed. He knew that the desires of a courtier are an abyss that can never be filled up: and therefore, instead of lucrative rewards, he recompensed their adherence to his person by honours. In short, he proved himself in every respect the father of his people: he reformed the laws, encouraged commerce, and invited into his dominions the arts and sciences. These he endeavoured to promote both from interest and inclination: his mornings were dedicated to study, part of the day to the review of his troops, and his evenings to society. In those hours of vacant hilarity he always threw aside the king. The persons who made at this time the most shining figure at his court, either for wit or learning, were the Marquis d'Argens, Maupertuis, the Baron Polnitz, and Wolfius.

The Marquis d'Argens was graceful in person, regularly featured, and had an extreme vivacity in his eye. I mention these trifling particulars only because gallantry constituted the leading part of his character, and for this he was happily formed by nature. He always endeavoured to unite in himself the man of pleasure and the philosopher, and only by this means called in the assistance of sentiment to refine his enjoyments; in other words, all his philosophy consisted in epicurism. He was formed for society, spoke infinitely better than he wrote, and wrote infinitely better than he lived. A man of pleasure often leads the most miserable life that can be conceived. Such was his case; he considered every abatement in his enjoyments as insupportable; passed his day between rapture and disappointment, between the extremes of agony and bliss; and often felt a pang as poignant for want of appetite, as the wretch who wants a meal. In these intervals of spleen he usually kept his bed, and only rose to some varied mode of enjoyment.

The King was delighted with this Frenchman's wit, and pleased with his conversation; but was too wise to give him any other place at court than that of superintendent of the pleasures. He was empowered to invite singers and dancers from abroad, to be master of the ceremonies on all court entertainments, and on those occasions to give laws to the King himself; who never chose to be distinguished from the rest of his subjects, when in pursuit of pleasure.

Maupertuis was a man of very different disposition. He had led in youth a life of academic severity, and practised and praised temperance. He was possessed of some genius, but more industry; had read and digested a great deal, and was one of that cast of characters which are content that there should be subordination in the literary world. He was perfectly acquainted with mathematics, and had read some poetry: from the one his writings have borrowed grace, from the other solidity. However, they all want that characteristic of true genius, originality; and while the reader can observe in them nothing to be censured, they have little that can be the subject of praise. What Maupertuis wanted in wit, he made up by prudence. This is a happy succedaneum to genius, and few who are possessed of the one in a very great degree are found to enjoy the other. No levities ever carried him beyond the bounds of decency; no speech of his ever betrayed the least dislike of the King's conduct, or his measures; hence he was regarded at first as a harmless good-natured man, and this by degrees grew into esteem; so that he had the good sense to make himself at last the principal favourite.

Baron Polnitz was formed in the school of adversity. He had been in his youth the sport of fortune; he travelled Europe without money, and all the friends he made were owing to his address. The reader will readily conceive that he was now and then obliged to act the *chevalier d'industrie.* It must be owned, his integrity in those juvenile adventures has more than once been called in question. But, as a companion, with the exception of Voltaire, perhaps none of his cotemporaries could exceed him. Though in his writings he appears a servile encomiast, in conversation he always mixed something of the misanthropist, which gave an air of shrewdness to his observations, and a strain of singularity to his manner. He had learned to read mankind, not by precept but experience; and as the needy generally see the worst side of those they converse with, he regarded human nature in the most disadvantageous points of view.

Wolfe had long been a professor in the University of Halle, in Saxony; but, indulging a metaphysical turn of thinking, he happened to differ from the modes of speculation at that time established in the schools, for which he was expelled the university. Distress alone was a sufficient recommendation to the King of Prussia's protection; he came over to the Court of Berlin, and was graciously received. Whatever opinion his Prussian Majesty might have had of this professor in his youth, he soon altered his sentiments, and regarded him rather as a learned visionary than a man of wisdom. The truth is, his performances are little more than trifling refinements on the opinions of Leibnitz; who being very erroneous himself, cannot be expected to have bequeathed precision to his followers.

From the joint efforts of these men, and of some others, too tedious to mention, the King was resolved to establish a society for the promotion of science and the belles lettres. The studies of the academy were divided into four different departments, each, however, serving to illustrate or advance the other. The first for metaphysics; the second for mathematics and experimental philosophy; the third for the languages and belles lettres; and the fourth, for the study and propagation of religion. Maupertuis was chosen president, and the King himself became a member, and gave in his papers in turn.

Such was a picture of the Court of Berlin at the time Voltaire accepted his Majesty's invitation. When the King was apprised of his arrival in his dominions, he went to meet him, attended only by one domestic, some miles out of town, and gave him the most cordial reception. He found Voltaire even more than his hopes or his works had described him. An easy fluency of animated observation generally composed his conversation; he had for some time thrown aside the man of wit, for the more substantial character of the man of wisdom; he had refined by study all that paradox of which he was once so fond; he assumed neither the character of a misanthrope, like Polnitz, nor of an undistinguishing admirer of the human species, like D'Argens. The King perceived he was possessed of more historical learning than Maupertuis, and more sprightly sallies of imagination than himself, even in his gayest moments. But, while I thus describe Voltaire's superiority, his faults must not be concealed. He was perfectly conscious of his own excellence, and demanded a deference from his brother poets which they did not choose to indulge. This at first raised some jealousies, and the King perceived them; but such was his address, so nicely did he divide his favours and his marks of esteem among these rival wits, that each thought himself the favourite, and all contributed to render the Court of Berlin the most polite in Europe.

But, whatever favours the King bestowed on others, Voltaire enjoyed the strongest marks of his friendship and esteem. To him he communicated his writings, desired his advice with regard to his future designs, and made him a partner in the secrets of his government. He was offered the most honourable and lucrative employments; but these he refused, alleging that it was not riches but friendship that he sought from his connexions with kings, and that he came not to impoverish the court, but to improve it. When he had rested some days after the fatigues of his journey, he thought it his duty to write to his old friend, Cardinal Fleury, and at the same time sent him a performance ascribed to the King of Prussia, entitled "Anti-Machiavel." The letter and the book the Cardinal received with the most extreme satisfaction, and returned Voltaire his acknowledgments in a well written epistle, in which he informed him of the pleasure he found in his present; adding, that if the author of this fine performance was not a king, at least he deserved to be one; and that if such a man had been born in the humblest station, his merits would have raised him to the greatest. This letter Voltaire communicated to Frederick, and it was, perhaps, one cause of the alliance which soon succeeded between the Courts of France and Prussia. The greatest events often rise from the slightest causes. * * * *

END OF THE MEMOIRS OF M. DE VOLTAIRE.

THE LIFE

OF

RICHARD NASH, ESQ.

T

PREFACE.

The following Memoir is neither calculated to inflame the reader's passions with descriptions of gallantry, nor to gratify his malevolence with details of scandal. The amours of coxcombs and the pursuits of debauchees are as destitute of novelty to attract us as they are of variety to entertain; they still present us but the same picture, a picture we have seen a thousand times repeated. The life of Richard Nash is incapable of supplying any entertainment of this nature to a prurient curiosity. Though it was passed in the very midst of debauchery, he practised but few of those vices he was often obliged to assent to. Though he lived where gallantry was the capital pursuit, he was never known to favour it by his example, and what authority he had was set to oppose it. Instead, therefore, of a romantic history filled with warm pictures and fanciful adventures, the reader of the following account must rest satisfied with a genuine and candid recital compiled from the papers he left behind, and others equally authentic; a recital neither written with a spirit of satire nor panegyric, and with scarcely any other art than that of arranging the materials in their natural order.

But though little art has been used, it is hoped that some entertainment may be collected from the life of a person so much talked of, and yet so little known, as Mr. Nash. The history of a man who for more than fifty years presided over the pleasures of a polite kingdom, and whose life, though without anything to surprise, was ever marked with singularity, deserves the attention of the present age; the pains he took in pursuing pleasure, and the solemnity he assumed in adjusting trifles, may one day claim the smile of posterity. At least such a history is well calculated to supply a vacant hour with innocent amusement, however it may fail to open the heart, or improve the understanding.

Yet his life, how trifling soever it may appear to the inattentive, was not without its real advantages to the public. He was the first who diffused a desire of society and an easiness of address among a whole people, who were formerly censured by foreigners for a reservedness of behaviour and an awkward timidity in their first approaches. He first taught a familiar intercourse among strangers at Bath and Tunbridge, which still subsists among them. That ease and open access first acquired there, our gentry brought back to the metropolis, and thus the whole kingdom by degrees became more refined by lessons originally derived from him.

Had it been my design to have made this history more pleasing at the expense of truth, it had been easily performed; but I chose to describe the man as he was, not such as imagination could have helped in completing his picture; he will be found to have been a weak man, governing weaker subjects, and may be considered as resembling a monarch of Cappadocia, whom Cicero somewhere calls, "the little king of a little people."

But while I have been careful in describing the monarch, his dominions have claimed no small share of my attention. I have given an exact account of the rise, regulation, and nature of the amusements of the city of Bath; how far Nash contributed to establish and refine them, and what pleasure a stranger may expect there upon his arrival. Such anecdotes as are at once true and worth preserving are produced in their order, and some stories are added, which, though commonly known, more necessarily belong to this history than to the places from whence they have been extracted. But it is needless to point out the pains that have been taken, or the entertainment that may be expected from the perusal of this performance. It is but an indifferent way to gain the reader's esteem, to be my own panegyrist; nor is this preface so much designed to lead him to beauties, as to demand pardon for defects.

LIFE OF RICHARD NASH, ESQ.

HISTORY owes its excellence more to the writer's manner than to the materials of which it is composed. The intrigues of courts, or the devastation of armies, are regarded by the remote spectator with as little attention as the squabbles of a village, or the fate of a malefactor, that fall under his own observation. The great and the little, as they have the same senses and the same affections, generally present the same picture to the hand of the draughtsman: and whether the hero or the clown be the subject of the memoir, it is only man that appears with all his native minuteness about him; for nothing very great was ever yet formed from the little materials of humanity.

Thus no one can properly be said to write history, but he who understands the human heart, and its whole train of affections and follies. Those affections and follies are properly the materials he has to work upon. The relations of great events may surprise indeed; they may be calculated to instruct those very few who govern the million beneath: but the generality of mankind find the most real improvement from relations which are levelled to the general surface of life, which tell—not how men learned to conquer, but how they endeavoured to live—not how they gained the shout of the admiring crowd, but how they acquired the esteem of their friends and acquaintance.

Every man's own life would perhaps furnish the most pleasing materials for history, if he only had candour enough to be sincere, and skill enough to select such parts as once making him more prudent, might serve to render his readers more cautious. There are few who do not prefer a page of Montaigne or Colley Cibber, who candidly tell us what they thought of the world and the world thought of them, to the more stately memoirs and transactions of Europe, where we see kings pretending to immortality, that are now almost forgotten, and statesmen planning frivolous negotiations that scarcely outlive the signing.

It were to be wished that ministers and kings were left to write their own histories: they are truly useful to few but themselves; but for men who are contented with more humble stations, I fancy such truths only are serviceable as may conduct them safely through life. That knowledge which we can turn to our real benefit should be most eagerly pursued. Treasures which we cannot use but little increase the happiness or even the pride of the possessor.

I profess to write the history of a man placed in the middle rank of life; of one whose vices and virtues were open to the eye of the most undiscerning spectator; who was placed in public view without power to repress censure or command adulation; who had too much merit not to become remarkable, yet too much folly to arrive at greatness. I attempt the character of one who was just such a man as probably you or I may be; but with this difference, that he never performed an action which the world did not know, or ever formed a wish which he did not take pains to divulge. In short, I have chosen to write the life of the noted Mr. Nash, as it will be the delineation of a mind without disguise, of a man ever assiduous without industry, and pleasing to his superiors without any superiority of genius or understanding.

Yet, if there be any who think the subject of too little importance to command attention, and who would rather gaze at the actions of the great than be directed in guiding their own, I have one undeniable claim to their attention. Mr. Nash was himself a King. In this particular, perhaps no biographer has been so happy as I. They who are for a delineation of men and manners may find some satisfaction that way, and those who delight in adventures of kings and queens may perhaps find their hopes satisfied in another.

It is a matter of very little importance who were the parents, or what was the education, of a man who owed so little of his advancement to either. He seldom boasted of family or learning, and his father's name and circumstances were so little known, that Dr. Cheyne used frequently to say that Nash had no father. The Duchess of Marlborough one day rallying him in public company upon the obscurity of his birth, compared him to Gil Blas, who was ashamed of his father. "No, madam," replied Nash, "I seldom mention my father in company; not because I have any reason to be ashamed of him, but because he has some reason to be ashamed of me."

However, though such anecdotes be immaterial, to go on in the usual course of history, it may be proper to observe, that RICHARD NASH, Esq., the subject of this memoir, was born in the town of Swansea, in Glamorganshire, on the 18th of October, in the year 1674. His father was a gentleman whose principal income arose from a partnership in a glass-house; his mother was niece to Colonel Poyer, who was killed by Oliver Cromwell, for defending Pembroke Castle against the rebels. He was educated under Mr. Maddocks at Carmarthen School, and from thence sent to Jesus College, Oxford, in order to prepare him for the study of the law. His father had strained his little income to give his son such an education; but from the boy's natural vivacity, he hoped a recompense from his future preferment. In college, however, he soon showed that though much might be expected from his genius, nothing could be hoped from his industry. A mind strongly turned to pleasure always is first seen at the university: there the youth first finds himself freed from the restraint of tutors, and being treated by his friends in some measure as a man, assumes the passions and desires of riper age, and discovers in the boy what are likely to be the affections of his maturity.

The first method Mr. Nash took to distinguish himself at college was not by application to study, but by his assiduity to intrigue. In the neighbourhood of every university there are girls who with some beauty, some coquetry, and little fortune, lie upon the watch for every raw youth, more inclined to make love than to study. Our hero was quickly caught, and went through all the mazes and adventures of a college intrigue, before he was seventeen: he offered marriage, the offer was accepted, but the whole affair coming to the knowledge of his tutors, his happiness, or perhaps his future misery, was prevented, and he was sent home from college, with necessary advice to him, and proper instructions to his father.

When a man knows his power over the fair sex, he generally commences their admirer for the rest of life. That triumph which he obtains over one only makes him the slave of another, and thus he proceeds conquering and conquered, to the closing of the scene. The army seemed the most likely profession in which to display this inclination for gallantry; he therefore purchased a pair of colours, commenced a professed admirer of the sex, and dressed to the very edge of his finances. But the life of a soldier is more pleasing to the spectator at a distance than to the person who makes the experiment. Nash soon found that a red coat alone would never succeed, that the company of the fair sex is not to be procured without expense, and that his scanty commission could never procure him the proper reimbursements. He found, too, that the profession of arms required attendance and duty, and often encroached upon those hours he could have wished to dedicate to softer purposes. In short, he soon became disgusted with the life of a soldier, quitted the army, entered his name as a student in the Temple books, and here went to the very summit of second-rate luxury. Though very poor, he was very fine; he spread the little gold he had in the most ostentatious manner, and though the gilding was but thin, he laid it on as far as it would go. They who know the town cannot be unacquainted with such a character as I describe; one who, though he may have dined in private upon a banquet served cold from a cook's shop, shall dress at six for the side box; one of those whose wants are only known to their laundress and tradesmen, and their fine clothes to half the nobility; who spend more in chair hire than housekeeping, and prefer a bow from a lord to a dinner from a commoner.

In this manner Nash spent some years about town, till at last, his genteel appearance, his constant civility, and still more, his assiduity, gained him the acquaintance of several persons qualified to lead the fashion both by birth and fortune. To gain the friendship of the young nobility, little more is requisite than much submission and very fine clothes; dress has a mechanical influence upon the mind, and we naturally are awed into respect and esteem at the elegance of those whom even our reason would teach us to contemn. He seemed early sensible of human weakness in this respect; he brought a person genteelly dressed to every assembly: he always made one of those who are called very good company, and assurance gave him an air of elegance and ease.

When King William was upon the throne, Mr. Nash was a member of the Middle Temple. It had been long customary for the Inns of Court to entertain our monarchs upon their accession to the crown, or some such remarkable occasion, with a revel and pageant. In the earlier periods of our history, poets were the conductors of these entertainments: plays were exhibited, and complimentary verses were then written; but by degrees the pageant alone was continued, Sir John Davis being the last poet that wrote verses upon such an occasion, in the reign of James I.

This ceremony, which has been at length totally discontinued, was last exhibited in honour of King William, and Mr. Nash was chosen to conduct the whole with proper decorum. He was then but a very young man; but we see at how early an age he was thought proper to guide the amusements of his country, and be the *Arbiter Elegantiarum* of his time; we see how early he gave proofs of that spirit of regularity for which he afterwards became famous, and showed an attention to those little circumstances, of which, though the observance be trifling, the neglect has often interrupted men of the greatest abilities in the progress of their fortunes.

In conducting this entertainment, Nash had an opportunity of exhibiting all his abilities, and King William was so well satisfied with his performance, that he made him an offer of knighthood. This, however, he thought proper to refuse; which in a person of his disposition seems strange. "Please your Majesty," replied he, when the offer was made him, "if you intend to make me a knight, I wish it may be one of your Poor Knights of Windsor, and then I shall have a fortune at least able to support my title." Yet we do not find that the King took the hint of increasing his fortune; perhaps he could not; he had at that time numbers to oblige, and he never cared to give money without important services.

But though Nash acquired no riches by his late office, yet he gained many friends, or, what is more easily obtained, many acquaintances, who often answer the end as well. In the populous city where he resided, to be known was almost synonymous with being in the road to fortune. How many little things do we see, without merit or without friends, push themselves forward into public notice, and by self-advertising attract the attention of the day! The wise despise them, but the public are not all wise. Thus they succeed, rise upon the wing of folly or of fashion, and by their success give a new sanction to effrontery.

But besides his assurance, Mr. Nash had in reality some merit and some virtues. He was, if not a brilliant, at least an easy companion. He never forgot good manners, even in the highest warmth of familiarity, and, as I hinted before, never went in a dirty shirt to disgrace the table of his patron or his friend. These qualifications might make the furniture of his head; but for his heart, that seemed an assemblage of the virtues which display an honest, benevolent mind, with the vices which spring from too much good-nature. He had pity for every creature's distress, but wanted prudence in the application of his benefits. He had generosity for the wretched in the highest degree, at a time when his creditors complained of his justice. He often spoke falsehoods, but never had any of his harmless tales tinctured with malice.

An instance of his humanity is told us in The Spectator, though his name is not mentioned. When he was to give in his accounts to the Masters of the Temple, among other articles, he charged "For making one man happy, 10*l*." Being questioned about the meaning of so strange an item, he frankly declared, that happening to overhear a poor man declare to his wife and a large family of children that 10*l*. would make him happy, he could not avoid trying the experiment. He added, that if they did not choose to acquiesce in his charge, he was ready to refund the money. The Masters, struck with such an uncommon instance of good-nature, publicly thanked him for his benevolence, and desired that the sum might be doubled, as a proof of their satisfaction.

Another instance of his unaccountable generosity, and I shall proceed. In some transactions with one of his friends, Nash was brought in debtor twenty pounds. His friend frequently asked for the money, and was as often denied. He found at last that assiduity was likely to have no effect, and therefore contrived an honourable method of getting back his money without dissolving the friendship that subsisted between them. One day, returning from Nash's chamber with the usual assurance of being paid to-morrow, he went to one of their mutual acquaintance, and related the frequent disappointments he had received, and the little hopes he had of being ever paid. "My design," continues he, "is that you should go and try to borrow twenty pounds from Nash, and bring me the money. I am apt to think he will lend to you, though he will not pay me. Perhaps we may extort from his generosity what I have failed to receive from his justice." His friend obeyed, and going to Nash, assured him, that unless relieved by his friendship, he should certainly be undone; he wanted to borrow twenty pounds, and had tried all his acquaintance without success. Nash, who had but some minutes before refused to pay a just debt, was in raptures at thus giving an instance of his friendship, and instantly lent what was required. Immediately upon the receipt, the pretended borrower goes to the real creditor, and gives him the money, who met Mr. Nash the day after. Our hero upon seeing him immediately began his usual excuses, that the billiard-room had stripped him; that he was never so damnably out of cash, but that in a few days——"My dear sir, be under no uneasiness," replied the other, "I would not interrupt your tranquillity for the world; you lent twenty pounds yesterday to our friend of the back stairs, and he lent it to me; give him your receipt, and you shall have mine." "Perdition seize thee!" cried Nash, "thou hast been too many for me. You demanded a debt, he asked a favour; to pay thee would not increase our friendship; but to lend him was procuring a new friend, by conferring a new obligation."

Whether men, at the time I am now talking of, had more wit than at present, I will not take upon me to determine; but certain it is, they took more pains to show what they had. In that age, a fellow of high humour would drink no wine but what was strained through his mistress's smock. He would eat a pair of her shoes tossed up in a fricasee; he would swallow tallow candles instead of toasted cheese, and even run naked about town, as it was then said, to divert the ladies. In short, that was the age of such kind of wit as is the most distant of all others from wisdom.

Mr. Nash, as he sometimes played tricks with others, upon certain occasions received very severe retaliations. Being at York, and having lost all his money, some of his companions agreed to equip him with fifty guineas, upon this proviso, that he would stand at the great door of the Minster in a blanket, as the people were coming out of church. To this proposal he readily agreed; but the Dean passing by, unfortunately knew him. "What!" cried the divine, "Nash in masquerade?" "Only a Yorkshire penance, Mr. Dean, for keeping bad company," said Nash, pointing to his companions.

Some time after this, he won a wager of still greater consequence, by riding naked through a village upon a cow. This was then thought a harmless frolic; at present it would be looked upon with detestation.

He was once invited by some gentlemen of the navy on board a man-of-war, that had sailing orders for the Mediterranean. This was soon after the affair of the revels, and being ignorant of any design against him, he took his bottle with freedom. But he soon found, to use the expression then in fashion, that he was absolutely "bitten." The ship sailed away before he was aware of his situation, and he was obliged to make the voyage in the company where he had spent the night.

Many lives are often passed without a single adventure, and I do not know of any in the life of our hero that can be called such, except what we are now relating. During this voyage, he was in an engagement, in which his particular friend was killed by his side, and he himself wounded in the leg. For the anecdote of his being wounded we are solely to trust to his own veracity; but most of his acquaintance were not much inclined to believe him, when he boasted on those occasions. Telling one day of the wound he had received for his country, in one of the public rooms at Bath (Wiltshire's, if I do not forget), a lady of distinction that sat by, said it was all false. "I protest, madam," replied he, "it is true; and if I cannot be believed, your ladyship may, if you please, receive farther information, and feel the ball in my leg."

Nash was now fairly for life entered into a new course of gaiety and dissipation, and steady in nothing but in pursuit of variety. He was thirty years old, without fortune, or useful talents to acquire one. He had hitherto only led a life of expedients; he thanked chance alone for his support, and having been long precariously supported, he became, at length, totally a stranger to prudence or precaution. Not to disguise any part of his character, he was now by profession a gamester, and went on from day to day, feeling the vicissitudes of rapture and anguish, in proportion to the fluctuations of fortune.

At this time London was the only theatre in England for pleasure or intrigue. A spirit of gaming had been introduced in the licentious age of Charles II., and had by this time thriven surprisingly. Yet all its devastations were confined to London alone. To this great mart of every folly, sharpers from every country daily arrived for the winter; but were obliged to leave the kingdom at the approach of summer, in order to open a new campaign at Aix, Spa, or the Hague. Bath, Tunbridge, Scarborough, and other places of the same kind here, were then frequented only by such as really went for relief: the pleasures they afforded were merely rural; the company splenetic, rustic, and vulgar. In this situation of things, people of fashion had no agreeable summer retreat from the town, and usually spent that season amidst a solitude of country squires, parsons' wives, and visiting tenants, or farmers; they wanted some place where they might have each other's company, and win each other's money, as they had done during the winter in town.

To a person who does not thus calmly trace things to their source, nothing will appear more strange, than how the healthy could ever consent to follow the sick to those places of spleen, and live with those whose disorders are ever apt to excite a gloom in the spectator. The truth is, the gaming-table was properly the salutary font to which such numbers flocked. Gaming will ever be the pleasure of the rich, while men continue to be men; while they fancy more happiness is being possessed of what they want, than they experience pleasure in the fruition of what they have. The wealthy only stake those riches which give no real content, for an expectation of riches in which they hope for satisfaction. By this calculation, they cannot lose happiness, as they begin with none; and they hope to gain it, by being possessed of something they have not had already.

Probably upon this principle, and by the arrival of Queen Anne there, for her health, about the year 1703, the city of Bath became in some measure frequented by people of distinction. The company was numerous enough to form a country-dance upon the bowling-green: they were amused with a fiddle and hautboy, and diverted with the romantic walks round the city. They usually sauntered in fine weather in the grove, between two rows of sycamore-trees. Several learned physicians, Dr. Jorden and others, had even then praised the salubrity of the wells, and the amusements were put under the direction of a master of the ceremonies.

Captain Webster was the predecessor of Mr. Nash. This I take to be the same gentleman whom Mr. Lucas describes in his history of the lives of the Gamesters, by which it appears that Bath, even before the arrival of Nash, was found a proper retreat for men of that profession. This gentleman, in the year 1704, carried the balls to the Town-hall, each man paying half-a-guinea each ball.

Still, however, the amusements of this place were neither elegant, nor conducted with delicacy. General society among people of rank or fortune was by no means established. The nobility still preserved a tincture of Gothic haughtiness, and refused to keep company with the gentry at any of the public entertainments of the place. Smoking in the rooms was permitted; gentlemen and ladies appeared in a disrespectful manner at public entertainments in aprons and boots. With an eagerness common to those whose pleasures come but seldom, they generally continued them too long; and thus they were rendered disgusting by too free an enjoyment. If the company liked each other, they danced till morning; if any person lost at cards, he insisted on continuing the game till luck should turn. The lodgings for visitants were paltry, though expensive; the dining-rooms and other chambers were floored with boards, coloured brown with soot and small-beer, to hide the dirt; the walls were covered with unpainted wainscot; the furniture corresponded with the meanness of the architecture; a few oak chairs, a small looking-glass, with a fender and tongs, composed the magnificence of these temporary habitations. The city was in itself mean and contemptible; no elegant buildings, no open streets, nor uniform squares! The pump-house was without any director; the chairmen permitted no gentlemen or ladies to walk home by night without insulting them; and to add to all this, one of the greatest physicians of his age conceived a design of ruining the city, by writing against the efficacy of the waters. It was from a resentment of some affronts he had received there, that he took this resolution; and accordingly published a pamphlet, by which he said, "he would cast a toad into the spring."

In this situation of things it was that Nash first came into that city, and hearing the threat of this physician, he humorously assured the people, that if they would give him leave, he would charm away the poison of the doctor's toad, as they usually charmed the venom of the tarantula, by music. He therefore was immediately empowered to set up the force of a band of music, against the poison of the doctor's reptile. The company very sensibly increased; Nash triumphed, and the sovereignty of the city was decreed to him by every rank of people.

We are now to behold this gentleman as arrived at a new dignity, for which nature seemed to have formed him: we are to see him directing pleasures, which none had better learned to share; placed over rebellious and refractory subjects, that were to be ruled only by the force of his address, and governing such as had been long accustomed to govern others. We see a kingdom beginning with him, and sending off Tunbridge as one of its colonies.

But to talk more simply, when we talk at best of trifles. None could possibly conceive a person more fit to fill this employment than Nash. He had some wit, as I have said once or twice before; but it was of that sort which is rather happy than permanent. Once a week he might say a good thing: this the little ones about him took care to divulge; or if they happened to forget the joke, he usually remembered to repeat it himself. In a long intercourse with the world he had acquired an impenetrable assurance; and the freedom with which he was received by the great, furnished him with vivacity which could be commanded at any time, and which some mistook for wit. His former intercourse among people of fashion in town had let him into most of the characters of the nobility; and he was acquainted with many of their private intrigues. He understood rank and precedence with the utmost exactness; was fond of show and finery himself, and generally set a pattern of it to others. These were his favourite talents, and he was the favourite of such as had no other.

But to balance these which some may consider as foibles, he was charitable himself, and generally shamed his betters into a similitude of sentiment, if they were not naturally so before. He was fond of advising those young men who, by youth and too much money, are taught to look upon extravagance as a virtue. He was an enemy to rudeness in others, though in the latter part of his life he did not much seem to encourage a dislike of it by his own example. None talked with more humanity of the foibles of others, when absent, than he, nor kept those secrets with which he was entrusted more inviolably. But above all (if moralists will allow it among the number of his virtues), though he gamed high, he always played very fairly. These were his qualifications. Some of the nobility regarded him as an inoffensive, useful companion, the size of whose understanding was, in general, level with their own; but their little imitators admired him as a person of fine sense, and great good breeding. Thus people became fond of ranking him in the number of their acquaintance, told over his jests, and Beau Nash at length became the fashionable companion.

His first care when made Master of the Ceremonies, or King of Bath, as it is called, was to promote a music subscription of one guinea each, for a band, which was to consist of six performers, who were to receive a guinea a week each for their trouble. He allowed also two guineas a week for lighting and sweeping the rooms; for which he accounted to the subscribers by receipt.

The pump-house was immediately put under the care of an officer, by the name of the pumper; for which he paid the corporation an annual rent. A row of new houses was begun on the south side of the gravel-walks, before which a handsome pavement was then made for the company to walk on. Not less than seventeen or eighteen hundred pounds were raised this year and in the beginning of 1706 by subscription, and laid out in repairing the roads near the city. The streets began to be better paved, cleaned, and lighted; the licences of the chairmen were repressed, and by an Act of Parliament procured on this occasion, the invalids, who came to drink or bathe, were exempted from all manner of toll, as often as they should go out of the city for recreation.

The houses and streets now began to improve, and ornaments were lavished upon them even to profusion. But in the midst of this splendour, the company still were obliged to assemble in a booth to drink tea and chocolate, or to game. Mr. Nash undertook to remedy this inconvenience, and by his direction, one Thomas Harrison erected a handsome assembly-house for these purposes. A better band of music was also procured, and the former subscription of one guinea was raised to two. Harrison had three guineas a week for the room and candles, and the music two guineas a man. The money Mr. Nash received and accounted for with the utmost exactness and punctuality. To this house were also added gardens for people of rank and fashion to walk in; and the beauty of the suburbs continued to increase, notwithstanding the opposition that was made by the corporation; who at that time looked upon every useful improvement, particularly without the walls, as dangerous to the inhabitants within.

His dominion was now extensive and secure, and he determined to support it with the strictest attention. But in order to proceed in everything like a King, he was resolved to give his subjects a law, and the following Rules were accordingly put up in the pump-room:—

RULES TO BE OBSERVED AT BATH.

1. "That a visit of ceremony at first coming, and another at going away, are all that is expected or desired by ladies of quality and fashion,—except impertinents.

2. "That ladies coming to the ball appoint a time for their footmen coming to wait on them home, to prevent disturbance and inconveniences to themselves and others.

3. "That gentlemen of fashion never appearing in a morning before the ladies in gowns and caps, show breeding and respect.

4. "That no person take it ill that any one goes to another's play or breakfast, and not theirs;—except captious by nature.

5. "That no gentleman give his ticket for the balls to any but gentlewomen.—N.B. Unless he has none of his acquaintance.

6. "That gentlemen crowding before the ladies at the ball, show ill-manners; and that none do so for the future,—except such as respect nobody but themselves.

7. "That no gentleman or lady take it ill that another dances before them;—except such as have no pretence to dance at all.

8. "That the elder ladies and children be content with a second bench at the ball, as being past or not come to perfection.

9. "That the younger ladies take notice how many eyes observe them.—N. B. This does not extend to the Have-at-alls.

10. "That all whisperers of lies and scandal be taken for their authors.

11. "That all repeaters of such lies and scandal be shunned by all company,—except such as have been guilty of the same crime.—N.B. Several men of no character, old women and young ones of questioned reputation, are great authors of lies in these places, being of the sect of levellers."

These laws were written by Mr. Nash himself, and by the manner in which they are drawn up, he undoubtedly designed them for wit. The reader, however, it is feared, will think them dull. But Nash was not born a writer; for whatever humour he might have in conversation, he used to call a pen his torpedo: whenever he grasped it, it benumbed all his faculties.

But were we to give laws to a nursery, we should make them childish laws; his statutes, though stupid, were addressed to fine gentlemen and ladies, and were probably received with sympathetic approbation. It is certain they were in general religiously observed by his subjects, and executed by him with impartiality; neither rank nor fortune shielded the refractory from his resentment.

The balls, by his directions, were to begin at six, and to end at eleven. Nor would he suffer them to continue a moment longer, lest invalids might commit irregularities, to counteract the benefit of the waters. Everything was to be performed in proper order. Each ball was to open with a minuet, danced by two persons of the highest distinction present. When the minuet concluded, the lady was to return to her seat, and Nash was to bring the gentleman a new partner. This ceremony was to be observed by every succeeding couple; every gentleman being obliged to dance with two ladies till the minuets were over, which generally continued two hours. At eight the country-dances were to begin; ladies of quality, according to their rank, standing up first. About nine o'clock a short interval was allowed for rest, and for the gentlemen to help their partners to tea. That over, the company were to pursue their amusements till the clock struck eleven. Then the master of the ceremonies entering the ball-room, ordered the music to desist by lifting up his finger. The dances discontinued, and some time allowed for becoming cool, the ladies were handed to their chairs.

Even the royal family themselves had not influence enough to make him deviate from any of these rules. The Princess Amelia once applying to him for one dance more, after he had given the signal to withdraw, he assured her royal highness, that the established rules of Bath resembled the laws of Lycurgus, which would admit of no alteration, without an utter subversion of all his authority.

He was not less strict with regard to

the dresses in which ladies and gentlemen were to appear. He had the strongest aversion to a white apron, and absolutely excluded all who ventured to appear at the assembly dressed in that manner. I have known him on a ball night strip even the Duchess of Q——, and throw her apron at one of the hinder benches among the ladies' women: observing, that none but Abigails appeared in white aprons. This from another would be an insult; in him it was considered as a just reprimand, and the good-natured duchess acquiesced in his censure.

But he found more difficulty in attacking the gentlemen's irregularities; and for some time strove, but in vain, to prohibit the use of swords. Disputes arising from love of play were sometimes attended with fatal effects. To use his own expression, he was resolved to hinder people from doing "what they had no mind to;" but for some time without effect. However, there happened about that time a duel between two gamesters, whose names were Taylor and Clarke, which helped to promote his peaceable intentions. They fought by torch-light in the grove; Taylor was run through the body, but lived seven years after, at which time his wound breaking out afresh, it caused his death. Clarke from that time pretended to be a Quaker, but the orthodox brethren never cordially received him among their number; and he died at London, about eighteen years after, in poverty and contrition. From that time it was thought necessary to forbid the wearing of swords at Bath, as they often tore the ladies clothes, and frighted them, by sometimes appearing upon trifling occasions. Whenever, therefore, Nash heard of a challenge given or accepted, he instantly had both parties arrested. The gentlemen's boots also made a very desperate stand against him; the country squires were by no means submissive to his usurpations, and probably his authority alone would never have carried him through, had he not reinforced it with ridicule. He wrote a song upon the occasion, which, for the honour of his poetical talents, the world shall see.

FRONTINELLA'S INVITATION TO THE ASSEMBLY.

Come, one and all, to Hoyden Hall,
For there's the assembly this night;
None but prude fools
Mind manners and rules;
We Hoydens do decency slight.
Come, trollops and slatterns,
Cocked hats and white aprons,
This best our modesty suits;
For why should not we
In dress be as free
As Hogs-Norton squires in boots?

The keenness, severity, and particularly the good rhymes of this little *morçeau*, which was at that time highly relished by many of the nobility at Bath, gained him a temporary triumph. But to push his victories, he got up a puppet-show, in which Punch came in booted and spurred, in the character of a country squire. He was introduced as courting his mistress, and having obtained her consent to comply with his wishes, upon going to bed, he is desired to pull off his boots. "My boots!" replies Punch; "why, madam, you may as well bid me pull off my legs. I never go without boots; I never ride, I never dance, without them, and this piece of politeness is quite the thing at Bath. We always dance at our town in boots, and the ladies often move minuets in riding-hoods." Thus he goes on, till his mistress, grown impatient, kicks him off the stage.

From that time few ventured to be seen at the assemblies in Bath in a riding-dress; and whenever any gentleman, through ignorance or haste, appeared in the rooms in boots, Nash would make up to him, and bowing in an arch manner, would tell him that he had "forgot his horse." Thus he was at last completely victorious.

"Dolisque coacti
Quos neque Tydides nec Larissæus Achilles
Non anni domûere decem."

He began therefore to reign without a rival, and like other kings had his mistresses, flatterers, enemies, and calumniators. The amusements of the place, however, wore a very different aspect from what they did formerly. Regularity repressed pride; and that, lessened, people of fortune became fit for society. Let the morose and grave censure an attention to forms and ceremonies, and rail at those whose only business it is to regulate them; but, though ceremony is very different from politeness, no country was ever yet polite that was not first ceremonious. The natural gradation of breeding begins in savage disgust, proceeds to indifference, improves into attention, by degrees refines into ceremonious observance; and the trouble of being ceremonious at length produces politeness, elegance, and ease. There is, therefore, some merit in mending society, even in one of the inferior steps of this gradation; and no man was more happy in this respect than Nash. In every nation there are enough who have no other business or care but that of buying pleasure; and he taught them who bid at such an auction, the art of procuring what they sought, without diminishing the pleasure of others.

The city of Bath, by such assiduity, soon became the theatre of summer amusements for all people of fashion; and the manner of spending the day there must amuse any but such as disease or spleen had made uneasy to themselves. The following is a faint picture of the pleasures that scene affords. Upon a stranger's arrival at Bath he is welcomed by a peal of the Abbey bells, and, in the next place, by the voice and music of the city waits. For these civilities, the ringers have generally a present made them of half-a-guinea, and the waits of half-a-crown, or more, in proportion to the person's fortune, generosity, or ostentation. These customs, though disagreeable, are however liked, or they would not continue. The greatest incommodity attending them is the disturbance the bells must give the sick. But the pleasure of knowing the name of every family that comes to town recompenses the inconvenience. Invalids are fond of news, and upon the first sound of the bells everybody sends out to inquire for whom they ring.

After the family is thus welcomed to Bath, it is the custom for the master of it to go to the public places, and subscribe two guineas at the assembly-houses towards the balls and music in the pump-house, for which he is entitled to three tickets every ball night. His next subscription is a crown, half-a-guinea, or a guinea, according to his rank and quality, for the liberty of walking in the private walks belonging to Simpson's assembly-house; a crown or half-a-guinea is also given to the booksellers, for which the gentleman is to have what books he pleases to read at his lodgings, and at the coffee-house another subscription is taken for pen, ink, and paper, for such letters as the subscriber shall write at it during his stay. The ladies, too, may subscribe to the booksellers, and to a house by the pump-room, for the advantage of reading the news, and for enjoying each other's conversation.

Things being thus adjusted, the amusements of the day are generally begun by bathing, which is no unpleasing method of passing away an hour or so.

The baths are five in number. On the south-west side of the Abbey Church is the King's Bath, which is an oblong square; the walls are full of niches, and at every corner are steps to descend into it: this bath is said to contain 427 tons and 50 gallons of water; and on its rising out of the ground over the springs, it is sometimes too hot to be endured by those who bathe therein. Adjoining to the King's Bath, there is another, called the Queen's Bath; this is of a more temperate warmth, as borrowing its water from the other.

In the south-west part of the city are three other baths, viz.: the Hot Bath, which is not much inferior in heat to the King's Bath, and contains 53 tons, 2 hogsheads, and 11 gallons of water; the Cross Bath, which contains 52 tons, 3 hogsheads, and 11 gallons; and the Leper's Bath, which is not so much frequented as the rest.

The King's Bath (according to the best observations) will fill in about nine hours and a half; the Hot Bath in about eleven hours and a half; and the Cross Bath in about the same time.

The hours for bathing are commonly between six and nine in the morning, and the baths are every morning supplied with fresh water; for when the people have done bathing, the sluices in each bath are pulled up, and the water is carried off by drains into the river Avon.

In the morning the lady is brought in a close chair, dressed in her bathing clothes, to the bath; and, being in the water, the woman who attends presents her with a little floating dish like a basin; into which the lady puts a handkerchief, a snuff-box, and a nosegay. She then traverses the bath; if a novice, with a guide; if otherwise, by herself; and having amused herself thus while she thinks proper, calls for her chair, and returns to her lodgings.

The amusement of bathing is immediately succeeded by a general assembly of people at the pump-room; some for pleasure, and some to drink the hot waters. Three glasses at three different times is the usual portion for every drinker; and the intervals between every glass are enlivened by the harmony of a small band of music, as well as by the conversation of the gay, the witty, or the forward.

From the pump-room the ladies, from time to time, withdraw to a female coffee-house, and from thence return to their lodgings to breakfast. The gentlemen withdraw to their coffee-houses, to read the papers, or converse on the news of the day, with a freedom and ease not to be found in the metropolis.

People of fashion make public breakfasts at the assembly-houses, to which they invite their acquaintances, and they sometimes order private concerts; or, when so disposed, attend lectures on the arts and sciences, which are frequently taught there in a pretty superficial manner, so as not to tease the understanding, while they afford the imagination some amusement. The private concerts are performed in the ball-rooms; the tickets a crown each.

Concert breakfasts at the assembly-house sometimes make also a part of the morning's amusement here, the expenses of which are defrayed by a subscription among the men. Persons of rank and fortune who can perform are admitted into the orchestra, and find a pleasure in joining with the performers.

Thus we have the tedious morning fairly over. When noon approaches, and church (if any please to go there) is done, some of the company appear upon the parade, and other public walks, where they continue to chat and amuse each other, till they have formed parties for the play, cards, or dancing for the evening. Another part of the company divert themselves with reading in the booksellers' shops, or are generally seen taking the air and exercise, some on horseback, some in coaches. Some walk in the meadows round the town, winding along the side of the river Avon and the neighbouring canal; while others are seen scaling some of those romantic precipices that overhang the city.

When the hour of dinner draws nigh, and the company are returned from their different recreations, the provisions are generally served with the utmost elegance and plenty. Their mutton, butter, fish, and fowl, are all allowed to be excellent, and their cookery still exceeds their meat.

After dinner is over, and evening prayers ended, the company meet a second time at the pump-house. From this they retire to the walks, and from thence go to drink tea at the assembly-houses, and the rest of the evenings are concluded either with balls, plays, or visits. A theatre was erected in the year 1705, by subscription, by people of the highest rank, who permitted their arms to be engraven on the inside of the house, as a public testimony of their liberality towards it. Every Tuesday and Friday evening is concluded with a public ball, the contributions to which are so numerous, that the price of each ticket is trifling. Thus Bath yields a continued rotation of diversions, and people of all ways of thinking, even from the libertine to the methodist, have it in their power to complete the day with employments suited to their inclinations.

In this manner every amusement soon improved under Mr. Nash's administration. The magistrates of the city found that he was necessary and useful, and took every opportunity of paying the same respect to his fictitious royalty that is generally extorted by real power. The same satisfaction a young lady finds upon being singled out at her first appearance, or an applauded poet on the success of his first tragedy, influenced him. All admired him as an extraordinary character; and some who knew no better, as a very fine gentleman. He was perfectly happy in their little applause, and affected at length something particular in his dress, behaviour, and conversation.

His equipage was sumptuous, and he usually travelled to Tunbridge in a post chariot and six greys, with out-riders, footmen, French-horns, and every other appendage of expensive parade. He always wore a white hat; and, to apologize for this singularity, said, he did it purely to secure it from being stolen; his dress was tawdry, though not perfectly genteel; he might be considered as a Beau of several generations, and in his appearance he, in some measure, mixed the fashions of the last age with those of the present. He perfectly understood elegant expense, and generally passed his time in the very best company, if persons of the first distinction deserve that title.

But I hear the reader now demand, what finances were to support all this finery, or where the treasures that gave him such frequent opportunities of displaying his benevolence, or his vanity? To answer this, we must now enter upon another part of his character,—his talents as a gamester; for by gaming alone, at that period of which I speak, he kept up so very genteel an appearance. When he first figured at Bath, there were few laws against this destructive amusement. The gaming-table was the constant resource of despair and indigence, and frequent ruin of opulent fortunes. Wherever people of fashion came, needy adventurers were generally found in waiting. With such Bath swarmed; and among this class Mr. Nash was certainly to be numbered in the beginning, only with this difference, that he wanted the corrupt heart too commonly attending a life of expedients; for he was generous, humane, and honourable, even though by profession a gamester.

A thousand instances might be given of his integrity, even in this infamous profession, where his generosity often impelled him to act in contradiction to his interest. Wherever he found a novice in the hands of a sharper, he generally forewarned him of the danger; whenever he found any inclined to play, yet ignorant of the game, he would offer his services, and play for them. I remember an instance to this effect, though too nearly concerned in the affair to publish the gentleman's name of whom it is related. In the year 1725, there came to Bath a giddy youth, who had just resigned his fellowship at Oxford. He brought his whole fortune with him there; it was but a trifle; however he was resolved to venture it all. Good fortune seemed kinder than could be expected. Without the smallest skill in play, he won a sum sufficient to make any unambitious man happy. His desire of gain increasing with his gains, in the October following he was at all, and added four thousand pounds to his former capital. Mr. Nash, one night, after losing a considerable sum to this undeserving son of fortune, invited him to supper. "Sir," cried this honest, though veteran gamester, "perhaps you may imagine I have invited you, in order to have my revenge at home; but I scorn so inhospitable an action. I desired the favour of your company to give you some advice, which, you will pardon me, sir, you seem to stand in need of. You are now high in spirits, and drawn away by a torrent of success; but there will come a time, when you will repent having left the calm of a college life for the turbulent profession of a gamester. Ill runs will come, as sure as day and night succeed each other. Be therefore advised, remain content with your present gains; for be persuaded, that had you the Bank of England, with your present ignorance of gaming, it would vanish like a fairy dream. You are a stranger to me; but to convince you of the part I take in your welfare, I'll give you fifty guineas, to forfeit twenty every time you lose two hundred at one sitting." The young gentleman refused his offer, and was at last undone!

The late Duke of B. being chagrined at losing a considerable sum, pressed Mr. Nash to tie him up for the future from playing deep. Accordingly, the Beau gave his Grace a hundred guineas, to forfeit ten thousand whenever he lost a sum to the same amount at play, in one sittting. The duke loved play to distraction, and soon after, at hazard, lost eight thousand guineas, and was going to throw for three thousand more, when Nash, catching hold of the dice-box, entreated his Grace to reflect upon the penalty if he lost; the duke for that time desisted; but so strong was the furor of play upon him, that soon after, losing a considerable sum at Newmarket, he was contented to pay the penalty.

When the late Earl of T——d was a youth, he was passionately fond of play, and never better pleased than with having Mr. Nash for his antagonist. Nash saw with concern his lordship's foible, and undertook to cure him, though by a very disagreeable remedy. Conscious of his own superior skill, he determined to engage him in single play for a very considerable sum. His lordship, in proportion as he lost his game, lost his temper too; and as he approached the gulf, seemed still more eager for ruin. He lost his estate: some writings were put into the winner's possession; his very equipage was deposited as a last stake, and he lost that also. But, when our generous gamester had found his lordship sufficiently punished for his temerity, he returned all; only stipulating, that he should be paid five thousand pounds whenever he should think proper to make the demand. However, he never made any such demand during his lordship's life; but some time after his decease, Mr. Nash's affairs being in the wane, he demanded the money of his lordship's heirs, who honourably paid it without any hesitation.

But whatever skill Nash might have acquired by long practice in play, he was never formed by nature for a successful gamester. He was constitutionally passionate and generous. To acquire a perfection in that art, a man must be naturally phlegmatic, reserved, and cool; every passion must learn to obey control; but he frequently was unable to restrain the violence of his, and was often betrayed by this means into unbecoming rudeness, or childish impertinence; was sometimes a minion of fortune, and as often depressed by adversity. While others made considerable fortunes at the gaming-table, he was ever in the power of chance; nor did even the intimacy with which he was received by the great, place him in a state of independence.

The considerable inconveniences that were found to result from a permission of gaming, at length attracted the attention of the legislature, and in the twelfth year of George II. the most prevalent games at that time were declared fraudulent and unlawful. Every age has had its peculiar modes of gaming. The games of Gleek, Primero, In-and-In, and several others now exploded, employed our sharping ancestors; to these succeeded the Ace of Hearts, Pharaoh, Basset, and Hazard, all games of chance like the former. But though in these the chances seemed equal to the novice, in general those who kept the bank were considerable winners. The Act, therefore, passed upon this occasion, declared all such games and lotteries illicit, and directed that all who should set up such games should forfeit two hundred pounds, to be levied by distress on the offender's goods; one-third to go to the informer, the residue to the poor. The Act further declared, that every person who played in any place, except in the royal palace where his majesty resided, should forfeit fifty pounds, and should be condemned to pay treble costs in case of an appeal.

This law was scarcely made, before it was eluded by the invention of divers fraudulent and deceitful games; and a particular game, called Passage, was daily practised, and contributed to the ruin of thousands. To prevent this, the ensuing year it was enacted, that this and every other game invented, or to be invented with one die, or more, or any other instrument of the same nature, with numbers thereon, should be subject to a similar penalty; and at the same time, the persons playing with such instruments should be punished as above.

This amendment of the law soon gave birth to new evasions; the game of Rolly-Polly, Marlborough's Battles, but particularly the E O, were set up; and, strange to observe, several of those very noblemen who had given their voices to suppress gaming were the most ready to encourage it. This game was at first set up at Tunbridge. It was invented by one C——k, and carried on between him and one Mr. A——e, proprietor of the assembly-room at that place; and was reckoned extremely profitable to the bank, as it gained two and a half per cent. on all that was lost or won.

As all gaming was suppressed but this, Nash was now utterly destitute of any resource that he could expect from his superior skill and long experience in the art. The money to be gained in private gaming is at best but trifling, and the opportunity precarious. The minds of the generality of mankind shrink with their circumstances; and Nash, upon the immediate prospect of poverty, was now mean enough (I will call it no worse) to enter into a confederacy with those low creatures to evade the law, and to share the plunder. The occasion was as follows. The profits of the table were, as I observed, divided between C——k the inventor, and A——e the room-keeper. The first year's profits were extraordinary, and A——e, the room-keeper, now began to wish himself sole proprietor. The combinations of the worthless are ever of short duration. The next year, therefore, A——e turned C——k out of his room, and set up the game for himself. The gentlemen and ladies who frequented the wells, unmindful of the immense profit gained by these reptiles, still continued to game as before; and the keeper was triumphing in the success of his politics, when he was informed, that C——k and his friends had hired the crier to cry the game down. The consequences of this would have been fatal to A——e's interest; for by this means frauds might have been discovered, which would deter even the most ardent lovers of play. Immediately, therefore, while the crier was yet upon the walks, he applied to Mr. Nash to stop these proceedings, and at the same time offered him a fourth share of the bank, which Nash was mean enough to accept. This is the greatest blot in his life; and this, it is hoped, will find pardon.

The day after, the inventor offered one-half of the bank; but this Mr. Nash thought proper to refuse, being pre-engaged to A——e. Upon which, being disappointed, he applied to one Mr. J——e, and under his protection another table was set up, and the company seemed to be divided equally between them. I cannot reflect without surprise at the folly of the gentlemen and ladies, in suffering themselves to be thus parcelled out between a pack of sharpers, and to be defrauded of their money, without even the show of opposition. The company thus divided, Mr. Nash once more availed himself of their parties, and prevailed upon them to unite their banks, and to divide the gains into three shares, of which he reserved one to himself.

Nash had hitherto enjoyed a fluctuating fortune; and had he taken the advantage of the present opportunity, he might have been for the future not only above want, but even in circumstances of opulence. Had he cautiously employed himself in computing the benefits of the table, and exacting his stipulated share, he might have soon grown rich; but he entirely left the management of it to the people of the rooms; he took them (as he says in one of his memorials upon this occasion) to be honest, and never inquired what was won or lost; and it is probable they were seldom assiduous in informing him. I find a secret pleasure in thus displaying the insecurity of friendships among the base. They pretended to pay him regularly at first; but he soon discovered, as he says, that at Tunbridge he had suffered to the amount of two thousand guineas.

In the meantime, as the E O table thus succeeded at Tunbridge, Mr. Nash was resolved to introduce it at Bath, and previously asked the opinion of several lawyers, who declared it no way illegal. In consequence of this, he wrote to Mrs. A——e, who kept one of the great rooms at Bath, acquainting her with the profits attending such a scheme, and proposing to have a fourth share with her and Mr. W——, the proprietor of the other room, for his authority and protection. To this Mr. W—— and she returned for answer, that they would grant him a fifth share; which he consented to accept. Accordingly, he made a journey to London, and bespoke two tables, one for each room, at the rate of fifteen pounds each table.

The tables were no sooner set up at Bath, than they were frequented by a greater concourse of gamesters than those at Tunbridge. Men of that infamous profession, from every part of the kingdom, and even other parts of Europe, flocked here to feed on the ruins of each other's fortune. This afforded another opportunity for Nash to become rich; but, as at Tunbridge, he thought the people here also would take care of him, and therefore he employed none to look after his interest. The first year they paid him what he thought just; the next, the woman of the room dying, her son paid him, and showed his books. Some time after the people of the rooms offered him one hundred pounds a year each for his share, which he refused; every succeeding year they continued to pay him less and less, until at length he found, as he pretends, that he had thus lost not less than twenty thousand pounds.

Thus they proceeded, deceiving the public and each other, until the legislature thought proper to suppress these seminaries of vice. It was enacted, that after the 24th of June, 1745, none should be permitted to keep a house, room, or place, for playing, upon pain of such forfeitures as were declared in former acts instituted for that purpose.

The legislature likewise amended a law, made in the reign of Queen Anne, for recovering money lost at play, on the oath of the winner. By this Act, no person was rendered incapable of being a witness; and every person present at a gaming-table might be summoned by the magistrate who took cognizance of the affair. No privilege of parliament was allowed to those convicted of having gaming-tables in their houses. Those who lost ten pounds at one time were liable to be indicted within six months after the offence was committed; and being convicted, were to be fined five times the value won or lost, for the use of the poor. Any offender, before conviction, discovering another, so as to be convicted, was to be discharged from the penalties incurred by his own offences.

By this wise and just Act, all Nash's future hopes of succeeding by the tables were blown up. He had now only the justice and generosity of his confederates to trust to; but that he soon found to be a vain expectation; for, if we can depend on his own memorials, what at one time they confessed, they would at another deny; and though upon some occasions they seemed at variance with each other, yet when they were to oppose him, whom they considered as a common enemy, they generally united with confidence and success. He now therefore had nothing but a lawsuit to confide in for redress; and this is ever the last expedient to retrieve a desperate fortune. He accordingly threw his suit into Chancery, and by this means the public became acquainted with what he had long endeavoured to conceal. They now found that he was himself concerned in the gaming-tables, of which he only seemed the conductor; and that he had shared part of the spoil, though he complained of having been defrauded of a just share.

The success of his suit was what might have been naturally expected: he had but at best a bad cause, and as the oaths of the defendants were alone sufficient to cast him in Chancery, it was not surprising that he was nonsuited. But the consequence of this affair was much more fatal than he had imagined: it lessened him in the esteem of the public; it drew several enemies against him, and in some measure diminished the authority of any defence he could make. From that time (about the year 1745) I find this good-natured but misguided man involved in continual disputes, every day calumniated with some new slander, and continually endeavouring to obviate its effects.

Upon these occasions his usual method was, by printed bills handed about among his acquaintance, to inform the public of his most private transactions with some of those creatures with whom he had formerly associated; but these apologies served rather to blacken his antagonists than to vindicate him. They were in general extremely ill written, confused, obscure, and sometimes unintelligible. By these however it appeared, that W—— was originally obliged to him for the resort of company to his room; that Lady H., who had all the company before W——'s room was built, offered Nash a hundred pounds for his protection; which he refused, having previously promised to support Mr. W——. It appears by these apologies, that the persons concerned in the rooms made large fortunes, while Nash still continued in pristine indigence; and that his nephew, for whom he had at first secured one of the rooms, was left in as great distress as he.

His enemies were not upon this occasion contented with aspersing him, as a confederate with sharpers; they even asserted, that he embezzled the subscriptions of gentlemen and ladies, which were given for useful or charitable purposes. But to such aspersions he answered by declaring, to use his own expression, before God and man, that he never diverted one shilling of the said subscriptions to his own use; nor was he ever thought to have done it till new enemies started up against him.

Perhaps the reader may be curious to see one of these memorials, written by himself; and I will indulge his curiosity, merely to show a specimen of the style and manner of a man whose whole life was passed in a round of gaiety and conversation, whose jests were a thousand times repeated, and whose company was courted by every son and daughter of fashion. The following is particularly levelled against those who, in the latter part of his life, took every opportunity to traduce his character:—

"A MONITOR.

"'For the Lord hateth lying and deceitful lips.'
—*Psalm.*

"The curse denounced in my motto is sufficient to intimidate any person who is not quite abandoned in their evil ways, and who have any fear of God before their eyes; everlasting burnings are a terrible reward for their misdoings; and nothing but the most hardened sinners will oppose the judgment of heaven, being without end. This reflection must be shocking to such as are conscious to themselves of having erred from the sacred dictates of the Psalmist; and who, following the blind impulse of passion, daily forge lies and deceit, to annoy their neighbour. But there are joys in heaven which they can never arrive at, whose whole study is to destroy the peace and harmony and good order of society in this place."

This carries little the air of a bagatelle; it rather seems a sermon in miniature, so different are some men in the closet and in conversation. The following I have taken at random from a heap of other memorials, all tending to set his combination with the afore-mentioned parties in a proper light.

"E O was first set up in A——e's room, the profits divided between one C——k (the inventor of the game) and A——e.

"The next year A——e, finding the game so advantageous, turned C——k out of his room, and set the game up himself, but C——k and his friends hired the crier to cry the game down; upon which A——e came running to me to stop it, after he had cried it once, which I immediately did, and turned the crier off the walks.

"Then A——e asked me to go a fourth with him in the bank, which I consented to. C——k next day took me into his room which he had hired, and proffered me to go half with him, which I refused, being engaged before to A——e.

"J——e then set up the same game, and complained that he had not half play at his room; upon which I made them agree to join their banks, and divide equally the gain and loss, and I to go like share in the bank.

"I, taking them to be honest, never inquired what was won or lost, and thought they paid me honestly, till it was discovered that they had defrauded me of 2,000 guineas.

"I then arrested A——e, who told me I must go into Chancery, and that I should begin with the people of Bath, who had cheated me of ten times as much; and told my attorney that J——e had cheated me of 500, and wrote me word that I probably had it not under his hand, which never was used in play.

"Upon my arresting A——e, I received a letter not to prosecute J——e, for he would be a very good witness; I writ a discharge to J——e for 125*l.* in full, though he never paid me a farthing, upon his telling me if his debts were paid he was not worth a shilling.

"Every article of this I can prove from

A—e's own mouth, as a reason that he allowed the bank-keepers but 10 per cent. because I went 20, and his suborning . . . to alter his informations.

"RICHARD NASH."

This gentleman's simplicity, in trusting persons whom he had no previous reasons to place confidence in, seems to be one of those lights in his character which, while they impeach his understanding, do honour to his benevolence. The low and timid are ever suspicious; but a heart impressed with honourable sentiments, expects from others sympathetic sincerity.

But now that we have viewed his conduct as a gamester, and seen him on that side of his character, which is by far the most unfavourable, seen him declining from his former favour and esteem, the just consequence of his quitting, though but ever so little, the paths of honour; let me turn to those brighter parts, which gained him the affection of his friends, the esteem of the corporation which he assisted, and may possibly attract the attention of posterity. By his successes we shall find, that figuring in life proceeds less from the possession of great talents, than from the proper application of moderate ones. Some great minds are only fitted to put forth their powers in the storm, and the occasion is often wanting during a whole life for a great exertion: but trifling opportunities of shining are almost every hour offered to the little sedulous mind, and a person thus employed, is not only more pleasing, but more useful in a state of tranquil society.

Though gaming first introduced him into polite company, this alone could hardly have carried him forward, without the assistance of a genteel address, much vivacity, some humour, and some wit. But, once admitted into the circle of the beau monde, he then laid claim to all the privileges by which it is distinguished. Among others, in the early part of his life, he entered himself professedly into the service of the fair sex; he set up for a man of gallantry and intrigue; and, if we can credit the boasts of his old age, he often succeeded. In fact, the business of love somewhat resembles the business of physic; no matter for qualifications, he that makes vigorous pretensions to either is surest of success. Nature had bv no means formed Mr. Nash for a *beau garçon;* his person was clumsy, too large and awkward, and his features harsh, strong, and peculiarly irregular; yet even with those disadvantages, he made love, became a universal admirer of the sex, and was universally admired. He was possessed, at least, of some requisites of a lover. He had assiduity, flattery, fine clothes, and as much wit as the ladies he addressed. Wit, flattery, and fine clothes, he used to say, were enough to debauch a nunnery. But my fair readers of the present day are exempt from this scandal; and it is no matter now, what he said of their grandmothers.

As Nestor was a man of three ages, so Nash sometimes humorously called himself a beau of three generations. He had seen flaxen bobs succeeded by majors, which in their turn gave way to negligents, which were at last totally routed by bags and ramilies. The manner in which gentlemen managed their amours, in those different ages of fashion, were not more different than their periwigs. The lover in the reign of King Charles was solemn, majestic, and formal. He visited his mistress in state; languished for the favour, kneeled when he toasted his goddess, walked with solemnity, performed the most trifling things with decorum, and even took snuff with a flourish. The beau of the latter part of Queen Anne's reign was disgusted with so much formality; he was pert, smart, and lively; his billets-doux were written in a quite different style to that of his antiquated predecessor; he was ever laughing at his own ridiculous situation; till at last, he persuaded the lady to become as ridiculous as himself. The beau of the third age, in which Mr. Nash died, was still more extraordinary than either; his whole secret in intrigue consisted in perfect indifference. The only way to make love now, I have heard Mr. Nash say, was to take no manner of notice of the lady; which method was found the surest way to secure her affections.

However these things be, this gentleman's amours were in reality very much confined in the second and third age of intrigue; his character was too public for a lady to consign her reputation to his keeping. But in the beginning of life, it is said, he knew the secret history of the times, and contributed himself to swell the page of scandal. Were I upon the present occasion to hold the pen of a novelist, I could recount some amours in which he was successful. I could fill a volume with little anecdotes, which contain neither pleasure nor instruction; with histories of professing lovers, and poor believing girls deceived by such professions. But such adventures are easily written, and as easily achieved. The plan even of fictitious novel is quite exhausted; but truth, which I have followed here, and ever design to follow, presents in the affair of love scarce any variety. The manner in which one reputation is lost, exactly resembles that by which another is taken away. The gentleman begins at timid distance, grows more bold, becomes rude, till the lady is married or undone: such is the substance of every modern novel; nor will I gratify the pruriency of folly at the expense of every other pleasure my narration may afford.

Mr. Nash did not long continue a universal gallant; but, in the earlier years of his reign, entirely gave up his endeavours to deceive the sex, in order to become the honest protector of their innocence, the guardian of their reputation, and a friend to their virtue. This was a character he bore for many years, and supported it with integrity, assiduity, and success. It was his constant practice to do everything in his power to prevent the fatal consequences of rash and inconsiderate love; and there are many persons now alive, who owe their present happiness to his having interrupted the progress of an amour that threatened to become unhappy, or even criminal, by privately making their guardians or parents acquainted with what he could discover And his manner of disconcerting these schemes was such as generally secured him from the rage of the disappointed. One night when I was in Wiltshire's room, Nash came up to a lady and her daughter, who were people of no inconsiderable fortune, and bluntly told the mother *she had better be at home:* this was at that time thought an audacious piece of impertinence, and the lady turned away piqued and disconcerted. Nash, however, pursued her and repeated the words again, when the old lady, wisely conceiving there might be some hidden meaning couched under this seeming insolence, retired, and coming to her lodgings found a coach and six at the door, which a sharper had provided to carry off her eldest daughter.

I shall beg leave to give some other instances of Mr. Nash's good-nature on these occasions, as I have had the accounts from himself. At the conclusion of the treaty of peace at Utrecht, Colonel M. was one of the thoughtless, agreeable, gay creatures, that drew the attention of the company at Bath. He danced and talked with great vivacity; and when he gamed among the ladies, he showed that his attention was employed rather upon their hearts than their fortunes. His own fortune however was a trifle, when compared to the elegance of his expense; and his imprudence at last was so great, that it obliged him to sell an annuity arising from his commission, to keep up his splendour a little longer.

However thoughtless he might be, he had the happiness of gaining the affections of Miss L., whose father designed her a very large fortune. This lady was courted by a nobleman of distinction; but she refused his addresses, resolved upon gratifying rather her inclinations than her avarice. The intrigue went on successfully between her and the colonel, and they both would certainly have been married and been undone, had not Mr. Nash apprised her father of their intentions. The old gentleman recalled his daughter from Bath, and offered Nash a very considerable present for the care he had taken, which he refused.

In the meantime Colonel M. had an intimation how his intrigue came to be discovered, and, by taxing Nash, found that his suspicions were not without foundation. A challenge was the immediate consequence, which the king of Bath, conscious of having only done his duty, thought proper to decline. As none are permitted to wear swords at Bath, the colonel found no opportunity of gratifying his resentment, and waited with impatience to find Mr. Nash in town, to require proper satisfaction.

During this interval, however, he found his creditors become too importunate for him to remain longer at Bath; and his finances and credit being quite exhausted, he took the desperate resolution of going over to the Dutch army in Flanders, where he enlisted himself a volunteer. Here he underwent all the fatigues of a private sentinel, with the additional misery of receiving no pay, and his friends in England gave out that he was shot at the battle of ——.

In the meantime, the nobleman pressed his passion with ardour; but during the progress of his amour, the young lady's father died, and left her heiress to a fortune of fifteen hundred a year. She thought herself now disengaged from her former passion. An absence of two years had in some measure abated her love for the colonel; and the assiduity, the merit, and real regard of the gentleman who still continued to solicit her, were almost too powerful for her constancy. Mr. Nash, in the meantime, took every opportunity of inquiring after Colonel M., and found that he had for some time been returned to England, but had changed his name, in order to avoid the fury of his creditors, and was entered into a company of strolling players, at that time exhibiting at Peterborough.

He now therefore thought he owed the colonel, in justice, an opportunity of promoting his fortune, as he had once deprived him of an occasion of satisfying his love. Our Beau therefore invited the lady to be of a party to Peterborough, and offered his own equipage, which was then one of the most elegant in England, to conduct her there. The proposal being accepted, the lady, the nobleman, and Mr. Nash arrived in town just as the players were going to begin.

Colonel M., who used every means of remaining incognito, and who was too proud to make his distresses known to any of his former acquaintance, was now degraded into the character of Tom in the "Conscious Lovers." Miss L. was placed in the foremost row of the spectators, her lord on one side, and the impatient Nash on the other, when the unhappy youth appeared in that despicable situation upon the stage. The moment he came on, his former mistress struck his view; but his amazement was increased when he saw her fainting away in the arms of those who sat behind her. He was incapable of proceeding, and scarcely knowing what he did, he flew and caught her in his arms.

"Colonel," cried Nash, when they were in some measure recovered, "you once thought me your enemy, because I endeavoured to prevent you both from ruining each other; you were then wrong, and you have long had my forgiveness. If you love well enough now for matrimony, you fairly have my consent, and d—— him, say I, that attempts to part you." Their nuptials were solemnized soon after, and affluence added a zest to all their future enjoyments. Mr. Nash had the thanks of each, and he afterwards spent several agreeable days in that society which he had contributed to render happy.

I shall beg the reader's patience, while I give another instance, in which he ineffectually offered his assistance and advice. This story is not from himself, but told us partly by Mr. Wood, the architect of Bath, as it fell particularly within his own knowledge, and partly from another memoir to which he refers.

Miss Sylvia S—— was descended from one of the best families in the kingdom, and was left a large fortune upon her sister's decease. She had early in life been introduced into the best company, and contracted a passion for elegance and expense. It is usual to make the heroine of a story very witty and very beautiful, and such circumstances are so surely expected, that they are scarce attended to. But whatever the finest poet could conceive of wit, or the most celebrated painter imagine of beauty, were excelled in the perfections of this young lady. Her superiority in both was allowed by all who either heard or had seen her. She was naturally gay, generous to a fault, good-natured to the highest degree, affable in conversation, and some of her letters and other writings, as well in verse as prose, would have shone amongst those of the most celebrated wits of this, or any other age, had they been published.

But these great qualifications were marked by another, which lessened the value of them all. She was imprudent. But let it not be imagined that her reputation or honour suffered by her imprudence: I only mean, she had no knowledge of the use of money; she relieved distress by putting herself into the circumstances of the object whose wants she supplied.

She was arrived at the age of nineteen, when the crowd of her lovers and the continual repetition of new flattery had taught her to think she could never be forsaken, and never poor. Young ladies are apt to expect a certainty of success from a number of lovers; and yet I have seldom seen a girl courted by a hundred lovers that found a husband in any. Before the choice is fixed, she has either lost her reputation or her good sense; and the loss of either is sufficient to consign her to perpetual virginity.

Among the number of this young lady's lovers was the celebrated S——, who, at that time, went by the name of "the good-natured man." This gentleman, with talents that might have done honour to humanity, suffered himself to fall at length into the lowest state of debasement. He followed the dictates of every newest passion; his love, his pity, his generosity, and even his friendships were all in excess; he was unable to make head against any of his sensations or desires, but they were in general worthy wishes and desires, for he was constitutionally virtuous. This gentleman, who at last died in gaol, was at that time this lady's envied favourite.

It is probable that he, thoughtless creature, had no other prospect from this amour but that of passing the present moments agreeably. He only courted dissipation, but the lady's thoughts were fixed on happiness. At length, however, his debts amounting to a considerable sum, he was arrested and thrown into prison. He endeavoured at first to conceal his situation from his beautiful mistress; but she soon came to a knowledge of his distress, and took the fatal resolution of freeing him from confinement by discharging all the demands of his creditors.

Mr. Nash was at that time in London, and represented to the thoughtless young lady, that such a measure would effectually ruin both; that so warm a concern for the interests of Mr. S. would in the first place quite impair her fortune in the eyes of our sex, and what was worse, lessen her reputation in those of her own. He added, that thus bringing Mr. S. from prison would be only a temporary relief; that a mind so generous as his would become bankrupt under the load of gratitude; and instead of improving in friendship or affection, he would only study to avoid a creditor he could never repay; that though small favours produce good-will, great ones destroy friendship. These admonitions, however, were disregarded, and she found, too late, the prudence and truth of her adviser. In short, her fortune was by this means exhausted; and, with all her attractions, she found her acquaintance began to disesteem her in proportion as she became poor.

In this situation she accepted Mr. Nash's invitation of returning to Bath. He promised to introduce her to the best company there, and he was assured that her merit would do the rest. Upon her very first appearance, ladies of the highest distinction courted her friendship and esteem; but a settled melancholy had taken possession of her mind, and no amusements that they could propose were sufficient to divert it. Yet still, as if from habit, she followed the crowd in its levities, and frequented those places where all persons endeavoured to forget themselves in the bustle of ceremony and show.

Her beauty, her simplicity, and her unguarded situation soon drew the attention of a designing wretch, who at that time kept one of the rooms at Bath, and who thought that this lady's merit, properly managed, might turn to good account. This woman's name was dame Lindsey, a creature who, though vicious, was in appearance sanctified, and, though designing, had some wit and humour.

She began by the humblest assiduity to ingratiate herself with Miss S——; showed that she could be amusing as a companion, and, by frequent offers of money, proved that she could be useful as a friend. Thus by degrees she gained an entire ascendency over this poor, thoughtless, deserted girl; and in less than one year, namely about 1727, Miss S., without ever transgressing the laws of virtue, had entirely lost her reputation. Whenever a person was wanting to make up a party for play at dame Lindsey's, Sylvia, as she was then familiarly called, was sent for, and was obliged to suffer all those slights which the rich but too often let fall upon their inferiors in point of fortune.

In most, even the greatest minds, the heart at last becomes level with the meanness of its condition; but in this charming girl, it struggled hard with adversity, and yielded to every encroachment of contempt with sullen reluctance. But though in the course of three years she was in the very eye of public inspection, yet Mr. Wood, the architect, avers, that he could never, by the strictest observations, perceive her to be tainted with any other vice than that of suffering herself to be decoyed to the gambling-table, and at her own hazard playing for the amusement and advantage of others. Her friend Mr. Nash, therefore, thought proper to induce her to break off all connexions with dame Lindsey, and to rent part of Mr. Wood's house, in Queen Square, where she behaved with the utmost complaisance, regularity, and virtue.

In this situation, her detestation of life still continued. She found that time would infallibly deprive her of part of her attractions, and that continual solicitude would impair the rest. With these reflections she would frequently entertain herself and an old faithful maid in the vales of Bath, whenever the weather would permit them to walk out. She would even sometimes start questions in company, with seeming unconcern, in order to know what act of suicide was easiest, and which was attended with the smallest pain. When tired with exercise, she generally retired to meditation, and she became habituated to early hours of sleep and rest; but when the weather prevented her usual exercise, and her sleep was thus more difficult, she made it a rule to rise from her bed, and walk about her chamber, till she began to find an inclination for repose.

This custom made it necessary for her to order a candle to be kept burning all night in her room; and the maid usually, when she withdrew, locked the chamber door, and pushing the key under it beyond reach, her mistress, by that constant method, lay undisturbed till seven o'clock in the morning, when she arose, unlocked the door, and rang the bell as a signal for the maid to return.

This state of seeming piety, regularity, and prudence continued for some time, till the gay, celebrated, toasted Miss Sylvia was sunk into a housekeeper to the gentleman at whose house she lived. She was unable to keep company, for want of the elegancies of dress, which are the usual passports among the polite; and was too haughty to seem to want them. The fashionable, the amusing, and the polite in society now seldom visited her; and from being once the object of every eye, she was now deserted by all, and preyed upon by the bitter reflections of her own imprudence.

Mr. Wood and part of his family were gone to London, and Miss Sylvia was left with the rest as a governess at Bath. She sometimes saw Mr. Nash, and acknowledged the friendship of his admonitions, though she refused to accept any other marks of his generosity than that of advice. Upon the close of the day on which Mr. Wood was expected to return from London, she expressed some uneasiness at the disappointment of not seeing him, took particular care to settle the affairs of his family, and then as usual sat down to meditation. She now cast a retrospect over her past misconduct, and her approaching misery; she saw that even affluence gave her no real happiness, and from indigence she thought nothing could be hoped but lingering calamity. She at length conceived the fatal resolution of leaving a life in which she could see no corner for comfort, and terminating a scene of imprudence in suicide.

Thus resolved, she sat down at her dining-room window, and with cool intrepidity wrote the following lines on one of the panes of the window:—

"O Death! thou pleasing end of human woe!
Thou cure for life! thou greatest good below!
Still mayst thou fly the coward and the slave,
And thy soft slumbers only bless the brave."

She then went into company with the most cheerful serenity, talked of indifferent subjects till supper, which she ordered to be got ready in a little library belonging to the family. There she spent the remaining hours preceding bed-time, in dandling two of Mr. Wood's children on her knees. In retiring from thence to her chamber, she went into the nursery to take her leave of another child, as it lay sleeping in the cradle. Struck with the innocence of the little babe's looks, and the consciousness of her meditated guilt, she could not avoid bursting into tears and hugging it in her arms; she then bid her old servant a good night, for the first time that she had ever done so, and went to bed as usual.

It is probable she soon quitted her bed, and was seized with an alternation of passions, before she yielded to the impulse of despair. She dressed herself in clean linen and white garments of every kind, like a bride-maid. Her gown was pinned over her breast, just as a nurse pins the swaddling-clothes of an infant. A pink silk girdle was the instrument with which she resolved to terminate her misery, and this was lengthened by another made of gold thread. The end of the former was tied with a noose, and the latter with three knots, at a small distance from one another.

Thus prepared, she sat down again and read; for she left the book open at that place in the story of Olympia, in the Orlando Furioso of Ariosto, where, by the perfidy and ingratitude of her bosom friend, she was ruined and left to the mercy of an unpitying world. This fatal event gave her fresh spirits to go through her tragical purpose; so, standing upon a stool, and flinging the girdle, which was tied round her neck, over a closet door that opened into her chamber, she remained suspended. Her weight, however, broke the girdle, and the poor despairer fell on the floor with such violence that her fall awakened a workman that lay in the house, about half an hour after two o'clock. Recovering herself, she began to walk about the room, as her usual custom was when she wanted sleep; and the workman imagining it to be only some ordinary accident, again went to sleep. She once more, therefore, had recourse to a stronger girdle made of silver thread, and this kept her suspended till she died. Her old maid continued in the morning to wait as usual for the ringing of the bell, and protracted her patience, hour after hour, till two o'clock in the afternoon; when the workmen at length entering the room through the window, found their unfortunate mistress still hanging and quite cold. The coroner's jury being impanelled, brought in their verdict lunacy, and her corpse was next night decently buried in her father's grave, at the charge of a female companion, with whom she had for many years an inseparable intimacy.

Thus ended a female wit, a toast, and a gamester; loved, admired, and forsaken: formed for the delight of society, fallen by imprudence into an object of pity. Hundreds in high life lamented her fate, and wished, when too late, to redress her injuries. They who once had helped to impair her fortune, now regretted that they had assisted in so mean a pursuit. The little effects she had left behind were bought up with the greatest avidity, by those who desired to preserve some token of a companion that once had given them such delight. The remembrance of every virtue she was possessed of was now improved by pity. Her former follies were few, but the last swelled them to a large amount; and she remains the strongest instance to posterity, that want of prudence alone almost cancels every other virtue.

In all this unfortunate lady's affairs Mr. Nash took a peculiar concern; he directed her when they played, advised her when she deviated from the rules of caution, and performed the last offices of friendship after her decease, by raising the auction of her little effects.

But he was not only the assistant and the friend of the fair sex; he was also their defender. He secured their persons from insult, and their reputations from scandal. Nothing offended him more than a young fellow's pretending to receive favours from ladies he probably never saw. Nothing pleased him so much as seeing such a piece of deliberate mischief punished. Nash and one of his friends, being newly arrived at Tunbridge from Bath, were one day on the walks, and, seeing a young fellow of fortune with whom they had some slight acquaintance, joined him. After the usual chat and news of the day was over, Mr. Nash asked him, how long he had been at the Wells and what company was there? The other replied, he had been at Tunbridge a month: but as for company, he could find as good at a Tyburn ball. Not a soul was to be seen, except a parcel of gamesters and strumpets, who would grant the last favour for a single stake at the Pharaoh bank. "Look you there," continued he, "that goddess of midnight, so fine at t'other end of the walks, by Jove she was mine this morning for half a guinea; and she there, who brings up the rear with powdered hair and dirty ruffles, she's pretty enough, but cheap, perfectly cheap: why, my boys, to my own knowledge, you may have her for a crown and dish of chocolate into the bargain—last Wednesday night we were happy." "Hold there, sir," cried the gentleman; "as for your having the first lady, it is possible it may be true, and I intend to ask her about it, for she is my sister; but as to your being happy with the other last Wednesday, I am sure you are a lying rascal. She is my wife, and we came here but last night." The buck vainly asked pardon; the gentleman was going to give him proper chastisement, when Mr. Nash interposed in his behalf, and obtained his pardon upon condition that he quitted Tunbridge immediately.

But Mr. Nash not only took care, during his administration, to protect the ladies from the insults of our sex, but to guard them from the slanders of each other. He, in the first place, prevented any animosities that might arise from place and precedence, by being previously acquainted with the rank and quality of almost every family in the British dominions. He endeavoured to render scandal odious, by marking it as the result of envy and folly united. Not even Solon could have enacted a wiser law in such a society as Bath. The gay, the heedless, and the idle, who mostly compose the group of water-drinkers, seldom are at the pains of talking upon universal topics which require comprehensive thought or abstract reasoning. The adventures of the little circle of their own acquaintance or of some names of quality and fashion make up their whole conversation. But it is too likely, that when we mention those, we wish to depress them, in order to render ourselves more conspicuous: scandal must therefore have fixed her throne at Bath preferable to any other part of the kingdom. However, though these endeavours could not totally suppress this custom among the fair, yet they gained him the friendship of several ladies of distinction who had smarted pretty severely under the lash of censure.

Among this number was the old Duchess of Marlborough, who conceived a particular friendship for him, and which continued during her life. She frequently consulted him in several concerns of a private nature. Her letting leases, building bridges, or forming canals, were often carried on under his guidance; but she advised with him particularly in purchasing liveries for the footmen; a business to which she thought his genius best adapted. As anything relative to her may please the curiosity of such as delight in the anecdotes and letters of the great, however dull and insipid, I shall beg leave to present them with one or two of her epistles, collected at a venture from several others to the same purpose.

"*To* MR. NASH, *at the Bath.*

"Blenheim, Sept. 18, 1724.

"Mr. Jennens will give you an account how little time I have in my power, and that will make my excuse for not thanking you sooner for the favour of your letter, and for the trouble you have given yourself in bespeaking the cloth, which I am sure will be good, since you have undertaken to order it. Pray ask Mrs. Jennens concerning the cascade, which will satisfy all doubts in that matter; she saw it play, which it will do in great beauty, for at least six hours together, and it runs enough to cover all the stones constantly, and is a hundred feet broad, which I am told is a much greater breadth than any cascade is in England; and this will be yet better than it is, when it is quite finished. This water is a great addition to this place, and the lake being thirty acres, out of which the cascade comes, and falls into the canal that goes through the bridge, it makes that look as if it was necessary, which before seemed so otherwise. I am your most humble servant,

"S. MARLBOROUGH."

"*To* MR. NASH, *at the Bath.*

"Marlborough-house, May, 17, 1735.

"SIR,—I have received the favour of yours of the 10th of May, with that from Mr. Harvey; and by last post I received a letter from Mr. Overton, a sort of a bailiff and a surveyor, whom I have employed a great while upon my estates in Wiltshire. He is a very active and very useful man of his sort. He writes to me, that Mr. Harvey has been with him, and brought him a paper, which I sent you. He says that, finding he was a man that was desirous to serve me, he had assisted him all he could, by informations which he has given; and that he should continue to assist him. I have writ to him that he did mighty well. There is likewise a considerable tenant of my Lord Bruce's, his name is Cannons, who has promised me his assistance towards recommending tenants for these farms. And if Mr. Harvey happens to know such a man, he may put him in mind of it. I am sure you will do me all the good you can. And I hope you are sure that I shall always be sensible of the obligations I have to you, and ever be your most thankful and obliged humble servant,

"S. MARLBOROUGH.

"Mr. Harvey may conclude to take any prices that were given you in the paper. But as I know that we have been scandalously cheated, if he finds that anything can be let better than it has been let, I do not doubt but he will do it."

The Duchess of Marlborough seems to have been not a much better writer than Mr. Nash; but she was worth many hundred thousand pounds, and that might console her. It may give splenetic philosophy, however, some scope for meditation, when it considers what a parcel of stupid trifles the world is ready to admire.

Whatever might have been Mr. Nash's other excellences, there was one in which few exceeded him; I mean his extensive humanity. None felt pity more strongly, and none made greater efforts to relieve distress. If I were to name any reigning and fashionable virtue in the present age, I think it should be charity. The numberless benefactions privately given, the various public solicitations for charity, and the success they meet with, serve to prove, that though we may fall short of our ancestors in other respects, yet in this instance we greatly excel them. I know not whether it may not be spreading the influence of Mr. Nash too widely to say, that he was one of the principal causes of introducing this noble emulation among the rich; but certain it is, no private man ever relieved the distresses of so many as he did.

Before gaming was suppressed, and in the meridian of his life and fortune, his benefactions were generally found to equal his other expenses. The money he got without pain he gave away without reluctance; and whenever unable to relieve a wretch who sued for assistance, he has been often seen to shed tears. A gentleman of broken fortune, one day standing behind his chair, as he was playing a game of picquet for two hundred pounds, and observing with what indifference he won the money, could not avoid whispering these words to another who stood by, "Heavens! how happy would all that money make me!" Nash, overhearing him, clapped the money into his hand; and cried, "Go and be happy."

About six-and-thirty years ago, a clergyman brought his family to Bath for the benefit of the waters. His wife laboured under a lingering disorder, which it was thought nothing but the Hot-wells could remove. The expenses of living there soon lessened the poor man's finances; his clothes were sold, piece by piece, to provide a temporary relief for his little family, and his appearance was at last so shabby, that, from the number of holes in his coat and stockings, Nash gave him the name of Doctor Cullender. Our beau, it seems, was rude enough to make a jest of poverty, though he had sensibility enough to relieve it. The poor clergyman combated his distresses with fortitude; and, instead of attempting to solicit relief, endeavoured to conceal them. Upon a living of thirty pounds a year he endeavoured to maintain his wife and six children; but all his resources at last failed him, and nothing but famine was seen in the wretched family. The poor man's circumstances were at last communicated to Nash; who, with his usual cheerfulness, undertook to relieve him. On a Sunday evening, at a public tea-drinking at Harrison's, he went about to collect a subscription, and began it himself by giving five guineas. By this means two hundred guineas were collected in less than two hours, and the poor family raised from the lowest despondence into affluence and felicity. A bounty so unexpected had a better influence even upon the woman's constitution than all that either the physicians or the waters of Bath could produce, and she recovered. But his good offices did not rest here. He prevailed upon a nobleman of his acquaintance to present the doctor with a living of 160*l.* a year, which made that happiness he had before produced, in some measure permanent.

In the severe winter of the year 1739 his charity was great, useful, and extensive. He frequently, at that season of calamity, entered the houses of the poor, whom he thought too proud to beg, and generously relieved them. The colliers were at this time peculiarly distressed; and in order to excite compassion, a number of them yoked themselves to a waggon loaded with coals, and drew it into Bath, and presented it to Mr. Nash. Their scheme had the proper effect. Mr. Nash procured them a subscription, and gave ten guineas towards it himself. The weavers also shared his bounty at that season. They came begging in a body into Bath, and he provided a plentiful dinner for their entertainment, and gave each a week's subsistence at going away.

There are few public charities to which he was not a subscriber, and many he principally contributed to support. Among others, Mr. Annesley, that strange example of the mutability of fortune, and the inefficacy of our laws, shared his interest and bounty. I have now before me a well-written letter, addressed to Mr. Nash, in order to obtain his interest for that unhappy gentleman: it comes from Mr. Henderson, a Quaker, who was Mr. Annesley's father's agent. This gentleman warmly espoused the young adventurer's interest, and, I am told, fell with him.

"London, October 23, 1756.

"My Good Friend,—When I had the honour of conversing with thee at Tunbridge, in September last, concerning that most singular striking case of Mr. Annesley, whom I have known since he was about six years old, I being then employed by the late Lord Baron of Altham, his father, as his agent. From what I know of the affairs of that family, I am well assured, that Mr. Annesley is the legitimate son of the late Lord Baron of Altham, and in consequence thereof is entitled to the honours and estates of Anglesey. Were I not well assured of his right to those honours and estates, I would not give countenance to his claim. I well remember, that thou then madest me a promise to assist him in soliciting a subscription, that was then begun at Tunbridge; but as that place was not within the limits of thy province, thou couldst not promise to do much there. But thou saidst, that in case he would go to Bath in the season, thou wouldst then and there show him how much thou wouldst be his friend.

"And now, my good friend, as the season is come on, and Mr. Annesley now at Bath, I beg leave to remind thee of that promise; and that thou wilt keep in full view the honour, the everlasting honour, that will naturally redound to thee from thy benevolence, and crown all the good actions of thy life. I say, now in the vale of life, to relieve a distressed young nobleman, to extricate so immense an estate from the hands of oppression; to do this, will fix such a ray of glory on thy memory, as will speak forth thy praise to future ages. This, with great respect, is the needful, from thy assured Friend,

"WILLIAM HENDERSON.

"Be pleased to give my respects to Mr. Annesley and his spouse."

Mr. Nash punctually kept his word with this gentleman. He began the subscription himself with the utmost liberality, and procured such a list of encouragers, as at once did honour to Mr. Annesley's cause and their own generosity. What a pity it was that this money, which was given for the relief of indigence only, went to feed a set of reptiles, who batten upon our weakness, miseries, and vice!

It may not be known to the generality of my readers, that the last act of the comedy called "Æsop," which was added to the French plot of Boursault by Mr. Vanbrugh, was taken from a story told of Mr. Nash upon a similar occasion. He had in the early part of life made proposals of marriage to Miss V——, of D——: his affluence at that time, and the favour which he was in with the nobility, readily induced the young lady's father to favour his addresses. However, upon opening the affair to herself, she candidly told him her affections were placed upon another, and that she could not possibly comply. Though this answer satisfied Mr. Nash, it was by no means sufficient to appease the father; and he peremptorily insisted upon her obedience. Things were carried to the last extremity, when Mr. Nash undertook to settle the affair; and desiring his favoured rival to be sent for, with his own hand presented his mistress to him, together with a fortune equal to what her father intended to give her. Such an uncommon instance of generosity had an instant effect upon the severe parent: he considered such disinterestedness as a just reproach to his own mercenary disposition, and took his daughter once more into favour. I wish, for the dignity of history, that the sequel could be concealed; but the young lady ran away with her footman, before half a year was expired, and her husband died of grief.

In general, the benefactions of a generous man are but ill bestowed. His heart seldom gives him leave to examine the real distress of the object which sues for pity; his good-nature takes the alarm too soon, and he bestows his fortune on only apparent wretchedness. The man naturally frugal, on the other hand, seldom relieves; but when he does, his reason, and not his sensations, generally find out the object. Every instance of his bounty is therefore permanent, and bears witness to his benevolence.

Of all the immense sums which Nash lavished upon real or apparent wretchedness, the effects, after a few years, seemed to disappear. His money was generally given to support immediate want, or to relieve improvident indolence, and therefore it vanished in an hour. Perhaps, towards the close of life, were he to look round on the thousand he had relieved, he would find but few made happy, or fixed by his bounty in a state of thriving industry: it was enough for him, that he gave to those that wanted; he never reflected that charity to some might impoverish himself without relieving them: he seldom considered the merit or the industry of the petitioner; or he rather fancied, that misery was an excuse for indolence and guilt. It was a usual saying of his, when he went to beg for any person in distress, that they who could stoop to the meanness of solicitation must certainly want the favour for which they petitioned.

In this manner, therefore, he gave away immense sums of his own, and still greater which he procured from others. His way was, when any person was proposed to him as an object of charity, to go round with his hat first among the nobility, according to their rank, and so on, till he left scarce a single person unsolicited. They who go thus about to beg for others, generally find a pleasure in the task. They consider, in some measure, every benefaction they procure as given by themselves, and have at once the pleasure of being liberal, without the self-reproach of being profuse.

But of all the instances of Nash's bounty, none does him more real honour than the pains he took in establishing an hospital at Bath, in which benefaction, however, Dr. Oliver had a great share. This was one of those well-guided charities, dictated by reason, and supported by prudence. By this institution, the diseased poor might recover health, when incapable of receiving it in any other part of the kingdom. As the disorders of the poor who could expect to find relief at Bath were mostly chronical, the expense of maintaining them there was found more than their parishes thought proper to afford. They therefore chose to support them in a continual state of infirmity, by a small allowance at home, rather than be at the charge of an expensive cure. An hospital therefore at Bath, it was thought, would be an asylum to those disabled creatures, and would, at the same time, give the physician a more thorough insight into the efficacy of the waters, from the regularity with which such patients would be obliged to take them. These inducements, therefore, influenced Dr. Oliver and Nash to promote a subscription towards such a benefaction. The design was set on foot so early as the year 1711, but was not completed till the year 1742. This delay, which seems surprising, was in fact owing to the want of a proper fund for carrying the work into execution. What I said above, of charity being the characteristic virtue of the present age, will be more fully evinced by comparing the old and new subscriptions for this hospital. These will show the difference between ancient and modern benevolence. When I run my eye over the list of those who subscribed in the year 1723, I find the subscriptions in general seldom rise above a guinea each person; so that, at that time, with all their efforts, they were unable to raise four hundred pounds; but in about twenty years after, each particular subscription was greatly increased—ten, twenty, thirty pounds, being the most ordinary sums then subscribed, and they soon raised above two thousand pounds for the purpose.

Thus, chiefly by the means of Dr. Oliver and Mr. Nash, but not without the assistance of the good Mr. Allen, who gave them the stone for building and other benefactions, this hospital was erected; and it is at present fitted up for the reception of one hundred and ten patients, the cases mostly paralytic or leprous.

The following conditions are observed, previous to admittance:—

"I. The case of the patient must be described by some physician or person of skill in the neighbourhood of the place where the patient has resided for some time; and this description, together with a certificate of the poverty of the patient, attested by some persons of credit, must be sent in a letter, post paid, directed to the registrar of the General Hospital of Bath.

"II. After the patient's case has been thus described, and sent, he must remain in his usual place or residence till he has notice of a vacancy, signified by a letter from the registrar.

"III. Upon the receipt of such a letter the patient must set forward for Bath, bringing with him this letter, the parish certificate, duly executed, and allowed by two justices, and three pounds caution-money, if from any part of England or Wales; but if the patient comes from Scotland or Ireland, then the caution-money to be deposited before admission is the sum of five pounds.

"IV. Soldiers may, instead of parish certificates, bring a certificate from their commanding officers, signifying to what corps they belong, and that they shall be received into the same corps, when discharged from the Hospital, in whatever condition they are. But it is necessary that their cases be described and sent previously, and that they bring with them three pounds caution-money.

"Note.—The intention of the caution-money is to defray the expenses of returning the patients after they are discharged from the Hospital, or of their burial in case they die there. The remainder of the caution-money, after these expenses are defrayed, will be returned to the person who made the deposit."

I am unwilling to leave this subject of his benevolence, because it is a virtue in his character which must stand almost single against an hundred follies; and it deserves the more to be insisted on, because it was large enough to outweigh them all. A man may be an hypocrite safely in every other instance but in charity: there are few who will buy the character of benevolence at the rate for which it must be acquired. In short, the sums he gave away were immense; and in old age, when at last grown too poor to give relief, "*he gave*," as the poet has it, "*all he had—a tear:*" when incapable of relieving the agonies of the wretched, he attempted to relieve his own by a flood of sorrow.

The sums he gave and collected for the Hospital were great, and his manner of doing it was no less admirable. I am told that he was once collecting money in Wiltshire's room for that purpose, when a lady entered, who is more remarkable for her wit than her charity, and not being able to pass by him unobserved, she gave him a pat with her fan, and said, "You must put down a trifle for me, Nash, for I have no money in my pocket." "Yes, madam," says he, "that I will with pleasure if your grace will tell me when to stop;" then taking an handful of guineas out of his pocket, he began to tell them into his white hat—"One, two, three, four, five——" "Hold, hold!" says the duchess, "consider what you are about." "Consider your rank and fortune, madam," says Nash, and continues telling—"six, seven, eight, nine, ten." Here the duchess called again, and seemed angry. "Pray compose yourself, madam," cried Nash, "and don't interrupt the work of charity—eleven, twelve, thirteen, fourteen, fifteen." Here the duchess stormed, and caught hold of his hand. "Peace, madam," says Nash, "you shall have your name written in letters of gold, madam, and upon the front of the building, madam. Sixteen, seventeen, eighteen, nineteen, twenty." "I won't pay a farthing more," says the duchess. "Charity hides a multitude of sins," replies Nash; "twenty-one, twenty-two, twenty-three, twenty-four, twenty-five." "Nash," says she, "I protest you frighten me out of my wits. L—d, I shall die!" "Madam, you will never die with doing good; and if you do, it will be the better for you," answered Nash, and was about to proceed; but perceiving her grace had lost all patience, a parley ensued, when he, after much altercation, agreed to stop his hand, and compound with her grace for thirty guineas. The duchess, however, seemed displeased the whole evening, and when he came to the table where she was playing, bid him, "Stand farther, an ugly devil, for she hated the sight of him." But her grace afterwards having a run of good luck, called Nash to her. "Come," says she, "I will be friends with you, though you are a fool; and to let you see I am not angry, there is ten guineas more for your charity. But this I insist on, that neither my name nor the sum shall be mentioned."

From the hospital erected for the benefit of the poor, it is an easy transition to the monuments erected by him in honour of the great. Upon the recovery of the Prince of Orange, by drinking the Bath waters, Nash caused a small obelisk, thirty feet high, to be erected in a grove near the Abbey church, since called Orange Grove. This Prince's arms adorn the west side of the body of the pedestal. The inscription is on the opposite side, in the following words:—

"In memoriam sanitatis Principi Auriaco Aquarum thermalium potu, favente Deo, ovante Britannia, feliciter restitutæ, M.DCC.XXXIV." In English thus:—"In memory of the happy restoration of the health of the Prince of Orange, through the favour of God, and to the great joy of Britain, by drinking the Bath waters. 1734."

I find it a general custom at all baths and spas, to erect monuments of this kind to the memory of every prince who has received benefit from the waters. Aix, Spa, and Pisa abound with inscriptions of this nature, apparently doing honour to the prince, but in reality celebrating the efficacy of their springs. It is wrong, therefore, to call such monuments instances of gratitude, though they may wear that appearance.

In the year 1738, the Prince of Wales came to Bath, who presented Nash with a large gold enamelled snuff-box; and upon his departure, Nash, as king of Bath, erected an obelisk in honour of this prince, as he had before done for the Prince of Orange. This handsome memorial in honour of that good-natured prince is erected in Queen Square. It is enclosed with a stone balustrade, and in the middle of every side there are large iron gates. In the centre is the obelisk, seventy feet high, and terminating in a point. The expenses of this were eighty pounds; and Mr. Nash was determined that the inscription should answer the magnificence of the pile. With this view he wrote to Mr. Pope, requesting an inscription. I should have been glad to have given Nash's letter upon this occasion; the reader, however, must be satisfied with Pope's reply, which is as follows:—

"SIR,—I have received yours, and thank your partiality in my favour. You say words cannot express the gratitude you feel for the favour of his R.H., and yet you would have me express what you feel, and in a few words. I own myself unequal to the task; for even granting it possible to express an inexpressible idea, I am the worst person you could have pitched upon for this purpose, who have received so few favours from the great myself, that I am utterly unacquainted with what kinds of thanks they like best. Whether the P. most loves poetry or prose, I protest I do not know; but this I dare venture to affirm, that you can give him as much satisfaction in either as I can.

"I am, Sir, your affectionate servant,

"A. POPE."

What Mr. Nash's answer to this billet was I cannot take upon me to ascertain; but it was probably a perseverance in his former request. The following is the copy of Mr. Pope's reply to his second letter:—

"SIR,—I had sooner answered yours, but in the hope of procuring a properer hand than mine; and then in consulting with some whose office about the P. might make them the best judges what sort of inscription to set up. Nothing can be plainer than the enclosed; it is nearly the common sense of the thing, and I do not know how to flourish upon it; but this you would do as well or better yourself, and I dare say may mend the expression. I am truly, dear Sir, your affectionate servant,

"A. POPE.

"I think I need not tell you my name should not be mentioned."

Such a letter as this was what might naturally be expected from Mr. Pope. Notwithstanding the seeming modesty towards the conclusion, the vanity of an applauded writer bursts through every line of it. The difficulty of concealing his hand from the clerks at the post-office, and the solicitude to have his name concealed, were marks of the consciousness of his own importance. It is probable his hand was not so very well known, nor his letters so eagerly opened, by the clerks of the office, as he seems always to think; but in all his letters, as well as in those of Swift, there runs a strain of pride, as if the world talked of nothing but themselves. "Alas," says he, in one of them, "the day after I am dead, the sun will shine as bright as the day before, and the world will be as merry as usual!" Very strange, that neither an eclipse nor an earthquake should follow the loss of a poet!

The inscription referred to in this letter was the same which was afterwards engraved on the obelisk, and is as follows:—

"In memory of honours bestowed,
and in gratitude for benefits conferred in
this city
by his Royal Highness
Frederick, Prince of Wales,
and his Royal Consort,
in the year 1738,
this Obelisk is erected by
Richard Nash, Esq."

I dare venture to say, there was scarce a common councilman in the corporation of Bath but could have done this as well. Nothing can be more frigid, though the subject was worthy of the utmost exertions of genius.

About this period every season brought some new accession of honour to Nash; and the corporation now universally found that he was absolutely necessary for promoting the welfare of the city; so that this year seems to have been the meridian of his glory. About this time he arrived at such a pitch of authority, that I really believe Alexander was not greater at Persepolis. The countenance he received from the Prince of Orange, the favour he was in with the Prince of Wales, and the caresses of the nobility, all conspired to lift him to the utmost pitch of vanity. The exultation of a little mind, upon being admitted to the familiarity of the great, is inexpressible. The Prince of Orange had made him a present of a very fine snuff-box. Upon this some of the nobility thought it would be proper to give snuff-boxes too; they were quickly imitated by the middling gentry, and it soon became the fashion to give Nash snuff-boxes, who had in a little time a number sufficient to have furnished a good toy-shop.

To add to his honours, there was placed a full-length picture of him in Wiltshire's Ball-room, between the busts of Newton and Pope. It was upon this occasion that the Earl of Chesterfield wrote the following severe but witty epigram:—

"Immortal Newton never spoke
More truth, than here you'll find,
Nor Pope himself e'er penn'd a joke
More cruel on mankind.

"The picture placed the busts between
Gives satire its full strength;
Wisdom and Wit are little seen,
But Folly at full length."

There is also a full-length picture of Mr. Nash in Simpson's Ball-room, and his statue at full-length in the Pump-room, with a plan of the Bath Hospital in his hand. He was now treated in every respect like a great man; he had his levee, his flatterers, his buffoons, his good-natured creatures, and even his dedicators. A trifling, ill-supported vanity was his foible; and while he received the homage of the vulgar and enjoyed the familiarity of the great, he felt no pain for the unpromising view of poverty that lay before him: he enjoyed the world as it went, and drew upon content for the deficiencies of fortune. If a cringing wretch called him "his Honour," he was pleased; internally conscious that he had the justest pretensions to the title. If a beggar called him "my Lord," he was happy, and generally sent the flatterer off happy too. I have known him, in London, wait a whole day at a window in the Smyrna Coffee-house, in order to receive a bow from the Prince, or the Duchess of Marlborough, as they passed by where he was standing, and he would then look round upon the company for admiration and respect.

But perhaps the reader desires to know who could be low enough to flatter a man who himself lived in some measure by dependence. Hundreds are ready upon those occasions. The very needy are almost ever flatterers. A man in wretched circumstances forgets his own value, and feels no pain in giving up superiority to every claimant. The very vain are ever flatterers; as they find it necessary to make use of all their arts to keep company with such as are superior to themselves. But particularly the prodigal are prone to adulation, in order to open new supplies for their extravagance. The poor, the vain, and the extravagant are chiefly addicted to this vice: and such hung upon his good-nature. When these three characters are found united in one person, the composition generally becomes a great man's favourite. It was not difficult to collect such a group in a city that was the centre of pleasure. Nash had them of all sizes, from the half-pay captain in laced clothes, to the humble boot-catcher at the Bear.

I have before me a bundle of letters, all addressed from a pack of flattering reptiles, to "his Honour," and even some printed dedications in the same servile strain. In these, "his Honour" is complimented as the great encourager of the polite arts, as a gentleman of the most accomplished taste, of the most extensive learning, and, in short, of everything in the world. But, perhaps, it will be thought wrong in me to unveil the blushing muse, to brand learning with the meanness of its professors or to expose scholars in a state of contempt. For the honour of letters the dedications to Nash are not written by scholars or poets, but by people of a different stamp.

Among this number was the highwayman, who was taken after attempting to rob and murder Dr. Hancock. He was called Poulter, *alias* Baxter, and published a book, exposing the tricks of gamblers, thieves, and pickpockets. This he intended to have dedicated to Mr. Nash; but the generous patron, though no man loved praise more, was too modest to have it printed. However, he took care to preserve the manuscript among the rest of his papers. The book was entitled "The Discoveries of John Poulter, *alias* Baxter, who was apprehended for robbing Dr. Hancock of Salisbury, on Claverton Down, near Bath; and who has been admitted king's evidence, and discovered a most numerous gang of villains. Being a full account of all the robberies he committed, and the surprising tricks and frauds he has practised for the space of five years last past, in different parts of England, particularly in the west. Written wholly by Himself." The dedication intended to be prefixed is as follows, and will give a specimen of the style of a highwayman and a gambler :—

"*To the* HON. RICHARD NASH, ESQ.

"May it please your Honour,—With humblest submission I make bold to present the following sheets to your Honour's consideration and well known humanity. As I am industriously careful, in respect to his Majesty and good subjects, to put an end to the unfortunate misconducts of all I know, by bringing them to the gallows. To be sure some may censure, as if from self-preservation, I made this ample discovery; but I communicate this to your Honour and gentry, whether the life of one person being taken away, would answer the end, as to let escape such a number of villains, who has been the ruining of many a poor family, for whom my soul is now much concerned. If my inclinations were ever so roguish inclined, what is it to so great a number of villains, when they consult together. As your Honour's wisdom, humanity, and interest are the friend of the virtuous, I make bold to lay at your Honour's feet the following lines, which will put every honest man upon his defence against the snares of the mischievous; and am, with greatest gratitude, honoured Sir, your Honour's most truly devoted and obedient servant,

"JOHN POULTER, *alias* BAXTER.

"Taunton Gaol, June 2nd."

Flattery from such a wretch as this one would think but little pleasing; however, certain it is that Nash was pleased with it. He loved to be called "your Honour," and "Honourable," and the highwayman more than once experienced his generosity.

But since I have mentioned this fellow's book I cannot repress an impulse to give an extract from it; however foreign from my subject. I take the following picture to be a perfectly humorous description of artful knavery affecting ignorance on one hand, and rustic simplicity pretending to great wisdom and sagacity on the other. It is an account of the manner in which countrymen are deceived by gamblers, at a game called Pricking in the Belt, or the old Nob. This is a leathern strap folded up double, and then laid upon a table: if the person who plays with a bodkin pricks into the loop of the belt, he wins, if otherwise, he loses. However, by slipping one end of the strap, the sharper can win with pleasure.

There are generally four persons concerned in this fraud, one to personate a sailor called a leggbull, another called the capper, who always keeps with the sailor; and two pickers-up, or money-droppers, to bring in flats or bubbles. The first thing they do at a fair is to look for a room clear of company, which the sailor and capper immediately take, while the money-droppers go out to look for a flat. If they see a countryman whose looks they like, one drops a shilling or half-a-crown just before him, and picking it up again, looks the man in the face, and says, I have found a piece of money, friend; did you see me pick it up? The man says, Yes; then says the sharper, If you had found it I would have had half, so I will do as I would be done unto; come, honest friend, we will not part with dry lips. Then taking him into the room where the other two are, he cries, By your leave, gentlemen, I hope we don't disturb the company. No, cries the sailor, no, brothers; will you drink a glass of brandy, I don't like your weak liquors? and then begins a discourse, by asking the capper how far it is to London; who replies, I don't know; perhaps the gentleman there can tell you, directing his discourse to the flat. Perhaps the flat will answer, A hundred miles. The sailor cries, I can ride that in a day, ay, in four or five hours; for, says he, my horse will run twenty knots an hour for twenty-four hours together. Capper or the sailor's supposed companion, says, I believe, farmer, you have not got such a horse as the sailor has. The farmer cries, No, and laughs; and then the sailor says, I must go and get half a pint of brandy, for I am griped, and so leaves them. The capper, affecting a look of wisdom in his absence, observes, that it is an old saying, and a true one, that sailors get their money like horses, and spend it like asses; as for that there sailor, I never saw him till now, buying a horse of my man; he tells me he has been at sea, and has got about four hundred pounds prize money, but I believe he will squander it all away, for he was gaming just now with a sharping fellow and lost forty shillings at a strange game of pricking in a string. Did either of you ever see it, gentlemen? continued the capper; if you two are willing I will ask him to show it, for we may as well win some of his money as anybody else. The flat and the dropper cry, Do. Then in comes the sailor, staggering as if drunk, and cries, What cheer, brothers? I have just seen a pretty girl in the fair, and went in to drink with her; we made a bargain, and I gave her a six-and-thirty shilling piece, but an old b—h, her mother, came and called her away, but I hope she will come back to me presently. Then the capper laughs and says, Have you got your money of her again? The sailor says, No; but she will come to me, I'm sure; then they all laugh. This is done to deceive the flat; then says the capper, What have you done with the stick and the string, sailor? He answers, What, that which I bought of the boys? I have got it here, but will not sell it; and then he pulls out the old nob, saying, What do you think I gave for it? I gave but sixpence and as much brandy as the two boys could drink; it is made out of a monkey's hide, as the boys told me, and they told me there is a game to be played at it, which nobody can do twice together; I will go down aboard ship and play with my captain, and I do not fear but I shall win his ship and cargo. Then they all laugh, and the sailor makes up the old nob, and the capper lays a shilling, and pricks himself and wins. The sailor cries, You are a dab, I will not lay with you, but if you will call a stranger I will lay again. Why, if you think me a dab, I will get this strange gentleman, or this, pointing to the flat. Done, cries the sailor, but you shall not tell him. Then he makes up the nob, and capper lays a shilling; flat pricks, being permitted to go sixpence; to which he agreeing, wins; and capper says to the flat, Can you change me half-a-crown? This is done to find the depth of his pocket; if they see a good deal of gold, flat must win three or four times; if no gold, but twice. Sometimes, if the flat has no money, the sailor cries, I have more money than any man in the fair, and pulls out his purse of gold, and saith, Not one of you can beg, borrow, or steal half this sum in an hour for a guinea. Capper cries, I have laid out all mine; farmer, can you? I'll go your halves, if you think you can do it. The sailor saith, You must not bring anybody with you: then the dropper goes with the flat, and saith, You must not tell your friend it is for a wager; if you do, he will not lend it you. Flat goes and borrows it, and brings it to the sailor, shows it him, and wins the wager; then the sailor pinches the nob again, and the capper whispers to the flat, to prick out purposely this time, saying it will make the sailor more eager to lay on; we may as well win his money as not, for he will spend it upon whores. Flat, with all the wisdom in the world, loses on purpose, upon which the sailor swears, pulls out all his money, throws it about the room, and cries, I know no man can win for ever, and then lays a guinea, but will not let him prick, but throws down five guineas, and the capper urging the flat, and going his halves, the sailor saith, My cabin boy will lay as much as that; I'll lay no less than twenty guineas. The capper cries, Lay, farmer, and take up forty; which being certain of winning, he instantly complies with and loses the whole. When he has lost, in order to advise him, the dropper takes him by the arm, and hauls him out of doors, and the reckoning being in the meantime paid within, the capper and sailor follow after and run another way. When they are out of sight, the dropper saith to the flat, Go you back and play with the sailor for a shilling, whilst I go and borrow money; but when the flat goes to the house, he finds them gone, and then he knows that he is bit, but not till he has dearly paid for it.

By this fellow's discoveries, Mr. Nash was enabled to serve many of the nobility and gentry of his acquaintance: he received a list of all those houses of ill-fame which harboured or assisted rogues, and took care to furnish travellers with proper precautions to avoid them. It was odd enough to see a gamester thus employed in detecting the frauds of gamblers.

Among the Dedications there is one from a Professor of Cookery, which is even more adulatory than the preceding. It is prefixed to a work intituled "The Complete Preserver; or a new method of preserving fruits, flowers, and other vegetables, either with or without sugar, vinegar, or spirits, &c."

"*To the very* HON. RICHARD NASH, ESQ.

"HONOURED SIR,—As much as the oak exceeds the bramble, so much do you exceed the rest of mankind in benevolence, charity, and every other virtue that adorns, ennobles, and refines the human species. I have therefore made bold to prefix your name, though without permission, to the following work, which stands in need of such a patron, to excuse its errors, with a candour only known to such a heart as your own. The obligations I have received at your hands it is impossible for me ever to repay, except by my endeavours, as in the present case, to make known the many excellent virtues which you possess. But what can my wit do to recommend such a genius as yours: a single word, a smile from yourself, outweighs all that I, or perhaps the best of our poets, could express in writing, in the compass of a year. It would ill become my sex to declare what power you have over us; but your generosity is, even in this instance, greater than your desire to oblige. The following sheets were drawn up at my hours of leisure, and may be serviceable to such of my sex as are more willing to employ their time in laudable occupations and domestic economy, than in dress and dissipation. What reception they may receive from your Honour, I am incapable of telling; however, from your known candour and humanity, I expect the most favourable. I am, honoured Sir, your most obedient and obliged humble servant, "H. W."

A musician in his dedication still exceeds the other two in adulation. However, though the matter may be some impeachment on his sincerity, the manner in which it is written reflects no disgrace upon his understanding.

To RICHARD NASH, ESQ.

"SIR,—The kind partiality of my friend prevailed with me to present to the world these my first attempts in musical composition; and the generous protection you have been pleased to afford me, makes it my indispensable duty to lay them at your feet. Indeed, to whom could I presume to offer them, but to the great encourager of all polite arts; for your generosity knows no bounds; nor are you more famed for that dignity of mind, which ennobles and gives a grace to every part of your conduct, than for that humanity and beneficence which makes you the friend and benefactor of all mankind. To you, the poor and the rich, the diseased and the healthy, the aged and the young, owe every comfort, every conveniency, and every innocent amusement, that the best heart, the most skilful management, and the most accomplished taste can furnish. Even this age, so deeply practised in all the subtleties of refined pleasure, gives you this testimony: even this age, so ardently engaged in all the ways of the most unbounded charity, gives you this praise. Pardon me then, if, amidst the crowd of votaries, I make my humble offering, if I seize this opportunity of publicly expressing the grateful sentiments of my own heart and profound respect, with which I am, Sir, your most obliged, most devoted, and most obedient servant, "J. G."

I fancy I have almost fatigued the reader, and I am almost fatigued myself, with the efforts of these elegant panegyrists; however, I cannot finish this run of quotation, without giving a specimen of poetry, addressed to him upon a certain occasion; and all I shall say in its defence is, that those who are pleased with the prose dedications will not dislike the present attempt in poetry.

TO RICHARD NASH, ESQ.,
ON HIS SICKNESS AT TUNBRIDGE.

Say, must the friend of human kind,
Of most refined—of most diffusive mind;
Must Nash himself beneath these ailments grieve?
He felt for all—he felt—but to relieve,
To heal the sick—the wounded to restore,
And bid desponding nature mourn no more.
Thy quick'ning warmth, O let thy patron feel,
Improve thy springs with double power to heal:
Quick, hither, all-inspiring Health, repair,
And save the gay—and wretched from despair;
Thou only Esra's drooping sons canst cheer,
And stop the soft-eyed virgin's trickling tear;
In murmurs who their Monarch's pains deplore;
While sickness faints, and pleasure is no more.
O let not Death, with hasty strides, advance;
Thou, mildest Charity, avert the lance;
His threatening power, celestial maid! defeat;
Nor take him with thee, to thy well-known seat;
Leave him on earth some longer date behind,
To bless, to polish, and relieve mankind:
Come then, kind Health! O quickly come away,
Bid Nash revive—and all the world be gay.

Such addresses as these were daily offered to our titular King. When in the meridian of power, scarce a morning passed that did not increase the number of his humble admirers, and enlarge the sphere of his vanity.

The man who is constantly served up with adulation, must be a first-rate philosopher if he can listen without contracting new affectations. The opinion we form of ourselves is generally measured by what we hear from others; and when they conspire to deceive, we too readily concur in the delusion. Among the number of much applauded men in the circle of our own friends, we can recollect but few that have heads quite strong enough to bear a loud acclamation of public praise in their favour; among the whole list we shall scarce find one that has not thus been made, on some side of his character, a coxcomb.

When the best head turns and grows giddy with praise, is it to be wondered that poor Nash should be driven by it almost into a phrenzy of affectation? Towards the close of life he became affected. He chiefly laboured to be thought a sayer of good things; and by frequent attempts was now and then successful, for he ever lay upon the lurch.

There never perhaps was a more silly passion than this desire of having a man's jests recorded. For this purpose, it is necessary to keep ignorant or ill-bred company, who are only fond of repeating such stories; in the next place a person must tell his own jokes, in order to make them more universal; but what is worst of all, scarcely a joke of this kind succeeds, but at the expense of a man's good-nature; and he who exchanges the character of being thought agreeable for that of being thought witty, makes but a very bad bargain.

The success Nash sometimes met with led him on, when late in life, to mistake his true character. He was really agreeable, but he chose rather to be a wit; he therefore indulged his inclination, and never mattered how rude he was, provided he was thought comical. He thus got the applause he sought for; but too often found enemies, where he least expected to find them. Of all the jests recorded of him, I scarcely find one that is not marked with petulance: he said whatever came uppermost, and in the number of his remarks it might naturally be expected that some were worth repeating; he threw often, and sometimes had a lucky cast.

In a life of almost ninety years, spent in the very point of public view, it is not strange that five or six sprightly things of his have been collected, particularly as he took every opportunity of repeating them himself. His usual way when he thought he had said any thing clever, was to strengthen it with an oath, and to make up its want of sentiment by asseveration and grimace. For many years he thus entertained the company at the Coffee-house with old stories, in which he always made himself the principal character. Strangers liked this well enough; but they who were used to his conversation found it insupportable. One story brought on another, and each came in the same order that it had the day preceding. But this custom may be rather ascribed to the peculiarity of age, than a peculiarity of character. It seldom happens that old men allure, at least by novelty: age that shrivels the body contracts the understanding; instead of exploring new regions, they rest satisfied in the old, and walk round the circle of their former discoveries. His manner of telling a story, however, was not displeasing; but few of those he told are worth transcribing. Indeed, it is the manner which places the whole difference between the wit of the vulgar and of those who assume the name of the polite: one has in general as much good sense as the other; a story transcribed from one will be as entertaining as that copied from the other; but in conversation, the manner will give charms even to stupidity. The following is the story which he most frequently told, and pretty much in these words. Suppose the company to be talking of a German war, or Elizabeth Canning, he would begin thus:—"I'll tell you something to that purpose, that I fancy will make you laugh. A covetous old parson, as rich as the devil, scraped a fresh acquaintance with me several years ago at Bath. I knew him when he and I were students at Oxford, where we both studied damnationly hard; but that's neither here nor there. Well; very well. I entertained him at my house in John's Court. (No, my house in John's Court was not built then.) But I entertained him with all that the city could afford; the rooms, the music, and everything in the world. Upon his leaving Bath, he pressed me very hard to return the visit, and desired me to let him have the pleasure of seeing me at his house in Devonshire. About six months after, I happened to be in that neighbourhood, and was resolved to see my old friend, from whom I expected a very warm reception. Well: I knocks at his door, when an old queer creature of a maid came to the door, and denied him. I suspected, however, that he was at home; and going into the parlour, what should I see, but the parson's legs up the chimney, where he had thrust himself to avoid entertaining me. This was very well. My dear, says I to the maid, it is very cold, extreme cold indeed, and I am afraid I have got a touch of my ague; light me the fire, if you please. La! sir, says the maid, who was a modest creature to be sure, the chimney smokes monstrously; you could not bear the room for three minutes together. By the greatest good luck there was a bundle of straw in the hearth, and I called for a candle. The candle came. Well! good woman, says I, since you won't light me a fire, I'll light one for myself; and in a moment the straw was all in a blaze. This quickly unkennelled the old fox; there he stood in an old rusty night-gown, blessing himself, and looking like—a—hem—egad."

He used to tell surprising stories of his activity when young.—"Here I stand, gentlemen, that could once leap forty-two feet upon level ground, at three standing jumps, backward or forward. One, two, three, dart like an arrow out of a bow. But I am old now. I remember I once leaped for three hundred guineas with Count Klopstock, the great leaper, leaping-master to the Prince of Passau; you must all have heard of him. First he began with a running jump, and a most damnable bounce it was, that's certain: everybody concluded that he had the match hollow; when only taking off my hat, stripping off neither coat, shoes, nor stockings, mind me, I fetches a run, and went beyond him one foot three inches and three-quarters, measured, upon my soul, by Captain Pately's own standard!"

But in this torrent of insipidity, there sometimes were found very severe satire, strokes of true wit, and lines of humour, *cum flueret lutulentus, &c.* He rallied very successfully; for he never felt another's joke, and drove home his own without pity. With his superiors he was familiar and blunt; the inferiority of his station secured him from their resentment; but the same bluntness which they laughed at, was by his equals regarded as insolence —something like a familiar boot-catcher at an inn; a gentleman would bear that joke from him, for which a brother boot-catcher would knock him down.

Among other stories of Nash's telling, I remember one, which I the more cheerfully repeat, as it tends to correct a piece of impertinence that reigns in almost every country assembly. The principal inhabitants of a certain market-town at a distance from the capital, in order to encourage that harmony which ought to subsist in society, and to promote a mutual intercourse between the sexes, so desirable to both and so necessary for all, had established a monthly assembly in the town-hall, which was conducted with such decency, decorum, and politeness, that it drew the attention of the gentlemen and ladies in the neighbourhood, and a nobleman and his family continually honoured them with their presence. This naturally drew others, and in time the room was crowded with what the world calls good company; and the assembly prospered, till some of the newly admitted ladies took it into their heads that the tradesmen's daughters were unworthy of their notice, and therefore refused to join hands with them in the dance. This was complained of by the town ladies, and that complaint was resented by the country gentlemen; who, more pert than wise, publicly advertised that they would not dance with tradesmen's daughters. This the most eminent tradesmen considered as an insult on themselves, and being men of worth, and able to live independently, they in return advertised that they would give no credit out of their town, and desired all others to discharge their accounts. A general uneasiness ensued; some writs were actually issued out, and much distress would have happened, had not my lord, who sided with no party, kindly interfered and composed the difference. The assembly however was ruined, and the families, I am told, are not friends yet, though this affair happened thirty years ago.

Nothing debases human nature so much as pride. This Nash knew, and endeavoured to stifle every emotion of it at Bath. When he observed any ladies so extremely delicate and proud of a pedigree, as to only touch the back of an inferior's hand in the dance, he always called to order, and desired them to leave the room or behave with common decency; and when any ladies and gentlemen drew off, after they had gone down a dance, without standing up till the dance was finished, he made up to them, and after asking whether they had done dancing, told them they should dance no more unless they stood up for the rest; and on these occasions he always was as good as his word.

Nash, though no great wit, had the art of sometimes saying rude things with decency, and rendering them pleasing by an uncommon turn. But most of the good things attributed to him, which have found their way into the jest-books, are no better than puns. The smartest things I have seen are against him. One day in the Grove he joined some ladies, and asking one of them who was crooked, whence she came? she replied, "Straight from London." "Confound me, madam," said he, "then you must have been damnably warped by the way."

She soon, however, had ample revenge. Sitting the following evening in one of the rooms, he once more joined her company, and with a sneer and bow asked her if she knew her catechism, and could tell the name of Tobit's dog? "His name, sir, was Nash," replied the lady, "and an impudent dog he was." This story is told in a celebrated romance; I only repeat it here to have an opportunity of observing, that it actually happened.

Queen Anne once asked him, why he would not accept of knighthood? To which he replied, lest Sir William Read, the mountebank, who had been just knighted, should call him brother.

A house in Bath was said to be haunted by the devil, and a great noise was made about it, when Nash going to the minister of St. Michael's, intreated him to drive the devil out of Bath for ever, if it were only to oblige the ladies.

Nash used sometimes to visit the great

Doctor Clarke. The doctor was one day conversing with Locke, and two or three more of his learned and intimate companions, with that freedom, gaiety, and cheerfulness, which is ever the result of innocence. In the midst of their mirth and laughter, the doctor, looking from the window, saw Nash's chariot stop at the door. "Boys, boys," cried the philosopher to his friends, "let us now be wise, for here is a fool coming."

Nash was one day complaining in the following manner to the Earl of Chesterfield, of his bad luck at play. "Would you think it, my lord, that damned bitch fortune, no later than last night, tricked me out of five hundred. Is it not surprising," continued he, "that my luck should never turn—that I should thus eternally be mauled?"—"I don't wonder at your losing money, Nash," said his lordship, "but all the world is surprised where you get it to lose."

Dr. Cheyne once, when Nash was ill, drew up a prescription for him, which was sent in accordingly. The next day the doctor coming to see his patient, found him up and well; upon which he asked if he had followed his prescription. "Followed your prescription," cried Nash, "no. Egad, if I had, I should have broke my neck, for I flung it out of the two pair of stairs window."

It would have been well had he confined himself to such sallies; but as he grew old he grew insolent, and seemed, in some measure, insensible of the pain his attempts to be a wit gave others. Upon asking a lady to dance a minuet, if she refused he would often demand if she had got bandy legs. He would attempt to ridicule natural defects; he forgot the deference due to birth and quality, and mistook the manner of settling rank and precedence upon many occasions. He now seemed no longer fashionable among the present race of gentry; he grew peevish and fretful, and they who only saw the remnant of a man, severely returned that laughter upon him which he had once lavished upon others.

Poor Nash was no longer the gay, thoughtless, idly industrious creature he once was; he now forgot how to supply new modes of entertainment, and became too rigid to wind with ease through the vicissitudes of fashion. The evening of his life began to grow cloudy. His fortune was gone, and nothing but poverty lay in prospect. To embitter his hopes, he found himself abandoned by the great, whom he had long endeavoured to serve; and was obliged to fly to those of humbler stations for protection, whom he once affected to despise. He now began to want that charity which he had never refused to any; and to find that a life of dissipation and gaiety is ever terminated by misery and regret.

Even his place of master of the ceremonies (if I can trust the papers he has left behind him) was sought after. I would willingly be tender of any living reputation, but these papers accuse Mr. Quin of endeavouring to supplant him. He has even left us a letter, which he supposed was written by that gentleman, soliciting a lord for his interest upon the occasion. As I choose to give Mr. Quin an opportunity of disproving this, I will insert the letter, and to show the improbability of its being his, with all its faults both of style and spelling. I am the less apt to believe it written by Mr. Quin, as a gentleman who has mended Shakspeare's plays so often would surely be capable of something more correct than the following. It was sent, as it should seem, from Mr. Quin to a nobleman, but left open for the perusal of an intermediate friend. It was this friend who sent a copy of it to Mr. Nash, who caused it to be instantly printed, and left among his other papers. The letter from the intermediate friend to Nash is as follows:—

"London, Oct. 8, 1760.

"DEAR NASH,—Two posts ago I received a letter from Quin, the old player, covering one to my lord, which he left open for my perusal, which, after reading, he desired I might seal up and deliver. The request he makes is so extraordinary, that it has induced me to send you the copy of his letter to my lord, which is as follows:—

"'Bath, Oct. 3, 1760.

"'MY DER LORD,—Old Beaux Knash has mead himselfe so dissagreeable to all the companey that comes here to Bath that the corperatian of this city have it now under thier consideration to remove him from beeing master of the cereymoines, should he be continuead the inhabitants of this city will be rueind, as the best companey declines to come to Bath on his acc^{t}. Give me leave to show to your Lords'hip how he beheaved at the firs't ball he had here thiss season which was Tus'day last. A younge Lady was as'ked to dance a minueat she begg the gent^{m} would be pleased to exquise here as' she did not chuse to dance; upon thiss' old Nash called out so as to be head by all the companey in the room, G— dam yo Madam, what buisness have yo here if yo do not dance, upon which the Lady was so afrighted, she rose and danced, the ress'et of the companey was so much offended at the rudness of Nash that not one Lady more would dance a minueat that night. In country dances no person of note danced except two boys, Lords S— and T— the res't of the companey that danced waire only the families of all the haberdas'hers' machinukes and inkeepers in the three kingdoms brushed up and colected togither. I have known upon such an occaison as' thiss' seventeen Dutchess' and Contiss' to be at the opening of the ball at Bath now not one. This man by his' pride and extravagancis has outlived his' reasein it would be happy for thiss city that he was ded; and is now only fitt to reed Shirlock upon death by which he may seave his soul and gaine more than all the proffitts he can make, by his white hat suppose it was to be died red: The fav^{r} I have now to reques't by what I now have wrote yo, is that your Lordship will speke to Mr. Pitt for to recommend me to the corporeatian of this city to succede this old sinner as master of the cerremonies, and yo will much oblige, My Lord,

"'Your Lord^{s} and Hu^{e} Ob^{t} Servt.'

"N.B. There were some other private matters and offers in Quin's letter to my lord, which do not relate to you."

Here Nash, if I may be permitted the use of a polite and fashionable phrase, was humm'd; but he experienced such rubs as these, and a thousand other mortifications, every day. He found poverty now denied him the indulgence not only of his favourite follies, but of his favourite virtues. The poor solicited him in vain; for he was himself a more pitiable object than they. The child of the public seldom has a friend, and he who once exercised his wit at the expense of others, must naturally have enemies. Exasperated at last to the highest degree, an unaccountable whim struck him. Poor Nash was resolved to become an author; he who, in the vigour of manhood, was incapable of the task, now at the impotent age of eighty-six, was determined to write his own history! From the many specimens already given of his style, the reader will not much regret that the historian was interrupted in his design. Yet, as Montaigne observes, as the adventures of an infant, if an infant could inform us of them, would be pleasing, so the life of a beau, if a beau could write, would certainly serve to regale curiosity.

Whether he really intended to put this design in execution, or did it only to alarm the nobility, I will not take upon me to determine; but certain it is, that his friends went about collecting subscriptions for the work, and he received several encouragements from such as were willing to be politely charitable. It was thought by many, that this history would reveal the intrigues of a whole age; that he had numberless secrets to disclose; but they never considered, that persons of public character like him were the most unlikely in the world to be made partakers of those secrets which people desired the public should not know. In fact, he had few secrets to discover, and those he had are buried with him in the grave.

He was now past the power of giving or receiving pleasure, for he was poor, old, and peevish; yet still he was incapable of turning from his former manner of life to pursue happiness. The old man endeavoured to practise the follies of the boy: he spurred on his jaded passions after every trifle of the day: tottering with age, he would be ever an unwelcome guest in the assemblies of the youthful and gay, and he seemed willing to find lost appetite among those scenes where he was once young.

An old man thus striving after pleasure is indeed an object of pity; but a man at once old and poor, running on in this pursuit, might excite astonishment. To see a being both by fortune and constitution rendered incapable of enjoyment, still haunting those pleasures he was no longer to share in; to see one of almost ninety settling the fashion of a lady's cap, or assigning her place in a country dance; to see him, unmindful of his own reverend figure, or the respect he should have for himself, toasting demireps, or attempting to entertain the lewd and idle;—a sight like this might well serve as a satire on humanity; might show that man is the only preposterous creature alive who pursues the shadow of pleasure without temptation.

But he was not permitted to run on thus without severe and repeated reproof. The clergy sent him frequent calls to reformation; but the asperity of their advice in general abated its intended effects; they threatened him with fire and brimstone for what he had long been taught to consider as foibles, and not vices; so, like a desperate debtor, he did not care to settle an account, that, upon the first inspection, he found himself utterly unable to pay.

Thus begins one of his monitors:—"This admonition comes from your friend, and one that has your interest deeply at heart. It comes on a design altogether important, and of no less consequence than your everlasting happiness, so that it may justly challenge your careful regard. It is not to upbraid or reproach, much less to triumph or insult over your misconduct or misery; no, 'tis pure benevolence, it is disinterested good-will, prompts me to write. I hope, therefore, I shall not raise your resentment. Yet be the consequence what it will, I cannot bear to see you walk in the paths that lead to death without warning you of the danger, —without sounding in your ear the awful admonition, 'Return and live! Why do you such things? I hear of your evil dealings by all this people.' I have long observed and pitied you, and must tell you plainly, sir, that your present behaviour is not the way to reconcile yourself to God. You are so far from making atonement to offended justice, that each moment you are aggravating the future account, and heaping up an increase of His anger. As long as you roll on in a continued circle of sensual delights and vain entertainments, you are dead to all the purposes of piety and virtue. You are as odious to God as a corrupt carcase that lies putrefying in the churchyard. You are as far from doing your duty, or endeavouring after salvation, or restoring yourself to the Divine favour, as a heap of dry bones nailed up in a coffin is from vigour and activity. Think, sir, I conjure you, think upon this, if you have any inclination to escape the fire that will never be quenched. Would you be rescued from the fury and fierce anger of God? Would you be delivered from weeping and wailing, and incessant gnashing of teeth? Sure you would! But be certain, that this will never be done, by amusements which at best are trifling and impertinent, and for that, if for no other reason, foolish and sinful. 'Tis by seriousness, 'tis by retirement and mourning, you must accomplish this great and desirable deliverance. You must not appear at the head of every silly diversion, you must enter into your closet and shut the door, commune with your own heart and search out its defects. The pride of life and all its superfluity of follies must be put away. You must make haste and delay not to keep every injunction of heaven. You must always remember that mighty sinners must be mightily penitent or else mightily tormented. Your examples and your projects have been extremely *prejudicial*—I wish I could not say *fatal* and *destructive*—to many. For this there is no amends but an alteration of your conduct as singular and remarkable as your person and name. If you do not by this method remedy in some degree the evils that you have sent abroad, and prevent the mischievous consequences that may ensue, wretched will you be, wretched above all men to eternity. The blood of souls will be laid to your charge. God's jealousy like a consuming flame will smoke against you; as you yourself will see in that day, when the mountains shall quake, and the hills melt, and the earth be burnt up at His presence.

"Once more I exhort you as a friend; I beseech you as a brother; I charge you as a messenger from God in His own most solemn words, 'Cast away from you your transgressions, make you a new heart, and a new spirit; so iniquity shall not be your ruin.'

"Perhaps you may be disposed to contemn this and its serious purport, or to recommend it to your companions as a subject for raillery. Yet let me tell you beforehand, that for this as well as for other things, God will bring you to judgment. He sees me now I write. He will observe you while you read. He notes down my words; He will also note down your consequent procedure. Not then upon me—not upon me, but upon your own soul will the neglecting or despising my sayings turn. 'If thou be wise, thou shalt be wise for thyself; if thou scornest, thou alone shalt bear it.'"

Such repeated admonitions served to sting, without reforming him; they made him morose, but not pious. The dose was too strong for the patient to bear. He should have been met with smiles, and allured into reformation; if indeed he was criminal. But, in the name of piety, what was there criminal in his conduct? He had long been taught to consider his trifling profession as a very serious and important business. He went through his office with great gravity, solemnity, and care; why then denounce peculiar torments against a poor harmless creature, who did a thousand good things, and whose greatest vice was vanity! He deserved ridicule, indeed, and he found it; but scarce a single action of his life, except one, deserves the asperity of reproach.

Thus we see a variety of causes concurred to embitter his departing life. The weakness and infirmities of exhausted nature; the admonitions of the grave, which aggravated his follies into vices; the ingratitude of his dependants, who formerly flattered his fortunes; but particularly the contempt of the great, many of whom quite forgot him in his wants: all these hung upon his spirit and soured his temper, and the poor man of pleasure might have terminated his life very tragically, had not the corporation of Bath charitably resolved to grant him ten guineas the first Monday of every month. This bounty served to keep him from actual necessity, though far too trifling to enable him to support the character of a gentleman. Habit, and not nature, makes almost all our wants; and he who had been accustomed in the early parts of his life to affluence and prodigality, when reduced to a hundred and twenty-six pounds a year must pine in actual indigence.

In this variety of uneasiness his health began to fail. He had received from nature a robust and happy constitution, one indeed that was scarcely to be impaired by intemperance. He even pretended, among his friends, that he never followed a single prescription in the whole course of his life. However, in this he was one day detected on the parade; for boasting there of his contempt and utter disuse of medicine, unluckily the water of two blisters, which Dr. Oliver had prescribed, and which he then had upon each leg, oozed through his stockings, and betrayed him. His aversion to physic, however, was frequently a topic of raillery between him and Dr. Cheyne, who was a man of some wit and breeding. When Cheyne recommended his vegetable diet, Nash would swear that his design was to send half the world grazing like Nebuchadnezzar. "Ay," Cheyne would reply, "Nebuchadnezzar was never such an infidel as thou art. It was but last week, gentlemen, that I attended this fellow in a fit of sickness; there I found him rolling up his eyes to heaven and crying for mercy: he would then swallow my drugs like breast milk; yet you now hear him, how the old dog blasphemes the faculty." What Cheyne said in jest was true; he feared the approaches of death more than the generality of mankind, and was usually very devout while it threatened him. Though he was somewhat the libertine in words, none believed or trembled more than he did; for a mind neither schooled by philosophy nor encouraged by conscious innocence, is ever timid at the appearance of danger.

For some time before his decease nature gave warning of his approaching dissolution. The worn machine had run itself down to an utter impossibility of repair; he saw that he must die, and shuddered at the thought. His virtues were not of the great, but the amiable kind; so that fortitude was not among the number. Anxious, timid, his thoughts still hanging on a receding world, he desired to enjoy a little longer that life, the miseries of which he had experienced so long. The poor unsuccessful gamester husbanded the wasting moments with an increased desire to continue the game, and to the last eagerly wished for one yet more happy throw. He died at his house in St. John's Court, Bath, on the 12th of February, 1761, aged eighty-seven years, three months, and some days.

His death was sincerely regretted by the city, to which he had been so long and so great a benefactor. The day after he died, the mayor called the corporation together, when they granted fifty pounds towards burying their sovereign with proper respect. After the corpse had lain four days, it was conveyed to the Abbey church in that city, with a solemnity somewhat peculiar to his character. About five the procession moved from his house; the charity-girls, two and two, preceded; next the boys of the charity-school, singing a solemn occasional hymn. Next marched the city music, and his own band, sounding at proper intervals a dirge. Three clergymen immediately preceded the coffin, which was adorned with sable plumes, and the pall supported by the six senior aldermen. The masters of the assembly-rooms followed as chief mourners; the beadles of that hospital which he had contributed so largely to endow, went next; and last of all the poor patients themselves, the lame, the emaciated, and the feeble, followed their old benefactor to his grave, shedding unfeigned tears, and lamenting themselves in him.

The crowd was so great, that not only the streets were filled, but, as one of the journals in a rant expresses it, "even the tops of the houses were covered with spectators. Each thought the occasion affected themselves most; as when a real king dies, they asked each other, 'Where shall we find such another?' Sorrow sate upon every face, and even children lisped that their Sovereign was no more. The awfulness of the solemnity made the deepest impression on the minds of the distressed inhabitants. The peasant discontinued his toil, the ox rested from the plough; all nature seemed to sympathise with their loss, and the muffled bells rung a peal of bob-majors."

Our deepest solemnities have something truly ridiculous in them. There is somewhat ludicrous in the folly of historians, who thus declaim upon the death of kings and princes, as if there was anything dismal, or anything unusual, in it. "For my part," says Poggi, the Florentine, "I can no more grieve for another's death than I could for my own. I have ever regarded death as a very trifling affair, nor can black staves, long cloaks, or mourning coaches, in the least influence my spirits. Let us live here as long and as merrily as we can; and when we must die, why, let us die merrily too, but die so as to be happy."

The few things Nash was possessed of were left to his relations. A small library of well-chosen books, some trinkets and pictures, were his only inheritance. Among the latter (besides the box given him by the Prince of Wales) were a gold box, which was presented to him by the late Countess of Burlington, with Lady Euston's picture in the lid; an *étui*, mounted in gold, with a diamond to open it, and ornamented with another diamond at the top, given him by the Princess Dowager of Wales. He had also a silver terene, which was given him by the Princess Amelia; and some other things of no great value. The rings, watches, and pictures, which he formerly received from others, would have come to a considerable amount; but these necessity had obliged him to dispose of. Some family pictures, however, remained, which were sold by advertisement, for five guineas each, after Mr. Nash's decease.

It was natural to expect that the death of a person so long in the eye of the public must have produced a desire in several to delineate his character, or deplore his loss. He was scarcely dead, when the public papers were filled with elegies, groans, and characters; and before he was buried there were epitaphs ready made to inscribe on his stone. I remember one of those character writers, and a very grave one too, after observing, alas! that Richard Nash, Esq. was no more, went on to assure us, that he was "sagacious, *debonair*, and *commode;*" and concluded with gravely declaring, that "impotent posterity would in vain fumble to produce his fellow." Another, equally sorrowful, gave us to know, "that he was indeed a man;" an assertion which I fancy none will be so hardy as to contradict. But the merriest of all the lamentations made upon this occasion was that where he is called "a constellation of the heavenly sphere."

One thing, however, is common almost with all of them; and that is, that Venus, Cupid, and the Graces are commanded to weep; and that Bath shall never find such another.

But though he was satirized with the praises of those, there were some of real abilities who undertook to do justice to his character, to praise him for his virtues, and acknowledge his faults. I need scarcely mention that Dr. Oliver and Dr. King are of this number. They had honoured him with their friendship while living, and undertook to honour his memory when dead. As the reader may choose to compare their efforts, upon the same subject, I have subjoined them, and perhaps many will find in either enough, upon so unimportant a subject as Mr. Nash's life, to satisfy curiosity. The first published was that by Dr. Oliver, written with much good sense, and still more good-nature. But the reader will consider that he has assumed in his motto the character of a panegyrist, and spares his friend's faults, though he was too candid entirely to pass them over in silence :—

A FAINT SKETCH OF THE LIFE, CHARACTER, AND MANNERS OF THE LATE MR. NASH.

Imperium in Imperio.——
De mortuis nil nisi bonum.

Bath, February 13, 1761.

This morning died
RICHARD NASH, ESQ.
Aged eighty-eight.
He was by birth a gentleman, an ancient Briton;
By education, a student of Jesus College in Oxford;
By profession * * *
His natural genius was too volatile for any.
He tried the army and the law;
But soon found his mind superior to both—
He was born to govern,
Nor was his dominion, like that of other legislators,
Over the servility of the vulgar,
But over the pride of the noble and the opulent.
His public character was great,
As it was self-built and self-maintained:
His private amiable,
As it was grateful, beneficent, and generous.
By the force of genius
He erected the city of Bath into a province of pleasure,
And became, by universal consent,
Its legislator and ruler.
He planned, improved, and regulated all the amusements of the place;
His fundamental law was, that of good breeding;
Hold sacred decency and decorum,
His constant maxim:
Nobody, howsoever exalted
By beauty, blood, titles, or riches,
Could be guilty of a breach of it, unpunished—
The penalty, his disapprobation and public shame.
To maintain the sovereignty he had established,
He published Rules of behaviour,
Which from their propriety, acquired the force of laws;
And which the highest never infringed, without immediately undergoing the public censure.
He kept the Men in order; most wisely,
By prohibiting the wearing swords in his dominions;
By which means
He prevented sudden passion from causing
The bitterness of unavailing repentance.
In all quarrels he was chosen Umpire—
And so just were his decisions,
That peace generally triumphed,
Crowned with the mutual thanks of both parties.
He kept the Ladies in good humour; most effectually,
By a nice observance of the rules of place and precedence;
By ordaining scandal to be the infallible mark
Of a foolish head and a malicious heart,
Always rendering more suspicious
The reputation of her who propagated it,
Than that of the person abused.
Of the young, the gay, the heedless fair,
Just launching into the dangerous sea of pleasure,
He was ever, unsolicited (sometimes unregarded),
The kind protector:
Humanely correcting even their mistakes in dress,
As well as improprieties in conduct:
Nay, often warning them,
Though at the hazard of his life,
Against the artful snares of designing men,
Or an improper acquaintance with women of doubtful characters.

Thus did he establish his government on pillars
Of honour and politeness,
Which could never be shaken:
And maintained it for full half a century,
With reputation, honour, and undisputed authority,
Beloved, respected, and revered.
Of his private character, be it the first praise,
That while, by his conduct, the highest ranks became his subjects,
He himself became
The servant of the poor and the distressed:
Whose cause he ever pleaded amongst the rich,
And enforced with all the eloquence of a good example:
They were ashamed not to relieve those wants
To which they saw him administer with
So noble an heart, and so liberal an hand.
Nor was his munificence confined to particulars,
He being, to all the public charities of this city,
A liberal benefactor;
Not only by his own most generous subscriptions,
But, by always assuming, in their behalf, the character of
A sturdy beggar;
Which he performed with such an authoritative address
To all ranks, without distinction,
That few of the worst hearts had courage to refuse,
What their own inclinations would not have prompted them to bestow.

Of a noble public spirit
And
A warm grateful heart
The obelisk in the grove,
And
The beautiful needle in the square,
Are magnificent testimonies.

The One
Erected to preserve the memory of a
Most interesting event to his country,
The restitution of health, by the healing waters of this place,
To the illustrious Prince of Orange,
Who came hither in a most languishing condition:

The Other,
A noble offering of thanks
To the late Prince of Wales, and his royal Consort,
For favours bestowed,
And honours by them conferred, on this city.

His long and peaceful reign, of
Absolute power,
Was so tempered by his
Excessive good nature,
That no instance can be given either of his own cruelty,
Or of his suffering that of others to escape
Its proper reward.
Example unprecedented amongst absolute monarchs.

Reader.
This monarch was a man,
And had his foibles and his faults:
Which he would wish covered with the veil of good-nature,
Made of the same piece with his own:
But, truth forceth us unwillingly to confess,
His passions were strong;
Which, as they fired him to act strenuously in good,
Hurried him to some excesses of evil.

His fire, not used to be kept under by an early restraint,
Burst out too often into flaming acts,
Without waiting for the cool approbation of his judgment.
His generosity was so great,
That Prudence often whispered him, in vain,
That she feared it would enter the neighbouring confines of profusion:
His charity so unbounded,
That the severe might suspect it sometimes to be
The offspring of folly, or ostentation.

With all these,
Be they foibles, follies, faults, or frailties,
It will be difficult to point out
Amongst his cotemporary Kings of the whole earth,
More than One
Who hath fewer, or less pernicious to mankind.

His existence
(For life it scarcely can be called)
Was spun out to so great an age, that
The man
Was sunk, like many other heroes, in
The weakness and infirmities of exhausted nature;
The unwilling tax all animals must pay
For multiplicity of days.
Over his closing scene,
Charity long spread her all-covering mantle,
And dropped the curtain,
Before the poor actor, though he had played his part,
Was permitted to quit the stage.

Now may she protect his memory!
Every friend of Bath
Every lover of decency, decorum, and good breeding,
Must sincerely deplore
The loss of so excellent a governor;
And join in the most fervent wishes (would I could say hopes!)
That there may soon be found a man
Able and worthy
To succeed him.

The reader sees in what alluring colours Nash's character is drawn; but he must consider, that an intimate friend held the pencil; the Doctor professes to say nothing of the dead but what was good; and such a maxim, though it serves his departed friend, is but badly calculated to improve the living. Dr. King, in his Epitaph, however, is still more indulgent; he produces him as an example to kings, and prefers his laws even to those of Solon or Lycurgus.

EPITAPHIUM RICHARDI NASH, ARMIGERI.

H. S. E.

RICHARDUS NASH,

Obscuro loco natus,
Et nullis ortus majoribus:
Cui tamen
(O rem miram, et incredibilem!)
Regnum opulentissimum florentissimumque
Plebs, proceres, principes,
Liberis suis suffragiis
Ultrò detulerunt,
Quod et ipse summâ cum dignitate tenuit,
Annos plus quinquaginta,
Universo populo consentiente, approbante, plaudente.

Una voce præterea, unoque omnium ordinum consensu,
Ad imperium suum adjuncta est
Magni nominis Provincia:
Quam admirabili consilio et ratione
Per se, non unquam per legatos, administravit;
Eam quotannis invisere dignatus,
Et apud provinciales, quoad necesse fuit,
Solitus manere.

In tantâ fortunâ
Neque fastu turgidus Rex incessu patuit,
Neque, tyrannorum more, se jussit coli,
Aut amplos honores, titulosque sibi arrogavit;
Sed cuncta insignia, etiam regium diadema rejiciens,
Caput contentus fuit ornare
GALERO ALBO,
Manifesto animi sui candoris signo.

LEGISLATOR prudentissimus,
Vel Solone et Lycurgo illustrior,
Leges, quascunque voluit,
Statuit, fixit, promulgavit;
Omnes quidem cùm civibus suis,
Tum verò hospitibus, advenis, peregrinis,
Gratas, jucundas, utiles.

VOLUPTATUM arbiter et minister,
Sed gravis, sed elegans, sed urbanus,
Et in summâ comitate satis adhibens severitatis,
Imprimis curavit,
Ut in virorum et fœminarum cœtibus
Nequis impudenter faceret,
Neque in iis quod inesset
Impuritatis, clamoris, tumulti.

CIVITATEM hanc celeberrimam,
Delicias suas,
Non modò pulcherrimis ædificiis auxit,
Sed præclarâ disciplinâ et moribus ornavit:
Quippe nemo quisquam
To PREPON melius intellexit, excoluit, docuit.

JUSTUS, liberalis, benignus, facetus,
Atque amicus omnibus, præcipuè miseris et egenis,
Nullos habuit inimicos,
Præter magnos quosdam ardeliones,
Et declamatores eos tristes et fanaticos,
Qui generi humano sunt inimicissimi.

PACIS et patriæ amans,
Concordiam, felicem et perpetuam,
In regno suo constituit,
Usque adeò,
Ut nullus alteri petulanter maledicere,
Aut facto nocere auderet;
Neque, tanquam sibi metuens,
In publicum armatus prodire.

FUIT quanquam potentissimus,
Omnia arbitrio suo gubernans:
Haud tamen ipsa libertas
Magis usquam floruit
Gratiâ, gloriâ, auctoritate.
Singulare enim temperamentum invenit,
(Rem magnæ cogitationis,
Et rerum omnium fortasse difficillimam)
Quo ignobiles cum nobilibus, pauperes cum divitibus,
Indocti cum doctissimis, ignavi cum fortissimis
Æquari se putarent,
REX OMNIBUS IDEM.

QUICQUID PECCAVERIT,
(Nam peccamus omnes)
In seipsum magis, quàm in alios,
Et errore, aut imprudentiâ magis quam scelere, aut improbitate,
Peccavit;
Nusquam verò ignoratione decori, aut honesti,
Neque ità quidem usquam,
Ut non veniam ab humanis omnibus
Facilè impetrârit.

HUJUS vitæ morumque exemplar
Si cæteri reges, regulique,
Et quotquot sunt regnorum præfecti,
Imitarentur;
(Utinam! iterumque utinam!)
Et ipsi essent beati,
Et cunctæ orbis regiones beatissimæ.

TALEM virum, tantumque ademptum
Lugeant musæ, charitesque!
Lugeant Veneres, Cupidinesque!
Lugeant omnes juvenum et nympharum chori!
Tu verò, O BATHONIA,
Ne cesses tuum lugere
Principem, præceptorem, amicum, patronum;
Heu, heu, nunquam posthàc
Habitura parem!

The following translation of this Epitaph will give the English reader an idea of its contents, though not of its elegance:—

THE EPITAPH OF RICHARD NASH, ESQ.

Here lies

RICHARD NASH,

Born in an obscure village,
And from mean ancestors,
To whom, however,
Strange to relate,
Both the vulgar and the mighty,
Without bribe or compulsion,
Unanimously gave
A kingdom, equally rich and flourishing.
A kingdom which he governed
More than fifty years,
With universal approbation and applause.

To his empire also was added,
By the consent of all orders,
A celebrated province
Which he ever swayed with great prudence,
Not by delegated power, but in person.
He deigned to visit it every year,
And while the necessities of state demanded his presence,
He usually continued there.

In such greatness of fortune
His pride discovered itself by no marks of dignity;
Nor did he ever claim the honours of prostration.
Despising at once titles of adulation,
And laying aside all royal splendour,
Wearing not even the diadem,
He was content with being distinguished
Only by the ornamental ensign
Of a white hat;
A symbol of the candour of his mind.

He was a most prudent legislator,
And more remarkable even than Solon or Lycurgus
He at once established and authorized
Whatever laws were thought convenient,
Which were equally serviceable to the city,
And grateful to strangers,
Who made it their abode.

He was at once a provider and a judge of pleasures,
But still conducted them with gravity and elegance,
And repressed licentiousness with severity.
His chief care was employed
In preventing obscenity or impudence
From offending the modesty or the morals
Of the Fair Sex,
And in banishing from their Assemblies
Tumult, clamour, and abuse.

He not only adorned this city,
Which he loved,
With beautiful structures,
But improved it by his example;
As no man knew, no man taught, what was becoming
Better than he.

He was just, liberal, kind, and facetious;
A friend to all, but particularly to the poor.
He had no enemies,
Except some of the trifling great,
Or dull declaimers, foes to all mankind.

Equally a lover of peace and of his country,
He fixed a happy and lasting concord
In his kingdom,
So that none dare convey scandal, or injure by open violence the universal peace,
Or even by carrying arms appear prepared for war,
With impunity.

But though his power was boundless,
Yet never did liberty flourish more, which he promoted,
Both by his authority, and cultivated for his fame.
He found out the happy secret
(A thing not to be considered without surprise)
Of uniting the vulgar and the great,
The poor and the rich,
The learned and ignorant,
The cowardly and the brave,
In the bonds of society, an equal king to all.

Whatever his faults were,
For we have all faults,
They were rather obnoxious to himself than others;
They arose neither from imprudence nor mistake,
Never from dishonesty or corrupt principle;
But so harmless were they,
That though they failed to create our esteem,
Yet can they not want our pardon.

Could other kings and governors
But learn to imitate his example,
(Would to heaven they could!)
Then might they see themselves happy,
And the people still enjoying more true felicity.

Ye Muses and Graces mourn
His death;
Ye powers of Love, ye choirs of youth and virgins,
But thou, O Bathonia! more than the rest,
Cease not to weep,
Your king, your teacher, patron, friend,
Never, ah never, to behold
His equal.

Whatever might have been justly observed of Mr. Nash's superiority as a governor, at least it may be said, that few cotemporary kings have met with such able panegyrists. The former enumerates all his good qualities with tenderness, and the latter enforces them with impetuosity. They both seem to have loved him, and honourably paid his remains the last debt of friendship. But a cool biographer, unbiassed by resentment or regard, will probably find nothing in the man either truly great, or strongly vicious. His virtues were all amiable, and more adapted to procure friends than admirers; they were more capable of raising love than esteem. He was naturally endued with good sense; but by having been long accustomed to pursue trifles, his mind shrunk to the size of the little objects on which it was employed. His generosity was boundless, because his tenderness and his vanity were in equal proportion; the one impelling him to relieve misery, and the other to make his benefactions known. In all his actions, however virtuous, he was guided by sensation and not by reason; so that the uppermost passion was ever sure to prevail.

His being constantly in company had made him an easy though not a polite companion. He chose to be thought rather an odd fellow than a well-bred man; perhaps that mixture of respect and ridicule with which his mock royalty was treated, first inspired him with this resolution. The foundations of his empire were laid in vicious compliance, the continuance of his reign was supported by a virtuous impartiality. In the beginning of his authority, he in reality obeyed those whom he pretended to govern; towards the end, he attempted to extort a real obedience from his subjects, and supported his right by prescription. Like a monarch Tacitus talks of, they complied with him at first because they loved, they obeyed at last because they feared him. He often led the rich into new follies, in order to promote the happiness of the poor, and served the one at the expense of the other. Whatever his vices were, they were of use to society; and this neither Petronius, nor Apicius, nor Tigellius, nor any other professed voluptuary could say. To set him up, as some do, for a pattern of imitation, is wrong, since all his virtues received a tincture from the neighbouring folly; to denounce peculiar judgments against him is equally unjust, as his faults raise rather our mirth than our detestation. He was fitted for the station in which fortune placed him. It required no great abilities to fill it, and few of great abilities but would have disdained the employment. He led a life of vanity, and long mistook it for happiness. Unfortunately, he was taught at last to know that a man of pleasure leads the most unpleasant life in the world.

*A Letter from Mr. *** in Tunbridge to Lord **** in London, found among the papers of Mr. Nash, and prepared by him for the press.*

"MY LORD,—What I foresaw has arrived; poor Jenners, after losing all his fortune, has shot himself through the head. His losses to Bland were considerable, and his playing soon after with Spedding contributed to hasten his ruin. No man was ever more enamoured of play, or understood it less. At whatever game he ventured his money, he was most usually the dupe, and still foolishly attributed to his bad luck those misfortunes that entirely proceeded from his want of judgment.

"After finding that he had brought on himself irreparable indigence and contempt, his temper, formerly so sprightly, began to grow gloomy and unequal: he grew more fond of solitude, and more liable to take offence at supposed injuries; in short, for a week before he shot himself, his friends were of opinion that he meditated some such horrid design. He was found in his chamber fallen on the floor, the bullet having glanced on the bone, and lodged behind his right eye.

"You remember, my Lord, what a charming fellow this deluded man was once; how benevolent, just, temperate, and every way virtuous. The only faults of his mind arose from motives of humanity: he was too easy, credulous, and good-natured, and unable to resist temptation, when recommended by the voice of friendship. These foibles the vicious and the needy soon perceived, and what was at first a weakness they soon perverted into guilt; he became a gamester, and continued the infamous profession till he could support the miseries brought with it no longer.

"I have often been not a little concerned to see the first introduction of a young man of fortune to the gaming-table. With what eagerness his company is courted by the whole fraternity of sharpers; how they find out his most latent wishes, in order to make way to his affections by gratifying them, and continue to hang upon him with the meanest degree of condescension. The youthful dupe, no way suspecting, imagines himself surrounded by friends and gentlemen, and, incapable of even suspecting that men of such seeming good sense and so genteel an appearance should deviate from the laws of honour, walks into the snare, nor is he undeceived till schooled by the severity of experience.

"As I suppose no man would be a gamester unless he hoped to win, so I fancy it would be easy to reclaim him, if he was once effectually convinced, that by continuing to play he must certainly lose. Permit me, my lord, to attempt this task, and to show, that no young gentleman by a year's run of play, and in a mixed company, can possibly be a gainer.

"Let me suppose, in the first place, that the chances on both sides are equal, that there are no marked cards, no pinching, shuffling, nor hiding; let me suppose that the players also have no advantage of each other in point of judgment, and still further let me grant, that the party is only formed at home, without going to the usual expensive places of resort frequented by gamesters. Even with all these circumstances in the young gamester's favour, it is evident he cannot be a gainer. With equal players, after a year's continuance of any particular game it will be found that, whatever has been played for, the winnings on either side are very inconsiderable, and most commonly nothing at all. Here then is a year's anxiety, pain, jarring, and suspense, and nothing gained; were the parties to sit down and professedly play for nothing, they would contemn the proposal; they would call it trifling away time, and one of the most insipid amusements in nature; yet, in fact, how do equal players differ? It is allowed that little or nothing can be gained; but much is lost; our youth, our time, those moments that may be laid out in pleasure or improvement, are foolishly squandered away in tossing cards, fretting at ill-luck, or, even with a run of luck in our favour, fretting that our winnings are so small.

"I have now stated gaming in that point of view in which it is alone defensible, as a commerce carried on with equal advantage and loss to either party, and it appears, that the loss is great, and the advantage but small. But let me suppose the players not to be equal, but the superiority of judgment in our own favour. A person who plays under this conviction, however, must give up all pretensions to the approbation of his own mind, and is guilty of as much injustice as the thief who robbed a blind man because he knew he could not swear to his person.

"But, in fact, when I allowed the superiority of skill on the young beginner's side, I only granted an impossibility. Skill in gaming, like skill in making a watch, can only be acquired by long and painful industry. The most sagacious youth alive was never taught at once all the arts and all the niceties of gaming. Every passion must be schooled by long habit into caution and phlegm; the very countenance must be taught proper discipline; and he who would practise this art with success, must practise on his own constitution all the severities of a martyr, without any expectation of the reward. It is evident, therefore, every beginner must be a dupe, and can only be expected to learn his trade by losses, disappointments, and dishonour.

"If a young gentleman, therefore, begins to game, the commencements are sure to be to his disadvantage; and all that he can promise himself is, that the company he keeps, though superior in skill, are above taking advantage of his ignorance, and unacquainted with any sinister arts to correct fortune. But this, however, is but a poor hope at best, and, what is worse, most frequently a false one. In general, I might almost have said always, those who live by gaming are not beholden to chance alone for their support, but take every advantage which they can practise without danger of detection. I know many are apt to say, and I have once said so myself, that after I have shuffled the cards, it is not in the power of a sharper to pack them; but at present I can confidently assure your lordship that such reasoners are deceived. I have seen men both in Paris, the Hague, and London, who, after three deals, could give whatever hands they pleased to all the company. However, the usual way with sharpers is to correct fortune thus but once in a night, and to play in other respects without blunder or mistake, and a perseverance in this practice always balances the year in their favour.

"It is impossible to enumerate all the tricks and arts practised upon cards; few but have seen those bungling poor fellows who go about at coffee-houses, perform their clumsy feats, and yet, indifferently as they are versed in the trade, they often deceive us. When such as these are possessed of so much art, what must not those be, who have been bred up to gaming from their infancy, whose hands are not like those mentioned above, rendered callous by labour, who have continual practice in the trade of deceiving, and where the eye of the spectator is less upon its guard.

"Let the young beginner only reflect by what a variety of methods it is possible to cheat him, and perhaps it will check his confidence. His antagonists may act by signs and confederacy, and this he can never detect; they may cut to a particular card after three or four hands have gone about, either by having that card pinched, or broader than the rest, or by having an exceeding fine wire thrust between the folds of the paper, and just peeping out at the edge. Or the cards may be chalked with particular marks which none but the sharper can understand, or a new pack may be slipped in at a proper opportunity. I have known myself, in Paris, a fellow thus detected with a tin case, containing two packs of cards, concealed within his shirt sleeve, and which, by means of a spring, threw the cards ready packed into his hands. These and an hundred other arts may be practised with impunity and escape detection.

"The great error lies in imagining every fellow with a laced coat to be a gentleman. The address and transient behaviour of a man of breeding are easily acquired, and none are better qualified than gamesters in this respect. At first, their complaisance, civility, and apparent honour is pleasing; but upon examination few of them will be found to have their minds sufficiently stored with any of the more refined accomplishments which truly characterise the man of breeding. This will commonly serve as a criterion to distinguish them, though there are other marks which every young gentleman of fortune should be apprised of. A sharper, when he plays, generally handles and deals the cards awkwardly like a bungler; he advances his bets by degrees, and keeps his antagonist in spirits by small advantages and alternate success at the beginning: to show all his force at once, would but frighten the bird he intends to decoy; he talks of honour and virtue, and his being a gentleman, and that he knows great men, and mentions his coal-mines, and his estate in the country; he is totally divested of that masculine confidence which is the attendant of real fortune; he turns, yields, assents, smiles, as he hopes will be most pleasing to his destined prey; he is afraid of meeting a shabby acquaintance, particularly if in better company; as he grows richer he wears finer clothes; and if ever he is seen in an undress, it is most probable he is without money; so that seeing a gamester growing finer each day, is a certain symptom of his success.

"The young gentleman who plays with such men for considerable sums, is sure to be undone, and yet we seldom see even the rook himself make a fortune. A life of gaming must necessarily be a life of extravagance; parties of this kind are formed in houses where the whole profits are consumed, and while those who play mutually ruin each other, they only who keep the house or the table acquire fortunes. Thus gaming may readily ruin a fortune, but has seldom been found to retrieve it. The wealth which has been acquired with industry and hazard, and preserved for ages by prudence and foresight, is swept away on a sudden; and when a besieging sharper sits down before an estate, the property is often transferred in less time than the writings can be drawn to secure the possession. The neglect of business, and the extravagance of a mind which has been taught to covet precarious possession, bring on premature destruction: though poverty may fetch a compass and go somewhat about, yet will it reach the gamester at last; and though his ruin be slow, yet it is certain.

"A thousand instances could be given of the fatal tendency of this passion, which first impoverishes the mind, and then perverts the understanding. Permit me to mention one, not caught from report, or dressed up by fancy, but such as has actually fallen under my own observation, and of the truth of which I beg your lordship may rest satisfied.

"At Tunbridge, in the year 1715, Mr. J. Hedges made a very brilliant appearance. He had been married about two years to a young lady of great beauty and large fortune; they had one child, a boy, on whom they bestowed all that affection which they could spare from each other. He knew nothing of gaming, nor seemed to have the least passion for play; but he was unacquainted with his own heart; he began by degrees to bet at the tables for trifling sums, and his soul took fire at the prospect of immediate gain: he was soon surrounded with sharpers, who with calmness lay in ambush for his fortune, and coolly took advantage of the precipitancy of his passions.

"His lady perceived the ruin of her family approaching, but at first without being able to form any scheme to prevent it. She advised with his brother, who at that time was possessed of a small fellowship in Cambridge. It was easily seen that whatever took the lead in her husband's mind, seemed to be there fixed unalterably; it was determined, therefore, to let him pursue fortune, but previously take measures to prevent the pursuit being fatal.

"Accordingly, every night this gentleman was a constant attender at the hazard tables; he understood neither the arts of sharpers nor even the allowed strokes of a connoisseur, yet still he played. The consequence is obvious: he lost his estate, his equipage, his wife's jewels, and every other moveable that could be parted with, except a repeating watch. His agony upon this occasion was inexpressible; he was even mean enough to ask a gentleman, who sat near, to lend him a few pieces, in order to turn his fortune; but this prudent gamester, who plainly saw there were no expectations of being repaid, refused to lend a farthing, alleging a former resolution against lending. Hedges was at last furious with the continuance of ill-success, and pulling out his watch, asked if any person in company would set him sixty guineas upon it: the company were silent; he then demanded fifty; still no answer: he sunk to forty, thirty, twenty; finding the company still without answering, he cried out, 'By G—d it shall never go for less,' and dashed it against the floor, at the same time attempting to dash out his brains against the marble chimney-piece.

"This last act of desperation immediately excited the attention of the whole company; they instantly gathered round, and prevented the effects of his passion; and after he again became cool, he was permitted to return home, with sullen discontent, to his wife. Upon his entering her apartment, she received him with her usual tenderness and satisfaction; while he answered her caresses with contempt and severity; his disposition being quite altered with his misfortunes. 'But, my dear Jemmy,' says his wife, 'perhaps you don't know the news I have to tell: my mamma's old uncle is dead; the messenger is now in the house, and you know his estate is settled upon you.' This account seemed only to increase his agony, and looking angrily at her, he cried, 'There you lie, my dear, his estate is not settled upon me.'—'I beg your pardon,' says she, 'I really thought it was; at least you have always told me so.' 'No,' returned he, 'as sure as you and I are to be miserable here, and our children beggars hereafter, I have sold the reversion of it this day, and have lost every farthing I got for it at the hazard table.' 'What, all!' replied the lady. 'Yes, every farthing,' returned he, 'and I owe a thousand pounds more than I have to pay.' Thus speaking, he took a few frantic steps across the room. When the lady had a little enjoyed his perplexity: 'No, my dear,' cried she, 'you have lost but a trifle, and you owe nothing; our brother and I have taken care to prevent the effects of your rashness, and are actually the persons who have won your fortune: we employed proper persons for this purpose, who brought their winnings to me; your money, your equipage, are in my possession, and here I return them to you, from whom they were unjustly taken. I only ask permission to keep my jewels, and to keep you, my greatest jewel, from such dangers for the future.' Her prudence had the proper effect; he ever after retained a sense of his former follies, and never played for the smallest sums, even for amusement.

"Not less than three persons in one day

fell a sacrifice at Bath to this destructive passion. Two gentlemen fought a duel, in which one was killed, and the other desperately wounded; and a youth of great expectation and excellent disposition, at the same time ended his own life by a pistol. If there be any state that deserves pity, it must be that of a gamester; but the state of a dying gamester is of all situations the most deplorable.

"There is another argument which your lordship, I fancy, will not entirely despise: beauty, my lord, I own is at best but a trifle, but such as it is, I fancy few would willingly part with what little they have. A man with a healthful complexion, how great a philosopher soever he be, would not willingly exchange it for a sallow hectic phyz, pale eyes, and a sharp wrinkled visage. I entreat you only to examine the faces of all the noted gamblers round one of our public tables; have you ever seen anything more haggard, pinched, and miserable? And it is but natural that it should be so. The succession of passions flush the cheek with red, and all such flushings are ever succeeded by consequent paleness; so that a gamester contracts the sickly hue of a student, while he is only acquiring the stupidity of a fool.

"Your good sense, my lord, I have often had an occasion of knowing, yet how miserable is it to be in a set of company where the most sensible is ever the least skilful; your footman, with a little instruction, would, I dare venture to affirm, make a better and more successful gamester than you. Want of passions, and low cunning, are the two great arts; and it is peculiar to this science alone, that they who have the greatest passion for it, are of all others the most unfit to practise it.

"Of all the men I ever knew, Spedding was the greatest blockhead, and yet the best gamester; he saw almost intuitively the advantage on either side, and ever took it; he could calculate the odds in a moment, and decide upon the merits of a cock or a horse, better than any man in England; in short, he was such an adept in gaming, that he brought it up to a pitch of sublimity it had never attained before; yet, with all this, Spedding could not write his own name. What he died worth I cannot tell, but of this I am certain, he might have possessed a ministerial estate, and that won from men famed for their sense, literature, and patriotism.

"If, after this description, your lordship is yet resolved to hazard your fortune at gaming, I beg you would advert to the situation of an old and luckless gamester. Perhaps there is not in nature a more deplorable being: his character is too well marked, he is too well known to be trusted. A man that has been often a bankrupt, and renewed trade upon low compositions, may as well expect extensive credit as such a man. His reputation is blasted: his constitution worn, by the extravagance and ill hours of his profession; he is now incapable of alluring his dupes, and, like a superannuated savage of the forest, he is starved for want of vigour to hunt after prey.

"Thus gaming is the source of poverty, and still worse, the parent of infamy and vice. It is an inlet to debauchery, for the money thus acquired is but little valued. Every gamester is a rake, and his morals worse than his mystery. It is his interest to be exemplary in every scene of debauchery; his prey is to be courted with every guilty pleasure; but these are to be changed, repeated, and embellished, in order to employ his imagination, while his reason is kept asleep; a young mind is apt to shrink at the prospect of ruin; care must be taken to harden his courage, and make him keep his rank; he must be either found a libertine, or he must be made one. And when a man has parted with his money like a fool, he generally sends his conscience after it like a villain, and the nearer he is to the brink of destruction, the fonder does he grow of ruin.

"Your friend and mine, my lord, had been thus driven to the last reserve, for he found it impossible to disentangle his affairs, and look the world in the face; impatience at length threw him into the abyss he feared, and life became a burthen, because he feared to die. But I own that play is not always attended with such tragical circumstances: some have had courage to survive their losses, and go on content with beggary; and sure those misfortunes which are of our own production, are of all others most pungent. To see such a poor disbanded being an unwelcome guest at every table, and often flapped off like a fly, is affecting; in this case the closest alliance is forgotten, and contempt is too strong for the ties of blood to unbind.

"But, however fatal this passion may be in its consequence, none allures so much in the beginning; the person once listed as a gamester, if not soon reclaimed, pursues it through his whole life; no loss can retard, no danger awaken him to common sense; nothing can terminate his career but want of money to play, or of honour to be trusted.

"Among the number of my acquaintance, I knew but of two who succeeded by gaming; the one a phlegmatic heavy man, who would have made a fortune in whatever way of life he happened to be placed; the other who had lost a fine estate in his youth by play, and retrieved a greater at the age of sixty-five, when he might be justly said to be past the power of enjoying it. One or two successful gamesters are thus set up in an age to allure the young beginner; we all regard such as the highest prize in a lottery, unmindful of the numerous losses that go to the accumulation of such infrequent success.

"Yet I would not be so morose as to refuse your youth all kinds of play; the innocent amusements of a family must often be indulged, and cards allowed to supply the intervals of more real pleasure; but the sum played for in such cases should always be a trifle; something to call up attention, but not engage the passions. The usual excuse for laying large sums is, to make the players attend to their game; but, in fact, he that plays only for shillings will mind his cards equally well with him that bets guineas; for the mind habituated to stake large sums, will consider them as trifles at last; and if one shilling could not exclude indifference at first, neither will an hundred in the end.

"I have often asked myself, how it is possible that he who is possessed of competence, can ever be induced to make it precarious by beginning play with the odds against him; for wherever he goes to sport his money, he will find himself over-matched and cheated. Either at White's, Newmarket, the Tennis Court, the Cock Pit, or the Billiard Table, he will find numbers who have no other resource but their acquisitions there; and if such men live like gentlemen, he may readily conclude it must be on the spoils of his fortune, or the fortunes of ill-judging men like himself. Was he to attend but a moment to their manner of betting at those places, he would readily find the gamester seldom proposing bets but with the advantage in his own favour. A man of honour continues to lay on the side on which he first won; but gamesters shift, change, lie upon the lurch, and take every advantage, either of our ignorance or neglect.

"In short, my lord, if a man designs to lay out his fortune in quest of pleasure, the gaming table is, of all other places, that where he can have least for his money. The company are superficial, extravagant, and unentertaining; the conversation flat, debauched, and absurd; the hour unnatural and fatiguing; the anxiety of losing is greater than the pleasure of winning; friendship must be banished from that society the members of which are intent only on ruining each other; every other improvement, either in knowledge or virtue, can scarce find room in that breast which is possessed by the spirit of play; the spirits become vapid, the constitution is enfeebled, the complexion grows pale, till, in the end, the mind, body, friends, fortune, and even the hopes of futurity sink together! Happy, if Nature terminates the scene, and neither justice nor suicide are called in to accelerate her tardy approach. I am, my lord, &c."

Among other papers in the custody of Mr. Nash, was the following angry letter addressed to him in this manner:—

"*To* RICHARD NASH, ESQ.,
"*King of Bath.*

"SIRE,—I must desire your majesty to order the inclosed to be read to the great Mr. Hoyle, if he be found in any part of your dominions. You will perceive that it is a panegyric on his manifold virtues, and that he is thanked more particularly for spending his time so much to the emolument of the public, and for obliging the world with a book more read than the Bible, and which so eminently tends to promote Christian knowledge, sound morality, and the happiness of mankind."

(The inclosed we have omitted, as it contains a satire on gaming, and may probably give offence to our betters.)

"This author, however," (continues the letter writer,) "has not set forth half the merits of the piece under consideration, nor is the great care which he has taken to prevent our reading any other book, instead of this, been sufficiently taken notice of: beware of counterfeits; these books are not to be depended on unless signed by E. Hoyle, is a charitable admonition. As you have so much power at Bath, and are absolute, I think you should imitate other great monarchs, by rewarding those with honours who have been serviceable in your state; and I beg that a new order may be established for that purpose. Let him who has done nothing but game all his life, and has reduced the most families to ruin and beggary, be made a Marshal of the Black Ace; and those who are every day making proselytes to the tables, have the honour of knighthood conferred on them, and be distinguished by the style and title of *Knights of the four Knaves.*

"The moment I came into Bath, my ears were saluted with the news of a gentleman's being plundered at the gaming-table, and having lost his senses on the occasion. The same day a duel was fought between two gentlemen gamesters on the Downs, and in the evening another hanged himself at the Bear, but first wrote a note which was found near him, importing that he had injured the best of friends. These are the achievements of your Knights of the four Knaves. The Devil will pick the bones of all gamesters, that's certain. . . . Ay! and of duellers too, but in the meantime let none think that duelling is a mark of courage; for I know it is not. A person served under me in Flanders, who had fought four duels, and depended so much on his skill, the strength of his arm, and the length of his sword, that he would take up a quarrel for anybody; yet in the field I never saw one behave so like a poltroon. If a few of these gamesters and duellers were gibbeted, it might perhaps help to amend the rest. I have often thought that the only way, or at least the most effectual way, to prevent duelling would be to hang both parties—the living and the dead—on the same tree, and if the winner and the loser were treated in the same manner, it would be better for the public, since the tucking up of a few R——ls might be a warning to others, and save many a worthy family from destruction. I am yours, &c."

The author of this letter appears to have been very angry, and not without reason; for if I am rightly informed, his only son was ruined at Bath, and by sharpers. But why is Mr. Nash to be blamed for this? It must be acknowledged, that he always took pains to prevent the ruin of the youth of both sexes, and had so guarded against duelling, that he would not permit a sword to be worn in Bath.

As the heart of a man is better known by his private than his public actions, let us take a view of Nash in domestic life; among his servants and dependants, where no gloss was required to colour his sentiments and disposition, nor any mask necessary to conceal his foibles. Here we shall find him the same open-hearted, generous, good-natured man we have already described; one who was ever fond of promoting the interests of his friends, his servants, and dependants, and making them happy. In his own house no man perhaps was more regular, cheerful, and beneficent than Nash. His table was always free to those who sought his friendship, or wanted a dinner; and after grace was said, he usually accosted the company in the following extraordinary manner, to take off all restraint and ceremony: "Come, gentlemen, eat and welcome; spare, and the Devil choke you." I mention this circumstance for no other reason but because it is well known, and is consistent with the singularity of his character and behaviour.

As Mr. Nash's thoughts were entirely employed in the affairs of his government, he was seldom at home but at the time of eating or of rest. His table was well served, but his entertainment consisted principally of plain dishes. Boiled chicken and roast mutton were his favourite meats, and he was so fond of the small sort of potatoes, that he called them English pine-apples, and generally ate them as others do fruit, after dinner. In drinking he was altogether as regular and abstemious. Both in this and in eating, he seemed to consult Nature, and obey only her dictates. Good small beer, with or without a glass of wine in it, and sometimes wine and water, was his drink at meals, and after dinner he generally drank one glass of wine. He seemed fond of hot suppers, usually supped about nine or ten o'clock, upon roast breast of mutton and his potatoes, and soon after supper went to bed; which induced Dr. Cheyne to tell him jestingly, that he behaved like other brutes, and lay down as soon as he had filled his belly. "Very true," replied Nash, "and this prescription I had from my neighbour's cow, who is a better physician than you, and a superior judge of plants, notwithstanding you have written so learnedly on the vegetable diet."

Nash generally arose early in the morning, being seldom in bed after five; and to avoid disturbing the family and depriving his servants of their rest, he had the fire laid after he was in bed, and in the morning lighted it himself, and sat down to read some of his few but well-chosen books. After reading some time, he usually went to the pump-room and drank the waters; then took a walk on the parade, and went to the coffee-house to breakfast; after which, till two o'clock (his usual time of dinner) his hours were spent in arbitrating differences amongst his neighbours, or the company resorting to the wells; in directing the diversions of the day, visiting the new comers, or receiving friends at his own house; of which there was a great concourse till within six or eight years before his death.

His generosity and charity in private life, though not so conspicuous, was as great as that in public, and indeed far more considerable than his little income would admit of. He could not stifle the natural impulse which he had to do good, but frequently borrowed money to relieve the distressed; and when he knew not conveniently where to borrow, he has been often observed to shed tears, as he passed through the wretched supplicants who attended his gate.

This sensibility, this power of feeling the misfortunes of the miserable, and his address and earnestness in relieving their wants, exalts the character of Mr. Nash, and draws an impenetrable veil over his foibles. His singularities are forgotten when we behold his virtues, and he who laughed at the whimsical character and behaviour of this Monarch of Bath, now laments that he is no more.

END OF THE LIFE OF RICHARD NASH.

POEMS

THE TRAVELLER;

OR, A PROSPECT OF SOCIETY.

(1764.)

To the Rev. Henry Goldsmith.

Dear Sir,—I am sensible that the friendship between us can acquire no new force from the ceremonies of a Dedication; and perhaps it demands an excuse thus to prefix your name to my attempts, which you decline giving with your own. But as a part of this Poem was formerly written to you from Switzerland, the whole can now, with propriety, be only inscribed to you. It will also throw a light upon many parts of it when the reader understands that it is addressed to a man who, despising fame and fortune, has retired early to happiness and obscurity, with an income of forty pounds a year.

I now perceive, my dear brother, the wisdom of your humble choice. You have entered upon a sacred office, where the harvest is great and the labourers are but few; while you have left the field of ambition, where the labourers are many, and the harvest not worth carrying away. But of all kinds of ambition, what from the refinement of the times, from different systems of criticism, and from the divisions of party, that which pursues poetical fame is the wildest.

Poetry makes a principal amusement among unpolished nations; but in a country verging to the extremes of refinement Painting and Music come in for a share. As these offer the feeble mind a less laborious entertainment, they at first rival Poetry, and at length supplant her; they engross all that favour once shown to her, and though but younger sisters, seize upon the elder's birthright.

Yet, however this art may be neglected by the powerful, it is still in great danger from the mistaken efforts of the learned to improve it. What criticisms have we not heard of late in favour of blank verse and Pindaric odes, chorusses, anapests, and iambics, alliterative care and happy negligence! Every absurdity has now a champion to defend it: and as he is generally much in the wrong, so he has always much to say; for error is ever talkative.

But there is an enemy to this art still more dangerous,—I mean party. Party entirely distorts the judgment, and destroys the taste. When the mind is once infected with this disease, it can only find pleasure in what contributes to increase the distemper. Like the tiger, that seldom desists from pursuing man after having once preyed upon human flesh, the reader who has once gratified his appetite with calumny, makes ever after the most agreeable feast upon murdered reputation. Such readers generally admire some half-witted thing, who wants to be thought a bold man, having lost the character of a wise one. Him they dignify with the name of poet: his tawdry lampoons are called satires; his turbulence is said to be force, and his phrenzy fire.

What reception a poem may find, which has neither abuse, party, nor blank verse to support it, I cannot tell, nor am I solicitous to know. My aims are right. Without espousing the cause of any party, I have attempted to moderate the rage of all. I have endeavoured to show that there may be equal happiness in states that are differently governed from our own; that every state has a particular principle of happiness, and that this principle in each may be carried to a mischievous excess. There are few can judge better than yourself how far these positions are illustrated in this Poem. I am,

Dear Sir, your most affectionate Brother,

OLIVER GOLDSMITH.

REMOTE, unfriended, melancholy, slow,
Or by the lazy Scheld or wandering Po;
Or onward, where the rude Carinthian boor
Against the houseless stranger shuts the door;
Or where Campania's plain forsaken lies,
A weary waste expanding to the skies;
Where'er I roam, whatever realms to see,
My heart untravell'd fondly turns to thee;
Still to my brother turns, with ceaseless pain,
And drags at each remove a lengthening chain.
Eternal blessings crown my earliest friend,
And round his dwelling guardian saints attend:
Blest be that spot where cheerful guests retire
To pause from toil, and trim their evening fire:
Blest that abode where want and pain repair,
And every stranger finds a ready chair:
Blest be those feasts, with simple plenty crown'd,
Where all the ruddy family around
Laugh at the jests or pranks that never fail,
Or sigh with pity at some mournful tale;
Or press the bashful stranger to his food,
And learn the luxury of doing good.
But me, not destin'd such delights to share,
My prime of life in wandering spent and care;
Impell'd, with steps unceasing, to pursue
Some fleeting good, that mocks me with the view;
That, like the circle bounding earth and skies,
Allures from far, yet, as I follow, flies;
My fortune leads to traverse realms alone,
And find no spot of all the world my own.
E'en now, where Alpine solitudes ascend,
I sit me down a pensive hour to spend;
And plac'd on high above the storm's career,
Look downward where an hundred realms appear;
Lakes, forests, cities, plains extending wide,
The pomp of kings, the shepherd's humbler pride.
When thus Creation's charms around combine,
Amidst the store should thankless pride repine?

Say, should the philosophic mind disdain
That good which makes each humbler bosom vain?
Let school-taught pride dissemble all it can,
These little things are great to little man;
And wiser he, whose sympathetic mind
Exults in all the good of all mankind.
Ye glittering towns, with wealth and splendour crown'd;
Ye fields, where summer spreads profusion round;
Ye lakes, whose vessels catch the busy gale;
Ye bending swains, that dress the flowery vale;
For me your tributary stores combine:
Creation's heir, the world, the world is mine.
As some lone miser, visiting his store,
Bends at his treasure, counts, recounts it o'er;
Hoards after hoards his rising raptures fill,
Yet still he sighs, for hoards are wanting still:
Thus to my breast alternate passions rise,
Pleas'd with each good that Heaven to man supplies:
Yet oft a sigh prevails, and sorrows fall,
To see the hoard of human bliss so small;
And oft I wish amidst the scene to find
Some spot to real happiness consign'd,
Where my worn soul, each wandering hope at rest,
May gather bliss to see my fellows blest.
But where to find that happiest spot below
Who can direct, when all pretend to know?
The shudd'ring tenant of the frigid zone
Boldly proclaims that happiest spot his own;
Extols the treasures of his stormy seas,
And his long nights of revelry and ease:
The naked negro, panting at the line,
Boasts of his golden sands and palmy wine,
Basks in the glare, or stems the tepid wave,
And thanks his gods for all the good they gave.
Such is the patriot's boast where'er we roam;
His first, best country ever is at home.
And yet, perhaps, if countries we compare,
And estimate the blessings which they share,
Though patriots flatter, still shall wisdom find
An equal portion dealt to all mankind;
As different good, by art or nature given,
To different nations makes their blessing even.
Nature, a mother kind alike to all,
Still grants her bliss at labour's earnest call:
With food as well the peasant is supply'd
On Idra's cliffs as Arno's shelvy side;
And though the rocky-crested summits frown,
These rocks by custom turn to beds of down.
From art more various are the blessings sent;
Wealth, commerce, honour, liberty, content.
Yet these each other's power so strong contest,
That either seems destructive of the rest.
Where wealth and freedom reign, contentment fails;
And honour sinks where commerce long prevails.

Hence every state, to one lov'd blessing prone,
Conforms and models life to that alone.
Each to the fav'rite happiness attends,
And spurns the plan that aims at other ends:
Till carried to excess in each domain,
This fav'rite good begets peculiar pain.
  But let us try these truths with closer eyes,
And trace them through the prospect as it lies:
Here for a while my proper cares resign'd,
Here let me sit in sorrow for mankind;
Like yon neglected shrub at random cast,
That shades the steep, and sighs at every blast.
  Far to the right, where Apennine ascends,
Bright as the summer, Italy extends:
Its uplands sloping deck the mountain's side,
Woods over woods in gay theatric pride;
While oft some temple's mould'ring tops between
With venerable grandeur mark the scene.
  Could Nature's bounty satisfy the breast,
The sons of Italy were surely blest.
Whatever fruits in different climes were found,
That proudly rise, or humbly court the ground;
Whatever blooms in torrid tracts appear,
Whose bright succession decks the varied year;
Whatever sweets salute the northern sky
With vernal lives, that blossom but to die;
These, here disporting, own the kindred soil,
Nor ask luxuriance from the planter's toil;
While sea-born gales their gelid wings expand
To winnow fragrance round the smiling land.
  But small the bliss that sense alone bestows,
And sensual bliss is all the nation knows.
In florid beauty groves and fields appear;
Man seems the only growth that dwindles here.
Contrasted faults through all his manners reign:
Though poor, luxurious; though submissive, vain;
Though grave, yet trifling; zealous, yet untrue;
And e'en in penance planning sins anew.
All evils here contaminate the mind
That opulence departed leaves behind;
For wealth was theirs, not far removed the date
When commerce proudly flourish'd through the state:
At her command the palace learnt to rise,
Again the long-fall'n column sought the skies,
The canvas glow'd, beyond e'en nature warm,
The pregnant quarry teem'd with human form,
Till, more unsteady than the southern gale,
Commerce on other shores display'd her sail;
While nought remain'd of all that riches gave,
But towns unmann'd, and lords without a slave:
And late the nation found with fruitless skill
Its former strength was but plethoric ill.
  Yet still the loss of wealth is here supplied
By arts, the splendid wrecks of former pride;

From these the feeble heart and long-fall'n mind
An easy compensation seem to find.
Here may be seen, in bloodless pomp array'd,
The paste-board triumph and the cavalcade,
Processions form'd for piety and love,
A mistress or a saint in every grove.
By sports like these are all their cares beguil'd;
The sports of children satisfy the child.
Each nobler aim, represt by long control,
Now sinks at last, or feebly mans the soul;
While low delights succeeding fast behind,
In happier meanness occupy the mind:
As in those domes where Cæsars once bore sway,
Defac'd by time and tott'ring in decay,
There in the ruin, heedless of the dead,
The shelter-seeking peasant builds his shed;
And, wondering man could want the larger pile,
Exults, and owns his cottage with a smile.
My soul, turn from them, turn we to survey
Where rougher climes a nobler race display;
Where the bleak Swiss their stormy mansion tread,
And force a churlish soil for scanty bread.
No product here the barren hills afford,
But man and steel, the soldier and his sword:
No vernal blooms their torpid rocks array,
But winter lingering chills the lap of May:
No zephyr fondly sues the mountain's breast,
But meteors glare, and stormy glooms invest.
Yet, still, e'en here content can spread a charm,
Redress the clime, and all its rage disarm.
Though poor the peasant's hut, his feasts tho' small,
He sees his little lot the lot of all;
Sees no contiguous palace rear its head
To shame the meanness of his humble shed;
No costly lord the sumptuous banquet deal
To make him loath his vegetable meal;
But calm, and bred in ignorance and toil,
Each wish contracting fits him to the soil.
Cheerful at morn he wakes from short repose,
Breathes the keen air, and carols as he goes;
With patient angle trolls the finny deep;
Or drives his vent'rous plough-share to the steep;
Or seeks the den where snow-tracks mark the way,
And drags the struggling savage into day.
At night returning, every labour sped,
He sits him down the monarch of a shed;
Smiles by his cheerful fire, and round surveys
His children's looks, that brighten at the blaze;
While his lov'd partner, boastful of her hoard,
Displays her cleanly platter on the board:
And hapiy too some pilgrim, thither led,
With many a tale repays the nightly bed.
Thus every good his native wilds impart
Imprints the patriot passion on his heart;

And e'en those ills that round his mansion rise
Enhance the bliss his scanty fund supplies.
Dear is that shed to which his soul conforms,
And dear that hill which lifts him to the storms;
And as a child, when scaring sounds molest,
Clings close and closer to the mother's breast,
So the loud torrent and the whirlwind's roar
But bind him to his native mountains more.
Such are the charms to barren states assign'd;
Their wants but few, their wishes all confin'd.
Yet let them only share the praises due:
If few their wants, their pleasures are but few;
For every want that stimulates the breast
Becomes a source of pleasure when redrest;
Whence from such lands each pleasing science flies
That first excites desire, and then supplies;
Unknown to them, when sensual pleasures cloy,
To fill the languid pause with finer joy;
Unknown those powers that raise the soul to flame,
Catch every nerve, and vibrate through the frame.
Their level life is but a smouldering fire,
Unquench'd by want, unfann'd by strong desire;
Unfit for raptures, or, if raptures cheer
On some high festival of once a year,
In wild excess the vulgar breast takes fire,
Till, buried in debauch, the bliss expire.
But not their joys alone thus coarsely flow:
Their morals, like their pleasures, are but low;
For, as refinement stops, from sire to son
Unalter'd, unimprov'd the manners run,
And love's and friendship's finely pointed dart
Fall blunted from each indurated heart.
Some sterner virtues o'er the mountain's breast
May sit, like falcons cowering on the nest;
But all the gentler morals, such as play
Thro' life's more cultur'd walks, and charm the way,
These, far dispers'd, on timorous pinions fly.
To sport and flutter in a kinder sky.
To kinder skies, where gentler manners reign,
I turn; and France displays her bright domain.
Gay, sprightly land of mirth and social ease,
Pleas'd with thyself, whom all the world can please,
How often have I led thy sportive choir,
With tuneless pipe, beside the murmuring Loire?
Where shading elms along the margin grew,
And freshen'd from the wave the zephyr flew;
And haply, though my harsh touch, falt'ring still,
But mock'd all tune, and marr'd the dancer's skill,
Yet would the village praise my wondrous power,
And dance, forgetful of the noon-tide hour.
Alike all ages. Dames of ancient days
Have led their children through the mirthful maze,
And the gay grandsire, skill'd in gestic lore,
Has frisk'd beneath the burthen of threescore.

So blest a life these thoughtless realms display;
Thus idly busy rolls their world away;
Theirs are those arts that mind to mind endear,
For honour forms the social temper here.
Honour, that praise which real merit gains,
Or e'en imaginary worth obtains,
Here passes current: paid from hand to hand,
It shifts in splendid traffic round the land;
From courts to camps, to cottages, it strays,
And all are taught an avarice of praise.
They please, are pleas'd; they give to get esteem;
Till, seeming blest, they grow to what they seem.
But while this softer art their bliss supplies,
It gives their follies also room to rise;
For praise too dearly lov'd, or warmly sought,
Enfeebles all internal strength of thought,
And the weak soul, within itself unblest,
Leans for all pleasure on another's breast.
Hence ostentation here, with tawdry art,
Pants for the vulgar praise which fools impart;
Here vanity assumes her pert grimace,
And trims her robes of frieze with copper lace;
Here beggar pride defrauds her daily cheer,
To boast one splendid banquet once a year;
The mind still turns where shifting fashion draws,
Nor weighs the solid worth of self-applause.
To men of other minds my fancy flies,
Embosom'd in the deep where Holland lies.
Methinks her patient sons before me stand,
Where the broad ocean leans against the land,
And, sedulous to stop the coming tide,
Lift the tall rampire's artificial pride.
Onward methinks, and diligently slow,
The firm connected bulwark seems to grow;
Spreads its long arms amidst the watery roar,
Scoops out an empire, and usurps the shore.
While the pent ocean, rising o'er the pile,
Sees an amphibious world beneath him smile:
The slow canal, the yellow-blossom'd vale,
The willow-tufted bank, the gliding sail,
The crowded mart, the cultivated plain,—
A new creation rescued from his reign.
Thus while around the wave-subjected soil
Impels the native to repeated toil,
Industrious habits in each bosom reign,
And industry begets a love of gain.
Hence all the good from opulence that springs,
With all those ills superfluous treasure brings,
Are here display'd. Their much-lov'd wealth imparts
Convenience, plenty, elegance, and arts:
But view them closer, craft and fraud appear;
E'en liberty itself is barter'd here.
At gold's superior charms all freedom flies;
The needy sell it, and the rich man buys;

A land of tyrants, and a den of slaves,
Here wretches seek dishonourable graves,
And calmly bent, to servitude conform,
Dull as their lakes that slumber in the storm.
  Heavens! how unlike their Belgic sires of old!
Rough, poor, content, ungovernably bold;
War in each breast, and freedom on each brow:
How much unlike the sons of Britain now!
  Fir'd at the sound, my genius spreads her wing,
And flies where Britain courts the western spring;
Where lawns extend that scorn Arcadian pride,
And brighter streams than fam'd Hydaspes glide.
There all around the gentlest breezes stray;
There gentle music melts on every spray;
Creation's mildest charms are there combin'd,
Extremes are only in the master's mind!
Stern o'er each bosom Reason holds her state,
With daring aims irregularly great;
Pride in their port, defiance in their eye,
I see the lords of human kind pass by;
Intent on high designs, a thoughtful band,
By forms unfashion'd fresh from Nature's hand,
Fierce in their native hardiness of soul,
True to imagin'd right, above control,
While e'en the peasant boasts these rights to scan,
And learns to venerate himself as man.
  Thine, Freedom, thine the blessings pictur'd here;
Thine are those charms that dazzle and endear:
Too blest indeed, were such without alloy!
But foster'd e'en by Freedom ills annoy:
That independence Britons prize too high
Keeps man from man, and breaks the social tie;
The self-dependent lordlings stand alone,
All claims that bind and sweeten life unknown.
Here, by the bonds of nature feebly held,
Minds combat minds, repelling and repell'd;
Ferments arise, imprison'd factions roar,
Represt ambition struggles round her shore,
Till, over-wrought, the general system feels,
Its motions stop, or phrenzy fire the wheels.
  Nor this the worst. As nature's ties decay,
As duty, love, and honour fail to sway,
Fictitious bonds, the bonds of wealth and law,
Still gather strength, and force unwilling awe.
Hence all obedience bows to these alone,
And talent sinks, and merit weeps unknown:
Till time may come, when, stript of all her charms,
The land of scholars and the nurse of arms,
Where noble stems transmit the patriot flame,
Where kings have toil'd and poets wrote for fame,
One sink of level avarice shall lie,
And scholars, soldiers, kings, unhonour'd die.
  Yet think not, thus when Freedom's ills I state,
I mean to flatter kings, or court the great:

Ye powers of truth, that bid my soul aspire,
Far from my bosom drive the low desire.
And thou, fair Freedom, taught alike to feel
The rabble's rage and tyrant's angry steel;
Thou transitory flower, alike undone
By proud contempt or favour's fostering sun;
Still may thy blooms the changeful clime endure!
I only would repress them to secure:
For just experience tells, in every soil,
That those who think must govern those that toil;
And all that Freedom's highest aims can reach,
Is but to lay proportion'd loads on each.
Hence, should one order disproportioned grow,
Its double weight must ruin all below.
O then how blind to all that truth requires,
Who think it freedom when a part aspires!
Calm is my soul, nor apt to rise in arms,
Except when fast approaching danger warms;
But when contending chiefs blockade the throne,
Contracting regal power to stretch their own,
When I behold a factious band agree
To call it freedom when themselves are free,
Each wanton judge new penal statutes draw,
Laws grind the poor, and rich men rule the law,
The wealth of climes where savage nations roam
Pillaged from slaves to purchase slaves at home,
Fear, pity, justice, indignation start,
Tear off reserve, and bare my swelling heart;
Till half a patriot, half a coward grown,
I fly from petty tyrants to the throne.
Yes, brother, curse with me that baleful hour
When first ambition struck at regal power;
And thus polluting honour in its source,
Gave wealth to sway the mind with double force.
Have we not seen, round Britain's peopled shore,
Her useful sons exchanged for useless ore?
Seen all her triumphs but destruction haste,
Like flaring tapers brightening as they waste?
Seen opulence, her grandeur to maintain,
Lead stern depopulation in her train,
And over fields where scattered hamlets rose
In barren solitary pomp repose?
Have we not seen at pleasure's lordly call
The smiling long-frequented village fall?
Beheld the duteous son, the sire decayed,
The modest matron, and the blushing maid,
Forced from their homes, a melancholy train,
To traverse climes beyond the western main;
Where wild Oswego spreads her swamps around,
And Niagara stuns with thundering sound?
Even now, perhaps, as there some pilgrim strays
Through tangled forests and through dangerous ways,
Where beasts with man divided empire claim,
And the brown Indian marks with murderous aim;

There, while above the giddy tempest flies,
And all around distressful yells arise,
The pensive exile, bending with his woe,
To stop too fearful, and too faint to go,
Casts a long look where England's glories shine,
And bids his bosom sympathise with mine.
  Vain, very vain, my weary search to find
That bliss which only centres in the mind:
Why have I strayed from pleasure and repose,
To seek a good each government bestows?
In every government, though terrors reign,
Though tyrant kings or tyrant laws restrain,
How small, of all that human hearts endure,
That part which laws or kings can cause or cure!
Still to ourselves in every place consigned,
Our own felicity we make or find:
With secret course, which no loud storms annoy,
Glides the smooth current of domestic joy.
The lifted axe, the agonizing wheel,
Luke's iron crown, and Damien's bed of steel,
To men remote from power but rarely known,
Leave reason, faith, and conscience all our own.

THE DESERTED VILLAGE.

(1770.)

To Sir Joshua Reynolds.

Dear Sir,—I can have no expectations, in an address of this kind, either to add to your reputation, or to establish my own. You can gain nothing from my admiration, as I am ignorant of that art in which you are said to excel: and I may lose much by the severity of your judgment, as few have a juster taste in poetry than you. Setting interest therefore aside, to which I never paid much attention, I must be indulged at present in following my affections. The only dedication I ever made was to my brother, because I loved him better than most other men. He is since dead. Permit me to inscribe this Poem to you.

How far you may be pleased with the versification and mere mechanical parts of this attempt, I do not pretend to inquire; but I know you will object (and indeed several of our best and wisest friends concur in the opinion) that the depopulation it deplores is no where to be seen, and the disorders it laments are only to be found in the poet's own imagination. To this I can scarcely make any other answer than that I sincerely believe what I have written; that I have taken all possible pains, in my country excursions, for these four or five years past, to be certain of what I allege, and that all my views and inquiries have led me to believe those miseries real which I here attempt to display. But this is not the place to enter into an inquiry, whether the country be depopulating or not; the discussion would take up much room, and I should prove myself, at best, an indifferent politician, to tire the reader with a long preface, when I want his unfatigued attention to a long poem.

In regretting the depopulation of the country, I inveigh against the increase of our luxuries; and here also I expect the shout of modern politicians against me. For twenty or thirty years past it has been the fashion to consider luxury as one of the greatest national advantages, and all the wisdom of antiquity in that particular as erroneous. Still, however, I must remain a professed ancient on that head, and continue to think those luxuries prejudicial to states by which so many vices are introduced, and so many kingdoms have been undone. Indeed so much has been poured out of late on the other side of the question, that merely for the sake of novelty and variety, one would sometimes wish to be in the right. I am,

Dear Sir, your sincere Friend and ardent Admirer,

OLIVER GOLDSMITH.

SWEET AUBURN! loveliest village of the plain;
Where health and plenty cheered the labouring swain,
Where smiling spring its earliest visit paid,
And parting summer's lingering blooms delayed:
Dear lovely bowers of innocence and ease,
Seats of my youth, when every sport could please,
How often have I loitered o'er thy green,
Where humble happiness endeared each scene!
How often have I paused on every charm,
The sheltered cot, the cultivated farm,
The never-failing brook, the busy mill,
The decent church that topt the neighbouring hill,
The hawthorn bush, with seats beneath the shade,
For talking age and whispering lovers made!
How often have I blest the coming day,
When toil remitting lent its turn to play,
And all the village train, from labour free,
Led up their sports beneath the spreading tree,
While many a pastime circled in the shade,
The young contending as the old surveyed;
And many a gambol frolicked o'er the ground,
And sleights of art and feats of strength went round.
And still, as each repeated pleasure tired,
Succeeding sports the mirthful band inspired;
The dancing pair that simply sought renown,
By holding out, to tire each other down;
The swain mistrustless of his smutted face,
While secret laughter tittered round the place;
The bashful virgin's side-long looks of love,
The matron's glance that would those looks reprove.

These were thy charms, sweet village! sports like these,
With sweet succession, taught even toil to please:
These round thy bowers their cheerful influence shed:
These were thy charms—but all these charms are fled.
Sweet smiling village, loveliest of the lawn,
Thy sports are fled, and all thy charms withdrawn;
Amidst thy bowers the tyrant's hand is seen,
And desolation saddens all thy green:
One only master grasps the whole domain,
And half a tillage stints thy smiling plain.
No more thy glassy brook reflects the day,
But, choked with sedges, works its weedy way;
Along thy glades, a solitary guest,
The hollow-sounding bittern guards its nest;
Amidst thy desert walks the lapwing flies,
And tires their echoes with unvaried cries;
Sunk are thy bowers in shapeless ruin all,
And the long grass o'ertops the mouldering wall;
And, trembling, shrinking from the spoiler's hand,
Far, far away thy children leave the land.
Ill fares the land, to hastening ills a prey,
Where wealth accumulates, and men decay:
Princes and lords may flourish, or may fade;
A breath can make them, as a breath has made:
But a bold peasantry, their country's pride,
When once destroyed, can never be supplied.
A time there was, ere England's griefs began,
When every rood of ground maintained its man;
For him light labour spread her wholesome store,
Just gave what life required, but gave no more:
His best companions, innocence and health;
And his best riches, ignorance of wealth.
But times are altered; trade's unfeeling train
Usurp the land and dispossess the swain;
Along the lawn, where scattered hamlets rose,
Unwieldy wealth and cumbrous pomp repose,
And every want to opulence allied,
And every pang that folly pays to pride.
Those gentle hours that plenty bade to bloom,
Those calm desires that asked but little room,
Those healthful sports that graced the peaceful scene,
Lived in each look, and brightened all the green;
These, far departing, seek a kinder shore,
And rural mirth and manners are no more.
Sweet Auburn! parent of the blissful hour,
Thy glades forlorn confess the tyrant's power.
Here, as I take my solitary rounds
Amidst thy tangling walks and ruined grounds,
And, many a year elapsed, return to view
Where once the cottage stood, the hawthorn grew,
Remembrance wakes with all her busy train,
Swells at my breast, and turns the past to pain.
In all my wanderings round this world of care,
In all my griefs—and GOD has given my share—

I still had hopes, my latest hours to crown,
Amidst these humble bowers to lay me down;
To husband out life's taper at the close,
And keep the flame from wasting by repose:
I still had hopes, for pride attends us still,
Amidst the swains to show my book-learned skill,
Around my fire an evening group to draw,
And tell of all I felt, and all I saw;
And, as a hare whom hounds and horns pursue
Pants to the place from whence at first he flew,
I still had hopes, my long vexations past,
Here to return—and die at home at last.
  O blest retirement, friend to life's decline,
Retreats from care, that never must be mine,
How happy he who crowns in shades like these
A youth of labour with an age of ease;
Who quits a world where strong temptations try,
And, since 'tis hard to combat, learns to fly!
For him no wretches, born to work and weep,
Explore the mine, or tempt the dangerous deep;
Nor surly porter stands in guilty state,
To spurn imploring famine from the gate;
But on he moves to meet his latter end,
Angels around befriending Virtue's friend;
Bends to the grave with unperceived decay,
While resignation gently slopes the way;
And, all his prospects brightening to the last,
His heaven commences ere the world be past!
  Sweet was the sound, when oft at evening's close
Up yonder hill the village murmur rose.
There, as I past with careless steps and slow,
The mingling notes came softened from below;
The swain responsive as the milk-maid sung,
The sober herd that lowed to meet their young,
The noisy geese that gabbled o'er the pool,
The playful children just let loose from school,
The watch-dog's voice that bayed the whispering wind,
And the loud laugh that spoke the vacant mind;—
These all in sweet confusion sought the shade,
And filled each pause the nightingale had made.
But now the sounds of population fail,
No cheerful murmurs fluctuate in the gale,
No busy steps the grass-grown foot-way tread,
For all the bloomy flush of life is fled.
All but yon widowed, solitary thing,
That feebly bends beside the plashy spring:
She, wretched matron, forced in age, for bread,
To strip the brook with mantling cresses spread,
To pick her wintry faggot from the thorn,
To seek her nightly shed, and weep till morn;
She only left of all the harmless train,
The sad historian of the pensive plain.
  Near yonder copse, where once the garden smiled,
And still where many a garden-flower grows wild;

There, where a few torn shrubs the place disclose,
The village preacher's modest mansion rose.
A man he was to all the country dear,
And passing rich with forty pounds a year;
Remote from towns he ran his godly race,
Nor e'er had changed, nor wished to change, his place;
Unpractised he to fawn, or seek for power,
By doctrines fashioned to the varying hour;
Far other aims his heart had learned to prize,
More skilled to raise the wretched than to rise.
His house was known to all the vagrant train;
He chid their wanderings, but relieved their pain:
The long-remember'd beggar was his guest,
Whose beard descending swept his aged breast;
The ruined spendthrift, now no longer proud,
Claimed kindred there, and had his claims allowed;
The broken soldier, kindly bade to stay,
Sat by his fire, and talked the night away,
Wept o'er his wounds or tales of sorrow done,
Shouldered his crutch, and showed how fields were won.
Pleased with his guests, the good man learned to glow,
And quite forgot their vices in their woe;
Careless their merits or their faults to scan,
His pity gave ere charity began.
  Thus to relieve the wretched was his pride,
And e'en his failings leaned to virtue's side;
But in his duty prompt at every call,
He watched and wept, he prayed and felt for all;
And, as a bird each fond endearment tries
To tempt its new-fledged offspring to the skies,
He tried each art, reproved each dull delay,
Allured to brighter worlds, and led the way.
  Beside the bed where parting life was laid,
And sorrow, guilt, and pain, by turns dismayed,
The reverend champion stood. At his control
Despair and anguish fled the struggling soul;
Comfort came down the trembling wretch to raise,
And his last faltering accents whispered praise.
  At church, with meek and unaffected grace,
His looks adorned the venerable place;
Truth from his lips prevailed with double sway,
And fools, who came to scoff, remained to pray.
The service past, around the pious man,
With steady zeal, each honest rustic ran;
E'en children followed with endearing wile,
And plucked his gown, to share the good man's smile.
His ready smile a parent's warmth expressed;
Their welfare pleased him, and their cares distressed:
To them his heart, his love, his griefs were given,
But all his serious thoughts had rest in heaven.
As some tall cliff that lifts its awful form,
Swells from the vale, and midway leaves the storm,
Though round its breast the rolling clouds are spread,
Eternal sunshine settles on its head.

Beside yon straggling fence that skirts the way,
With blossom'd furze unprofitably gay,
There, in his noisy mansion, skilled to rule,
The village master taught his little school.
A man severe he was, and stern to view;
I knew him well, and every truant knew:
Well had the boding tremblers learned to trace
The day's disasters in his morning face;
Full well they laughed with counterfeited glee
At all his jokes, for many a joke had he;
Full well the busy whisper circling round
Conveyed the dismal tidings when he frowned.
Yet he was kind, or, if severe in aught,
The love he bore to learning was in fault;
The village all declared how much he knew:
'Twas certain he could write, and cypher too;
Lands he could measure, terms and tides presage,
And e'en the story ran that he could gauge:
In arguing, too, the parson owned his skill;
For e'en though vanquished, he could argue still;
While words of learned length and thundering sound
Amazed the gazing rustics ranged around;
And still they gazed, and still the wonder grew,
That one small head could carry all he knew.
But past is all his fame. The very spot
Where many a time he triumphed is forgot.
Near yonder thorn, that lifts its head on high,
Where once the sign-post caught the passing eye,
Low lies that house where nut-brown draughts inspired,
Where grey-beard mirth and smiling toil retired,
Where village statesmen talked with looks profound,
And news much older than their ale went round.
Imagination fondly stoops to trace
The parlour splendours of that festive place:
The white-washed wall, the nicely sanded floor,
The varnished clock that clicked behind the door;
The chest contrived a double debt to pay,
A bed by night, a chest of drawers by day;
The pictures placed for ornament and use,
The twelve good rules, the royal game of goose;
The hearth, except when winter chilled the day,
With aspen boughs and flowers and fennel gay;
While broken tea-cups, wisely kept for show,
Ranged o'er the chimney, glistened in a row.
Vain transitory splendours! could not all
Reprieve the tottering mansion from its fall?
Obscure it sinks, nor shall it more impart
An hour's importance to the poor man's heart.
Thither no more the peasant shall repair
To sweet oblivion of his daily care;
No more the farmer's news, the barber's tale,
No more the woodman's ballad shall prevail;
No more the smith his dusky brow shall clear,
Relax his ponderous strength, and lean to hear;

The host himself no longer shall be found
Careful to see the mantling bliss go round;
Nor the coy maid, half willing to be prest,
Shall kiss the cup to pass it to the rest.
  Yes! let the rich deride, the proud disdain,
These simple blessings of the lowly train;
To me more dear, congenial to my heart,
One native charm, than all the gloss of art;
Spontaneous joys, where Nature has its play,
The soul adopts, and owns their first-born sway;
Lightly they frolic o'er the vacant mind,
Unenvied, unmolested, unconfined.
But the long pomp, the midnight masquerade,
With all the freaks of wanton wealth arrayed,—
In these, ere triflers half their wish obtain,
The toiling pleasure sickens into pain;
And, e'en while fashion's brightest arts decoy,
The heart distrusting asks if this be joy.
  Ye friends to truth, ye statesmen who survey
The rich man's joys increase, the poor's decay,
'Tis yours to judge, how wide the limits stand
Between a splendid and a happy land.
Proud swells the tide with loads of freighted ore,
And shouting Folly hails them from her shore;
Hoards e'en beyond the miser's wish abound,
And rich men flock from all the world around.
Yet count our gains. This wealth is but a name
That leaves our useful products still the same.
Not so the loss. The man of wealth and pride
Takes up a space that many poor supplied;
Space for his lake, his park's extended bounds,
Space for his horses, equipage, and hounds:
The robe that wraps his limbs in silken sloth
Has robbed the neighbouring fields of half their growth;
His seat, where solitary sports are seen,
Indignant spurns the cottage from the green:
Around the world each needful product flies,
For all the luxuries the world supplies;
While thus the land adorned for pleasure all
In barren splendour feebly waits the fall.
  As some fair female unadorned and plain,
Secure to please while youth confirms her reign,
Slights every borrowed charm that dress supplies,
Nor shares with art the triumph of her eyes;
But when those charms are past, for charms are frail,
When time advances, and when lovers fail,
She then shines forth, solicitous to bless,
In all the glaring impotence of dress.
Thus fares the land by luxury betrayed:
In Nature's simplest charms at first arrayed,
But verging to decline, its splendours rise,
Its vistas strike, its palaces surprise;
While, scourged by famine from the smiling land,
The mournful peasant leads his humble band,

And while he sinks, without one arm to save,
The country blooms—a garden and a grave.
  Where then, ah! where, shall poverty reside,
To 'scape the pressure of contiguous pride?
If to some common's fenceless limits strayed
He drives his flock to pick the scanty blade,
Those fenceless fields the sons of wealth divide,
And even the bare-worn common is denied.
  If to the city sped—what waits him there?
To see profusion that he must not share;
To see ten thousand baneful arts combined
To pamper luxury, and thin mankind;
To see those joys the sons of pleasure know
Extorted from his fellow-creature's woe.
Here while the courtier glitters in brocade,
There the pale artist plies the sickly trade;
Here while the proud their long-drawn pomps display,
There the black gibbet glooms beside the way.
The dome where pleasure holds her midnight reign
Here richly deck'd admits the gorgeous train:
Tumultuous grandeur crowds the blazing square,
The rattling chariots clash, the torches glare.
Sure scenes like these no troubles e'er annoy!
Sure these denote one universal joy!
Are these thy serious thoughts?—Ah, turn thine eyes
Where the poor houseless shivering female lies.
She once, perhaps, in village plenty blest,
Has wept at tales of innocence distrest;
Her modest looks the cottage might adorn,
Sweet as the primrose peeps beneath the thorn;
Now lost to all; her friends, her virtue fled,
Near her betrayer's door she lays her head,
And, pinch'd with cold, and shrinking from the shower,
With heavy heart deplores that luckless hour,
When idly first, ambitious of the town,
She left her wheel and robes of country brown.
  Do thine, sweet Auburn,—thine, the loveliest train,—
Do thy fair tribes participate her pain?
Even now, perhaps, by cold and hunger led,
At proud men's doors they ask a little bread!
  Ah, no! To distant climes, a dreary scene,
Where half the convex world intrudes between,
Through torrid tracts with fainting steps they go,
Where wild Altama murmurs to their woe.
Far different there from all that charmed before,
The various terrors of that horrid shore;
Those blazing suns that dart a downward ray,
And fiercely shed intolerable day;
Those matted woods, where birds forget to sing,
But silent bats in drowsy clusters cling;
Those poisonous fields with rank luxuriance crowned,
Where the dark scorpion gathers death around,
Where at each step the stranger fears to wake
The rattling terrors of the vengeful snake,

Where crouching tigers wait their haplesss prey,
And savage men more murderous still than they;
While oft in whirls the mad tornado flies,
Mingling the ravaged landscape with the skies.
Far different these from every former scene,
The cooling brook, the grassy vested green,
The breezy covert of the warbling grove,
That only sheltered thefts of harmless love.
Good Heaven! what sorrows gloomed that parting day,
That called them from their native walks away;
When the poor exiles, every pleasure past,
Hung round the bowers, and fondly looked their last,
And took a long farewell, and wished in vain
For seats like these beyond the western main,
And shuddering still to face the distant deep,
Returned and wept, and still returned to weep.
The good old sire the first prepared to go
To new-found worlds, and wept for others' woe;
But for himself, in conscious virtue brave,
He only wished for worlds beyond the grave.
His lovely daughter, lovelier in her tears,
The fond companion of his helpless years,
Silent went next, neglectful of her charms,
And left a lover's for her father's arms.
With louder plaints the mother spoke her woes,
And blest the cot where every pleasure rose,
And kissed her thoughtless babes with many a tear,
And clasped them close, in sorrow doubly dear,
Whilst her fond husband strove to lend relief
In all the silent manliness of grief.
O luxury! thou curst by Heaven's decree,
How ill exchanged are things like these for thee!
How do thy potions, with insidious joy,
Diffuse their pleasures only to destroy!
Kingdoms by thee, to sickly greatness grown,
Boast of a florid vigour not their own.
At every draught more large and large they grow,
A bloated mass of rank unwieldy woe;
Till sapped their strength, and every part unsound,
Down, down they sink, and spread a ruin round.
Even now the devastation is begun,
And half the business of destruction done;
Even now, methinks, as pondering here I stand,
I see the rural virtues leave the land.
Down where yon anchoring vessel spreads the sail,
That idly waiting flaps with every gale,
Downward they move, a melancholy band,
Pass from the shore, and darken all the strand.
Contented toil, and hospitable care,
And kind connubial tenderness, are there;
And piety with wishes placed above,
And steady loyalty, and faithful love.
And thou, sweet Poetry, thou loveliest maid,
Still first to fly where sensual joys invade;

Unfit in these degenerate times of shame
To catch the heart, or strike for honest fame;
Dear charming nymph, neglected and decried,
My shame in crowds, my solitary pride;
Thou source of all my bliss, and all my woe,
That found'st me poor at first, and keep'st me so;
Thou guide by which the nobler arts excel,
Thou nurse of every virtue, fare thee well!
Farewell, and O! where'er thy voice be tried,
On Torno's cliffs, or Pambamarca's side,
Whether where equinoctial fervours glow,
Or winter wraps the polar world in snow,
Still let thy voice, prevailing over time,
Redress the rigours of the inclement clime;
Aid slighted truth with thy persuasive strain;
Teach erring man to spurn the rage of gain:
Teach him, that states of native strength possest,
Though very poor, may still be very blest;
That trade's proud empire hastes to swift decay,
As ocean sweeps the laboured mole away;
While self-dependent power can time defy,
As rocks resist the billows and the sky.

THE HERMIT: A BALLAD.

(1766.)

The following letter, addressed to the printer of the "St. James's Chronicle," appeared in that paper in June, 1767:—

SIR,—As there is nothing I dislike so much as newspaper controversy, particularly upon trifles, permit me to be as concise as possible in informing a correspondent of yours, that I recommended Blainville's Travels because I thought the book was a good one; and I think so still. I said I was told by the bookseller that it was then first published: but in that, it seems, I was misinformed, and my reading was not extensive enough to set me right.

Another correspondent of yours accuses me of having taken a ballad I published some time ago from one[1] by the ingenious Mr. Percy. I do not think there is any great resemblance between the two pieces in question. If there be any, his ballad is taken from mine. I read it to Mr. Percy some years ago; and he (as we both considered these things as trifles at best) told me with his usual good humour, the next time I saw him, that he had taken my plan to form the fragments of Shakespeare into a ballad of his own. He then read me his little Cento, if I may so call it, and I highly approved it. Such petty anecdotes as these are scarce worth printing: and, were it not for the busy disposition of some of your correspondents, the public should never have known that he owes me the hint of his ballad, or that I am obliged to his friendship and learning for communications of a much more important nature.

I am, Sir, yours, &c.
OLIVER GOLDSMITH.

(1) "The Friar of Orders Gray."—*Reliq. of Anc. Poetry,* vol. i. p. 243.

THE HERMIT.

"Turn, gentle Hermit of the dale,
And guide my lonely way
To where yon taper cheers the vale
With hospitable ray.

"For here forlorn and lost I tread,
With fainting steps and slow,
Where wilds, immeasurably spread,
Seem lengthening as I go."

"Forbear, my son," the Hermit cries,
"To tempt the dangerous gloom;
For yonder faithless phantom flies
To lure thee to thy doom.

"Here to the houseless child of want
My door is open still;
And though my portion is but scant,
I give it with good will.

"Then turn to-night, and freely share
Whate'er my cell bestows,
My rushy couch and frugal fare,
My blessing and repose.

"No flocks that range the valley free
To slaughter I condemn;
Taught by that Power that pities me,
I learn to pity them:

"But from the mountain's grassy side
A guiltless feast I bring,
A scrip with herbs and fruits supplied,
And water from the spring.

"Then, pilgrim, turn; thy cares forego;
All earth-born cares are wrong:
Man wants but little here below,
Nor wants that little long."

Soft as the dew from heaven descends
His gentle accents fell:
The modest stranger lowly bends,
And follows to the cell.

Far in a wilderness obscure
The lonely mansion lay,
A refuge to the neighbouring poor
And strangers led astray.

No stores beneath its humble thatch
Required a master's care;
The wicket, opening with a latch,
Received the harmless pair.

And now, when busy crowds retire
To take their evening rest,
The Hermit trimmed his little fire,
And cheered his pensive guest.

And spread his vegetable store,
And gaily pressed, and smiled;
And skilled in legendary lore
The lingering hours beguiled.

Around in sympathetic mirth
Its tricks the kitten tries;
The cricket chirrups in the hearth;
The crackling faggot flies.

But nothing could a charm impart
To soothe the stranger's woe;
For grief was heavy at his heart,
And tears began to flow.

His rising cares the Hermit spied,
With answering care opprest:
"And whence, unhappy youth," he cried,
The sorrows of thy breast?

"From better habitations spurned,
Reluctant dost thou rove?
Or grieve for friendship unreturned,
Or unregarded love?

"Alas! the joys that Fortune brings
Are trifling, and decay;
And those who prize the trifling things
More trifling still than they.

"And what is friendship but a name,
A charm that lulls to sleep,
A shade that follows wealth or fame,
But leaves the wretch to weep?

"And love is still an emptier sound,
The modern fair-one's jest;
On earth unseen, or only found
To warm the turtle's nest.

"For shame, fond youth, thy sorrows hush,
And spurn the sex," he said:
But, while he spoke, a rising blush
His love-lorn guest betrayed.

Surprised he sees new beauties rise,
Swift mantling to the view;
Like colours o'er the morning skies,
As bright, as transient too.

The bashful look, the rising breast,
Alternate spread alarms:
The lovely stranger stands confest
A maid in all her charms.

"And, ah! forgive a stranger rude,
A wretch forlorn," she cried;
"Whose feet unhallowed thus intrude
Where heaven and you reside.

"But let a maid thy pity share,
Whom love has taught to stray;
Who seeks for rest, but finds despair
Companion of her way.

"My father lived beside the Tyne;
A wealthy lord was he;
And all his wealth was marked as mine,—
He had but only me.

"To win me from his tender arms
Unnumbered suitors came,
Who praised me for imputed charms,
And felt or feigned a flame.

"Each hour a mercenary crowd
With richest proffers strove;
Amongst the rest young Edwin bowed,
But never talked of love.

"In humble, simplest habits clad,
No wealth nor power had he;
Wisdom and worth were all he had,
But these were all to me.

"And when beside me in the dale
He carolled lays of love,
His breath lent fragrance to the gale,
And music to the grove.

"The blossom opening to the day,
The dews of heaven refined,
Could nought of purity display,
To emulate his mind.

"The dew, the blossom on the tree,
With charms inconstant shine;
Their charms were his, but, woe to me!
Their constancy was mine.

"For still I tried each fickle art,
Importunate and vain;
And while his passion touched my heart,
I triumphed in his pain.

"Till quite dejected with my scorn
He left me to my pride,
And sought a solitude forlorn,
In secret, where he died.

"But mine the sorrow, mine the fault,
And well my life shall pay;
I'll seek the solitude he sought,
And stretch me where he lay.

"And there forlorn, despairing, hid,
I'll lay me down and die;
'Twas so for me that Edwin did,
And so for him will I."

"Forbid it, Heaven!" the Hermit cried,
And clasped her to his breast:
The wondering fair one turned to chide,—
'Twas Edwin's self that pressed.

"Turn, Angelina, ever dear;
My charmer, turn to see
Thy own, thy long-lost Edwin here,
Restored to love and thee.

"Thus let me hold thee to my heart,
And every care resign:
And shall we never, never part,
My life—my all that's mine?

"No, never from this hour to part,
We'll live and love so true,
The sigh that rends thy constant heart
Shall break thy Edwin's too."

THE HAUNCH OF VENISON.

A POETICAL EPISTLE TO LORD CLARE.

THANKS, my lord, for your venison, for finer or fatter
Never ranged in a forest, or smoked in a platter;
The haunch was a picture for painters to study,
The fat was so white, and the lean was so ruddy;
Though my stomach was sharp, I could scarce help regretting
To spoil such a delicate picture by eating;
I had thoughts in my chambers to place it in view,
To be shown to my friends as a piece of virtù;
As in some Irish houses, where things are so so,
One gammon of bacon hangs up for a show:
But, for eating a rasher of what they take pride in,
They'd as soon think of eating the pan it is fried in.
But hold—let me pause—don't I hear you pronounce
This tale of the bacon a damnable bounce?
Well, suppose it a bounce—sure a poet may try,
By a bounce now and then, to get courage to fly.
But, my lord, it's no bounce: I protest in my turn
It's a truth—and your lordship may ask Mr. Byrne.
To go on with my tale: as I gazed on the haunch,
I thought of a friend that was trusty and staunch;
So I cut it, and sent it to Reynolds undrest,
To paint it, or eat it, just as he liked best.
Of the neck and the breast I had next to dispose;
'Twas a neck and a breast that might rival Monroe's:
But in parting with these I was puzzled again,
With the how, and the who, and the where, and the when.
There's Howard, and Coley, and H—rth, and Hiff,
I think they love venison—I know they love beef.
There's my countryman Higgins—oh! let him alone,
For making a blunder, or picking a bone.
But hang it!—to poets who seldom can eat
Your very good mutton's a very good treat;
Such dainties to them their health it might hurt,
It's like sending them ruffles, when wanting a shirt.
While thus I debated, in reverie centred,
An acquaintance, a friend as he called himself, entered;
An under-bred, fine-spoken fellow was he,
And he smiled as he looked at the venison and me.
"What have we got here?—Why this is good eating!
Your own I suppose—or is it in waiting?"
"Why, whose should it be?" cried I with a flounce;
"I get these things often"—but that was a bounce:
"Some lords, my acquaintance, that settle the nation,
Are pleased to be kind—but I hate ostentation."
"If that be the case then," cried he, very gay,
"I'm glad I have taken this house in my way.

To-morrow you take a poor dinner with me;
No words—I insist on't—precisely at three;
We'll have Johnson, and Burke; all the wits will be there;
My acquaintance is slight, or I'd ask my Lord Clare.
And now that I think on't, as I am a sinner!
We wanted this venison to make out the dinner.
What say you—a pasty? It shall, and it must,
And my wife, little Kitty, is famous for crust.
Here, porter! this venison with me to Mile-end;
No stirring—I beg—my dear friend—my dear friend!"
Thus, snatching his hat, he brushed off like the wind,
And the porter and eatables followed behind.
  Left alone to reflect, having emptied my shelf,
And "nobody with me at sea but myself;"
Though I could not help thinking my gentleman hasty,
Yet Johnson, and Burke, and a good venison pasty,
Were things that I never disliked in my life,
Though clogged with a coxcomb, and Kitty his wife.
So next day, in due splendour to make my approach,
I drove to his door in my own hackney-coach.
  When come to the place where we all were to dine
(A chair-lumbered closet just twelve feet by nine),
My friend bade me welcome, but struck me quite dumb
With tidings that Johnson and Burke would not come:
"For I knew it," he cried: "both eternally fail;
The one with his speeches, and t'other with Thrale.
But no matter, I'll warrant we'll make up the party
With two full as clever, and ten times as hearty.
The one is a Scotchman, the other a Jew;
They're both of them merry, and authors like you;
The one writes the Snarler, the other the Scourge;
Some think he writes Cinna—he owns to Panurge."
While thus he describ'd them by trade and by name,
They entered, and dinner was served as they came.
  At the top a fried liver and bacon were seen;
At the bottom was tripe, in a swinging tureen;
At the sides there was spinach and pudding made hot;
In the middle a place where the pasty—was not.
Now, my lord, as for tripe, it's my utter aversion,
And your bacon I hate like a Turk or a Persian;
So there I sat stuck, like a horse in a pound,
While the bacon and liver went merrily round:
But what vex'd me most was that d——d Scottish rogue,
With his long-winded speeches, his smiles, and his brogue,
And, "Madam," quoth he, "may this bit be my poison,
A prettier dinner I never set eyes on;
Pray a slice of your liver, though may I be curst,
But I've eat of your tripe till I'm ready to burst."
"The tripe!" quoth the Jew, with his chocolate cheek;
"I could dine on this tripe seven days in a week:
I like these here dinners so pretty and small;
But your friend there, the doctor, eats nothing at all."
"O! ho!" quoth my friend, "he'll come on in a trice;
He's keeping a corner for something that's nice:

There's a pasty."—" A pasty!" repeated the Jew;
" I don't care if I keep a corner for't too."
" What the de'il, mon, a pasty!" re-echoed the Scot;
" Though splitting, I'll still keep a corner for that."
" We'll all keep a corner," the lady cried out;
" We'll all keep a corner," was echoed about.
While thus we resolved, and the pasty delayed,
With looks that quite petrified, entered the maid:
A visage so sad, and so pale with affright,
Waked Priam in drawing his curtains by night.
But we quickly found out—for who could mistake her?—
That she came with some terrible news from the baker:
And so it fell out, for that negligent sloven
Had shut out the pasty on shutting his oven.
Sad Philomel thus—but let similes drop—
And now that I think on't, the story may stop.
To be plain, my good lord, it's but labour misplaced,
To send such good verses to one of your taste;
You've got an odd something—a kind of discerning,
A relish, a taste—sickened over by learning;
At least, it's your temper, as very well known,
That you think very slightly of all that's your own:
So, perhaps, in your habits of thinking amiss,
You may make a mistake, and think slightly of this.

RETALIATION: A POEM.

(1774.)

Of old, when Scarron his companions invited,
Each guest brought his dish, and the feast was united;
If our landlord[1] supplies us with beef and with fish,
Let each guest bring himself, and he brings the best dish:
Our Dean[2] shall be venison, just fresh from the plains;
Our Burke[3] shall be tongue with the garnish of brains;
Our Will[4] shall be wild fowl, of excellent flavour,
And Dick[5] with his pepper shall heighten the savour;
Our Cumberland's[6] sweet-bread its place shall obtain,
And Douglas[7] is pudding, substantial and plain;

(1) The master of the St. James's coffee-house, where the Doctor, and the friends he has characterised in his poem, occasionally dined.
(2) Doctor Barnard, Dean of Derry and afterwards Bishop of Limerick.
(3) The Right Hon. Edmund Burke.
(4) Mr. William Burke, late secretary to General Conway, member for Bedwin, and a relative of Edmund Burke.
(5) Mr. Richard Burke, a barrister, and younger brother of the great statesman.
(6) Mr. Richard Cumberland, the dramatist.
(7) Dr. Douglas, canon of Windsor, an ingenious Scotch gentleman, who was made Bishop of Carlisle, and afterwards Bishop of Salisbury.

Our Garrick's[1] a salad, for in him we see
Oil, vinegar, sugar, and saltness agree;
To make out the dinner, full certain I am,
That Ridge[2] is anchovy, and Reynolds[3] is lamb,
That Hickey's[4] a capon, and, by the same rule,
Magnanimous Goldsmith a gooseberry fool.
At a dinner so various, at such a repast,
Who'd not be a glutton, and stick to the last?
Here, waiter, more wine! let me sit while I'm able,
Till all my companions sink under the table;
Then, with chaos and blunders encircling my head,
Let me ponder, and tell what I think of the dead.
Here lies the good Dean,[5] re-united to earth,
Who mixed reason with pleasure, and wisdom with mirth:
If he had any faults, he has left us in doubt;
At least, in six weeks I could not find 'em out;
Yet some have declared, and it can't be denied 'em,
That sly-boots was cursedly cunning to hide 'em.
Here lies our good Edmund,[6] whose genius was such,
We scarcely can praise it or blame it too much;
Who, born for the universe, narrowed his mind,
And to party gave up what was meant for mankind;
Though fraught with all learning, yet straining his throat
To persuade Tommy Townshend[7] to lend him a vote;
Who, too deep for his hearers, still went on refining,
And thought of convincing, while they thought of dining;
Though equal to all things, for all things unfit;
Too nice for a statesman, too proud for a wit,
For a patriot too cool, for a drudge disobedient,
And too fond of the *right* to pursue the *expedient.*
In short, 'twas his fate, unemployed, or in place, sir,
To eat mutton cold, and cut blocks with a razor.
Here lies honest William,[8] whose heart was a mint,
While the owner ne'er knew half the good that was in't;
The pupil of impulse, it forced him along,
His conduct still right, with his argument wrong;
Still aiming at honour, yet fearing to roam,
The coachman was tipsy, the chariot drove home;
Would you ask for his merits?—alas! he had none:
What was good was spontaneous, his faults were his own.
Here lies honest Richard,[9] whose fate I must sigh at;
Alas, that such frolic should now be so quiet!
What spirits were his! what wit and what whim!
Now breaking a jest, and now breaking a limb;
Now wrangling and grumbling to keep up the ball,
Now teasing and vexing, yet laughing at all!
In short, so provoking a devil was Dick,
That we wished him full ten times a day at Old Nick;

(1) David Garrick. (2) Counsellor John Ridge, a gentleman belonging to the Irish bar.
(3) Sir Joshua Reynolds. (4) An eminent Irish attorney. (5) See note 2, p. 594. (6) See note 3, p. 594.
(7) Mr. T. Townshend, M.P. for Whitchurch, afterwards Lord Sydney. (8) See note 4, p. 594.
(9) Mr. Richard Burke, see page 594. At different times he fractured both an arm and a leg.

But, missing his mirth and agreeable vein,
As often we wished to have Dick back again.
Here Cumberland lies, having acted his parts,
The Terence of England, the mender of hearts;
A flattering painter, who made it his care
To draw men as they ought to be, not as they are.
His gallants are all faultless, his women divine,
And comedy wonders at being so fine;
Like a tragedy-queen he has dizened her out,
Or rather like tragedy giving a rout.
His fools have their follies so lost in a crowd
Of virtues and feelings, that folly grows proud;
And coxcombs, alike in their failings alone,
Adopting his portraits, are pleased with their own.
Say, where has our poet this malady caught?
Or wherefore his characters thus without fault?
Say, was it that vainly directing his view
To find out men's virtues, and finding them few,
Quite sick of pursuing each troublesome elf,
He grew lazy at last, and drew from himself?
Here Douglas retires from his toils to relax,
The scourge of impostors, the terror of quacks:
Come, all ye quack bards, and ye quacking divines,
Come and dance on the spot where your tyrant reclines:
When satire and censure encircled his throne,
I feared for your safety, I feared for my own;
But now he is gone, and we want a detector,
Our Dodds[1] shall be pious, our Kenricks[2] shall lecture,
Macpherson' write bombast, and call it a style,
Our Townshend make speeches, and I shall compile;
New Lauders and Bowers[4] the Tweed shall cross over,
No countryman living their tricks to discover;
Detection her taper shall quench to a spark,
And Scotchman meet Scotchman, and cheat in the dark
Here lies David Garrick, describe me who can;
An abridgment of all that was pleasant in man.
As an actor, confessed without rival to shine:
As a wit, if not first, in the very first line:
Yet, with talents like these, and an excellent heart,
The man had his failings, a dupe to his art.
Like an ill-judging beauty, his colours he spread,
And beplastered with rouge his own natural red.
On the stage he was natural, simple, affecting;
'Twas only that, when he was off, he was acting.
With no reason on earth to go out of his way,
He turned and he varied full ten times a day:
Though secure of our hearts, yet confoundedly sick
If they were not his own by finessing and trick:

(1) The Rev. Dr Dodd, hanged for forgery in 1777.
(2) Dr. Kenrick, who read lectures at the Devil Tavern, under the title of "The School of Shakespeare," and one of Goldsmith's bitterest foes.
(3) James Macpherson, Esq. Goldsmith is alluding to his translation of Homer.
(4) William Lauder and Archibald Bower, Scotch writers.

He cast off his friends, as a huntsman his pack,
For he knew when he pleased he could whistle them back.
Of praise a mere glutton, he swallowed what came;
And the puff of a dunce, he mistook it for fame;
Till his relish grown callous, almost to disease,
Who peppered the highest, was surest to please.
But let us be candid, and speak out our mind:
If dunces applauded, he paid them in kind.
Ye Kenricks, ye Kellys,[1] and Woodfalls[2] so grave,
What a commerce was yours, while you got and you gave!
How did Grub-street re-echo the shouts that you raised,
While he was be-Rosciused, and you were bepraised.
But peace to his spirit, wherever it flies,
To act as an angel and mix with the skies:
Those poets who owe their best fame to his skill
Shall still be his flatterers, go where he will;
Old Shakespeare receive him with praise and with love,
And Beaumonts and Bens be his Kellys above.[3]
Here Hickey reclines, a most blunt, pleasant creature,
And slander itself must allow him good nature;
He cherished his friend, and he relished a bumper;
Yet one fault he had, and that one was a thumper.
Perhaps you may ask if the man was a miser:
I answer, No, no; for he always was wiser.
Too courteous, perhaps, or obligingly flat?
His very worst foe can't accuse him of that.
Perhaps he confided in men as they go,
And so was too foolishly honest? Ah no!

(1) Mr. Hugh Kelly, author of "False Delicacy," "Word to the Wise," "Clementina," "School for Wives," &c. &c.

(2) Mr. William Woodfall, printer of the Morning Chronicle.

(3) The following poems, composed in humorous revenge by Garrick, are found in Davies's "Life of Garrick."

JUPITER AND MERCURY: A FABLE.

HERE *Hermes*, says *Jove*, who with nectar was mellow,
Go, fetch me some clay; I will make an *odd fellow!*
Right and wrong shall be jumbled,—much gold and some dross;
Without cause be he pleased, without cause be he cross;
Be sure, as I work, to throw in contradictions,
A great love of truth, yet a mind turn'd to fictions!
Now mix these ingredients, which, warmed in the baking,
Turned to *learning* and *gaming*, *religion* and *raking*.
With the love of a wench, let his writings be chaste;
Tip his tongue with strange matter, his pen with fine taste;
That the rake and the poet o'er all may prevail,
Set fire to his head, and set fire to his tail:
For the joy of each sex, on the world I'll bestow it,
This *scholar*, *rake*, *Christian*, *dupe*, *gamester*, and *poet*;
Though a mixture so odd, he shall merit great fame,
And among brother mortals—be GOLDSMITH his name.
When on earth this strange meteor no more shall appear,
You, *Hermes*, shall fetch him—to make us sport here.

On Dr. Goldsmith's Characteristical Cookery.

A JEU D'ESPRIT.

ARE these the choice dishes the Doctor has sent us?
Is this the great poet whose works so content us?
This Goldsmith's fine feast, who has written fine books?
Heaven sends us good *meat*, but the *Devil sends cooks.*

Then what was his failing? come tell it, and burn ye.
He was—could he help it?—a special attorney.
Here Reynolds is laid, and, to tell you my mind,
He has not left a wiser or better behind.
His pencil was striking, resistless, and grand;
His manners were gentle, complying, and bland:
Still born to improve us in every part,
His pencil our faces, his manners our heart.
To coxcombs averse, yet most civilly steering:
When they judged without skill, he was still hard of hearing;
When they talk'd of their Raphaels, Corregios, and stuff,
He shifted his trumpet,[1] and only took snuff.

POSTSCRIPT.

[After the fourth edition of this Poem was printed, the publisher received the following epitaph on Mr. Whitefoord,[2] from a friend of the late Doctor Goldsmith.]

Here Whitefoord reclines, and, deny it who can,
Though he merrily lived, he is now a grave man.
Rare compound of oddity, frolic, and fun!
Who relished a joke, and rejoiced in a pun;
Whose temper was generous, open, sincere;
A stranger to flattery, a stranger to fear;
Who scattered around wit and humour at will;
Whose daily *bon mots* half a column might fill;
A Scotchman, from pride and from prejudice free;
A scholar, yet surely no pedant was he.
What pity, alas! that so liberal a mind
Should so long be to newspaper essays confined!
Who perhaps to the summit of science could soar,
Yet content "if the table he set on a roar;"
Whose talents to fill any station were fit,
Yet happy if Woodfall[3] confess'd him a wit.
Ye newspaper witlings! ye pert scribbling folks!
Who copied his squibs, and re-echoed his jokes;
Ye tame imitators, ye servile herd, come,
Still follow your master, and visit his tomb:
To deck it, bring with you festoons of the vine,
And copious libations bestow on his shrine;
Then strew all around it (you can do no less)
Cross-readings,[4] *ship-news*, and *mistakes of the press*.
Merry Whitefoord, farewell! for thy sake I admit
That a Scot may have humour,—I had almost said wit:
This debt to thy memory I cannot refuse,
"Thou best humoured man with the worst humoured Muse."

(1) Sir Joshua Reynolds was so deaf, as to be under the necessity of using an ear-trumpet in company.

(2) Mr. Caleb Whitefoord, author of many humorous essays. He was so notorious a punster, that Doctor Goldsmith used to say it was impossible to keep his company without being infected with the itch of punning.

(3) Mr. H. S. Woodfall, printer of the Public Advertiser, and the Woodfall of Junius.

(4) Mr. Whitefoord has frequently indulged the town with humorous pieces under those titles in the Public Advertiser.

AN ORATORIO.

THE PERSONS.

First Jewish Prophet.	*First Chaldean Priest.*
Second Jewish Prophet.	*Second Chaldean Priest.*
Israelitish Woman.	*Chaldean Woman.*

Chorus of Youths and Virgins.

SCENE—*The Banks of the River Euphrates near Babylon.*

ACT I.

FIRST PROPHET.

RECITATIVE.

YE captive tribes, that hourly work and weep
Where flows Euphrates murmuring to the deep,
Suspend your woes awhile, the task suspend,
And turn to God, your father and your friend.
Insulted, chained, and all the world our foe,
Our God alone is all we boast below.

AIR.

First Pro. Our God is all we boast below:
To Him we turn our eyes;
And every added weight of woe
Shall make our homage rise.

Second Pro. And though no temple richly drest,
Nor sacrifice, are here;
We'll make His temple in our breast,
And offer up a tear.
[*The first Stanza repeated by the* CHORUS.

ISRAELITISH WOMAN.

RECITATIVE.

That strain once more; it bids remembrance rise,
And brings my long-lost country to mine eyes.
Ye fields of Sharon, drest in flowery pride,
Ye plains where Kedron rolls its glassy tide,
Ye hills of Lebanon, with cedars crowned,
Ye Gilead groves, that fling perfumes around,—
How sweet those groves, that plain how wondrous fair,
How doubly sweet when Heaven was with us there!

AIR.

O Memory, thou fond deceiver,
Still importunate and vain,
To former joys recurring ever,
And turning all the past to pain.

Hence intruder most distressing,
Seek the happy and the free:
The wretch who wants each other blessing,
Ever wants a friend in thee.

SECOND PROPHET.

RECITATIVE.

Yet why complain? What though by bonds confined?
Should bonds repress the vigour of the mind?
Have we not cause for triumph, when we see
Ourselves alone from idol worship free?
Are not this very morn those feasts begun
Where prostrate error hails the rising sun?
Do not our tyrant lords this day ordain
For superstitious rites and mirth profane?
And should we mourn? Should coward virtue fly,
When vaunting folly lifts her head on high?
No; rather let us triumph still the more,
And as our fortune sinks, our spirits soar.

AIR.

The triumphs that on vice attend
Shall ever in confusion end;
The good man suffers but to gain,
And every virtue springs from pain:
As aromatic plants bestow
No spicy fragrance while they grow;
But crushed, or trodden to the ground,
Diffuse their balmy sweets around.

FIRST PROPHET.

RECITATIVE.

But hush, my sons, our tyrant lords are near;
The sound of barbarous pleasure strikes mine ear.
Triumphant music floats along the vale;
Near, nearer still, it gathers on the gale:
The growing sound their swift approach declares.
Desist, my sons, nor mix the strain with theirs.

Enter CHALDEAN PRIESTS *attended.*

FIRST PRIEST.

AIR.

Come on, my companions, the triumph display,
  Let rapture the minutes employ,
The sun calls us out on this festival day,
  And our monarch partakes in the joy.

SECOND PRIEST.

Like the sun, our great monarch all rapture supplies:
  Both similar blessings bestow;
The sun with his splendour illumines the skies,
  And our monarch enlivens below.

AIR.

CHALDEAN WOMAN.

Haste, ye sprightly sons of pleasure;
Love presents the fairest treasure:
  Leave all other joys for me.

A CHALDEAN ATTENDANT.

Or rather, love's delights despising,
Haste to raptures ever rising:
  Wine shall bless the brave and free.

FIRST PRIEST.

Wine and beauty thus inviting,
Each to different joys exciting,
  Whither shall my choice incline?

SECOND PRIEST.

I 'll waste no longer thought in choosing,
But, neither this nor that refusing,
  I 'll make them both together mine.

FIRST PRIEST.

RECITATIVE.

But whence, when joy should brighten o'er the land,
This sullen gloom in Judah's captive band?
Ye sons of Judah, why the lute unstrung?
Or why those harps on yonder willows hung?
Come, take the lyre, and pour the strain along;
The day demands it: sing us Sion's song.
Dismiss your griefs, and join our warbling choir,
For who like you can wake the sleeping lyre?

AIR.

Every moment as it flows
Some peculiar pleasure owes.
Come then, providently wise,
Seize the debtor ere it flies.

SECOND PRIEST.

Think not to-morrow can repay
The debt of pleasure lost to-day.
Alas! to-morrow's richest store
Can but pay its proper score.

SECOND PROPHET.

RECITATIVE.

Chained as we are, the scorn of all mankind,
To want, to toil, and every ill consigned,
Is this a time to bid us raise the strain,
Or mix in rites that Heaven regards with pain?
No, never. May this hand forget each art
That wakes to finest joys the human heart,
Ere I forget the land that gave me birth,
Or join to sounds profane its sacred mirth!

SECOND PRIEST.

Rebellious slaves! if soft persuasion fail,
More formidable terrors shall prevail.

FIRST PROPHET.

Why, let them come; one good remains to cheer:
We fear the Lord, and scorn all other fear.
[*Exeunt* CHALDEANS.

CHORUS OF ISRAELITES.

Can chains or tortures bend the mind
On God's supporting breast reclin'd?
Stand fast, and let our tyrants see
That fortitude is victory. [*Exeunt.*

ACT II.

ISRAELITES *and* CHALDEANS, *as before.*

FIRST PROPHET.

AIR.

O peace of mind, angelic guest,
Thou soft companion of the breast,
Dispense thy balmy store!
Wing all our thoughts to reach the skies,
Till earth, receding from our eyes,
Shall vanish as we soar.

FIRST PRIEST.

RECITATIVE.

No more. Too long has justice been delayed:
The king's commands must fully be obeyed;
Compliance with his will your peace secures;
Praise but our gods, and every good is yours.
But if, rebellious to his high command,
You spurn the favours offered from his hand,
Think, timely think, what terrors are behind;
Reflect, nor tempt to 'rage the royal mind.

AIR.

Fierce is the tempest howling
Along the furrowed main,
And fierce the whirlwind rolling
O'er Afric's sandy plain.
But storms that fly
To rend the sky,
Every ill presaging,
Less dreadful show
To worlds below
Than angry monarch's raging.

ISRAELITISH WOMAN.

RECITATIVE.

Ah me! What angry terrors round us grow!
How shrinks my soul to meet the threatened blow!
Ye prophets, skilled in Heaven's eternal truth,
Forgive my sex's fears, forgive my youth!
Ah! let us one, one little hour obey;
To-morrow's tears may wash the stain away.

AIR.

Fatigued with life, yet loth to part,
On hope the wretch relies;
And every blow that sinks the heart
Bids the deluder rise.
Hope, like the taper's gleamy light,
Adorns the wretch's way,
And still, as darker grows the night,
Emits a brighter ray.

SECOND PRIEST.

RECITATIVE.

Why this delay? At length for joy prepare,
I read your looks, and see compliance there.
Come on, and bid the warbling rapture rise,
Our monarch's fame the noblest theme supplies.
Begin, ye captive bands, and strike the lyre,
The time, the theme, the place, and all conspire.

CHALDEAN WOMAN.

AIR.

See the ruddy morning smiling,
Hear the grove to bliss beguiling;
Zephyrs through the woodland playing,
Streams along the valley straying.

FIRST PRIEST.

While these a constant revel keep,
Shall reason only teach to weep?
Hence, intruder! we'll pursue
Nature, a better guide than you.

SECOND PRIEST.

RECITATIVE.

But hold! see foremost of the captive choir,
The master prophet grasps his full-toned lyre.
Mark where he sits with executing art,
Feels for each tone, and speeds it to the heart;
See how prophetic rapture fills his form,
Awful as clouds that nurse the growing storm.
And now his voice, accordant to the string,
Prepares our monarch's victories to sing.

FIRST PROPHET.

AIR.

From north, from south, from east, from west,
Conspiring nations come;
Tremble, thou vice-polluted breast;
Blasphemers, all be dumb.

The tempest gathers all around,
On Babylon it lies;
Down with her! down, down to the ground
She sinks, she groans, she dies.

SECOND PROPHET.

Down with her, Lord, to lick the dust,
Before yon setting sun;
Serve her as she hath served the just!
'Tis fixed—It shall be done.

FIRST PRIEST.

RECITATIVE.

No more! when slaves thus insolent presume,
The king himself shall judge, and fix their doom.
Unthinking wretches! have not you, and all,
Beheld our power in Zedekiah's fall?

To yonder gloomy dungeon turn your eyes;
See where dethroned your captive monarch lies,
Deprived of sight, and rankling in his chain:
See where he mourns his friends and children slain.
Yet know, ye slaves, that still remain behind
More ponderous chains, and dungeons more confined.

CHORUS OF ALL.

Arise, all potent ruler, rise,
And vindicate thy people's cause;
Till every tongue in every land
Shall offer up unfeigned applause.

[*Exeunt.*

ACT III.

Scene as before.

FIRST PRIEST.

RECITATIVE.

Yes, my companions, Heaven's decrees are passed,
And our fixed empire shall for ever last:
In vain the madd'ning prophet threatens woe,
In vain rebellion aims her secret blow;
Still shall our name and growing power be spread,
And still our justice crush the traitor's head.

AIR.

Coeval with man
Our empire began,
And never shall fall
Till ruin shakes all.
When ruin shakes all,
Then shall Babylon fall.

SECOND PROPHET.

RECITATIVE.

'Tis thus the proud triumphant rear the head,
A little while and all their power is fled.
But, ha! what means yon sadly plaintive train,
That onward slowly bends along the plain?
And now, behold, to yonder bank they bear
A pallid corse, and rest the body there.
Alas! too well mine eyes indignant trace
The last remains of Judah's royal race.
Fall'n is our King, and all our fears are o'er,
Unhappy Zedekiah is no more.

AIR.

Ye wretches who by fortune's hate
In want and sorrow groan,
Come ponder his severer fate,
And learn to bless your own.

FIRST PROPHET.

You vain whom youth and pleasure guide,
Awhile the bliss suspend:
Like yours, his life began in pride;
Like his, your lives shall end.

First Prophet.

RECITATIVE.

Behold his wretched corse with sorrow worn,
His squalid limbs by ponderous fetters torn;
Those eyeless orbs that shock with ghastly glare,
Those unbecoming rags, that matted hair!
And shall not Heaven for this avenge the foe,
Grasp the red bolt, and lay the guilty low?
How long, how long, Almighty God of all,
Shall wrath vindictive threaten ere it fall!

Israelitish Woman.

AIR.

As panting flies the hunted hind,
  Where brooks refreshing stray;
And rivers through the valley wind,
  That stop the hunter's way:

Thus we, O Lord, alike distrest,
  For streams of mercy long;
Streams which cheer the sore opprest,
  And overwhelm the strong.

First Prophet.

RECITATIVE.

But whence that shout? Good heavens! Amazement all!
See yonder tower just nodding to the fall:
Behold, an army covers all the ground,
'Tis Cyrus here that pours destruction round:—
And now behold the battlements recline—
O God of hosts, the victory is thine!

Chorus of Captives.

Down with them, Lord, to lick the dust;
  Thy vengeance be begun;
Serve them as they have served the just,
  And let thy will be done.

First Priest.

RECITATIVE.

All, all is lost. The Syrian army fails;
Cyrus, the conqueror of the world, prevails.
The ruin smokes, the torrent pours along,—
How low the proud, how feeble are the strong!
Save us, O Lord! to Thee, though late, we pray;
And give repentance but an hour's delay.

First and Second Priest.

AIR.

O happy, who in happy hour,
  To God their praise bestow,
And own his all-consuming power,
  Before they feel the blow!

SECOND PROPHET.

RECITATIVE.

Now, now's our time! ye wretches bold and blind,
Brave but to God, and cowards to mankind,
Ye seek in vain the Lord unsought before,
Your wealth, your lives, your kingdom, are no more.

AIR.

O Lucifer, thou son of morn,
Of heaven alike and man the foe;
Heaven, men, and all,
Now press thy fall,
And sink thee lowest of the low.

FIRST PROPHET.

O Babylon, how art thou fallen!
Thy fall more dreadful from delay!
Thy streets forlorn
To wilds shall turn,
Where toads shall pant, and vultures prey.

SECOND PROPHET.

RECITATIVE.

Such be her fate. But hark! how from afar
The clarion's note proclaims the finish'd war!
Our great restorer, Cyrus, is at hand,
And this way leads his formidable band.
Give, give your songs of Sion to the wind,
And hail the benefactor of mankind:
He comes pursuant to divine decree,
To chain the strong, and set the captive free.

CHORUS OF YOUTHS.

Rise to transports past expressing,
Sweeter by remember'd woes;
Cyrus comes our wrongs redressing,
Comes to give the world repose.

CHORUS OF VIRGINS.

Cyrus comes, the world redressing,
Love and pleasure in his train;
Comes to heighten every blessing,
Comes to soften every pain.

SEMI-CHORUS.

Hail to him with mercy reigning,
Skilled in every peaceful art;
Who from bonds our limbs unchaining
Only binds the willing heart.

THE LAST CHORUS.

But chief to Thee, our God, defender, friend,
Let praise be given to all eternity;
O Thou, without beginning, without end,
Let us and all begin and end in Thee.

DRAMAS.

THE GOOD-NATURED MAN;

A COMEDY:

AS PERFORMED AT THE THEATRE ROYAL, COVENT GARDEN.

[1768.]

PREFACE.

When I undertook to write a comedy, I confess I was strongly prepossessed in favour of the poets of the last age, and strove to imitate them. The term "genteel comedy" was then unknown amongst us, and little more was desired by an audience than nature and humour, in whatever walks of life they were most conspicuous. The author of the following scenes never imagined that more would be expected of him, and therefore to delineate character has been his principal aim. Those who know anything of composition, are sensible that, in pursuing humour, it will sometimes lead us into the recesses of the mean; I was even tempted to look for it in the master of a spunging-house; but in deference to the public taste, grown of late, perhaps, too delicate, the scene of the bailiffs was retrenched in the representation. In deference also to the judgment of a few friends, who think in a particular way, the scene is here restored. The author submits it to the reader in his closet; and hopes that too much refinement will not banish humour and character from ours, as it has already done from the French theatre. Indeed the French comedy is now become so very elevated and sentimental, that it has not only banished humour and Moliere from the stage, but it has banished all spectators too.

Upon the whole, the author returns his thanks to the public for the favourable reception which "The Good-Natured Man" has met with; and to Mr. Colman in particular, for his kindness to it. It may not also be improper to assure any who shall hereafter write for the theatre, that merit, or supposed merit, will ever be a sufficient passport to his protection.

PROLOGUE.

WRITTEN BY DR. JOHNSON; SPOKEN BY MR. BENSLEY.

PRESS'D by the load of life, the weary mind
Surveys the general toil of human kind;
With cool submission joins the lab'ring train,
And social sorrow loses half its pain:
Our anxious bard, without complaint, may share
This bustling season's epidemic care,
Like Cæsar's pilot, dignified by fate,
Tost in one common storm with all the great;
Distrest alike, the statesman and the wit,
When one a borough courts, and one the pit,
The busy candidates for power and fame
Have hopes, and fears, and wishes, just the same;
Disabled both to combat, or to fly,
Must hear all taunts, and hear without reply.
Uncheck'd on both loud rabbles vent their rage,
As mongrels bay the lion in a cage.

Th' offended burgess hoards his angry tale
For that blest year when all that vote may rail;
Their schemes of spite the poet's foes dismiss
Till that glad night when all that hate may hiss.
"This day the powder'd curls and golden coat,"
Says swelling Crispin, "begg'd a cobbler's vote."
"This night our wit," the pert apprentice cries,
"Lies at my feet—I hiss him, and he dies."
The great, 'tis true, can charm the electing tribe;
The bard may supplicate, but cannot bribe.
Yet judg'd by those whose voices ne'er were sold,
He feels no want of ill-persuading gold;
But confident of praise, if praise be due,
Trusts without fear, to merit, and to you.

DRAMATIS PERSONÆ.

MEN.

Mr. Honeywood	Mr. Powell.
Croaker	Mr. Shuter.
Lofty	Mr. Woodward.
Sir William Honeywood	Mr. Clarke.
Leontine	Mr. Bensley.
Jarvis	Mr. Dunstall.
Butler	Mr. Cushing.
Bailiff	Mr. R. Smith.
Dubardieu	Mr. Holtom.
Postboy	Mr. Quick.

WOMEN.

Miss Richland	Mrs. Bulkley.
Olivia	Mrs. Mattocks.
Mrs. Croaker	Mrs. Pitt.
Garnet	Mrs. Green.
Landlady	Mrs. White.

Scene—London.

ACT THE FIRST.

Scene—*An Apartment in Young* Honeywood's *House.*

Enter Sir William Honeywood *and* Jarvis.

Sir Wil. Good Jarvis, make no apologies for this honest bluntness. Fidelity, like yours, is the best excuse for every freedom.

Jar. I can't help being blunt, and being very angry too, when I hear you talk of disinheriting so good, so worthy a young gentleman as your nephew, my master. All the world loves him.

Sir Wil. Say rather, that he loves all the world; that is his fault.

Jar. I am sure there is no part of it more dear to him than you are, though he has not seen you since he was a child.

Sir Wil. What signifies his affection to me; or how can I be proud of a place in a heart, where every sharper and coxcomb find an easy entrance?

Jar. I grant you that he is rather too good-natured; that he's too much every man's man; that he laughs this minute with one, and cries the next with another: but whose instructions may he thank for all this?

Sir Wil. Not mine, sure? My letters to him during my employment in Italy taught him only that philosophy which might prevent, not defend his errors.

Jar. Faith, begging your honour's pardon, I'm sorry they taught him any philosophy at all; it has only served to spoil him. This same philosophy is a good horse in the stable, but an arrant jade on a journey. For my own part, whenever I hear him mention the name on't, I'm always sure he's going to play the fool.

Sir Wil. Don't let us ascribe his faults to his philosophy, I entreat you. No, Jarvis, his good-nature arises rather from his fears of offending the importunate, than his desire of making the deserving happy.

Jar. What it rises from, I don't know. But, to be sure, everybody has it, that asks it.

Sir Wil. Ay, or that does not ask it. I have been now for some time a concealed spectator of his follies, and find them as boundless as his dissipation.

Jar. And yet, faith, he has some fine name or other for them all. He calls his extravagance, generosity; and his trusting everybody, universal benevolence. It was but last week he went security for a fellow whose face he scarce knew, and that he called an act of exalted mu—mu—munificence; ay, that was the name he gave it.

Sir Wil. And upon that I proceed, as my last effort, though with very little hopes to reclaim him. That very fellow has just absconded, and I have taken up the security. Now, my intention is to involve him in fictitious distress, before he has plunged himself into real calamity: to arrest him for that very debt; to clap an officer upon him, and then let him see which of his friends will come to his relief.

Jar. Well, if I could but any way see him thoroughly vexed, every groan of his would be music to me; yet, faith, I believe it impossible. I have tried to fret him myself every morning these three years; but, instead of being angry, he sits as calmly to hear me scold, as he does to his hair-dresser.

Sir Wil. We must try him once more, however, and I'll go this instant to put my scheme into execution: and I don't despair of succeeding, as, by your means, I can have frequent opportunities of being about him without being known. What a pity it is, Jarvis, that any man's good-will to others should produce so much neglect of himself, as to require correction! Yet we must touch his weaknesses with a delicate hand. There are some faults so nearly allied to excellence, that we can scarce weed out the vice without eradicating the virtue. [*Exit.*

Jar. Well, go thy ways, Sir William Honeywood. It is not without reason that the world allows thee to be the best of men. But here comes his hopeful nephew; the strange good-natured, foolish, open-hearted—And yet, all his faults are such that one loves him still the better for them.

Enter HONEYWOOD.

Hon. Well, Jarvis, what messages from my friends this morning?

Jar. You have no friends.

Hon. Well; from my acquaintance then?

Jar. (*Pulling out bills.*) A few of our usual cards of compliment, that's all. This bill from your tailor; this from your mercer; and this from the little broker in Crooked-lane. He says he has been at a great deal of trouble to get back the money you borrowed.

Hon. That I don't know; but I'm sure we were at a great deal of trouble in getting him to lend it.

Jar. He has lost all patience.

Hon. Then he has lost a very good thing.

Jar. There's that ten guineas you were sending to the poor gentleman and his children in the Fleet. I believe that would stop his mouth for a while at least.

Hon. Ay, Jarvis, but what will fill their mouths in the mean time? Must I be cruel, because he happens to be importunate; and, to relieve his avarice, leave them to insupportable distress?

Jar. 'Sdeath! Sir, the question now is how to relieve yourself; yourself.—Haven't I reason to be out of my senses, when I see things going at sixes and sevens?

Hon. Whatever reason you may have for being out of your senses, I hope you'll allow that I'm not quite unreasonable for continuing in mine.

Jar. You are the only man alive in your present situation that could do so. Every thing upon the waste. There's Miss Richland and her fine fortune gone already, and upon the point of being given to your rival—

Hon. I'm no man's rival.

Jar. Your uncle in Italy preparing to disinherit you; your own fortune almost spent; and nothing but pressing creditors, false friends, and a pack of drunken servants that your kindness has made unfit for any other family.

Hon. Then they have the more occasion for being in mine.

Jar. Soh! What will you have done with him that I caught stealing your plate in the pantry? In the fact; I caught him in the fact.

Hon. In the fact? If so, I really think that we should pay him his wages and turn him off.

Jar. He shall be turned off at Tyburn, the dog; we'll hang him, if it be only to frighten the rest of the family.

Hon. No, Jarvis; it's enough that we have lost what he has stolen; let us not add to it the loss of a fellow-creature!

Jar. Very fine! well, here was the footman just now, to complain of the butler: he says he does most work, and ought to have most wages.

Hon. That's but just; though perhaps here comes the butler to complain of the footman.

Jar. Ay, it's the way with them all, from the scullion to the privy-councillor. If they have a bad master, they keep quarrelling with him; if they have a good master, they keep quarrelling with one another.

Enter BUTLER, *drunk.*

But. Sir, I'll not stay in the family with Jonathan; you must part with him, or part with me; that's the ex—ex—exposition of the matter, sir.

Hon. Full and explicit enough. But what's his fault, good Philip?

But. Sir, he's given to drinking, sir, and I shall have my morals corrupted by keeping such company.

Hon. Ha! ha! he has such a diverting way—

Jar. Oh, quite amusing.

But. I find my wine's a-going, sir; and liquors don't go without mouths, sir; I hate a drunkard, sir.

Hon. Well, well, Philip, I'll hear you upon that another time; so go to bed now.

Jar. To bed! let him go to the devil.

But. Begging your honour's pardon, and begging your pardon, master Jarvis, I'll not go to bed, nor to the devil neither. I have enough to do to mind my cellar. I forgot, your honour, Mr. Croaker is below. I came on purpose to tell you.

Hon. Why didn't you show him up, blockhead?

But. Show him up, sir! With all my heart, sir. Up or down, all's one to me. [*Exit.*

Jar. Ay, we have one or other of that family in this house from morning till night. He comes on the old affair, I suppose. The match between his son that's just returned from Paris, and Miss Richland, the young lady he's guardian to.

Hon. Perhaps so. Mr. Croaker, knowing my friendship for the young lady, has got it into his head that I can persuade her to what I please.

Jar. Ah! if you loved yourself but half as well as she loves you, we should soon see a marriage that would set all things to rights again.

Hon. Love me! Sure, Jarvis, you dream. No, no; her intimacy with me never amounted to more than mere friendship—mere friendship. That she is the most lovely woman that ever warmed the human heart with desire, I own. But never let me harbour a thought of making her unhappy, by a connexion with one so unworthy her merits as I am. No, Jarvis, it shall be my study to serve her, even in spite of my wishes; and to secure her happiness, though it destroys my own.

Jar. Was ever the like? I want patience.

Hon. Besides, Jarvis, though I could obtain Miss Richland's consent, do you think I could succeed with her guardian, or Mrs. Croaker, his wife; who, though both very fine in their way, are yet a little opposite in their dispositions, you know?

Jar. Opposite enough, Heaven knows! the very reverse of each other: she, all laugh and no joke; he, always complaining and never sorrowful; a fretful poor soul, that has a new distress for every hour in the four and twenty—

Hon. Hush, hush, he's coming up, he'll hear you.

Jar. One whose voice is a passing-bell—

Hon. Well, well; go, do.

Jar. A raven that bodes nothing but mischief; a coffin and cross-bones; a bundle of rue; a sprig of deadly night-shade; a—(HONEYWOOD, *stopping his mouth, at last pushes him off.*) [*Exit* Jarvis.

Hon. I must own, my old monitor is not entirely wrong. There is something in my friend Croaker's conversation that entirely depresses me. His very mirth is quite an antidote to all gaiety, and his appearance has a stronger effect on my spirits than an undertaker's shop.—Mr. Croaker, this is such a satisfaction—

Enter CROAKER.

Cro. A pleasant morning to Mr. Honeywood, and many of them. How is this! you look most shockingly to-day, my dear friend. I hope this weather does not affect your spirits. To be sure, if this weather continues—I say nothing—But God send we be all better this day three months!

Hon. I heartily concur in the wish, though, I own, not in your apprehensions.

Cro. May be not. Indeed, what signifies what weather we have in a country going to ruin like ours? Taxes rising and trade falling. Money flying out of the kingdom, and Jesuits swarming into it. I know at this time no less than a hundred and twenty-seven Jesuits between Charing Cross and Temple Bar.

Hon. The Jesuits will scarce pervert you or me, I should hope.

Cro. May be not. Indeed, what signifies whom they pervert in a country that has scarce any religion to lose? I'm only afraid for our wives and daughters.

Hon. I have no apprehensions for the ladies, I assure you.

Cro. May be not. Indeed, what signifies whether they be perverted or no? The women in my time were good for something. I have seen a lady drest from top to toe in her own manufactures formerly. But now-a-days the devil a thing of their own manufacture's about them, except their faces.

Hon. But, however these faults may be practised abroad, you don't find them at home, either with Mrs. Croaker, Olivia, or Miss Richland.

Cro. The best of them will never be canonised for a saint when she's dead. By the bye, my dear friend, I don't find this match between Miss Richland and my son much relished, either by one side or t'other.

Hon. I thought otherwise.

Cro. Ah, Mr. Honeywood, a little of your fine serious advice to the young lady might go far: I know she has a very exalted opinion of your understanding.

Hon. But would not that be usurping an authority that more properly belongs to yourself?

Cro. My dear friend, you know but little of my authority at home. People think, indeed, because they see me come out in a morning thus, with a pleasant face, and to make my friends merry, that all's well within. But I have cares that would break a heart of stone. My wife has so encroached upon every one of my privileges, that I'm now no more than a mere lodger in my own house.

Hon. But a little spirit exerted on your side might perhaps restore your authority.

Cro. No, though I had the spirit of a lion! I do rouse sometimes. But what then? always haggling and haggling. A man is tired of getting the better before his wife is tired of losing the victory.

Hon. It is a melancholy consideration indeed, that our chief comforts often produce our greatest anxieties, and that an increase of our possessions is but an inlet to new disquietudes.

Cro. Ah, my dear friend, these were the very words of poor Dick Doleful to me not a week before he made away with himself. Indeed, Mr. Honeywood, I never see you but you put me in mind of poor Dick. Ah, there was merit neglected for you! and so true a friend! we loved each other for thirty years, and yet he never asked me to lend him a single farthing.

Hon. Pray what could induce him to commit so rash an action at last?

Cro. I don't know: some people were malicious enough to say it was keeping company with me; because we used to meet now and then and open our hearts to each other. To be sure I loved to hear him talk, and he loved to hear me talk; poor dear Dick! He used to say that Croaker rhymed to joker; and so we used to laugh.—Poor Dick! [*Going to cry.*

Hon. His fate affects me.

Cro. Ah, he grew sick of this miserable life, where we do nothing but eat and grow hungry, dress and undress, get up and lie down; while reason, that should watch like a nurse by our side, falls as fast asleep as we do.

Hon. To say a truth, if we compare that part of life which is to come, by that which we have past, the prospect is hideous.

Cro. Life at the greatest and best is but a froward child, that must be humoured and coaxed a little till it falls asleep, and then all the care is over.

Hon. Very true, sir; nothing can exceed the vanity of our existence, but the folly of our pursuits. We wept when we came into the world, and every day tells us why.

Cro. Ah, my dear friend, it is a perfect satisfaction to be miserable with you. My son Leontine shan't lose the benefit of such fine conversation. I'll just step home for him. I am willing to show him so much seriousness in one scarce older than himself. And what if I bring my last letter to the Gazetteer on the increase and progress of earthquakes? It will amuse us, I promise you. I there prove how the late earthquake is coming round to pay us another visit, from London to Lisbon, from Lisbon to the Canary Islands, from the Canary Islands to Palmyra, from Palmyra to Constantinople, and so from Constantinople back to London again. [*Exit.*

Hon. Poor Croaker! his situation deserves the utmost pity. I shall scarce recover my spirits these three days. Sure to live upon such terms is worse than death itself! And yet, when I consider my own situation,—a broken fortune, a hopeless passion, friends in distress, the wish but not the power to serve them—(*pausing and sighing.*)

Enter BUTLER.

But. More company below, sir; Mrs. Croaker and Miss Richland: shall I show them up? but they're showing up themselves. [*Exit.*

Enter MRS. CROAKER *and* MISS RICHLAND.

Miss Rich. You're always in such spirits.

Mrs. Cro. We have just come, my dear Honeywood, from the auction. There was the old deaf dowager, as usual, bidding like a fury against herself. And then so curious in antiques! herself the most genuine piece of antiquity in the whole collection.

Hon. Excuse me, ladies, if some uneasiness from friendship makes me unfit to share in this good-humour: I know you'll pardon me.

Mrs. Cro. I vow he seems as melancholy as if he had taken a dose of my husband this morning. Well, if Richland here can pardon you, I must.

Miss Rich. You would seem to insinuate, madam, that I have particular reasons for being disposed to refuse it.

Mrs. Cro. Whatever I insinuate, my dear, don't be so ready to wish an explanation.

Miss Rich. I own I should be sorry Mr. Honeywood's long friendship and mine should be misunderstood.

Hon. There's no answering for others, madam. But I hope you'll never find me presuming to offer more than the most delicate friendship may readily allow.

Miss Rich. And I shall be prouder of such a tribute from you, than the most passionate professions from others.

Hon. My own sentiments, madam: friendship is a disinterested commerce between equals; love, an abject intercourse between tyrants and slaves.

Miss Rich. And, without a compliment, I know none more disinterested, or more capable of friendship, than Mr. Honeywood.

Mrs. Cro. And, indeed, I know nobody that has more friends, at least among the ladies. Miss Fruzz, Miss Oddbody, and Miss Winterbottom, praise him in all companies. As for Miss Biddy Bundle, she's his professed admirer.

Miss Rich. Indeed! an admirer! I did not know, sir, you were such a favourite there. But is she seriously so handsome? Is she the mighty thing talked of?

Hon. The town, madam, seldom begins to praise a lady's beauty, till she's beginning to lose it—(*smiling.*)

Mrs. Cro. But she's resolved never to lose it, it seems; for, as her natural face decays, her skill improves in making the artificial one. Well, nothing diverts me more than one of these fine, old, dressy things, who thinks to conceal her age, by everywhere exposing her person; sticking herself up in the front of a side-box; trailing through a minuet at Almack's; and then, in the public gardens, looking for all the world like one of the painted ruins of the place.

Hon. Every age has its admirers, ladies. While you, perhaps, are trading among the warmer climates of youth, there ought to be some to carry on a useful commerce in the frozen latitudes beyond fifty.

Miss Rich. But, then, the mortifications they must suffer before they can be fitted out for traffic. I have seen one of them fret a whole morning at her hair-dresser, when all the fault was her face.

Hon. And yet, I'll engage, has carried that face at last to a very good market. This good-natured town, madam, has husbands, like spectacles, to fit every age, from fifteen to fourscore.

Mrs. Cro. Well, you're a dear, good-natured creature. But you know you're engaged with us this morning upon a strolling party. I want to show Olivia the town, and the things; I believe I shall have business for you for the whole day.

Hon. I am sorry, madam, I have an appointment with Mr. Croaker, which it is impossible to put off.

Mrs. Cro. What! with my husband? Then I'm resolved to take no refusal. Nay, I protest you must. You know I never laugh so much as with you.

Hon. Why, if I must, I must. I'll swear you have put me into such spirits. Well, do you find jest, and I'll find laugh, I promise you. We'll wait for the chariot in the next room. [*Exeunt.*

Enter LEONTINE *and* OLIVIA.

Leon. There they go, thoughtless and happy. My dearest Olivia, what would I give to see you capable of sharing in their amusements, and as cheerful as they are!

Oliv. How, my Leontine, how can I be cheerful, when I have so many terrors to oppress me? The fear of being detected by this family, and the apprehensions of a censuring world, when I must be detected—

Leon. The world, my love! what can it say? At worst it can only say that, being compelled by a mercenary guardian to embrace a life you disliked, you formed a resolution of flying with the man of your choice; that you confided in his honour, and took refuge in my father's house; the only one where yours could remain without censure.

Oliv. But consider, Leontine, your disobedience and my indiscretion; your being sent to France to bring home a sister, and, instead of a sister, bringing home—

Leon. One dearer than a thousand sisters. One that I am convinced will be equally dear to the rest of the family, when she comes to be known.

Oliv. And that, I fear, will shortly be.

Leon. Impossible, till we ourselves think proper to make the discovery. My sister, you know, has been with her aunt, at Lyons, since she was a child, and you find every creature in the family takes you for her.

Oliv. But mayn't she write, mayn't her aunt write?

Leon. Her aunt scarce ever writes, and all my sister's letters are directed to me.

Oliv. But won't your refusing Miss Richland, for whom you know the old gentleman intends you, create a suspicion?

Leon. There, there's my master-stroke. I have resolved not to refuse her; nay, an hour hence I have consented to go with my father to make her an offer of my heart and fortune.

Oliv. Your heart and fortune!

Leon. Don't be alarmed, my dearest. Can Olivia think so meanly of my honour or my love, as to suppose I could ever hope for happiness from any but her? No, my Olivia, neither the force, nor, permit me to add, the delicacy of my passion, leave any room to suspect me. I only offer Miss Richland a heart I am convinced she will refuse; as I am confident that, without knowing it, her affections are fixed upon Mr. Honeywood.

Oliv. Mr. Honeywood! You'll excuse my apprehensions; but when your merits come to be put in the balance—

Leon. You view them with too much partiality. However, by making this offer, I show a seeming compliance with my father's command; and, perhaps, upon her refusal, I may have his consent to choose for myself.

Oliv. Well, I submit. And yet, my Leontine, I own I shall envy her even your pretended addresses. I consider every look, every expression of your esteem, as due only to me. This is folly, perhaps: I allow it: but it is natural to suppose, that merit which has made an impression on one's own heart, may be powerful over that of another.

Leon. Don't, my life's treasure, don't let us make imaginary evils, when you know we have so many real ones to encounter. At worst, you know, if Miss Richland should consent, or my father refuse his pardon, it can but end in a trip to Scotland; and—

Enter CROAKER.

Cro. Where have you been, boy? I have been seeking you. My friend Honeywood here has been saying such comfortable things. Ah! he's an example indeed. Where is he? I left him here.

Leon. Sir, I believe you may see him, and hear him too, in the next room; he's preparing to go out with the ladies.

Cro. Good gracious! can I believe my eyes or my ears! I'm struck dumb with his vivacity, and stunned with the loudness of his laugh. Was there ever such a transformation! (*A laugh behind the scenes.* CROAKER *mimics it.*) Ha! ha! ha! there it goes: a plague take their balderdash! Yet I could expect nothing less, when my precious wife was of the party. On my conscience, I believe she could spread a horse-laugh through the pews of a tabernacle.

Leon. Since you find so many objections to a wife, sir, how can you be so earnest in recommending one to me?

Cro. I have told you, and tell you again, boy, that Miss Richland's fortune must not go out of the family; one may find comfort in the money, whatever one does in the wife.

Leon. But, sir, though, in obedience to your desire, I am ready to marry her, it may be possible she has no inclination to me.

Cro. I'll tell you once for all how it stands. A good part of Miss Richland's large fortune consists in a claim upon Government, which my good friend, Mr. Lofty, assures me the Treasury will allow. One half of this she is to forfeit, by her father's will, in case she refuses to marry you. So, if she rejects you, we seize half her fortune; if she accepts you, we seize the whole, and a fine girl into the bargain.

Leon. But, sir, if you will but listen to reason—

Cro. Come, then, produce your reasons. I tell you, I'm fixed, determined; so now produce your reasons. When I'm determined, I always listen to reason, because it can then do no harm.

Leon. You have alleged that a mutual choice was the first requisite in matrimonial happiness.

Cro. Well, and you have both of you a mutual choice. She has her choice—to marry you, or lose half her fortune; and you have your choice—to marry her, or pack out of doors without any fortune at all.

Leon. An only son, sir, might expect more indulgence.

Cro. An only father, sir, might expect more obedience: besides, has not your sister here, that never disobliged me in her life, as good a right as you? He's a sad dog, Livy, my dear, and would take all from you. But he shan't, I tell you he shan't, for you shall have your share.

Oliv. Dear sir, I wish you'd be convinced, that I can never be happy in any addition to my fortune which is taken from his.

Cro. Well, well, it's a good child, so say no more: but come with me, and we shall see something that will give us a great deal of pleasure, I promise you; old Ruggins, the curry-comb maker, lying in state: I am told he makes a very handsome corpse, and becomes his coffin prodigiously. He was an intimate friend of mine, and these are friendly things we ought to do for each other. [*Exeunt.*

ACT THE SECOND.

Scene—CROAKER'S *House.*

MISS RICHLAND *and* GARNET.

Miss Rich. Olivia not his sister? Olivia not Leontine's sister? You amaze me!

Gar. No more his sister than I am; I had it all from his own servant: I can get anything from that quarter.

Miss Rich. But how? Tell me again, Garnet.

Gar. Why, madam, as I told you before, instead of going to Lyons to bring home his sister, who has been there with her aunt these ten years, he never went further than Paris: there he saw and fell in love with this young lady—by the bye, of a prodigious family.

Miss Rich. And brought her home to my guardian as his daughter?

Gar. Yes, and daughter she will be.

If he don't consent to their marriage, they talk of trying what a Scotch parson can do.

Miss Rich. Well, I own they have deceived me—And so demurely as Olivia carried it too!—Would you believe it, Garnet, I told her all my secrets; and yet the sly cheat concealed all this from me?

Gar. And, upon my word, madam, I don't much blame her: she was loth to trust one with her secrets, that was so very bad at keeping her own.

Miss Rich. But, to add to their deceit, the young gentleman, it seems, pretends to make me serious proposals. My guardian and he are to be here presently, to open the affair in form. You know I am to lose half my fortune if I refuse him.

Gar. Yet, what can you do? For being, as you are, in love with Mr. Honeywood, madam—

Miss Rich. How! idiot, what do you mean? In love with Mr. Honeywood! Is this to provoke me?

Gar. That is, madam, in friendship with him; I meant nothing more than friendship, as I hope to be married; nothing more.

Miss Rich. Well, no more of this. As to my guardian and his son, they shall find me prepared to receive them: I'm resolved to accept their proposal with seeming pleasure, to mortify them by compliance, and so throw the refusal at last upon them.

Gar. Delicious! and that will secure your whole fortune to yourself. Well, who could have thought so innocent a face could cover so much 'cuteness!

Miss Rich. Why, girl, I only oppose my prudence to their cunning, and practise a lesson they have taught me against themselves.

Gar. Then you're likely not long to want employment, for here they come, and in close conference.

Enter CROAKER *and* LEONTINE.

Leon. Excuse me, sir, if I seem to hesitate upon the point of putting to the lady so important a question.

Cro. Lord! good sir, moderate your fears; you're so plaguy shy, that one would think you had changed sexes. I tell you we must have the half or the whole. Come, let me see with what spirit you begin. Well, why don't you? Eh! what? Well, then—I must, it seems—Miss Richland, my dear, I believe you guess at our business; an affair which my son here comes to open, that nearly concerns your happiness.

Miss Rich. Sir, I should be ungrateful not to be pleased with anything that comes recommended by you.

Cro. How, boy, could you desire a finer opening? Why don't you begin, I say? [*To* Leontine.

Leon. 'Tis true, madam, my father, madam, has some intentions—hem—of explaining an affair—which—himself—can best explain, madam.

Cro. Yes, my dear; it comes entirely from my son; it's all a request of his own, madam. And I will permit him to make the best of it.

Leon. The whole affair is only this, madam; my father has a proposal to make, which he insists none but himself shall deliver.

Cro. My mind misgives me, the fellow will never be brought on (*aside*). In short, madam, you see before you one that loves you, one whose whole happiness is all in you.

Miss Rich. I never had any doubts of your regard, sir; and I hope you can have none of my duty.

Cro. That's not the thing, my little sweeting; my love! No, no, another-guess lover than I: there he stands, madam, his very looks declare the force of his passion—Call up a look, you dog! (*aside*)—But then, had you seen him, as I have, weeping, speaking soliloquies and blank verse, sometimes melancholy, and sometimes absent.

Miss Rich. I fear, sir, he's absent now; or such a declaration would have come most properly from himself.

Cro. Himself, madam! he would die before he could make such a confession; and if he had not a channel for his passion through me, it would ere now have drowned his understanding.

Miss Rich. I must grant, sir, there are attractions in modest diffidence above the force of words. A silent address is the genuine eloquence of sincerity.

Cro. Madam, he has forgot to speak

any other language; silence is become his mother-tongue.

Miss Rich. And it must be confessed, sir, it speaks very powerfully in his favour. And yet I shall be thought too forward in making such a confession; shan't I, Mr. Leontine?

Leon. Confusion! my reserve will undo me. But, if modesty attracts her, impudence may disgust her. I'll try. (*Aside.*) Don't imagine from my silence, madam, that I want a due sense of the honour and happiness intended me. My father, madam, tells me, your humble servant is not totally indifferent to you—he admires you: I adore you; and when we come together, upon my soul I believe we shall be the happiest couple in all St. James's.

Miss Rich. If I could flatter myself you thought as you speak, sir—

Leon. Doubt my sincerity, madam? By your dear self I swear. Ask the brave if they desire glory? ask cowards if they covet safety——

Cro. Well, well, no more questions about it.

Leon. Ask the sick if they long for health? ask misers if they love money? ask——

Cro. Ask a fool if he can talk nonsense! What's come over the boy? What signifies asking, when there's not a soul to give you an answer? If you would ask to the purpose, ask this lady's consent to make you happy.

Miss Rich. Why indeed, sir, his uncommon ardour almost compels me—forces me to comply. And yet I'm afraid he'll despise a conquest gained with too much ease; won't you, Mr. Leontine?

Leon. Confusion! (*aside.*) Oh, by no means, madam, by no means. And yet, madam, you talked of force. There is nothing I would avoid so much as compulsion in a thing of this kind. No, madam, I will still be generous, and leave you at liberty to refuse.

Cro. But I tell you, sir, the lady is not at liberty. It's a match. You see she says nothing. Silence gives consent.

Leon. But, sir, she talked of force. Consider, sir, the cruelty of constraining her inclinations.

Cro. But I say there's no cruelty. Don't you know, blockhead, that girls have always a roundabout way of saying yes before company? So get you both gone together into the next room, and hang him that interrupts the tender explanation. Get you gone, I say; I'll not hear a word.

Leon. But, sir, I must beg leave to insist—

Cro. Get off, you puppy, or I'll beg leave to insist upon knocking you down. Stupid whelp! But I don't wonder: the boy takes entirely after his mother.

[*Exeunt* Miss Rich. *and* Leon.

Enter MRS. CROAKER.

Mrs. Cro. Mr. Croaker, I bring you something, my dear, that I believe will make you smile.

Cro. I'll hold you a guinea of that, my dear.

Mrs. Cro. A letter; and, as I knew the hand, I ventured to open it.

Cro. And how can you expect your breaking open my letters should give me pleasure?

Mrs. Cro. Poo! it's from your sister at Lyons, and contains good news; read it.

Cro. What a Frenchified cover is here! That sister of mine has some good qualities, but I could never teach her to fold a letter.

Mrs. Cro. Fold a fiddlestick! Read what it contains.

CROAKER, *reading.*

"*Dear Nick,*—An English gentleman, of large fortune, has for some time made private, though honourable proposals to your daughter Olivia. They love each other tenderly, and I find she has consented, without letting any of the family know, to crown his addresses. As such good offers don't come every day, your own good sense, his large fortune, and family considerations, will induce you to forgive her.

"Yours ever,

"RACHAEL CROAKER."

My daughter Olivia privately contracted to a man of large fortune! This is good news, indeed. My heart never foretold me of this. And yet, how slily the little baggage has carried it since she came home; not a word on't to the old ones for the world. Yet I thought I saw something she wanted to conceal.

Mrs. Cro. Well, if they have concealed their amour, they shan't conceal their wedding; that shall be public, I'm resolved.

Cro. I tell thee, woman, the wedding is the most foolish part of the ceremony. I can never get this woman to think of the most serious part of the nuptial engagement.

Mrs. Cro. What would you have me think of, their funeral? But come, tell me, my dear, don't you owe more to me than you care to confess? Would you have ever been known to Mr. Lofty, who has undertaken Miss Richland's claim at the Treasury, but for me? Who was it first made him an acquaintance at Lady Shabbaroon's rout? Who got him to promise us his interest? Is not he a backstairs favourite, one that can do what he pleases with those that do what they please? Is not he an acquaintance that all your groaning and lamentation could never have got us?

Cro. He is a man of importance, I grant you. And yet what amazes me is, that, while he is giving away places to all the world, he can't get one for himself.

Mrs. Cro. That perhaps may be owing to his nicety. Great men are not easily satisfied.

Enter French Servant.

Ser. An expresse from Monsieur Lofty. He vil be vait upon your honours instammant. He be only giving four five instruction, read two three memorial, call upon von ambassadeur. He vil be vid you in one tree minutes.

Mrs. Cro. You see now, my dear. What an extensive department! Well, friend, let your master know, that we are extremely honoured by this honour. Was there anything ever in a higher style of breeding? All messages among the great are now done by express.

Cro. To be sure, no man does little things with more solemnity, or claims more respect than he. But he's in the right on't. In our bad world, respect is given where respect is claimed.

Mrs. Cro. Never mind the world, my dear; you were never in a pleasanter place in your life. Let us now think of receiving him with proper respect—(*A loud rapping at the door*),—and there he is, by the thundering rap.

Cro. Ay, verily, there he is! as close upon the heels of his own express, as an endorsement upon the back of a bill. Well, I'll leave you to receive him, whilst I go to chide my little Olivia for intending to steal a marriage without mine or her aunt's consent. I must seem to be angry, or she too may begin to despise my authority. [*Exit.*

Enter LOFTY, *speaking to his* Servant.

Lof. "And if the Venetian ambassador, or that teasing creature the Marquis, should call, I'm not at home. Dam'me, I'll be pack-horse to none of them." My dear madam, I have just snatched a moment—"And if the expresses to his grace be ready, let them be sent off; they're of importance."—Madam, I ask a thousand pardons.

Mrs. Cro. Sir, this honour—

Lof. "And, Dubardieu! if the person calls about the commission, let him know that it is made out. As for Lord Cumbercourt's stale request, it can keep cold: you understand me."—Madam, I ask ten thousand pardons.

Mrs. Cro. Sir, this honour—

Lof. "And, Dubardieu! if the man comes from the Cornish borough, you must do him; you must do him, I say."—Madam, I ask ten thousand pardons.—"And if the Russian ambassador calls; but he will scarce call to-day, I believe."—And now, madam, I have just got time to express my happiness in having the honour of being permitted to profess myself your most obedient, humble servant.

Mrs. Cro. Sir, the happiness and honour are all mine: and yet, I'm only robbing the public while I detain you.

Lof. Sink the public, madam, when the fair are to be attended. Ah, could all my hours be so charmingly devoted! Sincerely, don't you pity us poor creatures in affairs? Thus it is eternally; solicited for places here, teased for pensions there, and courted everywhere. I know you pity me. Yes, I see you do.

Mrs. Cro. Excuse me, sir. "Toils of empires pleasures are," as Waller says.

Lof. Waller, Waller, is he of the house?

Mrs. Cro. The modern poet of that name, sir.

Lof. Oh, a modern! We men of business despise the moderns; and as for the ancients, we have no time to read them. Poetry is a pretty thing enough for our wives and daughters; but not for us. Why now, here I stand that know nothing of books. I say, madam, I know nothing of books; and yet, I believe, upon a land-carriage fishery, a stamp act, or a jag-hire, I can talk my two hours without feeling the want of them.

Mrs. Cro. The world is no stranger to Mr. Lofty's eminence in every capacity.

Lof. I vow to gad, madam, you make me blush. I'm nothing, nothing, nothing in the world; a mere obscure gentleman. To be sure, indeed, one or two of the present ministers are pleased to represent me as a formidable man. I know they are pleased to bespatter me at all their little dirty levees. Yet, upon my soul, I wonder what they see in me to treat me so! Measures, not men, have always been my mark; and I vow, by all that's honourable, my resentment has never done the men, as mere men, any manner of harm—that is, as mere men.

Mrs. Cro. What importance, and yet what modesty!

Lof. Oh, if you talk of modesty, madam, there, I own, I'm accessible to praise: modesty is my foible: it was so the Duke of Brentford used to say of me. "I love Jack Lofty," he used to say: "no man has a finer knowledge of things; quite a man of information; and when he speaks upon his legs, by the Lord he's prodigious, he scouts them; and yet all men have their faults; too much modesty is his," says his grace.

Mrs. Cro. And yet, I dare say, you don't want assurance when you come to solicit for your friends.

Lof. Oh, there indeed I'm in bronze. Apropos! I have just been mentioning Miss Richland's case to a certain personage; we must name no names. When I ask, I am not to be put off, madam. No, no, I take my friend by the button. A fine girl, sir; great justice in her case. A friend of mine—borough interest—business must be done, Mr. Secretary.—I say, Mr. Secretary, her business must be done, sir. That's my way, madam.

Mrs. Cro. Bless me! you said all this to the Secretary of State, did you?

Lof. I did not say the Secretary, did I? Well, curse it, since you have found me out, I will not deny it. It was to the Secretary.

Mrs. Cro. This was going to the fountain-head at once, not applying to the understrappers, as Mr. Honeywood would have had us.

Lof. Honeywood! he! he! He was, indeed, a fine solicitor. I suppose you have heard what has just happened to him?

Mrs. Cro. Poor dear man! no accident, I hope?

Lof. Undone, madam, that's all. His creditors have taken him into custody. A prisoner in his own house.

Mrs. Cro. A prisoner in his own house? How! At this very time? I'm quite unhappy for him.

Lof. Why, so am I. The man, to be sure, was immensely good-natured. But then I could never find that he had anything in him.

Mrs. Cro. His manner, to be sure, was excessively harmless; some, indeed, thought it a little dull. For my part, I always concealed my opinion.

Lof. It can't be concealed, madam; the man was dull, dull as the last new comedy! a poor impracticable creature! I tried once or twice to know if he was fit for business; but he had scarce talents to be groom-porter to an orange-barrow.

Mrs. Cro. How differently does Miss Richland think of him! for, I believe, with all his faults, she loves him.

Lof. Loves him! Does she? You should cure her of that by all means. Let me see; what if she were sent to him this instant, in his present doleful situation? My life for it, that works her cure. Distress is a perfect antidote to love. Suppose we join her in the next room? Miss Richland is a fine girl, has a fine fortune, and must not be thrown away. Upon my honour, madam, I have a regard for Miss Richland; and rather than she should be thrown away, I should think it no indignity to marry her myself. [*Exeunt.*

Enter OLIVIA *and* LEONTINE.

Leon. And yet, trust me, Olivia, I had every reason to expect Miss Richland's refusal, as I did everything in my power to deserve it. Her indelicacy surprises me.

Oliv. Sure, Leontine, there's nothing so indelicate in being sensible of your merit. If so, I fear I shall be the most guilty thing alive.

Leon. But you mistake, my dear. The same attention I used to advance my merit with you, I practised to lessen it with her. What more could I do?

Oliv. Let us now rather consider what is to be done. We have both dissembled too long.—I have always been ashamed—I am now quite weary of it. Sure I could never have undergone so much for any other but you.

Leon. And you shall find my gratitude equal to your kindest compliance. Though our friends should totally forsake us, Olivia, we can draw upon content for the deficiencies of fortune.

Oliv. Then why should we defer our scheme of humble happiness, when it is now in our power? I may be the favourite of your father, it is true; but can it ever be thought, that his present kindness to a supposed child will continue to a known deceiver?

Leon. I have many reasons to believe it will. As his attachments are but few, they are lasting. His own marriage was a private one, as ours may be. Besides, I have sounded him already at a distance, and find all his answers exactly to our wish. Nay, by an expression or two that dropped from him, I am induced to think he knows of this affair.

Oliv. Indeed! But that would be a happiness too great to be expected.

Leon. However it be, I'm certain you have power over him; and I am persuaded, if you informed him of our situation, that he would be disposed to pardon it.

Oliv. You had equal expectations, Leontine, from your last scheme with Miss Richland, which you find has succeeded most wretchedly.

Leon. And that's the best reason for trying another.

Oliv. If it must be so, I submit.

Leon. As we could wish, he comes this way. Now, my dearest Olivia, be resolute. I'll just retire within hearing, to come in at a proper time, either to share your danger, or confirm your victory. [*Exit.*

Enter CROAKER.

Cro. Yes, I must forgive her; and yet not too easily, neither. It will be proper to keep up the decorums of resentment a little, if it be only to impress her with an idea of my authority.

Oliv. How I tremble to approach him!—Might I presume, sir,—if I interrupt you—

Cro. No, child, where I have an affection, it is not a little thing that can interrupt me. Affection gets over little things.

Oliv. Sir, you're too kind. I'm sensible how ill I deserve this partiality. Yet, Heaven knows, there is nothing I would not do to gain it.

Cro. And you have but too well succeeded, you little hussy, you! With those endearing ways of yours, on my conscience, I could be brought to forgive anything, unless it were a very great offence indeed.

Oliv. But mine is such an offence—When you know my guilt—Yes, you shall know it, though I feel the greatest pain in the confession.

Cro. Why, then, if it be so very great a pain, you may spare yourself the trouble; for I know every syllable of the matter before you begin.

Oliv. Indeed! then I'm undone.

Cro. Ay, miss, you wanted to steal a match, without letting me know it, did you? But I'm not worth being consulted, I suppose, when there's to be a marriage in my own family. No, I'm nobody. I'm to be a mere article of family lumber; a piece of cracked china to be stuck up in a corner.

Oliv. Dear sir, nothing but the dread of your authority could induce us to conceal it from you.

Cro. No, no, my consequence is no more; I'm as little minded as a dead Russian in winter, just stuck up with a pipe in its mouth till there comes a thaw—It goes to my heart to vex her. [*Aside.*

Oliv. I was prepared, sir, for your anger, and despaired of pardon, even while I presumed to ask it. But your severity shall never abate my affection, as my punishment is but justice.

Cro. And yet you should not despair neither, Livy. We ought to hope all for the best.

Oliv. And do you permit me to hope, sir? Can I ever expect to be forgiven? But hope has too long deceived me.

Cro. Why then, child, it shan't deceive you now, for I forgive you this very moment; I forgive you all; and now you are indeed my daughter.

Oliv. O transport! this kindness overpowers me.

Cro. I was always against severity to our children. We have been young and giddy ourselves, and we can't expect boys and girls to be old before their time.

Oliv. What generosity! but can you forget the many falsehoods, the dissimulation——

Cro. You did indeed dissemble, you urchin, you; but where's the girl that won't dissemble for a husband? My wife and I had never been married, if we had not dissembled a little beforehand.

Oliv. It shall be my future care never to put such generosity to a second trial. And as for the partner of my offence and folly, from his native honour, and the just sense he has of his duty, I can answer for him that——

Enter LEONTINE.

Leon. Permit him thus to answer for himself (*kneeling*). Thus, sir, let me speak my gratitude for this unmerited forgiveness. Yes, sir, this even exceeds all your former tenderness. I now can boast the most indulgent of fathers. The life he gave, compared to this, was but a trifling blessing.

Cro. And, good sir, who sent for you, with that fine tragedy face, and flourishing manner? I don't know what we have to do with your gratitude upon this occasion.

Leon. How, sir! Is it possible to be silent, when so much obliged? Would you refuse me the pleasure of being grateful? of adding my thanks to my Olivia's? of sharing in the transports that you have thus occasioned?

Cro. Lord, sir, we can be happy enough without your coming in to make up the party. I don't know what's the matter with the boy all this day; he has got into such a rhodomontade manner all this morning!

Leon. But. sir, I that have so large a part in the benefit, is it not my duty to show my joy? is the being admitted to your favour so slight an obligation? is the happiness of marrying my Olivia so small a blessing?

Cro. Marrying Olivia! marrying Olivia! marrying his own sister! Sure the boy is out of his senses! His own sister!

Leon. My sister!

Oliv. Sister! How have I been mistaken! [*Aside.*

Leon. Some cursed mistake in all this, I find! [*Aside.*

Cro. What does the booby mean? or has he any meaning? Eh, what do you mean, you blockhead, you?

Leon. Mean, sir—why, sir—only, when my sister is to be married, that I have the pleasure of marrying her, sir; that is, of giving her away, sir—I have made a point of it.

Cro. Oh, is that all? Give her away. You have made a point of it. Then you had as good make a point of first giving away yourself, as I'm going to prepare the writings between you and Miss Richland this very minute. What a fuss is here about nothing! Why, what's the matter now? I thought I had made you at least as happy as you could wish.

Oliv. Oh yes, sir; very happy.

Cro. Do you foresee anything, child? You look as if you did. I think if anything was to be foreseen, I have as sharp a look-out as another; and yet I foresee nothing. [*Exit.*

Oliv. What can it mean?

Leon. He knows something, and yet for my life I can't tell what.

Oliv. It can't be the connexion between us, I'm pretty certain.

Leon. Whatever it be, my dearest, I am resolved to put it out of fortune's power to repeat our mortification. I'll haste and prepare for our journey to Scotland this very evening. My friend Honeywood has promised me his advice and assistance. I'll go to him, and repose our distresses on his friendly bosom; and I know so much of his honest heart, that if he can't relieve our uneasiness, he will at least share them. [*Exeunt.*

ACT THE THIRD.

Scene—Young HONEYWOOD'S *House.*

Bailiff, HONEYWOOD, Follower.

Bail. Lookye, sir, I have arrested as good men as you in my time: no disparagement of you neither: men that would go forty guineas on a game of cribbage. I challenge the town to show a man in more genteeler practice than myself.

Hon. Without all question, Mr. ——. I forget your name, sir.

Bail. How can you forget what you never knew? he! he! he!

Hon. May I beg leave to ask your name?

Bail. Yes, you may.

Hon. Then, pray, sir, what is your name?

Bail. That I didn't promise to tell you. He! he! he! A joke breaks no bones, as we say among us that practise the law.

Hon. You may have reason for keeping it a secret, perhaps?

Bail. The law does nothing without reason. I'm ashamed to tell my name to no man, sir. If you can show cause, as why, upon a special capus, that I should prove my name—But, come, Timothy Twitch is my name. And, now you know my name, what have you to say to that?

Hon. Nothing in the world, good Mr. Twitch, but that I have a favour to ask, that's all.

Bail. Ay, favours are more easily asked than granted, as we say among us that practise the law. I have taken an oath against granting favours. Would you have me perjure myself?

Hon. But my request will come recommended in so strong a manner, as, I believe, you'll have no scruple (*pulling out his purse*). The thing is only this. I believe I shall be able to discharge this trifle in two or three days at farthest; but as I would not have the affair known for the world, I have thoughts of keeping you, and your good friend here, about me till the debt is discharged; for which I shall be properly grateful.

Bail. Oh! that's another maxum, and altogether within my oath. For certain, if an honest man is to get anything by a thing, there's no reason why all things should not be done in civility.

Hon. Doubtless, all trades must live, Mr. Twitch; and yours is a necessary one. (*Gives him money.*)

Bail. Oh! your honour; I hope your honour takes nothing amiss as I does, as I does nothing but my duty in so doing. I'm sure no man can say I ever give a gentleman, that was a gentleman, ill usage. If I saw that a gentleman was a gentleman, I have taken money not to see him for ten weeks together.

Hon. Tenderness is a virtue, Mr. Twitch.

Bail. Ay, sir, it's a perfect treasure. I love to see a gentleman with a tender heart. I don't know, but I think I have a tender heart myself. If all that I have lost by my heart was put together, it would make a—but no matter for that.

Hon. Don't account it lost, Mr. Twitch. The ingratitude of the world can never deprive us of the conscious happiness of having acted with humanity ourselves.

Bail. Humanity, sir, is a jewel. It's better than gold. I love humanity. People may say, that we in our way have no humanity; but I'll show you my humanity this moment. There's my follower here, little Flanigan, with a wife and four children; a guinea or two would be more to him than twice as much to another. Now, as I can't show him any humanity myself, I must beg leave you'll do it for me.

Hon. I assure you, Mr. Twitch, yours is a most powerful recommendation. (*Giving money to the* Follower.)

Bail. Sir, you're a gentleman. I see you know what to do with your money. But to business: we are to be with you here as your friends, I suppose. But set in case company comes.—Little Flanigan here, to be sure, has a good face; a very good face; but then, he is a little seedy, as we say among us that practise the law. Not well in clothes. Smoke the pocket-holes.

Hon. Well, that shall be remedied without delay.

Enter Servant.

Ser. Sir, Miss Richland is below.

Hon. How unlucky! Detain her a moment. We must improve my good friend little Mr. Flanigan's appearance first. Here, let Mr. Flanigan have a suit of my clothes—quick—the brown and silver—Do you hear?

Ser. That your honour gave away to the begging gentleman that makes verses, because it was as good as new.

Hon. The white and gold then.

Ser. That, your honour, I made bold to sell, because it was good for nothing.

Hon. Well, the first that comes to hand then. The blue and gold then. I believe Mr. Flanigan will look best in blue.

[*Exit* Flanigan.

Bail. Rabbit me, but little Flanigan will look well in anything. Ah, if your honour knew that bit of flesh as well as I do, you'd be perfectly in love with him. There's not a prettier scout in the four counties after a shy-cock than he: scents like a hound; sticks like a weasel. He was master of the ceremonies to the black Queen of Morocco, when I took him to follow me. (*Re-enter* FLANIGAN.) Heh, ecod, I think he looks so well, that I don't care if I have a suit from the same place myself.

Hon. Well, well, I hear the lady coming. Dear Mr. Twitch, I beg you'll give your friend directions not to speak. As for yourself, I know you will say nothing without being directed.

Bail. Never you fear me; I'll show the lady that I have something to say for myself as well as another. One man has one way of talking, and another man has another, that's all the difference between them.

Enter MISS RICHLAND *and her* Maid.

Miss Rich. You'll be surprised, sir, with this visit. But you know I'm yet to thank you for choosing my little library.

Hon. Thanks, madam, are unnecessary; as it was I that was obliged by your commands. Chairs here. Two of my very good friends, Mr. Twitch and Mr. Flanigan. Pray, gentlemen, sit without ceremony.

Miss Rich. Who can these odd-looking men be! I fear it is as I was informed. It must be so. [*Aside.*

Bail. (*after a pause.*) Pretty weather; very pretty weather for the time of year, madam.

Fol. Very good circuit weather in the country.

Hon. You officers are generally favourites among the ladies. My friends, madam, have been upon very disagreeable duty, I assure you. The fair should, in some measure, recompense the toils of the brave.

Miss Rich. Our officers do indeed deserve every favour. The gentlemen are in the marine service, I presume, sir.

Hon. Why, madam, they do—occasionally serve in the fleet, madam. A dangerous service!

Miss Rich. I'm told so. And I own it has often surprised me, that while we have had so many instances of bravery there, we have had so few of wit at home to praise it.

Hon. I grant, madam, that our poets have not written as our soldiers have fought; but they have done all they could, and Hawke or Amherst could do no more.

Miss Rich. I'm quite displeased when I see a fine subject spoiled by a dull writer.

Hon. We should not be so severe against dull writers, madam. It is ten to one but the dullest writer exceeds the most rigid French critic who presumes to despise him.

Fol. Damn the French, the parle vous, and all that belongs to them.

Miss Rich. Sir!

Hon. Ha, ha, ha! honest Mr. Flanigan. A true English officer, madam; he's not contented with beating the French, but he will scold them too.

Miss Rich. Yet, Mr. Honeywood, this does not convince me but that severity in criticism is necessary. It was our first adopting the severity of French taste, that has brought them in turn to taste us.

Bail. Taste us! By the Lord, madam, they devour us. Give monseers but a taste, and I'll be damned but they come in for a bellyful.

Miss Rich. Very extraordinary this!

Fol. But very true. What makes the bread rising? the parle vous that devour us. What makes the mutton fivepence a pound? the parle vous that eat it up. What makes the beer threepence-halfpenny a pot?——

Hon. Ah! the vulgar rogues; all will be out. (*Aside.*) Right, gentlemen, very right, upon my word, and quite to the purpose. They draw a parallel, madam, between the mental taste and that of our senses. We are injured as much by the French severity in the one, as by French rapacity in the other. That's their meaning.

Miss Rich. Though I don't see the force of the parallel, yet I'll own, that we should sometimes pardon books, as we do our friends, that have now and then agreeable absurdities to recommend them.

Bail. That's all my eye. The king only can pardon, as the law says: for, set in case——

Hon. I'm quite of your opinion, sir. I see the whole drift of your argument. Yes, certainly, our presuming to pardon any work is arrogating a power that belongs to another. If all have power to condemn, what writer can be free?

Bail. By his habus corpus. His habus corpus can set him free at any time: for, set in case——

Hon. I'm obliged to you, sir, for the hint. If, madam, as my friend observes, our laws are so careful of a gentleman's person, sure we ought to be equally careful of his dearer part, his fame.

Fol. Ay, but if so be a man's nabbed, you know—

Hon. Mr. Flanigan, if you spoke for ever, you could not improve the last observation. For my own part, I think it conclusive.

Bail. As for the matter of that, mayhap—

Hon. Nay, sir, give me leave in this instance to be positive. For where is the necessity of censuring works without genius, which must shortly sink of themselves? what is it, but aiming an unnecessary blow against a victim already under the hands of justice?

Bail. Justice! Oh, by the elevens, if you talk about justice, I think I am at home there: for, in a course of law——

Hon. My dear Mr. Twitch, I discern what you'd be at, perfectly; and I believe the lady must be sensible of the art with which it is introduced. I suppose you perceive the meaning, madam, of his course of law.

Miss Rich. I protest, sir, I do not. I perceive only that you answer one gentleman before he has finished, and the other before he has well begun.

Bail. Madam, you are a gentlewoman, and I will make the matter out. This here question is about severity, and justice, and pardon, and the like of they. Now, to explain the thing——

Hon. Oh! curse your explanations. [*Aside.*

Enter Servant.

Ser. Mr. Leontine, sir, below, desires to speak with you upon earnest business.

Hon. That's lucky. (*Aside.*) Dear madam, you'll excuse me and my good friends here, for a few minutes. There are books, madam, to amuse you. Come, gentlemen, you know I make no ceremony with such friends. After you, sir. Excuse me. Well, if I must. But I know your natural politeness.

Bail. Before and behind, you know.

Fol. Ay, ay, before and behind, before and behind.

[*Exeunt* Honeywood, Bailiff, *and* Follower.

Miss Rich. What can all this mean, Garnet?

Gar. Mean, madam! why, what should it mean, but what Mr. Lofty sent you here to see? These people he calls officers are officers sure enough; sheriff's officers; bailiffs, madam.

Miss Rich. Ay, it is certainly so. Well, though his perplexities are far from giving me pleasure, yet I own there is something very ridiculous in them, and a just punishment for his dissimulation.

Gar. And so they are. But I wonder, madam, that the lawyer you just employed to pay his debts, and set him free, has not done it by this time. He ought at least to have been here before now. But lawyers are always more ready to get a man into troubles than out of them.

Enter SIR WILLIAM HONEYWOOD.

Sir Wil. For Miss Richland to undertake setting him free, I own, was quite unexpected. It has totally unhinged my schemes to reclaim him. Yet it gives me pleasure to find that, among a number of worthless friendships, he has made one acquisition of real value; for there must be some softer passion on her side that prompts this generosity. Ha! here before me: I'll endeavour to sound her affections.—Madam, as I am the person that have had some demands upon the gentleman of this house, I hope you'll excuse me, if before I enlarged him, I wanted to see yourself.

Miss Rich. The precaution was very unnecessary, sir. I suppose your wants were only such as my agent had power to satisfy.

Sir Wil. Partly, madam. But I was also willing you should be fully apprised of the character of the gentleman you intended to serve.

Miss Rich. It must come, sir, with a very ill grace from you. To censure it after what you have done, would look like malice; and to speak favourably of a character you have oppressed, would be impeaching your own. And sure, his tenderness, his humanity, his universal friendship, may atone for many faults.

Sir Wil. That friendship, madam, which is exerted in too wide a sphere, becomes totally useless. Our bounty, like a drop of water, disappears when diffused too widely. They who pretend most to this universal benevolence, are either deceivers or dupes: men who desire to cover their private ill-nature by a pretended regard for all; or men who, reasoning themselves into false feelings, are more earnest in pursuit of splendid, than of useful virtues.

Miss Rich. I am surprised, sir, to hear one, who has probably been a gainer by the folly of others, so severe in his censure of it.

Sir Wil. Whatever I may have gained by folly, madam, you see I am willing to prevent your losing by it.

Miss Rich. Your cares for me, sir, are unnecessary. I always suspect those services which are denied where they are wanted, and offered, perhaps, in hopes of a refusal. No, sir, my directions have been given, and I insist upon their being complied with.

Sir Wil. Thou amiable woman! I can no longer contain the expressions of my gratitude, my pleasure. You see before you one who has been equally careful of his interest; one, who has for some time been a concealed spectator of his follies, and only punished in hopes to reclaim him—his uncle!

Miss Rich. Sir William Honeywood! You amaze me. How shall I conceal my confusion? I fear, sir, you'll think I have been too forward in my services. I confess I——

Sir Wil. Don't make any apologies, madam. I only find myself unable to repay the obligation. And yet, I have been trying my interest of late to serve you. Having learnt, madam, that you had some demands upon Government, I have, though unasked, been your solicitor there.

Miss Rich. Sir, I'm infinitely obliged to your intentions. But my guardian has employed another gentleman, who assures him of success.

Sir Wil. Who? The important little man that visits here? Trust me, madam, he's quite contemptible among men in power, and utterly unable to serve you. Mr. Lofty's promises are much better known to people of fashion, than his person, I assure you.

Miss Rich. How have we been deceived! As sure as can be, here he comes.

Sir Wil. Does he? Remember I'm to continue unknown. My return to England has not yet been made public. With what impudence he enters!

Enter LOFTY.

Lof. Let the chariot—let my chariot drive off; I'll visit to his grace's in a chair. Miss Richland here before me! Punctual, as usual, to the calls of humanity. I'm very sorry, madam, things of this kind should happen, especially to a man I have shown everywhere, and carried amongst us as a particular acquaintance.

Miss Rich. I find, sir, you have the art of making the misfortunes of others your own.

Lof. My dear madam, what can a private man like me do? One man can't do everything; and then, I do so much in this way every day. Let me see; something considerable might be done for him by subscription; it could not fail if I carried the list. I'll undertake to set down a brace of dukes, two dozen lords, and half the lower house, at my own peril.

Sir Wil. And, after all, it's more than probable, sir, he might reject the offer of such powerful patronage.

Lof. Then, madam, what can we do? You know I never make promises. In truth, I once or twice tried to do something with him in the way of business; but, as I often told his uncle, Sir William Honeywood, the man was utterly impracticable.

Sir Wil. His uncle! then that gentleman, I suppose, is a particular friend of yours.

Lof. Meaning me, sir?—Yes, madam, as I often said, my dear Sir William, you are sensible I would do anything, as far as my poor interest goes, to serve your family: but what can be done? there's no procuring first-rate places for ninth-rate abilities.

Miss Rich. I have heard of Sir William Honeywood; he's abroad in employment: he confided in your judgment, I suppose.

Lof. Why, yes, madam, I believe Sir William had some reason to confide in my judgment; one little reason, perhaps.

Miss Rich. Pray, sir, what was it?

Lof. Why, madam—but let it go no further—it was I procured him his place.

Sir Wil. Did you, sir?

Lof. Either you or I, sir.

Miss Rich. This, Mr. Lofty, was very kind indeed.

Lof. I did love him, to be sure; he had some amusing qualities; no man was fitter to be a toast-master to a club, or had a better head.

Miss Rich. A better head?

Lof. Ay, at a bottle. To be sure, he was as dull as a choice spirit; but, hang it, he was grateful, very grateful; and gratitude hides a multitude of faults.

Sir Wil. He might have reason, perhaps. His place is pretty considerable, I'm told.

Lof. A trifle, a mere trifle among us men of business. The truth is, he wanted dignity to fill up a greater.

Sir Wil. Dignity of person, do you mean, sir? I'm told he's much about my size and figure, sir.

Lof. Ay, tall enough for a marching regiment; but then he wanted a something—a consequence of form—a kind of a—I believe the lady perceives my meaning.

Miss Rich. Oh, perfectly; you courtiers can do anything, I see.

Lof. My dear madam, all this is but a mere exchange; we do greater things for one another every day. Why, as thus, now: let me suppose you the First Lord of the Treasury; you have an employment in you that I want; I have a place in me that you want: do me here, do you there: interest of both sides, few words, flat, done and done, and it's over.

Sir Wil. A thought strikes me. (*Aside.*) Now you mention Sir William Honeywood, madam; and as he seems, sir, an acquaintance of yours, you'll be glad to hear he's arrived from Italy. I had it from a friend who knows him as well as he does me, and you may depend on my information.

Lof. The devil he is! If I had known that, we should not have been quite so well acquainted. [*Aside.*

Sir Wil. He is certainly returned; and, as this gentleman is a friend of yours, he can be of signal service to us, by introducing me to him: there are some papers relative to your affairs, that require dispatch and his inspection.

Miss Rich. This gentleman, Mr. Lofty, is a person employed in my affairs: I know you'll serve us.

Lof. My dear madam, I live but to serve you. Sir William shall even wait upon him, if you think proper to command it.

Sir Wil. That will be quite unnecessary.

Lof. Well, we must introduce you, then. Call upon me—let me see—ay, in two days.

Sir Wil. Now, or the opportunity will be lost for ever.

Lof. Well, if it must be now, now let it be. But damn it, that's unfortunate; my Lord Grig's cursed Pensacola business comes on this very hour, and I'm engaged to attend—another time——

Sir Wil. A short letter to Sir William will do.

Lof. You shall have it; yet, in my opinion, a letter is a very bad way of going to work; face to face, that's my way.

Sir Wil. The letter, sir, will do quite as well.

Lof. Zounds! Sir, do you pretend to direct me in the business of office? Do you know me, sir? Who am I?

Miss Rich. Dear Mr. Lofty, this request is not so much his as mine; if my commands—but you despise my power.

Lof. Delicate creature! your commands could even control a debate at midnight: to a power so constitutional, I am all obedience and tranquillity. He shall have a letter: where is my secretary? Dubardieu! And yet, I protest I don't like this way of doing business. I think if I spoke first to Sir William—but you will have it so. [*Exit with* Miss Richland.

Sir Wil. (*Alone.*) Ha! ha! ha!—This, too, is one of my nephew's hopeful associates. O vanity, thou constant deceiver, how do all thy efforts to exalt, serve but to sink us! Thy false colourings, like those employed to heighten beauty, only seem to mend that bloom which they contribute to destroy. I'm not displeased at this interview: exposing this fellow's impudence to the contempt it deserves, may be of use to my design; at least, if he can reflect, it well be of use to himself.

Enter JARVIS.

Sir Wil. How now, Jarvis, where's your master, my nephew?

Jar. At his wit's ends, I believe: he's scarce gotten out of one scrape, but he's running his head into another.

Sir Wil. How so?

Jar. The house has but just been cleared of the bailiffs, and now he's again engaging, tooth and nail, in assisting old Croaker's son to patch up a clandestine match with the young lady that passes in the house for his sister.

Sir Wil. Ever busy to serve others.

Jar. Ay, anybody but himself. The young couple, it seems, are just setting out for Scotland; and he supplies them with money for the journey.

Sir Wil. Money! how is he able to supply others, who has scarce any for himself?

Jar. Why, there it is: he has no money, that's true; but then, as he never said *No* to any request in his life, he has given them a bill, drawn by a friend of his upon a merchant in the city, which I am to get changed; for you must know that I am to go with them to Scotland myself.

Sir Wil. How?

Jar. It seems the young gentleman is obliged to take a different road from his mistress, as he is to call upon an uncle of his that lives out of the way, in order to prepare a place for their reception, when they return; so they have borrowed me from my master, as the properest person to attend the young lady down.

Sir Wil. To the land of matrimony! A pleasant journey, Jarvis.

Jar. Ay, but I'm only to have all the fatigues on't.

Sir Wil. Well, it may be shorter, and less fatiguing, than you imagine. I know but too much of the young lady's family and connexions, whom I have seen abroad. I have also discovered that Miss Richland is not indifferent to my thoughtless nephew; and will endeavour, though I fear in vain, to establish that connexion. But, come, the letter I wait for must be almost finished; I'll let you further into my intentions, in the next room. [*Exeunt.*

ACT THE FOURTH.

Scene—CROAKER'S *House.*

Lof. Well, sure the devil's in me of late, for running my head into such defiles, as nothing but a genius like my own could draw me from. I was formerly contented to husband out my places and pensions with some degree of frugality; but, curse it, of late I have given away the whole Court Register in less time than they could print the title-page: yet, hang it, why scruple a lie or two to come at a fine girl, when I every day tell a thousand for nothing. Ha! Honeywood here before me! Could Miss Richland have set him at liberty?

Enter HONEYWOOD.

Mr. Honeywood, I'm glad to see you abroad again. I find my concurrence was not necessary in your unfortunate affairs. I had put things in a train to do your business; but it is not for me to say what I intended doing.

Hon. It was unfortunate indeed, sir. But what adds to my uneasiness is, that while you seem to be acquainted with my misfortune, I myself continue still a stranger to my benefactor.

Lof. How! not know the friend that served you?

Hon. Can't guess at the person.

Lof. Inquire.

Hon. I have; but all I can learn is, that he chooses to remain concealed, and that all inquiry must be fruitless.

Lof. Must be fruitless!

Hon. Absolutely fruitless.

Lof. Sure of that?

Hon. Very sure.

Lof. Then I'll be damned if you shall ever know it from me.

Hon. How, sir!

Lof. I suppose now, Mr. Honeywood, you think my rent-roll very considerable, and that I have vast sums of money to throw away; I know you do. The world, to be sure, says such things of me.

Hon. The world, by what I learn, is no stranger to your generosity. But where does this tend?

Lof. To nothing; nothing in the world. The town, to be sure, when it makes such a thing as me the subject of conversation, has asserted, that I never yet patronised a man of merit.

Hon. I have heard instances to the contrary, even from yourself.

Lof. Yes, Honeywood; and there are instances to the contrary, that you shall never hear from myself.

Hon. Ha! dear sir, permit me to ask you but one question.

Lof. Sir, ask me no questions; I say, sir, ask me no questions; I'll be damned if I answer them.

Hon. I will ask no further. My friend! my benefactor! it is, it must be here, that I am indebted for freedom, for honour. Yes, thou worthiest of men, from the beginning I suspected it, but was afraid to return thanks; which, if undeserved, might seem reproaches.

Lof. I protest I do not understand all this, Mr. Honeywood: you treat me very cavalierly. I do assure you, sir—Blood! sir, can't a man be permitted to enjoy the luxury of his own feelings, without all this parade?

Hon. Nay, do not attempt to conceal an action that adds to your honour. Your looks, your air, your manner, all confess it.

Lof. Confess it, sir! Torture itself, sir, shall never bring me to confess it. Mr. Honeywood, I have admitted you upon terms of friendship. Don't let us fall out; make me happy, and let this be buried in oblivion. You know I hate ostentation; you know I do. Come, come, Honeywood, you know I always loved to be a friend, and not a patron. I beg this may make no kind of distance between us. Come, come, you and I must be more familiar—indeed we must.

Hon. Heavens! Can I ever repay such friendship? Is there any way?—Thou best of men, can I ever return the obligation?

Lof. A bagatelle, a mere bagatelle! But I see your heart is labouring to be grateful. You shall be grateful. It would be cruel to disappoint you.

Hon. How! teach me the manner. Is there any way?

Lof. From this moment you're mine. Yes, my friend, you shall know it—I'm in love.

Hon. And can I assist you?

Lof. Nobody so well.

Hon. In what manner? I'm all impatience.

Lof. You shall make love for me.

Hon. And to whom shall I speak in your favour?

Lof. To a lady with whom you have great interest, I assure you: Miss Richland.

Hon. Miss Richland!

Lof. Yes, Miss Richland. She has struck the blow up to the hilt in my bosom, by Jupiter!

Hon. Heavens! was ever anything more unfortunate! It is too much to be endured.

Lof. Unfortunate, indeed! And yet I can endure it, till you have opened the affair to her for me. Between ourselves, I think she likes me. I'm not apt to boast, but I think she does.

Hon. Indeed! But, do you know the person you apply to?

Lof. Yes, I know you are her friend and mine: that's enough. To you, therefore, I commit the success of my passion. I'll say no more; let friendship do the rest. I have only to add, that if at any time my little interest can be of service—but, hang it, I'll make no promises—you know my interest is yours at any time. No apologies, my friend, I'll not be answered; it shall be so. [*Exit.*

Hon. Open, generous, unsuspecting man! He little thinks that I love her too; and with such an ardent passion!—But then it was ever but a vain and hopeless one; my torment, my persecution! What shall I do? Love, friendship; a hopeless passion, a deserving friend! Love, that has been my tormentor; a friend, that has, perhaps, distressed himself to serve me. It shall be so. Yes, I will discard the fondling hope from my bosom, and exert all my influence in his favour. And yet to see her in the possession of another!—Insupportable! But then to betray a generous, trusting friend!—Worse, worse! Yes, I'm resolved. Let me but be the instrument of their happiness, and then quit a country, where I must for ever despair of finding my own. [*Exit.*

Enter OLIVIA *and* GARNET, *who carries a Milliner's Box.*

Oliv. Dear me, I wish this journey were over. No news of Jarvis yet? I believe the old peevish creature delays purely to vex me.

Gar. Why, to be sure, madam, I did hear him say, a little snubbing before marriage would teach you to bear it the better afterwards.

Oliv. To be gone a full hour, though he had only to get a bill changed in the city! How provoking!

Gar. I'll lay my life, Mr. Leontine, that had twice as much to do, is setting off by this time from his inn; and here you are left behind.

Oliv. Well, let us be prepared for his coming, however. Are you sure you have omitted nothing, Garnet?

Gar. Not a stick, madam—all's here. Yet I wish you could take the white and silver to be married in. It's the worst luck in the world, in anything but white. I knew one Bett Stubbs, of our town, that was married in red; and, as sure as eggs is eggs, the bridegroom and she had a miff before morning.

Oliv. No matter. I'm all impatience till we are out of the house.

Gar. Bless me, madam, I had almost forgot the wedding ring!—The sweet little thing—I don't think it would go on my little finger. And what if I put in a gentleman's night-cap, in case of necessity, madam? But here's Jarvis.

Enter JARVIS.

Oliv. O Jarvis, are you come at last? We have been ready this half-hour. Now let's be going. Let us fly!

Jar. Ay, to Jericho; for we shall have no going to Scotland this bout, I fancy.

Oliv. How! what's the matter?

Jar. Money, money, is the matter, madam. We have got no money. What the plague do you send me of your fool's errand for? My master's bill upon the city is not worth a rush. Here it is; Mrs. Garnet may pin up her hair with it.

Oliv. Undone! How could Honeywood serve us so! What shall we do? Can't we go without it?

Jar. Go to Scotland without money! To Scotland without money! Lord, how some people understand geography! We might as well set sail for Patagonia upon a cork jacket.

Oliv. Such a disappointment! What a base, insincere man was your master, to serve us in this manner! Is this his good-nature?

Jar. Nay, don't talk ill of my master, madam. I won't bear to hear anybody talk ill of him but myself.

Gar. Bless us! now I think on't, madam, you need not be under any uneasiness: I saw Mr. Leontine receive forty guineas from his father just before he set out, and he can't yet have left the inn. A short letter will reach him there.

Oliv. Well remembered, Garnet; I'll write immediately. How's this! Bless me, my hand trembles so, I can't write a word. Do you write, Garnet; and, upon second thought, it will be better from you.

Gar. Truly, madam, I write and indite but poorly. I never was 'cute at my learning. But I'll do what I can to please you. Let me see. All out of my own head, I suppose!

Oliv. Whatever you please.

Gar. (*Writing.*) Muster Croaker—Twenty guineas, madam?

Oliv. Ay, twenty will do.

Gar. At the bar of the Talbot till called for. Expedition—Will be blown up—All of a flame—Quick dispatch—Cupid, the little god of love.—I conclude it, madam, with Cupid: I love to see a love-letter end like poetry.

Oliv. Well, well, what you please, anything. But how shall we send it? I can trust none of the servants of this family.

Gar. Odso, madam, Mr. Honeywood's butler is in the next room: he's a dear, sweet man; he'll do anything for me.

Jar. He! the dog, he'll certainly commit some blunder. He's drunk and sober ten times a day.

Oliv. No matter. Fly, Garnet; anybody we can trust will do. (*Exit* GARNET.) Well, Jarvis, now we can have nothing more to interrupt us; you may take up the things, and carry them on to the inn. Have you no hands, Jarvis?

Jar. Soft and fair, young lady. You, that are going to be married, think things can never be done too fast; but we, that are old, and know what we are about, must elope methodically, madam.

Oliv. Well, sure, if my indiscretions were to be done over again——

Jar. My life for it, you would do them ten times over.

Oliv. Why will you talk so? If you knew how unhappy they make me——

Jar. Very unhappy, no doubt: I was once just as unhappy when I was going to be married myself. I'll tell you a story about that——

Oliv. A story! when I'm all impatience to be away. Was there ever such a dilatory creature!——

Jar. Well, madam, if we must march, why, we will march, that's all. Though, odds bobs, we have still forgot one thing; we should never travel without—a case of good razors, and a box of shaving-powder. But no matter, I believe we shall be pretty well shaved by the way. [*Going.*

Enter GARNET.

Gar. Undone, undone, madam. Ah, Mr. Jarvis, you said right enough. As sure as death, Mr. Honeywood's rogue of a drunken butler dropped the letter before he went ten yards from the door. There's old Croaker has just picked it up, and is this moment reading it to himself in the hall.

Oliv. Unfortunate! We shall be discovered.

Gar. No, madam; don't be uneasy; he can make neither head nor tail of it. To be sure he looks as if he was broke loose from Bedlam about it, but he can't find what it means for all that. O lud, he is coming this way all in the horrors.

Oliv. Then let us leave the house this instant, for fear he should ask further questions. In the meantime, Garnet, do you write and send off just such another.

[*Exeunt.*

Enter CROAKER.

Cro. Death and destruction! Are all the horrors of air, fire, and water, to be levelled only at me? Am I only to be singled out for gunpowder-plots, combustibles, and conflagration? Here it is—an incendiary letter dropped at my door. "To Muster Croaker, these with speed." Ay, ay, plain enough the direction: all in the genuine incendiary spelling, and as cramp as the devil. "With speed." O, confound your speed. But let me read it once more. (*Reads.*) "Muster Croaker, as sone as yow see this, leve twenty gunnes at the bar of the Talboot tell caled for, or yowe and yower experetion will be al blown up." Ah, but too plain. Blood and gunpowder in every line of it. Blown up! murderous dog! all blown up! Heavens! what have I and my poor family done, to be all blown up? (*Reads.*) "Our pockets are low, and money we must have." Ay, there's the reason; they'll blow us up, because they have got low pockets. (*Reads.*) "It is but a short time you have to consider; for if this takes wind, the house will quickly be all of a flame." Inhuman monsters! blow us up, and then burn us! The earthquake at Lisbon was but a bonfire to it. (*Reads.*) "Make quick dispatch, and so no more at present. But may Cupid, the little god of love, go with you wherever you go." The little god of love! Cupid, the little god of love, go with me! Go you to the devil, you and your little Cupid together. I'm so frightened, I scarce know whether I sit, stand, or go. Perhaps this moment I'm treading on lighted matches, blazing brimstone, and barrels of gunpowder. They are preparing to blow me up into the clouds. Murder! we shall be all burnt in our beds; we shall be all burnt in our beds!

Enter Miss Richland.

Miss Rich. Lord, sir, what's the matter?

Cro. Murder's the matter! We shall all be blown up in our beds before morning.

Miss Rich. I hope not, sir.

Cro. What signifies what you hope, madam, when I have a certificate of it here in my hand? Will nothing alarm my family? Sleeping and eating, sleeping and eating, is the only work from morning till night in my house. My insensible crew could sleep, though rocked by an earthquake, and fry beef-steaks at a volcano.

Miss Rich. But, sir, you have alarmed them so often already; we have nothing but earthquakes, famines, plagues, and mad dogs, from year's end to year's end. You remember, sir, it is not above a month ago, you assured us of a conspiracy among the bakers, to poison us in our bread; and so kept the whole family a week upon potatoes.

Cro. And potatoes were too good for them. But why do I stand talking here with a girl, when I should be facing the enemy without? Here, John, Nicodemus, search the house. Look into the cellars, to see if there be any combustibles below; and above, in the apartments, that no matches be thrown in at the windows. Let all the fires be put out, and let the engine be drawn out in the yard, to play upon the house in case of necessity. [*Exit.*

Miss Rich. (*Alone.*) What can he mean by all this? Yet, why should I inquire, when he alarms us in this manner almost every day? But Honeywood has desired an interview with me in private. What can he mean? or, rather, what means this palpitation at his approach? It is the first time he ever showed anything in his conduct that seemed particular. Sure he cannot mean to—but he's here.

Enter Honeywood.

Hon. I presumed to solicit this interview, madam, before I left town, to be permitted——

Miss Rich. Indeed! Leaving town, sir?

Hon. Yes, madam; perhaps the kingdom. I have presumed, I say, to desire the favour of this interview,—in order to disclose something which our long friendship prompts. And yet my fears——

Miss Rich. His fears! What are his fears to mine! (*Aside.*) We have indeed been long acquainted, sir; very long. If I remember, our first meeting was at the French ambassador's.—Do you recollect how you were pleased to rally me upon my complexion there?

Hon. Perfectly, madam: I presumed to reprove you for painting; but your warmer blushes soon convinced the company that the colouring was all from nature.

Miss Rich. And yet you only meant it in your good-natured way, to make me pay a compliment to myself. In the same manner you danced that night with the most awkward woman in company, because you saw nobody else would take her out.

Hon. Yes; and was rewarded the next night, by dancing with the finest woman in company, whom everybody wished to take out.

Miss Rich. Well, sir, if you thought so then, I fear your judgment has since corrected the errors of a first impression. We generally show to most advantage at first. Our sex are like poor tradesmen, that put all their best goods to be seen at the windows.

Hon. The first impression, madam, did indeed deceive me. I expected to find a woman with all the faults of conscious flattered beauty; I expected to find her vain and insolent. But every day has since taught me that it is possible to possess sense without pride, and beauty without affectation.

Miss Rich. This, sir, is a style very unusual with Mr. Honeywood; and I should be glad to know why he thus attempts to increase that vanity, which his own lessons have taught me to despise.

Hon. I ask pardon, madam. Yet, from our long friendship, I presumed I might have some right to offer, without offence, what you may refuse without offending.

Miss Rich. Sir! I beg you'd reflect: though, I fear, I shall scarce have any power to refuse a request of yours, yet you may be precipitate: consider, sir.

Hon. I own my rashness; but as I plead the cause of friendship, of one who loves —don't be alarmed, madam—who loves you with the most ardent passion, whose whole happiness is placed in you——

Miss Rich. I fear, sir, I shall never find whom you mean, by this description of him.

Hon. Ah, madam, it but too plainly points him out; though he should be too humble himself to urge his pretensions, or you too modest to understand them.

Miss Rich. Well; it would be affectation any longer to pretend ignorance; and I will own, sir, I have long been prejudiced in his favour. It was but natural to wish to make his heart mine, as he seemed himself ignorant of its value.

Hon. I see she always loved him. (*Aside.*) I find, madam, you're already sensible of his worth, his passion. How happy is my friend, to be the favourite of one with such sense to distinguish merit, and such beauty to reward it!

Miss Rich. Your friend, sir! What friend?

Hon. My best friend—my friend Mr. Lofty, madam.

Miss Rich. He, sir!

Hon. Yes, he, madam. He is, indeed, what your warmest wishes might have formed him; and to his other qualities he adds that of the most passionate regard for you.

Miss Rich. Amazement!—No more of this, I beg you, sir.

Hon. I see your confusion, madam, and know how to interpret it. And, since I so plainly read the language of your heart, shall I make my friend happy, by communicating your sentiments?

Miss Rich. By no means.

Hon. Excuse me, I must; I know you desire it.

Miss Rich. Mr. Honeywood, let me tell you, that you wrong my sentiments, and yourself. When I first applied to your friendship, I expected advice and assistance; but now, sir, I see that it is in vain to expect happiness from him, who has been so bad an economist of his own; and that I must disclaim his friendship who ceases to be a friend to himself. [*Exit.*

Hon. How is this! she has confessed she loved him, and yet she seemed to part in displeasure. Can I have done anything to reproach myself with? No; I believe not: yet, after all, these things should not be done by a third person: I should have spared her confusion. My friendship carried me a little too far.

Enter CROAKER, *with the Letter in his hand, and* MRS. CROAKER.

Mrs. Cro. Ha! ha! ha! And so, my dear, it's your supreme wish that I should be quite wretched upon this occasion? Ha! ha!

Cro. (*Mimicking.*) Ha! ha! ha! And so, my dear, it's your supreme pleasure to give me no better consolation?

Mrs. Cro. Positively, my dear; what is this incendiary stuff and trumpery to me? Our house may travel through the air like the house of Loretto, for aught I care, if I am to be miserable in it.

Cro. Would to Heaven it were converted into a house of correction for your benefit! Have we not everything to alarm us? Perhaps this very moment the tragedy is beginning.

Mrs. Cro. Then let us reserve our distress till the rising of the curtain, or give them the money they want, and have done with them.

Cro. Give them my money!—And pray, what right have they to my money?

Mrs. Cro. And pray, what right then have you to my good humour?

Cro. And so your good humour advises me to part with my money? Why then, to tell your good humour a piece of my mind, I'd sooner part with my wife. Here's Mr. Honeywood; see what he'll say to it. My dear Honeywood, look at this incendiary letter, dropped at my door. It will freeze you with terror; and yet lovey here can read it—can read it, and laugh!

Mrs. Cro. Yes, and so will Mr. Honeywood.

Cro. If he does, I'll suffer to be hanged the next minute in the rogue's place, that's all.

Mrs. Cro. Speak, Mr. Honeywood; is there anything more foolish than my husband's fright upon this occasion?

Hon. It would not become me to decide, madam; but, doubtless, the greatness of his terrors now will but invite them to renew their villany another time.

Mrs. Cro. I told you he'd be of my opinion.

Cro. How, sir! do you maintain that I should lie down under such an injury, and show neither by my tears, nor complaints, that I have something of the spirit of a man in me?

Hon. Pardon me, sir. You ought to make the loudest complaints, if you desire redress. The surest way to have redress is to be earnest in the pursuit of it.

Cro. Ay, whose opinion is he of now?

Mrs. Cro. But don't you think that laughing off our fears is the best way?

Hon. What is the best, madam, few can say; but I'll maintain it to be a very wise way.

Cro. But we're talking of the best. Surely the best way is to face the enemy in the field, and not wait till he plunders us in our very bed-chamber.

Hon. Why, sir, as to the best, that—that's a very wise way too.

Mrs. Cro. But can anything be more absurd than to double our distresses by our apprehensions, and put it in the power of every low fellow, that can scrawl ten words of wretched spelling, to torment us?

Hon. Without doubt, nothing more absurd.

Cro. How! would it not be more absurd to despise the rattle till we are bit by the snake?

Hon. Without doubt, perfectly absurd.

Cro. Then you are of my opinion?

Hon. Entirely.

Mrs. Cro. And you reject mine?

Hon. Heavens forbid, madam! No, sure, no reasoning can be more just than yours. We ought certainly to despise malice if we cannot oppose it, and not make the incendiary's pen as fatal to our repose as the highwayman's pistol.

Mrs. Cro. Oh! then you think I'm quite right?

Hon. Perfectly right.

Cro. A plague of plagues, we can't be both right! I ought to be sorry, or I ought to be glad. My hat must be on my head, or my hat must be off.

Mrs. Cro. Certainly, in two opposite opinions, if one be perfectly reasonable, the other can't be perfectly right.

Hon. And why may not both be right, madam? Mr. Croaker in earnestly seeking redress, and you in waiting the event with good humour? Pray, let me see the letter again. I have it. This letter requires twenty guineas to be left at the bar of the Talbot inn. If it be indeed an incendiary letter, what if you and I, sir, go there; and, when the writer comes to be paid for his expected booty, seize him?

Cro. My dear friend, it's the very thing; the very thing. While I walk by the door, you shall plant yourself in ambush near the bar; burst out upon the miscreant like a masked battery; extort a confession at once, and so hang him up by surprise.

Hon. Yes, but I would not choose to exercise too much severity. It is my maxim, sir, that crimes generally punish themselves.

Cro. Well, but we may upbraid him a little, I suppose? [*Ironically.*

Hon. Ay, but not punish him too rigidly.

Cro. Well, well, leave that to my own benevolence.

Hon. Well, I do; but remember that universal benevolence is the first law of nature.

[*Exeunt* Honeywood *and* Mrs. Croaker.

Cro. Yes; and my universal benevolence will hang the dog, if he had as many necks as a hydra.

ACT THE FIFTH.

Scene—an Inn.

Enter OLIVIA *and* JARVIS.

Oliv. Well, we have got safe to the inn, however. Now, if the post-chaise were ready——

Jar. The horses are just finishing their oats; and, as they are not going to be married, they choose to take their own time.

Oliv. You are for ever giving wrong motives to my impatience.

Jar. Be as impatient as you will, the horses must take their own time; besides, you don't consider, we have got no answer from our fellow-traveller yet. If we hear nothing from Mr. Leontine, we have only one way left us.

Oliv. What way?

Jar. The way home again.

Oliv. Not so. I have made a resolution to go, and nothing shall induce me to break it.

Jar. Ay; resolutions are well kept, when they jump with inclination. However, I'll go hasten things without. And I'll call, too, at the bar, to see if anything should be left for us there. Don't be in such a plaguy hurry, madam, and we shall go the faster, I promise you. [*Exit.*

Enter Landlady.

Land. What! Solomon, why don't you move? Pipes and tobacco for the Lamb there.—Will nobody answer? To the Dolphin: quick. The Angel has been outrageous this half-hour. Did your ladyship call, madam?

Oliv. No, madam.

Land. I find, as you're for Scotland, madam—But that's no business of mine; married, or not married, I ask no questions. To be sure we had a sweet little couple set off from this two days ago for the same place. The gentleman, for a tailor, was, to be sure, as fine a spoken tailor as ever blew froth from a full pot. And the young lady so bashful, it was near half an hour before we could get her to finish a pint of raspberry between us.

Oliv. But this gentleman and I are not going to be married, I assure you.

Land. May be not. That's no business of mine; for certain, Scotch marriages seldom turn out.—There was, of my own knowledge, Miss Macfag, that married her father's footman—Alack-a-day, she and her husband soon parted, and now keep separate cellars in Hedge-lane.

Oliv. A very pretty picture of what lies before me. [*Aside.*

Enter LEONTINE.

Leon. My dear Olivia, my anxiety, till you were out of danger, was too great to be resisted. I could not help coming to see you set out, though it exposes us to a discovery.

Oliv. May everything you do prove as fortunate. Indeed, Leontine, we have been most cruelly disappointed. Mr. Honeywood's bill upon the city has, it seems, been protested, and we have been utterly at a loss how to proceed.

Leon. How! an offer of his own too. Sure, he could not mean to deceive us?

Oliv. Depend upon his sincerity; he only mistook the desire for the power of serving us. But let us think no more of it. I believe the post-chaise is ready by this.

Land. Not quite yet: and, begging your ladyship's pardon, I don't think your ladyship quite ready for the post-chaise. The north road is a cold place, madam. I have a drop in the house of as pretty raspberry as ever was tipt over tongue. Just a thimble-full to keep the wind off your stomach. To be sure, the last couples we had here, they said it was a perfect nosegay. Ecod, I sent them both away as good-natured—Up went the blinds, round went the wheels, and drive away post-boy, was the word.

Enter CROAKER.

Cro. Well, while my friend Honeywood is upon the post of danger at the bar, it must be my business to have an eye about me here. I think I know an incendiary's look; for wherever the devil makes a purchase, he never fails to set his mark. Ha! who have we here? My son and daughter! What can they be doing here?

Land. I tell you, madam, it will do you good; I think I know by this time what's good for the north road. It's a raw night, madam.—Sir——

Leon. Not a drop more, good madam. I should now take it as a greater favour, if you hasten the horses, for I am afraid to be seen myself.

Land. That shall be done. Wha, Solomon! are you all dead there? Wha, Solomon, I say! [*Exit, bawling.*

Oliv. Well, I dread lest an expedition

begun in fear, should end in repentance.—Every moment we stay increases our danger, and adds to my apprehensions.

Leon. There's no danger, trust me, my dear; there can be none. If Honeywood has acted with honour, and kept my father, as he promised, in employment till we are out of danger, nothing can interrupt our journey.

Oliv. I have no doubt of Mr. Honeywood's sincerity, and even his desire to serve us. My fears are from your father's suspicions. A mind so disposed to be alarmed without a cause, will be but too ready when there's a reason.

Leon. Why, let him, when we are out of his power. But believe me, Olivia, you have no great reason to dread his resentment. His repining temper, as it does no manner of injury to himself, so will it never do harm to others. He only frets to keep himself employed, and scolds for his private amusement.

Oliv. I don't know that; but, I'm sure, on some occasions, it makes him look most shockingly.

Cro. (*Discovering himself.*) How does he look now?—How does he look now?

Oliv. Ah!

Leon. Undone!

Cro. How do I look now? Sir, I am your very humble servant. Madam, I am yours. What, you are going off, are you? Then, first, if you please, take a word or two from me with you before you go. Tell me first where you are going; and when you have told me that, perhaps I shall know as little as I did before.

Leon. If that be so, our answer might but increase your displeasure, without adding to your information.

Cro. I want no information from you, puppy: and you too, good madam, what answer have you got? Eh! (*A cry without, Stop him!*) I think I heard a noise. My friend Honeywood without—has he seized the incendiary? Ah, no; for now I hear no more on't.

Leon. Honeywood without! Then, sir, it was Mr. Honeywood that directed you hither?

Cro. No, sir, it was Mr. Honeywood conducted me hither.

Leon. Is it possible?

Cro. Possible! Why, he's in the house now, sir; more anxious about me than my own son, sir.

Leon. Then, sir, he's a villain.

Cro. How, sirrah! a villain, because he takes most care of your father? I'll not bear it. I tell you I'll not bear it. Honeywood is a friend to the family, and I'll have him treated as such.

Leon. I shall study to repay his friendship as it deserves.

Cro. Ah, rogue, if you knew how earnestly he entered into my griefs, and pointed out the means to detect them, you would love him as I do. (*A cry without, Stop him!*) Fire and fury! they have seized the incendiary: they have the villain, the incendiary in view. Stop him! stop an incendiary! a murderer! stop him! [*Exit.*

Oliv. Oh, my terrors! What can this tumult mean?

Leon. Some new mark, I suppose, of Mr. Honeywood's sincerity. But we shall have satisfaction: he shall give me instant satisfaction.

Oliv. It must not be, my Leontine, if you value my esteem or my happiness. Whatever be our fate, let us not add guilt to our misfortunes—Consider that our innocence will shortly be all that we have left us. You must forgive him.

Leon. Forgive him! Has he not in every instance betrayed us? Forced me to borrow money from him, which appears a mere trick to delay us; promised to keep my father engaged till we were out of danger, and here brought him to the very scene of our escape?

Oliv. Don't be precipitate. We may yet be mistaken.

Enter Postboy, *dragging in* JARVIS; HONEYWOOD *entering soon after.*

Post. Ay, master, we have him safe enough. Here is the incendiary dog. I'm entitled to the reward: I'll take my oath I saw him ask for the money at the bar, and then run for it.

Hon. Come, bring him along. Let us see him. Let him learn to blush for his crimes. (*Discovering his mistake.*) Death! what's here? Jarvis, Leontine, Olivia! What can all this mean?

Jar. Why, I'll tell you what it means:

that I was an old fool, and that you are my master—that's all.

Hon. Confusion!

Leon. Yes, sir, I find you have kept your word with me. After such baseness, I wonder how you can venture to see the man you have injured?

Hon. My dear Leontine, by my life, my honour—

Leon. Peace, peace, for shame; and do not continue to aggravate baseness by hypocrisy. I know you, sir, I know you.

Hon. Why, won't you hear me? By all that's just I knew not——

Leon. Hear you, sir! to what purpose? I now see through all your low arts; your ever complying with every opinion; your never refusing any request: your friendship as common as a prostitute's favours, and as fallacious; all these, sir, have long been contemptible to the world, and are now perfectly so to me.

Hon. Ha! contemptible to the world! that reaches me. [*Aside.*

Leon. All the seeming sincerity of your professions, I now find, were only allurements to betray; and all your seeming regret for their consequences, only calculated to cover the cowardice of your heart. Draw, villain!

Enter CROAKER, *out of breath.*

Cro. Where is the villain? Where is the incendiary? (*Seizing the* Postboy.) Hold him fast, the dog: he has the gallows in his face. Come, you dog, confess; confess all, and hang yourself.

Post. Zounds! master, what do you throttle me for?

Cro. (*Beating him.*) Dog, do you resist? do you resist?

Post. Zounds! master, I'm not he; there's the man that we thought was the rogue, and turns out to be one of the company.

Cro. How!

Hon. Mr. Croaker, we have all been under a strange mistake here; I find there is nobody guilty; it was all an error; entirely an error of our own.

Cro. And I say, sir, that you're in an error; for there's guilt and double guilt, a plot, a damned jesuitical, pestilential plot, and I must have proof of it.

Hon. Do but hear me.

Cro. What, you intend to bring 'em off, I suppose? I'll hear nothing.

Hon. Madam, you seem at least calm enough to hear reason.

Oliv. Excuse me.

Hon. Good Jarvis, let me then explain it to you.

Jar. What signifies explanations when the thing is done?

Hon. Will nobody hear me? Was there ever such a set so blinded by passion and prejudice? (*To the* Postboy.) My good friend, I believe you'll be surprised, when I assure you——

Post. Sure me nothing—I'm sure of nothing but a good beating.

Cro. Come then you, madam, if you ever hope for any favour or forgiveness, tell me sincerely all you know of this affair.

Oliv. Unhappily, sir, I'm but too much the cause of your suspicions; you see before you, sir, one that with false pretences has stepped into your family to betray it; not your daughter——

Cro. Not my daughter?

Oliv. Not your daughter—but a mean deceiver—who—support me, I cannot—

Hon. Help, she's going; give her air.

Cro. Ay, ay, take the young woman to the air; I would not hurt a hair of her head, whose ever daughter she may be—not so bad as that neither.

[*Exeunt all but* Croaker.

Cro. Yes, yes, all's out; I now see the whole affair: my son is either married, or going to be so, to this lady, whom he imposed upon me as his sister. Ay, certainly so; and yet I don't find it afflicts me so much as one might think. There's the advantage of fretting away our misfortunes beforehand: we never feel them when they come.

Enter MISS RICHLAND *and* SIR WILLIAM.

Sir Wil. But how do you know, madam, that my nephew intends setting off from this place?

Miss Rich. My maid assured me he was come to this inn; and my own knowledge of his intending to leave the kingdom, suggested the rest. But what do I see! my guardian here before us! Who, my dear sir, could have expected meeting you here? to what accident do we owe this pleasure?

Cro. To a fool, I believe.

Miss Rich. But to what purpose did you come?

Cro. To play the fool.

Miss Rich. But with whom?

Cro. With greater fools than myself.

Miss Rich. Explain.

Cro. Why, Mr. Honeywood brought me here, to do nothing now I am here; and my son is going to be married to I don't know who, that is here: so now you are as wise as I am.

Miss Rich. Married! to whom, sir?

Cro. To Olivia, my daughter, as I took her to be; but who the devil she is, or whose daughter she is, I know no more than the man in the moon.

Sir Wil. Then, sir, I can inform you; and, though a stranger, yet you shall find me a friend to your family. It will be enough at present to assure you, that both in point of birth and fortune, the young lady is at least your son's equal. Being left by her father, Sir James Woodville——

Cro. Sir James Woodville! What, of the west?

Sir Wil. Being left by him, I say, to the care of a mercenary wretch, whose only aim was to secure her fortune to himself, she was sent to France, under pretence of education; and there every art was tried to fix her for life in a convent, contrary to her inclinations. Of this I was informed upon my arrival at Paris; and, as I had been once her father's friend, I did all in my power to frustrate her guardian's base intentions. I had even meditated to rescue her from his authority, when your son stept in with more pleasing violence, gave her liberty, and you a daughter.

Cro. But I intend to have a daughter of my own choosing, sir. A young lady, sir, whose fortune, by my interest with those who have interest, will be double what my son has a right to expect. Do you know Mr. Lofty, sir?

Sir Wil. Yes, sir; and know that you are deceived in him. But step this way, and I'll convince you.

[Croaker *and* Sir William *seem to confer.*

Enter HONEYWOOD.

Hon. Obstinate man, still to persist in his outrage! insulted by him, despised by all, I now begin to grow contemptible, even to myself. How have I sunk by too great an assiduity to please! How have I overtaxed all my abilities, lest the approbation of a single fool should escape me! But all is now over; I have survived my reputation, my fortune, my friendships, and nothing remains henceforward for me but solitude and repentance.

Miss Rich. Is it true, Mr. Honeywood, that you are setting off, without taking leave of your friends? The report is, that you are quitting England. Can it be?

Hon. Yes, madam; and though I am so unhappy as to have fallen under your displeasure, yet, thank Heaven, I leave you to happiness; to one who loves you, and deserves your love: to one who has power to procure you affluence, and generosity to improve your enjoyment of it.

Miss Rich. And are you sure, sir, that the gentleman you mean is what you describe him?

Hon. I have the best assurances of it—his serving me. He does indeed deserve the highest happiness, and that is in your power to confer. As for me, weak and wavering as I have been, obliged by all, and incapable of serving any, what happiness can I find but in solitude? What hope, but in being forgotten?

Miss Rich. A thousand! to live among friends that esteem you, whose happiness it will be to be permitted to oblige you.

Hon. No, madam, my resolution is fixed. Inferiority among strangers is easy; but among those that once were equals, insupportable. Nay, to show you how far my resolution can go, I can now speak with calmness of my former follies, my vanity, my dissipation, my weakness. I will even confess, that, among the number of my other presumptions, I had the insolence to think of loving you. Yes, madam, while I was pleading the passion of another, my heart was tortured with its own. But it is over; it was unworthy our friendship, and let it be forgotten.

Miss Rich. You amaze me!

Hon. But you'll forgive it, I know you will; since the confession should not have come from me even now, but to convince you of the sincerity of my intention of—never mentioning it more. [*Going.*

Miss Rich. Stay, sir, one moment—Ha! he here—

Enter LOFTY.

Lof. Is the coast clear? None but friends. I have followed you here with a trifling piece of intelligence; but it goes no farther; things are not yet ripe for a discovery. I have spirits working at a certain board; your affair at the Treasury will be done in less than—a thousand years. Mum!

Miss Rich. Sooner, sir, I should hope.

Lof. Why, yes, I believe it may, if it falls into proper hands, that know where to push and where to parry; that know how the land lies—eh, Honeywood!

Miss Rich. It has fallen into yours.

Lof. Well, to keep you no longer in suspense, your thing is done. It is done, I say—that's all. I have just had assurances from Lord Neverout, that the claim has been examined, and found admissible. *Quietus* is the word, madam.

Hon. But how? his lordship has been at Newmarket these ten days.

Lof. Indeed! Then Sir Gilbert Goose must have been most damnably mistaken. I had it of him.

Miss Rich. He! why Sir Gilbert and his family have been in the country this month.

Lof. This month! it must certainly be so—Sir Gilbert's letter did come to me from Newmarket, so that he must have met his lordship there; and so it came about. I have his letter about me; I'll read it to you. (*Taking out a large bundle.*) That's from Paoli of Corsica; that from the Marquis of Squilachi.—Have you a mind to see a letter from Count Poniatowski, now King of Poland?—Honest Pon—(*Searching.*) Oh, sir, what, are you here, too? I'll tell you what, honest friend, if you have not absolutely delivered my letter to Sir William Honeywood, you may return it. The thing will do without him.

Sir Wil. Sir, I have delivered it; and must inform you, it was received with the most mortifying contempt.

Cro. Contempt! Mr. Lofty, what can that mean?

Lof. Let him go on, let him go on, I say. You'll find it came to something presently.

Sir Wil. Yes, sir; I believe you'll be amazed, if after waiting some time in the ante-chamber, after being surveyed with insolent curiosity by the passing servants, I was at last assured, that Sir William Honeywood knew no such person, and I must certainly have been imposed upon.

Lof. Good! let me die; very good. Ha! ha! ha!

Cro. Now, for my life I can't find out half the goodness of it.

Lof. You can't. Ha! ha!

Cro. No, for the soul of me! I think it was as confounded a bad answer as ever was sent from one private gentleman to another.

Lof. And so you can't find out the force of the message? Why, I was in the house at that very time. Ha! ha! It was I that sent that very answer to my own letter. Ha! ha!

Cro. Indeed! How? why?

Lof. In one word, things between Sir William and me must be behind the curtain. A party has many eyes. He sides with Lord Buzzard, I side with Sir Gilbert Goose. So that unriddles the mystery.

Cro. And so it does, indeed; and all my suspicions are over.

Lof. Your suspicions! What, then, you have been suspecting, you have been suspecting, have you? Mr. Croaker, you and I were friends; we are friends no longer. Never talk to me. It's over; I say, it's over.

Cro. As I hope for your favour I did not mean to offend. It escaped me. Don't be discomposed.

Lof. Zounds! sir, but I am discomposed, and will be discomposed. To be treated thus! Who am I? Was it for this I have been dreaded both by ins and outs? Have I been libelled in the *Gazetteer*, and praised in the *St. James's?* Have I been chaired at Wildman's, and a speaker at Merchant Tailors' Hall? Have I had my hand to addresses, and my head in the print-shops; and talk to me of suspects?

Cro. My dear sir, be pacified. What can you have but asking pardon?

Lof. Sir, I will not be pacified—Suspects! Who am I? To be used thus! Have I paid court to men in favour to serve my friends; the Lords of the Treasury, Sir William Honeywood, and the rest of the gang, and talk to me of suspects? Who am I, I say; who am I?

Sir Wil. Since, sir, you are so pressing for an answer, I'll tell you who you are. A gentleman, as well acquainted with politics as with men in power; as well acquainted with persons of fashion as with modesty; with Lords of the Treasury as with truth; and with all, as you are with Sir William Honeywood. I am Sir William Honeywood.

[*Discovering his ensigns of the Bath.*

Cro. Sir William Honeywood!

Hon. Astonishment! my uncle! [*Aside.*

Lof. So then, my confounded genius has been all this time only leading me up to the garret, in order to fling me out of the window.

Cro. What, Mr. Importance, and are these your works? Suspect you! You, who have been dreaded by the ins and outs; you, who have had your hand to addresses, and your head stuck up in print-shops. If you were served right, you should have your head stuck up in a pillory.

Lof. Ay, stick it where you will; for, by the Lord, it cuts but a very poor figure where it sticks at present.

Sir Wil. Well, Mr. Croaker, I hope you now see how incapable this gentleman is of serving you, and how little Miss Richland has to expect from his influence.

Cro. Ay, sir, too well I see it; and I can't but say I have had some boding of it these ten days. So, I'm resolved, since my son has placed his affections on a lady of moderate fortune, to be satisfied with his choice, and not run the hazard of another Mr. Lofty in helping him to a better.

Sir Wil. I approve your resolution; and here they come to receive a confirmation of your pardon and consent.

Enter MRS. CROAKER, JARVIS, LEONTINE, *and* OLIVIA.

Mrs. Cro. Where's my husband? Come, come, lovey, you must forgive them. Jarvis here has been to tell me the whole affair; and I say, you must forgive them. Our own was a stolen match, you know, my dear; and we never had any reason to repent of it.

Cro. I wish we could both say so. However, this gentleman, Sir William Honeywood, has been beforehand with you in obtaining their pardon. So, if the two poor fools have a mind to marry, I think we can tack them together without crossing the Tweed for it.

[*Joining their hands.*

Leon. How blest and unexpected! What, what can we say to such goodness? But our future obedience shall be the best reply. And as for this gentleman, to whom we owe—

Sir Wil. Excuse me, sir, if I interrupt your thanks, as I have here an interest that calls me. (*Turning to* HONEYWOOD.) Yes, sir, you are surprised to see me: and I own that a desire of correcting your follies led me hither. I saw with indignation the errors of a mind that only sought applause from others; that easiness of disposition, which, though inclined to the right, had not courage to condemn the wrong. I saw with regret those splendid errors, that still took name from some neighbouring duty; your charity, that was but injustice; your benevolence, that was but weakness; and your friendship, but credulity. I saw with regret great talents and extensive learning only employed to add sprightliness to error, and increase your perplexities. I saw your mind with a thousand natural charms; but the greatness of its beauty served only to heighten my pity for its prostitution.

Hon. Cease to upbraid me, sir: I have for some time but too strongly felt the justice of your reproaches. But there is one way still left me. Yes, sir, I have determined this very hour to quit for ever a place where I have made myself the voluntary slave of all, and to seek among strangers that fortitude which may give strength to the mind, and marshal all its dissipated virtues. Yet ere I depart, permit me to solicit favour for this gentleman; who, notwithstanding what has happened, has laid me under the most signal obligations. Mr. Lofty—

Lof. Mr. Honeywood, I 'm resolved upon a reformation as well as you. I now begin to find that the man who first invented the art of speaking truth, was a much cunninger fellow than I thought him. And to prove that I design to speak truth for the future, I must now assure you, that you owe your late enlargement to another; as, upon my soul, I had no hand in the matter. So now, if any of the company has a mind for preferment, he may take my place, I'm determined to resign. [*Exit.*

Hon. How have I been deceived!

Sir Wil. No, sir, you have been obliged to a kinder, fairer friend, for that favour. To Miss Richland. Would she complete our joy, and make the man she has honoured by her friendship happy in her love, I shall then forget all, and be as blest as the welfare of my dearest kinsman can make me.

Miss Rich. After what is past it would be but affectation to pretend to indifference. Yes, I will own an attachment, which I find was more than friendship. And if my entreaties cannot alter his resolution to quit the country, I will even try if my hand has not power to detain him. [*Giving her hand.*

Hon. Heavens! how can I have deserved all this? How express my happiness, my gratitude? A moment like this overpays an age of apprehension.

Cro. Well, now I see content in every face; but Heaven send we be all better this day three months!

Sir Wil. Henceforth, nephew, learn to respect yourself. He who seeks only for applause from without, has all his happiness in another's keeping.

Hon. Yes, sir, I now too plainly perceive my errors; my vanity, in attempting to please all by fearing to offend any; my meanness, in approving folly lest fools should disapprove. Henceforth, therefore, it shall be my study to reserve my pity for real distress; my friendship for true merit; and my love for her, who first taught me what it is to be happy.

EPILOGUE.*

SPOKEN BY MRS. BULKLEY.

As puffing quacks some caitiff wretch procure
To swear the pill, or drop, has wrought a cure;
Thus, on the stage, our playwrights still depend
For Epilogues and Prologues on some friend,
Who knows each art of coaxing up the town,
And make full many a bitter pill go down.
Conscious of this, our bard has gone about,
And teased each rhyming friend to help him out.
An Epilogue, things can't go on without it;
It could not fail, would you but set about it.
Young man, cries one (a bard laid up in clover),
Alas! young man, my writing days are over;
Let boys play tricks, and kick the straw, not I;
Your brother doctor there, perhaps, may try.
What I! dear sir, the doctor interposes;
What, plant my thistle, sir, among his roses!

* The author, in expectation of an Epilogue from a friend at Oxford, deferred writing one himself till the very last hour. What is here offered, owes all its success to the graceful manner of the actress who spoke it.—GOLDSMITH.

No, no, I've other contests to maintain ;
To-night I head our troops at Warwick-lane.
Go ask your manager—Who, me ! Your pardon ;
Those things are not our forte at Covent-garden.
Our author's friends, thus placed at happy distance,
Give him good words indeed, but no assistance.
As some unhappy wight at some new play,
At the pit door stands elbowing away ;
While oft, with many a smile, and many a shrug,
He eyes the centre, where his friends sit snug ;
His simpering friends, with pleasure in their eyes,
Sink as he sinks, and as he rises rise :
He nods, they nod ; he cringes, they grimace ;
But not a soul will budge to give him place.
Since then, unhelped, our bard must now conform
"To 'bide the pelting of this pitiless storm,"
Blame where you must, be candid where you can,
And be each critic the *Good-natured Man.*

END OF THE GOOD-NATURED MAN.

SHE STOOPS TO CONQUER;

OR,

THE MISTAKES OF A NIGHT.

A COMEDY.

To SAMUEL JOHNSON, LL.D.

DEAR SIR,—By inscribing this slight performance to you, I do not mean so much to compliment you as myself. It may do me some honour to inform the public, that I have lived many years in intimacy with you. It may serve the interests of mankind also to inform them, that the greatest wit may be found in a character, without impairing the most unaffected piety.

I have, particularly, reason to thank you for your partiality to this performance. The undertaking a comedy not merely sentimental was very dangerous; and Mr. Colman, who saw this piece in its various stages, always thought it so. However, I ventured to trust it to the public; and, though it was necessarily delayed till late in the season, I have every reason to be grateful.

I am, dear Sir, your most sincere friend and admirer,

OLIVER GOLDSMITH.

PROLOGUE,

BY DAVID GARRICK, ESQ.

Enter MR. WOODWARD, *dressed in black, and holding a handkerchief to his eyes.*

Excuse me, sirs, I pray—I can't yet speak—
I'm crying now—and have been all the week.
"'Tis not alone this mourning suit," good masters:
"I've that within"—for which there are no plasters!
Pray, would you know the reason why I'm crying?
The Comic Muse, long sick, is now a-dying!
And if she goes, my tears will never stop;
For as a player, I can't squeeze out one drop:
I am undone, that's all—shall lose my bread—
I'd rather, but that's nothing—lose my head.
When the sweet maid is laid upon the bier,
Shuter and I shall be chief mourners here.
To her a mawkish drab of spurious breed,
Who deals in sentimentals, will succeed!
Poor Ned and I are dead to all intents;
We can as soon speak Greek as sentiments!
Both nervous grown, to keep our spirits up.
We now and then take down a hearty cup.

What shall we do? If Comedy forsake us,
They'll turn us out, and no one else will take us.
But why can't I be moral?—Let me try—
My heart thus pressing—fixed my face and eye—
With a sententious look, that nothing means,
(Faces are blocks in sentimental scenes)
Thus I begin: "All is not gold that glitters,
"Pleasure seems sweet, but proves a glass of bitters.
"When Ignorance enters, Folly is at hand:
"Learning is better far than house and land.
"Let not your virtue trip; who trips may stumble,
"And virtue is not virtue, if she tumble."

I give it up—morals won't do for me;
To make you laugh, I must play tragedy.
One hope remains—hearing the maid was ill,
A Doctor comes this night to show his skill.
To cheer her heart, and give your muscles motion,
He, in Five Draughts prepar'd, presents a potion:
A kind of magic charm—for be assur'd,
If you will swallow it, the maid is cur'd:
But desperate the Doctor, and her case is,
If you reject the dose, and make wry faces!
This truth he boasts, will boast it while he lives,
No poisonous drugs are mixed in what he gives.
Should he succeed, you'll give him his degree;
If not, within he will receive no fee!
The College *you*, must his pretensions back,
Pronounce him Regular, or dub him Quack.

DRAMATIS PERSONÆ.

MEN.	
Sir Charles Marlow	Mr. Gardner.
Young Marlow (*his son*)	Mr. Lee Lewes.
Hardcastle	Mr. Shuter.
Hastings	Mr. Dubellamy.
Tony Lumpkin	Mr. Quick.
Diggory	Mr. Saunders.

WOMEN.	
Mrs. Hardcastle	Mrs. Green.
Miss Hardcastle	Mrs. Bulkley.
Miss Neville	Mrs. Kniveton.
Maid	Miss Williams.

Landlord, Servants, &c. &c.

ACT THE FIRST.

Scene—*A Chamber in an old-fashioned House.*

Enter Mrs. Hardcastle *and* Mr. Hardcastle.

Mrs. Hard. I vow, Mr. Hardcastle, you're very particular. Is there a creature in the whole country but ourselves, that does not take a trip to town now and then, to rub off the rust a little? There's the two Miss Hoggs, and our neighbour Mrs. Grigsby, go to take a month's polishing every winter.

Hard. Ay, and bring back vanity and affectation to last them the whole year. I wonder why London cannot keep its own fools at home! In my time, the follies of the town crept slowly among us, but now they travel faster than a stage-coach. Its fopperies come down not only as inside passengers, but in the very basket.

Mrs. Hard. Ay, your times were fine times indeed; you have been telling us of them for many a long year. Here we live in an old rumbling mansion, that looks for all the world like an inn, but that we never see company. Our best visitors are old Mrs. Oddfish, the curate's wife, and little Cripplegate, the lame dancing-master; and all our entertainment your old stories of Prince Eugene and the Duke of Marlborough. I hate such old-fashioned trumpery.

Hard. And I love it. I love everything that's old: old friends, old times, old manners, old books, old wine; and I believe, Dorothy (*taking her hand*), you'll own I have been pretty fond of an old wife.

Mrs. Hard. Lord, Mr. Hardcastle, you're for ever at your Dorothys and your old wifes. You may be a Darby, but I'll be no Joan, I promise you. I'm not so old as you'd make me, by more than one good year. Add twenty to twenty, and make money of that.

Hard. Let me see; twenty added to twenty makes just fifty and seven.

Mrs. Hard. It's false, Mr. Hardcastle; I was but twenty when I was brought to bed of Tony, that I had by Mr. Lumpkin, my first husband; and he's not come to years of discretion yet.

Hard. Nor ever will, I dare answer for him. Ay, you have taught him finely.

Mrs. Hard. No matter. Tony Lumpkin has a good fortune. My son is not to live by his learning. I don't think a boy wants much learning to spend fifteen hundred a year.

Hard. Learning, quotha! a mere composition of tricks and mischief.

Mrs. Hard. Humour, my dear; nothing but humour. Come, Mr. Hardcastle, you must allow the boy a little humour.

Hard. I'd sooner allow him a horse-pond. If burning the footmen's shoes, frightening the maids, and worrying the kittens be humour, he has it. It was but yesterday he fastened my wig to the back of my chair, and when I went to make a bow, I popt my bald head in Mrs. Frizzle's face.

Mrs. Hard. And am I to blame? The poor boy was always too sickly to do any good. A school would be his death. When he comes to be a little stronger, who knows what a year or two's Latin may do for him?

Hard. Latin for him! A cat and fiddle. No, no; the alehouse and the stable are the only schools he'll ever go to.

Mrs. Hard. Well, we must not snub the poor boy now, for I believe we shan't have him long among us. Anybody that looks in his face may see he's consumptive.

Hard. Ay, if growing too fat be one of the symptoms.

Mrs. Hard. He coughs sometimes.

Hard. Yes, when his liquor goes the wrong way.

Mrs. Hard. I'm actually afraid of his lungs.

Hard. And truly so am I; for he sometimes whoops like a speaking trumpet—(*Tony hallooing behind the scenes*)—O, there he goes—a very consumptive figure, truly.

Enter TONY, *crossing the stage.*

Mrs. Hard. Tony, where are you going, my charmer? Won't you give papa and I a little of your company, lovee?

Tony. I'm in haste, mother; I cannot stay.

Mrs. Hard. You shan't venture out this raw evening, my dear; you look most shockingly.

Tony. I can't stay, I tell you. The Three Pigeons expects me down every moment. There's some fun going forward.

Hard. Ay; the alehouse, the old place: I thought so.

Mrs. Hard. A low, paltry set of fellows.

Tony. Not so low, neither. There's Dick Muggins the exciseman, Jack Slang the horse doctor, little Aminadab that grinds the music box, and Tom Twist that spins the pewter platter.

Mrs. Hard. Pray, my dear, disappoint them for one night at least.

Tony. As for disappointing them, I should not so much mind; but I can't abide to disappoint myself.

Mrs. Hard. (*detaining him.*) You shan't go.

Tony. I will, I tell you.

Mrs. Hard. I say you shan't.

Tony. We'll see which is strongest, you or I. [*Exit, hauling her out.*

Hard. (*solus.*) Ay, there goes a pair that only spoil each other. But is not the whole age in a combination to drive sense and discretion out of doors? There's my pretty darling Kate! the fashions of the times have almost infected her too. By living a year or two in town, she is as fond of gauze and French frippery as the best of them.

Enter Miss Hardcastle.

Hard. Blessings on my pretty innocence! drest out as usual, my Kate. Goodness! What a quantity of superfluous silk hast thou got about thee, girl! I could never teach the fools of this age, that the indigent world could be clothed out of the trimmings of the vain.

Miss Hard. You know our agreement, sir. You allow me the morning to receive and pay visits, and to dress in my own manner; and in the evening I put on my housewife's dress to please you.

Hard. Well, remember, I insist on the terms of our agreement; and, by the by, I believe I shall have occasion to try your obedience this very evening.

Miss Hard. I protest, sir, I don't comprehend your meaning.

Hard. Then to be plain with you, Kate, I expect the young gentleman I have chosen to be your husband from town this very day. I have his father's letter, in which he informs me his son is set out, and that he intends to follow himself shortly after.

Miss Hard. Indeed! I wish I had known something of this before. Bless me, how shall I behave? It's a thousand to one I shan't like him; our meeting will be so formal, and so like a thing of business, that I shall find no room for friendship or esteem.

Hard. Depend upon it, child, I'll never control your choice; but Mr. Marlow, whom I have pitched upon, is the son of my old friend, Sir Charles Marlow, of whom you have heard me talk so often. The young gentleman has been bred a scholar, and is designed for an employment in the service of his country. I am told he's a man of an excellent understanding.

Miss Hard. Is he?

Hara. Very generous.

Miss Hard. I believe I shall like him.

Hard. Young and brave.

Miss Hard. I'm sure I shall like him.

Hard. And very handsome.

Miss Hard. My dear papa, say no more, (*kissing his hana*), he's mine; I'll have him.

Hard. And, to crown all, Kate, he's one of the most bashful and reserved young fellows in all the world.

Miss Hard. Eh! you have frozen me to death again. That word *reserved* has undone all the rest of his accomplishments. A reserved lover, it is said, always makes a suspicious husband.

Hard. On the contrary, modesty seldom resides in a breast that is not enriched with nobler virtues. It was the very feature in his character that first struck me.

Miss Hard. He must have more striking features to catch me, I promise you. However, if he be so young, so handsome, and so everything as you mention, I believe he'll do still. I think I'll have him.

Hard. Ay, Kate, but there is still an obstacle. It's more than an even wager he may not have you.

Miss Hard. My dear papa, why will you mortify one so? Well, if he refuses, instead of breaking my heart at his indifference, I'll only break my glass for its flattery, set my cap to some newer fashion, and look out for some less difficult admirer.

Hard. Bravely resolved! In the mean time I'll go prepare the servants for his reception: as we seldom see company, they want as much training as a company of recruits the first day's muster. [*Exit.*

Miss Hard. (*Alone*). Lud, this news of papa's puts me all in a flutter. Young, handsome: these he put last; but I put them foremost. Sensible, good-natured; I like all that. But then reserved and sheepish; that's much against him. Yet can't he be cured of his timidity, by being taught to be proud of his wife? Yes, and can't I—But I vow I'm disposing of the husband before I have secured the lover.

Enter Miss Neville.

Miss Hard. I'm glad you're come, Neville, my dear. Tell me, Constance, how do I look this evening? Is there anything whimsical about me? Is it one of my well-looking days, child? Am I in face to-day?

Miss Nev. Perfectly, my dear. Yet now I look again—bless me!—sure no accident has happened among the canary birds or the gold fishes. Has your brother or the cat been meddling? or has the last novel been too moving?

Miss Hard. No; nothing of all this. I have been threatened—I can scarce get it out—I have been threatened with a lover.

Miss Nev. And his name—

Miss Hard. Is Marlow.

Miss Nev. Indeed!

Miss Hard. The son of Sir Charles Marlow.

Miss Nev. As I live, the most intimate friend of Mr. Hastings, my admirer. They are never asunder. I believe you must have seen him when we lived in town.

Miss Hard. Never.

Miss Nev. He's a very singular character, I assure you. Among women of reputation and virtue he is the modestest man alive; but his acquaintance give him a very different character among creatures of another stamp: you understand me.

Miss Hard. An odd character indeed. I shall never be able to manage him. What shall I do? Pshaw, think no more of him, but trust to occurrences for success. But how goes on your own affair, my dear? has my mother been courting you for my brother Tony as usual?

Miss Nev. I have just come from one of our agreeable *tête-à-têtes.* She has been saying a hundred tender things, and setting off her pretty monster as the very pink of perfection.

Miss Hard. And her partiality is such, that she actually thinks him so. A fortune like yours is no small temptation. Besides, as she has the sole management of it, I'm not surprised to see her unwilling to let it go out of the family.

Miss Nev. A fortune like mine, which chiefly consists in jewels, is no such mighty temptation. But at any rate, if my dear Hastings be but constant, I make no doubt to be too hard for her at last. However, I let her suppose that I am in love with her son; and she never once dreams that my affections are fixed upon another.

Miss Hard. My good brother holds out stoutly. I could almost love him for hating you so.

Miss Nev. It is a good-natured creature at bottom, and I'm sure would wish to see me married to anybody but himself. But my aunt's bell rings for our afternoon's walk round the improvements. *Allons!* Courage is necessary, as our affairs are critical.

Miss Hard. "Would it were bed-time, and all were well." [*Exeunt.*

SCENE—*An Alehouse Room. Several shabby Fellows with punch and tobacco.* TONY *at the head of the table, a little higher than the rest, a mallet in his hand.*

Omnes. Hurrea! hurrea! hurrea! bravo!

First Fel. Now, gentlemen, silence for a song. The 'squire is going to knock himself down for a song.

Omnes. Ay, a song, a song!

Tony. Then I'll sing you, gentlemen, a song I made upon this alehouse, the Three Pigeons.

SONG.

Let schoolmasters puzzle their brain
  With grammar, and nonsense, and learning,
Good liquor, I stoutly maintain,
  Gives *genus* a better discerning.
Let them brag of their heathenish gods,
  Their Lethes, their Styxes, and Stygians,
Their Quis, and their Quæs, and their Quods,
  They're all but a parcel of Pigeons.
    Toroddle, toroddle, toroll.

When methodist preachers come down,
  A-preaching that drinking is sinful,
I'll wager the rascals a crown,
  They always preach best with a skinful.
But when you come down with your pence,
  For a slice of their scurvy religion,
I'll leave it to all men of sense,
  But you, my good friend, are the Pigeon.
    Toroddle, toroddle, toroll.

Then come, put the jorum about,
  And let us be merry and clever,
Our hearts and our liquors are stout,
  Here's the Three Jolly Pigeons for ever.
Let some cry up woodcock or hare,
  Your bustards, your ducks, and your widgeons;
But of all the *gay* birds in the air,
  Here's a health to the Three Jolly Pigeons.
    Toroddle, toroddle, toroll.

Omnes. Bravo, bravo!

First Fel. The 'squire has got spunk in him.

Second Fel. I loves to hear him sing, bekeays he never gives us nothing that's low.

Third Fel. O damn anything that's low, I cannot bear it.

Fourth Fel. The genteel thing is the

genteel thing any time: if so be that a gentleman bees in a concatenation accordingly.

Third Fel. I likes the maxum of it, Master Muggins. What, though I am obligated to dance a bear, a man may be a gentleman for all that. May this be my poison, if my bear ever dances but to the very genteelest of tunes; "Water Parted," or "The minuet in Ariadne."

Second Fel. What a pity it is the 'squire is not come to his own. It would be well for all the publicans within ten miles round of him.

Tony. Ecod, and so it would, Master Slang. I'd then show what it was to keep choice of company.

Second Fel. O he takes after his own father for that. To be sure old 'Squire Lumpkin was the finest gentleman I ever set my eyes on. For winding the straight horn, or beating a thicket for a hare, or a wench, he never had his fellow. It was a saying in the place, that he kept the best horses, dogs, and girls, in the whole county.

Tony. Ecod, and when I'm of age, I'll be no bastard, I promise you. I have been thinking of Bet Bouncer and the miller's grey mare to begin with. But come, my boys, drink about and be merry, for you pay no reckoning. Well, Stingo, what's the matter?

Enter Landlord.

Land. There be two gentlemen in a post-chaise at the door. They have lost their way upo' the forest; and they are talking something about Mr. Hardcastle.

Tony. As sure as can be, one of them must be the gentleman that's coming down to court my sister. Do they seem to be Londoners?

Land. I believe they may. They look woundily like Frenchmen.

Tony. Then desire them to step this way, and I'll set them right in a twinkling. (*Exit* Landlord.) Gentlemen, as they mayn't be good enough company for you, step down for a moment, and I'll be with you in the squeezing of a lemon.

[*Exeunt mob.*

Tony (*solus*). Father-in-law has been calling me whelp and hound this half year. Now, if I pleased, I could be so revenged upon the old grumbletonian. But then I'm afraid—afraid of what? I shall soon be worth fifteen hundred a year, and let him frighten me out of *that* if he can.

Enter Landlord, *conducting* MARLOW *and* HASTINGS.

Mar. What a tedious uncomfortable day have we had of it! We were told it was but forty miles across the country, and we have come above threescore.

Hast. And all, Marlow, from that unaccountable reserve of yours, that would not let us inquire more frequently on the way.

Mar. I own, Hastings, I am unwilling to lay myself under an obligation to every one I meet, and often stand the chance of an unmannerly answer.

Hast. At present, however, we are not likely to receive any answer.

Tony. No offence, gentlemen. But I'm told you have been inquiring for one Mr. Hardcastle in these parts. Do you know what part of the country you are in?

Hast. Not in the least, sir, but should thank you for information.

Tony. Nor the way you came?

Hast. No, sir; but if you can inform us——

Tony. Why, gentlemen, if you know neither the road you are going, nor where you are, nor the road you came, the first thing I have to inform you is, that—you have lost your way.

Mar. We wanted no ghost to tell us that.

Tony. Pray, gentlemen, may I be so bold so as to ask the place from whence you came?

Mar. That's not necessary towards directing us where we are to go.

Tony. No offence; but question for question is all fair, you know. Pray, gentlemen, is not this same Hardcastle a cross-grained, old-fashioned, whimsical fellow, with an ugly face, a daughter, and a pretty son?

Hast. We have not seen the gentleman; but he has the family you mention.

Tony. The daughter, a tall, trapesing, trolloping, talkative maypole; the son, a pretty, well-bred, agreeable youth, that everybody is fond of.

Mar. Our information differs in this. The daughter is said to be well-bred and beautiful; the son an awkward booby, reared up and spoiled at his mother's apron-string.

Tony. He-he-hem!—Then, gentlemen, all I have to tell you is, that you won't reach Mr. Hardcastle's house this night, I believe.

Hast. Unfortunate!

Tony. It's a damn'd long, dark, boggy, dirty, dangerous way. Stingo, tell the gentlemen the way to Mr. Hardcastle's! (*Winking upon the* Landlord.) Mr. Hardcastle's, of Quagmire Marsh, you understand me.

Land. Master Hardcastle's! Lock-a-daisy, my masters, you're come a deadly deal wrong! When you came to the bottom of the hill, you should have crossed down Squash Lane.

Mar. Cross down Squash Lane!

Land. Then you were to keep straight forward, till you came to four roads.

Mar. Come to where four roads meet?

Tony. Ay; but you must be sure to take only one of them.

Mar. O, sir, you're facetious.

Tony. Then keeping to the right, you are to go sideways till you come upon Crackskull Common: there you must look sharp for the track of the wheel, and go forward till you come to farmer Murrain's barn. Coming to the farmer's barn, you are to turn to the right, and then to the left, and then to the right about again, till you find out the old mill—

Mar. Zounds, man! we could as soon find out the longitude!

Hast. What's to be done, Marlow?

Mar. This house promises but a poor reception; though perhaps the landlord can accommodate us.

Land. Alack, master, we have but one spare bed in the whole house.

Tony. And to my knowledge, that's taken up by three lodgers already. (*After a pause, in which the rest seem disconcerted.*) I have hit it. Don't you think, Stingo, our landlady could accommodate the gentlemen by the fire-side, with——three chairs and a bolster?

Hast. I hate sleeping by the fire-side.

Mar. And I detest your three chairs and a bolster.

Tony. You do, do you? then, let me see—what if you go on a mile further, to the Buck's Head; the old Buck's Head on the hill, one of the best inns in the whole county?

Hast. O ho! so we have escaped an adventure for this night, however.

Land. (*apart to* TONY). Sure, you ben't sending them to your father's as an inn, be you?

Tony. Mum, you fool you. Let *them* find that out. (*To them.*) You have only to keep on straight forward, till you come to a large old house by the road side. You'll see a pair of large horns over the door. That's the sign. Drive up the yard, and call stoutly about you.

Hast. Sir, we are obliged to you. The servants can't miss the way?

Tony. No, no: but I tell you, though, the landlord is rich, and going to leave off business; so he wants to be thought a gentleman, saving your presence, he! he! he! He'll be for giving you his company; and, ecod, if you mind him, he'll persuade you that his mother was an alderman, and his aunt a justice of peace.

Land. A troublesome old blade, to be sure; but a keeps as good wines and beds as any in the whole country.

Mar. Well, if he supplies us with these, we shall want no farther connection. We are to turn to the right, did you say?

Tony. No, no; straight forward. I'll just step myself, and show you a piece of the way. (*To the* Landlord.) Mum!

Land. Ah, bless your heart, for a sweet, pleasant——damn'd mischievous son of a whore. [*Exeunt.*

ACT THE SECOND.

SCENE—*An old-fashioned House.*

Enter HARDCASTLE, *followed by three or four awkward* Servants.

Hard. Well, I hope you are perfect in the table exercise I have been teaching you these three days. You all know your posts and your places, and can show that you have been used to good company, without ever stirring from home.

Omnes. Ay, ay.

Hard. When company comes you are not to pop out and stare, and then run in again, like frighted rabbits in a warren.

Omnes. No, no.

Hard. You, Diggory, whom I have taken from the barn, are to make a show at the side-table; and you, Roger, whom I have advanced from the plough, are to place yourself behind my chair. But you're not to stand so, with your hands in your pockets. Take your hands from your pockets, Roger; and from your head, you blockhead you. See how Diggory carries his hands. They're a little too stiff, indeed, but that's no great matter.

Dig. Ay, mind how I hold them. I learned to hold my hands this way when I was upon drill for the militia. And so being upon drill——

Hard. You must not be so talkative, Diggory. You must be all attention to the guests. You must hear us talk, and not think of talking; you must see us drink, and not think of drinking; you must see us eat, and not think of eating.

Dig. By the laws, your worship, that's parfectly unpossible. Whenever Diggory sees yeating going forward, ecod, he's always wishing for a mouthful himself.

Hard. Blockhead! Is not a belly-full in the kitchen as good as a belly-full in the parlour? Stay your stomach with that reflection.

Dig. Ecod, I thank your worship, I'll make a shift to stay my stomach with a slice of cold beef in the pantry.

Hard. Diggory, you are too talkative.—Then, if I happen to say a good thing, or tell a good story at table, you must not all burst out a-laughing, as if you made part of the company.

Dig. Then ecod your worship must not tell the story of Ould Grouse in the gun-room: I can't help laughing at that—he! he! he!—for the soul of me. We have laughed at that these twenty years—ha! ha! ha!

Hard. Ha! ha! ha! The story is a good one. Well, honest Diggory, you may laugh at that—but still remember to be attentive. Suppose one of the company should call for a glass ot wine, how will you behave? A glass of wine, sir, if you please (*to* Diggory).—Eh, why don't you move?

Dig. Ecod, your worship, I never have courage till I see the eatables and drinkables brought upo' the table, and then I'm as bauld as a lion.

Hard. What, will nobody move?

First Serv. I'm not to leave this pleace.

Second Serv. I'm sure it's no pleace of mine.

Third Serv. Nor mine, for sartain.

Dig. Wauns, and I'm sure it canna be mine.

Hard. You numskulls! and so while, like your betters, you are quarrelling for places, the guests must be starved. O you dunces! I find I must begin all over again——But don't I hear a coach drive into the yard? To your posts, you blockheads. I'll go in the mean time and give my old friend's son a hearty reception at the gate. [*Exit* Hardcastle.

Dig. By the elevens, my pleace is gone quite out of my head.

Rog. I know that my pleace is to be everywhere.

First Serv. Where the devil is mine?

Second Serv. My pleace is to be nowhere at all; and so I'ze go about my business.

[*Exeunt* Servants, *running about as if frighted, different ways.*

Enter Servant *with candles, showing in* Marlow *and* Hastings.

Serv. Welcome, gentlemen, very welcome! This way.

Hast. After the disappointments of the day, welcome once more, Charles, to the comforts of a clean room and a good fire. Upon my word, a very well-looking house; antique but creditable.

Mar. The usual fate of a large mansion. Having first ruined the master by good housekeeping, it at last comes to levy contributions as an inn.

Hast. As you say, we passengers are to be taxed to pay all these fineries. I have often seen a good sideboard, or a marble chimney-piece, though not actually put in the bill, inflame a reckoning confoundedly.

Mar. Travellers, George, must pay in all places: the only difference is, that in good inns you pay dearly for luxuries; in bad inns you are fleeced and starved.

Hast. You have lived very much among them. In truth, I have been often surprised, that you who have seen so much of the world, with your natural good sense, and your many opportunities, could never yet acquire a requisite share of assurance.

Mar. The Englishman's malady. But tell me, George, where could I have learned that assurance you talk of? My life has been chiefly spent in a college or an inn, in seclusion from that lovely part of the creation that chiefly teach men confidence. I don't know that I was ever familiarly acquainted with a single modest woman—except my mother—But among females of another class, you know——

Hast. Ay, among them you are impudent enough of all conscience.

Mar. They are of *us*, you know.

Hast. But in the company of women of reputation I never saw such an idiot, such a trembler; you look for all the world as if you wanted an opportunity of stealing out of the room.

Mar. Why, man, that's because I do want to steal out of the room. Faith, I have often formed a resolution to break the ice, and rattle away at any rate. But I don't know how, a single glance from a pair of fine eyes has totally overset my resolution. An impudent fellow may counterfeit modesty; but I'll be hanged if a modest man can ever counterfeit impudence.

Hast. If you could but say half the fine things to them that I have heard you lavish upon the bar-maid of an inn, or even a college bed-maker——

Mar. Why, George, I can't say fine things to them; they freeze, they petrify me. They may talk of a comet, or a burning mountain, or some such bagatelle; but, to me, a modest woman, drest out in all her finery, is the most tremendous object of the whole creation.

Hast. Ha! ha! ha! At this rate, man, how can you ever expect to marry?

Mar. Never; unless, as among kings and princes, my bride were to be courted by proxy. If, indeed, like an Eastern bridegroom, one were to be introduced to a wife he never saw before, it might be endured. But to go through all the terrors of a formal courtship, together with the episode of aunts, grandmothers, and cousins, and at last to blurt out the broad staring question of, Madam, will you marry me? No, no, that's a strain much above me, I assure you.

Hast. I pity you. But how do you intend behaving to the lady you are come down to visit at the request of your father?

Mar. As I behave to all other ladies. Bow very low, answer yes or no to all her demands—But for the rest, I don't think I shall venture to look in her face till I see my father's again.

Hast. I'm surprised that one who is so warm a friend can be so cool a lover.

Mar. To be explicit, my dear Hastings, my chief inducement down was to be instrumental in forwarding your happiness, not my own. Miss Neville loves you, the family don't know you; as my friend you are sure of a reception, and let honour do the rest.

Hast. My dear Marlow! But I'll suppress the emotion. Were I a wretch, meanly seeking to carry off a fortune, you should be the last man in the world I would apply to for assistance. But Miss Neville's person is all I ask, and that is mine, both from her deceased father's consent, and her own inclination.

Mar. Happy man! You have talents and art to captivate any woman. I'm doom'd to adore the sex, and yet to converse with the only part of it I despise. This stammer in my address, and this awkward prepossessing visage of mine, can never permit me to soar above the reach of a milliner's 'prentice, or one of the duchesses of Drury-lane. Pshaw! this fellow here to interrupt us.

Enter HARDCASTLE.

Hard. Gentlemen, once more you are heartily welcome. Which is Mr. Marlow? Sir, you are heartily welcome. It's not my way, you see, to receive my friends with my back to the fire. I like to give them a hearty reception in the old style at my gate. I like to see their horses and trunks taken care of.

Mar. (*Aside.*) He has got our names from the servants already. (*To him.*) We approve your caution and hospitality, sir. (*To Hastings.*) I have been thinking, George, of changing our travelling dresses in the morning. I am grown confoundedly ashamed of mine.

Hard. I beg, Mr. Marlow, you'll use no ceremony in this house.

Hast. I fancy, George, you're right: the first blow is half the battle. I intend opening the campaign with the white and gold.

Hard. Mr. Marlow—Mr. Hastings—gentlemen—pray be under no constraint in this house. This is Liberty-hall, gentlemen. You may do just as you please here.

Mar. Yet, George, if we open the campaign too fiercely at first, we may want ammunition before it is over. I think to reserve the embroidery to secure a retreat.

Hard. Your talking of à retreat, Mr. Marlow, puts me in mind of the Duke of Marlborough, when we went to besiege Denain. He first summoned the garrison——

Mar. Don't you think the *ventre d'or* waistcoat will do with the plain brown?

Hard. He first summoned the garrison, which might consist of about five thousand men——

Hast. I think not: brown and yellow mix but very poorly.

Hard. I say, gentlemen, as I was telling you, he summoned the garrison, which might consist of about five thousand men——

Mar. The girls like finery.

Hard. Which might consist of about five thousand men, well appointed with stores, ammunition, and other implements of war. Now, says the Duke of Marlborough to George Brooks, that stood next to him—you must have heard of George Brooks—I'll pawn my dukedom, says he, but I take that garrison without spilling a drop of blood. So——

Mar. What, my good friend, if you gave us a glass of punch in the mean time; it would help us to carry on the siege with vigour.

Hard. Punch, sir! (*Aside.*) This is the most unaccountable kind of modesty I ever met with.

Mar. Yes, sir, punch. A glass of warm punch, after our journey, will be comfortable. This is Liberty-hall, you know.

Hard. Here's a cup, sir.

Mar. (*Aside.*) So this fellow, in his Liberty-hall, will only let us have just what he pleases.

Hard. (*Taking the cup.*) I hope you'll find it to your mind. I have prepared it with my own hands, and I believe you'll own the ingredients are tolerable. Will you be so good as to pledge me, sir? Here, Mr. Marlow, here is to our better acquaintance. [*Drinks.*

Mar. (*Aside.*) A very impudent fellow this! but he's a character, and I'll humour him a little. Sir, my service to you. [*Drinks.*

Hast. (*Aside.*) I see this fellow wants to give us his company, and forgets that he's an innkeeper, before he has learned to be a gentleman.

Mar. From the excellence of your cup, my old friend, I suppose you have a good deal of business in this part of the country. Warm work, now and then, at elections, I suppose.

Hard. No, sir, I have long given that work over. Since our betters have hit upon the expedient of electing each other, there is no business "for us that sell ale."

Hast. So, then, you have no turn for politics, I find.

Hard. Not in the least. There was a time, indeed, I fretted myself about the mistakes of government, like other people; but finding myself every day grow more angry, and the government growing no better, I left it to mend itself. Since that, I no more trouble my head about Hyder Ally, or Ally Cawn, than about Ally Croker. Sir, my service to you.

Hast. So that with eating above stairs, and drinking below, with receiving your friends within, and amusing them without, you lead a good pleasant bustling life of it.

Hard. I do stir about a great deal, that's certain. Half the differences of the parish are adjusted in this very parlour.

Mar. (*After drinking.*) And you have an argument in your cup, old gentleman, better than any in Westminster-hall.

Hard. Ay, young gentleman, that, and a little philosophy.

Mar. (*Aside.*) Well, this is the first time I ever heard of an innkeeper's philosophy.

Hast. So then, like an experienced general, you attack them on every quarter.

If you find their reason manageable, you attack it with your philosophy; if you find they have no reason, you attack them with this. Here's your health, my philosopher. [*Drinks.*

Hard. Good, very good, thank you; ha! ha! Your generalship puts me in mind of Prince Eugene, when he fought the Turks at the battle of Belgrade. You shall hear.

Mar. Instead of the battle of Belgrade, I believe it's almost time to talk about supper. What has your philosophy got in the house for supper?

Hard. For supper, sir! (*Aside.*) Was ever such a request to a man in his own house?

Mar. Yes, sir, supper, sir; I begin to feel an appetite. I shall make devilish work to-night in the larder, I promise you.

Hard. (*Aside.*) Such a brazen dog sure never my eyes beheld. (*To him.*) Why, really, sir, as for supper I can't well tell. My Dorothy and the cook-maid settle these things between them. I leave these kind of things entirely to them.

Mar. You do, do you?

Hard. Entirely. By the bye, I believe they are in actual consultation upon what's for supper this moment in the kitchen.

Mar. Then I beg they'll admit me as one of their privy council. It's a way I have got. When I travel, I always choose to regulate my own supper. Let the cook be called. No offence I hope, sir.

Hard. O no, sir, none in the least; yet I don't know how; our Bridget, the cook-maid, is not very communicative upon these occasions. Should we send for her, she might scold us all out of the house.

Hast. Let's see your list of the larder then. I ask it as a favour. I always match my appetite to my bill of fare.

Mar. (*To* HARDCASTLE, *who looks at them with surprise.*) Sir, he's very right, and it's my way too.

Hard. Sir, you have a right to command here. Here, Roger, bring us the bill of fare for to-night's supper: I believe it's drawn out—Your manner, Mr. Hastings, puts me in mind of my uncle, Colonel Wallop. It was a saying of his, that no man was sure of his supper till he had eaten it.

Hast. (*Aside.*) All upon the high rope! His uncle a colonel! we shall soon hear of his mother being a justice of the peace. But let's hear the bill of fare.

Mar. (*Perusing.*) What's here? For the first course; for the second course; for the desert. The devil, sir, do you think we have brought down a whole Joiners' Company, or the corporation of Bedford, to eat up such a supper? Two or three little things, clean and comfortable, will do.

Hast. But let's hear it.

Mar. (*Reading.*) For the first course, at the top, a pig and prune sauce.

Hast. Damn your pig, I say.

Mar. And damn your prune sauce, say I.

Hard. And yet, gentlemen, to men that are hungry, pig with prune sauce is very good eating.

Mar. At the bottom, a calf's tongue and brains.

Hast. Let your brains be knocked out, my good sir, I don't like them.

Mar. Or you may clap them on a plate by themselves. I do.

Hard. (*Aside.*) Their impudence confounds me. (*To them.*) Gentlemen, you are my guests, make what alterations you please. Is there anything else you wish to retrench or alter, gentlemen?

Mar. Item, a pork pie, a boiled rabbit and sausages, a Florentine, a shaking pudding, and a dish of tiff—taff—taffety cream.

Hast. Confound your made dishes; I shall be as much at a loss in this house as at a green and yellow dinner at the French ambassador's table. I'm for plain eating.

Hard. I'm sorry, gentlemen, that I have nothing you like, but if there be anything you have a particular fancy to——

Mar. Why, really, sir, your bill of fare is so exquisite, that any one part of it is full as good as another. Send us what you please. So much for supper. And now to see that our beds are aired, and properly taken care of.

Hard. I entreat you'll leave that to me. You shall not stir a step.

Mar. Leave that to you! I protest, sir, you must excuse me, I always look to these things myself.

Hard. I must insist, sir, you'll make yourself easy on that head.

Mar. You see I'm resolved on it. (*Aside.*) A very troublesome fellow this, as I ever met with.

Hard. Well, sir, I'm resolved at least to attend you. (*Aside.*) This may be modern modesty, but I never saw anything look so like old-fashioned impudence. [*Exeunt* Marlow *and* Hardcastle.

Hast. (*Alone.*) So I find this fellow's civilities begin to grow troublesome. But who can be angry at those assiduities which are meant to please him? Ha! what do I see? Miss Neville, by all that's happy!

Enter MISS NEVILLE.

Miss Nev. My dear Hastings! To what unexpected good fortune, to what accident, am I to ascribe this happy meeting?

Hast. Rather let me ask the same question, as I could never have hoped to meet my dearest Constance at an inn.

Miss Nev. An inn! sure you mistake: my aunt, my guardian, lives here. What could induce you to think this house an inn?

Hast. My friend, Mr. Marlow, with whom I came down, and I, have been sent here as to an inn, I assure you. A young fellow, whom we accidentally met at a house hard by, directed us hither.

Miss Nev. Certainly it must be one of my hopeful cousin's tricks, of whom you have heard me talk so often; ha! ha! ha!

Hast. He whom your aunt intends for you? he of whom I have such just apprehensions?

Miss Nev. You have nothing to fear from him, I assure you. You'd adore him, if you knew how heartily he despises me. My aunt knows it too, and has undertaken to court me for him, and actually begins to think she has made a conquest.

Hast. Thou dear dissembler! You must know, my Constance, I have just seized this happy opportunity of my friend's visit here to get admittance into the family. The horses that carried us down are now fatigued with their journey, but they'll soon be refreshed; and then, if my dearest girl will trust in her faithful Hastings, we shall soon be landed in France, where even among slaves the laws of marriage are respected.

Miss Nev. I have often told you, that though ready to obey you, I yet should leave my little fortune behind with reluctance. The greatest part of it was left me by my uncle, the India director, and chiefly consists in jewels. I have been for some time persuading my aunt to let me wear them. I fancy I'm very near succeeding. The instant they are put into my possession, you shall find me ready to make them and myself yours.

Hast. Perish the baubles! Your person is all I desire. In the mean time, my friend Marlow must not be let into his mistake. I know the strange reserve of his temper is such, that if abruptly informed of it, he would instantly quit the house before our plan was ripe for execution.

Miss Nev. But how shall we keep him in the deception? Miss Hardcastle is just returned from walking; what if we still continue to deceive him?——This, this way—— [*They confer.*

Enter MARLOW.

Mar. The assiduities of these good people teaze me beyond bearing. My host seems to think it ill manners to leave me alone, and so he claps not only himself, but his old-fashioned wife, on my back. They talk of coming to sup with us too; and then, I suppose, we are to run the gauntlet through all the rest of the family.—What have we got here?

Hast. My dear Charles! Let me congratulate you!—The most fortunate accident!—Who do you think is just alighted?

Mar. Cannot guess.

Hast. Our mistresses, boy, Miss Hardcastle and Miss Neville. Give me leave to introduce Miss Constance Neville to your acquaintance. Happening to dine in the neighbourhood, they called on their return to take fresh horses here. Miss Hardcastle has just stept into the next room, and will be back in an instant. Wasn't it lucky? eh!

Mar. (*Aside.*) I have been mortified enough of all conscience, and here comes something to complete my embarrassment.

Hast. Well, but wasn't it the most fortunate thing in the world?

Mar. Oh! yes. Very fortunate—a most joyful encounter—But our dresses, George, you know are in disorder— What if we should postpone the happiness till to-morrow?—To-morrow at her own house—It will be every bit as convenient—and rather more respectful—To-morrow let it be. [*Offering to go.*

Miss Nev. By no means, sir. Your ceremony will displease her. The disorder of your dress will show the ardour of your impatience. Besides, she knows you are in the house, and will permit you to see her.

Mar. O! the devil! how shall I support it? Hem! hem! Hastings, you must not go. You are to assist me, you know. I shall be confoundedly ridiculous. Yet, hang it! I'll take courage. Hem!

Hast. Pshaw, man! it's but the first plunge, and all's over. She's but a woman, you know.

Mar. And, of all women, she that I dread most to encounter.

Enter MISS HARDCASTLE, *as returned from walking, a bonnet, &c.*

Hast. (*Introducing them.*) Miss Hardcastle, Mr. Marlow. I'm proud of bringing two persons of such merit together, that only want to know, to esteem each other.

Miss Hard. (*Aside.*) Now for meeting my modest gentleman with a demure face, and quite in his own manner. (*After a pause, in which he appears very uneasy and disconcerted.*) I'm glad of your safe arrival, sir. I'm told you had some accidents by the way.

Mar. Only a few, madam. Yes, we had some. Yes, madam, a good many accidents, but should be sorry—madam—or rather glad of any accidents—that are so agreeably concluded. Hem!

Hast. (*To him.*) You never spoke better in your whole life. Keep it up, and I'll insure you the victory.

Miss Hard. I'm afraid you flatter, sir. You that have seen so much of the finest company, can find little entertainment in an obscure corner of the country.

Mar. (*Gathering courage.*) I have lived, indeed, in the world, madam; but I have kept very little company. I have been but an observer upon life, madam, while others were enjoying it.

Miss Nev. But that, I am told, is the way to enjoy it at last.

Hast. (*To him.*) Cicero never spoke better. Once more, and you are confirmed in assurance for ever.

Mar. (*To him.*) Hem! Stand by me, then, and when I'm down, throw in a word or two, to set me up again.

Miss Hard. An observer, like you, upon life were, I fear, disagreeably employed, since you must have had much more to censure than to approve.

Mar. Pardon me, madam. I was always willing to be amused. The folly of most people is rather an object of mirth than uneasiness.

Hast. (*To him.*) Bravo, bravo. Never spoke so well in your whole life. Well, Miss Hardcastle, I see that you and Mr. Marlow are going to be very good company. I believe our being here will but embarrass the interview.

Mar. Not in the least, Mr. Hastings. We like your company of all things. (*To him.*) Zounds! George, sure you won't go? how can you leave us?

Hast. Our presence will but spoil conversation, so we'll retire to the next room. (*To him.*) You don't consider, man, that we are to manage a little *tête-à-tête* of our own. [*Exeunt.*

Miss Hard. (*after a pause*). But you have not been wholly an observer, I presume, sir: the ladies, I should hope, have employed some part of your addresses.

Mar. (*Relapsing into timidity.*) Pardon me, madam, I—I—I—as yet have studied—only—to—deserve them.

Miss Hard. And that, some say, is the very worst way to obtain them.

Mar. Perhaps so, madam. But I love to converse only with the more grave and sensible part of the sex. But I'm afraid I grow tiresome.

Miss Hard. Not at all, sir; there is nothing I like so much as grave conversation myself; I could hear it for ever. Indeed, I have often been surprised how a man of sentiment could ever admire those light airy pleasures, where nothing reaches the heart.

Mar. It's——a disease——of the mind, madam. In the variety of tastes there must be some who, wanting a relish——for——um—a—um.

Miss Hard. I understand you, sir.

There must be some, who, wanting a relish for refined pleasures, pretend to despise what they are incapable of tasting.

Mar. My meaning, madam, but infinitely better expressed. And I can't help observing——a——

Miss Hard. (*Aside.*) Who could ever suppose this fellow impudent upon some occasions? (*To him.*) You were going to observe, sir——

Mar. I was observing, madam—I protest, madam, I forget what I was going to observe.

Miss Hard. (*Aside.*) I vow and so do I. (*To him.*) You were observing, sir, that in this age of hypocrisy—something about hypocrisy, sir.

Mar. Yes, madam. In this age of hypocrisy there are few who upon strict inquiry do not—a—a—a—

Miss Hard. I understand you perfectly, sir.

Mar. (*Aside.*) Egad! and that's more than I do myself.

Miss Hard. You mean that in this hypocritical age there are few that do not condemn in public what they practise in private, and think they pay every debt to virtue when they praise it.

Mar. True, madam; those who have most virtue in their mouths, have least of it in their bosoms. But I'm sure I tire you, madam.

Miss Hard. Not in the least, sir; there's something so agreeable and spirited in your manner, such life and force—pray, sir, go on.

Mar. Yes, madam. I was saying—— that there are some occasions, when a total want of courage, madam, destroys all the——and puts us——upon a—a—a—

Miss Hard. I agree with you entirely; a want of courage upon some occasions assumes the appearance of ignorance, and betrays us when we most want to excel. I beg you'll proceed.

Mar. Yes, madam. Morally speaking, madam—But I see Miss Neville expecting us in the next room. I would not intrude for the world.

Miss Hard. I protest, sir, I never was more agreeably entertained in all my life. Pray go on.

Mar. Yes, madam, I was——But she beckons us to join her. Madam, shall I do myself the honour to attend you?

Miss Hard. Well, then, I'll follow.

Mar. (*Aside.*) This pretty smooth dialogue has done for me. [*Exit.*

Miss Hard. (*Alone.*) Ha! ha! ha! Was there ever such a sober, sentimental interview? I'm certain he scarce looked in my face the whole time. Yet the fellow, but for his unaccountable bashfulness, is pretty well too. He has good sense, but then so buried in his fears, that it fatigues one more than ignorance. If I could teach him a little confidence, it would be doing somebody that I know of a piece of service. But who is that somebody?—That, faith, is a question I can scarce answer. [*Exit.*

Enter TONY *and* MISS NEVILLE, *followed by* MRS. HARDCASTLE *and* HASTINGS.

Tony. What do you follow me for, cousin Con? I wonder you're not ashamed to be so very engaging.

Miss Nev. I hope, cousin, one may speak to one's own relations, and not be to blame.

Tony. Ay, but I know what sort of a relation you want to make me, though; but it won't do. I tell you, cousin Con, it won't do; so I beg you'll keep your distance, I want no nearer relationship.

[*She follows, coquetting him to the back scene.*

Mrs. Hard. Well! I vow, Mr. Hastings, you are very entertaining. There's nothing in the world I love to talk of so much as London, and the fashions, though I was never there myself.

Hast. Never there! You amaze me! From your air and manner, I concluded you had been bred all your life either at Ranelagh, St. James's, or Tower Wharf.

Mrs. Hard. O! sir, you're only pleased to say so. We country persons can have no manner at all. I'm in love with the town, and that serves to raise me above some of our neighbouring rustics; but who can have a manner, that has never seen the Pantheon, the Grotto Gardens, the Borough, and such places where the nobility chiefly resort? All I can do is to enjoy London at second-hand. I take care to know every *tête-à-tête* from the Scandalous Magazine, and have all the fashions, as they come out, in a letter from the two Miss Rickets of Crooked Lane. Pray how do you like this head, Mr. Hastings?

Hast. Extremely elegant and *dégagée*, upon my word, madam. Your friseur is a Frenchman, I suppose?

Mrs. Hard. I protest, I dressed it myself from a print in the Ladies' Memorandum-book for the last year.

Hast. Indeed! Such a head in a side-box at the play-house would draw as many gazers as my Lady Mayoress at a City Ball.

Mrs. Hard. I vow, since inoculation began, there is no such thing to be seen as a plain woman; so one must dress a little particular, or one may escape in the crowd.

Hast. But that can never be your case, madam, in any dress. (*Bowing.*)

Mrs. Hard. Yet, what signifies my dressing when I have such a piece of antiquity by my side as Mr. Hardcastle: all I can say will never argue down a single button from his clothes. I have often wanted him to throw off his great flaxen wig, and where he was bald, to plaster it over, like my Lord Pately, with powder.

Hast. You are right, madam; for, as among the ladies there are none ugly, so among the men there are none old.

Mrs. Hard. But what do you think his answer was? Why, with his usual Gothic vivacity, he said I only wanted him to throw off his wig, to convert it into a *tête* for my own wearing.

Hast. Intolerable! At your age you may wear what you please, and it must become you.

Mrs. Hard. Pray, Mr. Hastings, what do you take to be the most fashionable age about town?

Hast. Some time ago, forty was all the mode; but I'm told the ladies intend to bring up fifty for the ensuing winter.

Mrs. Hard. Seriously. Then I shall be too young for the fashion.

Hast. No lady begins now to put on jewels till she's past forty. For instance, Miss there, in a polite circle, would be considered as a child, as a mere maker of samplers.

Mrs. Hard. And yet Mrs. Niece thinks herself as much a woman, and is as fond of jewels, as the oldest of us all

Hast. Your niece, is she? And that young gentleman, a brother of yours, I should presume?

Mrs. Hard. My son, sir. They are contracted to each other. Observe their little sports. They fall in and out ten times a day, as if they were man and wife already. (*To them.*) Well, Tony, child, what soft things are you saying to your cousin Constance this evening?

Tony. I have been saying no soft things; but that it's very hard to be followed about so. Ecod! I've not a place in the house now that's left to myself, but the stable.

Mrs. Hard. Never mind him, Con, my dear. He's in another story behind your back.

Miss Nev. There's something generous in my cousin's manner. He falls out before faces to be forgiven in private.

Tony. That's a damned confounded—crack.

Mrs. Hard. Ah! he's a sly one. Don't you think they are like each other about the mouth, Mr. Hastings? The Blenkinsop mouth to a T. They're of a size too. Back to back, my pretties, that Mr. Hastings may see you. Come, Tony.

Tony. You had as good not make me, I tell you. (*Measuring.*)

Miss. Nev. O lud! he has almost cracked my head.

Mrs. Hard. O, the monster! For shame, Tony. You a man, and behave so!

Tony. If I'm a man, let me have my fortin. Ecod! I'll not be made a fool of no longer.

Mrs. Hard. Is this, ungrateful boy, all that I'm to get for the pains I have taken in your education? I that have rocked you in your cradle, and fed that pretty mouth with a spoon! Did not I work that waistcoat to make you genteel? Did not I prescribe for you every day, and weep while the receipt was operating?

Tony. Ecod! you had reason to weep, for you have been dosing me ever since I was born. I have gone through every receipt in the Complete Huswife ten times over; and you have thoughts of coursing me through Quincy next spring. But, ecod! I tell you, I'll not be made a fool of no longer.

Mrs. Hard. Wasn't it all for your good, viper? Wasn't it all for your good?

Tony. I wish you'd let me and my good alone, then. Snubbing this way when I'm in spirits. If I'm to have any good, let it come of itself; not to keep dinging it, dinging it into one so.

Mrs. Hard. That's false; I never see you when you're in spirits. No, Tony, you then go to the alehouse or kennel. I'm never to be delighted with your agreeable wild notes, unfeeling monster!

Tony. Ecod! mamma, your own notes are the wildest of the two.

Mrs. Hard. Was ever the like? But I see he wants to break my heart, I see he does.

Hast. Dear madam, permit me to lecture the young gentleman a little. I'm certain I can persuade him to his duty.

Mrs. Hard. Well, I must retire. Come, Constance, my love. You see, Mr. Hastings, the wretchedness of my situation: was ever poor woman so plagued with a dear sweet, pretty, provoking, undutiful boy?

[*Exeunt* Mrs. Hardcastle *and* Miss Neville.

Tony. (*Singing.*) "There was a young man riding by, and fain would have his will. Rang do didlo dee."——Don't mind her. Let her cry. It's the comfort of her heart. I have seen her and sister cry over a book for an hour together; and they said they liked the book the better the more it made them cry.

Hast. Then you're no friend to the ladies, I find, my pretty young gentleman?

Tony. That's as I find 'um.

Hast. Not to her of your mother's choosing, I dare answer? And yet she appears to me a pretty well-tempered girl.

Tony. That's because you don't know her as well as I. Ecod! I know every inch about her; and there's not a more bitter cantankerous toad in all Christendom.

Hast. (*Aside.*) Pretty encouragement this for a lover!

Tony. I have seen her since the height of that. She has as many tricks as a hare in a thicket, or a colt the first day's breaking.

Hast. To me she appears sensible and silent.

Tony. Ay, before company. But when she's with her playmate, she's as loud as a hog in a gate.

Hast. But there is a meek modesty about her that charms me.

Tony. Yes, but curb her never so little, she kicks up, and you're flung in a ditch.

Hast. Well, but you must allow her a little beauty.—Yes, you must allow her some beauty.

Tony. Bandbox! She's all a made-up thing, mun. Ah! could you but see Bet Bouncer of these parts, you might then talk of beauty. Ecod, she has two eyes as black as sloes, and cheeks as broad and red as a pulpit cushion. She'd make two of she.

Hast. Well, what say you to a friend that would take this bitter bargain off your hands?

Tony. Anon.

Hast. Would you thank him that would take Miss Neville, and leave you to happiness and your dear Betsy?

Tony. Ay; but where is there such a friend, for who would take her?

Hast. I am he. If you but assist me, I'll engage to whip her off to France, and you shall never hear more of her.

Tony. Assist you! Ecod I will, to the last drop of my blood. I'll clap a pair of horses to your chaise that shall trundle you off in a twinkling, and may be get you a part of her fortin beside, in jewels, that you little dream of.

Hast. My dear 'squire, this looks like a lad of spirit.

Tony. Come along, then, and you shall see more of my spirit before you have done with me. (*Singing.*)

"We are the boys
That fears no noise
Where the thundering cannons roar."

[*Exeunt.*

ACT THE THIRD.

Enter Hardcastle, *alone.*

Hard. What could my old friend Sir Charles mean by recommending his son as the modestest young man in town? To me he appears the most impudent piece of brass that ever spoke with a tongue.

He has taken possession of the easy chair by the fire-side already. He took off his boots in the parlour, and desired me to see them taken care of. I'm desirous to know how his impudence affects my daughter. She will certainly be shocked at it.

Enter MISS HARDCASTLE, *plainly dressed.*

Hard. Well, my Kate, I see you have changed your dress, as I bade you; and yet, I believe, there was no great occasion.

Miss Hard. I find such a pleasure, sir, in obeying your commands, that I take care to observe them without ever debating their propriety.

Hard. And yet, Kate, I sometimes give you some cause, particularly when I recommended my modest gentleman to you as a lover to-day.

Miss Hard. You taught me to expect something extraordinary, and I find the original exceeds the description.

Hard. I was never so surprised in my life! He has quite confounded all my faculties!

Miss Hard. I never saw anything like it: and a man of the world too!

Hard. Ay, he learned it all abroad—what a fool was I, to think a young man could learn modesty by travelling. He might as soon learn wit at a masquerade.

Miss Hard. It seems all natural to him.

Hard. A good deal assisted by bad company and a French dancing-master.

Miss Hard. Sure you mistake, papa! A French dancing-master could never have taught him that timid look—that awkward address—that bashful manner—

Hard. Whose look? whose manner, child?

Miss Hard. Mr. Marlow's: his *mauvaise honte*, his timidity, struck me at the first sight.

Hard. Then your first sight deceived you; for I think him one of the most brazen first sights that ever astonished my senses.

Miss Hard. Sure, sir, you rally! I never saw any one so modest.

Hard. And can you be serious? I never saw such a bouncing, swaggering puppy since I was born. Bully Dawson was but a fool to him.

Miss Hard. Surprising! He met me with a respectful bow, a stammering voice, and a look fixed on the ground.

Hard. He met me with a loud voice, a lordly air, and a familiarity that made my blood freeze again.

Miss Hard. He treated me with diffidence and respect; censured the manners of the age; admired the prudence of girls that never laughed; tired me with apologies for being tiresome; then left the room with a bow, and "Madam, I would not for the world detain you."

Hard. He spoke to me as if he knew me all his life before; asked twenty questions, and never waited for an answer; interrupted my best remarks with some silly pun; and when I was in my best story of the Duke of Marlborough and Prince Eugene, he asked if I had not a good hand at making punch. Yes, Kate, he asked your father if he was a maker of punch!

Miss Hard. One of us must certainly be mistaken.

Hard. If he be what he has shown himself, I'm determined he shall never have my consent.

Miss Hard. And if he be the sullen thing I take him, he shall never have mine.

Hard. In one thing then we are agreed—to reject him.

Miss Hard. Yes: but upon conditions. For if you should find him less impudent, and I more presuming—if you find him more respectful, and I more importunate—I don't know—the fellow is well enough for a man—Certainly, we don't meet many such at a horse-race in the country.

Hard. If we should find him so——But that's impossible. The first appearance has done my business. I'm seldom deceived in that.

Miss Hard. And yet there may be many good qualities under that first appearance.

Hard. Ay, when a girl finds a fellow's outside to her taste, she then sets about guessing the rest of his furniture. With her, a smooth face stands for good sense, and a genteel figure for every virtue.

Miss Hard. I hope, sir, a conversation begun with a compliment to my good sense, won't end with a sneer at my understanding?

Hard. Pardon me, Kate. But if young Mr. Brazen can find the art of reconciling contradictions, he may please us both, perhaps.

Miss Hard. And as one of us must be mistaken, what if we go to make further discoveries?

Hard. Agreed. But depend on't I'm in the right.

Miss Hard. And depend on't I'm not much in the wrong. [*Exeunt.*

Enter TONY, *running in with a casket.*

Tony. Ecod! I have got them. Here they are. My cousin Con's necklaces, bobs and all. My mother shan't cheat the poor souls out of their fortin neither. O! my genus, is that you?

Enter HASTINGS.

Hast. My dear friend, how have you managed with your mother? I hope you have amused her with pretending love for your cousin, and that you are willing to be reconciled at last? Our horses will be refreshed in a short time, and we shall soon be ready to set off.

Tony. And here's something to bear your charges by the way (*giving the casket*); your sweetheart's jewels. Keep them: and hang those, I say, that would rob you of one of them.

Hast. But how have you procured them from your mother?

Tony. Ask me no questions, and I'll tell you no fibs. I procured them by the rule of thumb. If I had not a key to every drawer in mother's bureau, how could I go to the alehouse so often as I do? An honest man may rob himself of his own at any time.

Hast. Thousands do it every day. But to be plain with you; Miss Neville is endeavouring to procure them from her aunt this very instant. If she succeeds, it will be the most delicate way at least of obtaining them.

Tony. Well, keep them, till you know how it will be. But I know how it will be well enough; she'd as soon part with the only sound tooth in her head.

Hast. But I dread the effects of her resentment, when she finds she has lost them.

Tony. Never you mind her resentment, leave *me* to manage that. I don't value her resentment the bounce of a cracker. Zounds! here they are. Morrice! Prance! [*Exit* Hastings.

Enter MRS. HARDCASTLE *and* MISS NEVILLE.

Mrs. Hard. Indeed, Constance, you amaze me. Such a girl as you want jewels! It will be time enough for jewels, my dear, twenty years hence, when your beauty begins to want repairs.

Miss Nev. But what will repair beauty at forty, will certainly improve it at twenty, madam.

Mrs. Hard. Yours, my dear, can admit of none. That natural blush is beyond a thousand ornaments. Besides, child, jewels are quite out at present. Don't you see half the ladies of our acquaintance, my Lady Kill-daylight, and Mrs. Crump, and the rest of them, carry their jewels to town, and bring nothing but paste and marcasites back.

Miss Nev But who knows, madam, but somebody that shall be nameless would like me best with all my little finery about me?

Mrs. Hard. Consult your glass, my dear, and then see if, with such a pair of eyes, you want any better sparklers. What do you think, Tony, my dear? does your cousin Con. want any jewels in your eyes to set off her beauty?

Tony. That's as thereafter may be.

Miss Nev. My dear aunt, if you knew how it would oblige me.

Mrs. Hard. A parcel of old-fashioned rose and table-cut things. They would make you look like the court of King Solomon at a puppet-show. Besides, I believe, I can't readily come at them. They may be missing, for aught I know to the contrary.

Tony. (*Apart to* MRS. HARDCASTLE.) Then why don't you tell her so at once, as she's so longing for them? Tell her they're lost. It's the only way to quiet her. Say they're lost, and call me to bear witness.

Mrs. Hard. (*Apart to* TONY.) You know, my dear, I'm only keeping them for you. So if I say they're gone, you'll bear me witness, will you? He! he! he!

Tony. Never fear me. Ecod! I'll say I saw them taken out with my own eyes.

Miss Nev. I desire them but for a day, madam. Just to be permitted to show them as relics, and then they may be locked up again.

Mrs. Hard. To be plain with you, my dear Constance, if I could find them you should have them. They're missing, I assure you. Lost, for aught I know; but we must have patience wherever they are.

Miss Nev. I'll not believe it! this is but a shallow pretence to deny me. I know they are too valuable to be so slightly kept, and as you are to answer for the loss—

Mrs. Hard. Don't be alarmed, Constance. If they be lost, I must restore an equivalent. But my son knows they are missing, and not to be found.

Tony. That I can bear witness to. They are missing, and not to be found; I'll take my oath on't.

Mrs. Hard. You must learn resignation, my dear; for though we lose our fortune, yet we should not lose our patience. See me, how calm I am.

Miss Nev. Ay, people are generally calm at the misfortunes of others.

Mrs. Hard. Now I wonder a girl of your good sense should waste a thought upon such trumpery. We shall soon find them; and in the mean time you shall make use of my garnets till your jewels be found.

Miss Nev. I detest garnets.

Mrs. Hard. The most becoming things in the world to set off a clear complexion. You have often seen how well they look upon me. You *shall* have them. [*Exit.*

Miss Nev. I dislike them of all things. You shan't stir.—Was ever anything so provoking, to mislay my own jewels, and force me to wear her trumpery?

Tony. Don't be a fool. If she gives you the garnets, take what you can get. The jewels are your own already. I have stolen them out of her bureau, and she does not know it. Fly to your spark, he'll tell you more of the matter. Leave me to manage her.

Miss Nev. My dear cousin!

Tony. Vanish. She's here, and has missed them already. [*Exit* MISS NEVILLE.] Zounds! how she fidgets and spits about like a Catherine wheel.

Enter MRS. HARDCASTLE.

Mrs. Hard. Confusion! thieves! robbers! we are cheated, plundered, broke open, undone.

Tony. What's the matter, what's the matter, mamma? I hope nothing has happened to any of the good family!

Mrs. Hard. We are robbed. My bureau has been broken open, the jewels taken out, and I'm undone.

Tony. Oh! is that all? Ha! ha! ha! By the laws, I never saw it acted better in my life. Ecod, I thought you was ruined in earnest, ha! ha! ha!

Mrs. Hard. Why, boy, I *am* ruined in earnest. My bureau has been broken open, and all taken away.

Tony. Stick to that: ha! ha! ha! stick to that. I'll bear witness, you know; call me to bear witness.

Mrs. Hard. I tell you, Tony, by all that's precious, the jewels are gone, and I shall be ruined for ever.

Tony. Sure I know they are gone, and I'm to say so.

Mrs. Hard. My dearest Tony, but hear me. They're gone, I say.

Tony. By the laws, mamma, you make me for to laugh, ha! ha! I know who took them well enough, ha! ha! ha!

Mrs. Hard. Was there ever such a blockhead, that can't tell the difference between jest and earnest? I tell you I'm not in jest, booby.

Tony. That's right, that's right; you must be in a bitter passion, and then nobody will suspect either of us. I'll bear witness that they are gone.

Mrs. Hard. Was there ever such a cross-grained brute, that won't hear me? Can you bear witness that you're no better than a fool? Was ever poor woman so beset with fools on one hand, and thieves on the other?

Tony. I can bear witness to that.

Mrs. Hard. Bear witness again, you blockhead you, and I'll turn you out of the room directly. My poor niece, what will become of her? Do you laugh, you unfeeling brute, as if you enjoyed my distress?

Tony. I can bear witness to that.

Mrs. Hard. Do you insult me, monster? I'll teach you to vex your mother, I will.

Tony. I can bear witness to that.

[*He runs off, she follows him.*

Enter MISS HARDCASTLE *and* Maid.

Miss Hard. What an unaccountable creature is that brother of mine, to send them to the house as an inn! ha! ha! I don't wonder at his impudence.

Maid. But what is more, madam, the young gentleman, as you passed by in your present dress, asked me if you were the bar-maid. He mistook you for the bar-maid, madam.

Miss Hard. Did he? Then as I live, I'm resolved to keep up the delusion. Tell me, Pimple, how do you like my present dress? Don't you think I look something like Cherry in the Beaux Stratagem?

Maid. It's the dress, madam, that every lady wears in the country, but when she visits or receives company.

Miss Hard. And are you sure he does not remember my face or person?

Maid. Certain of it.

Miss Hard. I vow, I thought so; for, though we spoke for some time together, yet his fears were such, that he never once looked up during the interview. Indeed, if he had, my bonnet would have kept him from seeing me.

Maid. But what do you hope from keeping him in his mistake?

Miss Hard. In the first place I shall be seen, and that is no small advantage to a girl who brings her face to market. Then I shall perhaps make an acquaintance, and that's no small victory gained over one who never addresses any but the wildest of her sex. But my chief aim is, to take my gentleman off his guard, and, like an invisible champion of romance, examine the giant's force before I offer to combat.

Maid. But are you sure you can act your part, and disguise your voice so that he may mistake that, as he has already mistaken your person?

Miss Hard. Never fear me. I think I have got the true bar cant—Did your honour call?—Attend the Lion there—Pipes and tobacco for the Angel.—The Lamb has been outrageous this half-hour.

Maid. It will do, madam. But he's here. [*Exit* Maid.

Enter MARLOW.

Mar. What a bawling in every part of the house! I have scarce a moment's repose. If I go to the best room, there I find my host and his story: if I fly to the gallery, there we have my hostess with her curtsey down to the ground. I have at last got a moment to myself, and now for recollection. [*Walks and muses.*

Miss Hard. Did you call, sir? Did your honour call?

Mar. (*Musing.*) As for Miss Hardcastle, she's too grave and sentimental for me.

Miss Hard. Did your honour call? (*She still places herself before him, he turning away.*)

Mar. No, child. (*Musing.*) Besides, from the glimpse I had of her, I think she squints.

Miss Hard. I'm sure, sir, I heard the bell ring.

Mar. No, no. (*Musing.*) I have pleased my father, however, by coming down, and I'll to-morrow please myself by returning.

[*Taking out his tablets, and perusing.*

Miss Hard. Perhaps the other gentleman called, sir?

Mar. I tell you, no.

Miss Hard. I should be glad to know, sir. We have such a parcel of servants!

Mar. No, no, I tell you. (*Looks full in her face.*) Yes, child, I think I did call. I wanted—I wanted—I vow, child, you are vastly handsome.

Miss Hard. O la, sir, you'll make one ashamed.

Mar. Never saw a more sprightly malicious eye. Yes, yes, my dear, I did call. Have you got any of your—a—what d'ye call it in the house?

Miss Hard. No, sir, we have been out of that these ten days.

Mar. One may call in this house, I find, to very little purpose. Suppose I should call for a taste, just by way of a trial, of the nectar of your lips; perhaps I might be disappointed in that too.

Miss Hard. Nectar! nectar! That's a liquor there's no call for in these parts. French, I suppose. We sell no French wines here, sir.

Mar. Of true English growth, I assure you.

Miss Hard. Then it's odd I should not know it. We brew all sorts of wines in this house, and I have lived here these eighteen years.

Mar. Eighteen years! Why, one would think, child, you kept the bar before you were born. How old are you?

Miss Hard. O! sir, I must not tell my age. They say women and music should never be dated.

Mar. To guess at this distance, you can't be much above forty (*approaching*). Yet, nearer, I don't think so much (*approaching*). By coming close to some women they look younger still; but when we come very close indeed—(*attempting to kiss her*).

Miss Hard. Pray, sir, keep your distance. One would think you wanted to know one's age, as they do horses, by mark of mouth.

Mar. I protest, child, you use me extremely ill. If you keep me at this distance, how is it possible you and I can ever be acquainted?

Miss Hard. And who wants to be acquainted with you? I want no such acquaintance, not I. I'm sure you did not treat Miss Hardcastle, that was here awhile ago, in this obstropalous manner. I'll warrant me, before her you looked dashed, and kept bowing to the ground, and talked, for all the world, as if you was before a justice of peace.

Mar. (*Aside.*) Egad, she has hit it, sure enough! (*To her.*) In awe of her, child? Ha! ha! ha! A mere awkward squinting thing; no, no. I find you don't know me. I laughed and rallied her a little; but I was unwilling to be too severe. No, I could not be too severe, curse me!

Miss Hard. O! then, sir, you are a favourite, I find, among the ladies?

Mar. Yes, my dear, a great favourite. And yet hang me, I don't see what they find in me to follow. At the Ladies' Club in town I'm called their agreeable Rattle. Rattle, child, is not my real name, but one I'm known by. My name is Solomons; Mr. Solomons, my dear, at your service. (*Offering to salute her.*)

Miss Hard. Hold, sir; you are introducing me to your club, not to yourself. And you're so great a favourite there, you say?

Mar. Yes, my dear. There's Mrs. Mantrap, Lady Betty Blackleg, the Countess of Sligo, Mrs. Langhorns, old Miss Biddy Buckskin, and your humble servant, keep up the spirit of the place.

Miss Hard. Then it's a very merry place, I suppose?

Mar. Yes, as merry as cards, supper, wine, and old women can make us.

Miss Hard. And their agreeable Rattle, ha! ha! ha!

Mar. (*Aside.*) Egad! I don't quite like this chit. She looks knowing, methinks. You laugh, child?

Miss Hard. I can't but laugh, to think what time they all have for minding their work or their family.

Mar. (*Aside.*) All's well; she don't laugh at me. (*To her.*) Do you ever work, child?

Miss Hard. Ay, sure. There's not a screen or quilt in the whole house but what can bear witness to that.

Mar. Odso! then you must show me your embroidery. I embroider and draw patterns myself a little. If you want a judge of your work, you must apply to me. (*Seizing her hand.*)

Miss Hard. Ay, but the colours do not look well by candlelight. You shall see all in the morning. (*Struggling.*)

Mar. And why not now, my angel? Such beauty fires beyond the power of resistance.—Pshaw! the father here! My old luck: I never nicked seven that I did not throw ames ace three times following. [*Exit* Marlow.

Enter HARDCASTLE, *who stands in surprise.*

Hard. So, madam. So, I find *this* is your *modest* lover. This is your humble admirer, that kept his eyes fixed on the ground, and only adored at humble distance. Kate, Kate, art thou not ashamed to deceive your father so?

Miss Hard. Never trust me, dear papa, but he's still the modest man I first took him for; you'll be convinced of it as well as I.

Hard. By the hand of my body, I

believe his impudence is infectious! Didn't I see him seize your hand? Didn't I see him haul you about like a milkmaid? And now you talk of his respect and his modesty, forsooth!

Miss Hard. But if I shortly convince you of his modesty, that he has only the faults that will pass off with time, and the virtues that will improve with age, I hope you'll forgive him.

Hard. The girl would actually make one run mad! I tell you, I'll not be convinced. I am convinced. He has scarce been three hours in the house, and he has already encroached on all my prerogatives. You may like his impudence, and call it modesty; but my son-in-law, madam, must have very different qualifications.

Miss Hard. Sir, I ask but this night to convince you.

Hard. You shall not have half the time, for I have thoughts of turning him out this very hour.

Miss Hard. Give me that hour then, and I hope to satisfy you.

Hard. Well, an hour let it be then. But I'll have no trifling with your father. All fair and open, do you mind me.

Miss Hard. I hope, sir, you have ever found that I considered your commands as my pride; for your kindness is such, that my duty as yet has been inclination.

[*Exeunt.*

ACT THE FOURTH.

Enter HASTINGS *and* MISS NEVILLE.

Hast. You surprise me; Sir Charles Marlow expected here this night! Where have you had your information?

Miss Nev. You may depend upon it. I just saw his letter to Mr. Hardcastle, in which he tells him he intends setting out a few hours after his son.

Hast. Then, my Constance, all must be completed before he arrives. He knows me; and should he find me here, would discover my name, and perhaps my designs, to the rest of the family.

Miss Nev. The jewels, I hope, are safe?

Hast. Yes, yes, I have sent them to Marlow, who keeps the keys of our baggage. In the mean time, I'll go to prepare matters for our elopement. I have had the 'squire's promise of a fresh pair of horses; and if I should not see him again, will write him further directions. [*Exit.*

Miss Nev. Well! success attend you. In the mean time I'll go and amuse my aunt with the old pretence of a violent passion for my cousin. [*Exit.*

Enter MARLOW, *followed by a* Servant.

Mar. I wonder what Hastings could mean by sending me so valuable a thing as a casket to keep for him, when he knows the only place I have is the seat of a post-coach at an inn-door. Have you deposited the casket with the landlady, as I ordered you? Have you put it into her own hands?

Ser. Yes, your honour.

Mar. She said she'd keep it safe, did she?

Ser. Yes, she said she'd keep it safe enough; she asked me how I came by it; and she said she had a great mind to make me give an account of myself.

[*Exit* Servant.

Mar. Ha! ha! ha! They're safe, however. What an unaccountable set of beings have we got amongst! This little bar-maid though runs in my head most strangely, and drives out the absurdities of all the rest of the family. She's mine, she must be mine, or I'm greatly mistaken.

Enter HASTINGS.

Hast. Bless me! I quite forgot to tell her that I intended to prepare at the bottom of the garden. Marlow here, and in spirits too!

Mar. Give me joy, George. Crown me, shadow me with laurels! Well, George, after all, we modest fellows don't want for success among the women.

Hast. Some women, you mean. But what success has your honour's modesty been crowned with now, that it grows so insolent upon us?

Mar. Didn't you see the tempting, brisk, lovely little thing, that runs about the house with a bunch of keys to its girdle?

Hast. Well, and what then?

Mar. She's mine, you rogue you. Such fire, such motion, such eyes, such lips; but, egad! she would not let me kiss them though.

Hast. But are you so sure, so very sure of her?

Mar. Why, man, she talked of showing me her work above stairs, and I am to improve the pattern.

Hast. But how can you, Charles, go about to rob a woman of her honour?

Mar. Pshaw! phsaw! We all know the honour of the bar-maid of an inn. I don't intend to rob her, take my word for it; there's nothing in this house I shan't honestly pay for.

Hast. I believe the girl has virtue.

Mar. And if she has, I should be the last man in the world that would attempt to corrupt it.

Hast. You have taken care, I hope, of the casket I sent you to lock up? Is it in safety?

Mar. Yes, yes. It's safe enough. I have taken care of it. But how could you think the seat of a post-coach at an inn-door a place of safety? Ah! numskull! I have taken better precautions for you than you did for yourself——I have——

Hast. What?

Mar. I have sent it to the landlady to keep for you.

Hast. To the landlady!

Mar. The landlady.

Hast. You did?

Mar. I did. She's to be answerable for its forthcoming, you know.

Hast. Yes, she'll bring it forth with a witness.

Mar. Wasn't I right? I believe you'll allow that I acted prudently upon this occasion.

Hast. (*Aside.*) He must not see my uneasiness.

Mar. You seem a little disconcerted though, methinks. Sure nothing has happened?

Hast. No, nothing. Never was in better spirits in all my life. And so you left it with the landlady, who, no doubt, very readily undertook the charge.

Mar. Rather too readily. For she not only kept the casket, but, through her great precaution, was going to keep the messenger too. Ha! ha! ha!

Hast. He! he! he! They're safe, however.

Mar. As a guinea in a miser's purse.

Hast. (*Aside.*) So now all hopes of fortune are at an end, and we must set off without it. (*To him.*) Well, Charles, I'll leave you to your meditations on the pretty bar-maid, and, he! he! he! may you be as successful for yourself, as you have been for me! [*Exit.*

Mar. Thank ye, George: I ask no more. Ha! ha! ha!

Enter HARDCASTLE.

Hard. I no longer know my own house. It's turned all topsy-turvy. His servants have got drunk already. I'll bear it no longer; and yet, from my respect for his father, I'll be calm. (*To him.*) Mr. Marlow, your servant. I'm your very humble servant. (*Bowing low.*)

Mar. Sir, your humble servant. (*Aside.*) What's to be the wonder now?

Hard. I believe, sir, you must be sensible, sir, that no man alive ought to be more welcome than your father's son, sir. I hope you think so?

Mar. I do from my soul, sir. I don't want much entreaty. I generally make my father's son welcome wherever he goes.

Hard. I believe you do, from my soul, sir. But though I say nothing to your own conduct, that of your servants is insufferable. Their manner of drinking is setting a very bad example in this house, I assure you.

Mar. I protest, my very good sir, that is no fault of mine. If they don't drink as they ought, they are to blame. I ordered them not to spare the cellar. I did, I assure you. (*To the side scene.*) Here, let one of my servants come up. (*To him.*) My positive directions were, that as I did not drink myself, they should make up for my deficiencies below.

Hard. Then they had your orders for what they do? I'm satisfied!

Mar. They had, I assure you. You shall hear from one of themselves.

Enter Servant, *drunk.*

Mar. You, Jeremy! Come forward, sirrah! What were my orders? Were you not told to drink freely, and call for what you thought fit, for the good of the house?

Hard. (*Aside.*) I begin to lose my patience.

Jer. Please your honour, liberty and Fleet-street for ever! Though I'm but a servant, I'm as good as another man. I'll drink for no man before supper, sir, damme! Good liquor will sit upon a good supper, but a good supper will not sit upon ——hiccup——on my conscience, sir.

Mar. You see, my old friend, the fellow is as drunk as he can possibly be. I don't know what you'd have more, unless you'd have the poor devil soused in a beer-barrel.

Hard. Zounds! he'll drive me distracted, if I contain myself any longer. Mr. Marlow—Sir; I have submitted to your insolence for more than four hours, and I see no likelihood of its coming to an end. I'm now resolved to be master here, sir; and I desire that you and your drunken pack may leave my house directly.

Mar. Leave your house!——Sure you jest, my good friend! What? when I'm doing what I can to please you.

Hard. I tell you, sir, you don't please me; so I desire you'll leave my house.

Mar. Sure you cannot be serious? At this time o' night, and such a night? You only mean to banter me.

Hard. I tell you, sir, I'm serious! and now that my passions are roused, I say this house is mine, sir; this house is mine, and I command you to leave it directly.

Mar. Ha! ha! ha! A puddle in a storm. I shan't stir a step, I assure you. (*In a serious tone.*) This your house, fellow! It's my house. This is my house. Mine, while I choose to stay. What right have you to bid me leave this house, sir? I never met with such impudence, curse me; never in my whole life before.

Hard. Nor I, confound me if ever I did. To come to my house, to call for what he likes, to turn me out of my own chair, to insult the family, to order his servants to get drunk, and then to tell me, "This house is mine, sir." By all that's impudent, it makes me laugh. Ha! ha! ha! Pray, sir (*bantering*), as you take the house, what think you of taking the rest of the furniture? There's a pair of silver candlesticks, and there's a fire-screen, and here's a pair of brazen-nozed bellows; perhaps you may take a fancy to them?

Mar. Bring me your bill, sir; bring me your bill, and let's make no more words about it.

Hard. There are a set of prints, too. What think you of the Rake's Progress, for your own apartment?

Mar. Bring me your bill, I say; and I'll leave you and your infernal house directly.

Hard. Then there's a mahogany table that you may see your own face in.

Mar. My bill, I say.

Hard. I had forgot the great chair for your own particular slumbers, after a hearty meal.

Mar. Zounds! bring me my bill, I say, and let's hear no more on't.

Hard. Young man, young man, from your father's letter to me, I was taught to expect a well-bred modest man as a visitor here, but now I find him no better than a coxcomb and a bully; but he will be down here presently, and shall hear more of it. [*Exit.*

Mar. How's this? Sure I have not mistaken the house. Everything looks like an inn. The servants cry, coming; the attendance is awkward; the bar-maid, too, to attend us. But she's here, and will further inform me. Whither so fast, child? A word with you.

Enter MISS HARDCASTLE.

Miss Hard. Let it be short, then. I'm in a hurry. (*Aside.*) I believe he begins to find out his mistake. But it's too soon quite to undeceive him.

Mar. Pray, child, answer me one question. What are you, and what may your business in this house be?

Miss Hard. A relation of the family, sir.

Mar. What, a poor relation.

Miss Hard. Yes, sir. A poor relation, appointed to keep the keys, and to see that the guests want nothing in my power to give them.

Mar. That is, you act as the bar-maid of this inn.

Miss Hard. Inn! O law——what brought that in your head? One of the best families in the country keep an inn—Ha! ha! ha! old Mr. Hardcastle's house an inn!

Mar. Mr. Hardcastle's house! Is this Mr. Hardcastle's house, child?

Miss Hard. Ay, sure! Whose else should it be?

Mar. So then, all's out, and I have been damnably imposed on. O, confound my stupid head, I shall be laughed at over the whole town. I shall be stuck up in caricatura in all the print-shops. The *Dullissimo Maccaroni.* To mistake this house of all others for an inn, and my father's old friend for an innkeeper! What a swaggering puppy must he take me for! What a silly puppy do I find myself! There again, may I be hanged, my dear, but I mistook you for the bar-maid.

Miss Hard. Dear me! dear me! I'm sure there's nothing in my *behaviour* to put me on a level with one of that stamp.

Mar. Nothing, my dear, nothing. But I was in for a list of blunders, and could not help making you a subscriber. My stupidity saw everything the wrong way. I mistook your assiduity for assurance, and your simplicity for allurement. But it's over. This house I no more show *my* face in.

Miss Hard. I hope, sir, I have done nothing to disoblige you. I'm sure I should be sorry to affront any gentleman who has been so polite, and said so many civil things to me. I'm sure I should be sorry (*pretending to cry*) if he left the family upon my account. I'm sure I should be sorry if people said anything amiss, since I have no fortune but my character.

Mar. (*Aside.*) By Heaven! she weeps. This is the first mark of tenderness I ever had from a modest woman, and it touches me. (*To her.*) Excuse me, my lovely girl; you are the only part of the family I leave with reluctance. But to be plain with you, the difference of our birth, fortune, and education, makes an honourable connexion impossible; and I can never harbour a thought of seducing simplicity that trusted in my honour, of bringing ruin upon one whose only fault was being too lovely.

Miss Hard. (*Aside.*) Generous man! I now begin to admire him. (*To him.*) But I am sure my family is as good as Miss Hardcastle's; and though I'm poor, that's no great misfortune to a contented mind; and, until this moment, I never thought that it was bad to want a fortune.

Mar. And why now, my pretty simplicity?

Miss Hard. Because it puts me at a distance from one that, if I had a thousand pounds, I would give it all to.

Mar. (*Aside.*) This simplicity bewitches me, so that if I stay, I'm undone. I must make one bold effort, and leave her. (*To her.*) Your partiality in my favour, my dear, touches me most sensibly: and were I to live for myself alone, I could easily fix my choice. But I owe too much to the opinion of the world, too much to the authority of a father; so that—I can scarcely speak it—it affects me. Farewell. [*Exit.*

Miss Hard. I never knew half his merit till now. He shall not go, if I have power or art to detain him. I'll still preserve the character in which I *stooped to conquer;* but will undeceive my papa, who perhaps may laugh him out of his resolution. [*Exit.*

Enter TONY *and* MISS NEVILLE.

Tony. Ay, you may steal for yourselves the next time. I have done my duty. She has got the jewels again, that's a sure thing; but she believes it was all a mistake of the servants.

Miss Nev. But, my dear cousin, sure you won't forsake us in this distress? If she in the least suspects that I am going off, I shall certainly be locked up, or sent to my aunt Pedigree's, which is ten times worse.

Tony. To be sure, aunts of all kinds are damned bad things. But what can I do? I have got you a pair of horses that will fly like Whistle-jacket; and I'm sure you can't say but I have courted you nicely before her face. Here she comes, we must court a bit or two more, for fear she should suspect us.

[*They retire, and seem to fondle.*

Enter MRS. HARDCASTLE.

Mrs. Hard. Well, I was greatly fluttered, to be sure. But my son tells me it was all a mistake of the servants. I shan't be easy, however, till they are fairly married, and then let her keep her own fortune. But what do I see? fondling together, as

I'm alive. I never saw Tony so sprightly before. Ah! have I caught you, my pretty doves? What, billing, exchanging stolen glances and broken murmurs? Ah!

Tony. As for murmurs, mother, we grumble a little now and then, to be sure. But there's no love lost between us.

Mrs. Hard. A mere sprinkling, Tony, upon the flame, only to make it burn brighter.

Miss Nev. Cousin Tony promises to give us more of his company at home. Indeed, he shan't leave us any more. It won't leave us, cousin Tony, will it?

Tony. O! it's a pretty creature. No, I'd sooner leave my horse in a pound, than leave you when you smile upon one so. Your laugh makes you so becoming.

Miss Nev. Agreeable cousin! Who can help admiring that natural humour, that pleasant, broad, red, thoughtless (*patting his cheek*)—ah! it's a bold face.

Mrs. Hard. Pretty innocence!

Tony. I'm sure I always loved cousin Con.'s hazle eyes, and her pretty long fingers, that she twists this way and that over the haspicholls, like a parcel of bobbins.

Mrs. Hard. Ah! he would charm the bird from the tree. I was never so happy before. My boy takes after his father, poor Mr. Lumpkin, exactly. The jewels, my dear Con., shall be yours incontinently. You shall have them. Isn't he a sweet boy, my dear? You shall be married tomorrow, and we'll put off the rest of his education, like Dr. Drowsy's sermons, to a fitter opportunity.

Enter DIGGORY.

Dig. Where's the 'squire? I have got a letter for your worship.

Tony. Give it to my mamma. She reads all my letters first.

Dig. I had orders to deliver it into your own hands.

Tony. Who does it come from?

Dig. Your worship mun ask that o' the letter itself.

Tony. I could wish to know though (*turning the letter, and gazing on it*).

Miss Nev. (*Aside.*) Undone! undone! A letter to him from Hastings. I know the hand. If my aunt sees it, we are ruined for ever. I'll keep her employed a little if I can. (*To* MRS. HARDCASTLE.) But I have not told you, madam, of my cousin's smart answer just now to Mr. Marlow. We so laughed.—You must know, madam.—This way a little, for he must not hear us.

[*They confer.*

Tony. (*Still gazing.*) A damned cramp piece of penmanship, as ever I saw in my life. I can read your print hand very well. But here are such handles, and shanks, and dashes, that one can scarce tell the head from the tail.—"To Anthony Lumpkin, Esquire." It's very odd, I can read the outside of my letters, where my own name is, well enough; but when I come to open it, it's all——buzz. That's hard, very hard; for the inside of the letter is always the cream of the correspondence.

Mrs. Hard. Ha! ha! ha! Very well, very well. And so my son was too hard for the philosopher.

Miss Nev. Yes, madam; but you must hear the rest, madam. A little more this way, or he may hear us. You'll hear how he puzzled him again.

Mrs. Hard. He seems strangely puzzled now himself, methinks.

Tony. (*Still gazing.*) A damned up and down hand, as if it was disguised in liquor.—(*Reading.*) Dear sir,—ay, that's that. Then there's an M, and a T, and an S, but whether the next be an izzard, or an R, confound me, I cannot tell.

Mrs. Hard. What's that, my dear? Can I give you any assistance?

Miss Nev. Pray, aunt, let me read it. Nobody reads a cramp hand better than I. (*Twitching the letter from him.*) Do you know who it is from?

Tony. Can't tell, except from Dick Ginger, the feeder.

Miss Nev. Ay, so it is. (*Pretending to read.*) Dear 'Squire, hoping that you're in health, as I am at this present. The gentlemen of the Shake-bag club has cut the gentlemen of Goose-green quite out of feather. The odds—um—odd battle—um—long fighting—um—here, here, it's all about cocks and fighting; it's of no consequence; here, put it up, put it up. (*Thrusting the crumpled letter upon him.*)

Tony. But I tell you, miss, it's of all the consequence in the world. I would not lose the rest of it for a guinea. Here, mother, do you make it out. Of no consequence! (*Giving* MRS. HARDCASTLE *the letter.*)

Mrs. Hard. How's this?—(*Reads.*) "Dear 'Squire, I'm now waiting for Miss Neville, with a post-chaise and pair, at the bottom of the garden, but I find my horses yet unable to perform the journey. I expect you'll assist us with a pair of fresh horses, as you promised. Dispatch is necessary, as the *hag* (ay, the hag), your mother, will otherwise suspect us! Yours, Hastings." Grant me patience. I shall run distracted! My rage chokes me.

Miss Nev. I hope, madam, you'll suspend your resentment for a few moments, and not impute to me any impertinence, or sinister design, that belongs to another.

Mrs. Hard. (*Curtseying very low.*) Fine spoken, madam, you are most miraculously polite and engaging, and quite the very pink of courtesy and circumspection, madam. (*Changing her tone.*) And you, you great ill-fashioned oaf, with scarce sense enough to keep your mouth shut: were you, too, joined against me? But I'll defeat all your plots in a moment. As for you, madam, since you have got a pair of fresh horses ready, it would be cruel to disappoint them. So, if you please, instead of running away with your spark, prepare, this very moment, to run off with *me*. Your old aunt Pedigree will keep you secure, I'll warrant me. You too, sir, may mount your horse, and guard us upon the way. Here, Thomas, Roger, Diggory! I'll show you, that I wish you better than you do yourselves. [*Exit.*

Miss Nev. So now I'm completely ruined.

Tony. Ay, that's a sure thing.

Miss Nev. What better could be expected from being connected with such a stupid fool,—and after all the nods and signs I made him?

Tony. By the laws, miss, it was your own cleverness, and not my stupidity, that did your business. You were so nice and so busy with your Shake-bags and Goose-greens, that I thought you could never be making believe.

Enter HASTINGS.

Hast. So, sir, I find by my servant, that you have shown my letter, and betrayed us. Was this well done, young gentleman?

Tony. Here's another. Ask miss there, who betrayed you. Ecod, it was her doing, not mine.

Enter MARLOW.

Mar. So I have been finely used here among you. Rendered contemptible, driven into ill manners, despised, insulted, laughed at.

Tony. Here's another. We shall have old Bedlam broke loose presently.

Miss Nev. And there, sir, is the gentleman to whom we all owe every obligation.

Mar. What can I say to him, a mere boy, an idiot, whose ignorance and age are a protection?

Hast. A poor contemptible booby, that would but disgrace correction.

Miss Nev. Yet with cunning and malice enough to make himself merry with all our embarrassments.

Hast. An insensible cub.

Mar. Replete with tricks and mischief.

Tony. Baw! damme, but I'll fight you both, one after the other——with baskets.

Mar. As for him, he's below resentment. But your conduct, Mr. Hastings, requires an explanation. You knew of my mistakes, yet would not undeceive me.

Hast. Tortured as I am with my own disappointments, is this a time for explanations? It is not friendly, Mr. Marlow.

Mar. But, sir——

Miss Nev. Mr. Marlow, we never kept on your mistake till it was too late to undeceive you.

Enter Servant.

Ser. My mistress desires you'll get ready immediately, madam. The horses are putting to. Your hat and things are in the next room. We are to go thirty miles before morning. [*Exit* Servant.

Miss Nev. Well, well: I'll come presently.

Mar. (*To* HASTINGS.) Was it well done, sir, to assist in rendering me ridiculous? To hang me out for the scorn of all my acquaintance? Depend upon it, sir, I shall expect an explanation.

Hast. Was it well done, sir, if you're upon that subject, to deliver what I entrusted to yourself, to the care of another sir?

Miss Nev. Mr. Hastings! Mr. Marlow! Why will you increase my distress by this groundless dispute? I implore, I entreat you——

Enter Servant.

Ser. Your cloak, madam. My mistress is impatient. [*Exit* Servant.

Miss Nev. I come. Pray be pacified. If I leave you thus, I shall die with apprehension.

Enter Servant.

Ser. Your fan, muff. and gloves, madam. The horses are waiting.

Miss Nev. O, Mr. Marlow! if you knew what a scene of constraint and ill-nature lies before me, I'm sure it would convert your resentment into pity.

Mar. I'm so distracted with a variety of passions, that I don't know what I do. Forgive me, madam. George, forgive me. You know my hasty temper, and should not exasperate it.

Hast. The torture of my situation is my only excuse.

Miss Nev. Well, my dear Hastings, if you have that esteem for me that I think, that I am sure you have, your constancy for three years will but increase the happiness of our future connexion. If——

Mrs. Hard. (*Within.*) Miss Neville. Constance, why Constance, I say.

Miss Nev. I'm coming. Well, constancy, remember, constancy is the word. [*Exit.*

Hast. My heart! how can I support this? To be so near happiness, and such happiness!

Mar. (*To* TONY.) You see now, young gentleman, the effects of your folly. What might be amusement to you, is here disappointment, and even distress.

Tony. (*From a reverie.*) Ecod, I have hit it. It's here. Your hands. Yours and yours, my poor Sulky!—My boots there, ho!—Meet me two hours hence at the bottom of the garden; and if you don't find Tony Lumpkin a more good-natured fellow than you thought for, I'll give you leave to take my best horse, and Bet Bouncer into the bargain. Come along. My boots, ho! [*Exeunt.*

ACT THE FIFTH.

(SCENE *continued.*)

Enter HASTINGS *and* Servant.

Hast. You saw the old lady and Miss Neville drive off, you say?

Ser. Yes, your honour. They went off in a post-coach, and the young 'squire went on horseback. They're thirty miles off by this time.

Hast. Then all my hopes are over.

Ser. Yes, sir. Old Sir Charles has arrived. He and the old gentleman of the house have been laughing at Mr. Marlow's mistake this half hour. They are coming this way.

Hast. Then I must not be seen. So now to my fruitless appointment at the bottom of the garden. This is about the time. [*Exit.*

Enter SIR CHARLES *and* HARDCASTLE.

Hard. Ha! ha! ha! The peremptory tone in which he sent forth his sublime commands!

Sir Cha. And the reserve with which I suppose he treated all your advances.

Hard. And yet he might have seen something in me above a common innkeeper, too.

Sir Cha. Yes, Dick, but he mistook you for an uncommon innkeeper, ha! ha! ha!

Hard. Well, I'm in too good spirits to think of anything but joy. Yes, my dear friend, this union of our families will make our personal friendships hereditary; and though my daughter's fortune is but small—

Sir Cha. Why, Dick, will you talk of fortune to *me?* My son is possessed of more than a competence already, and can want nothing but a good and virtuous girl to share his happiness and increase it. If they like each other, as you say they do—

Hard. *If*, man! I tell you they *do* like each other. My daughter as good as told me so.

Sir Cha. But girls are apt to flatter themselves, you know.

Hard. I saw him grasp her hand in the warmest manner myself; and here he comes to put you out of your *ifs*, I warrant him.

Enter MARLOW.

Mar. I come, sir, once more, to ask pardon for my strange conduct. I can scarce reflect on my insolence without confusion.

Hard. Tut, boy, a trifle! You take it too gravely. An hour or two's laughing with my daughter will set all to rights again. She'll never like you the worse for it.

Mar. Sir, I shall be always proud of her approbation.

Hard. Approbation is but a cold word, Mr. Marlow; if I am not deceived, you have something more than approbation thereabouts. You take me?

Mar. Really, sir, I have not that happiness.

Hard. Come, boy, I'm an old fellow, and know what's what as well as you that are younger. I know what has passed between you; but mum.

Mar. Sure, sir, nothing has passed between us but the most profound respect on my side, and the most distant reserve on hers. You don't think, sir, that my impudence has been passed upon all the rest of the family.

Hard. Impudence! No, I don't say that—not quite impudence—though girls like to be played with, and rumpled a little too, sometimes. But she has told no tales, I assure you.

Mar. I never gave her the slightest cause.

Hard. Well, well, I like modesty in its place well enough. But this is over-acting, young gentleman. You may be open. Your father and I will like you all the better for it.

Mar. May I die, sir, if I ever——

Hard. I tell you, she don't dislike you; and as I'm sure you like her——

Mar. Dear sir—I protest, sir——

Hard. I see no reason why you should not be joined as fast as the parson can tie you.

Mar. But hear me, sir—

Hard. Your father approves the match, I admire it; every moment's delay will be doing mischief. So—

Mar. But why won't you hear me? By all that's just and true, I never gave Miss Hardcastle the slightest mark of my attachment, or even the most distant hint to suspect me of affection. We had but one interview, and that was formal, modest, and uninteresting.

Hard. (*Aside.*) This fellow's formal modest impudence is beyond bearing.

Sir Cha. And you never grasped her hand, or made any protestations?

Mar. As Heaven is my witness, I came down in obedience to your commands. I saw the lady without emotion, and parted without reluctance. I hope you'll exact no farther proofs of my duty, nor prevent me from leaving a house in which I suffer so many mortifications. [*Exit.*

Sir Cha. I'm astonished at the air of sincerity with which he parted.

Hard. And I'm astonished at the deliberate intrepidity of his assurance.

Sir Cha. I dare pledge my life and honour upon his truth.

Hard. Here comes my daughter, and I would stake my happiness upon her veracity.

Enter MISS HARDCASTLE.

Hard. Kate, come hither, child. Answer us sincerely and without reserve: has Mr. Marlow made you any professions of love and affection?

Miss Hard. The question is very abrupt, sir. But since you require unreserved sincerity, I think he has.

Hard. (*To* SIR CHARLES.) You see.

Sir Cha. And pray, madam, have you and my son had more than one interview?

Miss Hard. Yes, sir, several.

Hard. (*To* SIR CHARLES.) You see.

Sir Cha. But did he profess any attachment?

Miss Hard. A lasting one.

Sir Cha. Did he talk of love?

Miss Hard. Much, sir.

Sir Cha. Amazing! And all this formally?

Miss Hard. Formally.

Hard. Now, my friend, I hope you are satisfied.

Sir Cha. And how did he behave, madam?

Miss Hard. As most profest admirers do: said some civil things of my face, talked much of his want of merit, and the greatness of mine; mentioned his heart, gave a short tragedy speech, and ended with pretended rapture.

Sir Cha. Now I'm perfectly convinced, indeed. I know his conversation among women to be modest and submissive: this forward canting ranting manner by no means describes him; and, I am confident, he never sat for the picture.

Miss Hard. Then, what, sir, if I should convince you to your face of my sincerity? If you and my papa, in about half an hour, will place yourselves behind that screen, you shall hear him declare his passion to me in person.

Sir Cha. Agreed. And if I find him what you describe, all my happiness in him must have an end. [*Exit.*

Miss Hard. And if you don't find him what I describe—I fear my happiness must never have a beginning. [*Exeunt.*

SCENE *changes to the back of the Garden.*

Enter HASTINGS.

Hast. What an idiot am I, to wait here for a fellow who probably takes a delight in mortifying me. He never intended to be punctual, and I'll wait no longer. What do I see? It is he! and perhaps with news of my Constance.

Enter TONY, *booted and spattered.*

Hast. My honest 'squire! I now find you a man of your word. This looks like friendship.

Tony. Ay, I'm your friend, and the best friend you have in the world, if you knew but all. This riding by night, by the bye, is cursedly tiresome. It has shook me worse than the basket of a stage-coach.

Hast. But how? where did you leave your fellow-travellers? Are they in safety? Are they housed?

Tony. Five and twenty miles in two hours and a half is no such bad driving. The poor beasts have smoked for it: rabbit me, but I'd rather ride forty miles after a fox than ten with such varment.

Hast. Well, but where have you left the ladies? I die with impatience.

Tony. Left them! Why where should I leave them but where I found them?

Hast. This is a riddle.

Tony. Riddle me this then. What's that goes round the house, and round the house, and never touches the house?

Hast. I'm still astray.

Tony. Why, that's it, mon. I have led them astray. By jingo, there's not a pond or a slough within five miles of the place but they can tell the taste of.

Hast. Ha! ha! ha! I understand: you took them in a round, while they supposed themselves going forward, and so you have at last brought them home again.

Tony. You shall hear. I first took them down Feather-bed Lane, where we stuck fast in the mud. I then rattled them crack over the stones of Up-and-down Hill. I then introduced them to the gibbet on Heavy-tree Heath; and from that, with a circumbendibus, I fairly lodged them in the horse-pond at the bottom of the garden.

Hast. But no accident, I hope?

Tony. No, no. Only mother is confoundedly frightened. She thinks herself forty miles off. She's sick of the journey; and the cattle can scarce crawl. So if your own horses be ready, you may whip off with cousin, and I'll be bound that no soul here can budge a foot to follow you.

Hast. My dear friend, how can I be grateful?

Tony. Ay, now it's dear friend, noble 'squire. Just now, it was all idiot, cub, and run me through the guts. Damn *your* way of fighting, I say. After we take a knock in this part of the country, we kiss and be friends. But if you had run me through the guts, then I should be dead, and you might go kiss the hangman.

Hast. The rebuke is just. But I must hasten to relieve Miss Neville: if you keep the old lady employed, I promise to take care of the young one. [*Exit* Hastings.

Tony. Never fear me. Here she comes. Vanish. She's got from the pond, and draggled up to the waist like a mermaid.

Enter MRS. HARDCASTLE.

Mrs. Hard. Oh, Tony, I'm killed! Shook! Battered to death. I shall never survive it. That last jolt, that laid us against the quickset hedge, has done my business.

Tony. Alack, mamma, it was all your own fault. You would be for running away by night, without knowing one inch of the way.

Mrs. Hard. I wish we were at home again. I never met so many accidents in so short a journey. Drenched in the mud, overturned in a ditch, stuck fast in a slough, jolted to a jelly, and at last to lose our way. Whereabouts do you think we are, Tony?

Tony. By my guess we should come upon Crackskull common, about forty miles from home.

Mrs. Hard. O lud! O lud! The most notorious spot in all the country. We only want a robbery to make a complete night on't.

Tony. Don't be afraid, mamma, don't be afraid. Two of the five that kept here are hanged, and the other three may not find us. Don't be afraid.—Is that a man that's galloping behind us? No; it's only a tree.—Don't be afraid.

Mrs. Hard. The fright will certainly kill me.

Tony. Do you see anything like a black hat moving behind the thicket?

Mrs. Hard. Oh, death!

Tony. No; it's only a cow. Don't be afraid, mamma; don't be afraid.

Mrs. Hard. As I'm alive, Tony, I see a man coming towards us. Ah! I'm sure on't. If he perceives us, we are undone.

Tony. (*Aside.*) Father-in-law, by all that's unlucky, come to take one of his night walks. (*To her.*) Ah, it's a highwayman with pistols as long as my arm. A damned ill-looking fellow.

Mrs. Hard. Good Heaven defend us! He approaches.

Tony. Do you hide yourself in that thicket, and leave me to manage him. If there be any danger, I'll cough, and cry hem. When I cough, be sure to keep close. (MRS. HARDCASTLE *hides behind a tree in the back scene.*)

Enter HARDCASTLE.

Hard. I'm mistaken, or I heard voices of people in want of help. Oh, Tony! is that you? I did not expect you so soon back. Are your mother and her charge in safety?

Tony. Very safe, sir, at my aunt Pedigree's. Hem.

A A

Mrs. Hard. (*From behind.*) Ah, death! I find there's danger.

Hard. Forty miles in three hours; sure that's too much, my youngster.

Tony. Stout horses and willing minds make short journeys, as they say. Hem.

Mrs. Hard. (*From behind.*) Sure he'll do the dear boy no harm.

Hard. But I heard a voice here; I should be glad to know from whence it came.

Tony. It was I, sir, talking to myself, sir. I was saying that forty miles in four hours was very good going. Hem. As to be sure it was. Hem. I have got a sort of cold by being out in the air. We'll go in, if you please. Hem.

Hard. But if you talked to yourself you did not answer yourself. I'm certain I heard two voices, and am resolved (*raising his voice*) to find the other out.

Mrs. Hard. (*From behind.*) Oh! he's coming to find me out. Oh!

Tony. What need you go, sir, if I tell you? Hem. I'll lay down my life for the truth—hem—I'll tell you all, sir. [*Detaining him.*

Hard. I tell you I will not be detained. I insist on seeing. It's in vain to expect I'll believe you.

Mrs. Hard. (*Running forward from behind.*) O lud! he'll murder my poor boy, my darling! Here, good gentleman, whet your rage upon me. Take my money, my life, but spare that young gentleman; spare my child, if you have any mercy.

Hard. My wife, as I'm a Christian. From whence can she come? or what does she mean?

Mrs. Hard. (*Kneeling.*) Take compassion on us, good Mr. Highwayman. Take our money, our watches, all we have, but spare our lives. We will never bring you to justice; indeed we won't, good Mr. Highwayman.

Hard. I believe the woman's out of her senses. What, Dorothy, don't you know *me?*

Mrs. Hard. Mr. Hardcastle, as I'm alive! My fears blinded me. But who, my dear, could have expected to meet you here, in this frightful place, so far from home? What has brought you to follow us?

Hard. Sure, Dorothy, you have not lost your wits? So far from home, when you are within forty yards of your own door! (*To him.*) This is one of your old tricks, you graceless rogue, you. (*To her.*) Don't you know the gate, and the mulberry-tree; and don't you remember the horse-pond, my dear?

Mrs. Hard. Yes, I shall remember the horse-pond as long as I live; I have caught my death in it. (*To* TONY.) And is it to you, you graceless varlet, I owe all this? I'll teach you to abuse your mother, I will.

Tony. Ecod, mother, all the parish says you have spoiled me, and so you may take the fruits on't.

Mrs. Hard. I'll spoil you, I will.

[*Follows him off the stage. Exit.*

Hard. There's morality, however, in his reply. [*Exit.*

Enter HASTINGS *and* MISS NEVILLE.

Hast. My dear Constance, why will you deliberate thus? If we delay a moment, all is lost for ever. Pluck up a little resolution, and we shall soon be out of the reach of her malignity.

Miss Nev. I find it impossible. My spirits are so sunk with the agitations I have suffered, that I am unable to face any new danger. Two or three years' patience will at last crown us with happiness.

Hast. Such a tedious delay is worse than inconstancy. Let us fly, my charmer. Let us date our happiness from this very moment. Perish fortune! Love and content will increase what we possess beyond a monarch's revenue. Let me prevail!

Miss Nev. No, Mr. Hastings, no. Prudence once more comes to my relief, and I will obey its dictates. In the moment of passion fortune may be despised, but it ever produces a lasting repentance. I'm resolved to apply to Mr. Hardcastle's compassion and justice for redress.

Hast. But though he had the will, he has not the power to relieve you.

Miss Nev. But he has influence, and upon that I am resolved to rely.

Hast. I have no hopes. But since you persist, I must reluctantly obey you.

[*Exeunt.*

SCENE *changes.*

Enter SIR CHARLES *and* MISS HARDCASTLE.

Sir Cha. What a situation am I in! If what you say appears, I shall then find a guilty son. If what he says be true, I shall then lose one that, of all others, I most wished for a daughter.

Miss Hard. I am proud of your approbation, and to show I merit it, if you place yourselves as I directed, you shall hear his explicit declaration. But he comes.

Sir Cha. I'll to your father, and keep him to the appointment. [*Exit* Sir Charles.

Enter MARLOW.

Mar. Though prepared for setting out, I come once more to take leave; nor did I, till this moment, know the pain I feel in the separation.

Miss Hard. (*In her own natural manner.*) I believe these sufferings cannot be very great, sir, which you can so easily remove. A day or two longer, perhaps, might lessen your uneasiness, by showing the little value of what you now think proper to regret.

Mar. (*Aside.*) This girl every moment improves upon me. (*To her.*) It must not be, madam. I have already trifled too long with my heart. My very pride begins to submit to my passion. The disparity of education and fortune, the anger of a parent, and the contempt of my equals, begin to lose their weight; and nothing can restore me to myself but this painful effort of resolution.

Miss Hard. Then go, sir: I'll urge nothing more to detain you. Though my family be as good as hers you came down to visit, and my education, I hope, not inferior, what are these advantages without equal affluence? I must remain contented with the slight approbation of imputed merit; I must have only the mockery of your addresses, while all your serious aims are fixed on fortune.

Enter HARDCASTLE *and* SIR CHARLES *from behind.*

Sir Char. Here, behind this screen.

Hard. Ay, ay; make no noise. I'll engage my Kate covers him with confusion at last.

Mar. By heavens, madam! fortune was ever my smallest consideration. Your beauty at first caught my eye; for who could see that without emotion? But every moment that I converse with you steals in some new grace, heightens the picture, and gives it stronger expression. What at first seemed rustic plainness, now appears refined simplicity. What seemed forward assurance, now strikes me as the result of courageous innocence and conscious virtue.

Sir Cha. What can it mean? He amazes me!

Hard. I told you how it would be. Hush!

Mar. I am now determined to stay, madam; and I have too good an opinion of my father's discernment, when he sees you, to doubt his approbation.

Miss Hard. No, Mr. Marlow, I will not, cannot detain you. Do you think I could suffer a connexion in which there is the smallest room for repentance? Do you think I would take the mean advantage of a transient passion, to load you with confusion? Do you think I could ever relish that happiness which was acquired by lessening yours?

Mar. By all that's good, I can have no happiness but what's in your power to grant me! Nor shall I ever feel repentance but in not having seen your merits before. I will stay even contrary to your wishes; and though you should persist to shun me, I will make my respectful assiduities atone for the levity of my past conduct.

Miss Hard. Sir, I must entreat you'll desist. As our acquaintance began, so let it end, in indifference. I might have given an hour or two to levity; but seriously, Mr. Marlow, do you think I could ever submit to a connexion where I must appear mercenary, and you imprudent? Do you think I could ever catch at the confident addresses of a secure admirer?

Mar. (*Kneeling.*) Does this look like security? Does this look like confidence? No, madam, every moment that shows me your merit, only serves to increase my diffidence and confusion. Here let me continue——

Sir Cha. I can hold it no longer. Charles, Charles, how hast thou deceived me! Is this your indifference, your uninteresting conversation?

Hard. Your cold contempt; your formal interview! What have you to say now?

Mar. That I'm all amazement! What can it mean?

Hard. It means that you can say and unsay things at pleasure: that you can address a lady in private, and deny it in public: that you have one story for us, and another for my daughter.

Mar. Daughter! — This lady your daughter?

Hard. Yes, sir, my only daughter; my Kate; whose else should she be?

Mar. Oh, the devil!

Miss Hard. Yes, sir, that very identical tall squinting lady you were pleased to take me for (*courtesying*); she that you addressed as the mild, modest, sentimental man of gravity, and the bold, forward, agreeable Rattle of the Ladies' Club. Ha! ha! ha!

Mar. Zounds! there's no bearing this; it's worse than death!

Miss Hard. In which of your characters, sir, will you give us leave to address you? As the faltering gentleman, with looks on the ground, that speaks just to be heard, and hates hypocrisy; or the loud confident creature, that keeps it up with Mrs. Mantrap, and old Miss Biddy Buckskin, till three in the morning? Ha! ha! ha!

Mar. O, curse on my noisy head. I never attempted to be impudent yet, that I was not taken down. I must be gone

Hard. By the hand of my body, but you shall not. I see it was all a mistake, and I am rejoiced to find it. You shall not, sir, I tell you. I know she'll forgive you. Won't you forgive him, Kate? We'll all forgive you. Take courage, man. (*They retire, she tormenting him, to the back scene.*)

Enter MRS. HARDCASTLE *and* TONY.

Mrs. Hard. So, so, they're gone off. Let them go, I care not.

Hard. Who gone?

Mrs. Hard. My dutiful niece and her gentleman, Mr. Hastings, from town. He who came down with our modest visitor here.

Sir Cha. Who, my honest George Hastings? As worthy a fellow as lives, and the girl could not have made a more prudent choice.

Hard. Then, by the hand of my body, I'm proud of the connexion.

Mrs. Hard. Well, if he has taken away the lady, he has not taken her fortune; that remains in this family to console us for her loss.

Hard. Sure, Dorothy, you would not be so mercenary?

Mrs. Hard. Ay, that's my affair, not yours.

Hard. But you know if your son, when of age, refuses to marry his cousin, her whole fortune is then at her own disposal.

Mrs. Hard. Ay, but he's not of age, and she has not thought proper to wait for his refusal.

Enter HASTINGS *and* MISS NEVILLE.

Mrs. Hard. (*Aside.*) What, returned so soon! I begin not to like it.

Hast. (*To* HARDCASTLE.) For my late attempt to fly off with your niece let my present confusion be my punishment. We are now come back, to appeal from your justice to your humanity. By her father's consent, I first paid her my addresses, and our passions were first founded in duty.

Miss Nev. Since his death, I have been obliged to stoop to dissimulation to avoid oppression. In an hour of levity, I was ready to give up my fortune to secure my choice. But I am now recovered from the delusion, and hope from your tenderness what is denied me from a nearer connexion.

Mrs. Hard. Pshaw, pshaw! this is all but the whining end of a modern novel.

Hard. Be it what it will, I'm glad they're come back to reclaim their due. Come hither, Tony, boy. Do you refuse this lady's hand whom I now offer you?

Tony. What signifies my refusing? You know I can't refuse her till I'm of age, father.

Hard. While I thought concealing your age, boy, was likely to conduce to your improvement, I concurred with your mother's desire to keep it secret. But since I find she turns it to a wrong use, I must now declare you have been of age these three months.

Tony. Of age! Am I of age, father?

Hard. Above three months.

Tony. Then you'll see the first use I'll make of my liberty. (*Taking* MISS NEVILLE'S *hand.*) Witness all men by these presents, that I, Anthony Lumpkin, Esquire, of BLANK place, refuse you, Constantia Neville, spinster, of no place at all, for my true and lawful wife. So Constance Neville may marry whom she pleases, and Tony Lumpkin is his own man again.

Sir Cha. O brave 'squire!

Hast. My worthy friend!

Mrs. Hard. My undutiful offspring!

Mar. Joy, my dear George! I give you joy sincerely. And could I prevail upon my little tyrant here to be less arbitrary, I should be the happiest man alive, if you would return me the favour.

Hast. (*To* MISS HARDCASTLE.) Come, madam, you are now driven to the very last scene of all your contrivances. I know you like him, I'm sure he loves you, and you must and shall have him.

Hard. (*Joining their hands.*) And I say so too. And, Mr. Marlow, if she makes as good a wife as she has a daughter, I don't believe you'll ever repent your bargain. So now to supper. To-morrow we shall gather all the poor of the parish about us, and the mistakes of the night shall be crowned with a merry morning. So, boy, take her; and as you have been mistaken in the mistress, my wish is, that you may never be mistaken in the wife.

[*Exeunt Omnes.*

END OF SHE STOOPS TO CONQUER.

6/64

MISCELLANEOUS POEMS.

MISCELLANEOUS POEMS.

PROLOGUE.

Written and spoken by the Poet LABERIUS, *a Roman Knight whom* CÆSAR *forced upon the Stage.—Preserved by* MACROBIUS.

WHAT! no way left to shun th' inglorious stage,
And save from infamy my sinking age!
Scarce half alive, oppressed with many a year,
What, in the name of dotage, drives me here?
A time there was, when glory was my guide,
No force nor fraud could turn my steps aside;
Unawed by power, and unappalled by fear,
With honest thrift I held my honour dear:
But this vile hour disperses all my store,
And all my hoard of honour is no more;
For ah! too partial to my life's decline,
Cæsar persuades, submission must be mine,
Him I obey, whom Heaven itself obeys,
Hopeless of pleasing, yet inclined to please.
Here then at once I welcome every shame,
And cancel at threescore a life of fame:
No more my titles shall my children tell;
The old buffoon will fit my name as well:
This day beyond its term my fate extends,
For life is ended when our honour ends.

THE DOUBLE TRANSFORMATION. A TALE.

SECLUDED from domestic strife,
Jack Book-worm led a college life;
A fellowship at twenty-five
Made him the happiest man alive;
He drank his glass, and cracked his joke,
And freshmen wondered as he spoke.
Such pleasures, unalloyed with care,
Could any accident impair?
Could Cupid's shaft at length transfix
Our swain, arrived at thirty-six?
O! had the archer ne'er come down
To ravage in a country town!
Or Flavia been content to stop
At triumphs in a Fleet-street shop.
O, had her eyes forgot to blaze!
Or Jack had wanted eyes to gaze;
O! ———But let exclamations cease,
Her presence banished all his peace.
So with decorum all things carried;
Miss frowned and blushed, and then was —married.
Need we expose to vulgar sight
The raptures of the bridal night?
Need we intrude on hallowed ground,
Or draw the curtains closed around?
Let it suffice, that each had charms:
He clasped a goddess in his arms;
And, though she felt his usage rough,
Yet in a man 'twas well enough.
The honey-moon like lightning flew;
The second brought its transports too;
A third, a fourth, were not amiss;
The fifth was friendship mixed with bliss·
But, when a twelvemonth passed away,
Jack found his goddess made of clay;
Found half the charms that decked her face

Arose from powder, shreds, or lace:
But still the worst remained behind,
That very face had robbed her mind.
 Skilled in no other arts was she,
But dressing, patching, repartee;
And, just as humour rose or fell,
By turns a slattern or a belle.
'Tis true she dressed with modern grace,
Half naked at a ball or race;
But when at home, at board or bed,
Five greasy night-caps wrapped her head.
Could so much beauty condescend
To be a dull domestic friend?
Could any curtain lectures bring
To decency so fine a thing?
In short, by night 'twas fits or fretting;
By day 'twas gadding or coquetting.
Fond to be seen, she kept a bevy
Of powdered coxcombs at her levy:
The 'squire and captain took their stations,
And twenty other near relations:
Jack sucked his pipe and often broke
A sigh in suffocating smoke;
While all their hours were passed between
Insulting repartee or spleen.
 Thus as her faults each day were known,
He thinks her features coarser grown;
He fancies every vice she shows
Or thins her lip, or points her nose:
Whenever rage or envy rise,—
How wide her mouth, how wild her eyes!
He knows not how, but so it is,
Her face is grown a knowing phiz;
And, though her fops are wondrous civil,
He thinks her ugly as the devil.
 Now to perplex the ravelled noose,
As each a different way pursues,
While sullen or loquacious strife
Promised to hold them on for life,
That dire disease, whose ruthless power
Withers the beauty's transient flower—
Lo! the small pox, whose horrid glare
Levelled its terrors at the fair;
And, rifling every youthful grace,
Left but the remnant of a face.
 The glass, grown hateful to her sight,
Reflected now a perfect fright;
Each former art she vainly tries
To bring back lustre to her eyes;
In vain she tries her paste and creams,
To smooth her skin or hide its seams;
Her country beaux and city cousins,
Lovers no more, flew off by dozens;
The 'squire himself was seen to yield,
And even the captain quit the field.
 Poor madam, now condemned to hack
The rest of life with anxious Jack,
Perceiving others fairly flown,
Attempted pleasing him alone.
Jack soon was dazzled to behold
Her present face surpass the old:
With modesty her cheeks are dyed;
Humility displaces pride;
For tawdry finery is seen
A person ever neatly clean:
No more presuming on her sway,
She learns good-nature every day:
Serenely gay, and strict in duty,
Jack finds his wife a perfect beauty.

A NEW SIMILE. IN THE MANNER OF SWIFT.

LONG had I sought in vain to find
A likeness for the scribbling kind;
The modern scribbling kind, who write
In wit, and sense, and nature's spite;
Till reading, I forget what day on,
A chapter out of Tooke's Pantheon,
I think I met with something there
To suit my purpose to a hair:
But let us not proceed too furious,
First please to turn to God Mercurius!
You'll find him pictured at full length
In book the second, page the tenth:
The stress of all my proofs on him I lay,
And now proceed we to our simile.
 Imprimis, pray observe his hat,
Wings upon either side—mark that.
Well! what is it from thence we gather?
Why, these denote a brain of feather.
A brain of feather! very right,
With wit that's flighty, learning light;
Such as to modern bard's decreed;
A just comparison,—proceed.
 In the next place, his feet peruse,
Wings grow again from both his shoes;
Designed, no doubt, their part to bear,
And waft his godship through the air:
And here my simile unites;
For in the modern poet's flights,

I'm sure it may be justly said,
His feet are useful as his head.
Lastly, vouchsafe t' observe his hand,
Filled with a snake-encircled wand,
By classic authors termed Caduceus,
And highly famed for several uses.
To wit: most wondrously endued,
No poppy-water half so good;
For let folks only get a touch,
Its soporific virtue's such,
Though ne'er so much awake before,
That quickly they begin to snore.
Add too, what certain writers tell,
With this he drives men's souls to hell.
Now to apply begin we then:—
His wand's a modern author's pen:
The serpents round about it twined
Denote him of the reptile kind,
Denote the rage with which he writes;
His frothy slaver, venomed bites;
An equal semblance still to keep,
Alike, too, both conduce to sleep.
This difference only, as the god
Drove souls to Tart'rus with his rod,
With his goose-quill the scribbling elf,
Instead of others, damns himself.
And here my simile almost tript,
Yet grant a word by way of postscript.
Moreover Mercury had a failing:
Well! what of that? out with it—stealing;
In which all modern bards agree,
Being each as great a thief as he.
But even this deity's existence
Shall lend my simile assistance:
Our modern bards! why, what a pox
Are they—but senseless stones and blocks?

DESCRIPTION OF AN AUTHOR'S BEDCHAMBER.

Where the Red Lion, flaring o'er the way,
Invites each passing stranger that can pay,
Where Calvert's butt and Parson's black champagne
Regale the drabs and bloods of Drury-lane;
There, in a lonely room, from bailiffs snug,
The Muse found Scroggen stretched beneath a rug.
A window, patched with paper, lent a ray,
That dimly showed the state in which he lay;
The sanded floor that grits beneath the tread;
The humid wall with paltry pictures spread;
The royal Game of Goose was there in view,
And the Twelve Rules the royal martyr drew;
The Seasons, framed with listing, found a place,
And brave Prince William showed his lamp-black face:
The morn was cold, he views with keen desire
The rusty grate unconscious of a fire:
With beer and milk arrears the frieze was scored,
And five cracked teacups dressed the chimney board:
A night-cap decked his brows instead of bay;
A cap by night——a stocking all the day!

ELEGY ON THE DEATH OF A MAD DOG.

Good people all, of every sort,
Give ear unto my song;
And if you find it wondrous short,—
It cannot hold you long.

In Islington there was a man,
Of whom the world might say,
That still a godly race he ran,—
Whene'er he went to pray.

A kind and gentle heart he had,
To comfort friends and foes ;
The naked every day he clad,—
When he put on his clothes.

And in that town a dog was found,
As many dogs there be,
Both mongrel, puppy, whelp, and hound,
And curs of low degree.

This dog and man at first were friends;
But when a pique began,
The dog, to gain some private ends,
Went mad, and bit the man.

Around from all the neighbouring streets
The wondering neighbours ran,
And swore the dog had lost his wits,
To bite so good a man.

The wound it seemed both sore and sad
To every Christian eye ;
And while they swore the dog was mad,
They swore the man would die.

But soon a wonder came to light,
That showed the rogues they lied;
The man recovered of the bite,
The dog it was that died.

STANZAS. ON WOMAN.

When lovely Woman stoops to folly,
And finds too late that men betray,
What charm can soothe her melancholy,
What art can wash her guilt away?

The only art her guilt to cover,
To hide her shame from every eye,
To give repentance to her lover,
And wring his bosom—is, to die.

THE GIFT. TO IRIS, IN BOW-STREET, COVENT-GARDEN.

IMITATED FROM THE FRENCH.

Say, cruel Iris, pretty rake,
Dear mercenary beauty,
What annual offering shall I make
Expressive of my duty?

My heart, a victim to thine eyes,
Should I at once deliver,
Say, would the angry fair one prize
The gift, who slights the giver?

A bill, a jewel, watch, or toy,
My rivals give—and let 'em ;
If gems, or gold, impart a joy,
I'll give them—when I get 'em.

I'll give—but not the full-blown rose,
Or rose-bud more in fashion ;
Such short lived offerings but disclose
A transitory passion.

I'll give thee something yet unpaid,
Not less sincere than civil :
I'll give thee—ah! too charming maid,
I'll give thee—to the devil.

EPITAPH. ON THOMAS PARNELL.

This tomb, inscribed to gentle Parnell's name,
May speak our gratitude, but not his fame.
What heart but feels his sweetly moral lay,
That leads to truth through pleasure's flowery way?
Celestial themes confessed his tuneful aid;
And Heaven, that lent him genius, was repaid.
Needless to him the tribute we bestow,
The transitory breath of fame below :
More lasting rapture from his works shall rise,
While converts thank their poet in the skies.

EPILOGUE TO "THE SISTER."

SPOKEN BY MRS. BULKLEY.

WHAT ? five long acts—and all to make us wiser !
Our authoress sure has wanted an adviser.
Had she consulted me, she should have made
Her moral play a speaking masquerade ;
Warmed up each bustling scene, and in her rage
Have emptied all the green-room on the stage.
My life on't, this had kept her play from sinking ;
Have pleased our eyes, and saved the pain of thinking.
Well, since she thus has shown her want of skill,
What if I give a masquerade ?—I will.
But how ? ay, there's the rub ! [*pausing*]—I've got my cue ;
The world's a masquerade ! the masquers, you, you, you.
[*To Boxes, Pit, and Gallery.*
Lud ! what a group the motley scene discloses !
False wits, false wives, false virgins, and false spouses !
Statesmen with bridles on ; and, close beside 'em,
Patriots in partly-coloured suits that ride 'em.
There Hebes, turned of fifty, try once more
To raise a flame in Cupids of threescore.
These in their turn, with appetites as keen,
Deserting fifty, fasten on fifteen.
Miss, not yet full fifteen, with fire uncommon,
Flings down her sampler, and takes up the woman ;
The little urchin smiles, and spreads her lure,
And tries to kill, ere she's got power to cure.
Thus 'tis with all : their chief and constant care
Is to seem everything—but what they are.
Yon broad, bold, angry spark I fix my eye on,
Who seems t' have robbed his vizor from the lion,
Who frowns, and talks, and swears, with round parade,
Looking, as who should say, Dam'me ! who's afraid ? [*Mimicking.*
Strip but this vizor off, and sure I am
You'll find his lionship a very lamb.
Yon politician, famous in debate,
Perhaps, to vulgar eyes, bestrides the state ;
Yet, when he deigns his real shape t' assume,
He turns old woman, and bestrides a broom.
Yon patriot, too, who presses on your sight,
And seems, to every gazer, all in white,
If with a bribe his candour you attack,
He bows, turns round, and whip—the man's a black !
Yon critic, too—but whither do I run ?
If I proceed, our bard will be undone !
Well, then, a truce, since she requests it too :
Do you spare her, and I'll for once spare you.

INTENDED EPILOGUE TO "SHE STOOPS TO CONQUER."

Enter MRS. BULKLEY, *who curtsies very low as beginning to speak. Then enter* MISS CATLEY, *who stands full before her, and curtsies to the Audience.*

MRS. BUL. Hold, Ma'am, your pardon. What's your business here?
MISS CAT. The Epilogue.
MRS. BUL. The Epilogue?
MISS CAT. Yes, the Epilogue, my dear.
MRS. BUL. Sure you mistake, Ma'am. The Epilogue! *I* bring it.
MISS CAT. Excuse me, Ma'am. The Author bid *me* sing it.

RECITATIVE.

Ye beaux and belles, that form this splendid ring,
Suspend your conversation while I sing.
MRS. BUL. Why, sure the girl's beside herself! an Epilogue of singing?
A hopeful end indeed to such a blest beginning.
Besides, a singer in a comic set!—
Excuse me, Ma'am, I know the etiquette.
MISS CAT. What if we leave it to the House?
MRS. BUL. The House!—Agreed.
MISS CAT. Agreed.
MRS. BUL. And she whose party's largest shall proceed.
And first, I hope you'll readily agree
I've all the critics and the wits for me.
They, I am sure, will answer my commands:
Ye candid judging few, hold up your hands.
What! no return? I find too late, I fear,
That modern judges seldom enter here.
MISS CAT. I'm for a different set.—Old men, whose trade is
Still to gallant and dangle with the ladies.

RECITATIVE.

Who mump their passion, and who, grimly smiling,
Still thus address the fair with voice beguiling:

AIR.—*Cotillon.*

Turn, my fairest, turn, if ever
Strephon caught thy ravished eye.
Pity take on your swain so clever,
Who without your aid must die.
Yes, I shall die, hu, hu, hu, hu!
Yes, I must die, ho, ho, ho, ho!
Da capo.

MRS. BUL. Let all the old pay homage to your merit:
Give me the young, the gay, the men of spirit.
Ye travelled tribe, ye macaroni train,
Of French friseurs and nosegays justly vain,

Who take a trip to Paris once a year
To dress and look like awkward Frenchmen here,
Lend me your hands.—O fatal news to tell!
Their hands are only lent to the Heinel.

Miss CAT. Ay, take your travellers, travellers indeed!
Give me my bonny Scot, that travels from the Tweed.
Where are the chiels?—Ah, ah, I well discern
The smiling looks of each bewitching bairn.

AIR.—*A bonny young Lad is my Jockey.*

I'll sing to amuse you by night and by day,
And be unco' merry when you are but gay;
When you with your bagpipes are ready to play,
My voice shall be ready to carol away
With Sandy, and Sawney, and Jockey,
With Sawney, and Jarvie, and Jockey.

Mrs. BUL. Ye gamesters, who so eager in pursuit
Make but of all your fortune one *va toute:*
Ye Jockey tribe, whose stock of words are few;
"I hold the odds.—Done, done, with you, with you:"
Ye barristers, so fluent with grimace,
"My Lord,—your Lordship misconceives the case:"
Doctors, who cough and answer every misfortuner,
"I wish I'd been called in a little sooner:"
Assist my cause with hands and voices hearty;
Come, end the contest here, and aid my party.

AIR.—*Ballinamony.*

Miss CAT. Ye brave Irish lads, hark away to the crack,
Assist me, I pray, in this woful attack;
For sure I don't wrong you, you seldom are slack,
When the ladies are calling, to blush and hang back.
For you're always polite and attentive,
Still to amuse us inventive,
And death is your only preventive:
Your hands and your voices for me.

Mrs. BUL. Well, Madam, what if, after all this sparring,
We both agree, like friends, to end our jarring?

Miss CAT. And that our friendship may remain unbroken,
What if we leave the Epilogue unspoken?

Mrs. BUL. Agreed.

Miss CAT. Agreed.

Mrs. BUL. And now with late repentance
Un-epilogued the Poet waits his sentence.
Condemn the stubborn fool who can't submit
To thrive by flattery, though he starves by wit. [*Exeunt.*

ANOTHER INTENDED EPILOGUE TO "SHE STOOPS TO CONQUER."

TO BE SPOKEN BY MRS. BULKLEY.

THERE is a place, so Ariosto sings,
A treasury for lost and missing things:
Lost human wits have places there assigned them,
And they who lose their senses there may find them.
But where's this place, this storehouse of the age?
The Moon, says he:—but *I* affirm, the Stage:
At least in many things, I think, I see
His lunar and our mimic world agree.
Both shine at night; for, but at Foote's alone,
We scarce exhibit till the sun goes down:
Both prone to change, no settled limits fix:
And sure the folks of both are lunatics.
But in this parallel my best pretence is,
That mortals visit both to find their senses;
To this strange spot rakes, macaronies, cits,
Come thronging to collect their scattered wits.
The gay coquette, who ogles all the day,
Comes here at night, and goes a prude away.
Hither the affected city dame advancing,
Who sighs for operas, and doats on dancing,
Taught by our art her ridicule to pause on,
Quits the *ballet*, and calls for *Nancy Dawson.*
The gamester, too, whose wit's all high or low,
Oft risks his fortune on one desperate throw,
Comes here to saunter, having made his bets,
Finds his lost senses out, and pays his debts.
The Mohawk too, with angry phrases stored,
As "Dam'me, Sir," and "Sir, I wear a sword,"
Here lessoned for a while, and hence retreating,
Goes out, affronts his man, and takes a beating.
Here come the sons of scandal and of news,
But find no sense—for they had none to lose.
Of all the tribe here wanting an adviser,
Our Author's the least likely to grow wiser;
Has he not seen how you your favour place
On sentimental queens and lords in lace?
Without a star, a coronet, or garter,
How can the piece expect or hope for quarter?
No high-life scenes, no sentiment: the creature
Still stoops among the low to copy nature.
Yes, he's far gone:—and yet some pity fix,
The English laws forbid to punish lunatics.

FROM THE ORATORIO OF "THE CAPTIVITY."

SONG.

THE wretch condemned with life to part
Still, still on hope relies;
And every pang that rends the heart
Bids expectation rise.

Hope, like the gleaming taper's light,
Adorns and cheers our way;
And still, as darker grows the night,
Emits a brighter ray.

SONG, FROM THE SAME.

O MEMORY, thou fond deceiver!
Still importunate and vain;
To former joys recurring ever,
And turning all the past to pain;

Thou, like the world, opprest oppressing,
Thy smiles increase the wretch's woe,
And he who wants each other blessing
In thee must ever find a foe.

THE CLOWN'S REPLY.

JOHN TROT was desired by two witty peers
To tell them the reason why asses had ears.
"An't please you," quoth John, "I'm not given to letters,
Nor dare I pretend to know more than my betters:
Howe'er from this time I shall ne'er see your graces,
As I hope to be saved! without thinking on asses."

EPITAPH ON EDWARD PURDON.

HERE lies poor Ned Purdon, from misery freed,
Who long was a bookseller's hack.
He led such a damnable life in this world,
I don't think he'll wish to come back.

AN ELEGY ON THAT GLORY OF HER SEX, MRS. MARY BLAIZE.

GOOD people all, with one accord
Lament for Madam Blaize,
Who never wanted a good word,
From those who spoke her praise.

The needy seldom passed her door,
And always found her kind;
She freely lent to all the poor,—
Who left a pledge behind.

She strove the neighbourhood to please,
With manners wondrous winning;
And never followed wicked ways,—
Unless when she was sinning.

At church, in silks and satins new,
With hoop of monstrous size,
She never slumbered in her pew,—
But when she shut her eyes.

Her love was sought, I do aver,
By twenty beaux and more;
The king himself has followed her,—
When she has walked before.

But now her wealth and finery fled,
Her hangers-on cut short all;
The doctors found, when she was dead,—
Her last disorder mortal.

Let us lament, in sorrow sore,
For Kent-street well may say,
That had she lived a twelvemonth more,—
She had not died to-day.

SONG:

INTENDED TO HAVE BEEN SUNG BY MISS HARDCASTLE IN THE COMEDY OF "SHE STOOPS TO CONQUER."

AIR.—*The Humours of Ballamagairy.*

AH me! when shall I marry me?
Lovers are plenty, but fail to relieve me.
He, fond youth, that could carry me,
Offers to love, but means to deceive me.

But I will rally, and combat the ruiner;
Not a look nor a smile shall my passion discover.
She that gives all to the false one pursuing her
Makes but a penitent, and loses a lover.

PROLOGUE TO "ZOBEIDE," A TRAGEDY.

SPOKEN BY MR. QUICK IN THE CHARACTER OF A SAILOR.

In these bold times, when Learning's sons explore
The distant climates and the savage shore;
When wise astronomers to India steer,
And quit for Venus many a brighter here;
While botanists, all cold to smiles and dimpling,
Forsake the fair, and patiently—go simpling;
When every bosom swells with wondrous scenes,
Priests, cannibals, and *hoity-toity* queens;
Our bard into the general spirit enters,
And fits his little frigate for adventures.
With Scythian stores, and trinkets, deeply laden,
He this way steers his course, in hopes of trading;
Yet ere he lands he 'as ordered me before,
To make an observation on the shore.
Where are we driven? our reckoning sure is lost!
This seems a barren and a dangerous coast.
Lord, what a sultry climate am I under!
Yon ill-foreboding cloud seems big with thunder [*Upper gallery.*
There mangroves spread, and larger than I've seen 'em—[*Pit.*
Here trees of stately size, and turtles in 'em— [*Balconies.*
Here ill-conditioned oranges abound— [*Stage.*
And apples [*takes up one and tastes it*], bitter apples, strew the ground:
The place is uninhabited I fear:
I heard a hissing—there are serpents here!
Oh, there the natives are a dreadful race;
The men have tails, the women painted face.
No doubt they're all barbarians.—Yes, 'tis so;
I'll try to make palaver with them though: [*Making signs.*
'Tis best, however, keeping at a distance.
Good savages, our Captain craves assistance:
Our ship's well stored; in yonder creek we've laid her:
His honour is no mercenary trader.
This is his first adventure; lend him aid,
Or you may chance to spoil a thriving trade.
His goods, he hopes, are prime, and brought from far,
Equally fit for gallantry and war.
What! no reply to promises so ample?
I'd best step back—and order up a sample.

EPILOGUE.

SPOKEN BY MR. LEE LEWES, IN THE CHARACTER OF HARLEQUIN, AT HIS BENEFIT.

HOLD, Prompter, hold! a word before your nonsense!
I'd speak a word or two, to ease my conscience.
My pride forbids it ever should be said
My heels eclipsed the honours of my head;
That I found humour in a piebald vest,
Or ever thought that jumping was a jest. [*Takes off his mask.*
Whence, and what art thou, visionary birth?
Nature disowns and reason scorns thy mirth.
In thy black aspect every passion sleeps,
The joy that dimples, and the woe that weeps.
How hast thou filled the scene with all thy brood
Of fools pursuing, and of fools pursued!
Whose ins and outs no ray of sense discloses,
Whose only plot it is to break our noses;
Whilst from below the trap-door demons rise,
And from above the dangling deities.
And shall I mix in this unhallowed crew?
May rosined lightning blast me if I do!
No—I will act, I'll vindicate the stage:
Shakespeare himself shall feel my tragic rage.
Off, off, vile trappings! a new passion reigns!
The maddening monarch revels in my veins.
Oh for a Richard's voice to catch the theme!
"Give me another horse! bind up my wounds!—soft; 'twas but
 a dream."
Ay, 'twas but a dream, for now there's no retreating:
If I cease Harlequin, I cease from eating.
'Twas thus that Æsop's stag, a creature blameless,
Yet something vain, like one that shall be nameless,
Once on the margin of a fountain stood,
And cavilled at his image in the flood.
"The deuce confound," he cries, "these drumstick shanks;
They never have my gratitude nor thanks;
They're perfectly disgraceful! strike me dead!
But for a head; yes, yes, I have a head.
How piercing is that eye! how sleek that brow!
My horns!—I'm told horns are the fashion now."
Whilst thus he spoke, astonished, to his view,
Near, and more near, the hounds and huntsmen drew;
"Hoicks! hark forward!" came thundering from behind.
He bounds aloft, outstrips the fleeting wind;
He quits the woods, and tries the beaten ways;
He starts, he pants, he takes the circling maze.
At length his silly head, so prized before,
Is taught his former folly to deplore;
Whilst his strong limbs conspire to set him free,
And at one bound he saves himself,—like me.
[*Taking a jump through the stage-door.*

THE LOGICIANS REFUTED.

IN IMITATION OF DEAN SWIFT.

LOGICIANS have but ill defined
As rational the human mind;
Reason, they say, belongs to man,
But let them prove it if they can.
Wise Aristotle and Smiglecius,
By ratiocinations specious,
Have strove to prove with great precision,
With definition and division,
Homo est ratione prædìtum:
But for my soul I cannot credit 'em;
And must in spite of them maintain
That man and all his ways are vain,
And that this boasted lord of nature
Is both a weak and erring creature;
That instinct is a surer guide
Than reason—boasting mortals' pride;
And that brute beasts are far before 'em:
Deus est anima brutorum.
Who ever knew an honest brute
At law his neighbour prosecute,
Bring action for assault and battery,
Or friend beguile with lies and flattery?
O'er plains they ramble unconfined,
No politics disturb their mind;
They eat their meals and take their sport,
Nor know who's in or out at court;
They never to the levee go,
To treat as dearest friend a foe;
They never importune his Grace,
Nor ever cringe to men in place;
Nor undertake a dirty job,
Nor draw the quill to write for Bob;
Fraught with invective they ne'er go
To folks at Pater-Noster Row;
No judges, fiddlers, dancing-masters,
No pickpockets, or poetasters,
Are known to honest quadrupeds:
No single brute his fellow leads.
Brutes never meet in bloody fray,
Nor cut each other's throats for pay.
Of beasts, it is confessed, the ape
Comes nearest us in human shape:
Like man he imitates each fashion,
And malice is his ruling passion;
But both in malice and grimaces
A courtier any ape surpasses.
Behold him humbly cringing wait
Upon the minister of state;
View him soon after to inferiors
Aping the conduct of superiors:
He promises with equal air,
And to perfôrm takes equal care.
He in his turn finds imitators:
At court the porters, lacqueys, waiters,
Their master's manners still contract,
And footmen lords and dukes can act:
Thus at the court both great and small
Behave alike, for all ape all.

STANZAS

ON THE TAKING OF QUEBEC, AND DEATH OF GENERAL WOLFE.

AMIDST the clamour of exulting joys,
  Which triumph forces from the patriot heart,
Grief dares to mingle her soul-piercing voice,
  And quells the raptures which from pleasure start.

O Wolfe! to thee a streaming flood of woe,
  Sighing, we pay, and think e'en conquest dear;
Quebec in vain shall teach our breast to glow,
  Whilst thy sad fate extorts the heart-wrung tear.

Alive, the foe thy dreadful vigour fled,
  And saw thee fall with joy-pronouncing eyes:
Yet they shall know thou conquerest, though dead!
  Since from thy tomb a thousand heroes rise.

EPIGRAM

ON A BEAUTIFUL YOUTH STRUCK BLIND BY LIGHTNING.

SURE 'twas by Providence designed,
Rather in pity than in hate,
That he should be, like Cupid, blind,
To save him from Narcissus' fate.

A MADRIGAL.

WEEPING, murmuring, complaining,
Lost to every gay delight,
Myra, too sincere for feigning,
Fears the approaching bridal night.

Yet why impair thy bright perfection,
Or dim thy beauty with a tear?
Had Myra followed my direction,
She long had wanted cause of fear.

VERSES

IN REPLY TO AN INVITATION TO DINNER AT DR. BAKER'S.

"This *is* a poem! This *is* a copy of verses!"

YOUR mandate I got,
You may all go to pot;
Had your senses been right,
You'd have sent before night;
As I hope to be saved,
I put off being shaved;
For I could not make bold,
While the matter was cold,
To meddle in suds,
Or to put on my duds;
So tell Horneck and Nesbitt
And Baker and his bit,
And Kauffman beside,
And the Jessamy bride;
With the rest of the crew,
The Reynoldses two,
Little Comedy's face
And the Captain in lace.
(By the bye, you may tell him,
I have something to sell him;
Of use I insist,
When he comes to enlist.
Your worships must know
That a few days ago,
An order went out,
For the foot guards so stout
To wear tails in high taste,
Twelve inches at least:
Now I've got him a scale
To measure each tail,
To lengthen a short tail,
And a long one to curtail.)

Yet how can I when vext
Thus stray from my text?
Tell each other to rue
Your Devonshire crew,
For sending so late
To one of my state.
But 'tis Reynolds's way
From wisdom to stray,
And Angelica's whim
To be frolic like him.
But, alas! your good worships, how could they be wiser,
When both have been spoiled in to-day's Advertiser?

THRENODIA AUGUSTALIS.

SACRED TO THE MEMORY OF HER ROYAL HIGHNESS THE PRINCESS DOWAGER OF WALES.

1772.

ADVERTISEMENT.

THE following may more properly be termed a compilation than a poem. It was prepared for the composer in little more than two days; and may therefore rather be considered as an industrious effort of gratitude than of genius. In justice to the composer it may likewise be right to inform the public, that the music was composed in a period of time equally short.

OVERTURE.—*A solemn Dirge.*

Air.—Trio.

ARISE, ye sons of worth, arise,
  And waken every note of woe!
When truth and virtue reach the skies,
  'Tis ours to weep the want below.

Chorus.

When truth and virtue, &c.

MAN *Speaker.*

The praise attending pomp and power,
  The incense given to kings,
Are but the trappings of an hour—
  Mere transitory things:
The base bestow them; but the good agree
To spurn the venal gifts as flattery.
But when to pomp and power are joined
An equal dignity of mind;
When titles are the smallest claim;
When wealth and rank and noble blood
But aid the power of doing good;
Then all their trophies last—and flattery turns to fame.

Blest spirit thou, whose fame, just born to bloom,
Shall spread and flourish from the tomb;
How hast thou left mankind for Heaven!
Even now reproach and faction mourn,
And, wondering how their rage was born,
  Request to be forgiven!
Alas! they never had thy hate;
Unmoved in conscious rectitude,
Thy towering mind self-centred stood,
Nor wanted man's opinion to be great.

In vain, to charm thy ravished sight,
A thousand gifts would fortune send;
In vain, to drive thee from the right,
A thousand sorrows urged thy end:
Like some well-fashioned arch thy patience stood,
And purchased strength from its increasing load:
Pain met thee like a friend that set thee free;
Affliction still is virtue's opportunity!

SONG.—*By a* MAN.

Virtue, on herself relying,
  Every passion hushed to rest,
Loses every pain of dying,
  In the hopes of being blest.
Every added pang she suffers
  Some increasing good bestows,
And every shock that malice offers
  Only rocks her to repose.

WOMAN *Speaker.*

Yet, ah! what terrors frowned upon her fate—
Death with its formidable band,
Fever, and pain, and pale consumptive care,
Determined took their stand.
Nor did the cruel ravagers design
To finish all their efforts at a blow;
  But, mischievously slow,
They robbed the relic and defaced the shrine.
    With unavailing grief,
    Despairing of relief,

Her weeping children round
Beheld each hour
Death's growing power,
And trembled as he frowned.

As helpless friends who view from shore
The labouring ship, and hear the tempest roar,
While winds and waves their wishes cross,—
They stood, while hope and comfort fail,
Not to assist, but to bewail
The inevitable loss.
Relentless tyrant, at thy call
How do the good, the virtuous fall!
Truth, beauty, worth, and all that most engage,
But wake thy vengeance and provoke thy rage.

SONG.—*By a* MAN.

When vice my dart and scythe supply,
How great a king of terrors I!
If folly, fraud, your hearts engage,
Tremble, ye mortals, at my rage!

Fall, around me fall, ye little things,
Ye statesmen, warriors, poets, kings!
If Virtue fail her counsel sage,
Tremble, ye mortals, at my rage!

MAN *Speaker.*

Yet let that wisdom, urged by her example,
Teach us to estimate what all must suffer;
Let us prize death as the best gift of nature;
As a safe inn, where weary travellers,
When they have journeyed through a world of cares,
May put off life and be at rest for ever.
Groans, weeping friends, indeed, and gloomy sables,
May oft distract us with their sad solemnity;
The preparation is the executioner.
Death, when unmasked, shows me a friendly face,
And is a terror only at a distance;
For as the line of life conducts me on
To Death's great court, the prospect seems more fair.
'Tis Nature's kind retreat, that's always open
To take us in when we have drained the cup
Of life, or worn our days to wretchedness.
In that secure, serene retreat,
Where all the humble, all the great,
Promiscuously recline;
Where, wildly huddled to the eye,
The beggar's pouch and prince's purple lie,
May every bliss be thine!
And, ah! blest spirit, wheresoe'er thy flight,
Through rolling worlds or fields of liquid light,
May cherubs welcome their expected guest,
May saints with songs receive thee to their rest,
May peace, that claimed while here thy warmest love,
May blissful, endless peace, be thine above

SONG.—*By a* WOMAN.

Lovely, lasting Peace below,
Comforter of every woe,
Heav'nly born, and bred on high,
To crown the favourites of the sky;
Lovely, lasting Peace appear:
This world itself, if thou art here,
Is once again with Eden blest,
And man contains it in his breast.

WOMAN *Speaker.*

Our vows are heard! long, long to mortal eyes,
Her soul was fitting to its kindred skies;
Celestial-like her bounty fell,
Where modest want and patient sorrow dwell;
Want passed for merit at her door,
Unseen the modest were supplied,
Her constant pity fed the poor,
Then only poor, indeed, the day she died.
And, oh! for this, while sculpture decks thy shrine,
And art exhausts profusion round,
The tribute of a tear be mine,
A simple song, a sigh profound.
There Faith shall come, a pilgrim grey,
To bless the tomb that wraps thy clay;
And calm Religion shall repair
To dwell a weeping hermit there.
Truth, Fortitude, and Friendship shall agree,
To blend their virtues while they think of thee.

Air.—Chorus.

Let us, let all the world agree,
To profit by resembling thee.

PART II.

OVERTURE—*Pastorale.*

MAN *Speaker.*

Fast by that shore where Thames' translucent stream
Reflects new glories on his breast,
Where, splendid as the youthful poet's dream,
He forms a scene beyond Elysium blest,
Where sculptured elegance and native grace
Unite to stamp the beauties of the place;
While, sweetly blending, still are seen
The wavy lawn, the sloping green;
While novelty, with cautious cunning,
Through every maze of fancy running,
From China borrows aid to deck the scene:—
There sorrowing by the river's glassy bed,
Forlorn a rural bard complained,
All whom Augusta's bounty fed,
All whom her clemency sustained.
The good old sire, unconscious of decay,
The modest matron, clad in homespun grey,
The military boy, the orphaned maid,
The shattered veteran, now first dismayed;
These sadly join beside the murmuring deep,
And as they view the towers of Kew,
Call on their Mistress, now no more, and weep.

Chorus.

Ye shady walks, ye waving greens,
Ye nodding towers, ye fairy scenes,
Let all your echoes now deplore,
That she who formed your beauties is no more.

MAN *Speaker.*

First of the train the patient rustic came,
Whose callous hand had formed the scene.
Bending at once with sorrow and with age,
With many a tear and many a sigh between,
"And where," he cried, "shall now my babes have bread,
Or how shall age support its feeble fire?
No lord will take me now, my vigour fled,
Nor can my strength perform what they require;
Each grudging master keeps the labourer bare,
A sleek and idle race is all their care.
My noble Mistress thought not so:
Her bounty, like the morning dew,
Unseen, though constant, used to flow,
And as my strength decayed her bounty grew."

WOMAN *Speaker.*

In decent dress and coarsely clean,
The pious matron next was seen;
Clasped in her hand a godly book was borne,
By use and daily meditation worn;
That decent dress, this holy guide,
Augusta's care had well supplied.
"And ah!" she cries, all woe-begone,
"What now remains for me?
Oh! where shall weeping want repair
To ask for charity?
Too late in life for me to ask,
And shame prevents the deed,
And tardy, tardy are the times
To succour, should I need.
But all my wants, before I spoke,
Were to my Mistress known;
She still relieved, nor sought my praise,
Contented with her own.
But every day her name I'll bless,
My morning prayer, my evening song;
I'll praise her while my life shall last,
A life that cannot last me long."

SONG.—*By a* WOMAN.

Each day, each hour, her name I'll bless,
My morning and my evening song;
And when in death my vows shall cease,
My children shall the note prolong.

MAN *Speaker.*

The hardy veteran after struck the sight,
Scarred, mangled, maimed in every part,
Lopped of his limbs in many a gallant fight,
In nought entire—except his heart;
Mute for awhile, and sullenly distressed,
At last the impetuous sorrow fired his breast.
"Wild is the whirlwind rolling
O'er Afric's sandy plain,
And wild the tempest howling
Along the billowed main;

But every danger felt before,
The raging deep, the whirlwind's roar,
Less dreadful struck me with dismay,
Than what I feel this fatal day.
Oh, let me fly a land that spurns the brave,
Oswego's dreary shores shall be my grave;
I'll seek that less inhospitable coast,
And lay my body where my limbs were lost."

SONG.—*By a* MAN.

Old Edward's sons, unknown to yield,
Shall crowd from Cressy's laurelled field
To do thy memory right;
For thine and Britain's wrongs they feel,
Again they snatch the gleamy steel,
And wish the avenging fight!

WOMAN *Speaker.*

In innocence and youth complaining,
Next appeared a lovely maid,
Affliction o'er each feature reigning,
Kindly came in beauty's aid;
Every grace that grief dispenses,
Every glance that warms the soul,
In sweet succession charmed the senses,
While pity harmonised the whole.
"The garland of beauty" ('tis this she would say),
"No more shall my crook or my temples adorn;
I'll not wear a garland—Augusta's away,
I'll not wear a garland until she return;
But alas! that return I never shall see,
The echoes of Thames shall my sorrows proclaim,
There promised a lover to come, but, oh me!
'Twas Death,—'twas the death of my Mistress that came.
But ever, for ever, her image shall last,
I'll strip all the spring of its earliest bloom;
On her grave shall the cowslip and primrose be cast,
And the new blossomed thorn shall whiten her tomb!

SONG.—*By a* WOMAN.—*Pastorale.*

With garlands of beauty the Queen of the May
No more will her crook or her temples adorn;
For who'd wear a garland when she is away,
When she is removed and shall never return!
On the grave of Augusta these garlands be placed,
We'll rifle the spring of its earliest bloom;
And there shall the cowslip and primrose be cast,
And the new blossomed thorn shall whiten her tomb!

Chorus.

On the grave of Augusta this garland be placed,
We'll rifle the spring of its earliest bloom;
And there shall the cowslip and primrose be cast,
And the tears of her country shall water her tomb!

THE END